THE NEW BASICS

COOKBOOK

THE NEW BASICS

COOKBOOK

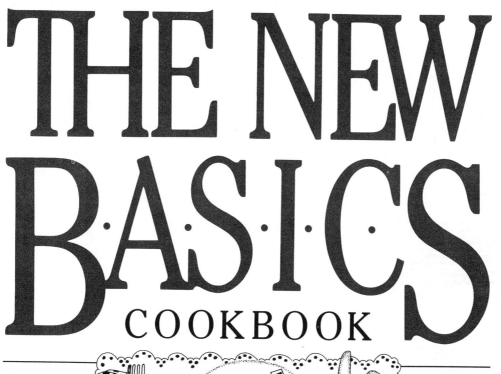

BY JULEE ROSSO & SHEILA LUKINS
ILLUSTRATED BY SHEILA LUKINS

WORKMAN PUBLISHING • NEW YORK

page 29: "Grilled Cumin Shrimp" is reprinted from the book
PLEASURES OF THE TABLE by Florence Fabricant. Published
in 1986 by Harry N. Abrams, Inc., New York. All rights reserved.

page 656: "The Chocolate Bread Pudding" is reprinted from the
book THE ARCADIA SEASONAL MURAL AND COOKBOOK
by Anne Rosenzweig with mural by Paul Davis. Published in 1986
by Harry N. Abrams, Inc., New York. All rights reserved.

page 670: "Lemon Poppy Seed Pound Cake." From p. 27 THE
CAKE BIBLE by Rose Levy Beranbaum. Copyright © 1988 by
Rose Levy Beranbaum. Reprinted by permission of William
Morrow and Company, Inc.

Library of Congress Cataloging-in-Publication Data

Rosso, Julee.
The new basics cookbook / by Julee Rosso & Sheila Lukins;
illustrated by Sheila Lukins.
p.   cm.
ISBN 0-89480-392-1
ISBN 0-89480-341-7 (pbk.)
1. Cookery, American. I. Lukins, Sheila. II. Title.
TX715.R8413   1989
641.5—dc19   88-51581
                                                 CIP

Art director and cover design by Paul Hanson
Book design by Lisa Hollander
  with Marcia Bujold, Regina Dalton-Fischel, and Lori Malkin
Back cover photo taken at Smallbone Inc.

Workman Publishing Company, Inc.
708 Broadway
New York, NY 10003

Manufactured in the United States of America
First printing October 1989
10 9 8 7 6 5

ACKNOWLEDGMENTS

In order to make all of our dreams come true, some of our very favorite people have been working with us from the beginning of *Basics* to the end. We're forever grateful to Sidney Burstein and Ellen Gibson White for their magic in the kitchen; Nancy Nordstrom and Ann Bloomstrand for their thorough curiosity, Kathie Ness for her recipe diligence, and Barbara Ottenhoff for her more than smooth style.

We sincerely thank the talented Susy Davidson, Rena Coyle, Fran Snyder, Stephanie Lyness, Lauren Jacobs, Candace Strong, Kathy Kelsh, Hadassah Gold, Sally Brazil, and Tess Platt for the terrific support and contributions. And thanks, too, to Steve Connolly, who taught us the way to make perfect pizza.

Our heartfelt gratitude goes to our creative colleagues and friends in the food business for sharing their favorite recipes with us, and who have inspired and encouraged us through the years; our cohorts, who were with us or there for us during so many of the Silver Palate years, especially Michael McLaughlin and Sarah Leah Chase; and our old and dear friends, who lovingly saw us through it all.

With love, we especially thank our friends at Workman—our very wonderful editor, Suzanne Rafer, who's seen us through thick and thin; art directors Paul Hanson and Charles Kreloff; designer Lisa Hollander, who with her crew—especially Lori Malkin, Marcia Bujold, and Regina Dalton-Fischel—made the book dance; Shannon Ryan, Mary Wilkinson, David Schiller, Cathy Dorsey, Amy Robbins, Ruth Hochbaum (and her staff at BPE) and Wayne Kirn for their help in moving the book along; Bert Snyder, Janet Harris, Andrea Glickson, and Annie Brody for seeing to it that all the work wasn't for naught; and of course to Peter and Carolan Workman. And, to Arthur Klebanoff, our dear friend. Thank you all, from the bottom of our hearts.

—*JULEE AND SHEILA*

With all our love and all our thanks

OUR NEXT CHAPTER

Since *The Silver Palate Cookbook* and *The Silver Palate Good Times Cookbook* were published, we've had a great time traveling around the U.S. and have been fortunate to meet and become friends with so many of you. It's been a real joy for us to share our passion for and curiosity about food, as well as our love for gracious entertaining.

We're often asked how we work together. Very, very well is our answer. In fact we have a creative relationship that just seems to keep getting better with age. Ideas for recipes sometimes come from an ingredient, a texture, a need to update a classic, or a dish we've tasted. But often a good idea arrives free-form—in the shower or during a walk. We talk it over and improve the concept, cook it, taste and critique it together, and decide which flavors, if any, need emphasizing; then we make the adjustments and taste it again. If we come up with something we can say we really love, we gamble that you will too.

We've become great friends over these past twelve years. We respect each other, finish each other's sentences, have ideas simultaneously, and have been known to show up in almost the same outfits. We just clicked long ago, and we're blessed with similar timetables, expectations, curiosities, and standards of taste.

But we are two different people, even though we're often confused one for the other. Sheila is married to Richard, and their teenage daughters, Annabel and Molly, hardly remember a time before The Silver Palate food shop. They live in Manhattan during the week and on weekends they retreat to a farm in Connecticut that has a rushing trout stream. Sheila loves her art, the opera, tending her garden, and scouting flea markets. Julee, recently married to Bill, divides her time between Manhattan and a cottage on Lake Michigan. She loves her herb and rose gardens, playing golf, grilling, sculpting, and collecting antique cookbooks.

Over the years, together and separately, we have been on the road again and again, both for business and for pleasure. We've given countless numbers of cooking classes and lectures on entrepreneurship, have signed thousands of books, and have worked with stores of every size and style to merchandise Silver Palate products. As the business expanded and the books were published in other countries, we traveled to Japan, France, Italy, Austria, Switzerland, and the Caribbean. With our professional colleagues, we've been lucky to be part of a renaissance in the food business in America.

Eventually, however, we determined that it was time to shift gears—not by any means to stop, but to reevaluate life's priorities, and to take time to smell the basil, not just purée it. It seemed the right time to sell The Silver Palate. For too long our schedules had kept us away from the people we wanted to share meals with—not just on weekends or at a special work-night dinner, but all of the time. We began to take a long, hard look at our own kitchens, rethinking and restocking them in keeping with all we had learned over the years.

Even without The Silver Palate, our schedules are still hectic, but we're in our own kitchens, setting our own moods, and cooking in our own styles. And meals with our families and friends have become the most rewarding and satisfying part of our day.

Selling the company also has freed us to do something that we have been wanting to do for the last few years—to write a basic cookbook that combines the information today's cooks need with irresistible recipes for the foods they want to prepare. THE NEW BASICS COOKBOOK reflects the exciting things we've learned over the years, as well as including our latest, and we think, greatest recipes. We hope you enjoy it.

—JULEE ROSSO AND SHEILA LUKINS

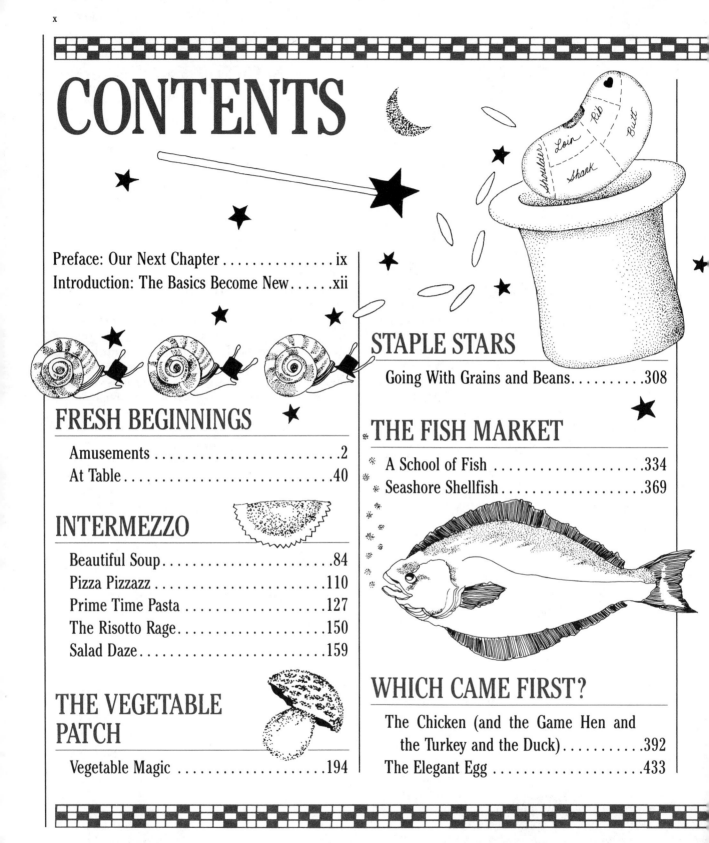

CONTENTS

FRESH BEGINNINGS

INTERMEZZO

THE VEGETABLE PATCH

STAPLE STARS

THE FISH MARKET

WHICH CAME FIRST?

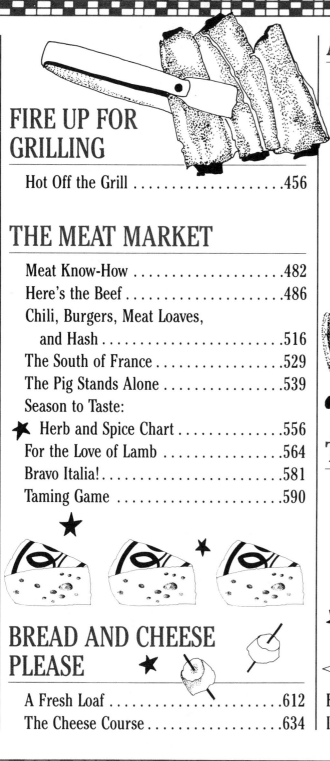

FIRE UP FOR GRILLING

THE MEAT MARKET

BREAD AND CHEESE PLEASE

AND EVERYTHING NICE

THE NEW BASICS

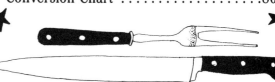

THE BASICS BECOME NEW

After being caught up in a whirlwind the past twenty years, with food fads and lifestyles changing faster than you can run a marathon, many people say that it is now time to take a breath, slow down, and hark back to a simpler time in America—to go back to basics. And we're all for it. At least in part. You see, after more than two decades as food professionals, and with all the exciting changes we have seen in the food world, we have no desire to take a step backward after coming so far. Instead we think a new and exciting version of those basics is what is needed.

Stimulated by this need plus our love for foods with strong, vibrant flavors, our concern for health and fitness, and our insatiable curiosity, we have delved into the newest ingredients, cooking techniques, and magical time-saving equipment. As we evaluated our pantries, it became clear that the best of the past two decades have become our staples—but the shelves are never so full that there isn't room for the latest find.

The true joy of cooking well for family and friends is no longer a weekend pastime. During the 1970s and '80s we spent our time in restaurants, take-out food shops, and more often than not, picking up fast food. Now we luxuriate in the search for the best and freshest of our bountiful ingredients. We want to know and be in control of what we're serving. The vast cornucopia of ethnic, exotic, and regional cuisines have become so accessible to us all, that borders are easily crossed and the most eclectic menus emerge. We're using more herbs, spices, garlic, lemon, and vinegar for colorful dishes with clean clear taste. We may still break rules, but that's the fun!

Cocktail hour has always been a regular gathering time, but today it has lightened up considerably. It serves the purpose of teasing and encouraging the appetite. Fundamental to the New Basics is balance—just a couple of light bites with a drink or glass of wine, nothing overwhelming, no heavy textures or flavors—even a full-blown cocktail party shouldn't leave the guests feeling leaden.

Soups and salads know no boundaries. They can begin a meal or be the meal any time of the year. The range of vegetables—found in the market and in our gardens—makes our heads spin. New varieties, hues, sizes, shapes—never have there been such choices. We've had to learn how to select them,

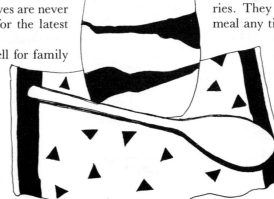

care for them, and prepare them, but the results have been great and now they are as important to us as the old favorites—the morel is as basic as the button mushroom; the spaghetti squash as basic as the zucchini, and cilantro as basic as parsley.

Pizzas have become a passion and we love to make them in sizes ranging from mini to maxi, depending on how and when they are being served. With dough always available in the freezer, we can easily prepare pizzas in no time, ad-libbing with our own favorite foods as toppings.

Pasta has become an integral part of our weekly menu, and at any given time there are sauces in the fridge or fresh vegetables in the crisper waiting to be tossed with steaming ribbons, tubes, or any of the dozens of attractive pasta shapes and flavors on the market.

Risotto, the staple of northern Italy, has become the rice of many moments in our kitchens. But other nutritious grains and beans have also been integrated into our diet, adding exciting flavors and textures that we had overlooked for too many years.

Fish and shellfish are regulars on our tables at home. We marvel at the delicate, yet rich flavors brought out by broiling, grilling, sautéing, and poaching. Today we see fish in our local shops that once were available only if we caught them ourselves, or if we were traveling in some other part of the world. Now they arrive in markets with their fragile flavors at their peak.

As we watch our cholesterol, we've taken more to chicken and less to eggs. So, while there was always a question as to which came first, there's no question at all as to which one wins the race. Chickens and their feathered friends are being cooked in more ways than ever, often shedding their skin to become lighter still. The trick today is to find the leanest birds around. And when you crave an egg and indulge, you want it to be either gloriously simple or a real flavor event— an omelet, frittata, strata, quiche, or a perfectly puffed soufflé.

The meat market abounds with leaner beef, veal, pork, lamb, and even tamed game, but we no longer see meat as the main event, and so are satisfied with smaller portions. We've been stimulated by the nuances of herbs and spices of many countries, although France and Italy still hold special places in our hearts and kitchens. We've adapted so many of their ways with flavorful cuts of meat that their basics have become ours.

Our sweet tooth, never completely satisfied, craves everything from the simplest perfect pear or poached peach to the most decadent chocolate terrine. It depends on our mood, the texture and tone of the meal, the season, and our current passion. When we want to indulge, the once trendy crème brûlée or tiramisu has found as comfortable a place in our kitchen as an old-fashioned berry cobbler or homemade apple pie.

And so our pantries have evolved, our kitchens feel refreshed. There's a microwave on the counter, a bowl of bright lemons on the table, pots of fresh herbs on the windowsill. Our spice racks overflow with so many new selections next to old favorites—cumin, coriander, cardamom line up with rosemary, tarragon, sage. Our vegetable crispers are packed with lush greens, peppers, beets, and eggplants in a rainbow of colors. There are always tomatoes ripening to perfection for a quick bruschetta, fresh or dried wild mushrooms to turn into a glorious risotto or pasta sauce, and pesto to spread on crostini.

Our food tastes better than ever to us. We think it has something to do with the fact that the basics have changed—and so have we.

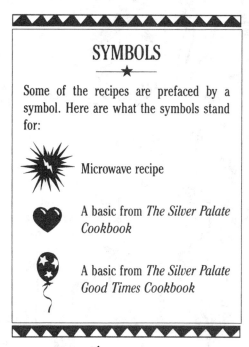

SYMBOLS

★

Some of the recipes are prefaced by a symbol. Here are what the symbols stand for:

Microwave recipe

A basic from *The Silver Palate Cookbook*

A basic from *The Silver Palate Good Times Cookbook*

FRESH BEGINNINGS

AMUSEMENTS

Amusements are really finger foods at their best. Never large enough to bring a conversation to a total stop, these bite-size little tastes are the perfect complement to a pre-dinner drink. Sometimes we like to amuse our guests with simple bowls of olives, chips, and dips, and pestos spread on rounds of toast or vegetables. Sometimes we crave a raw bar with every shellfish and sauce imaginable. Sometimes we want boards and baskets of crudités, pâtés, cheeses, and seafood mousses, or a bite of something warm and wonderful to pamper our guests perfectly. Other times only Champagne and caviar will do.

Whether the amusements *are* the party, or simply help to get the party rolling, these appetite teasers serve dozens of occasions perfectly. Cocktail parties are nothing more than drinks and two, three, or ten sorts of bite-size little tastes. If you have friends in for dinner or are gathering to go out, a cocktail with a little something to nibble on allows everyone to mix, mingle, and unwind.

SPICED PARTY NUTS

These make a great gift, and they're quick to prepare, so make some for yourself too. Always keep the batches to this size. The nuts need plenty of tossing and drying room.

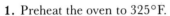

½ teaspoon ground cumin
½ teaspoon chili powder
½ teaspoon curry powder
½ teaspoon garlic salt
¼ teaspoon cayenne pepper
¼ teaspoon ground ginger
¼ teaspoon ground cinnamon
2 tablespoons olive oil
2 cups shelled whole almonds or pecan halves
1 tablespoon coarse (kosher) salt (optional)
Garlic salt (optional)

1. Preheat the oven to 325°F.
2. Mix the cumin, chili powder, curry powder, garlic salt, cayenne, ginger, and cinnamon in a bowl. Set aside.
3. Heat the oil in a nonstick skillet over low heat. Add the spice mixture and stir well. Simmer to mellow the flavors, 3 or 4 minutes.
4. Place the nuts in a mixing bowl, add the spice mixture, and toss well. Spread the nuts in a single layer on a baking sheet. Bake for 15 minutes, shaking the pan once or twice.
5. Remove the baking sheet from the oven, and using a rubber spatula, toss the nuts with any spices and oil that have accumulated on the bottom of the pan. Sprinkle with the coarse salt, and a bit more garlic salt if desired. Let rest for 2 hours in a cool place. Store in airtight jars.

2 cups

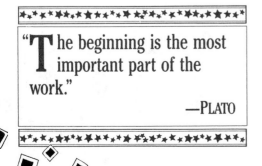

"The beginning is the most important part of the work."

—PLATO

CLASSIC TUSCAN CROSTINI

In Florence, *crostini* are a sign of hospitality. They greet you as prologues to a meal in homes and restaurants alike—tiny rounds of toast spread with anchovy paste, cheese, shellfish, or chicken liver pâté.

2 tablespoons unsalted butter
¼ cup extra virgin olive oil
1 pound chicken livers, trimmed, rinsed, and patted dry
1 cup chopped onions
½ cup Berta's Chicken Stock (see Index) or canned broth
½ cup dry white wine
3 cloves garlic, coarsely chopped
2 teaspoons crumbled dried sage leaves
2 teaspoons chopped fresh rosemary leaves
Freshly ground black pepper, to taste
3 tablespoons tiny capers, drained
4 anchovy fillets
1 ½ teaspoons tomato paste
Toasts made from thinly sliced French bread
Extra virgin olive oil, for assembling the crostini
Freshly grated Parmesan cheese, for garnish

1. Heat the butter and oil in a skillet over medium heat, and sauté the chicken livers and onions

until browned, about 10 minutes.

2. Add the stock, wine, garlic, sage, rosemary, and pepper to the skillet. Cook, stirring frequently, until the liquid has reduced by two thirds, 3 to 4 minutes.

3. Add the capers, anchovies, and tomato paste. Stir well, and cook 1 minute. Transfer the mixture to a food processor or blender, scraping the skillet well.

4. Purée the mixture until almost smooth. Remove it to a serving bowl, cover, and refrigerate at least 2 hours. Let the pâté stand at room temperature 30 minutes before serving.

5. To serve, lightly brush the toasts on one side with olive oil. Spread the liver mixture generously on the toasts, and sprinkle with Parmesan cheese.

2 cups; 16 to 24 crostini

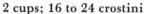

CROSTINI
♥

Crostini, Italian for "little crusts," originated as a clever way of using the very last bit of bread from yesterday's loaf. These small toasts are traditionally grilled over an open wood fire or under the broiler, drizzled with good olive oil, and topped with a mélange of mixtures from the simple to the complex. Crostini in one form or another are the invariable nibbles that precede a meal in Italy.

Crostini will stand up to almost anything you want to put on them. Some of our favorite savory crostini are: coarsely chopped olives, anchovy paste, caper butter, minced chicken livers, and chopped fresh herbs with capers.

OLIVADA CROSTINI

The perfect olive spread—pungent with capers and garlic—is topped with fresh mozzarella and roasted peppers and grilled ever so gently on bread slices for a delightful amusement.

1 red bell pepper, cored, halved, and seeded
1 yellow bell pepper, cored, halved, and seeded
1 narrow loaf Italian or French bread
2 balls (each about 6 to 8 ounces) fresh mozzarella cheese
1 cup Olivada (recipe follows)

1. Preheat the broiler.

2. Lay the peppers skin side up on a flat broiling pan, and place the pan 3 to 4 inches below the heat. Broil the peppers until the skins are charred (they should be black). Then place the peppers in a plastic bag, seal it with a twist tie, and set aside. Let the peppers steam in the bag for 20 minutes. Leave the broiler on.

3. Remove peppers from the bag and peel them. Slice them into thin strips, and set aside.

4. Slice the bread into twenty ¼-inch-thick slices. Place them under the broiler and toast for about 20 seconds on each side. Remove them from the broiler.

5. Slice the two mozzarella balls into twenty ¼-inch-thick pieces.

6. Spread a small amount of olivada on each piece of toast. Cover with a slice of cheese, and top with one yellow pepper strip and one red pepper strip, forming an X.

7. Broil for 30 seconds, and serve immediately.

20 hors d'oeuvres

OLIVES

Olives are an easy and attractive "bite" to serve with drinks. Choose a variety of black, purple, brown, and green, shriveled and plump, large and tiny. If they're preserved without a distinctive flavoring, toss them in a bit of good olive oil and add whatever herbs and flavoring ingredients strike your fancy.

ITALIAN

▲ **Alfonso** olives are huge, black, and delicious. Alfonsos also come from Spain, where they're green and usually stuffed, and South America, where they're not quite so black and have a meaty, sometimes mushy, texture.

▲ **Calabrese** are dull bronze-green and cracked. They are mellower than Sicilians.

▲ **Gaeta** are small, wrinkled, and black or mahogany-colored. They're sometimes packed with rosemary and have a mild earthy flavor.

▲ **Liguria,** brown-black to black, are slightly acidic and very flavorful.

▲ **Lugano** are salty and dark purple-black.

▲ **Sicilian** are small, cracked green ovals, sharp and bitter-tasting, and traditionally spiced with red pepper and oregano or fennel.

FRENCH

▲ **Niçoise** are purple-brown to brown to black. Small, tender, and shiny, they have more pit to meat than most olives and are redolent with the perfume of Provence, where they are grown.

▲ **Nyons** are small, round, and reddish brown.

Their taste is pleasantly bitter.

▲ **Picholine** are medium green in color, fresh-tasting, crisp and tender, and a little salty, too.

GREEK

▲ **Calamata** (Kalamata), purple-black and shiny, with an elegant almond shape, are considered superior olives. Small ones have the richest flavor.

▲ **Naphlion** (Naflion) are dark khaki-green, cracked and crisp, and taste fresh-fruity with a tart bite.

▲ **Royal** (Royal Victoria) are red to light brown to dark brown. Cured in olive oil and vinegar, they are like Calamatas in flavor and richness. Superbly luscious.

MOROCCAN

▲ **Morocco** olives are jet black, small, and shriveled like large raisins. They come packed with twigs and leaves.

CALIFORNIAN

Aside from the black olives packed in cans, California produces some of its own "ethnic" olives.

▲ **Dry-cured** are black, wrinkled, and tasty, with a meaty texture.

▲ **Greek-style black** have a purple tinge and firm flesh, with smoother, thicker skins than those grown in Greece.

▲ **Greek-style green** are cracked and fairly good.

▲ **Sicilian-style** are medium green and crisp.

OLIVADA

¾ *cup pitted black Italian or Calamata olives*
1 teaspoon minced garlic
1 tablespoon capers, drained
¼ *cup extra virgin olive oil*
1 tablespoon chopped fresh Italian
    (flat-leaf) parsley

Combine the olives, garlic, and capers in a food processor, and process for a few seconds to combine. With the motor running, slowly drizzle the olive oil through the feed tube, and process until smooth. Transfer the mixture to a bowl, and stir in the parsley. This will keep for 2 to 3 days, covered, in the refrigerator.

1 cup

CRAVING CAVIAR

We would bet that no one has ever served caviar and had any left over, nor has anyone ever had enough. Caviar is far too rare and precious a pleasure for most. When you decide to indulge, treat it tenderly.

You must always buy from a reputable dealer who specializes in caviar and therefore has the greatest turnover. Choose a well-known producer and read the label. Smell and taste the product if you can; caviar should never smell or taste fishy or salty. Malossol is the best grade and the least salty. Jet black, golden yellow, gray, or dark brown, the eggs should look shiny, translucent, firm, perfectly whole, and distinct.

Keep caviar refrigerated (never frozen) until 15 minutes before serving. Ideally, place the entire open tin on a bed of crushed ice, with the lid alongside. To avoid crushing the eggs, transfer the caviar to plates carefully with a bone, tortoise-shell, or mother-of-pearl spoon (stainless steel will do, too). Never use silver, as it gives the caviar a metallic taste.

Accompany caviar with fresh toast points (crusts removed), with or without sweet butter. This is not the time to bring out the packaged crackers or toasts or distract from the delicate flavor with lemon wedges, chopped egg, and sour cream. We like ours best with iced vodka, Champagne, aquavit, or dry white wine. Heavenly!

THE STURGEON DOES IT BEST

There are many types of fish eggs on the market, yet only eggs from the sturgeon can be labeled simply "caviar." Other fish roe processed in the same manner must be labeled with the name of the fish preceding the word "caviar." Sturgeon eggs come in several varieties:

▲ **Beluga** is gray and has the largest, best-quality, and mildest-flavored berry. The color is graded from 000 for the lightest gray (also the most prized) to 0 for the darkest.

▲ **Ossetra** is large grained and can be golden brown, bottle green, slate gray, or bluish white. Its flavor is more intense than the others'.

▲ **Sevruga** is the smallest grained and is dark gray to black. There are those who prefer sevruga above all others.

▲ **Keluga** caviar comes from northern Manchuria. The eggs are like beluga in size and gray, moist, and nonoily. The Chinese are striving to refine their processing of this caviar, and it may well be worth looking for in the future.

BUT OTHERS DO IT TOO

Salmon, whitefish, cod, flounder, shad, herring, scallops, crabs, and crawfish are all stuffed to the gills with eggs at spawning time. Cod has apple-pink roe, whitefish golden, and salmon Chinese red. Serving caviars of different colors is sheer drama.

▲ **Keta** is red salmon roe. It is bright orange-red and large grained.

▲ **Lumpfish** caviar is naturally sand-colored but is dyed either black or red. It is inexpensive and can be used as a substitute for the more expensive varieties in dips or as a garnish. It must be added to recipes just before serving, as the dye tends to run.

▲ **Whitefish** caviar comes from the Great Lakes and Canada. It has a mild, crisp, and clean taste and, because of its small grain, is not oily. Some whitefish caviar is flavored with chiles or liqueur.

▲ **Crab, flying fish, and cod** caviar are used in Japan for sushi. The crab roe has a bittersweet flavor and a crunchy texture. The flying fish produces a caviar with crunch and a fishy flavor.

Cod roe resembles anchovy paste in both flavor and texture. These roes are often dyed pale orange or yellow.

JUST A SPOONFUL...

▲ Top thinly sliced bread with cream cheese, a layer of smoked salmon, and salmon caviar

▲ Spoon caviar on broiled oysters

▲ Stuff baby new potatoes with sour cream and top with a little caviar

▲ Stir salmon or whitefish caviar into softened butter and put a dollop on grilled fish

▲ Garnish soup with a lemon slice or a spoonful of sour cream topped with a dab of caviar

▲ Spread black bread with sweet butter and then pressed roe. Sprinkle a few whole eggs over the top.

▲ Spoon caviar on lightly scrambled eggs

▲ Frost a small round of L'Explorateur or St.-André cheese with several brightly colored caviars

▲ Stuff raw mushroom caps with sour cream and caviar

▲ Spoon sour cream on cucumber slices and sprinkle with minced hard-cooked egg and a little salmon caviar

▲ Garnish a seafood salad or fish mousse with caviar

▲ Sprinkle paper-thin carpaccio with caviar

▲ Gently toss angel hair pasta with crème fraîche and caviar

▲ Make a vinaigrette with fruity olive oil, fine wine vinegar, and a generous spoonful of caviar—serve on a salad of simple greens

▲ Serve four different spoonfuls—golden whitefish, salmon, beluga, and sevruga—on chilled glass plates around toast points

▲ Spoon lobster salad into artichoke bottoms and crown with caviar

▲ Toss sliced cooked potatoes with fresh mayonnaise and fold in caviar just before serving

▲ Top potato pancakes with a dollop of sour cream and a spoonful of caviar

▲ Crown beef tartare with caviar

CAVIAR ARTICHOKE LEAVES

We use artichoke leaves instead of bread for these canapés. It's a light and elegant presentation for these bite-size amusements.

2 artichokes
½ cup sour cream
4 ounces red salmon caviar
1 tablespoon snipped fresh chives or
*   chopped fresh Italian (flat-leaf) parsley*

1. Wash the artichokes thoroughly, and trim away the tough outer leaves.

2. Place the artichokes in a saucepan, add an inch of water, and bring to a boil. Reduce the heat, cover, and simmer until tender, about 45 minutes. Remove the artichokes from the pan, and allow to drain and cool.

3. Place one of the artichokes in the center of a large plate. Peel the leaves away from the other artichoke (reserving the bottom for another use). Arrange the leaves in a circle around the whole artichoke. Place a small dollop of sour cream on the meaty part of each leaf. Top it with a few caviar eggs, and garnish with chives.

8 to 10 portions

TOMATO ARUGULA PROVENCAL

This robust combination is a perfect topping for pizza, pasta, small puff-tart hors d'oeuvres, or just spread on crusty toasted French bread.

20 ripe plum tomatoes
¼ cup extra virgin olive oil
½ teaspoon salt
1 easpoon freshly ground black pepper
8 cloves garlic, finely minced
1 large bunch arugula, well rinsed and patted dry, stems
    removed and leaves coarsely chopped (about 2 cups)
15 sun-dried tomatoes (packed in oil), drained and coarsely
    chopped
3 tablespoons freshly grated Parmesan cheese

1. Bring 4 quarts of water to a boil in a large pot. Drop the tomatoes into the water and leave for 20 seconds. Then drain and cool under cold water. Peel, core, and seed the tomatoes, and coarsely chop.

2. Heat the oil in a large skillet. Add the chopped tomatoes, salt, and pepper. Simmer over medium heat for 15 minutes. Add the garlic, and cook another 5 minutes. Then add the arugula, mix thoroughly, and remove from the heat.

3. Add the sun-dried tomatoes and Parmesan cheese to the mixture, and gently fold together. Let the mixture rest, covered, in the refrigerator for at least 4 hours before serving. This dish may be made up to 2 days ahead.

4 cups

CASUAL INDIAN SUMMER COCKTAIL PARTY

Elegant Eggplant Caviar
Crudités With Sorrel Mayonnaise and
Sesame Dip
Grilled Cumin Shrimp
Herbed Chèvre Bites
Classic Tuscan Crostini
Tomato Arugula Provençal
Spiced Party Nuts
Crocks of Black and Green Olives
Radishes With Sweet Butter

CAPONATA

Made subtly different from ratatouille by the addition of celery, Calamata olives, and capers, this is just the right consistency to fill One Bite Bread Cups and serve as canapés.

2 cups cubed peeled eggplant
1 teaspoon coarse (kosher) salt
4 tablespoons olive oil
1 cup chopped onion
½ cup chopped green bell pepper
½ cup chopped red bell pepper
¾ cup chopped celery
2 cups drained canned plum tomatoes, chopped (reserve the
    juice)
½ teaspoon coarsely ground black pepper
½ teaspoon dried oregano
½ teaspoon dried basil
1 tablespoon minced garlic
1 tablespoon chopped fresh Italian (flat-leaf) parsley
½ cup chopped pitted Calamata or Gaeta olives
2 tablespoons capers, drained

1. Place the eggplant in a colander, sprinkle it with the coarse salt, and let it drain for 1 hour.

2. Heat 2 tablespoons of the oil in a large flame-proof casserole or dutch oven. Pat the eggplant dry with paper towels, and add it to the casserole. Sauté over medium heat until soft and lightly browned, 10 minutes. Using a slotted spoon, remove the eggplant and set it aside. Add the remaining oil, then the onion, bell peppers, and celery to the casserole. Sauté over medium heat until the vegetables are softened, 10 minutes. Return the eggplant to the casserole.

3. Add the tomatoes, pepper, oregano, basil, garlic, parsley, olives, and capers. Simmer until the vegetables are tender, 45 minutes. If the mixture starts sticking while cooking, add the reserved juice from the tomatoes in small amounts. Serve hot or at room temperature.

4 cups

CAPONATA
—♥—

Caponata is an Italian ratatouille with very similar ingredients—basically tomato, eggplant, onion, garlic, black and green olives, red peppers, and artichoke hearts. Traditionally, each vegetable is cooked separately in olive oil to its optimum point, seasoned with herbs, and then combined with the others. We've broken tradition in *The New Basics* and melded the ingredients from the start. We think it's tastier than ever!

Caponata can be served warm or at room temperature (never cold, for the flavors won't be at their best). In Italy it is often served as part of an antipasto platter, but we don't like to limit it. Begin by using it as a bed for slivered sausages or poached eggs for a first course; or serve it with crusty bread, a green salad, and olives for lunch. Let your imagination soar.

TAPENADE SANS ANCHOVIES

We've made a less salty tapenade by eliminating the intense flavor of anchovies. Serve on toasted crostini alongside summer ripe tomatoes or mix with a bit of Light Lemon Mayonnaise and spread over thin slices of cold roasted veal.

1 cup pitted Niçoise or other black imported olives
1 tablespoon minced garlic
1 tablespoon capers, drained
3 tablespoons extra virgin olive oil
1 can (3¼ ounces) tuna packed in oil, drained
Juice of ½ lemon

Combine the olives, garlic, and capers in a food processor, and process to form a paste. With the motor still running, slowly add the olive oil through the feed tube and blend thoroughly. Then add the tuna and lemon juice, and continue processing until smooth.

1 cup

ELEGANT EGGPLANT CAVIAR

We love serving a bit of this full-flavored "caviar" on the end of crisp Belgian endive leaves, atop soft scrambled eggs for brunch, or spread on grilled peasant bread toast.

1 eggplant
½ cup walnut pieces
¼ cup minced onion
¼ cup minced fresh parsley
1 to 2 teaspoons minced hot finger chile pepper, depending on taste
1 clove garlic, minced
½ teaspoon salt
Freshly ground black pepper, to taste
2 tablespoons extra virgin olive oil
1 tablespoon fresh lemon juice

1. Prick the eggplant in several places with a fork. Place it on a microwave-safe dish and cook at full power (650 to 700 watts), uncovered, until soft and collapsed, 10 minutes. Set it aside to cool.
2. Arrange the walnut pieces on another microwave-safe dish and cook, uncovered, until fragrant and toasted, 2½ minutes. Chop fine.
3. Scrape the eggplant flesh into a wooden chopping bowl and coarsely chop.
4. Stir in the walnuts, onion, parsley, chile pepper, garlic, salt, and pepper. Then slowly beat in the oil and lemon juice. Adjust the seasonings if necessary.
5. Cover loosely and let stand at room temperature for several hours before serving.

1½ cups

Note: This recipe was cooked on High (full power,

650 to 700 watts) in a carousel microwave, using microwave-safe containers.

If your microwave is less powerful, you will have to allow for more cooking time (approximately 1½ times the amount called for—but watch carefully); if it does not have a carousel, you may have to rotate the dish while it is cooking.

BERTA'S CHOPPED LIVER

When Sheila's mother has the whole family over for Passover, she makes chopped liver to serve with drinks. Everyone eats so much of it, they barely have room for dinner. This is a once-a-year treat. Serve with plain crackers.

1 pound chicken livers
¼ cup rendered chicken fat (see page 279)
2 large onions, coarsely chopped
1 hard-cooked egg, coarsely chopped
Salt and freshly ground black pepper, to taste

1. Clean the chicken livers well. Bring a medium-size saucepan of water to a boil, and add the livers. Reduce the heat and simmer for 10 minutes. Drain and reserve.
2. Heat the chicken fat in a medium-size skillet. Add the onions and cook until wilted and lightly browned, 20 minutes. Remove from the heat.
3. Cut the chicken livers into small pieces and place them in a bowl. Add the onions and chicken fat, egg, and salt and pepper. Mix well.
4. Place the mixture in a food processor and pulse until it is almost smooth. Do not overprocess, as it should have a bit of texture. Transfer the mixture to a bowl and refrigerate, covered. (This can be made a day ahead.) Remove from the refrigerator 30 minutes before serving.

2 cups

Note: Chopped liver freezes well. Defrost it in the refrigerator one day before serving.

ANCHOVIES
★

In this country, we buy almost all our anchovies packed in oil or salt. In Italy or France, anchovies are more frequently served fresh and are very popular. Some fresh anchovies are available in this country, but the supply is extremely limited, as fresh anchovies are very fragile and have a shelf life of only about 48 hours.

Look for anchovies packed in good olive oil. Once you've opened a tin or jar of anchovies, store those you don't use covered with olive oil in the refrigerator, where they will keep perfectly for several months. If you buy them in salt, rinse them well before using.

BASIL ANCHOIDE

Serve this as a dipping sauce for a selection of vegetables—carrots, celery, haricots verts, cauliflower, zucchini, and hard-cooked eggs. For a truly wonderful crudité assortment, team it with a Tapenade served with toasted peasant bread and cherry tomatoes.

4 cloves garlic
3 cups loosely packed basil leaves
½ cup pine nuts (pignoli) toasted (see Index)
1 cup fresh Italian (flat-leaf) parsley leaves
2 cans (2 ounces each) anchovy fillets, drained
½ to ⅔ cup olive oil

1. Mash the garlic with the blade of a large knife.

2. Combine the basil, pine nuts, parsley, and anchovies in a food processor and purée. Add the garlic. With the motor running, pour in enough oil through the feed tube to make the mixture smooth, but not runny.

1½ cups

GUACAMOLE

Americans love the taste and buttery texture of avocados and always seem to finish off a bowl of guacamole, no matter how large. There really have not been many recipes using this fruit in other ways until recently. With southwestern cooking becoming so popular, the avocado becomes very versatile. For those who prefer a pure taste with just a bit of kick, we've made a very basic version of this dish (kids love this too). For those who love Hot Stuff, we've added jalapeños, garlic, more than a dash of Tabasco and fresh cilantro. If you can find fresh Mexican oregano, substitute it for the cilantro for a change of taste.

OLE GUACAMOLE

2 ripe avocados, halved and pitted
4 teaspoons fresh lemon juice
1 large ripe plum tomato, seeded and chopped
1 tablespoon chopped red onion
Salt and freshly ground black pepper, to taste
Dash of Tabasco or hot pepper sauce

1. Scoop the avocados into a bowl. Add the lemon juice, and mash the avocados coarsely.

2. With a fork, gently mix in the tomato, onion, salt and pepper, and Tabasco sauce. Serve within an hour or two at room temperature.

About 1½ cups

GUACAMOLE IS HOT!

3 large cloves garlic
1 jalapeño pepper, cored, seeded, and chopped
3 ripe avocados, peeled, halved, and pitted
3 tablespoons fresh lemon juice
2 plum tomatoes, seeded and chopped
2 scallions (green onions), white bulb and 3 inches green, diced
1 teaspoon Tabasco sauce
½ teaspoon salt
1 teaspoon freshly ground black pepper
2 tablespoons chopped cilantro (fresh coriander)

1. In a food processor, with the motor running, drop the garlic and jalapeño pepper down the feed tube. Process until finely chopped.

2. Add 1½ avocados and the lemon juice, and process until smooth. Transfer the mixture to a bowl.

3. Add the remaining avocados to the bowl and mash with a wooden spoon. Add the tomatoes, scallions, Tabasco, salt, pepper, and cilantro. Mix thoroughly with a fork. Serve within an hour or two at room temperature.

2 cups

HANDLING HOT PEPPERS

Hot peppers contain oils that can easily burn sensitive skin. When working with them, it is important to remember never to rub or touch your mouth, nose, ears, or eyes. And, when you are finished, be sure to wash your hands thoroughly with soap and water before continuing with a recipe. (Some people prefer wearing thin rubber gloves when working with hot peppers.)

THINK PESTO

Pesto comes from the Italian word *pestare*, meaning to pound or bruise. A handful of herbs or greens, a few nuts, a clove or two of garlic, and a little salt are placed in a mortar and ground to a paste with the pestle. Sharp, dry cheese is pounded in, then olive oil is beaten in with a wooden spoon or whisk. Most of us find it easier to make pesto in a blender or food processor, but these machines can overwork the tender leaves. If you are making just a small batch or want a truly superb pesto, make it the classic way—in a mortar with a pestle—if only once.

Basil pesto has become nearly as familiar as tomato sauce, but pestos also can be made with cilantro, mint, sage, parsley, arugula, and sorrel. Updating the term pesto even further, we use it to mean a group of concentrates of garlic, black beans, red beans, and sun-dried tomatoes. We like to have these flavor concentrates in the refrigerator and use them as dips and by the tablespoon to enhance a sauce, soup, or stew. They can also be frozen in an ice cube tray for longer storage.

▲ Use them to zip up sandwiches
▲ Spread them on pizza or nachos as a basic sauce
▲ Add a dash to a baked potato with butter or oil
▲ Lightly spread inside or under the skin of poultry before roasting
▲ Blend with butter and serve with grilled fish

BASIL PESTO

This puréed basil base makes a perfect *crostini* spread, or you can add ground pine nuts and Parmesan for a truly lush pesto.

4 cloves garlic, minced
2 cups fresh basil leaves, rinsed
    and thoroughly dried
⅓ cup extra virgin olive oil
½ teaspoon salt
½ teaspoon freshly ground black pepper

1. Place the garlic and basil in the bowl of a food processor. With the motor running, slowly drizzle in the oil through the feed tube, and process until the basil is puréed.
2. Transfer the pesto to a bowl and stir in the salt and pepper. Refrigerate, covered, until ready to use. This keeps in the refrigerator for 2 to 3 days.

¾ cup

CILANTRO PESTO

Dab this intense flavored pesto atop Black Bean Nachos, spoon a bit into guacamole, or spread lightly on a chicken fajita.

2 cups cilantro (fresh coriander) leaves
3 cloves garlic, minced
1 tablespoon fresh lemon juice
¼ cup extra virgin olive oil
½ teaspoon salt
½ teaspoon freshly ground black pepper

1. Place the cilantro leaves and garlic in the bowl of a food processor. With the motor running, slowly drizzle the lemon juice and the oil through the feed tube, processing until the cilantro is puréed.
2. Transfer the pesto to a bowl and stir in the salt and pepper. Refrigerate, covered, until ready to use. This will keep in the refrigerator for 2 days.

½ cup

RED BEAN PESTO

Blue corn chips, guacamole, and sour cream are perfect accompaniments for this nicely spiced bean paste.

5 ounces dried red kidney beans
2 cloves garlic
1 jalapeño pepper, cored and seeded
¼ cup water
½ cup corn oil
1 ½ teaspoons cider vinegar
½ teaspoon paprika
½ teaspoon freshly ground black pepper
¼ teaspoon chili powder
¼ teaspoon salt
Dash of Tabasco sauce

1. Cover the beans with cold water and soak overnight.

2. Drain the beans, place them in a saucepan, and cover with cold water. Bring to a boil, then lower the heat and simmer until the beans are tender, about 45 minutes. Drain, and cool completely.

3. In the bowl of a food processor, chop the garlic and jalapeño pepper. Add the beans. With the motor running, process the beans while slowly pouring the water and oil through the feed tube. Add the remaining ingredients and process until smooth. Adjust the seasonings to taste.

1 ½ cups

BLACK BEAN PESTO

These beans make a hot and spicy spread. Also use them in place of the red bean paste in the Three Layer Mexican Dip, or serve them in fajitas or on nachos. Black Bean Pesto can also be heated through and served as a side dish, garnished with sour cream and cilantro.

8 ounces dried black beans
1 quart water
1 bay leaf
1 ham hock
2 jalapeño peppers, seeded
2 cloves garlic
Stems from 1 bunch of cilantro (fresh coriander)
Salt and freshly ground pepper (optional)

1. Rinse and drain the beans thoroughly. Place them in a large saucepan or soup kettle, and add all the remaining ingredients. Bring to a boil, then reduce the heat and simmer, uncovered, for 1½ hours.

2. Remove and discard the ham hock and bay leaf. Using a slotted spoon, transfer the bean mixture, in batches, to the bowl of a food processor. Process, adding cooking liquid as necessary to form a smooth, thick paste. You will use a total of about 1 cup liquid.

3. Transfer the pesto to a bowl and stir in the salt and pepper, if needed. Refrigerate, covered, until ready to use. This will keep in the refrigerator for 2 to 3 days.

3 cups

> "**P**esto is the quiche of the '80s."
>
> —NORA EPHRON

ROASTED GARLIC PESTO

Sweetened from roasting, our garlic purée is splendid stirred into prepared mayonnaise for an instant aïoli. It also works wonders if rubbed under the skin of poultry before baking or added in a tiny amount to fluffy mashed potatoes.

15 heads garlic
2 tablespoons extra virgin olive oil
⅓ cup water

   1. Preheat the oven to 350°F.
   2. Remove the papery outer skin from the garlic heads, leaving the clusters of cloves intact.
   3. Brush a shallow roasting pan with 1 tablespoon of the oil. Place the garlic in the pan, and add the remaining oil and the water.
   4. Bake until the garlic cloves are very tender, 1 hour. If necessary, add a bit more water as they cook.
   5. Remove the garlic from the oven and allow to cool completely.
   6. Separate the cloves of garlic and pass them through a food mill. Discard the skins. (You may also slip the cloves out of their skins and purée them in a blender or food processor.) Refrigerate, tightly covered, until ready to use. This will keep in the refrigerator for 1 to 2 days.
   2 cups

FREEZING PESTO

All our pestos can be frozen in plastic containers for future use. They can also be frozen in ice cube trays; transfer the cubes to plastic bags and keep them in the freezer. They'll be perfect for flavoring sauces.

SUN-DRIED TOMATO PESTO

Spread this earthy flavored pesto on toasted *crostini*, use it to add depth to tomato soup, or mix it with a bit of mayonnaise and serve with grilled tuna steaks.

2½ tablespoons extra virgin olive oil
4 cloves garlic, minced
1 can (28 ounces) Italian plum tomatoes in purée
1 cup drained sun-dried tomatoes packed in oil, coarsely
   chopped, oil reserved
½ teaspoon salt
½ teaspoon freshly ground black pepper

   1. Heat the olive oil in a saucepan. Add the garlic, and cook gently for 3 minutes. Do not allow it to brown.
   2. Crush the plum tomatoes slightly, and add them, along with their purée, to the saucepan. Simmer, uncovered, over low heat until very thick, about 1 hour.
   3. Remove the pan from the heat and add the sun-dried tomatoes. Let the mixture rest, 5 minutes.
   4. Transfer the mixture to a food processor and process until smooth, slowly adding ¼ cup of the reserved sun-dried tomato oil through the feed tube. Transfer the pesto to a bowl and stir in the salt and pepper. Refrigerate, covered, until ready to use. This will keep in the refrigerator for 3 to 4 days.
   2½ cups

PEANUT PESTO

Serve our peanut paste as a dip for cocktail-size skewers of beef and chicken or thin it with a bit of broth and use it to sauce a pork roast. For a terrific quick first course, toss peanut paste with hot pasta and garnish the dish with chopped scallions.

1 cup unsalted roasted peanuts
½ cup soy sauce
¼ cup honey
⅓ cup water
3 cloves garlic, minced
½ cup sesame oil
½ teaspoon freshly ground black pepper

Place the peanuts in the bowl of a food processor, and process until finely ground. With the motor running, add the remaining ingredients, one at a time, through the feed tube. Process until a thick, smooth paste has formed. Transfer the mixture to a bowl, cover, and refrigerate until ready to use. This will keep in the refrigerator for 3 days.

1 ½ cups

ROQUEFORT SPREAD

Delicious on top of English biscuits, such as Carr's Table Water, or toasted crusty French bread. Serve with a glass of tawny port.

8 ounces Roquefort cheese, crumbled, at room temperature
¼ cup tawny port
¼ cup coarsely chopped walnuts

Place the Roquefort in a mixing bowl and stir well with a wooden spoon. Add the port, and stir until fairly smooth. Fold in the walnuts. Cover loosely with plastic wrap, and chill for 2 hours before serving.

1 cup

FRESH STARTS
★

Long ago, we realized that any vegetable or fruit slice sturdy enough to hold up under a dollop of seafood salad or a slice of pâté can replace the cracker or toast point for canapés. Consider slices of cucumber, radish, apple, pear, zucchini, cooked crisp potato, beet, and baby squash; crisp endive and radicchio leaves, yellow and red cherry tomato halves. You can even use cookie cutters and go wild with shapes. But don't stop there. Use tender spinach or basil leaves to wrap up succulent shrimp or little fingers of poached fish. Turn snow peas or mushroom caps into little boats for a delicate creamy cheese or seafood mousse.

Some of our favorites are:

▲ Cucumber slices with minced shrimp or scallops
▲ Finely chopped chicken, lobster, crab, or shrimp salad on endive leaves
▲ Egg salad on cucumber slices, topped with a little caviar and dill
▲ Curried shrimp or chicken salad on cucumber slices
▲ Snow peas stuffed with Boursin
▲ Pâté on apple or pear slices
   ▲ Shrimp wrapped with snow peas
   ▲ Tabbouleh on hollowed out cucumber or zucchini wedges
   ▲ Poached salmon wrapped in spinach leaves

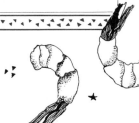

HERBED CHÈVRE BITES

We love cheese rolled in nuts and herbs—a great way to whet any appetite.

11 ounces chèvre, preferably Montrachet
1 tablespoon heavy or whipping cream
¼ cup finely chopped walnuts
¼ cup finely chopped fresh Italian (flat-leaf) parsley

1. In a bowl, mix the chèvre and cream thoroughly. Shape into rounded teaspoon-size balls, about ¾ inch in diameter.
2. Combine the walnuts and parsley in a shallow dish. Roll the cheese balls in the mixture, and chill, loosely covered, 2 to 3 hours before serving. Arrange on a plate or a flat basket decorated with lemon leaves.
12 hors d'oeuvres

Bowls of little red radishes are a classic summertime hors d'oeuvre in France. They are traditionally dipped into softened butter, then salt and served with small toasts and fresh young scallions. We like to leave an inch or two of stem and some pretty leaves at the top to use as a handle.

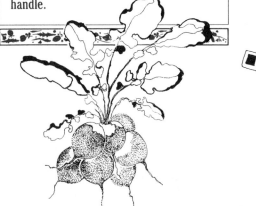

CANDACE'S BASIL CHEESE LOAF

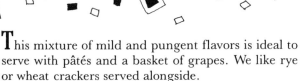

This mixture of mild and pungent flavors is ideal to serve with pâtés and a basket of grapes. We like rye or wheat crackers served alongside.

8 ounces cream cheese, at room temperature
4 ounces Roquefort cheese, at room temperature
1 cup loosely packed fresh spinach leaves, rinsed and thoroughly dried
¾ cup loosely packed fresh Italian (flat-leaf) parsley
¼ cup loosely packed fresh basil leaves
1 teaspoon minced garlic
¼ cup vegetable oil
¼ cup finely chopped walnuts
1 cup freshly grated Parmesan cheese
¼ cup slivered sun-dried tomatoes, patted dry

1. Combine the cream cheese and Roquefort in a bowl, and mix until smooth. Set aside.
2. Combine the spinach, parsley, basil, and garlic in the bowl of a food processor. With the motor running, slowly drizzle the oil through the feed tube; continue processing until smooth. Transfer the mixture to a bowl, add the walnuts and Parmesan, and mix thoroughly.
3. Line a 5½ x 2½-inch loaf pan with plastic wrap, leaving extra wrap hanging over the sides.
4. Spread one third of the cheese mixture evenly over the bottom of the pan. Next, spread half the pesto mixture, and arrange a layer of sun-dried tomatoes on top. Repeat the cheese, pesto, and tomato layers. Finish with the remaining third of the cheese mixture. Cover with the overhanging plastic wrap, and refrigerate for 24 hours.
5. To serve, allow the loaf to come just to room temperature, about 30 minutes. Invert it onto a platter, and provide a cheese-slicing knife. Have a basket of crackers and bread nearby.
6 to 8 portions

ONE BITE BREAD CUPS

These bite-size cups are just the right containers for vegetable, cheese, or pâté fillings.

12 very thin slices white bread
3 tablespoons olive oil (see Note)

1. Preheat the oven to 425°F.
2. Trim the crusts from the bread. Roll the bread slices with a rolling pin until very flat.
3. Press a slice of bread carefully into each cup of a small-cup muffin tin (1½-inch size). If the bread tears, press it back together with your fingers. Trim away the excess with a knife or scalloped cookie cutter.
4. With a small pastry brush, brush the bread with the oil. Bake until the cups are brown and crisp, 10 minutes. Remove the tin from the oven and cool for 5 minutes before removing to a rack. Allow to cool completely.
12 cups
Note: For a variation, use flavored oils such as herb, garlic, or chile.

JALAPENO CHEESE BITES

Sharp Cheddar and Monterey Jack make perfect cocktail bites when spiked with jalapeños.

2 fresh jalapeño peppers, cored, seeded, and minced
1½ cups grated Monterey Jack cheese
1½ cups grated sharp Cheddar cheese
2 tablespoons minced cilantro (fresh coriander)

Combine the jalapeños and cheeses in a mixing bowl, and blend well. Shape the mixture into rounded teaspoon-size balls, about ¾ inch in diameter, and roll them in the cilantro. Chill, loosely covered, 2 to 3 hours hours before serving.
12 to 14 hors d'oeuvres

CHEDDAR CHUTNEY BITES

Roll these spicy cheese bites in sweet chopped pecans. They're irresistible.

3 cups grated sharp Cheddar cheese
¼ cup mango chutney (pieces finely chopped)
¼ cup finely chopped pecans

Combine the cheese and chutney in a mixing bowl, and blend well. Shape the mixture into round teaspoon-size balls, about ¾ inch in diameter. Roll the balls in the chopped pecans. Cover and chill 2 to 3 hours before serving.
24 hors d'oeuvres

CARPACCIO AND RADISH CANAPES

Small cocktail pumpernickel rounds enhance the flavor of tissue-paper-thin daikon radish and luscious beef carpaccio, all topped with a creamy horseradish mustard sauce. Add some watercress leaves under the carpaccio for a refreshing bite.

1 cup Horseradish Mustard Sauce (recipe follows)
36 slices cocktail pumpernickel rounds
1 small daikon radish, sliced tissue-paper-thin
8 ounces carpaccio
1 tablespoon snipped fresh chives

1. Spread the mustard sauce on the bread slices, reserving a small amount for garnish.
2. Lay a slice of daikon radish on the bread, then a slice of carpaccio. Top with a small dollop of reserved horseradish mustard sauce, and sprinkle with the chives.
36 canápes

HORSERADISH MUSTARD SAUCE

½ cup Dijon mustard
¼ cup sour cream
¼ cup prepared white horseradish, well drained

Mix all the ingredients until well blended. Cover, and refrigerate for several hours before serving.

1 cup

WATERS RUN WILD

We thought we were drinking lots more clear, cool, wet water these days than ever before until we discovered that Caesar favored the water from Vichy, Michelangelo that from Fiuggi, and Peter the Great that from Bru in Belgium. Some prefer it from the tap, some in the bottle *sans gasse*, while still others want theirs to effervesce. Once we've found our water, we all seem to want our brand and nothing else.

Restaurants usually stock several waters, and water bars that carry hundreds of brands and conduct water tastings have sprung up on the West Coast (where over half of all the bottled water in America is consumed).

It's smart today to stock your bar with two or three types of water: a still, a bubbly, and perhaps one or two flavored with citrus. They may lighten a cocktail, spark a red or white wine spritzer, soften a fruit juice, or be served cool and crystal clear with just a twist or wedge of lemon or lime. On the top of our list are Evian and Vittel, but sparklers from natural French and Italian springs aren't far behind—Perrier and San Pellegrino.

SCANAPES

Serve these tidbits with shots of aquavit straight from the freezer and icy cold beer—that's the Scandinavian way.

8 ounces pickled herring fillets
¼ cup aquavit, chilled
¼ teaspoon sugar
Freshly ground black pepper, to taste
12 to 15 slices thin-sliced whole-grain or pumpernickel bread
¼ cup Caraway Dill Butter (recipe follows)
1 tart green apple, such as Granny Smith
Fresh dill sprigs, for garnish

1. Cut the herring fillets into 1-inch squares.
2. In a shallow bowl, toss the herring, aquavit, sugar, and pepper. Cover, and refrigerate 3 hours.
3. Cut the bread into small squares. Butter each with a very thin layer of Caraway Dill Butter.
4. Cut the apple into eight wedges, and cut each wedge crosswise in thin slices. Arrange three slices, overlapping, on each buttered bread square.
5. Drain the herring. Top each canapé with a square of herring and a sprig of dill.

50 canapés

CARAWAY DILL BUTTER

4 tablespoons (½ stick) unsalted butter, at room temperature
2 tablespoons chopped fresh dill
1 teaspoon caraway seeds, toasted and crushed (see Note)
1 teaspoon aquavit
¼ teaspoon salt
Freshly ground black pepper, to taste

Stir all the ingredients together in a small bowl. Cover, and refrigerate. The butter will keep for three days.

Note: Toast caraway seeds in a nonstick skillet over low heat, shaking the pan occasionally, until fragrant, 3 to 5 minutes.

¼ cup

> "**A** host is like a general: It takes a mishap to reveal his genius."
>
> —HORACE

POTTED MUSHROOMS

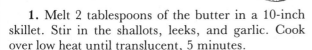

Make this on the day you plan to serve it—it will not hold longer than a day.

5 tablespoons unsalted butter
⅓ cup minced shallots
⅓ cup minced leeks, white part only
2 cloves garlic, minced
8 ounces cultivated mushrooms, finely chopped
2 teaspoons fresh thyme leaves
10 ounces fresh shiitake mushrooms, stems removed (reserve for another use), finely chopped
1 tablespoon finely snipped fresh chives
½ teaspoon salt
Freshly ground black pepper, to taste
Toast points, for serving

1. Melt 2 tablespoons of the butter in a 10-inch skillet. Stir in the shallots, leeks, and garlic. Cook over low heat until translucent, 5 minutes.

2. Add the cultivated mushrooms and the thyme. Cook, stirring occasionally, until the mushroom liquid has evaporated and the mixture is just moist, 10 minutes. Transfer the mixture to a bowl.

3. Add the remaining 3 tablespoons butter to the skillet, and stir in the shiitake mushrooms. Cook, stirring, until they are just beginning to stick to the pan, 5 minutes.

4. Pour off any juices that have accumulated in the bowl, and add the shiitakes to the mushroom mixture. Stir well, and season with the chives, salt, and pepper. Serve at room temperature accompanied by fresh toast points.

2 cups

SPICY POTTED SHRIMP

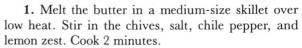

Lots and lots of shrimp—chunky yet spreadable. We've taken this traditionally English dish and spiced it up with chiles and Tabasco. Serve with toast points kept warm in pretty linen napkins.

5 tablespoons clarified butter (see Index)
1 tablespoon minced chives
¾ teaspoon salt
½ tiny hot fresh chile pepper, seeded and minced
½ teaspoon grated lemon zest
8 ounces medium-size shrimp, shelled, deveined, and coarsely chopped
Dash of Tabasco sauce (optional)

1. Melt the butter in a medium-size skillet over low heat. Stir in the chives, salt, chile pepper, and lemon zest. Cook 2 minutes.

2. Add the shrimp to the skillet and cook, stirring, over low heat for 3 minutes. Check the seasonings and add the Tabasco. Transfer to the bowl of a food processor and purée coarsely.

3. Pack the mixture into ramekins or a small bowl. Cover with plastic wrap, pressing it against the surface of the shrimp. Chill 4 hours or overnight.

1¼ cups

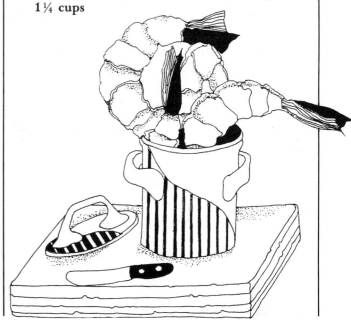

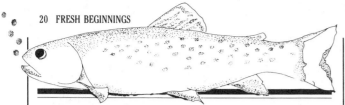

SMOKED TROUT MOUSSE

A delicate, smoky mousse to serve atop cucmber or black bread slices, or to offer as an accompaniment with crudités. It is also delicious on a bed of greens as a first course, spooned atop a grilled or broiled trout fillet with sliced tomato and purple onion, or as a full-blown black bread sandwich. In fact, we've found that this mousse is addictive!

1 cup ricotta cheese
1 cup coarsely flaked smoked trout
2 tablespoons prepared horseradish, drained
2 tablespoons chopped scallions (green onions)
1 tablespoon chopped fresh dill
2 teaspoons fresh lemon juice
Salt and freshly ground black pepper, to taste

1. In the bowl of a food processor, purée the ricotta until smooth (the consistency of sour cream). Scrape it into a bowl.

2. Fold in half the trout, then the horseradish, scallions, dill, and lemon juice. Season with salt and pepper, and fold in the remaining trout. Chill in small crocks.

2 cups

SALMON MOUSSE

This pâté is light, pretty, refreshing, and one of those foods that you enjoy time after time. It's been a favorite of ours for years. Serve it on toasts, black bread, or crackers.

1 envelope unflavored gelatin
¼ cup cold water
½ cup boiling water
½ cup mayonnaise
1 tablespoon fresh lemon juice
1 tablespoon finely grated onion
Dash of Tabasco sauce
¼ teaspoon sweet paprika
1 teaspoon salt
2 tablespoons finely chopped fresh dill
2 cups finely flaked poached fresh salmon or canned salmon, skin and bones removed
1 cup heavy or whipping cream

1. Soften the gelatin in the cold water in a large mixing bowl. Stir in the boiling water and whisk the mixture slowly until the gelatin has dissolved. Cool to room temperature.

2. Whisk in the mayonnaise, lemon juice, grated onion, Tabasco, paprika, salt, and dill. Stir to blend completely, and refrigerate until the mixture begins to thicken slightly, about 20 minutes.

3. Fold in the salmon. In a separate bowl, whip the cream until it is fluffy and forms peaks. Fold it gently into the salmon mixture.

4. Transfer the mixture to a 6- to 8-cup bowl or decorative mold. Cover, and chill for at least 4 hours.

12 or more portions

OYSTERS FIVE WAYS

A mini raw bar is a colorful way to present oysters. Line a large 2-inch-deep serving dish with chopped ice. Beg some seaweed from your fishmonger or use fresh rosemary, and arrange it over the ice. Place freshly opened oysters decoratively over the seaweed. Garnish with lemon wedges and a few pretty flowers. Place small bowls of the five sauces around the platters. Be sure to place a bowl nearby for shells.

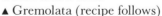

THE SAUCES

▲ Gremolata (recipe follows)
▲ Bloody Mary Sauce (recipe follows)
▲ Mignonette Sauce (recipe follows)
▲ Fresh Beet Horseradish (recipe follows)
▲ Golden American caviar

Spoon ¼ teaspoon of any of the various accompaniments on an oyster, and serve one or two of each on a small plate.

A RAW BAR

A raw bar of the freshest clams and oysters dazzles cocktail guests with hardly any effort on your part. Use trays, large baking sheets, a zinc bar, giant clam shells, oversize copper washtubs, halved wooden barrels, or plastic-lined baskets, and chock them full of crushed ice. Sprinkle the ice with seaweed, fresh herbs, and wild flowers. Shuck the clams and oysters and arrange them on the half shell on the ice. Tuck shells filled with toppings here and there. Include Mignonette Sauce, Gremolata, minced tomatoes, caviar, lemon and lime wedges, spicy cocktail sauce, and minced chile peppers, and have a good many pepper grinders about.

If a raw bar is grand for six, it's spectacular for sixty. Make it a splendid array of fruits from the sea and add cooked, but cold, scallops and mussels in shells, periwinkles, crawfish, and shrimp. For a "the-more-the-merrier" crowd, it's great to have waiters behind the raw bar shucking shells afresh.

Mountains of hot french fries and buckets of Champagne on ice go perfectly.

radishes with butter are great!

You can add cooked scallops

Don't forget to serve lots of lemon

cooked shrimp

cooked mussels

lemon juice

some cracked ice

clams

a bed of seaweed

oysters

horseradish sauce

a decorative bowl or tub

tartar sauce

mustard sauce

mignonette sauce

GREMOLATA

2 tablespoons chopped fresh Italian (flat-leaf) parsley
Finely grated zest of 1 lemon
2 cloves garlic, minced

Combine the parsley, lemon zest, and garlic in a small bowl and mix well.

¼ cup

BLOODY MARY SAUCE

¼ cup tomato purée
2 tablespoons vodka, chilled
1 teaspoon fresh lime juice
¼ teaspoon celery seeds
Pinch of salt
Freshly ground black pepper

Combine the tomato purée, chilled vodka, lime juice, celery seeds, and salt in a small bowl. Add a generous amount of black pepper, and stir.

¼ cup

MIGNONETTE SAUCE

¾ cup tarragon vinegar
2 tablespoons finely chopped shallots
1 jalapeño pepper, minced, with seeds
1 teaspoon grated lemon zest
½ teaspoon salt
¼ teaspoon freshly ground black pepper
½ ripe plum tomato, minced

Stir all the ingredients together in a small bowl. Cover, and chill until ready to serve.

1 cup

FRESH BEET HORSERADISH

1 cup grated peeled fresh horseradish (see Note)
1 small beet, cooked, peeled, and grated
2 tablespoons white vinegar
1 teaspoon sugar

Combine all the ingredients in a small bowl and stir well. Cover and refrigerate. This will keep for at least 2 weeks.

1 cup

Note: When working with fresh horseradish, keep in mind that the fumes are extremely strong and can overwhelm you. Keep your face far from the fumes.

SORREL MAYONNAISE

Lemony tart sorrel combined with the flavor of tarragon balance well in a lovely mayonnaise that is wonderful with crudités.

2 egg yolks
3 ounces fresh sorrel, washed, trimmed, and coarsely chopped
   (about 1 cup packed leaves)
2 tablespoons fresh tarragon leaves
2 tablespoons tarragon-flavored vinegar
½ teaspoon salt
Freshly ground black pepper, to taste
1 cup vegetable oil

Place the egg yolks in the container of a food processor and add the sorrel, tarragon, vinegar, salt, and pepper. Process until thick and smooth. With the motor running, slowly add the oil in a very thin stream through the feed tube, blending until incorporated. Transfer to a bowl, cover, and refrigerate. This mayonnaise will keep for 2 days.

1½ cups

THE CRUDITE CROWD

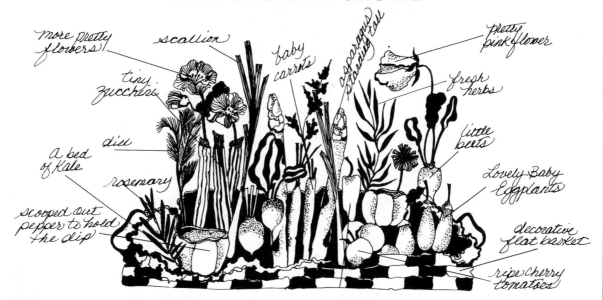

more pretty flowers!

scallion

tiny zucchini

baby carrots

asparagus standing tall

pretty pink flower

fresh herbs

dill

little beets

a bed of kale

rosemary

Lovely Baby Eggplants

scooped out pepper to hold the dip

decorative flat basket

ripe cherry tomatoes

With new vegetables showing up at the green market and in our ever-larger gardens, party crudités are more glorious than ever. Before you market, decide on your general color scheme and the container for the crudités. We prefer broad, flat dishes for the most dramatic presentation, but don't overlook other choices: a basket, an antique silver tray, a shallow copper pan, a Chinese bamboo steamer, a majolica ice bucket, a Lucite bowl, a lacquer tray.

AT THE MARKET

▲ Select two or three vegetables to be scooped out to act as containers for dips. They should stand up sturdily and contribute color. Try red cabbage, sweet peppers, or round squash.

▲ Purchase ¼ to ⅓ pound of each vegetable per person. That's generous, but the crudités should be lush, and there's always salad or soup to be made the next day with the leftovers.

▲ Buy a garnish, too. Scallions or chives, flowering herbs, vivid fruit, or delicate wild flowers tucked amid the vegetables help enliven them.

ASSEMBLY

▲ Line the container, if necessary to protect it, with foil or plastic wrap. Then arrange a blanket of greens over the bottom and let them spill over the sides. You can use red cabbage, kale, spinach, grape leaves, or any hearty green.

▲ Hollow out the vegetables that will hold the dips and nestle them in the greens.

▲ Use a mixture of blanched and raw vegetables in the assortment.

▲ Cut the larger vegetables into slices or strips and separate leaves so they all can be picked up and eaten easily.

▲ Arrange the vegetables in separate clumps to look the way they do when they are growing: baby carrots, beets, and radishes with their leafy tops on, asparagus set on end, mushrooms intact but with stems trimmed, squash "handles" left on, and new potatoes in their skins.

▲ At the very end, add the garnish. A little here, a little there, in varying textures and heights, emphasizes the natural garden look, but a single nosegay of herbs and flowers tucked off center among leafy greens is smashing, too.

HOMEMADE MAYONNAISE

During the reign of Henry IV of France, a sauce that had no other name than "cold sauce" was popular. One day, the Duke of Mayenne refused to leave his chicken salad with cold sauce to go to battle. France lost the battle, but the sauce, now named mayonnaise after the duke, became legendary.

Whether this tale is true or nothing but a culinary joke, it won't make any sense at all if the only mayonnaise you've ever tasted is store-bought. Homemade mayonnaise is so far superior to even the best commercial product, it's a wonder they share the same name. We find many cooks are afraid of making mayonnaise, so they never get to enjoy the real thing. Too bad, because making mayonnaise is really very easy.

Mayonnaise is simply an emulsion in which oil is suspended in egg yolks. The trick is to keep the suspension from breaking. The oil must be added very slowly in the beginning until the emulsion is established. Then the remaining oil is added in spoonfuls, and each spoonful is absorbed before another is added. Each egg yolk can absorb only ¾ cup of oil; if you add more than that, the emulsion will break and the ingredients will separate. But even then all is not lost. You can begin again with another egg yolk and add the broken mayonnaise first by drops and then by spoonfuls, as you did the oil in the first batch. Success is yours if you start with all the ingredients at room temperature and if you add the oil patiently and slowly.

Traditionalists rarely use a whisk, mixer, or food processor, using instead either a fork or a wooden spoon. But we use these gadgets because their performance is consistent. Home-made mayonnaise keeps in the refrigerator in a clean, covered jar for about a week. But it will probably disappear very quickly. For a basic home-made mayonnaise, see the index.

▲ **Apple-Horseradish Mayonnaise:** Mayonnaise with Granny Smith apple, lemon zest, fresh horseradish, and dill

▲ **Dill Mayonnaise:** Mayonnaise with Dijon mustard and lots of fresh dill

▲ **Rémoulade Sauce:** Mayonnaise with capers, cornichons, Dijon mustard, anchovy paste, parsley, and chives

▲ **Russian Dressing:** Mayonnaise with chili sauce, green pepper, pimiento, onion, horseradish, parsley, and cayenne

▲ **Sauce Aïoli:** Mayonnaise with crushed garlic cloves

▲ **Sauce Andalouse:** Mayonnaise with tomato and pimiento

▲ **Sauce Moutarde:** Mayonnaise with Dijon mustard

▲ **Sauce Niçoise:** Mayonnaise with tomato purée, red pepper, tarragon, and chives

▲ **Sauce Verte:** Mayonnaise with minced fresh greens, such as watercress, spinach, parsley, and/or scallions

▲ **Tartar Sauce:** Mayonnaise with sweet pickles, shallots, capers, parsley, tarragon, Dijon mustard, and lemon juice

▲ **Thousand Island Dressing:** Mayonnaise with chili sauce, green pepper, pimiento, chopped hard-cooked egg, and chives

▲ **Added extras:** Pink peppercorns, flavored vinegars, green chiles, pestos, citrus zest and juice, garlic, concentrated fruit juices, chutney, and sweet mustard all add sparkle to mayonnaise, too.

DILL MAYONNAISE

The perfect dip for lightly steamed asparagus spears.

1 whole egg
1 egg yolk
3 tablespoons fresh lemon juice
4 teaspoons Dijon mustard
¼ teaspoon salt
1½ cups oil, preferably safflower
⅓ cup chopped fresh dill

Combine the egg, egg yolk, lemon juice, mustard, and salt in the bowl of a food processor, and blend well. With the motor running, slowly add the oil through the feed tube. Then add the chopped dill and process just to mix well.

2 cups

GREEN GODDESS DIP

This classic dressing recipe is found in many cook-books. We prefer it a bit chunkier, to use as a dip, and have kept it out of the blender.

¾ cup mayonnaise
¾ cup sour cream
¼ cup fresh lemon juice
4 anchovy fillets, finely minced (optional)
¼ cup coarsely chopped fresh Italian (flat-leaf) parsley
1 clove garlic, finely minced
2 tablespoons thinly sliced scallions (green onions)
2 tablespoons snipped fresh chives
2 tablespoons finely chopped fresh tarragon leaves:
    or 2 teaspoons dried
Salt and freshly ground black pepper, to taste

Combine the mayonnaise, sour cream, and lemon juice in a bowl, and mix well. Stir in the remaining ingredients, and adjust the seasonings if necessary. Cover, and refrigerate for 3 to 4 hours before serving, so the flavors can mellow.

2 cups

RASPBERRY DIP

This blushing dip isn't shy, so don't you be. Try dipping vegetable favorites, shrimp or broiled chicken chunks, or drizzle the dip lightly over a berry or melon salad.

¾ cup fresh or frozen (thawed and drained) raspberries
¼ cup balsamic vinegar
¾ cup sour cream

1. Place the raspberries and vinegar in a small bowl and stir. Cover with plastic wrap and let sit for 30 minutes at room temperature.

2. Pour the raspberry mixture into the bowl of a food processor or blender, and process until smooth.

3. Place the sour cream in a medium-size serving bowl. Gently fold the raspberry mixture into the sour cream. Refrigerate until serving time.

About 1½ cups

SESAME DIP

Just right for asparagus or sugar snap peas.

1 egg yolk
½ cup sesame oil
½ cup corn oil
¼ cup soy sauce
1 teaspoon finely minced garlic
¼ cup peanut butter, at room temperature
1 tablespoon chile oil

1. Place the egg yolk in a medium-size bowl. Slowly add the sesame and corn oils, whisking constantly.

2. Add the soy sauce, garlic, peanut butter, and chile oil, and mix thoroughly. Chill, loosely covered, for at least 2 hours before serving.

1¾ cups

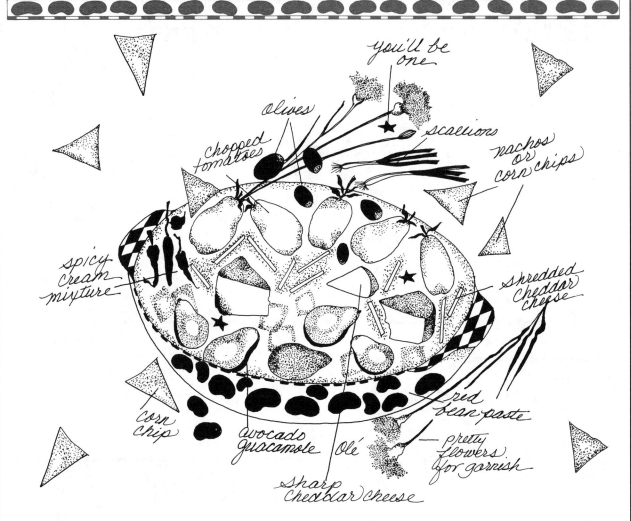

you'll be one

olives

chopped tomatoes

scallions

nachos or corn chips

spicy cream mixture

shredded Cheddar cheese

corn chip

avocado guacamole

Olé

red bean paste

pretty flowers for garnish

sharp Cheddar cheese

THREE LAYER MEXICAN DIP

A dip that everyone loves, it's simple to prepare ahead of time and bake at the last minute. Have plenty of taco chips on hand.

1 ½ cups Red Bean Pesto (see page 13)
1 ½ cups Guacamole (see page 11); use either version
1 ½ cups sour cream
½ teaspoon garlic powder
¼ teaspoon chili powder
¼ teaspoon ground cumin
¼ teaspoon salt
¼ teaspoon freshly ground black pepper

½ cup grated sharp Cheddar cheese
½ cup seeded and finely diced fresh plum tomatoes
¼ cup chopped pitted black olives
2 scallions (green onions), white bulb and 3 inches green, halved lengthwise and diced

1. Spread the bean pesto over the bottom of a 10-inch round glass baking dish. Cover it with the guacamole.

2. In a small bowl, combine the sour cream, garlic powder, chili powder, cumin, salt, and pepper. Mix thoroughly, and spread on top of guacamole.

3. Sprinkle the top with the cheese, tomatoes, olives, and scallions. Serve either chilled or hot (bake for 15 minutes in a preheated 425°F oven), with taco chips.

6 portions

DEVILED DEVILED EGGS

An American summertime tradition—a special treat in the era of cholesterol-watching. To make them even more so, we've spiced them up. Once in a while we have a devil-may-care attitude! Chile paste and Szechuan peppercorns are available in Asian grocery and vegetable markets.

6 hard-cooked eggs
¼ cup minced scallions (green onions)
3 tablespoons mayonnaise
2 teaspoons Dijon mustard
1 teaspoon soy sauce
1 teaspoon chile paste with garlic
1 teaspoon Szechuan peppercorns, toasted (see Note) and crushed
½ teaspoon sugar
Chopped scallions (green onions), for garnish

1. Shell the eggs and cut ¼ inch off the ends of each one; reserve these trimmings. Halve the eggs crosswise, and remove the yolks. Set the whites aside. Place the yolks and the trimmings in a bowl.
2. Add the remaining ingredients (except the chopped scallion garnish) to the bowl, and mash with a fork until just smooth but not mushy.
3. Spoon the mixture into the reserved whites, or pipe it in with a pastry tube. Sprinkle with the chopped scallions.

12 hors d'oeuvres

Note: Toast peppercorns in a small nonstick skillet over low heat, shaking the pan occasionally, until golden and fragrant, 3 to 5 minutes.

> "If you want to be witty, work on your character and say what you think on every occasion."
>
> —STENDHAL

CONFETTI NEW POTATOES

Potato salad in miniature. These pretty nibbles take some time to prepare, but your guests will love them, so be sure you make plenty.

20 small red new potatoes
2 ribs celery, finely chopped
2 scallions (green onions), white bulb and 3 inches green, quartered lengthwise and finely chopped
1 carrot, finely chopped
2 hard-cooked eggs, coarsely chopped
2 tablespoons finely chopped sweet gherkin pickles
4 tablespoons finely chopped fresh dill
2 tablespoons chopped fresh Italian (flat-leaf) parsley
½ teaspoon salt
¾ teaspoon coarsely ground black pepper
1 cup mayonnaise
1 cup sour cream

1. Fill a large saucepan with water, and bring to a boil. Drop the potatoes into the boiling water and cook until tender, 12 to 15 minutes. Drain, and set aside to cool.
2. When the potatoes are cool enough to handle, cut each in half. Cut a tiny slice off the bottom of each potato half so it can stand upright. Using the small scoop of a melon baller, very carefully scoop out the center of each potato half, leaving a firm potato shell. Place the scooped-out potato centers in a bowl. Reserve the shells.
3. Gently toss the potato centers with the celery, scallions, carrot, eggs, gherkins, 2 tablespoons of the dill, parsley, salt, and pepper.
4. Mix the mayonnaise and sour cream together, and fold into the potato salad. Adjust the seasonings, and with a small spoon, carefully mound into the potato shells.
5. Refrigerate, covered, until ready to serve. Sprinkle with the remaining 2 tablespoons dill before serving, and arrange on a decorative platter or in a flat basket.

40 hors d'oeuvres

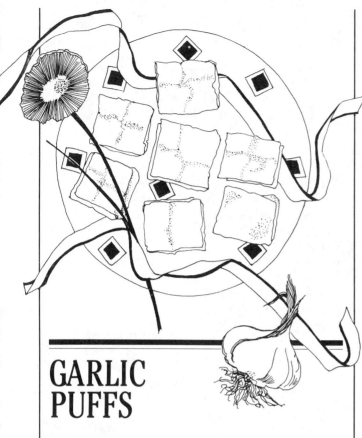

GARLIC PUFFS

Nutty, sweet garlic purée sandwiched between bite-size puff pastry squares. Great cocktail fare—plenty of flavor and light enough not to break an appetite.

*4 ounces fresh or frozen (thawed) puff pastry sheets**
½ cup Roasted Garlic Pesto (see page 14)
1 egg yolk
1 teaspoon water

1. Preheat the oven to 400°F.
2. Cut the puff pastry into four inch-wide strips. Roll out very thin (until about 2 inches wide). Prick all over with a fork.
3. Spread two pastry strips with the garlic pesto. Top with the remaining strips, and cut each strip "sandwich" crosswise into ten pieces. Arrange the puffs on baking sheets.
4. Mix the egg yolk and water together. With a pastry brush, brush each puff with egg wash. Bake until golden brown, 7 to 10 minutes.

20 puffs
*Available in the frozen foods section of most supermarkets.

DATE AND OLIVE WRAP-AROUNDS

These little hors d'oeuvres are cooked a dozen at a time, using any assortment of dried fruits. Figure one bacon slice is enough for four dried fruits. Assembly them early; then cook at the last minute.

Thin-sliced bacon
Pitted dates
Pitted prunes
Small dried figs
Dried apricot halves
Stuffed green olives

1. Halve each slice of bacon lengthwise and crosswise. One thin strip will be used for each hors d'oeuvre.
2. Cut each date, prune, and fig lengthwise through one side only, to open. Stuff each dried fruit with a small green olive, and wrap with a strip of bacon. Secure the bacon with a wooden toothpick.
3. Arrange 12 wrap-arounds around the inside edge of a 9-inch microwave-safe pie plate lined with a paper towel. Cook on full power (650 to 700 watts) uncovered, until the bacon is crisp, 5 to 6 minutes. Let stand 2 minutes; then drain on paper towels.
4. Repeat with the remaining ingredients, and serve.

Note: This recipe was cooked on High (full power, 650 to 700 watts) in a carousel microwave, using microwave-safe containers.

If your microwave is less powerful, you will have to allow for more cooking time (approximately 1½ times the amount called for—but watch carefully); if it does not have a carousel, you may have to rotate the dish while it is cooking.

> "The taste of an olive is older than meat, older than wine."
> —LAURENCE DURRELL

GORDON SINCLAIR'S ARTICHOKE FRITTERS

Trying to get a reservation at Gordon Restaurant was quite a feat—the phone line was constantly busy. We finally made it, though, and had a marvelous time at one of the hottest spots in Chicago. Gordon Sinclair has served these fritters since the restaurant opened in 1976. He says first-timers always order them because they've been much publicized. You'll see why.

1 cup unbleached all-purpose flour
1 teaspoon baking powder
Salt and freshly ground black pepper, to taste
1 cup milk
1 egg
1 teaspoon olive oil
3 cups corn or peanut oil
10 frozen artichoke hearts, thawed, drained, halved
    lengthwise, and patted dry
1 cup Béarnaise Sauce (see Index)

1. Combine the flour, baking powder, and salt and pepper in a mixing bowl. Mix well.
2. In another bowl, combine the milk, egg, and olive oil. Whisk this into the dry ingredients until well incorporated; do not overmix. Set the batter aside for 30 minutes.
3. Heat the corn oil to 375°F in a deep heavy skillet or flameproof casserole (see Note).
4. Using tongs, dip the artichoke hearts in the batter and then gently drop them in the hot oil. Fry a few at a time until golden brown, just a few seconds. Drain on paper towels and repeat with the remaining artichokes. Serve hot, with béarnaise sauce.

4 portions

Note: If you don't have a deep-fat thermometer, drop a 1-inch cube of bread in the oil. If it turns golden brown within 1 minute, the oil is hot enough. Remove the bread and proceed with the recipe.

FLORENCE FABRICANT'S GRILLED CUMIN SHRIMP

Florence found us months before we opened our little takeout food shop in 1977, when she was researching the renaissance of Columbus Avenue for a magazine article. What stumped us was her question, "And what have you decided on for a name, girls?" The girls hadn't, and Florence was under deadline. So, ever one to take the bull by the horns, Florence said, "Why don't you call it The Silver Palate," and it was sweetness to our ears.

About this recipe, Florence said, "When food was becoming my passion and was not yet my profession, my husband had a client in his law practice who gave him a sheaf of typewritten recipes. This was one of them. It has never failed to garner praise."

8 tablespoons (1 stick) unsalted butter
2 teaspoons ground turmeric
1½ teaspoons ground cumin
1 teaspoon ground coriander
1½ teaspoons salt
Juice of 2 lemons
2 pounds large shrimp, shelled and deveined

1. Preheat the broiler.
2. Melt the butter in a saucepan. Stir in the turmeric, cumin, coriander, salt, and lemon juice.
3. Arrange the shrimp in a single layer in a shallow broiling pan. Spread the butter mixture over them.
4. Broil under high heat until the shrimp are glazed and golden brown, about 8 minutes. Skewer with toothpicks and serve immediately.

12 hors d'oeuvres

CAJUN POPCORN

Though these are traditionally made with crawfish, we use shrimp. It's easy to prepare—and great with fresh Tartar Sauce.

1 pound large shrimp
1 cup unbleached all-purpose flour
1 tablespoon cayenne pepper
1 tablespoon chili powder
1 tablespoon ground cumin
1 teaspoon freshly ground black pepper
½ teaspoon salt
1 cup corn oil
Tabasco sauce, to taste

1. Peel and devein the shrimp. Cut them into ½-inch pieces.
2. Combine the flour, cayenne, chili powder, cumin, black pepper, and salt in a medium-size bowl.
3. Heat the oil in a large skillet. Dredge the shrimp in the flour mixture, shaking off any excess. Fry them quickly over high heat until brown and crisp, occasionally adding a dash of Tabasco for spice. Drain on paper towels, and serve immediately.

8 hors d'oeuvres

PLACES TO PARTY
~

Some of the best times are had in the most unusual places:

▲ In an art gallery
▲ In your kitchen
▲ On a boat
▲ On the beach under a full moon
▲ In a limousine on a mystery tour
▲ In the library—yours or theirs
▲ In a country barn
▲ In your office

BLACK BEAN NACHOS

These are hot! Serve them in wedges with drinks, or whole for lunch with some spicy guacamole on the side. Cool off with a chilled Dos Equis beer.

Corn oil
2 flour tortillas, 8 inches in diameter
2 chorizo or other spicy sausages
1 cup Black Bean Pesto (see page 13)
1 cup grated Monterey Jack cheese (see Note)
2 tablespoons chopped cilantro (fresh coriander)

1. Preheat the oven to 375°F.
2. Fill a medium-size heavy skillet with ½ inch corn oil. Heat it until the oil just starts to move. Then fry the tortillas, one at a time, until light golden brown, about 15 seconds on each side. Drain on paper towels.
3. Slice the chorizos into ¼-inch-thick rounds, and sauté them in a small skillet until crisp, about 5 minutes. Remove the sausages from the skillet, and drain on paper towels.
4. Place the tortillas on a baking sheet, and spread the pesto evenly over them. Arrange the sausage over the pesto, and sprinkle with the cheese. Top with the chopped cilantro.
5. Bake until brown, 20 minutes. Remove from the oven, and cut each tortilla into eight pieces. Serve immediately.

16 hors d'oeuvres

Note: Monterey Jack comes in several flavors—jalapeño, garlic, garlic and herb—as well as plain. Any one of them can be used.

RIO GRANDE NACHOS GRANDE

The first time we had nachos was in the old bar of the Jerome Hotel in Aspen—that was in the 1960s. Now the Jerome has been updated and upscaled, and we've learned to make nachos truly grand too, by adding broccoli, a fresh tomato sauce, and two kinds of cheese for a great meal. This is the way we think nachos deserve to be. If you wish yours a bit hotter, add a finely chopped jalapeño to the tomato sauce.

Corn oil
4 flour tortillas, 7½ to 8 inches in diameter
1 can (16 ounces) refried beans
2 cups broccoli florets, cooked
1 cup grated Monterey Jack cheese
1 cup grated sharp Cheddar cheese
1 cup Fresh Tomato Salsa (see Index)
2 jalapeño peppers, thinly sliced crosswise
2 scallions (green onions), white bulb and 3 inches green,
*   sliced thinly on the diagonal, for garnish*
1 cup sour cream (optional)

1. Preheat the oven to 350°F.

2. Fill a medium-sized skillet with ½ inch corn oil. Heat until the oil just starts to move, then fry the tortillas, one at a time, until light golden brown, about 15 seconds on each side. Drain on paper towels.

3. Arrange the tortillas on a baking sheet, and spread the refried beans evenly over them. Then layer the broccoli, both cheeses, and salsa over the beans. Arrange the jalapeño slices decoratively on top of the salsa. Bake until the cheese has melted and the nacho is heated through, 15 to 20 minutes.

4. Cut each tortilla into 6 wedges, but leave in a circle. Sprinkle with the sliced scallions and serve immediately. Pass the sour cream.

4 portions

NO MORE STICKY FINGERS

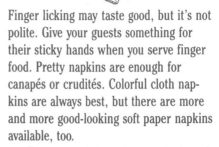

Finger licking may taste good, but it's not polite. Give your guests something for their sticky hands when you serve finger food. Pretty napkins are enough for canapés or crudités. Colorful cloth napkins are always best, but there are more and more good-looking soft paper napkins available, too.

For more substantial finger food, such as barbecued spareribs and chicken or shrimp in shells, finger bowls have stood the test of time. Use any small bowl and float a thin slice of lemon or a small flower in the water.

FRIED SPEARING

This dish, a quick tempura, can be made with any small fish such as whitebait, silversides, or spearing (fish about 3 inches long and ¼ inch thick).

5 tablespoons unbleached all-purpose flour
5 tablespoons cornstarch
⅔ cup water
1 teaspoon salt
Corn oil for deep-frying
1 pound spearing, whole and ungutted
Lemon wedges

1. Stir the flour, cornstarch, water, and salt together in a mixing bowl. Let stand 20 minutes.

2. Heat several inches of oil to 375°F in a deep-fryer.

3. Dip the fish in the batter; drain off any excess. Fry the fish in the hot oil until crisp and golden, 1 to 2 minutes. Drain on paper towels. Serve on a white cloth napkin with lots of lemon.

4 portions

THE WINE AND CHEESE PARTY

The wine and cheese party pairs fabulous food with wonderful drink. It's flexible—great for just a few or many, and it's brought off with minimum effort. If the party is small, buy almost as many cheeses as there are guests; if larger, figure on 4 to 6 ounces per guest, but buy whole cheeses or large pieces that weigh at least 12 ounces. Select as wide a range of cheeses as possible, from blue cheeses to goat cheeses to soft ripening to semihard to hard. Offer plenty of plain-tasting crackers or French bread, as well as apples, pears, and grapes, which go well with cheese.

If the cheeses and wines are to be brought out gradually, start with the mildest cheeses first and work up to the strongest ones. Or set up cheese and wine stations all about the room.

The following list is a general guide. Let your taste buds be the final judge.

CHEESE	WINE
BLUES	
Stilton	Ruby port
Roquefort	Beaujolais
Gorgonzola	Vino Nobile, Cabernet Sauvignon
Sweet Gorgonzola	Sauternes
Maytag Blue	Zinfandel
SOFT RIPENING	
Brie	Alsace Riesling, Bordeaux
Camembert	Merlot
Vacherin Mont d'Or	Cabernet Sauvignon, Pomerol
DOUBLE AND TRIPLE CREME	
L'Explorateur	Chardonnay
Brillat-Savarin	Beaujolais
St.-André	Tavel rosé, Pink Champagne
SEMIHARD CHEESES	
Appenzeller	Beaujolais
Cantal	Chardonnay
Cheddars	Beaujolais nouveau, Cabernet Sauvignon, tawny port

CHEESE	WINE
SEMISOFT CHEESES	
Morbier	Vouvray
Port-Salut	Mâcon-Villages
Reblochon	Beaujolais-Villages
Tomme de Savoie	Côtes du Rhône
Fontina	Chianti Classico
Munster	Alsace Riesling
Raclette	Alsace Riesling
Gouda	Red Rhône or Riesling
HARD CHEESES	
Parmigiano Reggiano	Vino Nobile, Barolo, Chianti Classico
Aged cow's-milk cheese	California Petite Sirah
Dry Jack cheese	Napa Gamay, Beaujolais
CHEVRES	
Montrachet	Zinfandel
Bucheron	Chardonnay
Banon	Sauvignon Blanc
Aged goat cheese	Sancerre
Crottin	Cabernet Sauvignon
Blue Capri	Beaujolais
Caprinio	Vin Santo

> "Champagne has the taste of an apple peeled with a steel knife."
> —ALDOUS HUXLEY

ROQUEFORT GOUGERES

Hot little cheese puffs are great with cocktails. Roquefort gives them a tangy and unexpected bite.

1 cup milk
8 tablespoons (1 stick) unsalted butter
1 teaspoon salt
1 cup sifted unbleached all-purpose flour
5 eggs
1½ cups slightly crumbled Roquefort cheese
2 tablespoons freshly grated Parmesan cheese

1. Preheat the oven to 375°F. Lightly butter a baking sheet.
2. Combine the milk, butter, and salt in a small saucepan, and bring to a boil. Remove the pan from the heat, and add the flour all at once. Whisk vigorously for a few minutes, then return the pan to medium heat and cook, stirring constantly, until the batter has thickened and is pulling away from the sides and bottom of the pan, 5 minutes or less.
3. Again remove the pan from the heat, and stir in 4 of the eggs, one at a time, making certain each egg is completely incorporated before adding the next. Stir in the Roquefort.
4. Drop the batter by teaspoons onto the prepared baking sheet.
5. Beat the remaining egg in a small bowl. Brush the top of each puff with beaten egg, and then sprinkle them with the Parmesan.
6. Place the baking sheet on the center rack of the oven, bake for 10 minutes, reduce the heat to 350°F

and bake until the gougères are puffed and well browned, another 5 minutes. Serve immediately.

40 to 50 hors d'oeuvres

BABY BEEF SKEWERED APPETIZERS

Both delicious and decorative, we've entwined each skewer with a sprig of rosemary, wrapping and tucking it between the beef, mushrooms, and peppers. Use 6-inch, wooden or bamboo cocktail skewers, which are light and easy to manage.

MARINADE
¼ cup soy sauce
2 tablespoons sesame oil
1 tablespoon Dijon mustard
1 tablespoon sugar
2 teaspoons minced garlic
1 teaspoon grated lemon zest
½ teaspoon dried red pepper flakes

8 ounces boneless beef rib steak, cut in 1-inch cubes
6 cultivated mushrooms, quartered
1 large yellow or orange bell pepper, cored, seeded, and cut into 1-inch pieces
2 tablespoons sesame seeds, toasted (see Index)
24 sprigs fresh rosemary or summer savory

1. In a medium-size bowl, stir all the marinade ingredients together. Add the cubed beef and the mushrooms; toss to coat, and let stand, loosely covered, at room temperature, for 1 hour.
2. Preheat the oven to 450°F. Lightly grease a baking sheet.
3. Thread each skewer with one piece of bell pepper, one beef cube, and one mushroom quarter.
4. Dip one side of each skewer in the sesame seeds; wrap or twist an herb sprig around each skewer. Arrange on the prepared baking sheet, and bake until sizzling, 5 minutes. Serve immediately.

24 hors d'oeuvres

THE LIVES OF THE PARTY

The classic cocktail party is making a grand comeback. The format is traditional but flexible enough to allow any host or hostess to add his or her own personal style. A cocktail party usually takes place in the early evening, lasts two to three hours, is filled with lots of finger food, and offers a full range of alcoholic and non-alcoholic drinks. It's a perfect and yet simple way to repay social obligations. Since people relax with drinks, it's also the perfect opportunity to mix different groups of friends.

COCKTAIL PARTY TIPS

▲ There are two types of cocktail parties to consider. One is a prelude to another event, such as a concert or dinner party. The food should be delicate, rich, and sometimes spicy to stimulate the appetite for what is to come. The second type is really a light buffet and is more substantial because it is a substitute for dinner. Be sure your invitation is clear.

▲ The most successful parties are those where the hosts welcome each guest, no matter how many, make each one feel special, and make meaningful introductions of one guest to another.

▲ If the party includes dinner, serve just a few hors d'oeuvres. If it's just cocktails, think big. We generally figure two or three bites per variety per person, but you should always plan on more than you think is necessary.

▲ Cocktail party food should be simple and easily eaten with the fingers (unless it's a buffet—then you can put out china and silverware). Arrange each kind of food on a separate tray so your guests will be able to identify each offering without having to study it.

▲ Garnish trays lavishly with greens, fresh herbs, and flowers.

▲ Keep the trays filled, or prepare two trays of each item—one to show and one ready to go.

▲ Place the food where you want the people to be. We plan food for each room, clustered in accessible locations. If the party is outside, use the same approach in different areas of the porch or yard.

▲ A two-hour party with twenty to forty guests should have six to ten somethings to nibble on. Two or three should be hot hors d'oeuvres and the rest cold or at room temperature. Plan a variety of textures from crisp to creamy, and flavors from subtle to spicy.

▲ Don't forget the music. Plan it ahead of time.

▲ Put large ashtrays out and keep them emptied. Stale tobacco doesn't go with food. If you would like to keep the party as smoke-free as possible, designate a room wherein guests may go to smoke.

▲ You can never have too much ice. Allow about ½ pound per person, 1½ pounds in the hot weather.

▲ For a small group, a serve-yourself bar will make your guests comfortable and give them reason to interact. A large party demands extras. Hire a bartender and waiters to freshen drinks, pass food, and whisk away debris.

▲ Cocktails don't have to mean hard liquor. You can choose your drink style, be it fruit punch, wines and waters, or beer.

▲ A bar set up on a hall table or living-room sideboard is more convivial than one centered in the kitchen.

▲ Plan on one drink per guest per hour. People drink Champagne more quickly, however.

THE COCKTAIL BAR

You can set up your cocktail bar well in advance. It doesn't have to be a full bar; if you want to offer just beer and wine choose good-quality red and white wines and perhaps a sparkling wine, too. The beer should be the best you can afford. Be sure to have plenty.

A full bar should include everything from hard liquor to red and white wine, beer, vermouth, club soda, mineral water, fruit juices, bitters, and grenadine. Most requests will be simple. Blender drinks are complicated; don't bring the machine out. There are a few aperitifs you might consider including. We like Lillet, Aberol, and Campari. Mixed with club soda, they offer a low-alcohol choice. We also like to pass one special drink on trays.

Try sangria with Champagne or frosty margaritas on a hot summer night. Offer tall glasses of French cider in the fall, or martinis on a snowy night. We think Champagne and tangerine juice is perfect for a spring evening.

Remember always to provide something refreshing for the non-drinker. Offer your own blend of fruit juices or nectars to mix with club soda or enjoy alone. Plan on at least three drinks, with or without liquor, for each person. One bottle of wine holds six glasses, so if only wine or Champagne is being served, count on half a bottle per person. Buy two white wines for every red, and buy a little extra—most liquor stores will take back unopened bottles if you ask beforehand.

Set up your bar and supplies in an easy-to-reach spot. If you expect more than sixteen people, consider hiring a bartender. When the mood is casual and the group small, the self-serve bar works well, after the first drink. The host should always break the ice by informing guests that they are free to

A GRAND COCKTAIL BUFFET

Carpaccio and Radish Canapés
Le Petit Aïoli
Roquefort Gougères
Olivada Crostini
Smoked Trout Mousse

Baked Party Ham With
Pineapple and Bourbon
Roast Fillet of Beef With
Black Peppercorns
Pinto Bean Chili
Lobster Salad à la Russe

Sautéed Baby Artichokes
Gazpacho Salad
Lemony Caesar Salad
American Picnic Potato Salad

Biscuits, Cornbread, and Muffins
With Fresh Mango Chutney
and Fruit Butters

Very Berry Fruit Salad With
Lemon Chèvre Dressing
Cookie Baskets

pour their own drinks. At the bar, have more ice than you think you will ever use.

Since we would never want to be caught short, for an open bar for forty, we would order:

Scotch, 3 bottles
Vodka, 3 bottles
Gin, 1 bottle
Rum, 1 bottle
Dry vermouth, 1 bottle
Sweet vermouth, 1 bottle
Campari, 1 bottle
Dubonnet, 1 bottle
Dry sherry, 2 bottles
Sweet sherry, 1 bottle
White wine, 10 bottles
Red wine, 5 bottles
Club soda, 12 large bottles
Tonic, 6 large bottles
Ginger ale, 6 large bottles
Tomato juice, 3 quarts
Orange juice, 4 quarts
Bitter lemon, 6 large bottles
Cola and diet cola, 24 cans, or
    12 large bottles
Waters, 6 large bottles natural,
    6 with bubbles

THE LARGE ESSENTIALS

1 silver or chrome cocktail shaker
1 large thick cocktail mixing glass
1 small ice bucket, large enough
    to hold two trays of ice
1 pair ice tongs
1 small decorative pitcher
1 double-sided jigger (1 jig-
    ger being 1½ ounces)
1 long-handled silver spoon
1 cocktail strainer
1 juicer
1 small cutting surface,
    marble or wood
1 paring knife
1 bottle opener

> " A toast to the Cocktail Party Where olives are speared and friends are stabbed."
> —ANONYMOUS

1 easy-to-use corkscrew
1 small mallet for crushing ice
1 pretty linen towel
Glass swizzle sticks

THE JIGGER

The jigger is a standard 1½-ounce measure used for making drinks. We have used this in most of our recipes.

THE LITTLE ESSENTIALS

1 lemon peeler for those twists
1 muddler for crushing sugar
    cubes and fruit
1 pepper grinder
Funny porcelain cork pourers
    (perhaps a stork?)
Extra corks or bottle stoppers
Cocktail toothpicks
    Pretty straws
        Small cocktail napkins
        Coasters

> " The best wine is the oldest, the best water the newest."
> —WILLIAM BLAKE

THE MUDDLER

A muddler is a little hardwood stick with a rounded bottom used for bruising mint leaves, crushing sugar with bitters for an old-fashioned, and lightly crushing other fruits.

VERY LARGE LUXURIES

1 Champagne cooler
1 silver or glass punch bowl and
    ladle

COCKTAIL GARNISHES

Large green martini olives with
    stems
Cocktail onions
Long-stemmed maraschino cher-
    ries
1 small branch of tiny dried chiles
Rose's lime juice, or fresh lime
    juice
Angostura bitters
Orange bitters
Lemons, limes, and oranges

GLASSWARE ESSENTIALS

Chic cocktail glasses, the new V-
    shaped martini style, 6 to 8
    ounces
Old-fashioned glasses with thick
    bottoms, 6 to 10 ounces
Highball glasses, 12 to 14 ounces
Sour glasses, 6 ounces
Champagne flutes, or tall tulip-
    shaped glasses
Long-stemmed all-purpose wine
    glasses, about 8 ounces

FAVORITE COCKTAILS

Elegant, sophisticated, glamorous—mixed drinks are for slowly sipping when romance is in the air and the strains of a gentle piano tune can be heard off in the distance.

CHAMPAGNE COCKTAIL

1 small sugar cube
Several dashes of orange bitters
¾ ounce Armagnac or Cognac
Chilled dry Champagne
Twist of lemon or orange zest

Place the sugar cube in the bottom of a champagne glass and sprinkle the bitters on top. Add the Armagnac. Fill the glass with Champagne and garnish with a twist.

1 cocktail

KIR ROYAL

1 to 2 teaspoons crème de cassis or
* Chambord*
Chilled dry Champagne

Place the crème de cassis in a champagne glass. Fill with Champagne. Stir.

1 cocktail

BLACK VELVET

Chilled stout
Chilled dry Champagne

Pour equal amounts of stout and Champagne into a champagne glass. Stir.

1 cocktail

PESCA BELLINI

Fresh puréed strawberries, apricots, and raspberries can also be mixed with Champagne with lovely results.

2 tablespoons puréed fresh peach
1 teaspoon peach schnapps
½ teaspoon fresh lemon juice
Chilled dry Champagne

Place the peach purée, schnapps, and lemon juice in a champagne glass. Fill to almost the top with Champagne and stir.

1 cocktail

DAIQUIRI

You can adjust the amount of sweetness to your taste.

4½ ounces light rum, preferably Bacardi
Juice of 1 lime
2 teaspoons Simple Sugar Syrup (see
* below)*

Pour the rum, lime juice, and sugar syrup into a cocktail shaker over crushed ice. Shake well and strain into a cocktail glass.

▲ For a frozen Daiquiri, place the rum, lime juice, and sugar syrup in a blender with 4 ounces of crushed ice. Blend well and pour into a cocktail glass. For a frozen banana or strawberry Daiquiri add ¼ cup sliced fruits to the mixture before blending.

1 cocktail

SIMPLE SUGAR SYRUP

Some cocktails call for sugar syrup. It's easy to make and lasts indefinitely in the refrigerator.

2 cups water
1 cup sugar

Combine the water and sugar in a saucepan. Simmer, stirring occasionally, until the sugar dissolves. Cool, and refrigerate in a closed jar. Use as needed.

3 cups

ICE BREAKERS

Today we find aperitifs a little more interesting and a lot more congenial than spirits.

▲ Extra dry, extra cold white wine is the basis of a dazzling array of "cocktails" that are lighter and more interesting than the usual party fare. We especially like Chablis, Riesling, Chenin Blanc, Mâcon Blanc, and Vouvray.

■ Stir a spoonful of framboise, Mirabelle, or Poire Williams into a glass of chilled white wine and garnish with a raspberry or slice of plum or pear, whichever is appropriate.

■ Fresh fruit makes a glass of white wine prettier and adds a little flavor of its own. Try a few green grapes, balls of fresh melon, or a slice of mango in the glass.

■ Stir a splash of crème de cassis in a glass of white wine for a lovely rosy Kir.

■ A sprig of mint is beautiful and tasty, too. Crush the sprig lightly in the bottom of the glass and pour in the chilled white wine.

■ Freeze strawberries or raspberries in ice cubes and float one or two in a glass of white wine mixed with a dash of berry purée.

■ Add a jigger of cranberry-raspberry, blackberry, or orange juice and a splash of seltzer to white wine.

▲ Dry sherry is delicious just slightly chilled, on the rocks or with a little soda. In a glass of Champagne, the way the Spanish do, it's pretty wonderful. A dash of port in Champagne is splendid too.

▲ Campari, that brilliantly red, slightly bitter Italian aperitif, is gaining popularity, especially in the summer. Try it with a splash of tonic or soda and a squeeze of fresh orange, lemon, or lime; or mixed with gin, dry vermouth, and lemon juice in a Negroni. One will do nicely.

▲ Pineau des Charentes is an aperitif made in France for over 400 years and only just beginning to be exported to America. It's a slightly sweet blend of white wine and Cognac that we adore.

▲ Garnish vermouth with a strip of orange or lemon zest. We like Lillet and Cinzano Rosso.

▲ Mix the artichoke-based Cynar or Italian Punt e Mes with tonic.

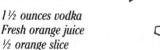
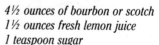

SCREWDRIVER

1½ ounces vodka
Fresh orange juice
½ orange slice

Place 3 ice cubes in a highball glass. Add the vodka, then fill to the top with orange juice. Stir with a long-handled spoon. Place the orange slice on the side of the glass.
1 cocktail

BRANDY ALEXANDER

1 ounce brandy
1 ounce white crème de cacao
1 ounce heavy or whipping cream
Whole nutmeg

Pour brandy, crème de cacao, and cream into a cocktail shaker over cracked ice. Shake well. Strain into a cocktail glass. Grate some whole nutmeg on top.
1 cocktail

WHISKEY SOUR

4½ ounces of bourbon or scotch
1½ ounces fresh lemon juice
1 teaspoon sugar

Place bourbon, lemon juice, and sugar over cracked ice in a large mixing glass. Stir with a long-handled spoon and strain into a sour glass. No garnish for this.
1 cocktail

MARTINI

4½ ounces gin (preferably Tanqueray)
1½ ounces dry French or Italian
  vermouth
Martini olives slightly bruised or a twist
  of lemon zest

Pour the gin and the vermouth over cracked ice in a cocktail shaker. Stir or shake. Strain into a chilled or frosted cocktail glass with an olive or two in the bottom.

▲ For an extra dry Martini use 6 ounces of gin and just a kiss of vermouth.

▲ If using lemon zest, twist it over the glass so the oils and aroma just fall in.

▲ For a Vodka Martini substitute vodka for gin. (Add little pickled onions and you have a Gibson.)

  1 cocktail

SWEET MANHATTAN

4½ ounces bourbon or rye
1½ ounces sweet Italian vermouth
Dash of Angostura bitters
Long-stemmed maraschino cherry
Twist of orange zest

Pour the bourbon and vermouth over cracked ice in a cocktail shaker. Add the bitters and stir with a long-handled spoon. Strain into a cocktail glass and dazzle with a long-stemmed cherry and an orange twist.

▲ For a dry Manhattan, substitute dry vermouth and garnish with a twist of lemon or lime.

▲ For a Rob Roy, substitute scotch for bourbon or rye, leave out the cherry, and add a twist of lemon instead of orange zest.

  1 cocktail

THE SEA BREEZE

1½ ounces vodka
⅓ cup fresh grapefruit juice
⅓ cup cranberry juice
Lime slice
1 tiny pink rose, on the stem,
  thorns removed

Place 3 ice cubes in a highball glass. Add the vodka, grapefruit juice, and cranberry juice. Stir with a long-handled spoon. Float the lime slice on top and garnish with the rose.

  1 cocktail

MARGARITA

Lime wedge
Coarse ground salt in a small plate
9 ounces tequila (preferably Cuervo Gold)
3 ounces fresh lime juice
1½ ounces Triple Sec
2 lime slices

1. Rub the rims of 2 cocktail glasses with the lime wedge, then dip them into the salt.

2. Pour the tequila, lime juice, and Triple Sec into a cocktail shaker over crushed ice. Shake well and strain half the mixture into each glass. Garnish each drink with a slice of lime.

  2 cocktails

WENDE'S BLOODY MARY

3 to 4 ounces vodka
1 tablespoon fresh lemon juice
½ teaspoon prepared white horseradish
½ teaspoon Worcestershire sauce
Dash of tabasco sauce
Dash of celery salt
Freshly ground black pepper
8 ounces tomato juice
1 celery rib with leaves, for garnish

Fill a highball glass with ice. Place all the ingredients except the celery in a large mixing glass. Stir well with a long-handled spoon. Pour into the highball glass and garnish with the celery.

  1 cocktail

OLD-FASHIONED

1 small cube of light brown or white
  sugar
1 teaspoon warm water
Dash of Angostura bitters
2 to 3 ice cubes
Twist of lemon zest
3 ounces rye
1 orange slice (in the winter try a blood
  orange)
Long-stemmed maraschino cherry

Place the sugar, water, and bitters in an old-fashioned glass. Crush with a muddler and spread the mixture around the sides a bit. Add the ice cubes and the lemon twist. Pour in the rye, stir, and decorate with the orange slice and cherry.

  1 cocktail

VERMOUTH CASSIS

2 ice cubes
3 ounces chilled dry French vermouth
3 ounces chilled sparkling water or club
  soda
2 tablespoons crème de cassis
Twist of lemon zest

Place the ice cubes in a highball glass and add the vermouth. Add the sparkling water, stir once, and drizzle in the cassis letting it float down onto the mixture. Garnish with the lemon twist.

  1 cocktail

AT TABLE

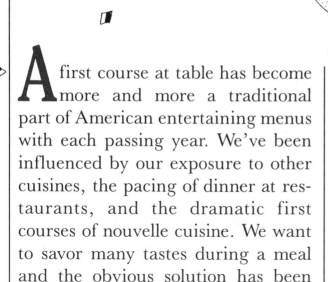

A first course at table has become more and more a traditional part of American entertaining menus with each passing year. We've been influenced by our exposure to other cuisines, the pacing of dinner at restaurants, and the dramatic first courses of nouvelle cuisine. We want to savor many tastes during a meal and the obvious solution has been more, but smaller, courses.

We love to have the first course on the table to greet family and friends as they enter the dining room. It always causes exclamation and sets a festive tone for the meal ahead. As much thought is put into the arrangement and garnish of the first course as into its preparation—sometimes more—but simplicity is always the key. It may be a gorgeous salad delicately sauced, an oversize lobster ravioli, miniature fish cakes topped with salsa, or a sliver of smoked fish on a beautiful plate combining high drama with great taste.

Some first courses are simply scaled down entrées, such as small servings of fresh pasta with a classic sauce, artful miniature pizzas, or individual cheese soufflés. But most first courses are specially designed to fit this opening role. Consider velvety foie gras, sheer slices of smoked salmon and melon on a black plate, or a salad composed of delicate greens. A first course offers the perfect opportunity to let your culinary imagination soar. Ours always does!

BRUSCHETTA

G reet friends as they sit down at table with a heaping plate of *bruschetta*. From Italy, where it is traditionally a workman's midday snack, bruschetta is thickly sliced country bread grilled over an open fire, then rubbed while warm with a clove of garlic, drizzled with exquisitely fruity green olive oil, and sprinkled with sea salt. Bruschetta can be embellished further with chunks of red ripe tomato, fresh basil, or arugula leaves, or slivers of salty Parmesan or rosy prosciutto with a grind or two of black pepper. Dressed simply or to the nines, bruschetta is a very warm way of breaking bread before a rustic meal.

VARIATIONS ON THE THEME

▲ Top with a couple of slices of perfectly ripe tomato and a few thin rings of red onion.

▲ Add a few slices of truffle, for a celebratory bruschetta.

▲ Pound garlic and hot pepper flakes together, season the mixture with salt and pepper, and moisten it with the juice of an orange and a little light olive oil. Spread over toasted bread.

▲ The French in Provence dip bread slices in oil, top them with crushed garlic and anchovies, and bake them in the oven until crisp.

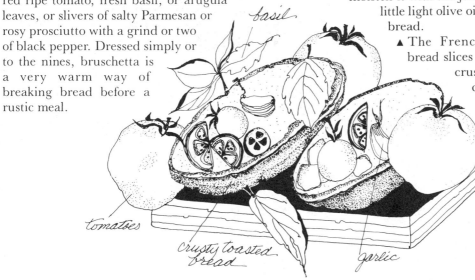

basil

tomatoes

crusty toasted bread

garlic

CLARK WOLF'S BRUSCHETTA

A nyone who knows Clark Wolf, a truly bi-coastal food consultant, is never ever bored. He is always full of surprises and fun, and he does it all with great style and substance.

Says Clark, "This is a recipe that evolved from the classic. It was the result of a fairly unrestrained shopping spree in the Italian Tuscan hill town of Cortona, in the spring of 1988. One delicious but expensive variation is to use a bit of truffled oil (oil infused with white Alba truffles). Another is to serve these alongside toasts slathered with an olive spread that has been seasoned with anchovies and capers.

The basic recipe may sound exotic, but can be made deliciously from ingredients found at almost any grocery. The trick is to do it in season, when the sun is warm and the tomatoes are red and ripe."

10 vine-ripened tomatoes, coarsely chopped
1 large yellow bell pepper, cored, seeded, and coarsely
    chopped
2 cloves garlic, finely slivered
½ cup coarsely chopped fresh Italian (flat-leaf) parsley
2 tablespoons finely snipped fresh chives
2 teaspoons finely chopped cilantro (fresh coriander)
1 teaspoon finely chopped fresh thyme leaves
3 fresh basil leaves, finely chopped (optional)
3 fresh sage leaves, finely chopped (optional)
8 Calamata or other imported black olives, pitted and
    chopped
1 tablespoon capers, drained and coarsely chopped
½ to 1 cup fragrant, fruity extra virgin olive oil
Salt and freshly ground black pepper, to taste
1 large country (peasant) bread with a good crust
2 large cloves garlic, halved

1. In a large bowl gently toss together the tomatoes, yellow pepper, slivered garlic, parsley, chives, cilantro, thyme, basil, sage, olives, and capers.

2. Pour in enough of the olive oil to cover. Season with salt and pepper and toss together gently. Let the mixture rest while you make the garlic toasts.

3. Cut the bread into ½-inch-thick slices and brown them on both sides under the broiler or on the grill.

4. Rub one side of each bread slice with the halved cloves of garlic, and then brush lightly with olive oil.

5. Place a slice of toast on each plate, and top it with a healthy spoonful of the tomato mixture.

12 portions

TUSCANY

In Tuscany, olive oil and bread are sacred gifts, and it is a grave sin to waste either of them. The Tuscans say you add years to your time in purgatory with the crumbs left on your plate.

ALICE WATERS' BRUSCHETTA

Whether a dish is simple or complicated, Alice Waters' integrity with ingredients, especially produce, has changed the way we in America eat today. From Alice: "I make this all the time for lunch or as a nice little late summer hors d'oeuvre when the tomatoes are perfectly ripe. It's quite beautiful, especially with a number of colors of tomato and basil. We've had available ripe green, yellow, and red tomatoes, along with opal and green basils."

1 loaf crusty sourdough country bread
Extra virgin olive oil
1 large garlic clove, halved
Ripe garden tomatoes (use 1 tomato per large slice of bread)
Red wine vinegar
Salt and freshly ground black pepper, to taste
Basil leaves
1 shallot, peeled and finely diced (optional)

1. Cut the bread into medium-thick slices. Either grill or toast them until they're nice and brown on both sides.

2. Drizzle toasts liberally with olive oil, and rub each slice with garlic.

3. Slice the tomatoes and arrange on top of the bread. Sprinkle with a splash of vinegar, salt, pepper, and a few basil leaves. Serve immediately. (If the tomatoes are not perfectly flavorful, macerate the finely diced shallot in the vinegar and sprinkle on top.)

OUR BASIC BRUSCHETTA

When we make bruschetta, we top it with a heady tomato mixture, made pungent with garlic, shallots, and the finest olive oil.

12 to 14 fresh ripe plum tomatoes (about 1 ¾ pounds)
2 tablespoons minced garlic
2 tablespoons minced shallots
1 cup fresh basil leaves
1 teaspoon fresh lemon juice
Salt and coarsely ground black pepper, to taste
⅓ cup plus ¼ cup extra virgin olive oil
3 cloves garlic, slivered
8 thick slices round peasant bread

1. Cut the tomatoes into ¼-inch dice and place in a bowl. Toss with the minced garlic and shallots.

2. Chop the basil coarsely and add to the tomatoes, along with the lemon juice, salt and pepper, and ⅓ cup olive oil. Set aside.

3. Heat the ¼ cup olive oil in a small skillet. Sauté the slivered garlic until golden, 2 to 3 minutes. Discard the garlic and reserve the oil.

4. Toast the bread and cut each slice in half. Arrange the slices on eight small plates. Brush the garlic-flavored oil over each slice, spoon the tomato mixture over the bread, and serve immediately. The mixture should be at room temperature.

8 portions

LE PETIT AIOLI

In summertime in the South of France, there is a traditional feast called The Grand Aïoli. In the towns of Lourdes, St. Rémy, Les Baux, and Bonnieux, look for the poster announcing the dates. Do participate in this village fête if you are there, for it is one of the few opportunities Americans have to celebrate with the very private French villagers and dine on some of the best this magical region has to offer.

Be ready to watch the "sunlight of Provence," as Frédéric Mistral described aïoli, ladled out in buckets to be eaten with thick slices of white cod, salmon, chicken, snails, herbed roast pork, crudités of potatoes, mushrooms, eggplant, fennel, artichokes, carrots, tomatoes, beets, celery, and rough country bread. As evening falls the after-dinner hour is devoted to pastries, bowls of mousse, and games of boules. A day like this will be cherished in your memory for a long time.

Aïoli is wonderful in miniature as a first course. Dot the table with several small bowls and plenty of crudités for dipping.

3 tablespoons minced garlic
4 egg yolks
2 tablespoons fresh lemon juice
½ teaspoon salt
2 ½ cups extra virgin olive oil

1. Smash the garlic cloves, using the blade of a large knife. Peel the garlic and chop very fine. You should have 3 tablespoons.

2. Combine the garlic with the egg yolks, lemon juice, and salt in the bowl of a food processor. With the motor running, slowly add the oil. Process until thick.

2 ¾ cups

IRENA CHALMERS' CURRIED MUSSELS AND CUCUMBERS POLONAISE

One of the wittiest, most charming, and most professional people we know, Irena Chalmers is tremendously accomplished.

"I love all the subtle flavors and complex tastes in this appetizer," Irena says, "and am always pleased when guests don't gobble it all—so I can have the leftovers as a salad the next day!"

3 pounds fresh mussels, well scrubbed
2 small cucumbers, peeled, seeded, and thinly sliced
3 teaspoons salt
2 tablespoons fresh lemon juice
⅓ cup heavy or whipping cream
½ cup sour cream
½ cup mayonnaise
¼ cup vegetable oil
1 tablespoon cider vinegar
1 teaspoon dried tarragon
¾ teaspoon curry powder
½ teaspoon freshly ground black pepper
Finely chopped fresh Italian (flat-leaf) parsley, for garnish

1. Remove the beards from the mussels. (Don't beard until right before you prepare this dish.)

2. Bring 1 inch of water to a boil in a large pot. Place a colander or steaming basket over the water, add the mussels, and cover. Steam until they open, about 5 minutes. Set aside to cool.

3. Toss the cucumbers with 2 teaspoons of the salt in a bowl, and chill, loosely covered, for 1 hour.

4. Drain the cucumbers and pat dry. Place them in a bowl and toss with the lemon juice and cream.

5. In another bowl, mix together the remaining 1 teaspoon salt and all the remaining ingredients, except the mussels and parsley. Add this to the cucumber mixture.

6. Remove the mussels from their shells and gently fold them into the cucumber mixture. Arrange in a serving bowl and garnish with the parsley.

4 to 6 portions

FELIPE ROJAS-LOMBARDI'S MUSSELS VINAIGRETTE

It seems so appropriate to have Felipe here with us. We have spent many happy hours at the Ballroom, his fabulous New York restaurant. In fact, we celebrated the publication of *The Silver Palate Good Times Cookbook* there.

5 pounds fresh mussels, well scrubbed
2 tablespoons plus ½ cup olive oil
½ cup dry white wine
4 sprigs fresh thyme or 1 teaspoon dried thyme leaves
8 ounces red new potatoes, cooked in their skins and quartered
1½ pounds ripe tomatoes, cut into bite-size chunks
½ onion, thinly sliced
¼ cup fresh or frozen (thawed) green peas
⅓ cup white wine vinegar
1 teaspoon coarse (kosher) salt
⅓ cup chopped fresh Italian (flat-leaf) parsley

1. Remove the beards from the mussels. (Don't beard until right before you prepare this dish.)

2. In a 12-inch skillet with a tight-fitting lid, combine 2 tablespoons of the olive oil, 2 tablespoons of the white wine, the thyme, and the cleaned mussels. Cover the skillet and steam the mussels over high heat until the shells are just opened, 5 to 8 minutes. Discard any mussels that have not opened, and set the rest aside.

3. Let the liquid in the skillet sit for a few minutes so that any sand or sediment settles at the bottom. Then carefully strain this liquid through a sieve lined with cheesecloth, leaving any residue in the skillet. Pour the liquid into a large bowl, and reserve.

4. Remove the mussels from their shells. Place the mussels in the bowl with the liquid.

5. Add the cooked potatoes, tomatoes, onion, peas, vinegar, salt, parsley, and the remaining ½ cup olive oil and remaining white wine. Toss gently, being careful not to damage the mussels. Serve at room temperature.

6 to 8 portions

FISHING FOR COMPLIMENTS

When you feel somewhere between the devil and the deep blue sea in searching for a starter course, look first to heavenly oysters, clams, scallops, and mussels on the half shell; shrimp, sardines, whitebait, herring, tuna, and salmon. Catch them as catch can (fresh from your local market—that is) and bring a fresh sea breeze to your table.

First-course seafood dishes should be half the size, if that, of a main-course portion, and delicately sauced if sauced at all. As with all first courses, the presentation is at least half the thrill. Scallops or shrimp can be nestled in curly greens, oysters in their primitive shells, and pink shrimp on a bed of crushed ice. Slivers of smoked salmon need just a spoonful of sauce and a feathery garnish of dill, and steamed mussels a quick sprinkle of chopped tomatoes and herbs. Seafood sets that smart, light pace you want for a starter. Thousands of dinner parties later, your guests will still adore it.

DEVILED MUSSELS

Mussels that have gone to the devil—unusual and addictive, with plenty of ginger added for a real zing.

3 dozen mussels
2 tablespoons olive oil
½ cup chopped onion
4 cloves garlic, minced
1 tablespoon grated lemon zest
1 teaspoon ground ginger
1 teaspoon dried red pepper flakes
1 teaspoon dried oregano
Freshly ground black pepper, to taste
2 cups chopped fresh tomatoes
2 tablespoons capers, drained
1 cup dry white wine
Chopped fresh parsley, for garnish

1. Remove the beards from the mussels. (Don't beard until right before you prepare this dish.)

2. Heat the oil in a large dutch oven or kettle. Stir in the onion, garlic, lemon zest, ginger, red pepper flakes, oregano, and black pepper. Cook until the onions are soft and the mixture is fragrant, about 5 minutes. Stir in the tomatoes, capers, and wine. Heat just to a simmer, and then add the mussels. Cover and cook, shaking once or twice, until the mussels have opened, about 5 minutes. Discard any unopened mussels.

3. Divide the mussels among four shallow bowls. Spoon the sauce over them, and sprinkle with parsley. Serve immediately.

2 portions

CELEBRATE!

If you've no reason to throw a party, it's fun to find one. Make it spontaneous: Celebrate something or someone—perhaps the first day of snow, the arrival of an out-of-town friend, the last strawberry from your garden, or the first tomato. Never lose sight of the real celebration—that of your family and friends gathered together.

COQUILLES FOR TWO

The tang of raclette cheese mixed with crème fraîche adds a new dimension to sweet bay scallops. Golden and bubbling hot, these coquilles are a warming start to a meal. Serve with a slightly chilled white Burgundy.

1 tablespoon unsalted butter
4 ounces bay scallops, rinsed and patted dry
Salt and freshly ground black pepper, to taste
½ cup crème fraîche (see Index)
1 ounce raclette cheese, shredded
2 tablespoons dried bread crumbs
1 tablespoon freshly grated Parmesan cheese
1 tablespoon unsalted butter, melted

1. Preheat the oven to 450°F.

2. Melt the butter in a small skillet over high heat. Cook the scallops just until cooked through, about 1 minute. Season with salt and pepper, and drain.

3. In a small bowl combine the crème fraîche, raclette, 1 tablespoon of the bread crumbs, and a pinch of salt and pepper. Stir in the scallops.

4. Divide the mixture between two shallow ½-cup ovenproof ramekins. Toss the remaining 1 tablespoon crumbs with the Parmesan cheese, and sprinkle over the scallops. Drizzle with the melted butter, and place on a small baking sheet.

5. Bake until bubbling and golden, 15 to 20 minutes. Serve immediately.

2 portions

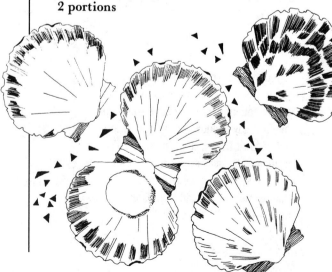

OYSTERS ROCKEFELLER

Oysters Rockefeller was created in the late nineteenth century at Antoine's restaurant in New Orleans—and myths aside, it was not originally made with spinach. Instead, the bed of scallions, tarragon, and celery made the oysters so green that chef Jules Alciatore associated them with greenbacks, and chose the obvious name for the time.

4 tablespoons (½ stick) unsalted butter, at room temperature
¼ cup dried bread crumbs
¼ cup sliced scallions (green onions)
¼ cup chopped celery
1 tablespoon chopped fresh tarragon leaves
¼ teaspoon salt
Freshly ground black pepper, to taste
Pinch of cayenne pepper
12 fresh oysters on the half shell

1. Preheat the broiler. Arrange the broiler rack 3 to 4 inches from the heat.

2. In the container of a food processor, purée the butter, bread crumbs, scallions, celery, tarragon, salt, black pepper, and cayenne until smooth.

3. With a small sharp knife, cut below each oyster to release it from its shell.

4. Arrange each oyster in its shell on a baking sheet. Spread some of the butter on each oyster.

5. Broil just until golden and crisp, 2 to 3 minutes. Serve immediately.

2 portions

SNAILS WITH HATS

This dish makes a wonderful first course and eliminates all the extra equipment associated with preparing escargots. The addition of mushrooms makes the overall texture of the dish more appealing, and the golden puff pastry adds elegance.

¼ cup Berta's Chicken Stock (see Index) or canned broth
4 tablespoons (½ stick) unsalted butter
2 cloves garlic, minced
1 tablespoon soy sauce
1 teaspoon sesame oil*
½ teaspoon Tabasco sauce
Freshly ground black pepper, to taste
20 fresh cultivated mushrooms, trimmed
16 to 20 canned snails, rinsed and drained
1 sheet frozen puff pastry, thawed
1 egg
1 tablespoon water

1. In a small saucepan, combine the stock, butter, garlic, soy sauce, sesame oil, Tabasco, and pepper. Add the mushrooms, and heat to a simmer. Cover, and cook 10 minutes. Then stir in the snails, and remove from the heat.

2. Divide the mixture among four ½-cup ovenproof ramekins.

3. Cut out four circles of puff pastry, about ½ inch wider than the diameter of the ramekins. Beat the egg and water together, and brush the rims of the ramekins and the edges of the pastry circles with this egg wash.

4. Cover each ramekin with a pastry circle, pressing the edges against the sides of the ramekins. Brush the tops with egg wash. Cut a small vent in the center of each, and chill 30 minutes.

5. Preheat the oven to 375°F.

6. Bake until the pastry tops are puffed and golden, 20 minutes. Serve immediately.

4 portions

*Available in Asian groceries and other specialty food shops.

A SNAIL'S PACE

Aristotle ate them. The Romans kept them and fed them herbs so they could feast on them year round. For us the taste of the snail is a little bit wild, a little bit bitter, and very, very addictive.

You can buy canned snails with a bag of clean shells attached—the best we've found are Ugma and Ile de France. Let them soak overnight in salted water with garlic and a bouquet garni. Then they can be sautéed in butter or olive oil and seasoned with herbs and garlic or baked with wine, fresh herbs, and butter. They are delicious stuffed in mushroom caps, covered with garlic butter, and broiled. Dredged in flour and seasoned with salt and pepper, they can be lightly sautéed in hot butter, then poured into beaten eggs to make a superb omelet.

As wonderful as canned snails are, fresh are better. You don't have to go to France to sample them fresh—now snails are being raised in America and are quite inexpensive, once you find a source. American snails are smaller than their European cousins and are raised in strictly controlled environments. A pound of fresh American snails equals about four dozen canned snails, but the fresh snails must be soaked, scrubbed, trimmed, and poached before they can be substituted for the canned snails in any recipe. Serving snails in shells requires special implements for each guest: *escargotières* (snail plates), snail pincers, and snail forks.

"I hate austere and chichi invitations. An invitation should let people know precisely what to expect—it should say something to me: what to wear, what's going to happen, et cetera. Better a mimeographed invitation than one that says too little."

—LIZ SMITH

CARACOLES AND RED BEANS

One of the most imaginative combinations we know of is this recipe from our friend Felipe Rojas-Lombardi. These snails and beans are wonderful served with a crusty bread and a good Spanish red wine.

1 pound (2 ¾ cups) dried red kidney beans; or 5 ¼ cups
*   canned red kidney beans, rinsed and drained*
4 teaspoons coarse (kosher) salt
6 tablespoons olive oil
1 large clove garlic, finely chopped
1 onion, finely chopped
¼ cup dry white wine
3 tablespoons unbleached all-purpose flour
1 teaspoon paprika
⅛ teaspoon ground cloves
⅛ teaspoon cayenne pepper
2 ½ cups homemade beef stock (see Index) or canned broth
1 can (14 ounces) snails, rinsed and drained
2 tablespoons balsamic vinegar
½ cup chopped fresh Italian (flat-leaf) parsley

1. If you are using dried beans, soak them overnight in a large pot filled with 3 quarts of cold water.

2. Place the pot containing the beans, soaking liquid, and 2 teaspoons of the coarse salt over high heat. Bring to a boil, reduce the heat, and simmer until the beans are tender but not mushy, 30 to 40 minutes. Drain and set aside. (Or substitute canned beans at this point.)

3. Heat 4 tablespoons of the olive oil in a skillet. Add the garlic and onion, and sauté over medium-low heat until translucent, 5 minutes. Add the wine and cook over medium heat until all the liquid has evaporated, 2 minutes.

4. Add the flour, paprika, cloves, and cayenne to the onions. Mix thoroughly, and add the beef stock. Stir with a wire whisk until smooth.

5. Bring the mixture to a gentle boil over medium heat, stirring frequently. Lower the heat to a simmer, add the remaining 2 teaspoons coarse salt, and cook the sauce for 10 minutes. Add the snails, stir, and cook 20 to 30 minutes longer, stirring occasionally. Remove from the heat and allow to cool.

6. In a serving bowl, combine the cooked (or canned) beans with the balsamic vinegar and mix well. Add the remaining 2 tablespoons olive oil, and toss. Then add the snail mixture and the chopped parsley, and toss again. Adjust seasonings if necessary, and serve. Serve warm or at room temperature.

6 to 8 portions

SALT COD

Those who hate salt cod have probably never had it prepared right. In spite of its appearance and name, salt cod does not need hours of cooking and it is not salty. If you want to serve it warm, fifteen minutes of poaching after an overnight soak is plenty. The longer it is cooked, the tougher, stringier, more tasteless and cottony it becomes. A perfectly cooked piece of salt cod is moist and tender; its taste, succulent, briny, and extremely delicate.

BRANDADE DE MORUE

This creamy combination of salt cod, garlic, and potatoes—a cherished tidbit in Mediterranean households for generations—was a revelation the first time we tasted it. It sounds simple, but it's actually a bit tricky to make. If you cook the salt cod too long it will become dry, and no matter how much cream and olive oil you add, you won't get the classic smooth texture that makes this such a magnificent dish. (Do look for thick white salt cod, with its skin; don't buy fish that is yellowing in the least.)

The cream and olive oil measurements are approximate. Use your eye and taste to judge exactly how much liquid to add. The brandade should be a bit chunky but not liquid. It is well worth careful watching, as a good brandade is magical. Serve it on toasted peasant bread.

8 ounces boneless salt cod
½ cup milk
1 potato, peeled and cut into 1-inch chunks
1 clove garlic, minced
Freshly ground black pepper, to taste
Pinch of cayenne pepper
¼ cup heavy or whipping cream
2 tablespoons extra virgin olive oil

1. Cover the salt cod with cold water and soak for 24 hours, changing the water twice. Drain, rinse, and drain again.

2. Place the milk and cod in a medium-size saucepan, and add water to cover. Heat to a boil, reduce the heat, and simmer 10 minutes. Drain. Break the fish into chunks in a large bowl.

3. Cook the potato in boiling water just until tender, about 20 minutes. Drain well, and add to the fish. Sprinkle with the garlic, black pepper, and cayenne.

4. Combine the cream and oil in a small saucepan, and heat almost to a simmer. Drizzle the mixture into the bowl, breaking up the fish and potato with a wooden spoon. Stir just until the liquid is incorporated. Transfer to a bowl, and serve warm.

1½ cups

CODFISH CAKES WITH PINEAPPLE SALSA

Spicy cod cakes cooled with the sweetness of pineapple. These would be great with any firm fish—a terrific variation for fish cakes.

8 ounces codfish fillet, skinned
¼ cup shredded coconut
¼ cup chopped onion
1 egg, lightly beaten
2 tablespoons dried bread crumbs
1 clove garlic, minced
1 teaspoon Worcestershire sauce
½ teaspoon dried thyme leaves, crumbled
½ teaspoon curry powder
½ teaspoon salt
¼ teaspoon dried red pepper flakes
Vegetable oil for deep-frying
1½ cups Pineapple Salsa (recipe follows)

1. Purée the codfish in a food processor until smooth. Transfer the purée to a mixing bowl.

2. Stir in the remaining ingredients (except oil and salsa), and shape the mixture into ten 2-inch patties.

3. Heat the oil to 360°F in a deep-fryer or large saucepan.

4. Fry the fish cakes, turning once, until deep golden, about 2 minutes. Drain on paper towels. Let stand 1 minute before serving with Pineapple Salsa.

8 to 10 portions

PINEAPPLE SALSA

Don't just serve this fruity salsa with codfish cakes. It makes a great topping for simply prepared fish and grilled poultry, and is just the right flavor for roasted duck too!

1 ½ cups chopped fresh pineapple
1 tablespoon chopped cilantro (fresh coriander)
1 tablespoon fresh lime juice
1 tablespoon sugar
1 teaspoon minced fresh ginger
Freshly ground black pepper, to taste

Stir all the ingredients together, cover, and chill until ready to serve. This will keep in the refrigerator for up to 2 days.

1 ½ cups

CILANTRO

Cilantro, Chinese parsley, and fresh coriander leaves are different names for the same herb. Cilantro looks like a lighter green and more delicate parsley and tastes slightly soapy. A few hate it, but most can't get enough of it. It is the essential herb for many Asian, Mediterranean, and Latin American dishes, and, best of all, it has become easier to find stateside every year. Coriander is the seed of the herb cilantro. It is pungent and essential for curries, couscous, and gingerbread but cannot be substituted for fresh cilantro.

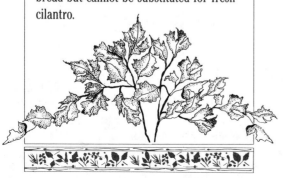

ESCABECHE OF FRESH SARDINES

Now that fresh sardines have become more readily available, we've turned these whole little fish into an escabèche. Serve them as a chilled appetizer. Lovely as a light luncheon dish, too.

SAUCE
1 tablespoon chopped orange zest
½ cup sun-dried tomatoes, chopped
12 large green Italian or other imported olives, pitted and coarsely chopped
½ cup balsamic vinegar
2 tablespoons olive oil
2 teaspoons sugar

¼ cup unbleached all-purpose flour
1 teaspoon salt
Freshly ground black pepper, to taste
1 pound fresh sardines (about 8 small fish), cleaned (see Note)
3 tablespoons olive oil

1. Blanch the orange zest in boiling water for 1 minute. Drain well.

2. Stir all the sauce ingredients together in a small saucepan. Set aside.

3. Toss the flour, salt, and pepper together in a shallow dish. Coat the sardines in the flour mixture.

4. Heat the oil in a large skillet over high heat. Fry the sardines, turning once, until golden and crisp, 5 minutes. Transfer them to a shallow dish.

5. Heat the sauce just to a simmer, and spoon it over the fish. Cover the dish loosely and refrigerate overnight, occasionally spooning the marinade over the fish.

4 portions

Note: To clean sardines, carefully slit the belly, remove the innards, and rinse under cold running water.

SMOKED FISH

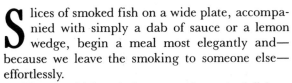

Slices of smoked fish on a wide plate, accompanied with simply a dab of sauce or a lemon wedge, begin a meal most elegantly and—because we leave the smoking to someone else—effortlessly.

You should buy only as much smoked fish as you will use within three days. Refrigerate it when you bring it home from the market. About 30 minutes before serving the first course, take the smoked fish out of the refrigerator and arrange the slices on plates. The thin slices are easier to separate when cold, but the fish should warm to room temperature before serving so that the rich fats can soften and the flavor will be at its peak. Smoked whole fish should be skinned and boned when they are cold and then left to warm a little before serving. Smoked fish is very rich, but fortunately, a little goes a long way. Plan on two large slices of smoked fish or half of a small trout per person.

Some of our favorites include:
▲ Smoked trout with a dollop of sour cream and snippets of fresh dill or chives
▲ Smoked sturgeon with buttered black bread, lemon wedges, and a spoonful of caviar
▲ Smoked trout with slices of Granny Smith apple and horseradish sauce
▲ Smoked mackerel with cucumbers, radishes, mint, and sour cream
▲ Smoked black bass drizzled with olive oil and sprinkled with chopped fresh basil and cilantro
▲ Smoked salmon with lemon juice, dill, capers, chopped red onion, and sour cream or caviar
▲ Smoked whitefish with diced tomatoes, black olives, and red onion
▲ Smoked trout with slices of honeydew, belgian endive chiffonade, dill, and a dollop of yogurt
▲ Smoked salmon with cucumber, unsalted butter, sweet honey mustard, and black bread

GEORGE LANG'S GRAVLAX CAFE DES ARTISTES

We have spent so many hours at Café des Artistes that it has almost become a second home for us. One of our favorite dishes is George Lang's "Salmon Four Ways." Small portions of smoked salmon, poached salmon, salmon tartare, and gravlax with a marvelous mustard dill sauce, are served at table on a wooden plank. We love this dish, but especially the gravlax. George was gracious enough to share the recipe for it with us.

2 pounds fresh center-cut salmon fillet, skin left on, halved lengthwise
2 tablespoons aquavit
⅓ cup coarse (kosher) salt
⅓ cup sugar
2 tablespoons freshly crushed (not ground) black peppercorns
4 ounces fresh dill sprigs

MUSTARD DILL SAUCE
1½ tablespoons white wine vinegar
1¾ tablespoons sugar
½ cup olive oil
5 to 6 tablespoons Dijon mustard
1 tablespoon chopped fresh dill
1 heaping tablespoon freshly ground white pepper

10 sprigs dill, for garnish
5 lemons, halved crosswise, for garnish

1. Wipe the salmon fillet dry with paper towels. Place one fillet half on top of the other, and trim so they are even in length. Then separate them and sprinkle each piece with 1 tablespoon of aquavit.

2. Combine the coarse salt, sugar, and crushed pepper in a small bowl, and rub some of this mixture into the skinless side of each piece.

3. Put one fillet half, skin side down, in a baking dish. Evenly distribute the dill over the fillet. Cover with the other half, skin side up. Sprinkle the remaining salt mixture over the top, and cover the salmon with foil.

4. Place a large platter or chopping board over the fillets, and weight it with a brick or heavy cans. Put the dish in the refrigerator and let the salmon marinate for at least 24 hours, and up to 36 hours, turning the salmon fillets over every 12 hours.

5. While the salmon is marinating, prepare the Mustard Dill Sauce: Whisk the vinegar and sugar together in a small mixing bowl until the sugar has dissolved. Slowly add the olive oil, whisking well until all the oil is incorporated. Blend in the mustard and chopped dill, and season with the white pepper. Cover, and refrigerate until needed.

6. After the salmon has finished marinating, remove the weights, foil, and dill. Using a stiff pastry brush, remove all of the seasoning mixture.

7. When you are ready to serve it, slice the salmon very thin on the bias. Put four or five slices on each serving plate, ladle a small portion of the Mustard Dill Sauce alongside, and garnish with a sprig of dill and a lemon half.

10 portions

Note: For best results, use only very fresh salmon. As an extra garnish, slice salmon skins into thin shreds and fry until crisp in a mixture of vegetable oil and butter; sprinkle on the gravlax at serving time. The same recipe can be applied to whitefish, king mackerel, salmon trout, and other oily fish suitable for marination.

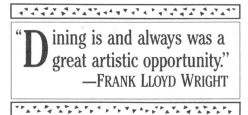

"**D**ining is and always was a great artistic opportunity." —FRANK LLOYD WRIGHT

GEORGE LANG ON CREATING SALMON FOUR WAYS

"When I opened the Café des Artistes in October of 1975, I wanted to invent a dish that would answer the following requirements and specifications:

1. It could be eaten as an appetizer, a main course, or an anytime snack.

2. It would have to be fish or seafood to get away from red meat.

3. It had to be a comfort food, but at the same time it had to have something about it to titillate the imagination and the palate.

4. The presentation would have to be the kind to start the gastric juices flowing, and also indicate the elegant informality of the Café des Artistes.

5. This new dish would have to be the type that both gluttons and thoughtful epicureans would dream about.

6. Since the seventies (and heaven knows, the eighties as well!) could be characterized as an age when people wanted to experience everything at the same time—and instantly—it would have to be several tastes and textures within one presentation.

7. Ever since I can remember, 'variation on a theme' was what gave me the most pleasure in music, love or food, and in this instance I was trying to come up with playful variations on a basic food."

TUNA "GRAVLAX"

For this recipe, it is important that you use very fresh tuna. For a more pronounced flavor, continue marinating the steaks for one more day, turning them once a day. Serve the tuna thinly sliced, on a bed of cucumber slices and garnished with wedges of lemon or lime.

2 tablespoons sugar
1 tablespoon coarse (kosher) salt
1 tablespoon wasabi (Japanese horseradish) powder*
1½ pounds fresh tuna fillet, cut into 2 steaks, each ¾ inch thick
¾ cup chopped scallions (green onions)
Thinly sliced cucumber, chilled
Lemon or lime wedges

1. Toss the sugar, salt, and wasabi powder together in a small bowl. Rub 1 tablespoon of this mixture into each side of the tuna steaks.

2. On a noncorrodible plate, sprinkle ¼ cup of the scallions. Cover with 1 steak. Sprinkle the steak with another ¼ cup scallions, and cover them with the remaining steak. Sprinkle with the remaining ¼ cup scallions.

3. Place a plate over the tuna, and set a 2-pound weight on top. Refrigerate for 24 hours, turning the steaks (together) every 8 hours. Some liquid will accumulate on the plate.

4. Pour off the liquid, scrape off the scallions, and slice the tuna on the diagonal (as you would for smoked salmon).

5. Serve tuna with crisp cucumber slices and wedges of lemon or lime.

10 to 12 portions

*Available in Asian groceries and other specialty food shops.

SALMON ARTICHOKE SHELLS

Easily prepared, this elegant first course sets the tone for a glorious evening of dining. Serve with icy Champagne.

4 large artichokes
½ cup crème fraîche (see Index) or sour cream
4 ounces red salmon caviar
8 slices smoked salmon
8 sprigs fresh dill
4 slices lemon

1. Place the artichokes in a large pot with an inch of water. Bring to a boil, reduce the heat, and simmer, tightly covered, until tender, about 45 minutes. Remove from the pot and allow to cool.

2. Peel the leaves away from the artichokes, and trim away the choke. Place an artichoke bottom in the center of each plate.

3. Spoon 2 tablespoons of crème fraîche onto each artichoke, and then 2 tablespoons of caviar on top of the crème fraîche. Arrange 2 slices of smoked salmon around each artichoke, and garnish with dill sprigs and lemon slices.

4 portions

> "There is so much good in the worst of us,
> And so much bad in the best of us,
> That it hardly becomes any of us
> To talk about the rest of us."
>
> —G.W. COOKE

SALMON PHYLLO PILLOWS

Phyllo pastry neatly wraps delicate salmon fillets that have been moistened with crème fraîche, to form little fish-shaped packages. Serve this new version of coulibiac golden brown and crispy for a light supper or luncheon dish.

8 ounces fresh spinach, stems removed, well rinsed and drained
½ bunch watercress, tough stems removed (about 1 cup)
6 tablespoons crème fraîche (see Index)
Salt and freshly ground black pepper
16 sheets phyllo pastry, 18 x 14 inches, thawed if frozen
6 tablespoons (¾ stick) unsalted butter, melted and cooled to room temperature
4 salmon fillets (about 6 ounces each), skinned
4 teaspoons chopped fresh dill

1. Preheat the oven to 375°F.
2. Place the spinach and watercress in a saucepan, and stir over medium heat until wilted, about 3 minutes. Drain, and squeeze to release liquid. Coarsely chop.
3. In a small bowl, combine the chopped spinach and watercress with 2 tablespoons of the crème fraîche, ¼ teaspoon of the salt, and ¼ teaspoon of the pepper. Set aside.
4. Unroll the phyllo and cover with a damp towel. Place one sheet on a flat surface, and brush with some of the melted butter. Repeat with three more sheets, placing one on top of another.
5. Fold the phyllo rectangle in half crosswise, and brush with more butter. With a short end facing you, spread one quarter of the spinach mixture over the center of the bottom half of the phyllo. Arrange 1 salmon fillet on top of the spinach, and sprinkle with a generous pinch of salt and pepper. Spread with 1 tablespoon crème fraîche. Sprinkle with 1 teaspoon dill. Fold the top half over the bottom and press the edges together lightly. Trim the corners to create a fish shape.

6. Repeat with the remaining ingredients to make three more "fish."
7. Arrange the fish on two lightly buttered baking sheets, and bake until golden, 12 minutes. Serve immediately.

4 portions

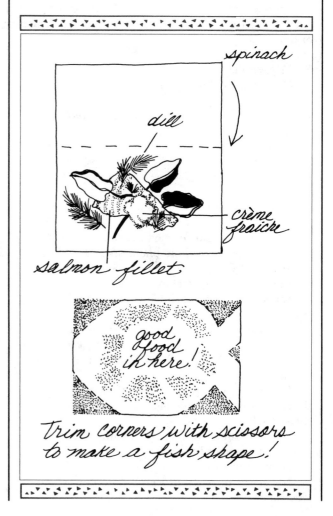

spinach

dill

crème fraîche

salmon fillet

good food in here!

Trim corners with scissors to make a fish shape!

BARRY WINE'S BEGGAR'S PURSES

Barry and Susan Wine have one of the most stunning restaurants in the country, New York's Quilted Giraffe. The food is always superb; the ideas behind the food, always brilliant. These Beggar's Purses, bursting with beluga caviar, are simply delicious.

CREPES

1½ cups milk
4 eggs
1⅛ cups pastry or unbleached all-purpose flour
½ teaspoon salt
½ cup (1 stick) clarified butter (see Index), melted

FILLING

48 chives, about 10 inches long
1¼ pounds beluga caviar, chilled
1 cup crème fraîche (see Index)
4 tablespoons (½ stick) unsalted butter, melted

1. Combine the milk, eggs, pastry flour, and salt in a mixing bowl. Whisk well, and then pour through a fine-mesh sieve into another bowl. Just before you cook the crepes, add 1 tablespoon of the clarified butter to the batter, and stir it in well.

2. Heat a crepe pan over medium-high heat until very hot. Lower the heat to medium. Brush the pan with a little of the melted butter, and when it sizzles, pour in 2 tablespoons of batter. Swirl the pan to form a crepe about 4½ inches in diameter. Cook just until the first side is set (do not brown), about 45 seconds to 1 minute, then turn the crepe and cook on the other side for 5 seconds. The crepes should be as thin as possible, with no holes. Remove the crepe from the pan and repeat the process, brushing the pan with butter as needed. Stack the cooked crepes as they are done, and when you have used up the batter (you should have 48 crepes), wrap them tightly in plastic wrap to keep them from drying out.

3. Bring a saucepan of water to a boil. Using tongs, dip a bunch of 12 chives in the boiling water and blanch for 10 seconds (this softens the chives). Repeat with the remaining chives, and place them on paper towels to dry.

4. Lay several crepes out on a piece of cooking parchment (no more than 12 at one time, so they won't dry out). Place 1 teaspoon of caviar in the center of each crepe, and top it with ⅓ teaspoon of the crème fraîche. Pull the edges of the crepe up around the filling, making small pleats to create a ruffle at the top. Holding the ruffled top with one hand, carefully tie a single chive around the neck, and make a double knot to hold it securely. Snip off any excess length of chive, and repeat with the remaining crepes and filling.

5. Brush the purses with the melted butter and serve them at room temperature, while the caviar is still cold.

12 portions

FOIE GRAS FOR TWO

Definitely a dish meant to begin a celebratory dinner. Have the Champagne chilled and ready.

2 tablespoons golden raisins
2 teaspoons capers, drained
3 tablespoons Madeira
¼ cup Berta's Chicken Stock (see Index) or canned broth
2 slices fresh duck foie gras (about 2 ounces each), ½ to ¾ inch thick

1. Combine the raisins and capers in a small bowl, add the Madeira and stock; soak for about 30 minutes.

2. Heat a small heavy skillet over medium-high heat until very hot. Add the foie gras; sauté until browned and cooked through, about 2 minutes per side. Transfer to two small plates and keep warm.

3. Pour off any fat in the skillet, and add the raisin/caper mixture. Stir well, scraping the pan, and cook just until heated through and very slightly thickened, 1½ to 2 minutes (watch this carefully). Pour over the foie gras and serve.

2 portions

FEAST ON FOIE GRAS

Exquisite, pale, fattened liver of goose or duck is called foie gras (*fwah-grah*), literally "fat liver." This luxurious food is bred in the southwest corner of France—Gascogne and the Périgord—and in the northeast in Alsace, as well as in Hungary, Israel, and most recently in the United States. Whether served cool from a terrine or in slices slightly seared, it is the most exquisite first course we know.

Imported foie gras: Most foie gras leaves France partially cooked, mixed with other ingredients, and processed in a tin or a jar. The foie gras can be whole, chopped, or puréed. The industry in France is strictly governed, and each tin sold must contain 75 percent foie gras. Truffles, eggs, and filler will make up the remaining 25 percent. Try not to buy foie gras with cornstarch or flour on the list of ingredients, for these are extenders and do the finished product no favors.

Domestic foie gras: The only fresh foie gras available in America (federal regulations forbid the importation of fresh European foie gras) is a very good product from D'Artagnan in upper New York State. This company is owned by our friends Ariane Daguin (daughter of the famous Gascon chef André) and the marketing wizard George Faison. Most stores will sell as much or as little as the customer desires. Or you can order it directly from D'Artagnan by calling (800) DARTAGNAN or in New Jersey (201) 792-0748.

A perfect foie gras should have a silken and velvety texture. It should taste as rich as butter and be firm with a slight give. It should smell sweet and have a creamy color. Brown edges or white spots indicate that it is getting old—do not eat it.

The classic wine for foie gras is Sauternes, the sweet white wine from Bordeaux. It provides a perfect balance for the acidity and richness of the foie gras. You could also serve this delicacy with chilled Champagne, or a light red Bordeaux.

ARIANE DAGUIN'S SAUTEED FOIE GRAS WITH GRAPE SAUCE

Ariane Daguin grew up in Auch, in the heart of Gascony, with foie gras all around her. Years ago we had dinner one night at André Daguin's restaurant in Auch. He proudly showed us his watch, which displayed the time in both France and New York. His daughter, Ariane, was a student at Columbia University then, and he told us that with a glance at his watch he could think of her and imagine what she was doing.

Ariane says to serve foie gras on warm plates and pour the sauce over it, making sure everyone gets an equal portion of both. "This is very important. Several European wars were started when the king got a smaller portion than his colleagues!"

1 fresh raw foie gras (about 1 ½ pounds), whole
Salt and freshly ground white pepper, to taste
1 cup red wine vinegar
1 cup strong chicken stock from chicken bouillon cubes (see Index)
1 bunch seedless green grapes, stems removed (about 32 grapes)
1 tablespoon confectioners' sugar

1. Cut the foie gras into slices ½ to ¾ inch thick. Sprinkle with salt and white pepper.

2. Place a nonstick skillet over high heat. When the pan is very hot, add the foie gras slices, in batches, and cook for 30 seconds on each side. Remove to paper towels and keep warm.

3. Pour off excess fat from the skillet, add the vinegar, and cook over high heat until reduced by half, 2 to 2½ minutes.

4. Add the stock and reduce by half again.

5. Add the grapes to the skillet and sprinkle with the sugar. Let the grapes caramelize for 30 seconds, then shake the pan vigorously to coat them with the sauce for another 10 to 15 seconds.

6. Serve slices of foie gras on warm plates, and pour the sauce over them.

8 portions

RASPBERRY CHICKEN LIVER SAUTE

These chicken livers are enhanced by a sauce of raspberry vinegar and red currant jelly. A risotto is an excellent entrée after this first course.

1 pound chicken livers
⅓ cup unbleached all-purpose flour
½ teaspoon salt
1 tablespoon freshly ground black pepper
2 tablespoons safflower oil
½ cup raspberry vinegar
3 tablespoons red currant jelly

1. Trim the livers and cut them apart. Rinse and pat them dry with paper towels. Combine the flour, salt, and pepper in a mixing bowl, and toss the livers in the mixture. Shake off any excess flour.

2. Heat the safflower oil in a large skillet, and cook the livers over medium-high heat until just cooked, 3 to 4 minutes. They should still be pink inside. Transfer to heated serving plates or a platter.

3. Add the vinegar and jelly to the skillet, and whisk well. Cook over high heat until reduced and syrupy, 2 to 3 minutes. Pour the sauce over the livers and serve immediately.

4 portions

CARPACCIO ON THE GREEN

We have enjoyed many versions of this dish in some of our favorite restaurants. The salad is simple to assemble, and we feel it should be brought into the home. Be sure to use the freshest, best-quality meat, and shave the Parmesan tissue-paper-thin with a vegetable peeler.

4 ounces filet mignon, in one piece (see Note)
12 Greek black olives, pitted and chopped
1 tablespoon capers, drained and chopped
1 clove garlic, minced
¼ cup extra virgin olive oil
1 bunch arugula, trimmed, rinsed, and dried (about 2 cups)
Salt and freshly ground black pepper, to taste
Large shavings from ¼-pound piece of aged Monterey Jack or Parmesan cheese

1. Chill the fillet, well wrapped, in the freezer until nearly frozen, 2 to 3 hours.

2. Combine the olives, capers, garlic, and oil in a small bowl.

3. Remove the fillet from the freezer, and cut it into paper-thin slices. Pound the slices even thinner between two sheets of waxed paper.

4. Arrange a bed of arugula on each of four salad plates, and place the fillet slices decoratively on the arugula. Sprinkle lightly with salt and pepper, and then spoon the oil mixture over the meat. Top with the cheese shavings, and serve immediately.

4 portions

Note: Your butcher can thinly slice the fillet for you, but be sure to use it the same day or it may discolor.

pepper, and 3 teaspoons of the mint. Set aside.

2. Arrange the melon slices, smoked salmon, prosciutto, and carpaccio decoratively on a dinner plate. Drizzle vinaigrette lightly over all, and garnish with the remaining chopped mint and the mint sprigs.

Note: Melons, salmon, and meat are for one portion. Increase accordingly. Vinaigrette yield: ½ cup

---

MEMORIES OF TUSCANY

Carpaccio on the Green

Ribollita
Olive Rosemary Country Bread
Chianti Classico

Sunny Lemon Sorbet

SUNSET MELON WITH SALMON AND PROSCIUTTO

This combination can take many forms: thinly sliced poached or smoked chicken breast may be substituted for the prosciutto and carpaccio, and thinly sliced sturgeon or other smoked whitefish may be substituted for the salmon.

VINAIGRETTE
3 tablespoons fresh orange juice
1 tablespoon raspberry vinegar
¼ cup olive oil
Salt and freshly ground black pepper, to taste
4 teaspoons chopped fresh mint leaves

3 very thin slices cantaloupe, rind removed
3 very thin slices honeydew melon, rind removed
4 very thin wedges watermelon, rind and seeds removed
2 thin slices smoked salmon
3 thin slices prosciutto
2 thin slices beef carpaccio (optional)
Mint sprigs, for garnish

1. Make the vinaigrette: Place the orange juice in a small bowl and whisk in the vinegar. Then slowly drizzle in the oil, whisking constantly. Add salt and

---

THINK CARPACCIO

▲ Beef carpaccio on a bed of arugula, topped with shavings of aged Parmesan, thinly sliced prosciutto, a drizzle of fruity olive oil and lemon juice, and a sprinkle of coarsely ground pepper

▲ Beef carpaccio on a bed of radicchio, topped with crumbled Gorgonzola, a drizzle of fruity olive oil and lemon juice, and a sprinkle of coarsely ground pepper

▲ Tuna carpaccio on a bed of thinly sliced tomatoes and red onions, sprinkled with chopped fresh basil leaves, drizzled with fruity olive oil and lemon juice, and sprinkled with coarsely ground pepper

▲ Salmon carpaccio on a bed of watercress topped with a layer of toasted, finely chopped hazelnuts, a drizzle of fruity olive oil and lemon juice, and a sprinkle of coarsely ground pepper

▲ Scallop carpaccio on a bed of endive, drizzled with fruity olive oil and lemon juice, and topped with a layer of chopped scallions, chopped fresh dill, and coarsely ground pepper

FOR SHEER JOY
CARPACCIO AND PROSCIUTTO

These two classic first courses from Italy set the stage in a striking way for what's to follow. Carpaccio, those thin, thin slices of the finest beef or fish; and transparent slices of prosciutto, that superbly cured Italian ham, are both light and can be easily followed by a pasta, fish, or robust meat course. Possible presentations are endless and the effort minimal.

CARPACCIO RENAISSANCE

Carpaccio was originally created at Harry's Bar in Venice for a countess who couldn't eat cooked meat. They took the very finest baby beef, quickly seared it, and trimmed the seared portion away.

We like the idea of slightly searing the beef. It tightens the meat for easier slicing, just as freezing it for two to three hours does. The beef is cut very thinly across the grain for the tenderest slices. Today poetic license has been taken, and we are seeing thinly sliced raw tuna, salmon, scallop, and black sea bass "carpaccios." When serving beef or fish uncooked, take care that it is very fresh. Buy only from the most reputable butcher and fishmonger.

Fish or beef carpaccio is delightful on beds of watercress, arugula, radicchio, endive, or chicory. The thin, delicate slices can then be topped with minced garlic or scallion, chopped Italian parsley or herbs, capers, tomatoes, or red onions. Drizzle it all with fruity olive oil, splash with lemon juice, and shower with freshly ground pepper.

PROSCIUTTO AND PARMA HAM

Prosciutto is simply the Italian word for ham. What we call prosciutto, the Italians call Parma ham. In Parma, Italy, they have bred an excellent strain of pigs just for prosciutto, feeding them the whey that is left over from the making of Parmesan, which gives the meat its very delicate flavor. The hams are seasoned, salt-cured, air-dried, and pressed so that the flesh is very firm. Our very favorite prosciutto is San Daniele, which actually comes not from Parma but from a little village near the mountains in the very north of Italy. There the pigs eat acorns, and the ham is very pale pink, very tender, sweet, and delicately flavored.

Prosciutto is available in Italian markets, of course, but it is being carried increasingly in the deli sections of city supermarkets. For first courses, prosciutto is sliced paper-thin, but it is also an important ingredient in all sorts of pastas, ragouts, and vegetable dishes. You can ask for thicker slices to cook with and dice these or cut them into strips.

SALTY PROSCIUTTO AND SWEET FRUITS

A first course of prosciutto, sliced transparently thin with a ribbon of white fat, is so sweet and tender that it is like a veil of flavor on the tongue rather than a texture. The fat holds much of the ham's perfume and is meant to be eaten along with the lean. As a first course, prosciutto is best served with slivers of the season's most refreshing fruits. The fruits may be quartered fresh figs, sweet melon slices, velvety persimmon wedges, perfect peaches, or plump plums. Prosciutto and fruit are dazzling when arranged on oversize plates and brought to the table, where they're drizzled with fresh lemon juice and sprinkled with fresh pepper.

Wedges of creamy cheese are sometimes served, or shavings of Parmesan are scattered over the fruit and prosciutto. Prosciutto is so delicate that it should be served with a crisp white wine; red would mask its subtlety.

FRUITS DE MER PASTA

This was inspired by a pasta sauce we first encountered in New Orleans' French Quarter; it impressed us because of its intense seafood flavor. The sauce clings to the linguine, and the sweet scallops and shrimp sit atop. A small portion of these rich flavors begins a meal nicely.

½ cup fish stock (see Index) or bottled clam juice
½ cup heavy or whipping cream
4 ounces medium-size shrimp, peeled and deveined
4 ounces bay scallops, rinsed and patted dry
1 teaspoon grated lemon zest
Salt and freshly ground black pepper, to taste
4 ounces linguine
2 tablespoons unsalted butter
2 ounces fresh crabmeat
1 tablespoon snipped fresh chives
1 teaspoon chopped fresh summer savory

1. In a small saucepan heat the stock, cream, 2 of the shrimp, ¼ cup of the scallops, and ½ teaspoon of the lemon zest. Bring to a boil, then reduce the heat and simmer just until the seafood is cooked, 1 minute.

2. Transfer the mixture to the container of a food processor; purée until smooth. Return the purée to the saucepan, bring to a boil, and reduce until slightly thick, about 2 minutes. Season with salt and pepper. Remove from the heat and keep warm.

3. Bring a large pot of water to a boil. Add the linguine and cook at a rolling boil just until tender.

4. Melt the butter in a small skillet. Stir in the remaining shrimp and scallops, and sauté just until cooked through, 1 to 2 minutes. Add the crabmeat and stir just until hot, 1 to 1½ minutes. Season with chives, savory, the remaining ½ teaspoon lemon zest, and salt and pepper. Keep warm.

5. Drain the linguine, and toss it in a bowl with the sauce until well coated. Arrange the linguine on two plates, and spoon the seafood over it. Serve immediately.

2 portions

LOBSTER RAVIOLI WITH FRESH TARRAGON

This oversize lobster ravioli with fresh tomato sauce is an elegant way to begin a meal. The spare stuffing of lobster chunks is simple and direct extravagance—just one on a plate will do nicely. If you make these raviolis in the summer and have access to lemon basil, use it instead of the tarragon—you will find it to be particularly well suited to the flavor of lobster. In the winter, when fresh tarragon may be hard to find, fresh chervil or parsley is a fine substitute.

1 tablespoon olive oil
5 large ripe tomatoes, peeled, seeded, and chopped
1 tablespoon chopped fresh tarragon leaves
Salt and freshly ground black pepper to taste
¼ cup heavy or whipping cream
12 ounces cooked fresh lobster meat, in large pieces
2 tablespoons freshly grated Parmesan cheese
Tarragon Pasta Dough (see Note)
Fresh tarragon leaves, for garnish
Orange and pink nasturtium blossoms, for garnish (optional)

1. Heat the olive oil in a large saucepan. Add the tomatoes, chopped tarragon, and salt and pepper, and simmer until slightly thick, 15 to 20 minutes. Add the cream, and cook an additional 5 minutes. Transfer to a food processor and purée until smooth. Place the purée in a saucepan.

2. In a small bowl combine the lobster, Parmesan, and ⅓ cup of the purée. Mix well.

3. Lay a sheet of pasta dough on a lightly floured counter or cutting board. Place portions of the lobster filling (approximately 3½ tablespoons for each ravioli) at least 5 inches apart on the pasta (you should have room for two). Lay another sheet of pasta on top, and press down lightly.

4. Using a pastry crimper, cut the dough into 4-inch squares, making sure that the filling is in the center of the squares. Repeat with the remaining dough. You should have enough extra dough to cover the filling on the third sheet of filling.

5. Bring a large pot of salted water to a boil. Drop in the ravioli, and cook until they rise to the surface, 2 to 3 minutes. Drain.

6. Heat the remaining tomato purée, and ladle enough onto each plate to form a pool. Place the ravioli in the center, and sprinkle fresh tarragon leaves on top. Garnish with a nasturtium blossom at the side of each ravioli.

6 portions

Note: To make Tarragon Pasta Dough, prepare our Pasta Dough recipe (see Index), laying fresh tarragon leaves on the dough sheets as described in Step 6. You will need ½ cup tarragon leaves.

RAVIOLI

Ravioli has grown up from the day it was created in Liguria—in both size and sophistication. A single, large ravioli on a plate in a pool of sauce may be filled with lobster and tarragon, foie gras, black truffles, pine nuts and garlic, scallops, zucchini and thyme, chicken livers and mushrooms, salmon and shrimp, or pork and ginger. It's a dramatic and warm opener.

SAGE BUTTER PASTA

This rich, wonderful sauce is made in a flash when you have fresh sage leaves on hand. It is meant to just veil the thinnest of ribbon pastas.

8 ounces linguine or angel hair pasta
1 cup (2 sticks) unsalted butter
2 tablespoons minced fresh sage leaves
Salt and freshly ground black pepper, to taste
¼ cup freshly grated Parmesan cheese
Freshly grated Parmesan cheese, for garnish

1. Bring a large pot of water to a boil. Add the pasta and cook at a rolling boil until tender.

2. While the pasta is cooking, melt the butter in a skillet. Add the sage and cook over low heat for 4 minutes.

3. Drain the pasta and toss it with the sage butter. Add salt and pepper, and the grated Parmesan. Toss well, and serve with extra Parmesan on the side.

4 portions

BASIL GNOCCHI WITH CREAMY TOMATO SAUCE

In no other region does French cooking influence Italian as much as in Piemonte. This *choux*-based gnocchi and creamy tomato sauce is a perfect example. It is a light dish, great for a first course or luncheon.

7 tablespoons unsalted butter
2½ cups water
1½ teaspoons salt
¾ teaspoon freshly ground black pepper
Ground nutmeg
¾ cup sifted unbleached all-purpose flour
4 eggs
1 tablespoon unsalted butter, at room temperature
¼ cup instant semolina
4 cloves garlic, finely chopped
½ cup coarsely chopped fresh basil leaves
½ cup freshly grated Parmesan cheese
3½ cups Creamy Tomato Sauce (recipe follows)

1. Combine 6 tablespoons of the butter, 1 cup of the water, 1 teaspoon of the salt, ¼ teaspoon of the pepper, and a pinch of nutmeg in a heavy saucepan and bring just to a boil. Remove the pan from the heat and add the flour all at once, stirring with a wooden spoon. Continue to stir vigorously until the mixture forms a smooth mass. Return the pan to low heat and cook, stirring, for about 1 minute.

2. Remove the saucepan from the heat and add the eggs one at a time, beating well after each addition. Remove the dough from the pan, rub it with the tablespoon of softened butter (this prevents a skin from forming), and set it, loosely covered, aside in a large mixing bowl.

3. Combine the remaining 1½ cups water, 1 tablespoon butter, ½ teaspoon salt, ½ teaspoon pepper, and a pinch of nutmeg in a saucepan and bring to a boil. Pour in the semolina in a steady stream, stirring constantly. Then add the garlic and continue to cook, stirring, until the semolina thickens, 2 to 3 minutes.

4. Beat the semolina into the dough. Add the basil and cheese, and mix thoroughly.

5. On a lightly floured surface, roll portions of dough into cylinders about ½ inch in diameter; cut the cylinders into 1½-inch lengths.

6. Bring a large pot of salted water to a boil. Reduce the heat to a slow boil and add the gnocchi; cook just until they rise to the surface, 2 minutes. Cook another 30 seconds.

7. Using a slotted spoon, remove the gnocchi to warmed bowls and serve immediately, topped with the hot Creamy Tomato Sauce.

6 portions

CREAMY TOMATO SAUCE

5 large ripe tomatoes (about 2½ to 3 pounds), peeled, seeded, and coarsely chopped
¼ cup finely chopped onion
2 cups heavy or whipping cream
Salt and freshly ground black pepper, to taste

1. Combine the tomatoes and the onion in a heavy saucepan, and cook over low heat, stirring occasionally, until the tomatoes have cooked to a sauce-like consistency, 10 to 15 minutes.

2. Raise the heat to medium, add the cream, and cook until the sauce is slightly thickened, 5 minutes. Season to taste with salt and pepper.

3½ to 4 cups

POTATO GNOCCHI

In Rome, Thursday is gnocchi day, when cooks use their old potatoes (because they have less water content) to make their own special gnocchi recipe.

The trick is to use as little flour as possible to hold the gnocchi together—for the less flour, the lighter the gnocchi—without using so little that they disintegrate in the boiling water.

You can use either waxy or floury potatoes. Waxy potatoes don't need any egg when mixed with the flour, but you may want to add an egg yolk when using floury potatoes to keep them from breaking in the water or sticking to each other.

Lightness is the key, whether the gnocchi are being flavored with spinach, tomatoes, or porcini mushrooms, whether they're baked with butter and sage or tossed with tomato sauce or pesto.

2 boiling potatoes (1 pound), unpeeled
Pinch of salt
1 egg yolk (optional)
¾ cup unbleached all-purpose flour
2 teaspoons olive oil
4 tablespoons (½ stick) unsalted butter
Salt and freshly ground black pepper, to taste
Freshly grated Parmesan cheese, for garnish
Snipped chives, for garnish

1. Place the potatoes in a saucepan, cover with cold water, and add the pinch of salt. Bring the water to a boil, reduce the heat, and simmer until the potatoes are tender, 40 minutes.

2. Drain the potatoes and return them to the pan. Shake the pan gently over low heat to dry the potatoes. Let stand just until the potatoes are cool enough to handle.

3. Peel the potatoes and cut them in chunks. Pass them through a ricer or food mill. Transfer to a lightly floured surface. Make a well in the center of the potatoes, and put the yolk in the well.

4. Sprinkle the potatoes with some of the flour and slowly work it in. Repeat until all the flour has been added and the mixture forms a smooth, slightly sticky, dough.

5. Divide the dough in fourths, and roll each piece into a 15-inch-long rope about ¾ inch in diameter. Using a floured knife, cut each rope into thirty pieces. The gnocchi can be cooked as is; or, to

PRIMO PASTA

We find perfect, piping hot pasta to be just about the most enjoyable way to begin a meal. The contrasting flavors, colors, textures, and temperatures make it a tempting and luscious plate. Remember, this is only a tasty beginning, so center a small mound of pasta on a grand plate and sauce it lightly. Pasta is a perfect opener for a chicken, fish, or meat entrée, and it takes the place of the starch in a menu in the most delightful way. We can't think of any pasta that wouldn't make a fine first course when served in small portions, so check the recipes in the pasta chapter for more ideas.

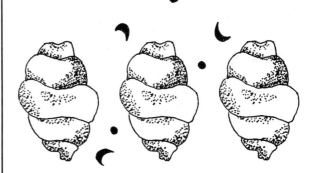

make decorative ridges, flour a dinner fork and roll the gnocchi under the tines.

6. Bring a large pot of salted water to a boil. Add the olive oil, and then drop the gnocchi into the boiling water.

7. When gnocchi rise to the surface, cook 30 seconds more. Drain in a colander.

8. Melt the butter in a large skillet, and add the gnocchi. Toss gently, and season with salt, pepper, and a generous grating of Parmesan cheese. Sprinkle with chives, and serve.

4 portions

Note: The dough can be frozen before cooking. After thawing, roll it out on a lightly floured surface to form the ropes.

ARUGULA

Arugula travels under a variety of names—rugula, roquette, rocket, or garden rocket. In Europe, arugula is nearly as common in the salad bowl as iceberg lettuce is here. This peppery green has a nutty flavor, compared by some to horseradish and by others to mustard greens. If you haven't tried arugula yet, toss a little to start with in your next salad. You will soon find you can't do without this pungent counterpoint in your greens.

ARUGULA PESTO PASTA

A pasta sauce from Rome, where the people are generous, warmhearted, and lusty. This sauce is based on a pesto made with peppery arugula, pine nuts, and mint—a choice for those who love intense flavors.

12 ounces linguine
4 cups fresh arugula leaves, rinsed and patted dry
1 cup fresh mint leaves, rinsed and patted dry
8 cloves garlic, minced
½ cup pine nuts (pignoli)
Salt and freshly ground black pepper, to taste
⅔ cup olive oil
Freshly grated Parmesan cheese, for garnish (optional)

1. Bring a large pot of water to a boil. Add the pasta and cook at a rolling boil just until tender.
2. While the pasta is cooking, combine the arugula, mint, garlic, ¼ cup of the pine nuts, and salt and pepper in a food processor and process until coarsely chopped. Do not over-process.
3. With the motor running, slowly add the olive oil in a steady stream; process until smooth.
4. Toast the remaining ¼ cup pine nuts (see page 77).
5. Drain the pasta and toss it with the pesto and the toasted nuts. Garnish with Parmesan cheese, if desired.

4 portions

PASTA WITH FRESH FENNEL AND SARDINES

This dish sums up what is best and most interesting in the cooking of Sicily. Sardines and wild fennel, typical foods of the ancient Romans, are softened with raisins and toasted pine nuts to dress the most contemporary of Italian foods, pasta. The dish is subtle, playing the soft, saline Mediterranean sardines against the pungent fennel from the mountains. Like most pasta dishes with fish, this does not get topped with cheese.

¼ cup olive oil
1 onion, cut into julienne
1 fennel bulb, cut into julienne
12 ounces spaghetti
½ cup golden raisins
½ cup toasted pine nuts (see page 77)
2 cans (4 ½ ounces each) sardines, drained
2 tablespoons chopped fresh Italian (flat-leaf) parsley

1. Heat the oil in a large skillet, and sauté the onion and fennel over low heat until soft, about 20 minutes.
2. Meanwhile, bring a large pot of water to a boil. Add the pasta and cook at a rolling boil just until tender.
3. Add the raisins and pine nuts to the skillet, and cook another 5 minutes.
4. Remove the skillet from the heat, add the sardines and parsley, and toss gently. Serve immediately over the drained hot spaghetti.

6 portions

WILD MUSHROOM PASTA SAUCE

Dried morels and cèpes plumped in Madeira and sautéed with fresh mushrooms: a wonderfully intense autumnal accent that does not depend on finding fresh wild mushrooms in the market.

To underline the earthy flavors, we sometimes add a few finely chopped chicken livers and Greek olives to the mushroom sauté.

1 ⅔ cups Madeira
1 ounce dried morels, rinsed
1 ounce dried cèpes, rinsed
2 tablespoons olive oil
1 tablespoon unsalted butter
2 tablespoons minced shallots
1 tablespoon plus 1 teaspoon minced garlic
1 ½ pounds fresh cultivated mushrooms, cleaned and thinly
  sliced
¼ cup chopped fresh parsley
Salt and freshly ground black pepper, to taste
1 pound angel hair pasta

1. Bring the Madeira to a boil in a saucepan. Add the dried mushrooms, remove from the heat, and set aside.

2. Heat the oil and butter in a large skillet. Add the shallots and 1 tablespoon garlic, and sauté over medium-low heat for 2 minutes. Add the fresh mushrooms, raise the heat slightly, and cook for 5 minutes.

3. Drain the dried mushrooms, reserving the Madeira. Coarsely chop the mushrooms and add them to the skillet. Cook over low heat, stirring occasionally, until the fresh mushrooms are fully cooked, about 20 minutes.

4. Add the reserved Madeira, the remaining 1 teaspoon garlic, the parsley, and salt and pepper. Cook another 2 minutes.

5. Meanwhile, bring a large pot of water to a boil. Add the pasta and cook at a rolling boil just until tender. Drain, and toss it with the mushroom sauce and serve immediately.

6 to 8 portions

HERBED CHEVRE PANZOTTI

Panzotti (meaning "pot-bellied") are triangular or round dumplings that are usually stuffed with cheese and spinach, chard, or borage. We make ours with a chèvre filling and serve them with Fresh Tomato Sauce. They also work well with a Red or Yellow Pepper Purée. Check the index for recipes for these sauces.

8 ounces soft chèvre, such as Montrachet
2 tablespoons heavy or whipping cream
1 tablespoon snipped fresh chives
1 tablespoon chopped shallots
1 tablespoon chopped fresh Italian (flat-leaf) parsley
½ teaspoon fresh marjoram leaves
Salt and freshly ground black pepper, to taste
Several dashes of Tabasco sauce
1 recipe Pasta Dough (rolled; see Index)

1. Crumble the chèvre into a mixing bowl, and stir it with a wooden spoon until creamy.

2. Add the cream, chives, shallots, parsley, marjoram, salt and pepper, and Tabasco. Mix thoroughly.

3. Lay a sheet of pasta on a counter or cutting board. Place the filling on top, in mounds of 2 heaping tablespoons each, placed at least 4 inches apart. Lay another sheet of dough over that, and press down lightly. If using herb pasta, try to place filling in center of herbs.

4. Use a 2½-inch round dough cutter to cut out the panzotti, making sure that the filling is in the center of each. Then seal the edges by crimping them with a fork. There should be a ¼-inch crimped edge all around. Continue until all the filling is used.

5. Bring a large pot of salted water to a boil. Reduce the heat to a slow boil, and drop in the panzotti. Cook until they rise to the surface, 2 to 3 minutes. Drain, and serve.

6 portions

CONFETTI VEGETABLE PATE

Bright and zesty, this green and orange pâté just looks like a signal for a party. It's truly the easiest vegetable pâté we know.

1 teaspoon plus 1 tablespoon unsalted butter
2 large leeks
4 carrots (about 12 ounces), peeled and cut into ¼-inch dice
1 bunch watercress, tough stems removed
4 ounces green beans, trimmed and cut into ¼-inch pieces
1 cup cooked long-grain rice
¼ cup chopped scallions (green onions)
2 tablespoons chopped fresh dill
1 teaspoon salt
Freshly ground black pepper, to taste
1 tablespoon cornstarch
4 large eggs
1½ cups half-and-half
2 cups Fresh Tomato Coulis (recipe follows)
Dill sprigs, for garnish
Thinly sliced cucumber, for garnish

1. Preheat the oven to 350°F. Grease the sides and bottom of a 9 x 5 x 3-inch loaf pan with the 1 teaspoon butter.
2. Trim the leeks, leaving about 1 inch of green. Halve them lengthwise, and rinse well. Cook the leeks in boiling water until soft, about 4 minutes. Rinse, drain, and pat dry. Line the prepared pan with the leek leaves in one layer, reaching almost to the top of the pan. Set the pan aside.
3. Melt the remaining 1 tablespoon butter in a skillet. Add the carrots and cook, stirring, until soft but not mushy, about 8 minutes. Transfer to a large bowl.
4. Cook the watercress in the same skillet, stirring, just until wilted, about 2 minutes. Drain and squeeze out excess moisture. Chop fine and add to the carrots.
5. Cook the green beans in boiling water until tender, about 4 minutes. Drain, rinse, and drain again.
6. Add the beans to the carrots and watercress, along with the rice, scallions, dill, salt, and pepper. Sprinkle with the cornstarch, and toss until it has been absorbed.
7. Lightly beat the eggs and half-and-half together until smooth. Stir into the vegetable mixture. Ladle the mixture into the prepared pan, and place it in a larger baking pan. Fill the larger pan with 1 inch of hot water.
8. Bake the pâté until the top is dry and firm to the touch, and a knife inserted in the center comes out clean, about 1 hour and 10 minutes. Cool on a rack for 2 hours. Then cover and chill for several hours.
9. Place a platter on top of the pâté and invert the platter and dish together. Unmold the pâté, and carefully cut it into ½- to ¾-inch-thick slices. Spoon the tomato coulis on the side. Garnish with fresh dill and cucumber slices.

12 portions

FRESH TOMATO COULIS

Fresh tomato and cucumber make a lovely flavor accent for the Confetti Vegetable Pâté, or atop grilled fish or chicken.

4 ripe plum tomatoes
½ large cucumber, peeled, seeded, and cut into ¼-inch dice
1 tablespoon snipped fresh chives
1 tablespoon chopped fresh dill
Salt and freshly ground black pepper, to taste
1 tablespoon olive oil

1. Purée 3 of the tomatoes in a food processor or blender until smooth. Transfer to a bowl.
2. Dice the remaining tomato and stir it, along with the cucumber, chives, and dill, into the purée. Season with salt and pepper.
3. Slowly stir in the oil until incorporated. Cover and chill until ready to serve.

2 cups

MOZZARELLA CASARECCIA ALLA GRIGLIA

We love eating at the restaurant Sole Mio in Chicago, where complex and robust dishes never cease to delight us. Paul LoDuca, one-time chef there, has shared a favorite with us.

3 tablespoons olive oil
1 teaspoon minced garlic
4 cups loosely packed fresh spinach leaves, well rinsed and
    patted dry
1 ripe tomato, cored and halved
1 ball fresh mozzarella cheese, about 8 ounces
1 cup Tomato Balsamic Vinaigrette (recipe follows)

1. Preheat the oven to 275°F.
2. Heat 2 tablespoons of the oil in a large skillet. Add the garlic and spinach, and sauté over medium heat until the spinach is just wilted, 4 to 5 minutes. Set aside.
3. Heat a heavy (preferably stainless steel) skillet until it is very hot. Add the tomato halves, cut side down, and sear until charred, about 2 minutes. Remove them from the pan, remove the skins, and set aside.
4. Clean the skillet and once again heat it until very hot. Cut the mozzarella into four ¾-inch-thick slices, and oil the slices with the remaining tablespoon of olive oil. Place the mozzarella slices in the

FRESH FROM THE GARDEN

Vegetables offer a great number of possibilities for openers. They can be served crisp and fresh with aïoli, grated and fried crisp in little pancakes, layered in a terrine and bound with a light custard, or baked in a colorful tart. Make the very most of your vegetable first course by arranging some fresh examples in your favorite basket or silver bowl and bringing them to the table as a lush and gorgeous centerpiece.

skillet, and sauté on one side only for 30 seconds. Carefully remove them from the skillet and invert two slices onto each plate. Place a tomato half in the center of each plate, next to the cheese, and arrange the spinach around the tomato.
5. Warm the plates in the oven until the cheese has melted, 8 to 10 minutes.
6. Remove the plates from the oven, drizzle with the vinaigrette, and serve immediately.
   2 portions

TOMATO BALSAMIC VINAIGRETTE

1 large ripe tomato, peeled, seeded, and chopped
1 tablespoon minced shallot
½ teaspoon minced garlic
½ cup tomato juice
¼ cup balsamic vinegar
¼ cup extra virgin olive oil
Salt and freshly ground black pepper, to taste

1. Place the chopped tomato in a heavy skillet, and cook over low heat until all the liquid evaporates. Remove it from the skillet, and allow it to cool.
2. Combine the tomato with the remaining ingredients, and mix well. Let stand, loosely covered, at least 2 hours before using, to blend the flavors.
   1 cup

CELERY ROOT PANCAKES

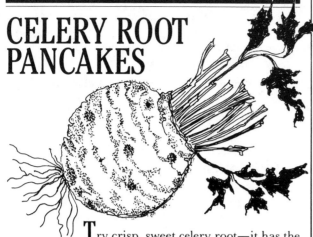

Try crisp, sweet celery root—it has the texture of a potato and the flavor of celery with a mild hint of parsley. These pancakes are a wintertime favorite in Scandinavia, where they are topped with a dab of sour cream and a dab of salmon or caviar. It's no wonder everyone roots for them!

1 celery root (about 8 ounces)
1 onion
¾ cup julienned red bell pepper, cut into 1-inch lengths
¾ cup cooked corn kernels, well drained
4 eggs, lightly beaten
5 tablespoons chopped cilantro (fresh coriander)
1 ½ teaspoons finely chopped fresh jalapeño pepper
3 tablespoons unbleached all-purpose flour
½ teaspoon baking soda
Salt and freshly ground black pepper, to taste
4 tablespoons (½ stick) unsalted butter
4 tablespoons olive oil
1 cup Avocado Purée (recipe follows), for garnish
½ cup crème fraîche (see Index), for garnish

1. Peel the celery root, and grate it on the largest holes of a grater. Place the gratings in a clean kitchen towel, and squeeze out any moisture. Transfer to a bowl.

2. Grate the onion coarsely. Place it in a clean kitchen towel, squeeze out any excess moisture, and add to the celery root.

3. Add the bell pepper, corn, eggs, 4 tablespoons of the cilantro, jalapeño pepper, flour, baking soda, and salt and pepper to the bowl. Toss gently with the celery root and onion until well mixed.

4. In a large skillet, heat 2 tablespoons of the butter with 2 tablespoons of the oil over medium heat.

5. Drop the celery root mixture by rounded ta-

blespoons into the skillet, and flatten slightly to form 2-inch pancakes. Sauté until golden, 2 minutes. Then turn and sauté until golden on the other side, 2 minutes. Place the cooked pancakes on paper towels and keep warm. Continue making pancakes, adding more butter and oil if necessary, until all the mixture has been used. (You should have 24 pancakes.)

6. Place three pancakes on each plate. Garnish with Avocado Purée and crème fraîche, and sprinkle with the remaining chopped cilantro. Serve immediately.

8 portions

AVOCADO PUREE

The velvety smooth texture and flavor of avocado purée complements crispy Celery Root Pancakes, Corn Crab Cakes, and a Best Western Omelet.

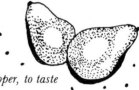

1 ripe avocado
2 tablespoons sour cream
2 tablespoons fresh lemon juice
Dash of Tabasco sauce
Salt and freshly ground black pepper, to taste

Peel the avocado, and purée it with the remaining ingredients in a food processor until smooth. Serve as a dipping sauce.

1 cup

Note: If you are not going to use the purée immediately, place the pit in a container with the purée; this will keep the purée from discoloring.

TRADE SECRET

If you are using half an avocado, leave the pit in the unused half, cover it with plastic wrap, and refrigerate. This will retard discoloration. If the avocado's cut surface should turn brown, gently scrape off the discoloration. The avocado should be fine underneath.

MOREL MUSHROOMS IN THE SQUARE

Woodsy, robust morels with shallots and fresh chives in the lightness of puff pastry—a sublime and elegant springtime first course.

2 ounces dried morels
2 cups Berta's Chicken Stock (see Index) or canned broth
Unbleached all-purpose flour
1 recipe Adrienne's Rough Puff Pastry (see Index), or 1
*   pound frozen puff pastry, thawed*
1 egg
1 teaspoon water
12 large shallots, peeled
1 cup (2 sticks) unsalted butter
5 teaspoons dried thyme leaves, crumbled
½ teaspoon freshly ground black pepper
1 teaspoon sugar
¼ cup Calvados or apple brandy
1 ¼ cups heavy or whipping cream
2 tablespoons snipped fresh chives

1. Place the morels in a strainer and rinse with cold water.

2. Bring the chicken stock to a boil in a medium-size saucepan. Drop in the morels, and simmer for 5 minutes. Remove the pan from the heat, and allow the morels to soak in the stock for 1 hour. Drain, reserving the morels and the soaking liquid separately.

3. Lightly flour a work surface and roll the puff pastry out to a thickness of ⅛ inch. Cut it into eight pieces approximately 3 ½ inches square.

4. Place the puff pastry squares on an ungreased baking sheet, and prick them all over with the tines of a fork. Whisk the egg and water together, and brush the top of each square with this egg wash. Cover the baking sheet with plastic wrap and refrigerate for at least 30 minutes.

5. Preheat the oven to 350°F.

6. Bake the pastry squares until puffed and golden, 25 to 30 minutes.

7. While the pastry is baking, cut each shallot in half lengthwise.

8. In a large heavy skillet, melt the butter over low heat. Add the shallots, sprinkle with the thyme and pepper, and cook for 7 minutes, shaking the pan

DINNER WITH HINTS OF THE PAST

Morel Mushrooms in the Square

———

Tournedos Rossini on a Celery Root
Bed
Beet and Coriander Purée
Fava Bean Purée
Côte de Beaune

———

Peaches and Cream Ice Cream
Orange Tuiles

frequently. Then sprinkle with the sugar and cook an additional 2 minutes, continuing to shake the pan. Using a slotted spoon, transfer the shallots to a bowl and keep warm.

9. Add the drained morels to the skillet and cook over low heat for 10 minutes, stirring frequently. Transfer them to the bowl with the shallots.

10. Add ¾ cup of the morel soaking liquid and the Calvados to the butter sauce in the skillet. Bring to a boil and continue boiling for 4 minutes, stirring well.

11. Add the cream and continue boiling, whisking constantly, until the sauce has reduced by half and thickened, about 10 minutes.

12. Gently remove the top half of the puff pastry shells. Place the bottom halves on plates, and top with the morels and shallots. Pour some cream sauce over each, sprinkle with chives, and place the top halves of the pastry shells over the filling, at an angle so that the filling shows. Serve immediately.

8 portions

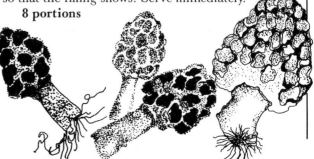

BLACK TIE ASPARAGUS

On a bed of thin green asparagus, softly scrambled eggs with some of your favorite caviar stirred in and the rest of your caviar quota atop. Just the right beginning for a festive dinner for two, or as the main event of a brunch, luncheon, or midnight supper. Just double the amount of ingredients.

If caviar isn't in the cupboard but other indulgences are, use smoked salmon, foie gras, or fresh white or black truffles.

4 thin asparagus spears, trimmed
1 teaspoon unsalted butter, melted
Freshly ground black pepper, to taste
1 tablespoon unsalted butter
1 egg
1 tablespoon heavy or whipping cream
1 tablespoon snipped fresh chives
Pinch of salt
1½ teaspoons good-quality
*   (not lumpfish) caviar*
Snipped fresh chives, for garnish

1. Blanch the asparagus in lightly salted boiling water for 2 minutes. Drain well, and arrange on a plate. Brush with the melted butter, sprinkle with pepper, and keep warm.
2. Melt the 1 tablespoon butter in a small skillet over low heat.
3. In a small bowl lightly beat the egg, cream, 1 tablespoon chives, salt, and pepper to taste.
4. Cook the egg in the skillet, stirring, over low heat until very soft and almost set, 1½ minutes. Stir in 1 teaspoon of the caviar, and spoon the eggs over the asparagus. Top with the remaining caviar, and garnish with chives. Serve immediately.
   1 portion

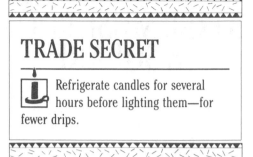

TRADE SECRET

Refrigerate candles for several hours before lighting them—for fewer drips.

FLAKY ASPARAGUS SANDWICH

A perfect first course or side vegetable to accompany stuffed Cornish game hens. When serving as a first course, place in the center of a large plate for a dramatic presentation.

1 recipe Adrienne's Rough Puff Pastry (see Index), or 1
*   pound frozen puff pastry, thawed*
1 pound thin asparagus (about 24 spears)
4 ounces haricots verts (thin, tender green beans), trimmed
2 tablespoons unsalted butter
4 tablespoons chopped shallots
Juice of 1 lemon, or to taste
Freshly ground black pepper, to taste
2 cups loosely packed fresh spinach leaves (trimmed), well
*   rinsed*

1. On a lightly floured surface, roll the dough out to form a 13-inch square. Trim the edges, and cut the dough into six 6 x 4-inch rectangles. Place the rectangles on a heavy baking sheet, cover, and chill for at least 30 minutes.
2. Preheat the oven to 350°F.
3. Trim the asparagus to 6-inch lengths. Bring a pot of salted water to a boil and add the asparagus. Simmer until crisp-tender, 2 to 3 minutes. Drain under cold water to stop the cooking process. Drain again, and set aside.
4. Bring another saucepan of salted water to a boil, and add the haricots verts. Cook until crisp-

tender, about 2 minutes. Drain, refresh in cold water, and drain again. Set aside.

5. Bake the chilled pastry rectangles until puffed and golden, 30 minutes. Remove the pastry from the oven, and set it aside to cool. When it is cool enough to handle, cut off the top third of each rectangle and set it aside.

6. Melt 1 tablespoon of the butter in a skillet, and add 2 tablespoons of the shallots. Cook until the shallots are soft, 2 to 3 minutes. Then add the asparagus and haricots verts; heat thoroughly, 1 to 1½ minutes. Remove from the heat, drain, and toss with lemon juice and black pepper to taste.

7. Melt the remaining 1 tablespoon butter in a saucepan, and add the remaining 2 tablespoons shallots and the spinach. Cook over medium-high heat, stirring, until the spinach has wilted, 3 minutes. Remove from the heat, drain, and toss with lemon juice and black pepper to taste.

8. Place a bed of spinach on the bottom of each pastry rectangle, and top it with some of the asparagus and haricots verts. Place the pastry top at an angle over each "sandwich," and serve immediately.

6 portions

THE BEST TABLE FOR THE BEST TALK

—■—

We think that the shape of a table shapes conversation. Those knights in King Arthur's court and the literary wits at the Algonquin figured it out for us—the round table makes for the best conversation. Think about it. You never see people standing and talking or huddled before a football play in a rectangle.

The art of conversation is fragile. A table that keeps people too far apart separates their remarks as well. Better an animated group, shoulder to shoulder, each member fully a part of a magic circle, than all the elbow room in the world.

STEAK TARTARE IN ARTICHOKE BOTTOMS

Buy your meat for steak tartare the day you plan to serve it. It should be of the best quality and very fresh. This presentation is a bit unusual and quite decorative.

4 large artichokes
8 ounces fresh beef sirloin, finely ground
1 tablespoon minced onion
1 tablespoon chopped fresh Italian (flat-leaf) parsley
2 teaspoons Dijon mustard
1 egg yolk
½ teaspoon salt
Freshly ground black pepper, to taste
4 attractive lettuce leaves, rinsed and patted dry
2 tablespoons snipped fresh chives
½ cup Calamata or other imported black olives
1 hard-cooked egg, coarsely chopped
⅓ cup tiny capers, drained
2 ripe plum tomatoes, cut into ¼-inch dice
Thinly sliced black bread, for serving

1. Place the artichokes in a large saucepan, and add an inch of water. Bring it to a boil; then reduce the heat, cover, and simmer until the artichokes are tender, about 45 minutes. Remove them from pot and set them aside to cool.

2. Peel the leaves away from the artichokes, and scoop out the fuzzy choke. Reserve the bottoms.

3. Combine the ground sirloin, onion, parsley, mustard, egg yolk, salt, and black pepper in a mixing bowl. Blend with a fork until just mixed. Cover, and refrigerate until ready to serve, but no more than 3 hours.

4. Arrange a lettuce leaf on each plate. Place an artichoke bottom in the center of the lettuce, and fill it with the steak tartare. Sprinkle with the chives.

5. Arrange the remaining ingredients in an attractive pattern around each artichoke bottom. Serve immediately, with thin slices of black bread.

4 portions

WHITE MISCHIEF

Sumptuous and beguiling—white, warm, creamy cheese is a seductive way to start a spectacular supper. Stratas, soufflés, simmered cheese rarebit, and a simple spinach and ricotta pie—what could be more scrumptiously spectacular?

ROQUEFORT TART PIPÉRADE

The sweetness of the peppers, brought about by long, slow cooking, plays off well against the slightly sharp taste of the cheese in the pastry. Delicious served in small, savory wedges.

PASTRY

1 ½ cups unbleached all-purpose flour
3 ½ tablespoons unsalted butter, cold, cut into small pieces
2 tablespoons Roquefort cheese, cold
3 tablespoons solid vegetable shortening, cold
4 tablespoons ice water

FILLING

¼ cup extra virgin olive oil
2 tablespoons unsalted butter
1 cup thinly sliced halved onions
2 yellow bell peppers, cored, seeded, and thinly sliced
2 red bell peppers, cored, seeded, and thinly sliced
1 tablespoon dried thyme leaves, crumbled
1 tablespoon dried rosemary, crushed
1 teaspoon freshly ground black pepper
½ teaspoon salt
½ cup finely slivered fresh basil leaves
¼ cup chopped fresh parsley
4 cloves garlic, finely minced

16 Niçoise or other imported black olives
1 teaspoon chopped fresh parsley, for garnish

1. Prepare the pastry 3 hours ahead: Place the flour in a medium-size bowl. Add the butter, cheese, and shortening, and using a pastry blender, two knives, or your fingertips, cut them into the flour until the mixture resembles coarse crumbs.

2. Using a fork, add enough of the ice water to the flour mixture to make a workable dough.

3. On a lightly floured work surface, form the dough into a ball. Wrap it in plastic wrap and refrigerate 3 to 4 hours.

4. Prepare the filling: Heat the oil and butter in a large heavy skillet over medium heat. Reduce the heat to low, and add the onions, both bell peppers, thyme, rosemary, black pepper, and salt. Simmer, uncovered, stirring frequently, until the vegetables are limp and the mixture resembles marmalade, 45 minutes.

5. Add the basil, parsley, and garlic and cook, stirring well, another 5 minutes. Adjust the seasonings. Remove the vegetables to a strainer and drain well.

6. Preheat the oven to 375°F.

7. On a lightly floured surface, roll the chilled dough out to form a circle ⅛ inch thick and 10 inches in diameter.

8. Transfer the dough to an 8-inch tart pan with removable bottom. Pat it into place and trim off any excess around the rim.

9. Prick the bottom of the crust well with a fork. Line the crust with aluminum foil, and fill it with dried beans or pie weights.

10. Bake the crust for 10 minutes. Then remove the weights and foil, and bake an additional 10 to 15 minutes. Cool slightly. Leave the oven on.

11. Spread the drained pepper mixture evenly in the crust, and arrange the olives decoratively on top. Bake until the crust pulls away from the sides of the pan, 15 minutes. Remove the tart from the oven, and let it rest for 2 minutes.

12. Carefully push the bottom up through the rim of the tart pan, and using a wide spatula, transfer the tart to a serving plate. Sprinkle with parsley, cut into wedges, and serve.

6 portions

ROSEMARY LEMON TART

A perfect lazy summer appetizer: the ripest tomatoes and the freshest rosemary, combined with a lemony chèvre filling in a Roquefort-accented crust. Serve this with a chilled Bandal rosé.

FILLING

11 ounces Montrachet chèvre
¼ cup heavy or whipping cream
2 tablespoons finely chopped fresh rosemary leaves
½ teaspoon dried thyme leaves
½ teaspoon coarsely ground black pepper
2 tablespoons grated lemon zest
½ teaspoon fresh lemon juice

PASTRY

1½ cups unbleached all-purpose flour
3½ tablespoons unsalted butter, cold
2 tablespoons Roquefort cheese, cold
3 tablespoons solid vegetable shortening, cold
4 tablespoons ice water

6 ripe plum tomatoes
Coarse (kosher) salt
¼ cup fresh rosemary leaves
Freshly ground black pepper, to taste
1 tablespoon extra virgin olive oil
Fresh rosemary sprigs, for garnish

1. Three to 4 hours before serving, prepare the filling and the pastry dough: Break the chèvre into chunks, and place them in a food processor. With the motor running, slowly add the cream through the feed tube, and process until smooth.

2. Transfer the mixture to a small bowl, and fold in the remaining filling ingredients. Cover, and refrigerate for 3 to 4 hours.

3. Next, make the dough: Place the flour in a medium-size bowl. Cut the butter, Roquefort, and shortening into pieces. Using two knives, a pastry blender, or your fingertips, cut the pieces into the flour until the mixture resembles coarse crumbs.

4. Add the water, 1 tablespoon at a time, mixing with a fork until the mixture forms a ball. Wrap the dough in plastic wrap, and refrigerate 3 to 4 hours.

5. When you are ready to assemble the tart, preheat the oven to 375°F.

6. Unwrap the chilled dough and place it on a lightly floured surface. Roll it out to form a circle about ⅛ inch thick.

7. Carefully lay the dough over an 8-inch fluted tart pan with removable bottom. Trim off any excess dough around the top of the rim. Prick the bottom of the crust with the tines of a fork. Line the crust with aluminum foil, and fill it with dried beans or pie weights.

8. Bake the crust for 10 minutes. Then remove the beans and foil, and bake until the crust is light brown, 10 to 15 minutes. Allow the crust to cool slightly. Leave the oven on.

9. Cut the tomatoes into ¼-inch-thick slices. Sprinkle them lightly with coarse salt, and place them on paper towels. Allow them to sit for 30 minutes (this removes excess liquid).

10. Using a rubber spatula, spread the chilled filling evenly in the cooled pie shell. Lay the tomato slices decoratively over the filling in a circular pattern, overlapping the slices. Sprinkle with the rosemary and pepper, and drizzle with the olive oil.

11. Bake the tart until the tomatoes are wilted and the crust has pulled away from the sides of the pan, 35 to 40 minutes. Remove the pan from the oven, and let it cool for 5 minutes.

12. Carefully push the bottom through the rim of the tart pan. Using a long metal spatula, gently slip the tart off the bottom and onto a serving platter. Garnish with the rosemary sprigs, and serve.

6 portions

TRADE SECRET

Stack large dinner plates at the start of the buffet table and silverware and napkins at the end. This way hands are freer to fill up the plates and aren't loaded down until the last moment.

CHAMPAGNE ANYTIME

Bubbly and splendid. Romantic and elegant. Champagne has always meant a celebration. The Champagne most celebrated throughout the world is Dom Pérignon, named for the seventeenth-century Benedictine monk credited as the father of Champagne.

Of all France's glorious vineyard regions, Champagne is the farthest north. Its cool climate and chalky soil are vital to this wine's sparkling perfection. In the heart of Champagne lie Reims and Epernay. Reims is best known for Taittinger, Pommery, Louis Roederer, Piper-Heidsieck, and Veuve Clicquot. From Epernay come Moët et Chandon, Dom Pérignon, and Perrier-Jouët.

Grapes for Champagne are the famous Burgundies: Chardonnay, Pinot Noir, and Pinot Meunier. Grapes are most often blended for the finest Champagnes; the exceptions are the light and delicate Blanc de Blancs, made from all Chardonnay grapes, and Blanc de Noirs, white wine made from black grapes.

The most important element in the creation of Champagne is *la méthode champenoise,* which turns still wine into sparkling wine. The still wine is infused with a mixture of cane sugar and citric acid and then bottled, corked, and stored on its side. The infusion slowly reacts with the natural yeasts in the wine, creating the second fermentation and producing a slightly higher alcohol content and carbon dioxide gas, which creates the sparkling bubbles we love so well. The method, no longer restricted to France, is used in making sparkling wines in the United States and Spain.

We have sung the praises of Champagne, but Shramsberg, from the Napa Valley in California, is a favorite sparkling wine and, we feel, the finest produced in California. The Blanc de Blancs is light and fruity, the Blanc de Noirs rich and exciting, and the Cuvée de Gamay an enchanting sparkling rosé.

We serve Champagne with oysters, caviar, and dessert, but no time has ever seemed inappropriate. Serve it chilled but not too icy to truly taste the full-bodied, elegant flavor.

Champagne is bottled in ten different sizes. It's a great pleasure to see them lined up smallest to largest and recite their names: Split, Pint, Quart, Magnum, Jeroboam, Rehoboam, Methusalem, Salmanasar, Balthazar, and Nebuchadnezzar—the equivalent of twenty quarts. *A votre santé!*

Julee
and
Bill
October
12

STAR STRATAS

Stratas make superb substitutes for the trickier soufflé. These savory custards can be prepared ahead of time and baked at the last minute for a beautiful first course or light after-theater supper.

8 ounces thinly sliced bacon
1 cup heavy or whipping cream
1 cup milk
5 eggs
1 teaspoon salt
Dash of Tabasco sauce
½ teaspoon freshly ground black pepper
1 tablespoon unsalted butter
8 slices good-quality white bread, crusts removed
1 pound Camembert cheese, rind removed
12 ounces sweet Gorgonzola or Saga blue cheese, rind removed
¼ cup finely chopped fresh rosemary leaves or 1 tablespoon dried, crumbled

1. Cut the bacon into ½-inch pieces. In a heavy skillet over medium heat, sauté the bacon until crisp. Drain on paper towels and reserve.

2. Whisk together the cream, milk, eggs, salt, Tabasco, and pepper in a medium-size bowl. Set aside.

3. Preheat the oven to 350°F.

4. Grease eight 1-cup soufflé dishes with the butter. Cut each slice of bread in half lengthwise, and put one piece in each soufflé dish. Sprinkle the bread evenly with half the cheeses, bacon, and rosemary. Repeat the layers.

5. Carefully pour the custard mixture over the bread and cheese layers, to reach ½ inch from the top of the soufflé dishes. Press the contents down gently with the back of a spoon, and set aside at room temperature, covered, for 30 minutes.

6. Line a baking sheet with aluminum foil. Place the soufflé dishes on the sheet, and bake until bubbling and golden on top, 30 minutes.

7. Remove the pan from the oven and let the stratas rest 10 minutes before serving.

8 portions

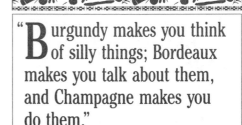

"Burgundy makes you think of silly things; Bordeaux makes you talk about them, and Champagne makes you do them."

—Brillat-Savarin

WELSH RABBIT

A classic dish that comes together perfectly in the microwave. Serve it on a thick slice of fresh multi-grain bread for a different twist.

8 ounces sharp Cheddar cheese, shredded
1 teaspoon cornstarch
½ teaspoon dry mustard
½ cup beer
1 teaspoon Worcestershire sauce
Freshly ground black pepper, to taste
1 egg yolk
4 thick slices multi-grain bread, toasted

1. Toss the cheese, cornstarch, and mustard in a mixing bowl.

2. Combine the beer, Worcestershire, and pepper in a 2-quart microwave-safe casserole and cook at full power, uncovered, 1 minute.

3. Whisk in the cheese mixture and cook 1 minute. Stir again, and cook another 30 seconds.

4. Whisk in the egg yolk. Cook 1 minute, stirring every 30 seconds until smooth. Spoon over toasted bread.

4 portions

Note: This recipe was cooked on High (full power, 650 to 700 watts) in a carousel microwave, using microwave-safe containers.

If your microwave is less powerful, you will have to allow for more cooking time (approximately 1½ times the amount called for—but watch carefully); if it does not have a carousel, you may have to rotate the dish while it is cooking.

DELICIOUS SCENTS

The scent in your home makes an important first impression. It's wonderful to be greeted by the smell of dinner cooking, but if all the food has been prepared ahead, you can plan the scent that will greet your guests.

▲ In winter, keep a small pan of apple juice with cloves and cinnamon simmering on the back burner.

▲ Place a bouquet of fresh herbs near the front door. Try mint in summer, for its refreshing scent, and rosemary in winter, for the aroma of pine.

▲ Put potpourri in small dishes and place them all around the house. Put some in a metal container on top of the radiator, too.

▲ Toss orange and lemon peels, cloves, cinnamon sticks, pine boughs, and cones into the fire.

▲ Burn fruitwood in the fireplace for a delicious scent.

▲ Place small bouquets of fragrant flowers throughout the party rooms. Try roses, jasmine, lilacs, wisteria, hyacinths, and gardenias.

SMOKED SALMON SOUFFLE

Don't wait for dinner—make these soufflés on a lovely Sunday morning. Or buy some great Irish smoked salmon and serve them as a late-supper treat after all the Saint Patrick's Day festivities have quieted down.

¼ cup freshly grated Parmesan cheese
2 eggs, separated
¼ cup heavy or whipping cream
2 tablespoons slivered smoked salmon
1 teaspoon snipped fresh chives
½ teaspoon grated lemon zest
½ teaspoon cornstarch
Pinch of salt
Freshly ground black pepper, to taste
Few drops of fresh lemon juice, ⅛ teaspoon

1. Preheat the oven to 375°F.

2. Butter four individual (5-ounce) ovenproof ramekins. Coat the bottom and sides with grated cheese, and shake out any excess.

3. In a mixing bowl stir together the egg yolks, cream, salmon, chives, lemon zest, cornstarch, salt, and pepper.

4. With an electric mixer, beat the egg whites with the lemon juice until firm but not dry. Gently fold the whites into the yolk mixture.

5. Fill the ramekins with the soufflé mixture, and arrange on a baking sheet.

6. Place the baking sheet in the oven, lower the heat to 350°F, and bake until puffed and golden, 10 minutes. Serve immediately.

4 portions

TOASTING PINE NUTS

To toast pine nuts, preheat the oven to 350°F. Spread out the nuts on a baking sheet and place them in the oven. Bake for 3 to 5 minutes. Check after 3 minutes. They go from browned to burned in a matter of seconds.

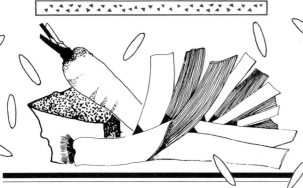

RICOTTA TORTE

Although classified as cheese, ricotta is in fact a by-product of cheesemaking. It is made from the whey after it has been separated from the curd—in this country generally from cow's milk. In Italy the genuine article is made from the whey of the ewe's milk that goes to make Pecorino cheese, and it is creamier and less crumbly than ours. We've smoothed this ricotta out with feta cheese and eggs.

*1 large leek (white part and 1 inch green), halved lengthwise
    and rinsed well*
*½ large carrot, peeled, cut in thin wide strips with a
    vegetable peeler*
1 package (10 ounces) frozen leaf spinach, thawed
6 ounces ricotta cheese
6 ounces feta cheese
3 large eggs, lightly beaten
¼ cup pine nuts (pignoli), toasted (see box)
3 tablespoons grated Parmesan cheese
2 tablespoons dried bread crumbs
¾ teaspoon dried thyme leaves, crumbled
¾ teaspoon salt
Freshly ground black pepper, to taste

1. Preheat the oven to 350°F. Butter a deep 1½-quart ovenproof casserole, and set it aside.

2. Blanch the leek and carrot strips in lightly salted boiling water for about 3 minutes. Rinse and drain. Pat dry.

3. Line the bottom and sides of the casserole with overlapping vegetable strips, alternating leek and carrot, starting in the center and radiating out like the spokes of a wheel.

4. Blanch the spinach in boiling salted water for 3 minutes. Drain well, and squeeze out excess moisture. Chop coarsely.

5. In a medium-size bowl, stir the spinach, ricotta and feta cheeses, eggs, pine nuts, Parmesan, bread crumbs, thyme, salt, and pepper until smooth. Pack the mixture into the prepared casserole.

6. Fold the ends of the vegetable strips over the mixture, adding more strips if necessary to cover. Cover the dish with foil.

7. Place the casserole in a larger ovenproof pan, and fill the pan with enough hot water to reach halfway up the sides of the casserole.

8. Bake 1 hour and 15 minutes. Remove the pan from the oven, and let the casserole stand for 10 minutes. Unmold the pie onto a serving plate. Cut into wedges and serve.

6 to 8 portions

ROSES

Nothing is more beautiful than antique vases filled with every pastel rose—pink, ecru, pale yellow, cream, and white. Buy roses at least two days ahead so they'll be in full bloom by the day of the party. When the roses start to fade, hang them upside down by their stems and let them dry. Dried roses keep their color and charm and make beautiful arrangements.

THE DINNER PARTY

Dinner parties are back. They always did surpass the night out in a restaurant as a way to share good food and conversation, but it took some of us a while to remember. Now that we do, we want to enjoy it as much as our guests. The key, we've found, is careful planning and organization.

THE INVITATION

▲ For the guest list, choose an interesting combination of people: some with similar interests, some who know each other, and some who will add another dimension to the party.

▲ Choose a date at least three to four weeks ahead of time to make sure guests will be available.

▲ Invitations set the tone of the party. For more formal dinners, we prefer to send printed or written invitations. The most formal are printed in black on heavy ecru cards. Semiformal invitations are also printed, but you fill in the date, time, place, and RSVP. Invitations by phone are very difficult these days, with so many people working. Invite by phone only for a small, casual dinner.

▲ Go to the post office to buy pretty stamps for your invitations. It shows your attention to detail and will surely be noticed.

▲ We like invitations that say "cocktails at 7:30; dinner at 8:30." One late guest can throw the most perfectly planned evening off, but the cocktail hour gives both hosts and guests a bit of grace. It is also the perfect time for guests who may not know each other to get to know each other, which makes dinner conversation more comfortable and interesting.

THE MENU

▲ When planning a menu, think very carefully about who your guests are and how many there will be. If there are some with dietary restrictions, such as a strict low-cholesterol diet or a vegetarian one, take it into consideration so that no one will feel he has to go hungry.

▲ We think the best menus reflect simple cooking with a special touch. Great fresh flavors should harmonize with textures throughout the courses. Plan food that is visually balanced, too, so that each course dazzles the eye as well as the palate.

A creamy soup should be followed by an entrée rich in texture but not heavily sauced. A highly seasoned first course should be followed by a more delicate main dish. A rich entrée should be preceded by a simple opener and followed by a light and tart dessert. Try not to repeat ingredients and flavors.

▲ The best way to plan a meal is to begin with knowing what ingredients are freshest in the market. Perhaps it's something that is in season for a short time, and you can choose to plan your menu around that special ingredient.

▲ The number of courses offered is completely up to you, but there should be at least three. Each one should be distinctive and special while balancing and complementing the others. Most important, do not plan a menu that calls for lots of last-minute preparation.

TIPS FOR THE CASUAL DINNER PARTY

- Invite guests by phone and mention names of others who are coming.
- Chill large bottles of water in wine buckets at either end of the table, or serve chilled water in pitchers so guests can help themselves.
- Serve soups and stews out of casseroles or large terrines, if attractive, right out of the oven.
- Let one person help you clear and serve so that the conversation isn't interrupted between courses by everyone getting up.
- Give a general seating rule, such as alternating boy and girl; anything more specific is unnecessary.
- If you're serving a buffet, be sure to offer large linen lap napkins, individual flat baskets, or stack tables so that guests can eat comfortably.

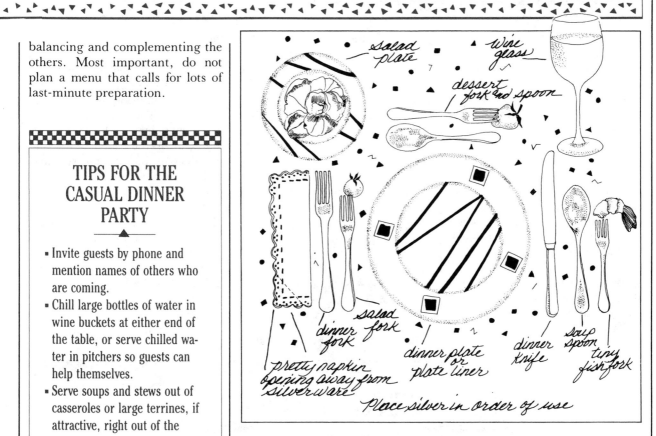

salad plate — wine glass — dessert fork and spoon — salad fork — dinner fork — pretty napkin opening away from silverware — dinner plate or plate liner — dinner knife — soup spoon — tiny fish fork

Place silver in order of use

SETTING THE SCENE

▲ As many as three days ahead, check that your silver is polished, glasses and dishes are sparkling, and linen is freshly washed and ironed. Lay out your serving platters and utensils and choose the most appropriate for each dish. If there's something you're missing, you'll have ample time to fill in.

▲ Collect and arrange your flowers ahead of time so that they will be in full bloom for the party.

▲ Check to see that the bar is fully stocked and choose the wines that will be served with dinner.

▲ Decide on music for the evening and have it ready. Choose light jazz or classical selections that can be played softly, remembering that vocals may compete with conversations.

▲ Shop for all your ingredients, except for those that must be purchased the day of the party. Prepare whatever dishes you can beforehand, starting in plenty of time so that you have the luxury of being at your most creative.

SETTING THE PLACE

▲ Set the table the day before. We love to iron our napkins open and either fold them softly or tie them with pretty ribbons. If you have a collection of napkin rings, use them and fan the top of the napkins to look like small bouquets.

▲ In the days of our youth we loved simple white dishes, but as we've matured we have come to love more ornate china. It is perfectly appropriate to mix sets of dishes as long as they share roughly the same weight and feel.

▲ Begin your setting with dinner plates or larger decorative plate liners. Arrange no more than three pieces of silverware on each side of the dinner plate. The service should be placed in the order of use for each course, beginning on the outside and working in. Forks go on the left, knives and spoons on the right. Knives always should be placed with the cutting edge toward the dinner plate.

▲ Place dessert forks and spoons just above the dinner plate—the spoon closest to the plate with handle facing right, the fork above the spoon with handle facing left.

▲ Set glasses to the right, above the knife, beginning with a water goblet, then a white-wine glass, and a red-wine glass if two wines are being served.

▲ Place the bread plate level with the glasses on the lefthand side,

above the forks. A butter knife should be placed along the top of the plate with the handle facing right. If a salad plate is set, put it slightly to the side and level with the top of the forks on the left. Place napkins to the left of the forks, or on the center of the dinner plate or liner if the first course will be served after everyone is seated.

▲ Appetizers, soups, or desserts in their bowls or on their plates should always be placed on a larger plate or liner, which is removed along with the empty dish.

▲ Now that the basic table is set, decide where you will place bread baskets, salt and pepper, butter dishes, and any other essentials.

CENTERPIECES

We love to arrange flowers, fresh herbs, vegetables, and fruits together in a centerpiece. Shiny purple eggplants or soft pale peaches nestled among flowers make the table come alive. Put the fresh flowers and herbs in small water tubes to keep them fresh and then arrange them with the vegetables and fruit. Your florist can supply you with the tubes.

▲ Line a basket with an antique lace cloth or napkin and fill it with small white eggplants and white lilacs or narcissus.

▲ Arrange stalks of rhubarb and quince blossoms in a large crystal vase.

▲ Stud a silver bowl of limes with pale, dainty verbena.

▲ Arrange daffodils and yellow peppers in a blue Fiestaware bowl.

▲ Tie bouquets of Queen Anne's lace and bunches of fresh sage together with celadon ribbon.

▲ Fill a white basket with small, shiny purple eggplants and clay pots of violets.

▲ Arrange red and orange peppers and Oriental poppies in an Indian basket.

▲ Serve blue corn chips in a turquoise bowl and decorate with cornflowers.

▲ Scatter sky-blue forget-me-nots in a bowl of blueberries.

▲ Arrange red anemones around a red lacquer bowl filled with long-stemmed strawberries.

▲ Place a lavender orchid alongside of a bowl of blackberries.

▲ Add bright red geraniums to baskets of plum tomatoes.

▲ Arrange little clay pots of hyacinths, crocus, fresh sage, and rosemary together in a shallow basket or wooden box.

THE DINNER

▲ The day of the party, begin early with any last-minute shopping and finish up as much cooking as possible.

▲ Have help arrive at least an hour ahead of guests so that you can discuss the timing of the evening. Make very clear how you would like everything served. Have ice buckets filled and wine ready.

▲ Be dressed at least 30 minutes before your guests arrive. Everything should be under control, so you can now enjoy a cocktail.

▲ When guests enter your home, their initial impression will remain throughout the evening. The mood is set: Have candles aglow, music playing, and perhaps pass a special cocktail or glasses of Champagne.

▲ Don't let time get away from you. Cocktails should last from 45 minutes to an hour and no longer.

▲ When you bring your guests into the dining room, the candles should be lit and the water glasses filled. Don't wait for people to ask for water. Nowadays it is almost impolite not to serve a water glass.

▲ Wine should be poured when the guests are seated. If you are serving both white and red, pour only the wine for the first course.

▲ The rule is serve from the left and clear from the right.

▲ There are several ways to serve the main course. If you want the food arranged in a certain way,

THE TOAST

Europeans toast and clink glasses whenever possible, and we're seeing it more and more in America. From simple clinking of glasses with a friend to clinking all around in a crowd, cheery shouts of salud, cin cin, skoal, and proost abound. It is always good manners to look the holder of the other glass directly in the eye before you take a sip.

More formal toasting is generally made by the host to an honored guest, but recently it has been extended to the host by a guest. What is said in a toast matters less than how it is said. For a toast to sound as if it just came to you in an affectionate flash, it will have to be prepared ahead of time. Know your message, how to open, and how to close. A quote is always nice. Be cheery, to the point, short and sweet. Mean what you say. If a toast isn't from the heart, it means nothing at all.

plate the entrée in the kitchen and serve each guest individually. Another option is French service: Large garnished platters are presented to each person, with the handles of the serving pieces facing the guests. Each person helps himself and the server moves on, ending with the hostess. The final choice is to serve family style, which we prefer with more casual entertaining. The main dish is served from the head of the table, with the host serving while the hostess adds the side dishes.

▲ Once the last course before dessert is finished, clear the table of breads, butters, salt, pepper, and any remaining condiments. If serving Sauternes, Champagne, or another dessert wine, replace glasses with fresh wine glasses.

▲ The ending to the meal need not be an overwhelmingly rich, sweet dessert. Something with a delicate touch of sweetness can be a very welcome finale. Consider ripe fresh fruits and a homemade sorbet. Desserts should complement the main course and blend well with the rest of the meal.

▲ We love to move to another room for coffee and after-dinner drinks. When weather permits, nothing is nicer than a porch or patio. This is the perfect time for guests to circulate and converse with people other than their dinner partners. Be sure to have decaffeinated coffee and tea and a lovely tray set up with a selection of brandies and liqueurs, accompanied by the appropriate glasses. As a treat, have small dishes of chocolate truffles, silver almonds, and sweet spiced nuts about.

INTERMEZZO

BEAUTIFUL SOUP

There is nothing quite like soup. It is seductive. It embraces your entire home with its heady aroma, and lovingly entices friends and family into the kitchen. Nourishing and comforting, it is beloved by both young and old.

A most versatile food, soup is the perfect way to balance a menu. Serve a light, appetite-stimulating consommé or bouillon to elegantly complement a rich main course, or if the main course is light, serve a more substantial puréed vegetable soup to round out the meal. Creamed soups, of course, hold a place in menus that don't feature cream sauces. Chilled fruit soups and gazpachos begin summer meals on a refreshingly festive note and still leave room for more. And sturdy, heartwarming vegetable, beef, or cheese soups—too filling to serve as starters—stand on their own as main dishes.

GOLDEN RAINBOW SOUP

A cool combo: two soups, each delicious on its own, combine to form a springtime treat in yellow and green.

5 cups Golden Pepper and Tomato Soup (recipe follows)
7 cups Sorrel Tarragon Soup (recipe follows)
⅔ cup crème fraîche (see Index), for garnish
8 whole fresh chives, with blossoms, for garnish (see Note)

1. Using two measuring cups, pour the chilled soups simultaneously into individual soup bowls, allowing about ¾ cup sorrel soup and ½ cup pepper soup for each serving. The colors should not combine.

2. Place a dollop of crème fraîche in the center of each bowl, and garnish with a whole chive.

8 portions

Note: If chives with blossoms aren't available, substitute a whole chive and another type of edible flower, such as nasturiums or spring violets.

GOLDEN PEPPER AND TOMATO SOUP

4 yellow bell peppers
3 pints ripe yellow cherry or
    pear tomatoes (2½ pounds)
½ cup fresh lemon juice
1 teaspoon ground ginger
½ teaspoon ground anise
½ teaspoon freshly ground black pepper
½ teaspoon sugar
½ cup heavy or whipping cream

1. Core and seed the peppers. Cut them lengthwise into ¼-inch-thick strips.

2. Cut the tomatoes in half.

3. In a medium-size heavy saucepan over low heat, combine the peppers, tomatoes, lemon juice, ginger, anise, pepper, and sugar. Cover, and simmer, stirring occasionally, for 50 minutes.

4. Transfer the soup, in batches, to a food processor and purée.

5. Pour the purée through a fine sieve into another bowl, to remove seeds and any tough pulp. Add the cream, and stir well. Refrigerate, covered, until chilled, at least 4 hours.

5 cups

RAINBOW SOUPS

Several years ago we began experimenting with the idea of serving two soups in the same bowl, and since then they've become one of our trademarks. "Rainbow soups" are a dramatic and nourishing way to begin an important meal, and the interplay between the flavors of two vegetable soups is intriguing.

The soups should complement—not conflict—with one another: neither one stronger, thicker, or richer than the other. Sometimes to get a good balance, you'll need more of one soup than the other. Each should have a clear, direct flavor.

For the soups to be poured together and meet without combining, they must be of similar consistency. Pouring from dry measuring cups, you simply pour one soup slowly down one side of the bowl while simultaneously pouring the other down the opposite side. Then garnish with thinly sliced radishes, carrots, a dollop of crème fraîche, scallions, chive blossom, finely minced red pepper, rouille, or pesto. Remember, too, that each soup in our Rainbow selection works on its own.

SORREL TARRAGON SOUP

1 cup (2 sticks) unsalted butter
2 large onions, halved crosswise and thinly sliced
5 large cloves garlic, crushed
14 ounces fresh sorrel leaves, rinsed and trimmed (12 cups tightly packed)
4 cups Berta's Chicken Stock (see Index) or canned broth
1 medium potato, peeled and cut into 6 pieces
1 cup loosely packed chopped fresh Italian (flat-leaf) parsley
1 tablespoon fresh lemon juice
2 teaspoons dried tarragon
1 teaspoon ground mace
1 teaspoon freshly ground black pepper
1 teaspoon salt
Pinch of cayenne pepper

1. In a heavy medium-size soup pot, melt the butter over low heat. Add the onions and garlic, cover, and cook, stirring occasionally, for 15 minutes.

2. Add the sorrel, stir well, and cook, covered, 5 minutes.

3. Add all the remaining ingredients, and bring to a boil. Reduce the heat, cover, and simmer 50 minutes.

4. Process the mixture, in small batches, in a food processor until smooth. Transfer the soup to a bowl and allow it to cool. Cover, and refrigerate until chilled, at least 4 hours.

7 cups

> "**O**f all the items on the menu, soup is that which exacts the most delicate perfection and the strictest attention."
> —AUGUSTE ESCOFFIER

FRESH SPRING RAINBOW SOUP

Both these soups work well on their own, but when combined they make for a vibrant and dazzling beginning to a spring menu. Garnish with more pink and green—magnificent!

5 cups Beet Vichyssoise (recipe follows)
5 cups Sweet Pea Soup (recipe follows)
½ cup crème fraîche (see Index) or sour cream
2 tablespoons snipped fresh chives
3 radishes, sliced paper-thin
6 whole fresh chives

1. Heat the vichyssoise and pea soup separately over low heat, until steaming.

2. Using two measuring cups, pour the soups simultaneously into individual serving bowls, so that the colors do not blend.

3. Garnish each serving with a dollop of crème fraîche, and sprinkle with the chopped chives and sliced radishes. Finally, lay one whole chive across each bowl. Serve immediately.

6 portions

BEET VICHYSSOISE

3 tablespoons unsalted butter
1 leek, well rinsed and thinly sliced
½ cup chopped onion
3 all-purpose potatoes, peeled and thinly sliced
1 beet, peeled and thinly sliced
2 cups Berta's Chicken Stock (see Index) or canned broth
2 teaspoons fresh lemon juice
1 cup heavy or whipping cream
½ cup milk
Salt and freshly ground black pepper, to taste

1. Melt the butter in a heavy saucepan. Add the leek and onion and cook over low heat until soft and translucent, 15 minutes.

2. Add the potatoes, beet, stock, and lemon juice. Bring to a boil, reduce the heat, and cover. Simmer until the potatoes and beet are tender, 40 minutes. Allow to cool slightly.

3. Process the soup in a blender or food processor until smooth. Return the soup to the saucepan and add the cream and milk. Season with salt and pepper, and set aside.

5 to 6 cups

SWEET PEA SOUP

6 tablespoons (¾ stick) unsalted butter
1½ cups chopped onions
7 cups frozen sweet peas
3 cups Berta's Chicken Stock (see Index)
    or canned broth
Salt and ground white pepper, to taste

1. Melt the butter in a large heavy saucepan. Add the onions and cook over low heat until soft and translucent, 15 minutes.

2. Add the peas and stock, and simmer 20 minutes longer. Allow to cool slightly.

3. Transfer the soup to a blender or food processor and process until smooth.

4. Put the soup through a food mill or fine strainer to remove any pea skins. Then return it to the saucepan, season with salt and white pepper, and set aside.

5 to 6 cups

FIREWORKS RAINBOW SOUP

A two-soup combo that creates the brilliance of the sunset—with some of the fire!

6 cups Tarragon Pea Soup (recipe follows)
3 cups Sweet Pepper Soup (recipe follows)
⅓ cup crème fraîche (see Index) or sour cream

1. Heat the two soups separately, until steaming.

2. Using two ladles or measuring cups, carefully pour the soups simultaneously into individual soup bowls, so that they swirl around each other but do not blend. If you like, use the handle of a spoon to form decorative swirls.

3. Garnish each serving with a dollop of crème fraîche, and serve immediately.

6 portions

TARRAGON PEA SOUP

4 tablespoons (½ stick) unsalted butter
1 onion, coarsely chopped
2 large cloves garlic, chopped
4 cups Berta's Chicken Stock (see Index)
    or canned broth
1 large Idaho potato, peeled and quartered
1½ pounds frozen sweet peas
¼ teaspoon cayenne pepper
½ teaspoon freshly ground black pepper
2 tablespoons dried tarragon

1. Melt the butter in a heavy saucepan over low heat. Add the onion and garlic, and cook gently until wilted, 10 minutes.

2. Add the stock and potato; bring to a boil. Reduce the heat and cook until the potato is just tender, about 15 minutes.

3. Add the peas, cayenne, and black pepper, and return to a boil. Then remove the pan from the heat and stir in the tarragon. Allow the soup to cool for 10 minutes.

4. Process the soup, in batches, in a food processor or blender until smooth. Pour the soup through a fine sieve or a food mill to remove any pieces of skin. Set aside.

6 cups

SWEET PEPPER SOUP

2 red bell peppers
10 ripe Italian plum tomatoes, quartered
4 tablespoons fresh lemon juice
½ teaspoon ground ginger
¼ teaspoon freshly ground black pepper

1. Core and seed the peppers. Cut them lengthwise into ¼-inch-thick strips.

2. Combine all the ingredients in a heavy saucepan over low heat. Cover, and simmer, stirring occasionally, until the peppers are tender, 30 minutes.

3. Purée the mixture, in batches, in a food processor or blender until smooth.

3 cups

ON THE TOP

The more complex the soup, the simpler the garnish. And although a garnish needn't duplicate an ingredient in the soup, it must complement or heighten the flavors. Try fresh minced herbs, minced scallions, grated Parmesan, a few whole shrimp, chopped hard-cooked eggs or nuts, a spoonful of caviar, a few berries, thin rounds of carrots, minced wild mushrooms, a slice of lemon, a dash of sherry, or a dollop of sour cream.

CREAM OF FENNEL SOUP

The flavor of this light fennel soup is enhanced with anisette. The fronds make a delicate garnish.

3 fennel bulbs with fronds
2 tablespoons olive oil
1 small onion, chopped
2 cups Berta's Chicken Stock (see Index) or canned broth
½ teaspoon salt
Freshly ground black pepper, to taste
2 tablespoons anise-flavored liqueur
½ cup heavy or whipping cream

1. Trim the fennel, removing the thin stalks and thick base. Reserve 2 tablespoons of the fronds. Coarsely chop the bulbs; you should have about 3½ cups.
2. Place the oil in a 2-quart microwave-safe cas-serole, and microwave on full power, uncovered, for 2 minutes. Stir in the onion and chopped fennel, cover, and cook 6 minutes, stirring after 3 minutes. The vegetables should be just crisp-tender.
3. Transfer the mixture to a food processor, add 1 cup of the stock, and purée until smooth. Pour the soup back into the casserole, and add the remaining 1 cup stock. Microwave, uncovered, 3 minutes.
4. Stir in the salt, pepper, liqueur, cream, and the reserved fronds. Cook, uncovered, 2 minutes. Whisk, and serve.

4 cups

Note: This recipe was cooked on High (full power, 650 to 700 watts) in a carousel microwave, using microwave-safe containers.

If your microwave is less powerful, you will have to allow for more cooking time (approximately 1½ times the amount called for—but watch carefully); if it does not have a carousel, you may have to rotate the dish while it is cooking.

BROCCOLI SPINACH SOUP

A great green soup, loaded with creamy flavor but no cream. This is a good soup to have in your repertoire, as it is seasonless.

2 heads broccoli (each about 2 pounds), tough stem ends
*   trimmed away*
4 tablespoons (½ stick) unsalted butter
1 large onion, diced
2 leeks, well rinsed and thinly sliced
1 carrot, peeled and diced
6 cloves garlic, minced
8 cups Berta's Chicken Stock (see Index) or canned broth
2 ripe plum tomatoes, coarsely chopped
¼ cup chopped fresh Italian (flat-leaf) parsley
1 bunch fresh spinach (about 8 ounces)
¼ teaspoon ground cardamom
¼ teaspoon ground nutmeg
Salt and freshly ground black pepper, to taste
¼ cup fresh lemon juice

1. Peel the broccoli stems with a vegetable peeler. Chop the florets, and thinly slice the stems. Reserve.

2. Melt the butter in a soup kettle. Add the onion, leeks, carrot, and garlic. Cook over low heat until wilted, 10 minutes.

3. Add the stock, reserved broccoli, tomatoes, and parsley. Bring to a boil, reduce the heat, and cover. Simmer for 25 minutes.

4. While the soup is simmering, wash the spinach leaves well and remove the stems. Discard any tough leaves.

5. Add the spinach leaves to the soup. Stir in the cardamom, nutmeg, and salt and pepper. Cook 1 minute longer and remove from the heat. Allow to cool slightly.

6. Purée the soup, in batches, in a blender or food processor. Return it to the pot and heat through. Add the lemon juice just before serving.

8 portions

CELERIAC VICHYSSOISE

The original potato and leek soup was created by Chef Louis Diat at the Ritz Carlton Hotel in New York in 1910—a memory of his mother's soup, made at the family home in Vichy, France.

We like the fresh flavor that celery root adds here.

4 tablespoons (½ stick) unsalted butter
3 cups diced onions
1 leek, well rinsed and diced
2 pounds potatoes, peeled and cut into large dice
2 pounds celeriac (celery root), cut into large dice
6 cloves garlic, halved
6 cups Berta's Chicken Stock (see Index) or
  canned broth
3 tablespoons fresh lemon juice
½ teaspoon celery seeds
Salt and freshly ground black pepper, to taste
3 cups milk
2 cups heavy or whipping cream
Snipped fresh chives, for garnish

1. Melt the butter in a large soup pot. Add the onions and leek, and cook over medium heat until the vegetables are wilted, 10 minutes.

2. Add the potatoes, celeriac, and garlic. Stir well, and cook 5 minutes. Then add the stock, lemon juice, celery seeds, and salt and pepper. Bring to a boil, reduce the heat, and cover. Simmer until the celeriac is tender, 30 minutes. Allow to cool slightly.

3. Purée the mixture, in batches, in a blender or food processor until fairly smooth. Do not overprocess.

4. Return the soup to the saucepan, add the milk and cream, and simmer until heated through. Serve garnished with chives.

10 to 12 portions

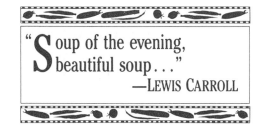

"Soup of the evening, beautiful soup..."
—LEWIS CARROLL

CREAM OF TOMATO SOUP

An old-fashioned tomato soup that can be made any time of the year. We always prefer Italian plum tomatoes for recipes that call for canned tomatoes; they are small and have the best flavor. (The pinch of sugar reduces the acidic taste of canned tomatoes.)

4 tablespoons (½ stick) unsalted butter
2 onions, thinly sliced
1 carrot, peeled and chopped
  6 cloves garlic, coarsely chopped
  2 cans (35 ounces each) plum tomatoes, with their juice
  8 large fresh basil leaves, slivered
  Pinch of sugar
Salt and freshly ground black pepper, to taste
4 cups Berta's Chicken Stock (see Index) or canned broth
½ teaspoon ground allspice
2 cups heavy or whipping cream

1. Melt the butter in a large soup pot. Add the onions, carrot, and garlic. Cook over medium heat until the vegetables have wilted, 10 minutes.

2. Add the tomatoes and their juice, basil, sugar, and salt and pepper. Cook for 5 minutes. Then add the stock and allspice, and slowly bring to a boil. Reduce the heat, partially cover, and simmer for 50 minutes.

3. Purée the soup, in batches, in a blender or food processor. Return it to the pot, add the cream, adjust the seasonings, and heat through.

8 to 10 portions

TOMATO LENTIL SOUP

A perfect one-dish meal, this vegetable soup cooks to a thick and luscious consistency after the lentils are added. Vegetarians can substitute vegetable broth for the chicken stock.

4 tablespoons (½ stick) unsalted butter
2 cups chopped onions
2 cups chopped celery
2 cans (35 ounces each) Italian plum tomatoes, with their juice
6 cups Berta's Chicken Stock (see Index) or canned broth
½ cup dried lentils
1 cup chopped fresh Italian (flat-leaf) parsley
½ cup dry red wine
4 cloves garlic, finely minced
½ teaspoon freshly ground black pepper
½ teaspoon salt
¼ teaspoon ground cloves

1. Melt the butter in a large soup pot. Add the onions and celery, and cook over low heat, stirring, until the vegetables are wilted, 10 minutes.

2. Purée the tomatoes with their juice in a blender, and add to the wilted vegetables.

3. Add the chicken stock and lentils, and bring to a boil. Reduce the heat and simmer, uncovered, stirring occasionally, for 20 minutes.

4. Add ½ cup of the parsley, along with the wine,

garlic, pepper, salt, and cloves. Stir well, and simmer another 25 minutes. Add the remaining ½ cup parsley, and simmer another 5 minutes. Serve the soup immediately.

8 portions

Note: If using canned or fresh chicken broth with a very mild flavor add a boullion cube to strengthen.

ARTICHOKE SOUP

A rich but delicate flavor comes through in this artichoke soup. The chicken broth is infused with the flavor of the artichokes as it simmers. Although removing pulp from leaves may take a while, it's worth the effort.

6 artichokes
1 cup sliced onion
4 cups Berta's Chicken Stock (see Index) or canned broth
2 cups water
½ cup heavy or whipping cream
1 tablespoon snipped fresh chives
1 tablespoon chopped fresh Italian (flat-leaf) parsley
Salt and freshly ground black pepper, to taste
Crème fraîche (see Index), for garnish (optional)

1. Wash the artichokes thoroughly.

2. Place the artichokes in a large pot. Add the onion, stock, and water, and bring to a boil. Reduce the heat, cover, and simmer until the artichokes are tender, about 45 minutes.

3. When the artichokes are done, remove them from the pot, reserving the liquid and onions. Let the artichokes cool.

4. Peel the leaves away from the artichokes; reserve the leaves. Scoop out and discard the fuzzy chokes, and dice the bottoms into ¼-inch pieces. Set aside.

5. Using a spoon, scrape the meaty pulp from the leaves and place it in a food processor. Add the reserved cooking liquid and the onions in small batches, and process until smooth. Return the mixture to the pot.

6. Add the cream, diced artichoke bottoms, chives, parsley, and salt and pepper. Heat through, and serve garnished with crème fraîche.

4 portions

CURRIED ZUCCHINI SOUP

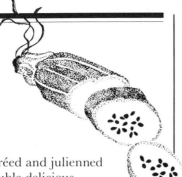

The combination of puréed and julienned zucchini makes for a double delicious zucchini experience.

5 tablespoons unsalted butter
2 onions, coarsely chopped
5 tablespoons curry powder
6 cups Berta's Chicken Stock (see Index) or canned broth
2 potatoes, peeled and cubed
1 teaspoon salt
1 teaspoon freshly ground black pepper
6 zucchini
1 ½ cups heavy or whipping cream
Snipped fresh chives, for garnish

1. Melt 4 tablespoons of the butter in a soup pot. Add the onions and curry powder, and cook, uncovered, over low heat, stirring occasionally, until the onions are wilted, about 15 minutes. Then add the stock and potatoes; simmer, uncovered, for 15 minutes. Season with the salt and pepper.

2. Slice 5 of the zucchini and add them to the soup pot. Simmer for 10 minutes.

3. Purée the soup, in batches, in a food processor or blender. While the machine is running, add the cream through the feed tube in a slow, steady stream. Pass the mixture through a food mill or a fine-mesh sieve, and return it to the pot. Keep it hot.

4. Julienne the reserved zucchini. Heat the remaining 1 tablespoon butter in a small skillet, add the julienned zucchini, and sauté over medium heat until just wilted, 1 minute. Add this to the soup, garnish it with chives, and serve.

8 portions

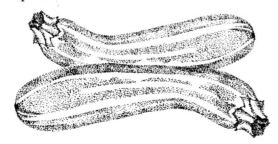

TRADE SECRET

Fresh herbs loose their distinctive flavor when cooked a long time. Add some extra just before serving.

YELLOW SQUASH POTATO SOUP

Yukon Gold potatoes are becoming more readily available in markets, and this soup was created to take advantage of their buttery texture and rich flavor. Under the skin, the potatoes are yellow in appearance, making for a truly golden soup. If you can't find Yukon Golds, substitute white potatoes.

3 yellow summer squash (about 1 ¾ pounds)
1 pound Yukon Gold potatoes
4 cups Berta's Chicken Stock (see Index) or canned broth
3 tablespoons unsalted butter, cut into small pieces
3 tablespoons chopped fresh dill
Salt and freshly ground black pepper, to taste
1 scallion (green onion), white bulb and 3 inches of green,
    thinly sliced on the diagonal, for garnish

1. Cut the squash into 2-inch pieces, leaving the skin on. Place in a large soup pot.

2. Peel the potatoes, cut them into 1-inch dice, and add to the squash.

3. Cover the vegetables with the stock, and bring to a boil. Reduce the heat, cover, and simmer until the squash is tender, 20 minutes. Then add the butter, 1 tablespoon of the dill, and salt and pepper. Remove from the heat.

4. Purée the soup in a blender or food processor until smooth. Return it to the soup pot and heat through, stirring in the remaining 2 tablespoons dill.

5. Sprinkle on the scallion just before serving.

4 portions

WILD MUSHROOM SOUP WITH MADEIRA

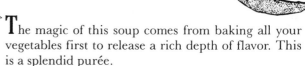

One ounce of dried wild mushrooms adds just the right amount of woodsy flavor to this soup. If morels are unavailable, substitute shiitakes or cèpes. This is a perfect soup to start off Thanksgiving dinner.

½ cup Madeira
2 ¾ cups Berta's Chicken Stock (see Index) or canned broth
1 ounce dried morels
3 leeks (white part only), well rinsed and dried
1 onion
4 tablespoons (½ stick) unsalted butter
3 tablespoons unbleached all-purpose flour
2 ¼ cups homemade beef stock (see Index) or canned broth
1 pound fresh cultivated button mushrooms, stems removed
Salt and freshly ground black pepper, to taste
Crème fraîche (see Index), for garnish
1 bunch snipped fresh chives (2 tablespoons), for garnish

1. In a small saucepan combine the Madeira, ½ cup of the chicken stock, and the morels. Bring to a boil, remove from the heat, and let stand for 30 minutes.

2. Dice the leeks and onion. Melt the butter in a large soup pot. Add the leeks and onion, and cook over low heat until wilted, about 10 minutes. Sprinkle with the flour, stir, and cook an additional 5 minutes.

3. Add the remaining 2 ¼ cups chicken stock, the beef stock, button mushrooms, morels and their soaking liquid, and salt and pepper. Simmer, uncovered, until the mushrooms are soft, 30 minutes. Allow the soup to cool slightly.

4. Purée the soup, in batches, in a blender or food processor. Return it to the pot and heat through over low heat. Serve garnished with a dollop of crème fraîche and snipped chives.

6 portions

BAKED WINTER SQUASH SOUP

The magic of this soup comes from baking all your vegetables first to release a rich depth of flavor. This is a splendid purée.

2 acorn squash (about 2 pounds each)
2 butternut squash (about 2 pounds each)
8 tablespoons (1 stick) unsalted butter
8 teaspoons dark brown sugar
3 carrots, peeled and halved
1 large onion, thinly sliced
10 cups Berta's Chicken Stock (see Index) or canned broth
¾ teaspoon ground mace
¾ teaspoon ground ginger
Pinch of cayenne pepper
Salt, to taste
Crème fraîche (see Index), for garnish
Snipped fresh chives, for garnish

1. Preheat the oven to 350°F.

2. Cut the four squash in half lengthwise. Scoop out and discard the seeds.

3. Place the squash halves, skin side down, in a shallow roasting pan. Place 1 tablespoon of the butter and 1 teaspoon of the brown sugar in the cavity of each squash half. Arrange the carrots and onion slices around the squash. Pour 2 cups of the stock in the pan, cover it tightly with aluminum foil, and bake for 2 hours.

4. Remove the pan from the oven, and allow the vegetables to cool slightly. Scoop the squash pulp out of the skins and place it in a soup pot. Add the carrots, onions, and the cooking liquid.

5. Add the remaining 8 cups chicken stock and the mace, ginger, cayenne, and salt. Stir well, and bring to a boil. Reduce the heat, and simmer, uncovered, for 10 minutes.

6. Purée the soup, in batches, in a blender or food processor until smooth. Return it to the pot, adjust the seasonings, and heat through. Serve each portion garnished with a dollop of crème fraîche and a sprinkling of chives.

12 portions

CARROT DILL SOUP

Fresh green dill and bright red pepper garnish this creamy carrot soup to perfection.

4 tablespoons (½ stick) unsalted butter
1 large onion, diced
2 ½ pounds carrots, peeled and diced
2 ribs celery, leaves included, diced
8 cups Berta's Chicken Stock (see Index)
    or canned broth
¼ cup plus 2 tablespoons chopped fresh dill
1 teaspoon salt
¼ teaspoon freshly ground black pepper
Pinch of cayenne pepper
6 teaspoons crème fraîche (see Index), for garnish
¼ cup finely diced red bell pepper, for garnish
6 dill sprigs, for garnish

1. Melt the butter in a soup kettle. Add the onion and cook over low heat until wilted, 10 minutes.

2. Add the carrots, celery, stock, ¼ cup dill, salt, black pepper, and cayenne. Bring to a boil, reduce the heat, and cover. Simmer until the carrots are tender, 40 minutes. Allow to cool slightly.

3. Purée the soup, in batches, in a blender or food processor. Return it to the kettle, stir in the remaining 2 tablespoons dill, and adjust the seasonings. Heat through.

4. Serve each bowl of soup garnished with a dollop of crème fraîche, a sprinkling of red pepper, and a sprig of dill.

6 portions

YELLOW PEPPER SOUP

Roasting brings out the full flavor of sweet yellow peppers before they're transformed into a warming soup.

*6 yellow bell peppers, cored, seeded,
    and halved lengthwise*
4 tablespoons (½ stick) unsalted butter
1 cup chopped onions
1 cup chopped leeks
½ teaspoon salt
½ teaspoon freshly ground black pepper
3 small boiling potatoes, peeled and sliced
5 cups Berta's Chicken Stock (see Index) or canned broth
2 tablespoons snipped fresh chives
*Toasted croutons (see facing
    page), for garnish (optional)*
*Extra virgin olive oil, for
    garnish (optional)*
*Freshly grated Parmesan cheese,
    for garnish*

1. Preheat the broiler.

2. Line a baking sheet with aluminum foil. Lay 6 of the pepper halves, cut side down, on the foil, and broil 2 inches from the heat until well charred, 5 to 10 minutes. Transfer the peppers to a plastic bag and seal the bag. Allow the peppers to steam in the bag for 10 minutes. Then remove them from the bag, and slip off and discard the skins. Coarsely chop the peppers, and set aside.

3. Melt the butter in a soup pot. Add the onions, leeks, salt, and pepper, and sauté over low heat until the vegetables are soft and translucent, 10 to 15 minutes.

4. Coarsely chop the remaining 6 pepper halves and add them to the pot, along with the potatoes, roasted peppers, and stock. Bring to a boil, then lower the heat and simmer, uncovered, until the vegetables are tender, 30 minutes.

5. Transfer the soup, in batches, to a food processor and process until smooth. Return it to the pot and heat through.

6. Serve the soup garnished with the chives, croutons, a splash of olive oil, and Parmesan cheese.

4 portions

SOUP BASICS

▲ Don't compromise on quality; lackluster ingredients will make a lackluster soup.

▲ Sauté vegetables in butter or oil before adding them to soup. This seals in their flavor and keeps them firm. Give onions a little extra time; slow cooking brings out their natural sweetness.

▲ You can make a very good soup with water, so the lack of a stock shouldn't stop you from trying a recipe. But a rich, homemade stock will add a depth of flavor that water cannot duplicate.

▲ Most soups (with the exception of delicate, fresh-fruit soups) improve with age and can be made a day or two in advance. And leftovers freeze well.

▲ It is a simple matter to defat a soup if you chill it first; the fat will solidify on top and can be easily removed with a spoon.

▲ To guard against burns, allow hot soup to cool slightly before puréeing.

▲ Leftovers make terrific soups. Sauté aromatic vegetables such as onions, carrots, and garlic in oil or butter, add bite-size pieces of leftover meats and vegetables along with a little stock or milk, and simmer until flavorful.

▲ The addition of wine frequently enhances the flavor of a soup. A not-too-dry sherry or Madeira blends well with subtle veal or chicken, while a little dry red table wine will complement the flavor of beef.

▲ To ensure that soups arrive at the table piping hot, serve them in tureens, lidded bowls, or well-heated cups. Serve cold soups ice cold in chilled bowls or goblets.

BAKED GARLIC AND ONION CREAM SOUP

This is heavenly! It's so full of flavor that just a little bowl is fine for a first course.

6 large onions, cut into ½-inch slices
2 heads garlic, cloves separated and peeled
5 cups Berta's Chicken Stock (see Index) or canned broth
1½ teaspoons dried thyme leaves
1 teaspoon coarsely ground black pepper
1 teaspoon coarse (kosher) salt
4 tablespoons (½ stick) unsalted butter
2 cups heavy or whipping cream
2 tablespoons chopped fresh Italian (flat-leaf) parsley, for garnish

1. Preheat the oven to 350°F.
2. Place the onions and garlic in a shallow roasting pan, and add 3 cups of the chicken stock. Sprinkle with the thyme, pepper, and coarse salt. Dot with the butter.
3. Cover the pan with aluminum foil and bake for 1½ hours. Stir once or twice while it is baking.
4. Remove the pan from the oven and purée the onions and garlic with the liquid, in batches, in a blender or food processor until smooth. With the motor on, gradually add the remaining 2 cups stock and the cream. Pour the soup into a large saucepan.
5. Adjust the seasonings and slowly heat through. Do not allow the soup to boil. Sprinkle with the parsley, and serve.
6 to 8 portions

PEANUT BUTTER PUMPKIN SOUP

This is a winner. It's so velvety and intensely flavored, just a cupful is wonderful! Pumpkin—or butternut squash if your garden is overflowing—never tasted so delicious.

4 tablespoons (½ stick) unsalted butter
4 cups canned pumpkin
2 cups cooked puréed sweet potatoes
1 cup smooth peanut butter
6 cups Berta's Chicken Stock (see Index) or canned broth
1 teaspoon freshly ground black pepper
1 teaspoon salt
Snipped fresh chives, for garnish
Sour cream, for garnish

1. Melt the butter in a soup pot over medium heat. Stir in the pumpkin, sweet potatoes, and peanut butter.
2. Add the stock, pepper, and salt, and stir well until smooth. Reduce the heat to a simmer and cook for 20 minutes.
3. Before serving, garnish the soup with chives and sour cream.
8 portions

SOUP CROUTONS

For a crisp, rich addition to soups, sauté small cubes or thin, decoratively shaped slices of bread in butter or olive oil with herbs or pepper flakes. Then dust them with cheese—freshly grated Parmesan, perhaps—while still hot. Serve the croutons in a small dish on the side and let guests help themselves; that way the croutons will stay crisp until the last moment.

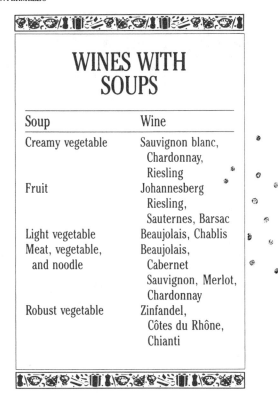

WINES WITH SOUPS

Soup	Wine
Creamy vegetable	Sauvignon blanc, Chardonnay, Riesling
Fruit	Johannesberg Riesling, Sauternes, Barsac
Light vegetable	Beaujolais, Chablis
Meat, vegetable, and noodle	Beaujolais, Cabernet Sauvignon, Merlot, Chardonnay
Robust vegetable	Zinfandel, Côtes du Rhône, Chianti

PROVENCALE FISH SOUP

Light and delicate and laced with Pernod (or other anise-flavored liqueur), this lovely fish soup has added sparkle supplied by crunchy fresh fennel.

4 cups fish stock (see Index)
1 can (16 ounces) peeled plum tomatoes, coarsely chopped, with their juice
2 tablespoons tomato paste
1 tablespoon anise-flavored liqueur (Pernod, Ricard, anisette)
2 cloves garlic, minced
¼ teaspoon saffron threads, crumbled
1 cup julienned fresh fennel bulb
½ teaspoon salt
Freshly ground black pepper, to taste
4 Garlic Croutons (see Index)

1. In a large saucepan, combine the stock, tomatoes, tomato paste, liqueur, garlic, and saffron. Bring to a boil, then lower the heat and simmer, uncovered, 30 minutes.

2. Strain the soup, pressing the solids against the strainer to extract all the liquid. Return the liquid to the saucepan and stir in the fennel. Simmer just until the fennel is crisp-tender, 2 to 3 minutes. Season with salt and pepper. Place a crouton in each bowl before ladling in the soup.

4 portions

SALMON CONSOMME

A consommé as crystal clear as the northern waters salmon love, this elegant first course is subtly flavored with asparagus, salmon, and dill. A lovely, light way to begin a special dinner.

4 cups fish stock (see Index), flour omitted
1 cup water
1 pound salmon trimmings (head, tail, bones)
2 egg whites, lightly beaten
1 cup sparkling white wine or Champagne
1 salmon fillet (3 ounces), poached and flaked
¾ cup minced fresh tomato
4 asparagus spears, blanched and cut into 3-inch julienne
2 tablespoons chopped fresh dill
½ teaspoon salt

1. Strain the stock into a saucepan, and add the water and salmon trimmings. Heat to a boil. Lower the heat and simmer, uncovered, 30 minutes. Strain; cool. Refrigerate for at least 2 hours.

2. Skim any fat off the chilled stock. In a medium-size saucepan, start heating the stock over very low heat. Stir in the egg whites and wine.

3. Now bring the stock to a boil. Once the egg whites have puffed and formed a crust on the surface,

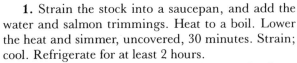

lower the heat and simmer over very low heat for 15 minutes. Do not stir the stock during this time.

4. Tilt the saucepan and ladle the consommé through a fine strainer lined with a damp lint-free towel, or through a coffee filter, into another pan.

5. Add the remaining ingredients and heat through. Serve in small glass cups.

8 small portions

SPRING HERB SOUP

A delicious light vegetable soup, enhanced during the last few minutes with fresh parsley and dill. The fresh flavors of the herbs dazzle!

2 tablespoons unsalted butter
1 cup loosely packed chopped celery leaves
1 small onion, chopped
1 medium potato (about 2½ ounces), peeled and diced
*   (1 cup)*
3 cups Berta's Chicken Stock (see Index) or canned broth
½ cup loosely packed dill sprigs, tough stems trimmed
½ cup loosely packed parsley sprigs, tough stems trimmed

1. Place the butter in a 2-quart microwave-safe casserole, and microwave on full power, uncovered, for 2 minutes. Stir in the celery leaves, onion, and potato, and cook another 3 minutes.

2. Stir in 2 cups of the stock. Cover the casserole, and cook 6 minutes.

3. Transfer the soup to a food processor, add the dill and parsley, and purée briefly, so there are still flecks of herbs. Return the soup to the casserole.

4. Add the remaining 1 cup stock, cover, and cook until heated through, 3 minutes. Serve immediately.

2 portions

Note: This recipe was cooked on High (full power, 650 to 700 watts) in a carousel microwave, using microwave-safe containers.

If your microwave is less powerful, you will have to allow for more cooking time (approximately 1½ times the amount called for—but watch carefully); if it does not have a carousel, you may have to rotate the dish while it is cooking.

STRACCIATELLA

An Italian classic, this is a spinach and egg soup done our way. For a bit of drama, present large shallow soup bowls filled with spinach chiffonade at the table. Ladle the steamy chicken broth into each bowl. It's a lovely moment, and a lovely way to begin a meal!

4 ounces fresh young spinach leaves, trimmed, well rinsed,
*   and dried*
¼ cup freshly grated Parmesan cheese
Freshly grated black pepper, to taste
1 egg
1 teaspoon fresh lemon juice
2 cups Berta's Chicken Stock (see Index) or canned broth
Salt, to taste
Freshly grated Parmesan cheese, for garnish

1. Cut the spinach into chiffonade (very thin strips). Divide it between two large soup bowls, and sprinkle with the cheese and a grating of pepper.

2. In a small bowl, beat the egg and lemon juice together.

3. Heat the stock just to a boil, then remove it from the heat. Stir in the egg mixture until the broth is ribbony and slightly thickened. Ladle over the spinach, and stir just until wilted.

4. Add salt, if needed, and serve immediately, with additional grated cheese on the side.

2 portions

CORN CHOWDER

An updated version of an Old West favorite— this is loaded with corn! The red pepper and cilantro give it a fresh new taste.

4 ounces sliced bacon, cut into 1-inch pieces
2 tablespoons unsalted butter
2 cups chopped onions
2 tablespoons unbleached all-purpose flour
4 cups Berta's Chicken Stock (see Index) or canned broth
2 large potatoes, peeled and cut into ¼-inch dice
1 cup half-and-half
4 cups cooked corn kernels, drained
¾ teaspoon coarsely ground black pepper
Salt, to taste
1 large red bell pepper, cut into ¼-inch dice
3 scallions (green onions), white bulb and 3 inches green, cut into ¼-inch slices
1 tablespoon chopped cilantro (fresh coriander), for garnish

1. Wilt the bacon in a large soup pot over low heat until fat is rendered, about 5 minutes. Add the butter and allow it to melt.

2. Add the onions and wilt over low heat for 10 minutes. Add the flour and cook, stirring, another 5 minutes.

3. Add the stock and potatoes. Continue cooking over medium-low heat until the potatoes are just tender, 12 to 15 minutes.

4. Add the half-and-half, corn, pepper, and salt. Cook 7 minutes, stirring occasionally.

5. Add the bell pepper and scallions, adjust the seasonings, and cook an additional 5 minutes. Serve immediately, garnished with cilantro.

6 portions

HOW TO REMOVE CORN KERNELS FROM THE COB

Hold the cob vertically over a wide, shallow bowl or pan. Using a sharp knife, slice straight down, cutting under the kernels and letting them fall into the bowl. When all the kernels have been removed, turn the knife over and with its dull side scrape the cob on all sides to extract the "milk."

If you want more creaminess than crunch, first score the kernels by slicing through the middle of each row, before cutting them off.

CHICKEN LITTLE'S SOUP

A rich and hearty chicken soup sweetened with parsnip and dill.

1 chicken (3½ pounds), rinsed, patted dry, and cut into small pieces
4 carrots, peeled
2 ribs celery, cut into 2-inch pieces
1 parsnip, peeled and halved
1 onion, halved
2 sprigs parsley
2 sprigs dill
1 or 2 stalks lemongrass cut into ½-inch pieces, or 2 strips (3 inches each) lemon zest
2 homemade chicken bouillon cubes (see Index)
10 cups water
2 tablespoons minced scallions (green onions)
2 tablespoons chopped fresh dill
1 teaspoon salt
Freshly ground black pepper, to taste

1. Place the chicken pieces in a large soup pot. Cut 2 of the carrots into 2-inch pieces and add them to the pot. Add the celery, parsnip, onion, parsley and dill sprigs, lemon grass, bouillon cubes, and water. Heat to a boil. Then lower the heat and simmer 1 hour, skimming when necessary.

2. Strain the soup, and discard the vegetables. Shred the meat from the chicken breasts and 1 thigh. Set the meat aside. Reserve the remaining chicken for another use.

3. Slice the remaining 2 carrots ¼ inch thick. Cook them in lightly salted boiling water for 7 minutes. Drain.

4. Combine the soup, shredded chicken, blanched carrots, scallions, chopped dill, salt, and pepper in a large saucepan and bring just to a boil. Serve.

6 to 8 portions

MARNO'S CHICKEN NOODLE SOUP

On a cold Sunday night, nothing tastes better than this rich soup made with just enough fresh noodles.

1 chicken (4 pounds), preferably a stewing hen
2 onions, halved
4 whole cloves
4 ribs celery, with leaves
4 carrots, peeled
3 parsnips, peeled
3 cloves garlic
6 sprigs dill
6 sprigs parsley
Salt and freshly ground black pepper, to taste
3 quarts water
1 homemade chicken bouillon cube (see Index)
Marno's Noodles (recipe follows; see Step 4)
1½ cups cooked peas
¼ cup chopped fresh dill
2 tablespoons chopped fresh parsley

1. Rinse the chicken well and place it in a large soup pot. Stud each onion half with a clove, and add them to the pot along with the celery, carrots, parsnips, garlic, sprigs of dill and parsley, and salt and

pepper. Add the water and bring to a boil. Reduce the heat, cover, and simmer for 2 hours. Occasionally skim off any foam that forms on top.

2. Remove the chicken from the soup and allow it to cool. Remove the skin and bones, and shred the meat. Reserve the meat, covered, in the refrigerator.

3. Strain the soup, discarding the vegetables, and return the liquid to the pot. Add the bouillon cube (for stronger flavor) and adjust the seasonings. Bring to a boil and cook, uncovered, for 10 minutes (to intensify the flavor). Set aside.

4. Make the noodles.

5. Before serving, bring the chicken broth to a gentle boil. Add the noodles and cook until they are tender, 4 minutes. Gently stir in the reserved chicken and the peas, chopped dill, and chopped parsley. Heat through and serve.

8 portions

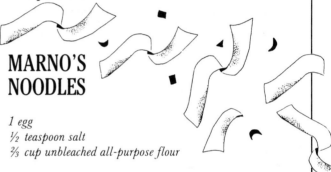

MARNO'S NOODLES

1 egg
½ teaspoon salt
⅔ cup unbleached all-purpose flour

1. Beat the egg and salt together in a bowl. Mix the flour in with a fork. Using your hands, form the mixture into a ball and knead it to form the dough.

2. Dust a work surface with flour, and roll the dough out to form a very thin rectangle approximately 18 x 9 inches. Dust the top of the dough lightly with flour.

3. Roll the dough up jelly-roll fashion, along the long side, to form an 18-inch-long roll. Slice crosswise into ¼-inch-wide rings.

4. Carefully shake out the rings to form long noodles, and let them rest on a baking sheet for 10 minutes before adding to the soup.

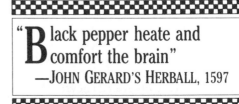

"**B**lack pepper heate and comfort the brain"
—JOHN GERARD'S HERBALL, 1597

GARDEN VEGETABLE SOUP

Make this soup when the tomatoes are ripe on the vine. The sharp accent of a chèvre garnish tops it all off.

3 leeks, well rinsed
2 cups water
2 tablespoons white wine vinegar
4 carrots, peeled
3 parsnips, peeled
6 large cloves garlic, minced
8 tablespoons (1 stick) unsalted butter
4 cups Berta's Chicken Stock (see Index) or canned broth
8 small red potatoes, quartered
12 ripe tomatoes, cut into 1-inch chunks
¼ cup coarsely chopped fresh Italian (flat-leaf) parsley
12 large fresh basil leaves, slivered
1½ tablespoons dried tarragon
1½ teaspoons freshly ground black pepper
1 teaspoon ground nutmeg
Salt, to taste
12 ounces hard chèvre, such as Crottin, rind removed, coarsely grated

1. Trim the leeks, leaving 1 inch of green. Cut the leeks in half lengthwise.

2. In a small bowl combine the water and vinegar. Soak the leeks for 15 minutes to remove sand. Rinse well under running water, and cut into fine dice. Place in a bowl.

3. Cut the carrots into fine dice. Add to the leeks.

4. Cut the parsnips into fine dice. Add to the vegetable bowl. Add the garlic.

5. Melt the butter in a heavy deep casserole over low heat. Add the diced vegetables and cook, covered, for 10 minutes, stirring occasionally.

6. Add the stock and potatoes and continue cooking, covered, for 10 minutes.

7. Add the tomatoes, parsley, basil, tarragon, pepper, nutmeg, and salt. Cover, and cook over medium heat for 15 minutes longer.

8. Remove the cover, reduce the heat to low, and cook another 30 minutes.

9. Serve topped with grated chèvre.

8 portions

WINTER VEGETABLE SOUP

Simple winter vegetables—leeks, celery, spinach, and potatoes—are cooked together for an elegant flavor. Half puréed, the texture is both smooth and chunky.

4 slices bacon, cut into 1-inch pieces
4 tablespoons (½ stick) unsalted butter
2 cups finely diced leeks (white part and 1 inch green)
1½ cups finely diced onions
1 cup finely diced celery
1½ teaspoons dried tarragon
½ teaspoon dried thyme
Salt and freshly ground black pepper, to taste
5 cups Berta's Chicken Stock (see Index) or canned broth
2½ cups finely diced potatoes (4 potatoes)
1 pound tender spinach, well rinsed, stems discarded, cut into ⅛-inch slivers
½ cup heavy or whipping cream

1. In a large soup pot, cook the bacon over low heat, until fat is rendered, 5 minutes. Remove the bacon with a slotted spoon, and discard.

2. Add the butter to the pot. When it has melted, add the leeks, onions, and celery. Cook over low heat until wilted, 15 minutes. Season with the tarragon, thyme, and salt and pepper. Stir well.

3. Add the stock and potatoes. Cover, and simmer until the potatoes are tender but not mushy, 15 to 20 minutes.

4. Add half the spinach. Simmer for 1 minute more.

5. Remove the soup from the heat. Purée half the amount in a blender or food processor, and return the purée to the soup pot.

6. Place the pot over low heat, and add the remaining spinach and the cream. Heat through, stirring well, but do not boil. Adjust the seasonings, and serve.

6 portions

****✦***✦***✦***✦*✦***✦*✦***✦***✦*✦***✦*✦***

SOUP WITH STYLE

It is so easy to serve soup with a sense of great style, turning the simplest preparation into something truly special. At times we like to place an elegant soup in a magnificent crystal or glass bowl. Other times we use a rustic, spectacularly colored country crock. Look around for dishes with great rims, unusual shapes, those that are clear and let you see to the bottom, and those that sparkle. Sometimes we like to make a very simple soup very grand in a shallow bowl with a broad, bold rim. Sometimes we don't use classic bowls at all, but substitute hollowed-out vegetables such as peppers, squash, or pumpkins—whatever tickles our fancy.

****✦***✦***✦***✦*✦***✦*✦***✦***✦*✦***✦*✦***

SPRING VEGETABLE SOUP

Without question, this is the freshest and prettiest vegetable soup we've ever tasted. Tender young or miniature vegetables create that just-picked, garden-fresh flavor. This soup makes a wonderful beginning, yet is substantial enough to make a meal.

4 tablespoons (½ stick) unsalted butter
6 large cloves garlic, coarsely chopped
4 pounds ripe plum tomatoes, coarsely chopped
3 cups Berta's Chicken Stock (see Index) or canned broth
2 teaspoons dried tarragon
1 teaspoon salt
½ teaspoon freshly ground black pepper
8 small red new potatoes, quartered
24 baby carrots, peeled
2 large bunches (16 to 20) radishes, stems removed
1 cup half-and-half
8 ounces young snow peas, stems removed
1 cup fresh asparagus tips, 2 inches long
  (12 to 16 asparagus)
12 large fresh basil leaves, slivered
¼ cup chopped fresh dill

1. Melt the butter in a large heavy soup pot over low heat. Add the garlic and cook for 5 minutes. Add the tomatoes, stock, tarragon, salt, and pepper. Cover, and simmer for 30 minutes. Remove from the heat and allow to cool slightly.

2. While the soup is simmering, fill a medium-size pot with water. Bring to a boil, and carefully drop in the potatoes. Cook for 10 minutes, drain, and reserve.

3. Fill another medium-size pot with water and add the carrots. Bring to a boil and cook until the carrots are just tender, 5 to 7 minutes. Then drop in the radishes and cook 1 minute. Drain and reserve.

4. Purée the tomato mixture, in batches, in a blender or food processor. Strain to remove any seeds. Return the purée to the pot, and stir in the half-and-half.

5. Before serving, heat the soup over low heat. When it is hot, add the reserved potatoes, carrots, and radishes, along

with the snow peas, asparagus tips, basil, and dill. Cook for 5 minutes.

6. Serve immediately, while the vegetables are just tender and brightly colored. Using a slotted spoon, divide the vegetables among eight soup bowls, mounding them a bit in the center of the bowl. Ladle the soup around the vegetables.

8 portions

WINTER BORSCHT

The rich ruby red of this hot borscht turns into a Valentine pink when sour cream is added.

2 pounds beets, well washed, with 1 inch of stem left on
Pinch of coarse (kosher) salt
2 tablespoons unsalted butter
2 tablespoons olive oil
2½ pounds short ribs of beef
6 cups homemade beef stock (see Index) or canned broth
3 cups water
1 onion, peeled and studded with 4 whole cloves
4 cloves garlic
4 sprigs fresh dill
3 cups finely shredded green cabbage
2 cups Great Northern or navy beans, cooked
2 carrots, peeled and cut into small dice
2 leeks (white part and 1 inch green), well rinsed and cut into julienne
1 parsnip, peeled and diced
4 cloves garlic, coarsely chopped
2 tablespoons tomato paste
4 cups Berta's Chicken Stock (see Index) or canned broth
2 teaspoons caraway seeds
½ cup chopped fresh dill
Salt and freshly ground black pepper, to taste
2 cups drained and coarsely chopped Italian plum tomatoes
¼ cup fresh lemon juice
Sour cream, for garnish
2 tablespoons chopped fresh dill, for garnish

1. Place the beets in a large saucepan, cover with cold water, and add the coarse salt. Bring to a boil, reduce the heat, and cover. Simmer until the beets are just tender, 40 minutes. Remove the beets with a slotted spoon. Strain and reserve the cooking liquid.

2. Slip the skins off the beets, and grate them coarsely. Reserve.

3. Heat the butter and oil in a heavy soup pot, and brown the short ribs on all sides, 12 to 15 minutes. Pour off the grease.

4. To the ribs in the soup pot add the beef stock, water, onion, garlic cloves, and dill sprigs. Bring to a boil, reduce the heat, and partially cover. Simmer for 1 hour.

5. Remove the onion and dill sprigs. Add the cabbage, cooked beans, carrots, leeks, parsnip, chopped garlic, tomato paste, chicken stock, and 2 cups of the reserved beet liquid. Partially cover and bring to a boil, then reduce the heat and cook 15 minutes.

6. Add the caraway seeds, chopped dill, salt and pepper, tomatoes, and reserved grated beets. Simmer, uncovered, for 15 minutes longer.

7. Remove the short ribs from the soup. Shred the meat from the bones and return the meat to the soup. Check soup for any loose bones, and discard. Add the lemon juice, and heat thoroughly. Serve garnished with a dollop of sour cream and some chopped dill.

10 to 12 portions

TRADE SECRET

For an unusual way to serve a cheese soup, cut the top quarter off of individual round loaves of country bread and hollow them out to make a bowl. Be careful not to cut through the bottom. Brush the insides with olive oil, and toast the "bowls" and their "lids" in a 350°F oven for 10 minutes, until a bit crusty. Ladle hot soup into your bread bowls and serve immediately on a plate liner.

SHORT RIBS VEGETABLE SOUP

A delicate yet highly flavored version of beef and vegetable soup that is somewhat Asian in presentation. Allow chilling time so that you can degrease the broth. Add fresh herbs just before serving.

4 pounds short ribs of beef, cut into pieces
1 onion, halved
4 cups homemade beef stock (see Index) or canned broth
2 ribs celery, cut into 1-inch julienne
2 carrots, peeled and cut into 1-inch julienne
1 leek (white part and 1 inch green), well rinsed and cut into
    1-inch julienne
8 fresh cultivated mushrooms, thinly sliced
2 tablespoons chopped fresh Italian (flat-leaf) parsley
1 tablespoon chopped fresh dill
Salt and freshly ground black pepper, to taste

1. Place beef ribs and onion halves in a large soup pot. Add the stock and enough water to cover the beef by 1½ inches.

2. Bring to a boil, reduce the heat, and cover. Simmer for 2 hours, skimming occasionally. The beef should be very tender and falling off the bones. (Do not overcook the beef, however, or it will lose its flavor.) Remove the short ribs and allow them to cool slightly. Shred the meat into small pieces and discard the bones. Wrap the meat well, and reserve.

3. Strain the broth into a large bowl and chill it, uncovered, until the fat rises to the top, 30 to 45 minutes. Skim and discard the fat. Or pour the broth through a gravy separator.

4. Return the defatted broth to the soup pot. Add the celery, carrots, and leek, and cook over medium heat for 2 minutes. Add the reserved beef.

5. Add the mushrooms and cook 3 minutes. Then stir in the parsley, dill, and salt and pepper. Serve immediately.

6 portions

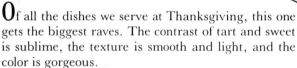

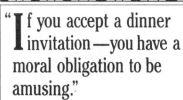

CANADIAN CHEESE SOUP

Of all the dishes we serve at Thanksgiving, this one gets the biggest raves. The contrast of tart and sweet is sublime, the texture is smooth and light, and the color is gorgeous.

10 tablespoons unsalted butter
1 carrot, peeled and finely diced
1 rib celery, finely diced
3 scallions (green onions), including green stems,
    thinly sliced
½ cup unbleached all-purpose flour
3½ cups Berta's Chicken Stock (see Index) or canned broth
1½ cups light ale
1 cup freshly grated Parmesan cheese
12 ounces sharp yellow Cheddar cheese, grated
5 ounces white Cheddar cheese, grated
    1 teaspoon ground white pepper
    2 tablespoons diced green bell pepper, for garnish
    2 tablespoons diced red bell pepper, for garnish

1. Melt the butter in a heavy pot over low heat. Add the diced vegetables, scallions, and flour, and cook, uncovered, for 5 minutes.

2. Add the stock and ale and bring to a slow simmer, stirring well.

3. Gradually whisk in the three cheeses and the white pepper. Simmer over low heat for 7 minutes. Do not boil.

4. Serve in a brightly colored soup tureen, garnished with the green and red peppers.

6 portions

ONION SOUP AU GRATIN

Caramelized sweet onions and nutty Gruyère make this French classic the perfect comfort food for a snowy winter day.

4 tablespoons (½ stick) unsalted butter
4 large onions, halved and thinly sliced
¼ cup sugar
Salt, to taste
½ teaspoon coarsely ground black pepper
6 cups homemade beef stock (see Index) or canned broth
2 tablespoons ruby port
4 large thick slices French bread, toasted
1 cup grated Gruyère cheese

1. Melt the butter in a soup pot. Add the onions and wilt over medium-low heat, covered, for 20 minutes, stirring occasionally.

2. Sprinkle the sugar over the onions, toss, and cook, uncovered, until caramelized, 10 minutes. Sprinkle with salt and pepper.

3. Add 3 cups of the stock and simmer, uncovered, over medium heat for 15 minutes. Then add the remaining 3 cups stock and the port; cook until the broth is rich in taste, another 30 to 40 minutes.

4. Preheat the broiler, or the oven to 350°F.

5. Divide the soup among four ovenproof bowls. Top each with a slice of toasted French bread, and sprinkle the cheese evenly on top. Place under the broiler until the cheese melts, or bake until the cheese has melted and the soup is bubbly.

4 portions

> "**T**he best kind of onion soup is the simplest kind."
>
> —AMBROSE BIERCE

SORREL SOUP

This is another recipe from our first cookbook that has become a basic in our kitchen. We love the light, refreshing lemony tartness of sorrel. Both the French and wild varieties will work in this soup. It's a snap to make, because with very light sautéing, sorrel melts almost into a purée to form a flavorful soup base. Cut the leaves into narrow strips so that the soup will not be stringy, and never use aluminum near sorrel— it will become wicked-tasting and turn an ugly color. Those cautions aside, you'll be hooked on sorrel soup once you've tried this one. It is great as a cool summertime soup and becomes very elegant when served hot as a first course.

4 tablespoons (½ stick) unsalted butter
2 large onions, thinly sliced
4 cloves garlic, chopped
12 ounces fresh sorrel leaves, rinsed and trimmed (10 cups tightly packed)
4 cups Berta's Chicken Stock (see Index) or canned broth
¾ cup chopped fresh Italian (flat-leaf) parsley
1 teaspoon salt
1 teaspoon freshly ground black pepper
2 teaspoons ground nutmeg
Pinch of cayenne pepper
1 cup sour cream, for garnish
Snipped fresh chives, for garnish

1. Melt the butter in a soup pot. Add the onions and garlic, cover, and cook over medium heat until tender and lightly colored, about 15 minutes.

2. Add the sorrel, cover, and cook until it is completely wilted, about 5 minutes.

3. Add the stock, parsley, salt, pepper, nutmeg, and cayenne, and bring to a boil. Reduce the heat, cover, and simmer for 50 minutes.

4. Transfer the soup to a blender or food processor, and purée until smooth.

5. If you are serving the soup hot, return it to the pot, taste and correct the seasoning, and stir over low heat until steaming, 5 to 7 minutes.

6. If you are serving it cold, transfer the soup to a bowl and allow it to cool. Cover, and refrigerate for at least 4 hours. Taste and correct the seasoning.

7. In either case, ladle the soup into bowls and garnish with sour cream and chives before serving.

6 portions

SPLIT PEA AND HAM SOUP

We've added lots of fresh vegetables to dress up our split pea soup. Adding a bit of sherry just before serving makes the taste special and lighter.

1 pound dried green split peas
5 cups Berta's Chicken Stock (see Index) or canned broth
5 cups water
1 meaty ham bone, or 2 smoked ham hocks
2 ribs celery, leaves included, diced
3 tablespoons chopped fresh Italian (flat-leaf) parsley
½ teaspoon crumbled dried tarragon leaves
4 tablespoons (½ stick) unsalted butter
1 cup diced peeled carrots
1 cup diced onion
1 leek (white part only), rinsed and sliced
1 cup slivered fresh spinach leaves
2 tablespoons dry sherry
½ teaspoon freshly ground black pepper

    1. Rinse the split peas in a strainer, and then combine them with the stock and water in a large soup pot. Bring to a boil.

    2. Add the ham bone, celery, 1 tablespoon of the parsley, and the tarragon. Reduce the heat to medium-low and simmer, partially covered, stirring occasionally, for 45 minutes.

    3. Melt the butter in a saucepan over medium-low heat. Add the carrots, onion, and leek. Cook until the vegetables are wilted, 10 minutes. Add them to the soup pot, along with the spinach. Simmer, partially covered, 30 minutes.

    4. Remove the soup from the heat. Remove the ham bone, and shred the meat from the bone, removing any excess fat. Return the meat to the soup.

    5. Add the sherry, pepper, and remaining 2 tablespoons parsley. Heat through, and serve immediately.

    6 portions

SOUPS TO START

A bowl of soup is a gracious and comforting invitation to a meal. Whether hot or cold, made with bright summer vegetables, aromatic spring herbs, or mellow winter roots, it will spark the appetite and soothe the soul.

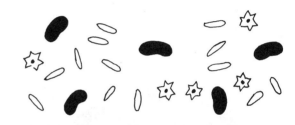

PASTA AND BEAN SOUP

A hearty one-dish meal for a cold winter night. Serve it with crusty bread, a green salad, and some good Chianti.

1 pound dried pinto beans (or kidney, Great Northern, or
    garbanzo beans)
½ cup olive oil
1½ cups chopped onions
3 tablespoons minced garlic
1 teaspoon dried oregano
1 teaspoon dried basil
3 bay leaves
1 can (6 ounces) tomato paste
1 can (28 ounces) tomato purée
10 cups water
Salt and freshly ground black pepper, to taste
1 cup orzo or other small pasta
¾ cup chopped fresh Italian (flat-leaf) parsley
Freshly grated Parmesan cheese, for garnish

1. Cover the beans with cold water and soak overnight.

2. Heat the olive oil in a large soup pot. Add the onions, garlic, oregano, basil, and bay leaves. Cook over low heat, stirring occasionally, until the onions and garlic are soft and translucent, 10 to 15 minutes.

3. Add the tomato paste and tomato purée, and cook another 5 minutes.

4. Stir in the water, cover partially, and cook over medium heat for 20 minutes.

5. Drain the beans and add them to the kettle with salt and pepper to taste. Reduce the heat, cover, and simmer until the beans are tender, about 1½ hours.

6. Add the orzo and continue to simmer until the pasta is tender, another 10 minutes. Stir in the parsley. If the soup seems too thick, thin it with a little water.

7. Ladle into soup bowls and serve garnished with Parmesan cheese.

12 portions

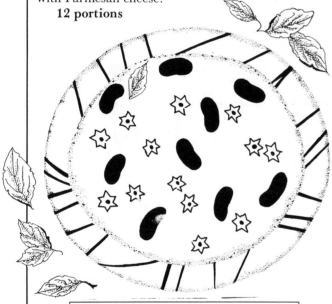

HEARTY SOUPS

These wonderfully thick and chunky soups are a meal in a bowl. Add a bit of warmed, crusty peasant bread, a fresh green salad, and a glass of wine for a glorious lunch or simple evening meal.

GAZPACHO

Gazpachos vary from Málaga to Córdoba to Segovia to Seville, and the recipes for them have consumed more conversation than all the El Grecos, Zurbaráns, cathedrals, and museums combined. (But not more than the bullfights.) Actually, we understand that in Spain gazpacho is eaten mostly by Americans—and some say its origin is a Polish *chlodnik,* a Turkish *cacik,* or a Greek *tarata.*

Wherever it truly originated, in an icy mug gazpacho is a great way to begin a summertime grilled menu. We've made this favorite—which appears in our first book—for years, and have been known to add a bit of vodka to our mugs so that it becomes a Spanish Bloody Mary. Olé!

½ cup red wine vinegar
½ cup extra virgin olive oil
6 large ripe tomatoes, coarsely chopped, with their juice
1½ cups canned tomato juice
3 eggs, lightly beaten
2 red bell peppers, cored, seeded, and coarsely chopped
2 onions, coarsely chopped
2 large shallots, peeled and coarsely chopped
2 large cucumbers, coarsely chopped
Pinch of cayenne pepper
Salt and freshly ground black pepper, to taste
½ cup chopped fresh dill

1. In a mixing bowl, whisk together the vinegar, olive oil, reserved fresh tomato juice, canned tomato juice, and eggs.

2. Purée the vegetables in small batches in a blender or a food processor, adding the tomato juice mixture gradually to keep the blades from clogging. Do not purée completely; the gazpacho should retain some of its crunch.

3. Stir in the cayenne, salt and pepper, and dill. Cover, and chill for at least 4 hours.

4. When you are ready to serve, stir the soup, taste and correct the seasoning, and ladle it into chilled soup bowls or mugs.

8 to 10 portions

GREEN GAZPACHO

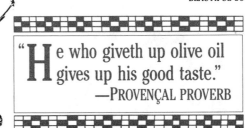

Cool, cool, cool—with seedless grapes. Perhaps it had something to do with the 99° heat we'd been suffering in New York City that led us to create Green Gazpacho. We suggest a small cup or mug for starters, topped with a little mint or lime zest.

1 cup green grapes
1 ripe avocado, pitted and peeled
¾ cup peeled and coarsely chopped cucumber
½ cup coarsely chopped green bell pepper
½ cup coarsely chopped celery
½ cup coarsely chopped scallions (green onions)
1½ cups white grape juice
1 tablespoon fresh lime juice
2 tablespoons chopped fresh mint leaves or lime zest
Salt and ground white pepper, to taste
8 sprigs mint, for garnish

   1. Purée the fruit and vegetables in small batches in a food processor, adding white grape juice as necessary to keep the blade from clogging. Do not purée completely; the gazpacho should be chunky.
   2. Transfer the mixture to a bowl, and add the remaining grape juice, lime juice, chopped mint, and salt and white pepper. Cover, and chill at least 4 hours.
   3. To serve, ladle the soup into chilled soup bowls or mugs and garnish with mint sprigs.
   6 portions

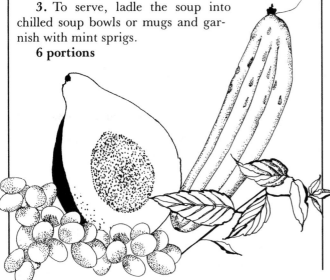

CHILLED AVOCADO SOUP

A lush, creamy summer soup lightened with low- or nonfat yogurt and flavored with thin slivers of fresh basil. We've topped it off with crisp chopped radishes for a lively bite.

4 ripe avocados, pitted and peeled
6 tablespoons fresh lemon juice
3 cups low-fat plain yogurt
3 cups Berta's Chicken Stock (see Index) or canned broth
4 large fresh basil leaves, slivered
¼ teaspoon freshly ground black pepper
Pinch of salt
4 large fresh basil leaves, for garnish
4 radishes, finely chopped, for garnish

   1. Set aside half of one of the avocados and place it in a small bowl. Sprinkle it with 1 tablespoon of the lemon juice, cover loosely, and refrigerate.
   2. Coarsely chop the remaining 3½ avocados, and place them in a large bowl. Add the remaining 5 tablespoons lemon juice, and toss.
   3. Add the yogurt, stock, slivered basil, pepper, and salt to the chopped avocados, and stir well. Then transfer the mixture to a food processor and process until fairly smooth, scraping down the sides of the bowl if necessary. Do not purée entirely; a bit of texture should remain. Remove the mixture to another bowl, cover, and chill for 2 hours.
   4. Sliver the basil for garnish right before you serve the soup. Dice the remaining avocado half. Divide the soup among individual soup bowls. Sprinkle the portions evenly with the diced avocado, and top with the radishes and slivered basil.
   6 to 8 portions

SUNSET BORSCHT

Sweet orange beets, orange peppers, and yellow tomatoes are beautifully presented in an unusual sunset-colored borscht. For a variation, garnish the soup with a dollop of crème fraîche or sour cream and a grating of orange zest. If you can't find orange beets, go with the red.

4 orange beets, peeled and sliced ½ inch thick
1 cup cherry tomatoes
1 orange bell pepper, cored, seeded, and cut into 1-inch
    pieces
6 ¼-inch-thick slices peeled fresh ginger
5 cups water
2 tablespoons fresh lemon juice
2 teaspoons sugar
1 teaspoon salt
Freshly ground black pepper, to taste
Snipped fresh chives, for garnish

1. Combine the beets, tomatoes, orange pepper, and ginger in a soup pot. Add the water, cover, and bring to a boil. Reduce the heat and simmer until tender, 30 minutes.
2. Transfer the mixture to a food processor or blender, in batches, and purée until smooth.
3. Transfer the borscht to a large bowl. Stir in the lemon juice, sugar, salt, and pepper. Refrigerate, covered, until chilled, 2 to 3 hours. Sprinkle with chives before serving.

6 portions

MINTY CUCUMBER SOUP

Here's that fresh, cool taste you like to begin a summer meal with. And please take note: There's no cream and plenty of flavor.

7 small cucumbers, peeled, halved, and seeded
1 clove garlic, minced
2 cups Berta's Chicken Stock (see Index) or canned broth
3 cups plain low-fat yogurt
2 teaspoons salt
1 teaspoon ground white pepper
1 ¼ cups fresh mint leaves
1 teaspoon fresh lemon juice
3 radishes, finely chopped, for garnish
6 sprigs mint, for garnish

1. Cut 6 of the cucumbers into 1-inch pieces. Cut the remaining cucumber into ¼-inch dice, and reserve, covered, in the refrigerator.
2. Combine the 6 cucumbers and the garlic in a food processor, and process for 30 seconds. Add the chicken stock, yogurt, salt, white pepper, ¾ cup of the mint leaves, and lemon juice. Process until smooth. Pass the mixture through a food mill or fine-mesh strainer into a mixing bowl.
3. Coarsely chop the remaining ½ cup mint leaves, and fold them into the soup. Chill, covered, for 3 hours.
4. To serve, ladle the chilled soup into individual bowls. Garnish with the radishes, reserved diced cucumbers, and a sprig of mint.

6 portions

ISLAND FRUIT SOUP

Yellow and orange fruits combine in one of the prettiest and tastiest soups we've ever created. Freshened and lightened with mint and sparkling water, this is a great way to begin a meal. The recipe can easily be doubled.

1 ¾ cups chopped fresh pineapple
¾ cup chopped ripe cantaloupe
¾ cup chopped ripe papaya
¾ cup unsweetened apricot nectar
¾ cup sparkling water
1 tablespoon chopped fresh mint leaves
Whole mint leaves, for garnish

1. Purée the fruit in a blender or food processor.
2. With the motor running, add the apricot nectar, sparkling water, and chopped mint. Transfer to a bowl, cover and chill at least 3 hours.
3. Serve in soup mugs or bowls, garnished with fresh mint leaves.

2 portions

STRAWBERRY SOUP

A perfect summer beginning—enriched with sweet fresh orange juice and Grand Marnier. Serve the soup on the same day it's made.

3 pints fresh strawberries, rinsed well and hulled
2 ½ cups fresh orange juice (4 or 5 oranges)
¼ cup Grand Marnier
3 tablespoons sugar (omit if berries are very sweet)
1 cup crème fraîche (see Index)

1. Purée all but 6 of the berries in a blender or food processor until smooth. Pour into a large bowl.
2. Add the orange juice, Grand Marnier, and sugar. Add the crème fraîche and whisk until well blended. Cover and chill for 1 hour.
3. Serve in shallow soup bowls or large balloon wine glasses. Slice the reserved strawberries, and carefully lay 3 slices on top of each serving.

6 portions

SPICED PLUM SOUP

This celebratory plum and red wine soup has a fabulous blush. We like it just as much warm as chilled. Serve it in balloon wine glasses to really set the tone for a festive menu.

4 cans (16 ounces each) plums in syrup
1 bottle Burgundy
1 teaspoon ground cinnamon
½ teaspoon ground nutmeg
½ teaspoon ground cloves
2 tablespoons sugar
¼ cup Cointreau
Grated zest of 2 lemons
Crème fraîche (see Index), for garnish
8 sprigs mint, for garnish

1. Drain the plums, reserving the liquid, and remove the pits.
2. In a medium-size soup pot, combine the plums and their liquid with the wine, cinnamon, nutmeg, cloves, and sugar. Bring to a boil, then reduce the heat and simmer, uncovered, for 30 minutes.
3. In a blender or food processor, purée the soup in small batches until smooth. Pass the soup through a sieve, to strain out any chunks, into a serving bowl.
4. Add the Cointreau and lemon zest. Mix well. Serve hot, or refrigerate at least 4 hours to serve cold.
5. Garnish each serving with a dollop of crème fraîche and a sprig of mint.

8 portions

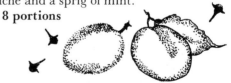

"I believe I once considerably scandalized her by declaring that clear soup was a more important factor in life than a clear conscience."

—SAKI

PIZZA PIZZAZZ

Pizza has come a long way from being sold by singing vendors on the streets of Naples. It may be difficult for us to pinpoint the reason for this: American teenagers, pizza delivery, or the terrific Los Angeles chef Wolfgang Puck. But pizza will never be the same again.

There are miniature pizzas for cocktails, unexpected brunchtime variations, first-course pizzas at the choicest dinner parties, double-crust or deep-dish pizzas for dinner, and folded calzones large enough to feed a football team. No matter how large or small, pizzas can be made everyone's way, for the toppings range from pepperoni to prosciutto, clams to caviar, anchovies to arugula and duck sausage. Anything goes on pizza, and we're crazy about it.

PIZZA KNOW-HOW

★

All in all, we still find the best pizza comes from home, not from the local pizzeria. Pizza must be fresh and hot to be good, and the topping ingredients should be the best, not budget. The secret, of course, to any great pizza begins with the crust.

CRUST

Our basic dough calls for all-purpose flour, which makes a crisp but tender crust. We allow our dough a good one hour rise to let it double in size. Once it rises, the dough is punched down, divided into balls, and left to rest for 15 to 20 minutes so that it can be stretched and shaped. Once you are proficient with the basic dough, you can branch out and add small amounts of other flours for different tastes and textures. A bit of whole-wheat flour gives the crust a nuttier taste, a little semolina flour makes a very crisp crust, and a bit of rye flour or cornmeal adds its own special taste and texture.

Pizza dough can be mixed and kneaded in a food processor, heavy-duty electric mixer, or by hand. If you're using the processor, you'll know the dough is thoroughly kneaded when it forms one or two balls on top of the blade. As long as you are making dough, you may as well make a double or triple batch, for the dough will keep perfectly in the freezer.

SHAPING A PIZZA

Shaping pizza dough is much easier than rolling out pie crust because the dough is elastic. It forgives. Any tears can be pinched together, any bumps pressed even, any unfortunate shape reformed. After the risen dough is punched down and kneaded briefly, let it rest for 15 to 20 minutes so that the gluten can relax and the dough can be spread thinly. To shape the dough, dust it lightly with flour and dust your work surface, too. Using your fingertips or the heel of your hand and working in a circular motion, flatten the dough into a 6- to 8-inch disk. Give the dough a few pats with the palm of your hand to even it, then flip it over. With the palm of your hand and working in a clockwise motion, begin to stretch the dough until it is 12 inches in diameter. If you find youself with a stubborn piece, shape it as thinly as possible, then let it rest for 10 to 15 minutes. The "relaxed" dough will be easier to shape. Finish by patting the edges all around with your fingertips to perfect the circle, then transfer to a pan that has been lightly dusted with cornmeal.

TOPPINGS

The list of vegetables that can go on a pizza is endless. Meats that top pizza are almost always cured—such as salamis, hard sausages, and hams—or are raw but blended with other flavorings, such as fresh sausage. Thin slices of smoked fish or fresh shellfish are also wonderful.

Most toppings can go directly on the pizza without any precooking if they cook in the same amount of time as the crust does and don't throw off a lot of water or fat as they cook. Seafood generally cooks quickly and can be added to the pizza raw. Cured meats in thin slices need no further cooking; they'll simply heat through. But fresh sausage must be precooked because it throws off quite a bit of fat. Vegetables generally also need precooking because either they won't cook through in time or they'll be swimming in their own juices if they do.

Grilling vegetables before using them as toppings adds excitement to pizza, but simple sautéing or blanching will do, too. Sautéing vegetables such as mushrooms, eggplant, and onions gives you the chance to add more flavor with a bit of olive oil or butter and herbs and other seasonings. Peppers—bell, chile, or Italian frying—are delicious roasted and peeled.

BASIC PIZZA DOUGH

A simple-to-prepare, classic pizza dough that is ideal for most toppings.

1 cup warm water
1 package active dry yeast or ¼ ounce compressed yeast
2 ½ to 3 cups unbleached all-purpose flour
2 tablespoons olive oil
½ teaspoon salt

1. Combine the water, yeast, and 1 ½ cups of the flour in a large bowl. Mix well. Add the oil, salt, and remaining flour. With your hands or a large wooden spoon, work the ingredients together until the dough holds its shape. (You may need a bit less flour, so add the last half gradually.)

2. Place the dough on a lightly floured surface and knead until it is smooth and elastic, 5 minutes. If the dough becomes sticky while you are kneading it, sprinkle a bit more flour over it.

3. Transfer the dough to a lightly oiled 2-quart bowl. Cover the bowl with plastic wrap or a kitchen towel, and let the dough rest until it has doubled in size, 1 hour.

4. When the dough has risen, place it on a lightly floured surface, divide it into two or more parts (see below) and roll them into balls. Cover them with a towel and let rest for 15 to 20 minutes. The dough is now ready to be shaped, topped, and cooked.
Two 12-inch pizzas (4 portions)
Four 6-inch pizzas (4 portions)
Eight 3-inch pizzas (8 appetizer portions)

WHOLE-WHEAT PIZZA DOUGH

Adding whole-wheat flour makes a dramatic difference to the Basic Pizza Dough, but don't use only whole-wheat flour in your dough. The flavor overwhelms and the dough does not press out well.

1 cup warm water
1 package active dry yeast or ¼ ounce compressed yeast
1 ½ cups unbleached all-purpose flour
1 cup whole-wheat flour
2 tablespoons olive oil
½ teaspoon salt

1. Combine the water, yeast, and all-purpose flour in a large bowl. Mix well. Add the whole-wheat flour, oil, and salt. With your hands or a large wooden spoon, work the ingredients together until the dough holds its shape. (You may need a bit less flour, so add the whole-wheat gradually.)

2. Place the dough on a lightly floured surface and knead until it is smooth and elastic, 5 minutes. If the dough becomes sticky while you are kneading it, sprinkle a bit more all-purpose flour over it.

3. Transfer the dough to a lightly oiled 2-quart bowl. Cover the bowl with plastic wrap or a kitchen towel, and let the dough rest until it has doubled in size, 1 hour.

4. When the dough has risen, place it on a lightly floured surface, divide it into two or more parts (see below), and roll them into balls. Cover them with a towel and let rest for 15 to 20 minutes. The dough is now ready to be shaped, topped, and cooked.
Two 12-inch pizzas (4 portions)
Four 6-inch pizzas (4 portions)
Eight 3-inch pizzas (8 appetizer portions)

TOMATO PIZZA DOUGH

Tomatoes in all forms work so well as pizza toppings, it should come as no surprise that they also make a nice variation in the pizza dough.

TOOLS OF THE TRADE

Wooden Pizza Peel

While traditionally pizza is baked in a wood-fired brick oven, a hot oven is all that is needed to produce a crisp crust. We find it absolutely necessary to preheat the oven to 500°F for an hour. For the best crust, bake it as close as possible to your oven floor.

We recommend a black steel pan for pizza because it retains heat best and delivers a brown, crisp crust. But almost any baking pan, including aluminum baking sheets, will give good results. All pans should be brushed with vegetable oil to keep the dough from sticking; if you want to add a little more texture to the crust, sprinkle the oiled pan with cornmeal.

Most likely you'll find that you already have the equipment needed to make pizza. But, if you bake them frequently, there are a few pieces you may be interested in acquiring. Pizza stones and baking tiles can bring a little of the traditional brick oven home. Unglazed quarry tiles can be bought from a ceramic tile store. They should be about a half-inch thick; thicker ones take too long to heat up and

those that are thinner break. Measure the floor or bottom rack of your oven before you buy tiles and allow for a 1-inch gap on all four sides so that the hot air can circulate. Most suppliers will cut tiles to fit. Baking stones are costlier than tiles, but they are also easier to get in and out of the oven. A baking stone for pizza should be at least 14 inches in diameter.

If you do decide to go with tiles or stones, your pizza utensil list will get a little longer, too. To get the pizza on and off the tiles, you are going to need a pizza peel, which is simply a flat paddle with a long handle; the back of a baking sheet works too, but you forfeit the distance the pizza peel gives you with its long handle. Some prefer to bake on a heavy wire-mesh circular pizza screen, because the pizza bakes directly on it and doesn't have to be coaxed off. Peels or baking sheets should be sprinkled well with cornmeal before the uncooked pizza goes on them. The pizza screen needs a good coating of olive or vegetable oil to make sure the dough doesn't stick.

---

1 cup good-quality tomato juice
1 package active dry yeast or ¼ ounce compressed yeast
2 ½ to 3 cups unbleached all-purpose flour
2 tablespoons olive oil
½ teaspoon salt

1. Combine the tomato juice, yeast, and 1 ½ cups of the flour in a large bowl. Mix well. Add the oil, salt, and remaining flour. With your hands or a large wooden spoon, work the ingredients together until the dough holds its shape. (You may need a bit less flour, so add the second half gradually.)

2. Place the dough on a lightly floured surface and knead until it is smooth and elastic, 5 minutes. If

the dough becomes sticky while you are kneading it, sprinkle a bit more flour over it.

3. Transfer the dough to a lightly oiled 2-quart bowl. Cover the bowl with plastic wrap or a kitchen towel, and let the dough rest until it has doubled in size, 1 hour.

4. When the dough has risen, place it on a lightly floured surface, divide it into two or more parts (see below), and roll them into balls. Cover them with a towel and let rest for 15 to 20 minutes. The dough is now ready to be shaped, topped, and cooked.

Two 12-inch pizzas (4 portions)
Four 6-inch pizzas (4 portions)
Eight 3-inch pizzas (8 appetizer portions)

LET'S TALK TOMATOES

We all know there's nothing better than the summer home-grown tomato, but let's be practical. The most dependable fresh tomato year-round is the meaty red plum tomato, although we also like the little yellow plums for variety. Another to consider for pizza is the sun-dried, with its wonderful concentrated taste. Sun-dried tomatoes packed in oil can be chopped, diced, or cut into thin strips, and the rosy oil adds wonderful flavor when drizzled over the top of a pizza. You can also buy sun-dried tomatoes loose and pack them yourself in olive oil or plump them in hot water.

BASIC TOMATO SAUCE FOR PIZZA

This is a good light base sauce for pizza because it is just the right thickness, and its flavorings will not overwhelm other toppings.

1 can (28 ounces) Italian-style tomato purée
1 large clove garlic, minced
1 teaspoon dried oregano or marjoram
4 fresh basil leaves or 1 teaspoon dried
1 bay leaf
Freshly ground black pepper, to taste

Place all the ingredients in a 3-quart saucepan. Cover and bring to a boil. Uncover, lower the heat, and simmer, stirring occasionally, 30 minutes.

3 cups (enough for two 12-inch pizzas)
Note: This sauce may be made ahead and frozen.

SPICY MEAT SAUCE FOR PIZZA

A full-flavored meat sauce that is a hearty addition to any pizza.

8 ounces hot Italian sausage meat
1 can (28 ounces) Italian-style tomato purée
2 teaspoons finely chopped fresh hot chile peppers, or more to taste
2 cloves garlic, minced
1 bay leaf
1 teaspoon freshly ground black pepper

1. Sauté the sausage meat in a skillet over medium heat until browned, breaking it up with a fork as it cooks. Drain and set aside.

2. Combine the remaining ingredients in a 3-quart saucepan, then stir in the reserved sausage. Cover, and bring to a boil. Uncover, lower the heat, and simmer for 30 minutes, stirring occasionally. Adjust the seasonings to taste.

About 3 cups
Note: This sauce may be made ahead and frozen if fresh sausage meat is used. (Do not refreeze meat.)

MARGHERITA PIZZA

We love this pizza for its taste and its colors; the red, white, and green of the Italian flag.

½ recipe Basic Pizza Dough (1 ball; see page 112)
1½ cups Basic Tomato Sauce for Pizza (see this page)
1½ cups grated mozzarella cheese
8 imported black olives
6 large fresh basil leaves
½ teaspoon salt (optional)
Pepper Pizza Oil, to taste (recipe follows)

1. One hour before cooking, preheat the oven to 500°F. When the oven is almost ready, lightly oil a pizza pan and sprinkle with cornmeal.

2. On a well-floured work surface, press out the

dough to form a 12-inch circle. Transfer the dough to the prepared pizza pan, and spread the sauce over it, leaving a ½-inch rim.

3. Sprinkle the mozzarella over the sauce, and arrange the olives and basil leaves decoratively over the cheese. Sprinkle with the salt and drizzle lightly with the oil. (The oil is very hot, so use it carefully.)

4. Bake until the crust is golden brown, 15 to 20 minutes.

2 portions

PEPPER PIZZA OIL

2 cups olive oil
¼ cup dried red pepper flakes

Combine the oil and dried red peppers in a bottle or other container. Mix well and set aside for 24 hours.

2 cups

Note: This can be stored at room temperature for 4 weeks—but watch out: the heat will increase.

HASH BROWN PIZZA

Forget baking up a quiche! Make brunch even more special with an exciting pizza variation on America's favorite breakfast potato dish.

2 small red new potatoes
12 large cloves garlic
2 tablespoons extra virgin olive oil
1 tablespoon plus 2 teaspoons chopped fresh rosemary leaves
½ teaspoon coarsely ground black pepper
½ recipe Basic Pizza Dough (1 ball; see page 112)
1 cup Onion Confit (see Index)
⅔ cup crumbled chèvre, such as Montrachet
Extra virgin olive oil

1. One hour before cooking, preheat the oven to 500°F.

2. Cook the potatoes in boiling salted water to cover for 10 minutes. Drain.

3. Slice the potatoes thinly, and place them and the garlic in a small roasting pan. Toss with the 2

tablespoons olive oil, 1 tablespoon rosemary, and black pepper. Bake them in the oven while it is preheating, shaking the pan occasionally, until golden brown, 40 minutes. Set aside.

4. Lightly oil a pizza pan and sprinkle with cornmeal. On a well-floured surface, press the dough out to form a 12-inch circle. Transfer it to the prepared pan, and spread the onion confit over it, leaving a ½-inch rim.

5. Lay the reserved potato mixture on top of the confit. Sprinkle with the chèvre and remaining 2 teaspoons rosemary.

6. Drizzle lightly with olive oil, and bake until the crust is golden brown, 15 to 20 minutes.

2 portions

A SHORT HISTORY OF PIZZA

It's impossible to date the first pizza, since it was never invented as such, but rather evolved over thousands of years. Starting from the flat rounds of bread that go as far back as Neolithic man (probably woman!), every people had a flat round of bread, and most spread some mixture of herbs and oil over them before or after baking. But pizza, as we know it, came into its own when the poorer Neapolitans started topping these humble rounds of dough with tomato.

The first pizzeria in America was opened on Spring Street in Manhattan in 1905. However, pizza never caught on in this country until after World War II, when GIs returning home from Naples refused to leave these delectable pies in Italy. But it took until the '70s and '80s for Americans to develop their own pizza styles. Now we can enjoy New England, Chicago, Tex-Mex, New Haven, and California pizzas.

SUNNYSIDE UP PIZZA

A great brunchtime pizza that can also be made with Whole-Wheat Pizza Dough.

6 slices bacon
½ recipe Tomato Pizza Dough (1 ball; see page 112)
½ cup sliced fresh plum tomatoes, cut ¼ inch thick
1 ½ cups grated Cheddar cheese
½ teaspoon freshly ground black pepper
1 large egg

1. One hour before cooking, preheat the oven to 500°F. When the oven is almost ready, lightly oil a pizza pan and sprinkle with cornmeal.

2. Cook the bacon in a skillet until it is half done. Transfer it to paper towels to drain, and set aside.

3. On a well-floured surface, press the dough out to form a 12-inch circle. Transfer the dough to the prepared pizza pan, and arrange half the tomato slices over the surface.

4. Sprinkle the Cheddar over the dough, leaving a 3-inch-wide well in the center (to hold the egg). Arrange the remaining tomato slices and the bacon over the cheese, and sprinkle with the pepper.

5. Bake the pizza for 3 minutes. Then remove it from the oven, crack the egg into the center, and return it to the oven. Bake until the egg is set and the crust is golden brown, another 12 to 15 minutes.

2 portions

LAZY SUNDAY BRUNCH

Mâche and Walnut Salad

Sunnyside Up Pizza
White Zinfandel

Poached Peaches
Lemon Lace Cookies

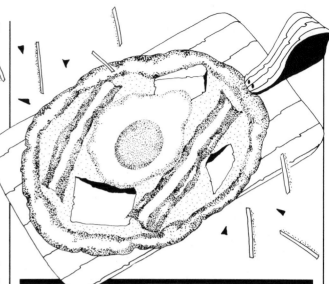

PORTOFINO PIZZA

Rich Mediterranean flavors are enlivened by a fresh egg baked on top of the pizza. This is also great when made with Tomato Pizza Dough.

½ recipe Basic Pizza Dough (1 ball; see page 112)
2 cups cubed mozzarella cheese (¼ -inch cubes)
6 anchovy fillets
12 Niçoise or other black imported olives
2 tablespoons chopped fresh oregano or 2 ½ teaspoons dried
1 large egg
5 sun-dried tomatoes, halved lengthwise
Fresh oregano leaves, for garnish

1. One hour before cooking, preheat the oven to 500°F. When the oven is almost ready, lightly oil a pizza pan and sprinkle with cornmeal.

2. On a well-floured surface, press the dough out to form a 12-inch circle. Transfer the dough to the prepared pizza pan and cover it with the mozzarella, leaving a well in the center and a ½ -inch outer rim. Arrange the anchovies and olives over the cheese, and sprinkle with the oregano.

3. Bake the pizza for 3 minutes. Then remove it from the oven, crack the egg into the center, and return it to the oven. Bake until the egg is set and the crust is golden brown, 15 minutes.

4. Remove the pizza from the oven, and place the sun-dried tomatoes around the egg. Garnish with oregano, and serve.

2 portions

FOUR SEASONS PIZZA

Each quarter of this pizza contains different ingredients, capturing the essence of each of the four seasons. Prepare everything ahead of time and assemble the pizza just before baking.

½ recipe Basic Pizza Dough
    (1 ball; see page 112)
Olive oil

SPRING

⅓ cup crumbled chèvre
¼ cup broccoli florets, lightly blanched
3 large shrimp, peeled, deveined, and halved lengthwise
1½ teaspoons chopped fresh dill

SUMMER

¼ cup Basic Tomato Sauce for Pizza (see page 114)
¼ cup cubed mozzarella cheese (¼-inch cubes)
¼ cup chopped ripe tomato
3 fresh basil leaves

AUTUMN

2 cups wild mushrooms
2 tablespoons olive oil
½ cup grated Italian Fontina cheese
½ teaspoon chopped fresh rosemary leaves
½ teaspoon finely grated lemon zest

WINTER

1 small Italian eggplant (see Step 3)
2 tablespoons olive oil
4 thin slices prosciutto
6 strips shaved Parmesan cheese (see Note)
4 fresh sage leaves

1. One hour before cooking, preheat the oven to 500°F. When the oven is almost ready, lightly oil a pizza pan and sprinkle with cornmeal.

2. Meanwhile, sauté the wild mushrooms (see "Autumn" ingredients): Heat the 2 tablespoons oil in a skillet. When it is hot, add the mushrooms and cook over high heat until deeply colored, 10 minutes. Set aside and clean the skillet.

3. Cut the eggplant (see "Winter" ingredients) into four thin lengthwise slices. Heat the 2 tablespoons oil in the skillet. When it is hot, add the slices and sauté them over medium heat, until lightly browned on both sides, 3 to 4 minutes per side. Set aside on paper towels.

4. On a well-floured surface, press the dough out to form a 12-inch circle, and transfer it to the prepared pizza pan. Using a knife, gently mark four equal wedges. For each quarter, arrange the ingredients of each season in the order given.

5. Drizzle the pizza lightly with olive oil, and bake until the crust is golden brown, 15 to 20 minutes.

2 portions

Note: For Parmesan shavings, scrape a whole wedge of Parmesan cheese carefully with a vegetable peeler.

HOW TO ROAST BELL PEPPERS

★

1. Preheat the broiler.

2. Slice the peppers in half lengthwise. Core them, and remove the seeds and ribs.

3. Lay the pieces skin side up on a flat broiling pan, and place the pan 3 to 4 inches below the heat. Broil the peppers until the skins are charred (they should be black). Then place the peppers in a plastic bag, seal it with a twist tie, and set aside. Let the peppers steam in the bag for 15 minutes.

4. Remove the peppers from the bag and slip off the charred skins.

5. Place the peppers in a storage jar, add olive oil to just cover, and store, covered, in the refrigerator. The peppers will keep for 1 week.

HAM AND CHEESE PIZZA

The classic Italian deli combination in a fun New Basics pizza.

1 recipe Basic Pizza Dough (2 balls; see page 112)
1 cup grated Swiss cheese
4 ounces thinly sliced baked ham
4 ounces thinly sliced mortadella
2 red bell peppers, quartered and roasted (see box)
½ teaspoon freshly ground black pepper
6 fresh basil leaves, slivered

1. One hour before cooking, preheat the oven to 500°F. When the oven is almost ready, lightly oil a pizza pan and sprinkle with cornmeal.

2. On a well-floured surface, press the balls of pizza dough out to form two 12-inch circles. Place one on the prepared pizza pan. Set the other aside.

3. Spread the Swiss cheese evenly over the dough in the pan, leaving ½-inch rim of dough. Cover the cheese with the ham and mortadella. Lay the roasted peppers over the top. Sprinkle with the pepper and slivered basil.

4. Carefully lay the second dough circle on top of the filling and pinch the edges of the two pieces together all around, making sure the edges are well sealed.

5. Use a fork to prick a few holes in the top layer, and bake until the crust is golden, 15 to 20 minutes.

2 to 3 portions

QUATTRO FORMAGGI AND PESTO PIZZA

The four classic Italian cheeses used in *quattro formaggi* are combined with our intense basil pesto for a real burst of summer.

½ recipe Basic Pizza Dough (1 ball; see page 112)
½ cup Basil Pesto (see Index)
½ cup freshly grated Parmesan cheese
½ cup grated provolone cheese
½ cup crumbled or cubed Gorgonzola cheese
½ cup cubed mozzarella cheese (¼ -inch cubes)
Extra virgin olive oil

1. One hour before cooking, preheat the oven to 500°F. When the oven is almost ready, lightly oil a pizza pan and sprinkle with cornmeal.

2. On a well-floured surface, press the dough out to form a 12-inch circle. Transfer the dough to the prepared pizza pan, and cover it with the pesto, leaving a ½-inch rim.

3. Arrange the cheeses separately, in four equal quarter sections, over the pesto.

4. Drizzle the pizza lightly with olive oil and bake until the crust is golden brown, 15 to 20 minutes.

2 portions

PIZZA CHEESE

MOZZARELLA: Fresh mozzarella is wonderful for flavor and melts easily. This cheese used to come only from Italy, where it was made with the milk of the water buffalo; now it is being made there and in the United States from cow's milk as well. Store fresh mozzarella covered in its own liquid in the refrigerator. Mozzarella and other soft cheeses melt so quickly that it's best to add them to pizza for just the last five minutes of cooking. Smoked mozzarella is wonderful with vegetable pizzas, and the saltier, firmer mozzarella available in supermarkets coast to coast is good on all kinds of pizza.

GRATING CHEESES: The most popular grating cheese in Italy is, of course, Parmesan. It has a sweet, nutty flavor and should be straw-colored with a firm texture. Real Parmesan is stamped "Parmigiano-Reggiano" on the rind; it's expensive but we think it's worth every penny. You can easily grate it yourself using the finest holes on a cheese grater, or peel thin shards off the wedge with a vegetable peeler. Freshly grated Pecorino Romano, adds intensity and interest to pizza.

AND KEEP IN MIND: Scamorza adds a pungent taste when melted. If you find the smoked or peppered varieties, try them for a pleasant change. For a full, sharp flavor try imported provolone; it combines well with other cheeses and melts well. If you are looking for a good melting cheese with a mild and creamy flavor, buy an imported Fontina. Some of the New England pizzas are good topped with their local white Cheddar, and the spicy flavors of Southwest or Tex-Mex pizzas combine well with Monterey Jack.

WILD MUSHROOM, GARLIC, AND MINT PIZZA

Mint makes this earthy pizza heavenly.

8 large cloves garlic
6 tablespoons extra virgin olive oil
Freshly ground black pepper, to taste
4 cups coarsely chopped fresh wild mushrooms (shiitake, portabello, oyster)
¼ teaspoon freshly ground black pepper
½ recipe Basic Pizza Dough (1 ball; see page 112)
1 cup coarsely grated or thinly sliced Fontina cheese
6 strips shaved Parmesan cheese (see Note, page 117)
1 tablespoon chopped fresh mint leaves
1 tablespoon chopped fresh Italian (flat-leaf) parsley
Extra virgin olive oil

1. One hour before cooking, preheat the oven to 500°F.

2. Place the garlic cloves in a small ovenproof dish, and sprinkle with 2 tablespoons of the olive oil and black pepper. Cover, and bake while oven is preheating, shaking the pan occasionally, until soft and golden, 40 minutes. Set aside.

3. Meanwhile, heat the remaining 4 tablespoons olive oil in a skillet. When it is hot, add the mushrooms and sauté over high heat for 10 minutes. Sprinkle with the pepper, and reserve.

4. Lightly oil a pizza pan and sprinkle with cornmeal. On a well-floured surface, press the dough out to form a 12-inch circle. Transfer it to the prepared pizza pan, and cover with the Fontina cheese, leaving a ½-inch rim.

5. Spoon the cooked mushrooms evenly over the Fontina. Arrange the roasted garlic and the Parmesan shavings on top of the mushrooms. Sprinkle with the mint and parsley.

6. Drizzle lightly with olive oil, and bake until the crust is golden brown, 15 to 20 minutes.

2 portions

PIZZAS PLUS

▼

Keep a supply of pizza dough in your freezer and you'll never be at a loss come dinnertime. A quick check in your pantry is sure to turn up a variety of delicious topping ingredients. And if you have some time to pick up a thing or two at the market, the possibilities are endless.

PIZZAS PLUS

▲ Small yellow plum tomatoes, red onion, hot sausage, Parmesan

▲ Goat cheese, fresh basil, pine nuts

▲ Grilled eggplant, fresh tomato, garlic Boursin

▲ Roasted garlic, caramelized onions, Fontina

▲ Sun-dried tomatoes, fresh herbs, fresh mozzarella

▲ Cilantro, fresh salsa, fresh roasted chiles, Monterey Jack

▲ Sautéed wild mushrooms, olive oil, garlic, parsley

▲ Fresh tomatoes, smoked mozzarella, fresh basil

▲ Shrimp, pesto, fresh tomatoes

▲ Gorgonzola, spinach, prosciutto

▲ Eggplant, roasted pepper, zucchini, tomatoes, fresh herbs

▲ Mozzarella, Fontina, tomatoes, basil, prosciutto, red onion, green pepper

▲ Smoked salmon, goat cheese, sour cream, golden caviar

▲ Red, yellow, and green peppers, Roasted Garlic Pesto, feta cheese, fresh herbs

▲ Shrimp, leeks, tomatoes, fresh mozzarella, garlic, fresh herbs

THE CLASSICS

Neapolitan: tomatoes, garlic, oregano or basil

Sardinian: red onions, anchovies, black olives, capers, marjoram

Sicilian: anchovies, provolone and mozzarella, tomato sauce, artichoke hearts, prosciutto, oregano

Romana Bianca: pancetta, onions, rosemary, mozzarella, black pepper

Ligurian: sweet onions, anchovies, black olives

Palermo: mozzarella, fresh herbs, black pepper, anchovies, olives

Provençal: tomatoes, onions, anchovies, Niçoise olives, fennel, herbs

Pissaladière: onions, anchovies, olives, black pepper

Tapenade: tapenade, mozzarella, tomatoes, sweet onions, oregano

Ratatouille: ratatouille, mozzarella, Parmesan

Fruits de Mer: Shrimp, squid, mussels, Niçoise olives, Tomato Coulis, garlic

Greek: tomatoes, green and hot peppers, spinach, feta cheese, Calamata olives, oregano, dill, hard-cooked eggs

Middle Eastern: ground lamb, raisins, pine nuts, tomatoes, onions, nutmeg

Spanish: sweet onions, red pepper, ham, uncooked eggs

Mexican: green pepper, Monterey Jack, garlic, plum tomatoes, hot chiles, hot Italian sausage, oregano, cilantro

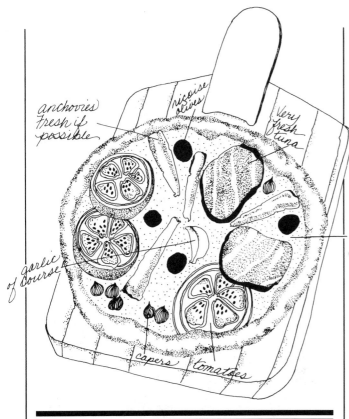

anchovies fresh if possible

niçoise olives

very fresh tuna

of garlic of course!

capers   tomatoes

TUNA NICOISE PIZZA

The fresh tuna atop a pizza makes the classic Niçoise even better. This is a summer snap to prepare when you have some Basic Tomato Pizza Sauce on hand. Try it with Tomato Pizza Dough, too.

½ recipe Basic Pizza Dough (1 ball; see page 112)
1 cup Basic Tomato Sauce for Pizza (see page 114)
6 slices ripe tomato
1 tablespoon capers, drained
12 Niçoise or other black imported olives, pitted
8 ounces fresh tuna, cut into 12 slices, ¼ inch thick, then
    into 2-inch squares
6 fresh basil leaves, slivered
½ teaspoon freshly ground black pepper
Extra virgin olive oil
4 fresh basil leaves, for garnish

1. One hour before cooking, preheat the oven to 500°F. When the oven is almost ready, lightly oil a pizza pan and sprinkle with cornmeal.
2. On a well-floured surface, press the dough out to form a 12-inch circle. Transfer it to the prepared pizza pan, and spread the tomato sauce over it, leaving a ½-inch rim.
3. Lay the tomatoes on top of the sauce. Sprinkle with the capers and olives. Then arrange the tuna evenly over the pizza.
4. Sprinkle the tuna with the slivered basil and black pepper.
5. Drizzle lightly with olive oil, and bake until the tuna is cooked and the crust is golden brown, 15 to 20 minutes. Garnish with whole basil leaves before serving.
   2 portions

Lots of other things (see recipe)

SMOKED SALMON AND CHEVRE PIZZA

Thin slices of smoked salmon, creamy chèvre and sour cream, and a sprinkling of leeks and dill top a pizza for the very essence of freshness.

½ recipe Basic Pizza Dough (1 ball; see page 112)
1 cup crumbled soft chèvre, such as Montrachet
2 tablespoons sour cream
½ cup julienned leeks
½ cup chopped fresh dill
6 thin slices smoked salmon
Olive oil

1. One hour before cooking, preheat the oven to 500°F. When the oven is almost ready, lightly oil a pizza pan and sprinkle with cornmeal.
2. On a well-floured surface, press the dough out to form a 12-inch circle. Transfer it to the prepared pizza pan, and cover it with ½ cup of the chèvre, leaving a ½-inch rim. Dot with 1 tablespoon of the sour cream.
3. Arrange ¼ cup of the leeks and ¼ cup of the dill over the cheese. Bake for 10 minutes.
4. Remove the pizza from the oven, and arrange the smoked salmon evenly over the top. Cover with the remaining ½ cup chèvre, 1 tablespoon sour cream, and ¼ cup each of leeks and dill. Drizzle lightly with olive oil, and bake until the crust is golden brown, 8 to 10 minutes.
   2 portions

FREEZING PIZZA DOUGH

To freeze dough, let the batch rise once, then punch it down and separate it into pieces, each large enough for one crust. Shape the pieces into balls, then flatten them into disks and wrap them separately in heavy plastic wrap or freezer bags. The dough will keep in the freezer up to four months. To thaw, place the dough in the refrigerator the night before you are going to use it, then let it warm completely to room temperature before shaping.

PURPLE FIG AND PINE NUT PIZZA

The sweet taste of fresh figs and onion confit are the perfect foil for the spinach and garlic sauté. The combination of colors and flavors in this pizza is extraordinary.

2 tablespoons extra virgin olive oil
1 ¼ pounds fresh spinach, trimmed, well rinsed, patted dry, and coarsely chopped
4 cloves garlic, coarsely chopped
Pinch of ground nutmeg
½ recipe Basic Pizza Dough (1 ball; see page 112)
1 cup Onion Confit (see Index)
¼ cup pine nuts (pignoli), toasted (see Index)
¼ cup golden raisins
3 ripe purple figs, quartered
2 teaspoons grated lemon zest
Extra virgin olive oil

1. One hour before cooking, preheat the oven to 500°F. When the oven is almost ready, lightly oil a pizza pan and sprinkle with cornmeal.

2. Heat the 2 tablespoons oil in a large nonstick skillet. Add the spinach, garlic, and nutmeg and cook until just wilted, 3 to 4 minutes. Drain well and set aside.

3. On a well-floured surface, press the dough out to form a 12-inch circle. Transfer it to the prepared pizza pan, and spread the onion confit over it, leaving a ½-inch rim. Top with the reserved spinach mixture.

4. Sprinkle the spinach with the pine nuts and raisins. Arrange the fig quarters decoratively on top, and sprinkle with the lemon zest.

5. Drizzle lightly with olive oil, and bake until the crust is golden brown, 15 to 20 minutes.

2 portions

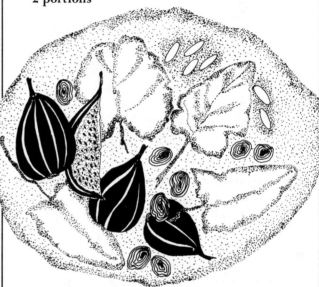

FENNEL CONFIT AND FONTINA PIZZA

For fennel-lovers, a pizza that is pure heaven. Fennel confit combines with fresh fennel for a splendid presentation. This topping also works well on Whole-Wheat Pizza Dough.

½ recipe Basic Pizza Dough (1 ball; see page 112)
1 cup grated Fontina cheese
1 cup Fennel Confit (see Index)
½ cup julienned fresh fennel bulb
10 small sprigs fennel
8 to 10 strips shaved Parmesan cheese (see Note, page 117)
Olive oil

1. One hour before cooking, preheat the oven to 500°F. When the oven is almost ready, lightly oil a pizza pan and sprinkle with cornmeal.

2. On a well-floured surface, press the dough out to form a 12-inch circle. Transfer it to the prepared pizza pan, and cover with the Fontina, leaving a ½-inch rim.

3. Spoon the fennel confit evenly over the cheese. Arrange the julienned fennel, fennel leaves, and Parmesan shavings evenly over the confit.

4. Drizzle lightly with olive oil, and bake until the crust is golden brown, 15 to 20 minutes.

2 portions

PRIMAVERA PIZZA

Fresh vegetables plus marinated artichokes arranged in colorful wedges make this a light, attractive lunchtime favorite.

1 small Italian eggplant
2 tablespoons extra virgin olive oil
½ recipe Basic Pizza Dough (1 ball; see page 112)
1 cup Basic Tomato Sauce for Pizza (see page 114)
1 cup cubed mozzarella cheese
⅓ cup sliced carrot rounds, cooked
⅓ cup broccoli florets, lightly blanched
⅓ cup coarsely chopped ripe tomato
⅓ cup marinated artichoke hearts, drained
1 teaspoon chopped fresh dill
1 teaspoon chopped fresh parsley
¼ teaspoon freshly ground black pepper
Extra virgin olive oil

1. One hour before cooking, preheat the oven to 500°F. When the oven is almost ready, lightly oil a pizza pan and sprinkle with cornmeal.

2. Cut the eggplant into four thin lengthwise slices. Heat the oil in a nonstick skillet, and when it is hot, add the slices and sauté them over medium heat until lightly browned on both sides, 3 to 4 minutes per side. Set aside on paper towels.

3. On a well-floured surface, press the dough out to form a 12-inch circle. Transfer the dough to the prepared pizza pan, and cover with the tomato sauce, leaving a ½-inch rim. Scatter the mozzarella over the surface.

4. Arrange the vegetables in five separate wedges, equal in size, filling the pizza. Sprinkle with the dill, parsley, and pepper.

5. Drizzle with olive oil, and bake until the crust is golden brown, 15 to 20 minutes.

2 portions

THE TRUE STORY OF MOZZARELLA DI BUFALA

Buffalo mozzarella has become a much-savored specialty in America. We are always warned to eat it within two or three days of purchasing or it will spoil. Henry Kaplan, one of the first great cheese importers in this country, told us the true story. In fact, most of the buffalo mozzarella that comes into this country is made with milk from both cows and water buffaloes. True mozzarella di bufala is a soft-ripening cheese that lasts for five to six weeks. It starts out chalky and becomes creamier the longer it sits. Ideally it should be quite spreadable when eaten. If you want true buffalo mozzarella, look for *"Mozzarella Volturna, prodotta con solo lati di bufala"* on the label. Let it ripen and enjoy it with the reddest of summer tomatoes, fresh basil, and extra virgin olive oil.

SPICY ROASTED PEPPER PIZZA

A delicious pizza for a snowy winter evening.

½ recipe Basic Pizza Dough (1 ball; see page 112)
1 cup Spicy Meat Sauce for Pizza (see page 114)
⅔ cup grated taleggio cheese
1 red bell pepper, quartered, roasted and peeled
*   (see page 118)*
1 yellow bell pepper, quartered, roasted and peeled
*   (see page 118)*
1 teaspoon chopped fresh rosemary leaves
Pepper Pizza Oil, to taste (see page 115)

1. One hour before cooking, preheat the oven to 500°F. When the oven is almost ready, lightly oil a pizza pan and sprinkle with cornmeal.

2. On a well-floured surface, press the dough out to form a 12-inch circle. Transfer the dough to the prepared pizza pan, and cover it with the meat sauce, leaving a ½-inch rim. Top with the cheese.

3. Arrange the roasted peppers around the pizza, alternating red and yellow. Sprinkle with rosemary.

4. Drizzle lightly with Pepper Pizza Oil, and bake until the crust is golden brown, 15 to 20 minutes.

2 portions

TRADE SECRET

Adding olive oil to pizza dough creates a crisp crust with a tender interior. Our friend and expert pizza-maker Steve Connolly usually brushes olive oil over the dough before cooking to keep it from drying out and to encourage a golden brown color. As soon as the pizza comes out, he swabs the edges with more oil to add a little moisture and flavor.

TRADITIONAL CALZONE

Sweet or spicy sausages, mozzarella and Romano cheeses, sun-dried tomatoes, Pepper Pizza Oil, and a wisp of fresh sage are combined to give us the robust spiciness we've come to expect from the southern Italian kitchen. We like to serve this straight from the oven.

1 tablespoon extra virgin olive oil
½ cup chopped onion
½ recipe Basic Pizza Dough (1 ball; see page 112)
1 cup chopped hot or sweet Italian sausage, cooked
1 cup ricotta cheese
1 cup cubed mozzarella cheese (¼ -inch cubes)
½ cup grated Romano cheese
2 sun-dried tomatoes, julienned
2 teaspoons chopped fresh sage or ¾ teaspoon dried
½ teaspoon freshly ground black pepper
1 tablespoon Pepper Pizza Oil (see page 115)
1 large egg, lightly beaten

1. One hour before cooking, preheat the oven to 500°F. When the oven is almost ready, lightly oil a pizza pan and sprinkle with cornmeal.

2. Heat the oil in a small skillet, and sauté the onion, over low heat, until soft, 5 minutes. Set it aside.

3. On a well-floured surface, press the dough out to form a 12-inch circle. Transfer the dough to the prepared pizza pan, and set aside.

4. Combine the remaining ingredients in a large bowl, add the reserved onion, and mix well with a fork.

5. Using a knife, lightly score a line down the center of the dough, and arrange the filling on one side of the line. Fold the other side over the filling, and pinch the edges together well, making sure the calzone is completely sealed.

6. Poke a few holes in the top of the calzone with the tines of a fork, and bake until it is golden brown, 20 to 25 minutes.

2 portions

PROSCIUTTO AND CHEESE CALZONE

Lusty pink prosciutto, black olives, and Fontina zested with oregano fill this wonderful calzone. Yum.

½ recipe Basic Pizza Dough (2 balls; see page 112)
¾ cup crumbled chèvre, such as Montrachet
½ cup grated Fontina cheese
5 to 6 slices prosciutto, shredded (1 cup)
1½ teaspoons chopped garlic
1 tablespoon fresh oregano leaves or 1 teaspoon dried
8 black imported olives, pitted and chopped
1 large egg, lightly beaten

1. One hour before cooking, preheat the oven to 500°F. When the oven is almost ready, lightly oil a pizza pan and sprinkle with cornmeal.

2. On a well-floured surface, press the dough out to form a 12-inch circle. Transfer the dough to the prepared pizza pan, cover loosely, and set it aside.

3. Combine the remaining ingredients in a large bowl, and mix well with a fork.

4. Using a knife, lightly score a line down the center of the dough, and arrange the filling on one side of the line. Fold the other side over the filling, and pinch the edges together well, making sure the calzone is completely sealed.

5. Poke a few holes in the top of the calzone with the tines of a fork and bake until it is golden brown, 20 to 25 minutes.

2 portions

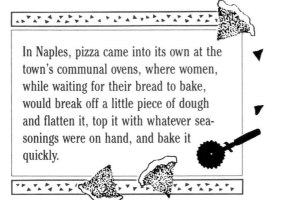

In Naples, pizza came into its own at the town's communal ovens, where women, while waiting for their bread to bake, would break off a little piece of dough and flatten it, top it with whatever seasonings were on hand, and bake it quickly.

PIZZA'S FIRST COUSIN

Any dish as grand as pizza is bound to attract innovators. A couple of centuries ago, some smart Neapolitan folded over a pizza and named it "calzone," the Italian word for trousers, because its half-moon shape looked very much like the trousers men were wearing at the time. The calzone, we imagine, immediately gained a loyal following among those who loved to eat pizza while strolling down Naples' walkways (an amusement still flourishing today). Calzones, like pizza, can be made small and tidy as appetizers, or large enough to feed a family. Most pizza toppings are wonderful in calzones, as long as they aren't too wet (in which case they'll come bubbling out when baked).

NUTTY CHEESE CALZONE

Fontina, mozzarella, provolone, Gorgonzola, and Parmesan melt nicely together, flavored with the mystery of rosemary and the surprising nuttiness of walnut halves.

½ recipe Basic Pizza Dough (2 balls; see page 112)
1 cup grated Fontina cheese
1 cup cubed mozzarella cheese (¼-inch cubes)
1 cup grated provolone cheese
½ cup crumbled Gorgonzola cheese
¼ cup freshly grated Parmesan cheese
½ cup coarsely chopped walnuts
2 teaspoons chopped fresh rosemary leaves
1 teaspoon finely chopped lemon zest
¼ teaspoon freshly ground black pepper
1 large egg, lightly beaten

1. One hour before cooking, preheat the oven to 500°F. When the oven is almost ready, lightly oil a pizza pan and sprinkle with cornmeal.

2. On a well-floured surface, press the dough out to form a 12-inch circle. Transfer the dough to the prepared pizza pan, and set it aside.

3. Combine the remaining ingredients in a large bowl, and mix well with a fork.

4. Using a knife, lightly score a line down the center of the dough, and arrange the filling on one side of the line. Fold the other side over the filling, and pinch the edges together well, making sure the calzone is completely sealed.

5. Poke a few holes in the top of the calzone with the tines of a fork, and bake until it is golden brown, 20 to 25 minutes.

2 portions

VEGETABLE FONTINA CALZONE

Fresh crunchy vegetables combine with melted Fontina in this very light calzone.

½ cup broccoli florets
½ cup sliced carrot rounds
2 tablespoons extra virgin olive oil
½ cup diced onion
½ cup diced fennel bulb
½ recipe Basic Pizza Dough (2 balls; see page 112)
½ cup diced roasted red bell peppers (see page 118)
½ cup grated Fontina cheese
1 teaspoon minced garlic
1 teaspoon chopped fresh dill

1. One hour before cooking, preheat the oven to 500°F. When the oven is almost ready, lightly oil a pizza pan and sprinkle with cornmeal.

2. Bring a saucepan of lightly salted water to a boil, add the broccoli, and simmer until crisp-tender, about 2 minutes. Drain, refresh under cold water, and drain again. Place them in a mixing bowl.

3. Bring another saucepan of lightly salted water

to a boil, add the carrot rounds, and simmer them until crisp-tender, 3 minutes. Drain, refresh under cold water, and drain again. Add them to the broccoli in the bowl.

4. Heat 1 tablespoon of the oil in a small skillet and sauté the onion over low heat until soft, 5 minutes. Using a slotted spoon, transfer the onion to the bowl.

5. In the same skillet, add the remaining tablespoon of oil and sauté the fennel until soft, 5 minutes. Remove it with a slotted spoon, and add to the other vegetables.

6. On a well-floured surface, press the dough out to form a 12-inch circle. Transfer the dough to the prepared pizza pan, cover loosely, and set aside.

7. Add the roasted peppers, Fontina, garlic, and dill to the cooked vegetables, and mix well with a fork.

8. Using a knife, lightly score a line down the center of the dough, and arrange the filling on one side of the line. Fold the other side over the filling, and pinch the edges together well, making sure the calzone is completely sealed.

9. Poke a few holes in the top of the calzone with the tines of a fork, and bake until it is golden brown, 20 to 25 minutes.

2 portions

OLIVE OIL FOR PIZZA

Many times a recipe will call for olive oil to be drizzled over the top of the pizza before it reaches the oven. For this we recommend a fruity, green, extra virgin olive oil for the best flavor. You don't need to use this premium olive oil in the dough, although you should use one that is of good quality with a pleasant, but not assertive, taste. We use corn oil to grease baking pans because its taste doesn't interfere.

PRIME TIME PASTA

Surely this has been the age of pasta. In the last decade we have seen that simple, humble staple rise to an extraordinary level. Every corner store now sells pasta in myriad shapes and colors and most restaurants have at least one pasta-of-the-day on the menu.

Pasta first came to this country with the immigrants from southern Italy at the turn of the century. But pasta seemed relegated to spaghetti houses and casseroles until the fairly recent surge of interest in northern Italian cuisine. A pasta revival quickly swept the country, and with it came a renewed interest in southern Italian food—the real stuff this time.

Now we won't be without it— pasta as first course, main course, even dessert; saffron pasta, whole-wheat pasta, beet pasta, black pepper pasta; pasta quills, shells, flat wide ribbons, thin thin angel hair, wheels, and butterflies; pasta with olive oil, walnuts, and Parmesan cheese, with cream, prosciutto, and fresh-shelled peas, with roasted peppers, tomatoes, and fresh basil, with shrimp, butter, and fresh lemon juice. We want our pasta every way, and maybe even every day.

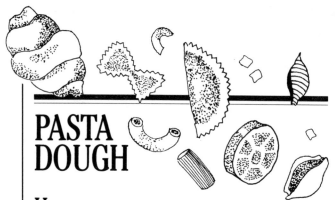

PASTA DOUGH

Homemade pasta dough is made even more special by rolling fresh herbs between the sheets just before passing it through the pasta machine for the last time. This is a very basic dough which can be machine-cut into strands of varying widths and also be used for pasta packages, such as ravioli and panzotti.

2 cups unbleached all-purpose flour
3 eggs
½ cup fresh herb leaves (optional)

1. Place the flour in a food processor, and with the motor running, add the eggs one at a time. Continue processing for 15 seconds.

2. Turn the dough out onto a lightly floured surface, and knead until it has formed a smooth, firm ball.

3. Cover with a kitchen towel and let rest for 30 minutes.

4. Divide the ball of dough into five pieces. Re-cover four of the pieces with the towel. Roll one piece slightly with a rolling pin. Flour the dough lightly on both sides.

5. Roll the dough through the widest setting of a pasta machine. Fold the pasta in thirds, and roll through the machine again. Repeat this four times, folding the dough each time.

6. Continue rolling the pasta through the machine, gradually making the opening smaller, until you arrive at the third-thinnest setting. At this point if you are adding herb leaves, such as parsley or tarragon, lay the leaves on half the sheet of dough, and then fold the other half over them. Run the dough through the machine one last time. It is now ready to be cut for pasta. Repeat with the remaining four pieces of dough.

About 1 pound pasta; enough for 4 to 6 portions

FRESH SUMMER TOMATO SAUCE

Tomatoes must be the sweet, honest, sun-ripened-to-almost-bursting garden variety for this classic sauce. When you are lucky enough to get them, then the simplest sauce with just a few herbs does them the greatest justice.

This sauce is to be found all through central Italy in the warm summer months; it is usually made in the morning and allowed to ripen at room temperature all day in a covered bowl. It's really a salad!

2 large ripe tomatoes
4 tablespoons olive oil
¼ cup chopped fresh basil leaves
¼ cup chopped scallions (green onions)
1 tablespoon chopped fresh oregano leaves
2 cloves garlic, minced
¼ teaspoon salt
Freshly ground black pepper, to taste
Freshly grated Parmesan cheese, for garnish

1. Bring a saucepan of water to a boil, and blanch the tomatoes in the water for 30 seconds. Then plunge the tomatoes into cold water (to stop the cooking). Drain the tomatoes, and peel them.

2. Remove the cores, and cut the tomatoes in half. Remove as many seeds as possible, and drain off the juices. Dice the tomato pulp.

3. Combine the diced tomatoes with 1 tablespoon of the olive oil in a mixing bowl. Add all the remaining ingredients, except the Parmesan, and toss to blend. (If not using the same day, cover, and refrigerate. Bring to room temperature before tossing with the pasta.)

4. To serve, add the remaining 3 tablespoons olive oil and toss with hot pasta. Sprinkle with grated Parmesan.

2 cups

PASTA PERFECT

PASTA SECCA AND PASTA FRESCA

Pasta, which literally means paste, comes as both *pasta secca* (dried pasta) and *pasta fresca* (fresh pasta). Dried pasta is just flour and water—but not just any flour. The best is made from the inner part of the grain of hard durum wheat, known—when ground—as durum semolina. The flour has a very high gluten content, which gives the pasta resiliency and allows it to cook *al dente,* tender, but still somewhat firm. Semolina produces a strong, fast-drying pasta containing more proteins and vitamins and less fat and calories than fresh pasta. The gluten acts as a shield to prevent the starches and nutrients from being left behind in the cooking water. A good pasta should not foam up when cooked. Look for a clear yellow color and a label that tells you it's made with semolina flour or durum wheat.

Fresh pasta is lighter and richer than dried because it is made with eggs and all-purpose flour. This is the traditional pasta of northern Italy, while dried pasta is traditional in southern Italy. When fresh pasta is dried, it is sold in nests and has a vivid yellow color.

Fresh pasta is not superior to packaged dried pasta. They are simply different and used with different sauces. A dried pasta will stand up to a robust sauce; delicate fresh pasta needs a gentler treatment. Both are wonderful.

Dried pasta is by far a better value than fresh, which has cost us as much as five dollars a pound. We can buy a one-pound box of imported dried linguine for just under two dollars, and since the dried costs so little, it makes sense to spend a little more on a really good imported brand. Dried pasta is easier to store; some say you should be able to keep it as long as five years, but there's little chance in our homes of ever finding out. Ideally, dried pasta should be used within six months. If fresh pasta isn't going to be eaten right away, it is best to let it dry completely and store it in a cool, dry place. There are a few commercial pasta producers who are packaging fresh pasta in airtight containers with a shelf life of three months.

COOKING PASTA

When cooking pasta, always start with at least one gallon of water for every pound of pasta. Depending on the pasta we may add one tablespoon of oil to keep the pasta from sticking to itself, but most Italians frown on this practice. In general, we do not salt the pasta water. Cook no more than two pounds of pasta at a time (double the water), for the water must be boiling rapidly during the cooking. If the water stops boiling, cover it until the boil returns. Stir as you add the pasta and continue to do so occasionally to keep it from sticking.

The real question is "When is it done?" First of all, we don't advise using the times printed on the box or package. Pasta should be tasted to know when it's done. Start testing fresh pasta after thirty seconds and dried pasta after four minutes. Fish a strand out and bite it. It should be firm yet tender, with just a tiny chalky white center. *Al dente,* so often used to describe perfectly cooked pasta, translates as "to the tooth," meaning it should feel pleasurable to the touch of your teeth—not too soft, not too hard, just right.

DRAINING PASTA

The easiest way to drain pasta is in a large colander, giving it a few quick shakes. Depending on the sauce, you may wish to retain a little of the water that remains on the pasta in order to dilute it. Warming the serving dish is added insurance that the pasta will be piping hot. Simply pour boiling water into the empty dish or set it in a warm oven until ready to use. Whatever method you choose, work as quickly as possible to get the pasta to its dish. Toss with the sauce and serve piping hot on warmed plates.

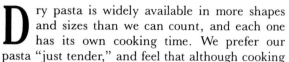

PASTA COOKING TIMES

Dry pasta is widely available in more shapes and sizes than we can count, and each one has its own cooking time. We prefer our pasta "just tender," and feel that although cooking times may vary a minute or two—depending on the manufacturer—our cooking times will produce the desired result. It's best to begin testing for doneness at the shortest given time.

NAME	DESCRIPTION	COOKING TIME
RIBBONS		
Fettuccine	"Little ribbons"; egg noodles	6 to 8 minutes
Lasagne	Long, wide strips, edges straight or curly	10 to 12 minutes
Lasagnette	Narrow lasagne	7 to 9 minutes
Linguine	"Little tongues"; long, narrow ribbons	6 to 8 minutes
Pappardelle	1-inch-wide noodles, edges straight or pinked	6 to 8 minutes
Tagliatelle	Egg noodles a bit wider than fettuccine	6 to 8 minutes

Sauces for thin ribbons: Oil and butter, light vegetable, light cream

Sauces for thick ribbons: Meat and game, hearty vegetable, heavier cream

NAME	DESCRIPTION	COOKING TIME
STRANDS		
Capelli D'Angelo	"Angel's hair"; the thinnest pasta	1 to 2 minutes
Cappellini	Thin strands, slightly thicker than angel's hair	3 to 4 minutes
Fusilli	Twisted or spiral-shaped strands	10 to 12 minutes
Spaghetti	Long, round, thin strands	10 to 12 minutes
Spaghettini	Very thin spaghetti	8 to 10 minutes
Vermicelli	"Little worms"; thin strands, slightly thicker than cappellini	4 to 6 minutes

Sauces for thin strands: Light vegetables, oil and butter; use in soups

Sauces for thicker strands: Seafood, heavier vegetable, creamy

NAME	DESCRIPTION	COOKING TIME
TUBES		
Bucatini	Thick-walled hollow spaghetti	12 to 14 minutes
Cannelloni	"Large reeds"; use for filling	7 to 9 minutes
Ditali	"Thimbles"; ½ inch long, smooth	8 to 10 minutes
Macaroni	Thick-walled tubes	8 to 10 minutes

NAME	DESCRIPTION	COOKING TIME
Manicotti	"Little muffs"; large tubes, use for stuffing	7 to 9 minutes
Penne	"Quills"; diagonally cut tubes, smooth or with ridges	10 to 12 minutes
Rigatoni	1½-inch-wide large tubes with ridges	10 to 12 minutes
Ziti	"Bridegrooms"; straight-cut narrow tubes	10 to 12 minutes

Sauces for small tubes: Creamy cheese; use in salads and in soups

Sauces for large tubes: Robust vegetable, chunky meat and game, heavier cream; can be stuffed

NAME	DESCRIPTION	COOKING TIME
SPECIAL SHAPES		
Agnolotti	Half-moon-shaped stuffed pasta	7 to 9 minutes
Cappelletti	"Little hats"; stuffed pasta	8 to 10 minutes
Cavatelli	Small lip-shaped shell with curly edges	8 to 10 minutes
Conchiglie	"Conch shells"	10 to 12 minutes
Farfalle	"Butterflies" or bow ties	10 to 12 minutes
Fiochetti	Bows	10 to 12 minutes
Orecchiette	"Little ears"	7 to 9 minutes
Orzo	Rice or oval-shaped pasta	7 to 9 minutes
Ravioli	1- to 2-inch squares stuffed with meat, cheese or vegetables, edges straight or pinked	7 to 9 minutes
Rotelle	"Little wheels"	8 to 10 minutes
Rotini	Little corkscrews	8 to 10 minutes
Ruote de carro	Cartwheels with spokes	8 to 10 minutes
Tortellini	"Little twists"; small pasta stuffed with meat, cheese or vegetables	10 to 12 minutes
Tortelloni	Larger tortellini	12 to 14 minutes

Sauces for small shapes: Light vegetable, light cream, vinaigrettes, butter and cheese; use for salads and in soups

Sauces for larger shapes: Heavier vegetable, robust sauces with beef or pork; can be stuffed

QUICK COOKED TOMATO SAUCE

One of the lightest, sweetest, and freshest-tasting tomato sauces we've ever created. Served with just one ounce of angel hair pasta per person, it is delicious, satisfying, and light.

½ cup olive oil
2 cloves garlic, finely slivered
2 cups diced fresh plum tomatoes
2 cups diced drained canned plum tomatoes
Pinch of nutmeg
Salt and freshly ground black pepper, to taste
4 tablespoons coarsely chopped fresh Italian (flat-leaf)
*   parsley*
3 cups halved and slivered onions

   1. Heat ¼ cup of the olive oil in a saucepan over low heat. Add the garlic and cook until it just softens, 1½ to 2 minutes. Do not brown.
   2. Add the fresh and canned tomatoes, nutmeg, and salt and pepper. Stir, and cook, uncovered, over medium heat for 10 minutes. Then add 2 tablespoons of the parsley and remove the pan from the heat. Keep warm.
   3. While the sauce is cooking, preheat the broiler. Line a baking sheet with aluminum foil. Spread the onions on the foil, and sprinkle with the remaining ¼ cup olive oil and black pepper to taste. Toss well. Place the onions 3 to 4 inches from the broiler heat, and cook until they are wilted and slightly brown, 5 to 6 minutes. Carefully stir the onions around a bit while they are broiling. Set aside.
   4. To serve, divide the tomato sauce among four bowls or plates, and place a serving of pasta (we prefer angel hair with this sauce) in the center of the sauce. Top with broiled onions, and sprinkle with the remaining 2 tablespoons parsley.
   4 portions
   Note: Try substituting cilantro for the parsley and adding 1 teaspoon chopped fresh jalapeño peppers. Or substitute slivered fresh basil for the parsley.

Legend has it that tortellini was created to honor Venus' belly button, after a Bolognese innkeeper spied on her through a keyhole and reported the rapturous details.

HEARTY TOMATO MEAT SAUCE

This rich meat sauce is heartily flavored by the pork and spareribs. They are what gives it the guts. Serve it over an equally hearty pasta, such as rigatoni.

4 tablespoons olive oil
6 sweet Italian sausages, cut in half
4 hot Italian sausages, cut in half
1 pound pork spareribs, cut into 2-inch lengths
8 ounces ground beef
8 ounces ground pork
1 ½ cups diced onions
5 large cloves garlic, minced
3 cans (35 ounces each) Italian plum tomatoes, with their
*   juice*
¾ cup tomato paste
½ cup dry red wine
1 cup chopped fresh Italian (flat-leaf) parsley
1 tablespoon dried oregano
1 ½ teaspoons freshly ground black pepper
Salt, to taste
Pinch of dried red pepper flakes
Pinch of sugar
Grated zest of 2 lemons

   1. Heat 2 tablespoons of the oil in a large skillet. Brown the sausages and spareribs in small batches, about 10 minutes each batch. Transfer them to a large heavy casserole, and set aside.
   2. Drain all but 3 tablespoons of the fat from the skillet, and add the ground beef and pork. Cook over

medium heat until lightly browned. Using a slotted spoon, transfer the ground meat to the casserole.

3. Add the onions and half the garlic to the skillet. Cook over medium heat for 5 minutes, stirring, and add to the meat in the casserole.

4. To the casserole add the tomatoes, tomato paste, wine, ½ cup of the parsley, remaining 2 tablespoons olive oil, oregano, pepper, salt, red pepper flakes, sugar, and half the lemon zest.

5. Bring the mixture to a boil, then reduce the heat and partially cover. Simmer over low heat for 2½ hours, stirring occasionally so the sauce doesn't stick to the bottom of the casserole.

6. Add the remaining garlic, ½ cup parsley, and lemon zest. Stir well, and cook, uncovered, for 1 hour, stirring occasionally. Adjust the seasonings and serve over your favorite pasta.

4 quarts; enough for 4 pounds pasta

Note: This sauce will freeze nicely for future use. Just be sure to use only fresh meat when preparing it.

HOW MUCH PASTA?

The usual pasta serving size is 4 ounces dried, but the cooked yield depends on the shape.

4 ounces uncooked = 2 cups cooked: spaghetti, vermicelli, capellini, linguine

4 ounces uncooked = 2½ cups cooked: elbow macaroni, conchiglie (seashells), rotini, ruote (cartwheels), mostaccioli, ziti, penne

4 ounces uncooked = 3 cups cooked: medium egg noodles, tagliatelle

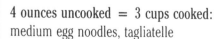

BOLOGNESE SAUCE

The traditional Bolognese sauce is most often made with ground beef, veal, or pork, and with a few chicken livers added for flavoring. And in Italy, the women get up early to put this sauce on the stove for a good, long simmer. Now with a much quicker cooking time and updated ingredients, it's become a New Basics favorite.

1 cup dry red wine
1 ounce dried cèpes or
    porcini mushrooms
1 tablespoon olive oil
1 pound ground beef
3 tablespoons unsalted butter
1 cup chopped onion
½ cup chopped celery
½ cup chopped carrot
½ cup chopped green bell pepper
8 ounces prosciutto, cut into julienne
4 cloves garlic
1 tablespoon unbleached
    all-purpose flour
½ cup homemade beef stock
    (see Index) or canned broth
1 tablespoon dried marjoram
1 tablespoon dried oregano
1 tablespoon dried basil
¼ teaspoon ground nutmeg
Salt and freshly ground black pepper, to taste
3 pounds (48 ounces) canned plum tomatoes, with their juice
3 tablespoons tomato paste
2 tablespoons minced garlic
½ cup chopped fresh Italian (flat-leaf) parsley
½ cup slivered fresh basil leaves

1. Bring the wine to a boil in a small saucepan. Add the cèpes; remove the pan from the heat, and set aside.

2. Heat the olive oil in a flameproof casserole or dutch oven. Add the beef, crumbling it into the casserole. Cook over medium-high heat, stirring occasionally, until browned. Using a slotted spoon, remove the meat and set it aside.

3. Melt the butter in the casserole. Add the onion, celery, carrot, and green pepper. Sauté over low heat until the vegetables are soft and translucent, 10 to 15 minutes.

4. Add the prosciutto and garlic cloves; sprinkle with the flour, stir, and cook another 5 minutes.

5. Drain the cèpes, reserving the wine, and coarsely chop them. Add them to the casserole.

6. Stir in the reserved beef, the beef stock, marjoram, oregano, basil, nutmeg, salt and pepper, plum tomatoes and their juice, and the reserved red wine. Partially cover the casserole and simmer, stirring occasionally, for 1 hour.

7. Then add the tomato paste, and cook, uncovered, for another 15 minutes.

8. Add the minced garlic, parsley, and fresh basil, and simmer another 15 minutes.

8 portions; enough for 2 pounds spaghetti

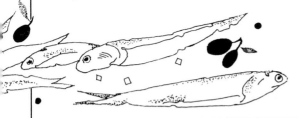

PUTTANESCA SAUCE

Our friend Bobbie's variation of the classic spicy puttanesca has been a favorite winter dinner basic. It is fast and easy and packs a very well-rounded-flavor bang. The secret is the olives. They must be imported, and although they're a job to pit, we just grin and bear it. You might want to make a double batch. It freezes nicely.

½ cup extra virgin olive oil
1 can (2 ounces) anchovy fillets, undrained
4 cloves garlic, crushed
1 can (35 ounces) plum tomatoes, drained
1 jar (2½ ounces) capers, drained
½ cup pitted imported black olives, coarsely chopped
Coarsely ground black pepper, to taste

1. Place the oil, anchovies, and garlic in a heavy medium-size saucepan. Mash thoroughly to form a paste.

2. Add the tomatoes, capers, and olives. Stir, and heat to simmering over medium heat. Reduce the heat to low, and simmer, uncovered, for 1 hour, stirring occasionally. Season with pepper.

2 portions; enough for 8 ounces capellini (very thin spaghetti)

AMATRICIANA SAUCE

The extraordinary flavor of this sauce—among the most popular in Italy—is based on the simplest of ingredients. We've added the smokiness of Canadian bacon as our secret contribution.

Serve this over bucatini, vermicelli, or spaghetti, with a gutsy red wine alongside and Pecorino Romano grated over all, for its sharp bite.

⅓ cup olive oil
4 onions, coarsely chopped
8 ounces sliced Canadian bacon or smoked ham, cut into
    ¾-inch squares
4 cloves garlic, crushed
2 cans (35 ounces each) plum tomatoes, drained
    (4 cups tomatoes)
2 teaspoons sugar
¾ cup dry red wine
Salt and freshly ground black pepper, to taste

1. Heat the oil in a medium-size heavy saucepan over medium-high heat. Add the onions, and sauté for 10 minutes.

2. Stir in the bacon and garlic, and sauté for 5 minutes more.

3. Stir in the tomatoes, sugar, and wine. Season to taste with salt and pepper. Simmer, uncovered, for 45 minutes, stirring occasionally.

6 portions; enough for 1 pound pasta

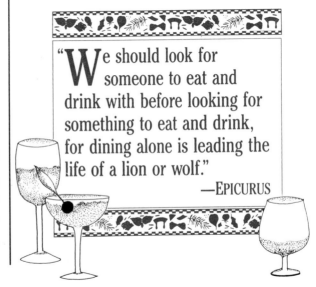

"We should look for someone to eat and drink with before looking for something to eat and drink, for dining alone is leading the life of a lion or wolf."
—EPICURUS

SAUCE FOR THE PASTA

So many of us make the mistake of drowning pasta in sauce, but we think sauces are flavorings and not the main show. We want to taste the pasta, so we feel the sauce should coat it as a vinaigrette coats the greens in a salad. If the sauce has a rich, concentrated flavor, a little goes a long way.

The shape of the pasta dictates the type of sauce to be used. The rule is simple: The longer the pasta, the thinner the sauce; the shorter the pasta, the thicker the sauce. Pastina and orzo are the exceptions, for they are very small, delicate pastas, best served in a light broth. Long, thin pasta goes well with light sauces that are smooth, whether based on oil or cream. There should be no chunks to slide off the surface of the pasta; you want the strands to stay separate and slippery. Light seafood sauces and tomato sauce work very well. Rich sauces laden with cream, butter, and cheese, or smooth meat sauces should be used with flat ribbon noodles, like fettuccine or pappardelle.

The tube pastas with holes and grooves, such as rigatoni, penne, and macaroni, are perfect for sauces that are substantial and chunky, with meats and vegetables to fill those tubes and grooves. They're also well suited for baked dishes because their thick walls stand up to prolonged cooking without falling apart.

One way of marrying the pasta to the sauce is to add the drained pasta directly to the pan of sauce while both are piping hot (obviously, making sure there's just enough in the pan to coat the pasta and not drown it). Combining and cooking the two together for just a moment allows the pores of the pasta to absorb the taste of the sauce, and the flavor spreads throughout. If this is a sauce that will be topped with grated Parmesan, add it now and it will further tie the sauce to the pasta.

Now we are aware of so many sauces, other than tomato, for pasta—both classics and our own inventions. When you create your own sauce, consider not only the flavors but also the textures, shapes, and overall look of the dish. And don't forget the season—the temperature outside, as well as what is fresh and at its peak in the market. Remember, the Italians are absolutely strict about the quality and freshness of their ingredients, and so, in the Italian tradition, should you be.

PASTA SAUCE RAPHAEL

One of the most popular pasta sauces we've ever served—with a few improvements. In this traditional way of making a sauce, all the vegetables are sautéed and simmered together, relinquishing their individual flavors to achieve a special new one. This was one of the most popular dishes in the *Silver Palate Cookbook*. We especially like it over tortellini. *Buon appetito!*

2 jars (6 ounces each) marinated
    artichoke hearts in oil
¼ cup olive oil
2 cups chopped onions
2 tablespoons minced garlic
½ teaspoon dried oregano
½ teaspoon dried basil
1 tablespoon coarsely ground black pepper
½ teaspoon salt
Pinch of dried red pepper flakes
1 can (28 ounces) plum tomatoes,
    with their juice
¼ cup freshly grated Parmesan cheese
¼ cup chopped fresh Italian (flat-leaf) parsley

1. Drain the artichoke hearts, reserving the marinade.

2. Heat the olive oil in a large saucepan. Add the onions, garlic, oregano, basil, black pepper, salt, red pepper flakes, and reserved artichoke marinade. Sauté over medium-low heat until the onions and garlic are soft and translucent, 10 minutes.

3. Add the tomatoes and simmer for 30 minutes.

4. Add the artichoke hearts, Parmesan, and parsley. Stir gently, and simmer another 5 minutes.

6 portions; enough for 1 pound pasta

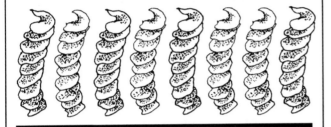

SPINACH AND THREE-CHEESE FUSILLI CASSEROLE

The region of Valle d'Aosta, filled with snowy mountains, is the area of Italy closest to Switzerland and France and has been strongly influenced by their culinary traditions. This three-cheese pasta casserole is indicative of just that influence. Serve it with a glorious green salad, crusty warmed peasant bread, and perfectly ripened pears—and you have a feast!

1 tablespoon extra virgin olive oil
1 pound spinach fusilli
1 cup heavy or whipping cream
½ cup dry white wine
Dash of Tabasco sauce
3 cups coarsely grated sharp Cheddar cheese
1 cup coarsely shredded Brie cheese, rind removed (see Note, page 139)
1½ cups coarsely shredded semisoft blue cheese, rind removed
2 tablespoons crumbled dried sage leaves
1 tablespoon dried thyme
2 teaspoons coarsely ground black pepper
2 large ripe plum tomatoes, thinly sliced
1 tablespoon chopped fresh Italian (flat-leaf) parsley
1 tablespoon freshly grated Parmesan cheese

1. Bring a large pot of water to a boil. Add the olive oil and fusilli. Cook at a rolling boil until just tender. Drain, rinse under cold water, drain again, and set aside.

2. Preheat the oven to 350°F.

3. Combine the cream, wine, and Tabasco in a heavy saucepan over low heat. Gradually add 1 cup of the Cheddar, the Brie, and the blue cheese, whisking constantly.

4. Gently whisk in the sage, thyme, and pepper. When the mixture is smooth, about 4 minutes, remove the pan from the heat.

5. Butter a 2½-quart ovenproof soufflé dish. Place one third of the fusilli in the dish. Pour one third of the cheese mixture over the fusilli, and sprinkle with one third of the remaining grated Cheddar. Repeat the layers until all the ingredients are used up.

6. Place the soufflé dish on a rack in the middle of the oven, and bake for 20 minutes. Then cover loosely with aluminum foil and bake another 15 minutes.

7. Remove the foil and arrange the tomato slices over the top of the casserole. Sprinkle with the parsley and Parmesan, and bake, uncovered, 10 minutes. Serve immediately or keep hot in a low oven until serving time.

8 portions

REHEATING PASTA

With the microwave oven has come the possibility of successfully reheating pasta, with or without sauce. The microwaves affect only the water molecules, thereby warming the pasta without drying it out. Microwave pasta in a covered dish on high power for about a minute; if the pasta is still cold, stir it and continue to microwave, checking it at 15-second intervals. You can also wrap pasta in aluminum foil and reheat it in a 350°F oven until hot. Check it after 15 to 20 minutes.

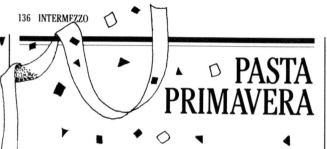

PASTA PRIMAVERA

Pasta Primavera has become the very essence of a vegetable pasta in this country—and we love it, even though it's not Italian at all. It was created in the early 1970s by Sirio Maccioni, owner of Le Cirque in New York. Here is our version.

1 small red bell pepper, cored, seeded, and cut into julienne
1 carrot, peeled and cut into julienne
1 small thin yellow summer squash, seeded and cut into julienne
4 ounces snow peas, trimmed and stringed
2 scallions (green onions), white bulb and 3 inches green
6 large ripe plum tomatoes
4 ounces fettuccine
2 teaspoons corn oil
1 tablespoon unsalted butter
2 tablespoons olive oil
½ cup dry white wine
4 tablespoons chopped fresh dill
Salt and freshly ground black pepper, to taste
2 tablespoons snipped fresh chives
4 whole chives, for garnish

1. Bring a medium-size pot of water to a boil. Drop in the bell pepper and carrot. Cook for 30 seconds. Add the squash and snow peas, and cook 1 minute more. Drain, rinse under cold water, pat dry, and reserve.

2. Cut the scallions on the diagonal into ¼-inch slices. Reserve.

3. Bring a small pot of water to a boil. Place the tomatoes, one at a time, on the end of a fork and dip them into the water for 30 seconds. Remove them from the water; peel off the skin. Cut into ½-inch dice.

4. Bring a large pot of water to a boil. Add the fettuccine and cook at a rolling boil until tender. Drain, rinse under cold water, and drizzle with the corn oil. Set aside.

5. Heat the butter and olive oil in a medium-size heavy saucepan over low heat. Add the tomatoes, wine, 2 tablespoons of the dill, and salt and pepper. Cook for 4 to 5 minutes, stirring gently.

6. Lightly toss the fettuccine with the tomato mixture. Add the reserved cooked vegetables, scallions, remaining 2 tablespoons dill, and snipped chives. Toss gently once more, and divide between two plates. Garnish each with 2 whole chives, and serve immediately.

2 portions

BROCCOLI AND GARLIC PENNE

This is pasta short-order cooking—fifteen minutes maximum—and very tasty.

1 pound penne
2 heads broccoli
¾ cup extra virgin olive oil
10 large cloves garlic, thinly sliced crosswise
Freshly ground black pepper, to taste
4 tablespoons (½ stick) unsalted butter
½ cup freshly grated Parmesan cheese

1. Bring a large pot of water to a boil. Add the penne, and cook at a rolling boil until the pasta is just tender. Drain, rinse under cold water, drain again, and reserve.

2. Cut the broccoli florets into fairly small pieces. Reserve the stems for another use. Bring a large saucepan of water to a boil. Add the broccoli, and simmer for 2 minutes. Drain, rinse under cold water, pat dry, and reserve.

3. Pour the oil into a large skillet, and heat over medium heat until it begins to ripple, about 1 minute. Add the garlic slices and cook, shaking the pan, until the garlic begins to brown around the edges, another minute.

4. Add the broccoli to the skillet, stir well, sprinkle with black pepper, and cook 2 minutes longer, shaking the skillet.

5. Add the butter and penne to the broccoli and cook, stirring often, until the penne is well mixed with the broccoli, oil, and garlic and the mixture is hot—3 to 4 minutes.

6. Place in a serving dish, sprinkle with the Parmesan cheese, and serve immediately. Pass the pepper mill.

8 portions

SHRIMP AND VEGETABLE PASTA

This festive pasta sauce combines blanching and marinating for the flavors to emerge—but it's a very simple sauce. Don't be embarrassed when the raves roll in. Just accept them graciously and save your secret.

2 pounds large shrimp, peeled and deveined
2 yellow bell peppers, cored, seeded, and cut into
    ¼-inch dice
2 red bell peppers, cored, seeded, and cut into
    ¼-inch dice
6 ripe plum tomatoes, cut into ½-inch dice
½ cup chopped fresh dill
2 tablespoons chopped fresh tarragon or 2 teaspoons dried
2 tablespoons chopped shallots
½ teaspoon dried red pepper flakes
1 teaspoon coarsely ground black pepper
1 teaspoon salt
½ cup fresh lemon juice
1 cup plus 1 tablespoon olive oil
¼ teaspoon hot chile oil*
1 head broccoli, cut into small florets (stems reserved for
    another use)
1½ cups cooked fresh peas or thawed frozen peas
1 pound linguine

1. At least 2 hours ahead, bring a large pot of water to a boil. Carefully drop in the shrimp and cook until just tender, 1 minute. Drain, rinse under cold water, drain again, and place in a large serving bowl.

2. Add the bell peppers, tomatoes, dill, tarragon, shallots, red pepper flakes, black pepper, salt, lemon juice, 1 cup of the olive oil, and the chili oil to the serving bowl. Toss well with the shrimp. Cover, and refrigerate.

3. When you are ready to serve, bring a large saucepan of water to a boil. Drop in the broccoli and cook for 1 minute. Drain, rinse under cold water, and drain again.

4. Toss the peas and broccoli with the shrimp and vegetables, and set aside.

5. Bring a large pot of water to a boil. Add the remaining 1 tablespoon olive oil, and the linguine. Cook at a rolling boil until just tender.

6. Drain the linguine and immediately toss with the shrimp and vegetable sauce. Serve at once.

6 portions

*Available in Asian groceries and other specialty food shops.

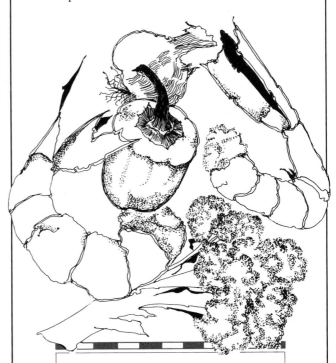

ONCE UPON A TIME

In the days when all the village bread was baked in a community oven, a young girl was sent down to the village with bread dough in baskets on the back of a donkey. It was a very hot afternoon and the oven was quite a long way from home. About halfway there, the girl met her young suitor, and he convinced her to rest with him in the shade of some trees. While the two young people rested together, the poor donkey was left standing in the sun with his load. Soon the dough began to melt and seep through the cracks and crevices of the baskets, and the hot sun dried it in long thin strands. The young girl returned home not with freshly baked bread but with spaghetti!

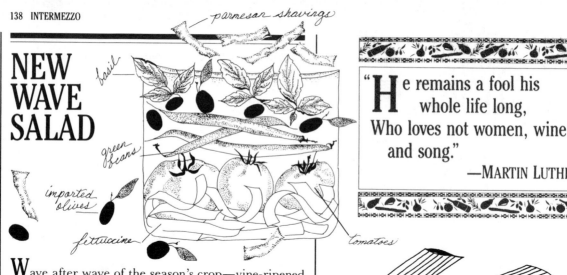

NEW WAVE SALAD

Wave after wave of the season's crop—vine-ripened tomatoes, snappy green beans, aromatic basil—combined with Italy's best—black olives, slivered Parmesan, and fettuccine. It will cause a tidal wave of compliments.

2 cups fresh basil leaves
1 tablespoon olive oil
8 ounces fettuccine
1 ½ cups Red Wine Basil Vinaigrette (see Index)
1 pound tender green beans, trimmed
6 ripe plum tomatoes, each cut into 8 pieces
2 cups Calamata or other imported black olives
2 tablespoons chopped fresh parsley
4 ounces Parmesan cheese, in one piece

1. Arrange the basil leaves in small stacks and roll them up lengthwise. Slice the stacks diagonally into slivers. Reserve ½ cup for the vinaigrette.

2. Bring a large pot of water to a boil. Add the oil and fettuccine and cook at a rolling boil until just tender. Drain, rinse under cold water, drain again, and place in a mixing bowl. Add ½ cup of the vinaigrette and toss well. Set aside.

3. Bring a saucepan of water to a boil, and add the beans. Simmer until just tender, 5 to 8 minutes. Drain, rinse under cold water, drain again, and set aside.

4. Place the pasta in a tall glass serving bowl. Cover with the tomatoes, and then the green beans. Cover the beans with the olives and remaining slivered basil. Sprinkle with the parsley, and pour the remaining 1 cup vinaigrette over the salad.

5. Scrape the Parmesan with a vegetable peeler or cheese server to make thin wide shavings. Place them on top of the salad. Toss well before serving.

8 portions

> "He remains a fool his whole life long, Who loves not women, wine and song."
>
> —MARTIN LUTHER

SUN-DRIED TOMATOES AND BASIL PASTA

The very best sun-dried tomatoes come from Liguria—smooth, sweet, plump, and tender. Others can be too acidic and therefore too sharp.

The tomatoes here are surrounded by basil and Brie in a "hot and cold" pasta sauce—the sauce is room temperature, the pasta hot.

8 ounces sun-dried tomatoes, slivered lengthwise, with their oil
1 cup Calamata or other imported black olives, pitted and halved
1 cup loosely packed fresh basil leaves, slivered
¼ cup grated lemon zest (about 8 lemons)
2 cloves garlic, finely minced
2 teaspoons coarsely ground black pepper
12 ounces Brie cheese, rind removed, coarsely shredded (see Note)
½ cup plus 1 tablespoon extra virgin olive oil
1 pound linguine or penne

1. Combine the sun-dried tomatoes, ¼ cup of the oil from the tomatoes, olives, basil, lemon zest, garlic, pepper, Brie, and ½ cup of the olive oil in a large

serving bowl. Cover, and let stand at room temperature for 4 hours.

2. Bring a large pot of water to a boil. Add the remaining 1 tablespoon olive oil and the linguine. Cook at a rolling boil until just tender.

3. Drain the pasta and immediately toss with the sauce. Serve at once.

6 portions

Note: Place the Brie in the freezer, well wrapped, for 1 hour before using. The rind will slice off easily and the cheese will be easier to shred.

MACARONI AND CHEESE

We've all had our share of macaroni and cheese over the years, from mother's own to school cafeteria to the frozen, dried, or canned versions. But lately we haven't had this classic often enough.

The trick to a terrific macaroni and cheese is the cheese. Most often Cheddar is used, but we've updated our version with a nutty Gruyère. If you're looking to give the dish added richness, replace some of the milk with an equal amount of evaporated milk.

1 pound penne
4 cups milk
4 tablespoons (½ stick) unsalted butter
6 tablespoons unbleached all-purpose flour
1 teaspoon paprika
Salt and freshly ground black pepper, to taste
12 ounces Gruyère cheese, grated (4 cups)

1. Bring a large pot of water to a boil. Add the penne and cook at a rolling boil until just tender. Drain, rinse under cold water, drain again and set aside in a large bowl.

2. Preheat the oven to 350°F.

3. Bring the milk just to a boil in a heavy saucepan and set aisde.

4. Meanwhile, melt the butter in another heavy saucepan. Add the flour, and whisk over low heat for 5 minutes. Do not brown. Remove from the heat.

5. Add the hot milk to the flour mixture, and whisk well. Add ½ teaspoon of the paprika, season

with salt and pepper, and return the pan to the heat. Cook over medium heat, whisking constantly, until the mixture thickens, 5 minutes. Add to the penne, and toss well to coat the penne completely.

6. Butter a 13 x 9 x 2-inch flameproof baking dish, and fill it evenly with the penne and sauce.

7. Distribute the grated cheese evenly over the penne, and sprinkle with black pepper and additional paprika.

8. Place the dish on a baking sheet, and bake until hot, 20 to 25 minutes.

9. Place the dish under the broiler, 4 inches from the heat, until the top is slightly golden and bubbling, 3 to 4 minutes. Serve immediately.

8 portions

Note: Other good melting cheeses may be substituted for Gruyère, such as Cheddar, mozzarella, or Jarlsberg. Or combine two of these cheeses. If you wish, add fresh shavings of Parmesan to the top of the casserole before you run it under the broiler.

THE MACARONI STORY

When in the late 1700s Yankee Doodle stuck a feather in his cap and called it macaroni, he was actually patting himself on the back for his fashion ingenuity, for macaroni was slang for chic (the most chic and popular dish of the day being macaroni).

Legend has it that in the late thirteenth century, German bakers made large figures out of noodle dough in the shapes of men, stars, birds, and seashells, which they called collectively "doughmen." These bakers went to Genoa, Italy, to sell their product, but the Italians found them too expensive and exclaimed "*ma caroni*," meaning "but it's too dear." So the Germans reduced the size and, with the size, the price. They made a bundle and the name stuck.

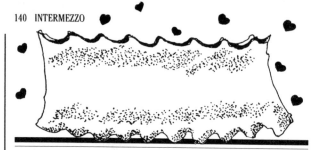

BEEF AND VEGETABLE LASAGNE

Lasagne is a specialty in the Emilia-Romagna region of Italy, where the pasta is made with only flour and eggs—brown-shelled, say the sticklers—to create the characteristic rich golden yellow sheets of dough. Our sauce, however, is more typical of Tuscany, with its abundance of tomato and nutmeg.

2 tablespoons olive oil
1 pound ground beef round
5 cups New Basic Tomato Sauce (see Index)
4 tablespoons chopped fresh Italian (flat-leaf) parsley
3½ cups ricotta cheese
1 cup chopped cooked spinach, well drained
¼ cup freshly grated Parmesan cheese
1 tablespoon dried oregano
¾ teaspoon ground nutmeg
Freshly ground black pepper, to taste
8 lasagne noodles, cooked until not quite tender
3 cups grated mozzarella cheese

1. Preheat the oven to 350°F.
2. Heat the olive oil in a skillet over medium heat. Add the beef, crumbling it into the skillet. Cook, stirring occasionally, until it is browned. Drain, and set aside.
3. Place the tomato sauce in a saucepan. Add the beef and 2 tablespoons of the parsley, and cook over medium heat for 5 minutes. Remove the pan from the heat.
4. In a mixing bowl, combine the ricotta, spinach, Parmesan, remaining 2 tablespoons parsley, oregano, nutmeg, and pepper. Stir well.
5. Place 2 cups of the tomato sauce in the bottom of a 13 x 9-inch baking dish. Arrange 4 lasagne noodles on top of the sauce. Spread half the ricotta mixture over the lasagne, and sprinkle with 1 cup of the mozzarella. Repeat the layers of sauce, noodles, ricotta, and mozzarella.

6. Top with the remaining 2 cups of sauce and 1 cup mozzarella, sprinkled evenly over the top.
7. Cover the dish loosely with aluminum foil, place it on a baking sheet, and bake for 45 minutes. Then remove the foil and bake an additional 20 minutes. Remove the dish from the oven and allow it to rest for 10 to 15 minutes before serving.

8 portions

Note: For individual frozen portions, cut the baked lasagne into eight pieces. Place in freezer containers with lids. Freeze when cool. To reheat, defrost and bake, covered with aluminum foil, at 350°F for 20 minutes.

GRATE PARMESAN

The best Parmesan cheese—not the grated, jarred supermarket variety—comes from the region of Emilia-Romagna and must have ''Parmigiano-Reggiano'' stamped on the rind. These huge wheels are the most famous and valuable of all the grana cheeses of Italy. The younger cheese is slightly moist, the aged drier and a bit chalky in appearance. In Italy, they serve the younger, two-year-old cheese as a table cheese, grate the three-year-old cheese over pasta, and stuff the four-year-old cheese into ravioli and tortellini. A wedge of Parmigiano-Reggiano should be straw yellow in color, crumble softly, and taste mellow, rich, and salty—never sharp. When we serve pasta, we always pass a wedge of Parmigiano-Reggiano along with a fine grater so everyone can grate their own. We think it's the only way.

SESAME CHICKEN AND ASPARAGUS PASTA

This is a pasta dish with a genuine Asian flavor. Garlic, soy, toasted sesame seeds, and sesame oil coat the linguine and chicken, and scallions and cucumbers provide the crunch. This is wonderful, so enjoy!

8 ounces linguine
3 cloves garlic, minced
1 tablespoon red wine vinegar
1 tablespoon brown sugar
6 tablespoons chunky peanut butter
¼ cup soy sauce
6 tablespoons sesame oil
3 tablespoons hot chile oil*
2 boneless and skinless cooked chicken breast halves
5 tablespoons sesame seeds, toasted (see Index)
1 pound thin asparagus, trimmed
3 scallions (green onions), white bulb and 3 inches green, cut into 2-inch julienne
1 small cucumber, halved, seeded, and cut into ¼-inch dice

1. Bring a large pot of water to a boil. Add the linguine, and cook at a rolling boil until just tender. Drain, rinse under cold water, drain again, and set aside in a large mixing bowl.

2. Place the garlic, vinegar, brown sugar, peanut butter, and soy sauce in a food processor. Process for 1 minute. With the motor running, slowly add the sesame and hot chili oils through the feed tube, and process until well blended.

3. Shred the chicken into 2-inch julienne, and toss with the linguine. Add the sauce and 4 tablespoons of the sesame seeds, and toss to coat well.

4. Cut the asparagus on the diagonal into 1-inch lengths. Blanch in a saucepan of boiling water for 1 minute. Drain, rinse under cold water, and pat dry.

5. Place the linguine and chicken in a large flat serving bowl, and arrange the asparagus on top. Sprinkle with the scallions, cucumber, and remaining 1 tablespoon sesame seeds. Serve at room temperature.

6 portions

*Available in Asian groceries and other specialty food shops.

Nothing Italians make shows their inventive genius, their playful love of design, their endless ingenuity, and their love of food better than the hundreds of ways they shape pasta. For many of these shapes there is a diminutive and a superlative as well—there are not just butterflies (*farfalle*) but little butterflies (*farfallette*) and bigger butterflies (*farfalloni*). Italy is the only country whose basic food is as visually varied and fanciful as its baroque facades and chapels. The Italians can't resist giving all of the ribbons, strands, and pasta shapes fanciful names; last told, the names numbered over three hundred. To dig into a delicious pasta or gaze into a golden clear consommé and find pasta butterflies, seashells, snails, cockscombs, thimbles, ribbons—even cupids, clowns' hats, priests' hats, trouts' eyes, sparrows' tongues, bow-ties, and little ears—is no small pleasure.

SQUID INK FETTUCCINE WITH MUSSELS, CLAMS, AND SQUID

Imagine having this sauce on a Mediterranean island like in Sardinia, where cork trees, olive groves, and huge palms grow, where bright pink flamingoes fly clattering into the air, where wild ponies play and wild boar and deer roam. And where you can enjoy some of the best seafood ever.

Here, mussels, clams, and squid are luxuriously tossed in a dill chive vinaigrette and dramatically presented on black squid ink pasta—it makes a grand presentation particularly by candlelight to emphasize the mysteries of the deep.

2 ½ pounds medium-size mussels, well scrubbed
2 tablespoons cornmeal
1 cup cold water
2 dozen littleneck clams, well scrubbed
2 quarts water
1 pound squid, cleaned, mantles cut into ¼-inch rounds,
  tentacles left whole
1 pound squid ink fettucine (see Note)
2 cups Dill Chive Vinaigrette (see Index)
2 tablespoons snipped fresh chives, for garnish
6 sprigs dill, for garnish

1. Place the mussels in a bowl and cover with cold water. Add the cornmeal and let soak for 1 hour. Drain, and rinse well in cold water. Beard the mussels.

2. Place the mussels in a pot, add the cold water, cover, and bring to a boil. Cook until the mussels open, 5 minutes. Remove the mussels, reserving the liquid, and remove the mussels from their shells. Reserve.

3. Place the clams in the mussel broth, bring to a boil, cover, and cook until the clams open, 4 to 5 minutes. Remove the clams from the liquid, and remove the clams from the shells. Reserve. Discard the liquid.

4. Fill a large pot with the 2 quarts water. Add the squid and bring to a boil. Reduce the heat and simmer, uncovered, until tender, 40 minutes. Do not overcook. Drain and reserve.

5. Bring a large pot of water to a boil. Add the fettuccine, and cook at a rolling boil until just tender. Drain the pasta and toss it with ½ cup of the vinaigrette.

6. Toss the mussels, clams, and squid with ½ cup of the vinaigrette.

7. Place the fettuccine on a decorative serving platter. Arrange the seafood on top, and drizzle ½ cup of vinaigrette over the seafood. Garnish with chives and dill. Serve at room temperature. Pass the remaining vinaigrette to those who'd like a bit more.

8 portions

Note: Squid ink pasta is available in Italian and other specialty food stores.

BASIL ALFREDO PASTA

We've added chèvre to our Alfredo sauce—you choose whether you want yours mild or sharp—and freshened it with lots of basil. A confetti of tomato makes this a perfect dinner party entrée.

2 cups heavy or whipping cream
1 cup coarsely chopped fresh basil leaves
1 teaspoon salt
9 ounces fresh spinach fettucine or 8 ounces dry
8 ounces chèvre, crumbled
½ cup diced seeded fresh plum tomatoes
½ cup slivered fresh basil leaves
Freshly ground black pepper, to taste

1. Bring the cream to a boil in a heavy saucepan. Reduce the heat and simmer, uncovered, until thick, 20 to 30 minutes. Then add the chopped basil and cook an additional 3 minutes. Remove the pan from the heat.

2. Bring a large pot of water to a boil. Add the salt and fettuccine, and cook at a rolling boil until just tender.

3. While the pasta is cooking, add half the chèvre to the basil sauce. Return the pan to low heat, stir, and heat through. Transfer to a warmed serving bowl.

4. Drain the pasta, add it to the sauce, and toss lightly. Top with the remaining goat cheese, tomato, slivered basil, and black pepper. Serve immediately.

4 portions

PITTI PALACE PASTA

Velvety rich chicken livers lightly sautéed with balsamic vinegar and rosemary—the taste of Tuscany. This rustic sauce demands a wider noodle; use tagliatelle, penne, or fusilli, for the sauce will cling!

1 pound chicken livers, trimmed, rinsed, and patted dry
½ cup unbleached all-purpose flour
1 teaspoon paprika
½ teaspoon salt
1½ teaspoons freshly ground black pepper
¼ cup olive oil
4 fresh ripe plum tomatoes, seeded and diced
¼ cup balsamic vinegar
¼ cup Berta's Chicken Stock (see Index) or canned broth
¼ cup dry red wine
1 tablespoon chopped fresh rosemary leaves or 1 teaspoon dried
8 ounces penne or tagliatelle

1. If the chicken livers are large, cut them in half.
2. Combine the flour, paprika, salt, and ½ teaspoon of the pepper in a mixing bowl.
3. Heat the oil in a large skillet. Dredge the livers in the flour mixture, and sauté until browned, about 5 minutes.
4. Raise the heat slightly, and add the tomatoes, vinegar, chicken stock, wine, and rosemary. Simmer until slightly thick, 5 minutes.
5. While the sauce is cooking, bring a large pot of water to a boil. Add the pasta, and cook at a rolling boil just until tender. Drain, and toss with the sauce. Add the remaining 1 teaspoon pepper, and serve immediately.

4 portions

ONE IF BY LAND PASTA

The basis for this pasta sauce is an unusual combination of smoked trout and spicy salami. The tartness of crème fraîche and vinegar holds this dish together.

4 ounces thinly sliced cervelat or other spicy salami, cut into 1-inch julienne
4 ounces smoked trout, flaked (about 1 cup)
½ red onion, slivered
½ green bell pepper, cut into 1-inch julienne
¼ cup chopped fresh dill
5 tablespoons crème fraîche (see Index)
2 tablespoons white wine vinegar
5 tablespoons olive oil
½ teaspoon salt
Freshly ground black pepper, to taste
8 ounces fusilli

1. Toss the cervelat, smoked trout, onion, bell pepper, and dill in a large bowl. Set aside.
2. Stir the crème fraîche and vinegar together in a small bowl. Whisk in the oil, salt, and pepper until smooth and thick.
3. Bring a large pot of water to a boil, and add the fusilli. Cook at a rolling boil until just tender. Drain, and toss with the cervelat mixture and the dressing until well coated. Serve immediately.

2 portions

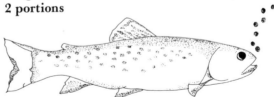

ROSEMARY

Rosemary is the ancient symbol of remembrance and friendship. Brides once carried sprigs of rosemary in their bouquets, and widows would toss a bough of it on the graves of their husbands.

PASTA WITH PROSCIUTTO AND PEAS

In northern
Italy this sauce would be made with cream and butter; in central Italy, with egg yolks and olive oil. We prefer the northern version, but either way, the flavor evokes the sensational essence of spring.

4 tablespoons (½ stick) unsalted butter
6 ounces prosciutto, cut into julienne
2 tablespoons unbleached all-purpose flour
2 cups heavy or whipping cream
1 cup cooked peas
1 teaspoon freshly ground black pepper
2 tablespoons freshly grated Parmesan cheese
2 tablespoons snipped fresh chives
1 tablespoon chopped fresh chervil, thyme, or Italian (flat-leaf) parsley
1 ½ pounds tortellini, or 1 pound fettuccine

1. Melt the butter in a heavy saucepan. Add the prosciutto, and sauté over low heat for 1 minute. Add the flour and cook for another 3 minutes, stirring.

2. Slowly add the cream, stirring with a wire whisk. Continue cooking until the sauce thickens, 5 to 7 minutes.

3. Add the peas, pepper, Parmesan, chives, and chervil. Bring to a simmer and keep warm.

4. Bring a large pot of water to a boil. Add the pasta, and cook at a rolling boil until just tender. Drain, and toss with the sauce. Serve immediately.

4 portions

POT ROAST PASTA

A *stracotto* is actually a stew, long simmered to concentrate the juices of the meat into a dense flavor. When spooned over tubular pasta, the bits of meat that have not disintegrated nestle into the cavities. Over flat noodles, the full-flavored sauce will cling to the tender ribbons.

3 tablespoons olive oil
2 pounds beef bottom round roast
1 ½ cups chopped onions
1 cup chopped carrots
1 cup chopped celery
4 cloves garlic, slivered, plus 1 teaspoon minced garlic
1 cup homemade beef stock (see Index) or canned broth
1 can (28 ounces) plum tomatoes, drained
3 tablespoons tomato paste
1 teaspoon freshly ground black pepper
½ teaspoon salt
½ teaspoon dried thyme leaves
1 bay leaf
½ cup dry red wine
¼ cup chopped fresh Italian (flat-leaf) parsley
1 pound penne or pappardelle

1. Heat the oil in a dutch oven over medium-low heat. Add the pot roast and brown on all sides. Remove the meat from the pan, and set aside.

2. Add the onions, carrots, celery, and slivered garlic and sauté until soft, 10 minutes. Remove the vegetables and set aside.

3. Set a rack in the bottom of the pot and place the roast on top. Pour the stock into the pot. Bring it to a boil, reduce the heat, cover, and simmer for 1 hour.

4. Preheat the oven to 350°F.

5. Remove the roast and the rack from the dutch oven, and cut the meat into ¼ -inch-thick slices (they

CARBOHYDRATES: WHAT'S ALL THE FUSS ABOUT?

C arbohydrates keep our motors running. Both brain and body thrive on glucose, which is what carbohydrates become when they are digested and broken down. Glucose is what our cells "eat," which makes carbohydrates the staff of life.

In some countries, carbohydrates make up 80 percent of the daily caloric intake. In the United States, carbohydrates make up about 40 percent, but nutritionists tell us our daily intake of carbohydrates should be up to 55 percent or more. We certainly don't need to add more carbohydrates to what we normally eat; we need to replace some of the protein and a lot more of the fat in our diets with carbohydrates.

The carbohydrates we are meant to eat are the complex—not the simple—variety. Simple carbohydrates, such as table sugar and honey, deliver energy but not nutrients; they are what nutritionists call empty calories. Simple carbohydrates pass quickly into the bloodstream, producing sugar shock—a quick burst rather than a steady pulse of energy.

Complex carbohydrates—found in grains, potatoes, pasta, fruits, vegetables, and milk products—provide energy and vitamins, minerals, some protein, and fiber. In fact, complex carbohydrates are our only fiber source. Complex carbohydrates are real stick-to-the ribs food, leaving you feeling satisfied with far fewer calories and less fat. Pasta falls under the category of complex carbohydrates. Dried pasta is made from durum wheat, which is easily digestible, goes into the bloodstream slowly, and gives energy for hours. That's why it's not only the classic night-before-the-marathon dinner but also appears regularly on health-conscious Americans' dinner tables. Four ounces of dried pasta (two cups cooked) has about 420 calories. Then it's up to you how many calories you add with the sauce.

will be quite rare). Return the slices to the pot, layering them evenly.

6. Crush the plum tomatoes slightly, and add them to the pot along with the tomato paste, the 1 teaspoon minced garlic, pepper, salt, thyme, bay leaf, red wine, and reserved vegetables. Bring to a boil, transfer to the oven, and bake, covered, until the meat falls apart, 1½ hours.

7. Remove the meat and bay leaf from the pot, and allow to cool slightly. Discard the bay leaf. Shred the meat and return it to the pot. Add the parsley, and heat through.

8. Bring a large pot of water to a boil. Add the pasta, and cook at a rolling boil until just tender. Drain. Serve the *stracotto* over the hot pasta.

6 portions

RABBIT RAGOUT PASTA

T his dish has its origins in sixteenth-century Tuscany, where wild hare was cooked with raisins, olives, prosciutto, garlic, and rosemary. It was a time when sweet-and-sour reigned supreme.

It is the essence of a *ragù*, a long-simmered meat sauce cooked until it falls apart with rich, earthy flavor, then tossed with a hearty pasta. It makes a wonderful autumnal feast.

1 rabbit (2 to 3 pounds), well-rinsed and patted dry
1 ½ cups dry red wine
8 cloves garlic, crushed, plus 1 tablespoon slivered garlic
2 bay leaves
½ teaspoon coarsely ground black pepper
4 tablespoons olive oil
2 leeks (white part and 2 inches green), well rinsed, dried,
  and chopped
4 ounces prosciutto, cut into julienne
2 tablespoons unbleached all-purpose flour
½ tablespoon brown sugar
5 cups homemade beef stock (see Index) or canned broth
3 tablespoons tomato paste
2 tablespoons chopped fresh rosemary leaves
1 teaspoon dried thyme leaves
Salt and freshly ground black pepper, to taste
¾ cup Calamata olives, pitted
½ cup golden raisins
2 tablespoons chopped fresh Italian (flat-leaf) parsley
½ teaspoon grated orange zest
1 pound fettuccine or rigatoni

1. Cut the rabbit into twelve pieces. Combine the wine, crushed garlic, bay leaves, and pepper. Pour this marinade over the rabbit, cover, and refrigerate for 24 hours.

2. Preheat the oven to 350°F.

3. Heat 2 tablespoons of the oil in an ovenproof casserole or dutch oven. Sauté the leeks over low heat until slightly soft, about 10 minutes. Add the prosciutto, and cook another 5 minutes. Remove the mixture from the casserole, and set aside.

4. Remove the rabbit from the marinade, and pat it dry with paper towels.

5. Heat the remaining 2 tablespoons oil in the casserole, and brown the rabbit on all sides. Sprinkle with the flour and brown sugar, and toss gently over high heat for 5 to 7 minutes.

6. Add the stock, tomato paste, rosemary, slivered garlic, thyme, and salt and pepper. Bring to a boil and then remove from the heat. Cover the casserole. Bake for 45 minutes.

7. Remove the casserole from the oven and let it cool slightly. Remove the rabbit from the sauce. Pull the meat from the bones and shred it into small pieces. Discard the bones, and return the meat to the sauce. Add the olives, raisins, parsley, and orange zest. Heat through.

8. Bring a large pot of water to a boil. Add the pasta and cook at a rolling boil until just tender. Drain, and toss with the sauce.

6 to 8 portions

MOREL AND SAGE RAVIOLI

Morels, plum tomatoes, toasted pine nuts, and Cognac form a rich sauce for fresh ravioli, topped with delicately fried sage leaves.

¼ cup Cognac
¼ cup Berta's Chicken Stock (see Index) or canned broth
1 ounce dried morels
1 cup fresh sage leaves
8 tablespoons (1 stick) unsalted butter
3 fresh plum tomatoes, cored and chopped
Safflower oil
1 pound fresh vegetable or cheese ravioli
½ cup pine nuts (pignoli), toasted (see Index)

1. Bring the Cognac and chicken stock to a boil in a small saucepan. Add the morels, cover, and remove from the heat. Soak for 30 minutes.

2. Select 12 nice sage leaves and set them aside; coarsely chop the remaining sage.

3. Drain the morels, reserving the liquid. Squeeze the morels to remove excess liquid. Slice them in half.

4. Melt the butter in a saucepan. Add the chopped sage and the morels, and cook over medium heat for about 5 minutes. Add the reserved morel liquid and the tomatoes; simmer until tender, an additional 5 minutes. Cover, and set aside.

5. Pour 2 inches of safflower oil into a small skillet. Heat the oil over medium heat until a small piece of bread browns easily in it but does not burn. Add the reserved sage leaves one by one, and cook until crispy, 5 to 10 seconds. They should be dark green, not black. Remove with a slotted spoon and drain on paper towels.

6. Cook the ravioli in a large pot of boiling water. Ravioli will float toward the top of the pot when done. Drain, and toss with the sage butter sauce and pine nuts. Serve immediately, topped with the sautéed sage.

4 portions

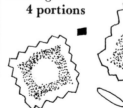
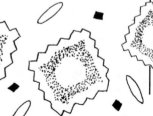

SPRING GREEN PASTA

Young asparagus, artichokes, tiny green peas, and green onions are tossed with orecchiette—pasta shaped like ears—in a pasta sauce popular in Michelangelo's Florence. We cherish this one.

4 cups cold water
½ lemon
6 baby artichokes
6 thin asparagus spears, trimmed,
    cut into 1-inch pieces
8 ounces orecchiette pasta
1 tablespoon olive oil
2 tablespoons unsalted butter
¼ cup chopped scallions (green onions)
2 cloves garlic, slivered
⅓ cup oil-cured black olives, pitted
⅓ cup tiny green peas
    (3 ounces; if using frozen, thaw)
4 tablespoons freshly grated Parmesan cheese
Salt and freshly ground black pepper, to taste

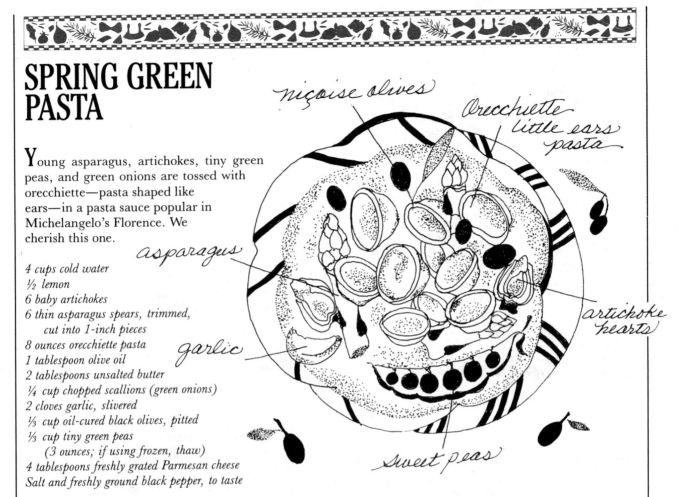

niçoise olives

Orecchiette little ears pasta

asparagus

garlic

artichoke hearts

Sweet peas

1. Fill a mixing bowl with the cold water, and squeeze the lemon juice into it. Drop the lemon half into the water as well. Set the bowl aside.

2. Using a sharp knife, trim off and discard the top ½ inch of each artichoke. Dip the cut tops into the acidulated water (to keep them from turning brown).

3. Pull the outer leaves off the artichokes, leaving a core of tender green leaves. Gently pry open the artichokes; using a small melon baller, scoop out and discard the chokes.

4. Cut the artichokes vertically into three or four slices, dropping them into the acidulated water as you work.

5. Bring a large saucepan of salted water to a boil. Drain the artichokes, and add them to the pan. Simmer for 10 minutes. Then drain the artichokes, reserving the cooking liquid, and rinse them under cold water. Set them aside.

6. Bring the reserved artichoke cooking liquid to a boil, and add the asparagus. Simmer for 3 minutes; then drain, again reserving the liquid. Rinse the asparagus under cold water, and set it aside.

7. Bring a large pot of fresh water to a boil. Add the orecchiette, and cook at a rolling boil until just tender.

8. Meanwhile, heat the olive oil and 1 tablespoon of the butter in a saucepan. Sauté the scallions and garlic for 3 minutes. Then stir in the olives, peas, reserved artichokes and asparagus, remaining 1 tablespoon butter, ⅓ cup of the reserved cooking liquid, and 3 tablespoons of the Parmesan. Stir well, and cook just until heated through, 2 minutes. Stir in 2 tablespoons of the pasta cooking water, and transfer the sauce to a heated serving bowl.

9. Drain the pasta, and toss it in the bowl with the sauce until well coated. Season with salt, pepper, and the additional 1 tablespoon grated Parmesan. Serve immediately.

4 portions

WINES WITH PASTA

Pasta Sauces	Wine
Cheese	Bardolino, Barbaresco, Gattinara
Creamy herb	Chardonnay, Chenin Blanc
Game	Chianti rufina, Barolo, Pinot Noir
Meat	Rubesco di Torgiano, Valpolicella
Seafood	Orvieto, Cortese di Gavi, Chardonnay
Robust tomato	Chianti, Zinfandel
Vegetable	Beaujolais, Zinfandel

ROASTED GARLIC AND WALNUT PASTA

In the Trastevere section of Rome, lusty peasant food is the style—food that is full of earthy flavors. This dish is based on one of the most memorable meals we've ever had in Rome.

1 head garlic
¼ cup Berta's Chicken Stock (see Index) or canned broth
½ cup walnut pieces
½ cup olive oil
3 tablespoons Roasted Garlic Purée (see Index)
1 tablespoon coarsely ground walnuts
8 ounces linguine
1 tablespoon chopped fresh parsley
Salt and coarsely ground black pepper, to taste

1. Preheat the oven to 350°F.

2. Remove the papery outer skin from the garlic head, leaving the cluster of cloves intact.

3. Place the garlic in a small roasting pan. Add the stock, and bake until the cloves are very tender, 1¼ hours. Remove from the oven and cool completely. Leave the oven on.

4. Spread out the ½ cup walnuts on a baking sheet and place in the oven. Toast, stirring once or twice, for 5 minutes. Set aside.

5. Heat the oil in a small skillet. Add the garlic purée and ground walnuts, and sauté over low heat for 5 minutes.

6. Meanwhile, bring a large pot of water to a boil. Add the linguine, and cook at a rolling boil until just tender. Drain.

7. Slip the cloves of roasted garlic out of their skins. Add them to the skillet along with the toasted walnuts, parsley, and salt and pepper. Stir well. Toss with the hot pasta, and serve immediately.

2 portions

FROM PLATE TO PALATE

★

People of all ages love to eat long ribbon pasta, but not all manage to eat it very gracefully. To those of you still having trouble, we have some sage advice. To begin, we find it easier if the pasta is served in a broad, flat bowl or a plate with a slight rim. Heat the plates before serving, so that no one feels he has to hurry to finish before the pasta cools. All you really need to eat pasta with is a fork.

Interestingly, the fork, as we know it, was invented in Venice just as pasta was becoming very fashionable. The elusive ribbons are best eaten slowly, just a few strands at a time. Slip a few onto the fork near the side of the plate and twirl them against the plate into a ball. The trick is to take small forkfuls and wind them tightly to avoid dangling strands. With practice everyone gets the knack.

VEGETABLE GARDEN LASAGNE

We don't know anybody who doesn't like lasagne, especially this one. For one thing, we've added extra vegetables—eggplant, red and green peppers. And with three cheeses—chèvre, mozzarella, and Parmesan—you'll never miss the meat!

1 eggplant
1 teaspoon coarse (kosher) salt
8 tablespoons olive oil
1 green bell pepper, cored, seeded, and cut into julienne
1 red bell pepper, cored, seeded, and cut into julienne
1 large onion, slivered
12 ounces fresh cultivated mushrooms, thinly sliced
¼ cup unbleached all-purpose flour
8 ounces lasagne noodles
3 cups New Basic Tomato Sauce (see Index)
1½ cups Béchamel Sauce (see Index)
¼ cup freshly grated Parmesan cheese
5 ounces chèvre
½ cup slivered fresh basil leaves
8 ounces mozzarella cheese, grated

1. Slice the eggplant into ¼-inch-thick rounds. Sprinkle them with the coarse salt, and let drain in a colander for 1 hour. Wipe off the salt and pat dry.

2. Heat 2 tablespoons of the olive oil in a large skillet. Add the bell peppers and onion, and sauté over medium-low heat until cooked through but not browned, 10 minutes.

3. Using a slotted spoon, remove the peppers and onion from the skillet. Add another 1 tablespoon olive oil, and sauté the mushrooms until cooked, 5 minutes.

4. Remove the mushrooms from the skillet, and add 3 more tablespoons olive oil. Dredge the eggplant with the flour, shaking off the excess, and sauté the slices on both sides, over medium heat, until lightly browned, adding more olive oil as needed. Transfer the cooked eggplant to paper towels.

5. Preheat the oven to 350°F.

6. Bring 4 quarts of salted water to a boil in a large pot. Add the lasagne, and cook at a rolling boil until just tender. Drain, rinse under cold water, and drain again.

7. Spread a small amount of tomato sauce on the bottom of a 13 x 9-inch baking dish. Arrange half the lasagne noodles over the sauce. Cover with the peppers, onion, mushrooms, and eggplant, in layers. Mix the béchamel and Parmesan together, and spoon half on top of the vegetables. Crumble the chèvre over the béchamel, and sprinkle with half the basil. Top with more tomato sauce, and then another layer of lasagne noodles. Spread the remaining béchamel over the lasagne, and sprinkle with the remaining basil. Top with the remaining tomato sauce. Sprinkle with the mozzarella.

8. Cover the dish with aluminum foil, and bake for 30 minutes. Uncover and bake until brown and bubbly, another 15 minutes.

6 portions

> "**W**ine is the pleasantest subject in the world to discuss. All its associations are with occasions when people are at their best; with relaxation, contentment, leisurely meals and the free flow of ideas."
>
> —HUGH JOHNSON

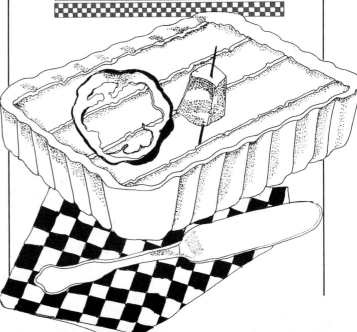

THE RISOTTO RAGE

Risotto, Italy's comfort food, is now creating quite a stir in American kitchens. This classic rice dish of northern Italy, called "the porridge of the gods" (and we can understand why), originated with the Venetians, who for centuries controlled the Po Valley, Italy's rice-producing region. Risotto quickly became popular in the neighboring regions of Piedmont and Lombardy, especially in the city of Milan, where they came up with their own recipe for ambrosia, *risotto alla milanese*. Risotto is Italian short-grain rice simmered and constantly stirred so that it gradually absorbs its flavorful cooking liquid. It has become a weekly ritual in Julee's house, for it is as marvelously versatile as pasta. Risotto serves equally well as an elegant, rich first course, a creamy, comforting main course, or a sophisticated accompaniment to meat, fish, and poultry entrées. Besides, it is nutritious, economical, and easy to prepare.

RISOTTO MILANESE

The legend behind this classic risotto dates back to 1574, when an artisan named Zafferano was working on the stained glass in Milan's Duomo. Because he added saffron to his paints, his coworkers teased Zafferano that one day he would probably go so far as to add saffron to his risotto. And so for his daughter's wedding feast, he did. Zafferano was not a rich man, but this bright yellow risotto, looking like golden coins, was his wedding present to the couple. Within a week it had become Milan's most fashionable dish—and so it has remained.

1 cup dry white wine
1 ounce dried porcini mushrooms
3 tablespoons olive oil
1½ cups chopped onions
2 cups Arborio rice
6 to 7 cups homemade beef stock (see Index) or canned broth
¼ teaspoon crushed saffron threads
1 tablespoon beef bone marrow (see Note)
Salt and freshly ground black pepper, to taste
Freshly grated Parmesan cheese, for garnish

1. Bring the white wine to a boil in a small saucepan. Add the porcini, then remove the pan from the heat and set aside.

2. In a heavy pot or flameproof casserole, heat the oil. Add the onions and sauté over low heat until soft, 5 minutes. Add the rice and cook, stirring, another 3 minutes.

3. Meanwhile, bring the stock to a boil in another saucepan. Reduce the heat and keep at a simmer.

4. Slowly add 1 cup of the hot stock to the rice. Stir, and allow it to simmer. When the stock has been absorbed, add another cup, stir, and simmer.

5. When half the stock has been added, add the wine, porcini, saffron, and marrow. Continue adding the remaining stock, ½ cup at a time, stirring constantly, until the rice is slightly creamy and just tender. Altogether the rice should cook for 25 to 30 minutes.

6. Season with salt and pepper, mix gently, and garnish with Parmesan cheese. Serve immediately.

8 portions

Note: In Italy Osso Buco, made with lamb shanks, is often served as an entrée after a risotto appetizer. Some of the cooked marrow is scooped from the shanks and added to the risotto preparation.

If you are not serving them both at the same meal, ask your butcher for beef marrow or soup bones, cut into 3-inch lengths. Roast the bones, covered with aluminum foil, in a preheated 350°F oven for 45 minutes to 1 hour. Cool them slightly and remove the marrow with a thin knife or the handle of a spoon.

FOR PERFECT RISOTTO

▲ Do not rinse the rice before cooking it. The starch that coats each grain is essential for making a creamy risotto.

▲ The proper pot is important. It should be heavy so that it doesn't bounce around on the burner while you stir, and it should heat evenly. Enameled cast-iron works well. The sides should be straight and the bottom flat to allow for even cooking.

▲ Keep the broth hot and the risotto at a lively simmer. If it cooks too quickly, the rice will be soft outside and chalky inside; if it cooks too slowly, the risotto will have a gluey texture.

▲ It you are adding seafood or vegetables that you want to remain crisp, sauté or blanch them beforehand and add them in the last minutes of cooking.

▲ Save the blanching water or the water you used to plump dried mushrooms and add it as part of the cooking liquid.

▲ Some vegetables, like zucchini, benefit from being sautéed with the rice. Their flavor marries with the rice and makes a wonderful dish.

▲ Start testing grains of rice for doneness after about 15 minutes of cooking. Remember the risotto is done when you like it.

RISOTTO PRIMAVERA

Celebrate spring with a colorful collection of lighter and lightly cooked vegetables that blend temptingly into a creamy risotto.

1 small yellow summer squash
¼ cup olive oil
1½ cups chopped onions
Salt and freshly ground black pepper, to taste
2 cups Arborio rice
6 to 7 cups Berta's Chicken Stock (see Index), defatted (see Note), or canned broth
12 ounces fresh spinach, well rinsed, trimmed, and chopped
2 ounces snow peas, trimmed
1 pound asparagus, tips only (reserve stems for other use)
2 ripe plum tomatoes, seeded and diced
2 tablespoons chopped fresh Italian (flat-leaf) parsley

1. Cut the squash in half lengthwise, then into ¼-inch-thick slices.

2. Heat the oil in a dutch oven over medium heat. Add the onions and salt and pepper, and sauté until soft, 5 minutes. Add the rice and cook, stirring, for another 5 minutes.

3. Meanwhile, bring the stock to a boil in another saucepan. Reduce the heat and keep it at a simmer.

4. Slowly add 1 cup of the hot stock to the rice. Stir, and allow it to simmer. When the liquid has been absorbed, add ½ cup of stock. Continue to add stock to the rice, ½ cup at a time, stirring constantly until almost all the stock has been added. This should take 15 minutes.

5. Add the spinach and stir. When it has wilted, add the snow peas, yellow squash, asparagus tips, and tomatoes. Continue cooking, adding the remaining stock in ¼-cup amounts, until the rice is slightly creamy and just tender, 3 to 5 minutes. Serve immediately, garnished with the chopped parsley.

6 portions

Note: To defat chicken stock, place it in the refrigerator and chill overnight. The fat will rise to the top and solidify. Carefully scrape it off the top, and discard.

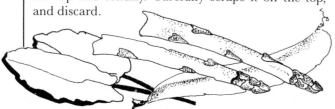

Other rices—converted, short grain, medium grain, and long grain—respond well to the risotto treatment. The texture won't be the same, but the flavor will be great.

SPRING GREEN RISOTTO

A wonderful fresh-tasting green and white risotto that mixes spinach (or perhaps arugula or watercress), thyme, and chives with the nuttiness of Parmesan. If you have Basil or Cilantro Pesto on hand, add 3 tablespoons. This risotto will be divine with any meal.

2 tablespoons olive oil
1 cup chopped onion
1 tablespoon minced garlic
1 cup Arborio rice
4 cups Berta's Chicken Stock (see Index) or canned broth
2 cups chopped fresh spinach
3 tablespoons snipped fresh chives
1 tablespoon chopped fresh thyme leaves
Salt and freshly ground black pepper, to taste
½ cup freshly grated Parmesan cheese

1. Heat the oil in a heavy saucepan or flameproof casserole. Add the onion and garlic, and cook over low heat until soft, 5 minutes. Then add the rice, stir, and cook another 3 minutes.

2. Meanwhile, bring the stock to a boil in another saucepan. Reduce the heat and keep it at a simmer.

3. Slowly add 1 cup of the hot stock to the rice, stirring constantly. Continue to stir, allowing the rice to simmer. When the stock has been absorbed, add ½ cup and allow it to simmer, stirring well until it has been absorbed.

4. Add the spinach, chives, and thyme. Continue cooking, adding stock, ½ cup at a time stirring

constantly, until the rice is slightly creamy and just tender. Altogether the rice should cook for 25 to 30 minutes.

5. Stir in the salt and pepper, and the Parmesan. Serve immediately.

4 portions

PESTO WALNUT RISOTTO

This risotto is as green as a spring field. The Italians say never to combine pesto and Parmesan—but in this dish, we say absolutely! Be sure to make plenty—this is a hard one to stop savoring.

1 ½ tablespoons olive oil
¾ cup chopped onion
1 cup Arborio rice
4 cups Berta's Chicken Stock (see Index) or canned broth
3 tablespoons Basil Pesto (see Index)
¾ cup freshly grated Parmesan cheese
½ cup chopped walnuts
Freshly ground black pepper, to taste

1. Heat the oil in a heavy saucepan or flameproof casserole. Add the onion and cook over low heat until soft, 3 minutes. Then add the rice and cook, stirring, another 3 minutes.

2. Meanwhile, bring the stock to a boil in another saucepan. Reduce the heat and keep it at a simmer.

3. Slowly add 1 cup of the hot stock to the rice, stirring constantly. Continue to stir, allowing the rice to simmer. When the stock has been absorbed, add ½ cup and allow it to simmer, stirring well until it has been absorbed. Continue adding the stock ½ cup at a time, stirring constantly, until almost all the stock has been added.

4. Add the pesto and continue cooking, adding the remaining stock in ¼ cups, stirring constantly, until the rice is slightly creamy and just tender. Altogether the rice should cook for 25 to 30 minutes. When all the stock has been absorbed, stir in the Parmesan, walnuts, and black pepper. Serve immediately.

4 portions

RISOTTO CON DUE FORMAGGI

If risotto with one cheese is good, with two cheeses it is better. You could also add three for perfection, or four for pure bliss. But two will do just fine for us in these days of cholesterol-watching. (And as far as that goes, the harder the cheese, the better.) For this kind of heaven, don't wait too long.

3 tablespoons olive oil
1 cup chopped onion
1 tablespoon minced shallots
½ cup chopped red bell pepper
2 cups Arborio rice
6 to 7 cups Berta's Chicken Stock (see Index) or canned broth
3 ounces taleggio cheese, coarsely chopped
3 ounces Fontina cheese, coarsely chopped
1 tablespoon chopped fresh rosemary leaves, or 1 teaspoon dried, crushed
Salt and freshly ground black pepper, to taste
2 tablespoons chopped fresh (flat-leaf) Italian parsley

MASTERING RISOTTO

There are two kinds of risotto. One is compact and sticky, like Risotto alla Milanese. The liquid not absorbed by the rice is evaporated, which makes a more closely bound rice dish. The second type is moist and is characteristic of the Veneto region. A small quantity of liquid is added at the end so that the risotto is slightly runny. This risotto is served with both fork and spoon. Both risottos are wonderful. Our recipes strive for a balance somewhere in between, but feel free to make yours as wet or as dry as you'd like. As a guide, use the looser Venetian-style risotto with seafood and delicate vegetables as a first or main course. Add heartier flavors, like game and wild mushrooms, to the stiffer risotto; serve it as an accompaniment or an entrée.

The rice for risotto is a short, round, pearl-centered grain, with a great capacity to absorb liquid, release its surface starch to add creaminess to the dish, and still hold its own shape. The best rice for risotto in Italy is called *superfini*. In this country, we look for Arborio rice.

FOR PERFECT RISOTTO

To make a good risotto, first quickly sauté the rice in hot olive oil until it is opaque and evenly coated with the oil. Have a pan of liquid simmering. Slowly add about 1 cup for 1 cup of rice, slightly more for 2 cups of rice. Stir the rice almost constantly, so that the grains don't stew in the liquid and become soggy. When you can see the bottom of the pot as you stir, add ½ cup liquid. Continue stirring until this too is absorbed. Add more liquid ½ cup at a time until the risotto is nearly done. As you get closer to doneness, add liquid ¼ cup at a time.

The first additions of liquid are absorbed quite quickly. As the rice plumps and nears completion, it will absorb the liquid more slowly. The rice is done when it is tender but firm to the bite, *al dente* like pasta.

While myths and rules about cooking risotto abound, a watchful eye, a little patience, and almost constant stirring is all that's really needed to make it perfect every time.

1. Heat the oil in a heavy saucepan or flameproof casserole. Add the onion, shallots, and bell pepper, and sauté over low heat until soft, 5 minutes. Then add the rice and cook, stirring, another 3 minutes.

2. Meanwhile, bring the stock to a boil in another saucepan. Reduce the heat and keep it at a simmer.

3. Slowly add 1 cup of the hot stock to the rice, stirring constantly. Continue to stir, allowing the rice to simmer. When the stock has been absorbed, add ½ cup and allow it to simmer, stirring well until it has been absorbed. Continue adding the stock ½ cup at a time, stirring constantly, until almost all the stock has been added.

4. Add the cheeses, rosemary, salt and pepper, and parsley. Stir, and continue cooking until the rice is slightly creamy and just tender. Altogether the rice should cook for 25 to 30 minutes. Serve immediately.

8 portions

CREAM OF TOMATO RISOTTO

When the creamy consistency of risotto is combined with fresh tomatoes, you get that old-fashioned cream-of-tomato-soup flavor without the cream. This is grand with baked country ham and a big green salad.

1 ½ tablespoons olive oil
¾ cup chopped onion
1 cup Arborio rice
4 cups Berta's Chicken Stock (see Index) or canned broth
¾ cup canned plum tomatoes, slightly crushed, with their juice
1 tablespoon chopped fresh rosemary leaves
½ cup freshly grated Parmesan cheese
Freshly ground black pepper, to taste

1. Heat the oil in a heavy saucepan or flameproof casserole. Add the onion and cook over low heat until soft, 3 minutes. Then add the rice and cook, stirring, another 3 minutes.

2. Meanwhile, bring the stock to a boil in another saucepan. Reduce the heat and keep it at a simmer.

3. Slowly add 1 cup of the hot stock to the rice, stirring constantly. Continue to stir, allowing the rice to simmer. When the stock has been absorbed, add ½ cup and allow it to simmer, stirring well until it has been absorbed. Continue adding the stock ½ cup at a time, stirring constantly, until almost all the stock has been added.

4. Add the tomatoes and rosemary. Continue cooking and stirring, adding the remaining stock in ¼-cup amounts, until the rice is slightly creamy and just tender. Altogether the rice should cook for 25 to 30 minutes.

5. When all the stock has been absorbed, stir in the Parmesan and black pepper. Serve immediately.

4 portions

"The trouble with eating Italian food is that five or six days later you're hungry again."
—GEORGE MILLER

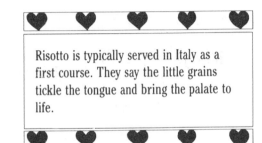

Risotto is typically served in Italy as a first course. They say the little grains tickle the tongue and bring the palate to life.

FRESH TOMATO RISOTTO

An easy and delicate "primavera" prepared in the microwave. Serve this alongside new spring lamb.

1 tablespoon olive oil
1 cup Arborio rice
3 cups Berta's Chicken Stock (see Index) or canned broth
½ cup water
⅓ cup dry white wine
6 small ripe plum tomatoes, halved, cored, and chopped
2 to 3 tablespoons chopped fresh basil leaves
Freshly ground black pepper, to taste
Freshly grated nutmeg, to taste
Grated aged hard chèvre, for garnish

1. Heat the oil in a deep 2½-quart microwave-safe casserole, uncovered, for 1 minute on full power (650 to 700 watts).

2. Stir in the rice. Cook 1 minute.

3. Stir in 2 cups of the stock, the water, and the wine. Cook 12 minutes, uncovered. Stir in the remaining 1 cup stock, the chopped tomatoes, and the basil. Cook 8 minutes.

4. Season with pepper and nutmeg, sprinkle with cheese, and serve immediately.

2 portions

Note: This recipe was cooked on High (full power, 650 to 700 watts) in a carousel microwave, using microwave-safe containers.

If your microwave is less powerful, you will have to allow for more cooking time (approximately 1½ times the amount called for—but watch carefully); if it does not have a carousel, you may have to rotate the dish while it is cooking.

RISOTTO WITH . . .

CUT-UPS:

▲ Eggplant, fresh tomatoes, goat cheese, basil
▲ Goose or chicken livers
▲ Shrimp, garlic, parsley
▲ Gorgonzola and sage
▲ Zucchini, sun-dried tomatoes, fresh basil
▲ Shreds of chicken, duck, or goose
▲ Fresh herb pesto
▲ Truffles
▲ Porcini mushrooms, prosciutto, red wine
▲ Spinach and goat cheese
▲ Lobster, mussels, oysters, prawns
▲ Four cheeses: Gorgonzola, Parmesan, Fontina, mozzarella
▲ Shrimp and peas
▲ Sausage and zucchini

TASTY LIQUIDS:

▲ Chicken, beef, fish, duck, or turkey stock
▲ Red wine or white wine
▲ Soaking liquid from dried wild mushrooms
▲ Vegetable juices

AND OTHER TASTY BITS:

▲ Vegetable purées
▲ Our pesto concentrates (see Index)
▲ Sun-dried tomato or black olive purée
▲ Juices and drippings from roasted meats and poultry

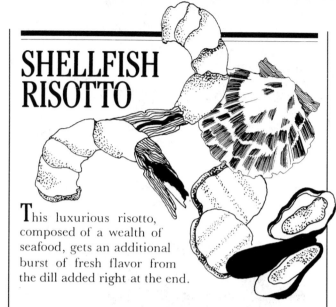

SHELLFISH RISOTTO

This luxurious risotto, composed of a wealth of seafood, gets an additional burst of fresh flavor from the dill added right at the end.

2 pounds mussels, well scrubbed and bearded (see Note)
½ cup dry white wine
3 tablespoons olive oil
½ cup chopped onion
2 tablespoons minced shallots
1 fennel bulb, tops removed, cut into julienne
2 cups Arborio rice
3 cups Berta's Chicken Stock (see Index) or canned broth
3 cups fish stock (see Index) or clam juice
8 ounces sea scallops
8 ounces large shrimp, peeled and deveined
1 teaspoon freshly ground black pepper
2 tablespoons chopped fresh dill

1. Place the mussels in a pot with the white wine, and bring to a boil. Lower the heat and simmer until the mussels open, about 5 minutes. Drain the mussels and strain the cooking liquid through several layers of cheesecloth. Remove the mussel shells and discard them. Set the mussels and reserved liquid aside.

2. Heat the oil in a large flameproof casserole or dutch oven. Sauté the onion and shallots over low heat until soft, 3 minutes. Add the fennel and sauté another 3 minutes. Add the rice and cook, stirring, 3 minutes longer.

3. Meanwhile, bring the chicken and stocks, and reserved mussel liquid to a boil in another saucepan. Reduce the heat and keep at a simmer.

4. Slowly add 1 cup of the hot liquid to the rice. Stir, and allow it to simmer. When the liquid has been absorbed, add ½ cup, stir, and simmer. Continue adding the liquid, ½ cup at a time, stirring constantly, until almost all the liquid has been added.

5. Add the scallops, shrimp, and reserved mussels. Continue cooking, adding liquid in ¼-cup amounts, until the seafood is cooked and the rice is slightly creamy and just tender. Altogether this should take 25 to 30 minutes.

6. Stir in the black pepper and dill. Serve immediately.

8 portions

Note: Do not beard mussels until you are going to cook them or they will die and spoil.

DUCK AND OLIVE RISOTTO

There is not much of a time difference between cooking risotto on top of the stove and cooking it in the microwave, but the amount of attention it requires is greatly reduced. We stir just five times, and the result is magical. The rice has a perfect moist yet creamy consistency. Not having to do all that stirring gives you time to whip up a salad, set the table, and open the wine.

1 tablespoon olive oil
1 leek (white part and 3 inches green), well rinsed, patted dry, and finely chopped
1 large shallot, minced
1 cup Arborio rice
3 cups Berta's Chicken Stock (see Index) or canned broth
½ cup water
⅓ cup dry white wine
1 cup shredded cooked duck meat or chicken dark meat
¼ cup slivered black Italian olives
¼ cup slivered green Italian olives
2 tablespoons freshly grated Parmesan cheese
Snipped fresh chives, for garnish

1. Heat the oil in a deep 2½-quart microwave-safe casserole, uncovered, for 2 minutes on full power (650 to 700 watts).

2. Stir in the leek and shallot. Cook 3 minutes.

3. Stir in the rice. Cook 1 minute.

4. Stir in 2 cups of the stock, the water, and the wine. Cook, uncovered, 12 minutes. Stir in the remaining 1 cup stock, the duck, and the olives. Cook 5 minutes.

5. Stir in the cheese, sprinkle with chives, and serve immediately.

2 portions

Note: This recipe was cooked on High (full power, 650 to 700 watts) in a carousel microwave, using microwave-safe containers.

If your microwave is less powerful, you will have to allow for more cooking time (approximately 1½ times the amount called for—but watch carefully); if it does not have a carousel, you may have to rotate the dish while it is cooking.

RISOTTO WAITS FOR NO MAN

Risotto should always be served good and hot! And the Italians take great care that it remain that way as they eat it. Risotto in Italy is served in a mound in the center of a wide bowl. They spread a bit of risotto toward the edge to cool, then eat it and continue on in a ring around the mound. The risotto in the center is still hot by the time they get to it.

ROSEMARY

Pick rosemary when in flower, finely chop the leaves and flowers, place them in jars or put the branches in whole, and cover with olive oil. Use both the herb and the oil for flavor.

RISOTTO WITH CANADIAN BACON, PORCINI, AND PEAS

A pink and green risotto that is so easy and flavorful that it's one of our favorite ways to entertain. We've also been known to whip up a batch and reheat it as needed for an instant meal.

If you prefer a variation, add just prosciutto and peas and eliminate the porcini. The mushrooms enrich the flavor, but with just prosciutto and peas, the risotto is light and very fresh-tasting. The trick is to barely cook the peas—just heat them through.

¾ cup dry red wine
½ ounce dried porcini mushrooms
3 tablespoons olive oil
4 cloves garlic, minced
6 ounces Canadian bacon, julienned
2 cups Arborio rice
6¼ cups homemade beef stock (see Index) or canned broth
1 tablespoon chopped fresh rosemary leaves or 1 teaspoon dried
1 teaspoon freshly ground black pepper
1½ cups frozen peas, thawed

1. Bring the wine to a boil in a small saucepan. Add the porcini, then remove the pan from the heat and set aside.

2. Heat the oil in a large flameproof casserole, and sauté 3 of the garlic cloves over low heat until soft, 3 minutes. Add the Canadian bacon, and sauté until lightly browned, another 3 minutes. Add the rice and cook, stirring, 3 minutes longer.

3. While the rice is cooking, bring the beef stock to a boil. Reduce the heat and keep it at a simmer.

4. Slowly add 1 cup of the hot stock to the rice. Stir, and allow it to simmer. When the stock has been absorbed, add ½ cup, stirring well, until it has been absorbed. Then add another ½ cup of stock.

5. When 2 cups of stock have been added, add the wine, porcini, rosemary, and pepper, and stir well. Continue adding the remaining stock, a little at a time, stirring constantly, until the rice is slightly creamy and just tender. Altogether the rice should cook for 25 to 30 minutes.

6. Stir in the peas and remaining 1 clove of minced garlic. Serve immediately.

8 portions

ONCE UPON A TIME

Often a dish we love to cook for guests has a history. When we take the time to explain the origins of a dish or an ingredient, we find we've launched some of our most interesting dinner conversations.

SALAD DAZE

With the recent availability of wonderful new lettuces and other vegetables, and with America's interest in fresh, healthy ingredients, salads have taken on a new look and a new importance. In fact, during summer heat waves when our flagging appetites demand something light and cool, we often make salads the focal point of our meals. The best salads are like marriages: The ingredients perfectly complement one another without any single taste overpowering the others. And salads give you the chance to really use your imagination while you play with combinations of textures, temperatures, and flavors, all on the same plate.

A GLOSSARY OF GREENS

GREEN	DESCRIPTION	COMBINE WITH	DRESSINGS, SEASONING
Arugula	A tender dark green with an aggressive peppery taste; small leaves are the mildest	Sweet mild lettuces such as Boston or Bibb	Olive oil and a flavorful vinegar such as balsamic or red wine
Belgian endive	Whitish, yellow-edged crunchy leaves; bitter tasting; good for salads or braising	Boston or Bibb lettuces, watercress, arugula, or radicchio	Mayonnaise, cream dressings, Walnut Vinaigrette and Roquefort cheese, or a citrus vinaigrette
Bibb lettuce	Pale to medium green; tender small heads with a sweet subtle taste	Boston, romaine, loose-leaf lettuces, Belgian endive, watercress, spinach, radicchio, or sorrel	Light, lemony mayonnaise or white wine or citrus vinaigrette
Boston lettuce	Pale green and red varieties; loose head with soft leaves; buttery flavor; can be sandy, wash well	Bibb or loose-leaf lettuces, endive, spinach, or watercress	Orange juice and olive oil vinaigrette, flavored with tarragon; white wine vinaigrette; or buttermilk dressing
Cabbage: Green	Pale green, tough, crisp leaves; strongly flavored	Bean or alfalfa sprouts; use in slaws with carrots, onions, bell peppers, and golden raisins	Creamy citrus or poppy seed dressing, vinaigrette with caraway seeds, rice wine vinaigrette with toasted sesame seeds, or sesame oil vinaigrette
Red	Purple leaves		
Chinese	Very light green, crinkly leaves on thick stem; more delicate flavor than other cabbages		
Chicory (Curly Endive)	Crisp, curly green leaves with pale heart; best when young, bitter when old	Bibb, Boston, loose-leaf lettuces, or radicchio	Hot bacon and red wine vinaigrette with garlic croutons
Cress	Resembles radish leaves and most often grows wild; has a hot peppery flavor	Adds zest to any mild green	Robust red wine garlicky vinaigrette
Dandelion	Use only pale young leaves, they become more pungent as they darken	Bibb, Boston, or loose-leaf lettuces	Warm, garlicky vinaigrette or white wine vinegar and olive oil

GREEN	DESCRIPTION	COMBINE WITH	DRESSINGS, SEASONING
Escarole	Green leaves with pale, yellowish-white heart (broader-leaved than chicory); look for crisp, light-colored leaves	Best alone	Garlic, lemon juice, and extra virgin olive oil, warm bacon and red wine vinaigrette
Frisée	Sweetest of the chicory family, with pale green, slender but curly leaves and a yellowish-white heart; mildly bitter	Arugula, baby oak leaf lettuce	Molly's Vinaigrette, Walnut Vinaigrette, or raspberry vinaigrette
Garden Cress	Small green leaves; spicy flavor resembling watercress	Adds spice to Bibb, romaine, loose-leaf lettuces, and spinach	Use as a garnish for salads and soups
Iceberg	Crisp, cool leaves; very mild flavor	Heightens most other greens	Russian, Roquefort, or French dressing; serve in wedges
Loose-leaf lettuce	Sprawling soft red or green leaves with a delicate, sweet flavor; best very young	Robust watercress, arugula, radicchio, fennel, or sorrel	Red, white, or cider vinaigrette, Lemon Chèvre Dressing
Mâche (Lamb's Lettuce, Corn Salad, Field Lettuce)	Light or deep green; delicate, sweet-nutty taste; may be very sandy, wash well; very perishable	Best alone or with Belgian endive	Raspberry, walnut, or citrus vinaigrette
Mesclun (Mesclum)	Mixture of tiny greens that may include arugula, chervil, chickweed, dandelion, and oak leaf lettuce, very delicate	Herbs and edible flowers	Light wine vinegar and a nut or olive oil
Radicchio	Brilliant, ruby-colored leaves in a small, tight head; peppery-tasting	Boston, loose-leaf lettuces, spinach, Belgian endive, or arugula	Walnut Vinaigrette; can stand a robust dressing
Romaine	Large head with long, crisp, succulent medium green or red leaves; a sweet nutty flavor	Bibb, spinach, arugula or watercress	Garlicky, anchovy, or red wine vinaigrette; great for Caesar salad
Watercress	Dark green, glossy leaves; spicy flavor	Romaine, Boston, loose-leaf lettuces, Belgian endive	Shallot Vinaigrette, Molly's Vinaigrette, or Walnut Vinaigrette

MACHE WITH BABY BEETS AND WALNUTS

The delicate flavor of mâche shines through clearly even in the presence of sweet beets and toasted walnuts.

¼ cup coarsely chopped walnuts
6 tiny beets, with 1 inch of stem, rinsed well
¼ cup walnut oil
1 tablespoon tarragon vinegar
1 tablespoon snipped fresh chives
1 teaspoon Dijon mustard
¼ teaspoon sugar
¼ teaspoon salt
Freshly ground black pepper, to taste
4 small bunches of mâche, trimmed (1 cup leaves), rinsed, and patted dry
1 small Belgian endive, julienned lengthwise

1. Preheat the oven to 350°F.
2. Spread out the walnuts in a small baking pan. Place the pan in the oven, and toast the nuts until they are lightly browned, 3 to 5 minutes. Check after 3 minutes and if the nuts are not done, shake the pan and continue to toast, watching carefully to prevent burning.
3. Place the beets in a small saucepan and add water to cover. Bring to a boil, reduce the heat, and simmer until tender, 20 to 25 minutes. Rinse the beets under cold water, drain, and slip off the skins. Trim off the stems.
4. In a small bowl, whisk together the oil, vinegar, chives, mustard, sugar, salt, and pepper. Stir in the beets and walnuts.
5. Arrange the mâche leaves on two salad plates, and top with the endive. Lightly dress each salad with the walnut vinaigrette, spooning on the walnuts and beets.

2 portions

MIXED BABY LETTUCE SALAD

Salads of wild greens are pretty, but we like to know what we're eating. Many new varieties of baby lettuces are available in markets today, and they are all well identified. Stay with the sweet types for this salad, and dress it lightly with a fruity vinaigrette. Scatter the flowers for garnish.

2 cups tiny frisée (curly endive) leaves
2 cups mâche lettuce leaves
1½ cups tiny red oak leaf lettuce leaves
1½ cups tiny green oak leaf lettuce leaves
1 cup tiny Lollo Rossa (ruffly red) lettuce leaves
½ cup Orange Raspberry Vinaigrette (recipe follows)
Edible flowers (such as nasturtium, borage, or violets), for garnish

1. Rinse the lettuces well, and spin dry. (Handle them very carefully.) Combine the lettuces in a large bowl, cover with a damp kitchen towel, and refrigerate for 30 minutes.
2. Toss the lettuces lightly with the vinaigrette, and garnish with the edible flowers. Serve immediately.

6 portions

ORANGE RASPBERRY VINAIGRETTE

3 tablespoons fresh orange juice
1 tablespoon raspberry vinegar
¼ cup light olive oil
Salt and freshly ground black pepper, to taste
2 teaspoons snipped fresh chives

Mix the orange juice and vinegar together in a small bowl. Slowly add the oil, whisking constantly until smooth. Season with salt and pepper, and stir in the chives.

½ cup

FLOWER POWER

We think flowers make a most appropriate and beautiful garnish for salads. Use your own good sense; some may tend to be too heavily scented and strong-tasting. Be sure to choose small flowers—that is when they are at their best.

Anise hyssop flowers: Purple or blue with an anise flavor; great with salads and fruit

Arugula flowers: Mild in taste; good in sandwiches and salads

Borage: Purple and pink flowers with a sweet cucumber-like taste; adds coolness to drinks

Calendula: Orange, white, or yellow blossoms with mild, slightly peppery taste; use the petals in salads

Chamomile: Delicate white flowers with yellow centers; mild and sweet for tea, salads, and as garnishes

Chive flowers: Light purple, globe-shaped flowers with a mild chive flavor

Chrysanthemums: Range in taste from faint peppery to mild cauliflower; blanch first and then scatter the petals on a salad. (Try the leaves in a vinaigrette.)

Daisies: Yellow and white flowers with yellow centers; mild, with a light mint or clover flavor. (Use just the petals; the centers are unpleasantly hard.)

Dandelion flowers: A slightly bitter taste; good for salads

Day lilies: Shades of orange and yellow; dramatic, slightly sweet-tasting bloom; use to decorate salads or cakes

Geraniums (Scented): Pink, red, white, or purple, with tastes ranging from lemon to rose to mint; use in salads or to garnish a cake. (Use the leaves sparingly; they are strong.)

Hollyhocks: Pastel colors; slightly sweet; particularly good stuffed

Honeysuckle: Pale red or yellow in color; tastes just like it smells

Lavender: Strongly flavored, purple-flowered member of the mint family, good for marinades, jellies, and garnishes. Use sparingly.

Marigolds: Yellow and orange; mildly peppery flavor is wonderful in salads, sauces, soups, or with fish or roasts. Use only the petals.

Mustard flowers: Yellow or white; a mild taste

Nasturtium flowers/leaves: Yellow, orange, red, rust, or dark brown with a peppery, radish-like flavor

Pansies: Multicolored, with a mild grape or clover taste

Rose petals: A taste as delicate as the smell of a rose; used for centuries in rose water, jellies and jams, teas, and as a crystallized decoration. Sprinkle the petals over salads.

Squash blossoms: Orange color, very mild zucchini-like flavor; a staple in Italian cooking, stuffed, sautéed, and fried.

Violas and **Violets:** Little bluish-purple flowers with a sweet taste; good in salads, honeys, or crystallized

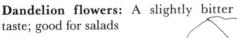

LEMONY CAESAR SALAD

This is a lovely light version of the classic. We like to tuck the walnut bread under a couple of big crisp leaves of romaine, so they are a surprise.

1 ½ tablespoons olive oil
¼ cup chopped walnuts
4 thin slices whole-grain bread
¼ cup Anchovy Spread (recipe follows)
½ large head romaine lettuce, rinsed and patted dry
1 cup Caesar Dressing (recipe follows)
4 ounces Parmesan cheese, in one piece

Lots of Lemon

1. Heat the olive oil in a small skillet. Add the walnuts, and sauté over medium heat until lightly toasted, 3 to 5 minutes. Set aside.

2. Toast the bread; then spread each slice with Anchovy Spread, and scatter with the toasted walnuts.

3. Tear the lettuce into pieces, and toss with the dressing.

4. Place a piece of prepared toast on each plate, and top with a portion of the lettuce and dressing. Using a vegetable peeler, shave thin slices of Parmesan over each portion. Serve immediately.

4 portions

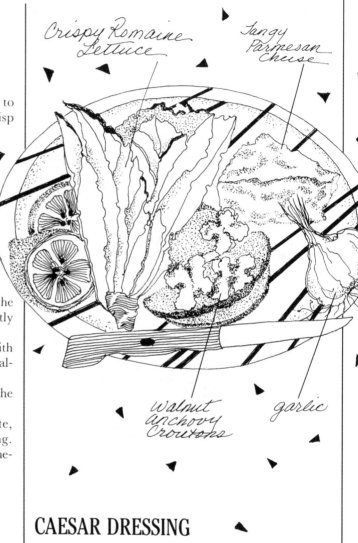

Crispy Romaine Lettuce

Tangy Parmesan Cheese

Walnut Anchovy Croutons

garlic

ANCHOVY SPREAD

12 anchovy fillets, drained
2 teaspoons Dijon mustard
1 teaspoon coarsely ground black pepper
2 tablespoons extra virgin olive oil
2 tablespoons unsalted butter, at room temperature
1 clove garlic, finely minced

1. Using a fork, mash the anchovies in a small bowl.

2. In another small bowl, whisk the remaining ingredients together. Add to the anchovies, and mix until a paste has formed.

About ¼ cup

CAESAR DRESSING

1 teaspoon grated lemon zest
3 tablespoons fresh lemon juice
2 cloves garlic, minced
1 teaspoon white wine vinegar
⅔ cup extra virgin olive oil
1 teaspoon coarsely ground black pepper
½ teaspoon salt

Combine the lemon zest, juice, garlic, and vinegar in a small bowl, and whisk well. Slowly add the olive oil, whisking constantly until smooth. Add the pepper and salt, and set aside.

1 cup

SALAD TIPS

▲ All ingredients must be of the best quality. Anything less can be masked in a cooked dish but not in a salad. Olive oil and vinegars should be the best you can afford. Vegetables and fruit must be perfectly ripe and fresh. Cooked ingredients must be done to perfection.

▲ Assertive tastes should be balanced with those that are mild. Taste the salad as you assemble it. Strong flavors can easily overpower those with milder nuances.

▲ Balance textures too—crunchy with soft, cooked with raw, succulent with crisp.

▲ Consider how the ingredients are cut or torn and how they will come together on a fork and in the mouth.

▲ Salads that accompany a meal should complement it. A substantial meal requires a light, refreshing salad; a light entrée, a heartier salad.

▲ Be thorough in rinsing and drying greens; nothing spoils a salad faster than a bit of sand or a puddle of water at the bottom of the bowl.

▲ The dressing for a salad is the tie that binds all ingredients together. A delicate green salad should be dressed with the lightest of vinaigrettes; a more robust salad will need a stronger dressing to bring it together.

▲ Add just enough dressing to coat the salad lightly. A heavy coating of oil or mayonnaise dulls the ingredients; let them take center stage.

▲ You'll be way ahead if you plan leftovers from other meals to work into main-course salads. Buy greens and salad vegetables accordingly.

CHICORY AND BACON SALAD QUATORZE

We have spent many daytime and nighttime hours at Quatorze—to us it's New York's perfect bistro. Peter Meltzer and Mark Di Giulio are always the most generous of hosts—the Champagne flowed the night that Julee and Bill announced their engagement!

This is their version of *salade frisée*, a Parisian bistro classic.

1 small shallot, peeled and finely chopped
1 tablespoon Dijon mustard
1 ½ tablespoons red wine vinegar
5 tablespoons extra virgin olive oil
Salt and freshly ground black pepper, to taste
⅓ pound slab bacon, cut into ½-inch cubes
12 croutons (½-inch cubes) cut from French-style bread (crust removed)
3 cups torn chicory leaves (2-inch pieces), rinsed and patted dry

1. Combine the shallot, mustard, and vinegar in a small bowl, and whisk well. Slowly add the olive oil, whisking constantly. Add the salt and pepper, and set aside.

2. Sauté the bacon in a small heavy skillet over medium heat until browned on all sides; about 5 minutes. Remove it with a slotted spoon and set aside. Add the croutons to the skillet, and sauté until bread is browned on all sides, about 5 minutes.

3. Return the bacon to the skillet, and heat it rapidly with the croutons, stirring constantly, until very hot.

4. Remove the skillet from the heat and quickly add the reserved dressing, stirring well. (There may be some spattering.)

5. Place the chicory in a salad bowl and toss it with the hot dressing, bacon, and croutons. Serve immediately.

2 portions

BELGIAN ENDIVE AND ROQUEFORT SALAD

A lovely luncheon or dinner appetizer. Also perfect served alongside roast lamb or baked chicken.

2 heads Belgian endive
¾ cup large walnut pieces
2 tablespoons chopped fresh Italian (flat-leaf) parsley
Coarsely ground black pepper, to taste
2 to 3 tablespoons Walnut Vinaigrette (see page 190)
4 ounces Roquefort cheese, coarsely crumbled

1. Rinse the endive; separate the leaves, and pat dry. Cut the leaves lengthwise into julienne strips.

2. Place the endive in a bowl, and add the walnuts, parsley, and pepper; toss together. Drizzle the vinaigrette over the salad, and toss gently.

3. Divide the salad among four plates, and scatter the cheese on top. Serve immediately.

4 portions

GREEN SALAD GARNISHES

▲ Tomato slices marinated in a balsamic vinaigrette
▲ Lemon slices
▲ Cooked baby beets, cut into rounds or julienne
▲ Toasted walnuts, sesame seeds, or pine nuts
▲ Capers
▲ Pomegranate seeds
▲ Orange sections
▲ Seedless or seeded table grapes
▲ Sliced red onions
▲ Fennel slices
▲ Cucumber slices
▲ Julienned green and red bell peppers
▲ Black or white truffle slivers
▲ Sliced hard-cooked eggs
▲ Small cherry or plum tomatoes

A WINTER GREEN SALAD

We love these bitter, crisp greens on a cold winter day. Julienned radicchio and Belgian endive add contrasting flavors and sparkle the colors.

2 cups arugula (tough stems removed)
2 cups watercress (tough stems removed)
1 cup torn red leaf lettuce leaves
1 cup torn romaine lettuce leaves
1 ½ cups julienned radicchio
1 ½ cups julienned Belgian endive
½ to ¾ cup Very Garlicky Vinaigrette (see page 189)

1. Rinse all the salad greens well, and spin or pat them dry. Combine the greens in a large bowl, cover with a damp kitchen towel, and refrigerate for about 30 minutes.

2. Toss the greens lightly with the vinaigrette, and serve immediately.

6 portions

ISLAND CHICKEN SALAD

We love the dazzling pink and yellow Caribbean feel of this luncheon salad.

½ cup dry white wine
½ teaspoon salt
1 tablespoon black peppercorns
1 lemon
5 sprigs thyme
1 whole chicken breast (about 1½ pounds), well rinsed and patted dry
½ ripe papaya
½ ripe mango
1 bunch watercress, rinsed, large stems trimmed
2 slices lime
½ cup Curry Mayonnaise (see page 191)

1. In a large saucepan combine the wine, salt, peppercorns, juice of half the lemon, and thyme sprigs. Add the chicken breast and enough water to cover. Heat the liquid to a boil, and skim off any scum that forms. Reduce the heat, and simmer for 10 minutes. Remove the pan from the heat, and allow the chicken to cool in the liquid for 45 minutes.

2. Meanwhile, peel the papaya and mango, and rub them with the other lemon half. Slice each into ½-inch wedges, and sprinkle with lemon juice.

3. Cutting down the backbone of the cooled chicken, remove the meat in one piece from each side of the breast. Cut each half lengthwise into 6 slices.

4. Arrange the watercress on two individual serving plates. Alternate slices of mango, papaya, and chicken in a fan pattern on the watercress. Garnish with a slice of lime and dollops of Curry Mayonnaise.

2 portions

LEMON CHICKEN SALAD

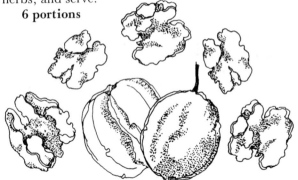

Create a pastel palette for a late spring luncheon or supper.

4 whole boneless, skinless chicken breasts (about 3 pounds), well rinsed and patted dry
¾ cup heavy or whipping cream
1 head Boston lettuce
1 head romaine lettuce
1 head Bibb lettuce
1 small head radicchio
1 large bunch watercress
1 cup walnut halves
2½ cups Light Lemon Mayonnaise (recipe follows)
Grated zest of 2 lemons
Fresh herbs (dill, tarragon, thyme, or chives), for garnish

1. Preheat the oven to 350°F.

2. Arrange the chicken breasts in a single layer in a shallow baking pan. Spread the cream evenly over them, and bake until done, 20 to 25 minutes; do not overcook them. Remove the pan from the oven, and allow the chicken to cool in the cream.

3. Rinse all the lettuces and the watercress. Choose the best leaves, and pat them dry.

4. Cut the whole chicken breasts in half lengthwise, then in half lengthwise again. Cut each piece into thirds on the diagonal. Divide the chicken evenly into 6 portions.

5. Arrange the salad greens decoratively on individual plates. Place the chicken pieces on top, and garnish with the walnuts. Add a dollop of Light Lemon Mayonnaise to each piece of chicken, and sprinkle with the lemon zest. Decorate with the fresh herbs, and serve.

6 portions

LIGHT LEMON MAYONNAISE

2 eggs
5 tablespoons fresh lemon juice
2 tablespoons Dijon mustard
1 cup corn oil
1 cup light olive oil
Grated zest of 2 lemons
Freshly ground black pepper, to taste
¼ cup finely chopped fresh dill, tarragon, or parsley
  (optional)

1. Combine the eggs, lemon juice, and mustard in a food processor or blender, and process for 15 seconds.

2. With the machine running, slowly pour the oils in through the feed tube. Process until the mayonnaise is thick. Transfer it to a bowl.

3. Lightly fold in the lemon zest and pepper. Add herbs if desired. Cover, and refrigerate at least 2 hours before serving (so the flavors will intensify).

2½ cups

WARM LEMON CHICKEN SALAD

The cool flavors of lemon and greens complement the crispy hot chicken. Perfection when dressed in even more lemon.

2 whole boneless, skinless chicken breasts (1½ pounds),
  well rinsed and patted dry
2 tablespoons frozen lemonade concentrate
2 tablespoons fresh lemon juice
1 cup arugula, rinsed and patted dry
1 cup romaine lettuce, rinsed and patted dry
1 cup watercress leaves, rinsed and patted dry
½ cup toasted almonds (see Index)
½ cup golden raisins
¾ cup unbleached all-purpose flour
1 teaspoon paprika
½ teaspoon salt
½ teaspoon freshly ground black pepper
1 cup corn oil
1 cup Lemon Dressing (recipe follows)

1. Slice the chicken breasts into thin 2-inch strips and place them in a shallow dish.

2. Combine the lemonade concentrate and lemon juice, stir well, and pour over the chicken. Marinate, loosely covered, at room temperature for 1 hour.

3. Tear the arugula and romaine into large pieces. Toss together with the watercress, almonds, and raisins. Set aside.

4. Combine the flour, paprika, salt, and pepper in a mixing bowl. Heat the oil in a skillet until bubbles form. Dredge the chicken in the flour mixture, shaking off any excess.

5. Fry the chicken in the oil until crisp, about 1 minute on each side. Drain on paper towels.

6. Toss the greens with the Lemon Dressing, and arrange on four serving plates. Top with the warm chicken, and serve immediately.

4 portions

LEMON DRESSING

1 egg
1 tablespoon frozen lemonade concentrate
2 tablespoons fresh lemon juice
2 tablespoons Dijon mustard
2 tablespoons white wine vinegar
¾ cup extra virgin olive oil
Salt and coarsely ground black pepper, to taste

Combine the egg, lemonade concentrate, lemon juice, mustard, and vinegar in a food processor. Process 30 seconds. Then, with the motor running, slowly add the olive oil through the feed tube and process until thick. Season with salt and pepper.

1 cup

"**C**hicken salad has a certain glamour about it. Like the little black dress, it is chic and adaptable and can be taken anywhere."

—LAURIE COLWIN

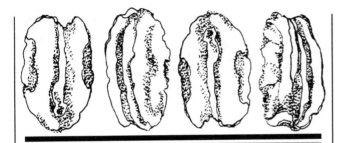

PECAN CHICKEN SALAD

We've poached our chicken breasts to keep them tender and moist for this salad. Green grapes and dill add fresh spring tastes. Pecans add the crunch.

3 pounds boneless, skinless chicken breasts, well rinsed and patted dry
3 cups water
1 homemade chicken bouillon cube (see Index)
1 pound seedless green grapes
1½ cups pecan halves
1 cup diced celery
1 cup chopped fresh dill
1½ cups sour cream
1½ cups mayonnaise
Salt and freshly ground black pepper, to taste
2 bunches watercress (optional)
Dill sprigs, for garnish

1. Preheat the oven to 350°F. Arrange the chicken breasts in a single layer in a shallow pan.

2. Bring the water to a boil and add the bouillon cube. Stir to dissolve. Pour enough bouillon in the baking pan to just cover the chicken breasts. Lay a sheet of cooking parchment or aluminum foil over the chicken, and bake until cooked through, 30 minutes. Allow the chicken to cool in the liquid; then discard the liquid.

3. Shred the chicken into bite-size pieces and place them in a large bowl. Add the grapes, pecans, celery, and chopped dill, and toss well.

4. In a separate bowl, mix the sour cream and mayonnaise together. Toss this into the chicken salad. Season with salt and pepper. Cover, and refrigerate for 2 hours.

5. Serve on a bed of watercress or other salad green, garnished with dill sprigs.

8 portions

MAYONNAISE

Homemade mayonnaise is so far superior to even the best commercial product that they are, for all intents and purposes, completely different foods. And we've discovered that with a food processor it is almost as easy to make your own as to open a jar of the commercial type.

Mayonnaise is essentially an emulsion in which the oil is suspended in the egg yolks. The trick is to make sure that the suspension holds, and therefore the oil must be added slowly so that the yolks can incorporate it without difficulty. Eggs can hold only so much oil in suspension— if the limit is exceeded, the bond will break and the ingredients will separate.

Our secrets are to be certain that yolks and oil are at room temperature, and to use a mild olive oil—if it is too fruity, it will overpower the mayonnaise. Now just go slowly, and you'll have perfect mayonnaise.

TARRAGON CHICKEN SALAD ♥

This is our signature chicken salad—lush and abundant. Lush because of the way the chicken breasts are baked for maximum moistness, and abundant because it's chunky with chicken, celery, and walnuts. It's elegant, and after all these years still tastes scrumptious to us.

4 boneless, skinless chicken breasts (3 pounds), well rinsed
    and patted dry
1 cup crème fraîche (see Index) or heavy or whipping cream
½ cup sour cream
½ cup mayonnaise
2 ribs celery, cut into 1-inch-long pencil strips
½ cup walnut halves
1 tablespoon crumbled dried tarragon
Salt and freshly ground black pepper, to taste

1. Preheat the oven to 350°F.

2. Arrange the chicken breasts in a single layer in a large baking pan and spread the crème fraîche evenly over them. Bake for 20 to 25 minutes. Remove from the oven and allow to cool in the cream.

3. Shred the meat into bite-size pieces and transfer it to a bowl. Discard the crème fraîche (or see Note).

4. Whisk the sour cream and mayonnaise together in a small bowl, and pour over the chicken.

5. Add the celery, walnuts, tarragon, and salt and pepper, and toss well.

6. Cover and refrigerate for at least 4 hours. Correct the seasoning before serving.

4 to 6 portions

Note: You can use the crème fraîche and accumulated juices from the baking pan to enrich soups or sauces.

> "Love, like a chicken salad or restaurant hash, must be taken with blind faith or it loses its flavor."
> —HELEN ROWLAND

LIGHT AUTUMN CHICKEN SALAD

A perfect luncheon dish for an October Sunday— delicate chicken breasts and light dill mayonnaise complemented by the licorice taste of fennel.

6 ribs celery, cut into large chunks
6 carrots, peeled and cut into large chunks
½ bunch parsley
1 leek, white part and 1 inch green, well
    rinsed and slit down the middle
½ teaspoon salt
1 large bunch dill
3 large fennel bulbs, halved
3 whole chicken breasts (about 3 pounds),
    well rinsed, patted dry, and halved
1 head romaine lettuce or other salad greens
1 cucumber, peeled and cut into ¼-inch-thick slices
2 cups Dill Mayonnaise (see Index)
Finely chopped fresh dill, for garnish

1. Fill a 6-quart stockpot with water. Add the celery, carrots, parsley, leek, and salt. Bring to a boil, and skim any scum that appears. Reduce the heat to low, and simmer for 30 minutes.

2. Add the dill to the broth. Slip the fennel into the broth, and cook at a gentle boil until just tender, about 15 minutes. Remove the fennel with a slotted spoon, and reserve.

3. Reduce the heat to a simmer, add the chicken breasts, and cook for 10 minutes. Remove the pot from the heat and allow the chicken to cool in the liquid for 20 to 25 minutes.

4. Separate the layers of the fennel bulbs. Slice each chicken breast lengthwise into three portions. On individual plates, alternate fennel and chicken on a bed of salad greens. Surround with cucumber slices, and fill each piece of fennel with Dill Mayonnaise. Sprinkle lightly with chopped dill, and serve.

6 portions

Note: Try to avoid putting the chicken in the refrigerator, as the meat will become slightly tough.

STORAGE

When preparing greens for storage, the basic thing to remember is that their high water content makes them highly perishable. Ideally, you should buy greens close to the time you are planning to use them, but if you store them as we suggest, they will keep for up to a week.

Greens can be a job to wash. They grow close to the ground, so it's not surprising to bring them home with what sometimes feels like an entire layer of topsoil. Often the leaves are tightly curled, and that just makes the sand and grit harder to clean out. We like to set aside a period of time right after we get home from the market for washing all our greens. That way we can put together a salad at a moment's notice.

Wash the greens carefully and thoroughly, and dry them completely before storing. A salad spinner, cotton tea towels, or paper towels all work well. If you're using towels, pat the greens gently to avoid bruising; if spinning, don't overload the spinner. Divide the dry greens among several plastic bags (do not pack them in, but rather allow them room to spread), wrapping each batch loosely in a paper towel before putting them in the bags. Then press all the air out of the bags (zipper-closed plastic bags work well for this) and store them in the crisper.

You can store greens unwashed, but they may not last as long. Since vegetables are often hosed down at the market to keep them fresh, we suggest that you shake them well to remove as much water as possible. Then store them in a plastic bag large enough to let the greens breathe.

TURKEY HASH SALAD

Try this salad the day after Thanksgiving—it's a great way to use those leftovers.

5 teaspoons Dijon mustard
⅓ cup red wine vinegar
1 cup light olive oil
12 small red new potatoes
½ teaspoon coarse (kosher) salt
2 teaspoons coarsely ground black pepper
12 large cloves garlic
8 ounces bacon, cut into ½-inch pieces
½ cup finely chopped red onion
¼ cup chopped fresh Italian (flat-leaf) parsley
3 cups coarsely shredded cooked turkey
1 bunch arugula, rinsed, trimmed, and patted dry
2 bunches watercress, rinsed, trimmed, and patted dry

1. Preheat the oven to 400°F.

2. Whisk the mustard and vinegar together in a small bowl. Slowly pour in ¾ cup of the olive oil, whisking constantly. Set the vinaigrette aside.

3. Prick the potatoes all over with the tines of a fork. Combine the remaining ¼ cup olive oil, coarse salt, and 1 teaspoon of the pepper in a bowl. Add the potatoes and toss until well coated with the mixture. Place the potatoes in a shallow roasting pan, and bake, uncovered, for 1 hour, turning occasionally.

4. Remove the potatoes from the oven and allow them to cool. Then cut them into ½-inch slices and place in a large bowl.

5. Place the garlic cloves in a small saucepan. Cover with water, bring to a boil, lower the heat, and simmer for 10 minutes. Drain, allow to cool, and peel.

6. Sauté the bacon in a heavy skillet until crisp. Transfer the bacon to paper towels to drain, reserving the fat.

7. Add the garlic cloves to the bacon fat in the

skillet, and cook over low heat for 2 minutes. Remove with a slotted spoon. Discard the fat.

8. Add the red onion, parsley, remaining 1 teaspoon of black pepper, and the vinaigrette to the potatoes. Toss gently.

9. Add the turkey, bacon, and garlic cloves. Gently fold all the ingredients together.

10. Arrange the arugula and watercress on a large serving platter, and place the salad on top. Serve immediately.

6 to 8 portions

NICOISE CORNISH HEN SALAD

These game hens are marinated in lemon juice, capers, a bit of olive oil, cinnamon, and brown sugar. Then they're roasted and served hot on a bed of cool haricots verts topped with a ripe tomato salad.

4 Rock Cornish hens (¾ to 1 pound each)
Juice of 1 orange
½ cup fresh lemon juice
¼ cup plus 1 tablespoon olive oil
2 large cloves garlic, finely minced
1 tablespoon tiny capers, drained
1 tablespoon dried thyme
1 tablespoon dark brown sugar
2 teaspoons ground cinnamon
1 teaspoon very coarsely ground black pepper
1 teaspoon salt
1 pound haricots verts (thin, tender green beans), trimmed
4 ripe tomatoes
½ teaspoon granulated sugar
¼ teaspoon freshly ground black pepper
1 large shallot, peeled and finely minced (2 tablespoons)

1. Rinse the hens under cold water, and pat dry. Quarter the hens, removing the backbone. Drizzle the orange juice over them (this refreshes them and removes any gamey odor).

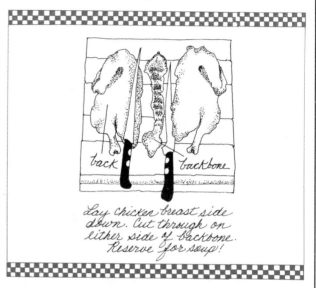

Lay chicken breast side down. Cut through on either side of backbone. Reserve for soup!

2. In a large bowl, combine the lemon juice, ¼ cup of the olive oil, garlic, capers, thyme, brown sugar, cinnamon, coarsely ground pepper, and salt. Stir well, and add the quartered hens. Coat them well with the marinade, cover, and marinate at room temperature for 1½ hours.

3. Bring 2 quarts of water to a boil in a large saucepan, and add the haricots verts. Simmer until just tender, 5 minutes. Drain, rinse under cold water, and drain again. Set them aside.

4. Preheat the oven to 425°F.

5. Seed, core, and cut the tomatoes into ½-inch dice. Place the tomatoes in a small glass or ceramic bowl, along with any juice. Sprinkle them with the remaining 1 tablespoon olive oil, granulated sugar, pepper, and shallot. Toss well, and set aside.

6. Arrange the hens in a single layer, skin side up, in a shallow roasting pan. Cover them with the marinade, and bake for 15 minutes. Then reduce the heat to 350°F, and bake for another 25 minutes, basting frequently.

7. Remove the pieces of white meat from the pan and keep warm. Continue baking the legs and thighs until the juices run clear when the meat is pricked with a fork, about 10 minutes.

8. Arrange the haricots verts on a large serving platter. Place the game hens on top, and sprinkle with the tomato mixture. Serve immediately.

8 portions

BUYING GREENS

◆

It may seem obvious, but the best gauge of freshness when choosing greens is how they look and smell: sparklingly fresh, with a good color and no wilted, dry, or yellowing leaves or tough or thick stems. They should not show excessive ripping or insect damage. And they should smell very, very fresh. Look at the stem base where the greens were cut. If it's very brown, slimy, or too dry, don't buy; the greens were harvested too long ago. And be sure to check the center of the head, if possible, because decay sometimes begins there.

Weight is another clue when choosing greens; the heavier the head or bunch the tighter, firmer, and fuller the leaves. Greens are almost all water—if they feel light, they're drying out.

FRUITS OF THE SEA SALAD

A light and lovely luncheon salad sparked with fresh dill. Serve this with thinly sliced black bread and a chilled Chablis.

DRESSING

6 tablespoons extra virgin olive oil
1 tablespoon plus 1 ½ teaspoons fresh lemon juice
1 ½ teaspoons Dijon mustard
¼ teaspoon salt
Freshly ground black pepper, to taste
Pinch of sugar
1 tablespoon chopped fresh dill

12 mussels, well scrubbed and bearded (see Note)
8 ounces medium-size shrimp, peeled and deveined
8 ounces salmon fillet, skinned, cut into 1 ½ -inch pieces
½ cup sliced peeled, seeded cucumber
½ cup slivered fresh fennel
½ cup thinly sliced red onion
2 heads Bibb lettuce, separated into leaves, rinsed and patted dry
1 bunch watercress, rinsed, patted dry, and large stems removed
Freshly ground black pepper, to taste

1. Make the dressing: In a small bowl, whisk together the oil, lemon juice, mustard, salt, pepper, and sugar. Whisk in the dill, and set aside.

2. In a shallow microwave-safe casserole large enough to hold the mussels in one layer, cook the mussels, covered, for 2 minutes on full power (650 to 700 watts),or until opened. Discard any that do not open. Remove the mussels from their shells, and transfer them to a bowl.

3. Discard any liquid in the casserole. Arrange the shrimp and salmon chunks in the casserole, cover, and cook 3 minutes on full power, until cooked through. Allow to cool slightly, then add to the mussels in the bowl.

4. Add the cucumber, fennel, and red onion to the bowl. Pour on the dressing, and toss gently.

5. On each of four plates, arrange the Bibb lettuce and watercress. Spoon the seafood salad on the greens, sprinkle with pepper, and serve.

4 portions

Notes: Do not beard mussels until you're ready to cook them or they will die and spoil.

This recipe was cooked on High (full power, 650 to 700 watts) in a carousel microwave, using microwave-safe containers.

If your microwave is less powerful, you will have to allow for more cooking time (approximately 1½ times the amount called for—but watch carefully); if it does not have a carousel, you may have to rotate the dish while it is cooking.

TUNA SALAD WITH GRAPES AND EGGS

We never tire of this salad. The coolness of the grapes offsets the bite of the red onion and zip of the lemon zest. Make it with water-packed tuna, plenty of black pepper, and a light mayonnaise.

1 can (6½ ounces) water-packed tuna, well drained
3 hard-cooked eggs, coarsely chopped
½ cup seedless green grapes, halved
2 tablespoons chopped red onion
1 teaspoon finely grated lemon zest
Freshly ground black pepper, to taste
3 tablespoons mayonnaise
2 tablespoons sour cream
8 decorative lettuce leaves, rinsed and patted dry
4 radishes, thinly sliced or finely chopped, for garnish

1. Combine the tuna, eggs, grapes, red onion, lemon zest, and pepper in a bowl. Toss gently with a fork.

2. Mix the mayonnaise and sour cream together, and toss this with the tuna salad. Serve on lettuce leaves, garnished with the radishes.

4 portions

CAJUN SHRIMP SALAD

Capers and cayenne spice up this shrimp salad. It's great stuffed in a tomato or avocado for a light and luscious luncheon.

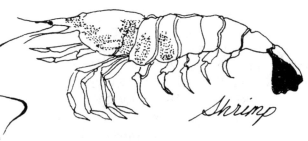

Shrimp

1½ pounds cooked shrimp, peeled and deveined
1 large yellow bell pepper, seeded, cored, and cut into ¼-inch dice
2 tablespoons capers, drained
1¾ cups Cajun Dressing (recipe follows)
1 teaspoon chopped cilantro (fresh coriander)
4 slices lemon

1. Toss the shrimp, bell pepper, and capers in a bowl.

2. Gently fold in 1½ cups of the dressing. Sprinkle with the cilantro, and garnish with the lemon slices. Serve the remaining dressing on the side.

4 portions

CAJUN DRESSING

2 eggs
2 tablespoons cider vinegar
1 teaspoon dry mustard
1 teaspoon minced garlic
½ teaspoon ground cumin
½ teaspoon cayenne pepper
½ teaspoon salt
1½ cups corn oil

Place the eggs, vinegar, mustard, garlic, cumin, cayenne, and salt in a food processor. Process briefly. Then, with the motor running, slowly pour the oil through the feed tube and process until thick and smooth.

1¾ cups

CRAB WITH CHORON SAUCE

A lovely tomato béarnaise mayonnaise accents luscious crabmeat. In a tomato or avocado, or on a bed of watercress, surrounded by tomatoes, yellow peppers, black olives, and cucumbers, this is a lovely luncheon version of a Crab Louis.

8 ounces fresh lump crabmeat, cartilage removed
1 ½ cups Sauce Choron (recipe follows)
1 teaspoon chopped shallots
1 teaspoon chopped fresh tarragon leaves
Salt and freshly ground black pepper, to taste
8 leaves green leaf lettuce, rinsed and patted dry
2 ripe avocados, halved and pitted
1 large yellow bell pepper, cored, seeded, and julienned
20 cherry tomatoes, halved
1 cup Calamata or other imported black olives
1 cucumber, peeled and sliced
1 cup Molly's Vinaigrette (see page 188)
Lemon slices, for garnish

1. Flake the crabmeat into large pieces, and gently toss it in a mixing bowl with the Sauce Choron, shallots, tarragon, and salt and pepper.
2. Lay two lettuce leaves on each plate. Fill one avocado half with one quarter of the crab mixture, and place it on the lettuce in the center of the plate. Surround it with bell pepper, cherry tomatoes, olives, and cucumber slices. Repeat with the remaining three plates.
3. Drizzle the vegetables with the vinaigrette, and garnish with lemon slices.

4 portions

SAUCE CHORON

2 tablespoons white wine vinegar
2 tablespoons dry white wine
1 tablespoon chopped shallots
1 tablespoon fresh chopped tarragon or 1 teaspoon dried
1 stick (8 tablespoons) unsalted butter
3 egg yolks
3 tablespoons tomato paste
Salt and freshly ground black pepper, to taste

1. Combine the vinegar, wine, shallots, and tarragon in a small saucepan. Boil over high heat until the mixture is reduced by half, about 1 minute. Remove from the heat, and set aside.
2. Melt the butter in another small saucepan over medium heat.
3. Combine the egg yolks and reserved shallot mixture in the top of a double boiler and place over hot, not boiling, water. Gradually whisk in the melted butter in a slow steady stream. Continue whisking until the sauce thickens. Remove the sauce from the heat and allow it to cool.
4. Whisk the tomato paste into the sauce 1 tablespoon at a time. Season with salt and pepper.

1 ½ cups

LOBSTER SALAD A LA RUSSE

This platter combines assorted blanched vegetables (don't limit yourself to our selection) and lobster meat, bathed in a light herb mayonnaise.

DRESSING
¾ cup mayonnaise
¼ cup watercress leaves
1 tablespoon fresh tarragon leaves
1 teaspoon tarragon vinegar
Freshly ground black pepper, to taste

1 ½ cups cauliflower florets, blanched
10 baby carrots, peeled and blanched
1 cup asparagus tips, blanched
8 ounces cooked lobster meat, cut into 1-inch chunks
Salt and coarsely ground black pepper, to taste
Snipped fresh chives, for garnish

1. Combine all the dressing ingredients in a food processor and purée until smooth.
2. Toss each vegetable in a small amount of the dressing, and arrange them separately on a platter.
3. Toss the lobster in the remaining dressing, and add it to the platter.
4. Season the vegetables with a sprinkling of salt, pepper, and chives.

4 portions

NEW BASIC COBB SALAD

Created by Robert Cobb at Hollywood's Brown Derby Restaurant in 1936, this salad of boiled eggs, bacon, blue cheese, tomatoes, and chicken is often layered. We chose to make it in the shape of a star, because we think Mr. Cobb has earned one!

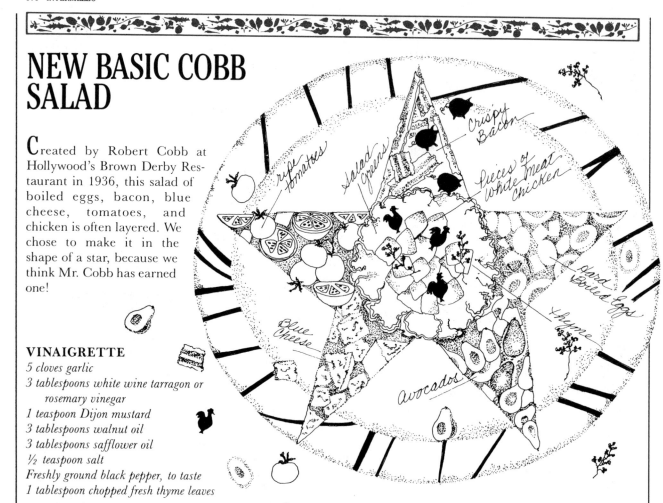

VINAIGRETTE
5 cloves garlic
3 tablespoons white wine tarragon or
*   rosemary vinegar*
1 teaspoon Dijon mustard
3 tablespoons walnut oil
3 tablespoons safflower oil
½ teaspoon salt
Freshly ground black pepper, to taste
1 tablespoon chopped fresh thyme leaves

½ cup white wine
Salt to taste
1 tablespoon peppercorns
1 lemon
5 sprigs thyme
1 whole chicken breast (about 1 ½ pounds), well rinsed and
*   patted dry*
1 large head salad greens (romaine, chicory, or red leaf
*   lettuce)*
4 tomatoes, peeled, seeded, and cut into ½-inch dice
4 hard-cooked eggs, cut into ½-inch squares
2 avocados, peeled and cut into ½-inch pieces
½ pound blue cheese, crumbled into large pieces
1 pound bacon, cooked and broken into large pieces
1 cup cut-up scallions (½-inch slices)

1. Prepare the vinaigrette: Smash the garlic cloves with the blade of a large knife, and peel them. Combine the vinegar and mustard in a medium-size bowl, and whisk well. Slowly add the oils, whisking constantly. Add the garlic, salt, pepper, and thyme.

2. In a large saucepan, combine the wine, salt, peppercorns, juice of half the lemon, and thyme. Add the chicken breast and enough water to cover. Bring to a boil, and skim off any scum that forms. Reduce the heat, and simmer 10 minutes. Remove the pan from the heat, and let the chicken cool in the poaching liquid for 40 to 45 minutes.

3. Cutting down the backbone, remove the meat in one piece from each side of the chicken breast. Cut each half into ½-inch cubes. Add the chicken to the vinaigrette, and toss well.

4. Tear the salad greens into small pieces and place a bed of greens on each plate. Place the chicken on top. Arrange the tomatoes, eggs, avocados, blue cheese, and bacon in individual triangles around the chicken, to form a star pattern. Sprinkle the scallions over the chicken. Serve the remaining vinaigrette separately.

4 portions

THE COMPOSED SALAD

When we were young, there was hardly a dinner without the omnipresent iceberg-lettuce-and-chopped-tomato salad laced with bottled dressing. It was Mom's way of ensuring that we ate something green by the end of the day. But we've come a long way. Today, salads are not only made with better tasting lettuces; they are, indeed, works of art.

Perhaps the most stunning are those we call composed salads, the word "composed" denoting "made up, fashioned, or created." Instead of being tossed in a bowl, each ingredient is artistically placed on the plate to create a visual feast of contrasting colors and shapes.

As with all good salads, a composed salad should begin with the best-quality, freshest ingredients. Start with what is in season and looks beautiful, and then try to balance flavor, color, shape, and texture. Greengrocers and supermarkets are filled with a variety of lettuces, fresh herbs, and edible flowers that allow you to experiment with sweet, peppery, mild, and bitter tastes, smooth and crinkly textures, as well as wonderful red, green, yellow—even blue and purple—colors. If your market is in an iceberg rut, do speak with the manager.

Any other additions to the salad are dictated by the place it holds in your menu. We make first-course salads with seafood or game on a bed of complementary greens. Other favorite additions include a ripe fruit with game, caviar with seafood, or cheese. A main-dish salad may be composed of steamed or grilled vegetables surrounded by thin slices of quickly seared fresh tuna, or it may feature a filling pasta or grain. (We like to serve main-course salads on a large platter rather than on individual plates to give a wonderful look of abundance). A salad served between main course and dessert can be a simple arrangement of greens with no added ingredients. Or, serve a simple platter of cheese and fruit alongside.

AMERICAN PICNIC POTATO SALAD

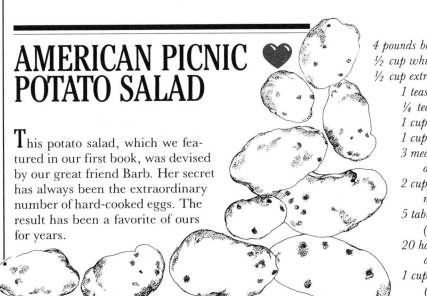

This potato salad, which we featured in our first book, was devised by our great friend Barb. Her secret has always been the extraordinary number of hard-cooked eggs. The result has been a favorite of ours for years.

4 pounds boiling potatoes
½ cup white wine vinegar
½ cup extra virgin olive oil
   1 teaspoon salt
   ¼ teaspoon freshly ground black pepper
   1 cup thinly sliced red onions
   1 cup celery strips (1 inch long, ¼ inch wide)
   3 medium cucumbers, peeled, seeded,
      and sliced
   2 cups mayonnaise, plus
      more if needed
   5 tablespoons Dijon or herb mustard
      (dill, tarragon, or basil)
  20 hard-cooked eggs, peeled
      and quartered
   1 cup chopped fresh Italian
      (flat-leaf) parsley

1. Peel the potatoes, dropping them into a kettle of cold salted water as you work. Then bring the water to a boil, and cook until the potatoes are tender but still firm, about 20 minutes.

2. Drain the potatoes and drop them into a mixing bowl; roughly slice them. Sprinkle the still-hot potatoes with the vinegar, olive oil, salt, and pepper.

3. Add the red onions, celery, cucumbers, mayonnaise, and mustard; toss gently to combine.

4. Add the eggs and parsley, and toss again. Cool to room temperature, cover, and refrigerate overnight. Before serving, toss again, correct the seasoning, and add more mayonnaise if needed.

20 portions

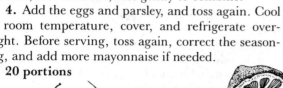

SUMMER LEMON POTATO SALAD

Yukon Gold potatoes have a rich buttery flavor and are available in many markets across the country. Combined with yellow wax beans, they turn this salad into a ray of sunshine.

2 pounds small yellow potatoes (Yukon Gold if possible), cut into 1-inch cubes
8 ounces wax beans, trimmed and cut into 1-inch pieces

DRESSING
¼ cup fresh lemon juice
2 tablespoons whole-grain mustard
1 egg yolk
1 tablespoon grated lemon zest
1 teaspoon salt
Freshly ground black pepper, to taste
⅓ cup extra virgin olive oil
⅓ cup snipped fresh chives

1. Place the potatoes in a medium-size saucepan, and cover with cold water. Bring to a boil, reduce the heat, and simmer until tender, 10 minutes. Drain, rinse under cold water, and drain again.

2. Bring a saucepan of lightly salted water to a boil, and add the beans. Reduce the heat, and simmer until tender, 5 minutes. Drain, rinse under cold water, and drain again.

3. Prepare the dressing: In a large bowl, whisk together the lemon juice, mustard, egg yolk, lemon zest, salt, and pepper. Slowly whisk in the oil. Then stir in the chives.

4. Toss the potatoes and beans in the dressing, and serve warm.

8 portions

POTATO SALAD

There should be no such thing as a bad potato salad—potatoes are just too good, and a great potato salad too easy to make. Potato salads can be very simple—just slices tossed with vinaigrette, fresh herbs, and maybe a little minced onion or shallot—or more complex, with hard-cooked eggs, blanched or raw vegetables, lemon zest, olives, anchovies, sun-dried tomatoes, garlic, lots of herbs, bits of seafood and poultry, mayonnaise, sour cream, crème fraîche, or a vinaigrette. We have just two simple rules for potato salad: Don't undercook or overcook the potatoes, and don't lose them in a quart of dressing. The potato makes this salad sublime, so let it shine through.

The new red potato comes close to being all-purpose for salads because it keeps its shape and texture when sliced or cubed and, with the skin left on, adds color. The mealier baking potatoes soak up dressing like a sponge and tend to crumble at the edges, but the salad is creamier and can be just as good.

COUNTRY HAM POTATO SALAD

Refreshing cubes of jicama add just the right crunch to this spicy entrée potato salad.

DRESSING
¾ cup mayonnaise
¼ cup Dijon mustard
2 tablespoons cider vinegar
1 tablespoon minced fresh chile pepper
1 teaspoon grated lime zest
1 teaspoon ground cumin
½ teaspoon salt
Freshly ground black pepper, to taste

2 pounds boiling potatoes, peeled and cut into 1-inch cubes
8 ounces baked ham, cut into ½-inch chunks
1 cup diced red onion
1 cup cubed (½ inch) peeled jicama
Snipped fresh chives, for garnish

1. Make the dressing: Combine all the dressing ingredients in a small bowl, and stir until smooth.
2. Place the potatoes in a medium-size saucepan and cover with cold water. Bring to a boil, then reduce the heat and simmer until tender, about 10 minutes. Drain, rinse under cold water, and drain again.
3. In a large bowl, toss the potatoes, ham, red onion, and jicama with the dressing. Season with salt and pepper and sprinkle on the chives.
6 to 8 portions

POTATO CHIP VEGETABLE SALAD

Warm, spicy, crusted cheese, sweet beets, carrots, cabbage, and crispy homemade potato chips compose a contrast of textures, temperatures, and flavors for this entrée salad. Arrange it beautifully on clear glass plates garnished with feathery dill sprigs.

½ cup lightly chopped rolled oats
2 cloves garlic, finely minced
2 tablespoons dried thyme
2 teaspoons coarsely ground black pepper
2 eggs
1 log (10 ounces) Montrachet chèvre, cut into 8 rounds
8 small beets with 1 inch of stem, washed
16 baby carrots with 1 inch of stem, peeled
½ cup fresh lemon juice
1 teaspoon salt
1 tablespoon sugar
⅓ large or 1 small (1 ½ pounds) green cabbage, cored and slivered
6 red new potatoes
2 cups corn oil
1 large head Boston lettuce leaves separated, rinsed and patted dry
2 cups Dill Mustard Vinaigrette (see page 189)
Coarse (kosher) salt (optional)
8 sprigs dill, for garnish

1. In a flat pie plate, combine the oats, garlic, thyme, and 1 teaspoon of the pepper. Stir well.
2. Beat the eggs in another pie plate.
3. Carefully dip the cheese rounds in the egg, and then roll them in the oatmeal mixture.
4. Place the cheese rounds on a foil-lined baking sheet, cover with plastic wrap, and refrigerate.
5. Place the beets in a medium-size saucepan. Cover with water, bring to a boil, and cook until tender when pierced with a fork, 10 to 15 minutes. Drain, allow to cool slightly, and slip off the skins.
6. Place the carrots in a medium-size saucepan. Cover with cold water, bring to a boil, and cook until tender, 6 to 8 minutes. Drain, rinse under cold water, and drain again. Set aside.
7. Place 2 cups of water, the lemon juice, salt, remaining 1 teaspoon pepper, and the sugar in a large saucepan. Bring to a boil, and add the cabbage.

Cover and cook over high heat for 4 to 5 minutes. Drain, refresh in a bowl of cold water for 2 minutes, and drain again. Set aside.

8. Cut the beets and carrots into ⅛-inch lengthwise slices. Set aside.

9. Slice the potatoes into slices 1/16 inch thick, placing them in cold water to prevent discoloration.

10. Preheat the oven to 350°F.

11. Heat the oil in a large skillet. Drain the potatoes and pat them dry on paper towels. When the oil sizzles when a drop of water is sprinkled on it, begin to fry the potato slices over medium heat. Fry them in small batches and drain on paper towels. Keep warm.

12. Bake the cheese rounds until they are heated through and the crust is a bit golden, 20 minutes.

13. To assemble the salad, lay out eight serving plates. Arrange the beets, carrots, cabbage, and lettuce leaves in a circle on each plate. Drizzle with the vinaigrette.

14. Using a spatula, carefully place a hot cheese round on the edge of each lettuce leaf.

15. Arrange the hot potato chips in the center of the salad. Sprinkle with coarse salt, and top with a sprig of dill. Serve immediately.

8 portions

GAZPACHO SALAD

When the tomatoes are ripe and the sun is hot, there's nothing quite as refreshing as icy cold gazpacho. And since we can't seem to get enough of it, we've made a salad out of that same great garden stuff.

1 cucumber, peeled and sliced
3 scallions (green onions), white bulb and 3 inches green,
*   coarsely chopped*
4 plum tomatoes, quartered
1 red bell pepper, cored, seeded, and coarsely chopped
1½ cups Gazpacho Dressing (recipe follows)

Combine all the vegetables in a bowl, and toss gently with the dressing.

4 portions

GAZPACHO DRESSING

2 shallots, peeled and minced
1 egg
¾ cup tomato juice
½ cup extra virgin olive oil
¼ cup red wine vinegar
Dash of Tabasco sauce
Salt and freshly ground black pepper, to taste
2 tablespoons chopped fresh dill

Combine all the ingredients and whisk until smooth. Refrigerate, loosely covered, until slightly thick, at least 1 hour.

1½ cups

COOL CUCUMBER SALAD

Thin slices of cucumber combine with yogurt and lots of mint for a cool, refreshing salad any time of the year. If black radishes or daikons are available, they're a great variation.

2 cucumbers
½ teaspoon coarse (kosher) salt
1 cup plain low-fat yogurt
1 tablespoon extra virgin olive oil
2 teaspoons white wine vinegar
Salt and freshly ground black pepper, to taste
2 tablespoons chopped fresh mint leaves
4 radishes, very thinly sliced, for garnish
Mint sprigs, for garnish

1. Peel the cucumbers, cut them in half lengthwise, and remove the seeds. Slice the halves into thin crescents. Lay them on paper towels, sprinkle with the coarse salt, and refrigerate, uncovered, for 1 hour.

2. Remove the cucumbers from the refrigerator and pat dry.

3. Combine the yogurt, oil, vinegar, salt and pepper, and mint in a small bowl. Blend thoroughly, and toss with the cucumbers. Decorate with the radishes and mint sprigs, and serve immediately.

6 portions

VERY BERRY SALAD

Our Lemon Chèvre Dressing has just enough tartness to beautifully accent the sweetness of the berries.

1 pint blackberries
1 pint raspberries
1 pint blueberries
¾ cup fresh orange juice
¼ cup fresh lemon juice
1 cup finely chopped fresh mint leaves
2 bunches watercress, rinsed, patted dry, and trimmed
Whole strawberries, for garnish
1 ⅓ cups Lemon Chèvre Dressing (recipe follows)

1. Pick over the berries gently, and remove any bruised ones. Rinse and pat dry.

2. Combine the berries in a medium-size bowl. Add the juices and mint, and toss gently.

3. Arrange the berries in the center of six plates, and place the watercress on one side. Garnish with a few strawberries, and spoon a generous dollop of dressing on top of the berries.

6 portions

LEMON CHÈVRE DRESSING

4 ounces mild soft chèvre, such as Montrachet
½ cup heavy or whipping cream
½ cup milk
Grated zest of 2 lemons
2 tablespoons fresh lemon juice
1 teaspoon poppy seeds

Combine the cheese, cream, and milk in a food processor, and process until smooth. Transfer the mixture to a bowl and fold in the lemon zest, juice, and poppy seeds. Cover and refrigerate until ready to serve.

1 ⅓ cups

PLAY THE MARKET FOR THE SEASON'S BEST, THEN HAVE A BALL

▲ Roasted slices of eggplant, roasted yellow peppers, and roasted garlic drizzled with extra virgin olive oil and balsamic vinegar

▲ Asparagus spears lightly blanched, dressed with Orange-Raspberry Vinaigrette and garnished with fresh raspberries and orange zest

▲ Thinly sliced cucumbers, radishes, and mandarin oranges in a fresh dill vinaigrette

▲ Smoked turkey, julienned cooked celery root, and walnuts in a rémoulade sauce on a bed of arugula

▲ Thin slivers of roast duck, poached fresh cranberries, and sliced fresh pears on a bed of frisée drizzled with raspberry vinaigrette and sprinkled with fresh thyme

▲ Bay scallops and shrimp, zucchini, and fresh peas in a light lemony mayonnaise, garnished with sliced scallion

▲ *Salade Niçoise* composed with haricots verts, plum tomatoes, red new potatoes, hard-cooked eggs, fresh grilled tuna, and anchovies drizzled with red wine vinegar and sprinkled with minced shallots

▲ Smoked salmon and smoked sturgeon slices, blanched baby carrots, and sliced avocado with a shallot vinaigrette

▲ Cold roast lamb, Belgian endive, and julienned fresh fennel in an herb vinaigrette, topped with slices of aged goat cheese

▲ Poached chicken breasts, seedless red grapes, and fresh tarragon in a tarragon mayonnaise

FRUIT SALADS

You don't really need a recipe for a fruit salad; almost any combination of ripe seasonal fruit can begin or end a meal on a sublime note. Slice, cube, or merely pit fresh fruit and combine at will. Taste and add a sprinkle of sugar or honey if the fruit needs it, spark it with a splash of fresh citrus juice, red or white wine, Champagne, or liqueur, and add citrus zest or a little fresh mint if you have it. Some of our favorite combinations include:

▲ Fresh blackberries, sliced purple figs, and a wedge of lime sprinkled with orange juice

▲ Cantaloupe and watermelon balls with chopped crystallized ginger in syrup

▲ Sliced pears drizzled with maple syrup

▲ Clementine sections in pomegranate juice, topped with pomegranate seeds

▲ Sliced strawberries and raspberries sprinkled with balsamic vinegar and powdered sugar

▲ Oranges drizzled with orange water and sprinkled with chopped crystallized ginger and pistachio nuts

▲ Pineapple chunks, kiwi slices, and strawberries drizzled with honey and candied lemon zest

▲ Sliced bananas and pink grapefruit sections sprinkled with brown sugar and lightly broiled

▲ Pitted peach and apricot halves, drizzled with wildflower honey, and grilled on a skewer

▲ Halved green grapes, honeydew melon balls, and diced kiwi drizzled with hot fudge sauce

▲ Pitted summer cherries with dollops of kirsch-flavored cream

▲ Sliced blood oranges, dusted with powdered sugar and garnished with candied violets

▲ Golden raspberries on a bed of sliced plums

▲ Fresh pineapple and casaba melon chunks drizzled with lime juice

▲ Grapefruit and tangerine sections and halved green grapes, drizzled with pomegranate syrup

▲ Raspberries, blackberries, and strawberries with orange juice and fresh mint

▲ Kiwi slices, strawberries, raspberries, and cantaloupe wedges sprinkled with poppy seeds and a citrus juice

▲ Raspberries, cherries, and strawberries sprinkled with framboise, rose petals, and powdered sugar

▲ Fresh pineapple chunks and halved black cherries garnished with lemon thyme

▲ Papaya and mango slices topped with diced candied lemon zest and garnished with lemon mint

▲ Baked bananas in banana liqueur, sprinkled with cinnamon sugar

▲ Lightly simmered fresh rhubarb and strawberries drizzled with Fraise eau-de-vie

▲ Sliced peaches drizzled with lemon juice and sprinkled with vanilla sugar

▲ Kumquats, prunes, and lemon slices poached in Zinfandel

▲ Honeydew melon and cantaloupe balls, halved green grapes, and diced cucumber with finely zested lime

▲ Papaya and watermelon chunks with candied ginger

▲ Cantaloupe balls, halved green grapes, and sliced carambolas, and avocados drizzled with honey and a bit of rum

▲ Diced cherimoya, fresh pineapple, and casaba melon tossed in a mixture of lemon and orange juice, and served in a pineapple half

▲ Sliced Bartlett pears and persimmons drizzled with honey and chopped pecans

▲ Banana slices sprinkled with toasted coconut and served with a dollop of crème fraîche and chopped macadamia nuts

PEAR AND BLUE CHEESE SALAD

Two great autumnal flavors—pears and blue cheese—accented by peppery watercress. Pretty heavenly for lunch with some country-style bread and a glass of Beaujolais.

1 cup coarsely chopped walnuts
8 ounces blue cheese
6 tablespoons heavy or whipping cream
4 firm ripe pears
1 lemon, halved
2 cups watercress sprigs, rinsed, patted dry, and trimmed
½ cup Walnut Vinaigrette (see page 190)
Freshly ground black pepper, to taste

1. Preheat the oven to 350°F.
2. Spread out the walnuts in a baking pan. Place in the oven and toast the nuts until they are lightly browned, 3 to 5 minutes. Check after 3 minutes and if the nuts are not done, shake the pan and continue to toast, watching carefully to prevent burning.
3. In a small bowl, coarsely mash the blue cheese with a fork. Add the cream, and gently stir until just combined.
4. Peel the pears, and rub them with a lemon half to prevent discoloration. Cut each pear in quarters, and cut out the core. Cut the quarters lengthwise into ¼-inch-thick slices, and sprinkle them with lemon juice.
5. Toss the watercress lightly with the vinaigrette, and arrange it on four individual serving plates. Place a dollop of the blue cheese mixture on each pear slice, and arrange them around the watercress in a spiral pattern. Sprinkle with the chopped walnuts, and season with black pepper.

4 portions

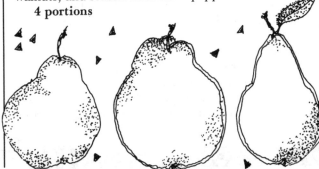

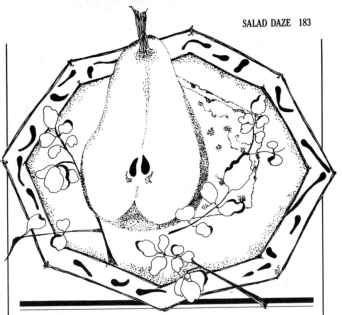

ASIAN PEAR WALDORF SALAD

Loved by the Japanese, crispy Asian pears resemble golden apples, but have the juiciness of the ripest pears. Slightly sweet, they mix beautifully with Bosc or Anjou pears for a very "new" Waldorf salad.

½ cup water
2 tablespoons fresh lemon juice
2 firm ripe pears (Bosc or Anjou)
2 Asian pears
2 ribs celery, split lengthwise, then in ½-inch pieces
2 carrots, peeled and cut into ¼-inch dice
1 cup walnut halves
1 cup golden raisins
2¾ cups Creamy Lime Dressing (see page 191)
1 tablespoon chopped fresh mint leaves
2 tablespoons shelled sunflower seeds

1. Mix the water and lemon juice in a large bowl. Core the pears and cut them into ½-inch pieces, tossing them into the bowl as you work (to prevent discoloration). Leave the pears in the bowl for 10 minutes, then drain and pat dry. Place them in a mixing bowl.
2. Add the celery, carrots, walnuts, and raisins to the pears. Toss with the lime dressing, cover, and refrigerate for 1 hour. Before serving, mix well and sprinkle with the mint and sunflower seeds.

10 to 12 portions

STRIKING OILS

The oils we use in the kitchen can be divided roughly into two categories—salad oils, which we use to flavor salad dressings, sauces, and marinades; and cooking oils, which we use to sauté and fry. Some oils may be used for either purpose, but others, because of their flavors or reactions to heat, are best confined to one or the other.

SALAD OILS

Salad oils, such as virgin olive, walnut, hazelnut, and Asian sesame oils, are characterized by strong flavors and often, but not always, by dark colors. Their smoking point—the temperature at which the oil smokes and breaks down chemically—is low; this makes them a bad choice for cooking. (Frying and sautéing require high heat; an oil that has been heated past its smoking point will give an unpleasant flavor to foods cooked in it.) Their intense flavors and aromas are best enjoyed as flavorings for cold foods, or as last-minute additions to hot dishes.

These oils are delicate and, particularly if unrefined, will turn rancid very quickly. Buy the oil in small bottles and store it away from heat and light. If you can't use the oil within two weeks, store it in the refrigerator. Refrigeration will cause the oil to become cloudy and solid, but it will quickly revert to its clear, liquid state if you let it stand several minutes at room temperature.

▲ **Olive oil:** Buying an olive oil can be a confusing experience. You'll find them in colors that vary from deep green to light amber and in flavors that range from downright bland to overpoweringly strong.

Olive oil is graded according to the process used to extract the oil, as well as by the amount of oleic acid it contains. The best oils, the extra virgin, superfine virgin, fine virgin, and virgin oils, are made from hand-picked olives that are "cold-pressed" (without the use of heat or chemicals) in huge, circular stone presses. The lesser-quality oils, labeled "pure," or simply "olive oil," are extracted from subsequent pressings of the olive residue using heat and chemical solvents. These oils are not nearly as flavorful as the virgin oils.

Olive oils have characteristic tastes, depending on where the olives were grown. Spanish, Greek, and southern Italian oils are heavier than those from Tuscany and Provence.

The strong flavor of a good olive oil is perfect for robust lettuces such as romaine, chicory, and arugula, but it is, by itself, too heavy for some foods. We often use a combination of olive oil and safflower or corn oil for our mayonnaises or when we are dressing delicate lettuces.

▲ **Nut oils:** Walnut and hazelnut oils are strong, deep-flavored oils with rich aromas. We like to combine them in a vinaigrette with a fruit or sherry vinegar, and then garnish the salad with toasted nuts or cheese. Endive and mâche go beautifully with hazelnut and walnut oils. We also use the oils in nutty desserts to intensify the flavor of the nuts. Their flavor is very strong, so you may want to mix them with a neutral oil such as corn or peanut.

Almond oil is a light oil with a delicately sweet flavor. We like it on salads with Champagne vinegar, on warm vegetables, or brushed on dark, whole-grain breads.

▲ **Asian sesame oil:** Amber-colored Asian sesame oil, not to be confused with its light-colored brother found in health-food stores, is a strong-tasting oil made from toasted sesame seeds. It is very often used as a flavoring in Asian cuisine, but never as a cooking oil. We like to use it in combination with a milder oil in salad dressings, along with red wine vinegar; the sweetness of the vinegar is a nice counterpoint to the gutsy oil.

▲ **Avocado oil:** An almost flavorless oil from California that we like to use with white wine or herb vinegars on salads.

▲ **Flavored oils:** Olive or grapeseed oils flavored with basil, rosemary, thyme, garlic, olives, peppers, dried wild mushrooms, sun-dried tomatoes, or dried chile peppers make superb vinaigrettes. We also toss the oils with steamed vegetables, drizzle them over pizza, serve them as simple accompaniments to grilled fish, or brush them over poultry and meats while grilling.

COOKING OILS

The best cooking oils are those with high smoking points and light flavors that will not intrude on the flavor of the food being cooked. Supermarket cooking oils such as corn, safflower, canola, and vegetable oils are usually refined chemically to lengthen their shelf life and to increase their stability during cooking, but the process also renders them nearly tasteless. Store cooking oils as you would salad oils, although refined oils spoil less readily.

▲ **Corn oil:** With a light flavor and a smoking point of about 440°F, corn oil is an excellent cooking oil. Unrefined corn oils found in health food stores have a stronger corn flavor than the refined oils. Corn oil is a good neutral oil to mix with olive oil in salad dressings or mayonnaises.

▲ **Safflower oil:** An almost flavorless oil with a smoking point of about 440°F; a very good choice for cooking.

▲ **Canola oil:** A very light-colored, flavorless oil with a smoking point of about 440°F. Very good for cooking.

▲ **Soy oil:** With a smoking point of about 440°F, refined soy oil is the major component of what is sold as vegetable oil. It is very pale in color and mild in flavor. Cold-pressed soy oil (sold in health-food stores) is darker and has a nutty flavor.

▲ **Sesame oil:** Light-colored, cold-pressed sesame oil has a smoking point of about 440°F and a light, nutty flavor that makes it a very good cooking oil. (Don't confuse it with dark-colored, strongly flavored Asian sesame oil, which is not a cooking oil.) We sometimes use sesame oil in salad dressings as well.

▲ **Peanut oil:** Peanut oil has a slightly lower smoking point than corn or safflower oil but is also a good cooking oil. Refined peanut oil has a very bland flavor, but if you can find the cold-pressed variety you will be rewarded with a mildly peanuty taste that is also good with fruit vinegars in fruit salads, or with balsamic vinegar in green salads.

▲ **Olive oil:** Due to their low percentages of oleic acid, virgin olive oils have very low smoking points that make them unsuitable for cooking. "Pure" olive oil, however, with a higher percentage of acid, is fine for cooking.

▲ **Coconut, palm, and palm kernel oils:** Generally not available to the retail consumer, these oils are widely used in commercial cookies and crackers. Unlike other cooking oils, they are high in saturated fats and should be avoided. Food manufacturers have lately gotten the message that these tropical oils are undesirable and are replacing them with polyunsaturated vegetable oils.

OILS AND CHOLESTEROL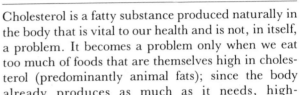

Cholesterol is a fatty substance produced naturally in the body that is vital to our health and is not, in itself, a problem. It becomes a problem only when we eat too much of foods that are themselves high in cholesterol (predominantly animal fats); since the body already produces as much as it needs, high-cholesterol foods can raise blood cholesterol to unhealthy levels. High cholesterol levels are associated with diseases of the heart and circulatory system.

Oils and fats are classified as saturated, polyunsaturated, or monounsaturated. Oils containing a high percentage of saturated fats are those that are solid at room temperature (such as butter and lard); they have been shown to raise blood cholesterol levels. Those containing a high percentage of monounsaturated or polyunsaturated fats are liquid at room temperature (most oils); they have been shown to *reduce* cholesterol in the blood. Recent studies have shown that monounsaturated fats may be particularly effective against high cholesterol.

BEST (Monounsaturated)	GOOD (Polyunsaturated)	WORST (Saturated)
Olive oil	Safflower oil	Palm oil
Canola oil	Sunflower oil	Coconut oil
Almond oil	Soy oil	Palm kernel oil
	Sesame oil	
	Corn oil	
	Peanut oil	
	Walnut oil	
	Margarine	

A SPLASH OF VINEGARS

Vinegar has long been a pantry staple in America. Now, however, we don't use it just for canning, pickling, and salad dressings. We use it much as we use lemon juice, salt, or pepper—as a flavor accent for sauces, stews, meat, fish, and vegetable dishes. Vinegar adds a zippy, clean taste that brings out the flavor of foods without adding fat or sodium (next time a sauce tastes flat, add a dash of vinegar—you won't miss the salt!). And the wide variety of vinegars available today gives us lots of tastes to play with.

The word vinegar is derived from the French *vinaigre,* meaning soured wine. Although fermented wine is a common base, vinegar can actually be made from anything that ferments, including grains, beer, fruits, molasses, and cider.

Vinegars will keep almost indefinitely if left unopened in a dark, cool place. Once opened, most vinegars will retain their flavors for a minimum of two to three months, and cider vinegar will be fine for up to six months. Keep vinegars tightly sealed after opening.

TYPES OF VINEGARS

▲ **Distilled vinegars:** Made from grains such as corn, rye, and barley, these vinegars have the harshest flavor. We use them primarily for pickling.

▲ **Malt vinegar:** An English favorite, this vinegar is made from ale and is often served with fish and chips. It is slightly sweeter than distilled vinegar. Its yeasty flavor combines well in salad dressings with neutral corn and peanut oils, or with robust nut and olive oils.

▲ **Cider vinegar:** A standard in most households, this tart, caramel-colored vinegar is made from apples. It is particularly good in dressings for salads of smoked meat or fish with strong-tasting lettuces. The fruitiness of the vinegar intensifies when cooked, making it a good choice for curries or sautéed fruits.

▲ **Rice vinegar:** Made in both China and Japan, this white vinegar has a sharp, clean taste that is somewhat mellower than that of distilled white vinegar. We use it in salads with a touch of Asian sesame oil—a particularly good combination with shredded green cabbage, spiced with hot chiles.

▲ **Wine vinegars:** Made from fermented red and white wines, sherry, or Champagne, these vinegars are the mildest and most versatile. We use them for salad dressings, marinades, sauces, and herb vinegars. Red wine vinegar is delicious in a mustardy vinaigrette on bitter lettuces or in an orange vinaigrette. We use white wine and Champagne vinegars in a beurre blanc sauce, in salad dressings with nut oils, or to accent vegetable salads.

Sherry vinegar is fuller and less acidic than other wine vinegars. Aged in wooden casks, the longer it is aged, the smoother it tastes. We like to combine sherry vinegar with olive, walnut, hazelnut, or peanut oils to emphasize its nutty taste; serve the vinaigrette with a salad of Belgian endive or smoked poultry. A dash of sherry vinegar will also pick up a creamy sauce for seafood or chicken, or a creamy soup.

▲ **Balsamic vinegar:** Once you've tasted this intense, sweet-tart vinegar, your pantry will never be without it. Unique to the area around Modena, Italy, balsamic vinegar is made from the unfermented juice (or must) of the white Trebbiano grape. This juice is boiled down to a sweet and intensely fruity syrup that is then aged in barrels made from a variety of woods (including chestnut, mulberry, juniper, oak, and cherry). The finished vinegar must be at least six years old. Fifty- and one-hundred-year-old balsamic is not unheard of, although pricing it would be like pric-

ing fine old wine. Younger bottles are much more affordable.

Balsamic vinegar makes a superb salad vinaigrette, of course. But, interestingly, the inhabitants of Modena often drink it as an after-dinner *digestif*, and we're passionate about using it in a fresh-fruit dessert—sprinkled on raspberries, peaches, strawberries, or melon with a little cracked black pepper or sugar. *Supremo.*

▲ **Herb vinegars:** Herb vinegars are good-quality wine or cider vinegars that have been infused with herbs. Our favorite herb vinegars are made with basil, tarragon, oregano, wild thyme, mint, rosemary, dill, chervil, chive blossoms, or savory.

A dash of herb vinegar is a delicious accent to vegetables, and it adds zip to bland lettuces such as butter, red leaf, iceberg, or Bibb. But don't use these vinegars indiscriminately. Consider the tastes: Tarragon vinegar will clash with arugula but will complement bitter Belgian endive; a mint vinegar will do nothing for Brussels sprouts but will add a nice contrast to fresh tomatoes or sautéed carrots; lemon or mint-flavored vinegar adds a welcome bite to mild-flavored chickpea or bulgur salads. We like to blend herb vinegars with olive and other neutral oils.

▲ **Fruit vinegars:** Fruit vinegars are made with good-quality white wine or cider vinegar and any of a variety of fruits: raspberries, blueberries, cranberries, blackberries, pears, peaches, oranges, lemons, limes, or strawberries. The fruits may also be mixed with a complementary herb or spice—try a lemon–thyme or cranberry–clove combination. Good-quality fruit vinegars taste of the essence of the fruit with which they are made.

Fruit vinegars are lovely in salad dressings with nut or olive oils. We like to use them with butter or mâche lettuces. Fruit salads are also enhanced by a touch of fruit vinegar. Next time you cook chicken breast, try deglazing the pan with a little raspberry or lemon vinegar.

FRUIT VINEGAR

Fruit vinegar punches up the taste of any fresh fruit salad or dessert. It makes a welcome house gift, so try to find the prettiest bottles.

1 quart cider or white wine vinegar
2 cups fresh or frozen cranberries or blueberries (not in syrup; thawed if frozen)
½ cup light clover honey
Whole cloves
Cinnamon sticks

1. Combine the vinegar and 1 cup of the berries in a medium-size saucepan. Bring to a boil, then lower the heat, and simmer, uncovered, for 2 minutes. Stir in the honey and remove from the heat. Pour the berry mixture through a fine-mesh strainer into a large measuring cup. Don't press down on the berries. Discard the berries.

2. Divide the remaining 1 cup berries between two decorative, clean 16-ounce bottles or four 8-ounce bottles. Place 4 whole cloves and one 4- to 6-inch cinnamon stick in each 16-ounce bottle; 2 cloves and one 3-inch cinnamon stick in each 8-ounce bottle. Pour the warm vinegar into the bottles to within 1 inch of the top. Prepare at least one week in advance so that the flavors can mellow.

1 quart

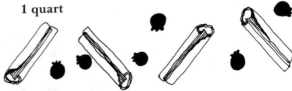

HERBED CIDER VINEGAR

When making herb vinegars, keep in mind that they should have an appealing taste, and also should be appealing visually. Look for the fullest, bushiest herb sprigs you can find. If the sprigs seem thin, add two per bottle; if they seem to overwhelm, trim them slightly. You can make herb vinegars in 8- to 16-ounce bottles.

Thyme sprigs
Rosemary sprigs
Large garlic cloves, peeled
Strips of lemon peel, 2 x ¼ inch
Cider vinegar

1. Place 1 sprig of thyme and 1 sprig of rosemary in each decorative, clean bottle.
2. Thread a garlic clove, lengthwise, and a strip of lemon peel, lengthwise, on a thin wooden skewer. Place 1 skewer in each bottle. Fill each bottle with cider vinegar. Let steep at least one week to bring out the flavors.

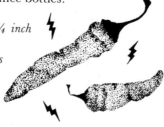

ENRAGED OIL

This sweet and savory oil makes for a great marinade, and also works well drizzled over grilling meats or vegetables. The number of herbs and spices given work well in 8- to 16-ounce bottles.

Strips of orange zest, 2 x ¼ inch
Bay leaves
Dried long red chile peppers
Whole allspice
Black peppercorns
Light olive oil

Place a strip of orange zest, 1 bay leaf, 1 chile pepper, 3 allspice, and 6 peppercorns in each decorative, clean bottle. Cover with the oil. Let steep at least two weeks to bring out the flavors.

> "**W**hat garlic is to salad, insanity is to art."
> —AUGUSTUS SAINT-GAUDENS

MOLLY'S VINAIGRETTE

With this simple preparation, Sheila's daughter Molly seems to come up with a perfect basic vinaigrette every time. Her method for incorporating the ingredients may be unusual, but works perfectly. Molly says, "For an Italian night, add a bit of Parmesan."

¾ cup extra virgin olive oil
⅓ cup red wine vinegar
2 teaspoons Dijon mustard
Pinch of salt
Pinch of freshly ground black pepper
1 teaspoon Parmesan cheese (optional)

Place all the ingredients except the cheese in a small bowl. Hold a wire whisk upright in the bowl, and rotate it between the palms of your hands until the vinaigrette is well blended. For an Italian accent, add Parmesan.

1 ¼ cups

MUSTARD VINAIGRETTE

Sweet flavored tarragon combines beautifully with the bite of mustard to dress summer greens or delicate chicken salads.

1 tablespoon Dijon mustard
3 tablespoons white wine or tarragon vinegar
1 teaspoon dried tarragon or 1 tablespoon fresh
½ teaspoon salt
½ teaspoon freshly ground black pepper
¾ cup extra virgin olive oil

Place the mustard in a small bowl. Add the vinegar, tarragon, salt, and pepper, and whisk well. Slowly drizzle in the olive oil, whisking constantly until the dressing is creamy.

1 cup

DILL CHIVE VINAIGRETTE

Light and lemony, this vinaigrette is the perfect addition to a fresh seafood salad.

⅔ cup fresh lemon juice
2 tablespoons Dijon mustard
Salt and freshly ground black pepper, to taste
1 cup light olive oil
2 tablespoons minced shallots
¼ cup snipped fresh chives
2 tablespoons chopped fresh dill

Place the lemon juice in a small bowl. Whisk in the mustard and salt and pepper. Slowly drizzle in the oil, whisking constantly until the vinaigrette has thickened. Fold in the remaining ingredients. Let the vinaigrette rest, covered, for 1 hour before using.

2 cups

SHALLOT VINAIGRETTE

Shallots add great sparkle to any salad, whether it's fresh vegetables or crispy greens.

2 tablespoons red wine vinegar
1 tablespoon Dijon mustard
½ cup extra virgin olive oil
1 tablespoon finely chopped shallots
Salt and freshly ground black pepper, to taste

Whisk the vinegar and mustard together in a small bowl. Slowly drizzle in the oil, whisking constantly. Add shallots and salt and pepper. Mix well, and let sit for 30 minutes for the flavors to develop.

¾ cup

DILL MUSTARD VINAIGRETTE

Lightly reminiscent of the Scandinavian classic, this vinaigrette is the perfect choice for seafood salads and tender, pale greens.

2 tablespoons Dijon mustard
½ cup tarragon vinegar
½ teaspoon freshly ground black pepper
Pinch of sugar
1 cup extra virgin olive oil
2 tablespoons chopped fresh dill

Whisk the mustard, vinegar, pepper, and sugar together in a small bowl. Slowly drizzle in the olive oil, whisking constantly until the vinaigrette has thickened. Stir in the fresh dill.

2 cups

VERY GARLICKY VINAIGRETTE

How we love garlic! This vinaigrette is perfect over hardy winter salads of arugula, watercress, and romaine lettuce—also great as a marinade for grilled chicken or flank steak. Drizzle a bit over sliced ripe tomatoes topped with slivered opal basil, and you'll be transported to Provence.

4 large cloves garlic, minced
2 tablespoons Dijon mustard
⅓ cup red wine vinegar
1 cup extra virgin olive oil
Salt and freshly ground black pepper, to taste

Combine the garlic, mustard, and vinegar in a small bowl. Whisk well. Slowly drizzle in the olive oil, whisking constantly until the dressing is quite thick. Season with salt and pepper.

1½ cups

RED WINE BASIL VINAIGRETTE

For the most robust greens, this vinaigrette is the way to go. In the summer, the basil perfumes luscious ripe tomatoes.

2 cloves garlic, crushed
2 tablespoons Dijon mustard
½ cup red wine vinegar
1 teaspoon freshly ground black pepper
1 cup extra virgin olive oil
½ cup slivered fresh basil leaves
½ cup chopped fresh parsley

Combine the garlic, mustard, vinegar, and pepper in a small bowl, and whisk well. Add the oil in a slow stream, whisking constantly until the vinaigrette has thickened slightly. Fold in the basil and parsley.

1 ½ cups

BASIL

Basil is Greek for "royal" or "kingly." The Greeks believed that only the sovereign himself, armed with his golden sickle, should be allowed to cut the basil. On the other hand, in Italy basil has always been a token of love. In Rumania, things are somewhat more defined. When a boy accepts a sprig of basil from his girl, he is engaged.

WALNUT VINAIGRETTE

An ideal vinaigrette for all the delectable new greens in the market. We love to serve this with Mâche With Baby Beets and Walnuts or slivered Belgian endive sprinkled with Roquefort.

2 tablespoons red wine vinegar
1 teaspoon Dijon mustard
¼ cup walnut oil
1 tablespoon safflower oil
Salt and freshly ground black pepper, to taste

Combine the vinegar and mustard in a small bowl, and whisk well. Slowly drizzle in the oils, whisking constantly until smooth. Season with salt and pepper.

½ cup

CUMIN VINAIGRETTE

The flavor of cumin and cider vinegar enlivens bean salads with a southwestern flair. Great to sprinkle on pan-fried catfish, too.

½ cup cider vinegar
1 tablespoon Dijon mustard
1 ½ teaspoons ground cumin
1 teaspoon minced garlic
1 teaspoon freshly ground black pepper
½ teaspoon salt
1 ½ cups extra virgin olive oil

Combine the vinegar, mustard, cumin, garlic, pepper, and salt in a small bowl. Whisk well. Slowly drizzle in the olive oil, whisking constantly until smooth.

2 cups

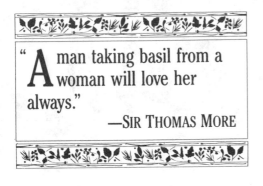

CURRY MAYONNAISE

A perfect dressing for chicken or seafood salads.

1 tablespoon safflower oil
½ onion, finely chopped
2 tablespoons curry powder
1 cup mayonnaise
Juice of 1 lime
2 tablespoons sour cream
2 tablespoons mango chutney

1. Heat the oil in a small skillet. Add the onion and sauté over low heat until soft, 8 to 10 minutes. Add the curry powder and cook, stirring, 5 minutes. Set aside and allow to cool thoroughly.

2. When they are cool, combine the curried onions with the mayonnaise, lime juice, sour cream, and chutney. Stir well. Refrigerate until ready to serve.

1½ cups

CREAMY LIME DRESSING

Toss a Waldorf salad with this creamy dressing or drizzle it over a sliced avocado, orange, and tomato salad. Chicken salad with cool green grapes combines beautifully with it, too.

5 tablespoons fresh lime juice
2 eggs
2 tablespoons Dijon mustard
1 cup corn oil
1 cup light olive oil
Grated zest of 2 limes
Freshly ground black pepper, to taste

Place the lime juice, eggs, and mustard in the bowl of a food processor, and process for 15 seconds. With the motor running, slowly pour the oils through the feed tube and process until the mayonnaise has thickened. Transfer it to a bowl, and fold in the lime zest and pepper. Cover and refrigerate until ready to use.

2¾ cups

BACON BUTTERMILK DRESSING

First select the tender-most spinach leaves and whitest button mushrooms, then toss lightly with this creamy dressing infused with chervil, garlic, and scallions. Delicious on a salad composed simply of fresh spinach leaves.

6 slices bacon, diced
1 cup mayonnaise
1 cup buttermilk
2 tablespoons minced scallions (green onions)
1 tablespoon minced fresh chervil
1 teaspoon minced garlic
½ teaspoon freshly ground black pepper
¼ teaspoon salt
¼ teaspoon paprika
Dash of Tabasco sauce

1. Sauté the bacon in a skillet until crisp. Drain on paper towels, and set aside.

2. In a mixing bowl, whisk all the other ingredients together; then add the bacon. Refrigerate, covered, for at least 1 hour before serving.

2 cups

THE
VEGETABLE
PATCH

VEGETABLE MAGIC

Traditionally vegetables have assumed the quietest corner of the plate, but now, they have taken on a great new importance. Markets are presenting with pride an array of vegetables at their freshest, and their healthful appeal has led to their taking center stage at many a dinner table. Vegetables, lightly cooked and presented with a touch of butter, a twist of lemon or a sprinkling of salt, and lots of pepper, are pure pleasure.

But, when combined with other fresh herbs and spices, garlic, cheeses, nuts, spicy peppers, tart vinegars, mellow wines, ripe fruits, and each other, they are extraordinary.

Always choose the sprightliest vegetables available. Their fresh quality will shine through.

OUR HEARTS BELONG TO ARTICHOKES

Artichokes are one of the most beautiful of all the vegetables, perhaps because they are immature thistles; if left longer on the stem, they would blossom into gorgeous flowers.

Because of their beauty and delicate taste, artichokes are most often served solo as a first course. Boiled or steamed whole, artichokes are ridiculously easy to prepare but look extravagant—all important for that opening note. The simplest way to serve them is hot with little bowls of melted butter or hollandaise sauce for dipping or completely cooled with a vinaigrette. Artichokes with their chokes removed or trimmed down to their meaty bottoms are the quintessential vegetable for stuffing. They take as well to simple savory mixtures in winter as to cool seafood salads in summer. Artichoke hearts are considered a delicacy not just for their rich taste but also for the labor of love needed to trim these prickly globes. Savor them sliced or sautéed.

BUYING

Freshness is everything with artichokes as with all green vegetables. A fresh artichoke will be silky, plump, compact, and heavy for its size. Old artichokes look old. The leaves are spread out as if about to bloom, and they are yellow and dry. If you're still not sure, hold the artichoke up to your ear and press the leaves; if it squeaks, it's fresh. If it's the heart that you're after, pick the roundest artichokes for they have the largest hearts. The season is blessedly long, from October through June, but artichokes are most plentiful in April and May.

Size does not indicate quality, just the size of the stem the artichoke grew on. At the peak of the season you should be able to buy large, medium, and small artichokes. Choose large artichokes for stuffing, medium for salads, and keep the small ones for fritters or pickling. Very fresh baby artichokes are delicious brushed with olive oil and grilled or sautéed. Frozen and canned artichoke hearts and bottoms are available year round and make great sense for busy cooks.

STORING

Store artichokes unwashed in a plastic bag in the refrigerator. They'll keep up to one week but are best cooked the same day you bought them.

PREPARING ARTICHOKES

▲

Two rules apply to artichokes: One, use stainless-steel knives to cut them and stainless-steel or enamel-coated pans to cook them. Two, rub the cuts with lemon juice to keep them from discoloring.

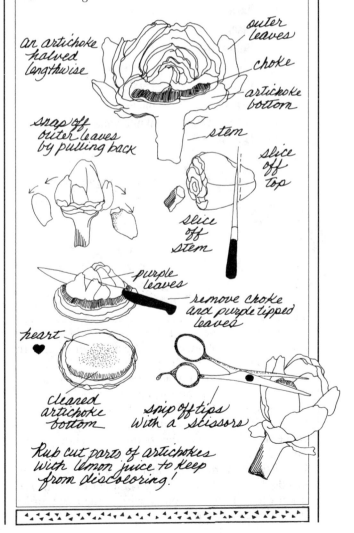

outer leaves

choke

artichoke bottom

an artichoke halved lengthwise

snap off outer leaves by pulling back

stem

slice off top

slice off stem

purple leaves

remove choke and purple tipped leaves

heart

cleared artichoke bottom

snip off tips with a scissors

Rub cut parts of artichokes with lemon juice to keep from discoloring!

YIELD

For whole artichokes as a first course, figure one large artichoke per person. If you are stuffing the artichokes, you could cut them in half and serve each person a half. Stuffed artichoke bottoms should be served one per person, and hearts one or two per person.

SEASON TO TASTE

When flavoring artichokes, think of some of our favorites:

Basil	Olive oil
Black pepper	Oregano
Butter	Parmesan
Chervil	cheese
Cream	Parsley
Garlic	Shallot
Ginger (fresh)	White wine
Lemon	

COOKING

▲ **Boiling:** Put the artichokes, stem side down, in a stainless-steel or enamel-coated pan in which they fit snugly so they don't bob up in the water. Cover with boiling water or fresh cold water and add a slice of lemon and ¼ teaspoon salt for each artichoke. Heat or return the water to boiling. Reduce the heat and boil gently, uncovered, 30 to 45 minutes. The artichoke is done when the bottom is tender when pierced with a knife and the leaves pull off easily. Using tongs, remove the artichokes and turn them upside down on a rack or in a colander to drain. Let drain a few minutes if you're serving them hot, or let them cool completely.

Boil artichoke hearts or bottoms with lemon slices in salted water to cover. Test for doneness by piercing them with a knife; it usually takes between 30 and 45 minutes. Drain and cool under cold running water.

▲ **Steaming:** Find a pan with a tight cover that will fit the artichokes standing upright. Pour in an inch of boiling water and a teaspoon of salt, cover the pan, and boil the artichokes gently until their bases are tender and the leaves pull off easily, 30 to 45 minutes. Keep a kettle of boiling water nearby because you may have to replenish the water several times. The denser bottom sitting in the water will cook faster than the tender leaves at the top—which is just the way it ought to be.

▲ **Sautéing:** Baby artichokes, if truly fresh and tender, can be sautéed whole or cut into halves or quarters lengthwise. Artichoke hearts and bottoms can be sautéed too, but first precook them until half-tender in boiling water to cover.

▲ **Baking:** Whole artichokes are better boiled or steamed, but if you want to cook them with a stuffing, baking is the answer. Trim whole artichokes and remove the chokes, spoon the stuffing into the center, and arrange them in a deep baking dish with a lid. Add enough broth or other cooking liquid to come 1 inch up the sides, and cover the dish. Bake at 350°F until the bottoms are tender, at least 45 minutes. You may want to remove the lid for the last 5 or 10 minutes to lightly brown the tops. Whole artichokes can also be precooked, halved or left whole, stuffed, and baked on a baking sheet or browned under the broiler.

Artichokes are a good source of vitamin A, vitamin C, calcium, iron, and potassium. They are moderately high in protein, high in carbohydrates, and low in fiber and fat.

SAUTEED BABY ARTICHOKES

We first enjoyed these tiny artichokes at Erminia, a New York restaurant presided over by the Latini family. They're becoming more common in the markets now, so when you see them (usually in the springtime), snap them up—the smallest you can find. They can range in size from one to three inches high. Just trim the stem and outer leaves—the rest can be eaten as the choke has not yet developed.

8 baby artichokes
3 tablespoons olive oil
1 tablespoon fresh lemon juice
Salt and freshly ground black pepper, to taste

1. Discard the stems and the tough outer leaves of the artichokes, and cut them into quarters.
2. Heat the olive oil in a skillet, and sauté the artichokes over medium heat, stirring constantly, for 10 minutes.
3. Add the lemon juice and salt and pepper, cover, and cook an additional 10 minutes. Serve as a side vegetable or as an appetizer.

4 portions

STUFFED ARTICHOKES

This giant thistle with its gray-green leaves cooks superbly in the microwave—so well, in fact, that the artichokes taste better and fresher than ever. We've stuffed them here with zucchini, bread crumbs, Parmesan, and mozzarella, flavored with garlic and oregano. A terrific first course.

2 large artichokes (about 12 ounces each)
½ lemon
¾ cup Berta's Chicken Stock (see Index) or canned broth
½ cup finely chopped zucchini
¼ cup dried bread crumbs
¼ cup grated Parmesan cheese
2 tablespoons butter, melted
1 ounce mozzarella cheese, shredded (¼ cup)
1 teaspoon dried oregano
1 clove garlic, minced
½ teaspoon salt
Freshly ground black pepper, to taste
Chopped fresh parsley, for garnish

1. Trim off the artichoke stems, cutting them flush with the bottom. Rub the cut with lemon. Using a sharp knife, slice 1 inch off the top of the artichokes. Rub the top with lemon.
2. Trim off the prickly point of each leaf with kitchen shears. Rub the leaves with lemon.
3. Arrange the artichokes upright on a microwave-safe plate. Pour in ½ cup of the stock, and cover with microwave-safe plastic wrap. Cook on full power (650 to 700 watts) until the stem end feels tender when pierced with the point of a knife, for 12 minutes. Let the artichokes stand 5 minutes. Reserve the liquid in the dish.
4. In a mixing bowl, stir together the zucchini, bread crumbs, Parmesan, melted butter, mozzarella, oregano, garlic, salt, pepper, and remaining ¼ cup stock.
5. Halve each artichoke lengthwise. Scrape out the fuzzy choke and the small leaves in the center. Arrange the two halves on a plate, stem ends facing the outer edge. Fill each half with the zucchini-crumb mixture, and cover loosely with microwave-safe plastic wrap.
6. Cook for 3 minutes at full power. Let stand 3 minutes, then sprinkle with parsley and serve.

2 portions
Note: This recipe was cooked on High (full power, 650 to 700 watts) in a carousel microwave, using microwave-safe containers.

If your microwave is less powerful, you will have to allow for more cooking time (approximately 1½ times the amount called for—but watch carefully); if it does not have a carousel, you may have to rotate the dish while it is cooking.

THE ASPARAGUS BED

T his most prized and elegant of all the world's vegetables is actually the young shoot of a perennial plant that appears in the first warm wet days of spring. Thick, thin, green, violet, white, tame, or wild—we enjoy asparagus either raw or cooked until just slightly limp. We adore them bright green and crisp for dipping in sauces. We cook them a little more for first courses and accompaniments and drizzle them with butter, vinaigrette, or hollandaise.

BUYING

The first maxim is the fresher, the better. Asparagus should be cut, cooked, and served without any dilly-dallying. The spring asparagus season is fleeting, so make sure you buy early and eat your fill. Check the stalk color and the tip for signs of freshness. Pick the greenest asparagus with straight, firm stalks; a duller khaki green indicates old age. The tips should be firm and tightly closed with a lavender tint. If the tips are opening up or look soggy, pass them by; old asparagus are stringy and taste bitter.

"**O**ut of the Earth I sing for them"
—TETON SIOUX POEM

STORING

Wrap asparagus, without cleaning first, in a plastic bag and store them in the crisper drawer of the refrigerator. They'll last a few days, but ideally you should eat them the same day or the day after. Asparagus can also be stored upright. Trim the bottom ends and place the asparagus in an inch of water in a deep, straight-sided container and cover the tops with a plastic bag. Don't snap or clean them until you're ready to cook.

YIELD

A half pound of asparagus per person will satisfy most as a first course or accompaniment; for an asparagus feast, perhaps the first asparagus of spring, buy ¾ to 1 pound per person. There are 15 to 20 medium-size stalks in a pound. One pound of asparagus, trimmed and cut into 1- to 2-inch lengths, will measure about three cups.

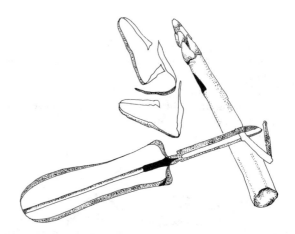

PREPARING

Snap off the ends by gently bending each stalk. The woody end should break off at just the right spot. Soak the stalks in cold water to loosen any dirt and refresh them. If they seem sandy, rinse them under cold water or soak in several changes of water.

Should you peel asparagus? Some think all asparagus should be peeled so the stalks will cook in the same time as the tender tips. We peel just the very fat stalks and those past their prime. Peel the stalks with a sharp vegetable peeler. Start at the bottom and peel gently toward the green tips. The trick is to take off a little more at the bottom and to let up toward the tip where the stalk is tender.

SEASON TO TASTE

Next time you cook asparagus, don't just think of butter. Make them extra special with some of the following:

Chive	Poppy seed
Lemon	Sage
Lemon balm	Savory
Nutmeg	Sesame oil and
Orange	seed
Parmesan	Tarragon
cheese	Thyme
Parsley	

COOKING

Size determines the cooking time, no matter what the cooking method. Asparagus, we think, should be cooked until crisp-tender. If you poke a stalk with a knife, you should feel a little resistance. The color should be bright green.

As with peelers and nonpeelers, there are people who always bundle asparagus and those who don't. The advantage of bundling is that asparagus can cook upright in a large pot with the tender tips above the water where they won't overcook. Bundling also makes it easy to pluck them out of the water and serve quickly. To bundle asparagus, tie stalks of equal size together with white kitchen string; tie securely but not too tightly.

To cook asparagus, bring water to a boil in a nonaluminum pot. If cooking bundled asparagus, stand the spears in 3 to 4 inches of boiling water. If cooking loose spears, use a shallow wide pot and lay the spears lengthwise in just an inch of water; they shouldn't be stacked more than three layers deep. Bring the water back to a gentle boil. Cooking times are approximate: 1 to 2 minutes for tiny spears, 3 to 5 minutes for small spears, 5 to 8 minutes for medium, and 10 to 12 minutes for large. As soon as the asparagus are done, pluck them out of the water and

drain for just a second on a kitchen towel or several layers of paper towels, then rush them to the table. If you want to serve them at room temperature or cold, gently run them under cold water to stop the cooking, and drain well.

Asparagus, cut into lengths or left whole, can also be gently sautéed in butter in a skillet. Cook over medium heat and turn the stalks often. Shave Parmesan cheese over the top.

VARIETIES OF ASPARAGUS

▲ **Green:** These stalks range from pencil-thin to very thick. Americans once had quite a few varieties of asparagus, but now most of it is simply green.
▲ **White:** This asparagus is preferred in Europe. The stalks are kept out of the sun; this prevents their turning green and makes them a little milder and more delicate. Some fresh white asparagus is showing up at markets stateside with more to come in the future, no doubt.
▲ **Violet:** This asparagus is best known in England and Italy. The stalks are thick and substantial.
▲ **Wild:** You'll probably have to hunt this variety yourself if you are ever to have a meal of it. Except in Italy and the South of France where wild asparagus is much more prolific, you won't find this asparagus at the market.

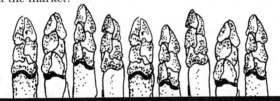

ASPARAGUS TIPS ORIENTAL

Whip up this stir-fry as soon as fresh asparagus comes into the market. It's very quick to prepare and makes a beautiful appetizer or side vegetable.

2 pounds asparagus, trimmed
2 tablespoons sesame oil
1 tablespoon soy sauce
1 tablespoon sesame seeds, toasted (see Index)
¼ cup cashews, toasted (see Index)
1 scallion (green onion), white bulb and 3 inches green,
    thinly sliced diagonally

1. Cut off the top 2 inches of the asparagus. Reserve the stems for another use.

2. Heat the sesame oil in a wok or a large skillet until quite hot. Add the asparagus tips and cook, over medium heat, tossing frequently, for 3 minutes.

3. Add the soy sauce, sesame seeds, and cashews. Cook over medium-high heat another 2 minutes. Garnish with the scallion, and serve immediately.

4 portions

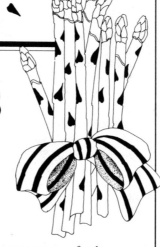

HERBED ASPARAGUS WITH PARMESAN CHEESE

One of our favorite ways to prepare fresh asparagus—cooked crisp-tender, tossed in herbs, and laced with Parmesan shavings. It's simple perfection. Don't forget the pepper grinder.

2 pounds pencil-thin asparagus, trimmed
4 tablespoons (½ stick) unsalted butter, at room temperature
1 tablespoon chopped fresh Italian (flat-leaf) parsley
1 tablespoon snipped fresh or freeze-dried chives
1 tablespoon chopped fresh dill
1 tablespoon chopped fresh rosemary
1 teaspoon coarsely ground black pepper
4 ounces Parmesan cheese, in 1 piece

1. Bring a large pot of water to a boil, and add the asparagus. Simmer until just tender, 1½ to 2 minutes. Drain and pat dry.

2. Combine the butter, chopped herbs, and pepper in a small bowl, and blend thoroughly.

3. Just before serving, melt the herb butter over medium heat in a large heavy skillet. Add the asparagus and toss gently to heat through, 2 minutes.

4. Transfer the asparagus to a warmed serving platter, and shave Parmesan cheese over it. Serve immediately.

6 portions

> "**I** stick to asparagus which still seems to inspire gentle thought."
>
> —CHARLES LAMB

ASPARAGUS AND SHIITAKE SAUTE

Quickly sautéed asparagus and wild mushrooms with a dash of ginger—this is a springtime treat. Don't feel guilty about how easy this is.

8 ounces pencil-thin asparagus, trimmed
8 ounces fresh shiitake mushrooms
4 tablespoons (½ stick) unsalted butter
⅓ cup minced shallots
2 tablespoons minced fresh ginger
½ teaspoon salt
Freshly ground black pepper, to taste
¼ cup dry vermouth
1 teaspoon slivered orange zest

1. Cut the asparagus spears in half lengthwise, and then into 1-inch pieces. (If the spears are thicker than a pencil, quarter them lengthwise.)

2. Remove the stems from the mushrooms, and reserve them for another use. Cut the mushrooms into ¼-inch-thick strips.

3. Melt the butter in a large skillet, and add the shallots and ginger. Cook over medium heat, stirring frequently, until golden, about 3 minutes.

4. Add the asparagus and mushrooms. Season with the salt and pepper, and cook 2 minutes, stirring.

5. Add the vermouth and cover the skillet. Cook 2 minutes, shaking the skillet once or twice. Then sprinkle the vegetables with the orange zest and cook 1 minute more. Serve immediately.

4 portions

ASPARAGUS WATERCRESS TIMBALES

Timbales, molded vegetable custards, have the consistency of a quiche. Once asparagus has been cooked for a while, it might lose some of its bright green color—so we've added watercress, both for its rich color and for its peppery flavor.

2 cups heavy or whipping cream
5 eggs
½ teaspoon dry mustard
½ teaspoon Worcestershire sauce
Dash of Tabasco sauce
2 cups chopped cooked asparagus
½ cup finely chopped watercress
½ cup grated Gruyère cheese
3 tablespoons grated Parmesan cheese

1. Preheat the oven to 350°F.
2. In a large bowl, combine the cream, eggs, mustard, Worcestershire, and Tabasco. Beat with a wire whisk until smooth.
3. Add the cooked asparagus, watercress, Gruyère, and Parmesan, and mix well.
4. Butter eight individual timbale molds (4-ounce size), and fill them three quarters full with the asparagus mixture.
5. Place the timbales in a baking pan with sides that are the same height as the molds. Fill the pan with hot (not boiling) water to reach three quarters of the way up the sides of the molds. Bake for 45 minutes.
6. Remove the timbales from the water, and let them rest for 5 minutes. To serve, invert them onto a serving platter or onto individual plates.

8 portions

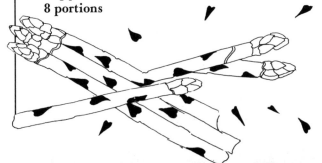

BABY WHITE ASPARAGUS SALAD

Though tiny in size, these slender white asparagus are big on flavor—sweet, nutty, and crunchy. They come ready to cook and are so delicious raw, steamed, or sautéed that they are quickly gaining in popularity. If they're not available in your area yet, you can bet they soon will be.

8 ounces baby white asparagus,* trimmed
8 ounces haricots verts (thin, tender green beans), trimmed
8 baby carrots, peeled
2 cups julienned cooked beets
¾ cup Shallot Vinaigrette (see Index)
1 tablespoon chopped fresh chervil or Italian (flat-leaf) parsley

1. Bring 2 quarts of water to a boil in a large saucepan. Add the asparagus, and cook until crisp-tender, 2 minutes. Remove them with tongs, rinse under cold water, and pat dry. Set them aside.
2. Add the haricots verts to the same water and cook until crisp-tender, 3 minutes. Remove them with tongs or a slotted spoon, rinse under cold water, and pat dry. Set them aside.
3. Cut the carrots into ½-inch-thick slices, and add them to the same water. Cook until crisp-tender, 5 minutes. Drain, rinse under cold water, and pat dry.
4. Divide the asparagus, haricots verts, and beets into eight portions. Divide the carrots into four portions. On each of four salad plates, arrange the asparagus, haricots verts, and beets in a spoke pattern. Place a mound of carrots in the center.
5. Drizzle with the vinaigrette, garnish with the chervil, and serve immediately.

4 portions

*Available through Michigan White, 8130 52nd St., Alto, MI 49302; (616) 868-7501.

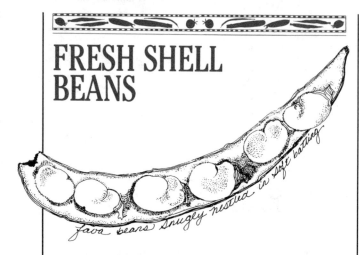

FRESH SHELL BEANS

fava beans snugly nestled in soft batting

These are the beans of summer porches and rocking chairs, for each one must be stripped from its shell before it is cooked. Lima beans are probably the best known of the fresh shell beans in this country, but our renewed interest in French and Italian cooking has perked our interest in their ways with fava beans. Fresh lima, cranberry, and fava beans have a buttery texture and delicate taste that must be tried to be believed. So buy a few pounds this summer, grab a friend and a couple of rocking chairs, and treat yourself to one of the lesser-known glories of summer.

BUYING

These beans are sweet and tender only if they are harvested when young and full of sugar. Just as with corn, sweet peas, and snap beans, the sugar changes to starch once the vegetables are picked from the stem. Choose the smallest pods for the tenderest, sweetest beans, and buy them only if they are really fresh. Look for velvety or shiny pods that are tightly closed and bulging with seeds.

These beans have some confusing nomenclature, so keep your eye out for them under another name. The smallest lima beans are called butter limas in some markets; large limas are often called Ford-hooks. Fava beans are called broad beans in England and by some Anglophiles here. In the South, cranberry beans are known as shellouts or shell beans.

STORING

Keep fresh shell beans unwashed in a plastic bag in the refrigerator up to two days, three days if you really must.

YIELD

The answer is as many as you can bear to shell. Ideally you'll buy at least ¾ pound per person. A pound of pods yields just 1½ to 2 cups of shelled beans.

COOKING

First, strip these beans out of their shells by pressing on the inside curve of the pod and splitting them open. You may need to run your thumbnail down the indentation to break it open. Pick the beans out and throw away the pods. Drop the beans into a large pot of boiling water and return to the boil. Reduce the heat and gently simmer until tender; for very fresh small beans that could be as quickly as 10 minutes. If the fava or lima beans are large and the skins are tough, quickly cool them under cold water and slip them out of their skins. Reheat the beans in butter just before serving.

The simplest way to serve shell beans is hot, tossed with butter, salt, and fresh pepper; or go a little farther south and combine them with crisp bacon, a little bacon fat, salt, and pepper. They're also wonderful with olive oil, garlic, and fresh herbs; toss these oil-and-herb-infused beans again with hot pasta and grated Parmesan cheese for a splendid dinner. You could also let the beans cool and toss them with a garlicky vinaigrette, or purée them in a food mill and reheat with butter or cream. In Italy and France, tiny, very fresh fava beans are served raw with salt. Diners shell them like peanuts and pop them into their mouths.

***

> "I saw him even now going the way of all flesh, that is to say towards the kitchen."
> —JOHN WEBSTER

FAVA BEANS WITH SOPRESSATA

Favas are so filled with fresh nutty flavor that just a few seconds of blanching are all they need. Try these beans marinated alongside sopressata sausage and you'll quickly understand why the fava season is so eagerly awaited along the Mediterranean—and at our house too.

3 cups shelled fava (broad) beans
2 tablespoons minced shallots
1 tablespoon minced garlic
1 tablespoon snipped fresh chives
½ tablespoon chopped fresh rosemary leaves
½ cup extra virgin olive oil
Salt and freshly ground black pepper, to taste
12 ounces sopressata sausage, thinly sliced
4 sprigs rosemary, for garnish

1. Rinse the beans thoroughly. Blanch them in a large saucepan of boiling water for 15 seconds. Drain, and rinse under cold water. Pat the beans dry.

2. Combine the beans, shallots, garlic, chives, rosemary, oil, and salt and pepper in a large bowl. Toss thoroughly, and cover the bowl. Marinate in the refrigerator for at least 12 hours.

3. Arrange the sausage on individual plates. Using a slotted spoon, scoop the beans onto the plates. Drizzle a bit of the marinade over the sausage, garnish with the rosemary sprigs, and serve.

4 portions

FAVA BEAN PUREE

The only time-consuming part of this wonderful dish is shelling the fava beans—but it's such a joy to see them nestled in their cozy cotton batting in the pods that it's really no trouble.

This flavorsome purée will explain the Europeans' passion for these beans. It's very rich, so you'll want only a spoonful per portion—perhaps alongside another vegetable purée.

3 cups shelled fava (broad) beans
2 tablespoons unsalted butter, melted
¼ cup heavy or whipping cream
Salt and freshly ground black pepper, to taste

1. Rinse the beans thoroughly. Add them to a large saucepan of boiling water. Reduce the heat and simmer until the beans are tender, 20 minutes.

2. Drain the beans, and pass them through a food mill. Add the melted butter, cream, and salt and pepper. Serve immediately.

4 portions

LIMAS AND SPINACH

We've combined these limas with two other vegetables, spinach and fennel. Garnished with fresh chives, this is a lovely side dish.

2 tablespoons olive oil
½ cup chopped fresh fennel bulb
½ cup chopped red onion
2 cups cooked baby lima beans, at room temperature
½ cup Berta's Chicken Stock or homemade vegetable stock
*   (see Index) or canned broth*
4 cups loosely packed trimmed spinach leaves
1 tablespoon white wine vinegar
½ teaspoon salt
Freshly ground black pepper, to taste
1 tablespoon snipped fresh chives

1. Cook the olive oil in a 2-quart microwave-safe casserole for 2 minutes at full power (650 to 700 watts). Stir in the fennel and onion, and cook 4 minutes. Remove the vegetables with a slotted spoon, and set aside.

2. Add the beans and stock to the casserole, cover, and cook 2 minutes.

3. Stir in the spinach. Cover, and cook until it has wilted, 2 minutes.

4. Stir in the reserved vegetables, vinegar, salt, and pepper. Cover, and let stand (out of the oven) for 30 seconds. Then sprinkle with the chives and serve.

4 portions

Note: This recipe was cooked on High (full power, 650 to 700 watts) in a carousel microwave, using microwave-safe containers.

If your microwave is less powerful, you will have to allow for more cooking time (approximately 1½ times the amount called for—but watch carefully); if it does not have a carousel, you may have to rotate the dish while it is cooking.

CRANBERRY BEAN SUCCOTASH

The Indians named it and we've updated their traditional corn dish with fresh cranberry beans, garlic chives, and shredded escarole. Great with grilled sausages, bratwurst, burgers, or ribs.

2 pounds cranberry beans
2 tablespoons unsalted butter
½ cup chopped onion
4 ounces Canadian bacon, cut into fine julienne
2 cups fresh corn kernels (about 3 ears)
2½ cups Berta's Chicken Stock (see Index) or canned broth
1 ripe tomato, diced
1 teaspoon salt
Freshly ground black pepper, to taste
2 cups shredded fresh escarole
½ cup chopped garlic chives (see Note)

1. Shell the beans and rinse them. Set aside.

2. Melt the butter in a medium-size saucepan.

Add the onion and Canadian bacon, and sauté over medium heat until the bacon is crisp at the edges, 5 minutes.

3. Add the reserved beans, corn, stock, tomato, salt, and pepper. Heat to a simmer. Cover, and cook over medium-low heat for 25 minutes.

4. Stir in the escarole. Cook 5 minutes.

5. Remove the pan from the heat and stir in the garlic chives. Cover the pan and let it stand for 10 minutes. Then season with salt and pepper to taste, and serve immediately.

4 to 6 portions

Note: Garlic chives are a bit stronger tasting than regular chives and appear to be more silvery in color than the bright green variety. If you can't find them, substitute regular chives.

SNAPPY GREEN BEANS

This common green bean was formerly known as the string bean, but the string has been bred out and now occurs only when the bean is overripe. Green, or snap beans are best when they are barely mature and thin; the seeds should be barely visible. They should also be crisp. Break one—if it doesn't snap, it's not fresh. Buy about ¼ pound per serving. Refrigerate beans unwashed in open or perforated plastic bags up to three days.

Cook these beans as simply as possible. First trim the stem end. Whether you trim the little tail at the other end is up to you, but it's not necessary. To boil beans, drop them in boiling water to cover and gently cook, uncovered, until crisp-tender and still bright green. Check after five minutes; no more than ten minutes is necessary. Steaming beans is just as easy and works equally well. Steam, covered, over an inch of boiling water, checking after five minutes. If you want to cook beans in the microwave, simply cover ½ pound of fresh beans in a dish and cook on high power four to seven minutes. We like green beans hot, tossed with butter and other seasonings, and also at room temperature, tossed with a well-seasoned vinaigrette.

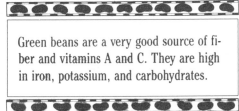

Green beans are a very good source of fiber and vitamins A and C. They are high in iron, potassium, and carbohydrates.

GREEN BEANS WITH ROQUEFORT AND WALNUTS

The bite of the cheese and the sweetness of the walnuts are perfect accents for fresh green beans. This is an easy sauté, and with such robust flavors it's a terrific main course for a light supper.

Choose beans that are crisp and vividly colored; this is the best way of telling that they were picked recently.

1 pound fresh, tender green beans
4 strips thick-sliced bacon or 2 slices slab bacon,
 ¼ inch thick
4 ounces Roquefort cheese, crumbled
1½ cups walnut halves, toasted (see Index)
Freshly ground black pepper, to taste

1. Bring a saucepan of water to a boil, and add the beans. Simmer until crisp-tender, about 3 minutes. Drain, rinse under cold water, and drain again. Set them aside.

2. Cut the bacon slices into ¼-inch-wide strips. Place them in a skillet and cook over medium heat until well cooked, 5 to 7 minutes. Remove the bacon with a slotted spoon (reserve the skillet), and set it aside to drain on paper towels.

3. Add the green beans to the skillet and heat through over medium heat, for 2 minutes. Add the Roquefort, and toss until the cheese just begins to melt, about 30 seconds. Sprinkle with the walnuts and lots of pepper, and serve immediately.

4 portions

GREEN BEANS PROVENCAL

These gutsy-flavored beans are the perfect accompaniment to a garlicky roasted chicken.

1 pound fresh, tender green beans
2 tablespoons olive oil
1 large onion, coarsely chopped
4 cloves garlic, finely chopped
4 large tomatoes, peeled, seeded, and coarsely chopped
½ cup dry white wine
½ cup pitted Niçoise olives
1 tablespoon fresh lemon juice
2 tablespoons coarsely ground black pepper

1. Bring a saucepan of water to a boil, and add the beans. Simmer until crisp-tender, about 3 minutes. Drain, rinse under cold water, and drain again. Set the beans aside.

2. Heat the oil in a large skillet over medium heat, and add the onion and garlic. Cook for 5 minutes. Then add the tomatoes and wine, and cook for 20 minutes.

3. Toss in the olives and the reserved beans; heat through, 3 minutes. Sprinkle with the lemon juice and pepper, and serve immediately.

4 to 6 portions

HARICOTS VERTS

We especially enjoy the slender delicate French green beans known as haricots verts. They cook in a minute, turn a deep, almost emerald, green, and they will never, ever taste like canned beans. If you see them, be sure to buy them to serve at dinner.

OIL-ROASTED HARICOTS VERTS, POTATOES, AND FENNEL

An unusual but very tasty combination of roasted vegetables.

2 fennel bulbs (about 1¼ pounds total)
1½ pounds small red new potatoes
1½ pounds haricots verts (thin, tender green beans)
⅔ cup olive oil
½ teaspoon coarse (kosher) salt
Freshly ground black pepper, to taste

1. Preheat the oven to 425°F.

2. Cut the tops off the fennel, and then cut the bulbs into quarters. Thinly slice the potatoes. Snap the ends off the beans.

3. Combine the fennel, potatoes, and oil in a mixing bowl and toss well. Spread the mixture (with the oil) out on a baking sheet, sprinkle with the coarse salt, and bake for 30 minutes.

4. Remove the baking sheet from the oven. Toss the beans with the cooked vegetables, and bake until lightly browned, 10 to 15 minutes. Sprinkle with pepper, and serve hot or at room temperature.

4 portions

HARICOTS VERTS IN MUSTARD SAUCE

These delicate green beans are prepared quickly in their rich mustard sauce. Just right to serve with a roast leg of lamb.

12 ounces haricots verts (thin, tender green beans)
2 tablespoons unsalted butter
2 tablespoons minced shallots
½ cup Berta's Chicken Stock (see Index) or canned broth
3 tablespoons heavy or whipping cream
2 tablespoons whole-grain mustard
Salt and freshly ground black pepper, to taste

1. Bring a saucepan of water to a boil, and add the green beans. Reduce the heat and simmer 3 to 5 minutes. Drain, rinse under cold water, and pat dry. Set aside.

2. Melt the butter in a medium-size saucepan, and add the shallots. Sauté over medium heat for 3 minutes.

3. Stir in the stock, cream, and mustard, and cook until the mixture is just slightly thickened, 5 minutes. Then add the beans and toss them in the sauce until well coated and heated through, 2 minutes.

4. Season the beans with salt and pepper, and serve immediately.

4 to 6 portions

BEET RED

We were just getting used to orange peppers and purple potatoes; then beets turned color on us, too. Now, alongside the familiar burgundy variety, we discover little baby beets, golden beets—even striped beets. We've tried them all and found there's more to these beets than just cosmetic changes. Baby beets are the tenderest beet imaginable. Golden beets are almost as orange as they are gold, and this color doesn't bleed—perfect for salads. Then there are the beets that are cherry red on the outside and striped on the inside—red and creamy white. This visually dramatic beet has a surprisingly mild flavor. Borscht has just become a whole new ball game.

BUYING

Beets are root vegetables. The best time to buy them is when they look like they've just been pulled from the earth—dusted with dirt and with their green tops attached. Choose small beets. Two inches is about as large as you will want them. If you can, pick beets of the same size so they will cook in the same time. The color should be deep and rich and the skin smooth and unbroken. Don't buy any that are bruised. If you can buy beets with the greens still attached, the beets will be fresher; and the greens can be cut off and cooked like spinach if they are crisp and fresh. Red-veined beet greens turn red at the tips instead of yellow as they wilt.

> Beets are rich in complex carbohydrates, vitamin C, and potassium. They have a moderate amount of protein and sodium, and they are low in fat.

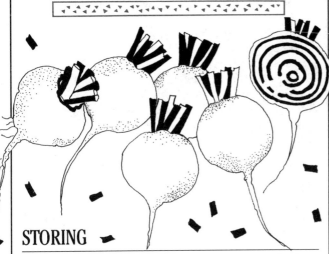

STORING

Handle beets carefully. If the skin is broken the beet will bleed, losing its sweetness and color. For the same reason, don't trim the greens close to the beet but leave an inch or two at the top; and leave the long thin root at the bottom alone. Store the unwashed beets in the refrigerator in an open plastic bag or a plastic bag with holes in it. They should last up to three weeks if they stay dry. The greens, if they are fresh to start with, can be refrigerated unwashed in a plastic bag up to three days.

YIELD

Ten 2-inch beets make about a pound—enough for four servings as a side dish.

COOKING

First, gently wash the beets to get rid of the dirt. Don't scrub or peel them. The skin must be unbroken or the beet will be flavorless and mushy when you cook it. Beets are root vegetables, like potatoes and yams; they take a while to cook and the size determines just how long that will be.

▲ **Boiling:** Put the beets in a pot and add cold water to cover. Heat to boiling, then reduce the heat, cover the pot, and simmer until tender. A 1½-inch beet will be done in about a half hour; larger beets can take up to an hour. Don't check for tenderness by poking them with a knife or fork until you are quite sure they are done. Best is to pluck one out and give it a very fast squeeze with your fingers.

Drain the beets and run them under cold water for just a minute. You can then trim the tops and bottoms and slip the skins off easily. Small beets can be served whole and larger beets sliced or chopped. If the beets have cooled off, you can simply reheat them in butter and serve them. Or you could use a little imagination and combine them with one or more of the other flavors they're great with—cucumbers, potatoes, apples, pears, sausages, balsamic vinegar, sour cream, oranges, mustard, horseradish, soy, lime, and mint. And that's the short list.

Baby beets can be steamed over boiling water, but anything larger is best boiled.

▲ **Baking:** Baked beets are long-time favorites of ours. Now it's become a favorite way to cook them because the flavor and the nutrients stay in the beet. Wrap each beet in aluminum foil and bake in a 350°F oven until tender. Or put the beets in a single layer in a buttered or oiled baking dish. Add ¼ inch water and cover the dish with the lid or aluminum foil. Bake at 350°F until tender, 1 to 1½ hours. Peel the beets as soon as you can touch them.

COOKING BEET GREENS

If you like cooked greens, you'll love cooked beet greens. They're pungent and stand up to cooking without getting mushy. First, trim any coarse stems and rinse the leaves well. Blanch in boiling water for about 2 minutes, then drain well and pat dry. Just before serving, sauté them for a few minutes in butter or olive oil. Minced shallots added to the sauté is a nice touch.

LITTLE FRENCH BEETS

This is a ruby version of *petits pois à la française*: beets cooked with radicchio leaves and flavored with balsamic vinegar and lemon zest. A perfect side vegetable with a fruit-stuffed loin of pork.

4 beets (about 12 ounces total)
2 slices bacon, cut into 1-inch pieces
¾ cup Berta's Chicken Stock or homemade vegetable stock
* (see Index) or canned broth*
1 small head radicchio, halved lengthwise
1 cup pearl onions
2 teaspoons unbleached all-purpose flour
2 tablespoons unsalted butter
2 tablespoons chopped fresh dill
1 tablespoon snipped fresh chives
2 teaspoons balsamic vinegar
1 teaspoon grated lemon zest
¾ teaspoon salt
½ teaspoon sugar
Freshly grated nutmeg, to taste
Freshly ground black pepper, to taste

1. Trim and peel the beets. Cut them in half, then into ¼-inch-thick slices. Set the beets aside.

2. Place the bacon in a microwave-safe 2-quart casserole, cover, and cook at full power (650 to 700 watts) for 3 minutes.

3. Stir the beets and broth into the casserole, cover, and cook 4 minutes. Stir, and cook 2 minutes.

4. Stir in the radicchio, onions, and flour. Cover, and cook 5 minutes.

5. Remove the casserole from the microwave, and stir in all the remaining ingredients. Serve immediately.

4 to 6 portions

Note: This recipe was cooked on High (full power, 650 to 700 watts) in a carousel microwave, using microwave-safe containers.

If your microwave is less powerful, you will have to allow for more cooking time (approximately 1½ times the amount called for—but watch carefully); if it does not have a carousel, you may have to rotate the dish while it is cooking.

BAKED BEETS

The flavor of these beets is wildly intense because none is lost in a cooking liquid. They can be baked ahead of time and then heated through at the last moment. They're wonderful with pork and ham.

8 beets (about 2 pounds total)
3 tablespoons unsalted butter
2 teaspoons raspberry vinegar
Finely grated zest of 1 orange
1 teaspoon caraway seeds
Salt and freshly ground black pepper, to taste
1 teaspoon snipped fresh chives

1. Preheat the oven to 350°F.

2. Trim the beets, leaving on 1 inch of stem. Rinse them well, but do not peel them.

3. Place the beets in a baking pan, and fill the pan with ¼ inch of water. Cover with aluminum foil, and bake for 1 hour. Then remove the foil and bake until the beets are tender, another 30 minutes.

4. Allow the beets to cool slightly, then peel and slice them into ¼-inch-thick rounds. Set them aside.

5. Melt the butter in a skillet over low heat. Add the beets, and toss to coat with the butter. Sprinkle with the raspberry vinegar, orange zest, caraway seeds, and salt and pepper. Cook, tossing gently, until the beets are heated through, 3 to 4 minutes.

6. Transfer the beets to a serving bowl, sprinkle with the chives, and serve immediately.

4 portions

HARVARD BEETS

Although both Harvard and Yale lay claim to having created Harvard beets, we prefer the story about them being devised in the seventeenth century in an English tavern called Harwood. One of its customers, a Russian, emigrated to Boston, opened a restaurant, and mispronounced the tavern's name when he put the beets on his menu.

In any case, this is one of America's favorite ways to eat beets—the light dressing of vinegar and orange juice emphasizes all that deeply rooted flavor nicely.

2 pounds beets, well rinsed
½ cup sugar
5 tablespoons red wine vinegar
¼ cup fresh orange juice
2 teaspoons cornstarch
Salt and freshly ground black pepper, to taste
1 tablespoon unsalted butter
Grated zest of 2 oranges

1. Place the beets in a medium-size saucepan, cover with cold water, and bring to a boil. Reduce the heat to a simmer, cover, and cook until tender, 40 to 50 minutes. Drain and rinse under cold water to cool. Slip off the skins, and cut the beets into ¼-inch dice. You should have 4 cups. Set them aside.

2. Combine the sugar, vinegar, orange juice, cornstarch, and salt and pepper in a heavy saucepan. Whisk well and bring to a boil over medium heat, whisking constantly until the mixture is clear and thickened, 4 to 5 minutes. Whisk in the butter and zest, and cook just until the butter has melted.

3. Remove the pan from the heat and pour the sauce over the beets. Toss gently. Serve hot or at room temperature.

4 to 6 portions

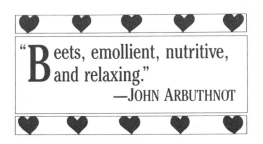

"**B**eets, emollient, nutritive, and relaxing."
—JOHN ARBUTHNOT

BEET AND CORIANDER PUREE

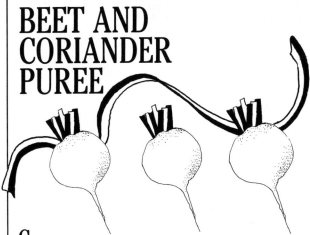

Coriander and cider vinegar add just the right amount of sweetness and tang to this ruby purée. Serve this vegetable alongside carrot purée to accompany roasted game birds and rabbit.

3¾ to 4 pounds tender young beets
1 cup (2 sticks) unsalted butter
1½ cups diced onions
½ cup cider vinegar
1 tablespoon sugar
2 teaspoons ground coriander
1 teaspoon salt

1. Trim the beets, leaving on 1 inch of stem. Rinse them well, but do not peel them.

2. Place the beets in a large saucepan, cover with cold water, and bring to a boil over high heat. Reduce the heat, cover the pan, and simmer until the beets are very tender, 50 to 60 minutes. Add additional water if necessary.

3. Drain the beets, and rinse them under cold water. Slip off the skins, and cut the beets into 1-inch pieces. Set them aside.

4. Melt the butter in a large saucepan over low heat. Add the onions, cover, and cook for 20 minutes. Then add the beets, vinegar, sugar, coriander, and salt. Stir well, and simmer, uncovered, stirring frequently, for 10 minutes.

5. Transfer the beet mixture, in batches, to a food processor and process until perfectly smooth.

6. Return the purée to a saucepan and stir well over low heat until heated through. (Or transfer the purée to an ovenproof serving dish, cover with aluminum foil, and heat in a preheated 350°F oven until steaming hot, 25 minutes.)

8 portions

STEAMED BEET GREENS

Take advantage of this special treat when you've bought beets for another dish. It's quick and easy—and yes, they do cook down that much!

8 cups loosely packed trimmed beet greens
4 tablespoons (½ stick) unsalted butter
3 tablespoons fresh lemon juice
6 tablespoons finely chopped shallots
Salt and freshly ground black pepper, to taste

1. Rinse the beet greens well, and leave the water clinging to the leaves.
2. Melt the butter in a medium-size skillet. Add the greens and lemon juice, cover, and cook over low heat for 5 minutes. Then add the shallots and salt and pepper. Stir well, cover, and cook until the greens have wilted, another 4 to 5 minutes. Adjust the seasonings if necessary, and serve immediately.

2 portions

SEASON TO TASTE

Some of our favorite flavors with beets include:

Allspice	Horseradish
Balsamic and	Lemon
cider vinegars	Nutmeg
Caraway seed	Orange
Celery seed	Red onion
Chive	Roquefort
Cinnamon	cheese
Clove	Tarragon
Dill	Walnuts

BROCCOLI BRUNCH

Those green heads of broccoli, sometimes purple these days, have become the giant of vegetables—and for good reason. Fresh green broccoli is available year round and is consistently of fine quality. It's always a good buy and its mild taste appeals to all. Agreeable broccoli lends itself to dozens of preparations, from crudités to stir-fries to elegant purées. But the best news from those in the know is that with all of its other attributes, it is also one of nature's healthiest foods. We may have taken broccoli for granted once, but now it's time to sit up and take a look at this darling of the cabbage patch.

BUYING

Choose only tight green broccoli heads on firm stalks. Broccoli on several slender stalks, rather than on one or two large stalks, will have tenderer stems for eating. Some markets cut up broccoli florets and sell them loose by weight for those who can't use the larger bundles.

STORING

Refrigerate unwashed broccoli in an open plastic bag or a bag with perforations, not in an airtight container. Or wrap it in damp paper towels and store it in the crisper drawer. Broccoli, if bought in good condition, will remain fresh for three to four days.

YIELD

A two-pound bunch of broccoli will serve four people generously.

PREPARING

Always rinse broccoli before you cook it. If you are serving it raw, crisp it in cold water for 10 minutes. But don't leave this vegetable soaking too long since the important vitamins in broccoli are water soluble.

Depending on how you're preparing broccoli, you may or may not want to separate the florets from the stalks. In either case, peel the stalks so they cook in the same time as the florets. If you do cut up broccoli, do so in uniform pieces so it cooks evenly.

SEASON TO TASTE

Try any of the following next time you prepare broccoli.

Basil	Lemon balm
Black pepper	Marjoram
Caraway seed	Mustard
Celery seed	Oregano
Cheddar cheese	Parmesan
Chile	cheese
Curry powder	Sesame oil and
Dill	seed
Garlic	Tarragon
Lemon	Thyme

COOKING

Don't overcook broccoli, regardless of how you're preparing it.

▲ **Boiling:** Some people like to boil broccoli in standing bunches so that the florets steam above the water while the stalks boil below. To do this, tie a bunch securely together and stand it upright in a pot of boiling water. Boil uncovered until tender.

If you've separated the florets from the stalks, the way you boil them depends on how thinly you sliced the stalks. If the stalks are in fairly thin slices, they can be cooked with the florets in boiling water to cover. If the stalks are in thick slices, drop them into the boiling water and cook about 3 minutes before adding the florets. The florets will be crisp-tender in just 2 to 3 minutes.

▲ **Steaming:** Steaming broccoli keeps the vitamins in the vegetable rather than in the cooking water. Bring an inch of water to the boil in a steamer. Put the peeled stems in the bottom of the steaming rack and the florets on the top. Cover and steam until crisp-tender. It will take 5 to 7 minutes.

▲ **Sautéing:** Peel the stems and cut into ½-inch pieces. Cut the florets into smaller florets, about an inch wide. Heat oil in a skillet or wok over medium heat. Add the broccoli and cook, stirring constantly, until crisp-tender. We like this sprinkled with Parmesan cheese.

▲ **Puréeing:** Peel the stems and boil or steam both stems and florets until tender. Purée in a food processor or food mill. Stir in defatted chicken broth, or 1 tablespoon cream and 2 tablespoons butter for every pound of broccoli. Reheat gently if necessary.

BROCCOLI SPINACH PUREE

If you have the misconception that purées are glorified baby foods, you're missing out on some of the most sophisticated vegetable flavors around. The potato provides the thickness here.

4 tablespoons (½ stick) unsalted butter
2 ribs celery, diced
1 onion, diced
1 small potato, peeled and diced
1 large bunch broccoli (2 pounds)
1½ cups Berta's Chicken Stock (see Index) or canned broth
3 cups slivered trimmed fresh spinach leaves, well rinsed
½ teaspoon nutmeg
Salt and freshly ground black pepper, to taste
1 tablespoon finely grated lemon zest

1. Melt the butter over low heat in a medium-size saucepan. Add the celery, onion, and potato. Cook, stirring occasionally, until wilted, 10 minutes.

2. While the vegetables are cooking, prepare the broccoli: Cut ½ inch off the bottom of the stem, and separate the stem from the head. Using a vegetable peeler, peel the entire stem. Cut the stem into thin slices crosswise, and then into quarters.

3. Reserve 1 cup of the florets from the head of broccoli. Chop the remainder of the head into small pieces.

4. Add the chopped stems and head to the wilted

vegetables, along with the chicken stock. Cover, and cook over low heat for 30 minutes.

5. Meanwhile, bring a small saucepan of water to a boil, and add the reserved florets. Simmer for 2 minutes; then drain, rinse under cold water, and set aside.

6. Add the spinach, nutmeg, and salt and pepper to the cooked vegetables, and cook for 1 minute.

7. Transfer the mixture to a food processor, in batches if necessary, and purée until smooth. Then transfer the purée to a warmed serving dish and fold in the lemon zest. Adjust the seasonings if necessary, garnish with the reserved broccoli florets, and serve immediately.

6 portions

Note: This can be prepared ahead. Skipping Step 5, proceed through Step 6. Purée the mixture, add the zest, and adjust the seasonings. Then, to reheat, place the purée in an ovenproof serving dish, cover with aluminum foil, and bake in a preheated 350°F oven for 15 to 20 minutes. Prepare the florets as described in Step 5. Remove the foil and garnish with the florets.

VEGETABLE PUREES
★

Vegetable purées provide an opportunity for blending unusual combinations of vegetables and of vegetables and fruits—often with unexpectedly exciting flavors and always with beautiful gem-like results.

Vegetable purées are often bonded with butter or sour cream, but we find that cheese and some of the starchier vegetables work well also; with them, add just a tiny bit of butter for the flavor.

Purées are so simple, delicious, and elegant—they shouldn't be missed. Try serving several in dollops of white, orange, green on each plate . . . and see if your guests can guess what the combinations are.

Cup for cup, raw broccoli has twice as much vitamin C as an orange and almost as much calcium as milk. It's also a good source of vitamins A, E, and K—and all at just 26 calories.

BROCCOLI PRIMAVERA

We toss lightly blanched broccoli with other fresh vegetables for this substantial salad. A pungent mustard vinaigrette tops them all off—remember to add it just before serving, to prevent the green vegetables from discoloring.

1 bunch broccoli (2 pounds)
3 carrots, peeled and cut into ¼-inch dice
1 yellow summer squash, halved lengthwise and cut into
*   ¼-inch-thick slices*
1 red bell pepper, cored, seeded, and cut into ¼-inch dice
1 cup frozen peas, thawed
Grated zest of 1 lemon
2 tablespoons chopped fresh Italian (flat-leaf) parsley
¾ cup Mustard Vinaigrette (see Index)

1. Trim the stems off the broccoli and reserve them for another use. Cut the top into small florets and set aside.

2. Bring a large saucepan of water to a boil. Add the carrots, and cook for 1 minute. Remove with a slotted spoon, rinse under cold water, and drain; set aside.

3. Add the squash to the same saucepan, and cook for 30 seconds. Remove with a slotted spoon, rinse under cold water, and drain; set aside.

4. Add the broccoli to the same saucepan, and cook for 30 seconds. Drain, rinse under cold water, and drain again. Pat all the vegetables dry with paper towels.

5. Combine the broccoli, carrots, squash, bell pepper, peas, lemon zest, and parsley in a salad bowl. Add the vinaigrette, toss gently, and serve.

6 portions

BROCCOLI AND WALNUT STIR-FRY

A quick Oriental stir-fry adds an enjoyable sesame taste to a winter broccoli preparation.

2 tablespoons sesame oil
½ cup coarsely chopped walnuts
4 cups broccoli florets
1 tablespoon soy sauce
2 tablespoons chopped red bell pepper

1. In a large skillet or wok, heat the oil until quite hot.
2. Add the walnuts and sauté for 1 minute. Add the broccoli and cook over medium heat, tossing frequently, until tender and crisp, 4 minutes.
3. Add the soy sauce and cook 1 more minute. Serve immediately, garnished with the bell pepper.

6 portions

BILLIONAIRE'S BROCCOLI

This dish makes use of only the very top of the stalks, the tiny green buds. Reserve the rest for soups or stir-fry.

1 large bunch broccoli (3 to 3½ pounds)
2 tablespoons olive oil
4 large cloves garlic, slivered
½ cup chopped scallions (green onions)
1 cup Berta's Chicken Stock or homemade vegetable broth
*   (see Index) or canned broth*
¼ teaspoon salt
Coarsely ground black pepper, to taste
Shaved or freshly grated Parmesan cheese, to taste

1. Using a sharp knife, carefully slice off the very tips (no more than ½ inch) of the broccoli florets; you should have about 3 cups.
2. Cook the oil in a 2-quart microwave-safe casserole for 2 minutes at full power (650 to 700 watts). Stir in the garlic, and cook until golden and crisp, 3 minutes.
3. Stir in the broccoli and scallions. Add the broth. Cover, and cook 5 minutes.
4. Season with the salt and pepper and sprinkle with cheese before serving.

4 portions

Note: This recipe was cooked on High (full power, 650 to 700 watts) in a carousel microwave, using microwave-safe containers.

If your microwave is less powerful, you will have to allow for more cooking time (approximately 1½ times the amount called for—but watch carefully); if it does not have a carousel, you may have to rotate the dish while it is cooking.

BROCCOLI RABE

Although broccoli rabe and broccoli share a name, there is little resemblance between them. Broccoli rabe never forms a head, just dark green leafy stalks with a few buds. Pungent, even bitter, in taste, broccoli rabe adds spark to other mild foods, such as potatoes and pasta. Cream smooths it and garlic and chiles support it.

Broccoli rabe is sold loosely tied in bunches. Look for those with the smallest stems and crisp fresh leaves. Rinse it thoroughly before cooking, then boil, steam, stir-fry, or sauté. Broccoli rabe cooks in just 2 to 5 minutes. Be sure to catch it while it is still crisp-tender or it turns to mush.

BROCCOLI RABE SOUFFLE

This soufflé matches up sweet roasted garlic and bitter broccoli rabe with happy results for an ideal luncheon or late-night-supper dish.

1 head garlic
1 tablespoon olive oil
2 cups broccoli rabe (leaves, stems, and florets) in 1-inch
  pieces
4 tablespoons (½ stick) unsalted butter
3 tablespoons unbleached all-purpose flour
1 ¼ cups milk
¾ teaspoon salt
Freshly ground black pepper, to taste
3 ounces Fontina cheese, cut into small cubes (¾ cup)
4 egg yolks
6 egg whites
Few drops of fresh lemon juice

1. Preheat the oven to 350°F.
2. Remove the papery outer skin of the garlic. Place the garlic head on a square of double-thickness aluminum foil. Drizzle it with the olive oil, and wrap it up in the foil. Bake for 1 hour.
3. Open the foil, and set the garlic aside until it is cool enough to handle.
4. Separate the garlic into cloves, and squeeze the garlic out of the skins into a small bowl. Stir until smooth; you should have about 2 tablespoons garlic purée. Cover, and set aside at room temperature. (The garlic may be prepared to this point a day in advance.)
5. Preheat the oven to 400°F. Butter an 8-cup soufflé dish.
6. Bring a saucepan of water to a boil, add the broccoli rabe, and simmer for 5 minutes. Drain, rinse under cold water, and drain again. Press out the excess moisture. Coarsely chop the broccoli rabe and set it aside.
7. Melt the butter over low heat in a medium-size saucepan. Add the flour, and whisk until smooth. Then whisk in the milk, salt, and pepper. Raise the heat to medium and cook, stirring, until the mixture is thick and boiling, about 2 minutes. Whisk in the garlic purée. Then add the cheese, and stir just until it has melted and the sauce is smooth. Set the sauce aside to cool slightly.
8. Whisk the egg yolks, one at a time, into the cooled sauce. Then stir in the broccoli rabe.
9. Beat the egg whites with the lemon juice until frothy; then continue beating until stiff but not dry. Stir one quarter of the whites into the sauce. Then quickly and gently fold in the remaining whites until smooth. Transfer the mixture to the prepared soufflé dish.
10. Bake until the soufflé is golden, puffed, and still moist inside, 30 minutes. Serve immediately.

8 portions

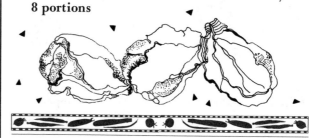

BRUSSELS SPROUTS

Don't neglect Brussels sprouts—when they are bought really fresh and cooked with care, they deliver a delicate and nutty taste. Brussels sprouts reach near Nirvana when baked with chestnuts, although a simple rolling in butter after they're cooked brings them close to perfection. They're great topped with mornay, béchamel, or hollandaise sauce, too. Still not convinced? Pull all the leaves off and sauté them with butter and shallots. You'll be surprised at what a subtle dish you've made.

BUYING

Unfortunately, the practice of packaging sprouts in little cartons (10 ounces each) is firmly entrenched. If possible, buy them loose or on the stalk at farmer's markets. In cartons or not, the heads should be firm, tight, and bright green. Pass by any that are yellowed and withered. The smallest sprouts make the best eating.

STORING

Don't wash sprouts before storing. Simply put them in an open plastic bag in the refrigerator and cook them within three days at most. If stored too long, Brussels sprouts will be strong and cabbagey tasting.

Brussels sprouts are high in fiber and carbohydrates, vitamins A and C, potassium, and iron. They are low in sodium, have no fat and no cholesterol.

YIELD

A 10-ounce carton will make three servings; one pound will feed four.

PREPARING

Trim the stem but not too much or you'll lose too many leaves. Pull off any yellowed or withered leaves. Cut an X in the stem of each sprout so that it will cook in the same time as the leaves. Except for the ones sold at farm stands, packaged Brussels sprouts have been rinsed before shipping and need just a quick rinse in cold water. If you have garden-fresh sprouts, soak them in cold salted water for 15 minutes to free them of any bugs.

COOKING

▲ **Boiling:** Pour about ½ inch of water into a wide saucepan and heat to boiling. Add the trimmed and X-ed sprouts and cover the pot. Boil gently until tender but still crunchy in the center, 8 to 10 minutes. (Check to make sure the water doesn't boil away.) Test by poking them with a knife or better yet by tasting them. Don't overcook Brussels sprouts. They shouldn't smell sulfurous (cabbagey). If you have sprouts of varying sizes, add the large ones first and cook for several minutes, then add the smaller ones. Drain, coat with butter, and season with salt and pepper.

If you like, add the drained sprouts to melted butter and a pinch of sugar in a skillet. Cook for just a minute, stirring constantly, until glistening.

▲ **Steaming:** Steam sprouts in a basket or on a rack over an inch of boiling water. Small sprouts may take just 6 to 8 minutes, medium sprouts 8 to 9 minutes, large ones 10 to 11 minutes.

▲ **Braising:** Melt about ¼ cup butter for every pound of sprouts in a skillet wide enough to hold them in a single layer. You can add a little chicken broth to the pan, too. Add the sprouts, cover the skillet, and cook over low heat until tender. Give the pan a shake occasionally to make sure they aren't sticking. Small sprouts can be braised without precooking, but larger sprouts are best if they are first blanched until half tender, then braised.

To braise sprouts in the oven, blanch all but the smallest until half tender. Coat with ¼ cup melted butter per pound of sprouts in a baking dish that holds them in a single layer. Cover the dish and bake at 350°F until tender, about 20 minutes.

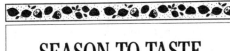

SEASON TO TASTE

Next time Brussels sprouts are on the menu, try them with:

Black pepper	Onion
Chestnut	Orange
Lemon	Parsley
Maple syrup	Shallot
Nutmeg	Thyme

VEGETABLE STRIPES

The pattern, colors, and glow of this presentation make it the vegetable dish to grace your Thanksgiving table. Sweetened kumquats are the special taste to mix with familiar Brussels sprouts, onions, and chestnuts, all glazed with dark brown sugar.

18 small white pearl onions
12 Brussels sprouts
12 fresh or jarred kumquats (if using jarred, rinse and drain
   them)
3 tablespoons unsalted butter
2 tablespoons (packed) dark brown sugar
12 fresh whole chestnuts, peeled (see box, How to Cook
   and Peel Chestnuts)
1 teaspoon crumbled dried rosemary leaves
½ teaspoon dried thyme leaves
Salt and freshly ground black pepper, to taste

1. Bring 2 quarts of water to a boil in a large saucepan. Cut a small X in the root end of each onion, and drop the onions into the water. Reduce the heat and simmer until tender but firm, about 10 minutes. Drain, rinse under cold water, and drain again. Peel and reserve.

2. Bring another 2 quarts of water to a boil. Cut a small X in the root end of each Brussels sprout. Drop the sprouts into the water, reduce the heat and simmer until tender but firm, about 10 minutes. Remove the Brussels sprouts with a slotted spoon, rinse under cold water, and drain. Set them aside.

3. Add the kumquats to the same water, and simmer for 4 minutes. Drain and set aside.

4. Melt 1 tablespoon of the butter in a skillet. Add the reserved onions and sprinkle with 1 tablespoon of the brown sugar. Cook the onions over medium-high heat, tossing frequently, until they are caramelized (brown and shiny), 3 minutes. Using a slotted spoon, remove them from the skillet and set aside.

5. Add 1 tablespoon of the butter to the skillet, and add the Brussels sprouts. Sprinkle them with the remaining 1 tablespoon brown sugar. Cook the sprouts, tossing frequently, until they are caramelized, 3 minutes.

6. Preheat the oven to 350°F.

7. In an 11 x 7-inch baking dish, arrange the onions, Brussels sprouts, kumquats, and chestnuts crosswise in rows of six, beginning and ending with the onions. Dot with the remaining 1 tablespoon butter, and sprinkle with the rosemary, thyme, and salt and pepper. Bake until the vegetables are heated through and tender, 15 to 20 minutes. Do not overcook.

6 portions

HOW TO COOK AND PEEL CHESTNUTS

Peeled whole chestnuts, packed in jars or cans, are available in many supermarkets and specialty food stores. For those who prefer to use fresh chestnuts, the methods to prepare them are simple, although a bit time consuming.

Using the tip of a small sharp knife cut an X in the flat side of the chestnut shells. Place them in a saucepan of boiling water to cover. Reduce the heat and simmer for 20 to 30 minutes, depending on the size of the chestnuts. Test for doneness by piercing a nut through the X with the tip of a knife. They should be tender. Drain the chestnuts, allow them to cool slightly, then peel off the shell and inner skin.

You can also roast chestnuts for peeling. Cut an X in the flat side of the shells. Place the chestnuts in a single layer on a baking sheet and roast them in a preheated 425°F oven until they are tender, 15 to 25 minutes. The shells will peel off easily and the nuts can be eaten out of hand or used in a recipe.

SAUTEED BRUSSELS SPROUT LEAVES

It may seem tedious, but separating the leaves of Brussels sprouts makes for a dish that is a pleasant change from boiling, braising, or steaming the whole buds. "Sweating" the leaves cooks them quickly and preserves their fresh flavor, allowing for more subtle combinations with other foods. Brussels sprout leaves are an ideal accompaniment to roast or braised pork and poultry, and in particular to delicate guinea hen.

1 pint Brussels sprouts
1 tablespoon unsalted butter
1 tablespoon olive oil
½ teaspoon dried thyme leaves
Salt and freshly ground black pepper, to taste
1 tablespoon chopped fresh Italian (flat-leaf) parsley
2 tablespoons chopped natural pistachio nuts

1. Carefully peel away the Brussels sprout leaves. Discard the cores.
2. Heat the butter and oil in a large skillet. Add the sprout leaves, thyme, and salt and pepper. Cook over medium heat, tossing frequently, until the leaves are wilted, about 15 minutes. Garnish with the chopped parsley and pistachios. Serve immediately.

4 portions

CABBAGES FOR KINGS

With so many light and flavorful ways to cook cabbage, and with dozens of varieties to choose from—pale green heads, crispy reds, snappy Savoys, and jewels from the Orient—it's sad to think that there are still cooks who see it as an odoriferous, unpleasant vegetable that should be avoided. Cabbage needn't be boiled to an overcooked pulp. Simply braised, steamed, and stir-fried—or served shredded and raw—it is just delicious.

VARIETIES OF CABBAGE

▲ **Green cabbage:** This is the most common variety. It has a mild flavor and can be eaten raw or cooked. Head sizes range from that of a large grapefruit to the size of a honeydew melon, to sometimes as big as a pumpkin.

▲ **Red cabbage:** This cabbage looks just like green cabbage except for its deep reddish purple color. Red cabbage takes longer to cook than green. It is often finely slivered and mixed with green in cole slaws.

▲ **Savoy cabbage:** This is certainly one of the prettiest vegetables. It is green with ruffled, deeply ridged and veined leaves. The lacy leaves often have a white trim, sometimes a reddish tint as well. Unlike the green and red head cabbages, the Savoy's leaves are loose. Some simply call it curly cabbage.

▲ **Chinese, celery, or Napa cabbage:** In appearance these cabbages, which fit under a very general heading of Chinese cabbage, are nothing at all like head cabbages. They look more like a cross between celery and lettuce, with long pearly stalks and rumpled celadon green leaves—very much like romaine lettuce. Their flavor is more delicate than head cabbage with a very fresh, slightly peppery taste. They are excellent in stir-fries or raw in salads.

▲ **Bok choy (*pak choi*):** This cabbage resembles Swiss chard with its long, thick-stemmed, light green to pearly white stalks. The flavor is very much like cabbage, just a bit fresher tasting. You can certainly eat bok choy raw, but it takes just a quick stir-fry to mellow the flavor a bit while retaining its crisp texture.

BUYING

If looking for head cabbage (green, red, or Savoy), choose firm, heavy heads with a bright fresh color. The brighter the leaves, the fresher the cabbage. Avoid those that have discolored, yellowing, or bruised leaves. Savoy cabbages will be loose leaved, but they should never be limp.

Chinese cabbages and bok choy should have crisp leaves and look fresh. Avoid those with discolored or mushy leaves.

STORING

Store cabbage in a plastic bag in the refrigerator. Never wash before storing. Green and red head cabbages will keep up to two weeks. Savoy and Chinese cabbages and bok choy are more perishable; they won't keep longer than a week.

If you use just part of a head, wrap the rest in plastic wrap. It will keep only for a couple of days—one reason to buy small heads.

YIELD

Head cabbages go a long way once you start slicing. A two-pound head cabbage will yield 9 to 10 cups when thinly sliced; a three-pound cabbage, 14 to 16 cups. A medium Chinese cabbage will make 6 cups sliced. A pound of cabbage will serve three people, depending on the recipe.

PREPARING

Peel off the tough outer leaves. Cut into quarters and cut away the core. Put the quarters, flat side down, on a cutting board and slice or shred crosswise. (Shredding is simply slicing very thin.)

If you need individual leaves for stuffing, cut out the core and blanch the whole head in boiling water until the leaves soften slightly and can be removed.

For raw cabbage salads, you can tame the taste by salting the shredded cabbage and soaking it in ice water up to an hour. Drain well.

COOKING

If you cook cabbage for a long time, it will undergo a chemical breakdown and release hydrogen sulfide, which can cause strong, lingering odors. Don't overcook cabbage.

▲ **Boiling:** Add the cabbage, quartered or sliced, to a large pot of boiling water. Cover the pot and gently boil until tender. This will take about 7 minutes for slices and 15 minutes for quarters. Red cabbage will need a couple of minutes more. The cabbage should still be a little crisp. Drain, toss with butter, and season with salt and pepper.

▲ **Steaming:** Heat about a half inch of water in a pan to boiling. Add the cabbage in quarters or thinly sliced, cover, and steam over low heat until tender. Shake the pan or stir every once in a while. Steaming cabbage preserves the texture and more of the vitamins than boiling does.

A little vinegar, red wine, or lemon juice added to the water for steaming red cabbage will set its bright color.

▲ **Braising:** Melt butter or bacon fat (about 6 tablespoons for two pounds of cabbage) in a large skillet. Add finely sliced cabbage and stir to coat. Cover the pan and cook, stirring occasionally, over low heat until tender, about 10 minutes for head cabbage and 4 to 5 minutes for Chinese cabbage. Season with salt and pepper. Sprinkle thyme and lots of black pepper over head cabbage and soy sauce over Chinese cabbage.

For a lighter braising, substitute a cup of chicken broth for the butter. The cabbage can also be braised in a covered baking dish in a 350°F oven; it will cook in 20 to 30 minutes.

▲ **Stir-frying:** Don't stir-fry head cabbage, just Chinese cabbage and bok choy. Trim the leaves from the stalks; cut the stalks into bite-size pieces and the leaves into 2-inch strips. Heat a tablespoon or two of peanut oil in a wok or heavy skillet over medium-high heat. Add the cabbage stalks and stir-fry until they just start to soften. Add a little liquid—broth mixed with a little soy sauce is great—and stir-fry a couple more minutes. Add the leaves and stir-fry until tender, 1 to 2 minutes. Serve hot.

SEASON TO TASTE

Enhance the flavor of cabbage with any of the following:

Basil	Ginger
Bacon	Marjoram
Black pepper	Nutmeg
Butter	Onion
Caraway seed	Sage
Cayenne	Savory
pepper	Sesame oil
Chile	Soy sauce
Dill	Vinegar
Fennel seed	Wine

STOMPING AT THE SAVOY

We love Savoy cabbage, especially for the way it turns electric green when lightly cooked. Here we've combined it with spaghetti and garnished it with crispy scallions for a lovely side dish or a luncheon entrée. Delicious served with Ruby Glazed Corned Beef or Confetti Corned Beef Hash.

½ small head Savoy cabbage
4 ounces spinach spaghetti or linguine
4 tablespoons (½ stick) unsalted butter
½ cup Berta's Chicken Stock (see Index) or canned broth
1 teaspoon salt
Freshly ground black pepper, to taste
¼ cup chopped scallions (green onions)

1. Core the cabbage and cut it into thin strips.
2. Bring a saucepan of water to a boil. Break the spaghetti into 2-inch lengths, and add it to the water. Cook until tender; then rinse under cold water and drain well.
3. Melt the butter in a large skillet over low heat, and stir in the cabbage. Cover and cook, stirring occasionally, until crisp-tender, 10 minutes.
4. Add the spaghetti and stock. Stir over low heat just until heated through, 2 minutes. Season with the salt and pepper, sprinkle with the scallions, and serve immediately.

2 to 4 portions

SWEET AND SOUR CABBAGE

Two of the best cabbage preparations cook together in this hearty winter dish. Sauerkraut, a German word, means sour "pickled" cabbage. The sweetness comes from the sauce of tomatoes, golden raisins, brown sugar, and ginger that surrounds the pork and beef inside the cabbage leaves.

1 head green cabbage (2 ½ pounds)
1 pound ground beef
8 ounces ground pork
¾ cup cooked white rice
⅓ cup sliced scallions
1 teaspoon salt
1 teaspoon caraway seeds
½ teaspoon dried thyme leaves
Freshly ground black pepper, to taste
1 can (15 to 16 ounces) stewed tomatoes
1 cup water
½ cup New Basic Tomato Sauce (see Index)
½ cup golden raisins
¼ cup (packed) dark brown sugar
1 tablespoon fresh lemon juice
1 teaspoon ground ginger
1 ½ cups prepared sauerkraut, rinsed and drained

1. Core the cabbage and cut it into thin strips.
2. Bring a large saucepan of water to a boil, and cook 8 large cabbage leaves (in batches if necessary) for 5 minutes. Transfer the leaves to a bowl of cold water to cool them, and then drain and set aside.
3. Combine the beef, pork, cooked rice, scallions, salt, caraway seeds, thyme, and pepper in a large bowl. Toss until thoroughly blended.
4. In another bowl, stir together the tomatoes, water, tomato sauce, raisins, brown sugar, lemon juice, and ginger.
5. Place 1 of the cooked cabbage leaves on a work surface. Spoon about ½ cup of the meat filling into the center. Fold up the bottom of the leaf to cover the mixture; then fold in the sides, and roll the filled part over onto the top. Repeat with the remaining leaves and filling.

6. Spoon 1 cup of the sauerkraut into a flame-proof casserole or dutch oven. Arrange a layer of cabbage rolls on top, seam side down, and then add the remaining sauerkraut. Top with the remaining rolls. (Or arrange the rolls in one layer if you are using a large casserole.) Pour the tomato mixture over the cabbage, and cover the casserole. Bring it just to a boil.

7. Transfer the casserole to the oven, and bake for 2 hours.

6 to 8 portions

> "**I**t's no use boiling your cabbage twice."
>
> —IRISH PROVERB

BOK CHOY STIR-FRY

Increasingly available in vegetable markets, bok choy (Chinese cabbage) is an excellent accompaniment to seafood and poultry.

1 head bok choy
1 tablespoon vegetable oil
1 clove garlic, minced
1 teaspoon minced fresh ginger
2 teaspoons soy sauce
1 teaspoon sesame oil
1 tablespoon sesame seeds, toasted (see Index)

1. Rinse and drain the bok choy, and pat it dry. Cut the leaves crosswise into ½-inch slices, and set aside. (Reserve the stems for another use.)

2. Heat the oil in a large skillet or wok over high heat until it ripples. Add the garlic and ginger. Cook 1 minute, stirring.

3. Add the bok choy and stir-fry until wilted and dark green, 2 minutes.

4. Stir in the soy sauce and sesame oil. Cook 1 minute. Sprinkle with the sesame seeds and serve immediately.

4 portions

RED CABBAGE BRAISED WITH VINEGAR AND BACON

Red cabbage is a good choice for braising. Slow cooking tones down its pungent, peppery qualities and softens its tough leaves.

1 pound bacon, cut into 1-inch pieces
2 cups chopped onions
1 head red cabbage (about 3 pounds), cored and finely slivered
3 Granny Smith or other tart apples, cored and cut into 1-inch cubes
1 cup golden raisins
¾ cup dry red wine
¾ cup red wine vinegar
3 tablespoons (packed) dark brown sugar
2 teaspoons caraway seeds
1 teaspoon dried thyme leaves
½ teaspoon freshly ground black pepper
½ teaspoon salt

1. Cook the bacon in a large deep skillet or dutch oven over low heat for 15 minutes.

2. Add the onions and cook until wilted, 10 minutes. Add the remaining ingredients and toss well.

3. Cover the skillet, and cook over medium heat for 1¼ hours, stirring occasionally. If necessary, add a bit more liquid. Adjust the seasonings and serve hot.

8 portions

CARDOONS

Like the artichoke, the cardoon is a thistle. But unlike the artichoke, the silvery stalk is eaten instead of the flower. Cardoons look like flattened celery and have a similar delicate although bittersweet taste.

You will most likely find cardoons in Italian markets from winter through early spring, although they have been showing up in some big-city supermarkets as well. Buy small stalks if you can; they'll be the most tender. If only large stalks are available, peel away the outer ribs and go for the smaller ones at the center. If the cardoon is not bitter, cut it into strips and eat it raw as the Italians do—dipped in a fruity olive oil. But most cardoons here are not as fresh and tender as the ones in Italy and they need to be boiled in water to cover until tender. Peel the tough strings from the outside as you would celery and cut it into 3- to 4-inch lengths first.

To store a cardoon, swaddle the base in a damp paper towel and wrap in a plastic bag. Refrigerate up to two weeks.

CARDOONS A LA GRECQUE

Cooking them in milk allows these delicious cardoons to retain their pale green color. Serve this at room temperature, but be sure to prepare it well ahead so that the flavors have time to richen.

1 bunch cardoons
6 cups water
2 cups milk
1 teaspoon salt
1 teaspoon sugar

DRESSING
½ cup walnut oil
½ cup fresh orange juice
2 tablespoons chopped fresh dill
1 tablespoon slivered orange zest
¾ teaspoon salt
Freshly ground black pepper, to taste

1. Trim the cardoons as you would celery. Scrape the ribbed side of each stalk with a sharp knife to remove strings and any brown skin. Cut them into ¼-inch-thick slices, dropping the slices in a bowl of cold water.

2. Combine the water, milk, salt, and sugar in a large saucepan and bring to a simmer. Add the sliced cardoons, and simmer for 15 minutes. Rinse under cold water and drain.

3. Stir the dressing ingredients together in a large bowl.

4. Toss the cardoons with the dressing. Let the mixture stand for several hours, loosely covered, at room temperature, stirring occasionally.

5. Serve as a side dish or appetizer, scooping up the cardoons with a slotted spoon.

4 portions

CRUNCHY CARROTS

Carrots have definitely recaptured our fancy. Available year round and far more common in the American diet than most other vegetables, for a long time we seemed to take them for granted. Then they were released from their plastic bags and began appearing in local markets with their lovely ferny green tops intact. Irresistible! Crispy fresh and chilled, they make for sweet crunchy snacking. They add sparkle and color to the dinner table and lend their intriguing flavor to salads, soups, stews, soufflés, and purées.

BUYING

Buy carrots that are smooth, firm, and nicely shaped. Choose small carrots—they'll be more tender and sweet. Don't buy carrots that are cracked, shriveled, or flabby. And if you have a choice, buy them with their green tops on; they'll be fresher than those packed in plastic bags.

STORING

Cut off the green tops if they're attached and refrigerate the carrots in a plastic bag in the crisper drawer. They should keep for a couple of weeks.

YIELD

A pound of carrots— 6 to 7 medium carrots or 12 to 13 small—will serve four people. Two medium carrots, shredded or sliced, equals 1 cup.

PREPARING

Scrub small carrots under cold running water and peel larger carrots with a vegetable peeler. Very large carrots will be less bitter and more tender if you take the core out: Trim the carrots, cut lengthwise in half, and cut out the core, starting at the large end.

Depending on how you are going to use them, carrots can be cooked whole or diced, quartered lengthwise for sticks, sliced crosswise into coins or diagonally for stir-fries, or julienned.

COOKING

Carrots should be cooked until just tender. You don't want them raw and you don't want them soft. To check, poke them with a sharp paring knife. It shouldn't slide right through the carrot; a little resistance is precisely what you want.

▲ **Boiling:** Pour enough water in a pot to cover the carrots and heat to boiling. Add the carrots, trimmed and whole, diced, sliced, or julienned, cover, and gently boil until tender. Thick slices will take 10 to 12 minutes, whole carrots a few minutes longer. Drain and toss with butter and chopped fresh herbs, such as dill, parsley, or mint.

Carrots can be cooked until nearly tender hours before serving and quickly reheated in butter or broth in a skillet at the last moment.

▲ **Steaming:** Steam carrots, covered, over 1 inch of boiling water until tender. Whole medium carrots will take 12 to 15 minutes, slices about 5 minutes.

▲ **Sautéing:** This method is ideal for thinly sliced or julienned carrots. Melt about ¼ cup butter per pound of carrots in a wide skillet. Add carrots and cook, stirring occasionally, over very low heat until tender.

▲ **Braising:** Melt about ¼ cup butter per pound of carrots in a skillet, add a couple tablespoons of water, fruit juice, or chicken broth, and then stir in the carrots. Cover the pan and cook over very low heat until tender. Unlike sautéing, braising will work as well with whole carrots as with thin slices. Make sure that the liquid doesn't evaporate, and that you stir occasionally.

▲ **Baking:** This method takes time but it's handy if the oven is already on. Put the carrots in a baking dish, sprinkle with a tablespoon of water or other cooking liquid, and dot with butter. Cover the dish and bake at 350° to 400°F until tender, 30 to 45 minutes.

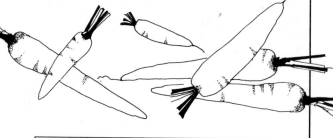

SEASON TO TASTE

♥

Carrots can carry an array of additional flavorings and not lose their individuality. Some of our favorites include:

Allspice	Dill
Anise	Ginger
Basil	Marjoram
Brown sugar	Mint
Caraway seed	Orange
Cardamom	Parsley
Chervil	Sage
Cinnamon	Savory
Clove	Maple syrup
Cumin	Tarragon
Curry powder	Thyme

PENNIES FROM HEAVEN

Sugar-glazed carrots sparkle like shiny new pennies and seem to be good luck with pork and game.

5 carrots, peeled and sliced ¼ inch thick
2 teaspoons sugar
½ teaspoon ground cinnamon
4 tablespoons (½ stick) unsalted butter
2 tablespoons fresh orange juice
Salt and freshly ground black pepper, to taste
10 dried pitted apricots, slivered
⅓ cup sliced almonds, toasted (see Index)

1. Place the carrots in a saucepan, cover with cold water, and bring to a boil. Reduce the heat and simmer for 10 minutes. Then rinse under cold water and drain.

2. Stir the sugar and cinnamon together until well mixed. Set aside.

3. Melt the butter in a skillet. Stir in the cooked carrots and the orange juice. Sprinkle with the sugar-cinnamon mixture, and cook over medium heat until the carrots are glazed and the sauce is slightly thickened, 5 minutes. Season with a pinch of salt and pepper.

4. Stir in the apricots and almonds, and cook just until heated through, 3 minutes. Serve immediately.

4 to 6 portions

CARROT PUREE

The simplicity of this preparation belies the depth of flavor that develops when sweet carrots are combined with orange juice, cardamom, and butter. A bit of cayenne provides just the right bite.

4 pounds carrots, peeled and cut into 1-inch rounds
8 tablespoons (1 stick) unsalted butter
1 ½ cups Berta's Chicken Stock (see Index) or canned broth, warmed
½ cup fresh orange juice
2 ½ teaspoons ground cardamom
1 ½ teaspoon salt
¼ teaspoon cayenne pepper

1. Place the carrots in a large saucepan, cover with water, and bring to a boil. Reduce the heat, cover, and simmer until the carrots are very tender, 30 minutes.

2. Drain the carrots and place them in a large mixing bowl. Add the remaining ingredients and stir well.

3. Transfer the mixture to a food processor in small batches, and purée until smooth.

4. Return the purée to a saucepan and cook over low heat, stirring, until heated through, 3 minutes. (Or transfer it to a baking dish, cover with aluminum foil, and bake in a preheated 350°F oven until steaming hot, 25 minutes.)

8 portions

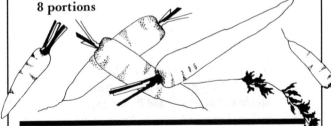

CARROT AND SQUASH PUREE

Yellow squash lighten this carrot purée in texture and flavor. Ginger and chives add the pizzazz!

2 cups water
2 homemade chicken bouillon cubes (see Index)
10 carrots, peeled and cut into ½-inch-thick slices
8 tablespoons (1 stick) unsalted butter
1 large onion, chopped
3 yellow summer squash, cut into ½-inch-thick slices
1 teaspoon dried thyme leaves
1 teaspoon ground ginger
1 teaspoon ground coriander
Salt, to taste
¼ cup snipped fresh chives

1. Bring the water to a boil in a large saucepan. Add the bouillon cubes, and stir until they have dissolved. Then add the carrots and additional water to cover. Bring to a boil again, reduce the heat, and cover. Simmer for 25 minutes. Drain the carrots, reserving the cooking liquid.

2. Melt the butter in a large saucepan. Add the onion and squash, and cook over medium-low heat until the onions have wilted and the squash skin is soft, about 15 minutes.

3. Add the cooked carrots, thyme, ginger, coriander, and salt. Mix well, and cook 5 minutes.

4. Transfer the mixture to a food processor, and purée. If it is too thick, add a little of the reserved carrot cooking liquid.

5. Transfer the purée to a warmed serving bowl, adjust the seasonings if necessary, and fold in the chives. Serve immediately.

6 portions

Note: To reheat, place the purée in an ovenproof serving dish. Cover with aluminum foil and bake in a preheated 350°F oven for 15 to 20 minutes.

> One 5½-inch carrot has 6,000 units of vitamin A. Only liver has more. Carrots also have vitamins B₁ and B₂, are high in carbohydrates and fiber, and have no fat. One crunchy carrot has only about 20 crunchy calories.

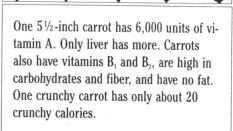

VEGETABLE BUNDLES

Julienned sweet carrots, nutty parsnips, and mildly oniony leeks all tied with a scallion and a sprig of dill. These look like presents on a plate, and are certainly not quiet vegetables.

3 carrots, peeled
2 parsnips, peeled
1 leek, well rinsed
2 scallions (green onions), just 4 inches green
4 tablespoons (½ stick) unsalted butter
1 shallot, peeled and minced
½ teaspoon dried tarragon
1 teaspoon chopped fresh dill
Freshly ground black pepper, to taste
4 sprigs dill, for garnish

1. Trim the carrots, parsnips, and leek to 5-inch lengths. Slice them into long julienne strips.

2. Fill a large saucepan with water and bring to a boil. Place the carrots in a metal basket or strainer, submerge them in the water, and cook for 20 seconds. Rinse under cold water and set aside to drain. Repeat with the parsnips, cooking them for 30 to 40 seconds; with the leeks, cooking them for 5 seconds; and with the scallion greens, cooking them for 45 seconds. (If you don't have a metal basket, remove each vegetable with a slotted spoon, then rinse, and drain.)

3. Evenly divide the carrots into four bundles, then add the parsnips and leeks to each bundle. Separate the scallion greens into four long strips, and use them to tie each bundle around the center, forming a knot. Set the bundles aside.

4. Melt the butter in a skillet. Add the shallot, tarragon, chopped dill, and pepper. Cook over medium heat for 1 minute. Then add the vegetable bundles, cover the skillet, and cook for 2 minutes.

5. Transfer the bundles to a warmed serving dish, and insert a sprig of dill behind each scallion knot. Spoon the herb butter over the bundles, and serve immediately.

4 portions

HEAD OF THE CLASS CAULIFLOWER

Slightly sweet and slightly nutty, snowy white cauliflower is a cabbage with a flower-like appearance. Although you can find it in the market in any season, it thrives in the cool temperatures from late fall to early spring.

We serve it year round in creamy purées, cut into florets and sautéed with plenty of fresh pepper ground over the top, or baked whole for an elegant presentation. And of course, the florets make wonderful crisp crudités, either raw or blanched for two minutes.

BUYING

Look for white or cream-colored heads that are heavy for their size with tightly packed florets. Old heads are crumbly and edged with brown.

Sometimes you can find Italian purple cauliflower at the market. Buy it for a change of pace. It, too, should be heavy with a fresh smell.

STORING

Refrigerate the whole head unwashed in a plastic bag. It should keep up to four days.

YIELD

A medium head of cauliflower will weigh about three pounds before trimming and when cooked will serve four people generously.

PREPARING

Turn the cauliflower stem side up and cut out the core with a small, sharp knife. Cut at an angle so that the core comes out in a cone and the head remains together. The dark green leaves will come off with the core. Any light green leaves still attached can stay since they are edible. To rid the cauliflower of unwanted bugs, soak it in cold salted water at least 10 minutes before cooking or serving raw. If it is to be cooked, cauliflower can be left whole or separated into florets.

COOKING

▲ **Boiling:** Cook the whole head, either stem side down or cut into florets, in at least 3 quarts water. Gently boil, covered or uncovered, until crisp-tender, 20 to 30 minutes for whole heads or 5 to 10 minutes for florets. For very white cauliflower, add a cup of milk or the juice of half a lemon to the cooking water.

▲ **Steaming:** Place the whole cauliflower head or florets in a steaming rack or basket over 1 inch of boiling water. Cover and steam until crisp-tender, at least 20 minutes for whole heads and 5 minutes for florets. Toss or coat boiled or steamed cauliflower with butter, salt, and pepper. Add Parmesan or herbs if you like.

▲ **Sautéing:** Boil or steam small cauliflower florets until barely tender, 2 to 3 minutes. Drain well and sauté in olive oil in a skillet over medium heat until crisp-tender. Sprinkle with chopped parsley.

▲ **Braising:** Boil or steam the whole head or the florets until barely tender. Put the cooked cauliflower in a buttered baking dish, dot with butter, and add enough water or broth to just cover the bottom of the dish. Sprinkle with cheese if you wish or combine the florets with a cheese or cream sauce. Cover tightly and bake at 350°F until tender, about 10 minutes for florets.

The whole head can also be braised without precooking. Drizzle with broth, olive oil, or butter. Cover the dish tightly, and bake at 350°F until tender, about 1¼ hours.

▲ **Deep-frying:** Boil or steam cauliflower florets until barely tender and drain well. Coat lightly with flour, then dip in fritter batter. Deep-fry in 375°F oil until golden brown.

Cauliflower is high on the list of anti-cancer vegetables—those cruciferous vegetables including cabbage, broccoli, and Brussels sprouts associated with lower cancer rates in those who eat them regularly. In addition, cauliflower is high in vitamin C, folic acid (a B vitamin), fiber, and carbohydrates.

SEASON TO TASTE

Here are some of our favorite seasonings for cauliflower:

Basil	Garlic
Black pepper	Gruyère cheese
Caper	Lemon
Caraway seed	Marjoram
Cheddar cheese	Mustard
Chervil	Nutmeg
Chile	Parmesan
Chive	cheese
Cumin	Parsley
Curry powder	Savory
Dill	

CAULIFLOWER ARUGULA PUREE

Just the right heady taste to serve with a rare shell steak. Lemon juice and arugula brighten the flavors of this wintery purée.

1 head cauliflower (about 3 pounds), trimmed and cut into florets
1 potato, peeled and cubed
1 bunch arugula (see Step 2)
2 tablespoons unsalted butter, at room temperature
1 teaspoon fresh lemon juice
1 teaspoon salt
Freshly ground black pepper, to taste

1. Bring a large pot of water to a boil, and add the cauliflower and potato. Cook until tender, 10 to 12 minutes. Drain, and set aside.

2. Bring another saucepan of water to a boil.

Trim the arugula, discarding the tough stems (you should have 2 cups leaves), and rinse it well. Cook until tender, 2 minutes. Then drain it thoroughly and chop coarsely.

3. Combine the cauliflower, potato, and arugula in a food processor, and purée. Add the butter, lemon juice, salt, and pepper, and process another 15 seconds.

4. Transfer the purée to the top of a double boiler and stir over simmering water until heated through, 10 minutes. Serve immediately.

4 portions

Note: You can also reheat the purée by placing it in an ovenproof casserole and baking it at 350°F until heated through, about 15 minutes.

BAKED CAULIFLOWER

A head of cauliflower, so like a snowy white bouquet, makes quite a dramatic presentation when served whole.

4 tablespoons (½ stick) unsalted butter, at room temperature
1 tablespoon chopped fresh dill
1 teaspoon grated lemon zest
1 clove garlic, minced
½ teaspoon ground cumin
¼ teaspoon salt
Freshly ground black pepper, to taste
1 head cauliflower (about 3 pounds)

1. Preheat the oven to 350°F.

2. In a small bowl, stir together the butter, dill, lemon zest, garlic, cumin, salt, and pepper. Blend well and set aside.

3. Trim all the leaves off the cauliflower, and cut the stem flush with the bottom of the head so it will sit steadily.

4. Spread the butter mixture evenly over the top and sides of the cauliflower. Place it in an ovenproof casserole just large enough to hold it, and cover the casserole tightly with aluminum foil.

5. Bake until fork-tender, 1¼ hours. Then transfer the cauliflower to a heated platter, spoon any pan juices over it, and bring it to the table whole for a dramatic presentation.

4 to 6 portions

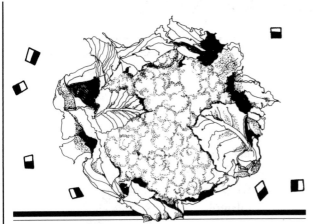

CAULIFLOWER AU GRATIN

A great alternative to potatoes, bubbling hot cauliflower is spiked with chèvre and crème fraîche. When served with Braised Lamb Shanks, the meaning of comfort foods is well understood.

1 head cauliflower (about 3 pounds), trimmed and cut into
    florets
2 tablespoons unsalted butter
2 tablespoons unbleached all-purpose flour
1 cup milk
1 cup crème fraîche (see Index)
2 ounces chèvre, crumbled (⅓ to ½ cup)
¼ cup snipped fresh chives
Pinch of salt
Pinch of cayenne pepper
Freshly ground black pepper, to taste

1. Preheat the oven to 350°F. Lightly butter a 12-inch gratin or shallow baking dish.

2. Bring a large pot of water to a boil, and add the cauliflower. Simmer until fork-tender, 10 minutes. Drain, and set aside.

3. Melt the butter in a small saucepan, and whisk in the flour. Stir until it forms a paste. Then gradually add the milk, stirring until smooth. Cook over low heat, stirring, until thick. Stir in the remaining ingredients and remove from the heat.

4. Arrange the cauliflower in the prepared dish, and pour the sauce over it. Bake until bubbling and golden, 40 minutes.

6 portions

CAULIFLOWER POLONAISE

A polonaise is a classic "Polish-style" garnish consisting of toasted bread crumbs, chopped parsley, and sieved hard-cooked egg.

4 tablespoons (½ stick) unsalted butter
5 tablespoons fresh bread crumbs
1 hard-cooked egg
2 tablespoons minced fresh parsley
1 head cauliflower (about 3 pounds), trimmed and cut into
    florets
Salt, to taste
Grated dry Monterey Jack or Parmesan cheese, to taste
Freshly ground black pepper, to taste

1. Melt 2 tablespoons of the butter in a small skillet, and add the bread crumbs. Cook over medium heat until lightly browned, 5 minutes. Set aside.

2. Press the hard-cooked egg through a sieve, or whirl it in a food processor until very finely minced.

3. Combine the crumbs, egg, and parsley in a small bowl, and mix well. Set it aside.

4. Bring a large pot of water to a boil, and add the cauliflower. Simmer until just tender, 6 to 8 minutes. Drain thoroughly and pat dry.

5. Melt the remaining 2 tablespoons butter in a large skillet, and lightly sauté the cauliflower until heated through, 3 to 4 minutes. Season with salt, and sprinkle with the reserved garnish. Toss to coat well.

6. Serve the cauliflower immediately, with a generous sprinkling of cheese and pepper.

4 to 6 portions

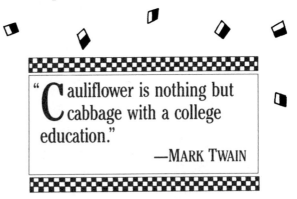

"Cauliflower is nothing but cabbage with a college education."
—MARK TWAIN

FRESH CELERY

Celery—some people love it; others, well . . . others just don't. We think it is indispensable for making savory soups and broths, crunchy salads, and flavorful stuffings. Pascal celery—the most common variety in markets through the year—is the crispest, strongest tasting, and greenest of all the celeries. Buy stalks that are firm, unwilted, and unblemished. The leaves should be fresh and green, not yellow or droopy.

Celery should keep refrigerated in a plastic bag seven to ten days. It must be rinsed well before using; the bottom is usually full of the black muck in which it grows. To crisp celery, trim the ribs and soak them in very cold water. If the ribs are tough, break off a small piece at the top without breaking through the strings, then tear the strings away by pulling the piece toward the bottom.

Celery is often eaten raw, but it can be boiled or braised as well.

SEASON TO TASTE

Match up any of these with celery for flavorful results.

Basil	Dill
Beef stock	Italian parsley
Black pepper	Nutmeg
Cardamom	Rosemary
Cilantro	Sesame oil
Coarse salt	Tarragon
Coriander	Thyme

BRAISED CELERY WITH DILL

A simple but tasty vegetable that deserves to stand on its own once in a while. Free it from tuna and chicken salad, and enjoy the results.

2 bunches celery (about 1 ½ pounds)
2 tablespoons unsalted butter
¾ cup homemade beef stock (see Index) or canned broth
2 tablespoons chopped fresh dill
Freshly ground black pepper, to taste

1. Trim the tops off the celery and cut the bunches into 4- to 5-inch lengths. Rinse well and pat dry.

2. Melt the butter in a deep skillet, and sauté the celery for 5 minutes.

3. Add the stock, 1 tablespoon of the dill, and the pepper. Cover, and cook over low heat until the celery is tender, 12 to 15 minutes. Garnish with the remaining 1 tablespoon dill, and serve.

4 portions

CELERY ROOT OR CELERIAC

Celery root is grown for the root and not the stalks. Even among the other root vegetables, its brown and knobby appearance wins no beauty contest. The taste is that of celery, only more pronounced, and the texture is firm and dense like that of a turnip. Europeans love this root; we in the United States are just starting to appreciate it. If you do find it at the market, buy the smallest ones, for the larger roots will be woody and tough.

Celery root can be peeled, julienned, blanched and combined with a tart dressing for a salad. It's also good boiled or braised and combines well with other vegetables, especially potatoes.

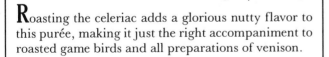

BAKED PUREE OF CELERIAC

Roasting the celeriac adds a glorious nutty flavor to this purée, making it just the right accompaniment to roasted game birds and all preparations of venison.

6 tablespoons fresh lemon juice
6 tablespoons water
4 large half-ripe pears
2 to 2 ¼ pounds celeriac (celery root), peeled and coarsely chopped
½ cup Berta's Chicken Stock (see Index) or canned broth
2 tablespoons sugar
1 teaspoon ground cardamom
Freshly ground black pepper, to taste
4 tablespoons (½ stick) unsalted butter
2 teaspoons chopped fresh Italian (flat-leaf) parsley

1. Preheat the oven to 375°F.

2. Mix the lemon juice and water together in a medium-size bowl.

3. Peel, core, and cut the pears into eighths. Place them in the acidulated water, add the celeriac, and toss well.

4. Drain the pears and celeriac, reserving the water, and transfer them to a shallow baking dish. Add the chicken stock and ¼ cup of the reserved lemon water.

5. Sprinkle with the sugar, cardamom, and pepper, and mix well.

6. Dot the mixture with the butter, cover, and bake for 1 ½ hours. Stir twice while baking.

7. Place the cooked pears and celeriac in a food processor, and add any pan juices. Purée until smooth. (If the mixture is too stiff, add a bit more stock.) Serve warm garnished with the parsley.

6 portions

SWEET CORN

Fresh sweet corn is one of the season's rewards and reason enough to weed the garden or watch the farmer's market closely. Once picked, corn is best boiled or roasted as soon as possible, for the moment the cob is snapped from its stalk, the sugar begins to turn to starch. Purists say to put the pot of water on to boil before you pick the corn.

Corn is the all-American vegetable and we say when it's available fresh, it's worth a daily trip to the market.

BUYING

Buy sweet corn in the summer, after the Fourth of July in most parts, when you know it's local and fresh. Most off-season corn travels too far a distance to be fresh; canned and frozen corn kernels are a better bet.

Fresh corn will have husks that are grass green, tightly wrapped, and even slightly damp. The silks at the top may be dry, but they shouldn't be brittle or rotting. Check the stem; if it's moist and not chalky or yellowed, the ear is fresh. Still not sure? Check the kernels at the top—they should be plump, even, and snug on the cob. Prick a kernel with your fingernail. If the juice looks like milk, the corn is new and sweet; if there's no juice, the corn is past its prime; and if the juice is clear, the corn is immature.

STORING

Keep the corn unshucked in plastic bags in the refrigerator. Eat it within a day.

YIELD

Plan on buying one or two ears per person. Two to three ears make a pound. Kernels cut from one medium-size ear of corn equal a scant ½ cup.

PREPARING

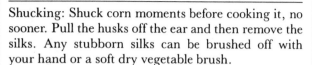

Shucking: Shuck corn moments before cooking it, no sooner. Pull the husks off the ear and then remove the silks. Any stubborn silks can be brushed off with your hand or a soft dry vegetable brush.

To cook corn in the husk, you still must remove the silk. Pull the husks down one by one until the corn is exposed, then pull off the silks. Carefully rewrap the corn in its husk and tie it at the top with kitchen string.

Cutting kernels: Shuck the corn and stand it on its stem on a cutting board or in a wide bowl. Using a sharp knife, cut off the kernels from top to the bottom, three or four rows at a time.

For creamed corn, slice each row of kernels in half, then scrape them off the cob with the back of a knife. If you like your corn off the cob or want to freeze a crop's worth of kernels, there are some very nifty corn-kernel cutters on the market.

COOKING

We think fresh sweet corn is best eaten on the cob, and when it's in season we do indulge frequently.

A note for all methods of cooking corn: Don't salt it until you are ready to serve it, for salt toughens the kernels.

▲ **Boiling:** Corn for boiling must be husked and all silks removed, but don't do that until you're ready to drop it in the water. If you are cooking more than one ear per person, cook up the first batch and remove it from the water, then add the second batch. Corn on the cob should be piping hot and freshly boiled. There are two methods for boiling corn. The first

is to heat a large pot of water (enough to cover the corn) to boiling, drop in the shucked corn, and boil 3 to 5 minutes. Some people add a pinch of sugar or a splash of milk to the water to bring up the sweetness, but that's unnecessary for truly fresh corn.

The second method is to put the shucked ears in a deep skillet and add enough cold water to cover the corn. Heat over high heat to a full rolling boil, then remove the corn and serve.

▲ **Roasting:** This is a delicious way to serve corn and especially handy if you already have the grill going. Remove the silks from the corn (see Preparing), replace the husks, and tie each one at the top. Soak the corn in cold water at least 10 minutes so that the husks don't burn up. Roast over hot coals, turning frequently to brown all sides. Small ears may be done in 15 minutes, larger ears in up to 30 minutes.

Corn can also be grilled shucked and wrapped in aluminum foil. It will steam in the foil and won't have that grilled flavor, but it can be spread with herb butter before it's wrapped. Turn the cobs several times. If the grill isn't going, the foil-wrapped corn can be baked at 425°F. It will cook in the same amount of time as corn on the grill.

▲ **Steaming:** Most people prefer to boil corn than steam it—it's quicker and easier and there's no difference in taste. Nonetheless, to steam corn, shuck and clean the ears and arrange them in a single layer on a steaming rack. Steam over 1 inch of boiling water until tender, 5 to 6 minutes.

▲ **Sautéing:** Shuck the corn and cut the kernels from the cobs. In a skillet over medium heat, melt 1 tablespoon of butter for every ear of corn. Add the kernels and cook, stirring frequently, until tender and cooked through, about 3 minutes. If you want, add a splash of cream at the last minute. Season generously with pepper and serve hot. Sautéed corn is good, but it's even better when we mix in other quick-cooking fresh vegetables. Diced red and green peppers make a beautiful dish.

Sweet corn is a high-carbohydrate, high-starch food. It is a good source of vitamins A, B, and C, and potassium. It has hardly any fat until you butter it and just a moderate amount of protein.

SEASON TO TASTE

Just in case butter, salt, and pepper aren't enough, here are a few other favorites to try on corn.

Basil	Lime
Chervil	Mint
Chile	Nutmeg
Chive	Oregano
Cilantro	Parsley
Cumin	Saffron
Curry powder	Sage
Lemon balm	Thyme

THE SWEETEST CORN ON THE COB

Everyone knows you should get the corn from the field to the pot as quickly as possible, for every moment it's off the stalk the sugars turn to starch. Some say to start the water boiling before you go and pick the corn. We've found that corn on the cob stays sweet and flavorful when we take a lesson from our own grilling method and leave it in its husk. So clean out the silk and retie the husks with kitchen string. Your guests will be surprised at the taste—so figure on them coming back for seconds, at least!

12 ears fresh sweet corn
Sugar (optional; see Step 2)
Jalapeño Lime Butter (recipe follows)

1. Break off the stems of the corn and peel back the husks, being careful not to pull them off. Remove the silk. Then rewrap the corn in the husks and tie with kitchen string.

2. While you are doing that, bring a large kettle of water to a boil. Add 1 teaspoon sugar for each quart of water.

3. Gently lower the corn—in batches if necessary—into the boiling water, and cook 3 to 5 minutes. Drain, and serve immediately with Jalapeño Lime Butter. Your guests can untie and unwrap the ears at the table.

6 portions

JALAPENO LIME BUTTER

Hot jalapeño peppers cooled down with fresh lime give this butter an extra sparkle.

1 small fresh jalapeño pepper
1 clove garlic
1 cup (2 sticks) unsalted butter, at room temperature
Grated zest of 2 limes
¼ teaspoon paprika

1. Cut the jalapeño in half, and carefully remove and discard the seeds.

2. Combine the pepper and garlic in a food processor, and process until finely minced. Add the remaining ingredients, and process until well blended.

3. Transfer the butter to a piece of plastic wrap and shape it into a small sausage. Wrap tightly, and refrigerate until firm. To serve, unwrap and cut into ⅛-inch-thick rounds.

1¼ cups

Note: This butter can be frozen in its sausage shape. It's also great on broiled fish.

JUNE'S SCALLOPED CORN

One of Julee's cravings, this corn dish—not quite a pudding, not quite a soufflé—is light and wonderful.

1 can (16 to 17 ounces) cream-style corn
1 cup milk
3 eggs, separated
3 tablespoons unsalted butter, melted
2 tablespoons sugar
1 tablespoon cornstarch
½ teaspoon salt
Freshly ground black pepper, to taste

1. Preheat the oven to 325°F. Butter a 2½-quart ovenproof casserole.

2. In a large bowl, stir together the corn, milk, egg yolks, butter, sugar, cornstarch, salt, and pepper.

3. Beat the egg whites in another bowl until stiff but not dry. Fold them into the corn mixture, and pour it into the prepared casserole.

4. Bake until golden, 45 minutes. (The mixture will be moist.) Serve immediately.

6 portions

BLUE CORN

Blue was the native American corn of the Southwest American Indians. Blue corn is still the corn of choice in the Southwest and it's making its way across the country in blue tortillas, blue chips, and ground blue meal for muffins, pancakes, and waffles.

For blue cornmeal, write to Casados Farm, P.O. Box 852, San Juan Pueblo, NM 87566; or Blue Corn Converter, 3825 Academy Parkway NE, Albuquerque, NM 87109.

CORN PUDDING

Vegetable puddings are like custards—they are bound with cream and eggs. They're good accompaniments for main courses that are not too rich.

For this one, find the freshest, sweetest corn and add chopped red pepper, parsley, and leeks. Yum!

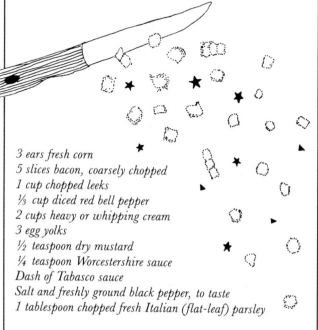

3 ears fresh corn
5 slices bacon, coarsely chopped
1 cup chopped leeks
⅓ cup diced red bell pepper
2 cups heavy or whipping cream
3 egg yolks
½ teaspoon dry mustard
¼ teaspoon Worcestershire sauce
Dash of Tabasco sauce
Salt and freshly ground black pepper, to taste
1 tablespoon chopped fresh Italian (flat-leaf) parsley

1. Fill a large pot with water and bring it to a boil. Drop the corn into the boiling water and cook for 5 minutes. Drain, and rinse the corn under cold water. When it is fully cooled, cut the kernels from the cob and set aside.

2. Preheat the oven to 350°F.

3. Sauté the bacon in a small skillet over medium heat until crisp. Remove it from the skillet and drain on paper towels. Add the leeks and red pepper to the skillet and sauté over medium heat for 5 minutes. Remove them from the skillet and set aside.

4. Combine the reserved corn with the cooked bacon, leeks, and red pepper in a bowl. Mix well, and then scatter over the bottom of a 6 x 4-inch baking dish.

5. Whisk together the cream, egg yolks, mustard, Worcestershire, Tabasco, salt and pepper, and parsley. Pour this into the baking dish and bake for 45 minutes. Serve immediately.

4 portions

> "Up from the meadows
> rich with corn.
> Clear is the cool
> September Morn."
> —JOHN GREENLEAF WHITTIER

CREAMY FRESH CORN

A classic summer favorite that matches up well to any grilled or broiled fish or chicken dishes.

1 ½ cups cooked fresh corn kernels
2 tablespoons unsalted butter
½ cup chopped onion
1 tablespoon unbleached all-purpose flour
¾ cup evaporated milk
Salt and freshly ground black pepper, to taste
¼ teaspoon paprika

1. Fill a large pot with water and bring it to a boil. Drop the corn into the boiling water and cook for 5 minutes. Drain, and rinse the corn under cold water. When it is fully cooled, cut the kernels from the cob and set aside.

2. Melt the butter in a saucepan. Add the onion and sauté over low heat for 5 minutes. Then add the flour, stir well, and cook another 5 minutes.

3. Raise the heat to medium, and while stirring with a wire whisk, slowly add the evaporated milk. Continue cooking and whisking until the sauce is thick, 4 to 5 minutes.

4. Stir in the corn, salt and pepper, and paprika, and cook another 3 minutes. Serve immediately.

2 or 3 portions

SWEET AND SOUR CORN RELISH

Great served alongside your favorite burgers, or with a bowl of chili and some Hot and Sassy Corn Bread.

5 ears fresh corn
1 ½ cups chopped red onions
1 cup chopped red bell pepper
3 cups white wine vinegar
½ cup sugar
1 teaspoon mustard seeds
1 teaspoon celery seeds
1 tablespoon coarse (kosher) salt
1 tablespoon coarsely ground black pepper

1. Cut the kernels off the ears of corn.

2. Combine the corn kernels with all the remaining ingredients in a large saucepan. Bring to a boil, then reduce the heat and simmer until the mixture thickens slightly, 40 minutes. Set aside to cool, then transfer the relish to storage jars and refrigerate until ready to serve, but no longer than 1 week.

6 cups

CORN FRITTERS

The coarse cornmeal gives these little corn cakes a delightful crunch. Serve in a basket lined with a bright linen napkin.

1 cup water
1 teaspoon sugar
½ teaspoon salt
½ teaspoon ground cumin
⅛ teaspoon cayenne pepper
Freshly ground black pepper, to taste
8 tablespoons (1 stick) unsalted butter
¾ cup unbleached all-purpose flour
¼ cup coarse yellow cornmeal
1 cup fresh corn kernels
3 large eggs
Vegetable oil for deep-frying

1. Combine the water, sugar, spices, and butter in a saucepan. Heat just until the butter has melted. Stir well, and remove the pan from the heat.

2. Add the flour and cornmeal to the saucepan, all at once, and whisk until the mixture is thick and smooth. Then stir in the corn.

3. Add the eggs one at a time, using a wooden spoon to beat well after each addition. The mixture will be thick.

4. Heat 1 inch of vegetable oil in a deep skillet until it reaches about 375°F on a deep-fryer thermometer. Drop the corn mixture by the dessert spoonful into the hot oil. Fry, turning once, until puffed and golden, 2½ minutes. As the fritters are cooked, set them aside on paper towels to drain. Serve immediately.

36 fritters, 6 to 8 portions

SILKY CORN CAKES

These little pancakes are delicate, rich, and lightly sweetened with maple syrup. They are delicious on their own, with just a sprinkling of powdered sugar.

¼ cup coarse yellow cornmeal
1 cup water
3 tablespoons unsalted butter
¾ cup unbleached all-purpose flour
½ teaspoon salt
½ teaspoon baking powder
¼ teaspoon baking soda
2 eggs, lightly beaten
½ cup milk
¼ cup sour cream
2 tablespoons maple syrup
½ cup fresh corn kernels

1. Combine the cornmeal and water in a small saucepan and cook, stirring over medium heat until thick and porridge-like, about 3 minutes. Then add the butter and stir until smooth. Set the mixture aside to cool slightly.

2. Combine the flour, salt, baking powder, and baking soda in a bowl, and mix well.

3. Stir the eggs, milk, sour cream, and maple syrup into the cooled cornmeal mixture. Then gently fold in the flour mixture and the corn. Stir thoroughly.

4. Lightly grease a griddle and place it over medium heat. Drop the batter by tablespoons onto the hot griddle and cook until the edges of the pancakes are dry, the tops are bubbling, and the undersides are golden, 1 minute. Turn, and cook 1 minute on the other side. Serve immediately.

36 pancakes, 6 to 8 portions

CORN POPOVERS

If you can, wait for local fresh corn to appear in the market in summer—that's when these popovers are just the best. Serve them hot out of the oven with lots of sweet butter or with one of our tangy flavored butters.

1 cup unbleached all-purpose flour
1 tablespoon coarse yellow cornmeal
1 teaspoon sugar
½ teaspoon salt
Freshly ground black pepper, to taste
1 cup milk
3 extra-large eggs, lightly beaten
½ cup fresh corn kernels, lightly mashed with a fork
1 tablespoon snipped fresh chives
1 tablespoon butter, melted and cooled to room temperature

1. Preheat the oven to 425°F. Butter a 12-cup popover pan or muffin tin.

2. In a medium-size bowl toss together the flour, cornmeal, sugar, salt, and pepper. Stir in the remaining ingredients until almost blended (some lumps should still remain).

3. Pour ¼ cup of the batter into each cup, and bake until puffed and deep golden, 25 to 30 minutes. Serve immediately.

6 portions

CUCUMBERS ARE COOL

There's nothing quite like a crisp slice of cucumber. A salad favorite, it adds a pleasant crunch without the effort of too much chewing. Cucumbers are great in combination with onions in a sweet vinaigrette or with yogurt and chopped radishes as a cool-down to accompany a spicy curry.

Typically, Americans buy the dark green slicing cucumbers, the plump, waxed 6- to 7-inch-long ones or the longer and thinner hothouse, or English, cucumbers. The young, unwaxed Kirbys are our pickling cucumbers. They're small with pale green bumpy skin. Eaten raw, Kirbys are crisp and refreshing. Gherkin cucumbers can be as tiny as a little finger; they're most often pickled sweet or tart with onions (cornichons).

 ## BUYING

Cucumbers are available year round, but the peak season is summer. Choose smaller cucumbers with firm dark green skins. Avoid those with soft spots or those that have yellowed or shriveled skins.

 ## STORING

Because cucumbers have so much water, they do not store well. Three to five days is about it. Store in a closed plastic bag in the refrigerator.

YIELD

Two medium cucumbers weigh ¾ to 1 pound. A pound of cucumbers, peeled, seeded, and sliced, will measure 2½ to 3 cups.

 ## PREPARING

If you have garden-fresh cucumbers, there is no need to peel them, but they should be scrubbed under cold water. The peel and seeds of store-bought cucumbers are often bitter because the cucumbers are past their prime. Slicing cucumbers are also coated with an edible wax to keep them fresher longer. Whether you need to peel and seed the cucumber really depends on how fresh it is. Cut off a slice and taste it. If it seems bitter, peel and seed it. If it tastes fresh and tender, whether to peel and seed it is up to you. Peel with a paring knife or vegetable peeler. To seed a cucumber, cut it lengthwise in half and scoop out the seeds with a teaspoon.

Most often cucumbers are eaten fresh, and there is no end to how you can eat them: sliced on buttered bread; mixed with sour cream; stuffed with vegetables or fish and rice; or served as the Greeks do with feta, olives, tomatoes, and onions.

Pull fork lengthwise along skin of cucumber

slice crosswise for pattern — dark green / pale green

 ## COOKING

Cooked cucumbers are a pleasant change of pace. They are as delicate hot as they are cold, which makes them naturals for elegant fish entrées. Because they contain so much water, cucumbers cook to mush if you don't watch them carefully, and they cool off in seconds. They should never be cooked over high heat, but rather simmered or sautéed gently. Cooked cucumbers are great with cream sauce, tossed with butter and lemon juice, or covered with hollandaise sauce.

▲ **Simmering:** Peel and seed the cucumbers and cut crosswise into large slices or leave in halves. Heat enough broth (water will dilute the taste) to barely cover the cucumbers in a skillet to simmering. Add the cucumbers and gently simmer just until heated through. Drain and toss with butter.

▲ **Sautéing:** Peel and seed cucumbers, then slice thick or into quarters. Heat about ¼ cup butter for every pound of cucumbers in a skillet over medium-low heat. Add the cucumbers and cook, stirring and tossing occasionally, until cooked through, 3 to 4 minutes. Sprinkle with chopped fresh parsley or dill, a sprinkling of salt, and plenty of pepper. Serve hot.

WENDE'S DILL PICKLES

From our dear friend Wende Sasse, who brought us Wende's Bloody Mary. Her pickle recipe makes quite a few, so save some for yourself and give the rest as gifts.

½ bushel (20 pounds) Kirby (pickling) cucumbers
1½ cups pickling spices
4 large bunches fresh dill, preferably with flowering heads
2 cups grape leaves packed in brine, drained
1 large head garlic, cloves separated and peeled
1 dried chile pepper, about 3 inches long
2½ cups cider vinegar
1¾ cups coarse (kosher) salt
10 quarts cold water
10 dill sprigs with flowering heads
10 large cloves garlic

1. Arrange one third of the cucumbers, pickling spices, dill, grape leaves, and garlic cloves from the whole head in a large crock. Repeat the layers two more times and top with the chile pepper.

2. Mix together the vinegar, coarse salt, and water. Pour this brine over the layers in the crock. Wrap a plate that is almost as wide as the crock with cheesecloth, and place it directly on top of the pickles. Weight the plate down with a large can or other heavy object. Place the crock in a cool place (do not refrigerate).

3. Let the pickles ferment in the brine for 2½ to 3 weeks, checking them every few days and skimming off any foam that rises to the surface. To check for doneness, cut a pickle in half; if it is green throughout, it is ready.

4. Transfer the pickles to sterile jars, and place a sprig of fresh dill and a clove of garlic in each jar.

5. Strain the brine into a large pot, bring it to a boil, and boil for 10 minutes. Pour the hot brine over the pickles so that they are covered, seal the jars, and process in a boiling water bath for 15 minutes. Allow the jars to cool to room temperature, and then store or give away.

10 quarts

MARINATED CUCUMBERS

Cool, translucent cucumbers the way our grandmothers fixed them: thin, thin, thinly sliced with vinegar, a dash of sugar, and a handful of chopped dill. A simple and refreshing summertime salad.

1 long seedless cucumber, peeled and cut into ⅛-inch-thick slices
1 cup tarragon vinegar
1 cup water
⅓ cup chopped scallions (green onions)
2 tablespoons chopped fresh dill
1 tablespoon sugar
1 teaspoon coarse (kosher) salt
Freshly ground black pepper, to taste

Combine all the ingredients in a large bowl and mix well. Cover, and refrigerate for at least 3 hours but no more than 6. Drain before serving.

6 portions

"The destiny of nations depends on their manner of eating."

—BRILLAT-SAVARIN

EGGPLANT GOES ELEGANT

We love eggplant. Once underappreciated in America, this beautiful, versatile vegetable is finally coming into its own, helped along by our growing appreciation of the many cuisines in which eggplant is essential. As children, we thought the popular Italian eggplant Parmesan was about the only way to prepare it, but thanks to Indian, Middle Eastern, and Asian influences, among others, we now serve eggplant puréed, grilled, sautéed, and as part of one of our favorite vegetable combinations, ratatouille.

VARIETIES OF EGGPLANT

Eggplants vary in color—from deep purple to pure white—and in size—some are small and slender, others plump and egg-shaped.

▲ **Deep purple:** This is the conventional eggplant found in most markets. It's properly called Western eggplant, but some call it Italian eggplant. It can be round, but is usually egg shaped. The skin is smooth, glossy, and delicate and the flesh is fine textured and sweet if fresh. This is the eggplant for which most recipes are written.

▲ **White:** This variety is smaller and firmer than the purple eggplant, with fewer seeds and what seems to us to be a sweeter flavor. It should be peeled before cooking, for the skin tends to be thick and tough.

▲ **Violet and striated:** These small, narrow eggplants, usually called Oriental or Japanese, are smoother than the larger varieties. They have a wonderful sweet taste, fine texture, and an attractive color.

▲ **Baby eggplants:** These are smaller versions of the other eggplants, so they can be found purple, white, and striped. The small size guarantees they'll be tender and sweet.

BUYING

Choose eggplants that are firm and heavy. The skin should be tight and have a nice healthy glow; the cap and stem should be green and fresh. Gently squeeze the eggplant. If soft, it's old and will be bitter when you cook it. If hard, the eggplant is underripe. If there's some give or spring, it's perfect.

STORING

Eggplants may look sturdy but they are not. Buy them no more than four or five days before preparing them. They are best stored in a plastic bag in the refrigerator.

YIELD

A medium purple eggplant typically weighs about 1½ pounds and will yield 4 cups of small cubes. A baby eggplant weighs about ¼ pound; buy at least one per person.

PREPARING

In the old days, most recipes called for salting eggplant, then draining off the bitter juices. Salting and draining still seem necessary for quick-cooking dishes where the excess water will turn it all to mush; but in longer-cooking stews, the water evaporates and doesn't cause a problem. Salting eggplant slices before frying will cut the amount of oil needed by two thirds—that seems worth it to us. Baking or roasting the eggplant whole circumvents the problem happily.

To salt eggplant, cut it into the shape called for in the recipe—slices, cubes, or halves—and spread on paper towels. Sprinkle generously but not heavily with salt and cover with more paper towels. Let stand at least 30 minutes; then rinse, drain, and pat dry.

Whether to peel or not depends on the dish. If you want whole slices, leave the peels on so they don't fall apart. If it's a long-cooking dish or a dip or purée, peel the eggplant with a vegetable peeler or sharp paring knife.

SEASON TO TASTE

Flavor eggplant with any of the following:

Basil	Mint
Black pepper	Onion
Chile	Oregano
Cinnamon	Parsley
Coriander	Rosemary
Curry powder	Savory
Dill	Sesame oil and
Garlic	seed
Lemon	Thyme
Marjoram	Vinegar

You can also coat the eggplant before sautéing. Dip either in seasoned flour, in an egg-and-milk mixture and then in seasoned flour, or in bread crumbs. (Again, resist the urge to add more oil.) Pieces should be browned, crisp, and tender. This preparation is nice topped with tomato sauce and chopped parsley and basil.

▲ **Baking:** Eggplant can be baked whole, halved, or sliced. First prick the whole eggplant to keep it from bursting. If baking halves, crosshatch the cut sides. Salt halves or slices if desired to drain out the water, then pat dry and brush all sides with olive oil. Preheat the oven to 400°F. Bake the eggplant, whole, halved, or sliced, on a baking sheet until tender, about 15 minutes for slices (turn halfway through) or up to 1½ hours for whole eggplant.

▲ **Grilling:** This is one of our favorites—great summertime fare. Oil small eggplants (baby ones are best) and grill, turning frequently, until tender when pierced with a knife or skewer. Or cut eggplants in thick slices or halves, salt if you want, and brush with oil. Then grill, turning often, until tender and browned. Sprinkle with fresh herbs.

COOKING

▲ **Broiling:** Cut the eggplant without peeling in ½-inch-thick slices. If the eggplant is large or a bit old, salt it, let stand at least 30 minutes, and dry the slices. Brush both sides of each slice with olive oil and arrange in a single layer on a baking sheet or broiler rack. Broil about 6 inches from the heat until the tops are lightly browned, then turn and broil the second side. Season and top with a sauce or splash of balsamic vinegar.

▲ **Sautéing:** Cut the eggplant into ½-inch slices or large cubes. Salt the eggplant if desired, let it drain, and pat dry.

Pour oil about ⅛ inch deep into a skillet. For 2 pounds of eggplant, you should use ½ to ¾ cup oil— no more—but you won't need it all at once. Add a bit more oil with each new batch. Eggplant will absorb all the oil you give it, so don't give it much.

Heat the oil over medium to medium-high heat. Add as many slices or cubes as will fit without crowding, and sauté until all sides are golden. If sautéing slices, turn several times, but if sautéing cubes, stir often.

ROASTED SWEET EGGPLANT

Thin slices of eggplant roasted until they're slightly charred, then sprinkled with balsamic vinegar. Don't hesitate to try this luscious preparation.

1 large eggplant
1 teaspoon coarse (kosher) salt
¾ cup olive oil
¾ cup balsamic vinegar
1 tablespoon sugar
Salt and freshly ground black pepper, to taste
2 tablespoons chopped fresh Italian (flat-leaf) parsley

1. Cut the eggplant lengthwise into ¼-inch-thick slices. Lay the slices on paper towels, sprinkle with the coarse salt, and set aside for 1 hour.

2. Preheat the broiler.

3. Shake or wipe any excess liquid off the eggplant slices. Brush them lightly on both sides with some of the olive oil. Place the eggplant on a broiler rack or baking sheet lined with aluminum foil, and broil the eggplant as close as possible to the heat for 3 minutes on each side. Transfer to a platter.

4. Combine the vinegar and sugar in a saucepan and heat until the sugar has dissolved, about 1 minute.

5. Drizzle the eggplant with the vinegar mixture and the remaining olive oil. Sprinkle with salt and pepper. Let it sit for 1 hour. Then serve, garnished with the parsley.

4 portions

Eggplants are low in calories, high in fiber and carbohydrates, and have little protein, almost no fat, and no cholesterol.

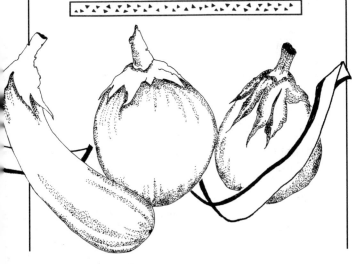

MARINATED WHITE EGGPLANT

Cook these dazzling white eggplants quickly in the microwave. Once tender, drizzle them with our garden-fresh marinade for an ideal accompaniment to grilled fish and meats.

MARINADE
¼ cup olive oil
1 tablespoon fresh lemon juice
1 ripe plum tomato, finely chopped
3 tablespoons chopped onion
2 tablespoons chopped fresh parsley
1 clove garlic, minced
Freshly ground black pepper, to taste

4 small white eggplants (about 5 ounces each)
Olive oil
Coarse (kosher) salt
Freshly ground black pepper, to taste

1. Stir the marinade ingredients together in a mixing bowl, and set aside.

2. Halve the eggplants lengthwise; rub them all over with olive oil. Arrange them, cut side up, in one layer on a microwave-safe plate. Cover with microwave-safe plastic wrap, and cook at full power (650 to 700 watts) until tender, about 7 minutes. Let stand, still covered, 5 minutes.

3. Lift the eggplant halves onto a platter, discarding any cooking liquid. Arrange them in one layer, cut side up. Sprinkle with salt and pepper, and spoon the marinade over them.

4. Let stand at least 1 hour before serving.

4 to 6 portions

Note: This recipe was cooked on High (full power, 650 to 700 watts) in a carousel microwave, using microwave-safe containers.

If your microwave is less powerful, you will have to allow for more cooking time (approximately 1½ times the amount called for—but watch carefully); if it does not have a carousel, you may have to rotate the dish while it is cooking.

ITALIAN RATATOUILLE (PEPERONATA)

New potatoes, bell peppers, red onion, basil, parsley, and oregano are added to eggplant and tomatoes for a ratatouille from the Italian Riviera.

2 small Italian eggplants (5 ounces each),
cut into 1-inch cubes
½ teaspoon salt
1 pound very small new potatoes (18 to 20)
4 tablespoons olive oil
1 green bell pepper, cored, seeded,
and cut into 1-inch squares
1 red bell pepper, cored, seeded,
and cut into 1-inch squares
1 red onion, coarsely chopped
4 cloves garlic, coarsely chopped
½ teaspoon salt
½ teaspoon freshly ground black pepper
6 ripe plum tomatoes, cubed
½ cup coarsely chopped fresh parsley
½ cup coarsely chopped fresh basil leaves
2 tablespoons fresh oregano leaves

GARNISH
2 tablespoons minced fresh basil leaves
1 tablespoon grated lemon zest
2 cloves garlic, minced

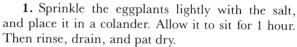

1. Sprinkle the eggplants lightly with the salt, and place it in a colander. Allow it to sit for 1 hour. Then rinse, drain, and pat dry.
2. Bring a large saucepan of water to a boil, and add the potatoes. Reduce the heat and simmer until just tender, about 25 minutes. Drain and set aside.
3. Preheat the oven to 350°F.
4. Heat 2 tablespoons of the oil in a large skillet, and add the bell peppers, red onion, and garlic. Sauté over medium-low heat for 5 minutes.
5. Remove the skillet from the heat and add the salt, pepper, tomatoes, parsley, basil, oregano, eggplants, and remaining 2 tablespoons oil. Stir well, and transfer the mixture to an ovenproof casserole. Cover, and bake 30 minutes. Stir in the reserved potatoes; and bake, uncovered, another 30 minutes, stirring once.

6. Combine the garnish ingredients in a small bowl, and stir it into the ratatouille just before serving. Serve hot or at room temperature.

8 to 10 portions

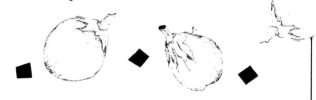

EGGPLANT GRUYERE PUREE

Sheila first had this wonderful vegetable in a farmhouse in the French countryside. The ingredients came from the larder—no special shopping necessary. It is perfect with roast leg of lamb.

2 eggplants
2 cloves garlic, slivered
2 tablespoons unsalted butter
¾ cup grated Gruyère cheese
1 egg, lightly beaten
2 tablespoons crème fraîche (see Index)
8 ounces fresh cultivated mushrooms, rinsed and thinly sliced
Salt and freshly ground black pepper, to taste

1. Preheat the oven to 375°F.
2. Cut small slits in the eggplants with the point of a sharp knife, and insert the garlic slivers in them. Wrap each eggplant well in aluminum foil, and bake for 1½ hours. Remove from the oven and allow to cool slightly. Leave the oven on.
3. Remove the foil and cut the eggplants in half lengthwise. Scoop the pulp and the garlic slivers into the bowl of a food processor. (Discard any bitter liquid that seeps out of the eggplant.) Add 1 tablespoon of the butter, cut into small pieces, and process until smooth. Transfer the purée to a bowl and fold in the cheese, egg, and crème fraîche.
4. Melt the remaining 1 tablespoon butter in a skillet. Add the mushroom slices and cook over medium heat for 5 minutes. Fold the mushrooms into the purée, and season with salt and pepper. Transfer the mixture to a 1-quart ovenproof baking dish, cover, and bake for 30 minutes. Serve immediately.

4 to 6 portions

FLAVORFUL FENNEL

We would like to see a taste for fennel develop among Americans as it has among Italians. They eat it raw and salted, much the way we eat celery, or they dip it in olive oil and season with pepper. They'll begin a meal with fennel (which they call *finocchio*) or serve it as a palate cleanser at the end. We think the taste does wonders for soups, salads, stews, and sauces.

Eat it raw, cut into wedges, shards, or sticks, and served with crumbly Parmesan cheese and chilled dry Marsala; with a mild goat cheese and olives; or with a light cream cheese and ripe figs for dessert. Fennel is the perfect accompaniment for fish, and because it's aromatic and crisp, it complements potatoes and grains extremely well.

BUYING

Buy fennel with firm stalks and bulbs. Avoid those that are cracked with brown bottoms or dried yellow tops. The short stalks look like celery growing from a white round bulb. Feathery, fern-like leaves grow from the stalks; save them for garnishing.

STORING

Store fennel in a plastic bag in the refrigerator up to five days. Fennel, like celery, will freeze and turn mushy if it gets too cold.

YIELD

For cooked or raw fennel, buy ½ to 1 bulb per serving.

PREPARING

Trim the stalks down to the bulb, trim the bottom, and peel off the wilted layer from the outside. The bulb can then be quartered or halved and sliced crosswise or into julienne strips.

COOKING

▲ **Boiling:** Boil fennel quarters, halves, or slices in just enough water or broth to cover it until crisp-tender, 7 to 10 minutes for slices. Drain, toss with lemon juice, olive oil, and fresh herbs.

▲ **Sautéing:** Quarter fennel bulbs and slice crosswise. Heat butter and/or olive oil in a skillet over medium-low heat. Add the fennel and cook, stirring occasionally, until crisp-tender, about 10 minutes. For variety, add garlic and onion to the fennel.

▲ **Braising:** Quarter or halve fennel and cut crosswise into ½-inch-thick slices. Cook in butter in a skillet about 5 minutes, then add about ½ cup broth and cover. Cook, stirring occasionally, over low heat until tender, 15 to 20 minutes. If there is still liquid in the pan, remove the cover and evaporate the liquid over medium-high heat. Try braised fennel sprinkled with Parmesan cheese.

To oven-braise fennel, cook trimmed whole bulbs in boiling water until barely tender. Let cool and quarter lengthwise. Arrange the quarters in an oiled baking dish, cover the dish, and bake at 375°F until tender, 20 to 25 minutes. If you want, sprinkle the fennel with Parmesan for the last 5 minutes of cooking time.

FRESH FENNEL CONFIT

We love this fennel confit atop pizza. If you make a larger batch, you can serve it as a vegetable to accompany roast lamb or Lemon and Ginger Pork Loin.

2 fennel bulbs
¼ cup olive oil
1 tablespoon unsalted butter
½ teaspoon coarsely ground black pepper
1 tablespoon Pernod liqueur

1. Trim the fennel bulbs, and cut them into long julienne strips (3 x ¼ inch).

2. Combine the oil and butter in a heavy saucepan over very low heat. Add the fennel and pepper, cover and cook, stirring occasionally, for 45 minutes.

3. Remove the cover, add the Pernod, and stir. Cook an additional 5 minutes.

1 cup

GREAT GARLIC

Yes, garlic really is a vegetable. It's a member of the lily family, which includes onions, shallots, leeks, and scallions—all vegetables as well. Although strongly flavored and most often used as seasonings, they all make delicious eating when cooked alone.

BUYING

Garlic heads or bulbs should be large, firm, and tight-skinned. Buy loose heads, which tend to be fresher than garlic packed in boxes. Old heads will be yellowed, soft, and sprouting.

STORING

If you store garlic in a cool, dry place, it will keep up to one month. Don't refrigerate it, and keep it out of the sun.

PREPARING

Garlic is as strong as you let it be: it's mildest as whole unpeeled cloves because no juice escapes; peeled whole garlic is a little stronger; sliced and minced cloves exude pungent juices; and mashed garlic lets loose with all the juices—it is the most powerful. Heat tames garlic's strength, but burned garlic is acrid and bitter.

To get peeled uncut cloves, you will have to fuss with each clove to get the papery skin off without cutting into the garlic and releasing the juices. If you have many cloves to peel, cover them with boiling water for a minute, then cool under cold water. The skins will slip off.

If the garlic is going to be sliced or minced, peeling garlic is much easier. Press each clove with the flat side of a knife until it breaks; the skin can then be slipped right off.

COOKING

Most of the garlic we buy is used as seasoning for other dishes, but cooked on its own, garlic has an incomparable nutty, sweet taste. Garlic cooked solo is most often roasted or baked in its skin, which keeps it from burning. Once cooked, the soft cloves are easily squeezed out of their skins.

The cloves can be separated from the head and roasted along with meats or vegetables. The heads can be baked whole, as well. Cut off the tip of the head, just exposing the cloves, and remove the outer layer of skin without separating the cloves. Put the head or heads in a small baking dish and coat with olive oil. Pour a little olive oil and broth into the dish and sprinkle the garlic with thyme, salt, and pepper. Bake, basting occasionally, at 350°F until very soft and tender, about 1¼ hours.

Elephant garlic is the wild ancestor of the cultivated leek. Its taste is milder than garlic, and although popular, is not a substitute for the real thing.

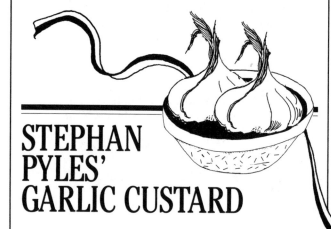

STEPHAN PYLES' GARLIC CUSTARD

This comes from one of the most imaginative and knowledgeable young chefs in America today. (Stephan is co-owner and chef of the Routh Street Cafe and Baby Routh in Dallas, and of Goodfellow's and Tejas in Minneapolis.)

In this unusual version of garlic custard, the cloves are cooked until they begin to "caramelize" in their cooking juices. The result is a gentle, rich custard with a heady aroma—utterly delicious. Serve it with roasted meats or poultry.

1 tablespoon olive oil
6 large cloves garlic
2 cups heavy or whipping cream
4 egg yolks
1 whole egg
Salt and freshly ground white pepper, to taste

1. Preheat the oven to 400°F. Lightly oil six ¾-cup ramekins, and set them aside.

2. Heat the olive oil in an ovenproof skillet, and add the garlic. Sauté over medium heat for 1 minute. Then transfer the skillet to the oven, and cook until the garlic is soft and lightly browned, 10 to 12 minutes. Remove the skillet from the oven, and reduce the temperature to 350°F.

3. Using a slotted spoon, transfer the garlic to a saucepan. Add the cream and bring to a boil. Remove the pan from the heat and allow the cream to cool slightly.

4. Transfer the cream and garlic to a blender and purée thoroughly, about 1 minute. Pour the purée into a mixing bowl.

5. Combine the egg yolks and whole egg in a small bowl, and beat well. Slowly whisk them into the cream mixture. Season with salt and white pepper. Divide the cream mixture among the prepared ramekins (about ½ cup in each). The ramekins should be about three quarters full.

6. Arrange the ramekins in a baking or roasting pan, and pour boiling water into the pan until it reaches halfway up the sides of the ramekins. Cover the ramekins with waxed paper, and then cover the pan tightly with aluminum foil—it should be airtight.

7. Place the pan in the oven, and bake until the custard is just set, 25 to 28 minutes. Serve immediately, or hold in the oven with the heat off and the door open for 10 to 15 minutes.

6 portions

"**G**arlic is the catsup of intellectuals."
—ANONYMOUS

If you have a head of garlic that is sprouting, don't throw it out. Separate the cloves and plant them close together in a pot or in your garden. The young shoots that will soon appear are garlic chives. They are mild with a faint garlic taste—perfect for eggs, salads, and sandwiches.

ROASTED GARLIC

Baked heads of garlic are luscious served as a vegetable alongside roasted meats. It's also delicious squeezed out of the skin and spread on thick slices of toasted peasant bread or Olive Rosemary Country Bread.

8 whole heads garlic
4 tablespoons (½ stick) unsalted butter
1 teaspoon dried thyme leaves
1 teaspoon coarsely ground black pepper
½ teaspoon coarse (kosher) salt
¾ cup Berta's Chicken Stock (see Index) or canned broth

1. Preheat the oven to 350°F.

2. Carefully remove the outer papery skin from the garlic heads, leaving the whole heads intact.

3. Arrange the garlic heads in a small baking dish so that they fit comfortably. Dot with the butter, thyme, pepper, and coarse salt. Pour the stock into the dish.

4. Cover the dish with aluminum foil and bake, basting frequently, for 1 hour. Uncover, and bake 15 minutes longer.

8 portions

JERUSALEM ARTICHOKES

This vegetable is neither from Jerusalem nor is it an artichoke. It's the knobby nut-brown tuber of a sunflower. It won't win any beauty contests, but the taste—between that of a potato and an artichoke—is definitely worth trying.

Buy only firm and unblemished tubers and store them in a cool, dry place up to a week. Jerusalem artichokes can be eaten raw, but we think they are much better cooked. Peel them or simply scrub them and trim any rootlets. Boil them in water to cover until tender. Jerusalem artichokes require about the same amount of cooking time as potatoes, 15 to 30 minutes, depending on how large the pieces are. You can cool them and slice or dice into salads, slice them and toss with butter and herbs, or purée them.

JERUSALEM ARTICHOKE PUREE

Combine the sweet, subtle taste of Jerusalem artichokes (not quite that of a potato nor of an artichoke—just mild and pleasing) with potatoes. The hazelnuts accent their nuttiness. This purée is just right with herb-roasted beef. Lemon and cayenne give it bite.

1 pound Jerusalem artichokes, peeled and sliced ¼ inch thick
1 potato (8 ounces), peeled and sliced ¼ inch thick
4 tablespoons (½ stick) unsalted butter
½ cup chopped onion
2 ounces hazelnuts (½ cup), toasted (see Index) and chopped
2 tablespoons heavy or whipping cream
Grated zest of 1 lemon
⅛ teaspoon cayenne pepper
Salt and freshly ground black pepper, to taste

1. Bring a large pot of water to a boil. Add the Jerusalem artichokes and potato, and cook until tender, about 20 minutes. Drain, and set aside.

2. Preheat the oven to 350°F.

3. Melt 2 tablespoons of the butter in a skillet, and sauté the onion over medium-low heat until golden, 7 to 10 minutes.

4. Combine the artichokes, potato, onion, remaining 2 tablespoons butter, hazelnuts, cream, lemon zest, and cayenne in a mixing bowl, and stir well. Transfer the mixture to a food processor, in batches if necessary, and purée until smooth.

5. Season the purée with salt and a generous grinding of pepper. Transfer it to an ovenproof casserole and bake just until the top is golden and the mixture is hot, 15 to 20 minutes.

6 portions

KOHLRABI

Kohlrabi, once tasted, can become an obsession, for it seems to exude freshness—almost a peppery version of broccoli. Kohlrabi is sometimes called cabbage turnip. It's a member of the cabbage family, but it does indeed look like a turnip with floppy leaves on thin stems growing from the top. You can find kohlrabi from May to December; the peak months are June and July. If they are very young and fresh, the leaves can be sautéed like greens, but the little pale green bulb is the sweetest part to our taste. Cut off the leaves and stems, peel the bulb, and eat it raw—sliced, diced, julienned, or grated—or boiled or steamed whole or in slices. Stuffed, the larger bulbs are just wonderful. Obviously we're kohlrabi fans. Trimmed of its leaves and refrigerated, kohlrabi will keep for five days.

Kohlrabi is a high-carbohydrate, high-potassium, high-fiber vegetable that is an excellent source of vitamins B and C. It is also high in calcium, iron, and phosphorus.

KOHLRABI PUREE

Instead of mashed potatoes, serve this puréed kohlrabi alongside your favorite meat loaf for a delicious change of pace.

4 kohlrabi bulbs with leaves
1 tablespoon olive oil
1 small onion, chopped
2 cloves garlic, minced
1 cup quartered small cultivated mushrooms
3 tablespoons Berta's Chicken Stock (see Index) or canned broth
1 tablespoon fresh lemon juice
1 teaspoon salt
Freshly ground black pepper, to taste

1. Trim and peel the kohlrabi bulbs, reserving the leaves (discard any that are yellow). Rinse the leaves, pat them dry, and coarsely chop. Set them aside. Cut the bulbs into 1-inch chunks.

2. Bring a saucepan of lightly salted water to a boil, and add the kohlrabi chunks. Reduce the heat and simmer until tender, about 15 minutes.

3. Meanwhile, heat the oil in a skillet. Add the onion and garlic, and sauté over medium-low heat until softened, about 5 minutes.

4. Add the mushrooms and the reserved kohlrabi leaves to the skillet. Cover, and cook 5 minutes. Then uncover, and cook, stirring, until all the liquid has evaporated, 3 minutes. Set the skillet aside.

5. Drain the kohlrabi chunks and place them in the bowl of a food processor. Add the mushroom mixture and all the remaining ingredients. Purée until smooth.

6. Transfer the purée to a saucepan and reheat over low heat, stirring, 2 minutes. (Or transfer it to a baking dish and bake in a preheated 350°F oven until steaming hot, 25 minutes.)

6 portions

KOHLRABI CAKES

Similar to potato pancakes, these kohlrabi cakes have a bite—they're spiked with ginger and hot red pepper. Minted Yogurt Sauce is the refreshing contrast.

4 kohlrabi bulbs
¼ cup chopped scallions (green onions)
2 eggs, lightly beaten
2 tablespoons dried bread crumbs
1 teaspoon salt
½ teaspoon ground ginger
¼ teaspoon dried red pepper flakes, crushed
Freshly ground black pepper, to taste
¼ cup olive oil
1 ⅓ cups Minted Yogurt Sauce (see Index)

1. Peel and shred the kohlrabi bulbs. Squeeze out any excess moisture.

2. Combine the kohlrabi, scallions, eggs, bread crumbs, salt, ginger, red pepper flakes, and black pepper in a mixing bowl. Stir until well blended.

3. Heat the oil in a large skillet, and drop the mixture into it by large spoonfuls. Sauté the cakes until golden, 3 to 4 minutes per side. Drain on paper towels.

4. Serve with Minted Yogurt Sauce.

4 portions

STUFFED KOHLRABI

Individually stuffed vegetables make a lovely presentation at any meal. We've enhanced the subtle sweet flavor of kohlrabi with shallots, seasonings, and parsley in this simple preparation.

4 kohlrabi bulbs
3 tablespoons unsalted butter
½ cup chopped shallots
½ teaspoon salt
Freshly ground black pepper, to taste
1 tablespoon chopped fresh parsley

1. Trim and peel the kohlrabi bulbs, reserving the leaves for another use.

2. Bring a saucepan of lightly salted water to a boil, and add the kohlrabi bulbs. Simmer until tender when pierced with a knife, 25 to 30 minutes. Then rinse under cold water, and drain. Set aside.

3. Preheat the oven to 350°F. Butter a baking sheet and set it aside.

4. Melt the butter in a small skillet, and sauté the shallots over very low heat, stirring occasionally, for 10 minutes. Set them aside.

5. Carefully scoop out the centers of the kohlrabi bulbs, leaving a shell ¼ inch thick (or slightly thicker). Mash or purée the kohlrabi centers, and combine the purée with the cooked shallots and the salt, pepper, and parsley. Fill the shells with the mixture, mounding it slightly.

6. Arrange the filled kohlrabi on the prepared baking sheet, and bake until the tops are golden, 30 minutes.

4 portions

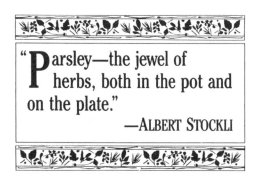

"**P**arsley—the jewel of herbs, both in the pot and on the plate."
—ALBERT STOCKLI

LEEKS

This tender, mild member of the lily family looks like an overgrown scallion, but it has a mild, almost sweet flavor that's all its own. Leeks add a depth of flavor to the stew or soup pot not achieved by onions alone. Served by themselves, leeks can be braised and eaten hot or cold—a favorite first course in French bistros. Sliced and gently sautéed in butter, they make a delicious filling for an omelet or quiche.

BUYING

Buy leeks that are no thicker than 1½ inches in diameter and quite straight from top to bottom. The tops should be bright green and fresh, not wilted and yellow.

STORING

Like scallions, leeks have a fairly short shelf life. Store them refrigerated in a plastic bag up to five days and rinse just before using.

YIELD

If you are serving the leeks as a first course or side dish, anticipate two medium leeks per person. Two pounds of leeks will yield 4 cups chopped but just 2 cups after cooking.

PREPARING

We've never met a leek that wasn't full of sand. It's not a lot of work to clean them, but one must be very thorough. Cut off the dark green tops and trim the root end. Only the light green and white of the leek is good eating. Some recipes call for just the white; save the light green part for stocks or use them in place of sautéed onions. Leeks can be cooked whole or sliced, chopped, or julienned.

To clean whole leeks, trim them, leaving 3 inches of green top. Cut an X in the root end. Soak for 30 minutes in a mixture of 10 cups water mixed with 1 tablespoon of vinegar. The sand will remain on the bottom of the bowl. Rinse the leeks thoroughly under cold water, fanning the leaves with your fingers.

If you are not using the leeks whole, cut each one in half lengthwise. Rinse under cold water, separating the leaves with your fingers, or plunge them up and down in a sinkful of cold water. Shake off the water and pat dry.

COOKING

▲ **Boiling:** Cook whole leeks in a large pot of boiling water until just tender, 10 to 12 minutes for medium leeks, and drain. Or lay them in a single layer in a wide pan, add cold water to cover, and boil until tender, 12 to 15 minutes. Drain, top with sauce, and serve hot.

If you are going to add the leeks to another dish or serve them at room temperature, run them under cold water to stop the cooking.

▲ **Steaming:** Steam whole leeks in a single layer over an inch of boiling water until tender, about 15 minutes for medium leeks.

▲ **Braising:** Melt 1 tablespoon of butter for every two leeks in a skillet over medium heat. Add the whole leeks and cook until they start to color. Add ½ cup broth, partially cover the skillet, and braise over low heat on top of the stove. Or arrange the leeks in a single layer in a baking dish, drizzle with about ¼ cup broth, and braise in a 350°F oven. The leeks are done when they are easily pierced with a knife. Oven-braising medium leeks takes about an hour, but start checking after 45 minutes. Skillet-braised leeks take even less time; a half hour is usually sufficient. Check the leeks every once in a while to make sure that enough liquid remains to keep them from scorching, and turn them occasionally so they will be evenly browned.

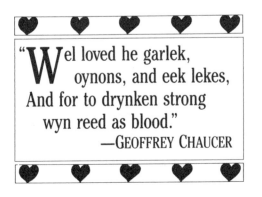

"**W**el loved he garlek,
    oynons, and eek lekes,
And for to drynken strong
    wyn reed as blood."
—GEOFFREY CHAUCER

LOTS OF LEEKS TART ▲

A tart chock-full of leeks, with just enough essence to hold it together—all on a thin crust of puff pastry.

*10 leeks (white bulb and ½ inch green), well rinsed and
    patted dry*
*⅓ pound Adrienne's Rough Puff Pastry (see Index), or
    frozen puff pastry, thawed*
1 egg yolk
1 teaspoon water
2 tablespoons unsalted butter
⅓ cup Berta's Chicken Stock (see Index) or canned broth
⅛ teaspoon freshly ground black pepper
1 teaspoon chopped fresh Italian (flat-leaf) parsley

1. Preheat the oven to 400°F.

2. Dice 9 of the leeks, reserving the tenth. Set them all aside.

3. Roll the pastry out on a lightly floured surface so that it will fit an 8-inch tart pan. Transfer the pastry to the tart pan, and prick the bottom all over with the tines of a fork.

4. Stir the egg yolk and water together, and using a pastry brush, brush this egg wash all over the pastry.

5. Bake the pastry for 7 minutes. Set it aside to cool. Leave the oven on.

6. Melt the butter in a large skillet, and sauté the diced leeks over medium heat until wilted, about 5 minutes. Add the stock and simmer until all the liquid has evaporated, 5 minutes.

7. Fill the cooled crust with the leek mixture. Slice the remaining leek into ¼-inch-thick rounds, and decorate the top of the tart with them, forming circles or a spiral. Sprinkle with the pepper and parsley, and bake until pale golden, 20 minutes. Serve hot or at room temperature.

4 portions

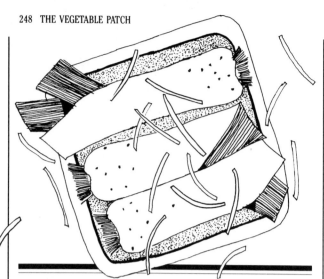

to 7 minutes. Transfer them to a warmed serving dish, fanning out the green ends decoratively. Keep warm.

5. Add the orange juice and 1 tablespoon of the zest to the skillet. Raise the heat to medium-high and whisk the sauce until it has thickened slightly, about 3 minutes.

6. Spoon the sauce over the leeks, and sprinkle with the remaining 1 tablespoon orange zest. Serve immediately.

6 portions

LEEKS WITH ORANGE GINGER SAUCE

Leeks become quite elegant when napped with a fresh orange ginger sauce. These are an ideal complement to roasted duck or sautéed duck breasts.

12 small to medium-size leeks
6½ quarts water
1 tablespoon white vinegar
6 tablespoons (¾ stick) unsalted butter
5 tablespoons grated fresh ginger
1 teaspoon ground ginger
1 cup fresh orange juice
2 tablespoons grated orange zest

1. Trim the root ends off the leeks. Cut an X in the bottom of each leek. Remove any tough or discolored leaves, and trim the tops, leaving 2 inches of green. Cut an X, lengthwise, through the green part.

2. Place 10 cups (2½ quarts) of the water in a large bowl, and add the vinegar and leeks. Soak for 30 minutes to remove any remaining sand. Rinse the leeks thoroughly under cold water.

3. Fill a large pot with the remaining 4 quarts water, and bring it to a boil. Add the leeks, reduce the heat, and simmer until just tender, 5 to 7 minutes. Drain the leeks and pat them dry.

4. Melt the butter in a large skillet over low heat. Add the fresh and ground ginger and cook for 1 minute, stirring. Then add the leeks and raise the heat to medium. Turning the leeks once or twice, cook until they are lightly browned on both sides, 5

MUSHROOMS

Growing up, it seemed to us that anything that wasn't a cultivated button mushroom had to be a hands-off toadstool. Who would have thought that there existed all those wonderful wild mushroom varieties? Once left to brave mushroom foragers with a better understanding than ours, shiitakes, morels, porcinis, and so many other rich-tasting wild mushrooms have been showing up in more markets each year—some now tamed, others still wild. The bounty is glorious; don't be shy in trying them all.

BUYING

Look for tight, firm mushrooms that are dry to the touch. The color should be solid, whether white, brown, or beige. An open cap is a sign of age—which isn't a bad trait in all mushrooms as long as they aren't wet or slimy. Try to buy mushrooms not more than a couple of days before using them; they're very perishable and must be fresh, especially if served raw.

STORING

Store mushrooms in the refrigerator in a paper bag or open container, covered loosely with a slightly damp paper towel. Keep them in one or two layers, if possible, instead of stacking them up. Never wash mushrooms until you are ready to use them. Soggy mushrooms have no use at all.

YIELD

One pound of fresh mushrooms will adequately serve three people. Buy 1½ pounds for four. Mushrooms are 90 percent water and shrink when cooked.

PREPARING

Thoroughly cleaning mushrooms is important. They can be very sandy and dirty, but if soaked in water they easily become waterlogged. If the mushrooms aren't too dirty, clean them with a moist paper towel—it is time consuming but worth the savings in flavor. Wild mushrooms especially can be full of sand. Rinse them quickly under warm water to loosen the dirt, then again under cold, and wipe with a moist cloth. Dry very gently by rubbing the mushrooms between paper towels.

Mushrooms should never be peeled, but the stems usually need trimming. If the stem is woody or very soft, remove it and use just the caps.

Mushrooms can be kept whole or sliced, quartered, or diced. If you are slicing mushrooms to cook them, cut thick slices to keep them from falling apart when the water is cooked out of them. Always slice lengthwise across the cap and stem because the mushroom won't hold together if sliced crosswise.

COOKING

▲ **Sautéing:** There are two very different methods of sautéing mushrooms: The first method delivers a mushroom with great flavor and acceptable texture; the second method delivers the best texture and good flavor.

Old-school method: Melt ¼ cup of butter (or a combination of butter and oil) in a skillet over low to medium heat. Add a pound of mushrooms, whole, sliced, or chopped, when the butter foams. Sauté, stirring the mushrooms occasionally, until all the liquid evaporates and the mushrooms brown, about 10 minutes for sliced mushrooms. Whole mushrooms will take about 5 minutes longer. Season with salt and pepper and serve.

New-school method: Heat ¼ cup of oil in a skillet over high heat. Add the mushrooms and sauté, stirring and tossing constantly, until browned, about 2 minutes. By sautéing over high heat, the liquid is prevented from escaping and the mushrooms will be full and firm. Toss with a little butter if you want the flavor; season, and serve.

▲ **Braising:** This method is best for mushroom caps, especially the large meaty ones. Melt 2 tablespoons of butter in a skillet, add the mushrooms, and sauté about 5 minutes. Add enough liquid, wine or broth, to cover the bottom of the pan. Cover with a tight-fitting lid and simmer gently over low heat until the mushrooms are tender, about 5 more minutes. Remove the lid and turn up the heat to evaporate any remaining liquid.

▲ **Baking:** Arrange whole mushrooms in a single layer in a baking dish. Add 1 cup broth mixed with a little wine for every pound, and dot the tops with butter. Bake at 350°F until tender and browned, about 20 minutes.

▲ **Broiling:** Larger mushrooms are best for broiling because they won't dry out, and for stuffing they hold more and are less tedious to fill. Coat mushroom caps lightly with olive oil or butter mixed with oil. Arrange, cap side up, on an oiled broiler rack or baking sheet. Broil 4 inches from the heat for about 2 minutes. Turn the mushrooms, drizzle with butter or fill each one with stuffing, and broil until tender, 2 to 5 minutes.

▲ **Grilling:** Brush the largest, wildest, meatiest mushroom caps you have with good olive oil and grill over medium coals, turning frequently, until tender. Season and serve hot.

SEASON TO TASTE

Next time you prepare mushrooms, sprinkle on any of the following for extra flavor:

Balsamic vinegar	Parsley
Black pepper	Olive oil
Coriander seed	Rosemary
Garlic	Shallot
Lemon	Sherry and port (dry)
Marjoram	Tarragon
Marsala	Thyme
Nutmeg	Wine

MUSHROOMS, WILD & TAME

Many mushroom varieties that were once only found wild now have been tamed and are being farmed. When cultivated, a mushroom often doesn't have flavor as rich as its wild equivalent. But it will be delicious, nonetheless, and certainly more readily available.

NAME	DESCRIPTION	PREPARATION
Angel trumpet (not related to black trumpet)	White to almost transparent; delicate flavor. Tame.	Very subtle taste; sauté in butter and a drop of lemon juice
Chanterelle (Girolle)	Trumpet-shaped; mild flavor. Wild.	Complements chicken, game hens, veal, eggs; combine with creamy pasta sauces, or sauté in butter with shallots
Cremini, (Roman)	Cocoa-colored versions of the cultivated button; more intense flavor than button mushrooms. Tame.	Versatile: sauté, roast, or grill; sprinkle with olive oil and lemon juice
Cultivated commercial (button)	White or cream-colored; mild flavor. Tame.	Versatile: serve raw in salads; sautéed in butter and/or oil with herbs; cooked in soups, stews, and atop grills
Enoki (Enoki-take)	Tiny white caps with very long, sprout-like stems; fruity with a fresh tang. Both wild and tame.	Raw in salads or sandwiches; stir-fried or sautéed gently in whole bunches
Fairy ring	Taupe with little brown rings on stems; delicate flavor. Wild.	Cook simply with poultry or seafood; excellent in veal stews or in soups
Hen-of-the-Woods	Gray-brown, spoon-shaped fluffy clusters with feathery edges; rich flavor. Tame.	Long, slow cooking will give a just-tender texture
Matsutake	Grows wrapped in a veil; spicy, earthy flavor. Wild.	Sauté simply or grill

NAME	DESCRIPTION	PREPARATION
Morel	Cone-shaped with a spongy beige to dark brown cap; meaty texture with an earthy nut-like taste. Wild.	Cook simply with poultry in cream sauces, or sauté with garlic and butter
Oyster (Pleurotte)	Beige colored fans; mild flavor, silky texture. Both wild and tame.	Cook as for button mushrooms; use in cream sauces and gratins
Pom Pom (Forest, Coral, Lobster)	Cauliflower-like leaves; taste is reminiscent of seafood. Tame.	Bake at high heat, sliced or whole; enhanced by butter, lemon juice, parsley, and pepper
Porcini (Cèpe, Boletus)	Large taupe to brown, parasol-shaped caps with thick stems; deep, meaty, smoky flavor. Wild.	Separate caps and stems. Sauté, braise, grill or broil; wonderful in extra virgin olive oil
Portobello	Taupe to brown, looks like a thatched roof; milder than porcini but with some depth of flavor. Both wild and tame.	Stuff, grill, broil, or roast with extra virgin olive oil
Shiitake	Large, tawny, parasol-shaped caps with cream-colored inside; rich, meaty, smoky flavor. Both wild and tame.	Separate caps and stems. Cook simply with game or poultry; stir-fry or bake
Trompettes-des-Morts (Horns of Plenty)	Black trumpet-shaped; deep, nutty flavor. Wild.	Wonderful stuffed in pork loins and poultry
Wood Ear (Cloud Ear, Tree Ear)	Usually black or brown, nearly transparent, ear-shaped; mild and nutty flavor. Tame.	Classic in Chinese soups and stir-fries; can hold up to longer cooking for a tender texture

CREAMED MUSHROOMS

Cultivated mushrooms dressed up for a special occasion with a bit of cream and a bit more Madeira. Lovely on toast or a puff pastry square. This is a great first course, or luncheon or supper fare.

2 tablespoons unsalted butter
1 tablespoon minced shallots
2 teaspoons unbleached all-purpose flour
12 ounces fresh cultivated mushrooms, sliced
¾ cup heavy or whipping cream
¼ cup Madeira
½ teaspoon dried thyme leaves
Salt and freshly ground black pepper, to taste
1 teaspoon snipped fresh chives

1. Melt the butter in a skillet. Add the shallots and cook over low heat for 5 minutes. Sprinkle the shallots with the flour; then add the mushrooms, cream, Madeira, and thyme and stir.

2. Simmer the mushrooms over low heat until the sauce has thickened slightly, 25 minutes. Season with salt and pepper, garnish with the chives, and serve.

2 portions

TRADE SECRET

Add the liquid from steeping dried mushrooms to soups or sauces. It's great!

APRICOT CHANTERELLES

Chanterelles are expensive, seasonal, and not yet cultivated commercially. When you are lucky enough to find them in your market, indulge!

In this recipe, the subtle apricot flavor of the wild mushroom is heightened by the addition of dried apricots. It is an elegant preparation that can begin a special dinner. Without the toast, it can serve as a vegetable.

½ cup dried apricots, halved
½ cup Berta's Chicken Stock (see Index) or canned broth
3 tablespoons unsalted butter
2 shallots, peeled and sliced ¼ inch thick
8 ounces fresh chanterelles, halved
Salt and freshly ground black pepper, to taste
1 tablespoon snipped fresh chives
4 to 6 slices bread, toasted

1. Combine the apricots and stock in a small bowl, and set aside to soak for 30 minutes.

2. Melt the butter in a medium-size skillet, and sauté the shallots over medium-low heat for 3 minutes. Add the chanterelles, lower the heat, and cook, tossing gently, for 2 minutes.

3. Add the apricots and stock. Cover the skillet, and cook over medium heat for 2 minutes. Then uncover the skillet and simmer until the mushrooms are tender, 4 minutes.

4. Season the mushrooms lightly with salt and pepper, and sprinkle with the chives.

5. Place a slice of toast on each plate, and spoon some of the mushroom mixture and cooking liquid over the toast. Serve at once.

4 to 6 portions

ENOKI SAUTE

A bunch of enoki mushrooms sautéed intact makes a delightful and dramatic presentation as a first course or a side vegetable. Serve them on dishes of contrasting colors so that they stand out. If you can find chives with blossoms, garnish each plate with one.

2 bunches fresh enoki mushrooms (from two 3 ½ -ounce
    packages)
1 tablespoon unsalted butter
1 tablespoon soy sauce
1 tablespoon fresh lemon juice
Snipped fresh chives

   1. Trim about ½ inch off the bottom of the bunches, leaving the mushrooms attached.
   2. Melt the butter in a small skillet over medium-high heat. Add the enoki and sauté until golden on one side, 2 minutes. Turn the mushrooms over, and pour the soy sauce and lemon juice over them. Cook 2 minutes.
   3. Lift the mushrooms onto two plates, and spoon the cooking liquid over them. Sprinkle with chives, and serve immediately.
   2 portions

"**N**ature alone is antique and the oldest art a mushroom."
—THOMAS CARLYLE

BROILED MUSHROOMS

D on't be limited by these mushrooms. In the fall, search the markets for all the exciting varieties available. Remember to wipe fresh mushrooms carefully with a damp paper towel to clean them—don't soak them with water.

1 pound fresh shiitake or oyster mushrooms (pleurottes),
    stems removed
6 tablespoons fresh lemon juice
3 cloves garlic, finely minced
3 tablespoons coarsely chopped fresh Italian (flat-leaf)
    parsley
2 tablespoons olive oil
Freshly ground black pepper, to taste

1. Preheat the broiler.

2. Clean the mushroom caps with a damp paper towel. (Discard the stems or reserve for stock.)

3. In a small bowl, combine 4 tablespoons of the lemon juice, the garlic, 2½ tablespoons of the parsley, and the oil and pepper. Mix well.

4. Line a 17 x 11-inch jelly roll pan with aluminum foil. Arrange the mushrooms, top side up, on the foil, and brush generously with the lemon juice mixture.

5. Place the mushrooms 4 inches from the heat and broil until just tender, 5 to 7 minutes.

6. To serve, sprinkle the mushrooms with the remaining 2 tablespoons lemon juice, ½ tablespoon parsley, and pepper to taste.

6 portions

1. Melt the butter in a skillet over medium heat. When it stops foaming, lower the heat and add the mushrooms. Turn them in the butter until well coated.

2. Sprinkle the mushrooms lightly with salt and pepper, and with the thyme leaves. Stir in the stock. Cover, and simmer until the mushrooms are tender, 2 minutes.

3. Uncover, and cook until most of the liquid has evaporated, 1 minute. Spoon the mushrooms over the croutons, garnish with the thyme sprigs, and serve.

4 portions

TROMPETTES DES MORTS SAUTE

We love these wild mushrooms. The black ones are the most familiar, but we have also seen snowy white ones. Although the preparation is simple, this is no ordinary mushrooms-on-toast.

2 tablespoons unsalted butter
4 ounces small fresh trompettes des morts
*   mushrooms (2 to 3 inches long)*
Salt and freshly ground black pepper, to taste
¼ teaspoon fresh thyme leaves or a pinch of dried
¼ cup homemade beef stock (see Index) or canned broth
4 large Garlic Croutons (see Index) or toasted bread slices
Small sprigs fresh thyme or chervil, for garnish

FRAGRANT ONIONS

A kitchen without onions can hardly be thought of as a functioning kitchen—onions are just that basic to our cuisine. There's hardly a recipe for soup, sauce, or stew that doesn't begin with "Sauté a medium onion" or a dish that isn't enhanced by their sweet pungency.

We are certain onions have never gone out of fashion in all of recorded history, for everyone seems to agree they bring out the best in so many dishes. But don't just think of onions as chopped flavorings. Prepare them baked, creamed, in stews, and as condiments—really get to know your onions.

VARIETIES OF ONIONS

Because there are so many varieties of onions, it is important to know the character and strength of each.

▲ **Chive:** These slender grass-like stalks are most often used like herbs. Chives are too delicate to stand up to heat. Simply snip and sprinkle over food before serving it.

▲ **Scallion or green onion:** A baby onion complete with a thin or roundish white bulb, a scallion is good sliced and added raw to dishes or cooked just enough to wilt it. The white bulb is a little stronger than the green tops.

▲ **Leek:** The sweet nutty leek resembles a fat scallion. It's quite versatile and for that reason we have given it a section of its own (see Leeks).

▲ **Shallot:** This onion is probably best characterized as a cross between garlic and onion. Its mild flavor is extraordinary in sauces and vinaigrettes. We think shallots are one of the essential onions to have in the kitchen at all times. They are becoming increasingly available.

▲ **Pearl onion:** A true pearl onion is small, not much more than an inch in diameter, with a papery white skin very much like that of garlic. Many cooks prepare them just once a year in cream sauce for Thanksgiving, but we like them sautéed and dropped into hearty stews all winter long.

To peel these little onions quickly, drop them into boiling water, boil for a minute, and cool under cold running water. Trim the tops and root ends, then slip off the skins.

▲ **Yellow onion:** This onion makes up more than 75 percent of the world's supply. When we call for an onion in a recipe, this is the onion we mean. Since they are strong and pungent, we almost always cook them. If we need raw onion for a dish, we choose a milder variety.

▲ **Red onion:** Also called purple onion, this onion originated in Italy and was once imported only at certain times of the year. It is now an American standard, and its delicious sweetness is perfect for salads and sandwiches. As a rule, don't cook red onions, for the color fades from the onion and bleeds into the other ingredients. But they're great sliced thick and grilled.

▲ **Sweet Bermuda and Spanish onions:** These onions are large and strong in flavor but not as pungent as yellow onions. They are sweet enough to be eaten raw—sliced on burgers or in salads—and they make wonderful onion rings and stuffed baked onions. The Bermuda onion is yellow or white with flattened ends; the Spanish is a big yellow or white globe.

▲ **Walla Walla, Maui, and Vidalia sweet onions:** These are other sweet onions named for where they are grown (Walla Walla, Washington, the island of Maui, and Vidalia, Georgia). They are all incredibly sweet and delicious and have a high water content, which makes them extremely perishable. Keep an eye out for them in their season and eat them right away. Mauis start the sweet onion season from April to June, Vidalias are available in May and June, and Walla Wallas end the season in July and August.

 **BUYING**

Leeks, scallions, and chives are always sold fresh; look for crisp stalks and bright green color.

All other onions are cured after harvesting to develop the papery skins that protect the flesh. Look for dry, smooth, papery skins and hard, well-shaped onions. Don't buy onions with soft or sprouting tops. If they feel hollow or soft, they are starting to rot.

 STORING

Refrigerate fresh onions—scallions and chives—unwashed in plastic bags up to five days.

Store all other onions in a dry, dark, cool place, preferably in net bags or open baskets. They should keep up to four weeks. Refrigerating cured onions makes them moist and accelerates decay. Onions have a short life once they are cut; if you use half an onion one day, refrigerate the other half in plastic wrap and use it the next day.

 YIELD

One medium onion chopped will yield ¾ to 1 cup. One average shallot chopped will yield a generous tablespoon.

Onions are usually eaten in such small amounts that they make very little difference nutritionally, but the most nutritious ones are scallions, with four times the vitamin C and 5,000 times the vitamin A as other onions. If you eat onions by the pound, you'll be interested to know one pound has about 175 calories.

 PREPARING

Don't peel or cut onions until you are ready to use them. They lose flavor very quickly.

To chop an onion, cut a thin slice from the top—leave the root end alone. Peel off the skin and cut it in half through the root end. Lay an onion half, cut side down, on a work surface. Without cutting through the root end, first slice it parallel to the work counter, then lengthwise and finally crosswise to make small, even pieces. For a minced shallot or clove of garlic, the slices must be very thin, but for a coarsely chopped onion the slices can be much thicker.

Our advice for keeping tears at bay is to use a very sharp knife. It's the pungent juices that sting and a sharp knife will cut without crushing the onion and releasing the juices. It also gets the job done faster. If you have many onions to chop, do it in front of an open window or a fan. In our experience, soaking onions in cold water or slicing them under running water only makes for wet onions.

COOKING

▲ **Sautéing:** Sauté sliced or chopped onions (or small pearl onions) in butter and/or oil in a skillet over medium to high heat. Most recipes call for translucent or softened onions; others ask that they be cooked longer until golden. If you can't stir them frequently, turn down the heat and stir occasionally but don't let them burn or brown—they'll taste bitter.

▲ **Boiling:** Probably the best onions to boil are the small pearl onions. Peel (see Varieties of Onions for a quick peeling tip) and add them to enough boiling water to cover. Gently boil until tender but firm, 10 to 20 minutes; if overcooked, they fall apart and are mushy. Drain well and season or toss with melted butter or cream sauce.

▲ **Steaming:** Place peeled pearl onions or trimmed scallions in a single layer in a rack or basket over an inch of boiling water. Cover and steam until tender. Scallions will be done in no time, pearl onions in 10 to 20 minutes.

▲ **Braising:** Sauté peeled pearl onions in butter just to brown them, then add enough broth to cover the bottom of the pan. Simmer covered over low heat or bake covered at 350°F until tender.

▲ **Baking:** Onions can be baked in their skins. Rub well with olive oil and place them in a single layer in an oiled baking dish. Add a little broth to the bottom of the pan if you like. Bake at 375°F until tender, about 1½ hours for large onions. The baking temperature is flexible if you have other things in the oven at the same time—the onions will simply take more or less time to bake. Cut the baked onions in half and remove the skins, then drizzle with balsamic vinegar or herb butter.

FIVE CREAMED ONIONS

We've gathered our lilies, bathed them in cream, and dusted them with nutmeg, for a most extravagant combination.

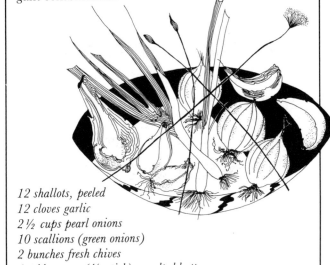

12 shallots, peeled
12 cloves garlic
2½ cups pearl onions
10 scallions (green onions)
2 bunches fresh chives
4 tablespoons (½ stick) unsalted butter
¼ cup unbleached all-purpose flour
2 cups heavy or whipping cream
Pinch of nutmeg
Salt and freshly ground black pepper, to taste

1. Place the shallots and garlic in a small saucepan. Add water to cover and bring to a boil. Reduce the heat and simmer until tender, 7 to 10 minutes. Drain, and set aside.

2. Cut a small X in the root end of each pearl onion, being careful not to cut completely through the end. Bring a saucepan of water to a boil. Drop in the onions, then reduce the heat and simmer until tender, about 15 minutes. Drain, peel, and set aside.

3. Trim the roots and the green stems from the scallions. Bring a saucepan of water to a boil. Drop in the scallions and cook for 5 minutes. Drain and reserve.

4. Snip the chives into small pieces. You should have 5 to 6 tablespoons. Set aside.

5. Melt the butter in a saucepan, and add the flour. Cook over low heat for 5 minutes, stirring occasionally. While stirring with a wire whisk, slowly add the cream in a steady stream. Continue cooking

and whisking until the sauce has thickened, 7 to 10 minutes. Add the nutmeg and salt and pepper.

6. Stir the shallots, garlic, pearl onions, scallions, and chives into the cream sauce. Heat through, 4 minutes, and serve immediately.

6 portions

Note: Creamed onions can be kept warm in a double boiler until ready to serve. Don't hold longer than 30 minutes.

"**E**at no onions nor garlic, for we are to utter sweet breath."

—WILLIAM SHAKESPEARE

ONION CONFIT

This is an aromatic and pungent sauce—a bit sweet, a bit sour, and just swell. It is wonderful as a condiment, added to pizza or hamburgers, or served with white-fleshed fish, lamb, poultry, or game.

¼ cup extra virgin olive oil
1 tablespoon unsalted butter
3 onions, slivered
½ teaspoon coarsely ground black pepper
1 tablespoon sherry vinegar

1. Heat the oil and butter in a heavy saucepan over low heat. Add the onions and pepper and cook until completely wilted, slowly stirring occasionally, 35 to 40 minutes.

2. Add the sherry vinegar, stir, and cook an additional 15 minutes. Cool, cover, and refrigerate for up to 3 days. Onion confit also freezes well.

1 cup

BAKED STUFFED ONIONS

Onions shouldn't be limited to soups and sauces. Served on their own, they make an excellent vegetable with roasted meats.

6 small yellow onions (about 1 ounce each), unpeeled
4 dried apricots, finely chopped
2 tablespoons dried bread crumbs
1 tablespoon unsalted butter, melted
2 teaspoons minced fresh rosemary leaves
¼ teaspoon salt
Freshly ground black pepper, to taste
2 teaspoons light olive oil

1. Preheat the oven to 375°F. Lightly oil a baking dish.

2. Place the whole unpeeled onions in a small saucepan, and cover with cold water. Bring to a boil, then reduce the heat and simmer for 10 minutes. Rinse under cold water, and drain.

3. Trim off the ends slightly, and cut the onions in half crosswise. Carefully peel off the skin. Then gently pull or scoop out the centers, leaving a ¼-inch-thick shell.

4. Mince the onion centers and place them in a mixing bowl. Add the apricots, bread crumbs, melted butter, rosemary, salt, and pepper; stir thoroughly. Fill each onion half with the apricot mixture, mounding it slightly. Arrange the onions in the prepared baking dish and drizzle them with the olive oil.

5. Bake until golden, 30 minutes. Serve the onions immediately.

6 portions

SWEET ONION RELISH

Sweet onions, fresh cauliflower, and golden raisins are tossed in a fresh pungent barbecue sauce for an unusual and exciting condiment. Serve with Venison Pâté and herbed meat loaves.

1 large sweet onion (about 8 ounces), such as Maui or Walla
    Walla, very thinly sliced
1 cup coarsely chopped cauliflower
½ cup golden raisins
3 tablespoons Fresh Tomato Paste (see page 299) or canned
    tomato paste
2 tablespoons light brown sugar
1 tablespoon soy sauce
1 tablespoon white wine vinegar
1 teaspoon Worcestershire sauce
1 teaspoon white peppercorns
1 teaspoon salt
Freshly ground black pepper, to taste
1 cup water

   1. Combine all the ingredients in a 2-quart microwave-safe casserole, and stir well.
   2. Cook, covered, at full power (650 to 700 watts) for 5 minutes. Stir, and cook another 5 minutes.
   3. Allow the relish to cool to room temperature, then refrigerate for up to 3 days.
   2½ cups
   Note: This recipe was cooked on High (full power, 650 to 700 watts) in a carousel microwave, using microwave-safe containers.
   If your microwave is less powerful, you will have to allow for more cooking time (approximately 1½ times the amount called for—but watch carefully); if it does not have a carousel, you may have to rotate the dish while it is cooking.

PARSNIPS

Parsnips belong to the carrot family, but they are creamy white and much fatter and larger than the carrot. While they can sometimes be quite assertive, especially if old and large, young parsnips have a sweet, nutty taste.

   Parsnips are usually tucked away in some forgotten corner of the vegetable section at the market. But out of sight should not be out of mind, for their flavor is often just what's needed for a soup, stew, or purée. Parsnips are an old-fashioned vegetable but perfect for the hearty dishes that get us through winter. So search them out at the market and enrich parsnip's nutty flavor with sugar, butter, olive oil, cream, or spices.

BUYING

Even though parsnips are available all year, peak season being fall and winter, it is often hard to find really good ones. If you do find them, buy them as you would carrots—firm, crisp, and free of cracks.

STORING

Store parsnips as you would carrots—in plastic bags in the refrigerator. If they were fresh when you bought them, they should keep two or three weeks.

YIELD

One pound of parsnips will serve three or four.

PREPARING

Trim the root ends and tops, then peel with a vegetable peeler. If the parsnips are large, cut them in half and remove the woody core. Parsnips can be cooked whole or in fairly large pieces, julienned, or diced.

COOKING

Sweet and nutty parsnips are ideal vegetables for soups and stews. Cut them in thick slices or chunks and drop them into the liquid for the last 30 minutes of cooking time. Or cut them into thick wedges and add them to a roast for the last hour of cooking time, basting the parsnips right along with the roast. However you cook them, keep in mind that they cook quickly and that an overcooked parsnip is not an edible parsnip.

▲ **Boiling:** Cover parsnip chunks with cold water and heat to boiling. Cover the pan and gently boil until tender. Check by piercing them with a knife or fork. Drain, coat with butter, and season. Two-inch chunks will take about 10 minutes. Boiled and steamed parsnips are delicious puréed and seasoned with salt and pepper and a dash of cinnamon or a sprinkle of chopped parsley.

▲ **Steaming:** Place the parsnips in quarters or large chunks in a steaming rack or basket. Steam, covered, over an inch of boiling water until tender. Two-inch chunks will take 7 to 10 minutes.

▲ **Baking:** Heat ¼ cup of butter in a baking dish. Add a pound of parsnips, peeled and quartered, and turn to coat with butter. Bake covered at 350°F until crisp-tender, 30 to 45 minutes, then remove the cover and continue to bake until lightly browned and tender, about 15 minutes longer. Turn once or twice during cooking, so the parsnips brown evenly. Season with thyme, salt, and pepper.

1. Preheat the oven to 375°F.
2. Combine the lemon juice and water in a large bowl.
3. Peel, core, and cut the apples into eighths, dropping the pieces into the acidulated water.
4. Place the parsnips in a shallow baking pan. Add the apples, using a slotted spoon, and ¼ cup of the acidulated water. Add the chicken stock.
5. Dot the parsnips and apples with the butter, and sprinkle with the brown sugar, coriander, and pepper. Cover the dish, and bake 1½ hours, stirring a few times during the baking.
6. Reduce the oven temperature to 350°F and transfer the parsnips and apples with their cooking liquid to a food processor and purée until smooth. Reheat if necessary, in a covered ovenproof dish, for 15 minutes. Serve garnished with the mint.

6 portions

PARSNIP AND APPLE PUREE

Nutty parsnips and tart Granny Smiths are baked to retain their most acute flavors, and then deliciously puréed together.

¼ cup fresh lemon juice
¼ cup water
4 large Granny Smith or other tart apples
2 pounds parsnips, peeled and coarsely chopped
¼ cup Berta's Chicken Stock (see Index) or canned broth
4 tablespoons (½ stick) unsalted butter, cut into pieces
2 tablespoons light brown sugar
1 teaspoon ground coriander
Freshly ground black pepper, to taste
Fresh mint sprigs, for garnish

PARSNIP AND POTATO MASH

Rich and sweet, this is the dish to serve alongside a batch of fried chicken, topped with creamy gravy.

1½ pounds parsnips, peeled and diced
1½ pounds boiling potatoes, peeled and diced
¼ cup heavy or whipping cream
3 tablespoons unsalted butter, at room temperature
1 egg yolk
Salt and freshly ground black pepper, to taste
1 scallion (green onion), white bulb and 3 inches green, very thinly sliced on the diagonal, for garnish
2 teaspoons coarsely chopped fresh parsley, for garnish

1. Place the parsnips in a saucepan, cover with cold water, and bring to a boil. Reduce the heat slightly, cover, and cook until very tender, 20 to 30

minutes. Drain the parsnips and return them to the saucepan. Shake over medium heat for 30 seconds to remove excess moisture. Set them aside.

2. While the parsnips are cooking, place the potatoes in a saucepan, cover with cold water, and bring to a boil. Reduce the heat slightly, cover, and cook until very tender, 20 to 30 minutes. Drain the potatoes and return them to the saucepan. Shake over medium heat for 30 seconds to remove excess moisture.

3. Transfer the parsnips and potatoes to the bowl of an electric mixer. Beat on medium speed, gradually adding the cream, butter, egg yolk, and salt and pepper. Beat until smooth. Then adjust the seasonings if necessary, garnish with the scallion and parsley, and serve.

6 portions

Note: To reheat, place the mixture in an ovenproof dish, dot with additional butter, and cover. Bake in a preheated 350°F oven for 15 to 20 minutes.

PARSNIPS JULIENNE

The flavor of parsnips is enhanced when baked with butter and brown sugar. Serve this as a side vegetable with Ruby Glazed Corned Beef.

1 ½ pounds parsnips, peeled and julienned
4 tablespoons (½ stick) unsalted butter, cut into pieces
¼ cup (packed) light brown sugar
¼ teaspoon ground nutmeg
Freshly ground black pepper, to taste
½ cup Berta's Chicken Stock (see Index) or canned broth
2 teaspoons chopped fresh Italian (flat-leaf) parsley

1. Preheat the oven to 350°F.
2. Arrange the parsnips in a shallow baking dish, and dot with the butter. Sprinkle with the brown sugar, nutmeg, and pepper. Pour the stock into the dish and cover with aluminum foil.
3. Bake for 45 minutes, shaking the dish once during the baking.
4. Stir well and adjust the seasonings if necessary. Sprinkle with the chopped parsley before serving.

4 to 6 portions

THE PEA PATCH

Peas have a gentleness about them that is reminiscent of a warm spring rain. A mountain of shelled fresh peas tossed lightly with butter and mint is the first of the gardener's rewards, for peas are a cool-weather crop and can never withstand the heat of the summer sun. Fortunately, shelled fresh peas freeze well so we need never be without.

Cousins to the shell pea are those peas with edible pods—the snow pea (or sugar pea as some call it) and the sugar snap pea, which is actually a cross between the snow pea and the shell pea. Snow peas are flat; sugar snap peas, rounder. Both are sweet and available year round thanks to the mild winters in the southern states.

BUYING

Freshness is everything when buying peas. Like corn, they are full of sugar when fresh, and the sugar starts turning to starch the moment they are picked. Shell peas should have bright green and shiny pods that are well filled (but not stuffed) with peas. Never buy peas in dry or yellowing pods or peas that have already been shelled. The best way to check for freshness is to open a pod and eat a pea. It should taste sweet—not starchy.

Snow peas are dull green and flat. Sugar snap peas are slightly darker and the pods are rounder. Snow peas are always a little limp, but sugar snap peas should be very crisp. Look for bright color with no sign of dryness or yellowing. Buy the smallest pods for they will be the sweetest. Frozen snow and sugar snap peas are not a good substitute since they get mushy when frozen, but frozen shelled peas are usually very good.

STORING

Shell peas are best eaten immediately after picking. If you must store them, refrigerate the peas unshelled in plastic bags. Four days is about the maximum storage for shell peas; a week for snow and sugar snap peas.

SEASON TO TASTE

*Flavor your fresh spring peas
with any of the following:*

Bacon	Nutmeg
Basil	Pearl onion
Caraway seed	Savory
Chervil	Sesame
Chive	Shallot
Dill	Tarragon
Lemon	Thyme
Mint	

YIELD

You will need to shell a pound of peas for one cup, which will serve two people. Edible-pod peas (sugar snap or snow peas) go much further. A pound will serve four.

PREPARING

To shell peas, snap off the stem end of the pod and pull the string down, then press on the seam and pop it open. Run your finger down the pod, pushing the peas out.

To prepare sugar snap and snow peas, rinse the peas well, snap off the stem end, and remove the string. Sugar snaps have a string on both sides of the pod; both should be removed. Sugar snaps should be left whole, but snow peas can be sliced on the diagonal for stir-frying.

COOKING

Shell peas are usually best cooked very briefly—although it's hard to keep from eating them raw when they are very fresh and sweet. Snow peas and sugar snaps are wonderful for crudités or tossed in a fresh garden salad. Because snow peas are always a little limp, crisp them by soaking them in ice water for 30 minutes.

SHELL PEAS

▲ **Boiling:** Bring ¼ to ½ inch of water to boiling in a saucepan. Add the shelled peas, cover the pan, and turn the heat down to low. Simmer until the peas are just tender and still bright green, 5 to 10 minutes. Drain and toss with butter. Add a little cream if you want, or chopped fresh herbs, especially mint.

SNOW AND SUGAR SNAP PEAS

▲ **Boiling:** Bring a large pot of water to a boil. Drop in the peas and boil, uncovered, until just tender and still bright green, 2 to 3 minutes. Drain. Be careful not to overcook these peas or the sweetness will be lost. If you are not serving them hot, stop the cooking by running cold water over them. Steaming fades the color of the peas and we don't recommend it.

▲ **Sautéing:** This method brings out the bright green color, but the peas must be watched carefully so they don't overcook and brown. Melt 1 tablespoon of butter for each cup of peas in a skillet over medium heat. Add the peas and cook, stirring frequently, just until tender, 2 to 3 minutes. Sugar snap peas especially may be a little tough and require blanching before sautéing. Because they will be cooked further, blanch them for just a minute, then cool under cold running water and dry very well.

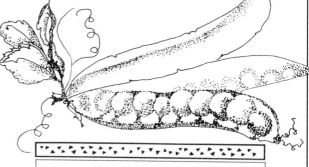

"**Y**ou may crown the month of May with lilac, put in her ears ear-rings of cherries, dress her in tender young leaves—all very well, but it will be nothing without a neck-lace of green peas."
—ANONYMOUS

CREAMY PEAS

Young, tender peas remind us of springtime in Florence, where they seem the sweetest, so we've combined them with two other Italian favorites, basil and Parmesan. Now, everyone will finish their peas.

2 cups heavy or whipping cream
1 tablespoon unsalted butter
1 tablespoon minced shallots
½ cup grated Parmesan cheese
½ cup slivered fresh basil leaves
Dash of Tabasco sauce
2 cups cooked peas

1. Bring the cream to a boil in a saucepan. Then lower the heat and simmer until it has reduced slightly, 2 to 4 minutes.

2. Melt the butter in a small skillet, and sauté the shallots over medium-low heat until translucent, 2 to 3 minutes.

3. Add the cooked shallots and the cheese to the cream, and continue cooking until slightly thickened, 2 to 3 minutes.

4. Add the basil, Tabasco, and peas. Heat through, 2 minutes, and serve immediately.

4 portions

SWEET PEA AND MINT PUREE

Sweet peas just barely cooked so that the purée tastes very fresh—with just a bit of cream to make it smooth.

4 cups peas
3 tablespoons unsalted butter
½ cup chopped onion
½ cup Berta's Chicken Stock (see Index) or canned broth
¼ cup heavy or whipping cream
1 cup fresh mint leaves
Salt and freshly ground black pepper, to taste

1. Bring a saucepan of water to a boil. Add the peas, and simmer until crisp-tender, 3 to 5 minutes. Drain, rinse under cold water, and drain again. Set the peas aside.

2. Melt the butter in a saucepan, and sauté the onion over medium-low heat until soft but not browned, about 5 minutes.

3. Add the stock and cream, raise the heat to medium, and cook until reduced by half, 5 minutes.

4. Add the mint and peas. Cook for 1 minute, and remove from the heat.

5. Transfer the mixture to the container of a food processor and purée until smooth. Then pass the purée through a food mill. Season with salt and pepper, and transfer to the top of a double boiler placed over simmering water. Reheat and serve.

4 portions

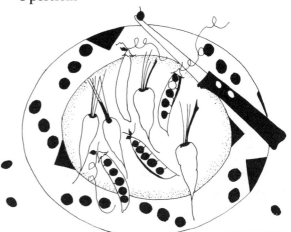

NEW AMERICAN PEAS AND CARROTS

Tender young carrots and fresh sweet sugar snap peas are our contemporary version of those basic vegetables. Be sure not to overcook the pea pods. Sauté them until they surrender their fresh, watery crispness but are still crunchy. The carrots too should retain a bit of their crunch.

8 ounces baby carrots, peeled
8 ounces sugar snap peas, trimmed
3 tablespoons Lime Ginger Butter (see Index), cut into pieces
2 teaspoons sugar
Salt and freshly ground black pepper, to taste
Snipped fresh chives, for garnish

1. Bring a saucepan of water to a boil. Add the carrots, and simmer 7 minutes. Drain, rinse under cold water, and drain again.

2. Meanwhile, bring another saucepan of lightly salted water to a boil. Add the snap peas, and simmer 3 minutes. Drain, rinse under cold water, and drain again.

3. Combine the carrots, snap peas, Lime Ginger Butter, and sugar in a 10-inch skillet. Toss over medium heat until the vegetables are glazed and heated through, 3 to 4 minutes.

4. Season with salt and pepper, sprinkle with chives, and serve.

4 portions

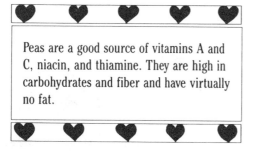

Peas are a good source of vitamins A and C, niacin, and thiamine. They are high in carbohydrates and fiber and have virtually no fat.

SESAME SNOW PEAS

A fast and delectable sauté of snow peas flavored with sesame oil and sesame seeds. Great with At Home Peking Duck.

3 tablespoons sesame oil
1 pound snow peas, trimmed
10 thin scallions (green onions), white bulb and 2 inches green
2 tablespoons pine nuts (pignoli)
1 tablespoon sesame seeds, toasted (see Index)
Salt and freshly ground black pepper, to taste

1. Heat the sesame oil in a large skillet or a wok. Add the snow peas and scallions and sauté over medium heat, tossing frequently, for 3 minutes.

2. Add the pine nuts, sesame seeds, and salt and pepper. Cook an additional 2 to 3 minutes. Serve immediately.

4 portions

PEPPERS ARE HOT

Peppers come in endless variety from fiery red to cool white to royal purple, from sweet and mild to incendiary. Experts say there are over 1,000 varieties. Latin American and Near Eastern cuisines have brought an explosion of peppers into our national cuisine—and confusion abounds. We adopted the name chile from Mexico, pimento from the Spanish, and kept the word "pepper" from the English. Add to that our inexperience and mislabeling of varieties, and we have a peck of peppers nearly impossible to sort out. But we are nothing if not intrepid. Follow along.

Capsicum is the botanical classification of all peppers. Peppercorns are not part of the capsicum genus at all; they are *Piper nigrum,* whether white or black. Pepper is the word used for the capsicum in both the United States and Europe. Chile is the Mexican word for both hot and sweet peppers. Chile is often misspelled "chili" in the United States, but to us chili can only mean a big pot of stewed stuff—beans, meat, or vegetables—delicious. In the States, chile or chile pepper always means a hot pepper. *Pimiento* is the Spanish name for pepper, but we use it to indicate the roasted red sweet peppers packed in jars or stuffed in green olives.

We are calling these 1,000 varieties of the capsicum family sweet peppers and chile peppers, and are providing a glossary for both. Of course, we can't cover all the peppers, so we've chosen the ones we think are important to today's cooking.

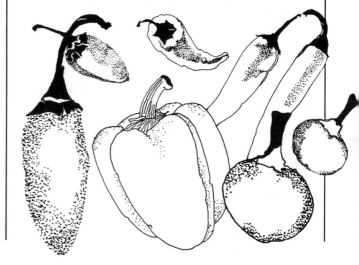

SWEET PEPPERS

This category includes both the familiar bell peppers and the elongated Italian (or frying) peppers. The bells are named for their color—green, red, yellow, orange, ivory, purple, and black or chocolate brown. All bell peppers start out green. Some will remain green, but others ripen to their characteristic color, becoming sweeter as they do so. Bell peppers other than red and green are imported for the most part from the Netherlands. They are often even sweeter than the red and frequently more expensive.

Bell peppers are available year round. Our summer crop comes mostly from California. The colorful imported peppers appear at the end of August as the California crop is finishing. They are inexpensive to start, when supplies are plentiful, but the price goes way up by October and stays up through February and March, which is the end of their season. Florida peppers start coming in during March.

Sweet peppers are prized for both their color and flavor. They are roasted, skinned, and bathed in olive oil; essential for ratatouille and Hungarian goulash; sliced into salads; minced for relishes; pickled; and stuffed as well.

Italian frying peppers look like elongated bell peppers and are pale yellow-green. They have more flavor and less bite than green bell peppers. They, too, are available year round.

▲ **Buying:** Buy sweet peppers with glossy, tight skins. They should be firm to the touch, with no soft spots. If you are buying peppers to roast and peel, buy those with the smoothest sides.

▲ **Storing:** Refrigerate sweet peppers, unwashed, in the crisper drawer up to one week. Wrap any cut pieces in plastic and use them as soon as possible. Because the other colored peppers are riper than the green, they won't keep as long.

▲ **Preparing:** Preparation depends upon how you intend to use the pepper. Before slicing or dicing, first cut the pepper in half through the stem end; then cut the stem away, shake out the seeds, and trim the pithy ribs on the inside with a small paring knife.

For stuffed peppers, choose sturdy peppers with thick, firm walls. Cut a sliver from the bottom so that it stands flat, then cut off a slice from the top for the lid. Use your fingers or a knife to remove the seeds and ribs.

Roasted peppers have a velvety texture and a rich, soft but intense flavor. When you roast a pepper, you must also skin it. For this technique, see Roasted Red Peppers on page 267.

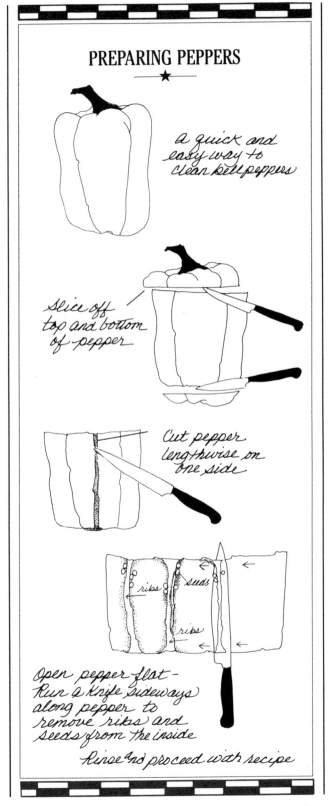

PREPARING PEPPERS

a quick and easy way to clean bell peppers

slice off top and bottom of pepper

Cut pepper lengthwise on one side

ribs seeds ribs

Open pepper flat—Run a knife sideways along pepper to remove ribs and seeds from the inside

Rinse and proceed with recipe

CHILE PEPPERS

When we originally marketed our Real Hot Pepper Chutney over a decade ago in the Southwest, people said, "It's not hot enough." We marketed the same chutney in Boston, and nostrils flared. One man's passion is another man's poison.

Not only do regional tastes differ but individual tastes do as well. Some people go for the burn, but we like deep flavor that develops by layering various levels of warmth. Our advice for cooking with chile peppers is to always taste them and the dish you are adding them to. Two peppers, even from the same plant, can be radically different in heat. You'll never know without tasting. As a general rule, the longer and thinner the pepper is, the hotter it will be. You can turn down the heat of a pepper by cutting it in half and removing the pithy ribs and all the seeds. Most of the flavor, not the heat, is in the outer wall, the fleshy part.

▲ **Buying:** The same criteria apply to buying fresh chile peppers as to sweet peppers. The skins should be tight and glossy and the pepper firm with no bruises or soft spots.

▲ **Storing:** Store fresh chiles in a paper bag in the refrigerator. Most will keep up to two weeks.

▲ **Caution:** Although we've said it before, it is well worth repeating that you must take precautions when working with hot peppers. It's best to wear rubber gloves or cover your hands with plastic sandwich bags before touching chile peppers, then wash your hands thoroughly when you are through. Never rub your eyes or touch your face. Peppers can cause second-degree burns, and it takes a good 12 hours for the pain to subside. Don't risk it.

KNOW YOUR CHILES

We have arranged this list from the hottest chiles to the mildest.

▲ **Habanero** are tiny chiles, squat and fat, with a neon orange color. Researchers at Texas A&M University state the habanero is 1,000 times hotter than the jalapeño. Use just a little and keep your hands covered when working with them.

▲ **Cascabelle** are tiny peppers shaped like fat cones or bullets. They are colored fire-engine red, bright orange, or creamy yellow-green. They are incredibly hot, second only to the habanero.

▲ **Serrano** look like fat little pinkie fingers with a slight point at the end. They are colored red or green and are very hot. Serrano is the chile of choice for

Mexican cooks, who mix them into everything good—from guacamole to beans. To cool their fire, remove the ribs and seeds. They are also milder roasted than fresh.

▲ **Santaka and Thai** are the size of a small fingernail. They are often sold on the branch or as a whole plant with hundreds of peppers that dry and keep for years—simply pick them as needed. They are extremely hot, and the heat doesn't soften, even after cooking.

▲ **Cayenne** are slim and twisted with a long point. They are colored red, green, and yellow-green and range from 3 to 6 inches in length. Most cayenne chiles are dried for cayenne pepper. The fresh cayennes are fiery hot. The smaller and more pointed the pepper, the hotter it will be.

▲ **Jalapeño** are plump little barrels with thick green skins. Most are as big as a thumb. They are hot but manageable and the most available of all the fresh chiles. If you've only had jalapeños fresh, try them roasted; they are a little less hot and have wonderful flavor.

▲ **Fresno** are shaped like the jalapeño and are as hot, but they have a lighter green or bright red skin.

▲ **Chimayo** are shaped like long cones that are slightly collapsed. They are very hot and up to now available mainly in the Southwest.

▲ **Sucette de Provence** are long peppers shaped like snap beans with a long, tapering end. The color ranges from fiery red to orange red. This chile is very hot.

▲ **Hot Portugal** are long and bean shaped with collapsed walls and an orange-red color. They are very hot.

▲ **Santa Fe Grande** are cone shaped with smooth skin. They can be deep red or yellow streaked with orange. They are very hot. Use them fresh or roast and peel them.

▲ **Hungarian wax (banana pepper)** are long, tapering cones with a creamy yellow skin. Some are very mild; others are medium-hot. Taste them before you add them to a dish. These peppers are wonderful pickled. Look for them in big jars with Hungarian labels.

▲ **Surefire** are elongated, cone-shaped peppers with a slight curve or twist. They can be deep red or bright yellow and have medium heat.

▲ **Ancho (poblano)** are cone shaped with a long tip. They have a very shiny skin, colored green or red. They have medium heat but wonderful flavor. We like them best roasted and peeled.

▲ **Mexi-bell** look exactly like a bell pepper but they

have some heat. They are wonderful peppers for stuffing.

▲ **Red cherry** look like cherry tomatoes with thick, deep red skin. They are medium hot. We like them fresh but especially pickled.

▲ **Anaheim** are elongated and coneshaped with a slight twist. They can be red or green and are mild to medium-hot. They are favorites for stuffing.

▲ **Hot shot** are thick-skinned, elongated cones colored deep red. They are barely hot.

▲ **Pepperoncini (Tuscan peppers)** are shaped like long cones and colored almost neon red. They have mild heat. We like them best pickled and added to an Italian antipasto.

THE NUTRITIONAL PEPPER

— ★ —

Peppers are rich in vitamins A, C, and E. Red peppers have ten times more vitamin A than green, and chile peppers have less nutritional value than sweet. Vitamin levels are decreased when peppers are cooked and disappear when they are dried.

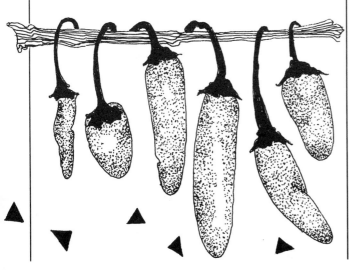

VARIATIONS ON THE PEPPER

▲ **Cayenne** is a dried, crushed spice named for the capital city of French Guiana, once the major growing region for cayenne peppers. It is orange-red in color and very hot. In current parlance, it is often simply called ground red pepper.

▲ **Crushed red pepper** is flaked, dried red peppers, called pizza pepper in some neighborhoods. The same pepper is available in whole dried pods—they are simply called dried red peppers.

▲ **Paprika** is ground and dried sweet red peppers, popularized by Hungarians who still make the best. Paprika is available sweet, moderately hot, and hot.

CONDIMENTS

▲ **Chile oil** is a fiery oil used by the drop in Asian cooking.

▲ **Chili powder** is ground dried chiles mixed with cumin, ginger, cayenne, oregano, and dried mustard. There is no one formula for chili powder, so try different brands until you find one you like. The best we've found are special blends from small producers.

▲ **Curry powder** is dried chiles ground with spices and herbs. Like chili powder, curry powder varies dramatically from brand to brand. Keep trying until you find one you like. Curry powder should never be harsh.

▲ **Harissa** is a fiery paste used in North African cooking.

▲ **Mandram** is a West Indian mix of chile peppers, cucumber, shallot, chive, lemon or lime juice, and Madeira.

▲ **Pickled peppers** are bottled whole or sliced. They can be eaten right out of the jar, layered in sandwiches, or added to sauces and dips. Most are very mild.

▲ **Pimento** is the Anglicization of pimiento, the name for the sweet, thick-walled, red peppers that are roasted and bottled.

▲ **Salsa** is simply the Mexican word for sauce. In this country, salsa or salsa picante means a table sauce of chiles, tomatoes, onions, cilantro, garlic, and salt. The salsa market is said to be expanding 15 to 20 percent every year.

▲ **Tabasco** is powdered chile peppers mixed with vinegar and salt. It's also called pepper sauce, red sauce, and hot red pepper sauce.

STUFFED POBLANO CHILES

These are hot! All the flavors and colors of the Southwest are mingled in these chiles, which we temper with cooling sour cream.

2 large or 3 medium poblano (ancho) chiles, halved
    lengthwise and seeded
¾ cup fresh or frozen corn kernels, thawed if frozen
¼ cup chopped red onion
¼ cup chopped celery
¼ cup chopped red bell pepper
2 tablespoons chopped cilantro (fresh coriander)
2 ounces sharp Cheddar cheese, shredded (¾ cup)
1 fresh jalapeño pepper, seeded and minced
1 tablespoon dried bread crumbs
½ teaspoon salt
Freshly ground black pepper, to taste
Sour cream or crème fraîche (see Index)

1. Preheat the oven to 375°F. Oil a baking sheet.
2. Arrange the pepper halves on the baking sheet.
3. Combine all the remaining ingredients except the sour cream in a mixing bowl, and toss thoroughly. Fill the pepper halves with this mixture.
4. Bake until the peppers are tender and the filling is heated through, 30 minutes.
5. Serve immediately, topped with a dollop of sour cream.

4 portions

"Nothing is so strong as gentleness, nothing so gentle as real strength."
—FRANCIS DE SALES

SIX PEPPER SLAW

Fresh orange, yellow, red, green, and purple peppers sparkled with a toasted caraway and jalapeño pepper dressing. It's vivid in both look and taste—yummy!

1 red bell pepper
1 orange bell pepper
1 green bell pepper
1 purple bell pepper
1 yellow bell pepper
1 red onion

DRESSING
1 fresh jalapeño pepper, cored, seeded, and minced
2 tablespoons tarragon vinegar
1 tablespoon Dijon mustard
2 teaspoons sugar
1 teaspoon salt
¼ teaspoon Tabasco sauce
Freshly ground black pepper, to taste
¼ cup vegetable oil
2 tablespoons peanut oil
1 tablespoon caraway seeds, toasted (see Index) and crushed
2 teaspoons grated lime zest

1. Core, seed, and slice all the peppers into long julienne strips. Cut the red onion lengthwise into thin strips. Toss the pepper strips and onion together in a medium-size bowl. Set aside.
2. Make the dressing: In a medium-size bowl, stir together the jalapeño pepper, vinegar, mustard, sugar, salt, Tabasco, and black pepper. Slowly add both oils, whisking until the dressing is smooth and thick.
3. Toss the vegetables with the dressing. Sprinkle with the caraway seeds and lime zest, and toss until blended.
4. Cover and refrigerate at least 3 hours. Stir before serving.

6 portions

ROASTED RED PEPPERS

Keep plenty of these velvety-smooth roasted peppers in your refrigerator. They are so delicious and useful, you'll wonder how you ever got through a week without them.

6 red bell peppers
2 tablespoons fresh lemon juice
1 teaspoon coarsely ground black pepper

1. Preheat the broiler.
2. Halve the peppers lengthwise, and remove the seeds. Place them skin side up on a broiler pan.
3. Broil the peppers 2 to 3 inches from the heat. Watch carefully, and when the skin blackens, turn the peppers until the skins are black all over.
4. Using tongs, transfer the peppers to a plastic bag, and seal it well with a twist tie. Let the peppers steam in the bag for 15 to 20 minutes. Then remove them from the bag and peel off the skin.
5. Place the peppers in a shallow dish, drizzle them with the lemon juice, and sprinkle with the black pepper.

6 portions

HOT PEPPER SANDWICH

Instead of the hot red cherry peppers we remember in sausage and pepper sandwiches, here a hot chile is tempered (but not too much) by a sweet banana pepper and nutty Jarlsberg cheese.

1 sweet banana (Hungarian wax) pepper
1 mildly hot long chile pepper
1 scallion (green onion), white bulb and 3 inches green
2 ounces Jarlsberg cheese, shredded (¾ cup)
Freshly ground black pepper, to taste
1 small loaf French or Italian bread
1 tablespoon unsalted butter, at room temperature

1. Preheat the oven to 350°F.
2. Slice the banana pepper in half lengthwise and remove the seeds. Slice it crosswise into thin strips. Seed and chop the chile pepper. Thinly slice the scallion.
3. Combine the peppers, scallion, cheese, and black pepper in a small bowl, and toss to mix.
4. Halve the bread lengthwise. Remove some of the insides, making a long indentation in each half. Butter the bread lightly, and fill it with the pepper mixture. Close the sandwich and wrap it in foil, leaving the top uncovered. Brush the top lightly with butter; sprinkle it with black pepper.
5. Place the sandwich on a baking sheet, and bake until golden and crisp, about 30 minutes. Cut it in half and serve it hot.

1 or 2 portions

RED PEPPER AND GINGER MARMALADE

Sweet red bell peppers are simmered with garlic, ginger, sugar, and orange juice and zest to create a slightly sweet condiment with a bite to it. Great served with grilled chicken or beef, sausages, lamb, on a sandwich, in a potato, or with game. Try to always have some on hand—it's addictive.

12 medium to large red bell peppers (about 3 pounds)
4 tablespoons (½ stick) unsalted butter
½ cup extra virgin olive oil
3 rounded tablespoons minced garlic (10 cloves)
½ cup coarsely grated fresh ginger
Grated zest of 3 oranges
¾ cup fresh orange juice
3 tablespoons sugar
2 teaspoons freshly ground black pepper

1. Core and seed the peppers, and cut them into ¼-inch-wide lengthwise strips (you should have 12 cups).

2. Heat the butter and oil in a heavy flameproof casserole. Add the garlic and ginger, and cook over low heat for 5 minutes. Add the peppers, and stir well to coat.

3. Mix in the orange zest, juice, sugar, and pepper. Stir gently and cover. Cook over medium-low heat, stirring occasionally, until the peppers are wilted and their skins are soft, 25 minutes.

4. Remove the cover and continue cooking over low heat, stirring frequently, until most of the liquid has evaporated, 2 hours.

5. Serve hot or at room temperature. This keeps, covered tightly, in the refrigerator for up to 4 days.

4 cups

2. Combine the orange and pepper pieces in a food processor and process until smooth. (There may still be small flecks of red pepper.)

3. Transfer the purée to a deep 2-quart microwave-safe casserole, and stir in the remaining ingredients. Cook at full power (650 to 700 watts) for 2 minutes. Stir, and cook until thick, about another 4 minutes.

4. Allow the marmalade to cool to room temperature, and then cover and refrigerate.

1⅓ cups

Note: This recipe was cooked on High (full power, 650 to 700 watts) in a carousel microwave, using microwave-safe containers.

If your microwave is less powerful, you will have to allow for more cooking time (approximately 1½ times the amount called for—but watch carefully); if it does not have a carousel, you may have to rotate the dish while it is cooking.

HOT-PEPPER AND ORANGE PRESERVE

This deep orange marmalade is sweet and hot and ready in six minutes. If you see blood oranges in the market, use them for their bright red color. This is delicious with savory biscuits and spicy breakfast patties.

½ navel orange
1 to 1½ hot fresh red chile peppers
1 cup sugar
¼ cup water
2 tablespoons fresh lemon juice

1. Quarter the orange half and remove the seeds; do not remove the peel. Carefully remove the stem and seeds from the chile pepper, and quarter it.

THREE PEPPER SAUCES

These three sauces, each one bright and beautiful, can be served in a variety of ways. Alone or spooned next to each other on a small plate, they are perfect garnishes for Swiss Chard Strudel, Corn Crab Cakes, and Ricotta Torte. Each has a distinct flavor.

GREEN PEPPER SAUCE

2 tablespoons olive oil
1 leek (white part and 1 inch green), well rinsed, patted dry, and chopped
2 cloves garlic, minced
1 green bell pepper, cored, seeded, and chopped
¼ cup chopped fresh basil leaves
½ cup Berta's Chicken Stock (see Index) or canned broth
¼ teaspoon salt
Freshly ground black pepper, to taste

1. Cook the oil in a 2-quart microwave-safe casserole at full power (650 to 700 watts) for 2 minutes.

2. Stir in the leek and garlic. Cook 3 minutes.

3. Stir in the green pepper and basil. Cover, and cook 4 minutes.

4. Transfer the mixture to a food processor, and add the broth. Purée until smooth. Season with the salt and pepper, and serve immediately (or briefly reheat later in the microwave.)

1½ cups

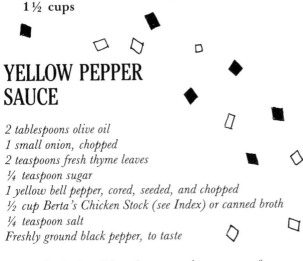

YELLOW PEPPER SAUCE

2 tablespoons olive oil
1 small onion, chopped
2 teaspoons fresh thyme leaves
¼ teaspoon sugar
1 yellow bell pepper, cored, seeded, and chopped
½ cup Berta's Chicken Stock (see Index) or canned broth
¼ teaspoon salt
Freshly ground black pepper, to taste

1. Cook the oil in a 2-quart microwave-safe casserole at full power (650 to 700 watts) for 2 minutes.

2. Stir in the onion, thyme, and sugar. Cover, and cook 4 minutes.

3. Stir in the yellow pepper. Cover, and cook 4 minutes.

4. Transfer the mixture to the container of a food processor, and add the broth. Purée until smooth. Season with the salt and pepper, and serve immediately (or briefly reheat later in the microwave.)

1½ cups

RED PEPPER SAUCE

2 tablespoons olive oil
1 small onion, chopped
1 tablespoon tomato paste
1 tablespoon balsamic vinegar
1 red bell pepper, cored, seeded, and chopped
½ cup Berta's Chicken Stock (see Index) or canned broth
¼ teaspoon salt
Freshly ground black pepper, to taste

1. Cook the oil in a 2-quart microwave-safe casserole at full power (650 to 700 watts) for 2 minutes.

2. Stir in the onion, tomato paste, and vinegar. Cook 3 minutes.

3. Stir in the red pepper. Cover, and cook 4 minutes.

4. Transfer the mixture to the container of a food processor, and add the broth. Purée until smooth. Season with the salt and pepper, and serve immediately (or briefly reheat later in the microwave.)

1½ cups

Note: These recipes were cooked on High (full power, 650 to 700 watts) in a carousel microwave, using microwave-safe containers.

If your microwave is less powerful, you will have to allow for more cooking time (approximately 1½ times the amount called for—but watch carefully); if it does not have a carousel, you may have to rotate the dish while it is cooking.

TRADE SECRET

Keep roasted and peeled peppers covered with a bit of olive oil in the refrigerator for at least a week to serve with eggs or on ham sandwiches or grilled toast.

"A little bad taste is like a nice splash of paprika."
—DIANA VREELAND

REAL HOT PEPPER CHUTNEY

In twenty minutes you'll have a glistening *hot* pepper chutney that's great to serve with food from the grill, or with a Best Western Omelet.

1 green bell pepper, cored and seeded
1 red bell pepper, cored and seeded
4 fresh jalapeño peppers
¾ cup white wine vinegar
½ cup granulated sugar
½ cup (packed) brown sugar
½ cup crystallized ginger, slivered
½ cup golden raisins
2 cloves garlic, minced

1. Cut each bell pepper into 8 long strips. Cut the strips crosswise into ¼-inch-wide slices.
2. Remove the stems from the jalapeños and cut them in half lengthwise. Cut them crosswise into ¼-inch-thick slices (with seeds).
3. Stir the peppers and all the remaining ingredients together in a 4-quart microwave-safe casserole.
4. Cook, uncovered, at full power (650 to 700 watts) until thick, 20 minutes. This keeps for up to two weeks, covered, in the refrigerator.

2½ cups

Note: This recipe was cooked on High (full power, 650 to 700 watts) in a carousel microwave, using microwave-safe containers.

If your microwave is less powerful, you will have to allow for more cooking time (approximately 1½ times the amount called for—but watch carefully); if it does not have a carousel, you may have to rotate the dish while it is cooking.

ALL EYES ARE ON POTATOES

Mashed potatoes with whole milk, melting butter, and salt and pepper—served just to the right of the meat loaf and left of the string beans—was the best meal in the world and a good part of growing up.

French- or home-fried, baked, boiled, scalloped, or in salads, potatoes are the starch of choice in so many homes. Serve them up—white or sweet, waxy or starchy—to garner praise any time of the year. They're just too versatile to ever be out of fashion.

VARIETIES OF POTATO

We never see just one kind of potato at the market; there are always at least three or four—new potatoes, red potatoes, white potatoes, and russets. The only important fact to know is what potato is best for what preparation. Some potatoes are great baked; some aren't. Some make wonderful fries or potato salad; others don't. It all depends on how much starch a potato has. We'll describe the most common potatoes and how they are best used.

▲ **New potatoes:** A new potato is simply harvested before it reaches maturity and sent directly to the market instead of being stored. There is just one potato crop each year but several harvests. New potatoes are dug up in the spring and early summer—the year's first harvest. A new potato can have a skin that is red or light brown, but the smaller the better. We've had them as small as your thumbnail and they're quite irresistible.

The crop of new potatoes comes on the market in the late spring and stays through most of the summer, although some new red potatoes grown in warmer climates appear in the produce section sometime in February. A "new" potato in the supermarket from November to January is most likely not new at all—it's been in storage. Don't pay new potato prices for old potatoes.

Like so many other vegetables, such as corn and peas, a potato's natural sugars begin turning to starch as soon as it's picked. Because new potatoes are sent immediately to market, they are low in starch and still fairly sweet. They are firmer and moister than stored potatoes, so they are best steamed or boiled. They make poor baked potatoes.

▲ **Mature potatoes:** Mature potatoes can be used in many ways that new potatoes cannot—mainly, baking and frying. Mature potatoes can be divided roughly into two categories: russets and all-purpose potatoes. Russets, which includes Idahos, are usually long in shape and called baking potatoes because that's what they do best. They are the starchiest of all the potatoes, which makes for a fluffy baked potato and French fry.

All-purpose potatoes can be round or long in shape and brown or red in color. They are lower in starch and moister than baking potatoes, which makes them perfect for boiling, roasting, and slicing into salads.

BUYING

Buy potatoes that are firm, smooth, well shaped, and heavy for their size. Size is unimportant unless you are serving them baked, but baking potatoes all make generous single servings. Don't buy potatoes with cracks, discoloring, withered skin, or sprouting eyes. Check carefully for any green tinge on the skin. Potatoes that have a green cast have been exposed to light; they'll taste bitter and can make you sick.

STORING

All potatoes should be kept in a cool, well-ventilated place. Air circulation is important to the life of a potato because it keeps them dry. They should keep at least two weeks.

If you've bought potatoes in plastic bags, take them out and put them in a net bag or basket. If you have very hot and humid summers and your potatoes sprout before you can get to them, you can refrigerate them in paper bags for a short while as long as they stay dry.

YIELD

One medium potato will serve one person adequately. It takes about three medium potatoes to make a pound. Eight to ten small new potatoes make a pound and will serve three people.

PREPARING

Potatoes should be scrubbed or peeled just before cooking. If you're cooking them in their skin, scrub them well (a vegetable brush helps immensely) but be careful not to tear or break the skin. You will lose a lot of the potato's vitamins by peeling it, but there are times when peel you must. Do so with a vegetable peeler and drop them immediately into a bowl of cold water to keep them from browning. Potatoes with a few eyes or sprouts can be used—just cut around and remove them.

COOKING

Follow this advice and you'll never be disappointed when cooking potatoes: starchy dry potatoes—bake or french fry; semistarchy, moist—roast or boil; new potatoes—boil or steam. Beyond that, the sky is the limit—with butter and parsley or dill, plain, au gratin, twice baked and stuffed with cheese, or sausage, or peppers and onions. The list goes on and on, but don't forget the standards: old-fashioned mashed, french fries, or roasted wedges.

▲ **Boiling:** Scrub or peel potatoes. Cut them into even pieces if they are large and put them in a pot. Cover with plenty of cold water and salt it. Heat to boiling, then turn down the heat a bit and gently boil, covered or uncovered, until tender when pierced with a knife, 15 to 30 minutes depending on how large the potatoes are. Drain well, then return the potatoes to the pan and toss over low heat to evaporate any remaining water. Add butter if you want and toss to coat the potatoes. Sprinkle with parsley or dill and serve.

▲ **Steaming:** Scrub small new potatoes and put them in a steaming rack or basket over 1 inch of boiling water. Steam covered until tender when pierced with a knife, 15 to 30 minutes, depending on size.

▲ **Baking:** The first rule is use the right potato—a russet (sometimes labeled simply Idaho).

Scrub the potatoes and pat dry, then prick the skins several times with a fork. Bake the potatoes directly on the rack at 375°F for 1 to 1½ hours, depending on the size. To test for doneness, squeeze them (with an oven mitt or quickly with your fingers). If the potato gives and feels soft, it is done. Serve baked potatoes immediately or the skins turn soft and limp.

Don't bake potatoes wrapped in foil. It steams them, making the skin soft and the center moist and dense.

▲ **Roasting:** There is nothing like the taste of potatoes cooked in the oven and basted with the drippings of a roast. But they can also be roasted by themselves on top of the stove or in the oven. The methods are so simple, we think they should be in everyone's basic repertoire.

Oven roasting: Scrub all-purpose or new potatoes and cut lengthwise into quarters—or halves if small. Place them in a large baking dish or roasting pan where they will have plenty of room. Add at least ¼ cup of olive oil or oil mixed with melted butter—enough to coat the potatoes and the dish liberally—and turn to coat the potatoes well. Roast at 350° to 375°F, turning occasionally, until they are crisp and browned on the outside and tender at the center, 1 to 1½ hours. Whole cloves of garlic in their skins can be roasted right along with the potatoes, and the potatoes can be sprinkled with dried herbs, salt, and pepper halfway through cooking.

Pan roasting: Prepare the potatoes as for oven roasting. Heat ¼ inch of olive oil in a heavy skillet large enough to hold the potatoes in a single layer over medium-high heat. Add the potatoes and turn to coat with oil. Cover the skillet and cook 15 minutes, turning the potatoes when the underside is browned. Remove the cover and continue to cook, turning the potatoes as needed, until crisp and browned on the outside and tender at the center, about 15 more minutes. As for oven-roasted potatoes, whole cloves of garlic in their skins can be cooked with these potatoes and they can also be seasoned halfway through cooking.

Roasting with meat: Add the scrubbed and quartered potatoes to the roasting pan about 1 hour before the roast should be done. Baste them with the pan juices and turn several times to brown evenly.

> "**W**hat I say is that, if a fellow really likes potatoes, he must be a pretty decent sort of fellow."
> —A. A. MILNE

BASIC MASHED POTATOES

Whichever way you like them, mashed potatoes are one of the best things in life.

4 Idaho potatoes (8 ounces each), peeled and cubed
4 tablespoons (½ stick) unsalted butter, at room temperature
½ cup milk, heated
¼ cup sour cream
Salt and coarsely ground black pepper, to taste
Chopped fresh Italian (flat-leaf) parsley, for garnish

1. Place the potatoes in a saucepan, cover with cold water, and bring to a boil. Reduce the heat slightly and cook until the potatoes are tender, 20 to 30 minutes. Drain the potatoes, return them to the saucepan, and shake the pan over low heat to remove the remaining moisture, 10 to 15 seconds.

2. Transfer the potatoes to the bowl of an electric mixer, or to a mixing bowl. (Or you can press the potatoes through a ricer into a mixing bowl.) Begin mashing with the mixer or by hand, and add the butter, hot milk, sour cream, and salt and pepper. Continue beating until smooth; make sure there are no lumps.

3. Garnish with parsley and serve immediately.

4 portions

Note: To reheat mashed potatoes, place them in the top of a double boiler over simmering water, and stir until heated through.

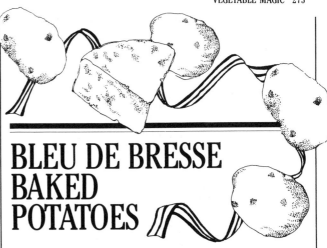

GARLIC MASHED POTATOES

When plain mashed potatoes just won't do, add garlic. Don't overbeat the potatoes—a lump or two makes them real down home!

3 pounds all-purpose potatoes, peeled and cubed
1 large head garlic
5 tablespoons heavy or whipping cream
4 tablespoons (½ stick) unsalted butter, at room temperature
1 egg yolk
½ teaspoon coarsely ground black pepper
Salt, to taste
1 tablespoon chopped fresh Italian (flat-leaf) parsley,
*   for garnish*

1. Place the potatoes in a large saucepan, cover with cold water, and bring to a boil. Reduce the heat slightly and cook until tender, 20 minutes.

2. While the potatoes are cooking, peel the paper-like outer skin off the garlic and separate the cloves. Place them in a small saucepan, cover with water, and bring to a boil. Lower the heat and simmer until the garlic is very soft, 15 minutes. Drain and allow to cool.

3. Drain the potatoes and return them to the saucepan. Shake over medium heat to remove the remaining moisture, 10 to 15 seconds. Set the potatoes aside.

4. Slip the skins off the garlic, and combine the garlic cloves and the cream in a food processor. Purée.

5. Transfer the potatoes to the bowl of an electric mixer, and add the puréed garlic, butter, egg yolk, pepper, and salt. Beat until just smooth. Garnish with the parsley, and serve immediately.

6 portions

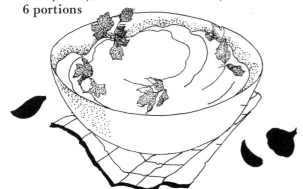

BLEU DE BRESSE BAKED POTATOES

These potatoes are just about a meal on their own. Serve them with a crispy green salad and a Beaujolais-Villages.

4 Idaho potatoes (8 ounces each) scrubbed and patted dry
2 tablespoons unsalted butter
2 large cloves garlic, very finely minced
½ cup sour cream
2 ounces Bleu de Bresse or other mild blue cheese
1 tablespoon chopped fresh parsley
1 tablespoon plus 2 teaspoons snipped fresh chives
Salt and freshly ground black pepper, to taste
Paprika, to taste

1. Preheat the oven to 375°F.

2. Prick the potatoes all over with the tines of a fork, and place them on a baking sheet. Bake for 1¼ hours.

3. Melt the butter in a skillet, add the garlic, and cook over very low heat for 1½ minutes; do not let it brown. Set it aside.

4. Remove the potatoes but leave the oven on. Allow the potatoes to cool slightly. Then cut a lengthwise slit in the top of each potato and carefully remove the pulp, leaving the skin intact. Place the pulp in a mixing bowl, and set the skins aside.

5. Mash the potatoes with a fork. Add the garlic butter, sour cream, cheese, parsley, 1 tablespoon chives, and salt and pepper. Mix thoroughly, and then carefully stuff the mixture back into the potato skins, mounding it slightly. Sprinkle the top lightly with paprika.

6. Arrange the potatoes on a baking sheet, and bake for 15 minutes. Sprinkle with the remaining 2 teaspoons chives and serve immediately.

4 portions

SAUSAGE BAKED POTATOES

Have the Sunday papers waiting alongside these delicious breakfast potatoes. The eggs and sausage make them an early-morning one-dish meal.

4 Idaho potatoes (8 ounces each), scrubbed and patted dry
2 tablespoons olive oil
4 sweet Italian sausages, meat removed from casing
1 cup diced onion
2 tablespoons chopped fresh Italian (flat-leaf) parsley
6 tablespoons heavy or whipping cream, warmed
¼ cup sour cream
2 egg yolks
Salt and freshly ground black pepper, to taste

1. Preheat the oven to 375°F.
2. Prick the potatoes all over with the tines of a fork, and place them on a baking sheet. Bake for 1¼ hours.
3. Meanwhile, heat the oil in a skillet. Add the sausage meat and cook over medium heat until browned, breaking the meat apart as it cooks.
4. Using a slotted spoon, transfer the cooked sausage to a mixing bowl. Add the onion to the skillet and cook over medium heat until it is wilted and lightly colored, 5 minutes. Add the onion to the sausage. Toss in the parsley, and set aside.
5. Remove the potatoes from the oven, but leave the oven on. Set them aside to cool slightly. When they are cool enough to handle, cut an oval section of skin off the top, and carefully scoop out the pulp, leaving a shell of skin. Set the shells aside, and place the potato pulp in a mixing bowl.
6. Mash the potatoes, adding the cream, sour cream, egg yolks, and salt and pepper. Gently stir in the sausage and onion mixture. Stuff the potato shells with the filling, mounding it slightly.
7. Place the potatoes on a baking sheet, and return them to the oven to heat through, 15 minutes.
   4 portions

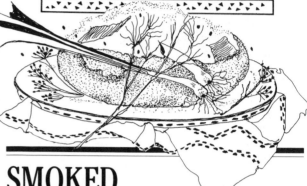

TRADE SECRET

When baking potatoes, make a few extra to use for hash browns the next morning. Always leave the skins on.

SMOKED SALMON BAKED POTATOES

Baked potatoes rise to new heights in this dish. Serve them with Double-Boiler Scrambled Eggs and pink champagne for a post-theater supper.

4 Idaho potatoes (8 ounces each), scrubbed and patted dry
4 slices smoked salmon
2 scallions (green onions), white bulb and 3 inches green,
    thinly sliced on the diagonal
½ cup sour cream
4 tablespoons (½ stick) unsalted butter, at room temperature
1 tablespoon chopped fresh dill
Salt and freshly ground black pepper, to taste
Chopped fresh dill, for garnish

1. Preheat the oven to 375°F.
2. Prick the potatoes all over with the tines of a fork, place them on a baking sheet, and bake for 1¼ hours.
3. Shred the salmon into small pieces and place in a bowl with the scallions. Set aside.
4. When the potatoes are done, remove them from the oven and allow to cool slightly. (Leave the oven on.) Then cut a slit lengthwise along the top, and carefully remove the insides, leaving a thin shell.

5. Place the potato pulp in a bowl and mash it with a fork. Add the sour cream, butter, dill, and salt and pepper. Blend well. Gently mix in the reserved salmon and scallions. Carefully stuff the mixture back into the potato skins, mounding it slightly.

6. Place the potatoes on a baking sheet, return them to the oven, and bake for 15 minutes. Sprinkle with fresh dill, and serve immediately.

4 portions

CRISPY BAKED SKINS

We love munching on these in restaurants, but they're easy and fun to make at home. Be sure the skins are nice and crispy.

2 Idaho potatoes (8 ounces each), scrubbed and patted dry
2 teaspoons unsalted butter
Freshly ground black pepper, to taste

1. Preheat the oven to 375°F.
2. Prick the potatoes all over with the tines of a fork. Place them on a baking sheet and bake until the skin is very crisp, 1½ hours.
3. Cut a long oval shape out of the top of each potato. Remove the inside of the potatoes and save for another use.
4. Put 1 teaspoon of the butter inside each potato skin, and return them to the oven for 5 minutes. Sprinkle with pepper and serve immediately.

2 portions

MINTY ROASTED POTATOES

Our very favorite potatoes are roasted and then tossed with lots of garlic and fresh mint. Be sure to hide them before you serve them, or you'll have less than expected!

8 red new potatoes scrubbed and patted dry
¼ cup olive oil
Coarse (kosher) salt, to taste
Freshly ground black pepper, to taste
4 cloves garlic, finely chopped
2 tablespoons coarsely chopped fresh mint leaves or Italian (flat-leaf) parsley

1. Preheat the oven to 350°F.
2. Prick the potatoes with the tines of a fork and arrange them on a baking sheet. Bake for 1½ hours.
3. Cut the potatoes into quarters and place them in a serving bowl. While they are still hot, toss them with the oil, coarse salt, pepper, and garlic.
4. Gently toss in the mint. Serve hot or at room temperature.

4 portions

SEASON TO TASTE

Potatoes welcome a range of flavors. When you're in the mood for more than butter, salt, and pepper, try any of the following:

Basil	Mint
Caraway seed	Mustard
Cardamom	Nutmeg
Cayenne	Olive oil
pepper	Onion
Cheese	Oregano
Chive	Parsley
Cilantro	Rosemary
Dill	Tarragon
Fennel	Thyme
Garlic	Vinegar

OVEN-BAKED FRENCH FRIES

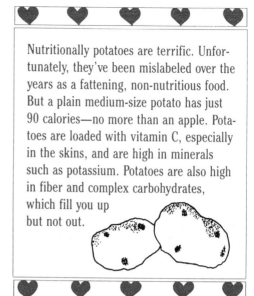

In the mid-1800s crescent-shaped fried potato chips were first sold on the Pont Neuf in Paris as *pommes frites Pont Neuf*. The popularity spread first to England as "chips" and then to America as "french fries."

Serve these with your favorite ketchup, malt vinegar, or a wedge of lemon.

4 Idaho potatoes (8 ounces each)
1 tablespoon white wine vinegar
4 tablespoons (½ stick) unsalted butter
¼ cup corn oil
Coarse (kosher) salt, to taste

1. Peel the potatoes and cut them into ¼-inch-thick lengthwise strips. Place the strips in a bowl of cold water mixed with the vinegar. (The potatoes should be totally submerged.) Soak for 1 hour.
2. Preheat the oven to 400°F.
3. Drain the potatoes and thoroughly pat them dry.
4. Heat the butter and oil in a saucepan, add the potatoes, and toss to coat. Then transfer the potatoes to a strainer and let them drain. Arrange them on two baking sheets.
5. Bake the potatoes until golden on the bottom, 20 minutes. Then turn them over and bake until they are golden all over, another 15 to 20 minutes.
6. Remove the potatoes from the oven and place them on paper towels to drain. Sprinkle with coarse salt and serve immediately.

4 portions

Note: Allow 1 potato per person when making french fries.

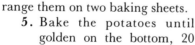

Nutritionally potatoes are terrific. Unfortunately, they've been mislabeled over the years as a fattening, non-nutritious food. But a plain medium-size potato has just 90 calories—no more than an apple. Potatoes are loaded with vitamin C, especially in the skins, and are high in minerals such as potassium. Potatoes are also high in fiber and complex carbohydrates, which fill you up but not out.

UPPER CRUST POTATOES

Among the most precious standbys in the kitchen, the potato gratin is perfect with all grilled and roasted meats, poultry, and game. Different textures can be achieved by coarsely or thinly grating, dicing, or julienning the potatoes. This is a winner, particularly when there's a chilly wind outside.

3 pounds Idaho potatoes (about 6)
1 ½ cups heavy or whipping cream
2 tablespoons unsalted butter
¼ cup finely chopped shallots
2 teaspoons minced garlic
2 bay leaves
1 ½ teaspoons finely chopped fresh rosemary leaves
¾ cup cream cheese, at room temperature
½ cup milk
½ teaspoon paprika
Salt and freshly ground black pepper, to taste
¾ cup freshly grated Parmesan cheese
¼ cup dried bread crumbs
2 tablespoons chopped fresh Italian (flat-leaf) parsley

1. Preheat the oven to 375°F. Oil the bottom of a shallow 2-quart baking dish.

2. Peel and very thinly slice the potatoes. Place them in a mixing bowl and add ¾ cup of the cream. Toss to mix. Set aside.

3. Melt the butter in a skillet, and add the shallots and garlic. Sauté over low heat for 3 to 4 minutes; do not brown.

4. Add the bay leaves and rosemary to the skillet. Whisk in the cream cheese, milk, and remaining ¾ cup cream. Simmer, whisking constantly, until smooth, 2 to 3 minutes. Then add the paprika and salt and pepper. Discard the bay leaves and pour the mixture over the potatoes; toss gently.

5. Arrange the potato mixture in a baking dish, spreading it out evenly. Sprinkle it first with the Parmesan, and then with the bread crumbs.

6. Bake until the potatoes are tender and the top is golden brown and bubbly, 1 to 1¼ hours. Sprinkle with the parsley and serve immediately.

8 portions

THE NEWEST POTATO ON THE BLOCK

Yukon Gold potatoes, just beginning to be distributed around the country, are one of the nicest things to happen to spuds we know.

The Yukon Gold has a creamy texture and golden flesh—a combination that makes it taste and look buttery. So much so, it makes it easy to skip the butter entirely, which is great for all of us watching our fat intake. Yukon Golds are harvested small, medium, and large, but all have the same great taste. These potatoes are good baked, but they make the creamiest mashed potatoes imaginable, the crispest deep orange French fries, and the best potato salad ever!

ROSEMARY POTATO GALETTE

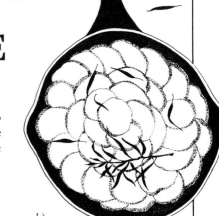

Be sure to present this beautiful potato tart whole, and slice it into wedges at the table. Everyone will be dazzled.

4 Idaho potatoes (8 ounces each)
8 tablespoons (1 stick) unsalted butter
1½ teaspoons chopped fresh rosemary leaves or Italian (flat-leaf) parsley
¾ teaspoon dried thyme leaves
Freshly ground black pepper, to taste
Coarse (kosher) salt, to taste

1. Peel the potatoes and slice them very thin, dropping the slices into a bowl of cold water as you proceed. When they are all sliced, drain and pat dry.

2. Melt 2 tablespoons of the butter in a 10-inch nonstick skillet. Swirl the butter to coat the surface; then remove the skillet from the heat. Arrange one third of the potato slices in a spiral, starting in the center and overlapping, so that the bottom of the skillet is covered.

3. Cut 2 tablespoons of the butter into small pieces and sprinkle them over the potatoes. Then sprinkle the potatoes with ½ teaspoon of the rosemary, ¼ teaspoon of the thyme, and salt and pepper. Repeat, making two more layers of potatoes, butter, and seasonings, pressing each layer down with a spatula.

4. Place the skillet over medium-low heat, and cook until the bottom is crisp and golden brown, 45 minutes. Then invert the galette onto a flat plate and slip it back into the skillet. Continue cooking until the other side is golden, 10 to 15 minutes.

5. Invert the galette again onto a serving platter. Cut it into wedges and serve immediately.

6 to 8 portions

HERBY STEAMED POTATOES

Don't overcook these tiny gems of summer. Their perfect waxy texture is heightened by a touch of butter and the freshest herbs.

12 very small red new potatoes scrubbed
1 cup water
1 tablespoon unsalted butter
Coarse (kosher) salt, to taste
Coarsely ground black pepper, to taste
1 tablespoon chopped fresh Italian (flat-leaf) parsley or fresh dill

1. If you like, use a vegetable peeler to remove a thin stripe of red skin around the center of each potato; even it off with a small paring knife if necessary.

2. Place the potatoes and water in a saucepan and bring to a boil. Reduce the heat to medium, cover, and cook, shaking the pan occasionally, until the potatoes are tender, 30 minutes.

3. Drain the potatoes and return them to the saucepan. Shake it over low heat to remove the remaining moisture, 10 to 15 seconds. Then remove the pan from the heat, add the butter, salt, pepper, and parsley, and toss well. Transfer the potatoes to a bowl and serve immediately.

4 portions

HOME-FRIES

When you're baking potatoes for dinner, make a few extra so you can have these gutsy home-fries in the morning. Olive oil and lots of black pepper make them perfect with steak, too.

4 Idaho baking potatoes (8 ounces each), scrubbed and patted dry
3 tablespoons olive oil
1 large onion, halved and thinly sliced
Coarsely ground black pepper, to taste
Coarse (kosher) salt, to taste

1. Preheat the oven to 350°F.

2. Rinse the potatoes and pat them dry. Prick them with the tines of a fork. Place the potatoes on a baking sheet, and bake for 1 hour. Allow them to cool.

3. Leaving the skins on, cut the potatoes into ½-inch-thick slices.

4. Heat 2 tablespoons of the oil in a large skillet. Add the onion and cook over medium-high heat, turning them with a metal spatula, until they are wilted and lightly browned, 8 to 10 minutes. Then add the potatoes and cook, turning with the spatula, until they are crisp and brown (add the remaining 1 tablespoon oil if necessary), 10 minutes.

5. Season with pepper and coarse salt, and serve.

4 portions

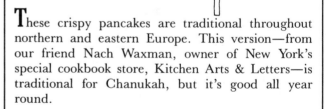

NACH WAXMAN'S POTATO LATKES

These crispy pancakes are traditional throughout northern and eastern Europe. This version—from our friend Nach Waxman, owner of New York's special cookbook store, Kitchen Arts & Letters—is traditional for Chanukah, but it's good all year round.

8 Idaho potatoes (8 ounces each), scrubbed and patted dry
2 onions
2 eggs, lightly beaten
¼ cup unbleached all-purpose flour
¾ teaspoon baking powder
Coarsely ground black pepper, to taste
Corn oil
2 tablespoons rendered chicken fat (optional)

1. Using a hand grater or a food processor, coarsely grate the (unpeeled) potatoes and place them in a glass or ceramic bowl. Let them sit for 15 to 20 minutes. The potatoes will release liquid and turn red.

2. Grate the onions into another bowl, and set them aside.

3. Transfer the potatoes to a large colander, and let them drain for 10 minutes. Then spray them hard with water for 2 to 3 minutes, working the shreds with your fingers. The reddish starch will wash out and the potatoes will be white. Squeeze them to remove as much water as possible, and transfer them to a clean mixing bowl.

4. Using a fork, stir the onions into the potatoes. Then add the eggs, flour, baking powder, and pepper, and mix thoroughly.

5. Heat ⅛ inch of corn oil and chicken fat in a large nonstick skillet over medium-high heat. Using a slotted spoon, drop level spoonfuls of the potato mixture into the hot oil. Sauté them until golden brown on both sides, pressing them lightly with the spatula when you turn them, 1½ to 2 minutes per side. As they are cooked, drain the pancakes on brown paper bags and keep them warm. Add more oil to the skillet as needed for additional batches. Serve the pancakes immediately, piping hot.

8 portions

TO RENDER CHICKEN FAT

Although chicken fat, with its high cholesterol count, has fallen out of favor, it does add great flavor to certain dishes. Many butchers sell rendered chicken fat. To render it yourself, remove all large pieces of fat from a chicken and place them in the top of a double boiler over slowly boiling water. Cook until the fat becomes liquid. Remove from the heat and strain. Cool and refrigerate, or freeze, until ready to use.

SCALLOPED HAM AND POTATOES

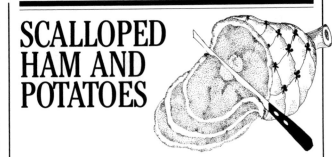

Garlic spices up the cream in this dish—a perfectly luxurious way to turn leftover baked ham into a weekend luncheon or a Sunday-night supper.

4 cups heavy or whipping cream
2 cloves garlic, slivered
1 teaspoon dried thyme leaves
1 teaspoon salt
½ teaspoon freshly ground black pepper
1 pound baked ham, sliced
2 pounds all-purpose potatoes, peeled and thinly sliced
1 large onion, thinly sliced
1 tablespoon chopped fresh Italian (flat-leaf) parsley

1. Preheat the oven to 350°F.

2. Combine the cream, garlic, thyme, salt, and pepper in a heavy saucepan. Bring to a boil, reduce to a simmer, and cook until the sauce has reduced by one third, 10 to 12 minutes.

3. Layer half the ham slices in a 14 x 8-inch baking dish. Then layer half the potatoes, followed by half the onion. Pour half the reduced cream mixture over these layers. Repeat the layering.

4. Place the dish in the center of a rimmed baking sheet (in case it bubbles over). Bake on the center rack of the oven until the potatoes are tender and the top is golden brown and bubbly, 1 hour.

5. Remove the dish from the oven and let it rest for 10 minutes before serving. Sprinkle with the chopped parsley.

8 portions

Note: There are lots of variations to this dish:

▲ Sprinkle freshly grated Parmesan cheese over the onion layers before adding the cream.

▲ Lay strips of red bell pepper between the first ham and potato layers.

▲ Sprinkle fresh dill over both onion layers.

▲ Place a layer of thinly slivered green cabbage between the first ham and potato layers.

POTATO PIE CHEZ LOUIS

A favorite recipe from David Liederman's popular New York restaurant, Chez Louis. It's particularly terrific served with his recipe for roast chicken (check the index for that one).

4 ½ to 5 pounds large Idaho baking potatoes, peeled and halved crosswise
4 cloves garlic
4 tablespoons unsalted butter
4 tablespoons light olive oil
Salt and freshly ground black pepper, to taste

1. Place the potatoes and 2 cloves of the garlic in a large saucepan, cover with cold water, and bring to a boil. Reduce the heat and simmer until the potatoes are tender, 25 to 30 minutes.

2. While the potatoes are cooking, heat the butter and olive oil in a small skillet. Add the remaining 2 cloves garlic and cook over medium-low heat until the garlic is golden brown, 2 minutes; do not let it burn. Discard the garlic and set the oil and butter mixture aside.

3. Drain the potatoes and set them aside until they are cool enough to handle. Then cut them into ¼-inch-thick slices.

4. Preheat the oven to 450°F.

5. Heat some of the butter-oil mixture in a large nonstick skillet. Sauté the potatoes, in batches, until they are lightly browned. (Add more butter/oil as needed.) While they are sautéing, season the potatoes with salt and pepper.

6. Arrange the potatoes in a heavy ovenproof 9-inch skillet, pressing them down firmly with the back of a spoon or a clean dish towel. Transfer the skillet to the oven, and bake until the potatoes are crispy and browned, about 10 minutes.

7. Slide a spatula under the pie and invert it onto a warmed plate. Serve immediately.

6 portions

Spring and summer is new potato time. They are sold as small as peas or as large as golf balls. Steam little red new potatoes in their jackets; they are so sweet and moist they need very little beyond a pinch of salt and pepper and a chopped fresh herb. Toss them hot with just enough butter or cream to coat them lightly, or let them cool and slice them for salad with fresh herbs and vinaigrette—not with mayonnaise.

LACY POTATO NESTS

Crisped in the oven, these are a great nesting place for vegetables, stews, or purées.

1 all-purpose potato (about 8 ounces), peeled
2 teaspoons olive oil
2 teaspoons dried rosemary leaves, crushed
¼ teaspoon salt
Freshly ground black pepper, to taste

1. Preheat the oven to 350°F. Line a 12-cup muffin tin with aluminum foil, letting the foil come out over the edges of the cups. Brush the foil with oil.

2. Coarsely grate the potato into a colander. Rinse it well under cold water. Drain, and gently squeeze out as much moisture as possible.

3. Transfer the potato to a mixing bowl, and add the olive oil, rosemary, salt, and pepper. Stir well. Divide the mixture among the prepared muffin cups. Using the back of a spoon, gently press the mixture into the bottom and halfway up the sides of the cups.

4. Bake until golden, 30 minutes. Cool the nests in the muffin tin for 10 minutes. Then carefully remove them by lifting up the edges of the foil. Peel off the foil (they are very fragile).

5. Before using them, crisp the nests in a preheated 350°F oven for 5 minutes.

12 nests

SWEET SWEET POTATOES

A lthough they share the name potato, there are many differences between a white potato and a sweet potato. Obviously, color is one. Sweet potatoes are indeed sweeter and are grown in warmer climates; white potatoes grow best in cool climates. The two of them have kept much of the world alive and continue to do so to this day.

We grow two main types of sweet potatoes in the United States. Although we refer to the more slender, deeper-orange-fleshed variety as a yam, it's really not. The true yam is a much larger vegetable that is generally found in specialized produce markets.

Sweet potatoes are often called the near perfect food because of their high nutritional value. They are loaded with vitamin A. In fact, one sweet potato has twice the amount of vitamin A a person needs in one day. It has equally impressive amounts of potassium and calcium as well.

There is just one crop of sweet potatoes each year. They are kiln dried and stored so that we have a steady supply all through the year. The new crop comes in starting late August. From August to October, you'll get the freshest and moistest potatoes. In June and July, you will get the potatoes that have been stored all winter and spring.

BUYING

Buy small or medium sweet potatoes for they are the most tender. Choose them as you do white potatoes. They should be firm, heavy, and well shaped with no bruises or cuts. Many sweet potatoes have little hairs on them, which can be trimmed just before cooking. They do no harm. Don't buy sweets with strange twists or knobs—they are devilish to peel. In general, the darker the skin of the potato, the sweeter and moister its flesh.

STORING

Store sweet potatoes as you do white potatoes—in a cool, dry, well-ventilated place. They should last at least two weeks.

YIELD

One medium sweet potato will make one serving. It takes about three to make a pound.

PREPARING

Peeling sweet potatoes is much easier done after they are cooked than before, and more of the potato's vitamins and minerals will stay with the potato. The skins are very delicate so scrub them gently, then trim any hairs.

COOKING

▲ **Boiling:** Place the scrubbed potatoes in a large pot and cover with cold water. Cover the pot and gently boil until tender when pierced with a knife, 30 to 45 minutes. Drain and peel as soon as you can handle them. Reheat if they have cooled off or mash them with butter and orange juice with a little grated zest over low heat. Or spice them with cinnamon, nutmeg, and brown sugar or honey.

▲ **Baking:** Scrub and dry the potatoes. Pierce each one several times with a fork. Bake directly on the oven rack (you may want to put a piece of aluminum foil underneath to catch drips) at 400°F until soft when pinched, about 45 minutes. Serve with butter, brown sugar or honey, and spices.

Sweet potatoes can also be roasted and fried just like a white potato. They make great chips and wonderful hash browns as well.

yam

> "If beef's the King of Meat, Potato's the Queen of the Garden World."
> —OLD IRISH SAYING

NOT TOO SWEET POTATO PIE

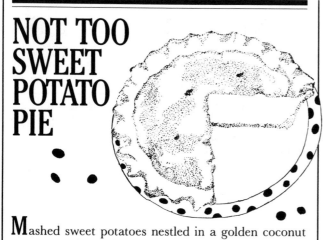

Mashed sweet potatoes nestled in a golden coconut crust are spiced with ginger and cardamom.

2 ½ cups flaked sweetened coconut
⅓ cup unsalted butter, melted
2 cups mashed cooked sweet potatoes
3 eggs, lightly beaten
½ cup sour cream
2 tablespoons fresh lemon juice
½ teaspoon ground ginger
½ teaspoon ground cardamom

1. Preheat the oven to 300°F.
2. Stir the coconut and butter together in a mixing bowl. Press the mixture into the bottom and up the sides of a 9-inch pie plate.
3. Bake just until light golden, 15 minutes. Remove the crust from the oven and raise the heat to 350°F.
4. Purée the remaining ingredients in a food processor until smooth.
5. Scrape the puréed potato mixture into the prepared crust. Bake until the top is dry and a knife inserted in the filling comes out clean, 30 minutes.
6. Cool on a rack.
8 portions

> "**D**on't let love interfere with your appetite. It never does with mine."
> —ANTHONY TROLLOPE

SWEET POTATO PANCAKES

These will astound you with their full, wonderful flavor. Potato pancakes have become very popular as a first course, or as a side dish topped with a bit of sour cream—so don't think of them just as a way of using up leftovers. Once again, some of the great old basics find a new presence in a menu.

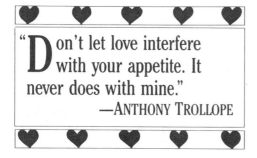

2 cups mashed cooked sweet potatoes
2 eggs, lightly beaten
½ cup coarsely grated onion
4 teaspoons unbleached all-purpose flour
1 teaspoon grated nutmeg
1 teaspoon curry powder
½ teaspoon freshly ground black pepper
½ teaspoon salt
¼ teaspoon cayenne pepper
8 tablespoons (1 stick) unsalted butter
4 tablespoons (¼ cup) solid vegetable shortening
Chunky Applesauce (see Index), cold

1. Combine the potatoes and eggs in a medium-size mixing bowl.
2. Put the grated onion in the center of a clean kitchen towel, and wring the liquid out of it. Add the onion to the bowl.
3. Add the flour, nutmeg, curry powder, black pepper, salt, and cayenne; stir well. Cover with plastic wrap and refrigerate for 1 hour.
4. Heat 2 tablespoons of the butter and 1 tablespoon of the shortening in a medium-size nonstick skillet over medium heat. Form the potato mixture into patties and add them to the hot skillet, three at a time. Spread them out to form pancakes ¼ inch thick and 3 inches in diameter. Brown them on one side, then turn and cook until the other side is golden brown. Arrange the cooked pancakes on a paper-towel-lined baking sheet, and keep them warm in the oven.
5. Repeat until all the potato mixture is used up, adding more butter and shortening as necessary. Serve with chilled applesauce.
10 to 12 pancakes, 5 to 6 portions

YUMMY CANDIED YAMS

These are a great classic favorite, but instead of serving them with cranberry sauce, bring out the Pineapple Chutney.

4 small yams (6 ounces each)
2 tablespoons unsalted butter
½ cup maple syrup
¼ cup bourbon
¼ cup Berta's Chicken Stock (see Index) or canned broth

1. Peel the yams and quarter them.
2. Place the yams in a saucepan, cover with cold water, and bring to a boil. Reduce the heat and simmer until they are just tender but still firm, 20 minutes. Drain well.
3. Melt the butter in a skillet. Add the maple syrup and bourbon and cook over low heat, stirring occasionally, until the mixture is slightly reduced, 15 minutes.
4. Add the yams and stir until lightly coated. Then add the stock and simmer over low heat for 10 to 15 minutes. Serve immediately.

4 portions

RADISHES FOR A PEPPERY CRUNCH

This peppery vegetable keeps surprising us in new shapes and colors. We all know the little red beauties we slice into salads or serve as a pre-dinner nibble. Recently we've been seeing more of two new radishes from opposite parts of the globe. Daikon radishes are a staple of Asian cooking. They look like oversize white carrots, weigh between 1½ and 2 pounds each, are as crisp and juicy as the common red radish, and taste just as peppery yet a little sweeter, too.

Black radishes come to us from the Slavic countries of Russia, Poland, and Hungary. These radishes can be short, round, and shaped like beets; or longer but still thick, shaped much like the daikon radish. They are indeed black on the outside, but like the familiar red radish, they are crisp and white on the inside. Black radishes taste very strong but are still usually eaten raw—just never solo. Thinly slice or grate black radishes and combine them with other vegetables for slaw. Thin slices are wonderful in sandwiches of roast beef or smoked ham.

THE RED AND THE BLACK

Red and black radishes look glorious together in paper-thin slices. Red radishes are usually sweet, but in late summer and fall they tend to be pungent, and black radishes can be a bit bitter—so we've added a little honey to the vinaigrette. It becomes a colorful salad that is crunchy and wonderfully refreshing.

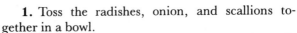

1 small black radish, peeled and sliced paper-thin
1 bunch red radishes (6 to 8), trimmed and sliced paper-thin
1 small onion, finely chopped
2 scallions (green onions), white bulb and 3 inches green, thinly sliced
2 tablespoons sour cream
1 tablespoon rice vinegar
2 teaspoons honey
½ teaspoon salt
Freshly ground black pepper, to taste

1. Toss the radishes, onion, and scallions together in a bowl.
2. In a second bowl stir the remaining ingredients together until well blended.
3. Toss the radishes with the dressing. Let stand, loosely covered, 1 hour, stirring occasionally, before serving.

4 portions

LEAFY GREEN SPINACH

Sometime, somewhere, some kid must have turned thumbs down and nose up to yet another plate of eat-it-it's-good-for-you overcooked spinach, whereupon the word went out once and for all that spinach and children were natural enemies. Ridiculous, we say. Spinach is not an acquired taste attained by adults. Eaten raw or briefly cooked, spinach is not only good for you—it also just plain tastes good. It is a deeply flavorful green to be enjoyed by the whole family.

BUYING

Look for the same qualities in spinach as you do lettuce. The leaves should be crisp and dark green with no sign of yellowing or wilting. Over-the-hill spinach tastes as bad as it looks. Try to buy spinach in bundles and not in bags—it will be fresher. If you must buy it bagged, open it up as soon as you get it home and sort through it for wet or rotting leaves.

Frozen spinach is a good reliable alternative for fresh, but only if you are cooking it.

STORING

Refrigerate spinach, unwashed, in plastic bags in the crisper drawer, but it won't last much longer than three or four days.

YIELD

One to 1½ pounds of fresh spinach will yield just 1 cup cooked, which serves two. Served raw in a salad, 1½ pounds of spinach will serve four.

Raw spinach has just 28 calories per cup and it's loaded with vitamins, namely A, B, and C.

SEASON TO TASTE

Spinach—quickly wilted and served with plenty of lemon wedges and freshly ground black pepper—divine! But don't stop there. Try some of our other favorites, too.

Basil	Lemon
Black pepper	Mint
Caraway seed	Nutmeg
Cheese:	Onion
Parmesan,	Oregano
feta, ricotta,	Parsley
and chevrè	Rosemary
Chervil	Shallot
Chive	Thyme
Dill	Watercress
Garlic	

PREPARING

First discard any yellow or wet and rotting leaves, then stem the leaves by folding the spinach leaf in half and pulling the stem up along the leaf until it naturally breaks off.

Spinach must be rinsed thoroughly because it's very sandy. Fill a sink with cold water, add the trimmed spinach and swish it around. Let it soak a minute or two and swish it some more. Lift the leaves out of the water, drain the sink, and fill it again with clean water. Add the spinach and swish some more. You may have to repeat this three or four times if you've gotten hold of some very sandy spinach.

If you are preparing the spinach for salad, wrap the leaves in paper towels and refrigerate to crisp them.

Never cook spinach in an aluminum pan, never serve it in silver, and chop it with a stainless-steel knife to keep it from discoloring.

COOKING

▲ **Steaming:** Trim and rinse spinach. Shake it lightly and put it with the water still clinging to the leaves in a heavy pan. Cover and cook over medium heat, shaking the pan once or twice, until wilted, 2 to 3 minutes. Drain off the excess water and season. You can also steam spinach in a basket over boiling water.

▲ **Sautéing:** Put the trimmed and rinsed spinach in a salad spinner and spin dry or pat dry with paper towels. Melt 2 to 3 tablespoons butter and/or oil in a heavy skillet over medium-low heat. Add the spinach and cook, stirring and tossing occasionally, until tender, 3 to 4 minutes. Season and serve hot.

SPINACH, BROCCOLI, AND BOURSIN TIMBALES

Boursin cheese gives an exciting flavor to this molded custard-like blend of spinach and broccoli.

½ cup Berta's Chicken Stock (see Index)
or canned broth
1 cup heavy or whipping cream
½ cup finely chopped cooked spinach
1 cup finely chopped cooked broccoli
2 ounces (3 tablespoons) Boursin cheese
5 eggs, lightly beaten
½ teaspoon dry mustard
½ teaspoon Worcestershire sauce
Dash of Tabasco sauce
¼ cup grated Parmesan cheese
3 tablespoons snipped fresh chives
8 fresh spinach leaves, well rinsed and trimmed

1. Preheat the oven to 350°F. Butter eight 4-ounce timbale molds or individual ramekins.

2. Combine the stock and cream in a small bowl, and set aside.

3. Combine the spinach, broccoli, Boursin, and ¼ cup of the stock mixture in a food processor and process until smooth. Set aside.

4. Combine the eggs, mustard, Worcestershire, Tabasco, and remaining 1¼ cups of the stock mixture in a mixing bowl. Whisk well. Fold in the spinach-broccoli mixture. Add the Parmesan and chives, and mix thoroughly.

5. Place the spinach leaves in a vegetable steamer over simmering water, and steam until just wilted, 1 minute. Drape a wilted spinach leaf along the bottom and sides of each prepared timbale, and fill the molds three quarters full with the spinach-broccoli mixture.

6. Place the molds in a baking or roasting pan with sides the same height as the molds. Fill the pan with hot (not boiling) water so that it reaches three quarters of the way up the sides of the molds. Bake for 45 minutes.

7. Remove the timbales from the water and let them rest for 5 minutes. Then invert them onto a serving platter or individual plates.

8 portions

DON'T SQUELCH SQUASH

All squash are gourds with seeds inside and protective skins outside. Summer squash are picked when they are immature and the skins and seeds are edible. Winter squash are picked fully mature; the skins are hard, protecting the flesh inside, and the seeds are large and woody. Squash are native to the Americas. In fact, the Incas had been cultivating them centuries before the first English settlers arrived. The seeds were rapidly dispatched back to England and the Indians' squash took Europe by storm. Now every year seems to bring a new variety to the market—one whose origins may be in Latin America, the Mediterranean, or the Orient. Squash has become a worldwide passion.

KNOW YOUR SUMMER SQUASH

▲ **Chayote (mirleton):** This squash is really a winter squash, but it is prepared in the same way as the summer varieties, so we've listed it here. Chayote is a relative newcomer to the markets in the United States, but has been a staple of Latin and Central American diets for centuries. The chayote is pear shaped with a thin, light green skin and very delicate taste. It has just one large seed; some cooks throw it away, others cook it along with the squash. Unlike summer squash, chayote cannot be eaten with the peel.

▲ **Pattypan:** This squash is also known as cymling or scalloped squash. It takes the prize for beauty with its small flying-saucer-shaped edge, like a pie crust with scallops. The skin is light green to creamy white. This tender squash can be cooked and eaten whole, but the shape lends itself to hollowing out and stuffing. Pattypans come small—just 2 to 3 inches across—to very large. Stick to the small ones for the best eating.

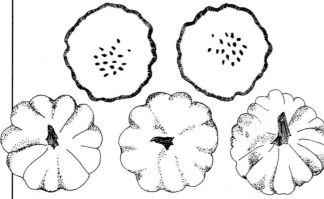

▲ **Yellow squash:** Banana yellow in color, this squash either is shaped with a crookneck or is straight and cylindrical like a zucchini. Most yellow squash have smooth thin skin, but some crooknecks have skin that is bumpy or pebbly. The skin is tender in either variety; the flesh, delicate and succulent. Yellow squash can be very small—babies really—or as long as a foot. Six to eight inches is standard; anything larger is overgrown and will be watery.

▲ **Zucchini:** This is probably the best known of all summer squash. The shape is long and cylindrical, and the skin can be dark green or striped green and yellow. All are tender and delicious when young, and every gardener knows they are watery and tasteless when overgrown. Because zucchini is so basic to American cooking, we've given the vegetable its own section. See Zillions of Zucchini.

BUYING

Buy only small, firm squash. Pattypans should be no larger than 3 inches; zucchini and yellow squash, 7 to 8 inches at most. Check for firmness, especially at the stem end, and avoid those with bruises or soft spots.

STORING

Refrigerate summer squash unwashed in plastic bags. These squash have tender skins, which don't give them much staying power. Use them within 4 to 5 days. Chayotes are more resilient because they have tougher (and inedible) skins; they should keep up to two weeks.

YIELD

Summer squash loses water as it cooks so you will need at least a pound to serve three. Buy at least one pattypan per person, two if they are small.

PREPARING

Peel chayote squash but don't peel the others—just scrub them gently with a vegetable brush to get rid of any dirt, and trim the ends.

COOKING

Summer squash can be eaten raw, sliced into salads or with crudités, but the flavor is so mild we wonder why bother. Summer squash is best cooked until crisp-tender; don't overdo it or the squash will be mushy and watery. Chayote squash are firmer and take longer to cook.

▲ **Steaming:** Cut the squash into thick slices or leave very small ones whole. Place them in a steaming basket or rack over an inch of boiling water. Steam covered just until tender. It won't take long, about 5 minutes. Toss with butter and season with salt and pepper and Parmesan cheese or chopped fresh herbs.

▲ **Sautéing:** Pattypans or very small squash can be sautéed whole; the others should be sliced thick or even grated. For whole squash or slices, melt butter in a heavy skillet, using 3 tablespoons for every pound; add the squash, and toss to coat with butter. Cover the skillet and cook, stirring occasionally, over low heat until tender, about 5 minutes. Season and sprinkle with parsley, chives, dill, or another fresh herb.

To sauté grated squash, first salt it and let it drain for at least 30 minutes; then squeeze out all the water by twisting it in a kitchen towel. Heat 3 to 4 tablespoons of butter or butter and olive oil in a large skillet over medium-high heat. Add the squash and sauté, tossing and stirring constantly, until tender, 3 to 4 minutes. Season with pepper (no salt) and serve. A thinly sliced onion sautéed until soft before adding the squash is delicious in this dish.

SEASON TO TASTE

The delicate flavor of summer squash combines well with any of the following seasonings:

Basil	Mint
Black pepper	Olive oil
Cheese (sharp)	Onion
Chive	Parsley
Cilantro	Savory
Crème fraîche	Tarragon
Dill	Thyme
Garlic	Vinegar

KNOW YOUR WINTER SQUASH

▲ **Acorn:** These are round, about the size of a large orange to that of a small melon; they are deeply ridged, which makes peeling them difficult at best. The skin is deep green, often mottled or streaked with orange. The flesh is pumpkin colored. They are the most common of all winter squash, probably because they bake so beautifully—moist, rich, and tender.

▲ **Buttercup:** This squash has an interesting shape —like a drum topped with a too small derby. The skin is dark green and usually striped with gray. The flesh is orange, very similar to that of a butternut squash.

▲ **Butternut:** This squash is shaped like a huge pear with buttery tan skin, weighing in at 2 to 3 pounds. It is nearly as popular as acorn squash. The flesh is moist and sweet.

▲ **Golden nugget:** This squash looks like a miniature pumpkin. Its small size (about ½ pound) makes it easy to handle and quick to cook. It has a good pumpkiny taste.

▲ **Hubbard:** These are huge, 8 to 15 pounds, and for that reason are often sold by the chunk. The flesh is stringier and drier than most winter squash, but they are wonderful baked or steamed.

▲ **Pumpkins:** Every child in America knows how to make a jack-o'-lantern, but few of us have eaten pumpkin that's not canned. In fact 99 percent of all pumpkins are sold for decorations.

Pumpkins for eating, called sweet, sugar, or cheese pumpkins, are small, have a deep, rich flavor, and meaty texture. Cook a pumpkin like other winter squash—baking it with butter and spices, puréeing or mashing it with orange zest and butter, or adding it diced or cubed to soups or hearty fall pastas. You might also enjoy combining pumpkin with rice, and layering it in gratins. You are in for a delicious taste treat!

▲ **Spaghetti:** Also called vegetable spaghetti, this squash is unlike the other winter squash. The cooked flesh can be pulled out in strands like orange spaghetti. It is shaped like a small watermelon but with yellow skin. Aside from its novelty, it's delicious, moist, and tender. The mild taste makes it perfect for combining with pasta sauces.

▲ **Turban:** These are small to medium squash in bizarre turban shapes and colors, often with bumpy skin. They are grown mostly as ornaments for the fall table, but they, of course, can be cooked like other winter squash.

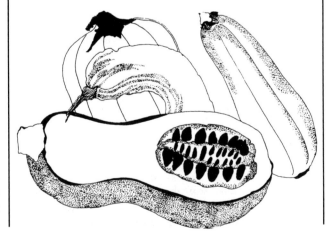

BUYING

Winter squash should be firm and heavy with no cracks or soft spots. Mottled or striped coloring is usual with winter squash. Acorn, butternut, and spaghetti squash are available year round; the others start coming in in early fall and stay through the winter.

STORING

Keep winter squash with the potatoes in a cool, well-ventilated, dry place. Most will keep at least one month. Don't refrigerate them, for they will get damp and soft.

YIELD

One pound of winter squash will make about two cups cooked, enough for two servings.

PREPARING

Winter squash are very hard and dense; you'll need a heavy knife to cut them. Cut off the stem first, then halve through the stem end. Scoop out all the seeds and string. Very large squash can be cut further into more manageable pieces. It's easier to peel winter squashes, if you must, after they are cooked. Spaghetti squash, as always, are the exception—cook them whole.

COOKING

▲ **Baking:** Most winter squash are best baked. Cut the squash into halves or quarters and place, cut side down, in a baking dish. Bake at 375° to 400°F until tender, at least 45 minutes (large chunks of Hubbard squash may take up to twice as long). Remove the squash from the oven, scoop out the flesh, and purée it. Or turn the pieces cut sides up, add butter (and brown sugar and spices, if you want), then return the squash to the oven and bake until the butter melts.

To bake spaghetti squash, pierce it deeply two or three times to keep it from exploding, and bake at 350°F until tender when pierced with a knife, about 1½ hours. Remove the squash from the oven and cut in half through the stem end. Use a fork to fluff and pull out the strings.

▲ **Steaming:** The squash should be cut into small pieces so that it steams in a relatively short time. Large pieces will be too soggy by the time they are tender. Chunks of acorn squash will steam tender in about 40 minutes. Let the squash cool enough to handle, then scrape the flesh from the skin and mash it or cut it into chunks. Combine with butter, spices, salt, and pepper.

Whole spaghetti squash can be steamed whole (pierce it several times first). Turn it occasionally and make sure the water in the bottom of the pan doesn't evaporate. It will take more than an hour even for a fairly small spaghetti squash.

SEASON TO TASTE

The stronger-flavored winter squash stand up to an array of hearty seasonings.

Brown sugar	Honey
Caraway seed	Mace
Cardamom	Nutmeg
Cinnamon	Nuts
Clove	Onion
Coriander	Oregano
Curry powder	Rosemary
Ginger	Thyme

BAKED TURBAN SQUASH

The striking mottled orange-and-green shell with its little chapeau serves as the container for this seasoned squash. (If you have the patience, shell the seeds and use them as you would pumpkin seeds. They are quite tasty.)

1 turban squash (about 3½ pounds)
½ cup shredded Cheddar cheese
¼ cup Berta's Chicken Stock (see Index) or canned broth
¼ cup minced scallions (green onions)
2 tablespoons unsalted butter
1 teaspoon minced orange zest
1 teaspoon salt
¼ teaspoon ground cinnamon
Freshly ground black pepper, to taste

1. Preheat the oven to 350°F.

2. Wrap the whole squash in a double thickness of aluminum foil, and set it on a baking sheet. Bake for 2 hours. Let it cool in the foil.

3. When the squash is cool enough to handle, unwrap it, and with a small sharp knife cut around the little "hat." Lift this off and set it aside.

4. Scoop out the seeds and discard them or save them for another use. Scoop the pulp into a mixing bowl, leaving a shell about ¼ inch thick. Add the remaining ingredients to the pulp, and stir until smooth.

5. Return the squash mixture to the shell, and top it with the "hat." Bake for 30 minutes. Serve it at the table in the shell.

4 to 6 portions

BUTTERNUT TIMBALES

It's hard to believe that butternut squash can be cooked in 6 minutes, but this microwave dish lets you enjoy it for dinner even when you don't get home from work until late.

½ butternut squash (about ¾ pound)
2 eggs, lightly beaten
⅓ cup chopped scallions (green onions)
¼ cup dried bread crumbs
1 teaspoon slivered lemon zest
½ teaspoon salt
½ teaspoon ground ginger
½ teaspoon ground cinnamon
Freshly ground black pepper, to taste
Dill or parsley sprigs, for garnish

1. Butter four 5-ounce microwave-safe timbales or individual ramekins. Set them aside.

2. Peel, seed, and shred the squash. You should have about 2½ cups.

3. Combine the squash with all the remaining ingredients except the dill sprigs, and mix until smooth. Divide the mixture among the prepared timbales.

4. Cook at full power (650 to 700 watts) until the tops are dry and the mixture feels firm to the touch, 6 minutes.

5. Let the timbales sit for 1 minute; then run a knife around the edge and unmold. Press a dill sprig into the top of each timbale before serving.

4 portions

Note: This recipe was cooked on High (full power, 650 to 700 watts) in a carousel microwave, using microwave-safe containers.

If your microwave is less powerful, you will have to allow for more cooking time (approximately 1½ times the amount called for —but watch carefully); if it does not have a carousel, you may have to rotate the dish while it is cooking.

SPAGHETTI SQUASH WITH CURRIED SQUASH SAUCE

Light, thin spaghetti squash becomes "pasta" to serve as a bed for a scrumptious curried yellow squash purée. It's a great golden first course or light entrée. Make sure you take the time to pull the spaghetti squash apart lightly, to make it really fluffy.

1 spaghetti squash (3 to 3 ½ pounds)
2 tablespoons unsalted butter
1 tablespoon curry powder
1 yellow summer squash, cubed
2 tablespoons snipped fresh chives
2 tablespoons freshly grated Parmesan cheese

1. Cut the spaghetti squash in half and scrape out the seeds. Place the squash skin side up in a large saucepan, cover by 2 inches with water, and bring to a boil. Lower the heat, cover, and simmer for 20 minutes.

2. While the spaghetti squash is cooking, prepare the curried squash: Melt the butter in a skillet, and add the curry powder and yellow squash. Sauté over medium heat until cooked, about 10 to 15 minutes. Pass the mixture through a food mill into a warmed bowl. Add the chives, and keep warm.

3. Using a fork, scoop out the center of the spaghetti squash; it will form spaghetti-like strands. Top it with the curried squash, sprinkle with the Parmesan, and serve immediately.

4 portions

SPAGHETTI SQUASH CASSEROLE

The texture of this squash is ideal for microwave cooking. Garlic, tomatoes, and mozzarella are just the right topping.

1 spaghetti squash (about 3 ½ pounds)
4 ripe tomatoes
3 tablespoons olive oil
2 cloves garlic, minced
1 teaspoon salt
Freshly ground black pepper, to taste
½ cup shredded mozzarella cheese
¼ cup grated Parmesan cheese
¼ cup chopped scallions (green onions)
Grated Parmesan cheese, for garnish

1. Prick the squash in three or four places with the tines of a fork. Place it on a microwave-safe plate, cover loosely with microwave-safe plastic wrap, and cook at full power (650 to 700 watts) for 9 minutes. Turn the squash over, and cook another 9 minutes. Then let it stand, still covered, for 5 minutes.

2. Using a sharp knife, cut a small X in the bottom of each tomato. Arrange the tomatoes on a microwave-safe plate and cover with a damp paper towel. Cook at full power for 4 minutes.

3. Let the tomatoes stand for 1 minute. Then peel, core, and coarsely chop. Pour off the excess liquid.

4. Place 1 tablespoon of the olive oil on a small microwave-safe plate, and cook at full power for 2 minutes. Then stir in the garlic and cook until it is crisp, 3 to 4 minutes.

5. Halve the squash and scrape out the seeds. Using a fork, scoop out the pulp and transfer the spaghetti-like strands to a 2 ½-quart microwave-safe casserole. Add the tomatoes, garlic and oil, salt, pepper, and remaining 2 tablespoons olive oil; toss well. Top with the mozzarella, Parmesan, and scallions.

6. Cook at full power until heated through, 4 minutes. Serve with additional Parmesan on the side.

4 portions
Note: This recipe was cooked on High (full power,

650 to 700 watts) in a carousel microwave, using microwave-safe containers.

If your microwave is less powerful, you will have to allow for more cooking time (approximately 1 ½ times the amount called for—but watch carefully); if it does not have a carousel, you may have to rotate the dish while it is cooking.

SWISS CHARD

Swiss chard seems to us two vegetables in one. It has long, flattened, celery-like stalks with large green leaves at the top. The two are cooked separately because the stalks take quite a bit longer than the leaves. Chard has become more familiar recently in the United States, right along with the popularization of other foods from the Mediterranean, where it is a much favored vegetable. Sautéed in olive oil with a sprinkle of vinegar or lemon juice at the end, it is served both hot and at room temperature as a salad. The taste is somewhat like spinach with a similar mildly earthy and slightly bitter flavor.

Buy Swiss chard that is crisp and green. Its season is June through October. Like spinach, if it's old and wilted to start with, it will only cook up bitter. Chard needs to be rinsed thoroughly—it's usually pretty sandy.

To prepare chard, cut the leaves from the stalks and string any large or tough stalks like celery. The stalks and leaves can be cooked separately, the leaves like spinach and the stalks like asparagus. Or they can be cooked together. Americans often boil chard, but we think the Mediterraneans have the better idea in sautéing it. To do so, cut the stalks in thick slices and toss with 2 tablespoons of olive oil per pound of chard in a large skillet. Cover and cook over low heat until tender, about 15 minutes. Cut the leaves into wide strips, stir them into the stalks, and cook, stirring occasionally, over medium heat until wilted and tender. Sprinkle with lemon juice or vinegar and season with salt and pepper.

SWISS CHARD STRUDEL

Don't think that strudel always means apples. Made with Swiss chard, nutty-flavored Jarlsberg, and fresh Parmesan cheese, all rolled up in phyllo pastry and baked until golden, this strudel is just right alongside Savory Short Ribs, Garden Vegetable Soup, or Eggplant Wrapped Moussaka.

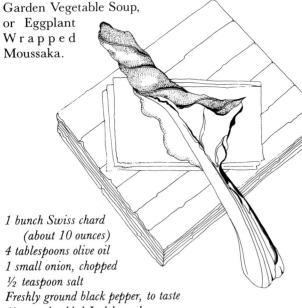

1 bunch Swiss chard
   (about 10 ounces)
4 tablespoons olive oil
1 small onion, chopped
½ teaspoon salt
Freshly ground black pepper, to taste
½ cup shredded Jarlsberg cheese
2 tablespoons plus 2 teaspoons dried bread crumbs
2 tablespoons grated Parmesan cheese
3 tablespoons unsalted butter, melted
6 sheets phyllo dough (about 16 x 12 inches each), thawed if frozen

1. Preheat the oven to 375°F.

2. Rinse and drain the chard. Remove the stems, trim and discard the woody bottoms, chop the rest, and set aside. Coarsely chop the leaves.

3. Heat 2 tablespoons of the oil in a skillet over low heat. Add the onion and sauté until wilted, about 5 minutes. Stir in the chard stems, and cook 3 minutes.

4. Stir in the chard leaves, and cook 3 minutes more. Drain off the excess liquid, and transfer the mixture to a bowl. Season with the salt and pepper. Stir in the Jarlsberg, 1 tablespoon of the crumbs, and the Parmesan. Set aside.

5. Stir the butter and remaining 2 tablespoons olive oil together in a small bowl.

6. Open 1 sheet of phyllo on a work surface. Brush it with some of the butter and oil mixture. Sprinkle with 1 teaspoon of the crumbs.

7. Top with 4 more sheets of phyllo, brushing each with butter and oil and sprinkling each with crumbs. Top with the remaining sheet, and brush it with butter and oil.

8. Spoon the filling along one short end of the phyllo, leaving about 1½ inches empty on each side. Fold the long sides in, overlapping the filling by 1½ inches, to enclose the ends of the filling.

9. Roll the phyllo and filling over onto itself to form a strudel roll. Place it on a baking sheet seam side down and brush the top with any remaining butter and oil. Bake until deep golden, 25 minutes. Let the strudel stand for 5 minutes before slicing and serving.

8 to 10 portions

TOMATO TIME

A tomato plucked from the vine, eaten on the spot with the warmth of the midday sun, will always be a vivid memory. There aren't enough summer meals to savor the perfection of their sun-warmed taste. When we were growing up, everyone had tomato plants and they were surely taken for granted. Now we marvel to see them on rooftops, fire escapes, and windowsills, knowing full well the joy these extreme efforts will bring.

To see a plump red tomato in the garden or at the greengrocer is pure pleasure and more and more varieties are coming into the markets year round from afar. If it's just the pale hothouse varieties that prevail, there's hope if you take them home and ripen them for two or three days. And in a pinch, we prefer either the canned Italian plum tomatoes, which are picked and preserved at their peak, or the robust sun-dried and oil-preserved tomatoes. They're both staples in our pantry, as you can see.

 ## KNOW YOUR TOMATOES

▲ **Globe or slicing tomatoes:** These are the familiar everyday tomatoes. They are good cooked but best sliced or cut up for salads. Most on the market are medium size, coming three or four to a pound, and are raised for their transportability, not their flavor. Growing them yourself or buying them at a local farm stand will yield a much more satisfying tomato.

▲ **Cherry tomatoes:** These bite-size tomatoes are available year round and the quality remains consistently good. Buy these in winter when the globe tomatoes are tasteless. Cherry tomatoes come both red and yellow. The red have more flavor than the yellow.

▲ **Plum, Italian, or Roma tomatoes:** These tomatoes have thick, meaty walls, small seeds, little juice, and rich flavor. They are the ideal cooking tomato. They are indeed plum shaped and are colored red, sometimes yellow. This is the only tomato rich enough to stand up to canning, and pretty much the only one we would buy in a can.

▲ **Yellow tomatoes:** Almost all red tomatoes have a counterpart colored yellow. The yellow tomatoes are always milder and less flavorful, but the color is such a knockout that we don't usually pass them by when we find them.

▲ **Green tomatoes:** These are immature tomatoes that haven't ripened. They are firmer and more acidic than red tomatoes, but they are still good eating—sliced and fried or cooked into relishes.

▲ **Tomatillos:** These yellow or green tomatoes wrapped in papery husks are the essential tomato of Mexican and southwestern cooking. Tomatillos are tart raw, but cooked they have a fresh, lemony, herbal flavor. They are firmer than red tomatoes even when dead ripe. Fresh tomatillos are a little more available nationwide each year and, like red tomatoes, their season is summer. Canned tomatillos are generally good. Look for *tomatillo entero, tomatito verde,* or "peeled green tomato" on the can.

 ## BUYING

Buy tomatoes that are firm but not hard with tight, unblemished skins. Tomatoes should give a little when squeezed. Plum tomatoes will be firmer than the others because they have less juice. Pick out the tomatoes with the deepest colors—deep red or deep yellow. Avoid the pink tomatoes of winter, for they have no taste and a mushy texture. Buy cherry tomatoes instead, which are generally of better quality year round, or pass the tomatoes by until their season begins again in early summer.

STORING

Don't refrigerate tomatoes—ever. Eat ripe tomatoes within a day or two. If you have more ripe tomatoes than you can use, cook them and keep them in the freezer. Most tomatoes at the market are underripe rather than overripe. To ripen tomatoes, put them in a closed paper bag, not on a sunny windowsill. Tomatoes, like apples, emit ethylene gas, which ripens them. To speed ripening, add an apple to the bag.

YIELD

Three medium globe tomatoes, seven or eight plum tomatoes, or about thirty cherry tomatoes make a pound. A pound of tomatoes, peeled and seeded, will yield about one cup of pulp.

PREPARING

A serrated knife is best for slicing tomatoes. If you are slicing them for salads or sandwiches, slice them lengthwise (through the stem end)—they'll be firmer and less juicy. Use only stainless-steel knives when cutting tomatoes and no aluminum or cast-iron pots when cooking them.

For stuffing tomatoes, either make a tomato shell by cutting a slice off the top and hollowing it out with a small spoon, or cut the tomato crosswise in half and hollow each half. Turn the tomatoes upside down on paper towels to drain a little before stuffing.

Peeling and seeding tomatoes: To peel tomatoes, drop them into a pot of boiling water for 1 to 2 minutes, depending on the size, then scoop them out and drop them in a bowl of ice water. Core the tomato by cutting out a small cone around the stem end, then slip off the skin. If it doesn't peel easily, return the tomato to the boiling water for 10 to 15 seconds more. To seed the tomato, cut it in half and gently squeeze the tomato over a bowl—or a sieve if you want to save the juice. The seeds should drop out. Pick out any stubborn seeds with your finger or a small spoon.

COOKING

▲ **Broiling:** Cut tomatoes crosswise in half and place, cut side up, on an oiled baking sheet or the broiler rack. Drizzle with a little olive oil or melted butter. Broil until the tops are lightly browned, 4 to 6 minutes. Season with salt and pepper and an herb if you want and broil 30 seconds longer.

▲ **Sautéing:** This method works best with plum, cherry, and green tomatoes. To sauté green tomatoes, slice them and dip each side in seasoned flour or cornmeal. Sauté in butter and/or olive oil over medium-high heat until browned on both sides. Serve hot.

To sauté cherry and plum tomatoes, stem the cherry tomatoes and keep them whole; cut plum tomatoes in half or in thick slices. Toss them about in hot butter and/or olive oil over medium heat just until heated through. Toss with a chopped fresh herb, salt, and pepper. Serve hot.

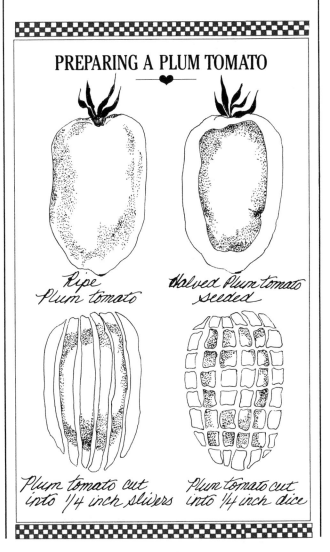

PREPARING A PLUM TOMATO

Ripe Plum tomato

Halved Plum tomato seeded

Plum tomato cut into 1/4 inch slivers

Plum tomato cut into 1/4 inch dice

TOMATO AND BREAD SOUP

This was once the porridge of Tuscany. Make sure the tomatoes and basil are fresh, the bread stale, and the garlic lavish. Serve it at room temperature. We like it with extra chopped basil on top.

2 tablespoons olive oil
2 tablespoons minced garlic
1 ½ tablespoons minced shallots
2 pounds ripe tomatoes, peeled, seeded, and chopped
¼ cup slivered fresh basil leaves
⅔ cup Berta's Chicken Stock (see Index) or canned broth
Salt and freshly ground pepper, to taste
5 slices day-old sourdough bread, sliced diagonally ¼ inch thick
Chopped fresh basil (optional)
Freshly grated Parmesan cheese (optional)

1. Heat the olive oil in a large saucepan. Add the garlic and shallots, and cook over medium-low heat until soft and translucent, 10 minutes.
2. Add the tomatoes, basil, stock, and salt and pepper. Stir, and simmer for 15 minutes.
3. Tear the bread into 1-inch pieces and add them to the soup. Let it cook for 1 minute, then remove from the heat and allow to rest at room temperature for 30 minutes. Serve sprinkled with the chopped basil and Parmesan cheese.

4 portions

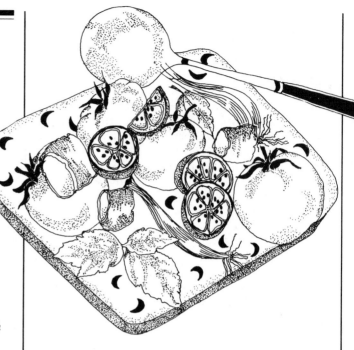

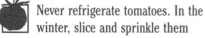

TRADE SECRET

 Never refrigerate tomatoes. In the winter, slice and sprinkle them with a bit of chopped shallots, a little sugar, and some oil to sweeten. Let rest for a couple hours before serving.

TOMATO BREAD SALAD

One of the simplest and most delicious salads there is, *panzanella* is a specialty of central Italy and in recent years has gained popularity in other regions as well. It is usually made at the peak of the tomato season, when stale country bread, sweet red onions, garlic, and herbs are added to ripe, juicy tomatoes. At first glance this rustic dish may seem a bit heavy, but trust us and the Italians—this is a lovely light summer salad.

3 pounds ripe plum tomatoes, cut into large cubes
2 cups thinly sliced red onions
1 cup slivered fresh basil leaves
⅔ cup extra virgin olive oil
Dash of red wine vinegar
Salt and coarsely ground black pepper, to taste
3 cups Herby Garlic Croutons (recipe follows)

1. Combine the tomatoes, red onions, basil, olive oil, vinegar, and salt and pepper in a large bowl.
2. Just before serving, toss in the croutons.
8 portions

HERBY GARLIC CROUTONS

3 tablespoons unsalted butter
3 tablespoons olive oil
3 cups stale bread cubes (about ½ inch thick)
2 large cloves garlic, minced
1 teaspoon chopped fresh parsley
1 teaspoon snipped fresh chives
1 teaspoon chopped fresh tarragon
3 tablespoons freshly grated Parmesan cheese

1. Heat the butter and oil in a large nonstick skillet. Add the bread cubes and cook over medium-high heat, tossing them constantly with a wooden spoon, for 3 to 4 minutes. Reduce the heat to medium-low.

2. Add the garlic and herbs. Continue to cook the croutons, tossing frequently, until golden brown, about 20 minutes. Transfer them to a bowl and toss with the Parmesan. Cool to room temperature, and store in an airtight container until ready to use.

3 cups

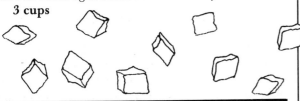

KAY'S FRESH TOMATO JUICE

Not only a quick and healthy pick-me-up but also a quick way to make use of stray veggies lurking in the bin.

3 ripe tomatoes (about 1½ pounds), quartered
1 rib celery with leaves, cut into 2-inch pieces
1 carrot, peeled and cut into 1-inch pieces
1 small onion, quartered
1 clove garlic
2 large fresh basil leaves
1 teaspoon Worcestershire sauce
¼ teaspoon salt (optional)
Freshly ground black pepper, to taste

1. Combine the tomatoes, celery, carrot, onion, garlic, and basil in a food processor, in batches if necessary, and purée until smooth.

2. Transfer the purée to a 4-quart microwave-safe bowl. Stir in the Worcestershire sauce. Cook at full power (650 to 700 watts), uncovered, for 6 minutes. Pass the mixture through a food mill, and season with salt and pepper.

3. Return the purée to the bowl and cook, uncovered, another 3 minutes. Chill and serve.

2½ cups

Note: This recipe was cooked on High (full power, 650 to 700 watts) in a carousel microwave, using microwave-safe containers.

If your microwave is less powerful, you will have to allow for more cooking time (approximately 1½ times the amount called for—but watch carefully); if it does not have a carousel, you may have to rotate the dish while it is cooking.

CAPERS

●

Capers are the unopened bud of a shrub that grows wild all over the Mediterranean, North Africa, and India. (The biggest and fleshiest grow in Sicily.) The green buds are picked by hand before sunrise, while they are still tightly closed, and then pickled.

We find ourselves using capers more and more, to add a bit of zip to *sauce verte,* piquant sauces, tuna, hamburgers, skate, trout, steak tartare, remoulade, hollandaise sauces, egg and cheese dishes, pizza, tomato salads, string beans, lamb, beef, and poultry. We've recently discovered giant caperberries from Spain, the size of cocktail olives with delicate, long stems. Put them in little bowls and serve as a condiment with roast suckling pig or alongside our Grand Gaucho Paella. Caperberries are available through De Choix Specialty Foods, 58–25 52nd Avenue, Woodside, NY 11377; telephone (718) 507-8080.

FRESH TOMATO SALADS

▲ Cut tomatoes in thick slices and arrange them on a plate. Drizzle with olive oil and sprinkle with chopped shallots and freshly ground pepper. Chopped fresh parsley, basil, marjoram, or oregano would be good too, as would a few drops of red wine vinegar. Let marinate about an hour, then season lightly with salt and serve. If you buy winter tomatoes, add a bit of sugar with the pepper before marinating.

▲ A very popular Mediterranean salad: coarsely chopped tomatoes and minced red onion dressed with extra virgin olive oil, lemon or lime juice, a little chopped fresh herb, and a grind or two of black pepper. The Portuguese add minced watercress and cilantro. The Greeks add a little basil and oregano, a lot of mint, a handful of black olives, and another handful of crumbled feta cheese. The Italians add basil, a little minced garlic, and fresh mozzarella in slices or little balls.

▲ Arrange sliced tomatoes on a bed of spinach and top with crumbled crisp bacon and Roquefort cheese.

▲ Serve sliced tomatoes and roasted red peppers with anchovies, sardines, herring, or flaked tuna on a bed of dressed arugula.

▲ Sprinkle sliced tomatoes with toasted sunflower or sesame seeds.

▲ Layer sliced tomatoes with thin slices of prosciutto and/or slices of fresh mozzarella, placing fresh basil leaves between each slice. Drizzle with extra virgin olive oil.

HOT TOMATO!

Baked tomatoes filled with corn, jalapeño and bell peppers, Monterey Jack, basil, and cilantro—one of the best stuffed tomatoes dishes we've tasted lately!

6 tomatoes, ripe but firm
1 cup fresh or frozen corn kernels, thawed if frozen
1 fresh jalapeño pepper, minced (2 teaspoons with seeds)
¼ cup chopped scallions (green onions)
¼ cup minced red bell pepper
3 tablespoons chopped fresh basil leaves
2 tablespoons chopped cilantro (fresh coriander)
4 ounces Monterey Jack cheese, shredded
½ teaspoon salt
Freshly ground black pepper, to taste
1 tablespoon stone-ground yellow cornmeal
1 tablespoon unsalted butter

1. Preheat the oven to 400°F. Lightly oil a baking sheet, and set it aside.

2. Slice off the top quarter of each tomato. Set the tops aside. Using a melon baller, scoop the centers out of 3 of the tomatoes, leaving a thin shell, and place the pulp in a mixing bowl. Scoop out and discard the pulp from the remaining 3 tomatoes (or save it for another use). Invert the tomato shells onto paper towels to drain.

3. Add the corn, jalapeño pepper, scallions, bell pepper, basil, cilantro, cheese, salt, and black pepper to the tomato pulp. Toss lightly until well mixed, and loosely fill the tomato shells with the mixture.

4. Sprinkle each tomato with ½ teaspoon of the cornmeal, and dot with ½ teaspoon of the butter. Arrange the tomatoes on the prepared baking sheet with the tops cut side down.

5. Bake until the crumbs are golden and the tomatoes are cooked through, 25 minutes. Place the "hats" back on top before serving.

6 portions

BAKED STUFFED TOMATOES

Yankee Doodle Tomato

A meal in a tomato—for luncheon or Sunday supper. We've put bacon, mushrooms, and spinach inside and baked it all together. Also lovely as a side vegetable with an herby omelet.

4 ripe tomatoes
6 fresh cultivated mushrooms, trimmed
4 slices thick bacon, cut into 1-inch pieces
2 shallots, peeled and minced
10 ounces fresh spinach, well rinsed and trimmed
2 tablespoons plus 2 teaspoons dried bread crumbs
½ teaspoon salt
Freshly ground black pepper, to taste
4 teaspoons unsalted butter

1. Preheat the oven to 400°F. Lightly oil a small baking sheet, and set it aside.

2. Slice off the top quarter of each tomato, and set the tops aside. Using a melon baller, scoop out the centers of 2 of the tomatoes, leaving a shell, and place the pulp in a medium-size mixing bowl. Scoop out and discard the pulp of the remaining 2 tomatoes (or save it for another use). Invert the tomato shells onto paper towels to drain.

3. Cut the mushrooms in half, and slice them ¼ inch thick. Set them aside.

4. Cook the bacon in a skillet over low heat until crisp, about 10 minutes. Using a slotted spoon, transfer the bacon to paper towels to drain. Pour off all but 2 tablespoons of the fat in the skillet.

5. Add the shallots and mushrooms to the skillet, and cook over medium heat until golden, 10 minutes. Using a slotted spoon, add them to the tomato pulp in the bowl.

6. Shake the excess water from the spinach, add it to the skillet, and wilt over low heat, 4 to 5 minutes. Drain the spinach, pressing out as much moisture as possible. Chop it coarsely and add it to the bowl.

7. Stir 2 tablespoons of the bread crumbs, the salt, and the pepper into the spinach mixture. Toss well.

8. Using a paper towel, gently pat dry the inside of the tomato shells. Spoon the spinach mixture loosely into the shells, and sprinkle each one with ½ teaspoon of the remaining bread crumbs. Top each with 1 teaspoon butter.

9. Arrange the tomatoes on the prepared baking sheet and place the tops alongside, cut side down. Bake until the crumbs are golden and the tomatoes are cooked through but still firm, 25 minutes. Place the "hats" on top before serving.

4 portions

SWEETLY STEWED TOMATOES

Not at all like the canned variety. This is a nice vegetable to have with a creamy cheesy pasta or risotto on a cold wintery night.

3 large ripe tomatoes
2 tablespoons unsalted butter
¼ cup sliced celery
1 small onion, diced
1 clove garlic, minced
1 tablespoon sugar
1 teaspoon grated lemon zest
1 tablespoon chopped fresh dill
¼ teaspoon salt
Freshly ground black pepper, to taste

1. Bring a saucepan of water to a boil, and blanch the tomatoes in it for 30 seconds. Then plunge them into cold water to stop the cooking. Peel, halve, and seed the tomatoes. Cut each half in half. Set them aside.

2. Melt the butter in a medium-size saucepan, and add the celery, onion, and garlic. Cover, and cook over low heat for about 5 minutes. Then stir in the tomatoes, sugar, and lemon zest. Re-cover the pan and cook, stirring occasionally, until the tomatoes are soft and the mixture is thick, 30 minutes.

3. Stir in the dill, salt, and pepper, and serve.

4 portions

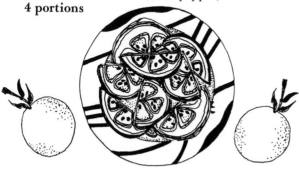

SEASON TO TASTE

A ripe summer tomato sprinkled with salt—what could be better? Perhaps nothing, but we think any of the following will please your palate as well:

Basil	Marjoram
Bay leaf	Mayonnaise
Black pepper	Onion
Cheese	Oregano
Chile pepper	Parsley
Chive	Rosemary
Cilantro	Savory
Dill	Tarragon
Garlic	Thyme
Lovage	Vinegar

FRESH TOMATO SALSA

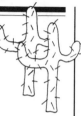

For nachos, chicken, fish, vegetables—or anytime you need a salsa with zip—this will do the trick.

4 large ripe plum tomatoes
¼ cup chopped scallions (green onions)
¼ cup chopped cilantro (fresh coriander)
1 tablespoon fresh oregano
2 cloves garlic, minced
1 teaspoon minced jalapeño pepper, or to taste
1 tablespoon olive oil
2 teaspoons fresh lime juice
Salt and freshly ground black pepper, to taste

1. Cut the tomatoes in half lengthwise and remove the seeds. Cut the halves into ¼-inch dice and place in a medium-size bowl.

2. Add the remaining ingredients to the bowl. Let sit, loosely covered, at room temperature, for the flavors to blend. Serve immediately or refrigerate and serve within 4 hours.

2 cups

TOMATO TIME KETCHUP

Here's a full-flavored tomato ketchup that went straight from grandma's recipe box into the microwave. The fresh flavor really leaps out, and it's smooth and thick, as a ketchup should be.

3 pounds ripe tomatoes, cored and quartered
½ cup cider vinegar
¼ cup sugar
½ teaspoon ground ginger
½ teaspoon salt
¼ teaspoon garlic powder
⅛ teaspoon ground cloves

1. Arrange the tomatoes packed tightly in a single layer in a 2½-quart microwave-safe casserole, and cover loosely with microwave-safe plastic wrap. Cook at full power (650 to 700 watts) for 40 minutes, stirring and breaking up the mixture with a wooden spoon every 10 minutes.

2. Allow the tomatoes to cool slightly. Then purée them in a food processor or blender. Strain the purée, pressing against the solids with a wooden spoon to extract as much pulp and juice as possible. You should have about 3 cups thick strained juice.

3. Return the juice to the casserole and stir in the remaining ingredients. Cook, uncovered and stirring every 10 minutes, until thick, 30 minutes.

2 cups

Note: This recipe was cooked on High (full power, 650 to 700 watts) in a carousel microwave, using microwave-safe containers.

If your microwave is less powerful, you will have to allow for more cooking time (approximately 1½ times the amount called for—but watch carefully); if it does not have a carousel, you may have to rotate the dish while it is cooking.

cube trays, then transfer to plastic bags and store in the freezer.

1 cup

Note: This recipe was cooked on High (full power, 650 to 700 watts) in a carousel microwave, using microwave-safe containers.

If your microwave is less powerful, you will have to allow for more cooking time (approximately 1½ times the amount called for—but watch carefully); if it does not have a carousel, you may have to rotate the dish while it is cooking.

TRADE SECRET

 When tomatoes are too soft to use in salads, chop them up with a couple of cloves of garlic and cook, covered, in the microwave on high for 3 minutes, stirring once. Freeze for a handy quick tomato sauce or for use in stews or soups.

FRESH TOMATO PASTE

A fresh tomato paste to make when there is an abundance of ripe, juicy tomatoes.

5 pounds large ripe tomatoes (6 or 7), cored and quartered

1. Place the tomatoes in a 4-quart microwave-safe bowl and cook, uncovered, at full power (650 to 700 watts) for 10 minutes. Stir, breaking up the tomatoes, and cook another 10 minutes. Stir again, and cook 20 minutes more.

2. Pass the mixture through a food mill and return it to the bowl. Cook for 30 minutes; stir, and cook another 15 minutes.

3. Transfer the mixture to a deep 2½-quart microwave-safe casserole. Cook 20 minutes, checking occasionally to make sure it does not burn. This will keep in the refrigerator for 3 days. Or, freeze in ice

HOT SUMMER TOMATO JAM

This is delicious—with an omelet or scrambled eggs, with spicy breakfast patties, with your favorite hamburger, or simply spread on toasted peasant bread.

6 allspice berries
6 whole cloves
½ teaspoon crushed dried red pepper flakes
¼ teaspoon mustard seeds
1½ pounds ripe plum tomatoes
1 cup sugar
½ cup cider vinegar
1 teaspoon salt
½ teaspoon freshly ground black pepper

1. Combine the allspice, cloves, red pepper flakes, and mustard seeds in a piece of cheesecloth. Tie it securely with a long piece of kitchen string, forming a spice bag. Leave the long string dangling.

2. Bring a large saucepan of water to a boil. Drop the tomatoes in the water and cook until the skins split, 1 to 2 minutes. Then plunge them into a bowl of cold water to stop the cooking. Pat the tomatoes dry, peel them, and cut into ¼-inch dice.

3. Place the tomatoes and all the remaining ingredients in a heavy saucepan. Add the spice bag, letting the string hang out of the pan. Slowly bring the mixture to a boil. Then reduce the heat and simmer for 30 minutes, stirring frequently.

4. Remove the pan from the heat and discard the spice bag. Let the jam cool, and then refrigerate.

1¼ cups

TURNIPS

T urnips, like parsnips, are another old-fashioned vegetable long due a revival. For starters, it's one of the prettiest of all the root vegetables, with rosy or violet tops and creamy white bottoms. Turnips are crisp and moist and have a mildly earthy taste—the perfect accompaniment for hearty fall and winter food, which is their peak season.

In France, baby turnips about the size of large cherry tomatoes are a favorite. They are as smooth as butter and delicious. These turnips don't have to be peeled, so they can show off their splendid coloring. Most of the turnips in our markets are too big for really good eating. Look for turnips no larger than an egg. Don't buy them at all if they are larger than two inches. Look for firm, unblemished skins and turnips that feel heavy for their size. If they feel light, they'll be woody when you cook them. If the turnips have the fresh greens still attached, separate the leaves and cook them like spinach.

Baby turnips can be cooked whole and unpeeled, but all others should be peeled and then quartered or cut into large chunks. They can be boiled or steamed (with broth for more flavor) until tender and tossed with butter, salt, and pepper. They are delicious

puréed with potatoes and carrots, too. We like them quartered and added along with potatoes and carrots to roast pork for the last hour of cooking. Still, a mixed sauté of carrots, rutabaga, turnips, and broccoli stalks has everything we want in a vegetable dish—vivid color, succulent texture, and great flavor. Cut the vegetables into julienne strips and blanch until barely tender, then sauté them all together in butter.

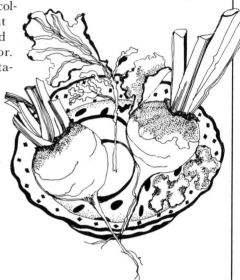

TURNIP AND PEAR SAUTE

T he flavors of this vegetable dish delight and surprise—the sweetness of the pears plays off the slightly bitter turnip. Walnuts add crunch, and lemon juice adds sparkle.

4 turnips (about 1 pound)
3 Seckel pears
3 tablespoons unsalted butter
1 shallot, peeled and thinly sliced
⅔ cup walnut halves
Salt and freshly ground black pepper, to taste
½ lemon
Chopped fresh parsley, for garnish

1. Peel the turnips and cut them in half lengthwise. Then cut them into ¼-inch-thick slices.

2. Cut the pears in half. Core them, and cut into ¼-inch-thick slices.

3. Melt the butter in a large skillet, and sauté the turnips until golden and crisp-tender, 6 to 8 minutes.

4. Add the pears and shallot. Cook, tossing the mixture, for 3 minutes. Then add the walnuts and cook until heated through, 2 minutes. Season with salt and pepper, squeeze the lemon over the mixture, and sprinkle with the parsley. Serve immediately.

4 to 6 portions

TURNIPS ANNA

This is a simply prepared winter vegetable that can take the place of potatoes. A perfect accompaniment to Fruit Stuffed Loin of Pork.

3 tablespoons unsalted butter
4 turnips (about 1 pound), peeled and very thinly sliced
1 shallot, peeled and minced
Salt and freshly ground black pepper, to taste

1. Preheat the oven to 425°F.

2. Melt the butter in a skillet and sauté the turnips just until coated in butter and partially cooked, 3 minutes.

3. In an 8-inch round cake pan (preferably non-stick), arrange a layer of overlapping turnip slices. Sprinkle with some of the shallot, and salt and pepper. Repeat with the remaining ingredients, ending with a layer of turnips.

4. Bake until crisp and golden, about 30 minutes.

4 portions

ZILLIONS OF ZUCCHINI

By far the most popular of the summer squash family, zucchini is also the most versatile. It has a mild flavor and tenderness that always takes up and harmonizes with other ingredients. It never obstructs. Perhaps that's why zucchini is such an important vegetable to dozens of cuisines around the world—Italian, French, and Japanese to name just a few. Its mildness pleases children, its versatility pleases food lovers, and its rapid cooking time pleases hurried chefs.

BUYING

Zucchini are available all year round, but the quality is best in late spring through summer. Buy zucchini that is firm and heavy for its size. The skin should be thin and tender—you can easily puncture it with your fingernail. Avoid those with bruises, soft spots, cuts, and scrapes. Don't buy large zucchini. Anything over 7 to 8 inches is too big. The tiny zucchini are very tender, but the medium 5 to 7 inchers work best for most dishes.

STORING

Refrigerate zucchini in a plastic bag up to three or four days. They keep better if dry; make sure there's no moisture on the zucchini or in the bag. Don't rinse them until you are ready to cook them.

YIELD

Three medium zucchini weigh about 1 pound. Each zucchini will serve one if cooked as a side dish. One medium zucchini, sliced, measures 2 cups; shredded, 1½ cups.

PREPARING

Scrub the zucchini under cold running water with a soft vegetable brush or rub them with your hands to remove any dirt. Be careful—the skin is very fragile. Peeling is unnecessary but the ends should be trimmed.

COOKING

We love stuffing baby zucchini with flavorful ingredients—garlic, fresh herbs, shallots, sharp cheeses, and plum tomatoes are just some of our favorites. But we also like sautéing zucchini with fresh thyme or basil and topping it with a fresh tomato sauce. Zucchini brushed with good olive oil, grilled, and sprinkled with pepper is delicious, too. Zucchini, like other summer squashes, has a high water content. Whichever way it's cooked, it should be done quickly so that it doesn't get soft and mushy.

▲ **Steaming:** Clean and trim zucchini. Leave small

ones whole but cut larger ones lengthwise in half or quarters or crosswise into thick slices. Steam in a steaming basket or rack over an inch of boiling water until crisp-tender. Zucchini slices cook in about 5 minutes. Halves and small whole zucchini need a bit more time, 8 to 10 minutes. Don't overcook zucchini. Check it by tasting it or piercing it with a knife.

You can also steam zucchini without a rack or basket by placing it in a pan with ½ inch of boiling water. Cover tightly and cook over medium heat, tossing occasionally.

▲ **Sautéing:** Clean and trim the zucchini, then cut into thick julienne strips, slices, chunks, quarters, or halves. Heat about 3 tablespoons butter and/or olive oil for every pound of zucchini in a large skillet over medium-high heat. Flavor the oil, if you want, with a crushed garlic clove for a minute, then remove it. Add the zucchini and sauté, turning frequently, until crisp-tender and just golden. You can sauté the zucchini with sliced onions for more flavor. One or two chopped fresh tomatoes and a sprinkle of chopped fresh herbs added at the last minute is good, too. To sauté grated zucchini, see Don't Squelch Squash.

▲ **Stuffing:** Rinse and trim the zucchini, then cut lengthwise in half and carefully scoop out the seeds and pulp, leaving a ¼- to ½-inch shell. Steam the shells until half tender. Stuff small zucchini with vegetable purées and large zucchini with cooked meat, cheese, or rice mixtures. Bake on an oiled baking sheet at 350°F until the stuffing and zucchini are heated through, 10 minutes for small zucchini, up to 30 minutes for larger zucchini with a heavy stuffing. Be careful that the zucchini doesn't overcook and fall apart.

ZUCCHINI FRITTI

Our philosophy with fried zucchini has always been the thinner the better.

This is a very simple zucchini fritti. Sometimes zucchini is boiled, sometimes dipped in batter, before it is fried—which robs it of its natural taste.

Squeeze lots of fresh lemon juice over a mountain of these in the center of the table, and let everyone eat them with their fingers as a starter. They're a great way to get the fun going.

½ cup olive oil
½ cup corn oil
¾ cup unbleached all-purpose flour
½ teaspoon paprika
½ teaspoon salt
½ teaspoon freshly ground black pepper
3 zucchini, cut into 3- to 4-inch-long julienne
Lemon wedges, for serving

1. Combine the oils in a skillet, and heat until hot but not smoking.

2. Stir together the flour, paprika, salt, and pepper in a mixing bowl.

3. Dredge the zucchini in the flour mixture, shaking off any excess. Sauté it in the hot oil, in batches, until golden and crisp. Drain on paper towels, and serve immediately with the lemon wedges alongside.

4 portions

ZUCCHINI SAUTE

Yellow and green summer squash in a lovely quick sauté that's anything but boring.

2 tablespoons unsalted butter
1 tablespoon olive oil
1 tablespoon minced shallots
2 yellow summer squash (8 ounces each), cut into 6-inch-long julienne
2 zucchini (8 ounces each), cut into 6-inch-long julienne
Salt and freshly ground black pepper, to taste
1 tablespoon chopped fresh dill
4 ounces Parmesan cheese, in one piece

1. Heat the butter and oil in a large skillet over low heat. Add the shallots, and sauté until soft and translucent, about 10 minutes.

2. Raise the heat to medium, add the yellow squash and zucchini, and cook, tossing frequently, until just wilted and slightly browned, 5 minutes.

3. Add the salt, pepper, and dill, and toss to mix. Transfer the squash to a warmed serving dish, and use a vegetable peeler to shave Parmesan cheese over it. Serve immediately.

4 portions

PROVENCAL RATATOUILLE

The most familiar ratatouille tastes fresh again. We've added a pesto cube—or *pistou* if you're a purist—and Niçoise olives. We have been known to take license with the classics!

1 eggplant (about 1 pound), cut into 1-inch cubes
1 teaspoon salt
2 tablespoons olive oil
2 leeks (white part and ½ inch green), well rinsed, patted dry, and cut into 1-inch pieces
2 zucchini (1 pound), cut into 1-inch cubes
3 cloves garlic, minced
3 tomatoes, diced
½ cup pitted Niçoise olives
6 tablespoons or 2 cubes (thawed) Basil Pesto (see Index)
6 anchovy fillets, rinsed and coarsely chopped
Freshly ground black pepper, to taste

1. Sprinkle the eggplant cubes lightly with the salt, and place them in a colander. Allow them to sit for 1 hour. Then rinse, drain, and pat dry. Set aside.

2. Preheat the oven to 350°F.

3. Heat the oil in a large skillet over low heat. Add the leeks and cook for 5 minutes. Stir in the zucchini and garlic, and cook 3 minutes.

4. Stir in the tomatoes, olives, basil pesto, anchovies, pepper, and reserved eggplant. Transfer the mixture to an ovenproof casserole, cover, and bake for 20 minutes. Stir the ratatouille, and bake another 25 minutes.

5. Serve hot or at room temperature.

6 portions

ASIAN RATATOUILLE

A classic Mediterranean combination—eggplant, zucchini, and garlic—with the surprise of sesame seeds and hot spices. All is lightened with cilantro, which is the parsley of China.

1 small eggplant (12 ounces to 1 pound), cut into ½-inch cubes
½ teaspoon salt
6 tablespoons sesame oil
2 ribs celery, cut diagonally into ¼-inch-thick slices
1 onion, halved, then cut into slivers
1 red bell pepper, cored, seeded, and julienned
2 small zucchini (6 ounces each), halved lengthwise and cut into ¼-inch-thick slices
8 ounces fresh cultivated mushrooms, thinly sliced
¾ cup Berta's Chicken Stock (see Index) or canned broth
2 tablespoons soy sauce
1 tablespoon dry sherry
1 teaspoon cornstarch
1 teaspoon minced garlic
1 teaspoon minced fresh ginger
2 teaspoons hoisin sauce*
1 tablespoon chopped cilantro (fresh coriander)
2 scallions (green onions), white bulb and 3 inches green, thinly sliced diagonally
2 tablespoons sesame seeds, toasted (see Index)

1. Sprinkle the eggplant with the salt and place it in a colander to drain for 30 minutes.

2. Preheat the oven to 350°F.

3. Heat 3 tablespoons of the sesame oil in a large flameproof casserole or dutch oven. Sauté the celery, onion, and bell pepper over medium-low heat until wilted, about 5 minutes. Remove the vegetables with a slotted spoon, and set aside.

4. Add the remaining sesame oil to the casserole. Sauté the zucchini, mushrooms, and eggplant until soft, about 5 minutes. Add the reserved onion, bell pepper, and celery, and remove from the heat.

5. Combine the stock, soy sauce, sherry, and cornstarch in a small bowl and blend well. Stir this into the vegetable mixture, cover the casserole, and transfer it to the oven. Bake for 40 minutes.

6. Stir in the garlic, ginger, and hoisin sauce. Re-cover, and bake the vegetables another 10 minutes.

7. Stir in the cilantro, garnish with the scallions and toasted sesame seeds, and serve.

6 to 8 portions

*Available in some supermarkets and in Asian groceries and specialty food shops.

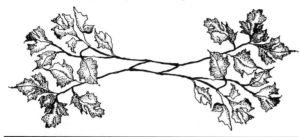

MEXICAN RATATOUILLE

Jalapeño pepper, a milder chile pepper, and cilantro take this ratatouille south of the border. It travels very well, as you'll see.

2 tablespoons vegetable oil
1 onion, chopped
2 yellow summer squash (6 ounces each), cut into ½-inch cubes
2 zucchini (6 ounces each), cut into ½-inch cubes
1 teaspoon dried oregano
¾ teaspoon salt
½ teaspoon ground cumin
Freshly ground black pepper, to taste
2 green (unripe) firm tomatoes, diced
1 fresh mild chile pepper, minced (2 teaspoons)
1 fresh jalapeño pepper, minced
¼ cup chopped cilantro (fresh coriander)

1. Preheat the oven to 350°F.

2. Heat the oil in a large skillet, and sauté the onion over medium heat for about 3 minutes. Add the yellow squash, zucchini, oregano, salt, cumin, and black pepper. Sauté 5 minutes, stirring.

3. Stir in the tomatoes and both chiles. Transfer the mixture to an ovenproof 2½-quart casserole, cover, and bake for 30 minutes.

4. Stir in the cilantro, and serve immediately or at room temperature.

4 to 6 portions

DILL ZUCCHINI PIE

A great way to use the abundance of zucchini available in late summer. The filling is spiced with pepper and dill, a counterpoint to the very fresh flavor of zucchini.

¾ cup whole-wheat flour
¾ cup unbleached all-purpose flour
1 tablespoon dried thyme leaves
¾ teaspoon coarsely ground black pepper
4½ tablespoons unsalted butter, cold
¼ cup solid vegetable shortening, cold
¼ cup ice water
3 small zucchini (6 to 8 ounces each), cut into ¼-inch-thick rounds
2 tablespoons coarse (kosher) salt
¼ cup olive oil
2 cups grated Gruyère cheese (about 8 ounces)
½ teaspoon grated nutmeg
⅓ cup chopped fresh dill
2 tablespoons chopped fresh Italian (flat-leaf) parsley
1 tablespoon extra virgin olive oil

1. Three to 4 hours ahead, prepare the tart crust: Combine the flours in a medium-size mixing bowl, and stir in the thyme and ½ teaspoon of the pepper. Cut the butter and shortening into small pieces, and using a pastry blender, two knives, or your fingertips, cut them into the flour mixture, until the mixture resembles coarse crumbs.

2. Add the ice water, 1 tablespoon at a time, mixing it in with a fork until the mixture forms a ball (you may need more than ¼ cup). Flatten the ball of dough slightly with your hands, cover it with plastic wrap, and refrigerate it for 3 hours.

3. Next, sprinkle the sliced zucchini with the coarse salt, and place it in a colander to drain for 1 hour.

4. When you are ready to cook the tart, preheat the oven to 375°F.

5. Roll the chilled dough out on a lightly floured surface to form a circle about ⅛ inch thick. Carefully lay the dough over a 9-inch tart pan with removable bottom and pat it in place, leaving a slightly thicker amount on the sides of the pan. Trim off any excess dough.

6. Prick the bottom of the crust with the tines of a fork, and line the crust with aluminum foil. Fill it with dried beans or pie weights.

7. Bake the crust for 10 minutes. Then carefully remove the beans and foil, and bake another 12 minutes. Allow the crust to cool slightly.

8. Rinse the zucchini and pat it dry. Heat the oil in a skillet, and sauté the zucchini over medium heat until lightly browned on both sides, 5 minutes. Drain it on paper towels.

9. Spread the cheese over the bottom of the pie shell. Arrange the zucchini over it in an overlapping circular pattern, covering the surface. Then sprinkle the zucchini with the nutmeg, remaining ¼ teaspoon pepper, dill, and parsley. Drizzle the top with the olive oil.

10. Bake the pie for 40 minutes. Let it rest 10 minutes. To serve, carefully remove the side of the pan and run a thin spatula under the crust to loosen it from the bottom of the pan.

4 to 6 portions

STUFFED SQUASH BLOSSOMS

Once seen mostly in Europe, delicate golden squash blossoms are becoming more available in our produce markets in summer. They are lovely stuffed with light-tasting cheese mixtures. In this preparation, the flowers form slightly crisp little packets around a silky filling.

1 cup fresh ricotta cheese
4 ounces fresh mozzarella cheese, shredded
1 tablespoon minced fresh chives
Freshly ground black pepper, to taste
25 squash blossoms, rinsed and drained
2 cups unbleached all-purpose flour
3 eggs
3 tablespoons milk
4 tablespoons clarified butter (see Index)
4 tablespoons olive oil

1. Stir the ricotta, mozzarella, chives, and pepper together in a mixing bowl. Fill each blossom with about 1 teaspoon of this mixture, and gently pinch or twist the ends shut.

2. Place the flour in one shallow bowl. Combine the eggs and milk in another shallow bowl, and blend well.

3. Heat 2 tablespoons of the clarified butter and 2 tablespoons of the oil in a skillet. Dip the blossoms first in the flour, then in the egg mixture, and sauté in batches until golden, about 2 minutes per side. As they are cooked, transfer the blossoms to a low (225°F) oven to keep warm. Continue cooking the blossoms, adding more butter and oil as needed. Serve immediately.

4 to 6 portions

Zucchini blossoms are a gardener's treat. In Europe they sell zucchini with blossoms attached; in the States, blossoms are available to gardeners and only occasionally are they seen in produce markets. Since every year we still have more zucchini in the garden than we know what to do with, we've started harvesting the blossoms in early summer. To save the summer crop completely, harvest just the male blossoms (long narrow stems) and leave the females (swollen stems) on the plant. Zucchini blossoms can be dipped in batter and deep-fried until crisp or stuffed with rice, seafood, vegetable, or cheese mixtures. The stuffed blossoms can be tied at the top, dipped in batter, and deep-fried, or folded to enclose the filling and baked on an oiled baking sheet until heated through.

STAPLE
STARS

GOING WITH GRAINS AND BEANS

Finally grains and beans are garnering the kind of respect they deserve. Perhaps it's because we are eating less meat that we have a new-found interest in these versatile, protein-filled foods. It's not that we never made bean or grain dishes. But for so long we served up the same ones, and in the same ways. Now that we better understand the wide range available to us, and their potential, we are experimenting more and more with exciting results. Minty bulgur tabboulehs, flavorful polentas, crunchy bean salads, velvety bean cakes and purées—the textures and flavors are outstanding. How could we have kept these great dishes out of the spotlight for so long? It's about time they took a bow.

BASIL BARLEY PROVENCAL

Barley, a grain of the grass family, was the first cereal cultivated as a foodstuff for man. Tossed with vegetables in Provençal style, its magic stretches across the ages. For your good health, you should add more grains and vegetables to your daily diet—and this is a great way to do it!

¼ cup extra virgin olive oil
1 large onion, cut into 1-inch pieces
2 zucchini (about 1 pound),
*   cut into 1-inch dice*
4 cloves garlic, coarsely chopped
½ cup Berta's Chicken Stock
*   (see Index) or canned broth*
6 ripe plum tomatoes, halved, seeded,
*   and cut into 1-inch dice*
Salt and freshly ground black pepper, to taste
1 cup cooked pearl barley
1 cup pine nuts, toasted (see Index)
1 cup (loosely packed) slivered
*   fresh basil leaves*
¼ cup (loosely packed) chopped fresh
*   Italian (flat-leaf) parsley*

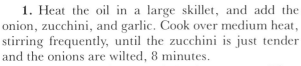

1. Heat the oil in a large skillet, and add the onion, zucchini, and garlic. Cook over medium heat, stirring frequently, until the zucchini is just tender and the onions are wilted, 8 minutes.

2. Add the stock and cook 2 minutes more. Then add the tomatoes and salt and pepper. Cook 1 minute, stirring frequently.

3. Add the barley, pine nuts, basil, and parsley to the skillet. Stir well, and cook until heated through, about 2 minutes. Adjust the seasonings if necessary, and serve immediately.

6 portions

BARLEY PILAF

Mushrooms and barley, traditionally an Old World soup, are combined here with pecans, golden raisins, and thyme and cooked to just the right texture in the microwave. Serve as a side dish with your favorite poultry.

4 tablespoons (½ stick) unsalted butter
1 cup sliced fresh cultivated mushrooms
1 small onion, finely chopped
½ cup chopped pecans
1 tablespoon fresh thyme leaves or 1 teaspoon dried
½ cup pearl barley
3 cups Berta's Chicken Stock (see Index) or canned broth
⅓ cup golden raisins

1. In a microwave-safe 2-quart casserole, melt 3 tablespoons of the butter at full power (650 to 700 watts) for 2 minutes.

2. Stir in the mushrooms, onion, pecans, and thyme. Cook 3 minutes.

3. Stir in the barley; cook 2 minutes.

4. Stir in the stock, raisins, and remaining 1 tablespoon butter. Cover, and cook 35 minutes. Let stand, covered, for 5 minutes before serving.

4 portions

Note: This recipe was cooked on High (full power, 650 to 700 watts) in a carousel microwave, using microwave-safe containers.

If your microwave is less powerful, you will have to allow for more cooking time (approximately 1½ times the amount called for—but watch carefully); if it does not have a carousel, you may have to rotate the dish while it is cooking.

MINTY TABBOULEH

The lightness of bulgur (cracked wheat) mixed with ripe plum tomatoes, cucumber, red onion, and lots of chopped parsley and mint makes for an extra-refreshing summertime salad that also keeps extremely well.

1 heaping cup bulgur
1 cup cold water
½ cup fresh lemon juice
⅔ cup extra virgin olive oil
1 cup coarsely chopped fresh mint leaves
1 cup coarsely chopped fresh Italian (flat-leaf) parsley
½ cup finely diced red onion
2 teaspoons minced garlic
1 teaspoon coarsely ground black pepper
½ teaspoon salt
4 ripe plum tomatoes, seeded and cut into ½-inch dice
1 large cucumber, peeled, seeded, and cut into ½-inch dice
Fresh mint leaves, for garnish

1. Combine the bulgur, water, lemon juice, and ⅓ cup of the olive oil in a large bowl. Mix well, and set aside for 30 minutes at room temperature. Then fluff the mixture with a fork.

2. Add the mint, parsley, red onion, garlic, pepper, salt, and remaining ⅓ cup olive oil. Toss well with a fork.

3. Add the tomatoes and cucumber, and toss again. Adjust the seasonings if necessary, and allow to stand, loosely covered, for at least 30 minutes for the flavors to come out.

4. Garnish with fresh mint leaves, and serve.

6 to 8 portions

KASHA VARNISHKES

Wouldn't our grandmothers be surprised to see this dish coming out of the microwave after 15 minutes of cooking, start to finish? Now that's modern!

3 ounces bow-tie pasta
1 tablespoon vegetable oil
½ cup whole-kernel kasha (roasted buckwheat groats)
1 egg, lightly beaten
1 cup Berta's Chicken Stock (see Index) or canned broth
3 tablespoons unsalted butter
15 fresh cultivated mushrooms, trimmed
1 shallot, peeled and thinly sliced
¼ cup chopped scallions (green onions)
½ teaspoon coarsely ground black pepper

1. Bring a large saucepan of water to a boil, and add the pasta. Cook until just tender; then drain, rinse under cold water, and drain again. Allow to cool to room temperature.

2. Cook the oil, uncovered, in a 2-quart microwave-safe casserole at full power (650 to 700 watts) for 2 minutes. Stir in the kasha, and cook until toasted and fragrant, 1½ minutes.

3. Remove the casserole from the oven and quickly add the beaten egg, stirring until it is almost cooked and the kernels are coated (this will take only a few seconds).

4. Return the casserole to the oven and cook 30 seconds. Stir to separate the kernels, breaking up any clumps with a fork.

5. Stir in the stock and cook, uncovered, until the liquid has been absorbed and the kernels are cooked through, 6½ minutes. Break up any clumps with a fork. Set the casserole aside.

6. Cook the butter in a microwave-safe pie plate for 1½ minutes. Then stir in the mushrooms and shallot, and cook 3 minutes. Remove the plate from the oven, and stir in the scallions and pepper.

7. Stir the mushroom mixture and the reserved pasta into the kasha, return the casserole to the oven, and cook just until heated through, 1 to 2 minutes.

4 portions

Note: This recipe was cooked on High (full power, 650 to 700 watts) in a carousel microwave, using microwave-safe containers.

If your microwave is less powerful, you will have to allow for more cooking time (approximately 1½ times the amount called for—but watch carefully); if it does not have a carousel, you may have to rotate the dish while it is cooking.

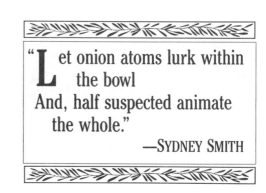

"**L**et onion atoms lurk within the bowl
And, half suspected animate the whole."
—SYDNEY SMITH

OUR BASIC POLENTA

Smooth and creamy polenta is light and delicious when made with milk. Fry it up for a real treat.

3 cups milk
1 tablespoon unsalted butter
1 teaspoon sugar
½ teaspoon salt
1 cup stone-ground yellow cornmeal
2 tablespoons unsalted butter, melted

1. Combine the milk, butter, sugar, and salt in a heavy saucepan and heat just to a simmer.
2. Slowly add the cornmeal in a thin stream, whisking constantly. Lower the heat and continue stirring with a wooden spoon until the mixture has thickened and leaves the sides of the pan, about 10 minutes.
3. Serve topped with melted butter.
6 portions

FRIED POLENTA

A favorite breakfast. Julee's grandmother made polenta once a week, and she'd serve it fried with a topping of maple syrup, brown sugar, or powdered sugar—or with lemon juice or berries.

¼ cup golden raisins
2 tablespoons maple syrup
1 recipe Polenta (above)
1 tablespoon unsalted butter
Maple syrup

1. Butter an 8½ x 4½-inch loaf pan.
2. Stir the raisins and syrup into the cooked polenta, and scrape the mixture into the prepared loaf pan. Cover, and refrigerate until firm, about 2 hours.
3. Unmold the chilled polenta and cut it into ½-inch-thick slices. Melt the butter in a skillet, and sauté the slices until golden on each side. (Add more butter if necessary.)
4. Serve hot, with maple syrup.
6 portions

POLENTA, SAUSAGE, AND TOMATO LAYERS

Layered levels of polenta, tomato sauce, hot Italian sausages, mozzarella, and Parmesan blend to form a warming casserole. This is a great Sunday night supper in front of a roaring fire—especially if you add a bottle of Chianti.

1 recipe Our Basic Polenta (see this page)
½ cup grated Parmesan cheese
1 tablespoon olive oil
4 hot Italian sausages (about ¾ pound), coarsely chopped
1½ cups Fresh Tomato Sauce (see Index)
8 ounces fresh mozzarella cheese, sliced ¼ to ½ inch thick

1. Preheat the oven to 375°F. Butter a 2½-quart flameproof casserole.
2. Combine the polenta and ¼ cup of the Parmesan in a mixing bowl. Stir thoroughly, and scrape the mixture into the prepared casserole.
3. Heat the oil in a medium-size skillet, and sauté the sausage over medium heat, breaking up the pieces with a wooden spoon, until browned and cooked through, about 10 minutes. Remove the skillet from the heat.
4. Sprinkle 2 tablespoons of the remaining Parmesan over the polenta. Add the sausage, using a slotted spoon, in an even layer. Then spoon on the tomato sauce. Sprinkle with the remaining 2 tablespoons Parmesan, and top with the mozzarella in an even layer.
5. Bake until bubbling, 30 minutes. Then place the casserole under the broiler and cook until browned, 3 minutes. Let it stand 10 minutes before serving.
6 portions

POLENTA WITH SWEET GORGONZOLA

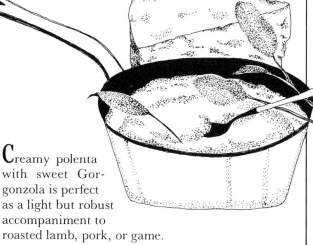

Creamy polenta with sweet Gorgonzola is perfect as a light but robust accompaniment to roasted lamb, pork, or game.

2 cups milk
8 tablespoons instant polenta
Salt and freshly ground black pepper, to taste
½ pound Gorgonzola cheese, rind removed
2 tablespoons heavy or whipping cream

1. Bring the milk to a boil in a saucepan. Add the polenta, salt and pepper. Reduce to a simmer and continue cooking, stirring constantly, for 5 minutes.

2. Tear the Gorgonzola into large pieces, and add them to the polenta along with the cream. Continue cooking until the cheese has melted, 2 to 3 minutes. Serve immediately.

4 portions

"They touched earth and grain grew."
—MARGARET ABIGAIL WALKER

CORNMEAL PROSCIUTTO STUFFING

The flavors of Tuscany are brought together in this cornmeal stuffing. Serve it hot out of the oven with a steaming casserole of Braised Rabbit Smothered With Onions and a Chianti Classico.

3 cups water
1½ teaspoons salt
1 tablespoon butter
1 cup stone-ground cornmeal
2 tablespoons olive oil
1 onion, diced
2 ribs celery, cut into ½-inch dice
2 cloves garlic, minced
1 tablespoon chopped fresh rosemary leaves
1 teaspoon crumbled dried sage
½ teaspoon dried thyme leaves
Freshly ground black pepper, to taste
4 ounces prosciutto, thinly sliced (but not paper-thin) and
  slivered
2 cups toasted white bread cubes
1 cup Berta's Chicken Stock (see Index) or canned broth

1. Preheat the oven to 375°F. Butter a baking sheet and a 2½-quart ovenproof casserole.

2. Combine the water, salt, and butter in a heavy saucepan and heat just to a simmer.

3. Slowly add the cornmeal in a thin stream, whisking constantly. Lower the heat and continue stirring with a wooden spoon until the mixture has thickened and leaves the sides of the pan, about 10 minutes. Remove from the heat.

4. Spread the mixture in a ½-inch-thick layer on the prepared baking sheet. Set it aside to cool to room temperature.

5. Heat the oil in a medium-size skillet, and sauté the onion, celery, and garlic over medium heat until softened and slightly colored, 10 minutes. Season with the rosemary, sage, thyme, and pepper.

6. Stir in the prosciutto and cook 2 minutes. Set the skillet aside.

7. Cut the cooled cornmeal mixture into 1-inch squares.

8. Toss the vegetable mixture, toasted bread cubes, and cornmeal squares in a large bowl. Add the chicken stock, and toss gently. Spoon the mixture into the prepared casserole, cover, and bake for 40 minutes.

6 portions

NUTTY QUINOA SALAD

The latest grain to land on our shores from South America, quinoa is very adaptable. We thought we'd update our favorite nutted wild rice recipe and see how good it would be. Though not ones to trade new friends for old, we have to admit we're very partial to the revision. The lightness of the quinoa gives magic to the flavors of the sweet orange juice, raisins, and mint. This is best served at room temperature, just great with a cold cucumber soup on a summer day or with an autumnal feast of roasted duck.

1 cup quinoa
2 cups water
½ cup golden raisins
¼ cup sesame oil
3 scallions (green onions), white bulb and 3 inches green, sliced
½ cup unsalted roasted peanuts
½ cup canned mandarin orange sections, drained
2 tablespoons chopped fresh mint leaves
2 teaspoons grated orange zest

1. Combine the quinoa and water in a large saucepan, and bring to a boil. Reduce the heat, cover, and simmer for 10 minutes. Then add the raisins and continue cooking until all the liquid has evaporated, 5 minutes. Remove the pan from the heat and spread the mixture out on a baking sheet. Let it cool completely.

2. In a large bowl, combine the quinoa and raisins with all the remaining ingredients. Toss gently and serve.

4 to 6 portions

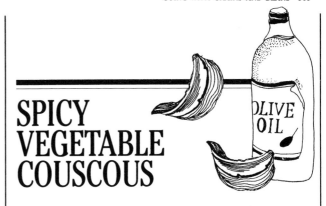

SPICY VEGETABLE COUSCOUS

On a cool, rainy summer afternoon, sometimes there is nothing more comforting than this easily prepared Middle Eastern classic. And if the weather suddenly takes a turn for the better, pack it up and bring it to the beach. It also tastes terrific cold.

2 tablespoons olive oil
½ cup diced yellow summer squash
½ cup diced zucchini
½ cup diced red onion
1 clove garlic, minced
1 cup cooked chick-peas (garbanzos)
½ teaspoon ground cumin
½ teaspoon curry powder
½ teaspoon dried red pepper flakes
½ teaspoon salt
Freshly ground black pepper, to taste
3 cups cooked couscous (cooked in Berta's Chicken Stock—see Index—or canned broth)
¼ cup chopped fresh parsley

1. Heat the oil in a large skillet, and sauté the squash, zucchini, red onion, and garlic for 5 minutes.

2. Stir in the chick-peas and spices. Then gently stir in the cooked couscous. Cook until hot, about 8 minutes. (Or spoon into a large casserole, dot with butter, and heat in a 350°F oven until hot, 15 minutes.) Garnish with the parsley before serving.

4 portions

GRAINS AT A GLANCE

GRAIN	DESCRIPTION	COOK	BEST
Pearl barley	Whole polished kernels; bland flavor and soft texture	Boil in plenty of salted water or simmer 1 part barley to 2 parts salted water, 45 minutes.	Added to soup, also mixed with vegetables as a main or side dish.
Buckwheat groats (kasha)	Whole kernels; mild nutty flavor and soft texture. Kasha is roasted buckwheat; the flavor is nuttier.	Simmer 1 part groats to 2 parts salted water, 15 minutes.	Important grain in Russian cooking. Kasha makes great pilaf.
CORN			
Cornmeal (polenta)	Ground corn kernels, white or yellow; sweet taste and soft texture	For cereal, simmer 1 part meal to 4 parts salted water, 30 minutes.	For cereal and polenta, also baking.
Hominy (posole)	Skinned white corn kernels; slightly sweet and firm texture	Soak overnight, then simmer 1 part hominy to 3 parts salted water, 2 ½ to 3 hours.	For cereal or side dishes.
Hominy grits (grits)	Ground hominy; available coarse, medium, and fine	Like cornmeal.	For cereal and baking.
Millet	Small, whole tan kernels; slightly nutty and chewy	Simmer 1 part millet to 2 parts salted water, 35 to 40 minutes.	Served like rice, also in soup.
OATS			
Oat groats	Whole oat grain; nutty flavor and chewy texture	Simmer 1 part groats to 2 parts salted water, 1 hour.	For cereal.
Oatmeal (also rolled oats and quick-cooking oatmeal)	Steamed, flattened, and flaked or cut oat groats; slightly nutty flavor and soft texture	Simmer 1 part oatmeal to 2 parts salted water. Check package directions for time.	For cereal and baking.
Steel-cut oats (Scottish or Irish oatmeal)	Sliced oat groats; nutty flavor and firm texture	Simmer 1 part oats to 2 parts salted water, 30 minutes.	For cereal and baking.
Quinoa	Pale yellow seed slightly larger than mustard seed; sweet flavor and soft texture	Rinse well, then simmer 1 part quinoa to 2 parts water, 12 to 15 minutes.	Served like rice, or as a base for salads.

GRAIN	DESCRIPTION	COOK	BEST
Rye groats	Whole rye kernels; sour taste and soft texture	Simmer 1 part groats to 2 parts salted water, 20 minutes.	For cereal and added to stews.

WHEAT

GRAIN	DESCRIPTION	COOK	BEST
Wheat berries	Unprocessed whole wheat kernels; hearty flavor and chewy texture	Soak overnight, then boil in plenty of salted water until tender, about 1 hour.	For salads and baking.
Cracked wheat	Crushed whole wheat kernels; flavor like wheat berries and firm texture	Simmer 1 part wheat to 2 parts salted water, about 40 minutes.	For cereal.
Bulgur	Cracked wheat that is hulled, steamed, and dried; nutty flavor and soft texture	Same as for cracked wheat.	Served like rice.
Bran	Outer coating of the wheat seed or germ		For baking.
Wheat germ	Seed of the wheat kernel		For baking and sprinkled over yogurt or cooked cereal.
Couscous (semolina grain)	Flour-coated semolina, which is ground durum wheat	Almost all couscous in U.S. markets is instant (precooked); follow package directions.	Served like rice.

> "**I**f it weren't for me people would have thought surreal was a breakfast food."
>
> —OISEAU

SUNSHINE CEREAL

Start the day off with the best—granola, bran, raisins, bananas, and yogurt!

½ cup Grape Nuts or natural granola cereal
¼ cup bran cereal
4 teaspoons sunflower seeds
1 tablespoon sliced almonds
2 tablespoons raisins
2 cups plain low-fat yogurt
1 small banana, peeled and sliced
Pinch of cinnamon
2 tablespoons honey
Sliced strawberries or other fresh fruit (optional)

Combine the cereals, 3 teaspoons of the sunflower seeds, and the almonds and raisins in a medium-size bowl. Stir well to mix, and then fold in the yogurt. Divide the cereal between two bowls, and top with the banana slices. Sprinkle with cinnamon, drizzle with the honey, and top with the remaining 1 teaspoon sunflower seeds. Add sliced strawberries on top of it all if you wish.

2 portions

BAYOU DIRTY RICE

Right from the Deep South, this spicy rice is full of meat and vegetables—just right for Sunday night supper.

6 slices bacon, diced
8 ounces ground pork
¾ cup chopped onion
½ cup chopped celery
½ cup chopped green bell pepper
½ cup chopped red bell pepper
1 tablespoon minced garlic
1 teaspoon cayenne pepper
1 teaspoon salt
1 teaspoon freshly ground black pepper
1 teaspoon ground cumin
½ teaspoon dried oregano
1 cup long-grain rice
2 cups Berta's Chicken Stock (see Index) or canned broth
8 ounces chicken livers, trimmed, rinsed, patted dry, and minced
2 tablespoons snipped fresh chives

1. Place a large heavy saucepan or dutch oven over medium heat, and sauté the bacon until slightly crisp, about 5 minutes. Remove the bacon from the pan and drain off all but 1 tablespoon of the fat.

2. Add the pork and sauté, breaking it up into small pieces, until it has changed color. Using a slotted spoon, remove the pork from the pan and add it to the bacon.

3. Add the onion, celery, bell peppers, and garlic to the pan. Sauté over low heat for 5 minutes. Then add the cayenne, salt, black pepper, cumin, and oregano. Stir, and cook an additional 3 minutes.

4. Stir in the rice and cook 5 minutes. Add the stock and the reserved bacon and pork. Bring to a boil; then reduce the heat, cover, and simmer for 10 minutes.

5. Stir in the chicken livers and cook, covered, 5 minutes. Serve immediately, garnished with the chives.

6 to 8 portions

RICE TIPS

▲ Add a tablespoon of butter or oil to the water when cooking rice to keep grains separate.

▲ If not used frequently, store rice, especially brown rice, in the refrigerator to keep it fresh.

▲ Simmer rice in broth or broth mixed with water for more flavor.

▲ Don't stir simmering rice; it mashes the grains and makes the rice gummy.

▲ If simmered rice is cooked but still watery, fluff it with a fork over low heat to evaporate the water.

▲ To bake rice, toss it with melted butter in a baking dish over medium heat, add water (same proportions as for simmered rice), and stir. Cover tightly and bake at 350° to 400°F until tender.

▲ Simmer rice in a heavy pan so the rice at the bottom doesn't scorch, and make sure the pan is large enough—rice triples or quadruples in bulk when cooked.

▲ To keep rice warm before serving, transfer the cooked rice to a baking dish, cover the dish, and keep warm in a low oven.

RED AND GREEN RICE

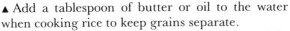

This is perfect with tender Lemon and Ginger Pork Loin.

2 ½ cups water
1 cup long-grain rice
1 tablespoon olive oil
1 tablespoon unsalted butter
1 clove garlic, minced
1 ½ cups coarsely chopped arugula
1 cup coarsely chopped watercress leaves
1 ½ cups julienned radicchio
1 tablespoon chopped fresh Italian (flat-leaf) parsley
Salt and freshly ground black pepper, to taste

1. Bring the water to a boil in a heavy saucepan. Add the rice, reduce the heat, and cook at a slow boil for 20 minutes.

2. While the rice is cooking, heat the oil and butter in a large skillet. Add the garlic, arugula, and watercress. Cook over medium heat, tossing con-

stantly, until the greens are slightly wilted.

3. Add the cooked rice to the skillet along with the radicchio, parsley, and salt and pepper. Stir gently until thoroughly blended. Serve immediately.

6 portions

MOROCCAN PILAF

The North African flavorings will make this pilaf the star of a meal.

2 tablespoons olive oil
⅓ cup blanched whole almonds
1 small onion, chopped
1 carrot, peeled and cut into ¼-inch dice
½ teaspoon ground cinnamon
1 cup long-grain rice
3 cups Berta's Chicken Stock (see Index) or canned broth
⅓ cup dried currants
Minced zest of 1 orange
¼ teaspoon cayenne pepper
1 ½ tablespoons snipped fresh chives

1. Preheat the oven to 375°F. Lightly oil a shallow 1½ quart ovenproof casserole.

2. Heat the oil in a large skillet, and sauté the almonds over medium heat until they are browned and fragrant, 3 minutes. Stir in the onion, carrot, and cinnamon. Cook 3 minutes.

3. Add the rice and cook, stirring, until translucent, 1 minute.

4. Stir in the stock, currants, orange zest, and cayenne pepper. Bring to a boil; remove from the heat.

5. Transfer the mixture to the prepared casserole and bake, uncovered, until the liquid has been absorbed and the rice is tender, about 45 minutes. Sprinkle with the chives, and serve.

4 to 6 portions

SEASON TO TASTE

Rice welcomes a wide range of flavorings. These are some of our favorites:

Basil	Lovage
Black pepper	Mint
Cheese	Nuts
Chile pepper	Olive
Chive	Onion
Cinnamon	Orange
Currants and raisins	Parsley
	Saffron
Dill	Tarragon
Fennel	Thyme
Garlic	Tomato
Lemon	

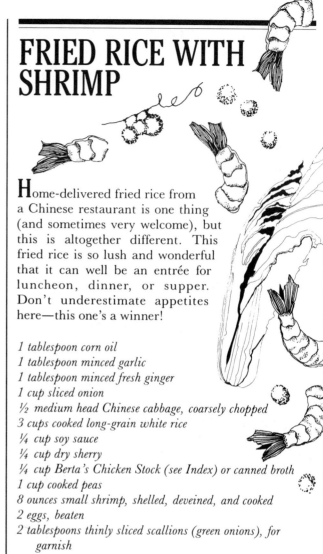

FRIED RICE WITH SHRIMP

Home-delivered fried rice from a Chinese restaurant is one thing (and sometimes very welcome), but this is altogether different. This fried rice is so lush and wonderful that it can well be an entrée for luncheon, dinner, or supper. Don't underestimate appetites here—this one's a winner!

1 tablespoon corn oil
1 tablespoon minced garlic
1 tablespoon minced fresh ginger
1 cup sliced onion
½ medium head Chinese cabbage, coarsely chopped
3 cups cooked long-grain white rice
¼ cup soy sauce
¼ cup dry sherry
¼ cup Berta's Chicken Stock (see Index) or canned broth
1 cup cooked peas
8 ounces small shrimp, shelled, deveined, and cooked
2 eggs, beaten
2 tablespoons thinly sliced scallions (green onions), for garnish

1. Heat the oil in a wok or a large skillet, and sauté the garlic, ginger, and onion over medium-low heat until soft, about 5 minutes.

2. Add the cabbage, raise the heat to medium, and sauté, stirring constantly, until limp, about 10 minutes.

3. Add the rice, soy sauce, sherry, and stock. Cook for 3 minutes, stirring constantly. Then add the peas and shrimp, and cook for 1 minute.

4. Make a small hole in the center of the rice mixture, and pour the eggs into the hole. Cook the eggs for about 1 minute, stirring with a fork; then gently fold the eggs into the rice.

5. Serve immediately, garnished with the scallions.

4 portions

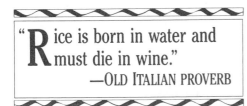

> "**R**ice is born in water and must die in wine."
> —OLD ITALIAN PROVERB

CALIFORNIA RED RICE SALAD

Wehani rice is a basmati-type hybrid grown in California. When cooked it turns a deep russet color. The flavor is earthy and complex.

1 cup Wehani or basmati rice
6 radishes, halved and sliced ¼ inch thick
½ cup diced red bell pepper
½ cup diced red onion
2 beets, cooked, peeled, and diced (about 1½ cups)
¼ cup snipped fresh chives
2 tablespoons chopped fresh dill

DRESSING
¼ cup white wine vinegar
2 tablespoons prepared horseradish
1 tablespoon whole-grain mustard
1 teaspoon sugar
1 teaspoon salt
Freshly ground black pepper, to taste
½ cup extra virgin olive oil

1. Cook the rice according to package directions or the chart on page 320; you should have about 3 cups. Allow it to cool to room temperature.

2. Combine the rice, radishes, bell pepper, red onion, beets, chives, and dill in a large bowl. Toss well.

3. Make the dressing: Whisk the vinegar, horseradish, mustard, sugar, salt, and pepper together in a small bowl. Gradually add the oil, whisking until smooth.

4. Pour the dressing over the rice mixture and toss until blended. Serve immediately, or cover and refrigerate for several hours to blend the flavors.

8 portions

TWICE THE RICE CASSEROLE

The nutty flavors of wild and brown rice are heightened by the addition of the pine nuts and sweet currants. This is a delicious wintertime accompaniment to any game or roasted poultry dish.

1 cup wild rice
1 cup brown rice
1 cup dried currants
½ cup pine nuts, toasted (see Index)
¼ cup chopped Italian (flat-leaf) parsley
2 tablespoons grated orange zest
¼ cup olive oil
2 tablespoons fresh orange juice
Salt and freshly ground black pepper, to taste
Freshly grated Parmesan cheese

1. Preheat the oven to 350°F.

2. Bring 3 cups water to a boil in a medium-size heavy saucepan. Add the wild rice, stir, and reduce the heat. Cover the pan, and simmer the rice for 35 minutes. (Wild rice can vary considerably in its cooking time. It should be just tender.) Drain the rice, if necessary, and transfer it to a large bowl.

3. Bring 2 cups water to a boil in a heavy saucepan. Add the brown rice, stir, and reduce the heat. Cover the pan, and simmer the rice for 20 minutes. The water should be totally absorbed and the rice just tender. Transfer the brown rice to the bowl with the wild rice.

4. Add the remaining ingredients, except the Parmesan cheese, to the rices, and toss to combine.

5. Transfer the rice mixture to an ovenproof casserole, cover tightly with aluminum foil, and bake until the rices are soft but not mushy, and the casserole is heated through, 20 to 30 minutes. Sprinkle with the Parmesan cheese and serve.

6 to 8 portions

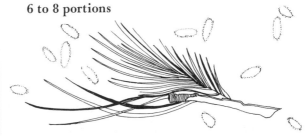

CHOOSING THE RIGHT RICE

RICE	DESCRIPTION	COOK	BEST
Aromatic long-grain rice (basmati from India and Pakistan; U.S. produces Texmati, wild pecan, Lundberg Royal, Wehani, Gourmet, and O Della)	Slender long grains colored white, tan, or deep brown; fragrant, delicate taste and light, fluffy texture	Rinse, then simmer covered 1 part rice to 1½ parts salted water, 15 to 20 minutes.	All-purpose but especially as a side dish—it's fragrant and delicious.
Glutinous rice (sweet, waxy, or sticky rice)	Polished white Oriental rice even shorter than Italian short-grain; slightly sweet and very sticky	Soak overnight, then simmer covered 1 part rice to 1 part salted water, 15 minutes.	For dim sum, sushi, and dessert puddings.
Italian short-grain rice (Arborio)	Polished white kernels a little longer than wide; bland taste and soft texture	Never rinse. Boil in plenty of salted water or simmer 1 part rice to 2 parts salted water or broth (add liquid gradually for risotto), 20 minutes.	For risotto.
Long-grain rice, white and brown	White is polished long kernels; brown has bran intact. White has bland flavor and firm texture; brown has a nuttier flavor and even firmer texture.	Boil in plenty of salted water or simmer covered 1 part rice to 2 parts salted water without stirring and adding a little butter to keep the grains from sticking, 15 to 20 minutes. Brown rice takes 15 to 30 minutes longer to cook than white.	For side dishes, casseroles, pilaf, salads.
Parboiled rice (Converted rice is trademark)	Looks just like long-grain white rice; bland flavor and firm texture, less sticky than long-grain	Same as for long-grain.	Same as for long-grain.

RICE	DESCRIPTION	COOK	BEST
Instant rice	Precooked, then dehydrated long-grain white rice; extremely bland and soft texture	Follow package directions.	We recommend none.
Medium-grain rice, white and brown	Slightly longer than short-grain rice	Rinse, then same as for long-grain rice.	All-purpose.
Wild rice	Not a rice but a seed of a native grass; long unpolished kernels; intense nutty, earthy flavor and firm, even chewy, texture	Rinse well, boil in plenty of salted water or simmer covered 1 part rice to 3 parts salted water, 45 minutes to 1 hour.	Combined with other rices and ingredients for salads, stuffing, and side dishes.

COOKING DRIED BEANS

▲ Essential with all beans is to first sort through them, picking out any small pebbles and withered beans. Then cover the beans with cold water and remove any that float. Rinse, several times if necessary, until the water runs clear.

▲ Not all beans need to be soaked before cooking. Place lentils and split peas in a pot, add 3 parts of cold water to 1 part of beans, and gently simmer, covered, 30 to 40 minutes. To test a bean for doneness, take several from the pot and taste them. The beans should be tender but not mushy. One bean is not enough of a sample. When cooking beans for salads, it's important that they keep their shape and not cook to a mush. Test often and cool immediately under cold water. For bean stews, soups, and purées, timing is not quite so critical.

▲ Dried beans other than lentils and split peas must be soaked before cooking. Small beans can soak for as little as four hours, but eight hours is always best. If you are really in a hurry, you can quick-soak beans by boiling them for one minute, cover-ing the pot, and letting them stand for an hour. Drain the beans and proceed with the recipe.

▲ To cook beans, discard the soaking water and cover with fresh cold water—3 parts of water to 1 part of beans. Exact measurements are not usually critical since you will discard the cooking water or can pour off any extra. Cooking times depend not on the kind of bean but on its size. Lentils, the size of a doll's buttons, need no soaking and have the shortest cooking time. Fava beans, kidney beans, and chick-peas are the largest and take the longest time—as much as three hours. Beans are tough customers; nonetheless, the water should be brought to a boil, then reduced to a *gentle simmer* to keep the beans in their jackets.

▲ How long a bean is stored affects cooking time, too. Beans stored less than a year are best; they take less time to cook and won't cook to a mush. But it's impossible to tell how long a bean has been stored. We can only recommend that you buy dried beans from a market with a steady turnover.

FULL OF BEANS SOUP

Mixed dried beans are widely sold prepackaged with instructions for making hearty winter soups. We appreciate the mixes, but we enjoy making our own combinations too. It is important to use some fairly specific proportions of each variety so that some remain whole while others purée into a thick rich base when cooking. Use about 1 cup light-colored beans such as navy, Great Northern, lima, or cranberry; ½ cup red beans such as kidney or pinto; ½ cup black-eyed peas or field peas; about ¼ cup mixed green and yellow split peas or lentils; and a few black turtle beans. Be adventurous and have fun with the combinations. This soup is great with Hot and Sassy Corn Bread!

2 cups mixed dried beans (about 1 ½ pounds)
2 ham hocks
4 large cloves garlic
10 cups water
¾ pound kielbasa sausage
2 cups canned crushed Italian plum tomatoes
2 onions, coarsely chopped
½ cup chopped fresh Italian (flat-leaf) parsley
¼ cup fresh lemon juice
1 teaspoon good-quality chili powder
½ teaspoon ground cumin
¼ teaspoon dried red pepper flakes, or more to taste
Salt and freshly ground black pepper, to taste
2 tablespoons chopped fresh Italian (flat-leaf) parsley, for garnish

1. Rinse and pick through the beans. Place them in a large heavy pot, cover with cold water, and soak overnight.

2. Drain the beans and return them to the pot along with the ham hocks, garlic, and water. Bring to a boil. Reduce the heat and simmer for 1½ hours, occasionally skimming off any foam that rises to the surface.

3. Cut the kielbasa into 1-inch slices, and then quarter the slices. Add the kielbasa to the soup and simmer for 1 hour longer, skimming when necessary.

4. Remove the ham hocks and allow them to cool. Shred the meat from the bone and set it aside.

5. Drain the crushed tomatoes, reserving the juice. To the soup add the crushed tomatoes, 1 cup of the juice, and the onions, ½ cup parsley, lemon juice, chili powder, cumin, red pepper flakes, and salt and pepper. Cook slowly for another 30 minutes, stirring occasionally.

6. Adjust the seasonings if necessary, and serve hot, garnished with the chopped parsley.

8 portions

"Still—in a way—nobody sees a flower—really—it is so small—we haven't time—and to see takes time, like to have a friend takes time."

—GEORGIA O'KEEFFE

CRUNCHY LENTIL SALAD

In this salad the smoky flavor of lentils is contrasted with crunchy sprouts and red onion, all flavored with orange and balsamic vinegar.

1 cup dried lentils
1½ cups crunchy fresh small sprouts
½ cup coarsely chopped fresh mint leaves
¼ cup minced red onion
¼ cup fresh orange juice
2 tablespoons extra virgin olive oil
1 tablespoon balsamic vinegar
1 teaspoon minced orange zest
1 teaspoon curry powder
1 teaspoon salt
Freshly ground black pepper, to taste

1. Bring a saucepan of lightly salted water to a boil, and add the lentils. Reduce the heat and simmer until crisp-tender, about 30 minutes.

2. Drain the lentils, rinse them under cold water, and pat dry. Place them in a salad bowl, and add all the remaining ingredients. Toss well to combine.

3. Cover and refrigerate for several hours (to develop the flavors) before serving.

4 to 6 portions

CURRIED CARROTS AND LENTILS

Carrots, golden raisins, and rich curry spices contribute to this colorful, flavorful dish. Serve it with lamb curry and lots of condiments.

½ cup dried red lentils
1 ½ cups water
3 carrots, peeled and cut
  into 2-inch pieces
½ cup chopped onion
¼ cup golden raisins
2 tablespoons unsalted butter
1 teaspoon salt
¾ teaspoon good-quality curry powder
½ teaspoon fennel seeds
Freshly ground black pepper, to taste

1. Combine the lentils and ½ cup of the water in a 2-quart microwave-safe casserole. Cover, and cook at full power (650 to 700 watts) for 5 minutes. (If the water foams and spills over, replace it with 1 or 2 tablespoons more water.)

2. Stir in the carrots and another ½ cup of the water. Cover, and cook 5 minutes.

3. Stir in the remaining ½ cup water and all the other ingredients. Cover, and cook 5 minutes.

4. Serve immediately.

4 to 6 portions

Note: This recipe was cooked on High (full power, 650 to 700 watts) in a carousel microwave, using microwave-safe containers.

If your microwave is less powerful, you will have to allow for more cooking time (approximately 1 ½ times the amount called for—but watch carefully); if it does not have a carousel, you may have to rotate the dish while it is cooking.

SEASON TO TASTE

Flavor up your next pot of beans with any of the following:

Bacon and ham hocks	Olive oil
	Onion
Bay leaf	Oregano
Cayenne pepper	Nutmeg
	Parsley
Celery	Rosemary
Chile pepper	Sage
Cilantro	Savory
Cumin	Sesame seed
Dill	Thyme
Garlic	Tomato
Lemon	Vinegar
Mint	Wine

ALL-AMERICAN BAKED BEANS

One of those American classics, first created in the Puritan era in Boston. No cooking was allowed on the Sabbath, so they served beans Saturday night for dinner, for Sunday breakfast with codfish cakes and Boston brown bread, and again for Sunday lunch.

1 pound dried navy or Great Northern beans
8 ounces slab smoked bacon, cut into ¼-inch cubes
1 cup chopped onions
2 cloves garlic, chopped
1½ cups (packed) dark brown sugar
2 cups ketchup
6 tablespoons maple syrup
6 tablespoons dark molasses
¼ cup Worcestershire sauce
½ teaspoon salt
¼ teaspoon freshly ground black pepper

1. Rinse and pick through the beans. Soak them overnight in a large pot of water.

2. Rinse the soaked beans well under cold water, and place them in a heavy saucepan. Cover with water and bring to a boil. Reduce the heat and simmer until tender, 45 minutes to 1 hour. Drain, reserving the cooking liquid.

3. Preheat the oven to 300°F.

4. Place a 2-quart flameproof casserole or dutch oven over medium heat and sauté the bacon until it is slightly crisp and fat is rendered, 5 minutes. Add the onions and garlic, and cook until wilted, 5 to 10 minutes.

5. Add the brown sugar and stir over medium-low heat until it has dissolved, about 5 minutes. Then stir in the ketchup, syrup, molasses, Worcestershire, salt, and pepper. Add the drained beans and mix well.

6. Cover the casserole and transfer it to the oven. Bake, stirring occasionally (making sure you scrape the bottom of the casserole), for 2½ hours.

7. Add ¾ cup of the reserved bean liquid, re-cover, and bake 30 minutes. Then remove the cover and bake until the sauce is thick and syrupy, another 10 to 15 minutes, stirring once. Serve hot.

10 to 12 portions

"**B**oston runs to brains as well as to beans and brown bread."
—WILLIAM COWPER BRANN

BLACK-EYED PEAS AND RICE

Dazzling Caribbean flavors highlight this dish. Sweet bell peppers and tomatoes counterpoint briny olives and salty anchovies; black-eyed peas are enhanced by the addition of allspice, cayenne, and crisp scallions. This is great with grilled fish.

8 ounces salt pork, rind removed, cut into ½-inch dice
2 red bell peppers, cored, seeded, and cut into 1-inch dice
6 ripe plum tomatoes, cut into ½-inch dice
1 onion, cut into ½-inch pieces
6 cloves garlic, finely chopped
1 cup converted rice
2 cups Berta's Chicken Stock (see Index) or canned broth
6 cups cooked black-eyed peas
1 cup pitted green olives
¼ cup capers, drained
6 anchovy fillets, drained and finely chopped
2 tablespoons dried oregano
1 teaspoon ground allspice
1 teaspoon coarsely ground black pepper
½ teaspoon cayenne pepper
½ teaspoon salt
¾ cup scallions (green onions), white bulb and 3 inches green, sliced on the diagonal
½ cup chopped fresh parsley

1. Place a large heavy flameproof casserole over low heat, and sauté the salt pork until the fat has been rendered, 7 to 10 minutes. Do not let it brown.

2. Add the peppers, tomatoes, onion, and garlic to the salt pork and cook over low heat for 5 minutes.

3. Add the rice and stir for 1 minute. Then add all the remaining ingredients except the scallions and parsley. Cover and cook until the rice is cooked and most of liquid has been absorbed, 20 minutes.

4. Add the scallions and parsley and gently mix. Serve hot.

8 portions

MISSISSIPPI CAVIAR

Mississippi Caviar, dressed up enough to go to the spiciest parties, is perfect for a summer barbecue buffet. Double or triple the recipe for company.

8 ounces dried black-eyed peas (about 1 ¼ cups), or
    about 4 cups cooked black-eyed peas
1 red bell pepper, cored, seeded, and diced
2 scallions (green onions), white bulb and 3 inches green,
    sliced
¼ cup olive oil
2 bottled jalapeño peppers in vinegar,
    drained and minced
2 tablespoons fresh lemon juice
1 tablespoon Dijon mustard
2 cloves garlic, minced
1 teaspoon salt
1 teaspoon dried thyme leaves
1 teaspoon sugar
¼ teaspoon Tabasco sauce
Freshly ground black pepper, to taste

1. If you are using dried beans, rinse and pick through them. Soak the beans overnight in a pot of cold water to cover.

2. Drain the beans and place them in a saucepan, cover with cold water, and bring to a boil. Reduce the heat and simmer until just tender, 30 to 45 minutes.

3. Drain the beans, rinse under cold water, and drain again. Place them in a large bowl, add the remaining ingredients, and toss until well blended.

4. Let the salad stand for several hours, stirring occasionally, to develop the flavors. Serve at room temperature.

6 portions

CANNELLINI FRESCA

These cannellini beans are prepared the way the people of Florence enjoy them: lavished with extra virgin olive oil, sage, and black pepper. Nothing could be simpler and nothing more is needed—just a salad, or a little steak, some bread, and some Chianti Classico.

1 cup dried cannellini beans
4 cups water
2 homemade chicken bouillon cubes (see Index)
2 sprigs fresh sage
2 cloves garlic, crushed
7 tablespoons extra virgin olive oil
1 ¼ teaspoons salt
Freshly ground black pepper, to taste
2 fresh sage leaves, minced
2 tablespoons minced scallions (green onions)

1. Rinse and pick through the beans. Place them in a pot, and cover with cold water. Soak for 4 hours.

2. Drain the beans and place them in a medium-size saucepan. Add the water, bouillon cubes, sage sprigs, garlic, 1 tablespoon of the oil, 1 teaspoon of the salt, and black pepper. Bring to a boil. Then lower the heat, cover, and simmer until the beans are tender, 1 hour. Allow them to cool in the liquid.

3. Using a slotted spoon, transfer the beans to a bowl. Add ¼ cup of the cooking liquid, the minced sage, scallions, 2 tablespoons of the olive oil, and remaining ¼ teaspoon salt. Toss well.

4. Drizzle the remaining olive oil over the beans just before serving at room temperature.

4 portions

THE NUTRITIONAL BEAN

In calories, both hamburger and dried beans are about 25 percent protein. But about 60 percent of the remaining hamburger's calories are fat and only 4 percent of the bean's calories are fat, and that little bit of fat is unsaturated—the cholesterol-lowering kind. The remaining calories in beans are complex carbohydrates, which experts tout as all important in reducing cholesterol and trimming fat. Dried beans also provide healthy amounts of vitamins A and B, iron, potassium, calcium, and phosphorus.

The protein in beans is incomplete, so beans must be combined with their protein complement or with a complete protein to deliver all nine amino acids the body needs. Protein complements are grains, and complete protein is provided by poultry, fish, meat, and dairy products. This sounds more complicated than it really is, because many popular bean dishes are already built around this principle. Consider chili (beans and beef), refried beans and tortillas, Boston baked beans (with pork), *pasta e fagioli* (beans and grain), and red beans and rice.

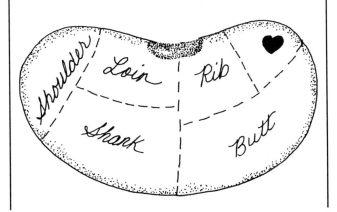

PENELOPE WISNER'S WHITE BEANS WITH STAR ANISE AND CHICKEN

We first met Penny Wisner many years ago when she was food editor of *House & Garden* magazine. She is now well ensconced in the Napa Valley, and we are delighted whenever our paths cross.

Penny says, "The success of this recipe depends on the quality of the cannellini beans. Mine are from Corti Brothers in Sacramento. (Corti will mail-order all over the States.) These beans are imported from Italy and are large and flavorful. Do not soak them ahead of time! This dish is great comfort food—good for Sunday night suppers. And the leftovers get better as the week progresses."

2 cups dried cannellini beans
5 whole star anise*
2 dried hot red chile peppers, about 2 inches long
3 cups Berta's Chicken Stock (see Index) or canned broth
Salt, to taste
3 large slices fresh ginger, lightly smashed
3 cloves garlic, lightly smashed
2 cups spicy white wine, such as Gewürtztraminer
1 whole head garlic
2 tablespoons plus ¼ cup olive oil
1 chicken (about 3 pounds), well rinsed, patted dry, and cut into serving pieces
2 tablespoons chopped cilantro (fresh coriander)

1. Rinse and pick through the beans, and place in a large saucepan. Add the star anise, dried red peppers, chicken stock, salt, ginger, smashed garlic cloves, and 1 cup of the wine. Bring to a boil, cover, and reduce the heat. Cook over very low heat, stirring occasionally, until the beans are tender, about 1½ hours.

2. Let the beans cool in the liquid. Remove the star anise, hot peppers, and ginger slices. (The dish can be made a day ahead to this point; cover and refrigerate until ready to proceed.)

3. Preheat the oven to 350°F.

4. Remove the papery outer skin of the garlic, leaving the head whole. Using a sharp knife, slice the top off the head, and open up most of the cloves. Place the garlic head in a small baking pan, drizzle it with the 2 tablespoons oil, and bake until completely cooked through and tender, 30 to 45 minutes. (Be careful not to let it burn.) Allow the garlic to cool, then peel the cloves and chop them into a rough paste. Stir the garlic paste into the beans. Reduce the oven heat to 325°F.

5. Heat the remaining ¼ cup oil in a heavy skillet and brown the chicken on all sides over medium-high heat, removing the pieces from the skillet as they are done. When all the chicken is browned, pour off the fat from the skillet and add the remaining 1 cup wine. Bring to a boil, scraping the brown bits off the bottom of the skillet, and boil for 1 to 2 minutes. Stir this into the beans.

6. Arrange the chicken in a large ovenproof casserole, and pour the beans over it. Cover and bake until the chicken is tender, about 45 minutes. Serve in bowls, as the dish will be stew-like, and sprinkle each serving with some of the cilantro.

4 portions

*Available in some supermarkets and in specialty food shops.

Summer savory has long been called the bean herb because it goes so well with all sorts of beans.

RED BEANS AND RICE

Around the globe peas and rice are married. In the Caribbean, each island has its own interpretation—all rich in spicy flavors. Here's our favorite, inspired by a dish we had many years ago at a little porch-front restaurant on St. Bart's. In New Orleans they squirt a little white vinegar atop the finished dish.

1 cup dried small
    red beans
1¾ cups Berta's
    Chicken Stock (see Index) or canned broth
1 cup drained crushed canned tomatoes
¾ cup water
1 tablespoon Worcestershire sauce
2 bay leaves
½ teaspoon salt
¼ teaspoon Tabasco sauce
4 ounces slab bacon, rind removed,
    cut into ½-inch cubes
1 small onion, minced
2 cloves garlic, minced
4 cups cooked white rice

1. Bring a large pot of water to a boil. Place the beans in a medium-size bowl, cover with the boiling water, and let stand for 2 hours.

2. Preheat the oven to 350°F.

3. Combine the stock, tomatoes, water, Worcestershire, bay leaves, salt, and Tabasco in a dutch oven, and bring to a boil. Drain the beans, and add them to the mixture. Stir in the bacon, onion, and garlic.

4. Cover the dutch oven and transfer it to the oven. Bake until the beans are tender, 1½ hours. Let the dish stand for 10 minutes before serving over the rice.

4 portions

BEAUJOLAIS NOUVEAU

★

There is much anticipation and then much celebration in France and in those American cities lucky enough to receive Beaujolais nouveau on November 15 of each year. Restaurateurs and wine merchants vie to be the first to stock it. Signs in windows advertise it and newspapers are filled with articles extolling its virtues, discussing its faults, and relating the inevitable dramas that come along with each new crop.

Beaujolais nouveau is made from Gamay grapes that are harvested, briefly fermented (they are not crushed), and bottled in time to leave the vineyards on or around November 15. The result is fruity, light, flirtatious, and lots of fun!

BLACK BEAN SALAD

Black Bean Salad is most definitely a New Basic. Its texture and taste complement Pan-Fried Catfish With Scallions, Country-Style Ribs, and Ellen's Fried Chicken. Fresh Tomato Salsa alongside adds just the right sparkle!

2 ½ to 3 cups cooked black beans
1 red bell pepper, cored, seeded, and cut into ¼-inch dice
3 scallions (green onions), white bulb and 3 inches green, sliced into ¼-inch rounds
2 ripe plum tomatoes, seeded and cut into ¼-inch dice
6 tablespoons extra virgin olive oil
3 tablespoons fresh lemon juice
5 tablespoons chopped cilantro (fresh coriander)
1 teaspoon coarsely ground black pepper
¾ teaspoon salt

Combine all the ingredients in a medium-size bowl and toss gently. Let the salad rest, loosely covered, at room temperature for at least 1 hour before serving.

6 portions

BLACK AND WHITE BEAN SALAD

Black turtle beans and white navy beans are combined with other colorful ingredients in this salad. Serve it with grilled ribs and Six Pepper Slaw for a great southwestern meal.

8 ounces dried black turtle beans
8 ounces dried white navy beans
1 cup chopped red onion
1 cup chopped red bell pepper
1 cup cooked corn kernels
¼ cup chopped cilantro (fresh coriander)
2 cups Cumin Vinaigrette (see Index)

1. Rinse and pick through the beans. Place them in separate pots or bowls of cold water to cover, and soak them overnight.

2. Drain the beans, and place them in separate saucepans. Cover with water and bring to a boil. Reduce the heat and simmer until tender, 45 minutes to 1 hour.

3. Drain the beans, rinse them under cold water, and pat dry. Combine the beans in a large bowl.

4. Add the remaining ingredients, toss gently to combine, and cover. Refrigerate for at least 1 hour before serving.

8 portions

THE BEST OF BEANS

BEAN	DESCRIPTION	SOAK	SIMMER	BEST
Aduki, or adzuki, beans	Small dark red Japanese beans; a little sweet with a delicate texture	yes	1 to 1 ½ hours	With Asian flavors, served with rice.
Black, or turtle, beans	Medium black-skinned ovals; rich earthy taste and soft texture	yes	1 ½ hours	In Mexican and Latin American soups, stews, and sauces; also salads with colorful vegetables and southwestern flavors.
Black-eyed peas	Medium creamy white ovals with a black spot; vegetable flavor and mealy texture	yes	1 hour	In salads and with rice, greens, and pork.
Chick-peas, or garbanzo beans	Large, round, wrinkled, tan peas; nutty flavor and crunchy texture	yes	2 to 3 hours	In soups and stews but also puréed for dips.
Fava or broad beans	Large, flat ovals; assertive taste and firm texture	yes, then peel	2 to 2 ½ hours	Puréed. (Peel these beans after soaking to remove the bitter skins.)
Kidney beans, red or white (white also called cannellini)	Large kidney-shaped beans; bland taste and soft texture but tough skins	yes	1 ½ to 2 hours	Stewed with other flavorful ingredients. Red kidney beans are most often used in chili. The white cannellini beans are essential for Italian bean stews with tomatoes, herbs, and bits of sausage.
Lentils	Small, flat, round, button shaped—green, brown, or pink; distinctive but mild taste with firm texture	no	30 to 40 minutes	Combined with grains or with vegetables in salads; also in soups and stews.
Lima beans	Flat, white ovals tinged with green; buy small dried limas for mild taste; all have soft, mushy texture	yes	1 ½ hours	In soups and stews.

BEAN	DESCRIPTION	SOAK	SIMMER	BEST
Pinto beans	Medium ovals mottled beige and brown; earthy flavor and mealy texture	yes	1 ½ to 2 hours	In stews and dips; important for Tex-Mex and Mexican bean dishes, especially refried beans, or *frijoles refritos*.
Red beans	Medium dark red ovals; taste and texture similar to kidney beans	yes	1 ½ to 2 hours	In soups and stews—the bean for red beans and rice.
Soybeans	Medium creamy white ovals; firm texture and extremely bland flavor	yes	3 to 4 hours	With other flavorful ingredients in stews.
Split peas	Small halved peas— green or yellow; earthy flavor and mealy texture	no	40 to 50 minutes	In soups.
White beans: small white, navy, or pea	Small white ovals	yes	1 ½ to 2 hours	In soups, stews, especially Boston baked beans and cassoulet; great puréed.
Great Northern	Medium white, kidney shaped All have delicate taste and firm texture.	yes	1 ½ to 2 hours	In stews, cassoulets, and bean salads.

THE
FISH
MARKET

A SCHOOL OF FISH

Finally—Americans are hooked on seafood. We're eating more of it than ever before, and for good reason: Fresh-flavored, quick to prepare, and healthy for us, fish and shellfish fit perfectly with today's lifestyle. Since improved methods of transportation now bring fresh seafood to our local markets from all over the world, we have a wide variety of choices. And, best of all, we've learned how to cook fish so that its subtle flavor is enhanced and more intriguing than ever before. Whether you catch it yourself or become a fish market regular, you'll learn how to tackle fish in the kitchen, if you follow our simple suggestions.

Start with some of the classics—Fish and Chips Forever, Rosy Red Snapper, Party Poached Salmon, or Sole Meunière—then let an ocean breeze catch your imagination. Make Reddened Catfish, Palm Beach Pompano, Chinese Black Sea Bass, or Tuna Tonnato. You'll be pleasantly surprised at how quickly you're out of the kitchen enjoying the compliments.

SHOPPING FOR FISH

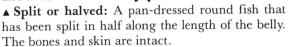

The single most important criterion for choosing seafood is that it be fresh. Its delicate flesh deteriorates very quickly once it leaves the water, and the sooner it is eaten the better. You can ensure freshness in two ways: Always inspect seafood carefully to determine good color, smell and texture; and, perhaps more importantly, foster a good relationship with a reliable fishmonger.

BUYING FISH

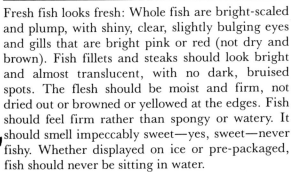

Fresh fish looks fresh: Whole fish are bright-scaled and plump, with shiny, clear, slightly bulging eyes and gills that are bright pink or red (not dry and brown). Fish fillets and steaks should look bright and almost translucent, with no dark, bruised spots. The flesh should be moist and firm, not dried out or browned or yellowed at the edges. Fish should feel firm rather than spongy or watery. It should smell impeccably sweet—yes, sweet—never fishy. Whether displayed on ice or pre-packaged, fish should never be sitting in water.

We think it best to select whole fish, with bones and gills intact, so that you can really see that it's fresh. Then, ask the fishmonger to clean and, if necessary, fillet it for you. Keep the head and usable trimmings for stock. (Fish stock is versatile, and once you begin keeping a supply in your freezer, you'll be surprised at how often it comes in handy.)

WHAT YOU'LL SEE AT YOUR FISH MARKET

▲ **Whole:** Not for the faint hearted, this refers to fish that has not been prepared in any way; it is sold with the head, scales, fins, guts—everything.
▲ **Drawn:** A whole fish that has been gutted and scaled, with the gills removed.
▲ **Dressed or Pan-Dressed:** A whole fish that has been gutted and scaled, and that also has gills, fins and head removed.
▲ **Split or halved:** A pan-dressed round fish that has been split in half along the length of the belly. The bones and skin are intact.
▲ **Butterflied:** Small round fish that have been pan-dressed, then boned and opened to lie flat.
▲ **Steaks:** Slices cut crosswise, ¾ to 1¾ inches thick, from a large round fish (such as a salmon) or flat fish (such as halibut), that include a section of backbone and skin. Steaks cut from very large fish, such as swordfish or tuna, are usually boneless and have been skinned.
▲ **Fillets:** The sides of either round or flat fish that are cut off the backbone. Fillets are boneless and may or may not be skinned.
▲ **Medallions:** Made from the fillet of a largish fish that has been cut at an angle into regular slices of an even thickness.
▲ **Chunks:** Trimmings cut from large fish, such as tuna and swordfish. Chunks make a quick meal of chowder or kabobs.

KEEPING FISH FRESH

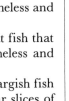

Unquestionably, seafood is best eaten within hours of buying it. But if you plan on storing fish longer than just a few hours, the best way to keep it fresh is to first dip it in a bowl of cold water to which you've added a squeeze of lemon juice to slow down decay. Carefully pat the fish dry. Unskinned, whole, gutted fish can be refrigerated directly on ice in a baking dish on the bottom shelf of the refrigerator (the coldest part), but drain the dish as often as necessary to ensure that the fish is never sitting in water. Wrap steaks and fillets in plastic wrap or waxed paper and refrigerate them on the bottom shelf in an ice-filled colander placed in a bowl; as the ice melts the water will drain away from the fish into the bowl. Or, refrigerate the fish in a baking dish surrounded by frozen ice packs. Stored correctly, fish will last up to four days.

COOKING FISH

Fish is very fragile and cooks quickly, so you must be careful to catch it before it becomes dry and overcooked. As a fish cooks, its translucent flesh turns opaque; when it's opaque at the thickest part (test by inserting the tip of a knife), or just slightly translucent at the very center, you know it's done. Do not wait for the flesh to flake—by that time it's already too dry. We swear by the Canadian Fisheries Cooking Theory, which estimates the total cooking time of any fish to be ten minutes for every inch of thickness, measured at the thickest part. This works for whole fish, steaks, or fillets, whether grilled, broiled, fried, poached, or baked. Try it—it's amazingly accurate.

starchy coating such as flour, cornmeal, bread crumbs, oat bran, or crushed crackers, and fry it in ¼ inch of oil until the flesh is opaque.

Fry over medium-high heat and use a heavy pan so as not to burn the coating. You may use butter or a combination of butter and oil, but clarified butter is really ideal because it imparts a wonderfully nutty, buttery flavor to the fish and doesn't burn. If you want to use straight olive oil, use one with a fairly mild flavor. Don't crowd the pan, or your fish will never brown.

The Cajun method of cooking blackened fish is very popular these days. It works well with redfish, pompano, red snapper fillets, or salmon steaks. The fish is seasoned with a spicy mixture of paprika, onion and garlic powders, pepper, and dried herbs, and then

fried in a superhot cast-iron pan until blackened on both sides.

A word of warning: Don't try to fry thawed fish. The fish will release so much water that it will steam, rather than brown, and fall apart. Save frozen fish for baking or poaching.

PAN FRYING

Pan frying is one of the most popular ways to prepare small fish, or firm-fleshed fillets, steaks, medallions, or butterflied fish. The outside becomes deliciously crisp and browned while the inside stays moist and tender. Steaks or fillets from fatty fish such as salmon, swordfish, or tuna can be simply seasoned and fried in about two tablespoons of hot oil. Small, whole fish, or fillets of lean fish such as flounder, snapper, or perch benefit from the protection of a light crust: Dip the fish in milk or buttermilk, dredge it in a

BAKING OR ROASTING

Baking is an ideal cooking technique for fish, as long as you provide some fat or moisture, either in the pan or in a stuffing, to keep the fish from drying out. Salmon, carp, tuna, halibut, bluefish, snapper, mackerel, bass, trout, mahimahi, and monkfish are all very good choices. We particularly like to bake whole fish, but steaks and fillets are fine as well.

To bake a whole fish, have the fishmonger remove the scales, guts, and fins; keep the head and tail intact unless the fish is very large. Ask him to remove the backbone if you are planning to stuff it. Then stuff the belly cavity with your favorite stuffing: crabmeat or other fish, nuts and crumbs, herbs, greens, or vegetables. Cut a few slits diagonally in one side of the fish and place lemon or lime wedges in the slits. Skewer the belly cavity closed with toothpicks and weave string around them to secure the stuffing. Lightly oil the fish and bake it in a preheated 400°F oven in an ovenproof dish, or on a baking sheet lined with aluminum foil, until it is just opaque. The side with the lemon wedges should be facing up.

BROILING

Broiling is a particularly successful technique for fattier fish such as salmon, swordfish, mackerel, or shad, since it adds very little additional fat. Use whole fish, butterflied fish, steaks, and fillets.

To broil a whole fish, preheat the broiler for at least 15 minutes so that it is very hot. Oil the fish well on both sides and rub it with salt and pepper. Slash the skin in two or three places with a sharp knife, and, if you like, stuff the cavity with herbs, shellfish, lemons, or limes. Broil the fish on an oiled rack, 4 to 6 inches from the heat for large fish, and 2 to 4 inches from the heat for small fish, until the flesh is opaque. Depending on the thickness of the fish, you may not need to turn it.

When broiling fillets or steaks, choose cuts that are at least ¾ inch thick; any thinner than that and they may dry out. Preheat the broiler as for a whole fish. Put the fish in a shallow baking dish and drizzle it with just enough liquid (such as lemon juice, white wine, or vermouth) to keep it from drying out. Broil 4 inches from the heat. Thick steaks will need to be turned once; thin steaks or fillets needn't be turned at all.

POACHING

Poaching is a lovely way to cook firm-fleshed whole fish or fillets, and it is particularly kind to lean fish such as halibut, whose delicate flesh may dry out over high, dry heat. It is also a classic method for preparing fish that is to be served cold.

You may poach fish in water, but we like to use either a fish stock, made from fish bones, wine, aromatic vegetables and herbs, or a court bouillon, made by simmering a combination of water, wine or vinegar, and herbs and vegetables for 30 minutes. The choice of vegetables, herbs, and wine or vinegar is determined by the flavor of the fish and how it is to be served. If you use stock, it may be reduced to make a sauce after poaching.

To poach a whole fish, place the fish on the rack of a fish poacher. Tie a whole fish loosely to a lightly oiled rack with kitchen string to prevent it from slipping off should the rack tilt when you lift it. You may also want to wrap whole fish in cheesecloth for ease of handling. Set the rack in the poacher with the warm court bouillon or stock (hot liquid will cook the outside flesh before the inside is cooked through) and

bring the liquid to a simmer. Cover the pot and simmer the fish very gently until it is just opaque in the center. Begin timing the fish from the moment that the liquid comes to a simmer, and remove the fish immediately from the poaching liquid when it is cooked through, as it will continue to cook slightly as it cools. You may want to skin the fish and remove the fatty brown layer before serving.

Fillets don't need to be poached in a fish poacher. If you use a skillet, one that is nonstick is best—fillets tend to stick to the bottom of the pan and since they are delicate, will be difficult to remove once cooked.

STEAMING

This is an excellent way to cook delicately flavored fish because the fish cooks in its own juices, therefore retaining more of its flavor. Almost any firm-fleshed fish can be steamed; steam it whole, if small, or filleted, steaked, butterflied, or cut into medallions.

A Chinese steamer is ideal for this, but if you don't have one, you can improvise with a colander or steamer basket set over boiling water. Bring 1 to 2 inches of water to a boil in a wok (if using a Chinese steamer) or in a pot large enough to hold the colander or steamer basket. If you are using the Chinese steamer, oil the fish and put it on a plate. Then put the plate over the wok, cover, and steam the fish until firm, and opaque in the cen-

ter. The advantage of using a Chinese steamer is that you can flavor the fish while it is steaming on the plate with herbs, spices, and flavorful oils and liquids.

COOKING EN PAPILLOTE

This French technique is perfectly suited to fish because the parchment or foil packaging allows the fish to steam gently in its own juices. The package inflates with the steam during cooking, providing each diner with a delightful puffed package filled with tantalizing smells. Use fairly thin fillets or medallions when cooking en papillote.

The package can be made from foil or parchment, although it is indisputable that parchment allows for a better presentation. Cut either foil or parchment into a rectangle or heart shape, and brush the edges with oil. Arrange a thin fillet in the center of one half of the foil or parchment, along with precooked or quick-cooking vegetables (try a dice or julienne of leek, carrot, peppers, snow peas, cabbage or Swiss chard), a few tablespoons of liquid (often wine), oil or butter, and herbs or spices. (Or try soy sauce, ginger, sesame oil, and wine.) Then fold the remaining half of the foil or parchment shape over the fish and seal the package by folding in the edges. Cook the packages in a 400°F oven for 8 to 10 minutes.

DEEP-FAT FRYING

Lean, firm-textured fish are best for deep-fat frying, and include cod, haddock, lemon sole, flounder, whiting, and perch. Mildly flavored vegetable, peanut, or corn oil, all of which can be heated to a suitable temperature without breaking down are suitable for frying fish. Use a heavy pot that is deep enough to hold 2 to 3 inches of oil and still be only half full. Cut uniformly sized pieces of fish, no more than 1½ inches thick—any thicker and they will still be raw by the time the coating is cooked. Sprinkle the fish with salt and dip it in any of the following combinations: milk and then flour; flour, then milk, then bread crumbs; or milk, then flour, then beaten egg, then lightly herbed bread crumbs or cracker crumbs. Some people dip the fish in wine or cider before dredging in flour.

Heat the oil to between 350° and 375°F. If it is any hotter the coating will burn before the fish is cooked; if the oil is cooler the coating will absorb too much oil. Place a single layer of coated fish in the pot. Do not crowd the fish—the fish will cool the oil anyway, and if you cook too many at a time you won't be able to get the temperature back up quickly. Cook the fish, turning them occasionally so that they brown evenly, until the coating is browned and crisp and the fish is cooked through (you may have to test one or two; the timing depends upon the size of the fish).

FISH SCHOOL

FISH	WATER	FAT*	TEXTURE/ FLAVOR	SUBSTITUTIONS	THE WAY WE LIKE IT
ABALONE There are eight species in the waters off the California coast: black, green, pink, red, white, flat, threaded, and pinto.	Salt	Lean	Rubbery, sweet	Squid, octopus, geoduck	Slice into steaks, pound to tenderize, grill, bread and fry, steam, or use in chowder (do not overcook)
ANCHOVY A small blue-green sea fish with silver-gray sides.	Salt	Fatty	Soft/salty	Herring, sardines	Grill or pan fry
ANGLERFISH (Also called cotte or monkfish.) Very ugly fish, usually sold without its huge, toothy head for aesthetic reasons. Smooth, scaleless skin; dense, pure white flesh.	Salt	Lean	Succulent, sweet, lobster-like flavor	Lobster, shark, swordfish	Pan fry, grill, sauté, roast, or use in soups or stews
BARRACUDA In Atlantic waters, barracuda over 5 pounds are poisonous. Pacific barracuda are safe to eat; prized for firm, sweet flesh. Identified by its pointed snout and row of low, sharp, pointed teeth.	Salt	Lean	Mild	Swordfish, mahimahi	Broil or grill
BASS, BLACK Not a true bass, but a member of the sunfish family. Found in 49 states. Most widely distributed species are smallmouth and largemouth black bass. More delicate texture than true bass.	Fresh	Lean	Firm, mild	Other black bass species, grouper, halibut, snapper, tilefish, monkfish, porgy, orange roughy, ocean perch	Grill, poach, fry, broil, or grill
BASS, LARGEMOUTH/SMALLMOUTH Both widely sold species of black bass. They thrive in lakes and rivers and ponds. The largemouth may reach 20 pounds; the smallmouth is generally no more than twelve.	Fresh	Lean	Firm, mild	Black bass species, halibut, orange roughy, tilefish, grouper, mahimahi, porgy, ocean perch	Bake, grill, broil, poach or fry

*Fish in this chart are categorized as lean (under 2 percent fat), moderately fatty (2 to 6 percent fat), or fatty (over 6 percent fat).

FISH	WATER	FAT*	TEXTURE/ FLAVOR	SUBSTITUTIONS	THE WAY WE LIKE IT
BASS, STRIPED					
(Also called rockfish or striper.) Steely blue to olive green with a distinctive horizontal stripe along its side and a silvery white belly.	Salt, spawns in fresh water	Moderately fatty	Medium firm, mild	Grouper, black cod	Poach, bake, grill, stuff, fry, broil, or stew; use raw in sashimi
BLACK SEA BASS					
A bottom-feeding fish of the Atlantic, it is known as *loup de mer* in France and is favored by the Chinese.	Salt	Moderately fatty	Tasty, firm, and delicate	Grouper, black cod, striped sea bass	Grill, poach, broil or serve raw in carpaccio with a lemon-soy sauce
BLACKFISH					
(Also called tautog.) Found in Atlantic waters, dull gray or green skin.	Salt	Lean	Firm, mild	Mahimahi	Very good for chowders
BLOWFISH					
(Also called puffer, globefish, sea squab, the famous fugu of Japan.) Mildly to very toxic species. Our Atlantic species rarely poisonous. Meat resembles chicken.	Salt	Lean	Firm, plump, sweet, similar to frog's leg	Monkfish	Bread and pan fry. Plan 4 to 6 per person
BLUEFISH					
A superb, spirited game fish found around the world. Very abundant in Atlantic waters. Rapacious eaters.	Salt	Fatty	Dark meat with distinctive flavor, somewhat oily	Mackerel, kingfish, whitefish, lake trout, rainbow trout, pompano	Use acidic marinade, then broil, grill, or bake
BUFFALOFISH					
Member of the sucker family. Abundant all over America. Round-lipped mouth built for sucking in food.	Fresh	Moderately fatty	Sweet, firm white flesh	Carp	Split and fry
BUTTERFISH					
Found in Atlantic waters from Nova Scotia to Cape Hatteras. Small body—less than 10 inches long—and fine-scaled.	Salt	Fatty	Firm, sweet, and true to its name	Mackerel	Butterfly and broil or bake
CARP					
Originally from Asia, carp is fished in the Great Lakes and the Mississippi River. Skin is greenish brown.	Fresh	Moderately fatty	Strong flavor, bony	Buffalofish	Pan fry

FISH	WATER	FAT*	TEXTURE/ FLAVOR	SUBSTITUTIONS	THE WAY WE LIKE IT
CATFISH					
Channel, white, and blue catfish are the most popular species in America. Aquafarming has tamed the taste, and this is becoming one of America's favorite fish.	Fresh	Moderately fatty	Medium firm, sweet	Trout	Bake, broil, grill, poach, fry, or deep-fry
COD					
Most common species are Atlantic cod, hake, haddock, pollack, and tomcod. It is the most popular fish worldwide.	Salt	Lean	Delicate, mild, sweet, firm white flesh	Scrod, sable, lingcod, flounder	Poach, broil, grill, pan fry or use in chowder
DRUM					
(Also called croakers.) A very large family including weakfish, red drums, and black drums. Red drums are the popular redfish used in Cajun cooking.	Salt	Lean	Delicate, mild-flavored	Grouper, snapper	Poach, broil, sauté, pan fry, or grill
FLOUNDER					
General flatfish name that includes, among others, fluke, sanddab, and plaice. See also halibut, sole, and turbot.	Salt	Lean	Mild	Flatfish substitute for one another	Pan fry, broil, or sauté
GROUPER					
Member of sea bass family. Vary in size and texture. Common species are the Warsaw grouper, red grouper, black grouper, and the Nassau grouper.	Salt	Lean	Firm, mild, and wonderful	Black sea bass, snapper, halibut, walleye, pike, tautog, tilefish, buffalofish	Pan or deep-fry, grill, poach, broil, bake; very good in chowder
HADDOCK					
A member of the cod family. Much smaller than Atlantic cod. Finnan haddie is smoked haddock.	Salt	Lean	Sweet, lean, mild, softer flesh than Atlantic cod	Other cods and flounders	Best to stuff and poach or bake
HALIBUT					
Member of family of flounders. The Atlantic halibut is the largest. Pacific halibut is similar to Atlantic. Greenland halibut is inferior in texture and taste to both the others.	Salt	Lean	Mild, sweet, medium firm flesh	Grouper, cod, snapper, turbot	Steaks or fillets: grill, broil, or poach

*Fish in this chart are categorized as lean (under 2 percent fat), moderately fatty (2 to 6 percent fat), or fatty (over 6 percent fat).

FISH	WATER	FAT*	TEXTURE/ FLAVOR	SUBSTITUTIONS	THE WAY WE LIKE IT
HERRING					
In America, mostly found pickled or cured, as kippers or Bismarck herring.	Salt	Fatty	Salty and oily	Whitebait, sardines, anchovies	Best to grill, smoke, bake, or pickle
JOHN DORY					
The delicate St. Peter's fish.	Salt	Lean	Lean, mild, sweet	Flounder, sole	Lightly sauté, use delicate sauce, broil
MACKEREL					
In the same family as tuna. From the North Atlantic, the North Sea, and the Mediterranean and Hawaiian waters; the most popular are Atlantic wahoo, Spanish, and king mackerel, or kingfish.	Salt	Fatty	Flesh varies from white to red, depending on species. Oily, strong-flavored	Bluefish, rainbow trout, brook trout, whitefish, lake trout, sea trout	Marinate in citrus juices and broil or grill
MAHIMAHI					
(Also called dolphinfish—no relation to mammal.) Found in tropical seas. Very tough, inedible skin.	Salt	Lean	Firm white flesh, mild flavor	Snapper, ono, salmon, sea trout, cod	Fillets: grill, poach, broil, or bake
MULLET					
Silvery-skinned fish found all over the world (the highly prized French *rouget* is mullet). Most common species are the striped and silver mullet.	Salt	Fatty	Mild, firm white flesh	Mackerel, pompano, sablefish, salmon, whitefish, sardines	Grill or smoke
OCEAN PERCH					
A red-skinned fish that actually is not a perch, but belongs to the rockfish family.	Salt	Lean	Delicate flavor, somewhat flaky	Snapper, orange roughy, cod	Steam, fry, bake, or broil
ORANGE ROUGHY					
A deep-water fish from New Zealand with bright orange skin.	Salt	Lean	Medium, very mild	Sole, cod, snapper, flounder	Pan fry, broil, grill, bake, or poach
PIKE					
Long, tapered, spotted fish of which the most common species are northern pike and muskellunge.	Fresh	Lean	Medium firm, flaky	Cod, snapper	Stuff and poach, roast, or grill
POMPANO					
A silvery-skinned fish, most common in Florida, that is flat as a pancake.	Salt	Fatty	Mild, distinctive taste	Kingfish, swordfish, bluefish, mackerel, snapper	Sauté, broil, bake, or grill

FISH	WATER	FAT*	TEXTURE/ FLAVOR	SUBSTITUTIONS	THE WAY WE LIKE IT
PORGY Found in Atlantic, Mediterranean, and Pacific waters, these silver-skinned fish are often called sea bream.	Salt	Moderately fatty	Firm, flaky	Cod, snapper	Grill, steam, or bake
RED SNAPPER Found from North Carolina to Brazil. Its rose-red color is distinctive. The most expensive of the snapper family.	Salt	Lean	Medium firm, mild and sweet	Grouper, halibut, other snapper, orange roughy, sole, cod, lingcod	Bake, broil, grill, or stew in chowders
SABLEFISH (BLACK COD) Not a cod at all, this nearly black-skinned fish is found in northern Atlantic waters. Smoked Canadian black cod is a specialty of the Pacific Northwest.	Salt	Fatty	Soft, delicate, and buttery white meat.	Salmon, bluefin tuna, black bass, sturgeon	Broil, smoke, steam, or sauté
SALMON Common species are Atlantic, chum, king, pink, silver, and sockeye. Silver skin; flesh ranges from light orange to orange-red.	Salt, spawns in fresh water	Fatty	Firm, distinctive flavor	Whitefish, trout, sea trout	Poach, grill, broil, bake, sauté, or use in mousses
SARDINE General term for small herring, including Pacific and Atlantic sardines. Blue-green skin. Common in Mediterranean.	Salt	Fatty	Soft, darkish flesh	Anchovies, mackerel	Grill them fresh or pan fry
SCROD A small cod (see Cod).					
SHAD The largest member of the herring family. Mostly fished in the Atlantic. Famous for roe.	Salt, spawns in fresh water	Fatty	Soft and rich	Salmon, trout	Bake, broil, grill, sauté, smoke; sauté the roe
SHARK Blue and mako. Blue shark is prized by the Chinese. Mako, common on the Atlantic coast of the U.S., is similar to more expensive swordfish.	Salt	Lean	Firm, mild-flavored	Swordfish, ono (wahoo), tuna	Skewer and grill steaks

*Fish in this chart are categorized as lean (under 2 percent fat), moderately fatty (2 to 6 percent fat), or fatty (over 6 percent fat).

FISH	WATER	FAT*	TEXTURE/ FLAVOR	SUBSTITUTIONS	THE WAY WE LIKE IT
SKATE					
A member of the ray family. Large, thin wings are edible.	Salt	Lean	Sweet meat, mild-flavored	Monkfish, flatfish	Poach, sauté, steam
SMELT					
Very small, silvery fish.	Salt and fresh	Moderately fatty	Sweet, tender	Herring, sardine	Fry and eat whole
SOLE					
Dover, lemon, gray, petrale, English soles—all flatfish members of the flounder family.	Salt	Lean	Sweet	Other flounder and sole	Poach, sauté, bake, or steam
STURGEON					
Includes green, white, and Atlantic sturgeon. Very often sold smoked. Famous for its roe (caviar).	Salt and fresh	Fatty	Firm white flesh. Taste varies with species.	Shark, marlin, swordfish	Sauté, bake, fry, or smoke
SUNFISH					
(Also called bream.) Outnumber all other fish caught by sport fishermen. Includes bluegills, redear, rock bass, and pumpkin seeds. Skin is not edible.	Fresh	Lean	Lean, firm, delicate flavor, sweet aroma	Snapper, black bass	Pan fry, deep fry, or broil
SWORDFISH					
Found in warm waters throughout the world. Very large fish with long "sword."	Salt	Moderately fatty	Firm, mild	Ono (wahoo), shark, tuna, marlin	Grill, bake, or broil
TILEFISH					
Found in very deep water off the continental shelf.	Salt	Lean	Firm, tender flesh	Lobster, scallops	Bake, broil, or deep-fry
TROUT, BROOK					
Considered to be the finest trout. Olive skin with red spots.	Fresh	Moderately fatty	Delicate flavor	Shad, catfish, lake trout, salmon, rainbow trout	Pan fry, poach, bake, smoke
TROUT, LAKE					
Found mostly in northern U.S. Gray-blue to green color. Not a member of the trout family.	Fresh	Fatty	Rich, mild flesh	Trout, salmon, catfish	Pan fry, poach, bake, grill, steam
TROUT, RAINBOW					
Found throughout the U.S., but mainly in Idaho. Dark, spotted, silvery olive skin.	Fresh	Moderately fatty	Delicate flavor	Brook trout, lake trout, salmon	Pan fry, poach, bake, smoke

FISH	WATER	FAT*	TEXTURE/ FLAVOR	SUBSTITUTIONS	THE WAY WE LIKE IT
TUNA, BLUEFIN A member of the mackerel family. Found in warm waters of the Atlantic. Red flesh. Largest of the tunas.	Salt	Moderately fatty	Firm, distinctive	Swordfish, shark, ono (wahoo), any other tuna, marlin	Grill, broil, poach; use raw in sushi
TUNA, YELLOWFIN Also a member of the mackerel family. Found in warm waters. Lighter-colored flesh than bluefin. Silver-gray skin. Called ahi in Hawaii.	Salt	Moderately fatty	Firm, mildly distinctive	Swordfish, shark, ono (wahoo), any other tuna, marlin	Grill, broil, or poach
TURBOT Highly regarded European member of flounder family. Usually large.	Salt	Lean	Firm, sweet, delicate	Mahimahi, other flounder	Poach, grill, broil, or bake
WALLEYED PIKE (Also called yellow pike.) Not a pike but a perch.	Fresh	Lean	Sweet, white, fine flakes	Flounder, sole, cod, rainbow trout, brook trout	Pan fry, grill, bake, or broil
WEAKFISH (Also known as gray or sea trout.) Its delicate weak mouth is often torn by hooks.	Salt	Fatty	Fine, white flesh	Snapper, salmon, trout	Stuff and bake whole
WHITEBAIT 5 or 6 species of tiny saltwater fish such as herring, anchovy, smelt, and silversides.	Salt	Fatty	Delicate	Smelts	Dust with flour and deep-fry
WHITEFISH Found in deep lakes of the U.S. Most common is lake whitefish. Member of the salmon and trout family.	Fresh	Fatty	White flesh, bony, delicate, sweet and nutty	Trout, salmon, sunfish	Bake, broil, grill, or fry
YELLOWTAIL SNAPPER Caught off the Florida Keys, in the West Indies, and off the South American coast. Member of the snapper family. Yellowish skin.	Salt	Lean	Medium firm, sweet, fine texture	Snapper, grouper, cod, sole	Grill, broil, or sauté

*Fish in this chart are categorized as lean (under 2 percent fat), moderately fatty (2 to 6 percent fat), or fatty (over 6 percent fat).

PREPARING FISH

FLAT FISH

To skin a flat fish

Lay the fish flat to Remove skin

Cut a slit just above the tail through the skin— not the flesh. Hold the fish down with one hand and release a bit of skin from the flesh. with the knife flat. Holding the tail down pull the skin in one piece toward the head.

spine

dark skin Light skin is underneath fish

To fillet a flat fish

Lay the fish on a flat board

Cut through the skin diagonally behind the head. Place the knife between the flesh and the backbone, laying your free hand on top of the fish. Keep the knife flat.

Skin fillet like a roundfish.

Slide the knife along the backbone from head to tail releasing the flesh. Turn fish over to do other side.

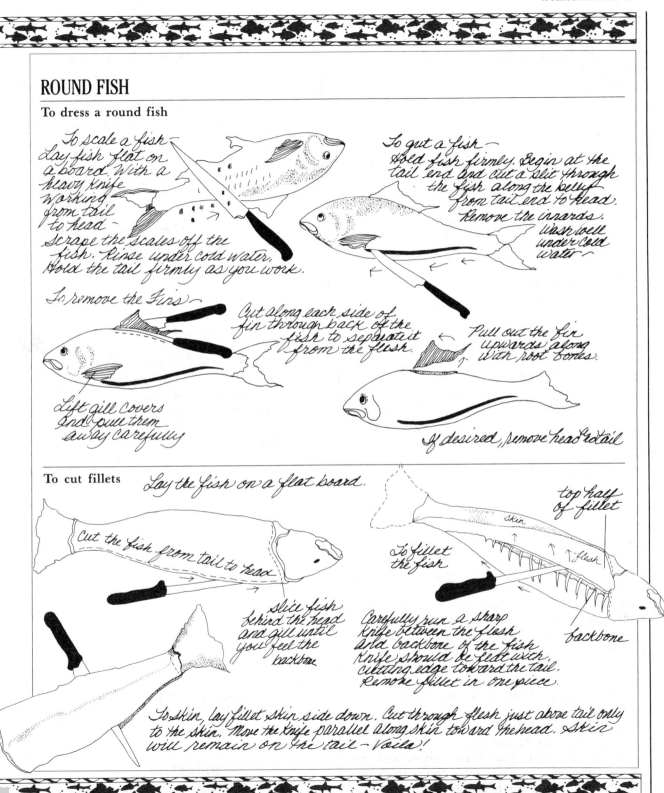

ROUND FISH

To dress a round fish

To scale a fish —
Lay fish flat on a board. With a heavy knife working from tail to head — scrape the scales off the fish. Rinse under cold water. Hold the tail firmly as you work.

To gut a fish —
Hold fish firmly. Begin at the tail end and cut a slit through the fish along the belly from tail end to head. Remove the innards. Wash well under cold water —

To remove the fins —

Cut along each side of fin through back of the fish to separate it from the flesh.

Pull out the fin upwards along with root bones.

Lift gill covers and pull them away carefully

If desired, remove head & tail

To cut fillets

Lay the fish on a flat board.

Cut the fish from tail to head

top half of fillet

skin

flesh

To fillet the fish

Slice fish behind the head and gill until you feel the backbone

Carefully run a sharp knife between the flesh and backbone of the fish. Knife should be felt with cutting edge toward the tail. Remove fillet in one piece.

backbone

To skin, lay fillet skin side down. Cut through flesh just above tail only to the skin. Move the knife parallel along skin toward the head. Skin will remain on the tail — Voila!

CHINESE BLACK SEA BASS

Here is our version of a longtime Chinese favorite, baked wtih fresh ginger, garlic, sesame seeds, and soy. You'll find it most addictive.

2 whole black sea bass (about 1 pound each), cleaned

MARINADE
1 tablespoon soy sauce
2 teaspoons minced fresh ginger
½ teaspoon sesame oil

SAUCE
2 tablespoons unsalted butter
1 tablespoon sesame seeds
1 teaspoon minced fresh ginger
1 teaspoon minced garlic
1 tablespoon soy sauce
1 tablespoon fresh lemon juice
1 teaspoon cornstarch
½ cup water
¼ cup chopped scallions (green onions)

1. On each side of the fish, make three diagonal cuts 2½ inches long and ½ inch deep.
2. Stir the marinade ingredients in a small bowl, and spoon it over the fish, making sure it seeps into the cuts. Let the fish stand in the marinade, uncovered, at room temperature, for 1 hour.
3. Preheat the oven to 400°F.
4. Make the sauce: Melt the butter in a small skillet, and sauté the sesame seeds until golden, 1 minute. Stir in the ginger and garlic; cook 1 minute. In a small bowl, combine the soy sauce, lemon juice, cornstarch, and water; stir until smooth. Stir this into the butter mixture, and heat to a simmer, stirring. Cook until slightly thickened, 1 minute. Set aside and keep warm.
5. Arrange the fish in a baking pan, and bake until it flakes easily, 15 minutes.
6. Stir any accumulated pan juices and the chopped scallions into the sauce. Spoon the sauce over the fish or serve alongside.

2 portions

STRIPED BASS WITH PESTO

Striped bass is an ideal fish for baking with a robust pesto. Angel hair pasta topped with a light tomato sauce makes a delicious and colorful accompaniment.

1 whole striped bass (1 ½ pounds), cleaned
1 cup Basil Pesto (see Index)
6 thin lemon slices
3 tablespoons chopped shallots

1. Preheat the oven to 400°F.
2. Rinse and dry the fish thoroughly.
3. Spread the pesto over the outside and the inside of the fish. Place the fish in a baking dish, arrange the lemon slices over the top, and sprinkle with the shallots.
4. Bake until the thickest part of the fish flakes easily when tested with a fork, 20 to 25 minutes.

2 portions
Note: Bake fish 10 minutes for every inch of thickness, measured at the thickest part.

SUPPER BY THE SEA

Fava Beans With Sopressata

Striped Bass With Pesto
Baked Stuffed Tomatoes
Chardonnay or Orvieto

Blushing Pears

NEW BASIC BOURRIDE

fennel seeds

Silken, garlicky, with a generous portion of absolutely fresh and wonderful fish. The trick is not to let the sauce boil, for it will curdle. Be traditional and serve this over thick slices of French bread sautéed in olive oil.

fennel

6 boiling potatoes, peeled and halved
3 cups fish stock (see Index)
1 medium leek, trimmed, well rinsed, dried, and cut into
    3 inch julienne
1 teaspoon salt
Freshly ground black pepper, to taste
2½ pounds fillets of white non-oily fish, such as red
    snapper, whitefish, or monkfish cut into 3-ounce pieces
2 cups Le Petit Aïoli (see Index)
1½ teaspoons water-packed green peppercorns, drained and
    crushed
Chopped fennel tops or Italian (flat-leaf) parsley, for
    garnish

1. In a medium-size saucepan, cover the potatoes with cold water and bring to a boil. Cook until tender, 25 minutes. Drain and keep warm.

2. In a large deep skillet or kettle, heat the fish stock, leek, salt, and pepper just to a simmer. Arrange the fish pieces in one layer in the liquid, folding the fillets if they are thin. Cover, and simmer until cooked through, about 10 minutes. Transfer the fish to a platter, spoon a small amount of broth over them, and keep warm.

3. Place 1 cup of the aïoli in a medium-size bowl. Slowly add 1 cup of the hot broth, stirring until smooth. Pour this back into the skillet and add the peppercorns. Heat over low heat just until slightly thickened, 2 to 3 minutes. Do not boil.

4. Arrange pieces of fish and 2 potato halves in each of six shallow bowls; then ladle the thickened broth into the bowl. Sprinkle with chopped fennel tops. Serve the remaining aïoli alongside.

6 portions

FRENCH RIVIERA SUPPER

Mâche and Walnut Salad

New Basic Bourride
Olive Rosemary Country Bread
Bandol rosé

Lemon Meringue Tartlets

REDDENED CATFISH

A very easy way to bake catfish without losing that sweet taste, yet giving it some spice too. The sauce cools it down, and the contrast in flavor is fantastic.

½ cup dried bread crumbs
1 tablespoon grated lemon zest
2 teaspoons paprika
2 teaspoons dried oregano
2 teaspoons coarse (kosher) salt
1 teaspoon dried red pepper flakes
¼ cup half-and-half
1 egg
¼ teaspoon sugar
6 catfish fillets (about 3½ ounces each), skinned
1 cup Lime Watercress Sauce (recipe follows)

1. Preheat the oven to 450°F. Lightly grease a baking sheet and set aside.

2. On a plate, toss the bread crumbs, lemon zest, paprika, oregano, salt, and red pepper flakes until well mixed. In a shallow bowl, lightly beat the half-and-half, egg, and sugar.

3. One at a time, dip the fillets first in the egg mixture and then in the crumb mixture.

4. Arrange the fillets on the prepared baking sheet, and bake until sizzling and cooked through, 12 to 14 minutes. Serve immediately with the sauce alongside.

4 portions

LIME WATERCRESS SAUCE

This sauce should be prepared on the day it is to be served.

1 egg yolk
½ cup minced watercress leaves
¼ cup chopped scallions (green onions)
2 tablespoons fresh lime juice
1 tablespoon Dijon mustard
½ teaspoon salt
Freshly ground black pepper, to taste
¾ cup vegetable oil
2 teaspoons grated lime zest

1. Purée the egg yolk, watercress, scallions, lime juice, mustard, salt, and pepper in a food processor until smooth.
2. With the machine running, slowly add the oil in a thin stream through the feed tube, and process until the sauce is thick and smooth. Transfer to a bowl, and stir in the lime zest. Cover and refrigerate until ready to use.

1 generous cup

"**B**ut now through friendly
 seas they softly run,
Painted the mid-sea blue or
 the shore-sea green,
Still patterned with the vine
 and grapes in gold."
—JAMES ELROY FLECKER

PAN-FRIED CATFISH WITH SCALLIONS

Catfish, long a southern favorite, is now very popular from coast to coast. In the South it is being farmed in shallow pools, which gives it a flavor that is mild and delicate. We love it atop cilantro-laced black beans and sweet roasted peppers . . . you will, too. Place some lime wedges alongside—catfish, cilantro, and lime were made for each other.

½ cup olive oil
18 scallions (green onions), white bulb and 5 inches green
1 teaspoon coarsely ground black pepper
1 teaspoon dried thyme leaves
1 tablespoon chopped fresh parsley
1 cup milk
1 cup yellow cornmeal
1 cup unbleached all-purpose flour
½ teaspoon cayenne pepper
Salt and freshly ground black pepper, to taste
6 catfish fillets (2 to 2½ pounds total)
1 cup (2 sticks) unsalted butter, clarified (see Index)
2 tablespoons chopped cilantro (fresh coriander)
Lemon Roasted Peppers (recipe follows)
Black Bean Salad (see Index)

1. Heat the olive oil in a large skillet over medium heat. Add the scallions, and cook, turning them with tongs, until just wilted, 2 minutes. Sprinkle them with the pepper and thyme as they cook. Remove the scallions from the skillet, sprinkle them with the parsley, and set aside.
2. Pour the milk into a glass pie plate. Mix the cornmeal, flour, cayenne, and salt and pepper together in a second pie plate.
3. Dip the catfish fillets first in the milk, then in the cornmeal mixture.
4. Melt the butter in a large skillet over medium heat. Sauté the fish until golden on both sides, 3 minutes per side.
5. Place the catfish on a serving platter, and garnish each fillet with three scallions. Sprinkle with the chopped cilantro. Serve with Lemon Roasted Peppers and Black Bean Salad.

6 portions

LEMON ROASTED PEPPERS

Make these peppers an hour in advance to give them time to marinate in the lemon juice.

6 red bell peppers, halved lengthwise, cored, and seeded
2 tablespoons fresh lemon juice
1 teaspoon coarsely ground black pepper

1. Preheat the broiler.
2. Place the bell peppers skin side up on a broiler pan, and broil 2 to 3 inches from the heat, until the skins are black. Turn the peppers to blacken the skins all over.
3. Using tongs, transfer the peppers to a plastic bag, seal it, and let the peppers steam in the bag for 15 to 20 minutes. Then remove them from the bag and peel off the skin.
4. Place the peppers in a shallow dish, drizzle with the lemon juice, and sprinkle with the black pepper. Loosely cover and let sit at room temperature until ready to serve.

6 portions

DOVER SOLE WITH BASIL CHIFFONADE

Dover sole, napped with a lemon butter sauce and garnished with slivered fresh basil is simple to prepare yet quite complex in flavor.

2 tablespoons unsalted butter
2 tablespoons olive oil
2 tablespoons fresh lemon juice
4 Dover sole fillets (6 ounces each)
Salt and freshly ground black pepper, to taste
¼ teaspoon paprika
½ cup slivered fresh basil leaves

1. Preheat the broiler. Cover a baking sheet with aluminum foil.
2. Melt the butter in a small saucepan. Add the olive oil and lemon juice, and cook over low heat for 5 minutes. Cover and remove from the heat.
3. Lay the fish fillets on the prepared baking sheet, brush them with a bit of the butter sauce, and sprinkle with salt, pepper, and paprika.
4. Broil the fish as close to the heat as possible for 4 minutes. Transfer it to a platter, top with the lemon butter sauce and fresh basil, and serve immediately.

4 portions

JOHN DORY ON A BED OF GREENS

A light preparation for this fish, also known as St. Peter's fish. Look for it in the market or ask your fishmonger to let you know when he has it, as it tends to be a bit hard to find.

2 tablespoons unsalted butter
½ cup loosely packed slivered fresh basil leaves
2 cups loosely packed slivered fresh spinach leaves
2 John Dory (St. Peter's fish) fillets, (about 6 ounces each)
Salt and freshly ground black pepper, to taste
1 lemon half

1. Melt the butter on full power (650 to 700 watts) for 2 minutes in a 10-inch microwave-safe pie plate. Quickly add the basil and spinach, stirring until slightly wilted.

2. Arrange the fillets in the dish, spooning the greens on top. Season with salt and pepper. Cook 4 minutes. Drizzle with lemon juice and serve.

2 portions

Note: This recipe was cooked on High (full power, 650 to 700 watts) in a carousel microwave, using microwave-safe containers.

If your microwave is less powerful, you will have to allow for more cooking time (approximately 1½ times the amount called for—but watch carefully); if it does not have a carousel, you may have to rotate the dish while it is cooking.

ROUND FISH VS. FLAT FISH

Round fish, such as salmon or snapper, and flat fish, such as sole or flounder, have very different bone structures and consequently, are prepared differently and yield different cuts. We find it helpful to think of round fish as three-dimensional, with a plump, cylindrical shape, and eyes that lie on either side of the head. The backbone runs along the center of the fish, separating the two thick fillets on either side. A row of bones lines the top of the backbone, and two more lines of bones fan out from the bottom of the backbone around the viscera. Round fish can either be filleted or cut into steaks.

Flat fish such as sole are, not surprisingly, flat, sort of two-dimensional, with both eyes on the top of the head. The backbone runs through the center of the fish, and two lines of bones fan out on either side, separating the thin top and bottom fillets of the fish. Flat fish can be filleted and, if very large, like halibut or turbot, cut into steaks.

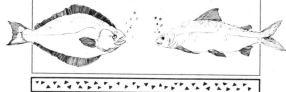

GREY SOLE BAKED IN FOIL

A lovely light meal. Sole is cooked on a bed of sorrel and topped with fresh tomatoes, scallions, and haricots verts. The aroma that rises as diners open their packets is splendid.

1 bunch fresh sorrel, rinsed, trimmed and coarsely chopped
    (3½ to 4 cups)
4 grey sole fillets (6 ounces each)
2 tablespoons dry white wine
2 tablespoons fresh lemon juice
2 ripe plum tomatoes, cored and chopped
8 scallions (green onions), white bulb and 1 inch green,
    halved lengthwise
⅓ pound haricots verts (thin, tender green beans), trimmed
Salt and freshly ground black pepper, to taste
2 tablespoons snipped fresh chives

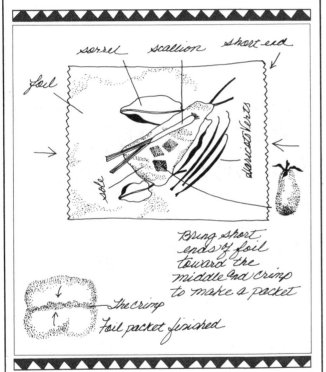

1. Preheat the oven to 400°F.

2. Divide the sorrel among four pieces of aluminum foil large enough to hold a fillet. Arrange each piece of fish on top of the sorrel, and sprinkle with the wine and lemon juice. Top the fillets with the tomatoes and scallions. Place a small bundle of haricots verts next to the fish, and sprinkle salt and pepper over all.

3. Seal the packets, and set them on a baking sheet. Bake for 10 minutes. Remove the packets from the oven, set them on plates, and serve immediately (allow your guests to open the packets at table—carefully, as steam will billow out). Pass the chives.

4 portions

SOLE MEUNIERE

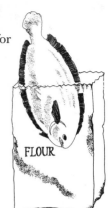

The simplest of preparations for the sweetest of fish—a classic.

1 lemon half (cut lengthwise)
2 lemon or grey sole fillets
    (6 to 7 ounces each)
Salt and freshly ground black pepper,
    to taste
Flour for dredging
3 tablespoons unsalted butter
1 tablespoon olive oil
2 tablespoons chopped fresh parsley

1. Cut the lemon in half again lengthwise, and then slice the wedges crosswise into paper-thin slices. Remove any seeds. Set aside.

2. Season the fillets lightly with salt and pepper, and dredge them thoroughly in flour. Shake off any excess flour.

3. Heat 2 tablespoons of the butter and the oil in a large skillet over medium-high heat. When the butter stops foaming, add the fillets. Cook, turning once, until golden and cooked through, 5 minutes. Transfer to dinner plates and keep warm.

4. Lower the heat under the skillet, and swirl in the remaining 1 tablespoon butter and the lemon slices. Sprinkle with the parsley, and season lightly with salt and pepper. Spoon the sauce over the fillets, and serve immediately.

2 portions

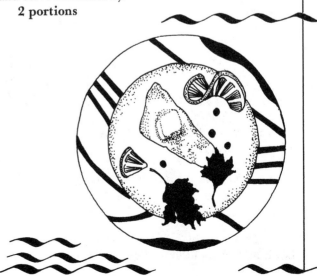

FISH AND CHIPS FOREVER

flounder · onions · lemons

Deep-fried flounder with the lightest batter imaginable, the unmistakable flavor of lemon, and the thinnest onion slices. We always squeeze drops of fresh lemon atop just before serving.

1 cup milk
2 tablespoons fresh lemon juice
¾ cup unbleached all-purpose flour
1 teaspoon salt
½ teaspoon cayenne pepper
¼ teaspoon baking soda
Freshly ground black pepper, to taste
1 egg
2 tablespoons club soda
2 teaspoons grated lemon zest
Vegetable oil for deep-frying
8 flounder fillets (3 ounces each)
Flour for dredging
Salt, to taste
2 onions, thinly sliced and separated into rings
1 or 2 firm lemons, sliced paper-thin, seeds removed, and patted dry

1. Combine the milk and lemon juice in a small bowl, and let stand until slightly textured and thick, 5 minutes.

2. In a second bowl, toss the flour, salt, cayenne, baking soda, and pepper. Stir in the milk mixture, egg, club soda, and lemon zest. Let stand, uncovered at room temperature, 20 minutes.

3. Heat the oil to 360°F in a deep-fryer.

4. Coat the fillets lightly in flour seasoned with salt and pepper. Stir the batter; then dip the fillets in it. Let any excess drip off. Fry the fillets, in batches if necessary, just until golden and crisp, 3 minutes per side. Keep warm in a low (250°F) oven.

5. Flour the onion rings, and dip them in the batter. Let any excess drip off. Flour the lemon slices. Fry the onions along with several floured lemon slices, in batches, until deep golden and crisp. Serve immediately.

4 portions

ORANGE ORANGE ROUGHY

Closely related to the Australian salmon, we thought this tender, tasty white fish would take to the flavor of orange, and we were right.

¼ cup fresh orange juice
4 orange roughy fillets (about 6 ounces each)
2 tablespoons safflower or olive oil
1 tablespoon dried tarragon
1 tablespoon coarsely ground black pepper
Grated zest of 2 oranges

1. Preheat the oven to 325°F.

2. Pour the orange juice into a shallow baking dish large enough to hold the fish in one layer.

3. Brush the fish lightly with oil on both sides, and place the fillets in the baking dish.

4. Combine the tarragon, pepper, and orange zest in a small bowl, and sprinkle over the fish, patting it lightly to form a thin crust.

5. Bake until the fish flakes easily when tested with a fork, 20 to 25 minutes.

6. Using a long metal spatula, carefully transfer the fish to a serving dish. (The fish may release a lot of liquid while cooking; just discard it.) Serve immediately.

4 portions

SPICED MONKFISH

A simple preparation, this fish is made special by its robust crust of cracked pepper, fennel seeds, thyme, and lemon zest.

1 tablespoon cracked or coarsely ground black pepper
1 teaspoon fennel seeds, crushed
1 teaspoon dried thyme leaves, crumbled
½ teaspoon salt
1 teaspoon grated lemon zest
1 tablespoon unsalted butter, melted
½ teaspoon Dijon mustard
2 monkfish fillets (about 7 ounces each)
Large lemon wedges

1. Preheat the oven to 325°F.
2. Stir the spices, herbs, and lemon zest together, and sprinkle on a plate.
3. Combine the butter and mustard; brush over the fillets. Then roll the fillets in the spice mixture to coat well. Arrange on a baking sheet.
4. Bake until fragrant and cooked through, 30 minutes. Slice each fillet on an angle to form thick medallions. Arrange, overlapping, on two plates, and serve with lemon wedges alongside.

2 portions

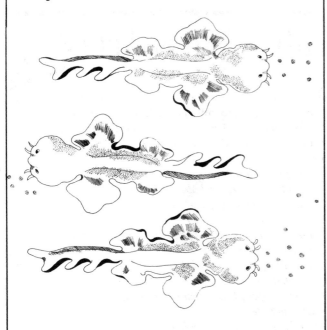

ABOUT FROZEN FISH

It would be wonderful if we could always get beautiful, fresh seafood. But sometimes the "fresh" seafood just isn't, and, much as we hate to say it, in that case you're better off buying frozen. If you do, look for packages that are frozen solid; seafood that has been thawed and refrozen will suffer in texture and flavor. Avoid torn packaging, ice crystals, and seafood that shows white patches or discoloration (both signs of freezer burn that dehydrates fish and gives it a cottony texture). And try to cook frozen seafood as soon as possible after you buy it.

We can't wholeheartedly recommend freezing fish at home because home freezers just don't get cold enough to do the job properly. You'll have the most success with whole, cleaned fish with the head still on because the skin protects the flesh. Unskinned fillets will freeze better than skinned for the same reason. In any event, the most important thing is that the fish be sealed against contact with air. To that end, you may wrap the fish tightly in either heavy plastic wrap or aluminum foil, pressing out the air as you wrap. Whole fish can be frozen, completely submerged in a brine solution (⅓ cup salt to 1 gallon water), in an airtight plastic container. Cover the container with the lid, and freeze. Oily fish may be frozen for up to two months and lean fish for up to three.

Thaw frozen fish on a plate or in a baking dish in the refrigerator, draining it often—don't allow it to sit in accumulated liquid. You should count on about 24 hours to thaw steaks, fillets or small fish; larger fish will take longer.

STAR FISH

This dish is beautiful in both presentation and flavor. Sweet white-fleshed orange roughy is sautéed, then topped with slices of golden star fruit in a sauce composed of cinnamon, orange zest, and dry vermouth. A swirl of butter enriches the sauce at the last minute, and makes you a star.

2 orange roughy fillets (about 6 ounces each)
Salt and freshly ground black pepper, to taste
Flour for dredging
2 tablespoons olive oil
1 carambola (star fruit), sliced ¼ inch thick
4 strips orange zest, 2 inches long, julienned
Pinch of ground cinnamon
⅓ cup dry vermouth
2 tablespoons unsalted butter, cold, cut in quarters

1. Season the fillets lightly with salt and pepper. Dredge them in the flour, shaking off any excess.
2. Heat the oil in a skillet. Sauté the fillets over medium heat until golden and cooked through, 3 minutes per side. Set aside and keep warm.
3. Pour off the fat from the skillet, and stir in the carambola and orange zest. Sprinkle with the cinnamon. Stir over low heat 2 minutes. Then stir in the vermouth, and cook until slightly reduced, another 2 minutes. Swirl in the butter, one piece at a time, stirring until the sauce is thick and smooth; spoon over the fillets, and serve.

2 portions

SEASON TO TASTE

These are some of our favorite flavors with fish:

Anise	Lemon
Basil	Lime
Borage	Marjoram
Caraway seed	Orange
Chervil	Oregano
Chives	Parsley
Cilantro	Pernod
Dill	Rosemary
Fennel	Saffron
Garlic	Sage
Ginger	Savory
Herbed	Tarragon
vinegars	Thyme

ROSY RED SNAPPER

Red snapper in a pool of saffron sauce, topped with chopped tomato and chervil. It's as electric in appearance as a summer sunset, and an exciting combination of tastes and textures.

1 cup heavy or whipping cream
⅓ cup fish stock (see Index) or bottled clam juice
1 tablespoon tomato paste
½ teaspoon anchovy paste
Freshly ground black pepper, to taste
Pinch of saffron threads
1 small ripe tomato, seeded and diced
1 tablespoon chopped fresh chervil or parsley
2 red snapper fillets (about 6 ounces each)
Salt, to taste
2 tablespoons fresh lemon juice

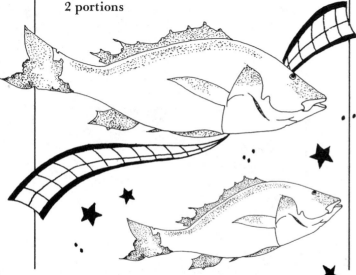

Skate Wings

1. Make the sauce: In a small saucepan, heat the cream, stock, tomato paste, anchovy paste, and pepper just to a simmer. Cook until reduced to ¾ cup, about 10 minutes. Do not allow the mixture to boil. Stir in the saffron and set aside; keep warm.

2. Preheat the broiler. Oil a shallow pan and set aside.

3. Toss the chopped tomato and chervil together in a small bowl.

4. Season the fillets lightly with salt, pepper, and lemon juice. Arrange in one layer in the prepared pan. Broil just until cooked through, 5 minutes.

5. Pour a pool of sauce on each dinner plate, and arrange the fillets in the center. Sprinkle each fillet with the tomato-chervil mixture, and serve.

2 portions

SOY-BAKED SNAPPER

This simple preparation allows the sweet taste of the snapper to come through—with just a bit of a "snap" from the garlic.

2 small red snappers (about 1 ½ pounds each), cleaned and left whole
¼ cup soy sauce
1 tablespoon Asian sesame oil
2 cloves garlic, minced

1. Cut three slits, about ½ inch deep and 2 inches apart, diagonally in the sides of each fish; don't cut down to the bone. Arrange the fish in one layer in an ovenproof casserole.

2. Combine the soy, sesame oil, and garlic in a small bowl. Stir well, and spoon over the fish, making sure the mixture seeps into the slits. Let the fish stand, loosely covered, at room temperature, for 30 minutes.

3. Preheat the oven to 425°F.

4. Bake the fish until it is cooked through and the skin is lightly crisp, 30 minutes. Serve immediately.

2 portions

GINGER SKATE

Skate, one of the least expensive and most ignored fish, is finally coming into its own, as well it should. Its flavor is reminiscent of scallops. The French have classically prepared skate with a *beurre noir*. We've taken poetic license and added a bit of ginger. This is sublime!

1 ½ pounds skate wings, skinned and filleted, cartilage removed, cut into 4 pieces
Salt and freshly ground black pepper, to taste
About 1 cup milk
Flour for dredging
4 tablespoons (½ stick) unsalted butter
2 teaspoons walnut oil or light olive oil
1 tablespoon capers, drained
1 teaspoon minced fresh ginger
2 teaspoons chopped fresh parsley

1. Preheat the oven to 400°F.

2. Season the fish lightly with salt and pepper. Place the milk in one shallow dish and the flour in another. Dip the fish first in the milk and then in the flour, and shake off any excess flour.

3. Melt 2 tablespoons of the butter in a large skillet and sauté the fish over medium-high heat, 1 minute per side. Transfer the fish to a baking sheet, and bake until cooked through, 8 minutes.

4. In the same skillet, whisk the remaining 2 tablespoons butter with the walnut oil, capers, and ginger. Cook over medium-high heat until foaming and light brown, 2 to 3 minutes. Then whisk in the parsley and remove from the heat.

5. Arrange the fish on two plates, and pour the *beurre noir* over.

2 portions

Note: This method of saucing with *beurre noir* works equally well with thin scallops of chicken or veal.

PIQUANTE BLUEFISH

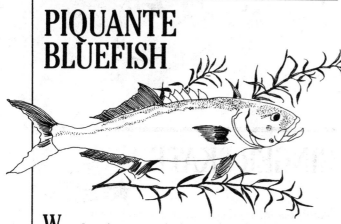

We often hear people lamenting that they love to fish when the blues are running—they're great sport—but they often give them away because they don't like the oiliness of the fish.

Marinating bluefish in lemon helps reduce the oiliness of this favorite fish. And combined with a salsa of yellow cherry tomatoes, tart green apple, yellow peppers, and scallions, it becomes truly a special summertime dish.

1 teaspoon plus 2 tablespoons olive oil
2 tablespoons fresh lemon juice
1 tablespoon snipped fresh chives
2 teaspoons capers, drained
1½ teaspoons finely chopped fresh rosemary leaves
Freshly ground black pepper, to taste
¼ teaspoon sugar
Pinch of salt
2 bluefish fillets (6 to 7 ounces each)
¼ cup cracker crumbs
1¼ cups Salsa Piquante (recipe follows)

1. In a small bowl, stir together the 1 teaspoon olive oil, lemon juice, chives, capers, rosemary, pepper, sugar, and salt. Spoon this mixture over both sides of the fillets. Cover, and refrigerate 1 hour, turning once.

2. Preheat the oven to 450°F.

3. In a large ovenproof skillet, heat the remaining 2 tablespoons olive oil. Coat the fillets with the cracker crumbs, and sauté them in the oil just until light golden, 1 minute per side. Then spoon 2 tablespoons salsa over each fillet, and transfer the skillet to the oven. Bake until the fish is sizzling and cooked through, 10 minutes. Serve immediately, with the remaining salsa on the side.

2 portions

SALSA PIQUANTE

The combination of these flavors is really wonderful. Don't save the salsa only for bluefish—it will enliven any whitefish or chicken, or would be terrific on fajitas or a grilled veal chop. This is a winner!

1 cup yellow cherry tomatoes, halved
½ cup diced yellow bell pepper
½ cup finely diced tart green apple
2 tablespoons minced scallions (green onions)
2 tablespoons fresh lemon juice
1 tablespoon extra virgin olive oil
1 tablespoon capers, drained and minced
2 teaspoons finely chopped fresh rosemary leaves
½ teaspoon salt
¼ teaspoon sugar
Freshly ground black pepper, to taste

Stir all the ingredients together in a bowl, crushing the tomatoes lightly with the back of a spoon. Cover, and refrigerate at least 1 hour.

2 cups

MARINATING FISH

★

Allowing fish to stand for a short time (no more than an hour) in an appropriate marinade is a subtle way to add flavor. Centuries ago, the original marinade was sea water, used as a preservative. We like to marinate fish in a flavorful oil with an acid such as lemon or lime juice, vinegar, or wine, and herbs or spices. Or sometimes we go Asian with sesame oil, soy sauce, and ginger.

A whole fish cooked on the bone with head and tail intact makes a wonderfully grand presentation. But keeping the fish whole has other benefits as well: The bones add flavor to the flesh and keep it moist, and the skin of most fish has an underlying layer of fat that seeps into the fish as it cooks to give it added richness.

BARBARA ENSRUD'S BAKED BLUEFISH

We met Barbara, author of *American Vineyards,* when we first opened The Silver Palate. She was a great neighborhood customer and has become a great friend. Here's her description of this recipe:

"Red wine with fish can be a delectable match. If I want to prove it to skeptics, I often do it with this dish. Bluefish, because it is fairly strong in flavor and slightly oily, should be as fresh as possible. It needs a fruity red wine with good acidity, something like one of the lighter red Burgundies—a 1985 Volnay or Santenay, for instance, or an Oregon Pinot Noir."

1 tablespoon olive oil
½ cup chopped red onion
½ cup chopped red bell pepper
½ cup chopped yellow bell pepper
¼ cup dry white wine or dry vermouth
¼ cup dried black currants
¼ cup sliced almonds, toasted (see Index)
¼ cup chopped fresh Italian (flat-leaf) parsley
2 cloves garlic, minced
Salt and freshly ground black pepper, to taste
1 whole bluefish (1 ½ to 2 pounds), boned, head and tail left on
3 thin lemon wedges
Parsley sprigs, for garnish
Lemon wedges, for garnish

1. Preheat the oven to 350°F. Lightly oil a roasting pan large enough to hold the fish and set aside.
2. Heat the oil in a skillet over medium heat, and sauté the red onion and both peppers until soft but not brown, about 7 minutes. Add the wine and simmer briefly until reduced, 2 to 3 minutes. (White wine is used for its acidity as a reducing liquid; red wine would add too much flavor.)
3. Add the currants, almonds, chopped parsley, garlic, and salt and pepper, and stir well. Remove from the heat and keep warm.
4. Rinse the fish and pat it dry. Stuff the cavity of the fish with some of the vegetable mixture, and close the cavity with toothpicks. Make three slashes on one side of the body and insert a lemon wedge into each.
5. Place the fish in the prepared roasting pan, and bake until it flakes easily when tested with a fork, 25 to 30 minutes.
6. Serve on a warmed platter, garnished with the remaining vegetable mixture, sprigs of parsley, and lemon wedges.

2 portions

BROILED PERCH

A simple way to prepare perch. They are seasoned with lime ginger butter right before serving—no sauce is necessary.

4 perch fillets (about 6 ounces each), skinned
Salt and freshly ground black pepper, to taste
5 tablespoons Lime Ginger Butter (see Index), chilled
Chopped fresh parsley, for garnish

1. Preheat the broiler.
2. Lightly season the fillets with salt and pepper, and broil until cooked through, about 5 minutes.
3. Cut the butter into twelve thin slices. Arrange three slices, overlapping, on each fillet, sprinkle with parsley, and serve.

4 portions

PALM BEACH POMPANO

Pompano, one of the favorites of all seafood lovers, is accented here with sweet juicy crabmeat and brought to perfection with fresh citrus. All is cooled with fresh mint. Lovely.

4 pompano fillets (about 6 ounces each)
Salt and freshly ground black pepper, to taste
8 ounces fresh lump crabmeat, cartilage removed
1 large orange, peeled, segmented, seeds removed
1 sweet grapefruit, peeled, segmented, seeds removed
¼ cup fresh orange juice
2 tablespoons unsalted butter, at room temperature
3 tablespoons dried bread crumbs
Chopped fresh mint leaves, for garnish

1. Preheat the oven to 350°F. Butter a baking dish.

2. Arrange the fillets in one layer in the baking dish. Sprinkle lightly with salt and pepper.

3. Divide the crabmeat among the four fillets, arranging it on top of the fish. Then arrange a row of alternating orange and grapefruit segments on each fillet. Drizzle orange juice over each.

4. Blend the butter and bread crumbs, and sprinkle over the citrus segments.

5. Bake until the fillets are cooked through and the crumbs are crisp and golden, 15 minutes. Sprinkle with fresh mint, and serve immediately.

4 portions

WINES WITH SMOKED FISH

FISH	WINE
Gravlax	Aquavit, Gewürztraminer, Pouilly-Fuissé
Herring	Chenin Blanc, Aquavit
Salmon	Tokay d'Alsace, Sparkling Blanc de Noirs, Sauvignon Blanc, Pouilly-Fuissé
Trout	Chardonnay, Chenin Blanc
Whitefish	Pinot Blanc

PARTY POACHED SALMON

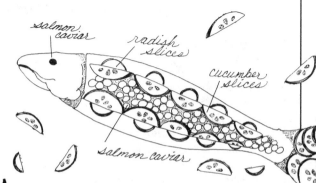

salmon caviar
radish slices
cucumber slices
salmon caviar

A beautiful presentation for a spring or summer luncheon, this salmon is poached in a blush Zinfandel and then decorated with a refreshing mosaic pattern of cucumbers, radishes, and salmon caviar. Be sure to fill the eye cavity of the fish with caviar.

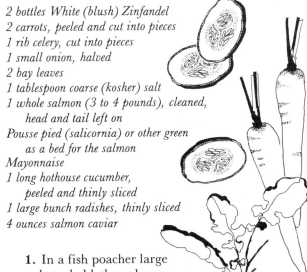

2 bottles White (blush) Zinfandel
2 carrots, peeled and cut into pieces
1 rib celery, cut into pieces
1 small onion, halved
2 bay leaves
1 tablespoon coarse (kosher) salt
1 whole salmon (3 to 4 pounds), cleaned,
    head and tail left on
Pousse pied (salicornia) or other green
    as a bed for the salmon
Mayonnaise
1 long hothouse cucumber,
    peeled and thinly sliced
1 large bunch radishes, thinly sliced
4 ounces salmon caviar

1. In a fish poacher large enough to hold the salmon, combine the Zinfandel, carrots, celery, onion, bay leaves, and coarse salt. Cover, bring to a boil, and simmer 30 minutes. (The poacher can be placed across two burners on a conventional stove.)

2. Push the vegetables to the side of the poacher, or remove them temporarily if necessary. Place the salmon on the poaching tray and gently lower it into the liquid. Return the vegetables if removed.

3. Add enough water to just cover the fish, and bring just to a simmer. Cover, and cook 30 minutes, or 10 minutes for each inch of thickness measured at the thickest part of the fish. (Check periodically to make sure that the liquid is barely simmering.)

4. Remove the poacher from the heat, uncover partially, and allow to cool to room temperature. Refrigerate the salmon overnight in the poaching liquid.

5. Several hours before serving, arrange a bed of the pousse pied on a serving platter large enough to hold the fish. (If you are using an exotic green, wait until nearer to serving time and lay it around the salmon.)

6. Gently lift the salmon out of the poacher, and slide it carefully onto the platter. Peel off the top skin, and scrape off any grayish brown flesh, if desired.

7. Spread a thin (⅛-inch) layer of cold mayonnaise over the body of the salmon. Decorate with lengthwise rows of sliced cucumbers, radishes, and the caviar. Remove the eye and fill the cavity with caviar. Refrigerate until serving time.

6 to 8 portions

SALMON WITH POTATO FANS

This dish can be prepared with other potatoes, but Yukon Golds add an intensely buttery, rich flavor. The thin slices can be further cut into small circles to resemble the scales of a fish.

1 tablespoon unsalted butter, at room temperature
1 Yukon Gold potato, peeled and thinly sliced
Salt and freshly ground black pepper, to taste
4 teaspoons minced shallots
2 salmon fillets (about 5 ounces each)

1. Preheat the oven to 350°F.

2. Spread the butter in a medium-size ovenproof skillet. Arrange the potato slices, overlapping, in the skillet in the shape of the two salmon fillets, leaving space between the two. Sprinkle with salt, pepper, and the shallots.

3. Season the fillets with salt and pepper, and arrange them, skin side up, on the potatoes.

4. Cook over medium heat for 5 minutes, then transfer the skillet to the oven, and bake just until the salmon is cooked through and the potatoes are golden, 10 minutes. Using a spatula, gently lift the potatoes and fillets from the skillet and transfer them to two plates, potato side up. Serve immediately.

2 portions

A SPRING CELEBRATION FOR ONLY TWO

Sautéed Foie Gras for Two

Salmon With Potato Fans
Asparagus Watercress Timbales
Sauternes or Gewürztraminer

Almond Cheesecake

SALMON WITH SESAME BUTTER

The unique flavor of lime juice combined with soy sauce and sesame seeds sets these salmon steaks apart.

MARINADE
2 tablespoons fresh lime juice
1 tablespoon vegetable oil
1 tablespoon soy sauce

4 salmon steaks (about 8 ounces each)
1 tablespoon sesame seeds
½ teaspoon celery seeds
Sesame Butter (recipe follows), chilled

1. Combine the marinade ingredients in a shallow bowl. Add the salmon, and turn to coat well in the mixture. Let stand, loosely covered, 1 hour.
2. Preheat the oven to 350°F.
3. Spread out the sesame and the celery seeds in a small baking pan. Place the pan in the oven and toast the seeds until they are lightly browned, 3 to 5 minutes. Check after 3 minutes and if the seeds are not done, shake the pan and continue to toast, watching carefully to prevent burning. Remove from the oven and set aside.
4. Preheat the broiler.
5. Broil the salmon steaks 5 minutes per side. Serve with 1 to 2 slices of sesame butter, each about ¼ inch thick on top. Sprinkle with the toasted sesame and celery seeds.
4 portions

SESAME BUTTER

8 tablespoons (1 stick) unsalted butter, at room temperature
2 tablespoons toasted sesame seeds (see above for toasting)
2 tablespoons minced chives or scallions (green onions)
2 teaspoons sesame oil
2 teaspoons soy sauce
Freshly ground black pepper, to taste

Stir all ingredients together in a small bowl until smooth. Shape into a cylinder and roll in aluminum foil or waxed paper. Chill until firm.
About ¾ cup

CANNED SALMON

There are five different kinds of canned salmon on the market. Chinook, or king, salmon has a soft, rich flesh that varies in color from deep red to white, depending on the grade. It is often labeled as "Royal Chinook" and is a good choice for salads. Sockeye, or "red," salmon is firm-fleshed and deep orange in color; it works well in a variety of dishes. Coho, or silver, salmon is pink-fleshed and fine-textured; it's fine for cooking, but we wouldn't use it in salads. Pink salmon is very fine-textured and light pink in color; we like to use it in sandwiches. Chum salmon is very light-colored, sometimes almost gray, and is inferior to other canned salmons.

SALMON CROQUETTES WITH SORREL MAYONNAISE

This recipe uses canned salmon. After flaking the salmon, either remove the soft bones or crush them with a fork and incorporate them into the mixture. The skin and bones are a good source of Omega-3, a possible cholesterol-reducing agent.

1 can (15 ½ ounces) pink salmon
¾ cup dried bread crumbs
½ cup mayonnaise
½ cup chopped onion
¼ cup minced yellow bell pepper
¼ cup minced celery
¼ cup chopped fresh parsley
1 egg
2 teaspoons grated lemon zest
1 teaspoon Dijon mustard
1 teaspoon Worcestershire sauce
6 drops of Tabasco sauce
¼ teaspoon salt
¼ cup peanut oil
1 ½ cups Sorrel Mayonnaise (see Index)

1. In a mixing bowl, combine half the salmon with ½ cup of the bread crumbs and the mayonnaise, onion, bell pepper, celery, parsley, egg, lemon zest, mustard, Worcestershire, Tabasco, and salt. Mix well, then gently stir in the remaining salmon. Shape into twelve 2-inch croquettes. Coat the croquettes in the remaining ¼ cup bread crumbs.

2. Heat the oil in a large skillet. Cook the croquettes over medium-high heat, turning once, until they are browned and crisp, about 6 minutes. Drain on paper towels. Serve with Sorrel Mayonnaise.

4 portions

PAN-FRIED TROUT WITH SAGE AND ALMONDS

The sage and almond coating adds exceptional flavoring to simple pan-fried trout.

¼ cup unbleached all-purpose flour
¼ cup sliced almonds (with skins), toasted (see Index)
3 tablespoons dried sage leaves
1 teaspoon salt
Freshly ground black pepper, to taste
4 brook trout (about 1 pound each), cleaned, heads and tails left on
6 tablespoons peanut or olive oil

1. Place the flour, almonds, sage, salt, and pepper in a food processor and process until fine. Sprinkle the mixture on a plate, and coat each trout well with it. Sprinkle the cavities of the fish lightly with additional salt and pepper.

2. Divide the oil between two large skillets, and place over medium-high heat. Sauté the trout, turning once, until golden and crisp, 10 minutes.

4 portions

Note: It is easier to cook trout this way if it is whole. However, if the fishmonger has filleted the trout for you (make sure he leaves the fillets attached), open each fish and sprinkle with additional crumbled dried sage leaves before frying.

POACHED TROUT

This cooking liquid is quite flavorful and can be frozen for later use as a court bouillon or as stock for poaching other fish or boiling lobster. It can also be the base of a soup or of a sauce for fish. Serve the trout with small potatoes.

3 cups water
1 cup dry white wine
2 tablespoons finely snipped fresh chives
2 tablespoons minced fresh basil leaves
1 tablespoon chopped fresh dill
1 tablespoon chopped fresh rosemary
1 tablespoon chopped fresh tarragon
1 teaspoon salt
Freshly ground black pepper, to taste
1 strip lemon zest, 2 inches by ½ inch
2 fresh brook trout (about 12 ounces each), cleaned, heads and tails left on
3 tablespoons unsalted butter, melted
Lemon wedges, for garnish

1. In a large pot or dutch oven, bring the water, wine, herbs, spices, and lemon zest to a boil. Lower the heat and simmer 10 minutes.

2. Gently lower the trout into the liquid. Simmer, partially covered, until firm to the touch, about 10 minutes (or 10 minutes per inch of thickness of the fish).

3. Using two spatulas, lift each trout out and place it on a dinner plate.

4. Blend the butter with 2 tablespoons of the cooking liquid (with as much of the herbs as you can retrieve), and spoon over the fish. Serve immediately, with lemon wedges alongside.

2 portions

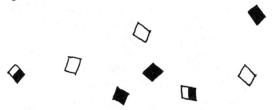

HOW MUCH FISH PER PERSON

When figuring out how much fish to buy, keep in mind that the richer the choice, the smaller the quantity. It is also important to consider what else is being served with the fish, and the richness of the sauce or garnish. The following list should be used as a general starting point.

FISH	PER SERVING
Drawn	¾ to 1 pound
Dressed	¾ pound
Split	½ to ¾ pound
Butterflied	⅓ to ½ pound
Steaks with bone	½ pound
Boned fillets and steaks	⅓ to ½ pound
Medallions	⅓ to ½ pound
Chunks	⅓ to ½ pound

FRESH FENNEL WHITEFISH

This is an easy way to steam fish—in the oven. The light anise flavor of Pernod and fennel provides a fresh accent to the delicate taste of the fish.

1 fennel bulb, trimmed, tops reserved
2 tablespoons unsalted butter
1 onion, cut in strips
2 cloves garlic, slivered
2 tablespoons Pernod liqueur
¼ teaspoon salt
¼ teaspoon freshly ground black pepper
1 fresh whitefish (about 2 pounds), cleaned and filleted
   (fillets remain attached)

1. Preheat the oven to 400°F. Cover a baking sheet with aluminum foil. Oil and set it aside.

2. Cut the fennel crosswise into 1-inch pieces.

3. Melt the butter in a skillet, and sauté the fennel, onion, and garlic until golden, 10 minutes. Stir in the Pernod, dissolving any browned bits in the bottom of the pan. Season with the salt and pepper, and set aside.

4. Lightly season the outside and the inside of the fish with salt and pepper.

5. Spoon half the fennel mixture in a strip on the prepared baking sheet, and arrange the fish on top of the fennel. Spoon half the remaining fennel into the cavity, and the remainder on top. Sprinkle with some chopped fennel tops. Cover with a second sheet of oiled foil. Fold and pinch the edges together to seal.

6. Bake until the fish is sizzling and cooked through, 30 minutes. Sprinkle with additional chopped fennel tops before serving.

3 to 4 portions

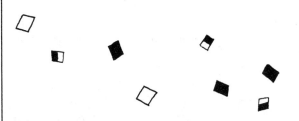

When you think of flavoring fish or shellfish, think fennel. Use the fronds, seeds, or slices of the bulb.

TUNA TONNATO

We've substituted succulent fresh tuna for veal and made a lighter tuna mayonnaise, easily prepared ahead, for a warm-weather classic. Delicious served with a Tomato Bread Salad and a chilled Orvieto wine.

MAYONNAISE
1 egg
1 egg yolk
2½ tablespoons fresh lemon juice
4 teaspoons Dijon mustard
½ cup olive oil
½ cup corn oil

TUNA SAUCE
½ cup canned tuna, drained
1½ tablespoons tiny capers, drained
4 flat anchovy fillets, drained
1 tablespoon fresh lemon juice
⅓ cup olive oil
2 teaspoons finely grated lemon zest
¼ teaspoon coarsely ground black pepper
Salt to taste

⅓ cup extra virgin olive oil
⅓ cup fresh lemon juice
½ teaspoon coarsely ground black pepper
8 fresh tuna steaks, 1 inch thick (about 6 ounces each)
2 tablespoons chopped fresh Italian (flat-leaf) parsley
1½ tablespoons tiny capers, drained
1 tablespoon finely grated lemon zest

1. Prepare the mayonnaise: Place the egg, egg yolk, lemon juice, and mustard in a food processor and process for 15 seconds. With the motor running, slowly pour in both oils through the feed tube and process until the mayonnaise has thickened. Transfer it to a bowl. Cover, and refrigerate, if you are making the mayonnaise ahead.

2. Prepare the tuna sauce: Combine the tuna, capers, anchovies, lemon juice, and oil in a food processor. Process until smooth, about 1 minute.

3. Fold the puréed tuna into the mayonnaise, along with the lemon zest, pepper, and salt. Cover, and refrigerate for at least 3 hours. (This can be made 1 day ahead.)

4. Mix the extra virgin oil, lemon juice, and black pepper in a shallow bowl just large enough to hold the tuna in a single layer. Add the tuna, coat it well with the marinade, cover, and refrigerate for 30 minutes, turning once.

5. Preheat the broiler.

6. Remove the tuna from the marinade and place it on a broiling pan. Broil 4 inches from the heat for 3 to 4 minutes on each side. Do not overcook. Set aside to cool to room temperature.

7. Arrange the cooled tuna steaks on a large serving platter or on individual plates. Spread 4 tablespoons of the tuna mayonnaise on top of each steak, and sprinkle with the parsley, capers, and lemon zest.

8 portions

WINES WITH FISH

FISH	WINE
Bass	Chardonnay, Orvieto
Bluefish	Chardonnay
Catfish	White Zinfandel
Cod	Bandol, Zinfandel
Flounder	Sauvignon Blanc
Grouper	Muscadet
John Dory	Fumé Blanc, Chablis
Monkfish	Montrachet
Perch	Chablis, Chenin Blanc
Pompano	Chardonnay
Salmon	Meursault
Sardines	Sancerre, White Rioja
Shad Roe	Puligny-Montrachet, Chardonnay
Skate	Puligny-Montrachet
Snapper	Pouilly-Fuissé
Sole	Sauvignon Blanc, Mâcon
Swordfish	Chardonnay, Beaujolais-Villages
Trout	Sancerre, Chenin Blanc

SHAD ROE WITH PROSCIUTTO

What a way to welcome spring! We've substituted prosciutto for the usual bacon to flavor our favorite shad roe. This dish is quite rich, so serve it with lightly steamed asparagus drizzled with fresh lemon juice.

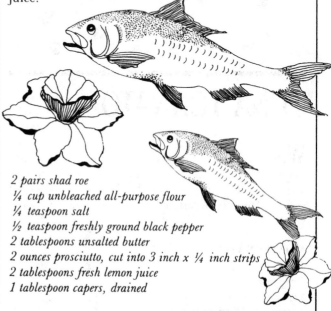

2 pairs shad roe
¼ cup unbleached all-purpose flour
¼ teaspoon salt
½ teaspoon freshly ground black pepper
2 tablespoons unsalted butter
2 ounces prosciutto, cut into 3 inch x ¼ inch strips
2 tablespoons fresh lemon juice
1 tablespoon capers, drained

1. Dip the shad roe in a bowl of cold water to rinse it, and gently pat dry with paper towels. Carefully cut away the membrane that connects each pair, separating them into two lobes.

2. Combine the flour, salt, and pepper, and dust the shad roe with the mixture.

3. Melt 1 tablespoon of the butter in a skillet. Add the shad roe, cover the skillet, and cook over low heat, turning the roe twice during the cooking until golden brown on the outside and a clamshell gray throughout the inside, 12 to 15 minutes. (It is important to cook the roe slowly to avoid breaking the fragile eggs.)

4. Transfer the roe to a serving platter. Add the remaining 1 tablespoon of butter and the prosciutto to the skillet. Cook over low heat for 1 minute. Then add the lemon juice and capers, and cook an additional minute. Pour the sauce over the shad roe, and serve immediately.

4 portions

BASQUE SWORDFISH

An unusual combination of potatoes, onions, bell pepper, and bacon tops these swordfish steaks. Drizzle chile oil over all, and broil your meal in 8 minutes. Serve with a crisp green salad and crusty bread.

2 swordfish steaks (about 8 ounces each), 1 inch thick
Salt and freshly ground black pepper, to taste
2 small potatoes, cooked and thinly sliced
1 small onion, thinly sliced
½ red bell pepper, cut into 1-inch squares
2 slices bacon, each cut into 3 pieces
Chile oil or cracked black pepper, to taste
Chopped fresh parsley, for garnish

1. Preheat the broiler. Oil a baking sheet.

2. Sprinkle the steaks lightly with salt and pepper, and place them on the prepared baking sheet.

3. Cover each steak with a layer of overlapping slices of potato, onion, and bell pepper. Arrange the bacon on top. Drizzle on a small amount of chile oil, or sprinkle with cracked pepper.

4. Broil until the vegetables are lightly charred and the fish is cooked through, 8 minutes. Sprinkle with parsley, and serve.

2 portions

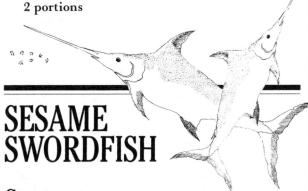

SESAME SWORDFISH

Crunchy toasted sesame seeds and fresh-tasting scallions complement a sautéed swordfish steak perfectly.

2 tablespoons sesame seeds
4 tablespoons sesame oil
4 swordfish steaks (8 ounces each)
1 cup fish stock (see Index)
5 scallions (green onions), white bulb and 3 inches green,
    thinly sliced on the diagonal

1. Preheat the oven to 350°F.

2. Spread out the sesame seeds in a small baking pan. Place in the oven and toast the seeds until they are lightly browned, 3 to 5 minutes. Check after 3 minutes and if the seeds are not done, shake the pan and continue to toast, watching carefully to prevent burning. Remove from the oven and set aside. Raise the oven temperature to 375°F.

3. Heat 3 tablespoons of the oil in a skillet until very hot. Quickly sear the swordfish on both sides, 1 minute per side. Transfer the fish to a baking dish, but retain the skillet.

4. Pour the fish stock into the baking dish, and bake until the fish flakes slightly, 5 minutes.

5. Add the remaining 1 tablespoon oil to the skillet, and sauté the scallions for 1 minute.

6. Serve the fish garnished with scallions and sesame seeds.

4 portions

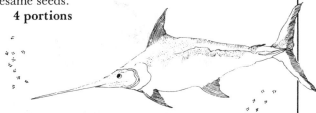

GROUPER NICOISE

We sing the praises of this fish. Although it looks like a marine monster, with its armor-plated head patterned with rust, vermilion, bronze, and gold, it tastes extraordinarily like lobster. Superb!

2 grouper fillets (about 6 ounces each)
Salt and freshly ground black pepper, to taste
Flour for dredging
1 tablespoon unsalted butter
Fresh Summer Tomato Sauce (see Index)
¼ cup Niçoise olives, pitted
1 tablespoon chopped fresh mint leaves

1. Season the fillets lightly with salt and pepper, and dredge in the flour. Shake off the excess.

2. Melt the butter in a skillet, and sauté the fillets just until golden, 1 minute per side. Cover with the tomato sauce, and sprinkle with the olives. Cover, and simmer until the fish is cooked through, 10 minutes. Sprinkle with fresh mint, and serve.

2 portions

HOW TO PEEL A TOMATO

Fill a saucepan with water and bring it to a boil. Cut a small X just through the skin on the bottom of the tomato. Place a tomato on the end of a long-handled fork, and hold it in the boiling water for 30 seconds. Then remove the tomato, dip it in cold water to cool it off, and peel off the skin starting at the X.

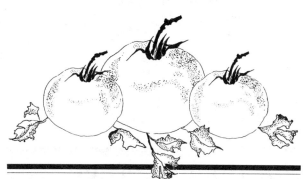

GAEL GREENE'S SWORDFISH WITH THE LAST OF THE GREAT TOMATOES

Gael has been a great inspiration, always furthering our love and appreciation of food through her magical writing. For years we've enjoyed reading Gael's entertaining restaurant reviews in *New York Magazine*.

Here's what Gael has to say about this recipe:

"I can never forget the class in James Beard's kitchen on the night we made his rolled leg of lamb, simmered and steamed in a big enameled cast-iron pot. It was studded with garlic and anchovies, as I recall, and served very rare with a garnish of minced black olives, minced lemon peel, finely chopped raw garlic, and snipped parsley. That night everything we made had garlic in it, except for the cassis sorbet. Much later, the man in my life, kissing the inside of my elbow, looked up at me with an unhappy expression and said, 'Do you know there is garlic oozing out of your skin?'

"I love the garnish so much that I do a version of it with this swordfish dish, which I like seared on the outside and just warm within."

TOMATO SAUCE

3 or 4 large ripe tomatoes
2 tablespoons finely minced shallots
2 tablespoons extra virgin olive oil
½ teaspoon fresh lemon juice
Pinch of sugar
1 teaspoon chopped cilantro (fresh coriander) or fresh Italian (flat-leaf) parsley

GARNISH

4 teaspoons finely minced garlic
1 teaspoon extra virgin olive oil
3 tablespoons minced pitted imported black olives (Greek or Moroccan)
4 teaspoons finely minced lemon zest
3 tablespoons chopped cilantro (fresh coriander) or fresh Italian (flat-leaf) parsley

2 pounds swordfish steak, 1 inch thick
1 cup dried bread crumbs
Salt and freshly ground black pepper, to taste
2 tablespoons unsalted butter, clarified (see Index)
2 tablespoons olive oil
Cilantro or parsley sprigs, for garnish

1. Make the sauce: Peel, seed, and chop the tomatoes, reserving the juice. Combine the tomatoes and their juice with the remaining sauce ingredients in a mixing bowl. Stir, and set aside.

2. For the garnish, combine the garlic and oil in a small bowl. Let rest for 5 minutes. Then add the remaining ingredients, stir, and set aside.

3. Cut the swordfish into 1-inch cubes. Combine the bread crumbs and salt and pepper in a plastic or paper bag. Add the swordfish, and shake to coat.

4. Heat 1 tablespoon of the clarified butter with 1 tablespoon of the olive oil in a nonstick skillet over medium heat. Sauté the swordfish until crusty brown on the outside and just warm within, about 2 minutes on each side. Cook the cubes in fairly small batches, adding butter and oil as needed.

5. Place a pool of tomato sauce in the center of four dinner plates, and arrange the swordfish cubes on the sauce. Sprinkle the olive garnish over the top, and decorate with a sprig of cilantro.

4 portions

SEASHORE SHELLFISH

Glorious shellfish is at last readily available around the country, dazzling our eyes as well as our palates. Glistening black and jade-green mussels abound. Shrimp and oysters range from tiny to large exotic species. And who can resist fresh lobsters, crawfish, and soft-shell and Dungeness crabs?

Transform the market's finest into exciting tastes, some traditional—Shrimp Scampi, New England Clam Chowder, Scalloped Oysters—and some that transcend to new heights—Soft-Shell Crab Sandwiches, Seafood Pepperpot, and Bayou Butter Crawfish.

SHOPPING FOR SHELLFISH

Since shellfish is often eaten raw, it is particularly important that it be super-fresh. Like fish, it will have a fresh, briny odor, never one that is "bad-smelling" or ammoniated. Mollusks bought in the shell (mussels, scallops, clams, and oysters) should always be alive and the shells should be tightly closed (except for scallops, which naturally hold their shells open), or should close quickly in response to gentle pressure. Avoid broken or cracked shells. Unless you are buying them already cooked, crabs, lobsters, and crayfish should be alive when purchased.

MUSSELS

The most commonly available mussel in America is the blue mussel, with its familiar purple-black shell. Choose ones with unchipped, closed shells and easy-to-spot beards. You may also encounter the exotic green-shelled mussel, now being imported from New Zealand, which does not taste substantially different from the blue mussel. The flesh of both ranges from creamy ivory to deep orange, edged with black.

SCALLOPS

There are hundreds of species of scallops throughout the world, but the two best-known in America are the large sea scallops and smaller bay scallops. Bay scallops are generally considered to be the more desirable of the two (perhaps, in part, because they are in short supply), and are very expensive. Sea and bay scallops range in color from ivory to tan with orange or pinkish tints.

If you are lucky, your fish market may sell scallops still in their shells, with the bright orange roe attached. (The delicate roe is completely edible and delicious.) Scallops that are not fresh have an unmistakably unpleasant sulphurous smell. Shucked scallops should be very firm; if they look like they are melting into one another, they are past their prime.

CLAMS

The two most popular types of clam found on the East Coast of America are the hardshell, also known by its Indian name quahaug or quahog, and the softshell, commonly referred to as a steamer. You'll find hardshell clams sold in a variety of sizes, from the smallest, called littlenecks (not to be confused with the West Coast clam of the same name), to cherrystones, to the large chowder clams. Smaller hardshell clams are usually eaten raw or, if large, they're used in chowders. Softshell clams are distinguished by their soft neck or "siphon" that protrudes from the shell, and are most often served steamed or fried.

The most popular West Coast clams are the native hardshell littlenecks, often eaten raw, and the impressively large geoducks (*gooey-ducks*), whose shell grows to be 7 inches across. The long, thick neck of the geoduck is either sliced and fried (some say it tastes like abalone) or ground up for chowder.

Clams are available in the shell or shucked. Shucked clams should be plump and fresh-smelling. Look for geoducks with short, fat, unwrinkled necks; after a few days out of the water the neck begins to dehydrate and shrivel.

OYSTERS

Oysters vary in appearance, flavor, and texture, depending on where they live and what they eat. There are an astonishing number on the market, named for the bays in which they are grown. Some of those you are likely to see are Blue Points, Chincoteagues, Cotuits, Malpêques and Wellfleets. And if you're lucky enough to live in the Northwest, you're probably familiar with the tiny sweet Olympia oyster, which is rarely sold outside its home territory.

Oysters are available in the shell or shucked. Shucked oysters should be packed in clear, not milky, liquid.

SQUID

Also called by their Italian name, calamari, squid have bright white flesh and red-brown spotted skin. Their eyes should be clear and their skin unbroken. The tentacles should be intact. Squid is available fresh or frozen. When estimating how much squid to buy, count on a yield of ¼ to ½ pound of clean flesh from a 10- to 12-inch-long squid.

SHRIMP

Although shrimp is in high demand in America, relatively little of it is sold fresh. Except around the Gulf, the Southeast, and the Northwest, the shrimp we see on the market has invariably been frozen and then thawed. It varies in color from pink to reddish brown to light gray. It is sold shelled or unshelled, but usually without the head because the head deteriorates very quickly. We prefer to buy them unshelled because the shells protect the meat.

Look for firm meat and shells that are firm and shiny and feel full. Black spots are a sign of aging. Cooked shrimp should be firm and bright white with a very mild odor.

SHRIMP SIZES:

Jumbo	10 per pound
Large	10 to 25 per pound
Medium	25 to 40 per pound
Small	40 to 60 per pound
Tiny	over 60 per pound

CRABS

The most commercially important crabs sold fresh in the United States are the blue crab (in both its hard- and soft-shell state), the Dungeness crab and the stone crab. You can buy blue crabs, with their blue-green shells and claws, all year long, but they are more readily available between June and October. Most blue crabs are harvested in the Chesapeake Bay. When blue crabs molt, they are sold as highly prized soft-shell crabs. Their peak season is June through August.

Dungeness crabs, found in the Pacific, are pinkish-yellow and weigh between 1¾ and 4 pounds. Their season is late fall to early winter.

Stone crabs from Florida have pink and white claws that are tipped with black. Only their claws are eaten. Their extremely hard shells must be hammered to crack them.

Crabs (including the softshell variety) should be very lively and wave their claws when you pick them up. When refrigerated, they will be more sluggish but should still be active. If you're in doubt, don't buy. You may want to ask your fishmonger to secure the claws with rubber bands to prevent your being pinched.

Crab is also sold frozen in the shell, or shelled and cooked. Cooked meat should be pure white, with some pink coloring. You should buy about 5 ounces of cooked crab per person.

Cooked, picked crabmeat is graded in three categories: Jumbo lump, or backfin, refers to large pieces of white meat from the body; flake, special, or body meat refers to smaller pieces of meat from the body; and claw meat refers to meat from the claws, which is typically brownish in color.

LOBSTER

Lobsters are sold by size, and the size doesn't much affect the quality of the meat. You'll find lobsters, weighing from about 1 pound to over 2½ pounds. When buying live lobsters, choose ones that appear very lively both in the water and when lifted from it.

CRAWFISH (CRAYFISH)

Crawfish (crayfish on the West Coast) are sweet freshwater shellfish that look like tiny lobsters. There are two types available in America—one from Louisiana and one from the West Coast—but the differences between the two are so minimal as to be unimportant. If you are lucky, you may be able to buy them live, in which case they should be very frisky. Or you may find whole, cooked crawfish, or raw or cooked tail meat.

NEW ENGLAND CLAM CHOWDER

This is, without question, the favored chowder of those on the northeastern seaboard. Serve this, steaming hot, from a tureen at the table. Or put the chunky ingredients—clams and potatoes—in soup bowls, and serve, ladling the smooth soup over top at table. A bit of theatrics while you're keeping the soup piping hot at the same time!

2 dozen cherrystone clams, well scrubbed
2 cups water
8 ounces slab bacon, cut into ½-inch dice
2 tablespoons unsalted butter
2 large onions, peeled and cut into ¼-inch dice
    (about 4 cups)
¼ cup unbleached all-purpose flour
6 potatoes, peeled and cut into ½-inch dice
    (about 4 cups)
1½ teaspoons dried thyme
Freshly ground black pepper, to taste
2 cups milk
2 cups heavy or whipping cream
3 tablespoons chopped fresh Italian (flat-leaf) parsley

1. Place the clams in a large soup pot along with the 2 cups water. Cover, and cook over medium heat until the clams open. Remove from the heat and allow to cool slightly. Discard any that don't open.

2. Remove the clams from their shells, and coarsely chop the clams. Strain; reserve the broth.

3. Cook the bacon in the soup pot over low heat until fat is rendered and the bacon is wilted and slightly browned on the edges, about 5 minutes.

4. Add the butter and onions, and cook, stirring, until the onions are wilted, 10 minutes. Add the flour and cook, stirring, another 5 minutes.

5. Add the reserved clam broth, potatoes, thyme, and pepper. Simmer 5 minutes longer.

6. Add the reserved chopped clams and simmer, stirring often, until they are tender, 12 to 15 minutes. Do not overcook, or the clams will be tough.

7. Add the milk and cream, and stir well over very low heat until hot. Do not boil, or the soup will curdle. Adjust the seasonings, stir in the parsley, and serve immediately.

10 to 12 portions

FREEZING SHELLFISH

Freeze shucked raw clams, oysters, or mussels in their liquor in an airtight plastic container for two to three months. Scallops may be frozen in the same manner, but their texture will hold up better if they are poached first. Freeze squid in plastic, as for fish, for up to two to three months. Cooked crab and lobster meat may be frozen in heavy airtight plastic bags for up to two months.

I'LL TAKE MANHATTAN CHOWDER

There are two different philosophies on clam chowder, and the twain shall never agree on which is best. But for the times you'd like your clams in a sweet tomato soup, here's our best.

6 slices bacon, cut into 1-inch pieces
2 tablespoons unsalted butter
1 cup chopped onions
½ cup chopped celery
½ cup chopped green bell pepper
½ cup chopped carrots
½ cup chopped leeks
24 cherrystone clams, shucked, in their liquid
1 can (15 ounces) plum tomatoes
1 cup Berta's Chicken Stock (see Index) or canned broth
1½ cups diced peeled potatoes
½ teaspoon dried thyme
Salt and freshly ground black pepper, to taste
2 tablespoons chopped fresh Italian (flat-leaf) parsley

1. In a large soup pot, sauté the bacon until it is soft and has rendered fat, about 5 minutes. Do not let it brown.

2. Add the butter. When it has melted, add the onions, celery, green pepper, carrots, and leeks. Cook over low heat until tender, about 10 minutes.

3. Drain the clams, reserving the liquid. Coarsely chop the clams, and set aside.

4. Add the reserved clam liquid, tomatoes, chicken stock, and potatoes to the pot. Cover, and simmer 15 minutes.

5. Add the clams, thyme, and salt and pepper. Cook, uncovered, until the clams are tender, 10 to 15 minutes.

6. Serve immediately, garnished with the parsley.

6 portions

THE LOIRE VALLEY WINES

Although the wines of the Loire Valley are less well known to the typical American consumer than those of other French wine districts, they are highly regarded in France. The wines are named for the varietal from which they are made:

▲ **Muscadet** is a fairly well-known, full-bodied white that is excellent served chilled with mussels, clams, shrimp, and lobster.

▲ **Sancerre** is a dry white made exclusively from the sauvignon blanc grape; stylish, light, and crisp, it is wonderful with seafood.

▲ **Vouvray,** one of the better-known whites from the Loire, made from the chenin blanc grape, is dry and soft, with just a hint of sweetness. Vouvray is just right served with hearty rillettes of duck or pork, and grilled boudin noir served with puréed celery root and pears, or our chunky applesauce.

STEAMED LITTLENECKS

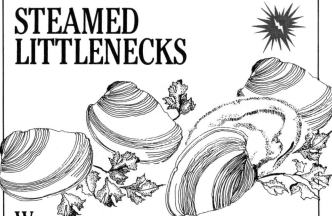

We love the microwave for steaming shellfish. In just 10 minutes you have a perfectly cooked dish, ready to put on the table. Serve this in shallow soup bowls, spooning the broth over clams—or serve it as an entrée over linguine or angel hair pasta.

2 dozen littleneck clams, well scrubbed
1 tablespoon salt
1 tablespoon cornmeal
½ cup dry white wine
½ cup water
4 tablespoons (½ stick) unsalted butter
2 shallots, peeled and chopped
2 tablespoons chopped fresh parsley
2 cloves garlic, minced
1 ripe plum tomato, diced

1. Place the clams in a large bowl and cover them with cold water. Sprinkle with the salt and cornmeal. Let stand 1 hour. Rinse, and drain.

2. In a microwave-safe casserole large enough to hold the clams in one layer, combine the wine, water, butter, shallots, parsley, garlic, and tomato. Stir well. Cook on full power (650 to 700 watts) uncovered, for 5 minutes.

3. Add the clams. Cover, and cook until the clams open, 5 to 6 minutes, stirring after 3 minutes. Discard any unopened clams.

2 to 4 portions

Note: This recipe was cooked on High (full power, 650 to 700 watts) in a carousel microwave, using microwave-safe containers.

If your microwave is less powerful, you will have to allow for more cooking time (approximately 1 ½ times the amount called for—but watch carefully); if it does not have a carousel, you may have to rotate the dish while it is cooking.

PORTUGUESE CLAMS

Steamed in a tangy broth touched with the fresh taste of cilantro. Lovely served with thick slices of country bread.

3 dozen littleneck clams (as small as you can find), well
*   scrubbed*
1 tablespoon cornmeal
1 tablespoon salt
1 cup dry white wine
3 tablespoons unsalted butter
2 tablespoons olive oil
2 cloves garlic, minced
1 teaspoon grated lemon zest
¼ cup chopped cilantro (fresh coriander)
Chopped cilantro, for garnish

1. Place the clams in a large bowl and cover them with cold water. Sprinkle with the cornmeal and salt. Let stand 1 hour. Rinse, and drain.

2. In a large skillet combine the wine, butter, oil, garlic, and lemon zest. Bring to a simmer over medium-low heat; cover, and cook 1 minute.

3. Add the clams and ¼ cup cilantro to the skillet. Cover and cook, shaking the skillet once or twice until the clams open, about 5 minutes. Discard any clams that haven't opened.

4. Spoon the clams and liquid into four shallow bowls. Sprinkle with the cilantro and serve.

4 portions

SCALLOPED OYSTERS

A Northeastern classic (originally called a chowder), this makes a lovely luncheon dish that should be accompanied by a bright green salad.

10 tablespoons (1 ¼ sticks) unsalted butter
2 shallots, peeled and finely chopped
1 ¾ cups saltine cracker crumbs
2 cups shucked oysters in their liquor
7 tablespoons heavy or whipping cream
½ teaspoon Worcestershire sauce
Dash of Tabasco sauce
½ teaspoon dried thyme leaves, crumbled
¼ teaspoon freshly ground black pepper
1 teaspoon chopped fresh Italian (flat-leaf) parsley
Salt, to taste

1. Preheat the oven to 350°F.

2. Melt the butter in a medium-size skillet. Add the shallots and wilt over medium heat for 5 minutes. Remove the skillet from the heat and using a fork, stir in the cracker crumbs.

3. Spread half the crumb mixture over the bottom of a 6 x 8-inch ovenproof baking dish.

4. Drain the oysters, reserving the liquor, and lay them evenly over the crumbs. Cover the oysters with the remaining crumb mixture.

5. In a small mixing bowl, combine the reserved oyster liquor, cream, Worcestershire, Tabasco, thyme, pepper, parsley and salt. Pour this over the oysters.

6. Bake on the center rack of the oven until brown and bubbly, 30 to 35 minutes.

6 portions

PREPARING CLAMS AND OYSTERS

Place clam or Oyster on a towel in the palm of your hand — Face hinge away from your body

insert the tip of a shucking knife between shells near the hinge

hinge

Try to hold the clam or oyster level so as not to lose the liquor.

Work knife back and forth to carefully pry the shells apart

— deep shell on bottom

Work the edge of an oyster shucker into the hinge of the shell — Proceed as for clams!

Move the knife along upper shell and carefully cut at the hinge. Discard top shell.

top shell

hinge

clam

Cut from underneath to free from the shell.

SHRIMP ON A BED OF LEEKS

Light and easy to prepare, this dish makes a meal. The leeks and shrimp still have a slight crispness to them, in both flavor and texture, when cooked in the microwave. It's delicious served over couscous in shallow soup plates.

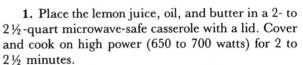

¼ cup fresh lemon juice
1 tablespoon olive oil
1 teaspoon unsalted butter
2 leeks (white part and ½ inch green), well rinsed and cut into fine julienne
½ cup coarsely chopped fresh Italian (flat-leaf) parsley
1 tablespoon chopped fresh rosemary
½ teaspoon sugar
¼ teaspoon freshly ground black pepper
4 ripe plum tomatoes, cut into 1-inch pieces
1 pound large shrimp, peeled and deveined

1. Place the lemon juice, oil, and butter in a 2- to 2½-quart microwave-safe casserole with a lid. Cover and cook on high power (650 to 700 watts) for 2 to 2½ minutes.

2. Add the leeks, parsley, and rosemary. Sprinkle with the sugar and pepper. Stir well, cover, and cook another 2½ minutes.

3. Add the tomatoes, stir, cover, and cook 2 minutes. Then add the shrimp, and toss well with the vegetables and liquid. Cover and cook, stirring once, until the shrimp are done but not overcooked, 4½ to 5½ minutes.

4 portions

Note: This recipe was cooked on High (full power, 650 to 700 watts) in a carousel microwave, using microwave-safe containers.

If your microwave is less powerful, you will have to allow for more cooking time (approximately 1½ times the amount called for—but watch carefully); if it does not have a carousel, you may have to rotate the dish while it is cooking.

SHRIMP SCAMPI

We never tire of these, and shrimp are always everyone's favorite. Your guests will adore you.

6 tablespoons (¾ stick) unsalted butter, at room temperature
¼ cup olive oil
1 tablespoon minced garlic
1 tablespoon minced shallots
2 tablespoons snipped fresh chives
Salt and freshly ground black pepper, to taste
¼ teaspoon paprika
2 pounds large shrimp, peeled and deveined

1. Preheat the broiler.
2. Combine the butter, olive oil, garlic, shallots, chives, salt and pepper, and paprika in a large bowl. Blend thoroughly.
3. Toss the shrimp in the mixture until thoroughly coated.
4. Broil the shrimp as close as possible to the flame for 2 minutes on each side. Serve immediately.
   4 portions

AN ITALIAN BUFFET

Pesto and Walnut Risotto

Shrimp Scampi
Sweet Pea and Mint Purée
Prosciutto and Onion Bread
Pinot Blanc

Red Berry Mousse

PREPARING SHRIMP

You may cook shrimp in their shells or peel them first. If you peel them, you will probably want to devein them as well, although it is not absolutely necessary, particularly for small shrimp.

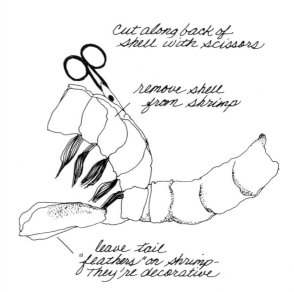

Cut along back of shell with scissors

remove shell from shrimp

leave tail "feathers" on shrimp—They're decorative

Peel a narrow strip on the back of the shrimp down to the tail

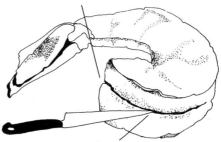

With tip of knife remove intestinal track—"deveining" Continue with recipe

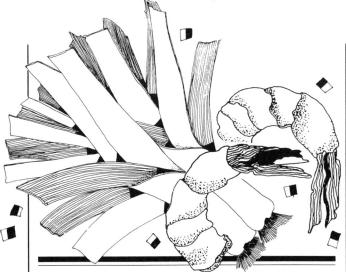

SHRIMP PROVENCAL

Not the typical French dish, but a more intense-tasting Italian version resplendent with sun-dried tomatoes and oil-cured olives.

2 tablespoons olive oil
1 leek (white part and 1 inch green), well rinsed and cut into ½-inch dice
1 rib celery, thinly sliced
1 cup dry white wine
1 tablespoon tomato paste
1 pound medium-size shrimp, peeled and deveined
12 oil-cured olives, pitted
½ cup slivered sun-dried tomatoes (packed in oil), drained
2 cloves garlic, minced
2 teaspoons herbes de Provence (see Note)
Salt and freshly ground black pepper, to taste
Chopped fresh parsley, for garnish

1. Heat the oil in a large skillet, and add the leek and celery. Sauté over low heat until soft, about 5 minutes.
2. Stir in the wine and tomato paste, and bring to a boil.
3. Stir in the shrimp, olives, sun-dried tomatoes, garlic, and herbs. Raise the heat to medium and cook just until the shrimp are cooked through, 2 to 3 minutes. Season with salt and pepper, sprinkle with parsley, and serve immediately.

4 portions

Note: Herbes de Provence is an aromatic blend of thyme, rosemary, lavender, and summer savory. It is available in many specialty food shops and some supermarkets.

BAYOU BUTTER CRAWFISH

Fresh crawfish from Louisiana are usually available between January and May—and the fresh are certainly the best! Roll up your sleeves, gather around the table, and eat away. Snap the head from the tail. Peel the shell off the tails in rings, and enjoy the sweet meat. Make sure you have finger bowls and lots of cold beer on hand!

3 quarts water
1 tablespoon salt
Freshly ground black pepper, to taste
2 teaspoons ground cardamom
2 teaspoons ground allspice
20 allspice berries, crushed
6 bay leaves
1 teaspoon ground cloves
1 teaspoon caraway seeds, crushed
1 lemon, halved
2 pounds crawfish, rinsed briefly in cold water

FLAVORED BUTTER
4 tablespoons (½ stick) butter, melted
1 teaspoon fresh lemon juice
¼ teaspoon ground allspice
¼ teaspoon ground cardamom
Salt and freshly ground black pepper, to taste
1 tablespoon chopped fresh parsley

To clean... twist center of tail and pull out the dark vein.

1. Heat the water in a large pot, and add the salt, a generous amount of pepper, and the cardamom, ground allspice and berries, bay leaves, ground cloves, and caraway seeds. Squeeze the lemon into the water and add the halves. Bring to a boil, then reduce the heat, cover, and simmer 15 minutes.
2. Add the crawfish all at once, and bring back to a boil. Reduce the heat again and simmer just until cooked through, 4 to 5 minutes.
3. Meanwhile, stir all the butter ingredients together in a small bowl.
4. Drain the crawfish and serve in a large bowl, with flavored butter on the side.

2 portions

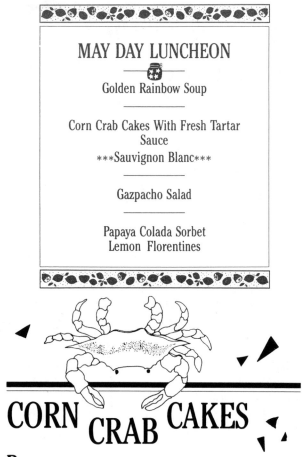

MAY DAY LUNCHEON

Golden Rainbow Soup

Corn Crab Cakes With Fresh Tartar
Sauce
Sauvignon Blanc

Gazpacho Salad

Papaya Colada Sorbet
Lemon Florentines

CORN CRAB CAKES

Blue crabs from the Chesapeake Bay are traditionally used in crab cakes. But because of their size—which makes them sweet, but scant—we sometimes save them for delicious bisques and sauces and instead use the Dungeness or Alaskan crab for cakes. Whichever you choose, lightness, plenty of crab, and a bit of a bite are the secrets of crab cakes.

1 pound fresh or frozen lump crabmeat, cartilage removed
1 cup cooked corn
½ cup finely diced onion
½ cup finely diced green bell pepper
½ cup finely diced celery
1 cup mayonnaise
½ teaspoon dry mustard
Pinch of cayenne pepper
Salt and freshly ground black pepper, to taste
1 egg, lightly beaten
1 ¼ cups saltine cracker crumbs
2 tablespoons olive oil
2 tablespoons unsalted butter
Tartar Sauce (recipe follows)

1. Combine the crabmeat, corn, onion, bell pepper, and celery in a mixing bowl, and toss well.

2. In another bowl, combine the mayonnaise with the mustard and cayenne pepper. Stir into the crabmeat mixture, and add salt and pepper. Then, using a rubber spatula, gently fold in the egg and ¼ cup of the cracker crumbs.

3. Form the crab mixture into eight patties. Carefully coat the patties with the remaining 1 cup cracker crumbs, and chill, covered, for at least 30 minutes, but no longer than a few hours.

4. Heat 1 tablespoon of the oil and 1 tablespoon of the butter in a medium-size skillet. Cook the crab cakes over medium heat until golden on both sides, about 3 minutes per side, adding more oil and butter as necessary. Serve immediately, with Tartar Sauce on the side.

4 portions

TARTAR SAUCE

We love tartar sauce with our fried flounder, crab cakes, and catfish! It's great when made fresh.

1 cup mayonnaise
2 tablespoons fresh lemon juice
1 teaspoon Worcestershire sauce
Dash of Tabasco sauce
¼ cup finely diced dill pickle
¼ cup chopped fresh Italian (flat-leaf) parsley
2 tablespoons finely minced shallots
2 tablespoons tiny capers, drained
Salt and freshly ground black pepper, to taste

Mix the mayonnaise, lemon juice, Worcestershire sauce, and Tabasco together in a bowl. Fold in the pickle, parsley, shallots, and capers. Season with salt and pepper, and refrigerate, loosely covered, at least 1 hour before serving (so the flavors will come out).

1 ½ cups

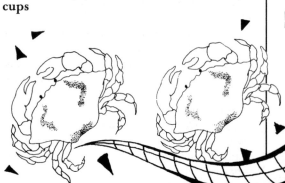

PREPARING CRABS

▼

SOFTSHELL | HARDSHELL

SOFTSHELL

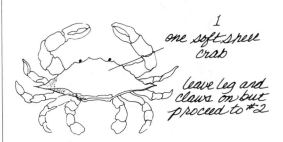

1

one soft shell crab

leave leg and claws on but proceed to #2

2

Turn crab over

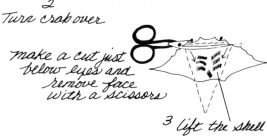

make a cut just below eyes and remove face with a scissors

3 Lift the shell to remove gills and innards

4

Back side up, remove the apron

5

Cook and enjoy your crab. What's left is edible!

HARDSHELL

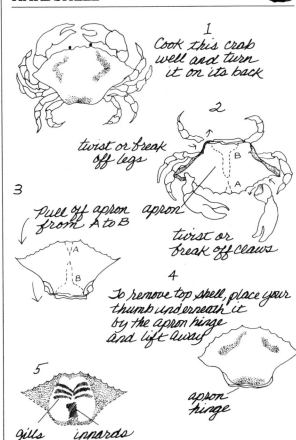

1

Cook this crab well and turn it on its back

2

twist or break off legs

apron

twist or break off claws

3

Pull off apron from A to B

4

To remove top shell, place your thumb underneath it by the apron hinge and lift away

apron hinge

5

gills   innards

Remove and discard the gills and innards

6

Break remaining crab in half lengthwise and pick out the meat

7

this is the delicious crab meat

THE WHITE WINES OF AMERICA

The chardonnay grape is California's grandest white varietal. Well-balanced, full-bodied wines, comparable to some of Burgundy's best, they range in style from light and delicate, resplendent with the fruity aromas of autumn apples and lush ripe melons, to the richer, more complex wines that are enhanced by aging in oak.

Chardonnays are perfect, lightly chilled, with white meats such as chicken, veal, and pork, and also with shellfish and fish. They are gutsy enough to stand up to a cream sauce and are a good accompaniment to full-flavored seafood dishes. Don't forget to put a bottle in the refrigerator as soon as the tips of spring asparagus poke through the ground.

The wines of the Sauvignon Blanc grape, also known as Fumé Blancs in America, are wonderfully dry and crisp full-bodied wines that we love to serve with seafood, and especially with shellfish. Well chilled, they complement all the glorious California goat cheeses that are currently available. Serve a selection of cheeses ranging from the creamy fresh to the harder aged varieties, along with ripe fruit and crusty bread for a simple summer luncheon.

Chenin Blanc is a lovely, light, fruity wine which is ideally suited to seafood and delicate poultry dishes.

We think it is never a bad idea to keep your favorites of these popular American whites on hand, for they can be called upon to make almost any dinner an occasion.

SOFTSHELL CRAB SANDWICH ALMONDINE

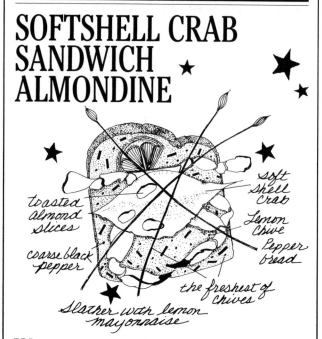

toasted almond slices

soft shell crab

Lemon Chive Pepper Bread

coarse black pepper

the freshest of chives

Slather with lemon mayonnaise

When it's softshell crab season, choose the smallest and sweetest and serve them this great new way. Lemony Almond Mayonnaise and toasted Lemon Chive Pepper Bread accent the sweet crabs beautifully. These sandwiches can go black tie or to a picnic.

½ cup unbleached all-purpose flour
Salt and freshly ground black pepper, to taste
4 small softshell crabs, cleaned
2 tablespoons unsalted butter
1 ¾ cups Almond Mayonnaise (recipe follows)
8 slices Lemon Chive Pepper Bread (see Index), ½ inch thick, toasted
⅓ cup slivered almonds, toasted (see Index)

1. Place the flour in a large bowl, and season it with salt and pepper. Lightly coat the crabs with the flour, shaking off any excess.

2. Melt the butter in a large skillet, and lightly sauté the crabs over medium heat, 3 to 4 minutes per side. Season them with additional salt and pepper as they cook.

3. Generously spread the mayonnaise over the 8 toast slices, and sprinkle them with the slivered almonds. Top four of the slices with the sautéed crabs, and set the remaining slices on top, at an angle. Serve immediately and pass the remaining mayonnaise.

4 portions

ALMOND MAYONNAISE

1 egg
1 teaspoon Dijon mustard
½ teaspoon salt
2 teaspoons fresh lemon juice
1 cup extra virgin olive oil
3 tablespoons finely grated lemon zest
3 tablespoons snipped fresh chives
¼ cup finely chopped toasted blanched almonds (see Index)

★ Combine the egg, mustard, salt, and lemon juice in a food processor, and process until blended. With the motor running, slowly drizzle in the olive oil through the feed tube, and blend until thickened. Transfer the mayonnaise to a small bowl, and stir in the lemon zest, chives, and almonds. Set aside.

1 ¾ cups

A CRAB BOIL

When setting out to boil crab, some like to flavor the water with traditional crab-boil spices, while others prefer the simple addition of wine, a bay leaf, a lemon wedge, and a clove or two of garlic. We have our own way—a mixture of flat beer, vinegar, and a bit of pickle juice, seasoned with mustard, paprika, salt, pepper, and a touch of garlic. Pile the crabs into a steamer in a large pot and let the liquid bubble for about 30 minutes. When the crabs turn bright red, you're ready to start cracking shells.

The best way to eat crab is off of newspaper at a large table with as many close friends as you can gather together. Accompany them with plenty of beer and iced tea. Have nutcrackers and hammers spread around—there's pickings for everyone.

BILLI BI

This velvety mussel soup offers a strong winey taste and a hint of saffron.

2 tablespoons unsalted butter
2 large shallots, peeled
  and chopped
2 dozen mussels, well scrubbed
  and bearded (see Step 3)
2 cups dry white wine,
  such as Chablis
2 egg yolks
½ cup crème fraîche (see Index)
Several saffron threads
Salt and freshly ground
  black pepper, to taste
Chopped fresh parsley,
  for garnish

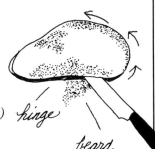

hinge

beard

1. Melt the butter in a 2-quart microwave-safe casserole on full power (650 to 700 watts), uncovered, for 2 minutes.
2. Stir in the shallots; cook for 2 minutes.
3. Beard the mussels right before cooking them, otherwise they will die and spoil. Add the mussels and wine. Cover, and cook until the mussels open, 6 minutes. Discard any unopened ones.
4. Using a slotted spoon, transfer the mussels to a bowl. Cover and keep warm.
5. Strain the cooking liquid, pressing against the shallots with a wooden spoon. Return the liquid to the casserole, and whisk in the egg yolks, crème fraîche, and saffron. Cook, uncovered, whisking after each minute, until slightly thickened, 3 minutes. Season with salt and pepper.
6. Arrange the mussels (in their shells) in four soup plates. Pour the soup over them, sprinkle with parsley, and serve at once.

4 portions

Note: This recipe was cooked on High (full power, 650 to 700 watts) in a carousel microwave, using microwave-safe containers.

If your microwave is less powerful, you will have to allow for more cooking time (approximately 1 ½ times the amount called for—but watch carefully); if it does not have a carousel, you may have to rotate the dish while it is cooking.

SEAFOOD GUMBO

In the South, many stew-like dishes that contain tomatoes and sweet peppers are called gumbos, but actually they are Creole dishes. As any authentic gumbo cook will tell you, "if it ain't got okra, it ain't gumbo!" That's the difference. Serve this over white rice.

8 ounces kielbasa or Cajun sausage, cut into 1-inch slices
⅓ cup olive oil
1 pound okra, stems removed
2 cups diced onions
1 cup coarsely chopped red bell pepper
1 cup coarsely chopped green bell pepper
4 cloves garlic, finely minced
5 cups Berta's Chicken Stock (see Index) or canned broth
3 cups drained canned plum tomatoes, slightly crushed
1 teaspoon ground cumin
½ teaspoon cayenne pepper
½ teaspoon salt
½ teaspoon freshly ground black pepper
1 bay leaf
1 pound large shrimp, peeled and deveined
12 ounces sea scallops
12 ounces cooked lobster meat
8 ounces lump crabmeat, cartilage removed
2 tablespoons chopped fresh Italian (flat-leaf) parsley

1. In a large pot or dutch oven, sauté the sausage over medium heat until brown, about 15 minutes. Remove it from the pot and set aside.

2. Add half the oil to the pot. Then add the okra and cook over medium heat until slightly soft, about 15 minutes. Add the remaining oil, onions, bell peppers, and garlic. Stir, and cook another 10 minutes.

3. Add the chicken stock, tomatoes, cumin, cayenne, salt, black pepper, and bay leaf. Simmer, uncovered, for 30 minutes.

4. Add the shrimp and scallops to the gumbo and simmer another 5 minutes. Then add the lobster, crabmeat, and parsley, adjust the seasonings, and heat through, 2 to 3 minutes. Serve immediately.

8 portions

KEEPING SHELLFISH FRESH

Refrigerate live shellfish in a dry dish covered with moist seaweed (if you have access to it) or damp paper towels; do not store on ice, in water, or in plastic. Because oysters naturally open and close their shells, they need to be stored cupped-shell down so that their liquor doesn't drain out. Correctly refrigerated, clams and mussels will last up to two days and oysters somewhat longer, up to one week. Cleaned squid should be stored in leak-proof bags.

Cooked shellfish should be stored separately from raw to protect against any cross-contamination of bacteria from the raw shellfish.

BOBBIE'S "BOUILLABAISSE"

A true bouillabaisse can be an intimidating undertaking, but we do love a hearty fish soup on a cold winter's night. Our dear friends Bobbie and Bert have come up with this delicious version that is easy to prepare—just be sure you use the freshest seafood available. Serve with a spicy Rouille, the traditional Provençal red pepper sauce used to flavor soups.

2 dozen cherrystone clams, well scrubbed
¼ cup cornmeal
1 tablespoon plus 1 teaspoon salt
2 lobsters (1 ½ pounds each), boiled or steamed
4 slices bacon, cut into 1-inch pieces
2 carrots, peeled and sliced into ¼-inch-thick rounds
1 green bell pepper, cored, seeded, and diced
1 onion, diced
5 potatoes (about 1 pound), quartered
1 can (28 ounces) plum tomatoes, drained and coarsely
*   chopped*
1 cup water
1 cup dry red wine
1 bay leaf
½ teaspoon dried thyme leaves
Freshly ground black pepper, to taste
Pinch of sugar
2 dozen jumbo shrimp, shelled and deveined
2 pounds red snapper or scrod fillets (cut into 6 pieces each)
Chopped fresh basil leaves or parsley, for garnish
8 Garlic Croutons (recipe follows; optional)
1 ⅓ cups Rouille (recipe follows)

1. Place the clams in a large bowl and cover them with cold water. Sprinkle with the cornmeal and 1 tablespoon of the salt. Let stand 1 hour. Rinse, and drain.

2. Remove and crack the lobster claws. Remove the tails and halve them lengthwise. Discard the bodies, and reserve the tails and claws.

3. Sauté the bacon in a large kettle or dutch oven until crisp, 5 minutes.

4. Add the carrots, green pepper, onion, and potatoes. Cover, and cook, stirring, 10 minutes.

5. Stir in the tomatoes, water, wine, bay leaf, remaining 1 teaspoon salt, thyme, pepper, and sugar. Simmer, uncovered, 10 minutes.

6. Stir in the shrimp. Cover, and cook 3 minutes. Add the lobster and simmer an additional 2 minutes. Using a slotted spoon, transfer the lobster and shrimp to a large platter. Keep warm in a low (250°F) oven.

7. Add the clams and fish fillets to the kettle. Cover, and cook until the clams open and the fillets are cooked through, 10 to 12 minutes. Transfer them to the platter.

8. To serve, place an assortment of fish and shellfish in large individual bowls; then ladle the vegetables and soup over the fish. Sprinkle with the parsley, and slide a crouton into each bowl. Top with a dollop of rouille.

8 portions

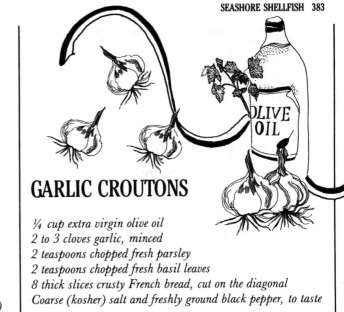

GARLIC CROUTONS

¼ cup extra virgin olive oil
2 to 3 cloves garlic, minced
2 teaspoons chopped fresh parsley
2 teaspoons chopped fresh basil leaves
8 thick slices crusty French bread, cut on the diagonal
Coarse (kosher) salt and freshly ground black pepper, to taste

1. Preheat the oven to 350°F.

2. In a small bowl, combine the olive oil, garlic, parsley, and basil. Stir well.

3. Spread 1 side of the French bread with generous amounts of the oil and herb mixture, then sprinkle with the coarse salt and pepper. Arrange the slices on a baking sheet, and bake until golden, 15 minutes.

8 croutons

ROUILLE

1 red bell pepper, roasted (see Index)
1 small hot red chile pepper, such as Santa Fe, cored and
*   seeded*
2 cloves garlic
1 egg yolk
½ teaspoon salt
Freshly ground black pepper, to taste
¾ cup olive oil
Few drops of fresh lemon juice

1. Place the roasted pepper in a food processor. Add the chile pepper, garlic, egg yolk, salt, and pepper. Purée until smooth. While the machine is running, slowly drizzle in the oil. Process until the mixture is thick and smooth.

2. Transfer the rouille to a bowl. Add the lemon juice. Season with additional salt and pepper, if desired.

About 1 ⅓ cups

> "In a bowl to sea went wise
>   men three,
> On a brilliant night in June;
> They carried a net, and their
>   hearts were set
> On fishing up the moon."
> —THOMAS LOVE PEACOCK

SEAFOOD PEPPERPOT

The sweetness of shrimp, crab, scallops, and grouper combined with sweet and hot peppers is a favorite of Caribbean residents and visitors alike. Each island has its own variation, depending on the herbs and spices grown there. This is great year-round—somehow those peppers just make a hot day feel cooler. Serve this over rice or another mild-flavored grain like barley.

1 pound bacon, cut into ½-inch pieces
1½ pounds okra, trimmed and sliced diagonally
2 tablespoons olive oil
2 red bell peppers, cut into ½-inch pieces
1 large onion, peeled and cut into ½-inch pieces
6 large cloves garlic, minced
2 cups canned plum tomatoes with their juice
3 fresh jalapeño peppers or other hot green chile peppers,
    cored, seeded, and finely minced (see Note)
4 teaspoons dried thyme
3 large bay leaves
1 teaspoon cayenne pepper
3 cups bottled clam juice
2 cups Berta's Chicken Stock (see Index) or canned broth
2 pounds grouper fillets, cut crosswise into 2-inch slices
1 pound sea scallops
1 pound large shrimp, peeled and deveined
8 ounces lump crabmeat, cartilage removed
Grated zest of 2 oranges
¼ cup chopped fresh Italian (flat-leaf) parsley

1. In a large heavy casserole, cook the bacon over medium heat until translucent. Add the okra and continue cooking until it is slightly brown and edges curl.

2. Add the olive oil, bell peppers, onion, and garlic. Continue cooking until the vegetables are soft, 7 to 10 minutes.

3. Add the tomatoes, chile peppers, thyme, bay leaves, and cayenne. Cook over medium-low heat for 15 minutes. Add the clam juice and chicken stock. Cook, partially covered, for 30 minutes.

4. Add the grouper and scallops and cook over medium-high heat for 2 minutes. Add the shrimp and cook an additional 3 minutes. Add the crabmeat and cook 1 minute more. Stir gently after each addition.

5. Gently fold in the orange zest, and sprinkle with the parsley. Serve immediately.

8 to 10 portions

Note: Wear rubber gloves when working with hot peppers, and be sure to wash your hands well when you're finished.

WINES WITH SHELLFISH

SHELLFISH	WINE
Clams, Crab, Lobster	Beaujolais-Villages, Sancerre, Sauvignon Blanc, Muscadet, Chardonnay, Tavel rosé
Mussels	Chablis, Fumé Blanc
Oysters	Champagne, Chardonnay
Scallops	Sauvignon Blanc, Pouilly Fumé
Shrimp	Pinot Blanc, Orvieto
Squid (calamari)	Soave, Riesling

LOBSTER BISQUE

A bisque is a thick cream soup containing shellfish. Here, a good deal of flavor comes from the lobster meat, but a good deal extra comes from the broth, in which the shells have simmered.

Lobster bisque is a bit of a project, and it obviously is expensive—but for that important dinner or celebration it is a truly elegant way to begin.

2 fresh lobsters (1½ pounds each), split and cleaned
12 tablespoons (1½ sticks) unsalted butter
1 cup diced peeled carrots
1 cup chopped onions
¼ cup coarsely chopped shallots
2 tablespoons chopped fresh Italian (flat-leaf) parsley
1 teaspoon dried tarragon
6 tablespoons brandy
2½ cups Berta's Chicken Stock (see Index) or canned broth
⅔ cup dry white wine
3 tablespoons Madeira
½ cup unbleached all-purpose flour
3 cups milk
3 cups half-and-half
2 ripe plum tomatoes, coarsely chopped
Pinch of cayenne pepper
Salt, to taste

1. Cut the lobster halves into three pieces each, and crack the claws.

2. Melt 6 tablespoons of the butter in a large saucepan over medium-low heat. Add the carrots, onions, and shallots and cook until the onions wilt, 5 to 7 minutes. Do not let them brown.

3. Add the lobster, parsley, and tarragon to the saucepan. Toss well, and cook over medium heat until the lobster shells turn red, 5 to 7 minutes.

4. Pour 4 tablespoons of the brandy over the lobsters and carefully ignite. When the flame goes out, add 1 cup of the chicken stock and the white wine. Simmer over low heat, partially covered, for 15 minutes. Remove from the heat.

5. Remove the lobster from the pan and allow to cool. Remove the meat from the shells and cut into ½-inch dice. Place the diced lobster in a small bowl and toss with the Madeira. Cover and reserve.

6. Coarsely crush the lobster shells, and reserve. Reserve the broth in the saucepan.

7. In a separate saucepan, melt the remaining 6 tablespoons butter. Add the flour, and blend with a wire whisk over low heat for 1 minute.

8. Bring the milk and half-and-half to a boil in another saucepan. Add this all at once to the flour mixture, and whisk constantly over low heat for 1½ minutes. Add this to the reserved broth.

9. Stir in the tomatoes, cayenne, and crushed lobster shells. Cover, and simmer over low heat for 15 minutes. Add the remaining 1½ cups chicken stock, cover, and simmer another 45 minutes. Season with salt if desired.

10. Pour the soup through a very fine strainer, pressing down on the shells and vegetables with the back of a spoon.

11. Return the soup to the saucepan and heat through. Stir in the remaining 2 tablespoons brandy and the reserved lobster meat. Serve immediately.

8 portions

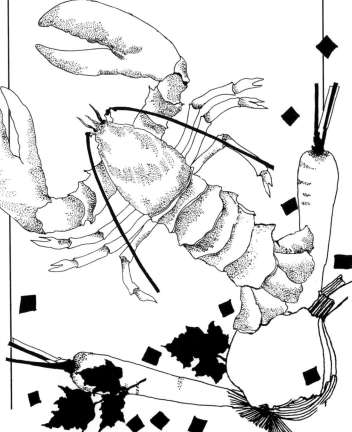

A BOILED LOBSTER LUNCH FOR TWO

These lobsters can be cooked in plain salted water. However, feel free to add chopped parsley, chives, basil, or tarragon; lemon peel; white wine; cracked pepper; and clam juice or fish stock to the cooking liquid for more flavor.

For a more humane approach, you may want to put these crustaceans out of their misery before boiling.

2 live lobsters (about 1 ¼ pounds each, preferably female; see Preparing Lobster box)
½ cup mayonnaise
¼ teaspoon salt
Freshly ground black pepper, to taste
¼ cup shredded lettuce, radicchio, or chicory leaves
¼ cup chopped fresh tomatoes
¼ cup chopped Kirby cucumber

1. Lower the lobsters carefully into a large pot of boiling salted water. Return to a boil and cook 6 minutes. Transfer the lobsters to a large bowl, and pour 1 cup of the cooking liquid over them. Allow to cool slightly.

2. Crack the lobster claws, cut through the underside of the tail, and remove the meat in large pieces. Halve the tail meat lengthwise. Discard the black vein behind the tail.

3. Lift out the tomalley (liver) and coral (eggs) if present. Transfer to a small bowl and mash with a fork or the back of a spoon while incorporating 2 tablespoons of the cooking liquid. Then whisk in the mayonnaise until smooth. (If there is no coral, simply combine the tomalley with the liquid and mayonnaise.) Season with salt and pepper.

4. Arrange the lobster meat artfully on a bed of crisp shredded greens. Surround with small mounds of tomato and cucumber. Set a small ramekin of sauce on the side of each plate.

2 portions

PREPARING LOBSTER

If you are planning to broil the lobster, you will want to kill it first. A reasonably humane way to do this is to grasp it by the tail to steady it, and then jab the tip of a large, sharp knife between the eyes—this will kill it instantly.

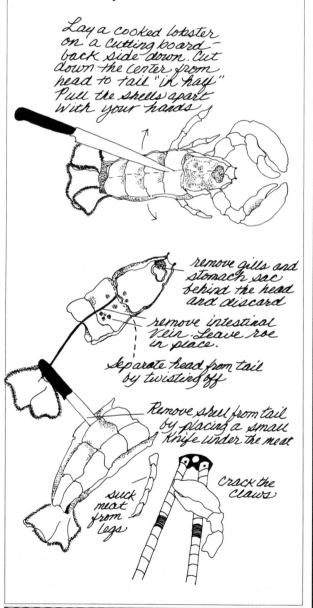

Lay a cooked lobster on a cutting board—back side down. Cut down the center from head to tail "in half." Pull the shells apart with your hands

remove gills and stomach sac behind the head and discard

remove intestinal vein. Leave roe in place.

Separate head from tail by twisting off

Remove shell from tail by placing a small knife under the meat

suck meat from legs

Crack the claws

LEMONY BROILED LOBSTERS

As kids, we always thought of lobster, especially broiled lobster, as *the* special going-out-to-dinner treat. Now lobsters are readily available in fish markets throughout the country and this at-home version of a classic favorite has a touch of lemon thyme and a grating of lemon zest to heighten the exquisite flavor of the dish.

2 live lobsters (about 1 ¼ to 1 ½ pounds each, preferably
*   female)*
5 tablespoons unsalted butter, melted
½ cup seasoned dried bread crumbs
¼ cup chopped fresh parsley
1 teaspoon grated lemon zest
1 teaspoon chopped fresh lemon thyme or thyme
Lemon wedges

   1. Prepare the lobsters by inserting the tip of a sharp knife into the flesh between the head and the body. (This severs the spinal cord.) Let stand 2 minutes.
   2. Crack the claws and remove any loose bits of shell.
   3. With the lobsters belly side up, use kitchen shears or a sharp chef's knife to halve each lobster lengthwise, cutting through the shell. You may leave little "hinges" of membrane or flesh to keep the halves attached for easier lifting. Fold back the sides and flatten to expose the flesh. Remove the coral, if present, and tomalley and place in a small bowl. Discard the black vein behind the tail.
   4. Stir 2 tablespoons of the butter, the bread crumbs, parsley, lemon zest, and thyme into the tomalley and coral (if there is any), mashing lightly until the mixture is smooth.
   5. Arrange the lobsters belly side up on a baking sheet or large broiler pan. Brush lightly with some of the remaining butter. Broil 2 minutes. Then brush with more butter, and broil until lobster meat is just opaque and the shells are red, about 1 ½ minutes. Sprinkle the crumb mixture in the cavities, and broil until the crumbs are golden and the tips of the shells are charred, 2 minutes.
   6. Serve immediately, with lemon wedges.
   2 portions

LOBSTER IN GREEN SAUCE "EL FARO"

Onion and garlic are mellowed by sherry and the crisp fresh taste of parsley for this emerald-green sauce. This dish was always a favorite at El Faro, a marvelous Spanish restaurant in Greenwich Village. A white Sangría is a perfect accompaniment.

2 live lobsters (about 1 ¼ pounds each)
3 tablespoons olive oil
3 tablespoons finely chopped white onion
1 teaspoon minced garlic
1 ½ tablespoons unbleached all-purpose flour
¾ cup fish stock (see Index) or bottled clam juice
¾ cup water
¼ cup finely chopped fresh parsley
2 tablespoons dry sherry
Chopped fresh parsley, for garnish

   1. Prepare the lobsters by inserting the tip of a sharp knife into the flesh between the head and the body. (This severs the spinal cord.) Let stand 2 minutes.
   2. Remove the claws and crack them. Remove the tails and cut them in half lengthwise, using a sharp chef's knife or kitchen shears. Discard the lobster bodies.
   3. Heat the oil in a skillet, and sauté the onion and garlic until slightly wilted, about 3 minutes.
   4. Add the lobster claws and tails, cover, and sauté, stirring occasionally, over medium heat, until the shells turn red, about 4 minutes. Remove the lobster from the skillet.
   5. Stir the flour into the skillet, forming a light paste. Whisk in the stock and water; simmer 5 minutes.
   6. Add the parsley, sherry, and the lobster and any accumulated juices to the skillet. Cover, and cook 3 minutes.
   7. Arrange the lobster in two shallow bowls. Spoon the sauce over it, and sprinkle with parsley.
   2 portions

CHOLESTEROL AND SEAFOOD

For years it has been vaguely understood that seafood was good for us. New studies indicate that not only is most seafood low in cholesterol, but fish oils have properties that thin the blood, lower cholesterol, and when eaten in conjunction with a healthy diet, can reduce the risk of heart disease by more than 50 percent. And although the official word on shellfish has vacillated over the past decade for those watching their cholesterol, shellfish now has the go-ahead; eat and enjoy.

OMEGA-3S

Although no one is sure why fish oils seem to prevent heart attacks, certain of their components, known as Omega-3 long-chain fatty acids, appear to be the best candidates for more research. Omega-3s may help prevent blood clots, a major cause of heart attacks, by thinning the blood. They may also lower cholesterol more effectively than polyunsaturated vegetable oils, and help lower the level of triglycerides, or blood fats, that can contribute to heart disease.

Fresh, fatty fish are the best source of Omega-3s, although lean fish are also considered to be very healthy food. Some of the best sources are tuna, mackerel, salmon, bluefish, mullet, rainbow trout, lake trout, herring, sablefish, shad, butterfish and pompano. Canned fish such as tuna, salmon, mackerel, and sardines are also excellent sources.

LOBSTER ROLL

The perfect summer extravaganza—large pieces of fresh lobster piled into grilled hot dog rolls with lemon mayonnaise. (The rolls that split along the top are the best to use here.)

1 pound cooked lobster meat, fresh or canned
2 ribs celery, diced
1 cup Light Lemon Mayonnaise (see Index)
1 tablespoon chopped fresh dill or tarragon
6 hot dog rolls
2 tablespoons unsalted butter

1. Cut the lobster meat into ½-inch pieces and place them in a mixing bowl. Add the celery, ¾ cup of the lemon mayonnaise, and dill. Toss thoroughly.

2. Toast the hot dog rolls under a broiler, and spread them with the butter and then extra mayonnaise. Heap the lobster mixture in the rolls. Serve immediately.

6 portions

LIME GINGER SCALLOP SAUTE

The sweet nuttiness of bay scallops (at their best in the fall), flavored with ginger and lime and then sautéed with toasted walnut halves—very enticing.

1 tablespoon olive oil
1 tablespoon unsalted butter
1 pound sea scallops, patted dry
3 tablespoons fresh lime juice
4 tablespoons Lime Ginger Butter (recipe follows), chilled
⅓ cup walnut halves, lightly toasted (see Index)
Chopped fresh parsley, for garnish

1. Heat the oil and butter in a large skillet over high heat. Add the scallops and stir until golden, about 2 minutes. Pour off the fat.

2. Stir in the lime juice and cook 1 minute. Then lower the heat and stir in the Lime Ginger Butter 1 tablespoon at a time. Cook just until a thick sauce forms. Stir in the walnuts, sprinkle with parsley, and serve.

2 portions

LIME GINGER BUTTER

4 tablespoons (½ stick) unsalted butter, at room temperature
2 teaspoons grated lime zest
1 teaspoon ground ginger
½ teaspoon salt
Freshly ground black pepper, to taste

Stir all the ingredients together in a small bowl until smooth. Shape into a cylinder 2½ inches in diameter, and wrap in foil or plastic wrap. Refrigerate until firm, about 1 hour.

About 5 tablespoons

CAJUN FRIED CALAMARI

We've spiced up our calamari with Cajun flavors. Dip it into a cool lime cilantro mayonnaise.

2 pounds calamari (squid), cleaned
1 ½ cups unbleached all-purpose flour
¼ cup ground cumin
¼ cup chili powder
1 teaspoon coarsely ground black pepper
½ teaspoon salt
2 cups corn oil
Tabasco sauce, to taste
¼ cup chopped cilantro leaves (fresh coriander)
1 cup Creamy Lime Dressing (see Index)

1. Rinse the calamari, cut them into ¼-inch-thick rings, and lay on paper towels to dry.

2. Combine the flour, cumin, chili powder, pepper, and salt in a shallow bowl.

3. Heat the oil in a large skillet. When it is very hot, dredge the calamari in the flour mixture, shake off any excess, and fry in the oil (in several batches) until brown and crispy. As the calamari are frying, sprinkle several dashes of Tabasco on them (depending on how spicy you want them to be). Drain on paper towels.

4. Stir the cilantro into the lime dressing and serve alongside the hot calamari.

4 portions

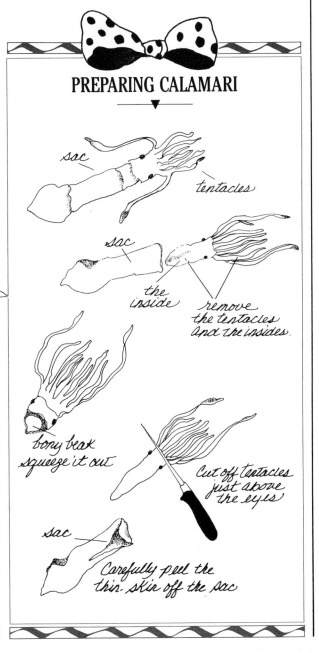

PREPARING CALAMARI

sac

tentacles

sac

the inside

remove the tentacles and the insides.

bony beak squeeze it out

Cut off tentacles just above the eyes

sac

Carefully peel the thin skin off the sac

Calamari Rings

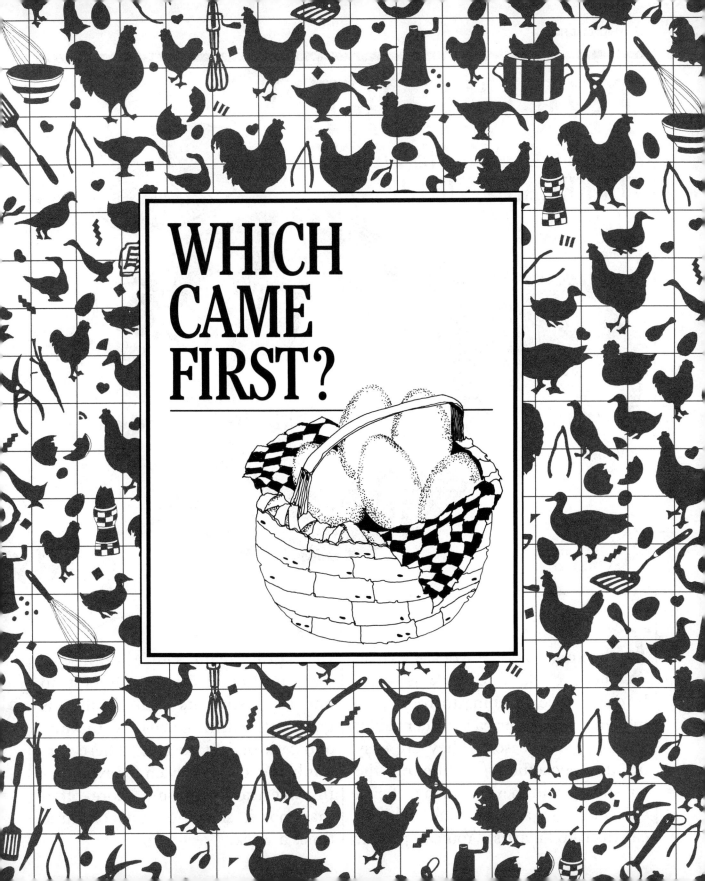

WHICH CAME FIRST?

THE CHICKEN
(AND THE GAME HEN AND THE TURKEY AND THE DUCK)

Chicken, capon, Rock Cornish hen, duck, and turkey—these birds have come home to roost permanently on America's dinner table, and for good reason. They are easy on the pocketbook, gentle on the waistline, and never boring, for a chicken is to a cook what a blank canvas is to an artist. You can poach, roast, grill, steam, sauté, or braise it; you can dress it down or dress it up and let it strut its stuff. Poultry is good hot, warm, or cold, with knife and fork or just fingers. There certainly is enough chicken for every pot in America today, and more often than not it shows up two or three times a week.

CHICKEN

Considering chicken breeds weren't developed and stabilized until the 18th century, the now nearly universal love for chicken has come on like a virtual rage, and chicken is still gaining in popularity. It's a particularly valued source of protein because it's lower in calories, saturated fat, and cholesterol than red meat. Calories can be reduced by 25 to 30 percent if you remove the fat at the opening of the cavities or trim fat from chicken parts and remove the fatty skin. In addition, broiling, roasting, poaching, steaming, microwaving, and sautéing in a nonstick pan deliver up flavorful poultry without additional fat and calories.

THE CHICKEN INDUSTRY

Today's chicken-breeding industry is a computerized and mechanized mass production of the plumpest, roundest birds imaginable. But do they have taste? Sadly, the answer is no.

Our response to these tasteless birds is twofold: We mask or enhance their flavor with imaginative seasonings, sauces, and marinades. We also pass them by when we can and search out free-range chickens. Free-rangers are not caged; they run free, strut and peck, take in the sunshine and fresh air. Though their diets are supplemented with protein, they are otherwise allowed to mature at their own rate, which is twice that of chickens bred in commercial farms. Free-range chickens are more expensive and difficult to find but are also as beautiful and tasty as chickens were in the old days. Although most of the chicken you will buy will be mass produced, if you know a source for free-rangers, do treat yourself occasionally. Roast this tasty bird simply, then dig in and savor.

A CHICKEN WHO'S WHO

▲ **Rock Cornish hens** are 5 to 6 weeks old and weigh between 1 and 2 pounds, most of them averaging about 1½ pounds. A special cross between two breeds of chicken, Rock Cornish hens are delicate, elegant miniatures that make an impressive and beautiful meal for a dinner party, or a perfect meal for two. They're wonderful roasted or split and grilled or broiled. The fresh hens are best if you can find them, but most are sold frozen in supermarkets. Figure one hen per person.

▲ **Broiler-fryers,** cut up in parts or whole, have garnered about 90 percent of the entire chicken market. Broiler-fryers are young, about 45 days old, and typically weigh between 3 and 4½ pounds. These tender birds are best broiled or fried, of course, but also can be roasted, steamed, or poached.

▲ **Roasters** are about 10 weeks old and weigh between 4½ and 8 pounds, with more meat per pound than smaller birds. Look for plump-breasted birds with creamy white or yellow skins and short bodies. These chickens are perfect for roasting, with or without stuffing, but the smaller roasters can also be cut up and sautéed, broiled, or poached.

▲ **Capons,** 10-week-old cocks that were caponized (or castrated) when young, weigh between 8 and 10 pounds. These birds live a lazy life and grow big and fat. As a result, they're delicate and tender, with an abundance of white meat; their flavor is milder than that of chicken, and their size makes them perfect for stuffing and roasting for a holiday table. Capons are specialty items, carrying a higher price per pound than chickens.

▲ **Fowl or stewing hens** are laying hens that have stopped laying. These tough old birds are typically 10 months or older and weigh between 3 and 7 pounds. Basically soup chickens, fowl are no longer easy to find. Because they're older birds, their meat is stringy but loaded with flavor. These chickens require slow, long, moist cooking or stewing to tenderize the meat and produce a strong, rich broth. Prepare them whole or cut up.

COOKING CHICKEN

SIMMERING

A technique most often used in making soup. Place a whole or cut-up chicken, along with herbs like dill, black pepper, bay leaf, and thyme; and vegetables like carrots, tomatoes, celery, leeks, garlic, onion, and parsnips in a large pot and cover them with cold water. Bring the water to a boil, skim the froth from the top and lower the heat. Simmer gently, uncovered or partially covered, 1 to 1½ hours for a young chicken or up to 3 hours for a stewing hen. Remove the chicken from the stock, let it cool, and take the meat off the bones. The meat can be returned to the strained stock for soup or used for salads, pot pies, and sandwiches. (Refrigerate any meat you are not using immediately.) You can then return the bones and skin to the stock and continue simmering for richer flavor. Strain and chill the stock so you can remove the layer of fat that rises to the surface. If the stock tastes weak, or if you want an especially strong stock for sauce, continue to simmer until it's as deep and rich as you desire.

POACHING

This gentle method of liquid cooking is best with chicken breasts and younger whole birds. The breasts or whole birds are poached in seasoned water, flavored broth, or white wine (or a combination of these), along with herbs and vegetables for flavor.

Heat to a low simmer enough liquid to cover the chicken, add the chicken, and cook partially covered until the flesh is just firm to the touch. Always keep the liquid below the boiling point; white meat is easily overcooked, making it dry and tough. Serve poached chicken hot with a sauce, or let it cool to room temperature and use it in salads. The cooking liquid (other than seasoned water) can be reduced and used as the base for a sauce. Whole chickens will cook in about an hour.

STEAMING

A fast and simple technique in which chicken pieces are cooked on a rack or steamer above simmering liquid in a covered pot. The liquid—broth, wine, or water—can be infused with complementary fresh herbs or garlic. A cut-up chicken will cook in 45 to 60 minutes. Use the meat for salads, or serve the chicken with a sauce.

ROASTING

To prepare a chicken for roasting, remove and set aside the giblets; rinse the bird well and pat it dry. Refresh it with juice from a lemon or orange. Season the bird inside and out with salt, pepper, and paprika, and tuck the flap of skin at the neck end under. Trussing (binding) a chicken makes for a slightly more elegant bird at the table, and is essential if the bird is stuffed, but we find it illogical to force the leg, which is the part that takes the longest to cook, against the body. The legs will cook faster if the bird isn't trussed.

Use a pan that fits the bird just right—without excess room and without squeezing it in—and use a rack in the pan so that the bird doesn't stew in its own juices.

In a 350°F oven, a 2½- to 3½-pound chicken will cook in 1½ to 1¾ hours; a 5- to 7-pound chicken in 2½ to 3 hours; a Rock Cornish hen in 1 to 1¼ hours. Stuffed birds require more cooking time; add approximately 20 minutes total. Baste the bird with pan juices every 20 minutes, and, if desired, add a small amount of liquid (water, broth, wine cider) to the bottom of the pan.

Check for doneness by piercing the flesh of the leg with the tip of a knife. If the juices run clear, the chicken is done. You can also check for doneness by twisting the leg. If it moves easily in its socket, the chicken is done.

FRYING

In general, chicken pieces are coated in seasoned flour or breading and fried in about a half inch of hot vegetable oil, starting with the dark meat; white meat fries in about two thirds the time it takes dark meat to cook. Do not crowd the pan or cover it. Fry in batches, and keep the cooked pieces warm in a low oven. Chickens for frying should be small and young; broiler-fryers are perfect of course.

BROILING

This method is well suited to chicken halves, quarters, and pieces if the bird isn't too large; broiler-fryers are ideal. Marinating the chicken for several hours before broiling, and basting it frequently keeps the chicken from drying out and adds flavor. You can marinate in highly flavored oils and citrus juices, in herbed yogurt and oil, or in sparkling fruit juices. If you're not using marinade, brush the skin with melted herb butter or seasoned oil during broiling.

Arrange the chicken pieces on a broiler pan skin side down. Broil 6 inches from the heat source for 15 to 20 minutes, then turn and broil the second side until the juices run clear when the piece is pierced. Remember, the white meat will be done before the dark.

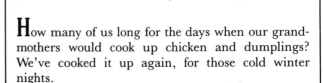

TRADE SECRET

 Turn leftover chicken, with the skin removed, and leftover baked potatoes into chicken hash. Chop, spice up, and sauté, then top with a poached egg.

CHICKEN AND DUMPLINGS

How many of us long for the days when our grandmothers would cook up chicken and dumplings? We've cooked it up again, for those cold winter nights.

1 chicken (3 to 4 pounds), cut into 8 pieces
1 teaspoon paprika
½ teaspoon salt
Freshly ground black pepper, to taste
1 tablespoon vegetable oil
1 rib celery, cut into 2-inch pieces
1 carrot, peeled and cut into 2-inch pieces
2 leeks (white part and 1 inch green), well rinsed and cut into 1-inch pieces
1 small onion, quartered
4 cups Berta's Chicken Stock (see Index) or canned broth

DUMPLINGS
1 cup unbleached all-purpose flour
1½ teaspoons baking powder
Freshly ground black pepper, to taste
2 tablespoons chopped fresh parsley
2 tablespoons solid vegetable shortening
⅓ cup milk
Chopped fresh parsley, for garnish

1. Rinse the chicken pieces well, and pat them dry. Combine the paprika, salt, and pepper in a small

bowl, and rub this mixture onto the chicken.

2. Heat the oil in a dutch oven, and cook the chicken over high heat until browned, about 10 minutes. Pour off the fat from the pan.

3. Add the vegetables and stock to the chicken, and bring to a boil. Lower the heat, cover, and simmer just until the chicken is tender and cooked through, about 45 minutes. Using a slotted spoon, transfer the chicken and vegetables to a platter and keep warm. Reserve the broth in the pot.

4. Make the dumplings: In a mixing bowl, stir together the flour, baking powder, pepper, and 2 tablespoons parsley. Using a pastry blender, two knives, or your fingertips, cut in the shortening until the mixture resembles coarse crumbs. Then add the milk, stirring just until the mixture is moistened. Gather the dough into a ball, knead it once or twice, and cut it into twelve pieces.

5. Bring the broth back to a simmer, and drop the dumplings into it. Cover, and simmer until they are puffed and cooked through, about 15 minutes.

6. To serve, arrange the chicken, vegetables, and dumplings in four shallow bowls. Ladle some broth into each bowl, and sprinkle with chopped parsley.

4 portions

THE WINES OF CHILE

Chilean weather and soil conditions are very good for growing grapes, and for the past several years, Chile has been coming out with some terrific wines. The Cabernets are smoky and full-flavored, with a delicious fruity, black currant taste. Their quality is uniformly good, but our favorites are from Cusiño-Macul and Los Vascos. We also like the big, oaky, honeyed flavor of the Sémillons of Undurraga and Santa Rita, and the wines produced by the Torres family. Try their steely Rieslings, delicate Gewürztraminers, or light Sauvignons.

CHICKEN POT PIE NOUVEAU

Sweet sugar snap peas and the lusty taste of rosemary make this a main event rather than a leftover. Baked as individual portions, this dish is easy to assemble and just right for company. A rich broth replaces the traditional cream sauce and a puff crust sits on top to lighten it even further. It's luscious.

2 to 2½ cups Berta's Chicken Stock or canned broth
2 cups sliced carrots (¼-inch-thick rounds)
4 sprigs fresh rosemary
4 ounces sugar snap peas, cut diagonally in half
1 cup tiny pearl onions
2 tablespoons unsalted butter
2 tablespoons unbleached all-purpose flour
8 ounces cooked chicken breast, cut into 1 x 3-inch strips (2 cups)
½ recipe Adrienne's Rough Puff Pastry (see Index)
1 egg
1 teaspoon water

1. Bring 1 cup of the chicken stock to a boil in a small saucepan. Add the carrots and 1 rosemary sprig, and boil for 4 minutes. Drain, reserving the liquid, and set aside. Discard the rosemary.

2. Bring a small saucepan of water to a boil. Add the snap peas and cook for 30 seconds. Drain, rinse under cold water, and add to the carrots.

3. With the tip of a paring knife, make a small incision at the root end of each onion; be careful not to cut through completely so that the onion does not fall apart in cooking. Bring a saucepan of water to a boil, add the onions, and cook until just tender, 10 minutes. Drain, rinse under cold water, and peel. Set aside.

4. Melt the butter in a saucepan, add the flour, and cook, whisking over medium-low heat, 3 to 4 minutes. Add the reserved carrot liquid and enough of the remaining stock to make 2 cups. Cook, whisking, until thickened, another 3 to 4 minutes. Add a sprig of rosemary, cover, and set aside to cool.

5. Lightly butter four individual (1½-cup) ramekins. Place a portion of the cooked chicken in each, followed by a portion of the snap peas, onions, and carrots. Pour the thickened sauce over each mixture,

and insert half a rosemary sprig in each. Cover the ramekins, and place them in the refrigerator.

6. On a cool floured surface, roll the pastry out to form a rectangle ¼ inch thick. Cut it into four rectangles.

7. Whisk the egg and water together, and brush the outside rim of each ramekin with this egg wash. Set a pastry rectangle on top, draping the excess dough over the sides and pressing around the outside to seal. Trim the dough to make a neat edge, and chill in the freezer for 20 minutes.

8. Preheat the oven to 475°F.

9. Transfer the ramekins to the oven, and bake until the pastry is puffed and well browned, 15 to 18 minutes. Serve immediately, in the ramekins.

4 portions

CHICKEN FRICASSEE

A classic chicken fricassee, made more delicate by julienning the vegetables. For a touch of elegance, substitute fresh wild mushrooms for the domestic ones.

2 chickens (2 to 2½ pounds each), each cut into 8 pieces
10 tablespoons (1¼ sticks) unsalted butter
1 tablespoon olive oil
2 carrots, peeled and chopped
2 ribs celery, with leaves, chopped
1 onion, chopped
2 cloves garlic, chopped
3 sprigs Italian (flat-leaf) parsley
3 sprigs dill
4 cups water
2 cups Berta's Chicken Stock (see Index) or canned broth
1 zucchini, cut into 2-inch julienne
1 carrot, peeled and cut into 2-inch julienne
1 leek (white part only), well rinsed and cut into 2-inch julienne
6 ounces fresh cultivated mushrooms, cleaned and sliced
¼ cup unbleached all-purpose flour
½ cup heavy or whipping cream
Salt and freshly ground black pepper, to taste
2 shallots, peeled and finely chopped
3 tablespoons chopped fresh Italian (flat-leaf) parsley

1. Rinse the chicken pieces well and pat them dry.

2. Heat 4 tablespoons of the butter with the oil in a heavy dutch oven. Brown the chicken in small batches until golden on both sides. Using tongs, remove the chicken as it is done and set it aside.

3. When all the chicken has been browned, pour off most of the fat from the dutch oven. Return the chicken to the pot, along with the chopped carrots, celery, onion, garlic, and the parsley and dill sprigs. Add the water and stock, and bring to a boil. Reduce the heat, cover, and simmer for 30 minutes.

4. Remove the chicken to a serving platter and keep warm. Strain the broth, discarding the vegetables if desired, and return the broth to the pot. Bring it to a boil and reduce by half; this will take about 10 minutes. Remove the fat by skimming or by pouring the liquid through a gravy separator. Reserve 2 cups of the liquid (freeze any excess for another use).

5. While the broth is reducing, melt another 4 tablespoons of the butter in a large skillet. Add the julienned zucchini, carrot, and leek, and the mushrooms. Sauté quickly until just tender, 3 minutes. Set the vegetables aside.

6. Melt the remaining 4 tablespoons butter in a heavy saucepan. Add the flour, and whisk constantly over low heat for 3 minutes. Then add the 2 cups reserved broth and the cream, whisking constantly until the sauce has thickened. Season with salt and pepper, and remove from the heat.

7. Add the sautéed vegetables, shallots, and 2 tablespoons of the chopped parsley to the sauce. Pour it over the chicken, and sprinkle the remaining 1 tablespoon parsley on top. Serve immediately.

6 portions

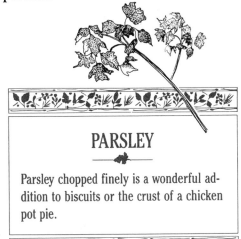

PARSLEY

Parsley chopped finely is a wonderful addition to biscuits or the crust of a chicken pot pie.

COQ AU VINO BIANCO

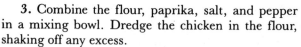

There are many traditional variations on *coq au vin* in France—in the Jura they add morels; the Alsatian version is bound at the last minute with egg yolks and cream and served with noodles; in Provence cooks add tomatoes, black olives, and red peppers; in Normandy the wine becomes cider; in Flanders, beer. And of course the original is the Burgundian chicken stew with red wine, onions, mushrooms, and *lardons*. We've decided to make it lighter with white wine—and Italian wine at that. We like to make this peasant dish a day in advance, to give time for the flavors to meld.

2 cups tiny pearl onions
2 tablespoons unsalted butter
1 cup coarsely chopped onion
¾ cup unbleached all-purpose flour
½ teaspoon paprika
½ teaspoon salt
½ teaspoon freshly ground black pepper
1 chicken (3½ to 4 pounds), well rinsed,
    cut into 8 serving pieces
2 tablespoons olive oil
6 slices bacon, cut into 1-inch pieces
1 teaspoon sugar
1 pound fresh cultivated mushrooms,
    stems discarded, caps quartered
1 bay leaf
2 cups dry Italian white wine, such as
    Soave or Orvieto
1 cup Berta's Chicken Stock (see Index)
    or canned broth
½ teaspoon dried thyme
2 tablespoons chopped fresh
    Italian (flat-leaf) parsley

1. Using a sharp knife, make a small X in the root end of each pearl onion. Bring a saucepan of water to a boil, add the pearl onions, lower the heat, and simmer about 10 minutes. Drain, rinse under cold water, and peel.

2. Melt the butter in a large flame-proof casserole. Add the chopped onion, and sauté over low heat, until soft and translucent, about 10 minutes. Using a slotted spoon, remove the onions and set aside.

3. Combine the flour, paprika, salt, and pepper in a mixing bowl. Dredge the chicken in the flour, shaking off any excess.

4. Add the olive oil to the casserole, and brown the chicken on all sides. Return the chopped onions to the pot.

5. Cook the bacon in a skillet over medium-low heat until it is lightly colored and the fat is rendered. Remove the bacon with a slotted spoon, and add it to the chicken.

6. Add the pearl onions to the skillet and cook them, over medium heat, tossing constantly, until lightly browned. Sprinkle them with the sugar, and continue cooking until the onions are caramelized, 3 to 5 minutes. Add them to the chicken.

7. Add the mushrooms to the skillet, and cook over medium heat until tender, about 5 minutes; add them to the chicken.

8. Add the bay leaf, wine, stock, and thyme to the casserole. Cover, and bring to a boil. Reduce to a simmer and cook until the juices run clear when the meat is pierced with a fork, 30 minutes.

9. Transfer the chicken and vegetables to a warmed platter. Bring the remaining liquid to a boil and reduce until it is slightly thick, about 10 minutes. Pour the sauce over the chicken, and serve garnished with the chopped parsley.

4 portions

"**P**oultry is for the cook what canvas is for the painter."

—BRILLAT-SAVARIN

BUYING AND STORING CHICKEN

In general you want a chicken with moist skin, tender flesh, and a fresh smell. Avoid chickens with dry, hard, bruised, or scaly skin. Of course, it's impossible to get a sniff of chicken wrapped tightly in plastic, until you get it home. At the supermarket, check the expiration date. If you buy mass-produced birds, you may want to try chickens from several producers and stick with one that pleases you.

Skin color is a regional preference. In the Midwest, people like their chickens with creamy white skin; in the Northeast and West, yellow skin is preferable. The feed makes the difference in skin color, but the chickens taste the same.

As a rule of thumb, buy ¾ to 1 pound bone-in chicken for each serving. A 3½-pound bird will feed four comfortably, but a 1½-pound Rock Cornish hen will feed just one hungry person. For chicken parts, a half breast or two drumsticks or thighs per person is sufficient.

At home, remove the chicken from its wrapping and rinse it thoroughly with cold water. Set aside the package of innards and remove any lumps of fat and tissue in the cavity and around the openings. If you are cooking the chicken right away, refresh the bird by squeezing fresh lemon or orange juice over the skin and in the cavity.

If you aren't going to cook the chicken immediately, wrap it loosely in foil or waxed paper, keeping the ends open, and refrigerate it for up to 48 hours. To freeze chicken, seal it airtight in a heavy plastic bag or freezer wrap. Mark the date on the package and freeze it for up to 3 months. Thaw frozen chicken in the refrigerator; a 3½-pound chicken will thaw in about a day. Do not refreeze uncooked chicken.

Remove the liver from the giblets. If you aren't using it immediately, see page 430 for storage information. The giblets may be frozen wrapped tightly in foil.

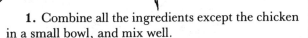

CHICKEN KIEV

This version of the famous Russian dish not only lightens the filling by using tangy yogurt instead of the traditional butter, but it also is made with the bone in to form a natural pocket.

½ cup plain yogurt
1 clove garlic, minced
3 tablespoons snipped fresh chives
½ teaspoon salt
Freshly ground black pepper, to taste
Pinch of cayenne pepper
4 skinless chicken breast halves, bone in, well rinsed and
    patted dry

1. Combine all the ingredients except the chicken in a small bowl, and mix well.

2. Holding a thin, sharp knife almost parallel to the bone, cut two diagonal slits in each breast, 2 inches apart, to form two pockets.

3. Lift the flap of each pocket, and fill it with some of the yogurt mixture. Arrange the breast halves in a baking dish, and spoon any remaining filling on top. Loosely cover and refrigerate for 1 hour.

4. Preheat the oven to 450°F.

5. Bake the chicken until it is crisp and browned, 35 minutes. Serve immediately.

4 portions

CHICKEN A LA KING

Who cannot conjure up memories of cold winter nights and warm, soothing chicken à la king? Now it can be served to company, with the addition of sugar snap peas, fresh red pepper, and garnishes of radish sprouts and enoki mushrooms.

Radish sprouts are available in some specialty produce markets. They're hot and spicy and provide a lively kick for chicken à la king. If they're unavailable, substitute small peppery garden cress. Enoki mushrooms show up often in Japanese food. White and tiny, about the size of large matchsticks, their clear fruity flavor makes a refreshing garnish.

5 tablespoons unsalted butter
1 cup fresh cultivated button mushrooms
½ red bell pepper, seeded and diced
3 ounces sugar snap peas
¼ cup unbleached all-purpose flour
2 ¼ cups Berta's Chicken Stock (see Index) or canned broth,
*   plus additional if needed*
3 to 4 cups cubed cooked chicken or turkey
½ cup sliced carrots, cooked
1 tablespoon snipped fresh chives
Salt and freshly ground black pepper, to taste
Cooked orzo, herbed rice, or individual brioches, for serving
Radish sprouts, for garnish
Enoki mushrooms, for garnish

1. Melt 1 tablespoon butter in a small skillet. Add the button mushrooms and sauté over medium-high heat until tender, 5 minutes. Set aside.

2. Bring a small saucepan of water to a boil, add the bell pepper, and cook for 2 minutes. Drain, rinse under cold water, and set aside.

3. Bring a small saucepan of water to a boil, add the snap peas, and cook for 1 minute. Drain, rinse under cold water, and set aside.

4. Melt the remaining 4 tablespoons of butter in a medium-size saucepan. Whisk in the flour and cook over low heat until smooth, 1 to 2 minutes. Slowly add the stock, whisking until smooth. Heat to a simmer, stirring, and cook until the mixture is thick and the flour taste has been cooked out, about 5 minutes. If it gets too thick, add a little extra stock.

5. Stir in the chicken, carrots, the reserved button mushrooms, bell pepper and snap peas, the chives, and the salt and pepper. Bring to a simmer and cook until heated through, 5 minutes. Thin the mixture with a little extra stock if necessary.

6. Serve over buttered orzo or herbed rice; or spoon into hollowed toasted individual brioches. Sprinkle each portion with radish sprouts and enoki mushrooms, and serve immediately.

4 portions

CHICKEN WITH GARLIC, LEMON, AND ROSEMARY

Lemons and rosemary infuse this chicken with their fresh and robust flavors.

2 heads garlic
1 large onion
1 roasting chicken (4 to 4 ½ pounds), with its giblets
1 teaspoon dried tarragon
Salt and freshly ground black pepper, to taste
2 lemons, halved
6 small sprigs fresh rosemary
2 tablespoons unsalted butter
2 tablespoons olive oil
1 cup Berta's Chicken Stock (see Index) or canned broth

1. Remove the paper-like outer skin from the garlic heads, and separate the cloves. Do not peel the cloves. Set them aside.

2. Cut the onion in half, and then in slivers. Set it aside.

3. Rinse the chicken well and pat it dry. Set the giblets aside. Sprinkle the cavity with the tarragon and salt and pepper. Place the lemons and the rosemary sprigs in the cavity, and tie the legs together.

4. Preheat the oven to 350°F.

5. Heat the butter and the oil in a dutch oven or large nonstick deep pan. Beginning with the breast, gently brown the chicken over medium heat. Turn the chicken with wooden spoons, or by carefully holding the ends of the legs, to brown it on all sides, 6 to 8 minutes per side. Try not to break the skin. It should be pale golden all over. Remove the chicken from the dutch oven, reserving the cooking juices.

6. Place the garlic cloves, slivered onion, and giblets (not the liver) in a shallow roasting pan. Place the chicken on top and pour the browning juices over it. Add the stock, and cover the pan with aluminum foil. Place it on the center rack of the oven, and bake for 30 minutes.

7. Remove the foil. Stir the garlic and onions around in the broth, and baste the chicken. Bake, uncovered, basting every 15 minutes, for 1 hour.

8. Remove the chicken from the pan. Discard the string, lemons, and rosemary. Slice the chicken, and serve it with the garlic cloves, onions, and pan juices. (The garlic cloves will be very sweet and soft.)

4 portions

ROAST CHICKEN CHEZ LOUIS

David Liederman has been a great friend over the years. As the David of David's Cookies, his fame has certainly spread worldwide. But, we are lucky enough to have his excellent restaurant, Chez Louis, in New York. When we go, we dine on this fabulous roast chicken.

One of the reasons his chicken is so good is because he grills it first to sear in the flavor. If you don't have a grill, sear the chicken in a skillet in 2 tablespoons of butter heated with 2 tablespoons of

vegetable oil, for about 6 minutes on each side. (Add an additional 2 tablespoons of each, if needed.)

From David: "After having eaten it all, or almost all; after parading through enough starred places to form my own constellation; and after having gained a hundred pounds on 'lighter nouvelle cuisine,' I decided I liked roast chicken the best. So Chez Louis was created. Now I've lost the hundred pounds and I'm much happier. The chicken we use in the restaurant is kosher and the garlic abundant."

MARINADE
½ cup extra virgin olive oil
1½ cups corn oil
7 cloves garlic
4 sprigs thyme
4 sprigs rosemary
Freshly ground black pepper, to taste

1 chicken (3 to 3½ pounds), well rinsed and patted dry
Salt and freshly ground black pepper, to taste
1 cup Berta's Chicken Stock (see Index) or canned broth
3 tablespoons unsalted butter
Watercress sprigs, for garnish

1. Place all the marinade ingredients in a large bowl and mix well. (There is enough for two chickens if you'd like). Place the chicken in the bowl, coat it with the marinade, and cover the bowl. Refrigerate, and marinate overnight, turning the chicken occasionally.

2. Prepare a charcoal grill. Preheat the oven to 450°F.

3. Season the chicken with salt and pepper.

4. Sear the chicken on the grill for about 3 minutes on each side. (See headnote for completing this step on top of the stove.) The chicken may be set aside for up to 2 hours before proceeding with the rest of this recipe.

5. Transfer the chicken to a heavy roasting pan, and roast, until the juices run clear when the meat is pricked with a fork, about 45 minutes.

6. Remove the chicken from the pan and let it rest for 10 minutes. Pour off the excess fat from the pan, and add the chicken stock. Cook over high heat for 1 to 1½ minutes, scraping up all the brown bits.

7. Add the butter to the pan juices, adjust the seasonings to taste, and cook, whisking over high heat for another minute.

8. Cut the chicken up, ladle some pan juices over each portion, and garnish with sprigs of watercress.

2 to 4 portions

CARVING POULTRY

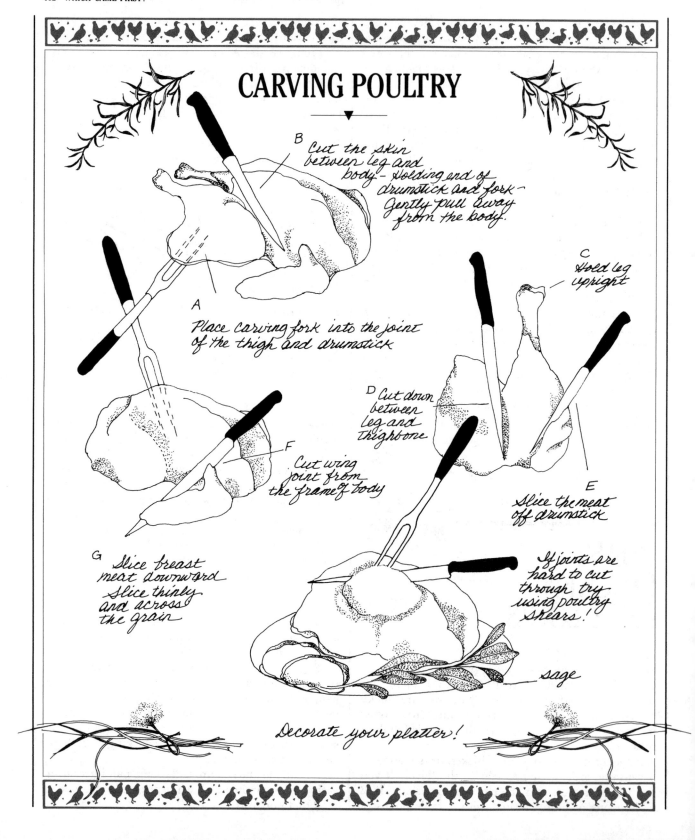

B Cut the skin between leg and body. Holding end of drumstick and fork. Gently pull away from the body.

C Hold leg upright

A Place carving fork into the joint of the thigh and drumstick

D Cut down between leg and thighbone

F Cut wing joint from the frame of body

E Slice the meat off drumstick

G Slice breast meat downward. Slice thinly and across the grain

If joints are hard to cut through try using poultry shears!

sage

Decorate your platter!

BOBBIE'S CHICKEN

One of our dearest friends created and perfected this chicken—aren't all sculptors perfectionists? We've had people stop us on the street to rave about this dish, and we always wish Bobbie and Bert were there to hear their praise. This is a good one!

1 roasting chicken (about 4½ pounds),
*   with its giblets*
1 lemon, halved
2 tablespoons dry mustard
2 tablespoons ground ginger
Salt and freshly ground black pepper, to taste
6 onions, quartered
2 homemade chicken bouillon cubes (see Index)
2¾ cups water

1. Preheat the oven to 425°F.

2. Rinse the chicken well and pat it dry. Squeeze the juice of the lemon all over the chicken and in the cavity.

3. Combine the mustard, ginger, and salt and pepper in a small bowl, and rub this mixture all over the chicken. Place the chicken in a roasting pan, and scatter 4 of the onions in the pan. Roast undisturbed for 30 minutes.

4. Meanwhile, combine the giblets (not the liver), the remaining 2 onions, the bouillon cubes, and 2 cups of the water in a small saucepan. Bring to a boil, then reduce the heat and simmer for 25 to 30 minutes. Set aside.

5. Reduce the oven temperature to 375°F, and pour the remaining ¾ cup water into the roasting pan. Roast the chicken 30 minutes more, basting occasionally with the pan juices.

6. Strain the giblet stock and pour ¾ cup of the stock into the roasting pan. Roast, basting occasionally, for 30 minutes more.

7. Remove the chicken from the pan, and cut it into serving pieces with a knife and fork (the chicken should be falling off the bone). Mix the chicken with the onions and juices in the pan, and pour in the remaining giblet stock. Cover the pan with aluminum foil and bake for 15 minutes. Serve the chicken on a large platter, surrounded by the juices.

4 portions

TRADE SECRET

Place flour in a small baking pan and bake at 350°F degrees until medium brown, about 5 minutes. This eliminates a floury taste when preparing gravies, sauces, or a "beurre manié."

CHICKEN GRAVY

This is great over the mashed potatoes that accompany your favorite chicken dish.

¼ cup chicken fat, pan drippings,
*   or unsalted butter*
½ cup chopped onion
1 teaspoon crumbled dried sage
1 teaspoon crumbled dried thyme
¼ cup unbleached all-purpose flour
2¼ cups milk
2 homemade chicken bouillon cubes (see Index)
½ teaspoon salt
Freshly ground black pepper, to taste
Chopped fresh parsley, for garnish

1. Heat the fat in a medium-size saucepan. Add the onion, sage, and thyme, and sauté over medium-low heat, about 3 minutes. Stir in the flour, and whisk over low heat until a paste has formed and the flour is lightly colored, 2 to 3 minutes.

2. Add the milk and bouillon cubes, and whisk until smooth. Bring to a boil, then reduce the heat and cook over low heat, stirring, about 10 minutes. Cook until the gravy is thick and the flour taste is cooked out, another 5 minutes. Thin slightly with extra milk if necessary.

3. Strain the gravy, season it with salt and pepper, and sprinkle with parsley.

2 cups

WINES WITH POULTRY

Poultry	Wine
Capon	Chardonnay
Roast chicken	Châteauneuf-du-Pape, Merlot
Robust chicken	Cabernet Sauvignon
Creamy chicken	Chardonnay
Fried chicken	Beaujolais
Spiced chicken	Zinfandel
Light chicken	Chablis, Sancerre
Chicken salads	Riesling (dry), Chenin Blanc
Roast duck	Vouvray
Duck stews	Pinot Noir
Rock Cornish hens	Vouvray, Merlot
Roast turkey	Zinfandel, Beaujolais
Turkey other ways	Beaujolais-Villages, Beaujolais nouveau
Chicken liver pâtés	Beaujolais-Villages, Sancerre, Vouvray
Foie gras	Sauternes, Gewürztraminer, Tokay d'Alsace

ORANGE ROASTED CAPON

Robust flavors of Italy and Spain perfume this luscious capon. Glazed with orange-flavored Cognac and surrounded by roasted baby carrots and pattypan squash, this dish is a proud focal point for an elegant dinner. Serve it with nutted wild rice and a tart green salad.

BASTING SAUCE

1 cup fresh orange juice
6 tablespoons (¾ stick) unsalted butter, melted
2 tablespoons minced orange zest
1 tablespoon finely chopped fresh rosemary

1½ pounds small onions (1½ to 2 inches in diameter), unpeeled
1 fennel bulb, trimmed and cut into thin strips
1 sprig fresh rosemary
1 head garlic, separated into cloves and peeled
¼ cup orange-flavored Cognac
2 tablespoons unsalted butter, melted
1 tablespoon slivered orange zest
Salt and freshly ground black pepper, to taste
1 capon (about 8½ pounds)
1 cup water
20 baby carrots, peeled
1 pound miniature pattypan or other squash

1. Combine the ingredients for the basting sauce in a small bowl. Set aside.

2. Preheat the oven to 350°F.

3. Bring a large saucepan of salted water to a boil, and add the onions. Cook for 20 minutes. Drain, cover with cold water until cool, and drain again. Peel the onions.

4. In a mixing bowl, toss the peeled onions with the fennel, rosemary, garlic, Cognac, butter, slivered orange zest, salt, and pepper.

5. Rinse the capon well, and pat it dry. Season it lightly, inside and out, with salt and pepper.

6. Fill the cavity of the capon with the onion mixture. Stuff 1 or 2 halved onions under the skin on each side of the breast. Place the capon in a roasting pan and add the water. Brush the capon liberally with the basting sauce.

7. Roast 1 hour and 20 minutes, basting every 20 minutes. Then remove the onions from the cavity and place them in the pan juices. Add the carrots and squash, turn all the vegetables to coat with the juices, and cook 1 hour.

8. Remove the pan from the oven and let it stand 15 minutes. Then carve the capon. Season the vegetables with salt and pepper, and arrange them around the carved meat on a platter. Degrease the pan juices, and pass them in a sauceboat.

8 portions

POULTRY ROASTING CHART

CUT	OVEN TEMPERATURE	INTERNAL TEMPERATURE	COOKING TIME
Chicken, unstuffed 4 to 7 pounds	350°F	180°F at inner thigh	20 minutes per pound (add 20 minutes if stuffed)
3 to 3½ pounds	450°F	180°F at inner thigh	13 to 15 minutes per pound (add 15 to 20 minutes if stuffed)
Capon, unstuffed 7 to 9 pounds	350°F	180°F at inner thigh	20 to 22 minutes per pound (add 20 to 25 minutes if stuffed)
Turkey, stuffed 16 to 24 pounds	325°F	180°F at inner thigh	12 to 15 minutes per pound
Rock Cornish hen, unstuffed ¾ to 1½ pounds	350°F	180°F at inner thigh	¾ to 1¼ hours (add 15 minutes if stuffed)
Duckling, unstuffed 4 to 5 pounds	400°F for 30 minutes, then 350°F		15 to 18 minutes per pound

▲ Based on poultry at room temperature when roasted.
▲ Roast turkey, capon, chicken, and duckling should rest 15 minutes before carving; internal temperature will rise 5° to 10°F.

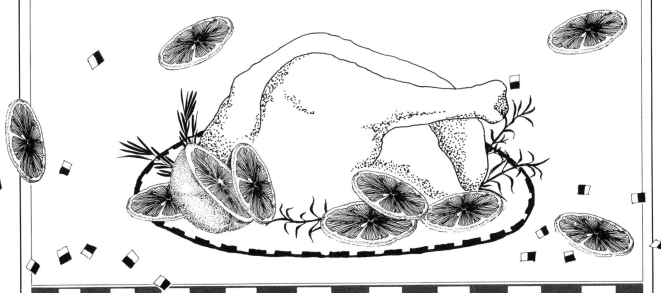

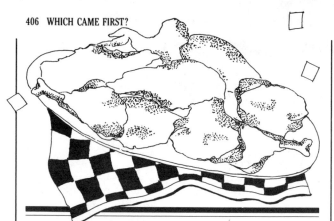

ELLEN'S FRIED CHICKEN

When Ellen White was chef at The Silver Palate, she made this chicken for store customers, but we were often lucky enough to get the first few pieces. It's been a favorite of ours for years.

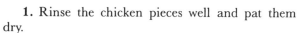

2 chickens (2½ to 3 pounds each), each cut into 8 pieces
4 eggs
¼ cup water
3 cups unbleached all-purpose flour
1 tablespoon paprika
2 teaspoons salt
1½ teaspoons freshly ground black pepper
3 cups corn oil
2 lemons

1. Rinse the chicken pieces well and pat them dry.
2. Beat the eggs and water together in a shallow bowl.
3. In another shallow bowl, stir together the flour, paprika, salt, and pepper.
4. Dip the chicken pieces first in the egg mixture, then in the flour. Coat them well, shaking off any excess.
5. Heat the oil in a deep-fryer or large deep skillet to 375°F. It should be hot, but not smoking.
6. Lower the heat slightly, and fry the chicken in the oil in small batches until golden and crisp all over, 10 to 15 minutes.
7. Drain the chicken on a cake rack or on paper towels. Serve hot or at room temperature, with lemon wedges.

6 to 8 portions

HOT CRUNCHY CHICKEN

Pecans and cornmeal provide the crunch in this spiced chicken—our version of a beach classic.

2 chickens (2½ pounds each), each cut into 8 pieces
1½ cups pecans
1 cup unbleached all-purpose flour
1 cup yellow cornmeal
4 teaspoons paprika
2 teaspoons salt
2 teaspoons freshly ground black pepper
2 teaspoons cayenne pepper
4 eggs
½ cup water
4 cups corn oil
1¼ cups Honey Pecan Butter (recipe follows; optional)

1. Rinse the chicken pieces well and pat them dry.
2. Chop the pecans fine in a food processor or blender. Combine the chopped pecans, flour, cornmeal, paprika, salt, pepper, and cayenne in a shallow bowl. Mix well.
3. In another shallow bowl, blend the eggs and water.
4. Dip the chicken pieces first in the egg mixture, and then in the dry mixture. Coat them well, shaking off any excess.
5. Heat the oil in a deep-fryer or heavy flameproof casserole to 375°F on a frying thermometer. It should be hot, but not smoking. Fry the chicken, a few pieces at a time, about 10 to 15 minutes. Drain the chicken on a rack.
6. If you are serving the chicken hot off the stove, serve Honey Pecan Butter alongside for dipping.

6 portions

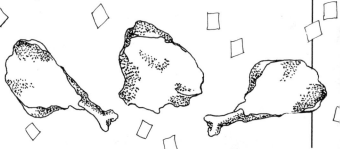

HONEY PECAN BUTTER

A perfect match for crunchy chicken when it's served piping hot—or try it atop waffles, hotcakes, or biscuits.

8 tablespoons (1 stick) unsalted butter, at room temperature
1 cup pecan halves
¼ cup light clover honey

Combine all the ingredients in a food processor. Pulse on and off several times to blend; the pecans should remain chunky. Transfer to a small bowl or individual ramekins, and serve.

1 ¼ cups

LEMON GINGER CHICKEN

A great chicken dish that combines three of our favorite flavors: lemon, ginger, and garlic. This is terrific hot from the oven—or at room temperature the next day.

1 chicken (2 ½ pounds), cut into 8 pieces
1 cup fresh lemon juice
4 cloves garlic, finely minced
4 teaspoons finely chopped fresh ginger
1 teaspoon lemon extract
1 cup unbleached all-purpose flour
2 teaspoons ground ginger
1 teaspoon paprika
1 teaspoon salt
1 teaspoon black pepper
2 cups corn oil
¼ cup Berta's Chicken Stock (see Index) or canned broth
¼ cup (packed) light brown sugar
2 lemons, sliced paper-thin

1. Rinse the chicken pieces well and pat them dry. Place the pieces in a large bowl.
2. Combine the lemon juice, garlic, fresh ginger, and lemon extract in a small bowl. Pour the mixture over the chicken, toss well, and cover the bowl. Refrigerate for 2 hours.

3. Preheat the oven to 350°F.
4. Remove the chicken from the bowl, reserving the marinade. Pat the pieces dry.
5. In a plastic or paper bag, combine the flour, ground ginger, paprika, salt, and pepper; shake the bag to mix well. Place the chicken pieces in the bag, two at a time, and shake them to coat with the mixture. Shake off any excess mixture, and set the pieces aside.
6. Heat the oil to 375°F in a deep-fryer. When it is ready, add the chicken, a few pieces at a time, and fry until golden and crisp, 5 to 7 minutes. As the pieces are done, place them, skin side up, in a shallow roasting pan.
7. Pour the stock and the reserved marinade into the baking pan. Sprinkle the brown sugar evenly over the chicken pieces, and pat it down slightly. Arrange the lemon slices over the chicken.
8. Bake until tender, 40 to 45 minutes; baste once after 20 minutes. Serve immediately.

2 portions

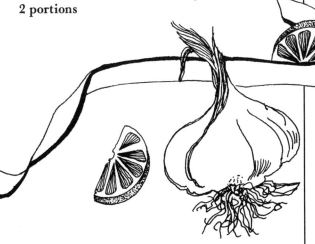

"I have often noticed that when chickens quit quarreling over their food they often find that there is enough for all of them. I wonder if it might not be the same with the human race."
—DON MARQUIS

CHICKEN BREASTS POSITANO

We first had a version of these lemony chicken paillards topped with a cool garlicky salad just off the Amalfi Drive in the lovely Italian seaside village of Positano. This is a wonderful entrée for a hot summer evening.

8 ripe tomatoes
1 small onion, cut lengthwise into fine slivers
3 cloves garlic, minced
2 cups extra virgin olive oil
Salt and freshly ground black pepper, to taste
2 tablespoons fresh lemon juice
1 teaspoon sugar
4 bunches arugula (about 6 to 7 cups with stems trimmed), rinsed and dried
3 whole boneless skinless chicken breasts, well rinsed and patted dry
2 cups stone-ground yellow cornmeal
2 teaspoons salt
½ teaspoon freshly ground black pepper
½ teaspoon good-quality chili powder
¼ teaspoon cayenne pepper
3 eggs
1 tablespoon water
Olive oil

1. Place a strainer over a medium-size saucepan. Holding the tomatoes over the strainer, remove the cores and seeds, letting them drop into the strainer. Press on the cores with the back of a spoon to extract the juice and discard what remains in the strainer. Dice the tomato pulp and add it to the saucepan. Add the onion, garlic, and oil, and stir. Season with salt and a generous amount of pepper. Stir in the lemon juice and sugar. Let the mixture stand, loosely covered, in a warm place (on top of the stove or in the oven with the pilot light on) for several hours.

2. Cut the arugula into slivers, and toss them with the tomato dressing, coating them well. Set the salad aside.

3. Cut each chicken breast in half along the breastbone line. Remove the fillets (the finger-size muscle on the back of each half), and reserve them for another use. Flatten each breast half with the flat end of a meat pounder until thin.

4. Place the cornmeal, salt, pepper, chili powder, and cayenne in a pie plate or shallow bowl, and mix well. Stir the eggs and water together in another shallow dish. Dredge the chicken pieces in the cornmeal mixture, shaking off any excess. Then dip them in the egg, and dredge them again in the cornmeal, pressing lightly to make sure it adheres well.

5. Heat ⅛ inch of the oil in a large heavy skillet, and sauté the chicken pieces until just cooked, about 2 to 3 minutes on each side.

6. To serve, place the chicken on individual plates or on a platter. Drain the arugula salad slightly, and arrange some on top of each portion; serve immediately.

6 portions

STUFFING STUFF

Black pepper	Marjoram
Celery	Onions
Chestnuts	Orange zest
Corn bread	Parsley
Dried apricots	Pecans
Dried cherries	Pistachios
Dried currants	Prunes
Firm-textured bread	Rosemary
Garlic	Sage
Granny Smith apples	Sausage
	Shallots
Grapes	Thyme
Hazelnuts	Walnuts
	Wild rice

SPRING-STUFFED CHICKEN BREASTS

The colors of spring—light green and pink—are rolled into chicken breasts for a delicate combination of flavors. Accented with lemon, parsley, and Madeira, this becomes a very special entrée.

6 whole boneless chicken breasts
4 leeks (white part and 1 inch green), halved lengthwise and well rinsed
7 tablespoons unsalted butter
12 ounces fresh cultivated mushrooms, sliced lengthwise
¾ cup coarsely chopped fresh Italian (flat-leaf) parsley
2 tablespoons chopped fresh rosemary leaves or 2 teaspoons crumbled dried
Grated zest of 2 lemons
12 thin slices prosciutto
12 thin slices (2½ x 1 inches) Monterey Jack cheese
Freshly ground black pepper, to taste
1 cup Madeira or dry sherry

1. Rinse the chicken pieces well and trim away any excess fat. Pat them dry. Place the breasts on a cutting surface skin side down. Remove the fillets (the finger-size muscle on the back of each breast half) and reserve them for another use. Place a piece of waxed paper or plastic wrap over each breast, and pound it with the flat side of a meat pounder until thin. Set the chicken aside.

2. Bring a saucepan of water to a boil. Add the leeks, and simmer for 1 minute. Drain, separate the leaves, and pat dry. Set them aside.

3. Melt 4 tablespoons of the butter in a skillet, and sauté the mushrooms over medium heat until just tender, 5 minutes. Drain well, and set aside.

4. Preheat the oven to 350°F.

5. Combine the parsley, rosemary, and lemon zest in a bowl; mix well.

6. To assemble the rolls, lay the chicken breasts flat, skin side down. Place one slice of prosciutto lengthwise on each side of the breasts. Divide the leeks evenly among the breasts, laying the leaves

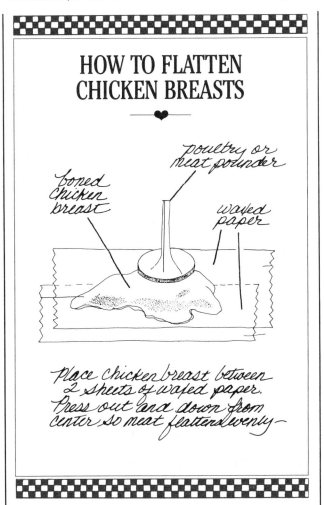

HOW TO FLATTEN CHICKEN BREASTS

boned chicken breast

poultry or meat pounder

waxed paper

Place chicken breast between 2 sheets of waxed paper. Press out and down from center so meat flattens evenly—

lengthwise. Arrange the mushrooms down the center of each breast. Sprinkle the parsley mixture over all, and top with 2 slices of cheese, lengthwise. Sprinkle with pepper.

7. Starting on one long side, roll the breasts carefully, making about three turns, to form a tight roll. Tie the roll together with kitchen string.

8. Line a shallow roasting pan with aluminum foil, and place the chicken rolls, seam side down, in the pan. Sprinkle the chicken with pepper, and place 1½ teaspoons of the remaining butter on top of each roll. Pour the Madeira into the pan.

9. Bake, basting frequently, until golden, 35 minutes.

10. To serve, slice the rolls into ½-inch-thick rounds. Arrange them decoratively on dinner plates, and spoon some of the pan juices over them.

6 portions

STUFFED WHOLE CHICKEN BREASTS

Little rolls of prosciutto, Jarlsberg, and chives are slipped under the skin of these butterflied chicken breasts. The cheese melts beautifully and the prosciutto adds a robust flavor. Serve this with our Spring Green Risotto.

1 whole bone-in chicken breast (about 1 pound)
Salt and freshly ground black pepper, to taste
2 thin slices prosciutto (about 1½ ounces total)
2 thin slices Jarlsberg cheese (about 2 ounces total)
3 tablespoons snipped fresh chives
1 tablespoon unsalted butter

1. Preheat the oven to 375°F.
2. Rinse the chicken well and pat it dry. Place the chicken breast, skin side up, on a work surface. Flatten it with the palm of your hand. Turn it over and remove the hard center breastbone, if desired, for easier carving. Season the chicken lightly with salt and pepper.
3. Lay the prosciutto slices flat on a work surface. Cover each with a slice of cheese and 1 tablespoon of the chives. Roll tightly to form two cylinders.
4. Stuff each roll under the skin, one on each side of the breast. Secure the skin on each side with a toothpick.
5. Melt the butter in a small ovenproof skillet, and brown the chicken on both sides. Sprinkle the top with the remaining 1 tablespoon chives.
6. Transfer the skillet to the oven, and bake 30 minutes.
7. Cut the breast in half, and serve.
1 to 2 portions

APPLE CHICKEN

Welcome autumn with a creamy combination of apples and chicken.

3 apples (Granny Smith, Golden Delicious, or McIntosh, or a combination)
½ lemon
2 tablespoons unsalted butter
1 tablespoon sugar
2 whole boneless skinless chicken breasts (1½ to 2 pounds total)
1 small onion, finely chopped (about ½ cup)
¼ cup apple cider vinegar
¼ cup heavy or whipping cream
¼ cup Berta's Chicken Stock (see Index) or canned broth
½ teaspoon salt

1. Core the apples, peel them, and cut them into ¼-inch-thick slices. Rub them with the lemon to prevent discoloration.
2. Melt 1 tablespoon of the butter in a skillet, and sauté the apples over medium-low heat, 5 to 7 minutes. Sprinkle them with the sugar, raise the heat, and cook over high heat until lightly browned on all sides, shaking the pan constantly to prevent the apple slices from sticking. Set the apples aside.
3. Rinse the chicken well and pat it dry. Cut each chicken breast in half along the breastbone line. Remove the fillets (the finger-size muscle on the back of each half) and reserve them for another use. Flatten each breast half with the flat end of a meat pounder until thin.
4. Melt the remaining 1 tablespoon butter in a large skillet. Raise the heat, add the chicken, and cook until it is lightly colored, about 2 minutes on each side. Remove the chicken from the skillet and set aside.
5. Add the onion to the skillet, cover, and cook until it is tender and slightly caramelized, 8 to 10 minutes. Uncover, raise the heat to high, and add the vinegar. Cook the mixture down to a syrup, about 1 minute. Then whisk in the cream, stock, and salt.
6. Return the chicken to the skillet and simmer gently in the sauce, basting often, until the sauce has thickened slightly and the chicken is cooked, 3 to 5 minutes. Do not overcook.
7. Remove the chicken breasts with a slotted spoon, and arrange them on a heated serving platter or individual plates. Add the apple slices to the skillet; cook over high heat until the sauce has reduced and the apples are thoroughly heated, about 1 minute.
8. Spoon the apples around the chicken, pour the sauce over, and serve immediately.
4 portions

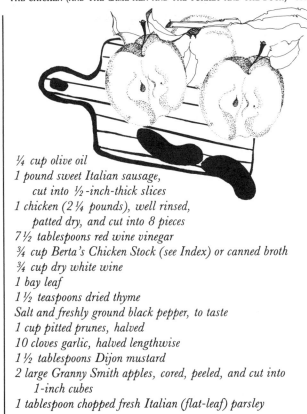

SEASON TO TASTE

Our favorite flavors with chicken include:

Anise	Marjoram
Basil	Onion
Bay leaf	Oregano
Black pepper	Paprika
Borage	Parsley
Chives	Rosemary
Cilantro	Saffron
Cinnamon	Sage
Cumin	Savory
Dill	Scallion
Fenugreek	Sesame oil
Garlic	Sesame seed
Ginger	Shallot
Hot chile	Tarragon
Lemon	Thyme
Lovage	

CHICKEN WITH SAUSAGE, PRUNES, AND APPLES

Chicken and sausages: We combine these luscious morsels with wine, prunes, garlic, and crisp tart apples. Begin the meal with Zucchini Watercress Soup.

¼ cup olive oil
1 pound sweet Italian sausage,
    cut into ½-inch-thick slices
1 chicken (2¼ pounds), well rinsed,
    patted dry, and cut into 8 pieces
7½ tablespoons red wine vinegar
¾ cup Berta's Chicken Stock (see Index) or canned broth
¾ cup dry white wine
1 bay leaf
1½ teaspoons dried thyme
Salt and freshly ground black pepper, to taste
1 cup pitted prunes, halved
10 cloves garlic, halved lengthwise
1½ tablespoons Dijon mustard
2 large Granny Smith apples, cored, peeled, and cut into
    1-inch cubes
1 tablespoon chopped fresh Italian (flat-leaf) parsley

1. Preheat the oven to 350°F.

2. Heat the oil in a flameproof casserole or dutch oven, and brown the sausage in small batches over medium heat. Using a slotted spoon, remove the sausage and set aside.

3. Brown the chicken pieces in the casserole until golden, and set them aside with the sausage. Pour off most of the fat. Add 4½ tablespoons of the vinegar to the casserole, and bring to a boil over medium heat, scraping up any brown bits. Then add the stock, wine, bay leaf, thyme, and salt and pepper. Cook 1 minute.

4. Add the prunes and garlic to the casserole, and cook 1 minute. Then return the sausage and chicken, mix them gently with the sauce, and cover the casserole. Transfer it to the oven, and bake for 40 minutes.

5. Using a slotted spoon, remove the chicken, sausage, and prunes to a heated serving platter, and keep warm. Add the mustard and the remaining 3 tablespoons vinegar to the casserole, and whisk well. Add the apples, and cook over medium-low heat until the apples and garlic are just tender, 5 to 7 minutes. Spoon the sauce over the chicken and sausage, sprinkle with the parsley, and serve.

4 portions

CHICKEN SAUTE WITH ASPARAGUS AND BALSAMIC SPLASH

The sweetness of aged balsamic vinegar holds this dish together in a shiny syrup sauce. A bit more sprinkled on before serving adds an extra sparkle.

2 chickens (2½ to 3 pounds each),
    well rinsed, patted dry, and quartered
2 cups balsamic vinegar
¼ cup fresh thyme leaves
3 tablespoons olive oil
3 sprigs fresh thyme
3 pounds asparagus
Balsamic vinegar, for garnish (optional)

1. Arrange the chicken pieces in a baking dish, and cover with the balsamic vinegar. Scatter the thyme over the chicken, and cover with plastic wrap. Refrigerate, and marinate for at least 8 hours.

2. Remove the chicken from the marinade, and pat the pieces dry. Strain the marinade and set it aside.

3. Heat 2 tablespoons of the oil in a deep heavy skillet, and sauté the chicken, in batches, over medium heat until lightly colored on each side, about 5 minutes. (Be careful: The marinated chicken will easily burn and may sputter when placed in the pan.)

4. Remove the chicken and pour off the fat; add the remaining 1 tablespoon of olive oil to the skillet. Return the dark-meat pieces to the skillet, cover, and cook over medium heat for about 10 minutes. Then turn the dark-meat pieces over, and add the white meat (wings and breasts) and sprigs of fresh thyme. Cover, and continue to cook until the juices run clear when the meat is pierced with a fork, 10 minutes.

5. Meanwhile, bring a large saucepan of water to a boil. Snap off and discard the tough lower stems of the asparagus. Blanch the asparagus in the boiling water until crisp-tender, 2 to 3 minutes. Drain, rinse under cold water, and set aside.

6. When the chicken is cooked, remove it from the skillet and set it aside, covered. Spoon the excess fat from the skillet, and return the skillet to the heat. Add the reserved marinade and the asparagus, and heat through, coating the asparagus thoroughly with the marinade, 1 to 2 minutes. Remove the asparagus and transfer it to heated serving plates or a platter; continue to boil the marinade down until it is reduced to a shiny syrup that coats the back of a spoon.

7. To serve, arrange the chicken next to the asparagus. Coat the chicken pieces with the sauce, and dribble several drops of balsamic vinegar over the asparagus, if desired.

8 portions

RHONE WINES

Lyons, one of the great gastronomic centers of France, rests at the head of the Rhône Valley, where the glorious Rhône grapes grow on steep cliffs, south from Lyons to Avignon. Rhône wines have not enjoyed the same glory as the wines from Bordeaux and Burgundy, although they are often confused with Burgundies. Because quality is not guaranteed with every Rhône wine, it is best to begin with those that are better known and set a standard for yourself. The two we recommend are Tavel and Châteauneuf-du-Pape. Tavel is considered one of the best rosés to come out of France. Made principally from the grenache grape, it has a lustrous, clear pink color and a full-bodied yet fresh taste. This wine should be enjoyed young and chilled. Tavel is in dramatic contrast to the full-bodied red Châteauneuf-du-Pape. Made of grenache and syrah grapes, this sturdy wine is excellent with roast chicken and other homey bistro foods we love so much today.

TRADE SECRET

When trimming and cleaning chicken, cook up the neck and backbone with a small amount of water, parsley, and carrot. Give it time on the stove to reduce and concentrate the flavors. Strain and freeze for a bit of strong stock.

CHICKEN MOLE

When thinking of *mole*, one generally thinks of chicken with chocolate sauce. There are many stories about the derivation of this Mexican festival dish, traditionally prepared with turkey, chiles, and chocolate. In fact, *mole* comes from the Nahuatl Indian word *molli*—a sauce made with chile peppers. The chocolate is not essential.

½ cinnamon stick (2 inches), broken into pieces
1 teaspoon cumin seeds
1 teaspoon aniseeds
1 teaspoon sesame seeds
½ teaspoon whole cloves
¼ cup shelled Toasted Pumpkin Seeds (recipe follows)
3 tablespoons olive oil
2 cloves garlic, minced
½ cup chopped onion
¾ cup Berta's Chicken Stock (see Index) or canned broth
¼ cup Basic Tomato Sauce (see Index)
1 large ripe plum tomato, coarsely chopped
2 tomatillos, papery skin peeled and cut into wedges (see Note)
4 boneless skinless chicken breast halves (about 6 ounces each), well rinsed and patted dry
Salt and freshly ground black pepper, to taste
1 teaspoon ground cinnamon

1. In a small dry skillet, toast the cinnamon stick, cumin, aniseeds, sesame seeds, and cloves over low heat, until fragrant and slightly browned, about 3 minutes. Place the mixture in a coffee or spice grinder, add half the pumpkin seeds, and grind to a powder. Set aside.

2. Heat 1 tablespoon of the oil in a small saucepan. Sauté the garlic and onion over medium heat, until translucent, 5 minutes. Stir in the stock, tomato sauce, and reserved spice mixture. Cook just until slightly thickened. Then stir in the chopped tomato and the tomatillos, and cook just until heated through, 2 to 3 minutes. Set aside and keep warm.

3. Season the chicken with salt and pepper. Sprinkle each side with a small amount of ground cinnamon; rub it into the surface.

4. Heat the remaining 2 tablespoons oil in a skillet, and sauté the chicken over medium heat, until cooked through, about 4 minutes per side. Transfer the chicken to four dinner plates, and spoon the sauce over it. Sprinkle with the remaining pumpkin seeds, and serve.

4 portions

Note: Tomatillos are somewhat firm Mexican green tomatoes with a lemony flavor. Often they are used, uncooked, in salsas. When cooked their flavor is enhanced. They can be found year-round in vegetable markets.

TOASTED PUMPKIN SEEDS

Seeds from 1 pumpkin, pulp and strings removed
2 tablespoons vegetable oil
Salt, to taste

1. Spread the seeds in a single layer on a baking sheet, making sure they are thoroughly cleaned of strings and pulp. Let them air-dry for at least 3 hours. Once dry, hull them.

2. Preheat the oven to 350°F.

3. Add the oil and salt to the seeds, and stir to coat them well. Place the baking sheet in the oven and toast, stirring the seeds every 5 minutes or so, until they are golden brown, about 25 minutes. Let the seeds cool, and then taste for salt; add more if necessary.

CHICKEN CURRY WITH ASIAN PEARS

The primary flavor here is curry—an aromatic, spicy combination of herbs and spices that's pleasantly confusing to the palate. We've added shiitake mushrooms, crisp Asian pears, and a dash of mango chutney. Serve with Rice Pilaf and let your guests add their own chutneys, grated coconut, currants, and nuts. Have a ball!

1 chicken (2½ pounds), well rinsed, patted dry, and
 quartered
Salt and freshly ground black pepper, to taste
1 tablespoon olive oil
½ cup chopped onion
1 tablespoon unsalted butter
2 Asian pears or Golden Delicious apples, cored, peeled, and
 sliced
8 ounces fresh shiitake mushrooms, sliced
2 tablespoons good-quality curry powder
2 tablespoons unbleached all-purpose flour
1 cup Berta's Chicken Stock (see Index) or canned broth
1 tablespoon mango chutney, large pieces coarsely chopped
¼ cup heavy or whipping cream
2 tablespoons chopped fresh Italian (flat-leaf) parsley, for
 garnish

FOR SERVING
1 cup mango chutney
1 cup shelled peanuts
1 cup dried currants
1 cup grated coconut

1. Sprinkle the chicken with salt and pepper.

2. Heat the oil in a large heavy skillet or dutch oven, and brown the chicken on all sides. Add the onion, lower the heat, cover, and cook until the juices run clear when a leg is pricked with a fork, 30 minutes.

3. Meanwhile, melt the butter in another skillet. Add the pears and sauté over medium heat for 3 minutes. Using a slotted spoon, remove them from the pan and set aside. Add the shiitake mushrooms, and sauté over low heat for 15 minutes. Set aside.

4. Remove the chicken from the skillet, and set it aside. Add the curry powder to that skillet, and cook over low heat for 10 minutes. Then add the flour and cook for an additional 3 minutes.

5. Add the stock, chutney and cream. Cook, stirring constantly, until the sauce has thickened, 2 minutes. Return the chicken to the skillet; add the pears and mushrooms. Heat through, about 3 minutes. Garnish with the chopped parsley. Pass dishes of chutney, peanuts, currants, and coconut.

4 portions

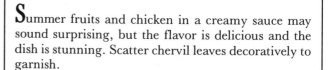

BLACKBERRY CHICKEN

Summer fruits and chicken in a creamy sauce may sound surprising, but the flavor is delicious and the dish is stunning. Scatter chervil leaves decoratively to garnish.

2 whole boneless skinless chicken breasts (about 2 pounds
 total)
2 tablespoons olive oil
2 tablespoons finely chopped shallots
¼ cup blackberry vinegar
¼ cup Berta's Chicken Stock (see Index) or canned broth
¼ cup heavy or whipping cream or crème fraîche (see Index)
1 tablespoon crème de cassis
10 fresh blackberries
Chervil leaves, for garnish

1. Rinse the chicken well and pat it dry. Cut each chicken breast in half along the breastbone line. Remove the fillets (the finger-size muscle on the back of each half) and reserve them for another use. Flatten each breast half with the flat end of a meat pounder until thin.

2. Heat the oil in a large skillet, add the breasts, and cook over medium heat until they are lightly colored, about 3 minutes per side. Remove from the skillet and set aside.

3. Add the shallots to the skillet and cook over low heat until they are translucent, about 5 minutes.

4. Add the vinegar, raise the heat, and cook, stirring occasionally, until it has reduced to a syrupy spoonful. Whisk in the stock, cream, and crème de cassis, and simmer for 1 minute.

5. Return the breasts to the skillet and simmer them gently in the sauce until they are just done, about 5 minutes; do not overcook.

6. Remove the breasts with a slotted spoon, and arrange them on a heated serving platter. Simmer the sauce gently until it has reduced and thickened slightly, 3 minutes. Add the blackberries; cook 1 minute. Pour the sauce over the breasts and serve immediately, garnished with chervil leaves.

4 portions

FREE-RANGE CHICKENS

At the tip-top of our pecking order for chickens are those known as free range, organic, natural, or barnyard. These chickens are fed grain and allowed to roam at will, pecking and scratching their days away. They are not cooped up just getting fat, and they taste the way chickens should. They're leaner, with skin that's creamy white in color and a texture that's neither spongy nor fluffy. There are many breeders in America who are raising free-range chickens; you may well have one in your area. Latch on to your source and become a regular customer. You'll be surprised how good roast chicken can be.

ROASTED CHICKEN LEGS WITH GLAZED SHALLOTS

We've removed the skin in this chicken dish without losing any of the chicken's rich, succulent flavor.

8 chicken legs (drumsticks and thighs)
1 tablespoon olive oil
18 large shallots, peeled
1 teaspoon sugar
½ cup Berta's Chicken Stock (see Index)
    or canned broth
¼ cup dry white wine
3 teaspoons chopped fresh rosemary leaves
2 teaspoons dried thyme
½ teaspoon coarsely ground black pepper
1 tablespoon chopped fresh Italian (flat-leaf) parsley

1. Preheat the oven to 375°F.

2. Remove the meat from each leg in two pieces. Divide each thigh in half. Reserve the leg bones for soup or stock. Skin the 32 chicken pieces, then rinse and pat them dry.

3. Heat the oil in a nonstick skillet. Add the shallots, and cook over medium heat for 7 minutes. Sprinkle with the sugar, and cook until the shallots are browned and caramelized, 3 minutes. Transfer the shallots to a shallow roasting pan.

4. Arrange the chicken pieces in the roasting pan. Combine the stock, wine, 2 teaspoons of the rosemary, 1 teaspoon of the thyme, and the pepper in a small bowl, and stir well. Pour over the chicken, cover the pan, and bake, stirring once, for 30 minutes.

5. Remove the cover, sprinkle the chicken with the remaining 1 teaspoon rosemary and 1 teaspoon thyme, and bake for another 25 minutes, basting and turning the chicken pieces twice.

6. Using a slotted spoon, transfer the chicken and shallots to a deep serving platter and keep warm. Strain the cooking liquid into a saucepan. Bring it to a boil, and cook until it is slightly reduced, 5 minutes. Pour the sauce over the chicken and shallots, and garnish with the parsley. Serve immediately.

6 portions

CHICKEN AND VEGETABLES WITH COUSCOUS

We've combined fresh garden vegetables, chicken, prunes, raisins, and rich Moroccan spices in this pungent chicken stew. Serve it over steamed couscous in large bowls, and savor the gravy.

2 chickens (2½ to 3 pounds each), each cut into 8 pieces
¼ cup olive oil
2 onions, cut into ¼-inch dice
6 cloves garlic, coarsely chopped
8 cups Berta's Chicken Stock (see Index) or canned broth
3 cinnamon sticks, each 3 inches long
2 teaspoons good-quality curry powder
2 teaspoons ground cumin
½ teaspoon ground turmeric
½ teaspoon freshly ground black pepper
½ teaspoon salt
2 carrots, peeled and cut into ¼-inch dice
2 zucchini, cut into ¼-inch dice
1 large white turnip, peeled and cut into ¼-inch dice
1 large red bell pepper, cored, seeded, and cut into ¼-inch dice
5 ripe plum tomatoes, seeded and cut into ½-inch dice
2 cups pitted prunes, halved
1 cup golden raisins
4 cups steamed couscous
2 tablespoons chopped fresh Italian (flat-leaf) parsley

1. Rinse the chicken pieces well and remove the skin (reserve the wings for another use). Pat the pieces dry.

2. Heat the oil in a large dutch oven. Cook the chicken in small batches until opaque and slightly golden on both sides. Do not overcook it. Using a slotted spoon, transfer the chicken to a dish and set it aside.

3. Add the onions and garlic to the dutch oven, and cook over low heat for 10 minutes. Then add the stock, cinnamon sticks, curry powder, cumin, turmeric, pepper, and salt. Slowly bring to a boil, then continue boiling for 5 minutes.

4. Reduce the heat to a simmer, and add the chicken legs and thighs, carrots, zucchini, turnip, and bell pepper. Simmer for 10 minutes. Then add the chicken breasts, tomatoes, prunes, and raisins, and simmer an additional 10 minutes.

5. Remove the cinnamon sticks, and serve the stew in deep bowls over steamed couscous, giving everyone plenty of broth. Garnish with the chopped parsley.

6 portions

TRADE SECRET

When cooking poultry that has been cut in pieces, remember that white meat cooks more quickly than dark.

MOROCCAN CHICKEN

Tangy preserved lemon and sweet dates enrich the sauce of this chicken dish. We use the dark meat because it resembles the flavor of the pigeons traditionally used in Moroccan tagines.

SPICE MIXTURE
3 cloves garlic, minced
2 tablespoons extra virgin olive oil
1½ teaspoons ground cumin
1 teaspoon ground ginger
1 teaspoon coarse (kosher) salt
½ teaspoon ground turmeric
½ teaspoon paprika
¼ teaspoon ground cinnamon
Freshly ground black pepper, to taste

4 chicken legs, rinsed well, patted dry, drumsticks and thighs separated
1 Preserved Lemon (see Index)
1 cup Greek olives, mixed green and black, pitted
10 dried dates, pitted and halved lengthwise

1. Combine all the ingredients for the spice mixture in a large bowl. Add the chicken pieces and coat them well with the mixture. Let the chicken stand, loosely covered, for 1 hour.

2. Place a deep heavy skillet over medium heat, and add the chicken, skin side down. Cover, and cook for 20 minutes (the chicken will cook in its own juices).

3. Meanwhile, discard the preserved lemon pulp, and cut the peel crosswise into ¼-inch-thick strips.

4. Turn the chicken pieces over, and sprinkle them with the lemon peel, olives, and dates. Cover, and cook another 20 minutes, adding a small amount of water if the mixture is too dry. Serve immediately.

4 to 6 portions

PEKING STIR-FRY

Shiitake mushrooms, chicken, and crisp vegetables—spiced with garlic, ginger, scallions, soy sauce, and chile oil—are stir-fried for this beautiful, light Oriental dish.

1 ounce dried shiitake mushrooms*
1½ cups Berta's Chicken Stock (see Index) or canned broth
½ cup peanut oil, plus more if needed
3 whole boneless, skinless chicken breasts, well rinsed,
*   patted dry, and cut lengthwise into ½-inch strips*
1 red bell pepper, cored, seeded, and cut into julienne
3 ribs celery, cut on the diagonal into julienne
10 scallions (green onions), white bulb and 4 inches green
2 carrots, peeled and cut into julienne
1 head bok choy (8 ounces), well rinsed and coarsely chopped
1 can (7 ounces) baby corn, drained
⅓ pound snow peas, trimmed and stringed
1 tablespoon finely minced fresh ginger
4 large cloves garlic, finely minced
2 tablespoons dry sherry
1½ tablespoons soy sauce
Dash of hot chile oil (optional)*
1 cup salted peanuts

1. Place the mushrooms in a small saucepan, add the chicken stock, and bring to a boil. Remove the pan from the heat, and let the mushrooms soak for 30 minutes. Then drain the mushrooms, reserving the liquid. Trim and discard the stems, and cut the mushroom tops in half. Set them aside.

2. Heat ¼ cup of the peanut oil in a large skillet or wok. When it is very hot, sauté the chicken strips, in small batches, until just cooked through and tender. Add more peanut oil as needed. Using a slotted spoon, remove the chicken from the skillet and keep warm.

3. Add the remaining ¼ cup peanut oil to the skillet. When it is very hot, sauté the bell pepper, celery, and scallions for 1 minute. Add the carrots and cook 1 minute more. Add the bok choy, corn, and snow peas, and cook 1 minute longer. Using a slotted spoon, remove all the vegetables from the skillet and set them aside, covered, to keep warm.

4. Add the reserved mushroom soaking liquid, ginger, garlic, sherry, soy sauce, and chile oil to the skillet. Cook over high heat to thicken the sauce slightly, 1 minute. Then return the vegetables to the skillet and quickly coat them with the sauce.

5. Place the chicken on a large serving platter, and arrange the vegetables on top of the chicken. Sprinkle with the peanuts, and serve immediately.

6 to 8 portions

*Available in Asian groceries and other specialty food shops.

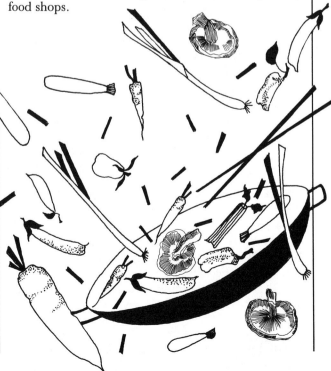

CHICKEN BREASTS WITH JULIENNE OF VEGETABLES

A light, quickly prepared, quickly cooked dish. The chicken breasts remain plump and moist and the vegetables retain their fresh flavors.

4 leeks (white part and 1 inch green), well rinsed and cut into fine julienne
1 carrot, peeled and cut into fine julienne
6 garlic cloves, sliced paper-thin
1 small hot finger chile pepper, thinly sliced, or a pinch of dried red pepper flakes
2 teaspoons chopped fresh dill
4 skinless boneless chicken breast halves (5 to 6 ounces each), well rinsed and patted dry
¼ teaspoon salt
Freshly ground black pepper, to taste

1. Toss the leeks, carrot, garlic, chile pepper, and 1 teaspoon of the dill in a bowl.

2. Sprinkle a thin layer of the mixed vegetables in a 9-inch glass pie plate.

3. Season the chicken breasts with the salt and pepper. Arrange them on top of the vegetables, around the edge of the pie plate. Sprinkle with the remaining vegetables, piling most of them in the center of the dish. Cover tightly with microwave plastic wrap and prick a tiny hole in the center.

4. Cook 8 minutes at full power (650 to 700 watts), or until the chicken is just firm to the touch. If the chicken seems undercooked, let it stand, covered, for 2 minutes. Remove the plastic wrap, sprinkle the vegetables with the remaining 1 teaspoon dill, and serve immediately.

4 portions

Note: This recipe was cooked on High (full power, 650 to 700 watts) in a carousel microwave, using microwave-safe containers.

If your microwave is less powerful, you will have to allow for more cooking time (approximately 1½ times the amount called for—but watch carefully); if it does not have a carousel, you may have to rotate the dish while it is cooking.

CHICKEN WITH SALSA

We consider this a perfect microwave dish. The ingredients are prepared ahead of time, and the meal is arranged and cooked directly on dinner plates.

SALSA
½ cup corn kernels, cooked
½ cup diced ripe tomato
2 tablespoons diced red bell pepper
2 tablespoons diced green bell pepper
2 tablespoons chopped cilantro (fresh coriander)
2 tablespoons red wine vinegar
2 tablespoons olive oil
1 clove garlic, minced
½ teaspoon ground cumin
¼ teaspoon salt
Freshly ground black pepper, to taste
Pinch of cayenne pepper

2 boneless skinless chicken breast halves (about 5 ounces each), well rinsed and patted dry
Salt and freshly ground black pepper, to taste

1. Stir all the salsa ingredients together in a small bowl, and set aside.

2. Remove the fillets (the finger-size muscle on the back of each breast half), and reserve them for another use. Flatten each half with the flat end of a meat pounder to a thickness of ¼ inch. Cut each breast half into four long strips. Lightly season them with salt and pepper.

3. Lightly oil two 10-inch dinner plates. Arrange four strips of chicken around the edge of each plate, and spoon the salsa over the chicken.

4. One at a time, cook each portion at full power (650 to 700 watts), uncovered, for 3 minutes. Serve immediately.

2 portions

Note: This recipe was cooked on High (full power, 650 to 700 watts) in a carousel microwave, using microwave-safe containers.

If your microwave is less powerful, you will have to allow for more cooking time (approximately 1½ times the amount called for—but watch carefully); if it does not have a carousel, you may have to rotate the dish while it is cooking.

HENS SOUTHWESTERN STYLE

A simple-to-prepare dish of Rock Cornish hens with a southwestern twist. The spices come through, adding great flavor, and the meat is perfectly moist. Delicious served with fresh Pineapple Salsa.

2 Rock Cornish hens (about 1½ pounds each), quartered and backbones removed
2 tablespoons fresh orange juice
1 tablespoon freshly grated orange zest
1 tablespoon white wine vinegar
1 clove garlic, minced
¾ teaspoon dried oregano
½ teaspoon salt
¼ teaspoon ground cinnamon
¼ teaspoon cayenne pepper
¼ teaspoon ground cumin
Freshly ground black pepper, to taste
1 cup Pineapple Salsa (see Index)

1. Rinse the hen pieces well and pat them dry.

2. Combine all the ingredients except the hens and salsa in a mixing bowl, and stir well. Coat the hen pieces thoroughly with this mixture.

3. Arrange the hen quarters in a glass 10-inch pie plate so that the thickest parts of the legs and thighs are against the rim and the breasts are in the center. Cover the pie plate loosely, and allow the dish to stand for 1 hour.

4. Cover the plate with microwave plastic wrap, and cook at full power (650 to 700 watts) for 10 minutes. Then turn the hen pieces over, re-cover the plate, and cook 2 minutes.

5. Allow the dish to stand for 1 minute. Then pile the hen quarters on a heated platter, and spoon some of the cooking juices over them. Serve with Pineapple Salsa on the side.

3 to 4 portions

Note: This recipe was cooked on High (full power, 650 to 700 watts) in a carousel microwave, using microwave-safe containers.

If your microwave is less powerful, you will have to allow for more cooking time (approximately 1½ times the amount called for—but watch carefully); if it does not have a carousel, you may have to rotate the dish while it is cooking.

> **"S**o much of our future lies in preserving our past."
> —PETER WESTBROOK

COQ AU VIN

With a microwave, you can have the long-simmered flavor of traditional coq au vin in half an hour. Use a hearty Burgundy of good quality, as its flavor infuses the whole dish.

2 slices bacon, cut into 1-inch pieces
20 fresh cultivated button mushrooms, stems trimmed
20 small pearl onions, peeled
2 cloves garlic, minced
½ teaspoon dried oregano
½ teaspoon dried thyme leaves
1 chicken (3½ pounds), well rinsed, patted dry, and cut into 8 pieces
1 cup Berta's Chicken Stock (see Index) or canned chicken broth
1 cup dry red wine
2 tablespoons tomato paste
½ teaspoon salt
Freshly ground black pepper, to taste
2 tablespoons unbleached all-purpose flour

1. Cook the bacon at full power (650 to 700 watts) in a microwave-safe 2½-quart casserole, uncovered, for 3 minutes. Stir in the mushrooms, onions, garlic, and herbs. Cook 2 minutes.

2. Arrange the chicken pieces on top of the vegetables, with the legs, thighs, and wings around the edge and the breasts in the center.

3. Combine the stock, wine, and tomato paste. Stir well, and pour over the chicken. Cover, and cook 12 minutes.

4. Using a slotted spoon, transfer the chicken and vegetables to a warmed platter.

5. Season the sauce with the salt and pepper. Place the flour in a small bowl, and add ¼ cup of the sauce, whisking until smooth. Whisk this mixture back into the remaining sauce and cook, uncovered, 2 minutes.

6. Return the chicken to the casserole, and arrange the vegetables on top. Cover, and cook 7 minutes. Let the dish stand 3 minutes, and then serve.

4 portions

Note: This recipe was cooked on High (full power, 650 to 700 watts) in a carousel microwave, using microwave-safe containers.

If your microwave is less powerful, you will have to allow for more cooking time (approximately 1½ times the amount called for—but watch carefully); if it does not have a carousel, you may have to rotate the dish while it is cooking.

Poultry provides complete protein and has less fat than beef, pork, or lamb. Most of the fat it does have is unsaturated. Small young birds, such as Rock Cornish hens, broiler-fryers, and small turkeys, have less fat (and fewer calories) than their more mature cousins. Wild game birds are also leaner than those raised domestically. Poultry is a good source of vitamins B_2, B_6, B_{12}, riboflavin, and niacin. It is also rich in zinc and magnesium.

CHICKEN, AVOCADO, AND CHEDDAR MELT

A New Basics version of a childhood favorite.

¼ cup mayonnaise
¼ cup ketchup
1 scallion (green onion), white bulb and 3 inches green, very thinly sliced on the diagonal
3 teaspoons chopped fresh Italian (flat-leaf) parsley
1 whole boneless skinless chicken breast (8 ounces), cooked
1 ripe avocado
4 slices whole-wheat bread, lightly toasted
4 large slices sharp Cheddar cheese, ⅛ to ¼ inch thick
Paprika, to taste

1. Mix the mayonnaise, ketchup, 1 teaspoon of the sliced scallion, and 2 teaspoons of the parsley in a bowl. Set aside.

2. Cut the chicken breast in half down the center. Cut each half into four thin long slices.

3. Peel the avocado, remove the pit, and slice each half lengthwise into four slices.

4. Place two slices of chicken on each piece of toast. Spread half the reserved dressing over the chicken. Lay the avocado slices over the dressing, and cover with the remaining dressing. Place a piece of Cheddar on top of each sandwich (the cheese should be large enough to cover the toast; or use several smaller pieces). Sprinkle lightly with the paprika and the remaining scallion slices.

5. Preheat the broiler.

6. Place the sandwiches in a broiling pan, and broil 3 inches from the heat until the cheese melts, 1½ minutes. Remove the pan from the broiler, and sprinkle the sandwiches with the remaining 1 teaspoon parsley. Serve immediately.

2 to 4 portions

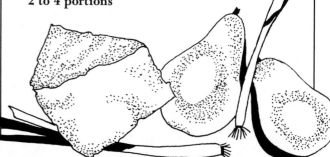

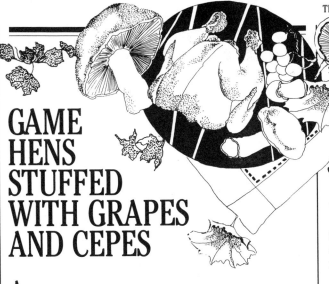

GAME HENS STUFFED WITH GRAPES AND CEPES

An elegant entrée for any dinner party, these game hens are easy to prepare. If cèpes are unavailable, porcini or morels make excellent substitutes.

1 cup Madeira
2 ounces dried cèpes, porcini, or morel mushrooms
1 cup seedless green or red grapes
8 tablespoons (1 stick) unsalted butter, at room temperature
½ cup seasoned dried bread crumbs
2 tablespoons chopped fresh parsley
¼ teaspoon dried thyme leaves
4 Cornish game hens
Salt and freshly ground black pepper, to taste

1. Bring the Madeira to a boil in a small saucepan. Add the cèpes, remove the pan from the heat, and set it aside.
2. Preheat the oven to 350°F.
3. Combine the grapes, 4 tablespoons of the butter, bread crumbs, parsley, and thyme in a mixing bowl, and toss well.
4. Rinse the hens well and pat them dry. Fill the cavities with the stuffing. Drain the cèpes, reserving the Madeira, and place 1 cèpe in each cavity.
5. Place the stuffed birds in a roasting pan. Dot them with the remaining 4 tablespoons butter, and sprinkle them with salt and pepper. Pour a small amount of the reserved Madeira (about ⅓ cup) into the pan. Bake for 1 hour, basting occasionally.
6. Remove the pan from the oven, and transfer the hens to a heated platter. Add the remaining cèpes and Madeira to the pan, and cook over low heat until the liquid is slightly reduced, about 5 minutes. Pour the sauce over the hens, and serve immediately.

4 portions

CORNISH HENS, SHOEMAKER'S STYLE

We've replaced the familiar chicken with Cornish game hens for this gutsy Italian classic. If you have an oval copper baking dish, use that and bring it right to the table from the oven.

¼ cup unbleached all-purpose flour
1 tablespoon minced fresh rosemary leaves
1 teaspoon salt
Freshly ground black pepper, to taste
2 Cornish game hens (about 3 pounds total), rinsed well, patted dry, and each cut into 8 pieces
3 tablespoons olive oil
2 shallots, minced
2 cloves garlic, minced
¾ cup dry white wine
¾ cup homemade beef stock (see Index) or canned broth
1 teaspoon anchovy paste
3 sprigs rosemary, cut into 1-inch pieces

1. Preheat the oven to 375°F.
2. Combine the flour, minced rosemary, salt, and pepper in a shallow bowl, and mix well. Dredge the hen pieces in the mixture, shaking off any excess.
3. Heat the oil in a large ovenproof skillet. Sauté the hen pieces over medium heat, turning once, until browned, 15 minutes. Transfer them to a plate.
4. Add the shallots and garlic to the skillet, and cook until golden, 2 minutes. Transfer them to a small plate. Pour off any fat, and return the hen pieces to the skillet.
5. In a small bowl, whisk the wine, stock, and anchovy paste together until smooth. Pour this mixture over the hens, and heat to a boil. Sprinkle with the reserved shallots and garlic, and with the pieces of rosemary sprigs. Transfer the skillet to the oven, and bake until the hens are deep golden and the sauce is slightly thickened, 30 minutes. Arrange the hen pieces on a warmed platter, and spoon the sauce over them. Serve immediately.

4 portions

TALKING TURKEY

———•———

It's easier to cook turkey than it used to be. Our traditional holiday bird, enormous and glittering in all its golden browned splendor, is marketed year-round in more modest forms. We're not always cooking for 20 or honoring abundance. We're seeing 4- and 6-pound broilers, which can be stuffed and roasted as well as cut up and grilled. We're also seeing turkey parts. This lean, tasty bird is gaining in popularity.

The greatest selection of turkeys is available at holiday time, and if you want to prepare a fresh turkey, Thanksgiving is the time to do so. Fresh turkey is much more succulent than frozen, but you must order one well in advance.

Wild turkeys are also wonderful. Their flesh is firm and dense and their aroma intriguing. They're smaller than most domesticated turkeys—usually 6 to 10 pounds, which is adequate for 6 to 8 persons. If you want a wild turkey, talk to your local butcher well in advance. He may be able to track one down given enough time.

Turkeys are categorized by ready-to-cook weight: small is 4 to 10 pounds; medium, 10 to 19 pounds; and large, 20 pounds and up. When buying a turkey or turkey parts for roasting, figure you will need about a pound per person. The younger the turkeys, the more tender the meat: A fryer-roaster is just 4 months old and most tender, a young hen or tom is 5 to 7 months old, and a yearling is a year old. Mature hens and toms over 15 months old are rarely found today.

A fresh turkey should be free of bruises, and the cavity should have a clean, fresh smell. At home, rinse well inside and out and pat dry, then refresh inside and out with fresh orange juice.

Thaw a frozen turkey in its original wrapper on a tray in the refrigerator. Be sure to allow the bird enough time to thaw completely; a 12-pound bird will need about 2 days, a 24-pound bird, 3 to 4.

Turkeys are ideal for stuffing, but never stuff the bird until you're ready to roast it. (Stuffing is the perfect moist environment for bacteria.) Be sure not to pack a turkey too tightly with stuffing; leave room for the stuffing to expand.

The perpetual problem with roasting turkey is to keep the breast meat moist and still have the legs cooked through. Our recommendation is to roast at 325°F, breast side up throughout, basting at least once an hour with pan juices and melted butter. To test for doneness, prick the skin at the thickest part of the thigh with the tip of a knife; the juices should run clear with no tinge of pink.

Remove the turkey to a heated platter; cover it loosely and let it stand for 15 minutes before carving. The juices will settle and slicing will go easier.

Carve the turkey at the table if you are a dependable carver or have one handy; otherwise, display it and then carve it in the kitchen.

Turkey pieces have brought this traditional holiday bird to the weekly dinner table. Turkey is now available in whole and half breasts, bone-in or boneless, turkey drumsticks, thighs, hind quarters (thigh and drumstick), wings and drumettes (half wings), as well as turkey breast cutlets, slices, and tenderloin. The dark meat—the thighs and drumsticks—and the wings should be braised or simmered slowly in flavorful broth. The breast can be roasted as if it were a whole turkey, and the breast cutlets or slices can be sautéed like veal or chicken cutlets, broiled, or cut up for stir-frying and kabobs.

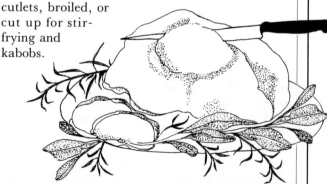

THANKSGIVING TURKEY

We've made the traditional meal a little lighter and a little crispier. Besides sausage, celery, and onions, the stuffing is flavored with toasted hazelnuts and dried Michigan cherries. We've left out the butter, and moistened the stuffing instead with tawny port and seasoned broth. The turkey is cooked on a bed of vegetables, which flavor the pan juices for the gravy—and we've added less flour than usual to the gravy. It's all new and delicious.

STUFFING
2 tablespoons vegetable oil
3 cups chopped celery with leaves
2 cups chopped onions
1 pound bulk country pork sausage, broken into small chunks
2 tart apples, cut into ½-inch cubes
1 cup hazelnuts, toasted, skinned, and chopped (see Index)
1 cup dried pitted cherries*
6 cups stale bread cubes
1 teaspoon salt
1 teaspoon dried thyme leaves
1 teaspoon crumbled dried sage leaves
Freshly ground black pepper, to taste
1 cup tawny port
1 cup Berta's Chicken Stock (see Index) or canned broth, well seasoned with salt and pepper

1 fresh turkey (18 to 20 pounds), with its giblets
3 ribs celery, halved crosswise
1 onion, quartered
1 large carrot, peeled and quartered
3½ cups water
8 tablespoons (1 stick) unsalted butter, melted
¾ cup tawny port
¼ cup unbleached all-purpose flour
Salt and freshly ground black pepper, to taste

1. Prepare the stuffing: Heat the oil in a large skillet. Sauté the celery and onions over low heat until softened but not browned, 10 minutes. Transfer the vegetables to a large mixing bowl.

2. Add the sausage to the skillet and cook, breaking up the sausage with a spoon, until it is cooked through and lightly browned, 10 minutes. Add the sausage to the vegetables in the bowl.

3. Stir the apples, hazelnuts, and cherries into the sausage mixture. Add the bread cubes, and toss lightly. Sprinkle with the salt, thyme, sage, and pepper. Toss lightly again. Add the port and stock, and toss until well blended.

4. Preheat the oven to 325°F.

5. Rinse the turkey well and pat it dry. Stuff the cavity loosely with about 7 cups of the stuffing. Skewer or sew the opening shut. Stuff the neck area with about 3 cups of stuffing. Secure the neck skin flap under the turkey. (Put any remaining stuffing in an ovenproof casserole and set it aside.)

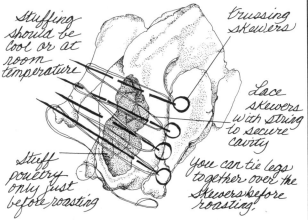

stuffing should be cool or at room temperature

trussing skewers

Lace skewers with string to secure cavity

Stuff poultry only just before roasting

You can tie legs together over the skewers before roasting!

6. Arrange a bed of the celery, onion, and carrot pieces in a large roasting pan. Gently place the turkey on the vegetables, and arrange the neck and gizzard alongside. Pour 3 cups water into the pan.

7. Roast the turkey for 4 hours, brushing it well with melted butter once an hour. After it has cooked for 4 hours, pour or brush ¼ cup of the port over the turkey. Bake 15 minutes. Repeat basting with port and baking three more times, until the turkey has cooked a total of 5 hours. (If you have reserved some extra stuffing in a casserole, stir in a bit of the pan juices and put it in the oven during the last hour, loosely covered. Bake for 45 minutes.)

8. Transfer the turkey to a heated platter, cover it loosely, and allow it to rest for 15 minutes.

9. While the turkey is resting, strain the pan juices into a saucepan. You should have 4 cups (add broth or water if necessary). Heat to a simmer.

10. Stir the flour and remaining ½ cup water together in a small bowl until smooth. Whisk this into the pan juices, and heat to a boil. Simmer 5 minutes. Season with salt and pepper, pour into a sauceboat, and serve along with the turkey.

16 portions (with leftovers)

*Available in the dried fruit section of top-quality supermarkets or in specialty food shops.

KNIFE AND FORK TURKEY SANDWICH

Luscious turkey slices replace the bread in this Thanksgiving weekend brunch or lunchtime sandwich.

2 large slices (¼ inch thick) cooked turkey
¼ cup leftover turkey stuffing
1 heaping tablespoon cranberry sauce
1 slice (⅛ inch thick) Vermont Cheddar cheese
¼ cup leftover turkey gravy (see page 423, Steps 9 and 10)

1. Preheat the oven to 350°F.
2. Assemble the "sandwich," using the turkey slices in place of bread: Place one slice of the turkey on a piece of aluminum foil. Spread the stuffing over the turkey. Spread the cranberry sauce over the stuffing, lay the slice of cheese over the cranberry sauce, and cover with the remaining turkey.
3. Wrap the foil loosely around the sandwich, place it on a baking sheet, and bake for 15 minutes.
4. While the sandwich is baking, heat the gravy in a small saucepan.
5. Unwrap the sandwich, transfer it to a plate, and pour the gravy over it. Serve immediately.

1 portion

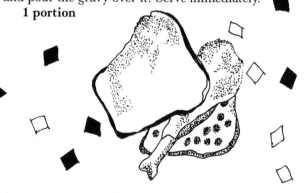

TURKEY BISTEEYA

Bisteeya, the great classical dish of Morocco, is one of the most spectacular dishes in the world. Traditionally it is a pigeon pie with eggs, almonds, lemon juice, an array of spices—all enclosed in a crackly crust of paper-thin layers of pastry wrapped up like a present. We've made it for parties for years, always with chicken, but why not turkey?

We usually serve this with Oranges Orientales or a bowl of pomegranate seeds on the side. A light Beaujolais or a Gamay-Beaujolais makes the occasion even more festive.

4 cups water
Zest of 1 lemon, cut into 8 strips
1 ½ teaspoons salt
2 small onions
1 cinnamon stick, 6 inches long
1 pound uncooked boneless turkey thigh, well rinsed, patted dry, and cut into 3 pieces
6 eggs
2 tablespoons fresh lemon juice
1 ½ teaspoons ground cinnamon
Freshly ground black pepper, to taste
5 ounces sliced almonds (about ¾ cup), toasted (see Index)
1 ½ tablespoons sugar
14 sheets (each 13 x 9 inches) phyllo dough, thawed if frozen
8 tablespoons (1 stick) unsalted butter, melted

1. Combine the water, 2 strips of the lemon zest, 1 teaspoon of the salt, onions, and cinnamon stick in a saucepan. Bring to a boil, cover, and cook 10 minutes.
2. Add the turkey, lower the heat, and simmer until cooked through, about 15 minutes. Remove the pan from the heat, and let the turkey stand in the liquid until it is cool enough to handle.
3. Reserve the cooking liquid. Shred the turkey and cut the onions into slivers. Set them aside.
4. In a mixing bowl, whisk together the eggs, lemon juice, ½ teaspoon of the ground cinnamon, remaining ½ teaspoon salt, the pepper, and ½ cup of the turkey cooking liquid.
5. Cook the egg mixture in a nonstick skillet over low heat, stirring, until dry clumps form, 3 to 4 minutes. Drain in a colander or strainer.
6. Combine the almonds, the remaining 6 strips of the lemon zest, the sugar, and the remaining 1 teaspoon ground cinnamon in a food processor. Process until the mixture resembles bread crumbs. Set aside.
7. Preheat the oven to 375°F. Butter a baking sheet.
8. Arrange 1 sheet of the phyllo on the prepared baking sheet. Brush it with some of the melted butter, and sprinkle with 1 teaspoon of the almond mixture.

Repeat with seven more sheets of phyllo, buttering and sprinkling almond mixture between them. Butter the top sheet.

9. Bake the phyllo layers 10 minutes. Allow to cool slightly. Leave the oven on.

10. Sprinkle the turkey and onion over the phyllo, leaving a 1-inch border around the edges. Cover with the drained egg mixture.

11. Set aside about 3 tablespoons of the almond filling. Sprinkle the remainder over the egg mixture.

Slowly pour ½ cup of the turkey cooking liquid over the egg mixture.

12. Cover the filling with 6 more sheets of phyllo, again brushing with melted butter and sprinkling 1 teaspoon almond mixture between the sheets. Sprinkle the top with the remaining almond mixture.

13. Bake until golden and crisp, 30 minutes. Let the bisteeya stand 5 minutes before cutting it into squares and serving.

6 portions

WINTER WINES

The slower pace of winter is perfect for formal entertaining, for wines that are generally heavier and more ceremonious. But choosing a wine for Thanksgiving or Christmas turkey dinner is difficult for most. The turkey itself is mild in flavor, but the traditional accompaniments—cranberries, sweet potatoes, Brussels sprouts, and stuffing—are strong-flavored mixtures of sweet and tart. A good rule is to stay with simple fruity wines, such as Beaujolais nouveau, white or red Zinfandel, or California Gewürztraminer. It all comes down to personal taste. Our favorite is a rich, fruity red California Zinfandel because it has the character to handle the aromatic side dishes. The Zinfandels we like are from Ridge Vineyards, Clos du Val, Ravenswood, and Burgess Vineyards. These are balanced enough to keep in the cellar for future celebrations, should you find one that you really like.

We like all our holidays accompanied with a bit of the bubbly—sparkling wines, especially Champagne. A good sparkling wine should have body, flavor, and aftertaste, and yet be light, fruity, and elegant. A vintage sparkling wine will have more color and body and a more complex bouquet than a non-vintage variety. Any sparkling wine should be chilled in the refrigerator for at least two hours before serving. Never place a sparkling wine in the freezer. If you need to chill the wine quickly, place the bottle in a bucket half-filled with ice and water for about 30 minutes. Ideally, the wine should be served between 42° and 48°F; if it's too cold the flavor and bouquet will be masked.

To uncork a sparkling wine, avoid the festive approach—with its loud pop and wasteful gush—and ease the cork out gently. Because the wine is under significant pressure, you should not take your hand from the cork until it is completely removed. Stand the bottle upright on a solid surface and remove the top half of the neck foil. Keep one hand over the cork and loosen the wire cage with the other hand. Grab the cage and cork firmly in one hand and, holding the bottle at a 45-degree angle, twist the bottle off the cork with the other hand. Do not twist the cork from the bottle; notice we said the bottle should be twisted from the cork. Hold the bottle at the same angle for a few seconds to allow the pressure to equalize, then commence pouring.

Remember to hold your glass by the stem instead of the bowl to keep your hands from warming the wine. We find that tall Champagne flutes support the bubbles for the longest time. The best sparkling wines have very tiny bubbles that rise steadily to the surface. The bubbles enhance the aroma and help spread the taste throughout your mouth. We like Iron Horse 1983 Blanc de Noirs for its good value, but when we really want to celebrate we drink Bollinger Tradition RD 1975 or Louis Roederer Cristal.

TURKEY IN THREE ACTS

Don't even think of serving this dish only in November. Turkey should be enjoyed all year long. It is versatile and exciting in many preparations. We've made the first act a luscious barley soup lightened with dill; the second act, a vegetable-stuffed breast; and the third, roasted legs and thighs. Serve the turkey with Maple Cranberry Sauce or Mango Chutney, and await the applause.

1 small fresh turkey (about 10 pounds), with its giblets (see Step 1)

BROTH
12 cups water
½ cup pearl barley
3 ounces haricots verts (thin, tender green beans), trimmed
2 parsnips, peeled and julienned
1 leek (white part and 1 inch green), rinsed and julienned
2 teaspoons salt
Freshly ground black pepper, to taste
¼ cup chopped fresh dill

STUFFING
2 tablespoons vegetable oil
2 cups chopped sweet potato (½-inch dice)
2 cups coarsely chopped mushrooms
1 cup chopped onion
1 cup fresh bread crumbs
1 cup Berta's Chicken Stock (see Index) or canned broth
¼ cup chopped fresh parsley
1 egg
1 tablespoon chopped fresh sage leaves
1 tablespoon chopped fresh rosemary leaves
1 teaspoon salt
1 teaspoon ground ginger
Freshly ground black pepper, to taste

BASTING SAUCE
8 tablespoons (1 stick) unsalted butter, melted
¼ teaspoon ground nutmeg
¼ teaspoon ground cloves
¼ teaspoon paprika
Freshly ground black pepper, to taste

1. Have the turkey cut as follows: drumsticks and thighs removed and separated, wings removed at the shoulder, breast boned and left in one large piece, carcass cut up. Rinse the pieces and pat them dry.

2. First, make the broth: Place the turkey wings, neck, giblets (except the liver), and carcass in a large soup pot, and add the water. Bring to a boil. Lower the heat and simmer about 1¼ hours, skimming when necessary.

3. Strain the broth; you should have about 10 cups. Return the broth to the pot, and stir in the barley. Simmer uncovered, 30 minutes. Then stir in the haricots verts, parsnips, and leek. Simmer 15 minutes. Season with the salt and pepper. Just before serving, stir in the dill.

4. Make the stuffing: Finely chop the turkey liver. Heat the oil in a large skillet. Add the sweet potato, mushrooms, onion, and turkey liver to the skillet. Cover, and cook 10 minutes. Allow to cool to room temperature.

5. Transfer the cooled mixture to a large bowl, and stir in the remaining stuffing ingredients.

6. Preheat the oven to 350°F.

7. Stuff and roast the turkey: Open the boned turkey breast, skin side down, on a work surface. Slide six lengths of kitchen string, long enough to wrap around the rolled breast, under the skin at 2-inch intervals. Sprinkle the breast lightly with salt and pepper.

8. Spoon the stuffing over the breast. Fold the breast over the stuffing and tie the strings to form a long roll. Tuck in any flaps of skin to help hold the stuffing. (You may need a hand tying the breast.)

9. Turn the roll over, and place it, skin side up, in a large roasting pan. Wrap a double thickness of aluminum foil around the turkey roll to hold it in place while it is roasting. Arrange the drumsticks and thighs around the roll.

10. Pour 1½ cups water into the pan. Stir together all the basting sauce ingredients, and brush this mixture over the turkey.

11. Bake 2 hours, basting every 15 minutes. Let the turkey stand, loosely covered, 15 minutes.

12. Slice the stuffed breast (removing the strings), and arrange the slices decoratively on a warmed platter. Carve the dark meat, and keep it warm in some of the pan juices.

13. To serve, begin with the soup course. Follow it with the sliced stuffed breast with a fruit relish. Act III is the carved dark meat with degreased pan juices, holiday vegetable, and potato.

8 to 10 portions

TURKEY STUFFING

There are hundreds of ways to make stuffing (called dressing or filling in some parts of the country). Stuffing can be moist or dry; in fact, people seem to have as strong opinions about moist or dry stuffing as about thin or thick pizza crust. Stuffing should be the way you like it, but never soggy.

Bread; corn bread; wild, brown, and white rice; or sweet and white potatoes can be used for the body of the stuffing. Sausage, oysters, onions, walnuts, chestnuts, pecans, hazelnuts, apples, pears, cranberries, dried apricots and prunes, or fresh or dried mushrooms will add flavor and texture. Butter, margarine, olive oil, rendered chicken fat, cream, broth, wine, brandy, or fruit or vegetable juices serve to moisten the mixture.

Sage is the traditional herb of Thanksgiving stuffing. (Try fresh sage in your next stuffing for a delightful difference.) But there's no law that states turkey and sage *must* go together; try fresh thyme, rosemary, marjoram, or winter savory instead.

Make the stuffing at your leisure and store it in the refrigerator; then stuff the bird just before roasting it. (Never stuff a turkey in advance; the risk of growing bacteria is too great.) Spoon the stuffing in loosely so there's room for it to expand. Stuffing that's packed in too tightly will come out of the bird compact and dense. You can fit about ½ cup stuffing in the cavity for every pound of turkey. Bake any extra in a buttered or oiled casserole covered loosely, basting it with a little of the turkey drippings if you want.

BOURBON TURKEY

In this unconventional dish, a mounded platter of glazed mahogany turkey pieces offers the flavors of the Far East in the marinade and of the American South in the glaze.

1 turkey or capon (10 pounds), cut up (see Step 1)

MARINADE
1 cup dry red wine
½ cup bourbon
½ cup dry sherry
⅓ cup soy sauce
3 tablespoons vegetable oil
2 tablespoons sugar
5 whole star anise
1 tablespoon minced fresh ginger
Freshly ground black pepper, to taste

GLAZE
1¼ cups bourbon
⅔ cup honey
⅔ cup ketchup
¼ cup (packed) brown sugar

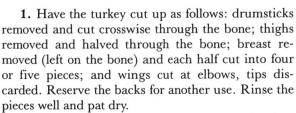

1. Have the turkey cut up as follows: drumsticks removed and cut crosswise through the bone; thighs removed and halved through the bone; breast removed (left on the bone) and each half cut into four or five pieces; and wings cut at elbows, tips discarded. Reserve the backs for another use. Rinse the pieces well and pat dry.

2. Stir all the marinade ingredients together in a large bowl. Add the turkey pieces and coat them in the mixture. Cover, and marinate for 1 hour.

3. Preheat the oven to 325°F.

4. Lift the turkey pieces from the marinade, and arrange them in one or two roasting pans. Pour ½ cup of the marinade (or 1 cup if using two pans) over the turkey.

5. Bake for 1 hour, turning and basting the pieces every 20 minutes. (If you are using two pans, rotate them after 30 minutes.)

6. Increase the oven temperature to 450°F.

7. Stir the glaze ingredients together in a bowl. Brush the turkey well with the glaze, and bake 30 minutes, brushing and turning every 5 minutes. (If you are using two pans, rotate them after 15 minutes.)

8. Mound the turkey on a large platter, and serve. This is great hot or at room temperature.

8 to 10 portions

TURKEY TIPS

▲ Buy a fresh turkey for Thanksgiving for a real taste treat.

▲ Wash thoroughly hands, utensils, and any surfaces or cloths that come in contact with the raw bird using hot soapy water. Hard plastic or acrylic boards—instead of wooden cutting boards—are best to use with all meats because they are nonabsorbent and will not provide a place for bacteria to grow.

▲ Use a meat thermometer when cooking turkey. Internal temperatures when done should be 170°F for the breast, 180°F for the thigh, and 160°F for the stuffing.

▲ When storing leftovers, remove any stuffing from the carcass and refrigerate the turkey and stuffing separately.

▲ Reheat leftovers thoroughly. Boil leftover gravy for 1 minute before serving.

TURKEY CROQUETTES

Moist and luscious patties of light and dark turkey chunks, egg, bread, onion, and parsley—these couldn't be easier. They're a good reason to cook turkey often, so you can use the leftovers!

3 slices whole-wheat bread, crusts removed
¼ cup milk
2½ cups coarsely chopped cooked turkey
1 cup coarsely chopped onion
2 eggs, lightly beaten
1 teaspoon dried thyme
Salt and freshly ground black pepper, to taste
2 cups seasoned dried bread crumbs
3 tablespoons chopped fresh Italian (flat-leaf) parsley
2 tablespoons paprika
3 tablespoons unsalted butter, melted
1 cup corn oil
2 tablespoons unsalted butter
Leftover turkey gravy (see page 423, Steps 9 and 10)

1. Soak the bread slices in the milk for 10 minutes. Then remove the bread, squeeze it dry, and shred it. Set it aside.

2. In a large mixing bowl, combine the turkey, shredded bread, onion, eggs, thyme, and salt and pepper. Toss well. Then transfer the mixture to a food processor, and using the pulse action, process until it is well blended but not completely puréed. Cover, and refrigerate for 1 hour.

3. Combine the bread crumbs, parsley, paprika, and melted butter in a 9-inch pie plate. Stir with a fork.

4. Shape the chilled turkey mixture into six large patties. Coat them with the bread crumb mixture, cover with plastic wrap, and return to the refrigerator for 1 hour more.

5. Heat ½ cup of the corn oil and 1 tablespoon of the butter in a large skillet. Cook the croquettes over medium heat, three at a time, until golden: 7 minutes on one side and 5 minutes on the other. Set them aside and keep warm. Repeat with the remaining croquettes, adding more oil and butter as necessary.

6. Heat the turkey gravy, and serve the hot croquettes topped with gravy.

6 portions

DUCK

Ducks are on the market year round. The duck is a heavy-framed bird with abundant fat, which makes it high in calories; however, half the fat is in the skin, which can be removed. The most common breed is Long Island duck, or duckling, also called White Pekin. A 5-pound, ready-to-cook duck feeds just two or three people. The duck you buy should have a plump, meaty breast and white or cream-colored fat and skin; the cavity should have a clean, fresh smell.

Duck meat is rich and flavorful. Ducks are best when roasted whole, but they can also be cut up into pieces. The legs and wings are wonderful braised with vegetables or beans; the breasts can be sautéed, grilled, broiled, or roasted in a hot oven for crisp skin and tender meat.

To roast a whole duck, simply remove the giblets; rinse the bird well and pat it dry. Pull out the excess fat from the cavity and from around the neck. Then prick the skin all over, but especially at the breast, without piercing the flesh. Season inside and out with salt and pepper and rub the inside with half a lemon. Place the duck, breast side up, on a rack in a roasting pan. Roast at 400°F for 30 minutes, then reduce the heat to 350°F and roast an additional 45 minutes, basting and pouring off the fat, until the skin is brown and crisp and the meat is done to your liking, with either slightly pink or clear juices when the thigh is pierced.

Rich duck meat is complemented by slightly acidic citrus sauces or by a slightly tart fresh cranberry sauce. Gin, too, is a great complement.

Wild ducks, such as mallard and teal, are sometimes available at local butchers or maybe as a gift from your neighborly hunter. They should be roasted slowly and basted with red wine and butter; cover the pan for two thirds of the cooking time to keep the birds from drying out.

DUCKLINGS STEWED IN RED WINE AND WINTER FRUITS

Figs, sweet potatoes, dried apricots, and cassis are succulent additions to our ducklings stewed in red wine. The sauce will thicken without adding flour. Serve with a robust winter green salad highlighted with julienned radicchio.

4 cups dry red wine
1 cup homemade beef stock (see Index) or canned broth
1 pound dried figs
3 pounds sweet potatoes
4 tablespoons (½ stick) unsalted butter
3 ducklings (4½ pounds each), well rinsed, patted dry, and each cut into 6 pieces
2 teaspoons coarsely ground black pepper
2 cups dried apricots
6 large cloves garlic
¼ cup crème de cassis
2 tablespoons dark brown sugar
2 tablespoons chopped fresh Italian (flat-leaf) parsley

1. Combine 3 cups of the wine and the stock in a saucepan, and bring just to a boil. Remove the pan from the heat, add the figs, and set aside.

2. Peel the potatoes, and cut them into balls with a melon baller; you should have about 4 cups. Place the potato balls in a large saucepan, cover with cold water, and bring to a boil. Lower the heat and simmer for 5 minutes, then drain the potatoes and set them aside.

3. Preheat the oven to 350°F.

4. Melt the butter in a large deep flameproof casserole or dutch oven. Brown the ducklings, a few pieces at a time, over medium heat. (While the ducks are browning, it may be necessary to pour off some of the fat. There should be no more than 4 tablespoons in the casserole.) As they are browned, transfer the pieces to a plate.

5. When all the duck has been browned, pour off any remaining fat from the casserole and return it to the heat. Add the remaining 1 cup wine and bring to a boil over medium heat, scraping up any brown bits in the casserole.

6. Return the duckling to the casserole, and sprinkle it with the pepper. Add the figs and their soaking liquid, the potatoes, and the apricots, garlic, crème de cassis, and brown sugar. Stir well, and bring to a boil over high heat.

7. Cover the casserole, transfer it to the oven, and bake for 30 minutes. Then stir it thoroughly, and bake another 30 minutes.

8. Arrange the duck, fruits, and vegetables on a large serving platter. Skim the grease from the sauce. Pour a bit of the degreased sauce over the duck, and sprinkle it with the parsley. Serve the remaining sauce on the side.

8 portions

TO SAVE CHICKEN AND DUCK LIVERS

To freeze chicken and duck livers, trim away any green spots and place them in a freezing container. Add milk to cover (it takes any bitterness out of the liver), snap on a tight-fitting lid, and freeze. You can continue to add fresh livers, with milk to cover, until you have as many as you need. Thaw the livers in the refrigerator at least a day before you plan to use them, then simply drain and pat dry.

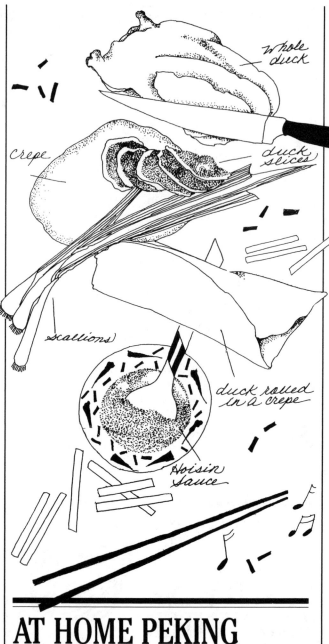

AT HOME PEKING DUCK

You no longer have to wait to be invited to a Chinese banquet to enjoy Peking Duck. When you realize that a lot of what appears to be complicated is really ceremony, this wonderful dish becomes very approachable. The scallion crepes are wonderful—use them often, duck or no.

1 duckling (4 to 4 ½ pounds)
¼ cup dry sherry
Salt
3 tablespoons honey
1 cup water
1 tablespoon ground ginger
1 ½ teaspoons freshly ground black pepper
3 tablespoons soy sauce
1 tablespoon sesame oil
8 Scallion Pancakes (recipe follows)
3 scallions (green onions), white bulb and 3 inches green, cut
    into 3-inch julienne
1 cucumber, peeled, seeded, and cut into 3-inch julienne
1 cup hoisin sauce or plum sauce*

1. In the morning of the day before you plan to serve it, prepare the duck: Rinse it well and remove all excess fat. Place the duck in a colander. Bring a kettle of water to a boil, and pour the boiling water over the duck until the skin turns white. Pat the duck dry; then rub it inside and out with the sherry and salt. Place it breast side down on a wire rack, and refrigerate it, uncovered, for 10 to 12 hours.

2. Turn the duck breast side up, brush it with 1 tablespoon of the honey, and refrigerate it overnight.

3. When you are ready to cook the duck, preheat the oven to 350°F.

4. Place the duck, breast side up, on a rack in a shallow roasting pan. Pour the water into the pan, cover the pan loosely with aluminum foil, and bake for 1 hour.

5. Remove the duck from the pan, and pour off the liquid in the pan. Prick the duck all over with the tines of a fork. Combine the ginger, pepper, 1 tablespoon of the soy sauce, and the sesame oil in a small bowl. Mix well, and coat the duck thoroughly with this mixture. Return the duck to the pan and bake, uncovered, for 30 minutes.

6. Raise the oven heat to 500°F. Combine the remaining 2 tablespoons honey and 2 tablespoons soy sauce, and coat the duck with this mixture. Bake until crisp and golden, 10 minutes.

7. Remove the duck from the oven, and allow it to cool slightly.

8. Slice the duck, with its skin, into ⅔-inch-thick slices, and arrange them on a large heated platter along with the pancakes, scallions, and cucumbers.

9. Each person rolls his or her own pancakes: Spread a pancake with hoisin sauce, top it with a slice or two of duck, and sprinkle with cucumber and scallions. Roll it up like a crepe, and eat with your fingers.

4 portions
*Available in Asian groceries and other specialty food shops.

SCALLION PANCAKES

1 cup unbleached all-purpose flour
⅔ cup water
⅔ cup milk
3 eggs
Pinch of salt
2 tablespoons unsalted butter, melted
2 scallions (green onions), white bulb and 3 inches green,
    thinly sliced lengthwise, then cut diagonally into
    ¼-inch pieces

1. Combine the flour, water, and milk in a food processor. Process for 15 seconds.

2. With the motor running, add the eggs, salt, and butter through the feed tube. Process until well blended. Transfer the batter to a bowl, and refrigerate, loosely covered, for 1 hour.

3. Fold the scallions into the batter.

4. Heat a nonstick crepe pan until quite hot. Add 3 tablespoons of batter, and tilt the pan so that the batter spreads evenly. Cook until the underside is lightly browned, 45 seconds to 1 minute. Flip the crepe over and cook another 15 seconds. Repeat with the remaining batter.

5. Stack the crepes as they are done between pieces of waxed paper. (If made in advance, reheat by removing all the waxed paper, wrapping the stacked crepes in aluminum foil, and placing them in a preheated 350°F oven until just warm, about 10 minutes.)

10 to 12 crepes

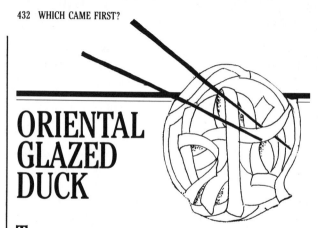

ORIENTAL GLAZED DUCK

This easily prepared duck is a showstopper when served with noodles that have been tossed with a light coating of our Sesame Dip.

1 duckling (5 pounds), excess fat removed, well rinsed, and
    patted dry
2 lemons, halved
Salt and coarsely ground black pepper, to taste
¾ cup soy sauce
¾ cup ketchup
⅓ cup clover honey
¼ cup corn oil
2 cloves garlic, finely chopped
1 tablespoon crumbled dried rosemary
2 scallions (green onions), white bulb and 3 inches green,
    thinly sliced diagonally, for garnish

1. Preheat the oven to 400°F.

2. Rub the duck inside and out with the juice of 1 lemon. Pat dry. Prick the skin all over with the tines of a fork. Sprinkle the outside and the cavity with salt and pepper. Place the second lemon in the cavity.

3. Place the duck, breast side up, on a rack in a shallow roasting pan, and bake for 30 minutes.

4. While the duck is roasting, make the glaze: Combine the soy sauce, ketchup, honey, oil, garlic, and rosemary in a small bowl. Mix well.

5. Reduce the oven temperature to 350°F. Pour off the fat that has accumulated in the roasting pan, and pour the glaze over the duck. Cook, basting frequently, another 45 minutes for medium-rare.

6. Remove the duck from the oven and let it rest for 15 minutes.

7. To serve, remove the duck from the roasting pan. Cut it in quarters, removing the backbone. Skim off any fat from the roasting pan, and reheat the glaze. Pour the glaze over the duck, and garnish with the sliced scallions.

2 portions

ARIANE DAGUIN'S MAGRET A LA D'ARTAGNAN

You'll notice that the ingredients list calls for three cups of hearty red wine but only two cups are used in the recipe. A good cook must always verify the quality of the ingredients—thus the third cup of wine!

2 whole magrets (duck breasts), well rinsed and patted dry
Salt and freshly ground black pepper, to taste
2 shallots, peeled and finely minced
3 cups hearty red wine
1 cup strong veal stock (see Index)
1 cup heavy or whipping cream

1. On the skin side of the duck breasts, score a crisscross pattern with the tip of a sharp knife. Sprinkle both sides with salt and pepper.

2. Place two nonstick skillets over the heat, and when they are very hot, add the duck breasts, skin side down. Cook for 10 minutes. Then reduce the heat, turn the breasts over, and cook another 5 minutes. Set the breasts aside and keep warm.

3. Pour off most of the fat from one of the skillets, leaving any brown particles and a bit of fat. Place the skillet over medium-low heat, add the shallots, and cook until golden but not brown, 2 minutes.

4. Raise the heat a bit and add 2 cups of the wine. Cook until the wine has reduced by half, 5 minutes. Then add the veal stock and reduce by half again, about 5 minutes. Finally, add the cream, but do not move or stir the pan.

5. Slice the reserved duck breasts into ¼-inch-thick slices, and arrange them in a fan pattern on eight warmed plates. Meanwhile the cream will have dispersed on its own in the sauce, which means it is ready. Pour the sauce over the duck, and serve immediately.

8 portions

THE ELEGANT EGG

Eggs have always seemed to us to be magic in a shell. Eggs puff soufflés, raise angel food cake to the heavens, bind sauces, clarify stocks, emulsify ordinary oil into silky mayonnaise, enrich pastries and breads, and smooth ice creams and custards. And that's just a short list. They show up in every meal of the day, but we still like ours best as a wake-up call in the morning for breakfast or brunch. Once thought of as the perfect food—low in calories yet packed with protein, vitamins, and minerals—the egg has toppled a bit from its pedestal now that we understand more about cholesterol, but when we do indulge, we savor it as a real treat.

ABOUT EGGS

Although some people eat the eggs of wild fowl, turkeys, geese, doves, and other birds, the egg of the chicken is the one most widely cultivated. Americans alone eat about 270 eggs per person each year. Not all of these eggs are scrambled or sunny-side up—we eat about two eggs each week in other products like cakes, ice cream, and pastry.

The average egg has just 75 calories and is a good source of protein, fat, calcium, iron, vitamins A and D, and riboflavin. Eggs are classed by grade and by size. Grades are AA, A, and B; most of the eggs at the market are grade A. Sizes range from jumbo to peewee and are determined not by the size of the shell but by weight per dozen. A dozen jumbo eggs weigh 30 ounces and a dozen medium eggs will tip the scales at 18. Chicken eggs are brown or white depending on the breed of laying hen, with the color of the shell having no effect on its flavor, performance, or nutritional value.

An egg yolk ranges from light yellow to gold in color (depending on the chicken feed) and makes up 30 percent of the total weight of the egg. A good egg has a yolk that is round and upstanding. As the egg ages, the yolk absorbs liquid from the white and flattens. If you keep an egg long enough, eventually the yolk and white will become one. The white of the egg will be thick and hold its shape when the egg is fresh, which is critical for good-looking poached and fried eggs.

STORAGE

The best way to store eggs is in the refrigerator in their original carton. Don't remove them to the egg storage area of your refrigerator because this is the warmest place. Make sure all your eggs are stored blunt end up to keep the yolk centered in the white. Since the shell is porous, eggs should never be stored near foods with strong aromas.

As the egg ages, it loses moisture through the shell and the moisture is replaced with air. A fresh egg will sink to the bottom of a glass of water; an old egg will float. To be sure of freshness you can buy eggs directly from the farm, but for most of us this is impractical. We compromise and buy just what we can use in about 10 days. The sell-by date on the end of a carton gives a date three to four weeks after grading; we try to use our eggs well before that date.

Separated whites and yolks can be stored as well. Egg whites will keep about a week in the refrigerator but much longer in the freezer. Freeze the egg whites in ice cube trays, then pop them out and keep them in a freezer bag. Yolks should be covered with water and will keep up to four days in the refrigerator; yolks do not freeze well. To use, gently remove them with a slotted spoon.

WATERCRESS SCRAMBLED EGGS

Watercress gives a peppery bite to these company-worthy scrambled eggs, and the dollop of sour cream is refreshing.

4 large eggs
1 tablespoon sour cream
Salt and freshly ground black pepper, to taste
½ cup coarsely chopped watercress leaves
2 teaspoons unsalted butter
Sour cream, for garnish
Watercress sprigs, for garnish

1. Lightly beat the eggs, sour cream, and salt and pepper in a bowl. Stir in the watercress.

2. Melt the butter in a nonstick skillet, and swirl to coat the bottom of the pan. Add the eggs and cook over low heat, stirring constantly with a fork. Cook until the eggs are set and soft, 2½ to 3 minutes; do not overcook. Garnish each portion with a dollop of sour cream and a sprig of watercress, and serve immediately.

2 portions

SPICY BREAKFAST PATTIES

Ground turkey from the supermarket makes great sausage, and these are so spicy and moist that you'll never miss the calories. Put one on a biscuit with a bit of scrambled eggs—you'll love it.

1 ¼ pounds ground turkey
½ cup minced onion
¼ cup chopped fresh basil leaves
¼ cup chopped fresh parsley
2 cloves garlic, minced
1 teaspoon salt
½ teaspoon dried thyme leaves
½ teaspoon ground ginger
½ teaspoon dried red pepper flakes, crushed
Freshly ground black pepper, to taste
2 tablespoons dried bread crumbs
1 egg, lightly beaten
2 tablespoons vegetable oil

1. Combine all the ingredients except the oil in a large mixing bowl, and stir well but do not overmix. Cover, and refrigerate for 1 hour.

2. Shape the turkey mixture into twelve patties about 2½ inches in diameter.

3. Heat the oil in a large skillet, and brown the patties, over medium heat, on both sides, about 2 minutes per side. Then reduce the heat to medium-low, cover the skillet, and cook, turning the patties occasionally, until they are crisp and cooked through, about 6 minutes. (You may have to do this in two batches.) Serve immediately.

12 patties

SCRAMBLED EGGS AND...

Perfect scrambled eggs are voluptuous and creamy, thick but uncurdled. The trick is very slow cooking; the longer it takes to scramble an egg the better it will be.

Softly scrambled eggs are the perfect bed for nestling all sorts of lovely treats, such as sautéed foie gras, blanched asparagus tips, caviar, smoked salmon or sable with fresh dill, crumbled chèvre with sliced olives, prosciutto, and thin shavings of truffle. In the minute or so before the eggs are cooked, we love to stir in extras like slivers of ham, crumbled crisp bacon, sautéed mushrooms, bits of smoked salmon, grated Parmesan cheese, sautéed tomatoes with basil, garden fresh herbs, sour cream with chives, crabmeat, herbed Boursin, capers, sautéed onions, grilled sausage, truffles, caviar, or finely chopped ratatouille.

DOUBLE-BOILER SCRAMBLED EGGS

The texture of these eggs is so soft and delicate—almost like a soufflé. Be sure you don't overcook. For a real treat, serve them in individual brioche—remove the tops, pull out some of the center bread, spoon in the eggs, and top with a dollop of crème fraîche and a spoonful of caviar.

4 eggs, lightly beaten
1 tablespoon sour cream
Salt and coarsely ground black pepper, to taste
1 teaspoon finely chopped herbs, such as chervil, dill, or tarragon (optional)
1 teaspoon unsalted butter

1. Lightly beat the eggs, sour cream, and salt and pepper in a mixing bowl. Fold in the herbs and stir to distribute them well.
2. Melt the butter in the top of a double boiler over simmering water, and swirl to coat the bottom of the pan.
3. Add the eggs and move them around with a soup spoon, bringing cooked eggs toward the center as they cook on the sides and bottom of the pan. Cook until the eggs are soft and still moist, 3 to 4 minutes. Do not overcook them. Serve immediately.

2 to 4 portions

SARABETH LEVINE'S GOLDILOX

We have known and loved Sarabeth for years—and love having breakfast at Sarabeth's Kitchen. But you must get there early, because lots of other New Yorkers love it too. These eggs are unsurpassed!

2 large eggs
1 teaspoon clarified butter (see Index)
2 ounces cream cheese, cut into ½-inch pieces, at room temperature
1 ounce Nova Scotia salmon, cut into ½-inch pieces

1. Place the eggs in a mixing bowl, and beat with a fork or a whisk for about 50 strokes. Strain the eggs into another bowl and set aside.
2. Melt the clarified butter in a nonstick skillet over medium heat. Pour in the eggs and reduce the heat to low.
3. Cook slowly, stirring gently with a rubber spatula once the eggs begin to firm up, using the spatula to free the eggs from the bottom of the pan.
4. When the eggs are almost cooked, distribute the cream cheese evenly over the top. Remove the pan from the heat, and fold in the salmon, trying not to break up the cheese cubes too much. Turn the eggs out onto a warm plate, and serve at once.

1 portion

BAKED EGGS ON ARTICHOKE BOTTOMS

Baked eggs served atop prosciutto and artichoke bottoms are perfect for an elegant brunch or a light luncheon. Place them in the center of large plates with a decorative rim. When buying the artichokes for this dish, be sure to choose large ones. An egg will nestle in the bottom of each.

4 large artichokes
2 tablespoons sour cream
4 slices prosciutto
4 eggs
¼ cup freshly grated Parmesan cheese
1 teaspoon freshly ground black pepper
1 tablespoon chopped fresh Italian (flat-leaf) parsley

1. Place the artichokes in a large saucepan, and add 1 inch of water. Bring it to a boil, reduce the heat, and cover. Cook until the artichokes are tender, about 45 minutes. Remove them from the pot and set them aside to drain and cool.

2. Preheat the oven to 375°F.

3. Peel away the artichoke leaves and remove the chokes. Set the leaves aside.

4. Place the artichoke bottoms on a baking sheet. Spread 1½ teaspoons of the sour cream on each bottom. Top with a folded slice of prosciutto. Break an egg on top of each, and then sprinkle with the cheese, pepper, and parsley.

5. Bake until the eggs are done to your liking, 15 to 20 minutes. Serve immediately surrounded by the leaves. Dip the leaves in the egg yolks.

4 portions

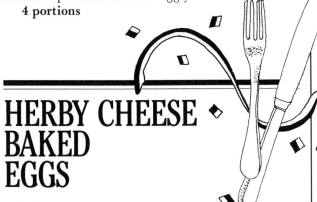

HERBY CHEESE BAKED EGGS

Vary the soft cheese in these eggs—there are so many pepper-and herb-flavored chèvres in the market now. As these eggs are baked in individual ramekins, you can serve breakast or brunch to a crowd and have all the eggs ready at the same time.

1 teaspoon unsalted butter
3 teaspoons heavy or whipping cream
1 egg
1 teaspoon herbed chèvre or Boursin cheese
Freshly ground black pepper, to taste
Fresh chervil leaves or chopped fresh Italian (flat-leaf)
    parsley, for garnish

1. Preheat the oven to 450°F.

2. Place the butter and 2 teaspoons of the cream in a ¾-cup ramekin. Carefully break the egg in the center. Dot the egg with the cheese, and spoon the remaining 1 teaspoon cream over the yolk. Season with pepper.

3. Place the ramekin in a small baking dish, and fill it with boiling water to reach halfway up the sides of the ramekin. Bake until the egg white is milky and the yolk is set, 7 to 10 minutes. Serve immediately, sprinkled with the fresh herbs.

1 portion

AFTER THE FLEA MARKET BRUNCH

Pickled Herring

Herby Cheese Baked Eggs
Beaujolais Nouveau

Spinach Salad With Bacon Buttermilk Dressing

Poached Peaches With Raspberry Peach Sauce

AVOCADO BAKED EGGS

Just the right dish for a Sunday brunch or a light lunch: layers of thinly sliced ham, ripe tomatoes, and creamy avocados topped with eggs, baked and served piping hot from the oven.

2 ripe plum tomatoes
¼ teaspoon salt
2 tablespoons unsalted butter
4 thin slices baked ham
2 teaspoons freshly grated Parmesan cheese
½ ripe avocado, peeled and cut into ½-inch pieces
2 tablespoons sour cream
4 eggs
Freshly ground black pepper, to taste
2 teaspoons chopped cilantro (fresh coriander) or fresh Italian
    (flat-leaf) parsley

1. Slice the tomatoes lengthwise into ¼-inch-thick slices. Place them on paper towels, sprinkle with salt, and let drain for 30 minutes.

2. Preheat the oven to 450°F, and bring a kettle of water to a boil.

3. Melt 1 tablespoon of the butter in a skillet, and sauté the ham until the slices are lightly browned. Place two slices each in the bottom of two individual oval ramekins, each 8 x 6 x 2 inches. Pat the tomato slices dry, and arrange them over the ham. Sprinkle with the Parmesan.

4. Scatter the avocado evenly over the cheese, and dot with the sour cream.

5. Break 2 eggs into each ramekin. Sprinkle them with pepper and dot with the remaining 1 tablespoon butter. Sprinkle with the cilantro.

6. Place the ramekins in a shallow roasting pan, and pour boiling water into the pan to reach three fourths of the way up the sides of the ramekins. Bake until the egg whites are milky and the yolks are set, 10 to 12 minutes.

2 portions

WHEN YOU WANT SHIRRED EGGS

A shirred egg is like a baked egg only the shirred egg is started on top of the stove and finished in the oven, and the baked egg is cooked completely in the oven. For shirred eggs, butter a flameproof pan and heat it over low heat, add the egg or eggs, and cook just until the white is set. Transfer the pan to the broiler or a 450°F oven, and broil or bake to set the top. We like to top shirred eggs with our own pesto mixed with a chopped plum tomato just before broiling or baking.

ORANGE EGGS BENEDICT

Inspired by Bradley Ogden's luscious breakfast at Campton Place in San Francisco, these orangey eggs are perfect to serve to your favorite weekend guests late on a Sunday morning.

8 slices Canadian bacon
4 Orange Scones (recipe follows)
8 eggs
2 cups Orange Hollandaise (recipe follows)
1 tablespoon chopped fresh mint leaves

1. Sauté the Canadian bacon in a nonstick skillet until slightly crisp. Set it aside to drain on paper towels.

2. Slice the scones in half, and toast them lightly. Set aside.

3. Fill two nonstick skillets with water and bring them to a gentle simmer. Carefully break an egg into a cup, and slide it into the simmering water. Repeat with the remaining eggs, one at a time. Cook over low heat 2 to 3 minutes, and then use a slotted spoon to transfer the poached eggs to a dish.

4. Place two scone halves on each plate. Top each with a slice of Canadian bacon, a poached egg, and some of the warm Orange Hollandaise sauce. Garnish with the mint, and serve immediately.

4 portions

ORANGE SCONES

2 cups unbleached all-purpose flour
2 teaspoons baking powder
½ teaspoon salt
4 tablespoons (½ stick) unsalted butter, chilled
2 eggs
⅓ cup heavy or whipping cream
2 tablespoons grated orange zest

1. Preheat the oven to 425°F.

2. Combine the flour, baking powder, and salt in a large mixing bowl. Using a pastry blender or two knives, work in the butter until it resembles coarse meal. Mix in the eggs one at a time, and then the cream and orange zest.

3. Turn the dough out onto a lightly floured surface and knead until smooth, about 2 minutes.

4. Roll out the dough until it is ¾ inch thick. Cut out the scones using a 3-inch round cookie cutter. Place them on a baking sheet and bake in the center of the oven until lightly golden and crusty, 15 to 20 minutes. Remove the scones from the oven and allow them to cool. You can prepare these 1 to 2 days ahead. Keep them wrapped in plastic wrap.

8 to 10 scones

ORANGE HOLLANDAISE

2 cups fresh orange juice
1 cup (2 sticks) unsalted butter
6 egg yolks
½ teaspoon salt

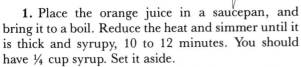

1. Place the orange juice in a saucepan, and bring it to a boil. Reduce the heat and simmer until it is thick and syrupy, 10 to 12 minutes. You should have ¼ cup syrup. Set it aside.

2. In another saucepan, melt the butter and heat until bubbling.

3. Place the egg yolks in a food processor and process for a few seconds. With the motor running, add the reduced orange juice and the salt. Then slowly add the butter in a thin stream. Process a few more seconds, until thick. Serve immediately.

2 cups

BAKED POTATOES AND EGGS

This simple dish is a delicious and satisfying way to start a cold winter morning.

2 Idaho baking potatoes
1 tablespoon unsalted butter
1 tablespoon heavy or whipping cream
Salt and freshly ground black pepper to taste
4 eggs
½ cup grated Cheddar cheese
1 tablespoon chopped fresh Italian (flat-leaf) parsley

1. Preheat the oven to 350°F.

2. Scrub the potatoes and dry with paper towels. Then prick them lightly all over with the tines of a fork. Bake them for 1 hour.

3. Remove the potatoes from the oven and allow them to cool slightly. Cut the potatoes in half lengthwise, and scoop out the pulp carefully, without tearing the skin. Reserve the four halves.

4. Mash or rice the potato pulp in a mixing bowl, and stir in the butter, cream, and salt and pepper.

5. Divide the potato mixture evenly among the potato halves, leaving an indentation in each for the egg.

6. Fill a small skillet with water and bring it to a simmer. Gently poach the eggs for 45 seconds (see tips, below). Remove them from the water with a slotted spoon.

7. Place one egg in the center of each potato. Top them with the cheese and parsley, and bake until the eggs are set, 10 to 15 minutes. Serve immediately.

4 portions

POACHED EGGS TIPS

A poached egg should look like a neat, trim oval with the egg yolk perfectly centered. Start with fresh eggs for the best results. Heat at least 2 inches of water in a deep skillet or saucepan to a gentle simmer. Occasionally we add 1 tablespoon of cider or white wine vinegar to the water to help the egg hold a nice shape. Some cooks like to create a whirlpool in the water by stirring it quickly, then dropping in the egg. We don't usually do this, but try it—it may work well for you.

Simmer eggs 3 minutes for soft yolks, 5 minutes for firmer yolks. (Any longer than 5 minutes and you may as well hard-cook them.) Poached eggs can be stored in cold water in the refrigerator up to two days and reheated in hot water for 10 seconds just before serving. Be sure to pat them dry first.

OMELET SAVVY

An omelet is nothing more than eggs, butter, and a little body English. Eggs are usually cooked over low heat so they don't become tough and leathery, but the omelet is the exception for it must be cooked quickly. Most recipes take longer to read than to do. Unfortunately, there are as many omelet techniques as there are omelets. You will eventually arrive at your own preferred technique but below, as a guideline, is ours.

OMELET TIPS

▲ Save your freshly laid eggs for frying if you are lucky enough to get them. Eggs should be at least two or three days old for omelets.

▲ Use a well-seasoned stainless steel or nonstick skillet with sloping sides, and use it just for omelets.

Never wash a stainless omelet pan—just scrub with coarse salt and paper towels after each use.

▲ Never make an omelet with more than three eggs. If you are making omelets for several people, mix and cook each one separately.

▲ Use two eggs per person for a plain omelet. For an omelet with a hearty garnish, three eggs for two people will be sufficient.

▲ Never beat the eggs far ahead of time. Just before slipping the eggs into the pan, beat them lightly with a fork until the yolks and whites are blended but still viscous.

▲ The French "varnish" the tops of their omelets with a piece of cold butter or "gild" them with a tablespoon of melted butter.

▲ A perfect omelet should be tender and firm on the outside with a creamy middle. If your omelet isn't perfect, it will still be good. Eat it and try again next week.

using a fork – swirl eggs with a circular motion

try to find a non stick omelet pan

carefully tilt the pan move eggs to the front of pan gently folding over

Tip pan and slide omelet onto plate

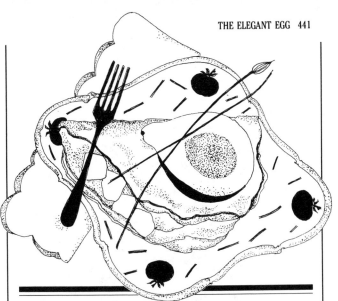

NEW BASIC OMELETTE NATURE

This plain omelet is not as *nature* as its classic cousin. We have taken the liberty of adding a few fresh herbs.

The ideal omelet-cooking motion is somewhat like rubbing your stomach while patting the top of your head. It is difficult at first, but after a little practice you'll develop the technique. The idea is to keep the mixture moving, incorporating air while keeping the center moist.

2 eggs
1 tablespoon half-and-half
1 tablespoon chopped fresh herbs, such as tarragon and/or chives
¼ teaspoon salt
Freshly ground black pepper, to taste
1 tablespoon unsalted butter

1. Lightly beat the eggs, half-and-half, herbs, salt, and pepper together in a small bowl.

2. Melt the butter in an 8-inch nonstick omelet pan over medium heat. When it has stopped foaming, raise the heat to high and pour in the egg mixture. Cook without stirring until the omelet starts to bubble around the edges, about 10 seconds. Then stir, gathering the mixture toward the center of the pan. Do not cut through the omelet; keep it in one piece. The entire process should take no more than 1½ minutes.

3. When the bottom is set but the top is still wet, carefully slide the omelet out of the skillet and onto a plate, until half of it is on the plate. Then flip the other half over the bottom half to form a half-circle. Serve at once.

1 portion

"**S**catter joy."
—RALPH WALDO EMERSON

AVOCADO OMELET

Two velvety textures combine with nutty flavored Jarlsberg for a luscious dish.

½ small ripe California avocado, peeled and diced
½ small plum tomato, seeded and diced
2½ tablespoons shredded Jarlsberg cheese
Salt and freshly ground black pepper, to taste
3 eggs
1 tablespoon snipped fresh chives
1 tablespoon unsalted butter

1. Toss the avocado, tomato, and cheese together in a small bowl. Season with a pinch of salt and pepper.

2. In a second bowl, lightly beat the eggs with the chives.

3. Melt the butter in an 8-inch nonstick omelet pan over medium heat. When it has stopped foaming, raise the heat to high, and pour in the eggs. Cook without stirring until the omelet starts to bubble around the edges, about 10 seconds. Then stir, gathering the mixture toward the center of the pan. When the bottom is set but the top is still slightly wet, spread the avocado mixture over half the omelet. Fold the remaining half over the avocado and cook until the filling is heated through, about 30 seconds. Slide the omelet onto a plate, and serve immediately.

1 to 2 portions

Note: Using a nonstick omelet pan reduces the amount of butter needed and allows you to cook over lower heat.

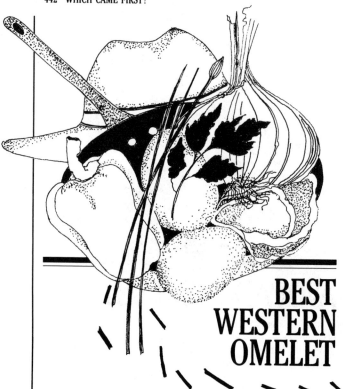

BEST WESTERN OMELET

An update on the omelet that's served in every diner and coffee shop throughout America—and that, unfortunately is a bit maligned today. This recipe brings it back to center. If you have access to aged Monterey Jack, this is the place to use it!

3 tablespoons crème fraîche (see Index) or shredded Monterey
    Jack or muenster cheese
1 tablespoon snipped fresh chives
Freshly ground black pepper, to taste
6 tablespoons diced Black Forest ham
2 eggs
2 tablespoons half-and-half
1 tablespoon chopped fresh parsley
2 tablespoons unsalted butter
¼ cup diced green bell pepper
¼ cup diced Vidalia or other sweet onion

1. Combine the crème fraîche, chives, pepper, and 2 tablespoons of the ham in a small bowl.

2. In another bowl, lightly beat the eggs, half-and-half, and parsley.

3. Melt the butter in a 10-inch nonstick omelet pan. When it has stopped foaming, stir in the bell pepper, onion, and remaining 4 tablespoons ham. Cook over medium heat, stirring, about 2 minutes.

4. Raise the heat to high, and add the egg mixture. Cook without stirring until the omelet starts to bubble around the edges, 10 seconds. Then stir, gathering the mixture toward the center of the pan. Cook until the bottom is set but the top is still slightly wet.

5. Spread the crème fraîche mixture over half the omelet, and fold the other half over it. Cook until the filling is heated through, 30 seconds. Slide the omelet halfway onto a plate, then flip it over itself and serve immediately.

1 portion

BREAKFAST ENTERTAINING

▲ Breakfast is an intimate meal—invite two or three guests at the most.

▲ Do as much as possible the night before. Prepare whatever food you know will hold. Get the kitchen cleaned up and ready to go. Set the table and locate that special jar of fruit conserve Aunt Sally sent last Christmas.

▲ Keep the menu simple. Remember this is breakfast not brunch. Something fruity and something starchy are required, although eggs and a small amount of meat or fish are certainly welcome, too.

▲ Use pretty accoutrements—cheerful placemats or tablecloth, nice china and glasses, cloth napkins. A fancy centerpiece would be out of place, but a few flowers here and there set the tone.

▲ Coffee or tea should be the best—freshly ground, freshly brewed, plentiful, and hot, hot, hot.

    Philosophical note: We cannot let this opportunity pass without saying that coffee and a Danish while discussing business is not breakfast, nor is it entertaining.

HERBED CHÈVRE OMELET

A lovely light omelet with fresh mint and a dab of sour cream.

2 tablespoons chopped toasted walnuts (see Index)
1½ tablespoons chèvre with herbs, crumbled
2 tablespoons chopped fresh mint leaves
1 tablespoon sour cream
2 eggs
¼ teaspoon salt
Freshly ground black pepper, to taste
1 tablespoon olive oil

1. Combine the walnuts, chèvre, 1 tablespoon of the mint, and the sour cream in a small bowl. Stir well and set aside.

2. In another bowl, lightly beat the eggs, salt, pepper, and remaining 1 tablespoon mint.

3. Heat the oil in an 8-inch nonstick omelet pan over high heat. Add the egg mixture, and cook without stirring until the omelet starts to bubble around the edges, 10 seconds. Then stir, gathering the mixture toward the center of the pan. Cook until the bottom is set but the top is still slightly wet.

4. Spread the chèvre filling over half the omelet. Fold the other half over the filling, and cook until heated through, 30 seconds. Slide the omelet onto a plate and serve immediately.

1 to 2 portions

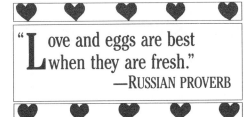

> "Love and eggs are best when they are fresh."
> —RUSSIAN PROVERB

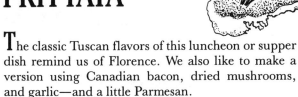

PROSCIUTTO AND MUSHROOM FRITTATA

The classic Tuscan flavors of this luncheon or supper dish remind us of Florence. We also like to make a version using Canadian bacon, dried mushrooms, and garlic—and a little Parmesan.

1½ tablespoons unsalted butter
⅓ cup thinly sliced shallots
¼ cup slivered prosciutto
Freshly ground black pepper, to taste
  2 ounces fresh pleurotes (oyster mushrooms) or
      other wild mushrooms, cut into ½-inch strips
  4 eggs
  ¼ cup coarsely chopped fresh Italian (flat-leaf)
      parsley, for garnish

1. Preheat the broiler.

2. Melt the butter in a 10-inch flameproof skillet. When it has stopped foaming, stir in the shallots, prosciutto, and pepper. Cook, over medium-high heat, stirring, until the shallots are golden and the prosciutto is nearly crisp, about 2 minutes. Then stir in the mushrooms, and cook 1 minute.

3. Lightly beat the eggs with the parsley and season with pepper. Lower the heat to medium-low and pour them into the skillet. Stir quickly, incorporating the mushroom mixture. Cook just until the bottom is set; the top should still be wet, 3 to 4 minutes.

4. Place the skillet under the broiler and cook just until the frittata is sizzling, puffed, and set, 1 to 2 minutes. Serve immediately.

2 portions

FRITTATAS

rittatas are to Italians what omelets are to the French. In a frittata (or tortilla in Spain) the filling is mixed with the eggs and the whole mixture is cooked slowly in a skillet until set, then quickly browned under the broiler. Frittatas are a bit drier than omelets, not so fussy in their timing, and much easier to make for a gang.

The filling ingredients are what make the frittata so wonderful, but it's the eggs that bind everything together.

Frittatas can be served hot right in the skillet or left to cool at room temperature. They can be cut into pie-shaped wedges for brunch or supper or little squares for appetizers. They're perfect for picnics, so don't pack a basket without one.

ARTICHOKE AND POTATO FRITTATA

This frittata of artichoke hearts and potatoes also features creamy fresh mozzarella and the sweet nuttiness of Parmesan.

½ cup (6 to 8) artichoke hearts (thawed if frozen), drained
2 tablespoons olive oil
1 small potato, cooked and cubed
1 teaspoon minced fresh rosemary leaves
Salt and freshly ground black pepper, to taste
3 eggs
¼ teaspoon salt
2 tablespoons shredded fresh mozzarella cheese
1 tablespoon freshly grated Parmesan cheese
Chopped fresh Italian (flat-leaf) parsley, for garnish

1. Bring a small saucepan of lightly salted water to a boil, and add the artichoke hearts. Lower the heat and simmer for 3 minutes; then rinse, drain, and pat dry. Set them aside.

2. Heat 1 tablespoon of the oil in a 10-inch flameproof skillet (preferably nonstick). Add the potato and rosemary, and sauté until golden and crisp, about 3 minutes. Add the artichoke hearts and sauté until golden, about 2 minutes. Sprinkle with a pinch of salt and pepper, and set aside.

3. Preheat the broiler.

4. Lightly beat the eggs with the ¼ teaspoon salt and pepper to taste. Heat the remaining 1 tablespoon oil in the same skillet. Pour in the eggs and cook, over medium-low heat, stirring lightly, just until the bottom is set, 3 to 4 minutes. The top should still be wet. Add the artichokes and potatoes; sprinkle with the cheeses. Place the skillet under the broiler and cook until the frittata is golden and sizzling, about 2 minutes. Sprinkle with parsley, and serve immediately.

1 to 2 portions

ASPARAGUS ARUGULA FRITTATA

Moist and chock-full of asparagus, arugula, and Gruyère, this makes a great brunch or luncheon dish.

3 eggs
2 tablespoons half-and-half
1 teaspoon minced fresh thyme leaves or ¼ teaspoon dried
¼ teaspoon salt
Freshly ground black pepper, to taste
4 asparagus spears
½ cup shredded Gruyère cheese
1 tablespoon dried bread crumbs
2 tablespoons unsalted butter
2 cups coarsely chopped arugula leaves

1. Preheat the broiler.

2. Beat the eggs, half-and-half, thyme, salt, and pepper together in a medium-size bowl. Set aside.

3. Cut the asparagus in half lengthwise and then in 1-inch pieces. Bring a saucepan of lightly salted water to a boil, add the asparagus, and reduce the heat. Simmer for 2 to 3 minutes. Then drain the asparagus and pat it dry.

4. Combine the asparagus with the Gruyère and bread crumbs in a mixing bowl; toss to combine.

5. Melt the butter in a 10-inch flameproof skillet over medium heat. When it has stopped foaming, add the arugula. Sauté the arugula until just wilted, 1 minute. Lower the heat to medium-low and pour in the egg mixture. Cook until the bottom is set; the top should still be wet, 3 to 4 minutes. Sprinkle with the asparagus mixture.

6. Place the skillet under the broiler and cook until the frittata is golden, 2 to 3 minutes. Serve immediately.

2 portions

HAPPY BIRTHDAY BRUNCH

Smoked Salmon and Leek Frittata
Sancerre or Soave

Chickory and Bacon Salad Quatorze
Sourdough Baguettes With Herbed Butter

Pear and Ginger Cobbler

SMOKED SALMON AND LEEK FRITTATA

Smoked salmon, leeks, and chèvre make a remarkable combination. Serve this with chilled Champagne. It's refreshing and delicious. Santé!

3 large eggs
2 tablespoons crème fraîche (see Index)
¼ teaspoon freshly ground black pepper
2 ounces smoked salmon, slivered (about ¼ cup)
2 tablespoons unsalted butter
1 leek (white part and 1 inch green), well rinsed, dried, and coarsely chopped (about ½ cup)
¼ teaspoon caraway seeds, crushed
3 tablespoons crumbled chèvre

1. Preheat the broiler.

2. Beat the eggs, crème fraîche, and pepper together in a mixing bowl. Stir in the smoked salmon.

3. Melt the butter in a 10-inch flameproof skillet over medium heat. When it has stopped foaming, stir in the leek and caraway. Cook, stirring, until the leeks are golden and soft, 2 to 3 minutes. Remove half the leeks with a slotted spoon, and set aside.

4. Lower the heat to medium-low, and stir in the egg mixture. Cook just until the bottom is set; the top should still be wet, 3 to 4 minutes. Sprinkle with the chèvre and reserved leeks.

5. Place the skillet under the broiler, and cook until the eggs are set and the cheese is slightly melted, 2 minutes. Serve immediately.

2 portions

FRENCH TOAST

The French call their special way of toasting bread *pain perdu*, or "lost bread," because it must be made with stale bread (bread that would have been tossed out, or "lost"). If the bread is too fresh, it will not only lose its shape but also absorb too much of the egg-and-milk mixture, which should be just a coating.

You may choose to use a good Italian or French loaf, challah, or croissants, but make sure the bread is at least two days old. Then, the simpler the better. Lightly beat eggs with milk or milk and cream, then mix in cinnamon, lemon or orange zest, a little orange liqueur, or a spoonful of fresh orange juice. Once the bread is fried in sweet butter to a golden brown, we love to have a number of toppings to choose from: warm maple syrup, fruit preserves, warm fruit compote, lemon juice and confectioners' sugar, fresh berries and wild honey, and lime juice and brown sugar.

PANCETTA AND GORGONZOLA STRATA

If you can't find pannetone—an Italian sweet cake with a bread-like texture—substitute an eggy bread such as challah.

8 ounces thinly sliced pancetta
(Italian bacon)
8 ounces pannetone
1¼ cups heavy or whipping cream
1¼ cups milk
1 teaspoon salt
Dash of Tabasco sauce
5 eggs
12 ounces sweet Gorgonzola cheese, rind removed, crumbled
12 ounces St.-André cheese, rind removed, crumbled
¼ cup fresh rosemary leaves, finely chopped, or 1 tablespoon dried rosemary, crumbled

1. Butter the bottom and sides of a 2½-quart soufflé dish, and set it aside.

2. Chop the pancetta into ½-inch pieces. Sauté them in a heavy skillet over medium-low heat until just crisp, 10 minutes. Drain on paper towels, and set aside.

3. Slice the pannetone into eight 1-inch-thick slices. Lightly toast them on both sides, and reserve.

4. Whisk together the cream, milk, salt, Tabasco, and eggs in a medium-size bowl. Set aside.

5. Lay 4 slices of the panettone in the prepared soufflé dish. Sprinkle them evenly with half of the remaining ingredients: Gorgonzola, Saint André, and rosemary, and half of the reserved pancetta. Cover with the remaining 4 slices, and then the remaining cheeses, rosemary, and pancetta.

6. Pour the egg mixture over the layers, cover, and set aside for 30 minutes.

7. Preheat the oven to 350°F.

8. Uncover the dish, and bake until the strata is bubbling and golden, 40 minutes.

9. Remove the dish from the oven and let it rest 10 minutes before serving.

8 portions

PUFFED AND GOLDEN SOUFFLES

Soufflés are magical, but we don't think you have to be a magician or even an exceptional cook to make them. Essential to success are the right dish, room temperature eggs, and a light hand. Choose a porcelain dish with straight sides made just for soufflés, or try a metal charlotte mold. If the dish is not deep enough to hold the soufflé as it rises, you can extend the side by fitting it with a collar of waxed paper or aluminum foil tied on with kitchen string. Butter the bottom and side of the dish and sprinkle with grated Parmesan cheese for a savory soufflé or granulated sugar for a dessert soufflé. The base of every soufflé is a béchamel or white sauce (made with butter, flour, and milk) with egg yolks added. You can make the base just before you beat the egg whites, but we get good results making the base ahead of time and holding it at room temperature.

For the best volume, the egg whites should be at room temperature before they're beaten until stiff but not dry. Gently fold the whites into the base, making sure the base has cooled to room temperature first, and pour the mixture into the dish. If you want a crown or high hat on the soufflé, gently cut a circle about 1½ inches deep and 1 inch in from the edge into the top with a table knife. Bake the soufflé without opening the oven for the minimum time indicated in the recipe. The soufflé should be golden, puffed, and set with the center slightly soft and custardy. A soufflé will fall quickly once it's out of the oven, so for maximum mileage get all diners to the table before you take it out.

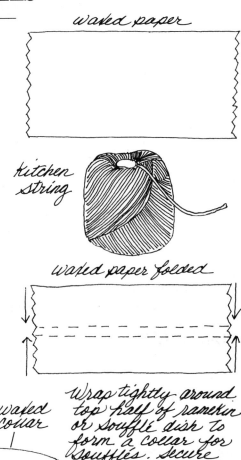

waxed paper

kitchen string

waxed paper folded

waxed collar

Wrap tightly around top half of ramekin or soufflé dish to form a collar for soufflés. Secure with kitchen string

Kitchen String

Ramekin or soufflé dish —

EASY EGG PREPARATIONS

For every egg that is eaten sauced and fancified, there are dozens prepared in the simple, basic ways. Early morning eggs are often served fried or soft-boiled; hard-cooked, they are lunchtime and salad favorites. And although coddled eggs are rarely called for, you don't want to be caught in the middle of a Caesar salad preparation and not know how to make one.

FRIED EGGS

Fried eggs are the cornerstone of a good country breakfast. Heat a skillet over medium-high heat. Add a pat of butter and when it begins to sizzle, gently slip the egg into the pan. You can baste the top with the hot butter to cook the film of white covering the egg yolk, or gently turn it a few seconds before it's done. Some people add a few drops of water to the pan just before the egg is done, cover the pan, and steam the top of the egg just to set it. Fried eggs easily become tough if cooked too long or over a heat that is too high.

SOFT-BOILED EGGS

The simplest way of all to cook an egg is to soft boil it—although these eggs are never really boiled, just simmered. Put the egg in a pan of boiling water and immediately adjust the heat so that the water is just gently simmering. Start timing. In three minutes the yolk will be slightly set; in four minutes set completely but very softly. Timing is all important for soft-boiled egg fans.

HARD-COOKED EGGS

First start with room temperature eggs if you can. Put the eggs in a pan and cover with enough cold water to measure an inch above the tops of the eggs. Bring the water to a boil. Now you have two choices: You can reduce the heat and simmer the eggs for 12 minutes or cover the pan, turn off the heat, and wait 15 to 20 minutes for hard-cooked.

When the time is up, immediately run the eggs under cool water. If you are going to peel them immediately, crack the shells and run them under cool water again. The eggs should peel easily. Hard-cooked eggs will keep in the refrigerator four to five days if left unpeeled.

CODDLED EGGS

The only time we ever coddle an egg is when we make Caesar salad. Let an egg warm to room temperature, then bring a pan of water to a boil and lower the egg into the water. Turn off the heat, cover the pan, and let set one minute, no more. Remove and shell immediately. These eggs are very runny with just a little of the white coagulated.

GRUYERE SOUFFLE

The simplest of light suppers: a tasty soufflé, a salad, some peasant bread, and a dry white wine. Sometimes we butter individual soufflé dishes, line them with transparent slices of ham and leaves of Parmesan, and then fill them with this cheese soufflé.

4 tablespoons (½ stick) unsalted butter
2 tablespoons freshly grated Parmesan cheese
3 tablespoons unbleached all-purpose flour
¼ teaspoon cayenne pepper
1 cup milk
3 egg yolks, at room temperature
1 cup shredded Gruyère cheese
4 ounces prosciutto, slivered
2 tablespoons snipped fresh chives
4 egg whites, at room temperature

1. Preheat the oven to 400°F.

2. Using 1 tablespoon of the butter, grease the bottom and sides of a 6-cup soufflé dish. Sprinkle it with 1 tablespoon of the Parmesan. Turn the dish so it is evenly coated. Set it aside.

3. Melt the remaining butter in a saucepan over medium heat. When it stops foaming, whisk in the flour to form a roux (a smooth paste). Whisk in the cayenne and milk.

4. Cook, stirring, until the mixture comes to a boil and is thick, 5 minutes. Transfer the mixture to a large bowl, and allow it to cool slightly.

5. Whisk in the yolks, Gruyère, prosciutto, chives, and remaining 1 tablespoon Parmesan.

6. Beat the egg whites in a mixer bowl until stiff. Stir a large spoonful of whites into the cheese mixture. Quickly and gently fold in the remaining whites, working so as not to deflate the volume. Transfer to the prepared dish.

7. Bake 20 minutes. Reduce the heat to 350°F, and bake until deep golden, puffed, and still slightly wet inside, 10 minutes. Serve immediately.

6 portions

CARIBBEAN CRAB SOUFFLE

You'll be picturing aquamarine water and windsurfers when you eat this moist and zesty crab soufflé. The sweet coconut tempers the hot spices.

½ cup unsweetened shredded coconut
4 tablespoons (½ stick) unsalted butter
⅓ cup minced celery leaves
1 clove garlic, minced
½ teaspoon curry powder
½ teaspoon dried thyme leaves
½ teaspoon dried red pepper flakes
½ teaspoon salt
Freshly ground black pepper, to taste
3 tablespoons unbleached all-purpose flour
1 ¼ cups milk
4 egg yolks
½ pound fresh crabmeat, cartilage removed
6 egg whites
¼ teaspoon fresh lemon juice

FOLDING IN EGG WHITES

You'll have the most success with folding in egg whites if you first mix in a quarter of the whites to lighten the batter. Then add the remaining whites and gently cut them into the batter with a rubber spatula. Turn the bowl as you mix and be patient and gentle.

Place spatula under ingredients and bring to the surface in a circular motion

1. Preheat the oven to 400°F, and butter an 8-cup soufflé dish. Set it aside.

2. Place a small nonstick skillet over low heat, and toast the coconut in it for 5 minutes. Set it aside.

3. Melt the butter in a saucepan over low heat. Stir in the celery, garlic, curry powder, thyme, red pepper flakes, salt, and pepper. Cook for 3 minutes.

4. Add the flour, and stir until smooth. Cook 1 minute.

5. Add the milk, and cook over medium heat, stirring, until the mixture comes to a boil and is thick and smooth. Set it aside to cool slightly.

6. Whisk the egg yolks, one at a time, into the sauce. Stir in the coconut and crabmeat.

7. Beat the egg whites and lemon juice in a mixer bowl until frothy. Continue beating until stiff but not dry. Stir one fourth of the whites into the crab mixture. Quickly and gently fold in the remaining whites, working so as not to deflate the volume. Transfer the mixture to the prepared soufflé dish, and place it on a rack in the bottom third of the oven.

8. Bake until golden, puffed, and still moist inside, 30 minutes. Serve immediately.

8 portions

ITALIAN QUICHE

A *quiche lorraine* gone Italian. If you prefer, substitute Canadian bacon and Jarlsberg for the salami and provolone.

Dough for 1 New Basic Pie Crust (see Index)
1 egg white, lightly beaten
1 cup milk
2 eggs
⅓ cup coarsely chopped fresh parsley
Pinch of salt
Freshly ground black pepper, to taste
Pinch of cayenne pepper
¼ cup slivered Genoa salami
¼ cup shredded provolone cheese
2 tablespoons freshly grated Parmesan cheese

1. Preheat the oven to 375°F.

2. Roll the crust dough out on a lightly floured surface to form an 11-inch circle. Press it into the bottom and sides of a 10-inch tart pan with removable bottom. Chill 30 minutes.

3. Prick the bottom and sides of the crust with a fork, and line it with foil. Bake 12 minutes. Then remove the foil and bake another 5 minutes. Brush with the beaten egg white, and bake 2 minutes. Remove the crust from the oven, and set it aside to cool slightly. Leave the oven on.

4. Lightly beat the milk, eggs, parsley, salt, black pepper, and cayenne together in a small bowl.

5. Sprinkle the crust with the salami and the cheeses. Pour the egg mixture into the crust and bake until puffed and golden, 25 minutes.

6 portions

BRUNCH BITS
★

Late morning brunches make any weekend celebratory. When preparing the menu, keep in mind that the food should be festive, yet comforting. Delicate, not sharp, flavors work best at this time of the day. Laden the table with fresh fruit, flowers, and pretty linen to ensure brightened spirits.

▲ Clear pitchers of freshly squeezed juices in sunshine colors are enticing. Be sure to add sprigs of mint.

▲ When serving more than four, choose a main course that does not have to be prepared at the last minute.

▲ Smoked fish platters are beautifully lightened with tissue-thin melon slices. Garnish with lemon halves instead of wedges.

▲ Instead of butter alone, serve a triple crème cheese along with a red berry jam, golden peach preserves, and a citrus marmalade with a bit of bite.

▲ Present bowls of plain and fruity yogurts alongside a selection of favorite toppings, including raisins, chopped nuts, granola, and melon chunks.

▲ Slice a French bread lengthwise, spread with butter, and toast under the broiler. Serve with thinly sliced country ham. Voila!

▲ Hot sweet potatoes are just the best in winter with Orange Butter, maple syrup, or brown sugar.

▲ Warm apple pie, farmstead Cheddar cheese, and hot chocolate make you a star on a January morning.

▲ Add a pinch of cinnamon to freshly ground coffee before brewing and serve with a pitcher of hot milk.

GREEN AND YELLOW QUICHE

All the tastes of late summer gardens are in this vegetable quiche. The custard is enriched with a cube of our basil pesto.

Dough for 1 New Basic Pie Crust (see Index)
1 egg white, lightly beaten
1 tablespoon olive oil
1 small zucchini (about 5 ounces), cut into small dice
1 small yellow summer squash (about 5 ounces), cut into small dice
¼ cup minced red bell pepper
Salt and freshly ground black pepper, to taste
1 cup half-and-half
2 eggs
⅓ cup shredded Gruyère cheese
3 tablespoons Basil Pesto (see Index and Note)
1 tablespoon cornstarch

1. Preheat the oven to 375°F.
2. Roll the dough out on a lightly floured surface to form an 11-inch circle. Press it into the bottom and sides of a 9-inch pie plate. Chill 30 minutes.
3. Prick the bottom and sides of the crust with a fork, and line it with foil. Bake 12 minutes. Then remove the foil and bake another 5 minutes. Brush the crust with the egg white, and bake 2 minutes. Remove the crust from the oven and set it aside to cool slightly.
4. Reduce the oven heat to 350°F.
5. Heat the oil in a skillet, and sauté the zucchini, yellow squash, and bell pepper over medium-high heat until golden, 5 minutes. Season with salt and pepper, and allow to cool slightly.
6. In a small bowl, whisk together the half-and-half, eggs, Gruyère, basil pesto, cornstarch, and salt and pepper to taste. Add the vegetable mixture, and stir well.
7. Pour the filling into the prepared crust, and bake until set, 25 minutes.

6 portions

Note: If you have frozen the basil pesto in ice cube trays, thaw 1 cube for this recipe.

SPRINGTIME QUICHE

This freshly flavored crustless quiche makes a perfect luncheon entrée served with a baby lettuce salad dressed with a lemony vinaigrette.

12 cups trimmed fresh spinach leaves
2 tablespoons unsalted butter
¾ cup chopped peeled shallots
3 plum tomatoes
1 cup milk
2 eggs
¾ cup shredded Monterey Jack cheese
¼ cup chopped fresh dill
2 teaspoons grated lemon zest
½ teaspoon salt
Freshly ground pepper, to taste
1 tablespoon dried bread crumbs
1 tablespoon freshly grated Parmesan cheese

1. Rinse the spinach well and place it in a large saucepan with just the water that clings to the leaves. Place the saucepan over low heat, and stir to wilt the spinach, 3 to 4 minutes. Drain well, squeezing out excess moisture. Chop coarsely, and set aside.
2. Preheat the oven to 350°F.
3. Melt the butter in a small skillet, and sauté the shallots over medium-low heat until translucent, 5 minutes. Set aside.
4. Halve the tomatoes and squeeze them, releasing and discarding the seeds and juice. Coarsely chop and set aside.
5. In a medium-size bowl, whisk together the milk, eggs, Jack cheese, dill, lemon zest, salt, and pepper. Stir in the reserved spinach, tomatoes, and shallots.
6. Thoroughly butter an 8-inch square baking pan. Add the filling, and sprinkle with the bread crumbs and Parmesan.
7. Bake until golden, 25 minutes. Let the quiche stand for 10 minutes before serving.

6 to 8 portions

YOGURT IN THE MORNING

Yogurt is cultured milk, much like butter-milk, sour cream, and crème fraîche, and develops from the action of acid-producing bacteria. Yogurt bacteria eat the milk sugar called lactose, which makes yogurt a wonderful milk substitute for those who are lactose intolerant.

Until the early '50s, yogurt couldn't be found in the United States except in ethnic markets. Today Americans eat more than one billion cups a year. We seem to have finally acquired a taste for it. Now you can buy yogurt plain (about 150 calories per cup); flavored, usually with lemon, vanilla, or coffee (200 to 250 calories per cup); with fruit on the bottom (raspberry has 225 to 300 calories per cup); Western style—flavored and with fruit on the bottom; or Swiss or French style, with fruit blended throughout. Cal-ories and nutrients differ from brand to brand, but if you want yogurt without the fat (whole milk yogurt has about 3.5 per-cent fat) you can opt for low-fat yogurt (with 1 to 2 percent fat) or skim milk yo-gurt (with .5 percent fat).

Yogurt is a light yet tasty way to begin the day. Start with plain nonfat or low-fat yogurt and add energy toppings:

Wheat germ	Chopped nuts
Bran	Sprinkles (more
Coconut flakes	for fun than
Sliced bananas	energy)
Granola	Fresh berries
Raisins	Orange sections

BUTTERMILK WAFFLES

Place a few of your favorite berries into the little waffle squares to make a decorative pattern. Serve this with a puréed fruit sauce on the side.

1 ½ cups unbleached all-purpose flour
½ cup whole-wheat flour
2 tablespoons (packed) light brown sugar
1 teaspoon baking soda
½ teaspoon ground cinnamon
¼ teaspoon salt
2 cups buttermilk
2 eggs, separated
⅓ cup unsalted butter, melted and cooled

1. Preheat a waffle iron and grease it lightly.
2. In a large mixing bowl, toss together the flours, brown sugar, baking soda, cinnamon, and salt.
3. In another bowl stir together the buttermilk, egg yolks, and butter.
4. Beat the egg whites in a mixer until stiff.
5. Stir the buttermilk mixture quickly into the dry ingredients, until almost blended. Then gently fold in the egg whites.
6. Cook the batter in the prepared waffle iron, using a generous ⅓ cup for each waffle, until crisp and golden, about 2 minutes. Serve immediately, with your favorite fruit sauce.

Twelve 5- to 6-inch waffles

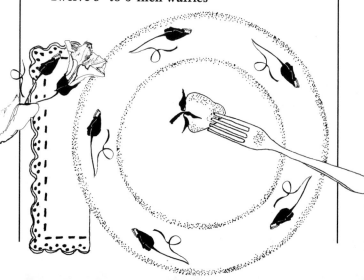

NEW BASIC BLUEBERRY PANCAKES

When blueberries are in season, this breakfast favorite is irresistible. Serve it with Orange Butter or spicy Blueberry Sauce.

1 cup unbleached all-purpose flour
1 ¼ teaspoons baking powder
¼ teaspoon ground cinnamon
¼ teaspoon freshly grated nutmeg
¼ teaspoon salt
¾ cup half-and-half
6 tablespoons milk
3 tablespoons (packed) light brown sugar
2 tablespoons unsalted butter, melted and cooled
1 egg
1 teaspoon vanilla extract
½ teaspoon grated lemon zest
¾ cup fresh blueberries
Unsalted butter for cooking the pancakes
Granulated or confectioners' sugar
1 cup Orange Butter (recipe follows)

1. In a medium-size mixing bowl, toss together the flour, baking powder, cinnamon, nutmeg, and salt.

2. In another bowl, stir the half-and-half, milk, brown sugar, butter, egg, vanilla, and lemon zest until smooth.

3. Stir the liquid into the dry ingredients until almost smooth; there may be some lumps. Fold in the blueberries, and let the batter stand, loosely covered, for 20 minutes.

4. Heat a griddle over medium-high heat, then butter it lightly. Gently drop the batter by heaping tablespoons (⅛ cup), and cook until the bottoms are golden and bubbles are popping on the surface, about 1 minute. Turn, and cook 1 minute on the other side. Repeat, using up all the batter. Sprinkle the pancakes with sugar, and serve with Orange Butter.

Eighteen 3-inch pancakes

FLAT AS A PANCAKE

A pancake is a flat cake cooked on a greased griddle until browned on both sides but still soft. The Native American Indians did not care for the settlers' *pannekoeken* for they already had their own soft cakes, which they made out of cornmeal. The settlers took up the cornmeal cakes, which eventually became johnnycakes, and added quite a few more as well, naming each one. The distinctions have all blurred and we don't know now what a griddlecake is that a flapjack isn't, but we do know we like them all.

ORANGE BUTTER

The sweet flavor of orange butter, heightened with vanilla and nutmeg, is great atop hot pancakes and waffles.

12 tablespoons (1 ½ sticks) unsalted butter, at room temperature
2 tablespoons confectioners' sugar
1 tablespoon grated orange zest
2 tablespoons orange-flavored liqueur
2 tablespoons fresh orange juice
¼ teaspoon vanilla extract
¼ teaspoon freshly grated nutmeg
Pinch of salt

Combine the butter, confectioners' sugar, and orange zest in a mixer bowl, and beat until light. Then slowly beat in the liqueur, juice, vanilla, nutmeg, and salt until smooth. Transfer to a crock, and serve immediately.

1 generous cup

Note: Orange Butter can be stored, covered, in the refrigerator. Before serving, bring it to room temperature and beat again with an electric mixer to lighten.

FIRE UP
FOR
GRILLING

HOT OFF THE GRILL

Everything tastes better when it's cooked on the grill! Just knowing there's an outdoor feast ahead makes guests arrive with a hearty appetite and the assurance that there will be a good time. Natives of Texas, South Carolina, Alabama, and Kansas City have known all along about the nuances of barbecue. And those of us who live in the North have come a long way from the once-a-year Fourth of July fête when we ate chicken, burgers, and ribs that all tasted the same—charred with a sweet and spicy sauce on top. Today, we want the great flavor of grilled food flavored by the brush of an herb, the smoke of fruitwood, a distinctive marinade, or a savory salsa. And each spring it seems we send our kitchen ovens into an earlier retirement as we get impatient for the taste of grilled whole chickens, giant shrimp in the shell, mussels, game, and every garden vegetable imaginable.

GRILLS

★

There are several different types of grills on the market, each with its own advantages and disadvantages. One piece of advice when buying any grill, however: Buy one that is sturdy, built of heavy metal, and constructed to last. You'll be glad you spent the extra money in the end.

THE BRAZIER

Not so long ago you could find one of these grills on every patio. An inexpensive introduction to outdoor cooking, the simplest braziers are shallow pans on legs fitted with a rack for holding the food as it cooks. You can also buy them with a partial hood and a rotisserie, and most are large enough to handle burgers for a yardful of hungry people. The advantage of the brazier is that it is very inexpensive. The disadvantage is that the heat cannot be adjusted so you may end up with overly charred food. The foods we recommend cooking on a brazier are those that are less than 1½ inches thick and cook quickly.

Hibachis—sort of mini-braziers—are perfect for city terraces and portable outdoor grill feasts.

THE COVERED GRILL

Usually kettle-shaped or rectangular, this grill has an advantage over simple braziers

in that it includes dampers—vents that open and close—in the grill pan and a hood to help you control the heat. It cooks foods more quickly and traps in the smoke for the flavor we love. We like this type of grill because of its versatility; you can use it like a brazier to grill, or cover it with the lid to roast or smoke foods.

There are also covered gas grills on the market; gas jets heat a layer of lava rocks (pieces of porous, volcanic rock), which in turn cook the food. The gas grill has the advantage of being very convenient and starting up quickly. We, however, find the heat of gas grills unpredictable and like to use a charcoal grill, which we can regulate to our liking. We also find that a charcoal grill gives food a better flavor.

INDOOR GAS COOKTOP OR ELECTRIC GRILL

Built-in indoor gas grills work on the same principle as the covered gas grills. They do not produce much smoke, so food cooked on them lacks the rich, smoky flavor possible from an outdoor grill. Built-in electric grills produce no smoke at all. But both gas and electric models are convenient and allow you to cook in your house at a very high heat, which gives food that wonderful crusty outside and juicy inside.

THE FIRE

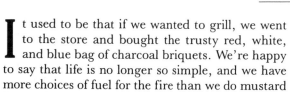

It used to be that if we wanted to grill, we went to the store and bought the trusty red, white, and blue bag of charcoal briquets. We're happy to say that life is no longer so simple, and we have more choices of fuel for the fire than we do mustard for our burgers.

The old-fashioned briquets are made from wood scraps that have been burned into carbon and then are mixed with fillers to lengthen their burning life. Hardwood charcoal, which we prefer to use, is made from chunks of wood that have been subjected to a long, slow process of carbonization; it contains no chemicals and burns hotter than briquets. It also sparks, so watch out. Hardwood charcoal is available in oak, maple, cherry, apple, hickory, mesquite, and alder woods.

To give your food a stronger, smoked flavor, you may want to add hardwood chips or chunks to the fire (hardwood *only*, please—softwood smoke is very unpleasant). Chunks are fist-size pieces of wood; chips are smaller and burn faster. Both are available in the same woods as the hardwood charcoal, and their flavoring is intense and smoky so use them sparingly. Both must be soaked in water before using: one hour for chips; two hours for chunks. Use wood chunks with a covered grill for foods that require lengthy cooking.

You may also want to use other flavoring agents on the fire, such as grapevines, nutshells, branches of herbs, garlic, orange or lemon zest, pumpkin and poppy seeds, or spices. Just make sure that the flavoring is compatible with the food being cooked. And anything that goes on the fire should be soaked briefly so it doesn't burn.

LIGHTING THE FIRE

We have a lot more choice these days as to how we want to light our fire. The old standby, charcoal lighter fluid, is currently the subject of a "heated" debate. Some people claim that the fluid leaves a chemical taste on the food. Others claim that since the fluid is highly volatile, it evaporates quickly, leaving no foreign taste whatsoever on the food. We prefer not to take chances and use kindling placed underneath the fuel to start the fire.

Another excellent option is the electric charcoal lighter. If you have an electrical outlet near the grill (or a very long, heavy-duty extension cord appropriate for outdoor use), it is a cinch to work the lighter in among the coals and let it heat for 7 to 10 minutes until the coals surrounding it are red-hot. Then remove the starter (if you let it heat for too long, it will burn itself out) and allow the other coals to catch.

The size of the fire depends upon the amount of food being cooked and its cooking time; you will clearly need more charcoal to grill a large piece of meat, such as a beef or pork roast, than to grill steaks or hamburgers. Mound the charcoal into a pyramid, light it by whatever method you wish, and allow it to burn for at least 30 minutes. It is ready when it is evenly covered with a layer of white ash.

Once the fire has reached the proper temperature, you will need to rearrange the coals depending on the food to be cooked. If you are cooking cuts of meat or fish that need only a short cooking time, such as chops, steaks, burgers, fish steaks, or fish fillets, scatter the charcoal evenly over the grill pan; this allows you to cook over direct heat. For long-cooking foods such as whole fish, turkeys, chickens, roasts, and ribs, you'll need to cook over indirect heat; push the coals away from the center of the grill pan to form a ring, and set a foil-lined drip pan in the center of the coals just below where the food will sit on the grill rack. Cover the grill when using indirect heat.

GRILLING POULTRY

Birds of all kinds and sizes are suited to grilling and smoking: Chicken, Rock Cornish game hen, capon, quail, duck, squab, grouse, guinea hen, pheasant, turkey, and partridge. Poultry is very versatile—you can cook it in pieces, butterflied and flattened, or whole. You can stuff it or marinate it. Since poultry has a tendency to dry out if left to its own devices, we always baste it like crazy. And we have found that poultry stays moister if cooked on the bone—and that the bone also adds flavor.

Poultry should be seared, skin side down to begin, and then cooked on a covered grill over direct heat until the meat at the bone is opaque and the juices from near the joint run yellow with just a trace of pink when pierced. (Remember that the dark meat will take substantially longer to cook than the light meat, so let the dark meat cook 15 minutes before adding the light meat to the grill.) If you are using a thermometer, cook poultry until it registers 170° to 175°F, and then let it stand off the heat for about 10 minutes; the temperature will continue to rise by 5 to 10 degrees.

If you are planning to grill split poultry, remove the backbone first—the bird will cook more evenly.

A WHOLE CHICKEN ON THE GRILL

Even without a spit, you can enjoy a moist, flavorful grilled chicken, complete with succulent juices. Don't truss this bird, because the legs won't cook evenly if they are pressed up against the body.

one whole chicken

one whole grill

½ cup fresh orange juice
½ cup red wine vinegar
½ cup tomato paste
1 teaspoon cayenne pepper
Freshly ground black pepper, to taste
1 whole chicken (2½ to 3 pounds),
    well rinsed, patted dry, and untrussed

1. Prepare hot coals for grilling.
2. Stir all the ingredients, except the chicken, together in a bowl until smooth.
3. Brush the chicken well with the sauce.
4. Grill the chicken over low heat, preferably covered, for about 1 hour and 10 minutes (turn the chicken a quarter turn and brush it with sauce every 15 minutes).
5. Let the chicken stand 10 minutes before carving and serving.

3 to 4 portions

Put down the lid—Chicken will be real moist!

CHICKEN IN QUARTERS

Delicious Oriental flavors marinate this chicken. The white meat will probably need less cooking time than the dark meat, so watch it carefully.

¼ cup sesame seeds, toasted (see Index)
¼ cup minced or grated fresh ginger
2 tablespoons sesame oil
2 tablespoons rice vinegar
1 teaspoon dried red pepper flakes
1 teaspoon Chinese five-spice powder
½ teaspoon salt
1 chicken (3 to 3½ pounds), well rinsed, patted dry, and quartered

1. In a bowl large enough to hold the chicken, stir all the ingredients, except the chicken, together. Add the chicken, and turn the pieces so they are well coated.

2. Cover the bowl loosely; refrigerate 6 hours or overnight.

3. Prepare hot coals for grilling.

4. Grill the chicken over medium heat, turning four or five times, until deep golden or lightly charred and cooked through, about 30 minutes. Be careful not to overcook it.

3 to 4 portions

CHICKEN BROCHETTES

Wittily laced with baby pattypans and zucchini, and entwined with sprigs of fresh rosemary, chicken brochettes become a star of any barbecue.

2 whole boneless skinless chicken breasts, well rinsed and patted dry
8 red or white pearl onions, unpeeled
8 tiny pattypan squash
8 tiny zucchini
¾ cup olive oil
⅓ cup fresh lemon juice
8 large cloves garlic
1 tablespoon chopped fresh rosemary leaves
Salt and freshly ground black pepper, to taste
8 cherry tomatoes, approximately the same size as the onions
8 long sprigs rosemary

1. Slice the chicken into 1½-inch-thick slices.

2. Bring a saucepan of water to a boil. With a

sharp knife, cut a small X in the root end of each onion. Drop the onions into gently boiling water and cook for 5 minutes. Drain, rinse under cold water, and peel.

3. Bring another saucepan of water to a gentle boil. Drop in the pattypan squash and zucchini, and cook for 3 minutes. Drain, rinse under cold water, and drain again.

4. Combine the olive oil, lemon juice, garlic, chopped rosemary, and salt and pepper in a large bowl. Add the chicken, pearl onions, pattypan, and zucchini. Toss well, cover loosely, and marinate in the refrigerator for 6 to 8 hours.

5. Prepare hot coals for grilling.

6. Roll up a piece of chicken and slide it onto a long metal skewer. Follow it with an onion, pattypan, zucchini, another piece of chicken, a cherry tomato, and a garlic clove from the marinade. Repeat with seven more skewers. Wrap a sprig of fresh rosemary around each skewer.

7. Place the skewers 3 inches from the coals and grill, turning once, 8 to 10 minutes.

4 portions

In Italy, butterflied, grilled chicken is called "chicken cooked the devil's way." A classic dish of Tuscany, the young chicken is cut in half down the back, opened up like a book, and gently flattened. It is brushed with the best olive oil, salt, and pepper and cooked on a grill over a wood fire until the skin is deliciously golden and crispy. Sometimes a tiny piece of chile pepper is added to the oil to give it a bite.

IT'S DONE!

▲ PEEKING: The most primitive test. One can peek by piercing the food with a long-handled fork or a metal or bamboo skewer, or by cutting into it with a sharp knife, and taking a look at the flesh. Use a knife only as a last resort because valuable juices will be lost in the process. Fish is done when the flesh is opaque or, if you like it less cooked, only very slightly transparent in the center. Steaks and chops are done when the center shows the meat to be cooked to your taste—rare, medium-rare, or well-done.

▲ FEELING: The way a piece of food feels when pressed with a finger is a very good indicator of doneness, but requires a little practice. This method is used by grill chefs for steaks, chops, fish, and poultry. Lightly press a piece of uncooked flesh to experience what really rare feels like; the flesh becomes progressively tighter and more resistant as it cooks.

NEW BASIC CHICKEN FAJITAS

These marinated chicken strips come to the table sizzling hot from the grill. Then it's up to everyone to get involved Mexican style and customize their own inside a corn or flour tortilla, using a fiery-hot sauce, chopped onions and tomatoes, sour cream or yogurt, guacamole, Black Bean Pesto, and shredded Monterey Jack. Then sprinkle them with freshly chopped parsley or cilantro—they're great for a Sunday afternoon lunch.

Juice of 4 limes
6 tablespoons olive oil
1 teaspoon dried oregano leaves
1 teaspoon coarsely ground black pepper
1 teaspoon salt
1 ½ pounds skinless boneless
   chicken breasts
2 large onions, halved lengthwise and
   cut into ¼-inch slivers
2 packages (7 ounces each) 6-inch corn
   or flour tortillas, at room temperature
1 ½ cups Guacamole Is Hot! (see Index)
8 ounces plain yogurt or sour cream
2 ripe plum tomatoes, seeded and cut into
   ¼-inch dice
¾ cup (12 tablespoons) Black Bean Pesto (see Index)
1 ½ cups grated Monterey Jack cheese
Tabasco or hot pepper sauce, to taste (optional)
1 tablespoon chopped fresh Italian (flat-leaf) parsley or
   cilantro (fresh coriander)

1. Combine the lime juice, 2 tablespoons of the olive oil, oregano, ½ teaspoon of the pepper, and ½ teaspoon of the salt in a glass bowl. Mix well, and add the chicken breasts. Cover loosely, and marinate, turning occasionally, for 2 hours.

2. Preheat the oven to 350°F, and prepare hot coals for grilling.

3. In a shallow roasting pan, combine the slivered onions with the chicken breasts and marinade. Cover the pan with aluminum foil, and bake until the chicken is just opaque, 15 to 20 minutes. Remove the chicken breasts to a platter, and set aside.

4. Transfer the onions to a heavy skillet, and add the remaining 4 tablespoons olive oil and any pan juices. Sprinkle with the remaining ½ teaspoon salt and ½ teaspoon pepper. Cook over medium heat, stirring often, until the onions are very soft and slightly browned, 15 minutes. Drain the onions and set them aside.

5. Place the chicken breasts over very hot coals, and grill until they are cooked through but still moist, about 2 minutes on each side. Slice them into strips 3 inches long and ½ inch wide.

6. Lay 12 prepared tortillas on a large platter and serve along with the chicken, onions, guacamole, yogurt or sour cream, tomatoes, black bean pesto, and cheese. Let each person fill a tortilla according to taste. Top with a dash of hot sauce and sprinkle with chopped parsley or cilantro. Fold or roll the tortillas and enjoy!

6 portions

MARY EMMERLING'S CHICKEN BARBECUE

We marvel at Mary—her taste superb, her eye for American country antiques unquestionable, and her passion relentless. She has taught America a great deal about style as she has traveled from one coast to the other writing, photographing, and searching for artisans.

½ cup apricot jam
2 tablespoons soy sauce
2 tablespoons dry white wine or dry sherry
2 tablespoons minced scallions (green onions)
2 tablespoons minced garlic
2 tablespoons minced fresh ginger
2 tablespoons fresh lemon juice
Salt and freshly ground black pepper to taste
1 chicken (2½ to 3 pounds), well rinsed, patted dry, and quartered

1. Combine all the ingredients except the chicken in a large bowl, and mix well.

2. Rinse the chicken pieces well and pat them dry. Place them in the bowl, and toss to coat with the marinade. Cover, refrigerate, and marinate at least 4 hours, turning occasionally.

3. Prepare hot coals for grilling.

4. Grill the chicken over medium-hot coals, basting frequently with the marinade, until the juices run clear when the meat is pricked with a fork, 15 minutes on each side. Serve immediately.

2 to 4 portions

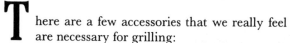

TOOLS OF THE TRADE

There are a few accessories that we really feel are necessary for grilling:

▲ A natural bristle, long-handled basting brush for applying thick sauces or for oiling the grill rack.

▲ A suction baster to use when applying marinades to food on the grill.

▲ Two flat metal spatulas.

▲ Heavy-duty, long-handled tongs to adjust the coals and turn and pick up the food; tongs won't break the food's outer crust as a fork will do, thus allowing the juices to escape.

▲ A hinged grill basket for grilling whole fish; this will save your life if you're cooking delicate-fleshed fish, which might fall apart when you turn it.

▲ Skewers in assorted lengths; these are great for making kabobs with chunks of vegetables, chicken, seafood, and meats. If you buy wooden skewers, soak them in water before using so they don't burn.

▲ A stiff, heavy wire brush to clean the grill rack between uses; last night's dinner will not burn off and its flavors will linger.

GRILLING BEEF

There are those who believe that the original method of cooking beef—over a fire—is still the best. And we agree. Grilling brings out its rich flavor, and there is nothing quite like eating a sizzling steak just off the grill.

Steaks are perfectly suited to grilling because they are flat and will cook uniformly. Well-marbled steaks need only a light brush of oil before grilling, but lean steaks such as round, London broil, or flank steak must be marinated before grilling and even then you should cook them rare so they do not become tough.

Trim most of the fat off the steak and lightly score the remainder with a sharp knife at 1-inch intervals. Thicker steaks will dry out less easily than thin ones; we like them 1½ to 3 inches thick. Rub the steaks with olive oil, sear them quickly on the oiled grill, and then cook them, turning once, until cooked the way you like them. Aged and well-marbled beef will cook more quickly than fresh, leaner steaks.

Hamburgers are terrific grilled. We like to flavor the meat with a variety of seasonings such as garlic, herbs, chiles, and spices, and we often add an egg, a dollop of mayonnaise, or a bit of butter or cream to keep the meat moist. Remember not to handle the meat too much because this toughens it—quickly mix in desired seasonings and gently shape into patties. If you are watching your cholesterol, try James Beard's trick of forming the hamburger around an ice cube; as the cube melts it bathes the meat in moisture. But be prepared for a rare burger.

Sear hamburgers and then grill them over medium-hot coals. We find that turning them several times during cooking will guarantee a nicely browned crust and juicy interior.

Our favorite cuts of beef for grilling are the tenderloin or filet mignon, T-bone, porterhouse, shell, rib, and New York steaks. We also like the less tender cuts such as London broil, round, and flank steaks as long as they are marinated before grilling.

VEAL

Veal is so lean these days that the only cut we trust to hold up to the high heat of grilling is a thick chop—about 1½ inches thick. Marinate the chops in olive oil, lemon juice, garlic, shallots, pepper, bay leaves, rosemary, and white wine. A dash of balsamic vinegar adds a tangy sweetness, if you like. Grill veal chops about 3½ to 4 inches from the fire, seven to nine minutes per side. Baste the chops frequently during cooking.

GRILLED MIXED GRILL

When we were testing this dish we enjoyed the flank steak, but we couldn't stop eating the grilled sausage. It's great looking and great tasting.

MARINADE
2 tablespoons soy sauce
1 tablespoon minced fresh ginger
1 tablespoon slivered lemon zest
2 teaspoons Asian sesame oil
1 clove garlic, minced
1 teaspoon coarsely ground black pepper
1 teaspoon brown sugar

1 flank steak (about 1½ pounds)
2 pounds hot Italian sausage, in 2 coils
Olive oil

1. In a shallow bowl large enough to hold the steak, stir the marinade ingredients together. Add the steak, and turn it in the marinade; rub marinade into the surface. Cover loosely, and refrigerate overnight.

2. Prepare hot coals for grilling.

3. Pierce each sausage coil with two skewers at right angles, to hold the shape and facilitate turning. Brush the sausages well with olive oil.

4. Grill the sausages over high heat until cooked through and lightly charred, about 7 minutes per side. Set aside, loosely covered with aluminum foil.

5. Remove the steak from the marinade, and grill it over high heat, 4 to 5 minutes per side.

6. Slice the steak thinly on the diagonal, and cut the sausages into large chunks. Serve immediately.

6 portions

SKIRT STEAK FAJITAS

The great sandwich of the southwest. We like to echo the flavors of the marinated steak and garnishes by serving our Black and White Bean Salad alongside. For a bit of cool, top with a dollop of sour cream.

1 ½ pounds beef skirt steak, trimmed
Juice of 2 limes
1 tablespoon olive oil
¼ cup chopped cilantro (fresh coriander)
1 small hot chile pepper, such as cascabelle, cored, seeded,
*   and minced*
1 clove garlic, minced
½ teaspoon ground cumin
¼ teaspoon salt
Freshly ground black pepper, to taste
Flour tortillas, warmed
1 ripe avocado, peeled and sliced
1 cup diced ripe tomatoes
½ cup diced red onion or sliced scallions
¼ cup sliced jalapeños (optional)
Fresh Tomato Salsa (see Index)

1. Cut the steak crosswise to create four pieces.

2. Stir the lime juice, oil, cilantro, chile pepper, garlic, cumin, salt, and pepper together in a medium-size bowl. Add the steak; turn to coat it in the mixture. Cover loosely, and let stand at room temperature for several hours or refrigerate overnight.

3. Prepare hot coals for grilling.

4. Arrange the steaks on the grill, close to the heat, and grill until lightly charred and cooked medium-rare, 3 to 4 minutes per side. Transfer the steaks to a cutting board, and let stand 1 minute.

5. Slice the steaks diagonally across the grain into ¼-inch-thick slices.

6. Place the steak strips on a large platter and serve with the warmed tortillas, avocado, tomatoes, onion, and jalapeños.

7. Spoon on salsa before folding and eating.

4 to 6 portions

SALSAS

In Spanish cuisine the word *salsa* means sauce, but in America it has come to mean any fresh, chunky condiment. More often than not a salsa begins with tomatoes, with peppers or tomatillos added. We make salsas with a variety of vegetables, or sometimes with fruits, or even with a combination of fruits and vegetables. Salsas are the freshest way around to top grilled food.

STUFFED HAMBURGERS WITH STYLE

America's favorite grill food, Italian style. Sun-dried tomatoes, capers, and mozzarella accent the beef perfectly to give these hamburgers pizzazz. If you keep them coming, you'll watch them disappear!

1 ½ pounds ground beef sirloin
½ cup chopped fresh Italian (flat-leaf) parsley
¼ cup finely chopped red onion
¼ cup tiny capers, drained
¼ cup Dijon mustard
2 ripe plum tomatoes, seeded and cut into ¼-inch dice
2 egg yolks
8 sun-dried tomato halves, coarsely chopped
2 teaspoons caraway seeds
1 teaspoon freshly ground black pepper
4 to 6 tablespoons coarsely grated
   mozzarella cheese (preferably
   fresh)

1. Prepare hot coals for grilling.

2. Combine all the ingredients except the cheese in a bowl, gently tossing with your hands. Do not overmix.

3. Divide the mixture in half, and make four patties out of one half. Make a small indentation in the center of each patty, and place some of the grated mozzarella in each. Top with the remaining meat to finish the patties.

4. Grill over hot coals for 3 minutes on each side for rare—or longer to taste.

4 portions

THE WINES OF SUMMER

Summer wines should be light, refreshing, and uncomplicated. Serve them chilled but not icy cold, so they are thirst-quenching yet not so cold as to lose their flavor. The fruity, crisp taste of Rieslings and Chenin Blancs are perfect. Dry, crisp rosés and chillable reds like Beaujolais are good with a meal of light meats and cold poultry.

Spicy, smoky flavors of foods cooked over an open fire call for a wine that can match that robust taste. We like to serve a fruity, light red, such as a Beaujolais, with ribs. Full-bodied, gutsy reds, such as Zinfandels or a Petite Sirah, will balance the flavors of steak, butterflied lamb, and our Grand Gaucho Paella. Pacific salmon steaks grilled on the beach should be served with glasses of crisp, chilled Chardonnay.

A Gewürztraminer teams up well with spicy foods. It is assertive enough to handle dishes with peppery sauces or southwestern spices. Shellfish and other seafoods go well with a steely Sauvignon Blanc. A spicy Beaujolais or a young Merlot or Cabernet is great with pasta and meat dishes.

Picnic wines should be casual and not at all fussy. Choose a Riesling or dry Chenin Blanc if you prefer a white, or a Beaujolais-Villages or Cabernet with heavier foods that demand a red. A tangy white Zinfandel seems perfect for warm weather's fried chicken, lobster salad sandwiches, and juicy, ripe tomatoes.

To launch a summer get-together in style, try serving a sparkling wine that is inexpensive yet good. We like the crisp, dry style of Segura Viudas Brut for less than $10 a bottle. The French Comte du Bailly Brut Crémant de Bourgogne is dry and a bargain at the same price. A tart, fruity, sparkling Vouvray is delicious with chicken salads.

GRILLING PORK

Pork is a natural on the grill whether as a chop, cooked quickly over high heat, or as a roast, cooked long and slow until the meat is tender enough to cut with a spoon. Remember that today's pork is leaner and more tender than it was years ago. It is best grilled on a covered grill to keep it moist. Sear and cook chops over direct heat, but cook roasts over indirect heat. We like to rub all cuts well with olive oil before cooking.

Our favorite cuts of pork to grill are ribs. We braise them first to rid them of excess fat so they don't cause flare-ups on the grill. Pork chops are also wonderful grilled—choose chops that are at least an inch thick so they don't dry out. The tenderloin is delicious either grilled whole or sliced into medallions and grilled in a flash. Boneless loin roasts are very easy to grill and very tender. For a real treat, try cooking a whole ham on the covered grill.

Cook pork until the internal temperature reaches 150° to 160°F. Then remove it from the grill and let it stand 15 minutes to finish cooking.

JIMMY SCHMIDT'S RATTLESNAKE RIBS

One of America's finest chefs, Jimmy Schmidt—of the Rattlesnake Club in Denver—has made these one of his signature dishes. The three sauces create deep hot flavor—these are real mean western ribs.

BRAISING LIQUID AND RIBS
4 quarts homemade beef stock (see Index)
    or canned broth
¾ cup red wine vinegar
1 tablespoon paprika
1 tablespoon cayenne pepper
1 ½ tablespoons ground cumin
3 tablespoons Tabasco sauce
1 ¼ tablespoons garlic powder
1 tablespoon ground ginger
1 cup tomato paste
¼ cup honey
1 tablespoon salt
4 slabs baby back ribs (1 ¼ pounds each)

SPICE MIXTURE
¼ cup garlic salt
1 tablespoon ground white pepper
½ cup paprika
¼ cup dry mustard
¼ cup red wine vinegar
¼ cup Worcestershire sauce
½ cup beer

3 cups Barbecue Sauce (recipe follows)

1. Combine all the braising liquid ingredients in a large pot. Stir well, and bring to a simmer over medium heat.

2. Add the ribs, and simmer until tender but not falling apart, about 1 hour and 45 minutes. When done, carefully transfer the ribs to a baking sheet.

3. Combine all the spice mixture ingredients in a medium-size bowl, and stir to form a paste. (Add more beer if it is too dry.)

4. Rub the paste over all surfaces of the ribs. Wrap each slab in aluminum foil, dull side out, and refrigerate until ready to cook. (These can be prepared up to 4 days in advance.)

5. Preheat the oven to 400°F, and prepare hot coals for grilling. Place the rack 3 to 4 inches from the heat.

6. Cover a baking sheet with aluminum foil, and arrange the ribs on the foil. Coat the ribs with 2 cups of the barbecue sauce, and bake on the center rack of the oven for 10 minutes.

7. Transfer the ribs to the grill, and cook long enough to char. Serve immediately, with the remaining 1 cup barbecue sauce on the side.

4 portions

BARBECUE SAUCE

1 cup chili sauce
1 cup ketchup
¼ cup steak sauce
1 tablespoon ground tamarind seeds or Worcestershire sauce
1 tablespoon finely pressed garlic
¼ cup finely grated fresh horseradish, or 2 tablespoons prepared, well drained
3 tablespoons dry mustard
1 tablespoon Tabasco sauce
1 tablespoon molasses
1 tablespoon jalapeño salsa (see Note)
1 tablespoon red wine vinegar

Combine all the ingredients in a medium-size bowl, and whisk until the sauce is well blended. Adjust seasonings to taste.

3 cups

Note: Most supermarkets carry salsas in varying degrees of hotness. For this dish, we recommend using one that packs a substantial wallop.

SKEWERED LAMB

We have updated the familiar lamb shish kabob by adding balsamic vinegar to a marinade. Baby artichokes, baby eggplants, and plum tomatoes combine to make a dazzling dish for the grill.

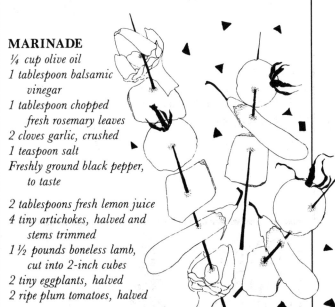

MARINADE

¼ cup olive oil
1 tablespoon balsamic vinegar
1 tablespoon chopped fresh rosemary leaves
2 cloves garlic, crushed
1 teaspoon salt
Freshly ground black pepper, to taste

2 tablespoons fresh lemon juice
4 tiny artichokes, halved and stems trimmed
1½ pounds boneless lamb, cut into 2-inch cubes
2 tiny eggplants, halved
2 ripe plum tomatoes, halved

1. Stir the marinade ingredients together in a large bowl.

2. Combine 6 cups water and the lemon juice in a medium-size saucepan and bring to a boil. Add the artichokes, lower the heat to medium, and cook until tender, 10 to 15 minutes. Drain well.

3. Add the lamb, artichokes, eggplants, and tomatoes to the marinade, and toss until well coated. Let stand, covered loosely, at room temperature, for 1 hour, stirring occasionally.

4. Prepare hot coals for grilling.

5. Thread four long metal skewers in this order: an artichoke half, a lamb chunk, an eggplant half, another lamb chunk, a tomato half, another lamb chunk, and finish with an artichoke half. (Reserve the marinade.)

6. Brush each skewer with marinade, and place them on the grill 4 to 5 inches above the coals. Grill, turning and basting frequently with the marinade, 12 to 15 minutes. Serve immediately.

4 portions

GRILLING LAMB

The most tender cuts of lamb come from the loin and rib sections, usually in the form of chops. We also like the leg because we feel that it is the most flavorful cut; it can be grilled whole or boned and butterflied. Most cuts of lamb benefit from a marinade; trim off the fat and marinate in oil flavored with herbs, garlic, lemon juice, wine, chiles, soy sauce, ginger—you name it.

We like our chops cut about 1½ inches thick. Trim the fat and marinate the chops. Score the remaining fat and sear over high heat. Then finish cooking over a lower heat.

Leg of lamb should be cooked over indirect heat on a covered grill. If the leg is butterflied, it will cook in about one quarter the time of a bone-in leg. We often make kabobs from cubed leg meat. Marinate the meat and skewer it, alternating with vegetables if you like, and then grill the skewers over direct heat. Let lamb stand five minutes before serving.

HONEY LAMB RIBLETS

The preparation is easy, the flavor of the lamb riblets succulent, the sauce pungent!

¼ cup honey
¼ cup Worcestershire sauce
3½ pounds lamb riblets, cut from the breast into 2 slabs

1. Prepare hot coals for grilling.
2. Stir the honey and Worcestershire sauce together in a small bowl, and brush the ribs on both sides with the mixture.
3. Grill the lamb over medium-high heat, turning and brushing four or five times with the sauce, until cooked through and fork-tender when pierced between the ribs, about 30 minutes.
4. Cut the lamb between the ribs. Serve with additional sauce if desired.

4 portions

LOIN LAMB CHOPS

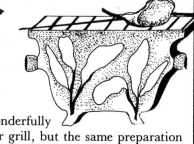

These chops are wonderfully tasty on the outdoor grill, but the same preparation serves equally well cooked under the broiler.

2 large cloves garlic, minced
2 tablespoons crumbled dried rosemary leaves
1 teaspoon coarsely ground black pepper
4 loin lamb chops (about 2 pounds total) 1½ inches thick

1. Stir the garlic, rosemary, and pepper together in a small bowl.
2. Press the herb mixture into the chops so they are well coated. Cover, and refrigerate for several hours or overnight.
3. Prepare hot coals for grilling.
4. Grill the chops over high heat, about 4 minutes per side for medium-rare. Serve immediately.

2 or 3 portions

BEER TIPS

Just as outdoor cooking encourages hearty appetites, it also seems to encourage mighty thirsts. Icy cold beer is always a popular answer, but it must be served just right.

▲ Store beer in a cool, dark area with the bottles in an upright position.

▲ If a beer is labeled unpasteurized, it should be kept refrigerated and consumed within one or two weeks.

▲ Once beer has been refrigerated, keep it there or iced until serving time; it will lose its flavor if warmed and rere-frigerated excessively.

▲ Serve beer in large glasses. If the beer is very foamy, we like to use a very tall, thin glass. Hold the glass at a 45-degree angle and pour the beer into the bottom to produce a small amount of froth. Then continue pouring slowly along the side. When full, straighten the glass to an upright position to add the head.

▲ Foods with spicy sauces should be paired with beers that have a strong character and full body.

▲ Grilled chicken with fresh herbs is complemented by a light, dry beer.

▲ Sausages and potato salads are great with strong brews. Serve a full-bodied ale for just the right touch.

▲ When a large pot of bean soup is simmering on the stove and the fire is crackling in the fireplace, it's time to bring out the hearty beers of winter. Serve a pork roast, a Bock beer, and crusty dark bread—then watch the snowflakes gently fall.

BUTTERFLIED LEG OF LAMB

This is the best way we know to grill lamb—it's easier to reach that perfect pinkness with a butterfly cut. If you're lucky you'll have leftovers, as it's just great cold the next day. Think of topping this, hot or cold, with herbed mayonnaise or aïoli. Just a little smidgen will do!

1 cup dry red wine
¾ cup soy sauce
4 large cloves garlic, crushed
½ cup chopped fresh mint leaves
2 tablespoons slightly bruised fresh rosemary leaves
*   or 1 tablespoon dried*
1 tablespoon coarsely ground black pepper
1 butterflied leg of lamb (4 to 5 pounds)

1. Combine the wine, soy sauce, garlic, mint, rosemary, and pepper in a small bowl, and mix well. Place the lamb in a nonreactive baking pan. Pour the mixture over the lamb, cover, and refrigerate for 6 hours, turning the lamb frequently.

2. Prepare hot coals for grilling.

3. Drain the meat, reserving the marinade. Grill the lamb 4 inches above the hot coals, basting frequently with the marinade, about 20 minutes on each side. Check the lamb for doneness frequently after 30 minutes' grilling.

4. Cut the lamb into very thin slices, and serve immediately.

8 portions

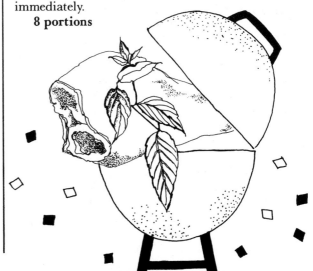

 # GRILLING SEAFOOD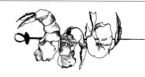

Seafood is sensational on the grill, whether you are cooking whole fish, steaks, fillets, or shellfish. We like to use oil marinades with lean fish; nothing too strong, and only for about 30 minutes so as not to overpower their delicate flavor. (An acidic marinade will cut the oiliness of fatty fish.) Herbs and wood chips add a light, smoky flavor to fish.

If you do a lot of fish grilling, you may want to invest in a hinged wire fish basket. The basket makes turning whole fish and fillets, which may fall apart on the grill, a snap. If you don't use a basket, oil the grill rack and turn the fish only once. Cook fillets and steaks with the skin on if you can. Or wrap the fish in aluminum foil before grilling.

Our favorite fish steaks to grill are salmon, sturgeon, swordfish, and tuna. We like steaks cut about 1½ inches thick, and we sometimes coat them with a crust of crumbs, black pepper, chopped almonds, or sesame seeds. Fish kabobs are also great on the grill, but the cubes of fish must be marinated before skewering to keep them moist.

Don't salt fish before grilling; salt draws moisture out of the flesh and may cause it to toughen. Grill steaks, fillets, small whole fish, shrimp, and scallops over high direct heat. Grill large, whole fish over indirect heat. And baste fish religiously as it cooks to keep it from drying out.

Fish cooks very fast on the grill and it is important not to overcook it. Count on a cooking time of 10 minutes per inch of thickness whether you are cooking a steak, fillet, or whole fish. When cooked, the flesh will turn opaque and will feel springy when pressed lightly with a finger. And remember that the fish will continue to cook slightly after it is removed from the grill.

Shellfish is also wonderful on the grill. We prefer to cook it in the shell so that the natural juices don't escape; oysters, mussels, and clams will open when cooked. Another delicious way to cook lobster is to split it down its length and grill it in the shell.

GRILLED LITTLE FISH

This method works well with trout, small bluefish, snappers, or sea bass. It is really a grilled papillote.

2 small whole fish (about 1 pound each), cleaned
Salt and freshly ground black pepper, to taste
1 lemon
12 small sprigs thyme

1. Prepare hot coals for grilling.
2. Cut three crosswise diagonal slits, about ½ inch deep and 2 inches apart, in each side of each fish; don't cut down to the bone.
3. Sprinkle the fish lightly with salt and pepper, and rub it into the slits.
4. Thinly slice the lemon; place 1 slice and 1 sprig of thyme in each slit.
5. Wrap each fish in aluminum foil.
6. Grill the fish over high heat turning once, until the flesh flakes easily when tested with a fork, about 10 minutes. Serve immediately.

2 portions

SWORDFISH STEAKS

When you are lucky enough to get great swordfish, the rule is to keep it simple. Grilled swordfish will be even tastier if it is marinated first. If you can get a good, hot wood fire going, we suggest cutting the swordfish thinner than 1½ inches (say, ½ inch thick), as they do in Sicily. It sears in the juices, cooks very quickly, and will taste even better than the usual inch-thick steaks.

Juice of 1 orange
Grated zest of ½ orange
1 tablespoon olive oil
½ teaspoon salt
½ teaspoon coarsely ground black pepper
2 swordfish steaks (6 ounces each), 1 ½ inches thick

1. In a bowl large enough to hold the steaks, stir all the ingredients, except the swordfish, together. Add the steaks, and turn them in the marinade. Cover loosely and refrigerate for several hours.

2. Prepare hot coals for grilling.

3. Oil the grill, and cook the steaks over high heat, about 3 to 4 minutes per side. The steaks should be seared on the outside and just cooked through.

2 portions

TUNA BROCHETTES

Tuna must be grilled quickly, since it will dry out badly if overcooked—so watch it carefully. Of course you can also grill tuna under an oven broiler.

MARINADE
¼ cup fruity olive oil
2 tablespoons fresh lemon juice
¼ cup chopped scallions (green onions)
1 tablespoon fresh thyme leaves
2 cloves garlic, minced
1 teaspoon salt
1 teaspoon fennel seeds, crushed
Freshly ground black pepper, to taste

1 ½ pounds fresh tuna, cut into 2-inch chunks
1 fennel bulb, trimmed and cut into 2-inch pieces
1 red onion, cut into 8 wedges

1. Whisk the marinade ingredients together in a large bowl until smooth. Add the tuna, fennel, and red onion, and turn in the marinade. Cover loosely, and refrigerate for several hours or overnight.

2. Prepare hot coals for grilling.

3. On four large metal skewers, thread the tuna chunks alternately with pieces of fennel and onion.

4. Oil the grill, and cook over medium heat about 3 to 4 minutes per side. Serve immediately.

4 portions

WINES WITH GRILLED FOODS

GRILLED FOOD	WINE
Chicken	Beaujolais, Chardonnay, Sauvignon Blanc
Fish	Fumé Blanc, Chardonnay
Hamburgers	Beaujolais-Villages
Lamb, or Pork Ribs	Zinfandel
Mixed Grill	Chianti, Merlot
Paella	Rioja red, Bandol red, Zinfandel, Beaujolais, Sangria
Steak	Zinfandel, Merlot
Vegetables	Bandol rosé, Sancerre, Beaujolais-Villages

PACIFIC NORTHWEST SALMON

Our good friends David and Niki Finholm learned this delicious preparation from the camp cook while on a fishing trip in Alaska.

8 tablespoons (1 stick) unsalted butter
⅓ cup honey
⅓ cup (packed) brown sugar
2 tablespoons fresh lemon juice
1 teaspoon natural liquid smoke flavoring
¾ teaspoon crushed dried red pepper flakes
1 center-cut salmon fillet (about 2 pounds), skin on, in 1 piece

1. Combine the butter, honey, brown sugar, lemon juice, liquid smoke, and red pepper flakes in a saucepan. Cook over medium heat, stirring, until smooth, 5 to 7 minutes. Cool to room temperature.

2. Arrange the salmon in a dish just large enough to hold it. Pour the cooled marinade over it, and let it stand for 30 minutes, turning once.

3. Prepare hot coals for grilling.

4. Oil the grill well, and cook the salmon, skin side up, over medium heat for 5 to 7 minutes. Then turn it over and cook until the fish flakes easily, another 5 to 7 minutes.

5. Transfer the fish to a platter, and serve immediately.

4 portions

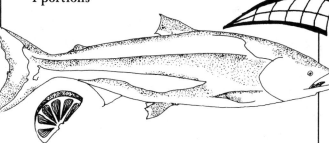

BILL'S PLANKED SALMON

American Indians were the first to plank salmon by nailing and cooking it on stakes placed around a fire. Today we cook it a bit faster, but the result is the same—a grilled fish that has the flavor of both the fire and the wood upon which it was planked. It's a fabulous and effortless way to cook fish for a crowd.

Find a 2-inch-thick fruitwood board, either wild cherry, peach, pear, or apple—or oak or cedar if you prefer. The wood is best when it's new, and it's even better if it contains a little sap for extra flavor. Cut the wood so that it is at least 2 inches wider than the fillet or fillets you're grilling (if you're grilling two fillets, you will want to lay them side by side). Prepare the coals for grilling as you normally would in a charcoal or gas grill. Lightly oil one side of the wood with olive oil and place it, oiled side down, on the hot coals. Char the wood well, and

then remove the board and flip it over.

Brush the charred side again with olive oil and a little lemon juice or vinegar. Position the grill rack 5 to 6 inches from the coals and lay the board, charred side up, on the rack. Lay the fillet or fillets skin side down on the board, and close the hood (or cover with a tent of aluminum foil to capture the smoke). Cook the salmon for 10 minutes per inch of thickness, measured at the thickest part, or until the flesh is opaque. Brush the fish well with oil, lemon juice, and parsley or dill just before it's done.

Use the entire board as a platter to serve the fish. The skin will stick to the board, so loosen the fish gently with a spatula. The flavor is lovely.

Planking works best with Atlantic, king, sockeye, and silver (coho) salmons. We have also used whitefish, bass, and lake trout very successfully.

SHRIMP

¼ cup olive oil
2 cloves garlic, minced
1 tablespoon chopped fresh rosemary leaves
½ teaspoon dried red pepper flakes
12 jumbo shrimp, in the shell

LOBSTER

¼ cup olive oil
1 tablespoon fresh lemon juice
1 tablespoon minced fresh tarragon or dill
1 teaspoon grated lemon zest
Freshly ground black pepper, to taste
4 lobster tails (about 3 pounds total), thawed if frozen

SAFFRON RICE

¼ cup olive oil
1 red onion, coarsely chopped
1 red bell pepper, cored, seeded, and coarsely chopped
1 green bell pepper, cored, seeded, and coarsely chopped
1 yellow bell pepper, cored, seeded, and coarsely chopped
6 cloves garlic, minced
4 cups long-grain white rice
8 cups Berta's Chicken Stock (see Index) or canned broth
1 ½ teaspoons saffron threads
1 cup small green Spanish olives
1 cup imported black olives
½ cup diced pimento

12 cherrystone clams, well scrubbed
1 pound mussels, well scrubbed and bearded (see Note)
1 pound garlic or hot Italian sausage, in 1 piece
1 ½ tablespoons olive oil
Chopped cilantro (fresh coriander), for garnish

A MIDSUMMER NIGHT'S SUPPER

★

Sorrel Soup

Pacific Northwest Salmon
Sweet Corn in the Husk
Eggplant on the Grill
∗∗∗Fumé Blanc∗∗∗

Strawberry Shortcake

GRAND GAUCHO PAELLA

Originally cooked outdoors and eaten directly out of the pan by the Spanish cowboys, paella has long been popular in the regions of France bordering Spain. There it is likely to include a wide variety of ingredients: snails, eels, duck, chicken, rabbit, codfish, crawfish, frogs, pork, artichoke hearts, green beans. It really is the perfect party dish, and we feel that it is time to take it back outdoors—to stand alongside the other great grill dishes. It is a memorable outdoor meal and well worth the effort!

RABBIT

½ cup dry red wine
¼ cup olive oil
2 cloves garlic, minced
Grated zest of ½ orange
½ teaspoon salt
Freshly ground black pepper, to taste
1 small rabbit (about 2 ½ pounds), well rinsed, patted dry, and cut into 8 pieces

---

1. Prepare the rabbit: Combine the wine, oil, garlic, orange zest, salt, and pepper in a mixing bowl. Stir well, and add the rabbit pieces. Cover, refrigerate, and marinate overnight, turning once or twice.

2. Prepare the shrimp: Combine the oil, garlic, rosemary, and red pepper flakes in a mixing bowl. Stir well, and add the shrimp. Cover, and refrigerate several hours.

3. Prepare the lobster: Combine the oil, lemon juice, tarragon, lemon zest, and pepper in a large bowl. Butterfly the lobster tails, cutting through the meat but not through the outer shell. Gently open each tail to expose the meat. Add the lobster tails to the marinade, and refrigerate for several hours; turn them occasionally and spoon marinade into the cavity while they are marinating.

4. Prepare hot coals for grilling.

5. About 1 hour before serving time, prepare the rice: Heat the oil in a large saucepan, and sauté the red onion, bell peppers, and garlic over medium heat for 10 minutes. Then stir in the rice and cook until translucent, 5 minutes. Add the stock and saffron, and bring to a boil. Then lower the heat and simmer, uncovered, until just tender, about 18 minutes. Stir in the olives and pimento, and transfer the rice to a large paella pan or an ovenproof platter. Keep it warm in a low (250°F) oven, or on the edge of the grill if it is large enough.

6. Remove the rabbit from the marinade, and grill over high heat, turning four or five times, for 10 to 20 minutes. Be careful not to overcook the smaller pieces. As it is cooked, add the rabbit to the rice.

7. Remove the shrimp from the marinade, and grill them over high heat, 2 minutes per side. Add them to the rice.

8. Grill the lobster tails over high heat, brushing them with any remaining marinade, 4 minutes per side. Add them to the rice.

9. Arrange the clams and mussels in one layer on the grill, and cook until just opened, 8 to 10 minutes. Add them to the rice.

10. Shape the sausage into a spiral and pierce it with two metal skewers at right angles, to secure the shape and facilitate turning. Brush the sausage with olive oil, and grill over high heat until lightly charred and cooked through, about 7 minutes per side.

11. Add the sausage to the rice, and arrange all the ingredients decoratively. Sprinkle the whole dish with lots of cilantro, and serve.

8 to 10 portions

Note: Do not beard mussels until right before you are ready to cook them or they will die and spoil.

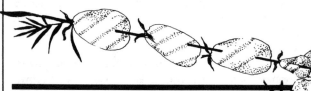

SPEARED PLUM TOMATOES

These grilled tomatoes are a bright addition to a summer barbecue—but please don't eat the bay leaves!

14 bay leaves, blanched
6 ripe but firm plum tomatoes, halved lengthwise
2 tablespoons olive oil
4 teaspoons coarsely ground black pepper
2 teaspoons grated lemon zest
1 teaspoon coarse (kosher) salt

1. Prepare hot coals for grilling.

2. Pierce the center of each bay leaf with the point of a sharp knife.

3. Starting and ending with a bay leaf, thread bay leaves alternately with tomato halves on two long metal skewers. Brush the tomatoes with the oil.

4. Mix the remaining ingredients together in a small bowl and sprinkle half the mixture over the tomatoes (on all sides).

5. Arrange the skewers on the grill over medium heat, and cook turning once, until cooked through but not soggy, about 10 minutes.

6. Transfer the skewers to a platter, and sprinkle the tomatoes with the remaining seasoning mixture.

4 to 6 portions

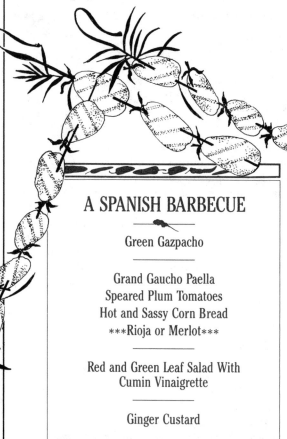

A SPANISH BARBECUE

Green Gazpacho

Grand Gaucho Paella
Speared Plum Tomatoes
Hot and Sassy Corn Bread
Rioja or Merlot

Red and Green Leaf Salad With
Cumin Vinaigrette

Ginger Custard

GRILLING VEGETABLES

A grill covered with vegetables is a wonderful thing to see. The interplay between different shapes, sizes, colors, and smells is magnificent. And you can grill just about any vegetable. Potatoes and unshucked (but desilked) corn may be wrapped in foil and cooked right in the coals. Eggplant, red onion, summer squash, and potatoes may be halved or sliced, brushed with oil, and grilled to sweet perfection. Tomatoes cut in half and heads of garlic are delicious grilled. Or you may cube and grill vegetables on skewers, but make sure that sizes and cooking times are compatible.

We generally cook vegetables over medium to medium-hot direct heat on a covered grill. They must be either marinated or basted well during cooking to protect against drying out.

TIPS FOR GRILLING VEGETABLES

▲ Grill soft or juicy vegetables in a hinged wire basket to facilitate turning.

▲ Foil-grilling is a convenient way to cook vegetables. Simply set vegetables requiring equivalent cooking times (such as cauliflower and broccoli florets or zucchini chunks and mushrooms) in an aluminum foil packet. Moisten with water, chicken stock, or herbed butter, and grill until done; the vegetables will gently steam in their juices.

▲ Shorten the grilling time of leeks, large fennel bulbs, and root vegetables such as potatoes, yams, and turnips by parboiling or precooking them in the microwave for a few minutes before grilling.

MAGNIFICENT MUSHROOMS

These grilled marinated Portobello mushrooms—giant-capped beauties—are so lush and rich that if you close your eyes, you might think you're eating filet mignon. And since they're not available as much as we'd like, do let them take the spotlight. On croutons they can be the entrée. If you can't find Portobello mushrooms, substitute porcini or cèpes with large flat caps.

4 large fresh Portobello mushrooms
   (about 5 ounces each), stems removed
½ cup walnut oil or fruity olive oil
2 cloves garlic, minced
1 teaspoon fresh thyme leaves
½ teaspoon salt
Freshly ground black pepper, to taste

CROUTONS
4 large slices peasant bread or other large country loaf
Olive oil
Minced garlic

Rosemary sprigs

1. Arrange the mushrooms in one layer in a large shallow bowl. Brush them on both sides with the oil. Sprinkle with the garlic, thyme, salt, and pepper. Cover loosely and refrigerate for 24 hours.

2. Prepare hot coals for grilling. Oil the grill.

3. Make the croutons: Brush both sides of the bread slices liberally with olive oil, and sprinkle with garlic. Grill over medium heat until golden and lightly charred, 5 minutes per side. Set aside and keep warm.

4. Dampen the sprigs of fresh rosemary and toss them on the fire. Arrange the mushrooms on the grill, cover, and cook until tender, 5 minutes per side.

5. Cut the mushrooms into thick slices and serve them on the croutons.

4 portions

SWEET CORN IN THE HUSK

The secret ingredient for grilled corn is spicy Albuquerque Butter. Slather the ears of corn with the butter, wrap them back up, and grill. The smoky flavor will come through.

4 ears fresh sweet corn, in their husks
½ cup Albuquerque Butter (recipe follows)

1. Prepare hot coals for grilling.

2. Soak the unhusked corn in a large bowl of cold water for 15 minutes. Then peel the husks halfway down, and remove and discard the silk.

3. Rub the exposed kernels with ¼ cup of the butter. Then replace the husks, and wrap each ear of corn in a double thickness of aluminum foil.

4. Arrange the corn directly on moderately hot coals. Turn them a quarter turn every 10 minutes, and cook for a total of 35 minutes.

5. Carefully remove the foil and husks, and serve the corn with the remaining Albuquerque Butter alongside.

2 to 4 portions

ALBUQUERQUE BUTTER

8 tablespoons (1 stick) unsalted butter, at room temperature
2 tablespoons minced scallions (green onions)
1 teaspoon salt
½ teaspoon ground cumin
½ teaspoon dried oregano leaves, crumbled
Freshly ground black pepper, to taste

Combine all the ingredients in a small bowl, and mix well. This will keep, covered, in the refrigerator for 2 days.

½ cup

GRILLING TIPS

★

▲ Use a hot fire for fish and shellfish and for searing meat and poultry; pack the coals close together and open the vents for greater air circulation.

▲ Use a cooler fire to finish meat and poultry after searing; allow a little space between coals and partially close the vents.

▲ For fatty foods or those requiring long cooking times, use a drip pan under the food.

▲ Buy top-quality ingredients for the best results.

▲ Remove food from the grill just before it's cooked; it will continue to cook off the fire.

▲ Bring food to room temperature before grilling.

▲ Brush the grill rack lightly with oil before using; this will prevent foods from sticking.

▲ Rub the food with olive, peanut, or corn oil, depending on the flavor desired.

MARINADES AND RUBS

—●—

Marinades have a multitude of uses. They tenderize the tough, moisten the dry, and enliven the bland. Although some foods taste fine grilled just as they are, almost everything will benefit from the additional flavor of a marinade. And for lean fish, beef, and game, a marinade is crucial.

Marinades are simply a combination of three ingredients: an acid (such as vinegar, tomatoes, buttermilk, yogurt, soy sauce, wine, or citrus juice), oil, and flavorings.

Acid is the tenderizing agent. The best candidates for high-acid marinades are tough meats such as flank steaks, round steaks, and shanks. Oil is a moisturizer, and the most popular oil used in marinades is olive oil. But experiment with sesame, nut, and herb-flavored oils.

Sugars are a common flavoring. Honey, molasses, and brown or granulated sugar take the sharp edge off a high-acid marinade, and meats basted with sweetened liquids develop a rich, brown crust.

The length of time a particular food is marinated depends on the strength of the marinade and the flavor and texture of the food. Fish should marinate no more than 30 minutes, and then only in a delicately flavored marinade that won't overpower it. Lean, strong-tasting venison can marinate in a hearty marinade overnight.

Keep foods well chilled while marinating (but remember to return to room temperature before grilling).

You may also add flavor to food by rubbing it before grilling with a dry rub such as fresh garlic, cracked peppercorns, and fresh herbs.

RUBY VEGETABLES

Miniature tender young vegetables look like precious gems and taste even better.

1 ½ cups olive oil
1 cup dry white wine
4 cloves garlic, crushed
1 cup coarsely chopped fresh Italian (flat-leaf) parsley
½ cup coarsely chopped fresh basil leaves
1 teaspoon salt
1 teaspoon freshly ground black pepper
12 tiny beets
12 tiny artichokes, stems trimmed
12 tiny eggplants
3 small heads radicchio, rinsed and patted dry

1. Combine the oil, wine, garlic, ½ cup of the parsley, basil, salt, and pepper in a mixing bowl. Cover, and let stand for at least 1 hour.

2. Clean the beets well, leaving on 1 inch of stem and trimming the roots. Place them in a saucepan, cover with water, and bring to a boil. Reduce the heat, cover, and simmer until just tender, 15 minutes. Drain the beets, and let them cool in a bowl of cold water. Then drain again, and slip off the skins.

3. Spread the beets, artichokes, and eggplants in a shallow roasting pan. Cut the heads of radicchio into quarters, and place them in a bowl. Pour 1 ½ cups of the marinade over the beets, artichokes, and eggplants, and 1 cup over the radicchio. Cover both dishes, and let them stand, turning the vegetables occasionally, for 4 hours.

4. Preheat the oven to 400°F, and prepare hot coals for grilling.

5. Uncover the roasting pan, place it in the oven, and bake, basting frequently with the marinade, until the vegetables are tender, 35 minutes. Allow them to cool slightly.

6. Thread the beets, artichokes, eggplants, and radicchio separately onto thin 16- to 18-inch-long skewers. Grill them over hot coals, turning and basting frequently with the marinade until lightly browned, 12 minutes.

7. Remove the vegetables from the skewers, and arrange them on a large serving platter. Garnish with the remaining ½ cup parsley, and serve.

8 portions

RED POTATOES AND RED ONIONS

New Basic pantry staples are stars on the grill! The smoky flavor makes a memorable potato salad and thickly sliced onions beg for burgers or a steak.

20 small red new potatoes, well scrubbed
4 tablespoons olive oil
6 red onions, cut into ½-inch slices
1 tablespoon red wine vinegar
1 tablespoon white wine
Coarse (kosher) salt, to taste
Coarsely ground black pepper, to taste
5 tablespoons chopped fresh Italian (flat-leaf) parsley

1. Preheat the oven to 350°F.
2. Prick the potatoes all over with the tines of a fork, and place them in a shallow roasting pan. Bake until tender, 45 to 50 minutes.
3. Meanwhile, prepare hot coals for grilling.
4. Allow the hot potatoes to cool slightly. Then coat them with 1 tablespoon of the olive oil, and thread them on thin metal skewers. Place the skewers over very hot coals and cook, turning once, until browned and tender. Remove them from the grill, and set aside.
5. Brush one side of the onion rings with 1 tablespoon of the olive oil, and place them, oiled side down, on the grill over very hot coals. Cook until brown and just tender; do not overcook. Remove the onions from the grill, using a spatula, and set them aside.
6. Remove the potatoes from the skewers, cut them in half, and place in a bowl.
7. Combine the remaining 2 tablespoons olive oil and the vinegar, wine, salt, pepper, and 4 tablespoons of the parsley in a small bowl. Pour over the potatoes, and toss carefully.
8. Arrange the potatoes in the center of a platter. Surround them with the grilled onion slices. Sprinkle the onions with additional salt and pepper and the remaining 1 tablespoon parsley. Serve at room temperature.

4 portions

GRILLED DINNER IN A HURRY

We've discovered two nontraditional ways to improve grilling results when a carefully timed meal is necessary. The first is to give the food a head start in the oven or on the stove, then finish it on the grill. Cook the dish anywhere from one third to two thirds done. Then, just before serving time, pop it on the grill for a crust, a char, and a smoky flavor. (Thirty minutes on the grill is enough time to give anything a smoky grilled flavor.) This technique has often been a lifesaver when we're cooking chicken, spareribs, and whole roasts.

The other method we discovered quite by accident as we were testing grilling recipes for this book: Fully cooked, grilled food reheats fabulously in the microwave! This makes it a terrific tool for plan-ahead grilling. When the fire is perfect and you have the time, you can grill several dinners worth of food, then refrigerate or freeze, and microwave when the hordes are hungry. Ironically, the oldest and newest cooking methods make perfect partners!

¼ cup fruity olive oil
2 tablespoons fresh lemon juice
¼ cup chopped scallions (green onions)
¼ cup chopped fresh basil leaves
2 cloves garlic, minced
1 teaspoon salt
1 teaspoon fennel seeds, crushed
Freshly ground black pepper, to taste

Whisk the oil and lemon juice together in a small bowl. Stir in the remaining ingredients, whisking until smooth. This will keep, covered and in the refrigerator, for 24 hours.

½ cup

EGGPLANT AND SQUASH ON THE GRILL

An assortment of summer vegetables can be grilled in advance, then arranged and garnished on large colorful platters. With crusty bread and a green salad, they make a light summer meal in themselves. With grilled fish or chicken, they are an appetizing accompaniment. Two favorites are eggplant and squash.

2 pounds tiny eggplants (6 to 8), halved lengthwise
2 pounds yellow summer squash (about 5 medium), trimmed
    and cut into thirds lengthwise
6 tablespoons Fennel Marinade (see Index)

1. Prepare hot coals for grilling.
2. Place the eggplants in a large bowl and the squash in another. Divide the marinade between the two bowls, tossing the vegetables to coat them well.
3. Arrange the eggplant halves and squash slices on the grill and cook (in batches if necessary) over medium heat, turning once, until fork-tender, 12 minutes for the squash, 15 to 20 for the eggplant. (If your grill can accommodate all the vegetables at once, begin the eggplant 3 to 4 minutes before adding the squash.)

6 to 8 portions

FENNEL MARINADE

Great for marinating vegetables for the grill, this is also good for swordfish steaks and poultry.

YOU'RE PLAYING WITH FIRE

TIPS ON GRILL SAFETY

▲ Never use a portable grill indoors.
▲ Never—ever—add lighter fluid directly to the fire or even to really hot coals.
▲ Line the drip pan with a double layer of aluminum foil to protect the bottom.
▲ Make sure you have adequate light for grilling.
▲ Make sure to turn off the gas grill or close the vents of a charcoal grill after use.
▲ Remove excess fat from food before cooking to guard against grease fires.
▲ If the fire flares up, move the food away from the area and let the grease burn off. Never use water to douse flare-ups; over time this practice will damage the grill.
▲ If using an extension cord, make sure that it is a heavy-duty type suitable for outdoor use, and keep it safely out of the way of guests who may trip over it.
▲ Keep the grill clean.

THE MEAT MARKET

MEAT KNOW-HOW

peppercorns growing

thyme

Black Peppercorn Crust

As important as knowing how to sauté, braise, roast, or stew meat is knowing which cut to buy for which dish. In years past we could rely on a neighborhood butcher to tell us not only what to buy but also exactly how to cook it. These days most of us buy our meat in supermarkets where the butchers are often behind the scenes. Certainly some savvy supermarkets are bringing back more personalized butcher services, but more often than not, we are on our own.

cooking to tenderize them and to extract the flavor. Muscles the animal uses infrequently (either because of where they are located on the animal or because the animal is young) will be tender. Cooking only toughens these tender cuts, so the less cooking the better. Use fast dry heat and cook rare to medium, never well-done (except for pork, which must be cooked through).

We really don't feel there are superior or inferior cuts of meat. A tender cut of meat will make an insipid stew because it lacks flavor; a roasted less tender cut will deliver a night's worth of chewing. But every cut can be a star if it's cooked right.

Fortunately, knowing the tender cuts from the less tender is easy because all these four-leggeds use their muscles in about the same way. The rib and loin sections are the least exercised and the most tender. This is where we get our succulent roasts, steaks, and chops. The shoulder, rump, and legs get the most exercise and deliver the most flavorful stews and braises. Veal (young beef) and lamb are slaughtered younger; thus more of their meat is tender. See the individual sections on meat for a diagram and discussion of specific cuts.

There is hope. Everything you need to know about a cut of meat is on the label. The catch is you need to know a few things about meat in order to make use of this information. Meat labels are now standardized and give the weight of the package, the price per pound, the cost, and the name of the cut. The name of the cut will always include the part of the animal the cut comes from.

Just three things determine how to cook a particular cut of meat: the quality of the cut (most supermarket meat is choice); the age of the animal (meat from a one-year-old lamb is tougher than that from a five-month-old), and the part of the animal from which the cut comes. All meat is muscle. The muscles the animal uses frequently will be tough but also flavorful; these cuts need long slow

STORING MEAT

Large cuts of meat generally will keep in the refrigerator four to five days. Remove any wrapping and rewrap the meat loosely so that it can breathe. Smaller pieces of meat shouldn't be refrigerated longer than two days before cooking; loosely rewrap these, too. The freezer is the answer for keeping meat longer, but to keep the meat from drying out it must be wrapped very well in heavy foil or freezer wrap.

COOKING IT RIGHT

Roasting is a dry-heat method of cooking reserved for the tenderest cuts. Place a large (at least two pounds) cut of meat with or without bones on a rack with the fat side up. The melting fat will baste the meat as it cooks, but the roast must be on a rack so that it doesn't stew in its own fat. If the roast has no fat (and some don't, such as veal or a well-rimmed leg of lamb), we like to cover it with a thin layer of fat or coat it lightly with oil or mustard. Don't cover the roast or add liquid to the pan because both will steam the meat. Bone-in roasts take less time to cook because the bone conducts heat.

The best cuts for roasting are beef rib, loin, sirloin, and tenderloin roasts; veal rib, loin, and sirloin roasts; lamb rib and loin roasts as well as leg; and pork—everything but the head, trotters, and tail can be roasted, but the loin, tenderloin, and fresh or cured ham are the best eating.

Two schools of roasting remain firm and entrenched. Some like to start a

roast at a high temperature to sear the outside and seal in the juices; others roast at a constant moderate (300° to 350°) temperature. According to some who have attempted to measure the difference in juiciness, there is simply no difference. You pick. Save the pan juices for gravy. All roasts should stand at least 15 minutes before carving to allow the juices to settle.

MEAT GRADES

BEEF	VEAL	LAMB	PORK
Prime	Prime	Prime	U.S. No. 1
Choice	Choice	Choice	U.S. No. 2
Good	Good	Good	U.S. No. 3
Standard	Standard	Utility	U.S. No. 4
Commercial	Utility	Cull	Utility

PAN GRAVY FOR ROASTS

★

Tilt the pan and collect all the fat and juices in one corner. Spoon off all but two to three tablespoons of fat and leave all the juices (they'll be darker and at the bottom of the pool). Place the pan over medium heat and whisk in flour, a tablespoon at a time, until a thin paste forms. Keep whisking until the paste is lightly browned, about three minutes, then gradually whisk in hot broth or stock. Cook, stirring or whisking constantly, until thickened and bubbly. If the gravy is too thick, whisk in a little more broth. Season with salt and pepper to taste, then pour the gravy into a sauceboat and serve hot.

Broiling is another dry-heat method for tender cuts. Steaks and chops can be broiled, but never whole roasts. For thin steaks or chops, adjust the broiler rack so that they are three inches from the heat; thicker cuts are more successful—grill them four inches from the heat. The best cuts are beef steaks and lamb chops cut from the rib and loin. Veal is very delicate and will dry out under intense heat. Pork must be cooked thoroughly and will be dry and tough on the outside before the center is cooked through.

Some less tender beef steaks can be broiled if they are first marinated (which starts breaking down tough muscle fibers), cooked just to rare or medium-rare, and then thinly sliced across the grain. Try flank (London broil) and skirt steaks.

Pan-broiling also uses fast dry heat, but the heat comes from the pan and not from a flame. Heat a dry heavy skillet over medium to medium-high heat until very hot. Pat the meat dry, add it to the skillet, and brown on both sides, checking the cen-

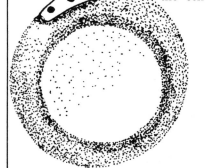

ter for doneness and adjusting the heat to maintain a lively sizzle. Pour off the drippings as they collect and turn the meat frequently. The best cuts are the same as for broiling.

DEGLAZING SAUCE FOR PAN-BROILING AND SAUTEING

▼

Remove the meat to a platter and cover it with foil to keep it warm. Add ¼ to ½ cup of stock, wine, or vegetable cooking liquid to the pan and heat over medium-high heat, scraping loose the browned bits on the bottom of the pan. Boil, stirring frequently, until the sauce is reduced to a thin syrup. If it reduces too much or if you want another spoonful or two, add more liquid. We like to add one to three teaspoons of very finely chopped shallots during the last 30 seconds of cooking.

Sautéing is just like pan-broiling except that a little fat is added to the pan first. Heat a tablespoon or two of butter or oil, or a combination of the two, in a heavy skillet over medium-high to high heat. (Oil will allow the butter to come to a higher temperature without burning.) Pat the meat dry, add it to the skillet, and cook without moving the pieces until the underside is brown. Turn and sauté the

second side. Don't crowd the pan or the pieces will steam and never develop their golden crisp crust. The best cuts are steaks and chops cut from the rib and loin sections of beef, veal, lamb, and pork.

Stir-frying is very much like sautéing, but the meat is cut into very thin strips and is kept almost constantly in motion in the pan to keep it from overcooking. A large wok or heavy skillet works best and the oil should be very hot. We like to stir-fry those not-so-tender steaks like flank because they can be thinly sliced across the grain and provide great flavor without great expense.

Braising is a moist-heat method of cooking for tough (or less tender) cuts of meat. A little liquid is added to the pan, the pan is tightly covered, and the meat is cooked in a slow oven or over low heat on top of the stove. Pot roast is a braised whole beef roast, but smaller cuts such as beef short ribs can be braised, too.

The best cuts are many: beef roasts cut from the shoulder (chuck), brisket, round, and rump, as well as short ribs; veal shanks, shoulder, breast, and rump roasts; lamb shanks, breast, and shoulder roasts; pork chops, steaks, and roasts from the shoulder (Boston butt) and arm.

It's best to brown the meat first to add flavor to the broth and give it an appetizing color. Sear a roast in a heavy skillet or dutch oven on top of the stove or in a roasting pan in a hot oven. Smaller cuts can be browned under the broiler. Once the meat is browned, put it in a dutch oven or a deep roasting pan with a tight-fitting lid. Add flavorful liquid such as wine or broth (or a combination of the two)—a little or a lot, but no more than half the level of the meat. Add aromatic vegetables (celery, carrots, onions) and herbs, too. Cover the pan tightly and cook the meat in a 325°F oven or over low heat on top of the stove, turning once or twice. The meat is done when it's tender to the fork. If you want to serve vegetables, add them in large pieces 45 to 60 minutes before the meat is done.

Braising yields a flavorful sauce, but it's usually too fatty to be served as is. We like to take the meat and vegetables out, strain the liquid, then let it sit for a minute so we can skim off the fat that rises to the top. If we find the sauce lacks flavor, we reduce it quickly over high heat to concentrate the flavors. If we want a thicker sauce, we add cornstarch, flour, beurre manié (flour and butter paste), or tomato paste and cook it quickly to thicken.

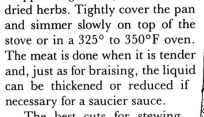

GETTING THE FAT OUT

- Limit portions to three ounces cooked. Meat is a nutritionally dense food, which means a little goes a long way and a lot goes too far.

- Trim the fat on the outside. Good-quality meat is marbled with enough interior fat to keep it moist and tasty.

- Pan-broil rather than sauté when possible to eliminate the extra cooking fat.

- Degrease sauces by letting them sit for a minute and spooning off the fat on the top. Make gravies or deglazing sauces with just a spoonful of fat (but all of the juices); throw away the rest.

- Use stocks, wine, vegetables, herbs, and seasonings for flavor rather than butter and cream.

Stewing is simmering small cubes of meat, usually one to two inches square, in enough flavorful liquid to cover. The meat can be browned or not and placed in a heavy pan with a tight-fitting lid. Add liquid to cover, aromatic chopped vegetables, and fresh or dried herbs. Tightly cover the pan and simmer slowly on top of the stove or in a 325° to 350°F oven. The meat is done when it is tender and, just as for braising, the liquid can be thickened or reduced if necessary for a saucier sauce.

The best cuts for stewing are beef shoulder (chuck), neck, shank, plate, and heel of round; veal shoulder and rump; lamb shoulder; and pork shoulder, arm (fresh picnic), hocks, and trotters.

Stews are fun and easy. We make them with whatever is on hand or with what appeals to us at the moment. If you're going to make a stew, you may as well make a lot because this is one leftover that's even better the next day.

Boiling is a misnomer. Meat that is truly boiled is incredibly tough no matter how long it's cooked, but, simmered gently in flavorful liquid with vegetables, "boiled" meat is a revelation. Choose a large roast and start it in cold stock. Add aromatic vegetables such as carrots, turnips, leeks, onions, and parsnips. Simmer gently uncovered or partially covered until tender and cooked through. The best cuts for simmering are beef chuck, round, and rump roast, and brisket—fresh and corned. Veal, lamb, and pork don't have enough flavor to make this an interesting dish.

HERE'S THE BEEF

Beef seems so purely American, it's hard to believe that it's actually yet another import. It was the Spaniards who brought the first cattle to this country in the sixteenth century, and while the settlers regarded them as the biblical beasts of burden, the Indians found them quite tasty. The Indians, in fact, were the first cattle herders, and they were the ones who moved the cattle across the Mississippi to the grasslands of the plains.

Railroads and refrigerated cars eventually made getting beef to the eastern markets easier. Beef's popularity continued to increase until it reached a peak in 1970. In recent years Americans, out of concern for a healthy diet, have cut back on their beef consumption. But the love is still there, and when you crave it, there's nothing to take its place!

ROAST FILLET OF BEEF WITH BLACK PEPPERCORNS

Our oven-roasted version of the French classic *steak au poivre*. The crunchy peppercorns accent the velvety texture of this premier beef. An important roast for important company.

1 beef fillet (3¼ pounds), rolled, fatted (see Note), and tied
2 cloves garlic, slivered
2 tablespoons coarsely crushed black peppercorns (see Note)
½ teaspoon dried thyme leaves
½ teaspoon coarse (kosher) salt

1. Preheat the oven to 425°F.
2. Using the tip of a sharp knife, cut slits all over the fillet and insert the garlic slivers into them.
3. Pat the pepper all over the beef, so that it is well coated. Sprinkle it with the thyme and coarse salt.
4. Place the fillet in a shallow roasting pan, and cook for 15 minutes. Reduce the heat to 350°F, and roast an additional 20 minutes for rare meat. (To test for doneness, insert an instant-reading meat thermometer in the thickest part of the roast. It should read 125° to 130°F for rare, 135° to 140°F for medium.)
5. Let the fillet rest 10 minutes before carving.
6 to 8 portions

Notes: Ask your butcher to fat the meat for you. A thin layer of fat imparts moisture to a lean cut of meat while it roasts. Remove the fat before slicing and serving.

The secret to this crust is the peppercorns. Place them on a board and crush them with the side of a wide chef's knife, pressing down hard with the palm of your hand. They will be just the right size.

A WINTER WONDERLAND DINNER

Oysters Rockefeller
Champagne

Roast Fillet of Beef With Black Peppercorns
Oil-Roasted Potatoes, Haricots Verts, and Fennel
Barolo or Cabernet Sauvignon

Mâche and Walnut Salad With Molly's Vinaigrette

Amaretto Soufflé With Chocolate Sauce

A PERFECTLY BROILED FILLET

An extremely quick and simple preparation, this fillet is just right served with our delicate Béarnaise Sauce. Minty Roasted Potatoes and Beet and Coriander Purée make the perfect meal.

4 filets mignons (8 ounces each), 2 inches thick
1½ teaspoons coarsely ground black pepper

1. Preheat the broiler.
2. Sprinkle the fillets well on both sides with the pepper.
3. Place the fillets 3 inches from the heat, and broil for 4 minutes. Turn, and cook another 3 minutes for rare meat. (For medium, cook an additional minute on each side.)
4 portions

GUIDE TO THE BEST CUTS

▼ **Shoulder or chuck:** Pot roasts and steaks can be bought bone-in or boneless and are best braised. We love chuck cut up for stews and chili, and ground chuck meat makes some of the best burgers.

Rib: Here lie the tender steaks and roasts, called rib, rib-eye, and in some parts Delmonico. The roasts roasted and the steaks broiled or grilled make luscious eating. No reason to avoid the bones in these steaks and roasts for they add flavor and make excellent gnawing, too.

★ ▶ **Loin and sirloin:** Closest to the rib is the short loin and closest to the rump is the sirloin.

Steaks from the short loin are called club, T-bone, and porterhouse; they're a little more tender (also more expensive) than sirloin steaks. Our favorite little parcel of meat from this section is the tenderloin, which is a separate boneless strip of tender meat that lies along the bone. The whole tenderloin is a luxury roast, but sliced into steaks, the tenderloin yields the celebrated chateaubriand, fillet steaks, tournedos, and filets mignons. Large roasts from the loin or tenderloin should be roasted rare to medium-rare; grill or broil the steaks or cut them into cubes for a very elegant stroganoff or fondue. Shell roast and shell strip steaks are the boneless meat of the sirloin. Ground sirloin and loin are used for steak tartare but make memorable burgers, too.

)● **Rump and round:** We like cuts from these parts braised, stewed, and boiled. They have terrific flavor but need long slow cooking to bring it out and make the meat tender. Rump is cut for both steaks and roasts; the round is cut just for roasts or ground for hamburger meat. The round itself has a descending order of tenderness: at the top, closest to the rump is top round, which is the tenderest; next comes eye of round and bottom round, which is the least tender. Remember, though, less tender doesn't mean less flavorful, which is why we like these roasts best for pot-au-feu and bollito misto.

◆◆ **Flank:** This cut lies below the loin and yields the flavorful flank steak, also called London broil. We like to marinate this steak and grill it or cook it very slowly with broth and vegetables for a heartwarming dinner. It's always a good buy.

▟▟ ▟ **Plate and skirt:** This cut is similar to flank, but it includes the bottom of the ribs (short ribs) and the strip of meat below it. We like short ribs braised and find good meat for stewing in the plate. The skirt steak, a boneless strip of meat on the inside of the plate, is much sought after for fajitas. We like it grilled and thinly sliced or slowly braised much like flank steak.

■ **Brisket:** Lying between the plate and the foreleg, brisket is a flavorful cut that needs long, slow cooking. It makes a superb pot roast and is often cured as corned beef. Sliced or shredded, brisket is ideal smoked and served in barbecue. Brisket can be bought in two cuts. The leaner first cut should not be allowed to overcook or it may dry out. The fattier second cut should be prepared a day in advance so that its juices may be easily skimmed before eating.

▟ **Shank and heel of round:** These cuts are at the bottom of the animal just above the legs. They are unsurpassed for making rich beef stock.

CARPETBAGGERS

A classic recipe from the nineteenth century, when oysters proliferated on both shores of the U.S. The taste combination is dramatic.

1 tablespoon unsalted butter
8 oysters, shelled
4 filets mignons (8 ounces each), 2 inches thick
1 teaspoon freshly ground black pepper
Chopped fresh Italian (flat-leaf) parsley, for garnish

1. Preheat the broiler.
2. Melt the butter in a small skillet. Add the oysters, and sauté over medium-low heat until the edges just begin to curl, about 1 minute. Set aside and allow to cool completely.
3. Make a slit in the side of each steak, and stuff 2 oysters into each pocket. Sprinkle the fillets with the pepper.
4. Place the meat on a broiling pan 3 inches from the heat. Broil for 4 minutes. Then turn and broil another 3 minutes for rare meat. (For medium, cook an additional minute on each side.) Garnish with parsley and serve immediately.

4 portions

GOOD TIMES ROAST BEEF

Instead of the usual standing rib roast, try a shell of beef for those very special occasions. We like ours cooked rare, so the flavor of the meat can be enjoyed to the fullest.

1 boneless beef shell roast (6½ pounds)
3 cloves garlic, slivered
½ teaspoon dried thyme leaves
Freshly ground black pepper, to taste
1 cup dry red wine
Yorkshire Pudding (optional; recipe follows)

1. Preheat the oven to 500°F.

2. With the point of a sharp knife, cut slits in the fat of the roast; insert the garlic slivers in the slits.

3. Place the meat on a rack in a roasting pan, and roast for 20 minutes. Then remove it from the oven, and lower the temperature to 375°F.

4. Sprinkle the meat with the thyme and pepper, and return it to the oven. Bake for an additional 30 minutes.

5. Remove the pan from the oven, and allow the roast to sit for 15 minutes before carving. (For rare meat a meat thermometer should read 130°F.) Remove ¼ cup of the pan drippings if you plan to make Yorkshire pudding.

6. Transfer the roast to a carving board. Add the wine to the roasting pan, and simmer over low heat, scraping up the pan drippings, until the sauce is slightly reduced, about 5 minutes. Carve, and serve with the sauce on the side.

8 to 10 portions

YORKSHIRE PUDDING

Just the right festive touch.

¼ cup roast beef pan drippings
1 cup unbleached all-purpose flour
¼ teaspoon salt
2 eggs
1 cup milk
1 tablespoon snipped fresh chives
1 teaspoon fresh thyme leaves or ¼ teaspoon dried

1. Preheat the oven to 450°F.

2. Spoon 1 teaspoon of the drippings into each cup of a 12-cup muffin tin. Place the tin in the oven to keep the drippings hot while the batter is being prepared.

3. Combine the flour and salt in a mixing bowl. Beat the eggs and milk together in another bowl. Make a well in the center of the flour, and pour in the egg mixture. Combine the ingredients with a few swift strokes.

4. Spoon the batter into the muffin cups (they should be filled about halfway). Sprinkle the tops with the chives and thyme. Bake until puffed and golden, 15 to 20 minutes. Serve immediately.

12 portions

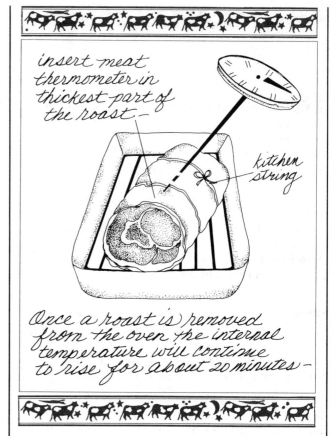

insert meat thermometer in thickest part of the roast —

kitchen string

Once a roast is removed from the oven the internal temperature will continue to rise for about 20 minutes —

SLICED SIRLOIN WITH SHALLOT WINE SAUCE

For a more delicate presentation, we pan fry our steak and slice it very thin. Here it's topped with a shallot wine sauce. If you prefer, just pan fry or broil the steak, and make the Shallot Chive Butter that follows, instead of the wine sauce.

3 tablespoons unsalted butter
2 tablespoons olive oil
1 sirloin steak (about 2 pounds), 2 inches thick
½ cup chopped peeled shallots
4 tablespoons snipped fresh chives
1 tablespoon red wine vinegar
¾ cup dry red wine
Salt and freshly ground black pepper, to taste

1. Place 2 tablespoons of the butter and the oil in a heavy skillet over medium heat. When the butter is sizzling, add the steak and cook for 8 minutes on each side for rare meat. Transfer the steak to a platter and keep warm.

2. Pour off all but 2 tablespoons of the fat in the skillet. Raise the meat to medium-high, and add the shallots and 3½ tablespoons of the chives. Stir, and cook for 15 seconds.

3. Add the vinegar and wine, and simmer for 1 minute. Stir in the remaining 1 tablespoon butter, season with salt and pepper, and remove from the heat.

4. Slice the steak crosswise into ½-inch-thick slices, and serve topped with the shallot wine sauce. Sprinkle with the remaining ½ tablespoon chives.

4 to 6 portions

Sirloin Steak

SHALLOT CHIVE BUTTER

This butter can be used for chicken, fish, and vegetables too.

8 tablespoons (1 stick) unsalted butter, at room temperature
4 teaspoons chopped shallots
4 teaspoons snipped fresh chives
Freshly ground black pepper, to taste

1. Combine all the ingredients in a bowl, and mix well. Place the mixture on a piece of plastic wrap, and form it into a log shape about 1 inch in diameter. Wrap well, and place in the refrigerator or freezer.

2. To serve, cut into ¼- to ½-inch rounds.
About ½ cup

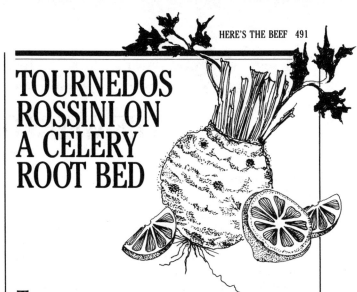

TOURNEDOS ROSSINI ON A CELERY ROOT BED

This is a most elegant, but easy, way to celebrate a special occasion: melt-in-your-mouth fillet with foie gras and truffle shavings on a slice of celeriac. Don't wait until you win the lottery!

2 tablespoons fresh lemon juice
2 small bulbs celeriac (celery root)
1 tablespoon unsalted butter
2 beef tournedos (5 to 6 ounces each)
Salt and freshly ground black pepper, to taste
2 slices foie gras, about 2 inches square and ¼ inch thick
1 cup Madeira Sauce (recipe follows)

1. Stir the lemon juice into 4 cups of water. Peel the celeriac, and cut it into ¼-inch-thick slices. As you work, drop the slices into the acidulated water to keep them from browning.

2. Bring a large saucepan of water to a boil. Drain the celeriac, and add it to the water; simmer until tender, 6 to 8 minutes. Drain.

3. Melt the butter in a medium-size skillet, and sauté the celeriac over medium heat until golden, about 1 minute per side. Arrange the slices, overlapping, in the center of two dinner plates, and keep warm.

4. Season the tournedos lightly with salt and pepper. Sauté them in the same skillet over medium heat, about 4 minutes per side for medium-rare. Arrange them on the sliced celeriac, and keep warm.

5. Sauté the foie gras in the same skillet over medium heat, about 1 minute per side. Place a slice on each tournedos.

6. Whisk the Madeira Sauce into the skillet, scraping up any browned bits. Bring it to a boil, and spoon over the fillets. Serve immediately.

2 portions

THE WINES OF BURGUNDY

The wines of Burgundy are named for the bottler and villages where they are grown. The most glorious of their wines are made from grapes grown along the rolling hills of the Côte d'Or, which is divided into the Côte de Nuits and the Côte de Beaune. One of the great reds is the delicate, velvety Gevrey-Chambertin from the Côte de Nuits. Another familiar red is the strong, full-bodied Nuits-Saint-Georges. Farther south we find Pommard, with its firm character and deep color, and the excellent Volnay. Among the best vineyards in Beaune are Les Grèves and Clos des Mouches.

Even farther south we encounter the magnificent whites—Meursault, Chassagne-Montrachet, and Puligny-Montrachet, regarded by some as the great dry white wines of the world. From the Mâconnais comes the lighter and fruitier Pouilly-Fuissé, a name very familiar to most Americans.

These wines are best drunk when young and are paler gold in color than the Montrachets. Unfortunately, they have become quite expensive.

The Beaujolais of southern Burgundy is one of the great all-purpose wines with wide general appeal. It is young, fruity, and easy to drink. Fleurie is extremely fruity and one of the most delightful, as is Moulin-à-Vent.

We love Beaujolais-Villages, too, and think it an excellent all-purpose wine to keep in your home. There are many selections and they are not terribly expensive. If you find a favorite, buy a case.

Chablis is another elegant white Americans know well. Among the seven vineyards producing the great Chablis whites are Les Clos, Blanchots, and Les Preuses. When choosing, be sure to look for a dry, full-bodied wine. Don't accept the sweeter wines that may be offered by the glass in many restaurants. Drink Chablis well chilled.

MADEIRA SAUCE

A rich and elegant sauce, filled with sliced truffles.

2 tablespoons unsalted butter
2 tablespoons unbleached all-purpose flour
2 cups homemade beef stock (see Index) or canned broth
6 tablespoons Madeira
1 tablespoon tomato paste
1 tablespoon caramel coloring (optional; see Note)
3 small white or black truffles, sliced
1 tablespoon truffle juice, if available
Salt and freshly ground black pepper, to taste

1. Melt the butter in a medium-size saucepan. Whisk in the flour and cook, stirring, over low heat for 3 minutes.
2. Add the beef stock, 4 tablespoons of the Madeira, and the tomato paste. Whisk until smooth, and bring to a boil. Reduce the heat and simmer until reduced to 1 cup, 30 minutes.
3. Whisk in the caramel coloring, truffles, juice, and remaining 2 tablespoons Madeira. Simmer 2 minutes. Season with salt and pepper.

1 cup

Note: Sauces are sometimes more appetizing when darker. To make a natural coloring, stir 2 tablespoons sugar and 1 tablespoon water in a small saucepan. Bring to a boil, and cook until the sugar turns a deep caramel color. Continue cooking until nearly black. (The mixture will be very hot.) Then remove it from the heat, and carefully add 2 tablespoons water. (The mixture will spurt.) Allow it to cool until the mixture is smooth. At this point the caramel has lost its sweetness. Stir the entire amount into the Madeira Sauce.

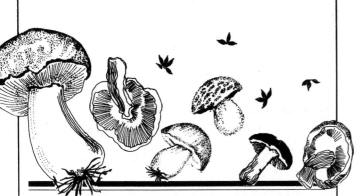

BEEF WELLINGTON FOR TWO

Once upon a time, it seemed as if every dinner party was built around Beef Wellington. Twenty years have passed, and beef is on the menu far less often—which is all the more reason to make it extra-special when it is. And this Wellington recipe is just that! Use the recipe for Potted Mushrooms. It goes well with the beef.

½ teaspoon coarsely ground black pepper
½ teaspoon salt
¼ teaspoon dried thyme leaves, crumbled
2 tournedos of beef (6 ounces each)
1 teaspoon Dijon mustard
1 tablespoon unsalted butter
¼ cup Potted Mushrooms (see Index)
1 sheet frozen puff pastry, 10 x 8 inches, ⅛ inch thick, thawed
1 egg
1 teaspoon milk

1. Preheat the oven to 425°F.

2. Toss the pepper, salt, and thyme in a small bowl. Rub the tournedos on all sides with the mustard, then sprinkle the spice mixture over them.

3. Melt the butter in a small skillet, and sear the tournedos on all sides, about 5 minutes. Cool to room temperature.

4. Arrange the tournedos on a small baking sheet, and cover them with the potted mushrooms.

5. Cut out two 4- to 5-inch circles of pastry. Drape each over one of the tournedos, and pinch the edges in four or five places to enclose the tournedos. Blend the egg and milk, and brush this glaze over the

pastry. Decorate the tops with cutouts made from pastry trimmings, if desired.

6. Bake 15 minutes for medium-rare. Serve immediately.

2 portions

NEW BASIC STEAK AU POIVRE

Shell strip steak, that juicy and tasty cut, seared quickly with green and black peppers, as the French have taught us. A dash of Cognac softens the aggressiveness of the pepper. For a treat, serve Red Pepper and Ginger Marmalade alongside.

1 boneless shell strip steak (about 1 pound)
4 teaspoons green peppercorns in brine, drained
2 teaspoons cracked black peppercorns (see Note with the Roast Fillet of Beef With Black Peppercorns, page 487)
1 tablespoon unsalted butter
2 tablespoons Cognac
¼ cup homemade beef or veal stock (see Index)
¼ cup heavy or whipping cream
Salt and freshly ground black pepper, to taste

1. Trim the steak, and cut it into two thick medallions. Using the side of a heavy cleaver, pound the medallions to flatten them slightly.

2. Press ½ teaspoon of the green peppercorns into each side of the steaks.

3. Sprinkle the cracked black pepper on a plate, and coat the steaks with the pepper.

4. Melt the butter in a medium-size heavy skillet, and sauté the steaks until browned on the outside but red and juicy on the inside, 2 to 3 minutes per side.

5. Pour off the fat from the skillet, and add the Cognac. Remove the skillet from the heat, and carefully light the Cognac. Flambé the steaks until the flames are extinguished. Transfer the steaks to two plates, and keep warm.

6. Add the stock, cream, and remaining 2 teaspoons green peppercorns to the skillet. Cook over high heat until thick, 2 to 3 minutes. Season the sauce with salt and pepper, pour it over the steaks, and serve.

2 portions

FLAMBEING

Flaming a dish with brandy or liqueur must be done very carefully. Use long kitchen matches (they work best), be sure not to lean over the dish while you're igniting it, and always remove it from the heat source first.

In order to flame, the brandy must be warmed first. Warm it in a small, heavy saucepan, remove it from the heat, then ignite it and pour it over the prepared dish, which is also off the heat. Or, skim the accumulated fat from the cooking liquids, add the brandy to the skillet, allow it to warm, then remove it from the heat, and ignite. The flame will die out quickly.

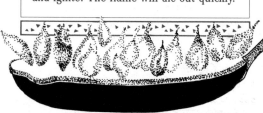

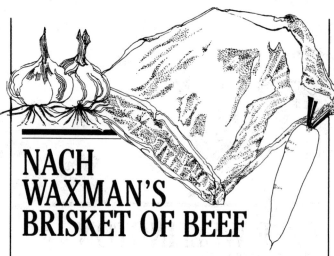

NACH WAXMAN'S BRISKET OF BEEF

How thrilled Julee was the day Nach Waxman opened Kitchen Arts & Letters in New York—a bookstore full of her obsession: cookbooks! And with an owner as passionate about the subject as she is. We're grateful to Nach for doing us all such a favor, and for sharing recipes as well. Here's how he describes this brisket:

"This is a traditional Eastern European dish of the utmost simplicity but with a flavor so distinctive and vigorous that few can believe how elementary it is or how few ingredients it contains. It is wonderful the day it is made, but even better on succeeding days—hot or cold. And it freezes well, with no loss of flavor."

Nach serves this with potato pancakes, fresh sauerkraut, and green tomato pickles.

1 first-cut brisket of beef (5 to 6 pounds; see Note)
1 to 2 teaspoons unbleached all-purpose flour
Coarsely ground black pepper, to taste
¼ cup corn oil
8 onions, thickly sliced and separated into rings
2 tablespoons tomato paste
1 ½ teaspoons coarse (kosher) salt
2 cloves garlic, quartered
1 carrot, peeled

1. Preheat the oven to 375°F.

2. Trim the brisket of most of its fat, and dust it very lightly with the flour. Sprinkle with pepper.

3. Heat the oil in a large heavy flameproof casserole. Add the brisket, and brown on both sides over medium-high heat until some crisp spots appear on the surface.

4. Transfer the brisket to a dish. Keeping the heat

medium-high, add the onions to the casserole and stir, scraping up the brown particles left from the meat. Cook until the onions have softened and developed a handsome brown color, 10 to 15 minutes.

5. Remove the casserole from the heat, and place the brisket, along with any juices that have accumulated, on top of the onions. Spread the tomato paste over the brisket as if you were icing a cake. Sprinkle with pepper and the coarse salt. Add the garlic and carrot, and cover tightly. Place the casserole on the middle rack in the oven, and bake for 1½ hours.

6. Remove the casserole from the oven, and transfer the meat to a carving board. Cut it into ⅛- to ¼-inch-thick slices. Return the slices to the pot, overlapping them at an angle so that you can see a bit of the top edge of each slice (in effect reassembling the brisket, slightly slanted). Correct the seasoning if necessary, and if absolutely necessary add 2 or 3 teaspoons of water to the casserole.

7. Cover, and return the casserole to the oven. Cook until the meat is brown and fork-tender, 1¾ to 2 hours longer.

8. Slice the carrot, and transfer the roast, onions, juice, and carrot slices to a heated platter. Serve at once.

8 portions

Note: First-cut brisket is leaner than the second cut and has only a thin layer of fat on its top side.

BEEF ROASTING CHART

CUT	OVEN TEMPERATURE	INTERNAL TEMPERATURE	COOKING TIME
Rib eye, boneless 3 pounds	350°F	130° for rare; 140°F for medium	12 to 13 minutes per pound for rare
Rib, bone in 4 to 6 pounds (low-heat method)	300°F	130°F for rare; 140°F for medium	25 minutes per pound for rare
Shell, boneless 5½ to 6½ pounds	500°F for 20 minutes, then 375°F	130°F for rare; 140°F for medium	8 to 10 minutes per pound for rare
Tenderloin 3 to 3½ pounds	425°F for 15 minutes, then 350°F	130°F for rare; 140°F for medium	11 to 12 minutes per pound for rare
Brisket, first cut 5 to 6 pounds	375°F		30 to 35 minutes per pound

▲ Based on meat at room temperature when roasted.
▲ Roast beef should rest 15 minutes before carving; internal temperature will rise 5° to 10°F.

> "**B**e moderate in order to taste the joys of life in abundance."
>
> —EPICURUS

SHREDDED BARBECUED BEEF

Serve these spicy barbecue sandwiches on old-fashioned poppy seed rolls along with Oven-Baked French Fries for an informal family get-together.

1 brisket of beef (about 5 pounds)
½ teaspoon natural liquid smoke flavoring
1 teaspoon salt
½ teaspoon paprika
½ teaspoon garlic powder
½ teaspoon dry mustard
8 to 10 poppy seed sandwich rolls
2 cups BBQ Sauce (recipe follows), hot

1. Preheat the oven to 325°F.

2. Place the brisket in a roasting pan, and brush with the liquid smoke.

3. Combine the salt and spices in a small bowl and mix well. Rub this into the brisket.

4. Cover the roasting pan, and bake until the brisket is fork-tender, about 3½ hours.

5. Remove the pan from the oven, and use two forks to pull the meat apart in the pan juices, shredding it coarsely.

6. For each sandwich, halve a poppy seed roll. Spoon about 2 tablespoons heated barbecue sauce over the bottom. Using a slotted spoon, pile about 1 cup of the shredded meat on the roll. Then pour 2 or 3 tablespoons sauce over the meat, and cover with the top half of the roll.

7. Serve with additional barbecue sauce on the side.

8 sandwiches

BBQ SAUCE

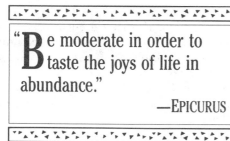

2 tablespoons vegetable oil
½ cup chopped onion
2 tablespoons minced garlic
1 teaspoon ground cumin
¼ teaspoon cayenne pepper
1 cup ketchup
½ cup malt vinegar
¼ cup soy sauce
¼ cup (packed) dark brown sugar
2 tablespoons Worcestershire sauce
¼ teaspoon natural liquid smoke flavoring

1. Heat the oil in a medium-size saucepan. Add the onion, garlic, cumin, and cayenne, and sauté over medium heat, 5 minutes.

2. Stir in the remaining ingredients and simmer, stirring, until slightly thickened, 10 minutes.

2 cups

WINES WITH BEEF

MEAT	WINE
Beef Stew	Burgundy, Châteauneuf-du-Pape, Beaujolais, Pinot Noir
Chili	Bandol, Zinfandel
Corned Beef	Zinfandel, Merlot
Fillet Steak	Pomerol, Vino Nobile di Montepulciano
Flank Steak	Cabernet Sauvignon, Shiraz, Beaujolais nouveau
Hamburger	Beaujolais-Villages
Meat Loaf	Zinfandel
Rib and Loin Steaks	Beaujolais-Villages
Roast Beef	Cabernet Sauvignon, Barolo, Pommard

RUBY GLAZED CORNED BEEF

This corned beef is easily prepared ahead and glazed with our Ruby Cumberland Sauce before baking. All dressed up in the dazzling sauce, the dish is elegant served with a Potato Galette.

1 fresh corned beef (10 ½ pounds)
2 large onions (1 pound total)
8 whole cloves
12 black peppercorns
6 large cloves garlic
2 large carrots, peeled and cut into 2-inch pieces
2 large ribs celery, cut into 2-inch pieces
½ cup whole-grain mustard
3 ½ cups Ruby Cumberland Sauce (recipe follows)
½ cup (packed) dark brown sugar

1. Place the corned beef in a large flameproof casserole or dutch oven, and add water to cover. Peel the onions and stud each one with 4 whole cloves. Add them to the casserole, along with the peppercorns, garlic, carrots, and celery. Bring to a boil over medium-high heat.

2. Reduce the heat to low, cover the casserole, and simmer until the beef is tender, 3 ¼ hours. While it is cooking, turn the beef over every hour.

3. Preheat the oven to 350°F.

4. Remove the corned beef from the casserole, and place it in a 17 x 12 x 2 ½-inch shallow roasting pan, fat side up. Trim off any excess fat.

5. Using a wide pastry brush or a spatula, spread the mustard evenly over the corned beef. Pour 2 ½ cups of the Ruby Cumberland Sauce over the beef, and sprinkle with the brown sugar.

6. Place the roasting pan on the middle rack of the oven, and bake, basting every 15 minutes, until the corned beef is glazed and has a deep, rich color, 45 minutes.

7. Transfer the corned beef to a platter, and spoon some sauce over the top. Serve the remaining sauce on the side.

8 to 10 portions

RUBY CUMBERLAND SAUCE

Our Ruby Cumberland Sauce is great as a glaze. You can also chill it and serve it with pâtés and game terrines, and with lamb or duck.

2 cups red currant jelly
½ cup ruby port wine
1 tablespoon finely slivered orange zest
1 ½ tablespoons finely slivered lemon zest
¼ cup fresh orange juice
¼ cup fresh lemon juice
½ cup finely chopped shallots
1 tablespoon dry mustard
1 ½ teaspoons ground ginger
1 ½ teaspoons coarsely ground black pepper
½ teaspoon salt

Combine all the ingredients in a small saucepan, and place over medium-low heat. Stir frequently until the jelly has melted. Remove the pan from the heat, and let the sauce stand for at least 30 minutes.

3 ½ cups

CORNED BEEF AND CABBAGE

Our corned beef and cabbage is too luscious to consider as just another weeknight meal. We love to present it on an antique blue and white serving platter, accompanied by a horseradish sauce made fluffy with the addition of whipped cream. Perfect with a spicy Zinfandel.

1 fresh corned beef (5 to 6 pounds)
2 onions, each studded with 3 whole cloves
4 carrots, peeled and halved
2 ribs celery, halved
4 sprigs Italian (flat-leaf) parsley
1 green cabbage (3 pounds), cored and cut into 6 wedges
12 small red new potatoes
6 small leeks (white part and 2 inches green), well rinsed
6 carrots, peeled and cut into 2½-inch lengths
Salt and freshly ground black pepper, to taste
4 tablespoons chopped fresh Italian (flat-leaf) parsley
2 cups Horseradish Cream Sauce (recipe follows)

1. Place the corned beef in a large soup kettle or dutch oven. Add the onions, halved carrots, celery, and parsley sprigs. Cover with cold water and bring to a boil. Then reduce the heat, cover, and simmer for 2¾ to 3 hours, turning the beef over in the broth every 30 minutes. When the meat is very tender, remove it from the kettle and keep warm.

2. Strain the broth and return it to the kettle. Add the cabbage, potatoes, leeks, cut-up carrots, salt and pepper, and 2 tablespoons of the chopped parsley. Bring to a boil; reduce the heat, cover, and simmer until the vegetables are tender, 30 minutes.

3. Arrange the beef on a warmed serving platter, and surround it with the cooked vegetables. Ladle broth over the beef and vegetables, and sprinkle with the remaining 2 tablespoons chopped parsley. Serve with the Horseradish Cream Sauce.

6 portions

HORSERADISH CREAM SAUCE

This is also delicious with smoked trout or fillet of beef.

¾ cup heavy or whipping cream
½ cup mayonnaise
½ cup prepared horseradish, drained
2 tablespoons Dijon mustard
Pinch of sugar
Salt and freshly ground black pepper, to taste

1. Whip the heavy cream in a bowl until it forms soft peaks.

2. Combine the mayonnaise, horseradish, and mustard in another bowl. Using a rubber spatula, fold in the whipped cream. Add the sugar, salt, and pepper. Stir well, and transfer to a serving bowl.

2 cups

ITALIAN STUFFED FLANK STEAK

Roasted red peppers, prosciutto, and a hot red cherry pepper provide a striking contrast to the flavor of flank steak. Try serving this at room temperature, cut into ¾-inch-thick slices and arranged on a serving platter garnished with crisp arugula and slivered Belgian endive, sprinkled with small black imported olives.

8 ounces fresh spinach, trimmed and well rinsed
½ cup dried bread crumbs
½ cup freshly grated Parmesan cheese
¼ cup olive oil
2 cloves garlic
3 red bell peppers, roasted (see Index)
1 flank steak (about 1½ pounds), butterflied
Salt and freshly ground black pepper, to taste
4 ounces thinly sliced prosciutto
1 fresh hot cherry pepper, cored, seeded, and minced

1. Preheat the oven to 350°F.

2. Place the spinach in a saucepan with just the water that clings to the leaves. Cover, and cook over medium heat until wilted, 5 minutes. Drain in a colander, and press out the excess moisture with the back of a spoon.

3. Combine the spinach, bread crumbs, Parmesan, olive oil, and garlic in a food processor and purée until thick and smooth. Transfer to a bowl.

4. Peel, core, and carefully seed the roasted peppers. Cut them in half.

5. Open the steak on a work surface, and season with salt and pepper. Arrange the prosciutto in one layer on the steak. Top with a layer of the roasted peppers. Then spread the spinach mixture over them, and sprinkle them with the minced cherry pepper.

6. Starting with a long side, roll the steak up jelly-roll style. Tie it with string at 2-inch intervals, and brush with a little olive oil. Season with salt and pepper. Place the steak in a shallow baking pan.

7. Bake 40 minutes for medium-rare. Cool slightly, or to room temperature, before slicing and serving.

4 to 6 portions

SKIRT STEAK STROGANOFF

Shiitake mushrooms and crème fraîche create a very special sauce for these sautéed beef strips. A tasty dish when served on buttered noodles.

2 pieces skirt steak (6 ounces each)
Salt and freshly ground black pepper, to taste
2 tablespoons unsalted butter
2 tablespoons minced peeled shallots
2 fresh shiitake mushrooms, stems discarded,
*   sliced ¼ inch thick*
¼ cup homemade beef stock (see Index)
*   or canned broth*
¼ cup crème fraîche (see Index)
2 teaspoons tomato purée
1 teaspoon Worcestershire sauce

1. Season the steaks lightly with salt and pepper.

2. Melt 1 tablespoon of the butter in a medium-size heavy skillet, and sauté the steaks until browned on the outside and pink and juicy on the inside, 2 to 3 minutes per side, depending on thickness. Transfer the steaks to a plate and keep warm.

3. Pour off the fat from the skillet. Add the remaining 1 tablespoon butter, and sauté the shallots and mushrooms over medium heat until just softened, 2 minutes.

4. Stir in the stock, crème fraîche, tomato purée, and Worcestershire sauce. Cook over high heat until slightly thick, 2 to 3 minutes. Add any juices that have accumulated from the steaks.

5. Quickly slice the steaks, across the grain and at an angle, into thin strips. Pour the sauce over them, and serve.

2 portions

A COZY SUPPER

Broccoli Spinach Soup

Skirt Steak Stroganoff
Barley Pilaf
***Pinot Noir or Châteauneuf-
du-Pape***

Baby Lettuce Salad With Creamy
Lime Dressing

Hot Lemon Mousse

SMOTHERED SKIRT STEAK

These steaks are rich and robust, with sautéed onions in a sauce evoking thoughts of a barbecue. Serve these with Six Pepper Slaw and Garlic Mashed Potatoes.

2 tablespoons unsalted butter
1 onion, sliced
¼ teaspoon garlic powder
¼ teaspoon salt
Freshly ground black pepper, to taste
2 pieces (6 ounces each) skirt steak
¼ cup homemade beef stock (see Index) or canned broth
1 teaspoon Worcestershire sauce
1 teaspoon tomato paste or ketchup

1. In a small heavy skillet (preferably cast iron), melt the butter. Add the onion, garlic powder, salt, and pepper. Cook over medium-low heat until the onions are wilted and slightly golden, about 15 minutes. Using a slotted spoon, remove the onions and set aside.

2. Increase the heat under the skillet to medium-high. Season the steaks with salt and pepper, and sauté them until browned on the outside and red and juicy on the inside, 2 to 3 minutes per side. Transfer to two plates, and keep warm.

3. Pour off the fat, and return the onions to the skillet. Stir in the remaining ingredients, and cook until heated through and just slightly thickened, 2 minutes. Spoon over the steaks, and serve.

2 portions

BEEF IS BASIC

Beef is a complete protein and among the most iron-rich foods in our American diet. Beef also has a healthy dose of zinc and B vitamins.

In response to our current tastes, beef has been bred leaner than it was 20 years ago. The fat is trimmed to ¼ inch, down from ½ inch, and of course, you can trim it even more. Portions are being cut down, too. Gone are the days, for most of us anyway, of the 16-ounce steak. Three ounces of protein is sufficient for the average adult. A 3-ounce portion of trimmed and cooked top round, top loin, eye of round, sirloin, or tenderloin provides only 155 to 177 calories. (That 16-ounce steak would provide even a he-man with his full daily allowance of calories.)

Our beef recipes aim to please, and all you'll need is a decent set of knives, a cutting board or butcher block, and a bit of TLC—for beef is no longer the meat we take for granted.

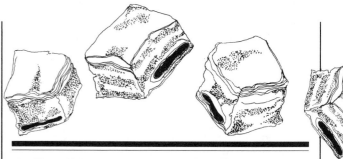

SAVORY SHORT RIBS

Short ribs are one of the tastiest cuts of beef—maybe because many markets are cutting the ribs shorter and using a higher quality of beef than years ago. But make sure you buy them on the bone—they're much more flavorful than boneless short ribs. Watch these disappear.

1 can (35 ounces) Italian plum tomatoes, drained and
    chopped
½ cup homemade beef stock (see Index) or canned broth
4 cloves garlic, minced
4 tablespoons chopped fresh Italian (flat-leaf) parsley
1 tablespoon chopped fresh rosemary leaves
½ teaspoon ground cinnamon
¼ cup olive oil
5½ to 6 pounds short ribs of beef
1 teaspoon coarsely ground black pepper
1 large onion, halved and slivered
½ cup dry red wine

1. Preheat the oven to 350°F.

2. In a bowl, mix together the tomatoes, stock, garlic, 3 tablespoons of the parsley, rosemary, and cinnamon. Set aside.

3. Heat the oil in a medium-size skillet, and brown the short ribs on all sides over medium heat, sprinkling with the pepper. Place the ribs in a shallow roasting pan.

4. Add the onion to the skillet and cook for 3 minutes, stirring. Add it to the short ribs. Pour the wine into the skillet and bring it to a boil, scraping up any brown bits. Pour the wine over the ribs and onion.

5. Pour the reserved tomato mixture over the ribs, and stir well. Cover the pan with aluminum foil, and bake 2½ hours. Baste two or three times while it is cooking.

6. Remove the foil and bake uncovered for 15 minutes.

7. Remove the pan from the oven. Skim off any grease, and serve the ribs topped with the thick tomato-onion sauce. Sprinkle with the remaining 1 tablespoon parsley.

6 portions

Note: When serving short ribs, allow approximately 1 pound per person.

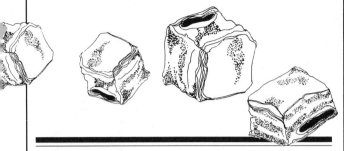

SPEEDY SHORT RIBS

A robust beef stew lightened by the flavor of tangerine cooks up in no time in the microwave.

2 tablespoons olive oil
½ cup chopped onion
2 teaspoons caraway seeds
2 pounds short ribs of beef, cut into 2 x 3-inch pieces
Olive oil
Salt and freshly ground black pepper, to taste
2 tablespoons unbleached all-purpose flour
½ teaspoon salt
1 cup homemade beef stock (see Index) or canned broth
½ cup dry white wine
¼ cup coarsely chopped fresh parsley
1 strip tangerine zest, about 2 inches long
20 fresh cultivated button mushrooms
¼ cup tomato sauce
¼ cup water

1. In a microwave-safe 3-quart casserole, cook the oil on full power (650 to 700 watts) for 2 minutes. Stir in the onion and caraway seeds; cook another 2 minutes.

2. Rub the short ribs lightly with olive oil, and season them with salt and pepper. Add them to the casserole and cook, uncovered, 8 minutes.

3. Sprinkle the meat with the flour, the ½ teaspoon salt, and pepper to taste. Stir until the flour is absorbed.

4. Pour the stock and wine over the meat, and sprinkle with the parsley. Add the tangerine zest. Cover, and cook 25 minutes, turning the meat after 10 minutes.

5. Stir in the mushrooms, tomato sauce, and water. Cover, and cook 15 minutes. Let stand 5 minutes before serving.

2 or 3 portions

Note: This recipe was cooked on High (full power, 650 to 700 watts) in a carousel microwave, using microwave-safe containers.

If your microwave is less powerful, you will have to allow for more cooking time (approximately 1½ times the amount called for—but watch carefully); if it does not have a carousel, you may have to rotate the dish while it is cooking.

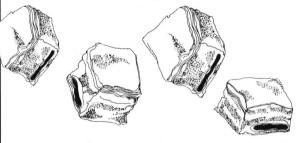

BAKED BBQ BEEF RIBS

When ribs are what you crave, these should certainly do the trick. They're easy to prepare, and the sauce can be made ahead of time—so make a large batch when company's coming.

3 pounds beef short ribs
2 cups BBQ Sauce (see page 496)

1. Preheat the oven to 350°F.

2. Arrange the ribs in one layer in a shallow baking or roasting pan. Cover the pan with aluminum foil, and bake for 1 hour.

3. Remove the pan from the oven, and brush the ribs well on all sides with barbecue sauce. Re-cover the pan, and bake for 1 hour.

4. Uncover the pan and bake, turning the meat and basting it well every 20 minutes, until it is fork-tender, 1 hour.

5. Serve the ribs with the remaining sauce on the side.

3 portions

A BISTRO DINNER

★

Brandade de Morue
Bandol Rouge

Manhattan Boiled Beef With
Horseradish Cream Sauce
Zinfandel

Pear Tatin

MANHATTAN BOILED BEEF

Often when chefs get together to talk food and compare notes, it is over a relatively simple meal—such as roast chicken or boiled beef. For it is these dishes, when done superbly, that elicit the greatest admiration for the cook. Of course the raw ingredients must be top-quality, but they are easy to find. This is a great way to treat family and good friends.

4 cups water
3½ cups homemade beef stock (see Index) or canned broth
4 ounces slab bacon, in 1 piece
½ cup celery leaves
2 sprigs parsley
2 bay leaves
2 cloves garlic, crushed
½ ounce dried mushrooms
4 leeks (white part and 1 inch green), rinsed well and tied together with string
3 carrots, peeled, halved lengthwise and crosswise
4 small turnips, peeled
1 parsnip, peeled, halved lengthwise and crosswise
1 beef eye of round (about 3½ pounds), tied

1. Combine the water, stock, bacon, celery leaves, parsley, bay leaves, garlic, and mushrooms in a flameproof casserole or dutch oven. Bring to a boil. Add the leeks, carrots, turnips, and parsnip, and simmer 20 minutes. Using a slotted spoon, remove the leeks (untie them) and parsnip and set them aside, loosely covered.

2. Simmer the remaining vegetables another 10 minutes. Then remove the turnips and carrots, cover loosely, and set aside with the leeks and parsnip. Cover the vegetables and refrigerate.

3. Add the beef to the casserole, cover partially, and bring to a boil. Reduce the heat and simmer, turning the beef twice and skimming when necessary, until tender, 3 to 4 hours. The beef should always be half immersed in water as it is cooking; add water to the casserole as needed. When the meat is tender, remove the casserole from the heat and set it aside; allow the beef to cool, uncovered, in the liquid. Then cover and refrigerate overnight.

4. Remove the beef from the liquid, and cut it into ½-inch-thick slices. Skim and strain the broth. Return the broth, sliced beef, and reserved vegetables to the casserole. Simmer gently until heated through, about 10 minutes.

5. Arrange the beef on a serving platter with the vegetables alongside. Spoon some of the broth over all, and serve any extra in a sauceboat.

6 portions

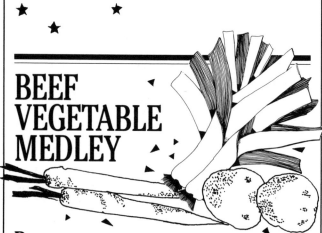

BEEF VEGETABLE MEDLEY

Parsnips, new potatoes, leeks, carrots, and tomatoes lighten this robust beef stew to make a contemporary classic. Be sure to use a good, "drinkable" Burgundy, and the aroma will have everyone in the kitchen long before dinnertime. Serve it with buttered noodles.

2 tablespoons olive oil
6 thick slices bacon, cut into 1-inch pieces
2 pounds boneless beef chuck, cut into 1-inch cubes
Freshly ground black pepper, to taste
10 small leeks (white part and 2 inches green), well rinsed
6 carrots, peeled and cut into 3-inch lengths
6 parsnips, peeled and cut into 3-inch lengths
2 tablespoons sugar
1 ½ cups homemade beef stock (see Index) or canned broth
1 ½ cups Burgundy
2 tablespoons unsalted butter
2 tablespoons red currant jelly
2 teaspoons dried thyme leaves
8 small red new potatoes, halved
6 cloves garlic, minced
6 ripe plum tomatoes, seeded and coarsely chopped
½ cup chopped fresh Italian (flat-leaf) parsley

1. Preheat the oven to 350°F.

2. Heat the olive oil in a large skillet. Add the bacon, and cook over medium heat until fat is rendered, 4 to 5 minutes. Using a slotted spoon, transfer the bacon to a heavy flameproof casserole.

3. Brown the beef in the same skillet, in small batches, over medium-high heat. Sprinkle the beef with pepper as it is cooking. Transfer the beef to the casserole with the bacon.

4. Place the leeks, carrots, and parsnips in the same skillet. Sprinkle them with the sugar and sauté over medium heat to caramelize them slightly, 6 to 8 minutes. Remove the vegetables from the skillet and set aside.

5. Add the stock and wine to the skillet and bring to a boil, scraping up any brown bits. Swirl in the butter, red currant jelly, and thyme. Cook for 1 minute, then pour over the meat in the casserole.

6. Add the potatoes and garlic to the casserole, and bring the mixture to a boil. Cover, transfer to the oven, and bake for 45 minutes.

7. Remove the casserole from the oven, and add the reserved vegetables. Add the tomatoes and all but 1 tablespoon of the parsley. Stir gently, adjust the seasonings, and return the casserole to the oven. Bake, uncovered, until the beef is tender, 45 minutes. Garnish with the remaining 1 tablespoon parsley, and serve.

6 portions

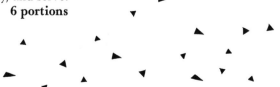

ROASTED PEPPER GOULASH

Red and yellow roasted peppers give this goulash a rich, deep flavor, and caraway seeds add the fresh nuttiness that Hungarians adore. We like it served over noodles tossed with butter and more caraway.

2 tablespoons olive oil
1 ½ pounds boneless beef chuck, cut into 1 ½ -inch chunks
1 cup chopped onion
3 fresh cherry peppers, cored, seeded, and minced
1 tablespoon chopped garlic
2 teaspoons caraway seeds
2 teaspoons paprika
2 cups homemade beef stock (see Index) or canned broth
¼ cup tomato purée
1 teaspoon coarse (kosher) salt
Freshly ground black pepper, to taste
2 roasted red bell peppers (see Index)
1 roasted yellow bell pepper (see Index)
½ cup crème fraîche (see Index)

1. Heat the oil in a flameproof casserole or dutch oven. Brown the beef over medium-high heat in batches if necessary. Using a slotted spoon, transfer the beef to a bowl and set aside.

2. Add the onion, cherry peppers, garlic, caraway, and paprika to the casserole. Cook over low heat, stirring, until just tender, 10 minutes.

3. Return the meat to the casserole. Add the stock and tomato purée. Cover, and simmer until tender, 1 ½ hours. Season with salt and pepper.

4. Meanwhile, cut the peppers into 1-inch squares.

5. Stir the peppers into the goulash, simmer, uncovered, 10 minutes. Then stir in the crème fraîche and serve.

4 portions

ABOUT VEAL

★

We used to eat almost all of our veal in Italian and French restaurants, where the chefs seemed able to create a magic with this meat that was beyond us. As it turned out, most of the magic was in the meat, for the veal available to the consumer was often more like young beef than calf. Recently, European methods of raising veal on milk alone and butchering the animals before six months of age have gained a foothold in America. Milk-fed veal is currently marketed nationwide. Look for Plume de Veau and Provimi Delft Blue. The meat of young milk-fed veal is ivory colored with just a blush of pink and the bones are creamy white and soft. Now it's up to us to learn how to cook it.

Veal is very lean and delicate and must be cooked more like poultry than beef. Roasting (don't sear it first) at a low temperature works well. Braising melds the flavor of veal with its accompanying vegetables and keeps the meat moist. Sautéing thin scallops or chops in butter or oil enhances both the delicate flavor and texture. Whatever you do with veal, do it gently and it won't disappoint you.

GUIDE TO THE BEST CUTS

▼ **Shoulder:** This is our favorite cut for veal stew meat, but the shoulder also yields wonderful chops and roasts (arm, blade, and rolled shoulder), all

VEAL CHOP WITH SUMMER SALAD

perfect for braising. Veal is quicker to cook than beef so you won't need half a day to put a succulent veal stew or braised chops on the table.

■ ★ Rib and loin: These luxurious roasts make spectacular entrées for entertaining: Check your pocketbook and look for a rib roast, crown roast, loin roast or rolled loin, double loin or saddle, sirloin roast, and rolled double sirloin. The veal on these roasts is very lean and care must be taken not to overcook it. We get good results by covering these roasts with a layer of fat (unsmoked bacon or salt pork) to baste the meat as it cooks and roasting them at a steady low heat (325°F). For everyday dining, though, the more important as well as affordable cut is the chops. Like the roasts, the chops are delicate and very lean. We find broiling much too harsh and sauté these chops instead. They cook in just minutes, so don't walk away.

)◆ Rump and leg: At the top of the leg is the rump, which is cut for standing rump roast and rolled rump roast—both of which should be braised. The leg itself is boned and tied for roasts but more often sliced for steaks, cutlets, and scallops. The steaks are best braised but the thinner boneless cutlets and scallops should be sautéed. Cutlets and scallops are endlessly versatile and quick to cook. Because they are so thin, there is no need to test for doneness when sautéing; simply take them out of the pan when both sides are golden.

♥ Breast: This is probably the least expensive cut but it is as wonderful eating as the rest of the animal. We like the breast stuffed, then baked slowly with herbs to enhance its flavor.

◗ Shank: The shanks are most frequently cut crosswise into thick slices so that they can be braised. They can stand up to longer cooking times and for that reason develop the most flavor. The velvety marrow inside the bone is icing on the cake.

Although this recipe has all the marks of being one of the great new entrées, it's actually a classic. We love these chops coated in Parmesan and bread crumbs, sautéed quickly, and topped with a crisp, cool salad of arugula, ripe tomatoes, and red onions. The counterpoints of cool and hot, crispy and moist, fresh and tart, work wonderfully. You can prepare the salad ingredients ahead of time, then coat the veal chops and sauté them at the last minute.

4 veal chops (8 ounces each), ¾ inch thick
½ cup seasoned bread crumbs (see Index)
½ cup freshly grated Parmesan cheese
4 ripe plum tomatoes, seeded and chopped
½ cup chopped red onion
1 cup chopped arugula leaves
5 tablespoons olive oil
Dash of red wine vinegar
Salt and freshly ground black pepper, to taste

1. Lay the veal chops between two pieces of waxed paper, and pound the meat as thin as possible up to ½ inch from the bone.

2. Combine the bread crumbs and Parmesan in a flat dish, and coat the chops thoroughly with the mixture.

3. Combine the tomatoes, red onion, arugula, 2 tablespoons of the olive oil, red wine vinegar, and salt and pepper in a bowl. Cover and set aside.

4. Heat the remaining 3 tablespoons olive oil in a skillet and brown the veal chops, 2 to 3 minutes on each side.

5. Transfer the chops to plates, and top each one with a large spoonful of the tomato and arugula salad. Serve immediately.

4 portions

VEAL MARENGO ROAST

The great appeal of this dish is the sublime combination of oranges, tomatoes, and olives with succulent veal roast. We've updated it by using robust sun-dried tomatoes and black olive purée.

1 veal shoulder roast (about 3½ pounds), tied
5 tablespoons Olivada (see Index)
¼ cup chopped sun-dried tomatoes
2 tablespoons orange marmalade
¾ cup California Cabernet Sauvignon
5 tablespoons water
4 cups red and yellow cherry tomatoes, mixed
Berta's Chicken Stock (see Index) or canned broth
15 Niçoise olives
1 tablespoon slivered orange zest
1 tablespoon cornstarch
Fresh mint sprigs, for garnish

   1. Cut 8 to 10 slits ¼ inch deep in the surface of the roast. Combine 4 tablespoons of the olivada, the sun-dried tomatoes, and the marmalade in a small bowl. Spread the mixture over the roast, pressing it into the slits. Cover loosely; let stand 3 hours.

   2. Preheat the oven to 350°F.

   3. Place the veal in a roasting pan. Pour the wine and 4 tablespoons of the water into the pan.

   4. Roast the veal 1 hour, basting every 15 minutes and adding water if necessary.

   5. Arrange the tomatoes around the roast, and cook another 15 minutes.

   6. Transfer the roast to a platter. Lift the tomatoes out with a slotted spoon, and arrange them around the roast. Cover loosely and keep warm.

   7. Pour the pan juices, plus enough chicken stock to make 2 cups, into a small saucepan. Stir in the olives, orange zest, and remaining 1 tablespoon olive purée. Heat to a simmer.

   8. Blend the cornstarch and remaining 1 tablespoon water in a samll bowl. Whisk this into the sauce, bring back to a simmer, and cook 1 minute.

   9. Slice the roast very thin and serve it with the sauce. Garnish with fresh mint.

   6 to 8 portions

VEAL ROASTING CHART

CUT	OVEN TEMPERATURE	INTERNAL TEMPERATURE	COOKING TIME
Rib 4 to 6 pounds	350°F	165° to 170°F	20 to 25 minutes per pound
Loin, bone in 4 to 6 pounds	350°F	165° to 170°F	20 to 25 minutes per pound
Loin, boned and rolled 3 to 5 pounds	350°F	165° to 170°F	25 to 28 minutes per pound
Breast, stuffed 6½ to 7½ pounds	350°F	165° to 170°F	20 to 25 minutes per pound

▲ Based on meat at room temperature when roasted.
▲ Roast veal should rest 15 minutes before carving; internal temperature will rise 5° to 10°F.

DINNER FOR A COOL SPRING EVENING

Sunset Melon With Salmon and
Prosciutto

Veal Marengo Roast
Sweetly Stewed Tomatoes
Potato Galette

Raspberry Angel Food Cake
Raspberry Amaretto Sauce

SALTIMBOCCA FOR TWO

Layers of the thinnest of veal scallopine, prosciutto, fresh sage, and Parmesan—a great light dinner for a special evening.

8 ounces veal scallopine (4 scallops), pounded thin
Salt and freshly ground black pepper, to taste
Unbleached all-purpose flour for dusting
4 tablespoons (½ stick) unsalted butter
¼ cup Parmesan cheese shavings (cut with a vegetable peeler)
4 thin slices prosciutto, cut to fit scallopine
4 fresh sage leaves
⅓ cup dry Italian white wine
1 teaspoon minced fresh sage leaves

1. Preheat the oven to 375°F.
2. Season the veal lightly with salt and pepper, and dust with flour, shaking off any excess.
3. Melt 2 tablespoons of the butter in a large skillet, and sauté the veal over medium-high heat until lightly browned, 1 minute per side. Transfer the scallops to a rimmed baking sheet or shallow pan, and reserve the skillet.

4. Sprinkle the cheese over the veal. Cover each scallop with 1 slice of prosciutto and a sage leaf. Bake until cooked through, 5 minutes.
5. Meanwhile, add the wine to the skillet and cook over high heat, scraping up any brown bits, until reduced to 3 tablespoons, 2 minutes. Then lower the heat and swirl in the remaining 2 tablespoons butter and the minced sage.
6. Arrange the veal on two plates, pour the sauce over, and serve immediately.
2 portions

FANCY VEAL BIRDS

Rolled veal stuffed with wild rice and apricots, simmered with shiitake mushrooms and onions in white wine. This is a classic dinner party dish, with lots of flavor.

¾ cup cooked wild rice
4 dried apricot halves, finely chopped
2 tablespoons dried currants
½ teaspoon salt
Freshly ground black pepper, to taste
1 pound veal scallopine (8 scallops), pounded thin
4 tablespoons (½ stick) unsalted butter
3 ounces fresh shiitake mushrooms, stems removed, sliced ¼ inch thick
¼ cup chopped onion
¼ teaspoon dried thyme leaves
Unbleached all-purpose flour for dusting
¾ cup California Sauvignon Blanc

1. Stir the rice, apricots, currants, ¼ teaspoon of the salt, and pepper together in a mixing bowl.
2. Lay the scallopine flat on a work surface, and spoon some of the rice filling onto the center of each one. Fold them up like envelopes, secure with string, and set aside.
3. Melt 2 tablespoons of the butter in a deep skillet, and sauté the mushrooms and onion over medium heat just until tender, 5 minutes. Season the mixture with the remaining ¼ teaspoon salt, pepper, and the thyme. Then remove it from the skillet and set aside.

4. Add the remaining 2 tablespoons butter to the skillet. Flour the veal rolls lightly, and brown them on all sides.

5. Pour the wine into the skillet, and spoon the mushroom mixture over and around the veal. Cover, and simmer 15 minutes.

6. Transfer the veal to a platter, and remove the strings. Spoon on the sauce, and serve.

4 portions

VEAL MARSALA

Veal scaloppine luxuriously sautéed with mushrooms and Marsala. A garnish of chives and a good grinding of black pepper make it perfect.

4 boneless veal cutlets (approximately 5 ounces each)
½ cup unbleached all-purpose flour
2 tablespoons unsalted butter
2 cups thinly sliced cultivated mushrooms
1 tablespoon olive oil
½ cup Marsala wine
Salt and freshly ground black pepper, to taste
1 tablespoon chopped fresh Italian (flat-leaf) parsley

1. Lay the veal between two pieces of waxed paper, and flatten each cutlet with the flat end of a meat pounder until thin. Dredge lightly with the flour.

2. Melt the butter in a skillet, add the mushrooms, and sauté over medium heat until nicely browned, 15 minutes. Remove the mushrooms from the skillet and set them aside.

3. Add the olive oil to the skillet and heat until very hot. Sauté the veal over high heat, about 1 minute on each side. (It needs very little cooking.) Remove it to a platter and keep warm.

4. Add the Marsala to the skillet and simmer until it has reduced slightly, 2 minutes. Add the reserved mushrooms, salt and pepper, and the parsley. Heat through and pour over the veal. Serve immediately.

4 portions

VEAL PICCATA

The lemony-est piccata of all! This is a veal dish we've always loved, for it is perfect for a light entrée any time of the year.

4 boneless veal cutlets (about 5 ounces each)
½ cup unbleached all-purpose flour
1 tablespoon olive oil
1 tablespoon unsalted butter
¼ cup dry white wine
1 tablespoon fresh lemon juice
Salt and freshly ground black pepper, to taste
1 tablespoon chopped fresh Italian (flat-leaf) parsley

1. Lay the veal between two pieces of waxed paper and flatten each cutlet with the flat end of a meat pounder until thin. Dredge lightly with the flour.

2. Heat the olive oil and butter in a large skillet. When it is very hot, sauté the veal over high heat until lightly browned, about 1 minute on each side. (It needs very little cooking.) Remove to a platter and keep warm.

3. Add the wine and lemon juice to the skillet and bring to a boil, scraping up any browned bits. Add salt and pepper and the parsley. Pour the sauce over the veal, and serve immediately.

4 portions

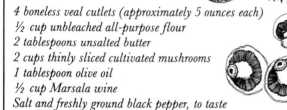

CHECKING UP ON VEAL

★

Three ounces of veal scallops sautéed in butter or oil has just 180 calories. Although veal is lean (10 to 15 percent fat), its cholesterol content is a bit higher than lamb and beef—about 84 milligrams for a three-ounce serving. Veal is a good source of protein, B vitamins (especially niacin), and zinc.

NEW BASICS VEAL PARMIGIANA

This veal dish was the first taste of Italian food for many of us, that is, besides spaghetti. We've made it our own with a little pesto, a very fresh-tasting tomato sauce, and Brie.

4 boneless veal cutlets (approximately 4 ounces each)
½ cup seasoned bread crumbs (see Index)
½ cup freshly grated Parmesan cheese
1 tablespoon olive oil
1 tablespoon unsalted butter
2 cups New Basic Tomato Sauce (see Index), heated
4 tablespoons Basil Pesto (see Index)
12 ounces Brie cheese, rind removed, cut into 4 slices (see Note)
8 fresh basil leaves

1. Preheat the broiler.
2. Lay the veal between two pieces of waxed paper and flatten each cutlet with the flat end of a meat pounder until thin.
3. Combine the bread crumbs and Parmesan in a flat dish, and stir well. Coat the veal with the mixture.
4. Heat the olive oil and butter in a large skillet, and sauté the veal for 2 minutes on each side.
5. Transfer the veal to a broiling pan or flameproof baking dish. Top each piece with ½ cup of the tomato sauce and 1 tablespoon of the pesto. Lay the slices of Brie on top.
6. Broil until the cheese has melted and is bubbling slightly, 1½ to 2 minutes. Garnish with the basil leaves and serve immediately.

4 portions

Note: To slice Brie, first place it in the freezer, well wrapped in plastic, for 30 minutes.

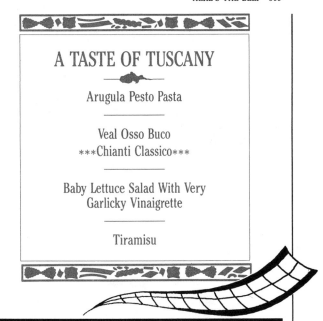

A TASTE OF TUSCANY

Arugula Pesto Pasta

Veal Osso Buco
Chianti Classico

Baby Lettuce Salad With Very
Garlicky Vinaigrette

Tiramisu

VEAL OSSO BUCO

Meaty veal shanks simmered until they're moist and succulent, shrouded in a rich tomato sauce. In Italy risotto Milanese traditionally is served alongside—the only time the risotto becomes a "side dish." This recipe, a longtime favorite of ours, was written up in our first book. We think it's well worth repeating.

1 cup unbleached all-purpose flour
Salt and freshly ground black pepper, to taste
16 sections of veal shank (12 to 14 pounds), 2 inches thick
¼ cup extra virgin olive oil
4 tablespoons (½ stick) unsalted butter
2 onions, coarsely chopped
6 large cloves garlic, chopped
½ teaspoon dried basil leaves
½ teaspoon dried oregano leaves
1 can (28 ounces) Italian plum tomatoes, drained
2 cups dry white wine
2 cups homemade beef stock (see Index) or canned broth
¾ cup chopped fresh Italian (flat-leaf) parsley
Grated zest of 2 lemons

1. Season the flour with salt and pepper, and dredge the pieces of veal shank in it. Shake off any excess.
2. Heat the oil and butter in a large flameproof casserole or dutch oven, and quickly sear the veal

over medium-high heat, browning it well on all sides. Transfer the veal to paper towels to drain.

3. Add the onions, garlic, basil, and oregano to the casserole and cook over medium heat, stirring occasionally, for 10 minutes.

4. Add the tomatoes, and salt and pepper to taste, and cook over medium-low heat for another 10 minutes. Skim off any excess fat.

5. Add the wine, raise the heat, and bring to a boil. Reduce the heat and simmer, uncovered, for 15 minutes.

6. Preheat the oven to 350°F.

7. Return the veal shanks to the casserole and add enough stock to just cover the meat. Cover the casserole, transfer it to the oven, and bake for 1½ hours. Then remove the lid and bake until the veal is very tender, another 30 minutes.

8. Just before serving, sprinkle with the chopped parsley and grated lemon zest.

6 to 8 portions

DILLED BLANQUETTE DE VEAU

This traditional creamy French stew has become one of our contemporary classics, freshened with sweet carrots and dill. It's pretty and sensational!

12 tablespoons (1½ sticks) unsalted butter
3 pounds boneless veal, cut into 1-inch cubes
8 tablespoons unbleached all-purpose flour
1 scant teaspoon freshly grated nutmeg
1½ teaspoons salt
1½ teaspoons freshly ground black pepper
3 cups diagonally sliced peeled carrots (slices ⅛ inch thick)
3 cups coarsely chopped onions
5 tablespoons finely chopped fresh dill
3 to 4 cups Berta's Chicken Stock (see Index) or canned broth
¾ cup heavy or whipping cream

1. Preheat the oven to 350°F.

2. Melt 8 tablespoons of the butter in a heavy flameproof casserole or dutch oven. Add the veal and cook over medium-low heat, turning frequently, until opaque but not browned, 5 to 10 minutes.

3. Stir 3 tablespoons of the flour together with the nutmeg, salt, and pepper in a small bowl, and sprinkle over the veal. Continue to cook over low heat, stirring, for 5 minutes. The flour and veal should not brown.

4. Add the carrots, onions, 3 tablespoons of the dill, and enough stock to just cover the meat and vegetables. Raise the heat to medium and bring just to a boil. Then cover the casserole, transfer it to the oven, and bake for 1½ hours.

5. Remove the casserole from the oven, and pour the stew through a strainer placed over a bowl. Reserve the solids and liquid separately.

6. Return the casserole to medium heat, and melt the remaining 4 tablespoons butter in it. Sprinkle in the remaining 5 tablespoons flour, and cook over low heat, whisking constantly, for 5 minutes.

7. Whisk the reserved cooking liquid slowly into the butter and flour mixture, and bring to a simmer. Cook slowly, stirring constantly, for 5 minutes.

8. Whisk in the cream, remaining 2 tablespoons dill, and additional salt, pepper, and nutmeg to taste. Return the veal and vegetables to the casserole, and simmer to heat through, about 5 minutes. Transfer to a deep serving dish and serve at once.

6 portions

WINES WITH VEAL

Veal	Wine
Chops	Gattinara, Cortese di Gavi, Fumé Blanc
Roasts	Beaujolais Fleurie, Barolo
Robust Stews	Valpolicella, Chianti Classico, Chardonnay
Scaloppine	Beaujolais, Cabernet Sauvignon
Calf's Liver	Riesling, Gewürztraminer

VEAL AND MUSHROOM STEW

The tenderness of delicate veal is featured in a luscious light stew that has the surprising color of plum tomatoes and the freshness of orange zest—perfect for a spring buffet.

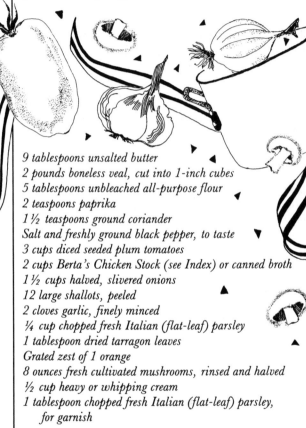

9 tablespoons unsalted butter
2 pounds boneless veal, cut into 1-inch cubes
5 tablespoons unbleached all-purpose flour
2 teaspoons paprika
1½ teaspoons ground coriander
Salt and freshly ground black pepper, to taste
3 cups diced seeded plum tomatoes
2 cups Berta's Chicken Stock (see Index) or canned broth
1½ cups halved, slivered onions
12 large shallots, peeled
2 cloves garlic, finely minced
¼ cup chopped fresh Italian (flat-leaf) parsley
1 tablespoon dried tarragon leaves
Grated zest of 1 orange
8 ounces fresh cultivated mushrooms, rinsed and halved
½ cup heavy or whipping cream
1 tablespoon chopped fresh Italian (flat-leaf) parsley,
    for garnish

1. Preheat the oven to 350°F.
2. Melt 4 tablespoons of the butter in a heavy flameproof casserole. Add the veal and cook, turning frequently, over low heat, about 5 minutes. Do not allow it to brown.
3. Stir 2 tablespoons of the flour together with the paprika, coriander, and salt and pepper in a small bowl. Sprinkle this over the veal and continue to cook over low heat, stirring, for 5 minutes. Do not let it brown.
4. Add 2 cups of the tomatoes, the chicken stock, onions, shallots, garlic, parsley, tarragon, and orange

zest. Bring to a boil. Cover, transfer to the oven, and bake until the veal is tender, 1¼ hours.
5. While the stew is cooking, melt 2 tablespoons of the butter in a skillet. Quickly sauté the mushroom halves over medium-high heat until golden brown, 4 to 5 minutes. Set them aside.
6. Remove the casserole from the oven, and pour the stew into a strainer placed over a bowl. Reserve the stew and the cooking liquid separately.
7. Place the casserole over medium heat, and melt the remaining 3 tablespoons butter in it. Sprinkle in the remaining 3 tablespoons flour, and cook over very low heat, whisking constantly, for 3 minutes.
8. Whisk the reserved cooking liquid slowly into the casserole and simmer slowly, stirring constantly, for 5 minutes.
9. Whisk in the cream and adjust the seasonings. Return the stew to the casserole. Gently stir in the remaining 1 cup tomatoes and the reserved mushrooms. Simmer until heated through, 5 minutes. Transfer to a deep serving dish, sprinkle with parsley, and serve.

6 portions

VELVETY VEAL

Delicate, smooth, and mild, veal has long been the favorite meat of great chefs around the world. Its subtle flavor makes it a perfect palette for creative cooks to work their magic. Europeans know how to cook veal to perfection and we're eager to learn. Veal piccata one night, parmigiana the next, perhaps osso buco or saltimbocca the night after. Veal marries perfectly with myriad vegetables and herbs as well as butter, cream, fragrant oils, wines, and flavorful stocks. It never overwhelms, it just supports, so that every time we cook veal, it seems new and exciting.

WINES OF AUSTRALIA

The Australian wine market is becoming very sophisticated, and the wines are beginning to show well on the American market. No matter how much the names may resemble those of California wines, these wines have a unique personality.

SHIRAZ: This varietal, of Persian origin, is often blended with the Cabernet grape to produce Cabernet Shiraz, a medium- to full-bodied wine with a delectable flavor. Serve it in winter with a rich veal stew or grilled meat. Try the wines from Penfolds Koonunga Hill, Virgin Hills, Chateau Le Amon, and Chateau Tahbilk.

CHARDONNAY: Be sure to drink Australian Chardonnays when they are young, for they are not bottled for long cellar storage. They have a rich flavor and tend to have a high alcohol content. The best come from New South Wales and South Australia. Look for the Rosemont Estate label, as well as Arrowfield, Petaluma, and Lake's Folly.

We also recommend the remarkable sparkling wines from Yellowglen Vineyards, as well as the late-harvest Rieslings, Sémillons, and Sauvignon Blancs from Petaluma, Rosemont, and Peter Lehmann.

RAGOUT OF VEAL

Chunky veal simmered in a lemony sauce with rosemary, nutty green olives, and artichoke hearts. The flavors contrast wonderfully.

4 large artichokes
½ lemon
2 tablespoons olive oil
½ cup chopped shallots
1½ pounds boneless veal, cut into 1½-inch cubes
Unbleached all-purpose flour for dusting
1½ cups Berta's Chicken Stock (see Index) or canned broth
½ cup large Italian or other imported green olives
1 large carrot, peeled and cut into ½-inch slices
Zest of 1 lemon, slivered
2 tablespoons unsalted butter, at room temperature
2 tablespoons unbleached all-purpose flour
2 teaspoons minced fresh rosemary leaves
1 tablespoon fresh lemon juice
Salt and freshly ground black pepper, to taste

1. Trim the stems off the artichokes, and rub the bottoms with the lemon half. Snap off all the leaves, and rub the edges with the lemon.

2. Bring a saucepan of lightly salted water to a boil. Add the artichokes, and simmer until crisp-tender, 20 minutes. Drain well, reserving 1 cup of the cooking liquid.

3. Trim the artichokes; scoop out the fuzzy chokes. Cut the bottoms into ½-inch slices, and set aside.

4. Heat the oil in a flameproof casserole or dutch oven and sauté the shallots over low heat for 3 minutes.

5. Lightly dust the veal cubes with flour. Add them to the casserole, and brown quickly over medium-high heat. Then stir in the reserved artichoke cooking liquid, stock, olives, carrot, and lemon zest. Cover, and simmer until tender, 1 hour.

6. Blend the butter and 2 tablespoons flour together in a small bowl. Whisk small bits of this beurre manié into the ragout just until thickened. Stir in the rosemary, lemon juice, and reserved artichoke slices. Simmer 10 minutes.

7. Season with salt and pepper and serve.

4 portions

Note: If you prefer, you can cook the artichokes whole (see Index). Then reserve the leaves and serve them as a first course on small plates, arranged in circles around small ramekins of vinaigrette.

The assertive flavor of rosemary is best released by mincing or crushing it in your hands and adding a little at a time.

MEDITERRANEAN BREAST OF VEAL

Greece and veal are not usually bedfellows, but sharp feta cheese, briny Calamata olives, and pungent rosemary complement and surprise. A hint of fresh mint in the stuffing subtly refreshes.

6 ounces feta cheese, crumbled
4 ounces Calamata olives (about 1 cup), pitted
1¼ cups dried bread crumbs
2 scallions (green onions), white bulb and 3 inches green, sliced
¼ cup chopped fresh mint leaves
2 eggs, lightly beaten
1 breast of veal (about 7½ pounds), trimmed, bones cracked, with a pocket cut for stuffing
¼ cup olive oil
Salt and freshly ground black pepper, to taste
1½ tablespoons fresh rosemary leaves or 2 teaspoons dried

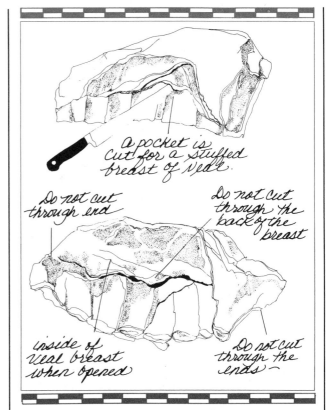

a pocket is cut for a stuffed breast of veal.

Do not cut through end

Do not cut through the back of the breast

inside of veal breast when opened

Do not cut through the ends —

1. Preheat the oven to 350°F.

2. Make the stuffing: In a mixing bowl, toss the cheese, olives, bread crumbs, scallions, mint, and eggs until well mixed. Fill the pocket in the veal with this mixture.

3. Arrange the veal in a roasting pan. Lightly brush the surface with olive oil, and sprinkle it with salt, pepper, and rosemary. Cover loosely with aluminum foil.

4. Bake 1½ hours. Uncover, and bake another 1½ hours.

5. Remove the veal from the oven, and let it stand for 20 minutes before carving (cut between the ribs).

6 portions

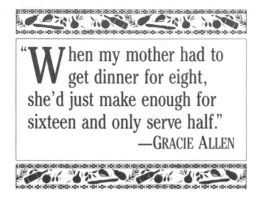

"**W**hen my mother had to get dinner for eight, she'd just make enough for sixteen and only serve half."
—GRACIE ALLEN

SWEET AND SOUR TONGUE

Sweet-and-sour sauces no longer mean simply lemon juice and sugar. The taste of this dish is pungent with the balsamic vinegar, cinnamon, ginger, and golden raisins.

1 smoked beef tongue (about 4 ½ pounds)
2 or 3 bay leaves
3 cloves garlic, slightly crushed
¼ cup balsamic vinegar
¼ cup sugar
1 ¾ cups homemade beef stock (see Index)
  or canned broth
2 cups tomato purée
1 cup dry red wine
1 strip lemon zest, 2 ½ x ½ inch
½ teaspoon ground cinnamon
½ teaspoon ground ginger
½ teaspoon salt
Freshly ground black pepper, to taste
½ cup golden raisins

1. Place the tongue in a very large, heavy saucepan and cover with cold water. Add the bay leaves and garlic, and bring to a boil. Lower the heat, cover partially, and simmer until fork-tender, 3 hours. Remove the tongue from the pan and set aside until cool enough to handle.

2. Meanwhile, make the sauce: Combine the vinegar and sugar in a heavy saucepan, bring to a boil, and cook until thick and bubbling, 2 to 3 minutes.

Then stir in the stock, tomato purée, wine, lemon zest, cinnamon, ginger, salt, and pepper. Simmer 10 minutes.

3. Stir in the raisins, and simmer another 10 minutes. Then set the sauce aside until the tongue has cooled.

4. Preheat the oven to 325°F.

5. With a paring knife, carefully loosen the skin at the back of the tongue, and peel toward the tip. Trim any fat at the back. Cut the tongue into slices ¼ to ½ inch thick.

6. Spoon half the sauce into a large shallow ovenproof casserole. Arrange the tongue in one layer, overlapping the slices. Pour the remaining sauce over the tongue, and cover the casserole loosely with aluminum foil.

7. Bake until bubbling and heated through, 1 hour.

6 to 8 portions

SAUTEED CALF'S LIVER WITH CARAMELIZED ONIONS

For an elegant presentation make sure the liver is thinly sliced—and be careful not to overcook it. Sweet balsamic vinegar flavors this light sauce enriched with caramelized onions.

8 ounces bacon, cut into 1-inch pieces
2 large onions, thinly sliced
2 pounds calf's liver, cut into ½-inch-thick slices
1 tablespoon unsalted butter (optional)
Freshly ground black pepper, to taste
Coarse (kosher) salt, to taste
3 tablespoons balsamic vinegar
3 tablespoons Berta's Chicken Stock (see Index) or canned broth

1. Sauté the bacon in a large skillet until crisp. Remove it with a slotted spoon, and set aside.

2. Add the onions to the skillet and cook over medium heat, stirring frequently, until wilted and golden, 20 to 25 minutes. Remove them with a slotted spoon and keep warm.

3. Raise the heat under the skillet to medium-high. When the bacon fat is hot, reduce the heat to medium and sauté the liver, a few slices at a time, for 1 to 2 minutes on each side for medium-rare. Add the butter to the skillet if necessary, and sprinkle the liver with pepper and coarse salt while it is cooking.

4. Slice the liver on the diagonal into about six slices per piece. Keep warm.

5. Add the vinegar and stock to the skillet and bring to a boil, scraping up any brown bits. Add the reserved onions and toss over medium heat for 30 seconds. Let them rest, off the heat, for an additional 30 seconds.

6. Arrange the liver on a serving platter or on individual dinner plates. Top with the onions and sprinkle with the reserved bacon.

6 portions

SEASON TO TASTE

A wide range of flavorings are well suited to veal. Some of our favorites include:

Basil	Marsala wine
Bay Leaf	Mint
Caper	Mustard
Chervil	Onion
Chive	Orange
Garlic	Parsley
Ginger	Rosemary
Lemon	Sage
Madeira	Savory
Marjoram	Thyme

SWEETBREADS AND ARTICHOKES ON TOAST

Sweetbreads must be handled with care, and their preparation takes a while, but the delicate flavor and texture make it worth the effort. If chive blossoms are in the market when you're shopping, grab them up for garnish. Edible violets would be beautiful too.

1 pound veal sweetbreads
1 tablespoon olive oil
1 tablespoon unsalted butter
1 tablespoon unbleached all-purpose flour
¾ cup dry white wine
¾ cup homemade beef stock (see Index) or canned broth
1 cup artichoke hearts (fresh, frozen and thawed, or canned in water and drained), quartered
¼ cup heavy or whipping cream
Salt and freshly ground black pepper, to taste
1 tablespoon snipped fresh chives
4 slices brioche or other rich egg bread, toasted
4 whole chives, for garnish

1. Place the sweetbreads in a bowl, cover with cold water, and soak for 1 hour.

2. Bring a saucepan of water to a boil, add the sweetbreads, and simmer for 5 minutes. Drain the sweetbreads and place them in a bowl of ice water; leave them for several minutes, until they are fully cooled. Then use a sharp knife to trim away all the membranes. Pat dry with paper towels, and slice into ½-inch pieces.

3. Heat the oil and butter in a large skillet. Add the sweetbreads, and sauté over medium heat until lightly browned, 1 minute each side. Using a slotted spoon, remove them from the skillet and keep warm.

4. Sprinkle the flour into the skillet. Add the wine, stock, and artichoke hearts. Stir, and cook until the sauce has thickened, 5 minutes. Add the cream, salt and pepper, and snipped chives. Cook an additional 2 minutes.

5. Place a slice of toasted brioche on each plate. Spoon the sweetbreads onto the toast, and top with the artichokes and sauce. Garnish each with a whole chive.

4 portions

CHILI, BURGERS, MEAT LOAVES, AND HASH

We loved them as kids and will never be so grown up that we lose our passion for the ground meat favorites—chili, hamburgers, meat loaves, and hash. They seem to us endlessly versatile and appealing in all their guises—mild or spicy, easy and casual or presented with panache. We know from long experience that everyone has a grand time when we bring out one of these age-old favorites. The compliments are always heartwarming.

CHILI FEVER

C hili, chili con carne, Texas red—whatever you affectionately call this savory mix of meat and heat—is one of those dishes that most people feel just misses when made by someone else, while their own recipe is a deeply held family secret that should win blue-ribbon honors.

Chili originated in Texas, where native cooks improved the cowboys' chuck-wagon stews with their incomparable blend of chiles and seasonings. The first chili joint opened its doors in Texas sometime before the turn of the century, and by the 1920s the Texans' bowl of red was a familiar sight just about anywhere west of the Mississippi.

Americans now have an abiding love for chili, both the eating and the making of it. It's always been a recipe people love to fiddle with. There is no consensus as to the correct degree of heat or what source should provide it—red pepper sauce, dried or fresh chiles, or cayenne pepper. But most everyone agrees that taste-bud-decimating hotness is way off base.

No one can agree, either, on which meat or beans are best, or if in fact, beans are needed at all. Many prefer a lean cut of beef; others go for the high-grade sirloin. Some mix in a little pork or chicken with the beef. Some cook cubed meat until meltingly tender; others start with the meat already ground. We're open to chili every which way—with meats, or with beans and vegetables—just as long as it's hearty and packed with flavor.

ITALIAN CHILI

T his chili borrows a few Italian flavors.

2 tablespoons peanut oil
1 cup chopped onion
1 cup chopped fennel bulb
1 fresh red chile pepper, seeded and minced (about 1 ½ teaspoons)
1 pound hot Italian sausages, halved lengthwise and cut into 1-inch pieces
1 ½ pounds skinless, boneless chicken thighs, rinsed, patted dry, and cut into 1-inch chunks
1 ¾ cups Berta's Chicken Stock (see Index) or canned broth
1 cup crushed tomatoes in purée
¼ cup tomato paste
1 tablespoon balsamic vinegar
1 tablespoon dried oregano
1 tablespoon ground cumin
1 ½ cups fresh or frozen (thawed) corn kernels (2 to 3 cobs)
4 ripe plum tomatoes, halved, seeded, and coarsely chopped
¼ cup chopped fresh basil leaves
Sour cream, for garnish

1. Heat the oil in a dutch oven. Add the onion, fennel, and chile, and cook, stirring, over medium heat, 5 minutes. Then add the sausages, and cook another 10 minutes, stirring occasionally.

2. Add the chicken pieces and cook, stirring, 10 minutes.

3. Tilt the pan, and spoon off all but 2 tablespoons fat. Stir the stock, crushed tomatoes, tomato paste, vinegar, oregano, and cumin into the pot. Bring to a boil, reduce the heat, and simmer, partially covered, for 30 minutes.

4. Stir in the corn, chopped tomatoes, and basil. Cook 5 minutes. Top each serving with a dollop of sour cream.

6 to 8 portions

VEGETABLE CHILI

Have a pot of chili ready when everyone comes over to watch the Super Bowl. This vegetable chili is just as gutsy as any made with meat. Everyone will love it!

¾ cup olive oil
2 zucchini, cut into ½-inch dice
2 onions, cut into ½-inch dice
4 cloves garlic, finely chopped
2 large red bell peppers, cored and cut into ¼-inch dice
1 can (35 ounces) Italian plum tomatoes, with their juice
1½ pounds ripe plum tomatoes, cut into 1-inch dice
2 tablespoons good-quality chili powder
1 tablespoon ground cumin
1 tablespoon dried basil
1 tablespoon dried oregano
2 teaspoons freshly ground black pepper
1 teaspoon salt
1 teaspoon fennel seeds
½ cup chopped fresh Italian (flat-leaf) parsley
1 cup canned dark red kidney beans, drained
1 cup canned chick-peas (garbanzos), drained
½ cup chopped fresh dill
2 tablespoons fresh lemon juice
1 cup sour cream
2 cups grated Monterey Jack cheese
4 scallions (green onions), white bulb and 3 inches green, sliced on the diagonal

1. Heat ½ cup of the oil in a large skillet over medium heat. Add the zucchini, and sauté until just tender, 5 to 7 minutes. Transfer the zucchini to a large flameproof casserole or dutch oven.

2. Heat the remaining ¼ cup oil in the skillet over low heat. Add the onions, garlic, and bell peppers. Sauté until just wilted, about 10 minutes.

Transfer the mixture to the casserole, along with the oil remaining in the skillet.

3. Place the casserole over low heat. Add the canned tomatoes and their juice, the fresh tomatoes, chili powder, cumin, basil, oregano, pepper, salt, fennel seeds, and parsley. Cook, uncovered, stirring often, for 30 minutes.

4. Stir in the kidney beans, chick-peas, dill, and lemon juice; cook for another 15 minutes. Stir well, and adjust the seasonings to taste. Serve with bowls of sour cream, grated cheese, and sliced scallions alongside.

8 portions

CHILI POWDER

Although the combination of chile peppers and oregano for seasoning has been traced to the Aztecs, the premixed blend is said to be the invention of early Texans. Chili powder today is a blend of dried chiles, red peppers, oregano, cumin, and garlic powder. Most chili powder is not particularly pungent, but you can make chili as hot as you like by adding cayenne pepper or ground dried chiles. Of course, we all have different sensitivities to hotness. When we are unsure of our guests' tolerance for heat, we keep the chili on the mild side and put a bottle of *picante* sauce, bowls of red pepper flakes and chopped jalapeños, and a tiny dish of cayenne on the table with the other chili condiments. Suggest to anyone not familiar with your chili to keep tasting it while increasing the heat just a pinch at a time.

HELL'S KITCHEN CHILI

A chunky beef chili perfected in our friend Sidney's kitchen, just off Ninth Avenue in the thirties, an area of New York City that's always "hot" in itself. Hopefully you'll have a square dance to go to or a calf to wrestle to work this off.

3 tablespoons peanut oil
1 onion, chopped
2 teaspoons good-quality chili powder
2 teaspoons ground cumin
1 teaspoon dried oregano
1 teaspoon dried red pepper flakes
2 pounds beef bottom round, cut into ½-inch cubes
2 cups crushed tomatoes
1¾ cups homemade beef stock (see Index) or canned broth
¼ cup tomato paste
2 slices Canadian bacon, minced
1 tablespoon sugar
Salt and freshly ground black pepper, to taste

GARNISHES
Chopped red, yellow, and orange bell peppers (mixed)
Minced watercress or arugula
Snipped fresh chives
Crumbled cooked bacon
Sour cream
Crumbled corn chips

1. Heat 2 tablespoons of the oil in a flameproof casserole or dutch oven. Add the onion, chili powder, cumin, oregano, and red pepper flakes. Cook over medium-low heat for 5 minutes.

2. Add the remaining 1 tablespoon oil, and brown the meat over high heat, in batches if necessary.

3. Stir in the tomatoes, stock, tomato paste, Canadian bacon, and sugar. Simmer, uncovered, until the beef is tender, 1¾ hours, covering the pot when the mixture becomes thick. Season with salt and pepper.

4. Serve the chili in a large bowl, surrounded by small bowls of the garnishes.

4 to 6 portions

PINTO BEAN CHILI

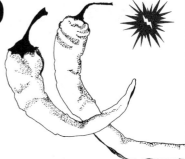

No longer an addition to a meat chili, these beans stand on their own. The texture of the beans is just right—cooked in the microwave for less than an hour.

1 cup dried pinto beans, soaked overnight in cold water, drained
3 cups Berta's Chicken Stock or homemade beef stock (see Index) or canned broth
1 cup New Basic Tomato Sauce (see Index)
¾ cup fresh or frozen (thawed) corn kernels (1 cob)
¾ cup diced zucchini
½ cup diced ripe tomato
¼ cup chopped scallions (green onions)
¼ cup chopped cilantro (fresh coriander)
2 tablespoons balsamic vinegar
2 cloves garlic, minced
1 teaspoon ground cumin
½ teaspoon dried oregano
½ teaspoon paprika
½ teaspoon salt
½ teaspoon sugar
¼ teaspoon cayenne pepper
Freshly ground black pepper, to taste

1. In a 2-quart microwave-safe casserole, cook the beans and stock, covered, at full power (650 to 700 watts) for 45 minutes. Remove from the oven and let stand 10 minutes.

2. Stir in the remaining ingredients, cover, and cook 5 minutes. Serve.

4 portions

Note: This recipe was cooked on High (full power, 650 to 700 watts) in a carousel microwave, using microwave-safe containers.

If your microwave is less powerful, you will have to allow for more cooking time (approximately 1½ times the amount called for—but watch carefully); if it does not have a carousel, you may have to rotate the dish while it is cooking.

SUPER BOWL LUNCH

●

Curried Zucchini Soup

●

Pinto Bean Chili
Roasted Red Pepper Biscuits
Tomato Bread Salad
Dos Equis Beer

●

Almond Sour Cream Cheesecake

BLACK BEAN VEGETABLE CHILI

A spicy, full-bodied black bean chili, made more contemporary with sweet corn. Make it as hot as you like, and serve three garnishes for cooling down—sour cream, scallions, and grated Monterey Jack.

1 eggplant, cut into ½-inch cubes
1 tablespoon coarse (kosher) salt
½ cup olive oil
2 onions, cut into ¼-inch dice
2 zucchini, cut into ¼-inch dice
1 red bell pepper, cored, seeded, and cut into ¼-inch dice
1 yellow bell pepper, cored, seeded, and cut into ¼-inch dice
4 large cloves garlic, coarsely chopped
8 ripe plum tomatoes, cut into 1-inch cubes
1 cup homemade vegetable broth (see Index)
1 cup chopped fresh Italian (flat-leaf) parsley
½ cup slivered fresh basil leaves
3 tablespoons best-quality chili powder
1½ tablespoons ground cumin
1 tablespoon dried oregano
1 teaspoon freshly ground black pepper
½ teaspoon dried red pepper flakes
Salt to taste (optional)
2 cups cooked black beans
1½ cups fresh or frozen (thawed) corn kernels (2 to 3 cobs)
½ cup chopped fresh dill
¼ cup fresh lemon juice
Sour cream, for garnish
Grated Monterey Jack cheese, for garnish
3 scallions (green onions), white bulb and 3 inches green, thinly sliced, for garnish

1. Place the eggplant in a colander. Toss it with the coarse salt, and let it sit for 1 hour to remove the moisture. Pat dry with paper towels.

2. Heat ¼ cup of the oil in a large flameproof casserole. Add the onions, zucchini, bell peppers, and garlic. Sauté over medium-low heat for about 10 minutes.

3. Place the remaining ¼ cup oil in a skillet, and cook the eggplant over medium-high heat until just tender, about 10 minutes. Using a slotted spoon, transfer the eggplant to the casserole.

4. Add the tomatoes, broth, ½ cup of the parsley, basil, and spices to the casserole. Cook over low heat for 30 minutes, stirring occasionally.

5. Add the black beans, corn, dill, and lemon juice. Cook another 15 minutes. Adjust the seasonings, and stir in the remaining ½ cup parsley. Serve hot, garnished with a dollop of sour cream, grated cheese, and scallions.

8 portions

JALAPEÑO CHILI

Hot, hot, hot! Lots of jalapeños and hot sausages, mixed with all our favorite chili ingredients. Have several varieties of iced Mexican beer on hand, to put out the fire.

1 pound hot Italian sausages, cut into 1-inch lengths
1 pound sweet Italian sausages, cut into 1-inch lengths
¼ cup olive oil
2 cups coarsely chopped onions
6 cloves garlic, minced (3 tablespoons)
2 pounds ground beef chuck
2 green bell peppers, cored, seeded, and coarsely chopped
2 red bell peppers, cored, seeded, and coarsely chopped
6 fresh jalapeño peppers (5 to 8 ounces total), cored, seeded, and cut into ⅛-inch dice (see Note)
3 cans (35 ounces each) Italian plum tomatoes, drained (5 cups tomatoes)
1 cup dry red wine
1 cup chopped fresh parsley
2 tablespoons tomato paste
6 tablespoons best-quality chili powder
3 tablespoons ground cumin
2 tablespoons dried oregano
1 tablespoon dried basil
2 teaspoons salt
½ tablespoon fennel seeds
2 teaspoons freshly ground black pepper
2 pounds ripe plum tomatoes, quartered
Grated Monterey Jack cheese, for garnish (optional)
Sour cream, for garnish (optional)
Sliced scallions (green onions), white bulb and 3 inches green, for garnish (optional)

1. Place a large heavy skillet over medium heat, and sauté the sausages until well browned. (If necessary, add ¼ cup water while browning.) Transfer the sausages to paper towels to drain.

2. Heat the oil in a deep, heavy, flameproof casserole over low heat. Add the onions and garlic, and cook until just wilted, 5 minutes.

3. Raise the heat to medium, and crumble in the ground chuck. Cook, stirring frequently to break up the pieces, until the meat is well browned.

4. Add the drained sausages, bell peppers, and jalapeño peppers to the casserole. Cook, stirring frequently, until the peppers are slightly wilted, 10 minutes.

5. Remove the casserole from the heat, and stir in the drained tomatoes, wine, parsley, tomato paste, and all the herbs and spices (do not add the fresh tomatoes).

6. Return the casserole to medium heat, and cook slowly, stirring frequently, 10 minutes. Then add the fresh tomatoes and cook another 10 minutes.

7. Serve the chili in bowls, garnished with cheese, sour cream, and scallions.

8 to 10 portions

Note: Remember, when working with hot peppers, it is best to wear rubber gloves. Do not rub your eyes, mouth, or other sensitive areas of your face, and be sure to wash your hands with soap and water immediately after dicing the peppers.

TONING DOWN THE HEAT

Condiments are the best way to soften the spiciness of your favorite chili. Put out a platter of raw celery and carrot sticks and individual bowls of chopped onions, soft tortillas, sour cream with lime wedges or mixed with lime juice and cilantro, grated Monterey Jack or Cheddar cheese, cole slaw, guacamole, and a big basket of corn bread. If your recipe doesn't include beans, have your favorites ready to go. We like chili over a bed of stewed pinto, kidney, or red beans, but we know people who always cook up a pot of rice.

AMERICA'S BEST

Everyone from one to one hundred knows just how they like their hamburgers. Some like ground sirloin, some round and some chuck; some add cream, others eggs. Hamburgers can be sautéed in an iron skillet sprinkled with a little salt, or broiled, or grilled. They can be prepared thick, thin, small, grand. Some mix in onion; others add herbs, grated cheese, lemon or lime juice. Some stretch the meat with bread crumbs, bulgur, vegetables, nuts, or cereals.

Once the burger is made, it's a question of what you like on top: grilled or raw onions, sliced tomatoes, melted Cheddar, bacon or ham, lettuce, mustard, ketchup, chili sauce, relish, herb butter, or just plain natural. The list goes on and on. One thing is sure—no matter who has the latest twist on the burger, you must have it your way.

A MEAL IN A BURGER

When you're eating alone and want to be really good to yourself, make up this New Basics staple. Of course, if company's coming, just multiply out the ingredient amounts, and be good to all your friends too.

6 ounces ground beef chuck or round
1 egg yolk
1 tablespoon cooked spinach, well drained and chopped
1 teaspoon grated onion
Salt and freshly ground black pepper, to taste
1 tablespoon grated Swiss or Cheddar cheese
Mayonnaise, to taste
Ketchup, to taste
1 sesame seed hamburger bun, toasted
1 slice ripe tomato

1. Preheat the broiler.

2. Combine the beef, egg yolk, spinach, onion, and salt and pepper in a bowl, and mix well.

3. Form three quarters of the meat mixture into a patty, reserving the remainder. Make an indentation in the center of the patty, and fill it with the cheese. Cover the cheese with the reserved meat, and form a finished patty.

4. Broil the patty for 2½ minutes on each side for a juicy rare burger—or longer according to taste.

5. Spread mayonnaise and ketchup on each side of the toasted bun. Place the burger on the bottom half, top it with the tomato slice, and cover it with the other half of the bun.

1 portion

MEADOW BURGERS

A burger with lots of healthy salad bar fixings. All the ingredients blend together beautifully for a flavorful—yet different—broiled treat.

8 ounces lean ground beef
1 cup finely chopped fresh spinach
½ cup finely grated peeled parsnip
½ cup cooked chick-peas (garbanzos), mashed
¼ cup chopped onion
1 teaspoon grated lemon zest
1 teaspoon salt
Freshly ground black pepper, to taste

1. Preheat the broiler.

2. Combine all the ingredients in a bowl, and mix until well blended. Shape the mixture into four 4-inch patties.

3. Broil the patties close to the heat source for 3 minutes per side for rare—or longer to taste. Serve immediately.

4 portions

KITCHEN TABLE FAMILY DINNER

★

Corn Chowder

★

Not So Sloppy Joe
All-American Baked Beans
Gazpacho Salad

★

Berta's Carrot Cake

NOT SO SLOPPY JOE

The origins of this dish are unknown (there probably wasn't even a Joe), and its rather messy appearance and tendency to drip off the roll surely make it "sloppy"—but it's delicious!

2 tablespoons olive oil
1 cup finely chopped onion
1 rib celery, minced
½ green bell pepper, cored, seeded, and chopped
½ teaspoon dried oregano
1 pound lean ground beef
½ cup ketchup
½ cup New Basic Tomato Sauce (see Index)
¼ cup water
2 tablespoons red wine vinegar
1 tablespoon Worcestershire sauce
1 tablespoon (packed) dark brown sugar
1 teaspoon salt
Freshly ground black pepper, to taste
Tabasco sauce, to taste (optional)
4 poppy seed rolls, halved and toasted, or 8 slices corn bread, toasted

1. In a 2½ quart microwave-safe casserole, cook the oil on full power (650 to 700 watts) for 2 minutes.

2. Stir in the onion, celery, bell pepper, and oregano. Cook 4 minutes.

3. Crumble in the ground beef, breaking it up with a spoon. Cook 2 minutes; stir again to break up any clumps, and cook another 3 minutes.

4. Stir in the remaining ingredients through the black pepper, and cook 4 minutes. Stir again, add the Tabasco, if using, and cook until bubbling and heated through, 2 minutes. Spoon over toasted poppy seed rolls, and serve.

4 portions

Note: This recipe was cooked on High (full power, 650 to 700 watts) in a carousel microwave, using microwave-safe containers.

If your microwave is less powerful, you will have to allow for more cooking time (approximately 1½ times the amount called for—but watch carefully); if it does not have a carousel, you may have to rotate the dish while it is cooking.

GOOD OLD MEAT LOAF

Saturday night dinner in the kitchen was often meat loaf when we were growing up. Many years later, we're still deciding whether it was best straight from the oven or the next day between white bread smothered with ketchup. Back then meat loaf was pretty standard stuff, but today it has become very chic as a great dish for playing with flavors. Meat loaf is just one of those foods we're most comfortable with—but comfort, we've learned, need not be boring.

CAJUN MEAT LOAF

Over the past several years the flavor of Cajun cooking has swept our country like wildfire. It should be hot, but not so hot that the flavors of the spices are lost.

2 tablespoons olive oil
8 ounces andouille or other Cajun sausage, finely chopped
1 cup chopped onion
1 red bell pepper, cored, seeded, and finely chopped
1 fresh cayenne or hot red chile pepper, seeded and minced (about 1½ teaspoons)
2 cloves garlic, minced
½ teaspoon dried thyme leaves
½ teaspoon dried oregano
½ cup New Basic Tomato Sauce (see Index) or good-quality canned
½ cup homemade beef stock (see Index) or canned broth
¼ cup fresh bread crumbs
2 pounds ground beef
1 teaspoon salt
Freshly ground black pepper, to taste

1. Heat the oil in a large skillet. Add the sausage, onion, bell pepper, cayenne pepper, garlic, thyme, and oregano. Cook over low heat, covered, for 15 minutes. Transfer the mixture to a bowl, and cool to room temperature.

2. Preheat the oven to 350°F.

3. Stir the tomato sauce, stock, and crumbs into the cooled mixture. Break up the ground beef and add it to the mixture. Season with the salt and pepper, and mix gently (do not overmix) until well blended.

4. Pack the mixture into a 9 x 5 x 3-inch loaf pan. Bake 45 minutes.

5. Remove the pan from the oven, and pour off some of the fat. Cover the loaf loosely and let it stand 10 minutes. Then slice and serve.

8 portions

SUNDAY BY THE FIRE

▼

Cream of Tomato Soup

▼

Market Street Meat Loaf
Garlic Mashed Potatoes
Six Pepper Slaw
Zinfandel

Little Boston Cream Pies

MARKET STREET MEAT LOAF

Venice, California's 72 Market Street is one hot restaurant. Several years ago we were served meat loaf and mashed potatoes, and we have never forgotten the wonderful flavors. This meat loaf is a hallmark of the New Basics.

It seems Tony Bill suggested including meat loaf on the menu at the restaurant. He discussed it with chef Leonard Schwartz who rolled his eyes thinking meat loaf was boring, but he began experimenting. Much to his surprise, Craig Claiborne came out for the recipe, *Vogue* magazine has termed it the "ultimate meat loaf" and "Good Morning America" flew him to New York to do the recipe on the show. Leonard says, "I suppose in the final analysis, Tony had a very good idea."

3 tablespoons unsalted butter
¾ cup finely chopped onion
¾ cup finely chopped scallions (green onions), white bulb and 3 inches green
½ cup finely chopped carrots
¼ cup finely chopped celery
¼ cup minced red bell pepper
¼ cup minced green bell pepper
2 teaspoons minced garlic
Salt, to taste
1 teaspoon freshly ground black pepper
½ teaspoon ground white pepper
¼ teaspoon cayenne pepper
1 teaspoon ground cumin
½ teaspoon freshly grated nutmeg
3 eggs, well beaten
½ cup ketchup
½ cup half-and-half
2 pounds lean ground beef chuck
12 ounces sausage meat (not fennel-flavored Italian sausage)
¾ cup fine fresh bread crumbs, toasted (see Index)

1. Preheat the oven to 375°F.
2. Melt the butter in a heavy skillet, and add the onion, scallions, carrots, celery, bell peppers, and garlic. Cook, stirring often, until the moisture from the vegetables has evaporated, 10 minutes. Set aside to cool; then refrigerate, covered, until chilled, at least 1 hour.

3. Combine the salt, black pepper, white pepper, cayenne, cumin, nutmeg, and eggs in a mixing bowl, and beat well. Add the ketchup and half-and-half. Blend thoroughly.
4. Add the chuck, sausage, and bread crumbs to the egg mixture. Then add the chilled vegetables and mix thoroughly with your hands, kneading for 5 minutes.
5. With damp hands, form the mixture into an oval approximately 17 x 4½ x 1½ inches—resembling a long loaf of bread.
6. Place the meat loaf in a baking dish, and place the dish inside a larger pan. Pour boiling water into the larger pan until it reaches halfway up the sides of the baking dish.
7. Place the pan in the oven and bake for 35 to 40 minutes.
8. Remove the baking dish from the water bath, and let the meat loaf rest for 20 minutes before slicing and serving.

8 to 10 portions

WHAT'S IN THE BEEF?

Now that Americans seem determined to get the fat out, they are starting with their favorite—ground beef. We still think you need some fat to make a good burger or meat loaf.

A high fat content, such as the 22 percent in most ground chuck, binds the beef and delivers both juiciness and flavor. For chili, beef with a lower fat content, such as ground round (about 15 percent fat), is really best. By law ground beef cannot be more than 30 percent fat. If hamburgers or meat loaf are on your weekly menu, you might look for beef graded select instead of choice; select has less fat than choice and is less expensive as well.

MEAT LOAF UN-DEUX-TROIS

A meat loaf of three layers—subtle yet complex enough to be served when company's coming.

4 ounces fresh spinach leaves
1½ pounds ground beef
1 pound ground veal
¾ cup chopped onion
6 tablespoons fresh bread crumbs
5 tablespoons milk
1 egg
1¼ teaspoons salt
Freshly ground black pepper, to taste
½ cup minced celery
½ teaspoon dried thyme leaves
½ cup shredded carrot
½ teaspoon ground cumin
1 tablespoon chopped fresh dill

1. Preheat the oven to 350°F.
2. Rinse the spinach leaves well and place them, with just the water clinging to the leaves, in a saucepan. Cook over medium-low heat, covered, until wilted, 3 minutes. Drain thoroughly, and then squeeze dry to remove as much moisture as possible. Chop the spinach, and set aside.
3. In a large bowl, gently toss the beef, one fourth of the veal, ½ cup of the onion, 4 tablespoons each of the crumbs and milk, the egg, 1 teaspoon of the salt, and pepper.
4. Divide the mixture in half. Into one half stir the celery and thyme. Into the other half stir the carrot and cumin. Set both mixtures aside.
5. In another bowl toss the remaining veal, ¼ cup chopped onion, 2 tablespoons crumbs, 1 tablespoon milk, ¼ teaspoon salt, the chopped spinach, pepper, and the dill.
6. Pat the mixture containing celery into a 9 x 5 x 3-inch loaf pan. Cover it with the spinach and veal mixture, and then top with the carrot mixture. Round the top slightly.
7. Bake 45 minutes. Remove the pan from the oven, and pour off some of the fat. Cover the loaf loosely, and let it stand 15 minutes. Then slice and serve.

8 portions

HERBED MEAT LOAF

Basil pesto, chives, and watercress give an intense herb flavor to this loaf. Hard-cooked eggs placed in the center make a decorative presentation.

1½ pounds ground beef
8 ounces ground veal
3 cubes Basil Pesto (see Index)
½ cup chopped watercress leaves
¼ cup snipped fresh chives
2 tablespoons chopped fresh oregano leaves
¼ cup milk
¼ cup fresh bread crumbs
1 teaspoon salt
Freshly ground black pepper, to taste
4 hard-cooked eggs

1. Preheat the oven to 350°F.
2. Toss all the ingredients except the eggs in a large bowl, mixing well.
3. Pack half the mixture into a 9 x 5 x 3-inch loaf pan. Arrange the eggs in a row down the center. Cover with the remaining meat mixture, rounding the top slightly.
4. Bake 45 minutes. Pour off some of the fat, and let the loaf stand, loosely covered, about 15 minutes. Then slice and serve.

8 portions

DON'T MASH THE HASH

Traditionally, hash has been made out of leftovers—cooked beef chopped or put through a meat grinder, yesterday's boiled potatoes diced fine, and for sizzle, a little onion. This cleaning-out-the-fridge meal was doused with gravy or maybe topped with a poached egg or, for the truly desperate, buried under ketchup.

Hash is centuries old, but its bad reputation seems to stick with it. We call a restaurant that serves so-so food a hash house. Making a hash of something is making a mess.

Because we like food that is both simple and delicious, we've come to believe it's high time to take a new approach to hash. We now make it from fresh ingredients, too, but feel there's no reason hash can't be pretty and taste good—even when made with leftovers. This all-American dish needs little to give it a bright taste and fresh look.

COZY TURKEY HASH

On Thanksgiving weekend (or any time you have the good luck to have leftover turkey or chicken), wake up palates with this perfect brunch dish. Served with a hot mulled apple cider, it's glorious.

2 cups cubed cooked turkey or chicken
1 ½ cups cubed cooked potato (white, sweet, or both)
¼ cup chopped onion
¼ cup chopped red bell pepper
¼ cup chopped mushrooms
3 tablespoons chopped fresh parsley
6 tablespoons heavy or whipping cream
1 egg, lightly beaten
1 clove garlic, minced
1 teaspoon Worcestershire sauce
1 teaspoon good-quality curry powder
½ teaspoon paprika
½ teaspoon salt
Freshly ground black pepper, to taste
1 tablespoon vegetable oil

1. Preheat the broiler.

2. Combine the turkey, potato, onion, bell pepper, mushrooms, and parsley in a large bowl. Toss well.

3. In another bowl, stir together the cream, egg, garlic, Worcestershire, curry powder, paprika, salt, and pepper.

4. Stir the cream mixture into the turkey, and let it stand for 30 minutes, stirring occasionally.

5. Heat the oil in a 10-inch ovenproof nonstick skillet over medium heat. Add the turkey mixture, cover, and cook until the bottom is set, 5 minutes.

6. Transfer the skillet to the broiler, and broil until the top is set and golden, 5 minutes. Serve immediately.

2 to 3 portions

CONFETTI CORNED BEEF HASH

This is a remarkable hash that's pretty enough to be the center of attention for brunch, lunch, or supper.

It's a great way to use leftovers, dicing red and green peppers, potatoes, corned beef, and onions for a charming confetti effect. To turn it into traditional Red Flannel Hash, add some diced cooked beets.

2 white boiling potatoes, cut into ¼-inch dice
6 tablespoons (¾ stick) unsalted butter
1 onion, cut into ¼-inch dice
1 red bell pepper, cored, seeded, and cut into ¼-inch dice
1 green bell pepper, cored, seeded, and cut into ¼-inch dice
1 pound cooked corned beef, cut into ¼-inch dice
5 tablespoons chopped fresh Italian (flat-leaf) parsley
1 teaspoon dried thyme
1 teaspoon coarsely ground black pepper
Salt, to taste
2 tablespoons olive oil
6 poached eggs (see Note)
2 scallions (green onions), white bulb and 3 inches green, thinly sliced

1. Place the diced potatoes in a saucepan, and cover with cold water. Bring to a boil, and simmer until just tender, about 10 minutes. Drain, transfer to a large bowl, and set aside.

2. Melt 4 tablespoons of the butter in a skillet, and add the onion and peppers. Cook over medium heat until wilted, 5 minutes. Add the vegetables to the potatoes in the large bowl.

3. Add the corned beef, 4 tablespoons of the parsley, the thyme, pepper, and salt to the vegetables. Stir well.

4. Heat the remaining 2 tablespoons butter and the oil in a 12-inch skillet. Add the hash, and spread it out evenly. Place a heavy lid or plate that is slightly smaller than the skillet on top of the hash, weighting it down. Cook over medium heat until the corned beef has browned slightly, 10 minutes. Remove the lid and turn the hash over with a large spatula. (This hash will not form a solid pancake shape.) Cook until the other side has browned slightly, 5 minutes.

5. Divide the hash among six plates, and top each portion with a poached egg. Sprinkle with the scallions and the remaining 1 tablespoon parsley.

6 portions

Note: To poach eggs, fill a nonstick skillet with water. Add 1 tablespoon of cider vinegar, and bring to a gentle simmer. Break an egg into a cup and carefully slide it into the simmering water. Cook for 2½ to 3 minutes. Remove the egg using a slotted spoon. Set it aside to keep warm, and poach the remaining eggs in the same water. (The vinegar helps the egg white hold a round shape.)

BRUNCH ON THE PORCH

Canadian Cheese Soup

Confetti Corned Beef Hash
Home Fries
Sweet and Sour Corn Relish

Lemon Shortbread Bars

FRANCES' CHORIZOS

Isabelle Nicholson, Julee's next-door neighbor on the beach in Saugatuck, is from a great big, loving Mexican family—fifteen children. And their mother, Frances, is some cook! We'd never thought of making our own chorizos until Frances taught us, and what a difference they make. Chorizos, spicy Spanish sausages, are delicious sautéed and used on Black Bean Nachos or shaped into hamburger-size patties and pan-fried with a poached egg on top for brunch. Add a dollop of sour cream and salsa.

1 pound ground pork (preferably pork butt)
½ cup cider vinegar
1 tablespoon coarse (kosher) salt
1 tablespoon minced garlic
1½ tablespoons good-quality chili powder
1½ tablespoons ground cumin

1. Place the ground pork in a glass or ceramic bowl. Add the cider vinegar and coarse salt, cover, and refrigerate overnight.

2. Add the garlic, chili powder, and cumin to the pork, and stir well. Let the mixture marinate 1 hour more.

3. Shape the meat into hamburger-size patties.

4. Heat a cast-iron skillet until quite hot. Add the patties, and sauté for 3 to 4 minutes on each side.

8 patties

THE SOUTH OF FRANCE

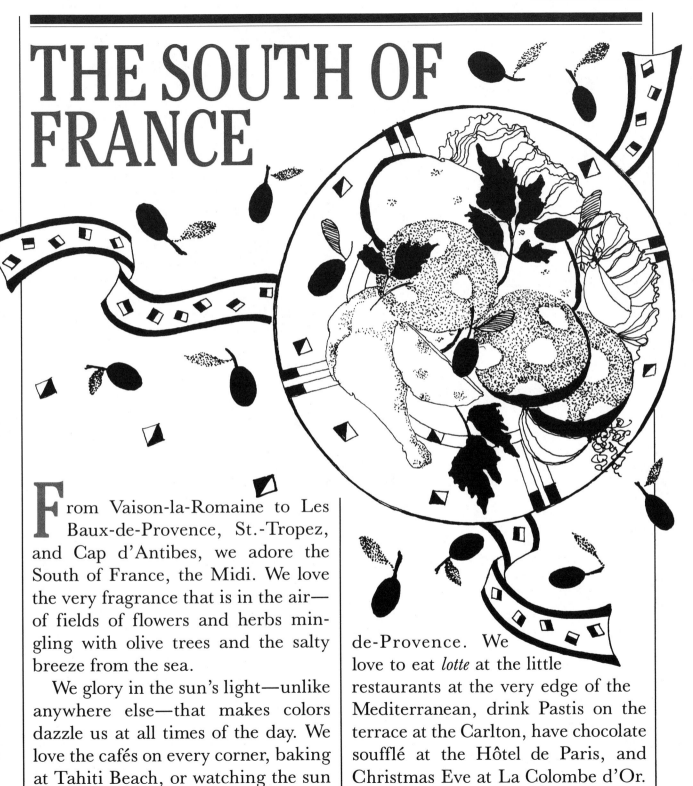

From Vaison-la-Romaine to Les Baux-de-Provence, St.-Tropez, and Cap d'Antibes, we adore the South of France, the Midi. We love the very fragrance that is in the air— of fields of flowers and herbs mingling with olive trees and the salty breeze from the sea.

We glory in the sun's light—unlike anywhere else—that makes colors dazzle us at all times of the day. We love the cafés on every corner, baking at Tahiti Beach, or watching the sun set on the white rocks in Les Baux- de-Provence. We love to eat *lotte* at the little restaurants at the very edge of the Mediterranean, drink Pastis on the terrace at the Carlton, have chocolate soufflé at the Hôtel de Paris, and Christmas Eve at La Colombe d'Or. It's all pure bliss.

SALADE NIÇOISE

Just the mention of *salade niçoise* evokes long, lazy lunches at cafés overlooking the sea on the French Riviera—lunches that are simply this salad, a long chewy baguette, and a bottle of chilled rosé.

Purists in Nice insist that a *salade niçoise* be served on a round or oval dish, not in a bowl, and consist only of raw vegetables, and no vinegar in the dressing. Our friend Julia Child, long a part-time resident of France, cannot conceive of this salad without each ingredient being tossed separately with extra virgin olive oil before it is added to the plate. We often partially prepare the plates, serving the capers, olives, eggs, and lemon in separate bowls, to allow for personal creativity at the table.

4 red new potatoes, well rinsed
8 ounces green beans, trimmed and halved lengthwise
1 can (6½ ounces) white-meat tuna
2 tablespoons chopped red onion
1 tablespoon tiny capers, drained
2 tablespoons plus 1½ teaspoons fresh lemon juice
2 tablespoons extra virgin olive oil
Freshly ground black pepper, to taste
2 teaspoons chopped fresh rosemary leaves
1 teaspoon minced garlic
Coarse (kosher) salt, to taste
2 ripe plum tomatoes
3 tablespoons chopped fresh Italian (flat-leaf) parsley
¼ cup black and green Niçoise olives (mixed)
1 hard-cooked egg, grated
8 lemon wedges

1. Preheat the oven to 350°F.

2. Prick the potatoes with the tines of a fork, and place them in a baking dish. Bake for 1 hour. Set aside to cool.

3. Bring a saucepan of water to a boil and add the beans. Simmer until just tender, 4 to 5 minutes. Drain, rinse under cold water, and drain again; pat dry with paper towels, and set aside.

HERBES DE PROVENCE

In Provence as well as throughout France, when fresh herbs are out of season, smart cooks use the traditional mixture of dried herbs that are the very essence of the region. Called herbes de Provence, it can be easily recreated here by combining 1 ounce each of dried thyme, bay leaves, rosemary, summer savory, lavender, cloves, and orange zest. Just remember to use the very best dried herbs you can find. Mix them well and store them in a tightly sealed opaque jar. Use the mixture sparingly until you understand the intricacies of its flavors.

4. Place the tuna in a mixing bowl, and break it into large chunks. Add the red onion, capers, 1 tablespoon of the lemon juice, 2 teaspoons of the olive oil, and pepper. Toss gently with a fork until well combined, and set aside.

5. Cut the cooked potatoes into ¼-inch-thick slices, and place them in a mixing bowl. Add 1 tablespoon of the olive oil, 1½ teaspoons lemon juice, rosemary, garlic, pepper, and coarse salt. Toss to combine, and set aside.

6. Cut the tomatoes into ¼-inch-thick slices and place them in a bowl. Sprinkle with pepper, coarse salt, and 2 tablespoons of the parsley.

7. Just before you are ready to serve the salad, toss the beans with the remaining 1 tablespoon lemon juice and 1 teaspoon olive oil.

8. Arrange the beans in four bunches on a large platter. Divide the potatoes, tuna, and tomatoes into four portions each, and arrange them next to the beans, with the potato and tuna portions surrounded by the tomato slices. Place the olives in the center of the platter, and sprinkle the salad with the grated egg, remaining 1 tablespoon parsley, and a bit more black pepper. Serve with lemon wedges.

4 portions

CASSOULET SALAD

For this salad we've taken the best elements of cassoulet—duck, sausage, and lots of garlic—and combined them with new potatoes, black olives, and a lusty vinaigrette on a contrasting bed of bright green Savoy cabbage leaves.

12 small red new potatoes (1½ to 2 inches in diamater)
¼ cup extra virgin olive oil
½ teaspoon salt
2 teaspoons coarsely ground black pepper
1 duckling (4½ pounds), ready to cook
1 orange, halved
Salt and freshly ground black pepper, to taste
8 ounces fresh French garlic sausages*
1 large head garlic
¾ cup chopped fresh Italian (flat-leaf) parsley
½ cup finely chopped red onion
½ cup Niçoise olives
1¼ cups Cassoulet Vinaigrette (recipe follows)
1 medium head Savoy cabbage

1. Preheat the oven to 400°F.
2. Prick the potatoes all over with the tines of a fork. Place the olive oil in a bowl, and roll the potatoes in it to coat them well; then sprinkle them with the salt and 1 teaspoon of the pepper.
3. Place the potatoes in a shallow baking pan and roast for 1 hour, uncovered, turning them occasionally.
4. Remove the potatoes from the oven, leaving the oven on. Allow them to cool slightly, then cut them into ½-inch-thick slices, and set aside.
5. Clean the duck well; rinse it under cold water, and pat dry. Prick the skin all over with the tines of a fork (this releases the fat while the duck is cooking). Rub the duck inside and out with the orange halves, and sprinkle generously with salt and pepper.
6. Place the duck breast side up in a roasting pan, and roast for 45 minutes.
7. While the duck is cooking, place the sausages in a medium-size saucepan and add 2 quarts of water. Bring to a boil, reduce the heat, and simmer for 40 minutes. Remove the sausages from the water and allow them to cool. Then remove the skin, and cut them into ½-inch rounds; cut the rounds in half crosswise. Set them aside.
8. Separate the garlic cloves (there should be about 24), but do not peel them. Place them in a small saucepan, cover with water, and bring to a boil. Reduce the heat, and simmer for 5 minutes. Drain the garlic cloves, allow them to cool slightly, then peel them.
9. After the duck has cooked for 45 minutes, turn it over, and add the garlic cloves to the pan. Roast for another 10 minutes.
10. Transfer the duck to a platter and allow it to cool. Remove the skin, and shred the meat into 2-inch pieces. Using a slotted spoon, remove the garlic cloves from the pan, and set them aside.
11. Add the potatoes, parsley, red onion, and olives to the vinaigrette, and toss gently to coat. Add the remaining 1 teaspoon coarsely ground pepper.
12. Then add the sausages, duck, and garlic cloves. Gently fold all the ingredients together.
13. Arrange the salad on a large platter, and surround it with bright green inner cabbage leaves.

8 portions

*Available in specialty food stores and many large supermarkets.

CASSOULET VINAIGRETTE

5 teaspoons Dijon mustard
½ cup red wine vinegar
¾ cup extra virgin olive oil

Combine the mustard and vinegar in a large bowl and whisk well. Slowly pour in the olive oil, whisking constantly.

About 1¼ cups

PATRICIA WELLS' ROAST LAMB WITH POTATO AND TOMATO GRATIN

We first met Pat in 1978, when she wrote about us for the food pages of *The New York Times*—our first big story! We liked her immediately and became fast friends, only to learn we would lose her to Paris. But an ocean has not come between us, and Pat and her husband, Walter, have become family. We're sure that those who have followed her wonderfully written *Food Lover's Guides* to Paris and France feel she is their friend, too.

"This dish—or variations of it—has become our 'house special' in Provence," Pat explains. "The recipe was originally offered to me by the village butcher, M. Roland Henny. As the lamb cooks, its wonderful juices drip into the gratin, a mixture of tomatoes, potatoes, and onions. While more traditional recipes call for baking the lamb right in the gratin, I like to let it sit an inch or so above it, on a sturdy cake stand or an oven rack that rests right on the gratin dish, so the lamb roasts, doesn't steam. Serve this with a solid red wine, such as a Côtes-du-Rhône-Villages or Châteauneuf-du-Pape."

7 cloves garlic, 1 halved, the rest coarsely chopped
2 pounds baking potatoes, peeled and very thinly sliced
Coarse (kosher) salt, to taste
Freshly ground black pepper, to taste
2 teaspoons fresh thyme leaves
2 large onions, very thinly sliced
5 ripe tomatoes, sliced
⅔ cup dry white wine
⅓ cup extra virgin olive oil
1 leg of lamb (6 to 7 pounds)

1. Preheat the oven to 400°F.

2. Rub the bottom of a large oval porcelain gratin dish (about 16 x 10 x 2 inches) with the garlic halves. Arrange the potatoes in a single layer in the dish, and season them with one third of the coarse salt, pepper, thyme, and chopped garlic. Place the sliced onions in a single layer on top of this, and season as you did the potatoes. Layer the tomatoes on top of the onions, and season with the remaining coarse salt, pepper, thyme, and chopped garlic. Add the white wine and the oil.

3. Trim the thicker portions of fat from the lamb. Season the lamb all over with coarse salt and pepper. Place the gratin dish in the oven, and set a sturdy cake rack or an oven rack directly on top of it. Set the lamb on the rack, so that the juices will drip into the gratin.

4. Roast, uncovered, for about 1¼ hours for rare lamb. Do not turn the lamb. Remove the lamb from the oven and let it sit for 20 minutes before carving. (Turn the oven off, open the door, and keep the gratin warm inside while the lamb rests.)

5. To serve, carve the lamb into thin slices and arrange them on warmed dinner plates or on a serving platter, with the vegetable gratin alongside.

8 to 10 portions

Tearing an herb's leaves seems to bring out more flavor than cutting them. There's added delight in your fingers smelling scrumptious.

MEDITERRANEAN HERO

crusty french bread

lettuce

parsley

tuna

Hard cooked eggs

tomato

purple onion

The great Mediterranean sandwich, *pan bagna,* is often called a Niçoise salad hero. The sandwich is made by splitting a crusty bread loaf in half, scooping out the insides, and drizzling one side with fruity olive oil. Now the mood is set. Add the summer's best tomatoes and red onions, lavishly sprinkle them with white-meat tuna, and a robust tomato sauce spiked with capers. Lighten the touch with crispy lettuce and a mimosa of eggs.

2 loaves French or sourdough bread
2 tablespoons extra virgin olive oil
4 ripe plum tomatoes, chopped
½ red onion, cut into ¼ -inch dice
Freshly ground black pepper, to taste
1 can (6½ ounces) white-meat tuna
2 cups Mediterranean Tomato Sauce (recipe follows)
3 hard-cooked eggs
4 leaves romaine lettuce, rinsed and patted dry
2 tablespoons chopped fresh Italian (flat-leaf) parsley

1. Cut the loaves of bread in half lengthwise, making the bottom half larger. Hollow the halves out, using your hands or a melon baller, to create a shell. Discard the insides, and place the tops aside.

2. Drizzle the olive oil over the bottom halves of the two breads. Layer the tomatoes and red onion over the bread, and season with pepper. Scatter the tuna over the onion, and press it down lightly. Then spread ⅓ cup of the tomato sauce over each loaf.

3. Slice 2 of the eggs, and arrange the slices over the tomato sauce. Slice the lettuce crosswise, and cover the eggs with the lettuce. Then spread the remaining tomato sauce over the lettuce.

4. Grate the remaining egg over the sauce, and sprinkle with the parsley. Replace the tops of the loaves, and press them down lightly.

5. To serve, cut into sandwich-size slices; or slice thinly for hors d'oeuvres.

6 to 8 portions

MEDITERRANEAN TOMATO SAUCE

½ cup extra virgin olive oil
1 can (2 ounces) anchovy fillets, undrained
4 large cloves garlic, crushed
1 can (35 ounces) plum tomatoes, drained
3 tablespoons capers, drained
1½ cups coarsely chopped pitted imported black olives
Freshly ground black pepper, to taste

1. Combine the olive oil, anchovies (with their oil), and garlic in a bowl, and mash to form a paste. Transfer the paste to a heavy saucepan.

2. Add the remaining ingredients, and stir well. Place over medium heat and bring to a simmer. Reduce the heat to low and cook, covered, stirring frequently, for 1 hour.

3. Allow the sauce to cool to room temperature.

Approximately 2 cups

SHEILA'S CASSOULET

The secret behind this legendary dish from Gascony is that all the elements are prepared separately. The magic begins when they are slowly baked together. The first crust that forms on top is buried in the beans toward the final hour of baking and a second crust forms to seal in the flavors of the aromatic mixture underneath. The effort will seem worthwhile when it is brought to the table.

8 ounces fresh pork rind
2 pounds dried white beans (Great Northern or flageolets),
  soaked overnight
1 duckling (4½ to 5 pounds)
Salt and freshly ground black pepper, to taste
1 pound lamb bones (approximately)
2¼ pounds boneless lamb stew meat,
  cut into 1-inch cubes
2 pounds boneless pork shoulder,
  cut into 1-inch cubes
1½ tablespoons dried thyme leaves
1 teaspoon ground allspice
1 to 2 tablespoons olive oil, if needed
⅓ cup rendered bacon fat
2 cups chopped onions
3 large carrots, peeled and chopped
2 cups dry white vermouth
1 can (6 ounces) tomato paste
5 cups homemade beef stock
  (see Index) or canned broth
5 bay leaves
9 large cloves garlic
1½ pounds fresh garlic sausage or kielbasa
1 pound salt pork
4 cups dried bread crumbs
1 cup chopped fresh parsley

1. Score the fat side of the pork rind with a sharp knife, and place it in a small saucepan. Cover it with cold water, bring to a boil, and simmer for 10 minutes. Drain, cover with cold water again, and repeat the process, this time simmering for 30 minutes. Reserve the pork rind and its second cooking water separately.

2. Drain the beans and place them in an 8-quart flameproof casserole with a lid. Cover them with water by at least 3 inches, and bring to a boil. Reduce the heat and cook briskly, uncovered, for 15 minutes. Remove the casserole from the heat and let the beans stand in the cooking liquid.

3. Preheat the oven to 450°F.

4. Cut the wing tips off the duck and set them aside, along with the neck, heart, and gizzard. (Save the liver for another use.) Pull all the fat out of the duck, and season the cavity with salt and pepper. Put the duck in a small roasting pan. Put the lamb bones in a second small pan, and place both pans in the oven. Roast, draining accumulated fat frequently, for 45 minutes.

5. Remove both pans from the oven; the duck should still be slightly underdone, and the lamb

bones should be well browned. Reserve the lamb bones. Reduce the oven temperature to 350°F. Drain the juices from the cavity of the duck into a large bowl, and set aside. Allow the duck to cool; then cover and refrigerate.

6. Brown the cubed lamb in a heavy skillet over medium-high heat, in batches, seasoning it with salt and pepper. Do not crowd the pan. Transfer the browned lamb to a large bowl and set aside.

7. Without cleaning the skillet, sauté the pork cubes and the reserved duck neck, giblets, and wing tips in the same fashion, seasoning with salt, pepper, 1½ teaspoons of the thyme, and the allspice. You may need to add 1 or 2 tablespoons olive oil if the skillet is particularly dry at this point. Set aside the browned pork in the same bowl as the lamb.

8. Do not clean the skillet. Melt the rendered bacon fat in the skillet and sauté the onions and carrots over medium-low heat, stirring, until tender, 20 minutes. Add them to the pot with the beans.

9. Using a slotted spoon, transfer the browned meats to the pot of beans. Add the lamb bones.

10. Add the vermouth, along with the juices that accumulated in the bowl of browned meats, to the skillet. Bring to a boil. Then lower the heat slightly and cook briskly, stirring, until the vermouth has reduced slightly and all browned cooking particles have dissolved, 4 to 5 minutes. Pour this into the beans.

11. Stir the tomato paste, the pork rind cooking liquid, the beef stock, reserved duck juices, remaining 1 tablespoon thyme, and the bay leaves into the beans. Chop 6 of the garlic cloves, and add them. Add additional water if necessary; the liquid should just cover the beans. Put the pork rind, fat side down, on top of the beans, and cover the casserole.

12. Place the casserole in the center of the oven and bake until the beans are completely tender, 2 to 2½ hours. Remove, uncover, and cool to room temperature, stirring occasionally. Then cover and refrigerate overnight.

13. The next day, bring a saucepan of water to a boil. Prick the skin of the garlic sausage all over with

a fork, add it to the water, and simmer for 30 minutes. Drain, and reserve.

14. Put the salt pork in a saucepan of cold water. Bring it to a boil, then lower the heat and simmer for 10 minutes. Drain, cover with cold water, and repeat, this time reserving the salt pork in its cooking water.

15. Remove the casserole from the refrigerator. Discard the lamb bones, bay leaves, duck neck and wing tips, and—if you can find them—the heart and gizzard.

16. Drain the salt pork; cut off the rind and discard it. Chop the salt pork into cubes, and place them in a food processor. Purée to a paste, dropping the 3 remaining garlic cloves through the feed tube while the motor is running. Stir the paste into the beans.

17. Skin the duck. Pull all the meat from bones, and cut the meat into chunks. Stir the duck meat into the beans. Skin the garlic sausage and cut it into rounds; stir them into the beans.

18. Preheat the oven to 325°F.

19. If the beans are too dry (they are about to cook for 1½ hours), stir in a cup or two of warm water. It is preferable that they be moist. Stir together the bread crumbs and parsley. Smooth the top of the beans, and sprinkle with half of the crumb and parsley mixture.

20. Bake for 45 minutes. Then remove the casserole from the oven, and stir the crust down into the beans. Sprinkle the remaining crumb and parsley mixture over the top, and bake until a crust has formed and browned well, 45 minutes. Serve hot from the oven.

Serves 12

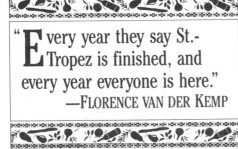

"Every year they say St.-Tropez is finished, and every year everyone is here."
—FLORENCE VAN DER KEMP

TRADE SECRET

When adding flour to stews as a thickener, sprinkle it over the meat and don't stir for 3 minutes; or first place the flour in a baking pan and cook it in a 350°F oven until it has browned slightly. Either method removes the floury taste.

MEDITERRANEAN LAMB STEW

This deeply flavorful lamb stew evokes all the gastronomic pleasures of the Mediterranean, especially when served in large rustic soup bowls over delicately steamed couscous. Accompany with sliced oranges and red onions atop a bed of watercress that has been drizzled with a red wine vinaigrette.

1 cup fresh orange juice
4 cloves garlic, coarsely chopped
5 tablespoons coarsely chopped fresh mint leaves
2 tablespoons extra virgin olive oil
1 tablespoon dried oregano
1 teaspoon freshly ground black pepper
2 pounds boneless lamb shoulder, cut into 1½-inch cubes
2 tablespoons olive oil
2 tablespoons unbleached all-purpose flour
1½ cups dry white wine
1½ cups homemade beef stock (see Index) or canned broth
2 tablespoons tomato paste
2 cups sliced carrots (1-inch lengths)
2 cups cooked Great Northern beans
2 cups diced seeded ripe plum tomatoes
1 cup large imported black olives, pitted
Finely slivered zest of 2 oranges

1. Combine the orange juice, garlic, 2 tablespoons of the mint, the extra virgin olive oil, oregano, and pepper in a large bowl. Mix well. Then add the lamb, toss well, and cover the bowl with plastic wrap. Marinate for 2 hours at room temperature.

2. Preheat the oven to 350°F.

3. Remove the lamb from the marinade, brushing off any pieces of garlic. Reserve the marinade. Pat the meat dry with paper towels.

4. Place the 2 tablespoons olive oil in a large dutch oven and brown the lamb, in small batches, over medium heat.

5. When all the lamb has been browned, discard any excess oil and return the lamb to the dutch oven. Sprinkle the flour over the meat and cook, stirring, over medium heat to brown the flour, 3 minutes.

6. Add the reserved marinade along with the wine, stock, tomato paste, and carrots. Cover the pot, transfer it to the oven, and bake for 40 minutes.

7. Add the cooked beans to the stew and bake, uncovered, 15 minutes.

8. Add the tomatoes and olives. Taste, and adjust the seasonings if necessary. Bake, uncovered, 10 minutes longer.

9. Remove the pot from the oven, and stir in the remaining 3 tablespoons mint and the orange zest. Serve immediately.

6 portions

BANDOLS FROM PROVENCE

There are moments in the summer when a *salade niçoise* or piperade tart can transport us to the South of France. The green beans are small and ripe for picking, and bright red tomatoes and peppers are bursting on the vine. This is the time we love to serve a chilled Bandol rosé. Somewhat more robust than a white Zinfandel, this fruity deep pink wine can stand up to the gutsy flavors of Provence-inspired dishes. Unfortunately, it is not easy to find these wines in the States, but persist! They are a lovely summer pleasure!

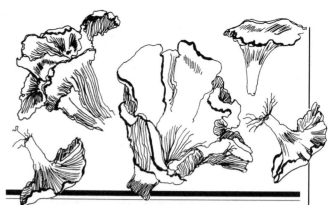

BEEF BOURGUIGNON

We've updated this rich winter classic by adding chanterelles, red pearl onions, and fresh rosemary. A dab of red currant jelly makes a shiny, rich brown sauce to cloak each chunky bite. This dish cries out for your best Burgundy—the better the wine, the better the stew!

8 ounces thick-sliced bacon, cut into small dice
3 pounds beef chuck, cut into 1-inch cubes
1 cup chopped onions
Salt and freshly ground black pepper, to taste
3 tablespoons unbleached all-purpose flour
3 cups Burgundy wine
3 cups homemade beef stock (see Index) or canned broth
2 tablespoons tomato paste
1 tablespoon chopped fresh rosemary leaves
3 to 4 carrots, peeled and cut into 1½-inch julienne (1½ cups)
2 cups red or white pearl onions
8 ounces fresh chanterelles or other wild mushrooms
1 tablespoon unsalted butter
1 tablespoon red currant jelly
2 tablespoons chopped fresh Italian (flat-leaf) parsley

1. Preheat oven to 350°F.

2. In a flameproof casserole or a dutch oven, sauté the bacon until crisp. Remove with a slotted spoon and drain on paper towels. Set bacon aside.

3. Pour off all but 1 tablespoon of the bacon drippings. Over medium-high heat, sauté the beef a few pieces at a time until browned on all sides.

4. Add the onions to the beef, and sprinkle with salt and pepper and the flour. Cook over high heat, stirring constantly, for 5 minutes.

5. Add the wine, stock, tomato paste, reserved bacon, and rosemary, and bring to a boil. Cover the casserole, transfer it to the oven, and bake until the meat is tender, about 2 hours.

6. Meanwhile, prepare the vegetables: Bring a small pot of water to a boil. Drop in the carrots and boil until tender, 5 to 7 minutes. Drain, rinse under cold water, and drain again. Reserve.

7. Make a small X in the root end of each pearl onion. Drop them into boiling water and cook for 5 minutes. Drain, rinse under cold water, and drain again. Peel and reserve.

8. Slice the chanterelles lengthwise. Melt the butter in a small skillet, add the chanterelles, and sauté over medium heat for 10 minutes. Set aside.

9. When the meat is cooked, transfer the casserole to a burner, and add the carrots, onions, chanterelles, and currant jelly. Heat through, about 7 minutes. Serve garnished with the chopped parsley.

6 portions

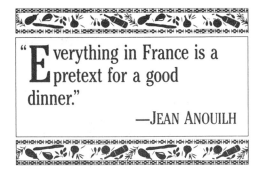

"**E**verything in France is a pretext for a good dinner."

—JEAN ANOUILH

TARTE NICOISE

The tastes of the Mediterranean—black olives, anchovies, garlic, red pepper, tomatoes, and thyme—combine in this tart to make a fabulous first course or luncheon dish . . . and it's gorgeous as well.

PASTRY
1 ¼ cups unbleached all-purpose flour
1 tablespoon fresh thyme leaves
½ teaspoon salt
Freshly ground black pepper, to taste
8 tablespoons (1 stick) unsalted butter, cold
2 teaspoons Dijon mustard
2 tablespoons ice water

FILLING
2 tablespoons extra virgin olive oil
4 red bell peppers, cored, seeded, and cut into ¼-inch-thick slices
1 cup sliced onion
½ teaspoon salt
Freshly ground black pepper, to taste

TOPPING
5 ripe plum tomatoes
10 anchovy fillets, rinsed and drained
15 oil-cured black olives, halved and pitted
4 cloves garlic, thinly sliced
1 tablespoon extra virgin olive oil
Freshly ground black pepper, to taste
1 tablespoon fresh thyme leaves

1. Make the pastry: In a medium-size bowl, toss the flour, thyme, salt, and pepper. Cut in the butter, 1 tablespoon at a time, with a pastry blender, two knives, or your fingertips until the mixture resembles coarse crumbs. Stir in the mustard and enough ice water for the mixture to hold together. Form it into a ball, cover with plastic wrap, and chill for 30 minutes.

2. Prepare the filling: Heat the oil in a large skillet. Stir in the bell peppers, onion, salt, and pepper. Cover, and cook, stirring occasionally, until soft and thick, 30 minutes. Transfer to a bowl and allow to cool to room temperature.

3. Preheat the oven to 375°F.

4. On a lightly floured surface, roll the chilled dough out to form an 11-inch circle. Transfer it to a 10-inch tart pan with removable bottom, and press the pastry into the bottom and sides. Using a slotted spoon, transfer the filling mixture to the tart pan, discarding any accumulated liquid in the bowl.

5. Prepare the topping: Halve the tomatoes lengthwise, and scoop out and discard the centers. Halve them again lengthwise. Arrange five rows of tomato strips, alternating with rows of anchovies, across the filling. Sprinkle the olives on top.

6. Combine the garlic and oil, and spoon over the tart. Sprinkle with pepper and thyme.

7. Bake until the filling is bubbling and the crust is golden, 35 minutes. Remove from the oven and let stand 10 minutes before serving.

8 portions

PEAR TATIN

Traditionally made with apples that have been caramelized, this luscious French dessert also works beautifully with pears. Serve it warm with a scoop of crème fraîche.

PASTRY
½ cup unbleached all-purpose flour
1½ teaspoons sugar
Pinch of salt
4 tablespoons (½ stick) unsalted butter, cold, cut into small pieces
1 tablespoon ice water

FILLING
4 tablespoons (½ stick) unsalted butter, at room temperature
6½ tablespoons sugar
4 ripe Bosc pears
¼ cup Poire Williams eau de vie

Crème fraîche (see Index)

1. Prepare the pastry: Combine the flour, sugar, and salt in a mixing bowl. Add the butter and using a pastry blender, two knives, or your fingertips, gently work it in until the mixture resembles coarse crumbs. Then sprinkle the ice water over the mixture and quickly work it into a dough. Gather it into a ball, flatten it slightly, cover with plastic wrap, and refrigerate for 30 minutes.

2. Roll the chilled dough between sheets of floured waxed paper to form a circle ⅛ inch thick. Carefully remove the top sheet of waxed paper and trim the dough to fit the top of an 8-inch skillet.

3. Moisten the edge of the circle with water, and use the pastry trimmings to make a decorative rim around the edges. Replace the top sheet of waxed paper, and freeze the dough for at least 1 hour.

4. Preheat the oven to 375°F.

5. Prepare the pear filling: Spread the butter on the inside of a heavy ovenproof 8-inch skillet. Sprinkle 4 tablespoons of the sugar over the butter.

6. Peel, quarter, and core the pears. Reserve one of the quarters. Arrange the remaining pear quarters in a tight circle around the skillet, cut sides down, with the wider ends facing the outside. Place the reserved quarter in the center, round side down.

7. Sprinkle another 1½ tablespoons sugar over the pears. Cook them over medium-high heat, swirling gently, until the sugar has caramelized and is a rich golden brown, 15 minutes. Do not let it burn.

8. Remove the crust from the freezer and place it snugly (with the rim down) over the pears in the skillet. With the point of a knife, cut a dime-size hole out of the center of the crust.

9. Place the skillet on a baking sheet, and bake the tart on the center rack of the oven until the crust is browned, 45 minutes.

10. Carefully remove the skillet from the oven, and place it briefly over high heat (to absorb any excess moisture and loosen any stuck caramel).

11. Place a wire cake rack over a flat plate, and invert them (together) over the tart. Invert, and carefully remove the skillet.

12. While the tart cools slightly, mix the Poire Williams with the remaining 1 tablespoon sugar in a small saucepan. Cook until the sugar has dissolved, 2 to 3 minutes. Then brush the mixture lightly over the pears.

13. Let the tart cool for 45 minutes. Then slide it onto a serving platter and serve with crème fraîche.

8 portions

"A color of blue reigns here that elsewhere is but a dream."
—COLETTE

THE PIG STANDS ALONE

"If you want a subject, look to pork!," writes Charles Dickens in *Great Expectations*. Although we no longer use "everything but the squeal," pork remains a universal favorite in America, offering a variety of cuts suitable for many preparations. Fresh pork, whether eaten as sautéed chops, a roasted loin, baked ribs, or fresh sausage, is mild-flavored and divinely succulent; it takes well to the flavors of sage, rosemary, thyme, ginger, juniper, and fresh and dried fruits. Smoked and cured, pork is a whole different eating experience. Lusciously pink, sweet, and salty, glazed with a honeyed mixture of mustard, cloves, apple juice, and bourbon, or studded with brandy-plumped dried fruits, ham is an indulgence and a feast for a king.

THIS LITTLE PIG WENT TO MARKET

The big news about pork these days is that pigs are being bred for much leaner meat than in the past. With 50 percent less fat than 20 years ago, pork now competes with chicken as a lean white meat. In fact, the tenderloin or a well-trimmed pork chop is now even *leaner* than chicken. The up side of this development is obvious—pork is no longer high on the cholesterol hit list.

When buying pork, look for meat that is pinkish white to pink in color (the color varies depending on the cut—loin meat is whiter than shoulder meat) and firm to the touch. As with beef, well-marbled pork will produce more tender results.

GUIDE TO THE UNCURED CUTS

▼■ **Shoulder** (includes the Boston butt and the picnic shoulder): The Boston butt, sold as both a bone-in and a boneless roast, or cut into cubes for kabobs or stew meat, is a well-marbled, flavorful cut, fine for braising, roasting, or stewing. The picnic shoulder (from which the hocks are cut) is relatively fatty, and it is also suitable for braising or roasting, or cubed as stew meat. We use shoulder meat principally in stews.

★ **Loin** (includes the blade, center rib, loin, and sirloin roasts; also chops, cutlets, and tenderloin): These tender, versatile cuts are excellent for roasting, sautéing, or grilling (much too lean for long stewing or braising). The tenderloin, the tenderest part of the pork, can be quickly roasted or cut into medallions and then sautéed or grilled. We like to serve the elegant crown roast for a fancy dinner; it is made by trimming two loins to expose the rib bones, tying the loins together, meaty sides facing out, and then forming the whole into a circle, or "crown."

≡ **Ribs** (spareribs, back ribs, and country-style ribs): These have been American favorites for generations. We love to grill them, braise them, and bake them with some of our favorite barbecue sauces. There are three types of ribs: the familiar spareribs are made up of breast and rib bones and don't have much meat on them; the type referred to as "back ribs" or "baby back ribs" are cut from the loin and are meatier than spareribs; and country-style ribs, cut from the blade end of the loin, are very meaty (they're actually more like chops), although they may not be as succulent as the others.

Fresh ham (includes the rump or butt, and the shanks): This cut is most often cured and smoked and sold as ready-to-eat ham, but when glazed and roasted fresh (uncured), it is particularly delicious.

Pig's feet: Rich in natural gelatin but containing very little meat, pig's feet are used mostly to add flavor and body to stocks. They may also be poached, braised, or stuffed.

THE CURED CUTS

Bacon and salt pork: What Americans call bacon is the fatty pork belly meat that has been cured and smoked. It can be bought in slabs, with the rind intact, or more commonly, in thin or thick slices. The curing and smoking process will determine the bacon's flavor. Canadian bacon is made from a section of boneless loin surrounded by a very thin layer of fat that is also cured and smoked. Salt pork is fat, most often from the belly, that is simply cured in coarse salt; it is added to stews and beans as a flavor enhancer.

Ham: A ham is correctly a leg of pork that has been wet- or dry-cured and has probably been smoked (the word itself is derived from the Old English word for thigh, *hamm*).

Wet-cured, or *brine-cured*, *hams* are cured in a solution of water, salt, preservatives, a variety of flavorings, and usually sugar. (Today's producers use a machine to inject the brine solution into the meat rather than soaking the hams in the brine.) Differences in brining solutions are responsible for the wide variation in ham tastes, causing some to be saltier, some sweeter, and some more watery tasting. Almost all brine-cured hams are also smoked over a hardwood such as hickory, apple, or maple (except so-called "boiling hams," which are cured but not smoked) and then they may be aged as well. If the smoking process brings the internal temperature of the ham to at least 155°F, it may be labeled "fully cooked" or "ready to eat." But we think hams have a much nicer flavor if heated through in a 350°F oven for 8 to 10 minutes per pound. Remember that although wet-cured hams are brined, they are not actually preserved (as are dry-cured hams) and they must be refrigerated just like fresh pork.

Dry-cured hams (Smithfields are undoubtedly the most famous) are processed by a different method than their wet-cured cousins, resulting in a saltier, stronger-tasting ham. Also known as country or southern-style, the hams are coated with a dry mixture of salt, sugar, and preservatives, which is allowed to remain on the ham for several weeks. This is a modified version of an age-old preserving process that works by drawing out moisture, thus dehydrating the meat to the point where spoilage-causing bacteria can no longer grow. This dehydration is also responsible for the concentrated, salty taste of the meat and its firm, dry texture. The hams are then smoked over a variety of woods such as hickory, apple, or sassafras, and aged. Whole dry-cured hams can be stored several months without refrigeration in a cool, dry place.

A dry-cured ham is not "ready to eat," and it requires a good deal of preparation. It must first be scrubbed with a stiff brush to remove any mold. Then it is soaked in several changes of cold water for 48 hours to leach out as much salt as possible, and scrubbed again. Finally, it is poached for several hours until fully cooked, and the softened rind is removed. At this point the ham is fine for eating, but we like to take it one step further and bake it with a wonderful marmalade glaze.

Ham is graded by the amount of added water and additives it contains: the highest grade, "ham," contains the lowest percentage; those labeled " . . . with natural juices" and " . . . water added" contain progressively greater amounts.

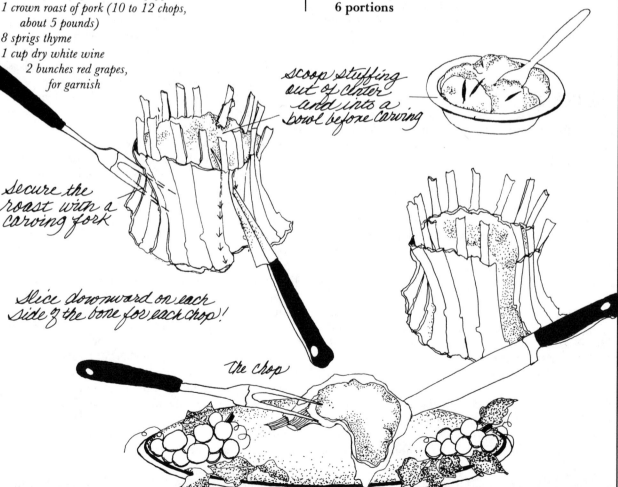

CROWNED ROAST

Fit for a king—and you too—a crown roast is practically a meal in itself. Stuffed with rice and prosciutto that have been generously flavored with fresh herbs, this is a dish for a very special occasion.

1 ½ tablespoons olive oil
1 pound ground pork
2 tablespoons minced garlic
8 ounces prosciutto, chopped
3 cups cooked wild rice
2 tablespoons chopped fresh rosemary leaves
2 tablespoons chopped fresh Italian (flat-leaf) parsley
Salt and freshly ground black pepper, to taste
1 crown roast of pork (10 to 12 chops,
    about 5 pounds)
8 sprigs thyme
1 cup dry white wine
    2 bunches red grapes,
        for garnish

1. Preheat the oven to 350°F.

2. Heat the oil in a nonstick skillet over medium heat. Add the ground pork, crumbling it with a wooden spoon. When lightly browned, add the garlic and cook 1 minute more. Remove from the heat and allow to cool slightly.

3. Combine the cooked pork mixture, prosciutto, cooked wild rice, rosemary, parsley, and salt and pepper in a mixing bowl. Toss well to combine.

4. Place the roast on a rack in a shallow roasting pan. Spoon the stuffing into the center of the crown. Drape the sprigs of thyme around the top.

5. Bake for 1 ½ hours, basting frequently with the wine.

6. Transfer the roast to a large platter, and garnish all around with grapes. Serve the stuffing and carve the chops at the table.

6 portions

scoop stuffing out of center and into a bowl before carving

Secure the roast with a carving fork

Slice downward on each side of the bone for each chop!

The chop

ROAST LOIN OF PORK WITH SAUSAGE STUFFING

The lean loin of pork is luscious when stuffed and roasted. Baked Beets and Chunky Applesauce complete the meal.

2 tablespoons olive oil
2 cups chopped onions
12 ounces sweet Italian sausage meat
8 ounces dried apricots, coarsely chopped
1 cup coarsely chopped fresh parsley
½ cup dried currants
3 cloves garlic, finely minced
Grated zest of 2 oranges
2 teaspoons fennel seeds
2 teaspoons dried thyme leaves
1 teaspoon freshly ground black pepper
½ teaspoon salt
1 boneless pork loin (4 pounds), with a pocket for stuffing cut lengthwise through the roast
2 cups bitter orange marmalade
1 cup Madeira
½ cup fresh lemon juice

1. Preheat the oven to 350°F.
2. Heat the oil in a large skillet. Add the onions and cook over medium heat, stirring, until wilted, 10 minutes. Add the sausage meat and cook it with the onions until browned. Using a slotted spoon, transfer the sausage mixture to a large mixing bowl. Allow to cool slightly.
3. Add the apricots, parsley, currants, garlic, orange zest, fennel seeds, 1 teaspoon of the thyme, ½ teaspoon of the pepper, and the salt to the sausage mixture. Stir well.
4. Fill the pocket in the roast with the stuffing, filling from both ends and using the handle of a wooden spoon to push the stuffing toward the center. Fill the pocket completely. Place the roast on a rack in a shallow roasting pan.
5. Stir the marmalade, Madeira, and lemon juice together in a bowl, and pour half the mixture over the pork. Sprinkle the roast with the remaining 1 teaspoon thyme and ½ teaspoon pepper.
6. Place the roasting pan on the middle rack in the oven, and cook, basting occasionally, for 45 minutes. (Add ½ cup water to the pan if the juices begin to dry up.) Then pour the remaining half of the marmalade mixture over the pork and bake, continuing to baste, until the internal temperature reads 150° to 160°F, another 45 minutes.
7. Remove the roast from the oven, and let it rest 15 minutes before slicing. Cut it into ½-inch-thick slices to serve.

8 portions

LEMON AND GINGER PORK LOIN

Lemon marmalade creates a glistening glaze on this roast pork. Fresh rosemary and ginger add a subtle spiciness.

1 boneless pork loin (3½ pounds)
Salt and freshly ground black pepper, to taste
2 teaspoons chopped fresh rosemary leaves
1 tablespoon minced fresh ginger
1 cup dry white wine
¾ cup lemon marmalade

1. Preheat the oven to 350°F.

2. Place the pork loin in a shallow roasting pan, and sprinkle it with salt, pepper, the rosemary, and the ginger. Pour the wine into the bottom of the pan. Cook, basting occasionally, for 1 hour.

3. Remove the pan from the oven. Place the marmalade in a small bowl, and add 3 tablespoons of the pan drippings; mix well and pour over the meat. Return the roast to the oven and cook, continuing to baste, until a meat thermometer reads 150° to 160°F, 30 to 45 minutes.

4. Let the meat rest for 15 minutes before slicing. Serve it with the pan juices.

6 portions

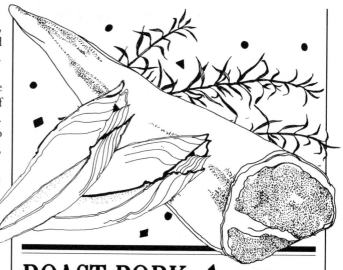

NEW BASICS MEAT AND POTATOES

Beat the meat and potatoes blues with any of the following:

Country Style Ribs
Red Beans and Rice

Lemon and Ginger Pork Loin
Risotto Primavera

Crowned Roast
Wild Rice

Grilled Mixed Grill
Polenta Tomato Casserole

The Pig Stands Alone Roast Pig
Black-Eyed Peas and Rice

Rattlesnake Ribs
Black and White Bean Salad

Roast Pork Romana
Roasted Garlic and Walnut Pasta

Asian Baby Back Ribs
Shrimp Fried Rice

ROAST PORK ROMANA

A roast loin of pork done with Italian flair—garlic, prosciutto, and in the background the lingering taste of rosemary.

1 boneless pork loin (about 2½ pounds)
2 tablespoons unsalted butter, at room temperature
2 ounces prosciutto, chopped
2 tablespoons chopped fresh rosemary leaves
1 tablespoon minced garlic
Freshly ground black pepper, to taste
6 small Belgian endives, halved lengthwise
2 cups Vin Santo or other sweet dessert wine

1. Preheat the oven to 350°F.

2. Using the tip of a sharp knife, cut slits 1 inch long and ¼ inch deep all over the surface of the roast.

3. Combine the butter, prosciutto, rosemary, and garlic in a small bowl, and mix thoroughly. Spread this over the surface of the roast, making sure it gets into the slits. Season the roast with pepper.

4. Place the roast in a small roasting pan, surround it with the endive, and pour the wine over it. Cook for 1¼ hours.

5. Remove the pan from the oven, and cover the roast loosely with aluminum foil. Let it stand for 15 minutes. Then transfer it to a platter and arrange the endive alongside. Serve it with the pan juices.

6 portions

PORK ROASTING CHART

CUT	OVEN TEMPERATURE	INTERNAL TEMPERATURE	COOKING TIME
Loin, stuffed or unstuffed 3 to 5 pounds	350°F	150° to 160°F	20 to 22 minutes per pound
Crown roast, stuffed 6 to 10 pounds	350°F	150° to 160°F	20 to 22 minutes per pound
Fresh whole ham 10 to 14 pounds	325°F	150° to 160°F	20 to 22 minutes per pound
Pork ribs 3 to 4 pounds	350°F		30 minutes per pound
Ham, bone in and fully cooked 12 to 14 pounds	350°F	130° to 140°F	10 to 12 minutes per pound

▲ Based on meat at room temperature when roasted.
▲ Roast pork and ham should rest 15 minutes before carving; internal temperature will rise 5° to 10°F.

PORK CHOPS NORMAND

Pork chops and apples are the perfect combination. We intensify this dish with Calvados and finish off the sauce with red currant jelly.

1 tablespoon olive oil
4 center-cut pork chops, about ¾ to 1 inch thick
⅛ cup dry white wine
2 Granny Smith apples, peeled and cored
1 tablespoon unsalted butter
¼ cup Calvados or apple brandy
2 tablespoons red currant jelly

1. Preheat the oven to 350°F.
2. Heat the oil in a large skillet, and sauté the pork chops over medium-high heat until lightly browned, 2 to 3 minutes per side. Transfer the chops to a baking dish. Add the wine to the skillet and bring to a boil, scraping up any brown bits. Pour the wine over the chops, cover the dish with aluminum foil, and bake for 20 minutes
3. Cut the apples into ⅛-inch-thick slices. Melt the butter in a skillet and sauté the apple slices over medium heat, until soft, 3 to 5 minutes. Add the Calvados and currant jelly, and continue cooking until the liquid forms a glaze on the apples, 1½ to 2 minutes.
4. Spoon the apples over the chops, and bake, uncovered, another 5 minutes.
4 portions

THE RED WINES OF AMERICA

★

Cabernet Sauvignon has taken its place as the leading grape of California wine production and deservedly so. Well suited to mellow aging, the Cabernet Sauvignons are spicy, herby, and tannic. When young, this grape is often blended with other Bordeaux grapes, such as Merlot and Cabernet Franc. We recall many years ago, when California wines began to blossom in America, the extraordinary Jordan and Sterling Cabernets served in a few fine restaurants in New York. This was but a preview of coming attractions, and we have not been disappointed since.

Heitz Cellars produces an extraordinarily intense Cabernet from Martha's Vineyard in the Napa Valley. Robert Mondavi produces both a brilliant Cabernet Reserve and an excellent Cabernet, Opus One. Created in collaboration with Baron Philippe de Rothschild, it is humbly described on the label as a "Red Table Wine." Others we enjoy are those from Ridge, Iron Horse, Joseph Phelps, and Conn Creek.

Cabernets are perfectly suited to full-flavored meat and game preparations. They are also wonderful with a simply prepared roast chicken. Though they can be as expensive as some of the fine Bordeaux wines, they can also compare in quality.

Merlot, fragrant and rich, is a bit softer than a Cabernet and should be enjoyed fairly young. Stag's Leap Wine Cellars produces an excellent Merlot, as does Clos du Val. For a nice change, try the wonderful Merlot produced at the Lynfred Wineries outside of Chicago. Moving east, Crossroads Winery on the northern fork of Long Island is excellent, as is the Merlot from Lenz Vineyards.

This smooth-bodied wine is quite versatile—lovely with braised rabbit, roasted guinea hens, and roasted leg of lamb, as well as grilled tuna and swordfish.

Pinot Noir, spicy and smooth, is a fairly new discovery for us. The intense flavor of this grape has always produced some of the great French Burgundies, but it has just recently come to life in America. Some bright stars are being produced in Oregon as complex, well-balanced, and elegant wines. Try the Pinot Noirs from Adelsheim, Knudsen Erath, and Oak Knoll. California boasts Carneros Creek, Calera "Jensen," and Acacia. We enjoy serving Pinot Noir with grilled salmon, partridge, pheasant, and highly flavored cheeses.

Zinfandel belongs to California and is virtually unknown in Europe. This extraordinary domestic grape produces wines that range from light-bodied cherry flavors to deep, strong, fruity, and peppery reds. The blush wines made from Zinfandel, which are called "white" Zinfandels, were the "hottest" wines of summer for several years. We still like the complex personalities of the red Zinfandels to serve with grilled steaks and veal chops. We even dress up an elegant burger alongside this wine. It is an excellent choice with pâtés, soft ripening cheeses, and spicy pork dishes. We recommend trying those from Ridge York Creek, Stony Brook Mountain, Grgich Hills, Burgess Cellars, and Clos du Val.

Sutter Home produces an excellent fresh white Zinfandel, as does Beringer. Chilled, these wines are lovely with mayonnaise-slathered lobster rolls, Lobster à la Russe, and ripe summer tomatoes. Serve a St.-André cheese and a bowl of ripe cherries for dessert. Also a pleasant treat for a summer evening accompanying a fresh vegetable couscous.

PORK CHOPS AND SCALLOPED POTATO CASSEROLE

This is hearty winter fare. All you need is a great green salad and some pumpernickel rolls to serve alongside.

2 cups heavy or whipping cream
1 clove garlic, thinly sliced
2 tablespoons whole-grain mustard
2 tablespoons Dijon mustard
2 teaspoons dried thyme leaves
3 cups thinly sliced peeled potatoes
2 tablespoons unsalted butter
6 loin pork chops
¼ cup dry white wine
1 cup thinly sliced onion
2 tablespoons chopped fresh Italian (flat-leaf) parsley
½ teaspoon freshly ground black pepper

1. Preheat the oven to 350°F.

2. Bring the cream and garlic to a boil in a large saucepan. Reduce the heat and simmer until reduced by a third, 5 to 8 minutes. Add both mustards and the thyme, and mix well. Set aside.

3. Fill a large pot with water and bring to a boil. Drop in the potatoes and cook for 30 seconds. Drain, rinse under cold water, and dry on paper towels.

4. Melt the butter in a skillet, and brown the chops over medium-high heat for 2 minutes on each side. Remove the chops from the skillet and set aside. Add the wine to the skillet and simmer for 30 seconds, scraping up any brown bits.

5. In a 12 x 8-inch flameproof baking dish, layer half the potatoes and onions; lay the pork chops on top, and pour the pan juices over them. Top with the remaining potatoes and onions, and then carefully pour the reduced cream over the top. (If it seems a bit dry, add a little more cream.) Sprinkle with the parsley and pepper.

6. Bake for 1¼ hours. Then place the dish under the broiler and cook until the top is brown and bubbly.

6 portions

SEASON TO TASTE

Flavors we love with pork and ham include:

Anise	Lemon and
Apple cider	orange
Black beans	marmalade
Brown sugar	Molasses
Caraway seed	Onions
Cardamom	Oregano
Cilantro	Red wine
Clove	vinegar
Dill	Rosemary
Garlic	Saffron
Ginger	Sage
Honey	Shallot
Jalapeño	Tarragon
pepper	Thyme

TUSCAN PORK CHOPS

Instead of the expected bread stuffing, we've used corn bread and flavored it with fennel, sage, and thyme. Apple cider adds a crisp autumnal flavor to this dish.

2 thick center-cut pork chops
    (about 1 ½ pounds total)
1 tablespoon olive oil
¼ cup diced fennel bulb
¼ cup chopped onion
1 ounce prosciutto, slivered
½ cup crumbled corn bread or corn muffin
Pinch of crumbled dried sage leaves
Pinch of crumbled dried thyme leaves
Freshly ground black pepper, to taste
½ cup plus 2 tablespoons Berta's Chicken
    Stock (see Index) or canned broth
2 tablespoons unsalted butter
¼ cup apple cider

   1. Cut a pocket in each chop: Insert the point of a small sharp knife into the flesh side of the chop. Make an internal horizontal cut in one direction without enlarging the outside opening. Remove the knife, and insert it again with the blade facing in the opposite direction. Make a second cut in the opposite direction without enlarging the opening.
   2. Heat the oil in a small skillet, and sauté the fennel and onion over medium heat for 3 minutes. Add the prosciutto; cook 2 minutes. Set aside 2 tablespoons of this mixture.
   3. Transfer the remaining contents of the skillet to a mixing bowl. Stir in the corn bread, sage, thyme, pepper, and 2 tablespoons chicken stock. Allow mixture to cool slightly.
   4. Fill each pocket with the stuffing mixture.
   5. Melt the butter in a skillet just large enough to hold the chops. Brown the chops, over medium-high heat, 2 minutes per side. Pour off the fat, and add the remaining ½ cup stock and the cider. Sprinkle the reserved stuffing mixture over the chops. Cover, and cook 15 minutes. Serve immediately.
   2 portions

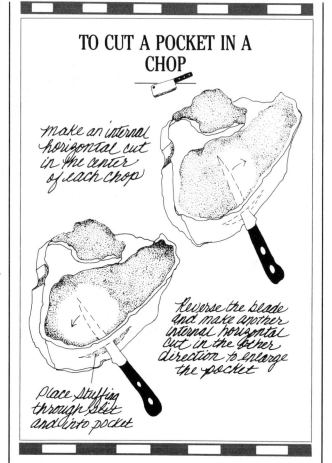

TO CUT A POCKET IN A CHOP

make an internal horizontal cut in the center of each chop

Reverse the blade and make another internal horizontal cut in the other direction to enlarge the pocket

Place stuffing through slit and into pocket

GINGER ALE PORK CHOPS

When just a little ginger won't do... The sweetness of raisins and cream mellow the lively flavor.

4 loin pork chops, about 1 inch thick
½ teaspoon ground ginger
1 tablespoon unsalted butter
¾ cup ginger ale
¼ cup minced fresh ginger
¼ cup slivered crystallized ginger
¼ cup coarsely chopped walnuts
¼ cup golden raisins
½ cup heavy or whipping cream

1. Preheat the oven to 350°F.

2. Sprinkle the pork chops all over with the ground ginger.

3. Melt the butter in a large skillet, and brown the pork chops over medium-high heat, 2 to 3 minutes per side. Transfer the chops to a flameproof baking dish.

4. Add the ginger ale, fresh ginger, and crystallized ginger to the skillet, and cook over high heat for 2 to 3 minutes. Pour this over the chops, transfer to the oven, and bake for 30 minutes.

5. Sprinkle the walnuts and raisins over the chops, and bake an additional 15 minutes.

6. Transfer the chops to a serving platter and keep warm. Add the cream to the baking pan and place it over high heat. Cook, scraping up the brown bits, until the sauce is slightly reduced and thickened, about 2 minutes. Pour the sauce over the chops, and serve immediately.

4 portions

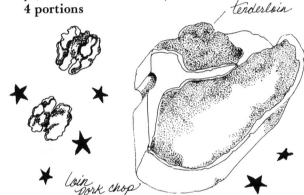

tenderloin

loin pork chop

A WINTER PIG ROAST

Ribollita

The Pig Stands Alone Roast Pig
Riesling or Zinfandel or Icy Cold Beer

Lemony Caesar Salad

Orange Flan
Very Ginger Snaps

THE PIG STANDS ALONE ROAST PIG

Years ago, Carlos, Sheila's friend from Venezuela, taught her how to roast this perfect—garlicky and crusty—suckling pig. We like to serve Yellow Pepper Soup for a starter, and then some red beans and rice alongside.

3 limes, halved
1 suckling pig (15 pounds), well cleaned
18 cloves garlic
2 tablespoons dried oregano leaves
⅓ cup capers with 3 tablespoons brine
2 tablespoons olive oil
1 teaspoon salt
1 teaspoon freshly ground black pepper
1 teaspoon good-quality curry powder
½ cup firmly packed cilantro (fresh coriander) leaves
1 tiny apple or crabapple, for garnish
Watercress sprigs, for garnish
Preserved or fresh kumquats, for garnish

1. Rub the lime halves all over the body of the pig, squeezing the juice liberally; rub the cavity with the limes too.

2. With the tip of a sharp knife, cut slits ¾ inch deep all over the body of the pig (do not prick the head). Cut 5 of the garlic cloves into 8 slivers each, and stuff the pieces into the slits.

3. Finely mince the remaining 13 garlic cloves, and place them in a medium-size bowl together with the oregano, capers, brine, olive oil, salt, pepper, and curry powder. Stuff half this mixture into the cavity of the pig, and rub the remainder all over the outside. Place the cilantro inside the cavity. Let the pig rest, covered, in the refrigerator for 24 hours.

4. Preheat the oven to 400°F.

5. Place the pig on a rack in a large roasting pan, and bake for 30 minutes. Then reduce the heat to 350°F and roast until the juices run clear when the meat is pricked with a knife, 3½ hours.

6. Place the apple in the pig's mouth, and serve on a large platter, decorated with the watercress and kumquats.

10 portions

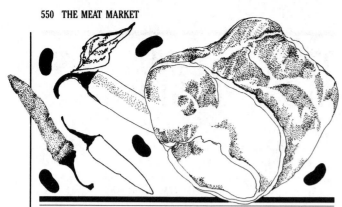

JONATHAN WAXMAN'S BARBECUED PORK WITH BLACK BEAN CAKES

Jonathan Waxman's style and flair with great regional ingredients have contributed greatly to many restaurants around the country today.

This fabulous pork dish is even better if you prepare it a day ahead—the flavors will intensify.

1 pork butt (4 to 6 pounds), cut into 2-inch cubes
2 cups sturdy red wine
6 tablespoons tequila
2½ to 3 tablespoons peeled and finely slivered fresh ginger
Salt and freshly ground black pepper, to taste
¼ cup olive oil, plus more if needed
3 onions, cut into 8 wedges each
2 heads garlic, cloves separated and peeled
12 shallots, peeled
4 tablespoons (½ stick) unsalted butter
2 bay leaves
1 bunch fresh thyme (about ½ cup)
4 ounces mixed fresh hot chile peppers (serrano, jalapeño),
  stems removed
1 tablespoon black peppercorns
Juice of 2 limes
16 Black Bean Cakes (recipe follows)
4 ripe plum tomatoes, finely chopped
1 cup crème fraîche (see Index)
Cilantro (fresh coriander) sprigs, for garnish
2 limes, cut into small wedges, for garnish

1. Place the pork in a large mixing bowl, and add the wine, tequila, and ginger. Toss, and marinate, loosely covered, in the refrigerator, for 1 to 2 hours.

2. Remove the pork from the marinade, and pat it dry with paper towels. Sprinkle the meat with salt and pepper. Reserve the marinade.

3. In a large heavy flameproof casserole, heat the olive oil until very hot. Very carefully add the pork, and cook over high heat, in batches, until it is a rich brown color. When all the pork is browned, return it to the casserole.

4. Add the onions, garlic, shallots, and butter to the casserole. Cook over high heat, stirring with a wooden spoon, until the vegetables are lightly browned, 5 to 7 minutes.

5. Discard any remaining fat in the casserole, and add the reserved marinade all at once. Continue to stir with a wooden spoon, scraping up any brown bits from the bottom of the casserole, 5 minutes. If the marinade reduces too quickly, add a bit of water.

6. Add the bay leaves, thyme, chiles, and peppercorns. Add enough water to cover the ingredients by 1 inch, and bring to a boil. Reduce the heat to low and simmer, stirring occasionally and skimming off the fat that rises to the surface, 2 to 3 hours. The length of cooking time will depend on the tenderness of the pork; it is ready when it is tender and almost falling apart.

7. Remove the pork (without the other ingredients) to a bowl. Strain the cooking liquid and pour it over the pork. (If you like, cover and refrigerate overnight at this point.)

8. Before serving, gently reheat the pork in its liquid, adding the juice of 2 limes. When heated, taste for seasoning.

9. Place 2 sautéed black bean cakes on each plate, and top with large spoonfuls of the pork mixture. Sprinkle the chopped tomato over the pork, and then add a dollop of crème fraîche. Garnish with cilantro sprigs and lime wedges.

8 portions

"Tis not the meat, but 'tis the appetite makes eating a delight."
—SIR JOHN SUCKLING

BLACK BEAN CAKES

2 cups dried black turtle beans, well rinsed
2 ham hocks
6 cloves garlic
2 bay leaves
Cilantro (fresh coriander) stems, tied in a bunch about
*   1-inch thick*
2 quarts water
Salt and freshly ground black pepper, to taste
4 tablespoons olive oil
2 tablespoons clarified butter (see Index)

1. Place the beans, ham hocks, garlic, bay leaves, and cilantro stems in a large heavy flameproof casserole. Add the water and bring to a boil. Reduce the heat, and simmer until the beans are tender, 1 hour and 20 minutes.

2. Drain the beans and remove the ham hocks, garlic, bay leaves, and cilantro. Transfer the beans to a food processor, and purée.

3. Season the purée with salt and pepper, and form it into 16 small cakes. Refrigerate, loosely covered, until ready to use, but at least 1 hour.

4. To cook the bean cakes, heat the oil and butter in a large heavy skillet. Add the cakes a few at a time, and sauté over medium heat until heated through, 2 minutes on each side. Use a metal spatula to turn them, as the cakes are a bit delicate to handle.

16 bean cakes

SANTA FE PORK STEW

Serve this one-dish meal in deep bowls with Hot and Sassy Corn Bread and a platter of watercress, sliced oranges, ripe tomatoes, and black olives.

3 tablespoons olive oil
3 pounds boneless pork shoulder, cut into 1 ½-inch cubes
2 ½ tablespoons unbleached all-purpose flour
2 sweet potatoes (1 ¼ pounds), peeled and cut into 1-inch
*   cubes*
1 ½ cups dry white wine
1 ½ cups Berta's Chicken Stock (see Index)
*   or canned broth*
½ cup red wine vinegar
1 ½ cups chopped onions
½ cup chopped fresh Italian (flat leaf) parsley
6 cloves garlic, finely minced
3 tablespoons tiny capers, drained
1 tablespoon plus 1 teaspoon ground cumin
2 cups cooked black beans
½ teaspoon freshly ground black pepper
½ cup chopped cilantro (fresh coriander)

1. Preheat the oven to 350°F.

2. Heat 2 tablespoons of the oil in a large skillet, and brown the pork in small batches. (Add extra oil if necessary.) Transfer the cooked meat to a flameproof casserole.

3. Sprinkle the flour over the pork and cook over medium heat, tossing well, for 3 minutes. Remove from the heat.

4. Add the potatoes, wine, stock, vinegar, onions, parsley, half the garlic, 2 tablespoons of the capers, and 1 tablespoon cumin to the casserole. Mix well, cover, and bake on the center rack of the oven for 1 hour.

5. Remove the casserole from the oven, and add the remaining garlic, 1 tablespoon capers, and 1 teaspoon cumin. Add the black beans and pepper, stir, and return to the oven. Bake, uncovered, 15 minutes.

6. Keep warm until ready to serve. Right before serving, stir the cilantro into the stew, adjust the seasonings, and return the casserole to the oven, uncovered, to heat through, 5 minutes. Serve immediately.

6 portions

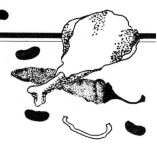

CARNIVAL FEIJOADA

This is our variation of the national feast dish of Brazil. Feijoada is as much an artistic production as is that earthy casserole from Gascony, the cassoulet. It is always best prepared one or two days in advance and reheated—allowing time for the flavors to merge even further.

Rice makes a grand accompaniment, and you might serve an array of condiments—orange slices, cooked green cabbage, and salsa—as they do in Brazil. Finish it off with a tomato salad, crusty bread, and icy cold beer for perfection.

1 pound dried black beans
6 cups water
1 pound prosciutto, in one piece
1 smoked or cooked turkey leg (about 1 pound)
1 pound hot Italian sausages, pricked
8 ounces slab bacon, in one piece
8 ounces chorizo sausages, cut into 2-inch pieces
1 pint cherry tomatoes
1 onion, chopped
2 small red chile peppers, halved, cored, and seeded
6 cloves garlic, slightly crushed
2 strips orange zest, 2½ x ¾ inch

1. Cover the beans with cold water and soak overnight; or cover them with boiling water and let stand 2 hours. Drain.
2. Preheat the oven to 350°F.
3. In a very large ovenproof kettle or dutch oven, combine the beans, 6 cups water, and all the remaining ingredients. Bring to a boil, skimming if necessary. Cover the kettle and transfer it to the oven. Bake 1½ hours. Then remove the cover and bake another 30 minutes, stirring twice.
4. Allow the mixture to cool slightly, then transfer the solids to a large bowl. Pour the liquid into a second bowl. Chill both, covered, overnight.
5. Skim most of the fat from the liquid. Slice the prosciutto, sausages, and bacon. Remove the meat from the turkey leg, and shred or cut it in pieces.
6. Heat the beans, meat, and liquid in a large pot until simmering. Serve in shallow bowls.
   10 to 12 portions

COUNTRY-STYLE RIBS

Couldn't be simpler—just a little Cinzano, regular basting, and some black pepper. Nice and moist, with the pork flavor coming clearly through.

1 piece pork loin country-style ribs (3 to 4 pounds), bones cracked (see Note)
Salt and freshly ground black pepper, to taste
1 cup sweet Italian red vermouth

1. Preheat the oven to 350°F.
2. Season the ribs lightly with salt and heavily with pepper. Place them in a baking pan, and cover loosely with aluminum foil. Bake for 30 minutes, then turn them over and bake another 30 minutes.
3. Pour the vermouth over the ribs, and cook, basting well every 10 minutes, for 1 hour. Turn the ribs over once, after 20 minutes. They should be well browned and fork tender. Slice between the bones and serve.
   4 portions
   Note: These come from the rib end of the loin of pork. They resemble a loin roast left on the bone. Have the butcher cut into and butterfly the loin portion on each "chop."

SOUTH-OF-THE-BORDER SUPPER

Fireworks Rainbow Soup
Carnival Feijoada
Rioja or Valpolicella

Sliced Oranges, Tomatoes, and
Watercress With Molly's Vinaigrette

Peaches and Cream Ice Cream

SUCCULENT RIBS

Some like them hot, some like them sweet, some like them with a runny sauce and some like them with a thick sauce, and some even like them with no sauce at all, but almost nobody just plain doesn't like ribs. We enjoy eating baby back ribs, which we find to be of consistently good quality and less fatty than other ribs. But fat aside, country-style ribs have a lot of wonderful meat on them. It's a tough choice. Whatever cut we're using, we like to cook them slowly in the oven first, about 30 to 40 minutes, to cook off some of the fat.

ASIAN BABY BACK RIBS

If you cannot find true baby back ribs, each slab weighing 14 to 16 ounces, then prepare this recipe using heavier ones. The result will be equally delicious, but the cooking time will be slightly longer. You can also substitute beef ribs, either long or short.

4 to 5 pounds baby back pork spareribs
2 tablespoons minced fresh ginger
1 tablespoon minced garlic
1 ½ cups ketchup
1 ½ cups soy sauce
½ cup honey
⅓ cup dry sherry
1 tablespoon chopped fresh rosemary leaves
2 tablespoons chopped scallions (green onions)

1. Arrange the ribs in a large baking dish. Combine the ginger, garlic, ketchup, soy sauce, honey, sherry, and rosemary in a small bowl. Mix thoroughly, and pour over the ribs. Loosely cover, and marinate overnight in the refrigerator.
2. Preheat the oven to 400°F.
3. Place a rack in a roasting pan and lay the ribs on top. Pour the marinade over them. Bake for 1 ¼ hours, basting frequently. Serve garnished with the chopped scallions.
6 portions

BAKED FRESH HAM WITH APPLEJACK GRAVY

This ham is not a ham. It is really a fresh pork roast, but it is the cut of meat that we normally associate with a ham.

Sliced thin and served with hot gravy, this is a wonderful centerpiece for a holiday buffet or sit-down dinner.

1 fresh ham (about 16 pounds; see Step 1)
4 cloves garlic, minced
¼ cup crumbled dried sage leaves
2 tablespoons crumbled dried thyme leaves
Freshly ground black pepper, to taste
1 pound sauerkraut, rinsed and drained
3 tart apples, peeled and diced
8 ounces fresh kale, stems removed, leaves coarsely chopped
¾ cup applejack or Calvados
½ cup water
Berta's Chicken Stock (see Index), or canned broth
3 tablespoons cornstarch
Salt, to taste

1. Have the butcher bone and butterfly the ham, leaving the skin on and scoring it in a diamond pattern.
2. Preheat the oven to 325°F.

3. Combine the garlic, sage, thyme, and pepper in a small bowl. Mix well.

4. In a large bowl toss the sauerkraut, apples, kale, ½ cup of the applejack, and all but 2 tablespoons of the herb mixture. Mix well.

5. Place the ham, skin side down, on a work surface. With a sharp knife make three or four long slashes about 2 inches deep into the meat. Spread the filling over the meat, pushing it into the cavities. Fold the two flaps over to form a large cylinder. Tie the roast with kitchen string at 2-inch intervals. (You may need help doing this.)

6. Rub the skin with the remaining herb mixture. Place the ham on a rack in a roasting pan, and cover with foil. Roast, uncovering and basting every 30 minutes, until a meat thermometer registers 160°F in the center of the roast, 2 to 2¼ hours. Transfer the roast to a platter, cover it loosely with foil, and let it rest 15 minutes. (The roast will continue to cook.)

7. Pour the pan juices into a bowl. Skim off and discard the fat. Place the roasting pan over low heat. Add the ½ cup water to the pan and scrape the bottom to dissolve any brown particles. Add this to the pan juices with enough stock or water to make 3 cups. Transfer this to a saucepan.

8. In a small bowl, combine the cornstarch and the remaining ¼ cup applejack; stir until smooth.

9. Heat the pan juices over low heat. Whisk in the cornstarch mixture, and bring to a boil. Boil 1 minute. Season with salt and pepper, and keep warm.

10. Slice the roast, and serve it with the gravy.

20 portions

BAKED PARTY HAM WITH PINEAPPLE AND BOURBON

It's rich with flavor, looks absolutely gorgeous, and when sliced paper-thin, will feed a throng. Surround the ham with breads, mustards, and chutneys—it's everybody's favorite sandwich.

1 ready-to-eat ham (12 to 14 pounds), bone in
Whole cloves
½ cup (packed) dark brown sugar, or more as needed
3 cans (5¼ ounces each) pineapple chunks, with their juice
1 cup bitter orange marmalade
1 cup bourbon

1. Preheat the oven to 350°F.

2. Peel the skin from the ham and trim the fat, leaving a ¼-inch layer. Using the tip of a sharp knife, score the fat in a diamond pattern.

3. Insert the cloves in the crossed point of each diamond, and pat the brown sugar evenly over the top of the ham. Place it in a shallow roasting pan, and bake for 30 minutes.

4. While the ham is baking, heat the pineapple chunks, juice, and marmalade together in a saucepan over medium-low heat. Remove the pan from the heat and add the bourbon.

5. Remove the ham from the oven, pour the pineapple sauce over it, and return it to the oven. Bake, basting frequently, another 1½ hours.

6. Remove the roasting pan from the oven and transfer the ham to a warm serving platter. Using a slotted spoon, transfer the pineapple to a saucepan. Skim accumulated fat from the cooking juices, or pour them through a gravy separator. Add the defatted juices to the pineapple, heat through, and pour into a bowl or sauceboat. Serve the ham with the sauce alongside.

20 to 25 portions

A WORLD OF HAM

▲ **Jambon de Paris** (what a Frenchman usually finds in his ham sandwich) is a boned, brined ham that is poached in stock and then pressed into a mold and steamed; it may be lightly smoked, or not smoked at all.

▲ **Jambon de Bayonne** is a strong-tasting, raw ham that is rubbed with a salt mixture, pickled in a wine-and-herb brine, lightly smoked, and then aged. It is served raw, thinly sliced, in sandwiches, as an appetizer, or to flavor cooked dishes.

▲ **Parma ham, or prosciutto,** is a dry-cured, unsmoked ham from Italy that is becoming increasingly well known in America for its delicate, velvety texture and delicious taste. It is eaten raw, often with ripe fruit, or used as a flavorful addition in cooked dishes.

▲ **Spech** is the smoked version of prosciutto; it is darker colored and has a stronger flavor.

▲ **Jamón serrano** is a raw ham, not dissimilar to prosciutto, made in Spain.

▲ **Presunto,** from Portugal, is similar to jamón serrano.

▲ **Westphalian ham** is a raw ham from Germany that is dry-cured, brined, and then smoked.

▲ **Mainz ham,** also from Germany, is brined, soaked in a mixture of brandy or wine lees, and then smoked.

▲ **York ham,** from England, is salted and then poached on the bone, as are excellent hams from Wiltshire and Suffolk.

▲ **Irish hams** are usually dry-cured, boned, and smoked over peat.

HAM STEAKS WITH FRESH TOMATO APPLE CHUTNEY

A light and refreshing way to prepare a basic favorite. Ripe tomatoes and tart apples make these ham steaks elegant enough to serve to company.

¾ cup apple cider or apple juice
¼ cup cider vinegar
½ cup golden raisins
1 ¼ cups chopped tomatoes
1 ¼ cups chopped and peeled Granny Smith or other
    tart apples
1 tablespoon dark brown sugar
1 tablespoon chopped crystallized ginger
Pinch of ground cloves
2 ready-to-eat ham steaks, 1 inch thick (1 pound each)
4 teaspoons grated orange zest

1. Preheat the oven to 375°F.

2. Combine the cider and vinegar in a saucepan, and bring to a boil. Remove the pan from the heat and add the raisins. Set aside for 15 minutes.

3. In a mixing bowl, toss together the tomatoes, apples, brown sugar, ginger, and cloves. Drain the raisins, reserving 1 cup of the juice, and add them to the mixture.

4. Place the ham steaks in a shallow flameproof baking dish that will hold them in one layer. Cover them with the tomato mixture. Sprinkle with the orange zest. Pour ½ cup of the reserved raisin liquid into the dish.

5. Cover the baking dish with aluminum foil, and bake, basting twice, for 35 minutes. Then remove the foil and bake, basting twice, for another 20 to 25 minutes.

6. Using a slotted spatula, transfer the ham and fruits to a serving dish. Keep warm. Add the remaining ½ cup reserved raisin juice to the baking dish, and bring it to a rapid boil. Boil until the juices have reduced slightly, 2 to 3 minutes. Serve the sauce in a gravy boat.

4 portions

SEASON TO TASTE: HERB AND SPICE CHART

A perfect tomato can taste of France, Italy, India, South America, or the American Southwest with just the right combination of fresh herbs and spices. Like a magic palette, they color the simplest of foods and turn ordinary dishes into extraordinary ones. They are the key to New Basics.

HERB OR SPICE	BEST USE	AVAILABLE	GROW (in average garden)
ALLSPICE			
Dried spice berries, slightly larger than peppercorns. Allspice tastes of cinnamon, cloves, and nutmeg—therefore, the name.	Excellent in spice cakes and cookies; plum, peach, and apple pies; breads; steamed puddings; and barbecue sauce, ketchup, pickles, sausages, pâtés, and corned beef.	Dried whole berries and ground	No
ANISE			
Small, licorice-flavored seeds.	Use in cookies, breads, and cakes.	Dried whole seeds and ground	No
BASIL			
Herb with sweet clove-like taste. Varieties include sweet basil, small-leaved bush basil, dark opal, and lemon basil.	Essential herb for Italian food, especially with eggs, tomatoes, pasta, chicken, fish, and shellfish.	Fresh sprigs and crumbled dried	Indoors and out
BAY LEAF			
Pungent, woodsy herb with sturdy leaves and faint cinnamon taste.	Essential for bouquet garni. Good with meat and/or bean stews, game, pot roasts; adds unusual note to rice pudding and custards.	Dried whole leaves	Indoors and out Bay is a perennial herb but will not overwinter in harsh climates.
BORAGE			
Leafy herb tasting faintly of cucumbers.	Young leaves are wonderful in salads—both green and fruit—with string beans, in fruit drinks and teas. Blue flowers are sweet tasting and a very pretty garnish.	In some vegetable markets	Indoors and out. Pick leaves when small and young; older leaves are tougher and hairy.

HERB OR SPICE	BEST USE	AVAILABLE	GROW (in average garden)
CARAWAY			
Nutty, licorice-flavored seeds.	Use with eggs, cheese spreads, and dips; with noodles; in rye bread, cole slaw, and sauerbraten; and with cooked vegetables— potatoes, beets, carrots, cabbage, turnips, and winter squash.	Dried whole seeds	Outdoors
CARDAMOM			
Fragrant cinnamon-like seed popular in baked goods and Indian cuisine.	Use in spice cakes and cookies, apple and pumpkin pies, curries; with winter squash and sweet potatoes.	Dried whole seeds and ground	No
CAYENNE			
Red pepper of the capsicum family most often used dried.	Use in any dish for a little heat, especially with eggs and cheese. Add cayenne by the pinch.	Dried whole pods, but more usually ground (also labeled simply "ground red pepper")	Outdoors
CELERY SEEDS			
Dried seed tasting strongly of celery.	Excellent in salads—potato, cole slaw, and vegetable.	Dried whole seeds	No
CHERVIL			
Delicate herb with subtle celery-licorice taste.	Excellent in green salads; with fish, shellfish, chicken, eggs, cream, peas, string beans, and tomatoes. Essential for *fines herbes*.	Fresh sprigs and crumbled dried	Indoors and out
CHILI POWDER			
Commercial mix of ground chile peppers, cumin, oregano, and other herbs and spices.	Use in bean and meat stews and soups; with eggs and cheese.	Ground	No
CHIVES			
Delicate herb with light onion or garlic taste. Decorative as well as useful garden herb.	Excellent in cream soups and sauces; with fish and shellfish, cheese, and eggs.	Fresh stalks; frozen and freeze-dried, minced, or chopped	Indoors and out

HERB OR SPICE	BEST USE	AVAILABLE	GROW (in average garden)
CINNAMON			
Spice bark of the cassia tree, sweet hot flavor.	Use in spice cakes, cookies, fruit and squash pies, custards; with fruit for sauce and conserves; carrots, winter squash, and sweet potatoes.	Dried whole sticks and ground	No
CLOVE			
Spice of winter holidays, pungent and sweet	A few whole cloves stuck in an onion flavor stocks, and more are pressed into the scored fat of a ham, but most are added ground to spice cakes and cookies, quick breads, fruit pies, and sauces. Use judiciously with sweet potatoes, winter squash, carrots, and pâtés.	Dried whole buds and ground	No
CORIANDER/CILANTRO			
Nutty-tasting seeds are called coriander. Cilantro is the herb and tastes refreshingly soapy.	Use whole seeds for pickles and ground for baking. Cilantro is an essential herb for Mexican, Latin American, and Asian cooking. Use with rice, dried beans, fish, shellfish, poultry, vegetables, salsas, and salads. Add the fresh herb at the last minute before serving.	Seeds: dried whole and ground Leaves: fresh	Outdoors. Hang cilantro flowers upside down over paper to gather seeds.
CUMIN			
Small, hot, bitter seed.	Essential spice for curry and chili powder mixtures. Good with curried vegetables, beans, fish, lamb, and poultry, as well as with cheese, sausages, chutney, and yogurt dip.	Dried whole seeds and ground	No

HERB OR SPICE	BEST USE	AVAILABLE	GROW (in average garden)
DILL			
Seeds and herb have delicate caraway taste. Seeds are the more pungent.	Both seeds and herb are used for pickles. Use seeds with rice and fish dishes and fresh dill leaves with eggs, fresh cheeses, yogurt, seafood, chicken, cucumbers, green beans, potatoes, tomatoes, and beets.	Seeds: dried whole Leaves: fresh and crumbled dried (dried leaves are sometimes labeled "dillweed")	Outdoors
FENNEL SEEDS			
Slight licorice flavor, similar to dill and anise.	Favorite for Scandinavian breads, cakes, cookies. Also good with oily fish (it cuts the oil), especially fish soup, and with vegetables, in salads and salad dressing.	Dried whole seeds	Outdoors
FILE POWDER			
Herb ground from sassafras leaves, tasting like sassafras or root beer.	Essential for gumbo.	Ground dried	No
FINES HERBES			
French herb blend of parsley, chives, tarragon, and chervil.	Good with fish, poultry, eggs, and cheese.	Crumbled dried leaves	Herbs grow well indoors and out. They can be dried and blended or combined fresh.
GINGER			
Versatile spice with bite and aroma. Important to dozens of cuisines from Jamaica to Germany to China.	Use ground dried judiciously in cakes, cookies, fruit and squash pies, custard, rice, and marinades. Use crystallized and preserved ginger in cakes and cookies. Use fresh sliced or grated in marinades and with fish, poultry, pork, and vegetables.	Dried ground, dried whole, crystallized, preserved, and fresh	No

HERB OR SPICE	BEST USE	AVAILABLE	GROW (in average garden)
HYSSOP			
Pungent herb with minty taste. Decorative garden plant.	Use flowers for garnish and young leaves in salads—both green and fruit.	Fresh sprigs in specialty markets	Outdoors
JUNIPER			
Strong spice berries the size of small blueberries. Most are used in the making of gin.	Use in marinades for fish, game, poultry, pork and beef, and in sauerkraut and choucroute.	Dried whole berries	No
LAVENDER			
Herb with fresh clean scent.	Excellent for sachets and potpourris but also good added judiciously to *herbes de Provence,* fruit, and iced tea.	Fresh sprigs and dried whole leaves in specialty markets	Best outdoors but will grow indoors
LEMON GRASS			
Straw-like stalk has woodsy, lemony flavor.	Essential herb of Indonesian and Near Eastern cooking. Use in fish, shellfish, chicken soup, salsas, and vinaigrettes. Low heat brings out the flavor.	Fresh and dried stalks in specialty markets	No
LEMON BALM			
Herb with sweet lemon flavor and citrusy scent.	Excellent in summer soups, salads, jellies and jams, and with fruit.	Fresh sprigs in specialty markets	Indoors and out
LOVAGE			
Herb with sharp celery taste.	Use judiciously in salads and stock or soup.	Fresh sprigs in specialty markets	Outdoors
MACE			
Lacy outer covering of nutmeg; flavor is similar to but slightly milder than nutmeg.	Good in spice cakes and cookies, custards, fruit desserts—especially plums, peaches, and apples—as well as with carrots, broccoli, Brussels sprouts, and cauliflower.	Dried blades and ground	No

HERB OR SPICE	BEST USE	AVAILABLE	GROW (in average garden)
MARJORAM Herb that is first cousin to oregano with similar but more delicate taste.	Use in almost any fish, meat, poultry, egg, or vegetable dish, and in tomato sauce.	Fresh sprigs, dried whole leaves, and crumbled dried	Indoors and out
MINT Herb with refreshing scent and cool taste. Of more than 30 varieties, peppermint and spearmint are best known. Lemon, orange, and apple mint have distinct fruit taste.	Use in Middle Eastern yogurt and grain dishes (tabbouleh), salads; with peas, beans, corn, and potatoes; in jellies, fruit salads, desserts, and iced tea.	Fresh sprigs and crumbled dried	Indoors and out
NUTMEG Sweet, nutty spice seed of the nutmeg tree, the size of an olive.	Best in cream sauces and soups, with vegetables—beans, broccoli, carrots, cauliflower, spinach, Brussels sprouts, onions —but especially for cakes, cookies, pies, pastries, custard, and of course, eggnog.	Whole seeds and ground Ground nutmeg quickly loses its flavor; buy whole nutmeg and grate as needed.	No
OREGANO Herb with pungent marjoram taste.	Use with fish, meat, poultry, dried beans, cheese, eggs; in vegetable soup; with tomatoes, mushrooms, peppers, summer squash, and eggplant. Essential herb for Italian, Greek, and Mexican cooking.	Fresh sprigs and crumbled dried	Indoors and out
PAPRIKA Ground spice of dried capsicum peppers.	Good in cooked salads—especially potato and egg—salad dressing, dips; with fish, shellfish, and poultry. Essential for goulash and paprikash.	Ground dried Hungarian paprika is most flavorful and available sweet or hot.	No

HERB OR SPICE	BEST USE	AVAILABLE	GROW (in average garden)
PARSLEY			
Crisp herb with celery flavor. Of two common varieties—Italian flat leaf and curly leaf—flat leaf has the stronger flavor. Use curly parsley for garnishing.	Excellent in soups, stocks, cream and tomato sauces, salads and salad dressings; with poultry, game, meats, fish, and shellfish, dried beans, and vegetables—from artichokes to zucchini.	Fresh sprigs and crumbled dried. Fresh parsley is readily available; dried parsley is pale and dusty in comparison.	Indoors and out
POPPY SEEDS			
Tiny blue-black seeds of the poppy flower. 900,000 make a pound.	Use for cakes, pastries, cookies, breads, with noodles and fresh fruit.	Whole seeds and ground paste	No
ROSEMARY			
Needle-like leaves with strong piny scent and flavor.	Best with game, poultry, and meats, especially grilled. Add judiciously to mushrooms, roasted potatoes, stuffing, olive oil breads and buns, and ripe melon.	Fresh sprigs and whole dried	Best outdoors but will grow indoors
SAFFRON			
Fragrant spice that is the dried stigmas of crocus. Expensive because they are handpicked (about 250,000 make a pound), but a little goes a long way. Too much saffron lends an unpleasant medicinal flavor.	Use in paella, bouillabaisse, risotto, tomato and cream soups, couscous; with seafood; in Swedish cakes and breads.	Dried whole stigmas and ground. Dried whole saffron threads are of better quality.	No
SAGE			
Herb with musky flavor. Silver-green leaves make sage a decorative garden plant.	Excellent and best known for poultry stuffing. Use judiciously with chicken, duck, goose, pork, sausages, cheese, eggplant, and dried bean stews and soups.	Fresh sprigs, dried whole leaves, crumbled dried, and ground	Best outdoors but will grow indoors

HERB OR SPICE	BEST USE	AVAILABLE	GROW (in average garden)
SALAD BURNET Lacy-leaved herb with a cucumber taste.	Use young small leaves in salads and with fresh cheeses.	Fresh sprigs in specialty markets	Outdoors
SAVORY This peppery herb has two varieties—summer and winter. Summer savory is the more delicate and best suited for cooking.	Europeans call savory the bean herb for its special affinity for limas, string beans, lentils, and dried beans. Also excellent in meatloaf and meatballs, sausages; with poultry, cheese, eggs, cauliflower, tomatoes, and onions.	Fresh sprigs and crumbled dried	Summer savory: indoors and out Winter savory: outdoors
TARRAGON Herb with mild licorice flavor. French tarragon has subtlest flavor.	Best with chicken, veal, fish, shellfish, eggs; in mayonnaise and salad dressings; with tomatoes, mushrooms, and carrots.	Fresh sprigs, dried whole leaves, and crumbled dried	Indoors and out
THYME Herb with tiny leaves and minty, tea-like flavor. Many varieties include lemon, orange, English, and French thyme.	Essential herb of the bouquet garni as well as fish and clam chowder, sausages, pâtés, and stuffing. Excellent with fish and shellfish, poultry, tomatoes, beans, eggplant, mushrooms, potatoes, and summer squash.	Fresh sprigs and crumbled dried	Indoors and out
TURMERIC Brilliant yellow ground spice.	Essential to mustard, curry powder, pickles, and relishes; also used in moderation for its yellow color in rice dishes.	Ground dried	No

FOR THE LOVE OF LAMB

There's no question about it, lamb is our favorite meat. And we're not fussy as to the cut—it can be as grand as a crown roast or saddle, as perfect as a juicy little chop, or as humble as succulent stew meat. Lamb seems equally at home on a silver platter or in a deep earthenware casserole, with elegant artichokes and asparagus or earthy potatoes and parsnips. Most often we like lamb prepared simply—a grilled chop rubbed with garlic and rosemary and roasted pink or a slowly braised shank. Lamb is no longer just the flavor of spring, and we fall in love with it again every season of the year.

ABOUT LAMB

◆

Lamb is coming into its own. No longer regarded as sheep or baby mutton, real lamb (from six weeks to a year old) is now treasured in America for its lean, light, tender, and luscious qualities just as it has been in Europe for centuries. Spring lamb now knows no season; it is available year round. The lamb for the Easter table is raised in Colorado, Iowa, New Jersey, Pennsylvania, and France, too. The supply for the rest of the year comes from those grassy lands down under—New Zealand and Australia. We prefer the domestic and French lamb because it hasn't been frozen and seems to us more flavorful.

There are four categories of lamb recognized in the United States: Baby or hothouse lamb is slaughtered between six and ten weeks of age. It's very small, about 20 pounds in all. The meat is whitish pink and very tender and the flavor very delicate because it is fed just mother's milk. True baby lamb is very hard to find unless you raise it yourself.

The second type is lamb slaughtered between five and six months when it reaches 50 to 60 pounds. This lamb feeds mostly on grasses and grains. The meat is light red, still young and tender, and if it is aged and cooked well, very delicious. This is the lamb we generally see at the market, and we find it pretty scrumptious.

Third is *pré-salé* lamb, the French favorite. This lamb feeds on the salt meadows near the coast of France and is usually very small. The meat is as delicate as it is rare. If you ever see the tiniest lamb chops imaginable, you are probably looking at *pré-salé* lamb.

The fourth category is mutton. At one year, lamb is yearling mutton; at two years, it is just mutton. Today it's difficult to find mutton, but this is the strongly-flavored lamb many are still trying to forget from years back.

You can generally tell the age of a lamb by the weight of the leg. The leg of a spring lamb weighs four to seven pounds; a winter leg, up to nine pounds. The more it weighs, the older the lamb is, the tougher the meat, the stronger the flavor, the thicker the fat, the darker the flesh. For true young lamb, look for bright pink and fine-grained flesh, creamy white fat, and spongy pink bones.

SALAD OF LAMB, BARLEY, AND GREEN BEANS

The classic flavors of lamb and mint balance each other here. The fresh taste of barley is a natural addition. This is a great way to use leftover lamb in quite a snazzy salad.

8 ounces green beans, trimmed
¼ cup plain low-fat yogurt
2 tablespoons chopped fresh basil leaves
½ teaspoon salt
Freshly ground black pepper, to taste
2 cups cooked barley
½ cup Fresh Mint Vinaigrette (see page 567)
1 pound leftover lamb, thinly sliced
Mint and basil sprigs, for garnish

1. Bring a saucepan of salted water to a boil. Add the beans, and simmer for 3 minutes. Rinse under cold water, drain well, and pat dry.

2. Toss the beans in a mixing bowl with the yogurt, basil, salt, and pepper. Loosely cover and refrigerate until ready to serve.

3. Toss the barley with ¼ cup of the vinaigrette. Loosely cover and refrigerate until ready to serve.

4. To serve, arrange the lamb slices on individual plates. Drizzle the remaining ¼ cup vinaigrette over the lamb. Arrange the bean mixture and the barley on the plates, and garnish with the mint and basil sprigs.

4 portions

RACK OF LAMB FOR TWO

For an elegant presentation, have the butcher French the bones: scrape away the thin strip of meat and fat from the ends to the eye, leaving the bare bones—which can be dressed at serving time with little paper booties. (This operation is not terribly difficult; you can perform it yourself.) Otherwise, leave the meat on the bones. Savor the eye of the rack in the traditional fork-and-knife manner, then tuck in your bib and attack those bones. In either case, have the chops cracked at the base for easy carving.

2 tablespoons coarsely ground cornmeal
1 teaspoon minced fresh rosemary leaves
1 clove garlic, minced
½ teaspoon coarse (kosher) salt
Freshly ground black pepper, to taste
1 rack of lamb for two (8 or 9 chops), cut in half
1 to 2 tablespoons Dijon mustard

1. Preheat the oven to 400°F.

2. Combine the cornmeal, rosemary, garlic, coarse salt, and pepper in a small bowl, and mix well.

3. Lightly brush the fat side of the racks with the mustard. Then coat the mustard with the cornmeal mixture.

4. Arrange the racks on a baking sheet, and cook 25 minutes for medium-rare. Slice the chops apart and serve immediately.

2 portions

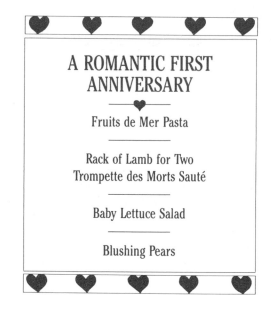

A ROMANTIC FIRST ANNIVERSARY

Fruits de Mer Pasta

Rack of Lamb for Two
Trompette des Morts Sauté

Baby Lettuce Salad

Blushing Pears

SPRING LAMB WITH FRESH MINT VINAIGRETTE

Frenched Leg of Lamb

For a spring or summer dinner, serve this leg of lamb at room temperature, drizzled with the vinaigrette. The flavors blend beautifully.

¼ cup chopped fresh mint leaves
¼ cup chopped fresh basil leaves
¼ cup chopped scallions (green onions)
2 tablespoons balsamic vinegar
1 tablespoon olive oil
1 teaspoon salt
Freshly ground black pepper, to taste
1 leg of lamb (about 7 pounds), trimmed of excess fat
1 cup Fresh Mint Vinaigrette (recipe follows)

1. In a small bowl, combine the mint, basil, scallions, vinegar, oil, salt, and pepper. Mix well, and rub over the lamb. Cover the lamb and refrigerate overnight.

2. Preheat the oven to 450°F.

3. Place the lamb on a rack in a roasting pan, and roast for 20 minutes. Then reduce the heat to 350°F, and roast another 1¼ hours for medium-rare.

4. Transfer the lamb to a platter, cover loosely with aluminum foil, and let it rest for 15 minutes. Then slice it thin, and serve with the vinaigrette.

8 portions

FRESH MINT VINAIGRETTE

⅔ cup olive oil
¼ cup white wine vinegar
2 teaspoons whole-grain mustard
1 teaspoon salt
Freshly ground black pepper, to taste
½ teaspoon sugar
⅓ cup chopped fresh mint leaves
2 ripe plum tomatoes, finely diced

Whisk the oil, vinegar, mustard, salt, pepper, and sugar together in a small bowl until smooth. Then stir in the mint and tomatoes. Serve immediately, or cover and refrigerate for up to 1 hour.

1½ cups

A SILVER ANNIVERSARY CELEBRATION

❤

Cream of Tomato Risotto

Herb-Crusted Lamb With Roast Potatoes
Green Beans Provençal
Cabernet Sauvignon

Arugula Salad With Red Wine Basil Vinaigrette

Very Lemon Tart

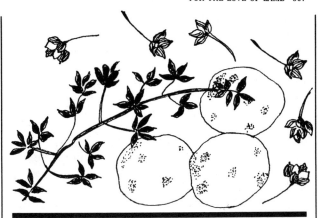

HERB-CRUSTED LAMB WITH ROAST POTATOES

The flavors of thyme, rosemary, black pepper, and coriander permeate the lamb and flavor the potatoes at the same time. Green Beans With Roquefort and Walnuts would make a perfect accompaniment.

1 leg of lamb (7 to 8 pounds)
2 large cloves garlic, slivered
5 tablespoons olive oil
2 tablespoons plus 2 teaspoons dried thyme leaves
2 tablespoons dried rosemary leaves
2 tablespoons plus 1 teaspoon coarsely ground black pepper
2 teaspoons ground coriander
30 small red new potatoes, quartered
2 tablespoons chopped fresh rosemary leaves
1 teaspoon coarse (kosher) salt
Rosemary sprigs, for garnish

1. Preheat the oven to 425°F.

2. Cut slits all over the lamb with the tip of a sharp knife, and insert the garlic slivers in the slits.

3. Brush the lamb all over with 2 tablespoons of the olive oil.

4. Combine the 2 tablespoons thyme, the dried rosemary, 2 tablespoons pepper, and coriander in a small bowl and mix well. Pat the herb mixture all over the lamb to form a crust. Place the lamb in a shallow roasting pan.

5. Place the potatoes in a large mixing bowl. Add the remaining 3 tablespoons olive oil, the fresh rosemary, the remaining 2 teaspoons thyme and 1 teaspoon pepper, and the coarse salt. Toss to mix well, and arrange around the lamb in the pan.

6. Place the pan on the center rack in the oven, and roast for 45 minutes. Then reduce the heat to 375°F, stir the potatoes slightly so they don't stick to the pan, and cook an additional 30 minutes.

7. Remove the pan from the oven, and insert an instant-reading meat thermometer in the thickest part of the meat. It should read 120°F for rare. Let the lamb rest, loosely covered, 15 minutes before carving. (The meat will continue to cook a bit more, and the temperature will rise to 135° to 140°F.) Place the roast on a serving platter, surrounded with the potatoes. Garnish with fresh rosemary sprigs.

8 portions

Note: For rare lamb allow 12 minutes per pound. For well-done lamb, allow 18 minutes per pound.

HOW TO TIE A BONELESS LEG OF LAMB

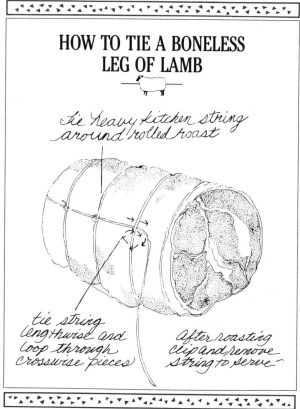

HOW TO CARVE A LEG OF LAMB
★

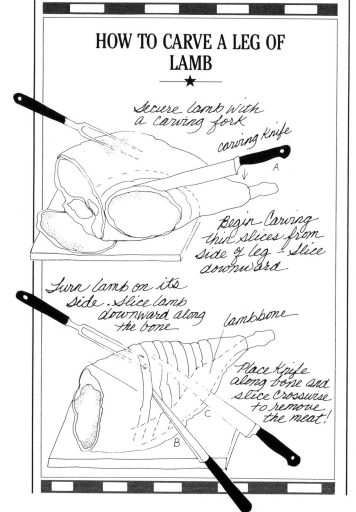

LAMB STUFFED WITH SPINACH AND CHEVRE

This is a truly elegant way to serve lamb. With each slice of pink meat comes a swirl of tart chèvre and sweet green spinach. It's also good the next day at room temperature, so plan on having a picnic.

1 tablespoon olive oil
2 tablespoons minced garlic
2 cups cooked spinach
8 ounces chèvre
Salt and freshly ground black pepper, to taste
1 butterflied leg of lamb (about 5 pounds after boning)
2 cloves garlic, slivered
½ teaspoon coarse (kosher) salt
½ teaspoon freshly ground black pepper
2 tablespoons fresh rosemary leaves

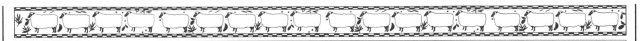

LAMB ROASTING CHART

CUT	OVEN TEMPERATURE	INTERNAL TEMPERATURE	COOKING TIME

Leg, bone in
  6 to 8 pounds
  (high-heat method)
	425° to 450°F for 20 to 45 minutes, then 350° to 375°F	135° to 140°F for rare; 150° to 155°F for medium	12 minutes per pound for rare

Leg, bone in
  6 to 8 pounds
  (low-heat method)
	325°F	135° to 140°F for rare; 150° to 155°F for medium	20 minutes per pound for rare; 25 minutes per pound for medium

Leg, boned, stuffed, and rolled
  4 to 6 pounds
  (high-heat method)
	400°F for 45 minutes, then 350°F	135° to 140°F for rare; 150° to 155°F for medium	12 minutes per pound for rare

Leg, boned, stuffed, and rolled
  4 to 6 pounds
  (low-heat method)
	325°F	135° to 140°F for rare; 150° to 155°F for medium	20 minutes per pound for rare; 25 minutes per pound for medium

Rib (rack) 2½ to 3 pounds	400°F	140° to 145°F for medium-rare	12 to 13 minutes per pound

▲ Based on meat at room temperature when roasted.
▲ Roast lamb should rest 15 minutes before carving; internal temperature will rise 5° to 10°F.

1. Preheat the oven to 425°F.

2. Heat the oil in a small skillet. Add the garlic and sauté over medium-low heat for 1 minute. Do not let the garlic brown.

3. Combine the garlic, spinach and chèvre in a bowl, and season with salt and pepper. Mix well.

4. Lay the lamb flat on a work surface, and spread it evenly with the spinach mixture. Roll the roast up lengthwise (jelly-roll style), and tie it at intervals with kitchen string.

5. Make small slits in the surface of the roast with the tip of a sharp knife, and insert the slivers of garlic in the slits. Sprinkle the roast with the coarse salt, pepper, and rosemary.

6. Place the roast in a shallow roasting pan and roast for 1 hour for rare meat (12 minutes per pound, 140°F on a meat thermometer inserted in the thickest part; for medium, allow 15 minutes per pound, about 155°F on a meat thermometer). Let the lamb rest for 15 minutes before carving. Cut it into ½-inch-thick slices, and serve.

6 to 8 portions

GUIDE TO THE BEST CUTS

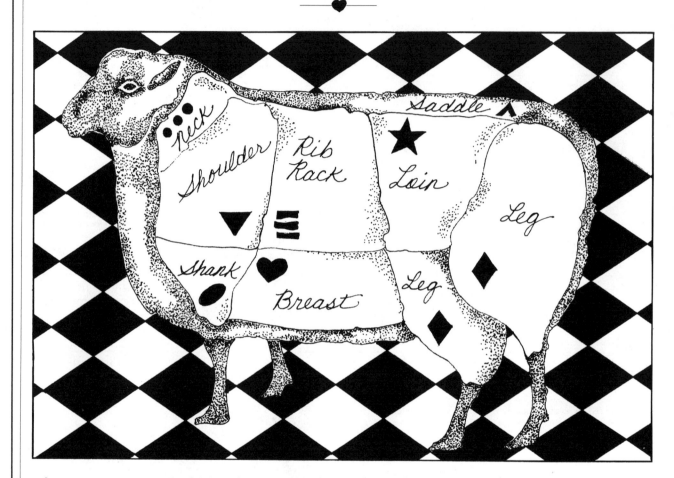

◆ **Leg:** This cut is the classic and it is available in a number of ways: American style (without the shank bone); French style (with the shank bone); boned, rolled, and tied; or boned and butterflied. The leg may be whole or with the first four inches removed for a three-quarter leg. The three-quarter leg is the one most often seen in retail meat cases. Unless we want to grill a butterflied leg, we buy it on the bone because the bones add a tremendous amount of flavor. Roast all legs of lamb, bone-in or boneless.

For a butterflied leg, the leg is trimmed of all fat and the fell (the membrane covering the leg), and then boned. The meat is spread open and pounded to even the thickness. When this cut is broiled or grilled, the thickest and densest portion will be rare, the medium-thick portion less so, and the thinnest well done. We've learned to get around this by cutting the meat into thick, medium-thick, and thin portions and then grilling it. We rearrange the meat into its butterfly shape on a platter before serving.

Rib: Meat from this section is served in a number of ways. The whole rack is a memorable roast; when two or more racks are tied together, they become a crown roast. The ribs are also cut into four-rib racks or single-rib chops. The eye section of the ribs is often removed and sliced into medallions, sometimes called noisettes. They are an impressive and quick-cooking entrée. All cuts from the rib are tender, and they are best roasted, broiled, or sautéed.

Loin or saddle: This cut starts at the end of the ribs and ends at the legs. Lamb has two loins and two fillets separated by a T-bone with flanks attached. A saddle weighs about 6 pounds untrimmed, but just 2¾ to 3½ pounds trimmed. It will serve six to eight people. The loin is also boned and tied for a roast or cut into chops. Some feel the loin is the choicest of all the cuts. We recommend roasting the roasts and broiling the chops.

Shoulder: This is a less expensive but delicious cut for roasting or braising. It can be left as a square-cut roast; with bones cracked and tied; or boned, rolled, and tied. Lamb shoulder is often sliced for chops, which are delicious braised.

Breast: Although a fatty cut, it is delicious boned and stuffed. Just trim it well and braise it gently.

Shanks: Both fore and hind shanks are some of the tastiest parts of a lamb. Each weighs about a pound and can be braised whole or cut crosswise into three or four pieces.

ORANGE LAMB STUFFED WITH MINT AND PECANS

Tender spring lamb stuffed with refreshing mint, spinach, and crunchy pecans. For an Italian rendition, substitute hazelnuts for the pecans.

1 leg of lamb, butterflied (5½ pounds after boning)
6 cloves garlic
3 tablespoons plus ½ cup olive oil
1 cup coarsely chopped pecans
1 pound spinach, cooked, well drained, and squeezed dry
2 cups coarsely chopped fresh mint leaves
Grated zest of 2 oranges
1 teaspoon dried thyme leaves
1 teaspoon freshly ground black pepper
½ teaspoon salt
¼ teaspoon ground cinnamon
1 egg, well beaten
1 cup fresh orange juice
1½ cups dry white wine
1 tablespoon Dijon mustard
1 tablespoon crumbled dried rosemary
1 teaspoon coarsely ground black pepper
8 sprigs mint, for garnish

1. Preheat the oven to 400°F.

2. Lay the lamb out on a flat surface, and trim off any small extra side pieces; reserve them for another use. Finely chop 4 of the garlic cloves.

3. Heat the 3 tablespoons olive oil in a small skillet over low heat. Add the chopped garlic and the pecans. Sauté until lightly browned, 4 to 5 minutes.

4. Transfer the garlic and pecans to a medium-size bowl, and add the spinach, mint leaves, orange zest, thyme, pepper, salt, and cinnamon. Pour in the egg and blend well.

5. With a narrow spatula or a knife, spread the stuffing over the lamb. Carefully roll the lamb up lengthwise, forming a long thin roast. Tie it at intervals with butcher's string. Place the lamb, seam side down, in a shallow roasting pan.

6. Mince the remaining 2 cloves garlic, and combine them in a medium-size bowl with the orange juice, 1 cup of the wine, remaining ½ cup olive oil, mustard, rosemary, and coarsely ground pepper.

Mix thoroughly, and pour over the lamb.

7. Roast the lamb for 20 minutes. Then reduce the heat to 350°F, baste the meat with the pan juices, and roast another 40 minutes for medium-rare. Remove the pan from the oven and let the lamb rest, loosely covered with aluminum foil, 15 minutes. Then transfer it to a heated platter.

8. Place the roasting pan over medium heat and add the remaining ½ cup white wine. Bring it to a boil, and cook, scraping up the brown bits in the pan, 3 minutes. Strain the sauce.

9. Cut the lamb into ¾-inch-thick slices, and garnish each serving with a mint sprig. Serve the sauce separately.

8 portions

LAMB OSSO BUCO

This dish is best made a day in advance, then finished the second day. It'll be richer and more flavorful.

3 pounds meaty lamb shanks (see Step 1)
1 cup dried small white beans, such as navy beans
¼ cup unbleached all-purpose flour
¼ teaspoon salt
Freshly ground black pepper, to taste
2 tablespoons olive oil
2 tablespoons capers, drained
4 tablespoons grated lemon zest
9 cloves garlic
4 sprigs oregano or 1 teaspoon dried
3 sprigs lemon balm or Italian (flat-leaf) parsley
1¾ cups Berta's Chicken Stock (see Index) or canned broth
3 cups water
3 carrots, peeled and cut into ¼-inch dice
¼ cup chopped fresh parsley

1. Have the butcher cut the lamb shanks crosswise into 2-inch-thick pieces.

2. Soak the beans in cold water to cover for 6 hours.

3. Preheat the oven to 350°F.

4. Toss the flour, salt, and pepper in a shallow bowl. Dredge the lamb pieces in the flour, coating all sides. Heat the oil in a dutch oven over medium-high heat, and brown the meat on all sides, in batches if necessary. Remove the meat and pour off the fat.

5. Drain the beans, and spoon them into the dutch oven. Place the browned lamb on top of the beans. Sprinkle with the capers and 2 tablespoons of the lemon zest. Crush 6 cloves of the garlic, and sprinkle them over the meat. Add the oregano, lemon balm, stock, and water. Heat to a boil. Cover, transfer to the oven, and bake until the lamb and beans are tender, 1½ hours.

6. Lift the lamb shanks onto a plate. Using a slotted spoon, transfer the beans to a bowl. Strain the cooking liquid into a second bowl. Cover everything and refrigerate overnight.

7. The next day, preheat the oven to 350°F.

8. Skim the grease off the reserved lamb liquid. Arrange the lamb and beans in a shallow ovenproof casserole. Heat 1 cup of the liquid and pour it over the lamb. Cover, and bake until hot, 35 minutes.

9. Combine the remaining lamb liquid and the carrots in a medium-size saucepan. Bring to a boil, and simmer 10 minutes. Then mince the remaining 3 cloves garlic and add them to the saucepan, along with the remaining 2 tablespoons lemon zest and the parsley.

10. Arrange the lamb and beans in four shallow bowls, ladle the carrot sauce over, and serve.

4 portions

A WINE TOUR OF BORDEAUX

Of all the French wines we know and have enjoyed, probably the most wonderful have been from Bordeaux in southwest France. Bordeaux is bordered by the Dordogne and the Garonne rivers, which meet slightly below the city and empty into the Gironde. Most of the great château vineyards are within view of the flowing rivers with the exception of the Pomerols and Saint-Emilions.

The regions of Médoc and Haute Médoc, to the north of Bordeaux, are most well known for great reds such as those from the districts of Margaux, Saint-Estèphe, Pauillac, and Saint-Julien. The climate of this area, located closest to the Gironde, is perhaps the most temperate and moist, and it produces the best conditions possible for growing the glorious harvest. These Bordeaux are delicate, yet they possess a rich, flowery bouquet. They age slowly and beautifully, sustaining great distinction. The château wine most notable from Margaux is Château Margaux; from Saint-Estèphe Château Cos d'Estournel; from Pauillac Château Mouton-Rothschild; and from Saint-Julien Château Léoville-Las-Cases, Château Léoville Poyferré, Château Léoville-Barton, Château Ducru-Beaucaillou, and Château Beychevelle.

When we visited the Médoc region we had lunch with the grape harvesters in the fields on the last day of the season. Simple roast pork, potatoes, and a salad were the fare, after starting off with a warm and creamy vegetable soup. The harvesters drank the younger wines, but we were treated to a fine aged vintage, delicate yet sturdy. We drove back to Bordeaux later that afternoon, after visiting Château Margaux and Château Mouton-Rothschild. Along the way we stopped at a little café in Pauillac, drank coffee and beer, and watched the sun set over the Gironde—a most glorious sight. Being so close to the water after hours of feeling enveloped by lush green vines and voluptuous, purple grapes was magical.

To the east of Bordeaux we are enthralled by the wines of Pomerol and Saint-Emilion. Pomerol is best known for the great Château Pétrus. This marvelous Bordeaux is made primarily from the Merlot grape blended with Cabernet Sauvignon. Growing conditions, soil, and climate vary from region to region and give each wine its distinctive taste. Somewhere between the delicate reds of the Haute Médoc and the full-bodied Saint-Emilions lie the Pomerols, well-balanced, smooth, and fruity.

The rich, full-bodied reds of Saint-Emilion are Château Cheval-Blanc and Château Ausone. Cheval-Blanc in particular is considered one of Bordeaux's great wines. Growing conditions and location make this robust wine perfection.

Traveling south from Bordeaux brings us to Graves and ultimately to Sauternes. Graves produces both red and white wines, the best known being from Château Haut-Brion. Haut-Brion red is on a par with the best from the Haute Médoc; its white is considered one of the best dry whites of Bordeaux.

With foie gras or with desserts we love Sauternes, the richest, most golden, and sweetest wine we know. The grapes must reach the perfect over-ripe state and be covered by a mold referred to as the "Noble Rot," which shrivels the grapes and intensifies their sweetness. Our very favorite Sauternes is produced by Château d'Yquem. It has an almost oily consistency and a deep golden color. It is not only one of the great wines of Bordeaux, but in its class, probably the greatest in the world.

While we are still in the southwest of France, it is hard not to recall a visit to Les Jacquets, the great oyster beds of Arcachon. Hosted by Monsieur Dupuch, we tasted the freshest and most glorious oysters, and drank Champagne—once again reminded of the maritime climate that contributes so dramatically to the great wines of Bordeaux.

SPRING LAMB AND VEGETABLE SAUTE

The very essence of spring, captured in less time than it takes to set the table.

2 teaspoons grated lemon zest
1 teaspoon minced garlic
½ teaspoon salt
Freshly ground black pepper, to taste
4 lamb noisettes (about 12 ounces total; see Note)
⅓ pound asparagus, trimmed and cut into 2-inch lengths
1 cup artichoke hearts, thawed if frozen
1 tablespoon olive oil
2 tablespoons dry white vermouth
2 tablespoons white wine vinegar
⅓ cup crème fraîche (see Index)
1 tablespoon chopped fresh dill
¼ cup fresh green peas

1. Combine 1 teaspoon of the lemon zest, the garlic, ¼ teaspoon of the salt, and pepper in a small bowl, and mix well. Rub this into the meat, and let it stand for 1 hour at room temperature.

2. Meanwhile, bring a saucepan of water to a boil, and add the asparagus. Simmer for 3 minutes. Drain, rinse under cold water, and drain again. Set aside, loosely covered.

3. Bring another saucepan of water to a boil, and add the artichoke hearts. Simmer for 3 minutes. Then drain, rinse under cold water, and drain again. Set aside, loosely covered.

4. Heat the oil in a skillet over high heat. Sauté the lamb 3 minutes per side for rare meat. Transfer the lamb to a platter, and keep warm. Discard the oil in the skillet.

5. Add the vermouth and vinegar to the skillet. Cook over medium-low heat until the liquid has reduced to 1 tablespoon, 1 to 2 minutes.

6. Stir in the crème fraîche, dill, remaining 1 teaspoon lemon zest and ¼ teaspoon salt, and pepper. Add the asparagus, artichoke hearts, and peas. Cook over high heat, adding any juices that have accumulated around the lamb, until the mixture is thick and the vegetables are coated. Season with salt and pepper.

7. Arrange the noisettes on two plates, and spoon the vegetables and sauce over and around them. Serve immediately.

2 portions

Note: A noisette is the trimmed meat from the eye of a loin lamb chop.

SEASON TO TASTE

Lamb can host a variety of seasonings. Next time you prepare it, consider:

Basil	Marjoram
Bay leaf	Mint
Black pepper	Onion
Chèvre (goat cheese)	Parsley
	Rosemary
Cinnamon	Saffron
Coconut	Sage
Coriander	Shallot
Cumin	Tarragon
Curry powder	Thyme
Dill	Raspberry
Garlic	vinegar
Ginger	Red wine
Lemon	Red wine
Lemon balm	vinegar

BRAISED LAMB SHANKS

In just a little over 30 minutes, these lamb shanks are braised to perfection in the microwave. Ask the butcher for the "foreshanks" if possible.

2 tablespoons plus 1 to 2 teaspoons olive oil
1 cup chopped red bell pepper
¾ cup chopped onion
2 cloves garlic, minced
2 sprigs fresh rosemary
    or ½ teaspoon crushed dried
½ teaspoon salt
Freshly ground black pepper, to taste
¾ cup dry red wine
1 tablespoon tomato paste
3 small lamb shanks (about 12 ounces each)
Salt and coarsely ground black pepper, to taste

Lamb Shank

1. In a 2-quart microwave-safe casserole, cook the 2 tablespoons oil at full power (650 to 700 watts) for 2 minutes.

2. Stir in the bell pepper, onion, garlic, rosemary, salt, pepper, wine, and tomato paste. Cook, uncovered, for 5 minutes.

3. Remove half the vegetable mixture and set it aside.

4. Lightly oil the shanks with the remaining oil. Sprinkle them with salt and coarsely ground pepper. Arrange the shanks in a triangle over the vegetables remaining in the casserole. Cover, and cook for 20 minutes. Then turn the shanks and cook for another 10 minutes.

5. Spoon the reserved vegetables over the shanks, cover, and cook for 2 minutes. Remove the casserole from the microwave, and let it stand for 5 minutes before serving.

2 to 3 portions

Note: This recipe was cooked on High (full power, 650 to 700 watts) in a carousel microwave, using microwave-safe containers.

If your microwave is less powerful, you will have to allow for more cooking time (approximately 1½ times the amount called for—but watch carefully); if it does not have a carousel, you may have to rotate the dish while it is cooking.

AN AUTUMN FEAST

Lobster Ravioli With Fresh Tarragon
Rosé

Braised Lamb Shanks
Eggplant Gruyère Purée
Billionaire's Broccoli
Merlot

Crispy Hot Apple Tart

A NEW NAVARIN OF LAMB

A stew always seems to make our guests relax. This is a springtime stew, with tender young lamb and tender young vegetables.

1 tablespoon olive oil
1¾ pounds boneless lamb, cut into 1½-inch chunks
1 tablespoon unbleached all-purpose flour
1 teaspoon sugar
1¼ cups homemade beef stock (see Index)
    or canned broth
½ cup dry red wine
2 tablespoons tomato paste
1 sprig rosemary or ¼ teaspoon dried
1 clove garlic, crushed
10 tiny orange or red beets, trimmed,
    ½ inch stem left on
10 tiny white turnips, trimmed
    (½ inch stem left on), and peeled
2 scallions (green onions), white bulb
    and 3 inches green, cut into 1-inch lengths
2 tablespoons unsalted butter

1. Heat the oil in a flameproof casserole or dutch oven, and brown the lamb in batches over medium-high heat. Return all the lamb to the pot, and sprinkle it with the flour and sugar. Cook, stirring, until absorbed, about 2 minutes.

2. Add the stock, wine, tomato paste, rosemary, and garlic. Stir well, and bring to a boil. Reduce the heat, cover, and simmer until the lamb is tender, 1½ hours.

3. Meanwhile, bring a saucepan of water to a boil, and add the beets. Simmer until tender, about 20 minutes. Drain, and set aside.

4. Bring a saucepan of water to a boil, and add the turnips. Simmer until tender, about 10 minutes. Drain, and set aside with the beets. When they have cooled a bit, rub off the skins.

5. Bring a small saucepan of water to a boil, and add the scallions. Simmer until tender, 3 minutes. Drain, and set aside with the beets and turnips.

6. Just before serving, melt the butter in a large saucepan and add the vegetables; cook over medium-low heat until heated through, 3 to 4 minutes.

7. Remove the rosemary sprig and spoon the navarin into individual bowls. Top each serving with some of the vegetables.

4 portions

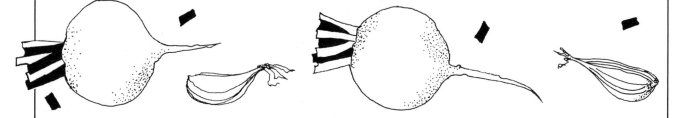

A GRIND OR TWO

P epper is not a grind to us. Freshly ground pepper is one of the most important seasonings in our kitchen.

White, black, and green peppercorns all come from the same plant—*Piper nigrum*. Green peppercorns are picked while still immature and then packed in brine or vinegar. They are pungent but not hot.

Left to mature, the berries turn red. When picked and dried, they shrivel and turn black. For white peppercorns, the dried berries are soaked and the outer covering removed. Black peppercorns have the strongest aroma and bite; white peppercorns are gentler.

Pink peppercorns are not a berry of the *Piper nigrum* plant but an altogether different species from Réunion Island in the Indian Ocean. Their pink color and faintly sweet flavor adds a spark to many dishes.

We prefer to buy all pepper as whole berries. They last about a year without losing flavor. Twist a grind or two over:
▲ Vegetable juices and Bloody Marys
▲ Salad dressing and greens
▲ Beef, pork, lamb, veal, rabbit, and venison
▲ Chicken, duck, goose, turkey, and game birds
▲ Flavored butter, mustard, mayonnaise, cheese, sour cream
▲ Eggs—deviled, poached, scrambled, stuffed, and boiled
▲ Barbecue sauce, Cajun gumbos, Tex-Mex fajitas
▲ Fresh garden tomatoes, beans, beets, carrots, squash, peas, broccoli, artichokes, asparagus
▲ Oysters, clams, fish
▲ Spice cake batter and cookie dough
▲ Soups, chowders, bisques
▲ Strawberries, melons, peaches

LAMB CURRY WITH CONDIMENTS

India, Morocco, France, Ireland —so many countries make their most basic and often most memorable dishes with lamb. It combines and adapts as well to mint jelly as it does to the golden dusky flavors of India.

2 tablespoons olive oil
3 pounds lamb shoulder, cut into 2-inch chunks
½ cup chopped onion
2 cloves garlic, minced
1 tablespoon minced fresh ginger
2 teaspoons best-quality curry powder
½ teaspoon freshly grated nutmeg
½ teaspoon ground cumin
½ teaspoon ground cardamom
¼ teaspoon ground cloves
¼ teaspoon cayenne pepper
2 cups homemade beef stock (see Index) or canned broth
1 cup New Basic Tomato Sauce (see Index)
¼ cup orange marmalade
¼ cup mango chutney
¼ cup cream of coconut
2 tablespoons fresh lemon juice
1 teaspoon salt
½ cup golden raisins
Toasted unsweetened coconut (see box), for garnish
3 to 4 cups cooked white rice

1. Heat 1 tablespoon of the oil in a flameproof casserole or dutch oven. Brown the lamb, in batches, over medium-high heat, and set aside.

2. Add the remaining oil and sauté the onion, garlic, and ginger over medium heat, 5 minutes. Then stir in all the spices.

3. Stir in the stock, tomato sauce, marmalade, chutney, cream of coconut, lemon juice, and salt. Return the lamb to the casserole.

4. Sprinkle the mixture with the raisins, and bring to a boil. Lower the heat, cover, and simmer for 1½ hours.

5. Sprinkle the curry with toasted coconut, and serve over rice.

4 to 6 portions

TOASTING COCONUT

To toast coconut in the oven: Preheat the oven to 325°F. Spread the coconut in a thin layer on a baking sheet and place on a center rack in the oven. Toast until golden brown, 7 to 10 minutes. Shake the pan a couple of times while toasting and start checking the coconut after 5 minutes to be sure it doesn't burn.

To toast coconut in the broiler: Preheat the broiler. Spread the coconut in a thin layer on a baking sheet. Broil 4 to 5 inches from the heat until golden brown, about 2 to 4 minutes. Be sure to watch the coconut very carefully as it can burn quickly.

MARRAKESH LAMB TAGINE

Tagines are the wonderfully flavored stews of Morocco. They are simmered slowly, and the rich flavors of the spices and saffron make a thick broth rarely tasted in other cuisines. Olives and soft preserved lemons heighten the flavors even further. Serve this over couscous in deep bowls.

SPICE MIXTURE

3 cloves garlic, minced
2 tablespoons olive oil
1½ teaspoons ground cumin
1 teaspoon ground ginger
1 teaspoon coarse (kosher) salt
½ teaspoon ground turmeric
½ teaspoon paprika
¼ teaspoon ground cinnamon
Freshly ground black pepper, to taste

3 pounds lamb shoulder, cut into 3- to 4-inch chunks
2 tablespoons olive oil
2 onions, thinly sliced
2 cups homemade beef stock (see Index) or canned broth
1 cup water
⅛ teaspoon crumbled saffron threads
15 Calamata or other imported black olives
2 Preserved Lemons (see Index), pulp discarded, skin slivered
¼ cup chopped cilantro (fresh coriander)
4 cups cooked couscous

1. Combine all the ingredients for the spice mixture in a large bowl, and stir well. Add the lamb, and turn to coat it well.

2. Lightly brown the lamb, in batches in the oil, over medium heat, in a flameproof casserole or dutch oven. Return all the meat to the casserole, and add the onions. Cook, stirring, 5 minutes. Then add the stock, water, and saffron. Bring to a boil, reduce the heat, and cover. Simmer for 1 hour.

3. Stir in the olives and slivered preserved lemons. Cover, and simmer another 30 minutes.

4. Spoon the tagine into soup bowls (preferably over steamed couscous), sprinkle with the cilantro, and serve.

4 to 6 portions

> "It's better to be a lion for a day than a sheep all of your life."
> —SISTER ELIZABETH KENNY

A SUN COUNTRY SUPPER

Sunset Melon With Salmon and Prosciutto
Champagne

Marrakesh Lamb Tagine
Moroccan Pilaf
Côte de Beaune

Baby Lettuce Salad With Lemon Chèvre Dressing

Key Lime Chiffon Pie

LAMB IN A GREEK WAY

Zucchini and lamb were made for each other—especially when seasoned with the spices that epitomize Greek cooking. Garlic, mint, oregano, and rosemary are mixed with pine nuts and currants to spice up the lamb filling, and are all baked together in zucchini shells.

4 zucchini, about 5 to 6 inches long
1 teaspoon coarse (kosher) salt
1 tablespoon olive oil
2 tablespoons minced garlic
1 pound ground lamb
½ cup pine nuts (pignoli)
3 ripe plum tomatoes, chopped
1 teaspoon dried oregano
1 tablespoon chopped fresh rosemary leaves
1 tablespoon chopped fresh mint leaves
¼ cup dried currants
Salt and freshly ground black pepper, to taste
¼ cup seasoned bread crumbs, homemade (see Index) or store-bought

1. Trim the ends off the zucchini. Cut the zucchini in half lengthwise; scoop out the pulp, leaving a ¼-inch-thick shell. Set aside the pulp. Sprinkle the interior of the shells with the coarse salt, and lay them, cut side down, on paper towels to drain for 30 minutes.

2. Preheat the oven to 350°F. Cover a baking sheet with aluminum foil.

3. Heat the oil in a skillet over low heat, and add the garlic. Sauté until soft, about 3 minutes.

4. Add the lamb and sauté until browned, stirring to break up the lumps. Then add the pine nuts, tomatoes, 1 cup of the reserved zucchini pulp, oregano, rosemary, mint, currants, and salt and pepper. Stir, and remove the skillet from the heat.

5. Cut a thin slice off the bottom of each zucchini shell so it will lie flat, and place them on the prepared baking sheet. Fill the shells with the lamb mixture. Sprinkle them with the bread crumbs, and bake for 30 minutes. Serve immediately.

4 portions

WINES WITH LAMB

MEAT	WINE
Leg Roasts and Racks of Lamb	Rubesco di Torgiano, Bordeaux, Cabernet Sauvignon
Moussaka and Curries	Zinfandel, Syrah, Valpolicella
Ragouts and Stews	Côte de Beaune
Lamb Stuffed With Vegetables	Merlot

EGGPLANT WRAPPED MOUSSAKA

We wrap our moussaka in eggplant slices and mold it in a round casserole. Apricots, currants, mint, and acorn squash add exciting new flavors to this dish, served with a Minted Yogurt Sauce.

2 teaspoons ground cumin
2 teaspoons ground ginger
2 teaspoons paprika
2 teaspoons ground cinnamon
½ teaspoon cayenne pepper
⅓ cup unbleached all-purpose flour
1 ¾ teaspoons salt
Freshly ground black pepper, to taste
¼ cup milk
1 large eggplant (about 1 ½ pounds), cut into
*   ¼-inch-thick slices*
2 tablespoons olive oil
1 onion, chopped
⅓ cup sliced almonds (with skins)
1 ½ pounds ground lamb
1 can (16 ounces) crushed tomatoes
1 cup homemade beef stock (see Index)
*   or canned broth*
½ cup chopped dried apricots
⅓ cup dried currants
3 tablespoons chopped fresh mint leaves
1 acorn squash (about 1 pound), halved,
*   seeded, and cooked until soft*
½ cup cooked white rice
2 teaspoons fresh lemon juice
1 ⅓ cups Minted Yogurt Sauce (recipe follows)

1. Preheat the oven to 375°F. Lightly grease two baking sheets and a 10-inch round, 2-inch-deep casserole (preferably glass).

2. Combine the cumin, ginger, paprika, cinnamon, and cayenne in a small bowl. Blend thoroughly.

3. Combine the flour, 1⅓ tablespoons of the spice mixture, 1 teaspoon of the salt, and pepper in a shallow bowl. Mix well. Pour the milk into another shallow bowl.

4. Dip each eggplant slice first in the milk, letting any excess drip off, and then in the flour mixture, pressing lightly so it is evenly coated. Shake off any

excess flour, and arrange the slices in a single layer on the prepared baking sheets. Bake until soft, 30 minutes (there may still be traces of flour on the eggplant). Remove the eggplant but leave the oven on.

5. Meanwhile, heat the oil in a large skillet. Stir in the onion and almonds, and cook over medium heat until the onion is soft and the almonds are toasted, 8 to 10 minutes. Add the lamb, raise the heat slightly, and cook, stirring and breaking up the meat, until browned, about 10 minutes. Pour off all but 2 tablespoons fat from the skillet.

6. Stir the remaining spice mixture into the meat, and cook 1 minute. Then stir in the tomatoes, stock, apricots, currants, and mint. Scoop the squash into the mixture in chunks. Stir in the rice, lemon juice, and remaining ¾ teaspoon salt. Remove the skillet from the heat.

7. Arrange a layer of cooked eggplant on the bottom and up the sides of the prepared casserole. Fill with the lamb mixture, and top with the remaining eggplant. Cover with aluminum foil, and bake 1 hour.

8. Remove the casserole from the oven and allow it to stand, still covered, for 15 minutes. Then uncover, and invert the moussaka onto a serving platter. Cut it into wedges, and serve with the Minted Yogurt Sauce.

6 to 8 portions

MINTED YOGURT SAUCE

1 ¼ cups plain low-fat yogurt
¼ cup chopped fresh mint leaves
1 tablespoon fresh lemon juice
¼ teaspoon salt
Freshly ground black pepper, to taste

Stir all the ingredients together in a bowl until smooth. Refrigerate, covered, until ready to serve.

1 ⅓ cups

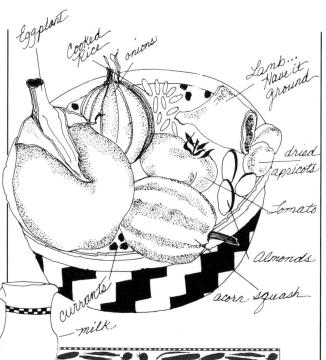

NEW BASICS MEAT AND POTATOES

Here are some of our favorite "lamb and" combinations:

Braised Lamb Shanks
Polenta With Sweet Gorgonzola

Eggplant Wrapped Moussaka
Minty Tabbouleh

Rack of Lamb for Two
Basil Barley Provençal

Lamb Curry With Condiments
Kasha Varnishkes

Spring Lamb With Fresh Mint
Vinaigrette
Vegetable Garden Lasagne

Lamb Stuffed With Spinach and
Chèvre
Crunchy Lentil Salad

BRAVO ITALIA!

The Italians have seduced us with their culinary spirit. The simplicity of their preparation of robust, luscious dishes is heavenly. Cooks in Italy take the very best from nature and with great creative talent, harmonize it all. To us, every meal seems a party—there's more contagious laughter at mealtime in Italy than anywhere else we know.

While appreciation of food is taken very seriously throughout the country, it is the region of Tuscany that beckons us most often. We're refreshed by the vistas of silvery green cypress, the sun-baked terra-cotta rooftops, and the quaint bridges spanning the Arno. Again and again we have been mesmerized by some new flavor, only to find out that it is a centuries-old tradition. Here, the trattorias and country kitchens are redolent with the flavors of basil, rosemary, garlic, olive oil, Parmesan, porcini, Chianti, and prosciutto.

Italian tastes have all become very dear to us, and their influence on our own cooking is clearly evident in this chapter as well as throughout this book.

WINES OF ITALY

Remember the days when ordering an Italian wine meant receiving a round green bottle wrapped in raffia with a long neck—a perfect candleholder once the wine was drunk? In retrospect, those were more the good old days of Italian wine bottle design than they were of Italian wine drinking. But things have changed. Today we are able to participate in very lively debates comparing some of the truly great Italian reds to those from France.

Italian wine-labeling laws now help you choose a good Italian wine. D.O.C. (*Denominazione di Origine Controllata*) indicates the wine has met the standard for quality control. D.O.C.G. (*Denominazione di Origine Controllata e Garantita*) is awarded to a wine only under the authority of the Ministry of Agriculture and Forestry, guaranteeing the wine is of the best quality.

Tuscany: This region is celebrated for its glorious Chianti. The vines that grow in abundance between Florence and Siena produce the fine Chianti Classico and Chianti Rufina. As many as five grapes are combined in the distinctive traditional formula: Sangiovese are used for the body of the wine; Canaiolo for sweetness and aroma; the whites Trebbiano and Malvasia lighten the color; while Colorino adds the ruby glow. An aged Chianti is a splendid, elegant wine.

Brunello di Montalcino is one of the great reds Italy has to offer. Similar in characteristics to some of the great Burgundies, this extraordinarily powerful fine wine, made from Brunello grapes (a variety of Sangiovese), should be decanted before serving.

Vino Nobile di Montepulciano is well worth buying. This rich, deep red wine was originally made from the Sangiovese grape by the nobles of the town.

Vin Santo, the "saintly" dessert wine, is made from delicately dried Trebbiano and Malvasia grapes. This golden nectar is the perfect dip for the hard little almond biscotti we love so dearly.

Piedmont: Piedmont is home to some of the finest wines Italy has to offer, among them two great reds from the Nebbiolo grape. Barolo, a powerful, robust red, is deep in color and strong in bouquet. The long aging process (many are aged for eight years) is important in softening the wine. Because of its strength and full body, this wine is best served with intensely flavored dishes such as game and red meats. We love Barolo served with our Rabbit Ragout Pasta.

Barbaresco, another great red, is a younger wine and lighter than Barolo. Quite strong in tannin when young, it becomes smooth and graceful when it's aged for the typical four years. Like its relative Barolo, Barbaresco is also excellent served with robust, flavorful dishes.

Gattinara, although not as magnificent as Barolo and Barbaresco, is also another popular red. Rich in bouquet, this rose-scented wine is high in tannin and delightful served with game birds and polenta.

Cortese di Gavi, a delightful white wine from southern Piedmont made from Cortese grapes, is gaining popularity in America. This dry white is best enjoyed while young.

Asti Spumante, familiar to many Americans, also hails from Piedmont. A sparkling white wine from Muscat grapes, Asti Spumante is both fruity and sweet. Bursting forth with a flowery bouquet, this wine says "Celebrate!"

Veneto: While not considered great, the red and white wines produced in the region around Venice are well liked, well known, and widely avail-

able in America. Soave, with its straw-like hue, is made from the familiar Trebbiano grape. Ask for dry Soave and serve it well chilled.

Bardolino, named for the town on the shore of Lake Garda, should be enjoyed while the wine is young to appreciate its charms. Serve this light and fruity red lightly chilled with creamy sweet Gorgonzola, ripe pears, and almonds.

Valpolicella is considered a delightful red when it is at its best. This fruity wine resembles a Beaujolais and is lovely served with antipasti laden with sausages and salamis. Try a glass with our fresh Fava Beans and Sopressata.

Umbria: This region is known for producing one of Italy's most charming white wines, Orvieto. The semisweet Orvietos are made from Trebbiano, Malvasia, Verdicchio, Verdello, and Procanico grapes. Orvieto is fruity yet delicate and should be enjoyed young. The dry Orvietos are made predominantly from Trebbiano grapes. Serve chilled with light seafood salads.

Rubesco di Torgiano, an excellent red from Umbria, resembles an even deeper and fuller-bodied Chianti. Enjoy it with hearty pastas and roast lamb.

Sicily: Sicily gives us Marsala, the sweet amber dessert wine that is also lovely served as an aperitif. While so many Americans use inexpensive versions of this wine for cooking, this was not its original raison d'être. It is a favorite of Italians, yet the finest varieties are becoming more difficult to find. Made from the must (grape juice syrup) of highly aromatic white wines and from dried grapes fermented with brandy, Marsala is a blended wine aged in casks for at least two years. Try to locate a fine aged Marsala and enjoy a satisfying new experience.

MINESTRONE

Minestrone, the quintessential Italian vegetable soup, varies from region to region throughout that country. In Milan it is made with rice and peas (not beans), in Genoa pesto is added, in Florence the beans are cooked separately and half of them puréed to thicken the soup, and in southern Italy minestrone is based on garlic.

While we generally serve minestrone as a hot first course, in Italy, in the summertime, we've enjoyed it at room temperature. In any season, though, it must be served with freshly grated Parmesan.

4 ounces salt pork, rind removed and cut into ¼-inch dice
2 tablespoons unsalted butter
4 cloves garlic, finely minced
2 carrots, peeled and cut into ¼-inch dice
1 onion, peeled and cut into ¼-inch dice
1 leek (white part and 1 inch green), well rinsed, quartered lengthwise, and cut into ¼-inch-thick slices
3 cups finely shredded green cabbage
2 zucchini, quartered lengthwise and cut into ¼-inch-thick slices
1 Idaho potato, peeled and cut into ¼-inch dice
4 cups Berta's Chicken Stock (see Index) or canned broth
2 cups homemade beef stock (see Index) or canned broth
2 tablespoons tomato paste
5 tablespoons chopped fresh Italian (flat-leaf) parsley
2 teaspoons dried oregano
1½ teaspoons dried basil
1 teaspoon coarsely ground black pepper
Salt, to taste
¾ cup dried red kidney beans, cooked and drained (about 2 cups)
4 ripe plum tomatoes, cut into ¼-inch dice
½ cup small pasta, such as tiny bow shapes or ditali (short macaroni)
Freshly grated Parmesan cheese, for garnish

1. Cook the salt pork in a large soup pot over low heat to render the fat, about 10 minutes. Do not let it brown. Add the butter, and when it has melted, add the garlic, carrots, onion, and leek and raise the heat slightly. Cover and wilt the vegetables for 10 minutes, stirring occasionally.

2. Add the cabbage, zucchini, potato, both stocks, and tomato paste. Bring to a boil. Reduce the heat and add 2 tablespoons of the parsley, oregano, basil, pepper, and salt. Simmer over medium heat for 15 minutes.

3. Add the kidney beans, tomatoes, and pasta. Simmer until the pasta is tender, 10 minutes. Adjust the seasonings and heat through. Stir in the remaining 3 tablespoons parsley before serving. Pass the Parmesan cheese alongside.

6 to 8 portions

RIBOLLITA

This is our version of a thick vegetable soup traditionally made a day or two ahead in Tuscan kitchens, then *ribollita,* or recooked. In addition to the best seasonal vegetables, classic ribollita contains white beans and *cavolo nero,* a dark green cabbage. For ours we use spinach.

This is really a meal. Just toss a little arugula with balsamic vinegar, pour a glass of Chianti Classico, and you're in heaven.

5 ½ cups Berta's Chicken Stock
    (see Index) or canned broth
½ cup dry white wine
8 ounces chicken wings
7 tablespoons olive oil
1 cup chopped leeks
2 cups chopped onions
1 cup chopped carrots
1 cup chopped celery
¾ cup chopped red bell pepper
¾ cup chopped green bell pepper
1 small yellow summer squash,
    sliced into ¼-inch rounds
1 small zucchini, sliced into ¼-inch rounds
2 cups diced green cabbage
2 cups chopped cooked spinach
1 tablespoon dried oregano
Salt and freshly ground black pepper, to taste
1 can (16 ounces) plum tomatoes, drained
1 can (16 ounces) dark red kidney beans, drained
    7 very thin slices white bread
    2 tablespoons minced garlic
    ⅓ cup freshly grated Parmesan cheese

1. In a large saucepan combine the stock, wine, and chicken wings. Bring to a boil, reduce the heat, and simmer for 25 minutes. Strain the stock, discarding the wings (or reserving them for another use), and set aside.

2. Preheat the oven to 350°F.

3. Heat 5 tablespoons of the oil in a large skillet. Add the leeks, onions, carrots, and celery. Sauté until slightly wilted, 10 minutes. Add the red and green peppers and sauté another 5 minutes. Then add the yellow squash, zucchini, and cabbage, and cook another 10 minutes.

4. Remove the skillet from the heat. Add the spinach, oregano, salt and pepper, tomatoes, and kidney beans.

5. Cut the crusts off the bread and lightly toast the slices.

6. Spread half the vegetable mixture in the bottom of a large ovenproof casserole. Layer the toast next, and then top with the remaining vegetable mixture.

7. In a small skillet, heat the remaining 2 tablespoons olive oil. Add the garlic and sauté until lightly browned. Spoon the garlic over the vegetables.

8. Add the reserved stock to the casserole, and sprinkle with the Parmesan cheese. Bake for 40 minutes. Serve piping hot.

6 portions

On the Italian Riviera, in Viareggio, there is a tradition that a good soup must always contain one stone from the sea. This stems from the days when an Italian fisherman's catch was scooped up in nets and landed all in the same pot. We like the thought.

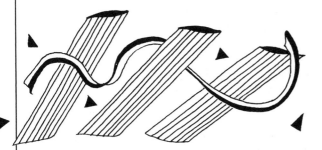

ITALIAN SAUSAGE AND PENNE

Broccoli florets and hot and sweet Italian sausages make a wonderful sauce for these hearty pasta quills. Sausage and penne is a traditional combination in Lucca and Siena, where the pork is very good. There they add a little tomato and cream to the sauce at the last moment.

5 tablespoons olive oil
4 cloves garlic, slivered
1 pound sweet and/or hot Italian sausages
4 cups broccoli florets, cut in both small and large pieces
12 ounces penne
¼ cup freshly grated Parmesan cheese
¾ teaspoon salt
½ teaspoon fennel seeds
Freshly ground black pepper, to taste
3 tablespoons chopped fresh fennel ferns (optional)

1. Heat 1 tablespoon of the oil in a large skillet. Add the garlic, and sauté over medium heat until it is golden and crisp, 3 to 5 minutes. Remove the garlic with a slotted spoon. Set it aside.

2. Remove 2 of the sausages from their casing and crumble the meat. Cut the remaining sausages into thirds. Add all the sausage to the same skillet, and cook over medium heat until browned, 3 to 4 minutes. Then cover, and simmer until cooked through, about 10 minutes. Remove the meat with a slotted spoon and set aside. Pour off all but 2 tablespoons fat.

3. Bring a large pot of lightly salted water to a boil. Add the broccoli, and blanch it for 3 minutes. Remove the broccoli with a slotted spoon, and drain, reserving the cooking liquid. Rinse the broccoli under cold water, drain again, and set aside.

4. Bring the broccoli cooking liquid to a boil again, and add the penne. Cook at a rolling boil until just tender. Drain, reserving ½ cup of the cooking liquid. Keep the penne warm in a covered bowl on top of the stove.

5. In a large saucepan, heat the sausage, broccoli, reserved ½ cup cooking liquid, and remaining 4 tablespoons olive oil.

6. Place the pasta in a heated serving bowl, and add the sausage mixture. Top with the Parmesan, salt, fennel seeds, pepper, and fennel ferns. Toss well, and sprinkle with the reserved garlic. Serve immediately, and pass the Parmesan.

4 portions

DUCK MEDITERRANEAN

Prepared in a Mediterranean style, these ducks are bathed in the flavor of green olives.

1 duck (about 3¾ pounds), well rinsed and patted dry
1½ cups Berta's Chicken Stock or homemade beef stock (see Index) or canned broth
1¾ cups dry white wine
4 sprigs oregano, thyme, rosemary, or Italian (flat-leaf) parsley
1 clove garlic, minced
½ teaspoon salt
Freshly ground black pepper, to taste
1 tablespoon whole-grain mustard
1 tablespoon unbleached all-purpose flour
1 cup green Greek or Italian olives, pitted

1. Cut the duck into pieces: Remove and discard the backbone. Remove the wings and reserve them for another use. Remove the legs, and separate the drumsticks from the thighs. Halve each breast crosswise.

2. Place the breast pieces in a 3-quart microwave-safe casserole, and cook at full power (650 to 700 watts), uncovered, for 5 minutes. Transfer the breast pieces to a plate, and pour the cooking liquid into a glass measuring cup.

3. Place the leg pieces in the casserole and cook for 4 minutes. Transfer them to the same plate, and pour the liquid into the measuring cup. Skim off any fat, and add enough broth to make ¾ cup.

4. Return all the meat to the casserole, and add the cooking liquid, 1½ cups of the wine, the oregano, garlic, salt, and a generous grinding of pepper. Cover, and cook at full power for 15 minutes. Stir, and cook another 20 minutes.

5. Remove the meat from the casserole and set it aside. In a small bowl, whisk together 1 cup stock, the remaining ¼ cup wine, and the mustard and flour. Stir this into the casserole, add the olives, and cook at full power, uncovered, for 3 minutes.

6. Stir the sauce until it is smooth; then add the duck, cover, and cook for 8 minutes. Serve immediately.

2 to 4 portions

Note: This recipe was cooked on High (full power, 650 to 700 watts) in a carousel microwave, using microwave-safe containers.

If your microwave is less powerful, you will have to allow for more cooking time (approximately 1½ times the amount called for—but watch carefully); if it does not have a carousel, you may have to rotate the dish while it is cooking.

> "**I**f you have no idea where you want to go, it makes little difference how fast you travel."
>
> —ITALIAN PROVERB

SICILIAN STYLE CHICKEN

All the robust flavors of southern Italy are combined in this gutsy chicken dish. Freshly chopped garlic and parsley intensify the kick at the last minute. Serve with pappardelle on the side to help savor the sauce and plenty of Chianti to drink.

½ cup Berta's Chicken Stock (see Index) or canned broth
½ cup dry white wine
1 ounce dried cèpes or morels
¼ cup olive oil
2 chickens (2½ to 3 pounds each), well rinsed, patted dry, and cut into 8 pieces each
12 cloves garlic
2 cups diced onions
¼ cup brandy
6 cups chopped drained canned Italian plum tomatoes
½ cup pitted Calamata or Niçoise olives
¼ cup coarsely chopped sun-dried tomatoes
4 ounces anchovy fillets, drained and coarsely chopped
3 tablespoons capers, drained
1 tablespoon red wine vinegar
2 bay leaves
2 tablespoons dried oregano
1 tablespoon dried basil
Freshly ground black pepper, to taste
½ cup chopped fresh Italian (flat-leaf) parsley

1. Combine the stock, wine, and dried mushrooms in a small saucepan. Bring to a boil, reduce the heat, and simmer 15 minutes. Set the mixture aside.

2. Heat the oil in a large dutch oven. Add the chicken in small batches, and sauté over medium heat on both sides. Transfer the chicken to a platter.

3. Mince 8 of the garlic cloves, and add them to the dutch oven along with the onions. Cook until tender, 5 minutes. Then return the chicken to the dutch oven. Add the brandy, and carefully flame, shaking the dutch oven slightly until the flame subsides.

4. Add the plum tomatoes, olives, sun-dried tomatoes, anchovies, capers, vinegar, bay leaves, oregano, basil, pepper, and reserved mushrooms and their soaking liquid to the chicken. Stir well, cover, and simmer over medium heat for 30 minutes, occasionally stirring gently.

5. While the chicken is cooking, mince the remaining 4 garlic cloves and combine them with all but 1 tablespoon of the parsley. Toss well and set aside.

6. Remove the dutch oven from the heat. Transfer the chicken to a serving platter, and keep warm. Add the reserved parsley mixture to the dutch oven, and simmer, uncovered, for 5 minutes. Spoon the sauce over the chicken, sprinkle with the remaining 1 tablespoon parsley, and serve.

6 to 8 portions

SAGE

Sage is among the greatest of Mediterranean herbs, and anyone who has been to Spain, Italy, or Greece can attest to the richness of flavor it imparts to their most important pasta, pork, lamb, chicken, vegetable, and cheese dishes. Perhaps sage is more popular in Europe, and used in a greater variety of dishes than it is here, because the Europeans understand how to use it sparingly. Too much sage overpowers a dish with a musty taste and smell.

TUSCAN CHICKEN

The more delicate tastes of Tuscany infuse this skillet-baked chicken. It goes right from oven to table. We love serving this dish with Our Basic Polenta and Olive Rosemary Country Bread.

1 chicken (3 to 4 pounds), well rinsed, patted dry, trimmed
*   of excess fat, and cut into 8 pieces*
¾ cup Chianti or other dry red wine
3 ribs celery, cut into 1½-inch pieces
6 shallots, peeled and quartered
15 oil-cured olives, pitted
⅓ cup golden raisins
¼ cup capers, drained
2 teaspoons dried sage leaves, crumbled
2 teaspoons dried rosemary, crumbled
1 teaspoon salt
Freshly ground black pepper, to taste
1 tablespoon olive oil
¾ cup homemade beef stock (see Index) or canned broth
¼ cup tomato paste

1. In a large bowl combine the chicken pieces, wine, celery, shallots, olives, raisins, and capers. Sprinkle with 1 teaspoon of the sage, 1 teaspoon of the rosemary, ½ teaspoon of the salt, and pepper. Mix well, cover, refrigerate, and marinate overnight.

2. Preheat the oven to 350°F.

3. Heat the oil in a heavy ovenproof skillet. Lift the chicken from the marinade, and sauté over medium heat until golden. Reserve the marinade.

4. While the chicken is sautéing, stir together the reserved marinade, the stock, tomato paste, remaining 1 teaspoon sage, 1 teaspoon rosemary, ½ teaspoon salt, and pepper to taste. When the chicken is browned, pour this mixture over it and bring to a boil.

5. Transfer the skillet to the oven and, basting and degreasing twice, bake 45 minutes. (Degrease by using a large metal spoon to carefully skim off any accumulated fat.)

6. Bring the skillet to the table, and serve immediately.

4 portions

> "**W**ine is sunlight, held together by water."
> —GALILEO

CAPRETTO ALLA ROMANO
(Baked Baby Goat, Roman Style)

At Nicola Civetta's New York restaurant, Primavera, a goat is roasted in the Roman style on Sunday nights. We have always enjoyed the flavors of this dish and were delighted that he shared the recipe with us.

1 rack of young goat (see Step 1)
½ cup dry white wine
Juice of 1 lemon
¼ cup extra virgin olive oil
2 cloves garlic, minced
1 sprig rosemary
1 sprig sage
Salt and freshly ground black pepper, to taste

1. Cut the ribs of the goat individually, approximately 2 inches thick, or have the butcher do this for you.
2. Mix the remaining ingredients in a large bowl, add the meat, and marinate at room temperature for at least 30 minutes, but no more than 4 hours.
3. Preheat the broiler.
4. Arrange the meat on a rack in a broiling plan, and broil until browned, approximately 3 minutes on each side. Serve immediately.

4 portions
Note: This can also be cooked on an outdoor grill.

SCHIACCIATA CON L'UVA
(Tuscan Grape Bread)

Since the days of the Etruscans, Florentines have been making this great round bread to celebrate the *vendemmia,* the harvest of the grapes.

The texture is more like a cake than a bread, and we've sweetened it with raisins soaked in Strega. You can use seedless grapes of course, but we like the crunch—a reminder of the crushing of the grapes! This is good with a roast, or toasted at breakfast, or anytime at all with a bottle of new wine.

SPONGE
¾ cup unbleached all-purpose flour
2 teaspoons sugar
1 package active dry yeast
½ cup warm water

½ cup large dark raisins
¼ cup Strega liqueur
¼ cup fruity olive oil
2 tablespoons fresh rosemary leaves
1 teaspoon aniseeds, crushed
1½ cups Concord grapes (with seeds)
2 cups unbleached all-purpose flour
6 tablespoons sugar
½ teaspoon salt
1 egg
Freshly ground black pepper, to taste

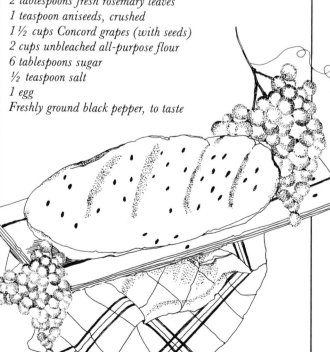

1. Make the sponge: Stir together the ¾ cup flour, sugar, yeast, and warm water in a bowl until smooth. Cover, and let stand in a warm place until doubled in bulk, 30 to 60 minutes.

2. While the sponge is rising, combine the raisins and Strega in a small bowl, and set aside to soak.

3. Heat the oil in a small skillet, and add the rosemary and aniseeds. Cook over low heat until fragrant, 5 minutes. Allow the mixture to cool slightly.

4. Toss the grapes with 2 tablespoons of the cooled herb-oil mixture, and set aside.

5. Place the 2 cups flour, 2 tablespoons of the sugar, and the salt and egg in a food processor. Add the sponge and the remaining 2 tablespoons herb-oil mixture. Pulse the processor on and off until the mixture forms a mass. Then process until it is soft and just slightly sticky, about 40 seconds.

6. Transfer the dough to a lightly floured surface, and knead 2 minutes. Drain the raisins, and work them into the dough; knead 1 minute. Let the dough rest in a warm place for 10 minutes.

7. Roll the dough out to form a rectangle about 14 x 10 inches, and transfer it to a baking sheet. Spoon the reserved grapes and their oil over the dough, leaving a ½-inch border all around. Sprinkle them with pepper and the remaining 4 tablespoons sugar. Cover the dough loosely, and let it rise in a warm place until doubled in bulk, 40 to 60 minutes.

8. Preheat the oven to 400°F.

9. Transfer the baking sheet to the oven, and bake until the loaf is puffed and deep gold, 25 minutes.

6 to 8 portions

"**I** fell in love for the first time in my life in Florence—with a town!"

—JANE GRIGSON

TIRAMISU

Venice's favorite dessert has become popular in chic Italian restaurants in America. The name means "pick me up," and it does indeed give us a lift! You can use ladyfingers or a *génoise* as a base—the latter being a little more elegant but also a bit more work. We prefer the peasant version.

3 egg yolks
2 tablespoons confectioners' sugar
2 tablespoons orange-flavored liqueur
1 tablespoon sweet Marsala
8 ounces mascarpone cheese
6 tablespoons strong coffee or espresso, cold
12 ladyfingers, broken into thirds
2 ounces milk chocolate, grated

1. Beat the egg yolks and confectioners' sugar together with an electric mixer until pale and thick. Slowly beat in 1 tablespoon of the liqueur and the Marsala. Add the mascarpone, and beat until the mixture is thick and smooth.

2. In a small bowl, combine the coffee and the remaining 1 tablespoon liqueur. Drop three ladyfinger pieces in the bottom of each of six wine glasses. Drizzle half the coffee mixture over the ladyfingers. Then spoon in half the mascarpone, and sprinkle with half the grated chocolate.

3. Repeat the layers with the remaining ladyfingers, coffee, mascarpone, and chocolate. Cover and chill for 2 hours before serving.

6 portions

TAMING GAME

In past years, the fall season in restaurants seemed the most exciting for the number and variety of great game entrées. We've nearly licked the platters clean of pheasant with lentils, venison chili, rabbit with tarragon and mustard sauce, roast quail with polenta, and casserole of wild duck. But game is too good to leave only to chefs and hunters. With farm-raised game available to home cooks and a few simple cooking tips, no one should have to go out for great game dinners. A rabbit in every pot and venison in every freezer seems to us a very fine thing, indeed.

ABOUT GAME

Today, most of the game we find in butcher shops, supermarkets, and restaurants has been raised on farms. This tame game delivers flavors more robust than those of our very domestic animals without being too wild. As the demand for full-flavored game increases, breeders are responding by raising the game in more natural environments.

Wild game is leaner, stronger tasting, and sometimes tougher than other meats. Most wild game has 5 to 7 percent fat, whereas a piece of prime well-marbled beef contains as much as 45 percent fat. The gamy flavor most associate with wild game comes not from its diet but from the aging process. If it looks to you like every hunting season is going to bring wild game to your kitchen, it will be well worth your while to study and experiment with ways of aging and preparing the animals for cooking. The rewards will be great. Keep in mind, too, that when working with wild game it is important to wear rubber gloves. Wild rabbits and other small game may harbor a bacterium that causes an infection called tularemia. Gloves should prevent any possible problems.

THE FLAVOR OF GAME

The age, size, species, sex, exercise patterns, water, feed, fresh air, and general well-being all affect the taste of a particular bird or animal. The way the animal was killed and the aging process further change the taste and texture of game. After that, it is up to the cook using technique, experience, and flavorings to bring this meat to the table. Especially with wild game, no one duck or deer will taste like another.

FREEZING GAME

If we have a choice, we prefer to cook game fresh, without freezing. Fattier meat freezes best, and

game, even when raised on farms, doesn't have much fat. But a bird in the freezer is still worth more than two in the bush. To freeze game, wrap the meat twice with aluminum foil or freezer wrap. Don't forget to label and date the package. Freeze it as quickly and at as low a temperature as possible. Plan to cook it within six months.

COOKING GAME

Aging game tenderizes the meat but produces a gamy taste that some do not like, yet others do. If you want to cut the gamy taste, by all means marinate the meat. A good marinade tenderizes the meat without entirely masking its flavor. Wine will bring out the tangy side of the flavor, and after marinating, the wine can be used to make a sauce for the meat. Buttermilk will mellow the meat, and olive oil and brandy both enhance the natural flavor. Marinating time depends on the size of the animal or cut. Small birds can be marinated for as little as 30 minutes, but a saddle of venison should marinate two to three days.

Because game is very lean, fat must be added to the meat if cooking with dry heat. Traditionally, strips of pork fat are seasoned with herbs and wine and run through large roasts with a larding needle. Birds and rabbits should be covered (barded) with bacon, thin sheets of pork fat, or caul (a lacy web of pork fat). The fat should be removed shortly before the meat is done to let the skin brown. Frequent basting with butter or olive oil will also help keep the meat moist.

Keep in mind that the goal of cooking game is not to have it taste like chicken or beef. The flavor of the meat and the leanness, not the fat, should come through. We've had great success braising game with fruit juices, wines, and spirits—they keep the meat moist and support the flavor without masking it.

VENISON

★

Most of the venison we see at the market is farm-raised in New Zealand, but all deer, once bagged, is venison. The best farm-bred venison is raised as wild, with nothing done to alter the feeding or breeding. The animal should be killed between one and two years of age (the older the tougher). If you have a hunter in the family, point him or her to the high pines where the wild deer have the best flavor.

The flavor of venison is rich and full. We like roasted venison best medium-rare, but whether rare or medium, it should be served hot out of the oven. Don't even give the roast the standard ten-to-fifteen-minute resting time, because the little fat there is on venison congeals quickly and makes unpleasant eating. For the same reason, spoon off all the fat from any pan gravy as well, and of course, trim all visible fat from the roast before cooking. All but the tenderest roasts and steaks should be cooked with moist heat—either braised or stewed. Heavy sauces or redolent marinades do venison no favors. Cook it simply and you won't be disappointed.

If that hunter you sent to the pines does come back with a deer, you are going to find yourself freezing a lot of it for later eating. Remove all the fat from the meat but leave the thin silverskin on. The silverskin must be removed before cooking, but it will protect the meat while in the freezer. Wrap the meat in two layers of aluminum foil or freezer paper. Make sure the packages are airtight, then label and date them. Venison frozen longer than six months will not be rewarding cooking or eating.

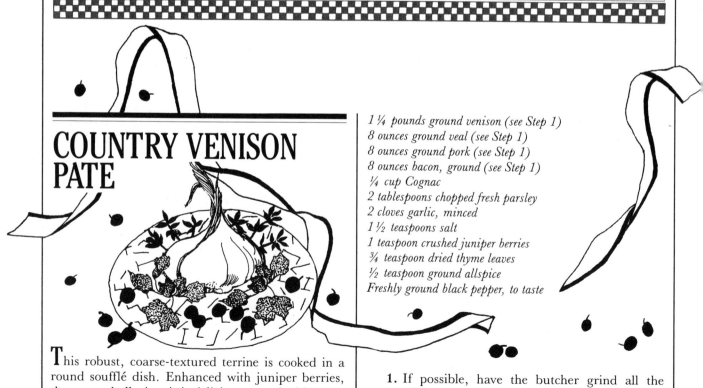

COUNTRY VENISON PATE

1¼ pounds ground venison (see Step 1)
8 ounces ground veal (see Step 1)
8 ounces ground pork (see Step 1)
8 ounces bacon, ground (see Step 1)
¼ cup Cognac
2 tablespoons chopped fresh parsley
2 cloves garlic, minced
1½ teaspoons salt
1 teaspoon crushed juniper berries
¾ teaspoon dried thyme leaves
½ teaspoon ground allspice
Freshly ground black pepper, to taste

This robust, coarse-textured terrine is cooked in a round soufflé dish. Enhanced with juniper berries, thyme, and allspice, it is delicious served with sweet onion relish and Ruby Cumberland Sauce.

1. If possible, have the butcher grind all the meats. Otherwise put them through a meat grinder; they should have the texture of raw hamburger.

2. In a large bowl mix all the ingredients, preferably by hand, until well blended. Cover, and refrigerate overnight.

3. Preheat the oven to 325°F.

4. Pack the mixture into a round 6-cup terrine or soufflé dish, and cover it with a double thickness of aluminum foil. Place the terrine in a larger pan, and fill the pan with enough hot water to reach halfway up the sides of the terrine.

5. Bake until the juices run clear, the internal temperature registers 150°F, and the pâté has pulled away from the sides of the terrine, about 2 hours.

6. Let the pâté cool to room temperature in the terrine. Then cover it, and refrigerate for at least 1 day to develop the flavor.

7. Remove any white fat that may have accumulated on top of the pâté. Unmold, and let it stand at room temperature for 30 minutes before slicing and serving.

10 to 12 portions

JUNIPER

Juniper berries are tiny blue berries that grow on prickly, waist-high bushes. The berries smell like a pine forest and are the principal flavoring of gin. In cooking, the berries are always crushed before using to release their perfume. Traditionally, juniper berries are added to marinades for pork and venison, pâtés, sauerkraut, and conserves. We combine them with allspice berries and black peppercorns, crush them all together, and dip both sides of venison steaks lightly in the mixture. This tenderizes the meat and complements its rich flavor. Juniper also combines wonderfully with bay leaves, fennel, marjoram, parsley, thyme, garlic, brandies, and wines.

SADDLE OF VENISON WITH DRIED MICHIGAN CHERRY SAUCE

Tender slices of rare venison fillet are slathered with the richest of sauces, made with bourbon, cranberry juice, and dried Michigan cherries. Cracked pepper and thyme are just the right seasonings. Since you have to hold this roast while you prepare the sauce, be sure to trim it of all visible fat before beginning. You don't want the fat congealing during the time it takes to finish the dish.

2 boneless venison fillets (2¼ pounds total), cut from a
*   3½-pound saddle, well rinsed, and patted dry*
1½ cups cranberry juice
2 tablespoons cracked or coarsely ground black pepper
2 tablespoons dried thyme leaves
1 tablespoon olive oil
¼ cup bourbon
¾ cup homemade beef stock (see Index) or canned broth
½ cup dried Michigan cherries (see Note)
1 tablespoon unsalted butter, at room temperature
1 tablespoon unbleached all-purpose flour
Salt and freshly ground black pepper, to taste

1. Trim any visible fat from the venison fillets. Arrange the fillets in a flat-bottomed bowl just large enough to hold them. Pour 1 cup of the cranberry juice over the meat, cover loosely, and refrigerate overnight.

2. Preheat the oven to 450°F.

3. Remove the venison from the marinade (discard the marinade). Sprinkle the fillets with cracked pepper and thyme.

4. Heat the oil in a large skillet, and brown the fillets on all sides over medium-high heat, about 5 minutes. Transfer the meat to a small baking sheet. Reserve the skillet.

5. Roast the venison for 15 minutes for medium-rare to rare. Remove it from the oven, cover, and set aside.

6. Place the skillet over medium heat, and add the bourbon. Simmer until the liquid has reduced to about 1 tablespoon, scraping up any browned particles. Stir in the stock, the remaining ½ cup cranberry juice, and the dried berries. Simmer for 5 minutes.

7. Stir the butter and flour together in a small bowl until a smooth paste (*beurre manié*) is formed. Add this to the sauce bit by bit, whisking well after each addition. Simmer until the sauce is smooth and thick enough to coat a spoon, about 3 minutes. Skim off any fat that may have accumulated around the fillets, and add any remaining juices to the sauce. Whisk again. Season with salt and pepper.

8. Cut the fillets into ¼- to ½-inch-thick slices. Spoon a pool of sauce onto each plate, and arrange the slices, overlapping, on the sauce. Serve immediately.

4 to 6 portions

Note: Many specialty food stores and fine supermarkets are now carrying these dried berries. They are wonderful additions in game dishes and also dress up fish in a spectacular way. If you can't find them locally, they can be ordered from American Spoon Foods, 411 East Lake Street, Petosky, Michigan 49770; (800) 222-5886.

If you can't find fresh venison where you live, order it from the Lucky Star Ranch in northern New York State. Those who enjoy their wild game mild and tender will relish the lean, dark red meat of the farmed fallow deer. Venison is low in both fat and cholesterol—even more reason to celebrate the holidays with it. Order three weeks in advance. Call (607)VENISON from 8 A.M. to 4 P.M. (E.S.T.) weekdays.

VENISON STEW

If you hunt deer or have a friend who does, you'll find that there will be plenty of meat that isn't tender enough for roasting. This autumnal stew is a great solution.

2 cups Berta's Chicken Stock
    (see Index) or canned broth
2 cups Madeira
1 cup dry red wine
1 cup red wine vinegar
½ cup plus 2 tablespoons olive oil
4 cloves garlic, coarsely chopped
2 teaspoons dried thyme
2 teaspoons freshly ground black pepper
8 juniper berries, crushed
1 bay leaf
3 pounds boneless venison shoulder, cut into 1½-inch pieces
8 ounces bacon, cut into 1-inch pieces
3 tablespoons unbleached all-purpose flour
1 rutabaga (about 2½ pounds), peeled and cut into ½-inch cubes
12 small white onions (about 1½ inches in diameter)
4 tablespoons (½ stick) unsalted butter
2 teaspoons sugar
2 cups pitted dates
1 large fennel bulb, julienned
3 tablespoons coarsely chopped fresh Italian (flat-leaf) parsley

1. In a large bowl, combine the stock, Madeira, red wine, vinegar, ½ cup of the olive oil, garlic, thyme, 1 teaspoon of the pepper, the juniper berries, and bay leaf. Stir well, and add the venison. Stir again, cover, and marinate at room temperature for 2 hours.

2. Preheat the oven to 350°F.

3. Drain the venison, reserving the marinade. Shake the garlic off the meat, and pat the meat dry.

4. Place a large flameproof casserole or dutch oven over medium heat, add the bacon, and cook until it is lightly browned and fat is rendered. Using a slotted spoon, remove the bacon and set it aside.

5. Add the venison to the casserole in batches, and brown it quickly over medium-high heat, adding the remaining 2 tablespoons olive oil if necessary.

6. Return all the meat to the casserole, sprinkle it with the flour, and stir well. Cook over medium heat for 2 to 3 minutes; then add the reserved marinade and cook another 2 minutes. Add the rutabaga and cover the casserole. Transfer it to the center rack of the oven, and bake for 45 minutes.

7. While the venison is cooking, place the onions in a saucepan and cover with water. Bring to a boil, reduce the heat, and simmer for 5 minutes. Drain the onions, and rinse them under cold water. Slip off the skins, but do not cut off the root end. Cut them in half lengthwise.

8. Melt 2 tablespoons of the butter in a skillet. Add the onions and cook over medium heat, shaking the skillet, for 2 minutes. Sprinkle 1 teaspoon of the sugar over them, and cook until they are caramelized, 1 minute. Remove the onions with a slotted spoon and set them aside. Set the skillet aside.

9. Add the onions and dates to the venison, and stir gently. Cover the casserole and continue baking until the meat is tender, another 15 minutes.

10. Meanwhile, add the remaining 2 tablespoons butter to the skillet. Add the fennel, and cook it over medium heat for 3 minutes. Sprinkle it with the remaining 1 teaspoon sugar and 1 teaspoon pepper. Cook until caramelized, 2 minutes, and set aside.

11. When the venison is cooked, gently fold in the cooked fennel, adjust the seasonings, and sprinkle with the parsley. Serve piping hot.

6 portions

PAN-FRIED VENISON STEAKS WITH WINTER VEGETABLES

Venison steaks are often given to friends by avid hunters. Do them proud by serving them with a julienne of rutabaga, carrots, and yams topped off with a creamy mustard sauce. A California Cabernet Sauvignon would be perfect with this.

4 venison steaks (about 2 pounds total)
1 cup olive oil
½ cup white wine vinegar
6 juniper berries
2 bay leaves
1 teaspoon freshly ground black pepper
1 cup julienned carrots
1 cup julienned rutabaga
1 cup julienned yams
⅓ cup vermouth or dry white wine
⅓ cup mustard, preferably half Dijon and half whole-grain
½ cup crème fraîche (see Index) or heavy or whipping cream
Salt and freshly ground black pepper, to taste
1 tablespoon chopped fresh Italian (flat-leaf) parsley

1. Trim the venison steaks of visible fat. Place the steaks in a shallow roasting pan. Combine the oil, vinegar, juniper berries, bay leaves, and pepper in a small bowl. Stir well, and pour over the steaks. Cover the pan, and marinate in the refrigerator, turning occasionally, for 6 hours.

2. Fill a saucepan with 1 inch of water and place a vegetable steamer over it. Bring the water to a boil. Add the carrots and rutabaga, cover, and steam for 5 minutes. Add the yams and steam an additional 5 minutes.

3. While the vegetables are steaming, prepare the meat: Heat a heavy skillet (preferably cast-iron) until quite hot. Remove the steaks from the marinade and sear them quickly on each side. Then cook an additional 2 to 3 minutes per side for rare meat, 4 to 5 minutes for medium.

4. Remove the steaks from the skillet and keep warm. Add the vermouth to the skillet and bring it to a boil, scraping up any browned bits. Then add the mustard, crème fraîche, and salt and pepper. Simmer, whisking constantly, until the liquid is reduced slightly, about 2 minutes.

5. Arrange the vegetables in a half circle on four plates. Place a steak next to the vegetables. Carefully pour the sauce over the steaks and vegetables, garnish with the parsley, and serve immediately.

4 portions

GAME ROASTING CHART

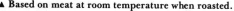

CUT	OVEN TEMPERATURE	INTERNAL TEMPERATURE	COOKING TIME
Venison tenderloin 1½ to 2 pounds	450°F	120° to 125°F for rare; 130° to 140°F for medium-rare	15 to 20 minutes per pound for rare, 25 minutes per pound for medium-rare
Venison saddle 5 to 6 pounds	450°F for 20 minutes, then 350°F	120° to 125°F for rare; 130° to 140°F for medium-rare	15 to 20 minutes per pound for rare, 25 minutes per pound for medium-rare

Rabbit
  2 to 3 pounds
Hare
  3 to 4 pounds
	400°F for 30 minutes,
	then 350°F
			18 to 20 minutes per
			pound

Goose 11 to 13 pounds	325°F	175° to 180°F at inner thigh	13 to 15 minutes per pound
Pheasant 2 to 4 pounds	350°F		40 to 45 minutes per pound
Guinea hen 2½ pounds	425°F for 30 minutes, then 350°F		30 to 35 minutes per pound
Grouse 14 ounces	500°F		18 minutes or 24 to 26 minutes per pound
Squab ¾ to 1 pound	425°F		30 minutes

▲ Based on meat at room temperature when roasted.
▲ Roast goose should rest 15 minutes before carving; internal temperature will rise 5° to 10°F.

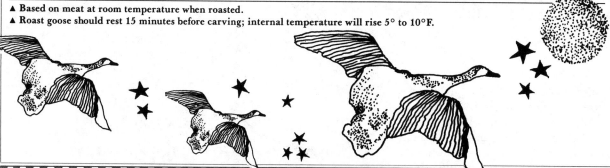

RABBIT AND HARE

Cooks agree that rabbit is a great alternative to chicken—more tender, with more flavor, lean and virtually fat-free, and so versatile that it can be substituted for chicken in most recipes. Rabbit is so popular today, most upscale markets keep it in stock year round.

Rabbit meat is very delicate and lean and takes on the flavor of the rabbit's diet. The close-textured flesh is similar to veal and chicken but sweeter. Because rabbits grow very quickly, they do not need hormones or chemicals to urge them on. Rabbit takes very well to marinades and slow simmering, but it's also delicious cooked quickly over fast heat. In fact, most people's favorite rabbit is grilled or fried. The best rabbits for quick cooking are under two months old. Rabbit with mustard sauce is a classic, but rabbit also loves rosemary, tomatoes, garlic, fennel, prosciutto, pine nuts, raisins, prunes, olives, and Cognac.

The hare is quite different from rabbit. In this country, hares are the American jackrabbit and the snowshoe rabbit. Their heavy hind legs and fleshy saddle are highly prized for the table. Hares are best eating under one year of age. A three-month-old hare will weigh about three pounds. To cook a young hare, first marinate it, then bard it with pork fat before roasting it slowly. Young hare should be served pink. An older hare is best stewed in a casserole and then deboned.

BRAISED RABBIT SMOTHERED WITH ONIONS

This recipe was inspired by a dish from Restaurante Du Marché in Paris. Blended with a bit of mustard, the onions create a rich, delicious sauce that is perfect with rabbit. Begin the meal with a Belgian Endive and Roquefort Salad and accompany all with Châteauneuf-du-Pape.

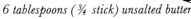

6 tablespoons (¾ stick) unsalted butter
3 tablespoons olive oil
3 rabbits (3 to 3½ pounds each), cut into 8 pieces each, well rinsed and patted dry
1 teaspoon coarsely ground black pepper
4 large onions, peeled, halved, and slivered
8 large cloves garlic, coarsely chopped
2 tablespoons dark brown sugar
1 tablespoon dried thyme leaves
2 teaspoons ground ginger
1 cup dry white wine
½ cup strong chicken stock (see Note)
½ cup homemade beef stock (see Index) or canned broth
Salt, to taste
5 tablespoons Dijon mustard
3 tablespoons chopped fresh Italian (flat-leaf) parsley

1. Preheat the oven to 350°F.
2. Heat 3 tablespoons of the butter and 1½ tablespoons of the oil in a large flameproof casserole. Brown the rabbit pieces, in batches over medium heat, sprinkling them with black pepper. Set them aside.
3. Add the remaining 3 tablespoons butter and 1½ tablespoons oil to the casserole. Add the onions and garlic, and cook over medium-low heat until wilted, about 15 minutes. Sprinkle with the brown sugar, thyme, and ginger; stir well.

4. Return the rabbit pieces to the casserole, and stir gently to mix with the onions. Add the wine, chicken and beef stocks, and salt. Bring to a boil. Then cover the casserole, transfer it to the oven, and bake until the meat is tender, 45 minutes to 1 hour.

5. Using a slotted spoon, remove the rabbit pieces from the casserole, and keep warm. Leave the oven on.

6. Place the casserole over low heat and whisk in the mustard (do not boil). Adjust the seasonings, and return the rabbit pieces to the casserole, stirring gently. Transfer the casserole to the oven and bake, uncovered, 10 minutes.

7. Serve directly from the casserole, or in a deep serving dish, sprinkled with the chopped parsley.

8 portions

Note: For strong stock, reduce 1 cup Berta's Chicken Stock (see Index) to ½ cup.

1. Combine the garlic, thyme, salt, pepper, and 1 tablespoon of the oil in a large bowl. Stir well, then add the rabbit pieces and turn to coat them well. Cover loosely, and let stand at room temperature for 2 hours.

2. Combine the beef stock and pitted olives in a food processor or blender, and purée until smooth. Transfer the mixture to a bowl, stir in the vinegar and tomato paste, and set aside.

3. Preheat the oven to 350°F.

4. Heat the remaining 1 tablespoon oil in a large ovenproof skillet. Sauté the rabbit over medium heat, turning it once or twice, until golden, 10 minutes.

5. Pour the olive sauce over the rabbit, and heat it to a simmer. Then transfer the skillet to the oven and bake for 1 hour, turning and basting the rabbit pieces every 10 minutes. Serve hot.

2 to 4 portions

RABBIT IN BLACK OLIVE SAUCE

Earthy, robust olives, balsamic vinegar, and tomato blend to create a luscious sauce for this richly satisfying dish. And it's an easy dinner to serve guests, since the sauce can be prepared ahead of time, while the rabbit is marinating—all you have to remember is to baste frequently while it's baking.

2 cloves garlic, minced
2 teaspoons fresh thyme leaves or ¾ teaspoon dried
½ teaspoon salt
Freshly ground black pepper, to taste
2 tablespoons olive oil
1 rabbit (about 2¾ pounds), cut into 8 or 10 pieces, well rinsed and patted dry
1 cup homemade beef stock (see Index) or canned broth
½ cup Gaeta or other small black Italian olives, pitted
3 tablespoons balsamic vinegar
1 tablespoon tomato paste

WINES WITH GAME

GAME	WINE
Goose	Pinot Noir, Châteauneuf-du-Pape
Grouse	Pommard, Riesling
Hare	Barbaresco, Shiraz
Partridge	Pinot Noir, Merlot
Pheasant	Brunello di Montalcino
Quail	Riesling, Gamay
Rabbit	Bordeaux, Gattinara
Venison	Barolo, Cabernet Sauvignon
Wild Duck	Gewürztraminer

HERB-ROASTED RABBIT AND POTATOES

Our roasted rabbit makes a Sunday autumnal lunch quite festive. Lots of garlic, bacon, and rosemary complement the rabbit's subtle flavor. Serve with a spicy Zinfandel.

8 red new potatoes, quartered
24 large cloves garlic
6 tablespoons olive oil
4 ounces slab bacon, rind removed and
*   cut into 1-inch cubes*
2 rabbits (2 pounds each), cut into 8 pieces each,
*   well rinsed and patted dry*
6 tablespoons fresh rosemary leaves
*   or 2 tablespoons dried*
2 teaspoons coarsely ground black pepper
Coarse (kosher) salt, to taste (optional)
6 sprigs rosemary, for garnish

1. Preheat the oven to 400°F.

2. Place the potatoes and garlic cloves in a large shallow roasting pan. Sprinkle with 1 tablespoon of the olive oil, and toss to coat. Bake for 30 minutes.

3. While the potatoes and garlic are roasting, combine the bacon and 2 tablespoons of the oil in a large skillet, and place over low heat. Cook just until the bacon begins to wilt. Then remove the bacon with a slotted spoon, and set it aside.

4. Sauté the rabbit, in batches if necessary, in the skillet, setting the pieces aside as they are browned. Reserve 2 tablespoons of the pan drippings.

5. Remove the roasting pan from the oven, and reduce the heat to 350°F.

6. Add the rabbit, rosemary, pepper, coarse salt, reserved pan drippings, and remaining 3 tablespoons oil to the roasting pan with the potatoes and garlic. Toss thoroughly, and return the pan to the oven. Bake for 20 minutes.

7. Sprinkle the reserved bacon over the top, and bake until the meat is tender and the vegetables are golden, another 20 minutes.

8. Arrange the mixture on a warmed platter, and garnish with the rosemary sprigs.

6 portions

OVEN-BRAISED HARE

The raspberry vinegar marinade cuts some of the gamy flavor, and the pomegranate seeds soften the wild rabbit.

1 hare (about 3 ¾ pounds), cut into 12 pieces, well rinsed
*   and patted dry*
1 ½ cups raspberry vinegar
2 tablespoons olive oil
2 ½ cups homemade beef stock (see Index) or canned broth
1 ⅓ cups pomegranate juice (about 5 pomegranates)
¼ cup sugar
1 cup pomegranate seeds

1. Place the hare pieces in a bowl just large enough to contain them. Pour 1 cup of the vinegar over the meat, and then add enough water to cover. Cover the bowl, and marinate the hare overnight in the refrigerator.

2. Preheat the oven to 350°F.

3. Drain the marinated meat, and pat it dry. Heat the oil in a flameproof casserole or dutch oven, and brown the hare over high heat, in batches if necessary. Keep the heat high so that the pieces are seared, not stewed.

4. When all the meat has been browned, add the stock and juice to the casserole, cover partially, and transfer to the oven. Bake for 1 hour and 20 minutes.

5. Stir the meat, cover the casserole tightly, and bake until tender, 40 minutes. Using a slotted spoon, transfer the hare to a large platter and keep warm.

6. Combine the remaining ½ cup vinegar and the sugar in a small saucepan, and bring to a boil. Cook until the mixture is thick and syrupy. Then pour it into the casserole, and place over high heat. Cook just until the sauce has thickened slightly. Strain it over the hare, sprinkle with the pomegranate seeds, and serve immediately.

4 portions

SOME OTHER GAME

——■——

WILD TURKEY

The wild turkey has a much deeper breast and longer legs than the domestic bird. It has a distinctive taste whether it's been raised on a game farm or is truly wild. The flesh is juicy and the bird is best stuffed and roasted. We like a stuffing of wild rice with rosemary and garlic or chestnuts with Madeira, garlic, and parsley. Sear the bird at 450°F for 20 minutes, then reduce the heat to 350°F and roast 15 minutes per pound, basting it every 15 minutes with butter.

SMALL GAME BIRDS

Ortolan, thrush, snipe, woodcock, reedbird, lark, plover, figpecker, coot, dove, quail, moorhen, and grouse—these small birds are the most loved game of many chefs. Their flavor comes from the nuts, berries, and insects they eat in the wild, but their tenderness comes from their tiny size. Half-pound birds are typically served two to a person, but some of these birds are even smaller and are served in fours and sixes. They're best roasted, sautéed, broiled, or grilled. Baste frequently and stop cooking when the juices still run slightly pink.

SQUAB

Squab are young tender pigeons raised on farms. Usually they are butchered at four weeks old and weigh about a pound, although the squab in the South are larger. These birds have a dark beefy flavor somewhat like liver.

To roast squab, first truss the bird and lay slices of bacon or pork fat over the breast. Roast at 400° to 425°F for 30 to 45 minutes, basting frequently. To broil the squab, cut out the backbone of the bird, open it up, and flatten the breastbone with the heel of your hand. Broil slowly about 20 minutes, turning once. As soon as they're done, brush them with raspberry or balsamic vinegar. You can also sauté the split squab for 15 to 20 minutes.

WILD DUCK WITH LENTILS

An old bistro favorite, this classic can be cooked in the microwave with excellent results. When buying the duck, be sure to ask your butcher for one that's tender and young.

1 wild duck (about 3¾ pounds), well rinsed and patted dry
1 onion, sliced
½ cup lentils, rinsed and drained
1 tablespoon fresh thyme leaves or chopped fresh Italian (flat-leaf) parsley
4 cups Berta's Chicken Stock, homemade beef stock (see Index), or canned broth
¼ cup tomato paste
1 tablespoon balsamic vinegar
1½ teaspoons salt
½ teaspoon paprika
Freshly ground black pepper, to taste

1. Cut the duck into pieces: Remove and discard the backbone. Remove the wings and split them at the "elbow" (cut them through the joint but do not separate the pieces). Remove the legs, and separate the drumsticks from the thighs. Halve each breast.

2. Arrange the pieces in a 3-quart microwave-safe casserole. Cook at full power (650 to 700 watts), uncovered, for 2½ minutes. Rearrange the pieces, and cook another 2½ minutes.

3. Discard any liquid that has accumulated in the casserole. Add the onion, lentils, and thyme. Stir the remaining ingredients together in a small bowl, and pour this mixture over the duck. Cover, and cook for 45 minutes. Let stand for 5 minutes before serving.

2 to 4 portions

Note: This recipe was cooked on High (full power, 650 to 700 watts) in a carousel microwave, using microwave-safe containers.

If your microwave is less powerful, you will have to allow for more cooking time (approximately 1½ times the amount called for—but watch carefully); if it does not have a carousel, you may have to rotate the dish while it is cooking.

DUCK

Many kinds of wild duck have wonderful flavor, but mallards, pintails, blacks, scoups, canvasbacks, and teals are easiest to find. Although these ducks are all different in the great outdoors, in the kitchen it doesn't much matter. The flavor of duck depends on the diet, the conditions it has endured, the size, and age. The older a duck is, the tougher it is. The smaller and early season ducks make the best eating to our minds. To check the age of a duck, press on the breastbone; if it's pliable, the duck is young. But even the youngest, plumpest wild duck can't be cooked like domestic duck. The meat is very lean and easily overdone. Cooked with care, wild ducks will charm the taste buds like few other birds with their dark, juicy, rich meat.

GUINEA HEN

This is another game bird people find tender and delicate. We think it falls somewhere between chicken and pheasant and cook it often, very much like chicken. The hens at the market weigh between 2 and 2½ pounds. They should be barded to protect the delicate breast meat and roasted. We like them best well-done, when the juices from the thigh run clear.

ROASTED GUINEA HEN

Simply prepared, our guinea hen is infused with the flavors of bacon and Madeira. Potatoes roast alongside garlic cloves and are refreshed by chopped Italian parsley just before serving.

1 guinea hen (2¼ to 2½ pounds), well rinsed and
*   patted dry*
1 orange, halved
1 teaspoon dried thyme leaves
½ teaspoon paprika
Salt and freshly ground black pepper, to taste
1 small onion, halved
4 sprigs Italian (flat-leaf) parsley
4 slices bacon
16 large cloves garlic
4 red new potatoes, cut into 6 pieces each
½ cup Madeira
1 tablespoon chopped fresh Italian (flat-leaf) parsley, for
*   garnish*

1. Preheat the oven to 425°F.

2. Rinse the hen well, and squeeze one of the orange halves inside and out, to refresh.

3. Pat the cavity dry, and sprinkle it with some of the thyme and paprika, and salt and pepper. Place the remaining orange half, the onion, and the parsley sprigs in the cavity and truss the hen. Sprinkle the outside with a little more thyme and paprika, and salt and pepper. Place the hen breast side up in a shallow roasting pan. Lay the bacon slices across the breast.

4. Distribute the garlic cloves and potatoes around the hen, and sprinkle them with the remaining thyme and paprika, and salt and pepper. Pour the Madeira into the pan and bake for 30 minutes, basting once.

5. Remove the bacon and reduce the heat to 350°F. Bake until golden brown, basting frequently, 50 to 60 minutes. The juices should run clear when the tip of a knife is inserted in the thickest part of the thigh. Remove the trussing string and discard the stuffing.

6. Place the hen on a platter, and surround it with the roasted garlic and potatoes; keep warm. Pour the pan juices through a gravy strainer, or carefully skim the fat from the juices. Heat through, and serve immediately with the hen. Garnish with the parsley before serving.

4 portions

CATALAN PHEASANT STEW

Dried fruits and olives are essential ingredients in the fine cooking of Spain, and Catalonia is rich with game birds. We've combined these intriguing flavors with Rioja wine and Spanish brandy in a long-simmering dish with an accent of orange.

4 small pheasants (about 1 to 1¼ pounds each), with their giblets, well rinsed and patted dry
4 tablespoons olive oil
6 cups water
3 bay leaves
4 strips of orange zest
2 cups Rioja wine, such as Marques de Riscal
¼ cup fresh orange juice
¼ cup Spanish brandy
6 plump dried figs, quartered
1 cinnamon stick, 3 to 4 inches
1 tablespoon tomato paste
1 teaspoon sugar
Salt and freshly ground black pepper, to taste
8 fresh figs
12 large green Greek or Italian olives
2 oranges, preferably blood oranges, peeled and cut into ½-inch-thick slices
¼ cup chopped cilantro (fresh coriander)

1. Trim off the pheasants' necks and feet, if attached, and the wings at the shoulder.

2. Heat 2 tablespoons of the oil in a flameproof casserole or dutch oven. Add the pheasant trimmings and brown well, over medium-high heat, about 10 minutes.

3. Add the water, bay leaves, and 2 strips of the orange zest, and heat to a boil. Reduce the heat and simmer for 1 hour, skimming when necessary. Strain the liquid; you should have about 2½ cups.

4. Transfer the strained liquid to a saucepan, and add the Rioja, orange juice, brandy, dried figs, cinnamon stick, tomato paste, sugar, and remaining 2 strips of orange zest. Heat to a boil, then reduce the heat and simmer for 30 minutes.

5. Strain the mixture, pressing the figs against the strainer with the back of a wooden spoon. Remove 3 figs from the strainer. Place them in a food processor or blender with some of the liquid, and purée until smooth. Mix this into the remaining liquid. You should have about 2¼ cups liquid in all.

6. Cut the pheasants up as follows: Remove the drumsticks and thighs in one piece. Leave the breast halves attached, removing only the backbone portion.

7. Heat the remaining 2 tablespoons oil in the same casserole. Season the pheasant with salt and pepper. Brown the breasts on all sides, and set them aside. Then brown the legs.

8. Add the reserved liquid to the legs in the casserole. Bring it to a boil, cover, and simmer for 10 minutes. Then add the breasts, stirring the mixture

gently. Cover, and simmer just until cooked through, 20 minutes.

9. Add the fresh figs and the olives. Simmer just until the figs are lightly cooked, 2 to 3 minutes.

10. Spoon the stew into shallow bowls, and garnish each serving with orange slices and chopped cilantro. Or serve the stew on a large platter, garnished with oranges and cilantro.

6 portions

PHEASANT

Pheasant is a lean, white-fleshed game bird that is raised commercially but rarely appears on American tables. This bird has the largest breast of all the game birds, but the meat is very lean and delicate and will be dry if overcooked. Farm-raised pheasant will remind one most of chicken because it's typically raised on corn. If allowed a more natural diet of insects and nuts, the meat will be pinker and more flavorful. The flesh of true wild pheasant is redder and tastes gamier. Most pheasants at the market are between one and three pounds; if you have a choice, buy the plumper females. A flexible breastbone indicates the bird's youth.

Except for the very young birds, which can be sautéed, or the older birds, which should be braised, pheasant seems best to us when we cover the breast with slices of bacon or pork fat and roast it at 375°F, basting often to keep it from drying out. The bird is done when the juices run pale pink; it usually takes 45 to 50 minutes. One pheasant will serve two generously. Serve with root vegetables, chestnuts, wild mushrooms, and cranberries or a tart currant sauce.

PHEASANT LENTIL SOUP

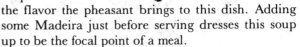

We tend to think of pheasant as being difficult to obtain and prepare—but ask your butcher for one in the fall and try this simply prepared soup. You will marvel at the flavor the pheasant brings to this dish. Adding some Madeira just before serving dresses this soup up to be the focal point of a meal.

4 tablespoons (½ stick) unsalted butter
3 small leeks (white part and 3 inches green), well rinsed and thinly sliced
2 or 3 large carrots, peeled and diced (2 cups)
2 large onions, diced (2 cups)
4 cloves garlic, finely minced
8 cups Berta's Chicken Stock (see Index) or canned broth
1 pheasant (about 1 ¾ pounds), well rinsed and halved
1 cup dried lentils
7 tablespoons chopped fresh Italian (flat-leaf) parsley
Salt and freshly ground black pepper, to taste
¼ cup Madeira

1. Melt the butter in a large soup pot over medium-low heat. Add the leeks, carrots, onions, and garlic, and cook until the vegetables are wilted, 15 minutes.

2. Add the stock, pheasant, lentils, 3 tablespoons of the parsley, and salt and pepper. Bring just to a boil, reduce the heat, and simmer, uncovered, 30 minutes.

3. Remove the pheasant and continue simmering the soup, uncovered, for 30 minutes. Meanwhile, shred the pheasant meat from the bones, and set aside.

4. Add the Madeira, remaining 4 tablespoons parsley, and the shredded meat to the soup. Adjust the seasonings and heat through, but do not boil. Serve immediately.

6 portions

PHEASANT POT PIE

carrots

juniper berries

succulent pieces of pheasant

golden crust

Golden puff pastry gently covers a wealth of pheasant, leeks, carrots, and pecans. The sauce is slightly thickened with tender prunes and spiked with green peppercorns. Spectacular in both presentation and flavor. Serve with a lightly chilled Chardonnay.

2 pheasants (2 pounds each), well rinsed and patted dry
Juice of 1 orange
6 slices bacon
1 ½ cups halved pitted prunes
2 cups Madeira
6 leeks (white part and 1 inch green), sliced in half
*   lengthwise and soaked (see Note)*
4 carrots, peeled and cut into 1-inch julienne
1 cup pecan halves
2 ¼ cups Berta's Chicken Stock (see Index) or canned broth
6 tablespoons cornstarch or potato starch
4 teaspoons green peppercorns in brine, drained and crushed
1 tablespoon dried thyme leaves
2 teaspoons dried oregano
4 juniper berries, crushed
Salt and freshly ground black pepper, to taste
½ cup chopped fresh Italian (flat-leaf) parsley, loosely
*   packed*
Grated zest of 1 orange
8 ounces puff pastry, thawed if frozen
2 egg yolks
1 teaspoon water

1. Preheat the oven to 350°F.

2. Rinse the pheasants well, and rub them, inside and out, with the orange juice. Pat dry with paper towels.

3. Place the pheasants breast side up in a shallow roasting pan. Lay 3 strips of bacon across each one, cover the pan with aluminum foil, and bake for 1 ¼ hours. Remove the bacon, and set the pheasants aside to cool, 30 minutes. Reserve the cooking juices in the roasting pan. Leave the oven on.

4. Combine the prunes and Madeira in a bowl, and allow them to soak for 30 minutes. Drain, reserving the prunes and liquid separately.

5. Slice the leeks into ½-inch pieces.

6. Bring a large saucepan of water to a boil. Add the leeks, and simmer for 1 ½ minutes to blanch them. Drain, pat dry, and set aside.

7. Bring another saucepan of water to a boil, and simmer the carrots until just tender, 3 minutes. drain, pat dry, and set aside with the leeks.

8. Carefully remove the skin from the cooled pheasants. Remove the meat from the bones, and shred it into pieces approximately 1 ½ x 1 inch. Place the meat in a large bowl and add the leeks, carrots, prunes, and pecans. Cover the bowl with plastic wrap and set it aside.

9. Place the roasting pan with the pan juices over low heat. Add the reserved prune soaking liquid and 1 ½ cups of the chicken stock. Cook, scraping up the brown bits in the pan, for 10 minutes. Then transfer the sauce to a heavy saucepan, bring it to a boil, and reduce it to a simmer.

10. Mix the cornstarch with the remaining ¾ cup chicken stock, and slowly add this to the sauce, whisking until it has dissolved and the sauce begins to thicken.

11. Add the green peppercorns, thyme, oregano, juniper berries, and salt and pepper. Simmer until the sauce is thick, 15 minutes.

12. Add the sauce to the bowl with the pheasants and vegetables, and toss gently to mix. Toss in the parsley and orange zest, and adjust the seasonings if necessary. Place the mixture in a 2-quart round soufflé dish or ovenproof casserole.

13. Roll the puff pastry out on a lightly floured surface to form a circle 2½ inches larger than the diameter of the soufflé dish. Blend the egg yolks with the water, and rub this egg wash around the rim of the soufflé dish, covering ½ inch on the inside and the outside of the rim. (Reserve the unused egg wash.) Carefully place the pastry over the dish, and crimp the edges on the inside and the outside to make a tight seal. Cut four small slits in the top so steam can escape. If you like, cut out some decorative shapes from leftover pastry and place them on top of the crust. Brush the entire crust with the remaining egg wash.

14. Place the soufflé dish on a baking sheet, and bake until the crust is golden, 45 minutes. Remove it from the oven and let it rest for 5 minutes before serving.

8 portions

Note: To soak leeks clean of sand, combine 10 cups water with 1 tablespoon cider vinegar. Place the halved leeks in the bowl and soak them for 20 minutes. Drain and rinse under cold water.

GROUSE

Grouse is also called ptarmigan, and in the North, partridge. Those who love it feel that it is the finest of all game birds. Unfortunately, grouse is notoriously difficult to bag and one grouse feeds just one person. We cook them very simply, without masking them with strong sauces or marinades.

The best and most basic way to prepare grouse is to split them down the back, flatten the breastbone, and rub all sides with butter. Broil 15 to 20 minutes, turning once. Accompany with crisp fried potatoes.

GROUSE ON TOAST

Our friend Ariane Daguin gave us the inspiration, the preparation, and the grouse for this recipe. This is the way the French love it—whether you're lucky enough to have wood grouse, black grouse, red grouse, or white grouse, this "less is more" preparation is best.

2 grouse (12 to 14 ounces each), well rinsed and patted dry
Salt and freshly ground black pepper, to taste
2 slices peasant bread, about ¾ inch thick, lightly toasted

1. Preheat the oven to 500°F.

2. Rinse the grouse well, and pat dry. Reserve the livers. Sprinkle the birds inside and out with salt and pepper.

3. Lay the bread slices in a shallow roasting pan, and the grouse on top of them. Place the livers alongside.

4. Bake for 18 minutes for fairly rare meat (which is how the French love it). The juices will soak into the bread while baking. Transfer the toast and grouse to a platter and serve immediately, with the livers on the side. Tip the grouse over the toast and livers to release juices from the cavity.

2 portions

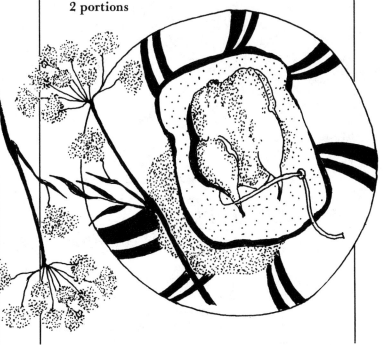

QUAIL

The tiny quail, called partridge in the South, is full of flavor with very rich and sweet meat. Our native quail, the bob-white, has long been replaced by farm-raised quail and in such large numbers that you should have no trouble finding them. Quail are small, between 6 and 8 ounces, and can be very dry if over-cooked. They are best done by roasting, grilling, gently braising, or sautéing over high heat. Sauté in butter or oil, turning to brown all sides and basting frequently. They will be done in just 15 to 20 minutes. Deglaze the pan quickly with a little port or Madeira for a wonderful sauce.

Figure on two of these little birds per serving and encourage everyone to eat them with their fingers to get every juicy morsel.

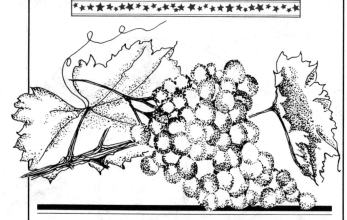

MICHAEL FOLEY'S QUAIL WITH GRAPES

Michael Foley, owner and chef of Printer's Row in Chicago, is one of the most enthusiastic and energetic people we know, and is a great advocate of midwest-ern ingredients, which star in his dishes.

STUFFING

3 slices white bread, crusts removed
1/3 cup milk
3 chicken livers or 8 quail livers
1 tablespoon brandy
Pinch of allspice
Salt and freshly ground black pepper, to taste

8 quail, boned (see Note), well rinsed and patted dry
8 grape leaves
8 thin sheets barding fat
4 tablespoons (1/2 stick) unsalted butter
2 tablespoons olive oil
1/2 cup Berta's Chicken Stock (see Index) or canned broth
2 tablespoons brandy
1 pound riesling or other seedless green grapes

1. Prepare the stuffing: Place the bread in a shallow bowl, pour the milk over it, and allow to soak for 10 minutes.

2. Combine the soaked bread and the chicken livers in a food processor, and pulse until puréed. Do not overprocess. Transfer the purée to a mixing bowl, and add the brandy, allspice, and salt and pepper. Mix gently.

3. Preheat the oven to 375°F.

4. Divide the stuffing mixture among the 8 quail, placing it in the boned breast cavity. Wrap the quail first in the grape leaves and then in the barding fat. Tie in place with kitchen string.

5. Heat the butter and oil in a heavy ovenproof skillet over medium-high heat. Brown the quail on all sides, 5 minutes. Then turn the quail breast side down, and transfer the skillet to the oven. Roast the quail, basting frequently, for 7 minutes. Turn them over and roast, basting frequently, another 7 minutes. The quail should not be overcooked.

6. Remove the quail from the skillet, unwrap them, and let them rest; keep them warm. Pour off the fat from the skillet, and place it over high heat. Add the stock and brandy, and bring to a boil. Then add the grapes, reduce the heat, and simmer gently for 3 minutes. (If necessary, add a bit of butter to smooth out the sauce.) Arrange 2 quail on each plate, and spoon the sauce over them.

4 portions

Note: Ask your butcher to bone the quail for you, keeping the legs intact.

QUAIL AND VEGETABLE RAGOUT

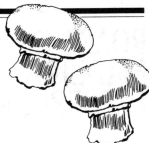

We've taken quail and prepared them in the style of coq au vin. The meat is delicate and succulent, and makes an elegant dish for an intimate dinner party.

6 quail, well rinsed and patted dry
2 cups tiny white pearl onions
1 cup Berta's Chicken Stock (see Index) or canned broth
8 ounces salt pork, rind removed, cut into ½-inch dice
12 large cloves garlic
12 large fresh cultivated mushrooms, rinsed, patted dry, and quartered
2 tablespoons unbleached all-purpose flour
2 cups good-quality Burgundy
2½ tablespoons chopped fresh Italian (flat-leaf) parsley
1 tablespoon red currant jelly
1 tablespoon dark brown sugar
1½ teaspoons dried thyme leaves
Salt and freshly ground black pepper, to taste
2 carrots, peeled and julienned

1. Quarter the quail, removing and reserving the backbones. Set the quartered pieces aside.

2. Place the onions in a saucepan, cover with water, and bring to a boil. Remove the pan from the heat, drain the onions, and rinse them under cold water. Slip off the skins, and set the onions aside.

3. Place the chicken stock in a small saucepan, and add the reserved backbones. Cover, and bring to a boil. Reduce the heat and simmer for 20 minutes. Strain the stock and set it aside.

4. Preheat the oven to 350°F.

5. Place the salt pork in a flameproof casserole or dutch oven and cook over medium heat, until just crisp. Using a slotted spoon, transfer the salt pork to paper towels to drain.

6. Add the quail pieces to the casserole, in batches if necessary, and brown them over medium-high heat on all sides. Set the pieces aside.

7. Add the onions and garlic to the casserole and sauté, stirring frequently, until browned, 10 minutes. Add the mushrooms and cook another 5 minutes. Sprinkle the vegetables with the flour, and cook 1 minute more.

8. Add the wine and ½ cup of the reserved chicken stock to the casserole. Bring to a boil and cook until the sauce has thickened, 3 to 4 minutes. Then reduce the heat and add 2 tablespoons of the parsley, the red currant jelly, brown sugar, thyme, and salt and pepper.

9. Mix the quail and the salt pork with the vegetables in the casserole, cover, and bake for 20 minutes.

10. While the quail is cooking, bring a saucepan of water to a boil, and add the carrots. Simmer for 2 minutes; then drain and set aside.

11. Add the carrots to the casserole, cover again, and bake another 10 minutes. Garnish with the remaining ½ tablespoon parsley before serving.

4 portions

GAME TIPS
★

▲ Always truss game birds for roasting. They just don't have enough fat to be cooked with an open cavity.

▲ Cover lean game for roasting with bacon, pork fat, or caul, and baste often.

▲ Don't overcook game. The meat is very lean and not nearly as forgiving of that extra five minutes as fattier chicken, pork, and beef. Game continues to cook, as do all roasts and birds, after it is removed from the heat. Stop cooking on the underside of done. You can always cook it longer, but never less.

▲ Game, especially small birds, cools down quickly, so serve it piping hot on warmed platters.

▲ Learn to test doneness by touch (looseness of the leg), smell, and sight. Birds cooked rare should have rosy pink juices and birds cooked well-done should have no trace of pink in their juices.

GEESE

Geese are available fresh during the Christmas season and frozen throughout the year although you may have to special-order one. Farm-raised geese are butchered at six to eight months of age when they weigh between 8 and 12 pounds. Look for the fresh, tender Toulouse goose in the market or ask your butcher for a recommendation. Because geese have less meat and more bone than chicken and turkey, you should allow 1½ pounds raw weight per person. The smaller and younger birds are preferred; the heavier birds are both older and tougher. Look for plumpness, a flexible breastbone, and pale, soft skin.

Farm-raised goose is very fatty and best either roasted on a rack in a slow oven or cooked on a spit over a pan to catch the drippings. Be sure to prick the skin of the goose all over (without piercing the flesh) to let the fat drain off as it melts. Remove the excess fat from the pan as it accumulates (save it for roasting potatoes). The goose is done when the thigh is pierced with a fork and the juices run clear with no tinge of pink. A meat thermometer inserted in the thickest part of the thigh should register 175° to 180°F. Goose is difficult to carve because of its complex bone structure; you may want to undertake this task in the kitchen.

Wild geese can be roasted much like the farm-raised geese if they are young, but they should first be covered with a layer of fat and basted frequently because they are leaner. Older wild geese are best braised in red wine or apple cider and served with red cabbage.

ROAST GOOSE WITH MADEIRA PEPPERCORN SAUCE

For an old-fashioned holiday menu serve this elegant roast goose with Braised Red Cabbage and Parsnips Julienned. Oysters Rockefeller are the perfect way to begin the meal.

1 cup pitted dried apricots, halved
1 cup pitted dried prunes, halved
½ cup Madeira
1 domestic goose (11 to 13 pounds),
*   ready to cook*
Juice of 1 orange
2 Granny Smith or other tart apples,
*   cored and coarsely chopped*
Grated zest of 1 orange
Coarse (kosher) salt, to taste
Coarsely ground black pepper, to taste
Paprika, to taste
8 slices bacon
1 ¼ cups Madeira Peppercorn Sauce (see Step 7; recipe
*   follows)*

1. Place the apricots and prunes in a large bowl, add the Madeira, and set aside for 30 minutes.

2. Preheat the oven to 325°F.

3. Rinse the goose well, removing all excess fat. Prick the skin all over with the tines of a fork) to help release fat while it cooks). Rub the goose, inside and out, with the orange juice.

4. Add the apples and orange zest to the apricots and prunes, and toss to combine.

5. Sprinkle the goose inside and out with coarse salt, pepper, and paprika. Stuff the cavity with the fruits, and close the opening with poultry skewers. Lay the bacon slices across the breast.

6. Place the goose, breast side up, on a rack in a shallow roasting pan and put it on the center rack in the oven. Roast for 1 ½ hours, removing the accumulated fat in the pan with a baster every 30 minutes.

7. Remove the bacon, and roast the goose, continuing to defat the pan, for 1 hour more. It is done when the temperature reads 175° to 180°F when an instant-read thermometer is inserted deep into the breast. Remove the goose from the roasting pan and

set the pan aside. Let the goose rest, covered loosely with aluminum foil, for 20 minutes before carving. While it is resting, make the sauce, to be served alongside.

6 portions

MADEIRA PEPPERCORN SAUCE

Pan drippings from roasted goose
2 shallots, peeled and chopped
¾ cup Berta's Chicken Stock (see Index) or canned broth
½ cup Madeira
1 tablespoon green peppercorns in brine, drained and slightly crushed
1 teaspoon cornstarch
Salt and freshly ground black pepper, to taste
½ teaspoon gravy enricher

1. Skim any remaining fat from the roasting pan, or remove it through a gravy separator. Scrape the browned pan drippings into a saucepan. Add the shallots, ½ cup of the stock, the Madeira, and the peppercorns. Simmer over low heat for 5 minutes.

2. Mix the cornstarch with the remaining ¼ cup chicken stock until smooth. Slowly drizzle this into the sauce, stirring rapidly. Add the salt, pepper, and gravy enricher. Stir, and simmer another 5 minutes. Serve hot, with the goose.

1¼ cups

PARTRIDGE

True partridge is not native to the United States, but some use the word for grouse and quail. The real birds are now being raised on farms and are prized for their tender and delicate flesh. Young partridge weighs about 1 to 1½ pounds; the older birds weigh between 2½ and 3 pounds and are best braised or stewed. Roast young partridges, barded with pork fat or bacon. Or sauté them and deglaze the pan with Madeira—luscious!

BAKED PARTRIDGE WITH SAVOY CABBAGE

Just remember to keep basting this partridge to prevent the breast from getting too dry. The pungency of cabbage and rosemary enhances the flavor of this game bird.

2 partridges (about 1 pound each), well rinsed, patted dry, and trussed
Salt and freshly ground black pepper
1 tablespoon olive oil, plus additional if needed
½ onion, sliced
3 cups very coarsely chopped Savoy cabbage (2-inch pieces)
2 cloves garlic
1 teaspoon dried rosemary leaves
1 cup dry white wine

1. Preheat the oven to 375°F.

2. Lightly season the partridges with salt and pepper to taste.

3. Heat the olive oil in an ovenproof skillet large enough to hold the two partridges. Brown the birds over medium heat on all sides. Set them aside.

4. Add the onion, cabbage, garlic, and rosemary to the skillet, adding more oil if necessary. Stir until wilted, 3 to 5 minutes. Season with ½ teaspoon salt and ½ teaspoon pepper. Add the white wine and bring it to a boil, stirring to dissolve any browned bits.

5. Return the partridges to the skillet. Spoon the vegetables over the birds.

6. Transfer the skillet to the oven, and bake 45 minutes, basting often with the pan juices. Let the birds stand for 5 minutes, then split them in half and serve with the vegetables and pan juices.

2 portions

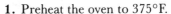

BREAD AND CHEESE PLEASE

A FRESH LOAF

No smell is more welcoming than that of freshly baked bread. Whether the loaf is simple or complex, the satisfaction that comes from baking and eating bread seems to be universal.

There are many different kinds of bread to choose from—yeast breads, quick breads, muffins, popovers, scones, and so on—that even if time is short, you can still turn out a successful loaf. Each one is unique and delicious.

YEAST BREADS

Inexperienced bakers are often intimidated by yeast breads, but there is no need for that to be the case today. Way back when, it was necessary to proof yeast first to see if it was still good. Today, as long as you refrigerate it and use it before the expiration date on the package, you can be sure the yeast is good. Dry yeast is probably the easiest to find in today's markets. It must be dissolved in water before it is mixed with flour. To dissolve yeast, simply sprinkle it over ¼ to ½ cup of lukewarm liquid and set it aside for 5 to 10 minutes. If you have a package of yeast that is older than the expiration date, you can proof it by adding a teaspoon of sugar or honey to the water; in 10 minutes the mixture will be bubbly and frothy if the yeast is still good.

The next important element in making yeast breads is developing the gluten. This is achieved by mixing and kneading the dough. If you are kneading by hand it may take longer than you'd like, but don't cheat. You need that elasticity with a bit of shine to make your best bread. Feel free to experiment with different flours. Rye flour, whole-wheat flour, and cornmeal add interesting tastes as well as textures to bread. But remember not to use these flours alone, for they have very little or no gluten to contribute to the bread. For yeast breads gluten is a must, which is why all yeast breads use a greater proportion of all-purpose or bread flour in relation to any other ingredients.

HOW YEAST BREAD RISES

Yeast, when mixed with flour or sugar and liquid, creates an alcoholic fermentation that converts the starch into carbon dioxide. Instead of letting the gas escape, the gluten captures it and stretches, making the dough rise. When the bread is put into the oven to bake, there is one last burst of fermentation, called "oven spring," and then the yeast dies. The gluten then sets and bakes to its browned, finished loaf.

MAKING CRUST

There are different ways of varying the crust on your breads:
▲ Bake the loaves free form on heated baking tiles or a baking stone for a heartier, crispier crust.
▲ Brush the loaves with water for a crispier crust.
▲ Brush the loaves with egg wash (egg mixed with milk) for a soft browned crust.
▲ Put the bread pans on the bottom rack or floor of the oven after 15 minutes of baking for a hard brown crust.
▲ Take the bread out of the pans and finish baking on the oven rack for the last 5 minutes for a crispier golden crust.
▲ Brush the loaves with butter as soon as they come out of the oven for a softer crust.
▲ Wrap the hot baked loaves in clean kitchen towels for a softer crust.
▲ Slash the top of the bread with a razor or very sharp knife just before they go into the oven so they crack attractively, rather than at random.

BAKING BREAD

If you are using a baking stone or tiles for free-form loaves, be sure to preheat the oven for at least 30 minutes to get the stone good and hot. Almost all breads are baked in the center of a preheated oven. When a loaf is done, it will pull away from the sides of the bread pan and sound hollow when you rap the bottom with a knuckle.

STORING BREAD

Let the bread cool completely on wire racks, then wrap well in plastic wrap or bags. The bread will lose its crispy crust, but it can be recrisped if put into a 350°F oven for 5 to 7 minutes. Bread freezes well—just make sure it's very well wrapped. You can thaw it either at room temperature or wrapped in aluminum foil (leave an opening at the top for steam to escape) in a 350° to 400°F oven.

RED-AND-YELLOW WHITE BREAD

We've added egg yolks for a richer flavor and spiked the taste with a bit of cayenne. They both add color, too, to this sandwich bread, perfect for slicing and toasting.

1 package active dry yeast
½ cup warm water
¼ teaspoon sugar
3 cups unbleached all-purpose flour
½ teaspoon salt
¼ teaspoon cayenne pepper
3 tablespoons unsalted butter, melted and cooled to room
    temperature
2 egg yolks, lightly beaten
5 to 6 tablespoons milk

1. Stir the yeast, warm water, and sugar together in a small bowl. Set the mixture aside until the yeast starts foaming, 5 to 10 minutes.

2. Combine the flour, salt, and cayenne in a large bowl. Stir in the yeast mixture, butter, egg yolks, and enough of the milk to form a mass of sticky dough. Let it stand for 10 minutes.

3. Transfer the dough to a lightly floured surface and knead until it is smooth and elastic, about 7 minutes. If the dough is sticky, sprinkle it lightly with more flour as you work.

4. Lightly oil a large bowl, and turn the dough in it to coat it with the oil. Cover the bowl loosely with a kitchen towel and let the dough rise in a warm place until doubled in bulk, about 45 minutes.

5. Oil a 9 x 5 x 3-inch loaf pan.

6. Punch the dough down and shape it into a loaf. Press it into the prepared pan. Cover it loosely and let the dough rise until it nearly fills the pan, 45 to 60 minutes.

7. Preheat the oven to 375°F.

8. Bake the bread until it is golden and the bottom sounds hollow when tapped with your finger, 35 to 40 minutes.

9. Remove the bread from the pan and let it cool on a wire rack.

1 loaf

SEEDED RYE BREAD

This is great for a hot corned beef sandwich. For a variation, use fennel seeds instead of caraway.

1 package active dry yeast
¾ cup plus 2 tablespoons warm water
¼ teaspoon sugar
2 cups unbleached all-purpose flour
1 cup rye flour
1 tablespoon caraway seeds
1 teaspoon salt
2 tablespoons vegetable oil
1 tablespoon honey
2 tablespoons yellow cornmeal
1 egg
1 tablespoon water
Caraway seeds, for sprinkling
Freshly ground black pepper, to taste

1. Stir the yeast, ¾ cup warm water, and sugar together in a small bowl. Set aside until the yeast starts foaming, 5 to 10 minutes.

2. Stir both flours, the caraway seeds, and the salt together in a large bowl. Add the yeast mixture, oil, honey, and remaining 2 tablespoons warm water. Stir until the mixture forms a mass. (If the dough seems too dry, add a small amount of water.)

3. Place the dough on a lightly floured surface and knead until it is smooth and elastic, 10 minutes.

4. Lightly oil a large bowl, and turn the dough in it to coat it with the oil. Cover the bowl loosely with a kitchen towel and let the dough rise in a warm place until doubled in bulk, about 45 minutes.

5. Punch the dough down and shape it into a ball. Return it to the oiled bowl, cover it loosely, and let it rise again until doubled, about 30 minutes.

6. Lightly butter a baking sheet. Sprinkle it with the cornmeal.

7. Punch the dough down and shape it into an 8-inch-long oval loaf. Place it on the baking sheet, cover it loosely, and let it rise until nearly doubled, about 30 minutes.

8. Meanwhile, preheat the oven to 375°F.

9. Beat the egg and water together, and brush this over the loaf. Sprinkle it with caraway seeds and pepper. Using a razor blade or a sharp knife, cut five slashes across the top.

10. Bake until the bread is deep golden and sounds hollow when the bottom is tapped with your finger, about 35 minutes. Remove it from the baking sheet and set it on a wire rack to cool.

1 loaf

BREAD SHOULDN'T KNEAD YOU

We used to think of bread baking as an all-day chore. Not that it took all our time, but we thought we had to be there with it. Then we discovered bread needed time, but it didn't really need us. Bread making will fall into your schedule. You can mix the dough in the morning, go play tennis or run errands, come home to punch it down, shape it, and leave it to rise again. If the rise is going too fast, put the dough in the refrigerator to slow it down. Cold doesn't kill yeast—heat does. When you are ready for the bread, just take it out of the refrigerator to continue its rise.

SOURDOUGH BAGUETTES

We like our baguettes thin, thin, thin! That way you get more crispy crust and a moist and holey inside.

This recipe makes use of wild yeast spores in the air to form the starter and raise the dough. It is a very lengthy process, but can be a very rewarding experience. If you would rather not risk the possibility of failure, add a package of active dry yeast to the starter in Step 1, wait for the mixture to bubble (within 10 minutes), and move on to Step 3.

STARTER
¾ cup skim milk
¼ cup low-fat buttermilk
¾ cup unbleached all-purpose flour
¼ cup whole-wheat flour
1 teaspoon sugar

4 cups unbleached all-purpose flour
1 cup warm water
½ teaspoon salt
2 tablespoons yellow cornmeal

1. Make the starter: Stir the starter ingredients together in a nonreactive bowl. Cover the bowl with a double thickness of cheesecloth, and tie a string or stretch a large rubber band around the rim to secure it. If the weather is warm, place the bowl near an open window; otherwise put it in a warm place.

2. Let the mixture stand until it is bubbling, 2 to 3 days. (If it turns moldy, discard it and start again.) You should have about 1 cup.

3. Divide the starter in half. One half will be used for the bread. The other half will be replenished and saved for future baking (see Note).

4. Scrape half the starter into a large bowl. Stir in 2 cups of the all-purpose flour and the warm water. Let the dough stand, loosely covered, until doubled in bulk, 4 to 6 hours (depending upon the strength of the starter and the possible addition of packaged yeast).

5. Stir in the salt. Slowly work in the remaining 2 cups flour, ½ cup at a time. Turn the dough out onto a lightly floured surface, and knead until it is smooth and elastic, 10 minutes.

6. Lightly oil a large bowl, and turn the dough in it to coat it with oil. Cover the bowl loosely, and let the dough rise in a warm place until doubled in bulk, up to 12 hours (again depending on the strength of the starter and the addition of packaged yeast).

7. Punch the dough down, knead it once or twice, and shape it into three loaves about 16 inches long. Butter a baking sheet and sprinkle it with the cornmeal. Arrange the loaves on the cornmeal.

8. Loosely cover the loaves, and let them rise until doubled in bulk, about 4 hours.

9. Preheat the oven to 450°F.

10. Using a razor blade or a sharp knife, slash the tops of the loaves crosswise in several places. Open the oven door and quickly spray the interior with a water mister. Place the bread in the oven and bake for 9 minutes, spraying the oven every 3 minutes. Then continue baking until the loaves are golden and sound hollow when tapped on the bottom, another 11 to 13 minutes.

3 loaves

Note: To replenish, add ½ cup all-purpose flour and ½ cup warm water to half the starter. Let the mixture stand, loosely covered, until it bubbles. Then refrigerate it in a nonreactive container, or freeze it. Use half this starter for the next baking, replenishing the other half.

OLIVE ROSEMARY COUNTRY BREAD

Lusty olives and rosemary make this bread special enough to plan a meal around. Serve it hot with a glorious Ribollita and an arugula salad for the most satisfying of meals. We also enjoy this bread toasted and slathered with a creamy sweet Gorgonzola cheese.

1 package active dry yeast
1 cup warm water
1 cup milk
2 tablespoons sugar
½ cup plus 2 tablespoons yellow cornmeal
3 tablespoons unsalted butter, at room temperature
⅔ cup coarsely chopped onion
2 tablespoons coarsely chopped fresh rosemary leaves
⅔ cup pitted Niçoise olives
2 teaspoons salt
1 tablespoon coarsely ground black pepper
2 cups whole-wheat flour
3 to 3½ cups unbleached all-purpose flour

1. Stir the yeast, warm water, and milk together in a large bowl. Let the mixture stand until the yeast has dissolved, 5 minutes.

2. Add the sugar, ½ cup cornmeal, butter, onion, rosemary, olives, salt, pepper, whole-wheat flour, and 2 cups of the all-purpose flour; beat well. Place the dough on a lightly floured surface and knead for 2 to 3 minutes, adding the remaining all-purpose flour as necessary to make a workable dough. Let the dough rest for 10 to 15 minutes.

3. Knead the dough again, until it is smooth and elastic, 10 minutes. (Sprinkle it with flour as you knead if necessary to keep it from sticking.)

4. Lightly oil a large bowl, and turn the dough in it to coat it with the oil. Cover the bowl with a kitchen towel and let the dough rise in a warm place until doubled in bulk, about 1½ hours.

5. Punch the dough down and divide it in half. Shape each half into a round loaf. Sprinkle a baking sheet with the remaining 2 tablespoons cornmeal, and place the loaves on it, seam side down. Cover with a kitchen towel and let rise again until barely doubled in bulk, about 45 minutes.

6. Meanwhile, preheat the oven to 350°F.

7. Bake the bread until it is well browned and sounds hollow when the bottom is tapped with your finger, about 45 minutes. Remove it from the baking sheet and set it on a wire rack to cool.

2 loaves

NEW BASIC SANDWICHES

▲ Sardines and crisp bacon with mayonnaise on whole-wheat toast

▲ Tapenade, sliced tomatoes, and arugula on sourdough bread

▲ Fried flounder, bacon, sliced tomato, and red onion rings on a toasted, buttered hot dog bun

▲ Thinly sliced shrimp, cucumber, and radishes with dill butter on pumpernickel bread

▲ Sliced ripe summer tomatoes, mayonnaise, salt, and pepper on fresh white bread with crusts removed

▲ Cream cheese, currants, and chopped pecans on cinnamon toast

▲ Bananas, bacon, and peanut butter drizzled with honey on raisin toast

▲ Thinly sliced Lemon Poppy Seed Pound Cake with cream cheese and sliced strawberries

▲ Cream cheese, golden caviar, orange nasturtium petals, and snipped chives on very thin slices of black bread

▲ Monterey Jack cheese and Jalapeño Chutney on toasted sourdough bread

▲ Scrambled egg, sliced ham, and sliced red onion with ketchup on toasted rye bread

▲ Grilled Italian sausage and warm Fennel or Onion Confit on a grilled roll

▲ Sliced roast lamb, Elegant Eggplant Caviar, and yogurt in pita garnished with chopped cucumber

▲ Sweet Gorgonzola cheese, sliced fresh purple figs, and fresh mint on grilled panettone

▲ Sliced roast lamb with fresh mint mayonnaise on toasted Grandma Clark's Soda Bread

▲ Roasted red and yellow peppers with sliced smoked ham on a thin baguette

▲ Sliced avocado, tomato, cucumber, and alfalfa sprouts with mayonnaise on toasted Multi-Grain Bread

▲ Hot tuna melt with chopped arugula, roasted red pepper, and sliced Parmesan cheese

▲ Hot steak sandwich with roasted shallots and tarragon mayonnaise on a thin baguette

▲ Sliced sweet onion on buttered white bread cut with a biscuit cutter and edges rolled in chopped fresh parsley

▲ Grilled cheese sandwich with sharp Cheddar cheese, sliced tomato, and crisp bacon

▲ Olivada, roasted pepper, and fresh mozzarella on a toasted baguette

▲ Thinly sliced roast pork with apple butter on Walnut Raisin Whole-Wheat Bread

▲ Corned beef and cole slaw on toasted Grandma Clark's Soda Bread

▲ Cajun Meat Loaf with ketchup on Hot and Sassy Corn Bread

▲ Egg salad and asparagus tips with dill mayonnaise on a croissant

▲ Sautéed garlic sausage, Onion Confit, and Dijon mustard on a thin baguette

▲ Hot pastrami and Six Pepper Slaw with a dollop of Pineapple Chutney on buttered black bread

▲ Sardines and egg salad on toasted rye bread

▲ Red Pepper and Ginger Marmalade topped with a fried egg on toasted Multi-Grain Bread

PROSCIUTTO ONION BREAD

Stuffed breads are beautiful and pungent, and great served with cheese and wine. A bit of whole-wheat flour adds depth to the flavor here.

1 package active dry yeast
½ cup warm water
¼ teaspoon sugar
2½ cups unbleached all-purpose flour
½ cup whole-wheat flour
¾ teaspoon garlic powder
½ teaspoon salt
⅓ cup water
1 tablespoon balsamic vinegar
3 tablespoons olive oil
1 cup chopped onion
6 ounces sliced prosciutto, slivered
¼ cup minced fresh sage leaves
Freshly ground black pepper, to taste
2 tablespoons yellow cornmeal

1. Stir the yeast, warm water, and sugar together in a small bowl. Let the mixture stand until the yeast starts foaming, 5 to 10 minutes.

2. In another bowl, mix the flours, garlic powder, and salt. Add the yeast mixture, ⅓ cup water, and vinegar, stirring until the mixture forms a mass.

3. Turn the dough out onto a lightly floured surface, and knead until it is smooth and elastic, 10 minutes.

4. Lightly oil a large bowl, and turn the dough in it to coat it with the oil. Cover the bowl loosely with a kitchen towel, and let the dough rise until doubled in bulk, about 1 hour.

5. Meanwhile, prepare the filling: Heat the oil in a skillet, and sauté the onion over medium heat until it is translucent, 5 minutes. Stir in the prosciutto and sage; cook 1 minute. Season generously with pepper, and allow to cool to room temperature.

6. Lightly butter a baking sheet, and sprinkle it with the cornmeal.

7. Punch the dough down. Transfer it to a lightly floured surface, and flatten or roll it out to form a 14 x 8-inch oval.

8. Spread the filling over the dough, leaving a 1-inch bare edge. Starting with a long end, roll it up tightly, jelly-roll style. Pinch the seams and ends well to seal them. Transfer the roll to the prepared baking sheet and cover it with a kitchen towel. Let it rise in a warm place until doubled in bulk, 1 hour.

9. Preheat the oven to 400°F.

10. Using a razor blade or a sharp knife, make four or five diagonal cuts ½ inch deep across the top of the bread.

11. Place the bread in the oven, and immediately spray the oven with a water mister. Bake 5 minutes and spray again. Then bake another 20 minutes.

12. Remove the bread from the baking sheet and set it on a wire rack to cool.

1 loaf

"**T**his is every cook's opinion—
No savory dish without an onion,
But lest your kissing should be spoiled
Your onions must be fully boiled."

—JONATHAN SWIFT

MULTI-GRAIN BREAD

Grains are becoming more and more popular because of their high fiber content. We've enhanced this bread with a finely ground seven-grain cereal made of wheat, millet, rye, oats, brown rice, and sesame and sunflower seeds.

1 package active dry yeast
½ cup warm water
¼ teaspoon sugar
1½ cups unbleached all-purpose flour
½ cup whole-wheat flour
¾ cup natural granola cereal
*¼ cup seven-grain cereal, finely ground**
1 teaspoon salt
⅓ cup water
2 tablespoons vegetable oil
2 tablespoons honey
⅔ cup cooked grain (brown rice, barley, cracked wheat,
    wheat berries, buckwheat groats, etc.), at room
    temperature

1. Stir the yeast, warm water, and sugar together in a small bowl. Let the mixture stand until the yeast starts foaming, 5 to 10 minutes.

2. In another bowl combine the flours, granola, seven-grain cereal, and salt. Stir well, and then add the yeast mixture, ⅓ cup water, oil, and honey. Stir until the mixture forms a mass.

3. Turn the dough out onto a lightly floured surface and knead it until smooth, about 10 minutes.

4. Lightly oil a large bowl, and turn the dough in it to coat it with the oil. Cover the bowl loosely with a kitchen towel, put it in a warm place, and let the dough rise until doubled in bulk, about 1 hour.

5. Lightly butter a 9 x 5 x 3-inch pan.

6. Punch the dough down and transfer it to a lightly floured work surface. Knead it once or twice and then flatten it out. Sprinkle the dough with the cooked grain, and knead again until the mixture is smooth and the grain well blended in. If sticky, sprinkle the surface with flour as you work.

7. Shape the dough into a loaf and place it in the prepared pan. Let it rise, loosely covered, until doubled in bulk, about 1 hour.

8. Preheat the oven to 375°F.

9. Bake the bread for 30 minutes. Remove from the loaf pan and return it to the oven on a baking sheet; bake another 5 minutes. Cool the bread on a wire rack.

1 loaf

*Available at health food stores and other specialty markets.

> We're lucky now that there is more and more interesting and healthy bread available in America—made by bakers who are just tired of the soft tasteless loaves widely distributed. Still, nothing compares to making your own. Some do it for therapy and some for love, and there is no good reason for not doing it because most bread baking isn't fussy or demanding.

CINNAMON RAISIN BREAD

One of our favorites for breakfast. Try it toasted, spread with creamy sweet butter, and sprinkled with cinnamon sugar.

1 package active dry yeast
½ cup warm water
¼ teaspoon plus 3 tablespoons sugar
2 ½ cups unbleached all-purpose flour
½ cup whole-wheat flour
1 ½ teaspoons ground cinnamon
½ cup walnut pieces, toasted (see Index) and chopped
5 tablespoons unsalted butter, melted and cooled to room temperature
⅓ cup water
1 cup raisins

1. Stir the yeast, warm water, and ¼ teaspoon sugar together in a small bowl. Let the mixture stand until the yeast starts foaming, 5 to 10 minutes.

2. Combine the flours, the remaining 3 tablespoons sugar, the cinnamon, and walnuts in a large bowl. Stir well.

3. Stir the yeast mixture, butter, and ⅓ cup water into the flour mixture. Then stir in the raisins or work them in by hand. Let stand 10 minutes.

4. Transfer the dough to a lightly floured surface and knead until it is smooth and elastic, about 7 minutes.

5. Lightly oil a large bowl, and turn the dough in it to coat it with the oil. Cover the bowl loosely with a kitchen towel and let the dough rise in a warm place until it is doubled in bulk, about 45 minutes.

6. Oil a 9 x 5 x 3-inch loaf pan.

7. Punch the dough down, and shape it into a loaf. Press it into the prepared pan and cover it loosely. Let the dough rise until it nearly fills the pan, 45 to 60 minutes.

8. Preheat the oven to 375°F.

9. Bake the bread until the top is browned and the bottom sounds hollow when tapped with your finger, 35 to 40 minutes.

10. Remove the bread from the pan and let it cool on a wire rack.

1 loaf

> "**I** always like to have the morning well-aired before I get up."
>
> —BEAU BRUMMELL

WALNUT RAISIN WHOLE-WHEAT BREAD

This loaf looks great served on an Early American bread board. The whole-wheat flour gives it a wonderful flavor, and the contrasting walnuts and raisins give it texture. Try lightly toasting thick slices and serving them with a sharp farmhouse Cheddar for breakfast.

1 package active dry yeast
1 cup warm water
1 cup milk
2 tablespoons sugar
½ cup plus 2 tablespoons yellow cornmeal
3 tablespoons unsalted butter, at room temperature
3 cups coarsely chopped walnuts
2 cups raisins
2 teaspoons salt
1 teaspoon coarsely ground black pepper
2 cups whole-wheat flour
2 ½ to 3 cups unbleached all-purpose flour

1. Combine the yeast, warm water, and milk in a large bowl. Let the mixture stand until the yeast has dissolved, 5 minutes.

2. Add the sugar, ½ cup cornmeal, butter, walnuts, raisins, salt, pepper, whole-wheat flour, and 2 cups of the all-purpose flour; beat well. Transfer the dough to a lightly floured surface and knead for 2 to 3 minutes, adding the remaining all-purpose flour as necessary to make it workable. Let the dough rest, covered loosely with a kitchen towel, for 10 to 15 minutes.

3. Knead the dough again, until it is smooth and elastic, 8 to 10 minutes. (Sprinkle it with extra flour if necessary to keep it from sticking.)

4. Oil a large bowl and turn the dough in it to coat it with the oil. Cover the bowl and let the dough rise in a warm place until doubled in bulk, about 1½ hours.

5. Punch the dough down and divide it in half. Shape the halves into round loaves. Sprinkle a baking sheet with the remaining 2 tablespoons cornmeal, and place the loaves on it, seam side down. Cover with the towel, and let them rise until doubled in bulk, about 45 minutes.

6. Preheat the oven to 350°F.

7. Place the baking sheet on the center rack of the oven, and bake until the bread is well browned and sounds hollow when the bottom is tapped with your finger, 45 minutes. Cool the bread on a wire rack.

2 loaves

> " Actually, the true gourmet, like the true artist, is one of the unhappiest creatures existent. His trouble comes from so seldom finding what he constantly seeks: perfection."
>
> —LUDWIG BEMELMANS

ANADAMA BREAD

Legend has it (according to one of many versions) that this bread was named by a disgruntled husband who shouted about his wife, "Anna, damn her." Maybe her version wasn't as good as ours is—nicely moistened with cream-style corn.

1 package active dry yeast
½ cup warm water
¼ teaspoon sugar
3 cups unbleached all-purpose flour
½ cup stone-ground yellow cornmeal
1 teaspoon salt
½ cup canned cream-style corn
¼ cup molasses
2 tablespoons unsalted butter, melted and cooled to room temperature

1. Combine the yeast, warm water, and sugar in a small bowl and set aside until the yeast starts foaming, 5 to 10 minutes.

2. Stir the flour, cornmeal, and salt together in another bowl.

3. In a third bowl, stir the corn, molasses, and melted butter together.

4. Add the yeast and corn mixtures to the flour, and stir until the mixture forms a mass. Turn the dough out onto a lightly floured surface, and knead until it is smooth and elastic, 10 minutes.

5. Lightly oil a large bowl, and turn the dough in it to coat it with the oil. Cover the bowl loosely with a kitchen towel, and let the dough rise in a warm place until it has doubled in bulk, 1 hour.

6. Lightly butter a 9 x 5 x 3-inch loaf pan.

7. Punch the dough down, and flatten it into a circle about 1 inch thick. Then roll it up and shape it into a loaf. Press it into the prepared pan, cover it loosely, and let it rise until doubled in bulk, about 1 hour.

8. Meanwhile, preheat the oven to 375°F.

9. Transfer the loaf pan to the oven, and bake until the bread is golden and sounds hollow when the bottom is tapped with your finger, 35 minutes.

10. Remove the loaf from the pan, and let it cool on a wire rack.

1 loaf

RAISIN PUMPERNICKEL ROLLS

Dark raisins burst forth from this slightly pale version of pumpernickel rolls—barley malt syrup, cocoa, and espresso powder lend both flavor and color.

1 package active dry yeast
½ cup warm water
¼ teaspoon sugar
1½ cups rye flour
1½ cups unbleached all-purpose flour
1 tablespoon caraway seeds, crushed
1 teaspoon salt
½ teaspoon ground coriander
½ cup water
¼ cup barley malt syrup*
2 tablespoons unsalted butter,
    at room temperature
1 tablespoon unsweetened cocoa
2 teaspoons instant espresso powder
1 cup raisins

1. Stir the yeast, warm water, and sugar together in a small bowl. Let the mixture stand until the yeast starts foaming, 5 minutes.

2. In another bowl, toss together the flours, caraway seeds, salt, and coriander.

3. In a third bowl, combine the ½ cup water, barley malt syrup, butter, cocoa, and espresso powder. Mix well.

4. Add the yeast mixture and the espresso mixture to the flour, and stir until the mixture forms a mass.

5. Turn the dough out onto a lightly floured surface and knead it for about 10 minutes. The dough may be stiff and slightly sticky. Let it rest 5 to 10 minutes, loosely covered with a kitchen towel if necessary, while kneading.

6. Lightly oil a large bowl, and turn the dough in it to coat it with the oil. Loosely cover the bowl, and let the dough rise in a warm place for about 1 hour.

7. Punch the dough down, and turn it out on a lightly floured surface. Flatten the dough and sprinkle it with the raisins. Knead the raisins in until they are evenly distributed in the dough. Shape the dough into 16 balls.

8. Arrange the dough balls on a buttered baking sheet and let them rise, loosely covered, until doubled in bulk, about 1 hour.

9. Preheat the oven to 375°F.

10. Spray the tops of the rolls with water, using a water mister or sprinkling with your fingertips. Bake until a crust has formed, about 18 minutes.

11. Cool the rolls on a wire rack.

16 rolls

*Available in health food stores.

RICH RUM STICKY BUNS

These irresistible sticky buns were first introduced in the *Silver Palate Good Times Cookbook*. We still think these pecany, sugary, sticky sticky buns are the very best.

DOUGH
1 cup warm milk
1 package active dry yeast
½ cup (packed) light brown sugar
5 to 5½ cups unbleached all-purpose flour
½ cup (1 stick) unsalted butter, at room temperature
2 eggs
1 tablespoon grated orange zest
2 tablespoons ground cinnamon
1 teaspoon salt

FILLING
3 tablespoons light brown sugar
3 tablespoons granulated sugar
2 teaspoons ground cinnamon
1 cup chopped pecans
½ cup golden raisins

TOPPING
1 cup (packed) light brown sugar
½ cup honey
1 cup (2 sticks) unsalted butter, melted
⅓ cup rum
1½ cup pecan halves

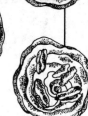

1. One day before serving, prepare the dough: Pour the milk into a large bowl. Stir in the yeast and brown sugar and let stand 5 minutes.

2. Beat in 2 cups of the flour, all the softened butter, the eggs, orange zest, cinnamon, and the salt until blended. Gradually stir in enough of the remaining flour to make a soft dough.

3. Transfer the dough to a lightly floured surface and knead until it is smooth and elastic, about 10 minutes.

4. Place the dough in a buttered large bowl and turn to coat it with butter. Loosely cover the bowl with plastic wrap and let the dough rise in the refrigerator overnight.

5. The following day, prepare the filling: Place the brown sugar, the granulated sugar, the cinnamon, and chopped pecans in a food processor and process until combined but still coarse and crumbly. Add the raisins and process very briefly to distribute the raisins evenly through the mixture. Set the filling aside.

6. Prepare the topping: Mix the brown sugar, honey, and melted butter in a small bowl. Stir in the rum and pecan halves. Set the topping aside.

7. Remove the dough from the refrigerator and punch it down. On a lightly floured surface, roll the dough out into a large rectangle, about ⅓ inch thick. Sprinkle the filling evenly over the dough and press it into the dough with a rolling pin. Starting at one long edge, roll up the dough as tightly as possible.

8. Lightly butter the sides of a 13 x 9-inch baking pan. Spread the topping evenly on the bottom.

9. Cut the dough crosswise into ¾-inch slices and arrange the slices in rows of three over the topping, leaving room for the buns to rise. You should be able to fit 12 to 14 slices in the pan. Cover and let rise until doubled, 45 minutes to 1 hour.

10. Preheat the oven to 350°F.

11. Bake the buns 25 to 30 minutes. Remove them from the oven and let cool 10 minutes. Invert the buns onto a large platter and serve immediately.

12 to 14 large buns

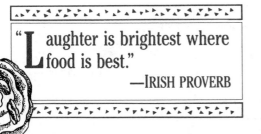

"**L**aughter is brightest where food is best."
—IRISH PROVERB

GRANDMA CLARK'S SODA BREAD

Grandma Clark's Irish eyes twinkled while she made this. This is the real thing from the "old country," and it's the best one we know of!

4 tablespoons (½ stick) unsalted butter
3 cups unbleached all-purpose flour
1½ teaspoons salt
1 tablespoon baking powder
1 teaspoon baking soda
¾ cup sugar
1½ cups dried currants
1¾ cups buttermilk
2 eggs, well beaten
2 tablespoons unsalted butter, melted and cooled to room
    temperature
1 tablespoon caraway seeds (optional)

1. Smear 2 tablespoons of the butter evenly over the bottom and sides of a 10-inch cast-iron skillet. Line the bottom of the skillet with a circle of waxed paper.

2. Preheat the oven to 350°F.

3. Sift the dry ingredients together in a large bowl. Add the currants and toss well to coat.

4. In another bowl, whisk together the buttermilk, eggs, and melted butter. Add this to the dry ingredients along with the caraway seeds, and mix just until blended. Do not overmix.

5. Spoon the batter into the prepared skillet, and smooth the top gently with a spatula. Dot the top with the remaining 2 tablespoons butter.

6. Place the skillet in the oven and bake until the bread is puffed and golden brown, about 1 hour. Cool in the skillet for 10 minutes and serve warm, or then transfer the bread to a wire rack to continue cooling. Cut the loaf into wedges to serve.

1 loaf

QUICK BREADS

Quick breads fall somewhere between cakes and yeast breads. They are quick because there is no waiting for the yeast to rise. They are leavened, instead, with baking powder or baking soda (except for popovers, which are leavened with eggs).

There are two kinds of quick breads—batter breads and dough breads. Batter breads are tea breads, muffins, popovers, and coffee cakes. Mix the dry ingredients thoroughly by hand to keep the texture light.

Dough breads are biscuits and scones. With these breads the fat should be chilled firm enough to cut into the dry ingredients and remain in tiny bits as in a pie crust. The dough is scooped onto a lightly floured surface, kneaded gently for just a minute to bring it together, shaped, and baked.

QUICK BREAD TIPS

When mixing quick breads, combine the wet and dry ingredients just until moistened. Too much mixing will develop the gluten in the flour and the bread will be tough with lots of air bubbles.

When adding plumped raisins or other dried fruit, first toss them very lightly with flour so they don't all sink to the bottom of the loaf.

Make sure your baking powder or baking soda is fresh—when you open a new carton, write the date on it and replace it after six months. The most common failure of quick breads is stale leavening.

BAKING QUICK BREADS

▲ Bake these breads in the center of a preheated oven with room between pans for the hot air to circulate. When the bread is ready, it will pull slightly away from the sides of the pan and a toothpick inserted into the center will come out clean.

▲ Remove biscuits and muffins from the pans immediately and cool on wire racks. Let loaves cool in the pans for 5 minutes, then remove and cool on wire racks.

▲ Slice bread only after it has cooled completely.

▲ Don't open the oven door until the minimum baking time has elapsed. This is especially crucial with popovers.

LEMON CHIVE PEPPER BREAD

We created this to serve toasted with soft-shell crabs or lobster sandwiches. It's also great with soup or salad, especially if you spread it with a little butter mixed with chives and lemon zest.

1 cup (2 sticks) unsalted butter, at room temperature
½ cup sugar
4 eggs, separated
⅓ cup fresh lemon juice
Grated zest of 2 lemons
3 cups unbleached all-purpose flour
4 teaspoons baking powder
1 tablespoon cracked or very coarsely ground black pepper
1 cup milk
Pinch of salt
¼ cup snipped fresh chives

1. Preheat the oven to 350°F. Butter a 9 x 5 x 3-inch loaf pan with 1 teaspoon of the butter.

2. Cream the remaining butter and the sugar together in a mixing bowl. Add the egg yolks one at a time, beating well after each addition. Then stir in the lemon juice and zest.

3. In another bowl, combine the flour, baking powder, and pepper. Stir one third of this mixture into the butter mixture. Then add ½ cup of the milk and mix it in. Continue, adding one third of the flour, the remaining ½ cup milk, and the remaining third of the flour, beating well after each addition. Do not overmix.

4. In another bowl, beat the egg whites with the pinch of salt until they form soft peaks. Fold the egg whites and the chives into the batter.

5. Pour the batter into the prepared loaf pan, and place on a rack in the middle of the oven. Bake until a skewer inserted in the center comes out clean, 50 to 60 minutes.

6. Let the bread cool for 5 minutes. Then remove it from the pan and set it on a wire rack to continue cooling.

1 loaf

LEMON BLUEBERRY BREAD

A fragrant tea cake with a crunchy top.

TOPPING
½ cup sugar
⅓ cup unbleached all-purpose flour
4 tablespoons (½ stick) unsalted butter, at room temperature
1 teaspoon grated lemon zest
½ teaspoon ground cinnamon

¾ cup sugar
½ cup milk
4 tablespoons (½ stick) unsalted butter, at room temperature
1 egg
2 cups unbleached all-purpose flour
2 teaspoons baking powder
¼ teaspoon salt
2 cups fresh blueberries
1 tablespoon grated lemon zest

1. Preheat the oven to 375°F. Oil a 9 x 5-inch loaf pan.

2. Stir the topping ingredients together in a small bowl until smooth. Set aside.

3. In a medium-size bowl, stir the sugar, milk, butter, and egg together until smooth.

4. In another bowl, toss the flour with the baking powder and salt. Stir this into the wet ingredients, and then fold in the blueberries and lemon zest.

5. Transfer the batter to the prepared loaf pan, and sprinkle with the topping. Bake until the topping is deep golden and has formed a thick crust, 50 minutes. Cool in the pan for 5 minutes, then transfer the bread to a wire rack to continue cooling.

1 loaf

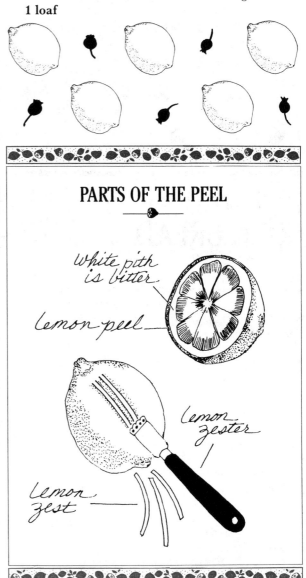

PARTS OF THE PEEL

White pith is bitter

lemon peel

lemon zester

lemon zest

CORN BREAD

★

Corn bread can be made with different cornmeals for varying textures. Coarse stone-ground cornmeal gives a rustic and gritty texture to the bread; fine yellow cornmeal makes a soft, tender bread. When making corn bread, add the liquid in two stages to avoid a lumpy batter because cornmeal doesn't absorb liquid quickly. For a dark, crisp crust, bake the batter in a preheated, greased cast-iron skillet. Serve fresh and hot with sweet butter and honey or Jalapeño Chutney.

HOT AND SASSY CORN BREAD

If Fats Waller were around, he'd write a song about this corn bread. Made with cornmeal, sweet corn kernels, and jalapeño pepper, this is just grand! And right up Fats' alley.

1 cup stone-ground yellow cornmeal
¾ cup unbleached all-purpose flour
¼ cup whole-wheat flour
1 teaspoon baking powder
¾ teaspoon salt
½ teaspoon baking soda
Freshly ground black pepper, to taste
1 cup canned cream-style corn
½ cup fresh or frozen corn kernels, thawed if frozen
½ cup sour cream
½ cup milk
2 eggs, lightly beaten
2 tablespoons vegetable oil
1 tablespoon (packed) light brown sugar
1 to 2 fresh jalapeño peppers, minced

1. Preheat the oven to 400°F. Butter an 8-inch square baking pan.

2. Toss the dry ingredients together in a mixing bowl.

3. In another bowl, stir the cream-style corn and all the remaining ingredients together until smooth. Add half the liquid mixture to the dry mixture, stirring just until blended. Add the remaining liquid and again stir until just blended. Pour the batter into the prepared pan.

4. Bake until the top is golden and a knife inserted in the center comes out clean, 25 minutes. Cool slightly in the pan before cutting into squares.

8 portions

POPOVERS

●

A popover is a crisp, golden balloon with a soft, moist, hollow center. Eggs are the only leavening in popovers. We add a bit of cheese or a fresh herb for flavor. Popovers are served hot and puffed right out of the oven. If you want to serve them a little later, just pierce the top with the tip of a knife to let the steam escape.

GOLDEN POPOVERS

These chive-laced popovers are easy to make and as light as air. They may taste special but you needn't wait for a special occasion to serve them.

3 tablespoons unsalted butter
4 eggs
1 cup unbleached all-purpose flour
Pinch of salt (optional)
Freshly ground black pepper, to taste
½ cup heavy or whipping cream
1 cup milk
¼ cup snipped fresh or freeze-dried chives

1. Preheat the oven to 400°F. Use 1 tablespoon of the butter to butter a 12-cup muffin tin.

2. Melt the remaining 2 tablespoons butter and set them aside.

3. Combine the eggs, flour, salt, and pepper in a food processor, and process until well blended, 10 seconds.

4. With the machine running, slowly pour the cream, milk, and melted butter through the feed tube. Process until smooth. Transfer the mixture to a bowl, and fold in the chives.

5. Fill the prepared muffin cups two thirds full with batter. Place the tin on a rack in the center of the oven, and bake for 35 minutes. Don't open the oven door while the popovers are baking or they may fall. Serve piping hot.

12 popovers

MUFFINS

Muffins have become the new breakfast. They are a wonderful way to eat fruit and fiber at the same time.

We like our muffins with rough, rounded tops and a dense, moist texture. Don't overbeat the batter or they will be tough and chewy. When adding a fruit or nut topping, be sure to press it firmly into the batter or it will be pushed off the muffin as it rises. Bake muffins in paper liners or well-oiled muffin cups. Muffins are ideal for preparing ahead because they freeze well.

ORANGE CURRANT BRAN MUFFINS

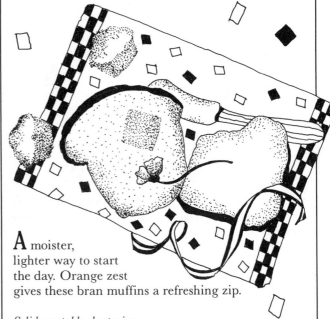

A moister, lighter way to start the day. Orange zest gives these bran muffins a refreshing zip.

Solid vegetable shortening
1 ½ cups oat bran
1 cup 100% bran cereal
1 tablespoon light brown sugar
1 tablespoon baking powder
½ teaspoon salt
½ cup dried currants
Grated zest of 1 orange
1 cup low-fat buttermilk
3 egg whites, lightly beaten
1 tablespoon safflower oil

1. Preheat the oven to 425°F. Lightly grease a twelve-cup muffin tin (with 2½-inch cups) with shortening. Set the tin aside.

2. Using a fork, mix both brans with the brown sugar, baking powder, and salt in a bowl. Stir in the currants and orange zest.

3. In another bowl, mix together the buttermilk, egg whites, and oil. Add this to the dry ingredients, stirring with a fork until moistened.

4. Pour the batter into the muffin cups, and bake for 17 minutes.

5. Transfer the muffins to a wire rack, and allow them to cool.

12 muffins

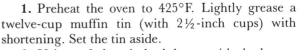

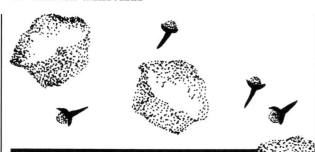

SWEET POTATO MAPLE MUFFINS

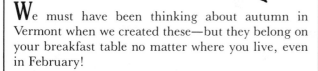

We must have been thinking about autumn in Vermont when we created these—but they belong on your breakfast table no matter where you live, even in February!

1 sweet potato
1½ cups unbleached all-purpose flour
Pinch of salt
2 teaspoons baking powder
1 teaspoon baking soda
1 teaspoon ground allspice
⅛ teaspoon ground cloves
6 tablespoons (¾ stick) unsalted butter,
    at room temperature
⅔ cup (packed) dark brown sugar
2 eggs, lightly beaten
½ cup milk
¾ cup maple syrup

1. Bring a saucepan of water to a boil, add the sweet potato, and simmer until tender, 20 to 25 minutes. Drain the potato and allow it to cool slightly; then peel it and cut it into several pieces.

2. Purée the potato in a food processor until smooth; you should have ½ cup. Set it aside.

3. Preheat the oven to 350°F. Generously butter two eight-cup muffin tins, or line them with paper liners.

4. In a large bowl, sift together the flour, salt, baking powder, baking soda, allspice, and cloves.

5. In another bowl, cream the butter and brown sugar together. Add the eggs and beat well. Then stir in the milk, maple syrup, and reserved sweet potato purée; mix thoroughly.

6. Make a well in the center of the dry ingredients, and pour the potato mixture into it. Stir just until the ingredients are incorporated—do not overmix.

7. Fill the cups about two thirds full with batter, and bake until a toothpick inserted in the center comes out clean, about 25 minutes. Transfer the muffins to a wire rack and allow them to cool.

16 muffins

ORANGE BRAN MUFFINS

Dark and moist bran muffins are a great way to greet the morning, toasted or not. Try them without butter on top—they really don't need it.

½ cup golden raisins
½ cup coarsely chopped dried apple slices
½ cup fresh orange juice
1 cup unbleached all-purpose flour
1 tablespoon baking powder
2 teaspoons baking soda
Pinch of salt
¾ cup sugar
½ teaspoon ground cinnamon
¾ cup bran flake cereal
1 egg
½ cup milk
⅓ cup vegetable oil

1. Combine the raisins, dried apples, and orange juice in a small bowl, and set aside to soak for 30 minutes.

2. Preheat the oven to 350°F. Line two eight-cup muffin tins with paper liners, or butter the cups generously.

3. In a large bowl, sift together the flour, baking

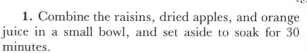

powder, baking soda, salt, sugar, and cinnamon. Add the bran cereal and mix thoroughly.

4. In another bowl, beat together the egg, milk, and oil.

5. Make a well in the center of the dry ingredients, and pour the egg mixture into it. Add the raisins, apples, and orange juice, and stir just until all the ingredients are incorporated—do not overmix.

6. Fill each cup about three quarters full with the batter, and bake until the muffins are well colored and a toothpick inserted in the center comes out clean, 18 to 20 minutes. Transfer the muffins to a rack and allow them to cool.

16 muffins

> "He that is of a merry heart hath a continual feast."
> —PROVERBS 15:15

DRIED CHERRY MUFFINS

From the northern woods of Michigan come the most delicious cherries imaginable. In fact, over 75 percent of our nation's cherries are grown here. Thank goodness they're now being dried again, as the Indians once did, for they give a most concentrated cherry flavor. We love to sit and snack on them, but buttermilk muffins seem to be the perfect wrapping—served warm, their flavor is at its peak.

1 cup dried cherries, pitted (about 8 ounces with pits)
1 cup buttermilk
1 ¾ cups unbleached all-purpose flour
2 teaspoons baking powder
1 teaspoon baking soda
Pinch of salt
8 tablespoons (1 stick) unsalted butter, at room temperature
¾ cup sugar
2 eggs, lightly beaten

1. Combine the cherries and buttermilk in a small bowl, and set aside to soak for 30 minutes.

2. Preheat the oven to 350°F. Generously butter 18 muffin cups or line them with paper liners.

3. In a large bowl, sift together the flour, baking powder, baking soda, and salt.

4. In another bowl, cream together the butter and sugar. Add the eggs and mix thoroughly.

5. Make a well in the center of the dry ingredients, and spoon the cherries and buttermilk into it. Then add the butter-sugar mixture. Mix until thoroughly blended—but do not overmix.

6. Fill the cups two thirds full with the batter, and bake until a toothpick inserted in the center comes out clean, 18 to 20 minutes. Transfer the muffins to a wire rack and allow them to cool.

18 muffins

BREAD BASKET BREAKFAST

Fresh Orange Juice

Dried Cherry Muffins
Orange Bran Muffins
Rich Rum Sticky Buns

Kiwi Lime Marmalade
Crock of Sweet Butter

Good Strong Coffee

NEW BASIC BISCUITS

This basic dough can be made sweet or savory: just adapt the recipe one way to make a great accompaniment to Spicy Breakfast Patties, another way for a fresh berry shortcake.

2 cups unbleached all-purpose flour
1 tablespoon baking powder
1 teaspoon sugar
½ teaspoon salt
5 tablespoons unsalted butter, cold
¾ cup half-and-half

1. Preheat the oven to 450°F.
2. In a large bowl, toss together the flour, baking powder, sugar, and salt. Cut the butter into small pieces, and cut it into the flour using two knives, a pastry blender, or your fingertips until the mixture resembles coarse crumbs.
3. Add the half-and-half, and stir gently until the mixture forms a mass. Gather it into a ball.
4. Transfer the dough to a lightly floured surface. Knead it for about 30 seconds, and then pat it out to form a ¾-inch-thick rectangle. Using a 2¾-inch cookie cutter, cut out 8 circles; use up all the dough.
5. Arrange the biscuits about 1 inch apart on a baking sheet. Bake until puffed and golden, 14 minutes. Transfer the biscuits to a wire rack and allow them to cool.

8 biscuits

SAVORY BISCUITS

To the flour mixture in Step 2 add 1 tablespoon snipped fresh chives, ¼ teaspoon paprika, and freshly ground black pepper to taste.

SWEET BISCUITS

Increase the sugar to 2 tablespoons and reduce the flour to 1¾ cups. Before baking, brush the tops of the biscuits with melted butter and sprinkle with additional sugar.

BISCUIT TIPS
★

Biscuits should rise to two times their original height when baked. They should be light, tender, and fluffy with a crisp, golden brown crust. Mix the dough gently so they don't become tough and chewy. If you don't have time or don't want to fuss with cutting the biscuits out, simply drop the batter from a spoon onto baking sheets. "Drop biscuits" won't rise as much but they taste every bit as good.

▲ For soft, fluffy biscuits, place them close together on the baking sheet.
▲ For crustier biscuits, place them at least an inch apart.
▲ For flakier biscuits, rub or cut the chilled butter into the flour (as if making pie dough) before adding the remaining ingredients.
▲ Buttermilk makes a tender biscuit with a slightly tart taste.
▲ Cream produces a light, buttery biscuit —perfect for shortcake.
▲ Grated orange or lemon zest adds a zippy flavor.
▲ To make biscuit splitting easier, roll the dough ¼ inch thick, then fold it in half and cut out the biscuits.

BUTTERMILK COUNTRY BISCUITS WITH HAM

An old Virginia treat at cocktail time—or at a buffet or for breakfast—these miniature ham-flavored biscuits are wonderful! Try spreading them with butter, sweet mustard, and thin slices of Baked Party Ham. They're also a nice treat with soup or salads.

2 cups unbleached all-purpose flour
1 tablespoon baking powder
1 teaspoon dried thyme leaves
1 teaspoon sugar
½ teaspoon ground ginger
¼ teaspoon ground nutmeg
¼ teaspoon baking soda
¼ teaspoon salt
Freshly ground black pepper, to taste
5 tablespoons solid vegetable shortening
½ cup minced cooked country ham (trimmed of all fat)
2 tablespoons minced green bell pepper
¾ cup buttermilk
4 tablespoons melted butter

1. Preheat the oven to 425°F.
2. In a large mixing bowl, toss together the flour, baking powder, thyme, sugar, ginger, nutmeg, baking soda, salt, and pepper. Using a pastry blender, two knives, or your fingertips, cut the shortening into the mixture until it resembles coarse crumbs.
3. Stir in the ham and green pepper. Add the buttermilk, and stir until the mixture forms a mass. Gather it into a ball.
4. Transfer the dough to a lightly floured surface and knead it for about 30 seconds. Then pat it out to form a ¾-inch-thick rectangle. Using a 1½-inch cookie cutter, cut out about 30 circles; use up all the dough.
5. Arrange the biscuits about 1 inch apart on a baking sheet. Brush the tops lightly with the melted butter. Bake until puffed and golden, 12 minutes. Transfer the biscuits to a wire rack and allow them to cool.

30 biscuits

TOMATO BASIL BISCUITS

These basil-flecked pink biscuits are great with a greens soup, grilled beef or fish, or an omelet.

1 cup unbleached all-purpose flour
Pinch of sugar
¼ teaspoon salt
2 teaspoons baking powder
4 tablespoons (½ stick) unsalted butter, cold
¼ cup half-and-half
2 ripe tomatoes, peeled, seeded, and coarsely chopped (½ cup)
⅓ cup coarsely chopped fresh basil leaves

1. Preheat the oven to 425°F.
2. In a large bowl, sift together the flour, sugar, salt, and baking powder. Cut the butter into ½-inch cubes, and with two knives, a pastry blender, or your fingertips work them into the flour until the mixture resembles coarse crumbs.
3. Add the half-and-half and the tomatoes, and stir to combine thoroughly. Incorporate the chopped basil.
4. Transfer the dough to a lightly floured surface, and knead it for about 30 seconds. Then pat it out until it is 1 inch thick, and cut out rounds with a 2-inch cookie cutter.
5. Arrange the biscuits about 1 inch apart on a baking sheet. Bake until puffed and golden, about 15 minutes. Transfer the biscuits to a wire rack and allow them to cool.

6 biscuits

JALAPENO CHEESE BISCUITS

Cheesy biscuits with a bit of a bite.

1 cup unbleached all-purpose flour
Pinch of sugar
¼ teaspoon salt
2 teaspoons baking powder
4 tablespoons (½ stick) unsalted butter, cold
6 tablespoons half-and-half
2 ounces Monterey Jack cheese with jalapeño peppers, grated (½ cup)

1. Preheat the oven to 425°F.

2. In a large bowl, sift together the flour, sugar, salt, and baking powder. Cut the butter into small pieces, and using two knives, a pastry blender, or your fingertips, work them into the flour until the mixture resembles coarse crumbs.

3. Add the half-and-half, and stir well. Then work in the grated cheese.

4. Transfer the dough to a lightly floured surface, and knead it for about 30 seconds. Then pat it out until it is 1 inch thick, and cut out rounds with a 2-inch cookie cutter.

5. Arrange the biscuits about 1 inch apart on a baking sheet. Bake until puffed and golden, about 15 minutes. Transfer the biscuits to a wire rack and allow them to cool.

6 biscuits

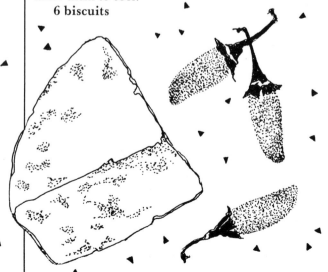

> "Beauty of style and harmony and grace and good rhythm depend on simplicity."
>
> —PLATO

ROASTED RED PEPPER BISCUITS

Light biscuits with bright red roasted peppers throughout. Serve them with sausage and eggs, with something cheesy, or with grilled meats.

1 cup unbleached all-purpose flour
Pinch of sugar
¼ teaspoon salt
2 teaspoons baking powder
4 tablespoons (½ stick) unsalted butter, cold
¼ cup half-and-half
1 red bell pepper, roasted (see Index), peeled, and cut into ½-inch pieces

1. Preheat the oven to 425°F.

2. In a large bowl, sift together the flour, sugar, salt, and baking powder. Cut the butter into ½-inch cubes, and using two knives, a pastry blender, or your fingertips, work the butter into the flour until the mixture resembles coarse crumbs.

3. Add the half-and-half, and stir to blend well. Then incorporate the roasted pepper.

4. Transfer the dough to a lightly floured surface and knead it for about 30 seconds. Pat it out until it is 1 inch thick, and cut out rounds with a 2-inch cookie cutter.

5. Arrange the biscuits on a baking sheet about 1 inch apart. Bake until puffed and golden, about 15 minutes. Transfer the biscuits to a wire rack and allow them to cool.

6 biscuits

DILL AND SMOKED SALMON BISCUITS

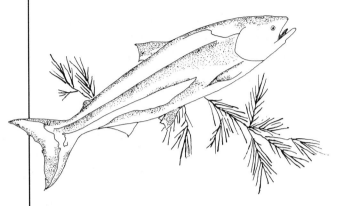

Serve these biscuits, warm out of the oven, at cocktail time or brunch. Be sure to have a fresh chèvre alongside.

2 ounces thickly sliced smoked salmon (see Step 2)
1 cup unbleached all-purpose flour
Pinch of sugar
¼ teaspoon salt
2 teaspoons baking powder
4 tablespoons (½ stick) unsalted butter, cold, cut into small
*   pieces*
6 tablespoons half-and-half
2 tablespoons finely chopped fresh dill

1. Preheat the oven to 425°F.

2. Cut the salmon into ½-inch cubes; you should have about ⅓ cup. Set it aside.

3. Sift the flour, sugar, salt, and baking powder together in a large bowl. Using your fingertips, two knives, or a pastry blender, work the butter into the flour until the mixture resembles oatmeal flakes. Add the half-and-half, and stir to combine thoroughly. Then work in the dill and salmon.

4. Transfer the dough to a lightly floured surface, and knead it for about 30 seconds. Pat it out until it is 1 inch thick, and cut out rounds with a 2-inch cookie cutter.

5. Arrange the biscuits about 1 inch apart on a baking sheet. Bake until puffed and golden, about 15 minutes. Transfer the biscuits to a wire rack and allow them to cool.

6 biscuits

MARY'S FRIED CAKES

The first American doughnuts did not have holes at all; they were quite literally little "nuts" of dough. Julee's grandmother Mary made them that way, and that's the way we still like them.

2½ cups unbleached all-purpose flour
2½ teaspoons baking powder
1 cup sugar
½ cup cooked mashed potatoes, warm
1 whole egg
1 egg yolk
¼ cup milk
2 tablespoons unsalted butter, melted and cooled to room
*   temperature*
1½ teaspoons freshly grated nutmeg
½ teaspoon salt
Vegetable oil for deep-frying
Confectioners' sugar, for dusting (optional)

1. Combine the flour and baking powder in a mixing bowl, and toss well with a fork.

2. In another bowl, stir the sugar and mashed potatoes together until smooth.

3. In a third bowl, beat the whole egg, egg yolk, milk, melted butter, nutmeg, and salt until well blended. Then stir in the potato mixture, and slowly beat in the flour mixture. Refrigerate for 30 minutes.

4. Roll the dough out on a lightly floured surface until it is ½ inch thick. Cut out rounds with a 1-inch cookie cutter.

5. Heat the oil to 375°F in a deep-fryer. Carefully drop the cakes into the hot oil, in batches, and cook, turning once, until deep golden, 2 minutes. Drain them on paper towels. Dust with confectioners' sugar if you like. Serve warm or at room temperature.

About 75 doughnuts

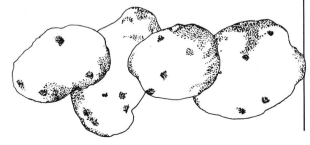

THE CHEESE COURSE

A cheese course during a dinner is a lovely way to prolong good wine and conversation while preparing the palate for dessert. We like to offer at least three cheeses; you may add more, depending on the number of guests and the type of meal being served. Balance the cheese course with the rest of the meal: Serve more extravagant cheeses with a light meal, and simple, light cheeses with a hearty meal.

Think of contrast in taste, texture, and color when selecting cheeses. Choose a representative from several families and try to include at least one familiar cheese, such as Brie or Camembert. If you buy about two ounces of each cheese per person, you will have plenty.

Cheese should always be served at room temperature—never cold—so be sure to take it out of the refrigerator in plenty of time. And don't cut cheeses before serving because the slices quickly dry out.

Add a selection of wonderful fresh fruits, too, making sure you have a knife for each cheese as well as knives for the fruit. Accompany all with crusty bread and crackers.

HARD CHEESES

In the past, we thought of hard cheeses as primarily for grating. Perhaps it was those many trips to Italy that changed our minds. Little bite-size pieces of sweet Parmigiano-Reggiano broken off a large wedge and eaten with ripe pears for dessert is one of the greatest treats we know. Shave these hard cheeses into tissue-thin slices to grace salads and enjoy the texture as well as the flavor.

These hard cheeses do not develop their great flavors until they have been aged for at least one year. As they age, the moisture evaporates and the taste intensifies. Buy a large piece because hard cheeses will keep for months if they are well wrapped in foil and stored in the lower part of the refrigerator.

▲ **Aged Cow's-Milk Cheese:** This less grainy, somewhat sweet hard cheese is produced by the Yerba Santa Goat Dairy in Lakeport, California. It is perfect for coarsely grating into lusty red bean casseroles as well as thinly sliced over peasant sourdough bread.

▲ **Asiago:** Originally made from sheep's milk, this straw-colored cheese is now made from cow's milk. A version is produced in Wisconsin. We much prefer the aged cheese to the young Asiago, which is somewhat bitter. Grate it over pasta tossed with a little butter and lots of black pepper.

▲ **Dry Jack Cheese:** Unfortunately, this cheese is still hard to find but it's well worth the search. The Rumiano Cheese Company in Crescent City, California, is the largest producer. Another resource is the Vella Cheese Company in Sonoma, California. They coat their Jack cheeses with cocoa and pepper dust in a vegetable oil base. The dry Jacks are wonderful grating cheeses and superb eaten on their own with ripe fruits and robust red wines. They are less grainy than Parmesan.

▲ **Grana Padano:** Aged for two years, this fine grating cheese has a grainy texture, straw-like color, and savory flavor. It is somewhat moister than Parmigiano-Reggiano. Serve as part of an antipasto with a crusty peasant loaf or grate over freshly cooked broccoli or baked zucchini.

▲ **Parmigiano-Reggiano:** This cheese has a sweet and nutty taste with a slightly grainy texture that melts in the mouth. It is expensive but we feel it's worth every penny. From the first of April through the eleventh of November, the cows of Parma eat fresh grass and produce the milk used to make this great Parmesan cheese, which is then aged with great care. Grate only as much as you need and store the remaining wedge airtight in the refrigerator. For dessert put the whole wedge on a plate, break off little bite-size pieces, and serve with perfectly ripe pears. In Italy, a great delicacy is fresh sweet Parmesan served with thin slices of raw artichoke bottoms laced with extra virgin olive oil. We agree!

▲ **Pepato:** A spicy cheese, pale yellow in color and studded with black peppercorns, it is wonderful grated over pasta.

▲ **Romano:** Many Romanos are made from sheep's milk and have a salty flavor. It lends a nice bite to pasta and is traditional to southern Italian cooking. It is often blended with grana to mellow its flavor.

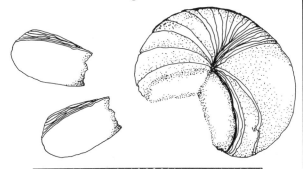

THE RACLETTE PARTY

▲

Chèvre, Bleu de Gex, and French Raclette
Country Venison Pâté
Basket of tiny boiled red new potatoes

▲

Pickled sour cherries, cornichons, and assorted imported olives

▲

Toasted Olive Rosemary Country Bread

▲

Côte de Beaune

SEMIFIRM CHEESES

The semifirm cheeses fall into several categories, including the Swiss and French "holey" cheeses with their nutty taste and mild fragrance. They are made from either sheep's or cow's milk and are pressed to achieve a firm yet supple texture.

The semifirm cheeses we enjoy the most are Gruyère, Emmentaler, Double Gloucester, Black Diamond, and Smoked Applewood Cheddar. The best known Cheddars vary greatly in color and sharpness. Depending on the age of the cheese, they can be very mild or sharp with great depth of character. Look for Cheddars that are *firm* and moist and keep well wrapped in the refrigerator. Fresh apple cider and sparkling grape juice are lovely to drink with these cheeses.

▲ **Appenzeller:** As this cheese ages, it is washed with spices and white wine, imparting a rich, fruity flavor. The wheel is much smaller than other Swiss cheeses, making it possible to fit a wedge on a cheese platter.

▲ **Cantal:** One of France's oldest cheeses, it is supple and nutty sweet. Its texture makes it an ideal cooking cheese, and it is delicious sliced on toasted whole-grain bread.

▲ **Cheddar:** The Cheddar family has a great range and large number of varieties. Eating Cheddars are best when aged at least six months. Although the color added to Cheddar to make it orange is quite natural, we find the white farmhouse varieties usually the best. Try a Double Gloucester made from the rich summer milk of English cows. Slightly sharp in taste, it pairs well with tawny port.

Wensleydale is a flaky white Cheddar with a slightly pungent taste. Huntsman is made from layers of Stilton and creamy orange Cheshire Cheddar. Canadians produce Black Diamond Cheddar, which is aged one to three years and coated with black wax. Serve this crumbly white cheese with Ruby Port, apples, and walnuts for dessert.

Smoked Applewood Cheddar from Meredith Mountain Farms in Delhi, New York, is permeated with the flavor of applewood; we found it quite extraordinary.

Hunter's Cheese, a Vermont Cheddar, is well aged, extra sharp in flavor, and made from raw milk. Tillamook raw-milk Cheddar is medium sharp in flavor and aged at least three months. These are great snacking cheeses.

APPLES WITH CHEESE

- ▲ Sliced with creamy Brie de Meaux
- ▲ With nutty Mimolette
- ▲ With smooth ashy Morbier
- ▲ With ripe Camembert and walnuts
- ▲ With smoky Applewood Cheddar and peanuts
- ▲ With dry Jack Cheese and pistachios
- ▲ With aged Gouda and roasted chestnuts
- ▲ Baked with a dollop of fresh chèvre
- ▲ Dipped in Emmentaler fondue
- ▲ With Stilton in the fall

▲ **Comté:** A French Gruyère from the mountainous region of Savoie, this cheese is firmer and drier than its Swiss relation. It has a nuttier flavor and gives excellent body to quiches and vegetable flans.

▲ **Emmentaler:** A true Swiss with a full nutty flavor, this cheese is slightly oily with holes completely through the body. It is perfect for melting over onion soup and gives a luscious boost to a quiche filling. Emmentaler is the perfect melting cheese to top a hot sandwich. Be sure the rind is stamped "Switzerland" in red to prove its authenticity.

▲ **Gruyère:** Named for the town where it has been made since the twelfth century, this deep nutty, full-flavored cheese is made only in the summer from cow's milk. It is the perfect base for cheese and vegetable tarts.

▲ **Mimolette:** One of the few cheeses from France that are bright in color, this large orange ball is nutty in flavor. Serve on pumpernickel with a glass of Beaujolais.

▲ **Uniekaas Light:** This Dutch cheese is mild, yellow, and semifirm with small holes. It has 25 percent less salt and 33 percent less fat than similar cheeses.

BLUE CHEESES

O f all the cheeses in the world, we might just love the blues the best. These cheeses of noble character are etched with delicate blue-green veins. Flavor-producing molds are injected during the cheese's curing process to create the veins. The cheeses age in caves where the dampness transforms the curds into a beautiful ivory color. They range from soft, creamy, and mild to intense and firm.

Although most blue cheeses are made from cow's milk, Roquefort is made from sheep's milk, and there are also some new blue goat's-milk cheeses being made in the States.

The grand trinity—Stilton, Roquefort, and Gorgonzola—are best served with fine aged port, fruity Beaujolais, or Vino Nobile from the Tuscan hill town of Montepulciano.

▲ **Bleu d'Auvergne:** Made in the style of Roquefort, this cow's-milk cheese is less salty and firmer with a sharp taste and aroma. This is the blue to use for salad dressing.

▲ **Bleu de Bresse:** This cheese from France is made in the style of Gorgonzola. It is a creamy dessert cheese with a mild flavor and aroma—lovely with dried apricots and dates.

▲ **Bleu de Gex:** This marvelous blue is a perfect melting cheese and would be fun to serve with a French Raclette and Chèvre Raclette for the ultimate Raclette party.

▲ **Bresse Blue:** Made in the style of the French soft blues, this Wisconsin cheese is getting rave reviews. Its creamy, mellow flavor complements other cheeses, and it is great served with a basket of polished, crisp fall apples.

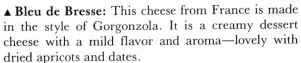

▲ **Gorgonzola:** One of Italy's oldest cheeses, Gorgonzola is rich and pungent with green veins and a golden curd. When young the cheese is sweet, creamy, and smooth. As it ages it becomes sharper and dry. Gorgonzola mixed with cream and mascarpone is spectacular with creamy polenta. Serve it for dessert with juicy ripe pears and a glass of Barolo wine.

Gorgonzola Dolce (sweet Gorgonzola) is eaten young when it is at its mildest. We like to make a creamy dressing with it and serve it over grilled radicchio.

▲ **Maytag Blue:** A smooth white cheese with heavy mold, Maytag Blue comes from Iowa and has the pleasant blue flavor we love. We think it the best of the domestic blues and serve it with salads and spicy Zinfandel.

▲ **Roquefort:** This blue is made from sheep's milk under the strictest of regulations. It must be aged for at least two months in the limestone caves of Cambalou in the South of France. When the cheese is first cut, it looks white on the inside. After it is exposed to the air the characteristic blue-green veins appear. We have had glorious moments eating Roquefort with crusty bread, sweet farmhouse butter, whole walnuts, and huge plump raisins.

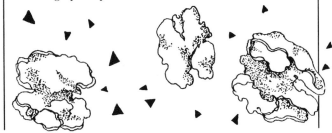

▲ **Saga Blue:** See Double- and Triple-Crème Cheeses. Wait until mid-November and drink a new Beaujolais with this incredible treat. We also love Saga Blue crumbled over a bitter Belgian endive salad napped with Walnut Vinaigrette.

▲ **Stilton:** Often referred to as the "King of Cheeses," Stilton is another favorite and is best eaten after four to six months of aging. Every September, when the "R"s return to the months, a small but venerable restaurant in London called Wiltons celebrates by ladening the bar with the freshest oysters and pouring chilled Champagne. For dessert they bring out a large aged Stilton, perfectly tied around the middle with a white linen napkin. They scoop out the Stilton with a spoon onto beautiful plates and serve it with luscious Bath Oliver biscuits and fine aged port. What a way to usher in autumn!

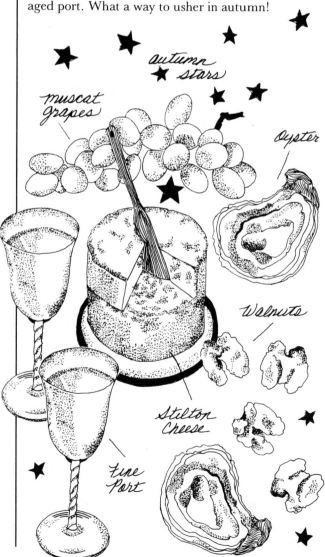

muscat grapes

autumn stars

oyster

Walnuts

Stilton Cheese

Fine Port

PLUMS WITH CHEESE

- ▲ With buttery ripe Explorateur
- ▲ With fruity Tomme de Savoie
- ▲ With Alpine Doux de Montagne
- ▲ With creamy Taleggio and whole almonds
- ▲ With tangy chèvre Raclette
- ▲ Stewed and served with creamy mascarpone
- ▲ For breakfast with creamy Havarti
- ▲ With mellow Monterey Jack

SEMISOFT CHEESES

Buttery and smooth in flavor, semisoft cheeses are tender to the touch. The mountain or monastery cheeses are members of this family. Some of the oldest traditions go back to the Trappist monks of the Middle Ages. Over the centuries, their rinds have been washed with wines, beers, and herb and spice infusions, and many are coated in wax. Some of our favorites are Morbier, Reblochon, Taleggio, Fontina, and Gouda.

Buy semisoft cheeses that are not cracked or dried out. Serve at room temperature to enjoy their full flavors and accompany with fruity white wine, such as Vouvray or Mâcon-Villages.

▲ **Creamy Havarti:** This cow's-milk cheese from Denmark is mild, smooth, and rindless. It comes plain or flavored with dill, chives, caraway, herbs, spices, or sometimes even jalapeño pepper. We find Havarti a lovely breakfast cheese.

▲ **Fleur de Lait:** A company in New Holland, Pennsylvania, Fleur de Lait makes three types of cheeses. The cheeses labeled "New Holland" are all natural and low in fat and sodium. They are available in natural, caraway, garlic and herb, garden vegetable, and jalapeño flavors, offering the cheese eater on a low-sodium diet a good-tasting "melter." The variety called Pyrenette is a semisoft cheese made in the style of the Pyrenees cheeses from the South of France. But the bulk of the Fleur de Lait production is in their Neufchâtel cheeses, which are soft, spreadable, and lower in fat than cream cheese. The variety of flavors ranges from natural to strawberry, chocolate, horseradish, and herbs and spices. They make excellent breakfast cheeses and can substitute for cream cheese in any recipe.

▲ **Fontina:** As this very special cheese from Italy ages, its nutty flavor becomes richer. Although more expensive, the real Fontina, Val d'Aosta, from northern Piedmont is well worth the price to experience the buttery texture and rich flavor reminiscent of truffles. Fontina is a superb cooking cheese as well. Add it to pasta dishes or slice it over polenta. At the end of a fine meal, serve it with pears and Chianti Classico.

▲ **Gaperon:** This delicious, supple, low-fat cheese is flavored with garlic and fresh black peppercorns. In earlier days a French farmer's wealth was judged by the number of Gaperons he had hanging from his kitchen rafters. Tied with a bright yellow cord, mini Gaperons are perfect for bringing along to a woodsy autumn picnic.

▲ **Gouda and Edam:** These are Holland's best-known cheeses. They are mild, smooth, and pale golden in hue. As the cheeses age, the flavors become more distinctive. Some are flavored with caraway or cumin seeds, but we prefer the simple aged Gouda with a character and texture of its own. Shred it over a simple omelet or use it for a grilled cheese sandwich.

▲ **Montflor:** Another of the low-fat cheeses, this tasty semisoft cheese is made from cow's milk. It has a washed rind and just 20 percent butterfat.

▲ **Morbier:** One of our favorite mountain cheeses, it is somewhat mild in flavor with a piquant aftertaste. It was originally made in the field by shepherds who cooked the morning milk in a skillet. The ash from the fire fell into the skillet and left a distinctive line when the evening milk was added to the top. It is still produced with morning and evening cow's milk with the edible ash in the center.

▲ **Munster:** True Munster is not found in our supermarkets. Originally produced by the Benedictine monks of the eighth century, this cheese is both rich and creamy. From the Vosges region of France, the distinctive orange-rinded cheese is fairly mild when young and becomes tangier as it ages. It is quite delicious served on a sandwich with garlic sausages.

▲ **Port-Salut:** This mild and creamy cow's-milk cheese was first made by Trappist monks. It has a low butterfat content and is best served simply with a crisp baguette and Mâcon-Villages wine.

▲ **Provolone:** Originally made from water buffalo's milk, this cheese is now produced from cow's milk. Young Provolone is mild; it becomes firmer and sharper with age. The cheese comes in many sizes and shapes, but our favorite is Provolone wrapped around a nugget of sweet butter. Serve it with roasted red peppers, sopressata salami, and crusty Italian bread.

"**I**f I had a son who was ready to marry, I would tell him, 'Beware of girls who don't like wine, truffles, cheese, or music.'"
—COLETTE

▲ **Pyrenees:** This family of cheeses come in many different shapes and are most often named for the region from which they come. One of the best known, Doux de Montagne, is shaped like a round, flat loaf of bread and coated with brown wax. The flavor is mild and a bit sweet; the texture, smooth and flecked with little holes. We feel this cheese can be served anytime. It's great with sparkling apple cider.

▲ **Raclette:** There are Raclettes from both France and Switzerland. We find the French Raclette more delicate in flavor and aroma. A half or quarter wheel of this cheese is warmed along the cut edge by a fire and scraped onto a waiting plate. Boiled potatoes are rolled in the soft cheese and eaten with thin slices of cured ham or bacon and cornichons. As the cheese warms, the flavor becomes more interesting. In Switzerland, baskets of pine cones and needles are kept by the fire to be added to the burning embers.

▲ **Reblochon:** This mild monastery cheese from Haute Savoie has a velvety smooth ivory interior. It continues to ripen in the refrigerator, so be sure to eat it when it's ready. Serve this luxurious cheese with a buttery green leaf salad and Beaujolais-Villages.

▲ **Taleggio:** One of our favorites for both eating and cooking, this fruity table cheese dates back to the tenth century. As it ages, the delicious creamy taste becomes stronger. We love to mix it in a risotto along with Fontina or melt it in an omelet.

▲ **Tilsit and Havarti:** These semisoft cheeses have a bit more character than Creamy Havarti. Drier, stronger, and more aromatic, they are perfect for snacking with a light, fruity beer.

▲ **Tomme de Savoie:** This rustic mountain cheese's strong fruity aroma may sometimes overpower the nutty flavor. Buy it in small wheels if possible. Serve after an entrée of Roast Chicken Chez Louis.

▲ **Tomme du Rouergue 20%:** A low-fat version of a semisoft cheese, Tomme du Rouergue 20% is soft and creamy with a sweet taste. Because low-fat cheeses tend to dry out more quickly, care must be taken in storing them properly. It is an excellent melting cheese and good for fondue and pasta dishes. This cheese has just 71 calories per ounce.

SOFT-RIPENING CHEESES

The snowy white rind is an edible and natural covering for these satiny cheeses that ripen from the outside rind toward the center. The traditional soft-ripening cheeses—Brie, Camembert, Coulommiers, Chaource, and Vacherin Mont d'Or—contain 50 percent butterfat and start off with a semisoft consistency. They are fully ripe and ready to serve when they have a creamy consistency throughout. Cheeses thicker than an inch will have a firmer core in the center, but if left to develop further, the edges will overripen. If the rind has a reddish tinge, it is fine to eat, but if a brownish tinge develops, the cheese is overripe and no longer good eating.

To ripen the cheese, leave it well wrapped at room temperature for a day or two. When it is ready, keep it in the refrigerator. Before serving, remove it from the refrigerator in time to come to room temperature and achieve its supple lusciousness, but always keep it well wrapped until ready to serve.

The soft-ripening cheeses are best with Cabernet Sauvignons, Merlots, Petite Sirahs, and fine aged ports.

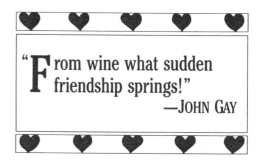

"From wine what sudden friendship springs!"
—JOHN GAY

▲ **Brie:** This cheese is probably the best known and most enjoyed of all French cheeses in America. The luscious aroma of Anjou pears wafts through the thin wheel covered with a downy white coat. A perfectly ripe Brie will ooze slightly when at room temperature. The most glorious is Brie de Meaux. Meaux, the center of Brie production in France, lies in the Lorraine region, where cheese makers use the best-quality milk and the cows are nourished on natural feed. Ideally, the butterfat content of any Brie should be between 50 to 60 percent. Check the label to make sure. Sixty percent Brie will take a bit longer to ripen.

There are several domestic Bries being produced today. The Kolb family in Lena, Illinois, has been producing fine Bries for over 50 years. Their Brie is available in eight-inch rounds weighing two pounds. We also see many fine varieties from California.

Toss Brie with hot pasta and let it melt into a sauce. Use it in stratas and to replace mozzarella in veal Parmesan. Treat Brie with tender care and reap the rewards.

▲ **Brie Henri IV:** This Brie is also called Coeur de Brie. It looks like a center-cut piece from a whole Brie, for it has no rind on the sides. The cheese has a smooth, spreadable texture and doesn't run like other Bries. The fresh-milk taste has a slight tang. Spread it on crusty bread and sprinkle a few drops of olive oil over the top.

▲ **Camembert:** Familiar throughout America, Camembert hails from the lush Normandy region of France where cows graze on grass nurtured by the salt air from the sea. The perfect Camembert is six weeks old, creamy and spreadable, with a floury rind speckled red and a fruity aroma. Delicious examples we enjoy eating are Milleret, which tasted slightly like a raw-milk Brie, and Royal Camembert— creamy, smooth, delicious. Don't cut Camembert before it is fully ripened or it will never reach its full potential. We have found a lovely Camembert from the Craigston Cheese Company in Massachusetts. New England cow's milk seems to be close to that of Normandy. Serve it with a California Merlot.

PEARS WITH CHEESE

- ▲ With Parmigiano-Reggiano
- ▲ With creamy sweet Gorgonzola and pecans
- ▲ With Italian Fontina and hazelnuts
- ▲ With Robiola del Bek and a grind of coarse pepper
- ▲ With Roquefort and walnuts
- ▲ With Maytag Blue
- ▲ With Caprini goat cheese and Vin Santo
- ▲ With a spoonful of Vacherin Mont d'Or

▲ **Chaource:** Similar in taste to Camembert and with the delicate aroma of mushrooms when ripe, Chaource comes from the Champagne region of France. Serve it with a full-bodied Chardonnay.

▲ **Chèvre Camembert:** This excellent soft-ripening cheese made from all goat's milk has a bit more tang than the cow's-milk variety. Serve it with a bowl of ripe melon balls, whole almonds, and tawny port.

▲ **Coeur Leger:** A product of France, Coeur Leger is the lowest-fat soft-ripened cheese with a full flavor on the market. The distinctive orange rind covers the creamy interior. It has a shelf life of 60 days if wrapped and stored in the refrigerator.

▲ **Coulommiers:** A member of the Brie family, this delicious cheese comes from the Ile-de-France region. Its taste is gentle when young and grows nuttier with a bit more tang as the cheese ages. A bit larger than Camembert and covered with a white rind, it is not often found in our country. If you do come across Coulommiers, serve it with ripe juicy peaches and plums.

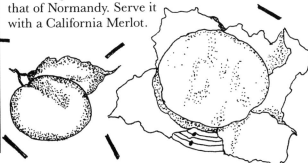

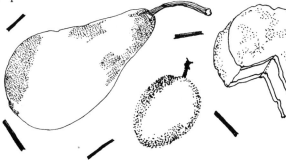

▲ **Vacherin Mont d'Or:** This voluptuous mountain cheese, made only after the cows have been fed the last cutting of grass before the snows, is the cheese we long for in November and December. Produced on both sides of the Swiss–French border, Vacherin is made from raw cow's milk with a 50 percent butterfat content. As the cheese is cured, it is brushed with white wine, which imparts an extraordinary flavor. Savor this satiny cheese with a spoon—the season is short.

COOKING WITH CHEESE

Because cheese reacts quickly to heat, it is best to cook it slowly over low heat. If you want to melt cheese, you must chop, grate, or shred it first. Add chopped or shredded cheese in small batches to batters or sauces so that it won't clump together.

When working with semisoft cheeses, refrigerate them until you need to chop or slice them. Use a heavy knife and a cutting board for the most control. A food processor can be used to chop or grate hard cheese, but use a hand grater with large holes for soft cheeses. We like to use a fine hand grater for Parmesan at the table, but a rotary hand grater is easier for large quantities of grated Parmesan. We also love Parmesan shavings, made by running a vegetable peeler along a large chunk of cheese. The long shards are delicious with carpaccio.

One quarter pound of semisoft or firm cheese will generally measure 1 cup when grated. Soft fresh cheeses have a high moisture content and measure closer to ½ pound per cup.

DOUBLE- AND TRIPLE-CREME CHEESES

There is nothing so lush and perfect as a thick buttery double- or triple-crème cheese served at the end of a grand meal. Their beguiling flavors can be very mild or wonderfully full bodied. The double crèmes have at least 60 percent butterfat and the triple crèmes between 70 and 75 percent. Buy these irresistible cheeses when fresh and light in aroma. Smooth and creamy, they tend to be very delicate. It is best to buy small whole cheeses and keep them very well wrapped in the refrigerator until an hour or two before serving.

▲ **Belletoile:** Similar in taste to Camembert and richer than Brie, this triple crème is perfect for spreading on little dessert crackers. Accompany the cheese with a bowl of fresh blackberries and a glass of Cointreau.

▲ **Brillat-Savarin:** This is one of the sweetest and mildest of the triple crèmes. We love it best and consider it the perfect cheese for dessert with fresh ripe purple figs and an icy cold bottle of Cristal Pink Champagne. Have candles glowing!

▲ **Corolle:** When we first began catering, we placed a whole Corolle on every buffet table. Its shape—like an oversized doughnut—makes it perfect for slicing and serving to a large group of people. The edges ripen to a creamy consistency but the center remains somewhat dry and chalky. The variations in texture along with its full flavor keep the double-crème Corolle a favorite. Serve it with a spicy Zinfandel.

▲ L'Explorateur: This extravagantly rich and buttery triple-crème cheese has a complex piquant taste. We find it best to buy the one-pound wheel as it ripens a little more slowly than the half-pound size and has a more delicious flavor. Serve this cheese in place of butter with dark bread and a bowl of ripe cherries on a lazy summer afternoon.

▲ Saga Blue: A rich white triple crème, Saga Blue was created by the Danes in the late 1970s. More like a fresh cheese, with its creamy Brie texture and mellow blue flavor, it's great for those who find more traditional blues too strong. Spread this delicious cheese on slices of crisp Asian pears, nibble walnuts, and drink a full-bodied Cabernet Sauvignon. Look, too, for Saga White and Saga with chives.

▲ St.-André: The thickness of this rich, buttery triple-crème cheese seems perfect for even ripening. Its crisp, clean flavor is ideal with ripe pineapples, mangoes, and papayas. Some varieties are made with lines of garlic or pepper running through the center. Serve them with a salad and crusty grilled bread.

> "Chardonnay is a red wine masquerading as a white, and Pinot Noir is a white wine masquerading as a red."
> —ANDRÉ TCHELISTCHEFF

Most chèvres are made from all goat's milk, but some are mixed with cow's milk and have a creamier consistency. Chèvres come in a multitude of shapes, ranging from pyramids and cones to logs and disks. They are dipped in brandy, wrapped in chestnut or grape leaves, rubbed with ash to prevent mold from forming, or left plain to develop a heavy mold coating. Some are laced with herbs and spices. There seems to be no end to the varieties. Try several to see which appeals to your taste. Serve chèvres with assertive Zinfandels or chilled Chardonnays.

▲ Aged Goat Cheese: This hard grating cheese (especially the fine variety from Yerba Santa Goat Dairy in Lakeport, California) is pale yellow in color, like Parmesan, but not salty. Its flavor is sweet and mellow with a slightly tangy bite. Grate it over hearty vegetable soups, shave pieces over carpaccio salad, or eat it in little chunks with ripe pears and tart apples.

▲ Banon: In this cheese, cow's milk is mixed with 25 percent goat's milk for a smoother, milder cheese—appealing to those who find other chèvres too strong. This French cheese is dipped in brandy, then beautifully wrapped with a chestnut leaf and tied up with raffia or a piece of straw. We love to roll a Banon in oatmeal, bake it, and serve it atop a salad of mixed baby greens.

▲ Blue Westfield Farm Capri: This velvety, creamy chèvre is produced in Hubbardston, Massachusetts. The delicate flavor is enhanced by the edible blue mold that forms on the outside. The cheese ripens from the outside in and will continue ripening in the refrigerator up to six weeks. Serve it with warm crusty bread, a Cabernet, and a big bowl of dried Michigan cherries.

CHEVRES

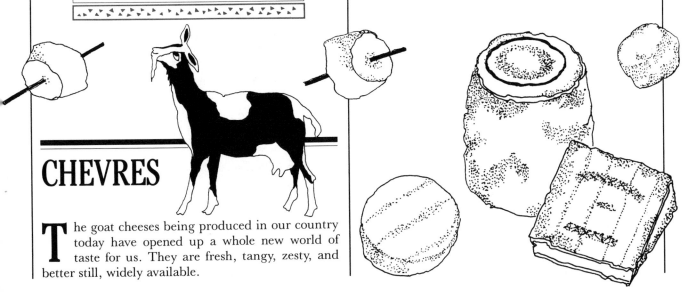

The goat cheeses being produced in our country today have opened up a whole new world of taste for us. They are fresh, tangy, zesty, and better still, widely available.

CHEVRE WITH . . .

- ▲ Spoon into a baked potato with lots of black pepper
- ▲ Top with your favorite preserves and serve on toast
- ▲ Mix with fresh fruit for a low-calorie, high-protein breakfast
- ▲ Make a cheesecake with fromage blanc instead of cream cheese
- ▲ Substitute for ricotta or feta in baked entrées
- ▲ Blend with a bit of cream and walnuts and serve with apples or pears

▲ **Boucheron and Lezay Bûche:** The two larger log-shaped French chèvres are named for their shape (*bûche* is a log). They are familiar to us and available in most cheese shops. Their somewhat buttery texture blends well with sweet red and black grapes. Served with whole-wheat and rye crackers, the tangy flavor is just the right foil for autumn's sweet harvest of Concord grapes.

▲ **Caprini Goat:** These soft, spreadable little logs from Italy make an irresistible spread for toasted raisin-walnut bread. Top it with kiwi-lime or fresh fig preserves. If the cheese is very fresh, serve it with ripe persimmons for dessert. Be sure to have a bottle of Vin Santo nearby.

▲ **Chavrous:** This cheese, from a little village in the South of France, has a smooth, spreadable texture and fresh, light flavor. It is milder than other chèvres and the flavor remains consistent as it ages. The cheese is packaged in resealable containers in a pyramid shape and lasts about two months.

▲ **Chèvre Raclette:** This is a new and exciting discovery for us. Produced in Savoie in the same manner as Raclette, it can be placed on a trivet by a roaring fire and spooned onto warm plates as it melts. Serve it with boiled new red potatoes, a crock of cornichons and sour cherries, and a coarse country-style pâté. A full-bodied red wine is the perfect accompaniment.

▲ **Cravet:** A lovely soft-ripening cheese from the Piedmont area of Italy, Cravet is perfect served with crusty bread and ripe pears. The texture becomes even silkier as it ripens.

▲ **Crottin:** These oversize buttons weigh between two and three ounces. As they age, they become quite hard. To keep them soft, cover them with extra virgin olive oil in a jar and add some fresh herb sprigs, a few peppercorns, and one or two dried chile peppers. They will keep for quite a while and are delicious served with crostini or thick slices of Olive Rosemary Country Bread. You can, of course, let the cheese age and grate it over fresh pasta or bake it and serve it warm with a winter salad of mixed greens.

▲ **Fresh Chèvre:** Unfortunately, this luscious spreadable treat has been hard to find in this country. Few things are better, though, than a dollop of it complementing a bowl of sweet berries on a warm summer morning or mixed with herbs, drizzled with oil, and spooned over crisp greens. Fresh chèvres are now being produced across the United States from Napa Valley to Maine. One of our favorites comes from Famtome Farms in Ridgeway, Wisconsin. Ask for them in your cheese shop.

PEACHES WITH CHEESE

- ▲ Sliced over fresh ricotta
- ▲ Mixed in sheep's-milk yogurt
- ▲ Dolloped with fresh chèvre
- ▲ Served in a bowl of ice water alongside sweet Gorgonzola
- ▲ With ripe Coulommiers
- ▲ With slices of *mozzarella di bufalo* and a bowl of toasted pine nuts (pignoli)
- ▲ With Blue Westfield Farm Capri

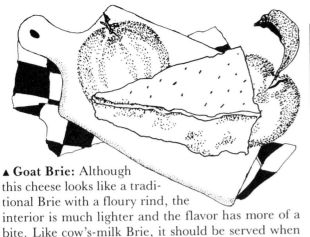

▲ Goat Brie: Although this cheese looks like a traditional Brie with a floury rind, the interior is much lighter and the flavor has more of a bite. Like cow's-milk Brie, it should be served when the center is somewhat runny. Be sure to let it warm to room temperature before serving.

▲ Laura Chenel's Chèvre: This cheese from Sonoma County encompasses all the best France and America have to offer. Laura Chenel studied cheese making in France and returned to America to produce some of the most innovative and personal cheeses available. Her little chèvre disks are creamy, moist, and tangy. They are too good to mix with other flavors, so enjoy them solo with good sourdough bread or with a salad.

▲ Montrachet: Of all the French chèvres, Montrachet is probably the most popular, versatile, and readily available in this country. This young mild cheese is the perfect introduction to the vast range of chèvres. Because of its creamy texture, it melts beautifully on pizzas, blends gently into soufflés, and replaces cream cheese in dips and spreads. We love to mix it with smoked salmon, scallions, lemon zest, and black pepper and spread it on thin black bread.

▲ Valençay: This pyramid-shaped chèvre is coated with edible wood ash. Soft and mild when young, this cheese becomes harder and tangier as it ages.

▲ Vermont Butter and Cheese Company: This domestic goat cheese producer seems to be meeting the demand for simplicity, freshness, and diversity. Crafted in the traditional French style, the cheeses are made in several different shapes. Some of the cheeses are soft ripened, while others are aged and are especially nice for melting. This company also produces fromage blanc—the French answer to cottage cheese—which is lightly whipped from skim milk. The silky texture and spreadability make it a great low-fat altenative to cream cheese. Fromage blanc contains no salt and has a mild and tangy flavor. It will keep in the refrigerator for about two weeks, and we find that freezing does not affect the flavor or texture.

SHEEP'S-MILK CHEESES

Sheep's-milk cheeses are usually grouped with chèvres for they both have a fuller flavor and saltier taste than cow's-milk cheese. One of the most famous sheep's-milk cheeses—Roquefort—we have grouped with the blues. Others come to us packed in brine or aged in a hard grating cheese.

If you have a sheep's-milk cheese packed in brine, you can slow down the aging process by replacing the brine with a solution of equal parts of milk and water that have been brought to a boil and cooled. Place the cheese in a clean jar and pour over the liquid. The liquid should completely cover the cheese. Cover the jar and keep it in the refrigerator. Dry cheese should be wrapped in foil or plastic and refrigerated as well. Before serving, let the cheeses sit at room temperature four to six hours. Serve with pita bread and olives and accompany with a fruity, dry white wine.

▲ Brebignal: Made in the Pyrenees of France, this cheese has the taste and texture of young Parmesan. It is mild enough to be a great table cheese but can be expensive since sheep give even less milk than goats.

▲ Feta: Essential to Greek salad, this cheese comes in chunks firm enough to hold their shape when sautéed but soft enough to crumble. Aged feta is salty and dry. Most prefer the mild young feta, although the flavor can get lost in cooked dishes. American and Danish feta cheeses are made from cow's milk with salt added and are less expensive varieties.

▲ Kasseri: A firm cheese that is fairly mild, Kasseri is wonderful as a picnic cheese. When aged, it becomes firmer and is excellent fried and served with ouzo.

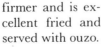
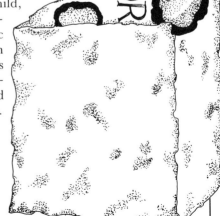

BERRIES WITH CHEESE

STRAWBERRIES

▲ Long-stemmed with ripe creamy Brie
▲ Sliced and juicy with fresh chèvre
▲ Dipped into fromage blanc with a little grated bittersweet chocolate
▲ Sliced with a dollop of mascarpone and drizzled with fraise eau-de-vie
▲ Sliced onto cottage cheese and spread over whole-wheat toast

RASPBERRIES

▲ Atop a bowl of fromage blanc sprinkled with rose water and tiny pink rose petals
▲ Drizzled with framboise eau-de-vie and dolloped with mascarpone
▲ Golden berries layered between slices of creamy Explorateur and garnished with nasturtium blossoms
▲ Puréed with a spoonful of sweet Gorgonzola on top
▲ Atop a creamy chèvre cheesecake glazed with raspberry jelly
▲ Golden raspberries with fresh cottage cheese and garnished with tiny leaves of lemon thyme
▲ Drizzled lightly with balsamic vinegar, sprinkled with sugar, and dolloped with sweet Gorgonzola

BLUEBERRIES

▲ Alongside a creamy Bleu de Bresse

▲ Studding the top of a ripe Brillat-Savarin
▲ Dazzling a fresh chèvre and sprinkled with cinnamon sugar
▲ Folded into fromage blanc with chopped pecans on top
▲ In luscious pancakes with a dollop of mascarpone
▲ Wild over farmer's cheese with a dollop of crème fraîche

FRAISES DES BOIS (WILD STRAWBERRIES)

▲ All alone or with just a spoonful of cream
▲ Layered in the middle of a small disk of fresh chèvre
▲ With a tiny spoonful of mascarpone or crème fraîche
▲ Atop ripe Corolle on walnut raisin toast

BLACKBERRIES

▲ Drizzled with fromage blanc for breakfast
▲ Sprinkled over Brousse de Brebis and dusted with confectioners' sugar for dessert

CHERRIES

▲ Drizzled with a bit of Grand Marnier and served with lush Belletoile
▲ In the center of a ripe Corolle
▲ With Brillat-Savarin and pink Champagne
▲ With oozing Brie and buttery cashews

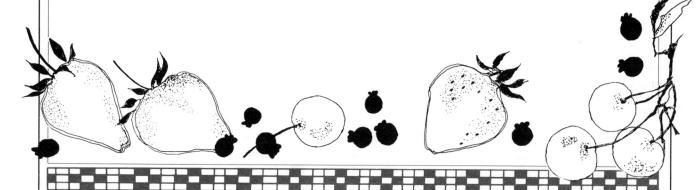

DESSERT OR MORNING CHEESES

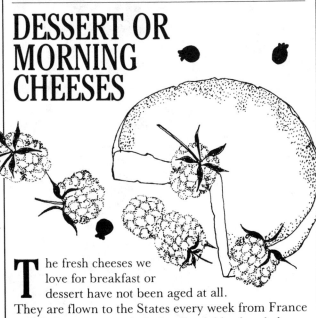

The fresh cheeses we love for breakfast or dessert have not been aged at all. They are flown to the States every week from France and Italy or are made in local neighborhood shops. Fresh American farm cheeses are seen more frequently, too. Seek out the creamy white cheeses, such as mascarpone, ricotta, and sweet Brousse de Brebis. Luscious fresh berries are all you need and, perhaps, a California Riesling or a glorious French Sauternes.

▲ **Brebioux:** This delicious cheese is made of all sheep's milk with a touch of Roquefort, which gives it a rich, delicate flavor. It is pleasantly light and fresher and milder than most sheep's-milk cheeses. Brebioux is packaged in a traditional cylindrical shape in a resealable container, which makes it easy to serve and store. Each cheese weighs about 5½ ounces. Don't let it sit around at room temperature. Serve it chilled.

▲ **La Bergère Brebiboum:** Another incredible product from La Bergère, this natural yogurt made from sheep's milk is the sweetest we've ever tasted. Serve it cold in little glass bowls garnished with sweet berries. You'll need no sugar or honey with this yogurt.

▲ **La Bergère Brousse de Brebis:** This is an excellent dessert cheese from Ste. Fromagère de St.-Georges. This low-fat (20 percent) sheep's-milk cheese is perfect with sweet biscuits, but it's also lovely for breakfast sprinkled with sugar, drizzled with honey, or spooned up with our Four-Berry Preserves.

▲ **Mascarpone:** The crème de la crème of dessert cheeses. We long to eat fresh mascarpone right from the container with a spoon. Its creamy fresh flavor is perfect for coeur à la crème or a delectable Tiramisu. Seek out the delicious fresh tortas made with layers of mascarpone and sweet Gorgonzola.

▲ **Ricotta:** We had a wonderful tasting of fresh ricottas with our friend Henry Kaplan, owner of De Choix Specialty Food. He treated us to the sweet, creamy ricotta alla panna flown in from Milan. This in no way resembles the ricotta you buy in supermarkets. Other fresh ricottas can be found in Italian cheese shops. Serve with fresh sweet berries for a luscious dessert.

▲ **Robiola del Bek:** This mild, creamy, and light cheese comes from Italy. It has a soft fresh taste that is savory but refined. Spread it over crusty slices of Italian bread and top with sliced tomatoes and fresh cucumbers sprinkled liberally with pepper. We like to spread Robiola on wheat toast with tart raspberry jam for a delectable breakfast. Some Robiolas come mixed with pear, pineapple, or walnuts.

KEEPING CHEESE FRESH

Store cheese in the produce or dairy compartment of your refrigerator. It will continue to age. Cheese should be wrapped airtight in plastic or aluminum foil; change the wrap every time you use it. Roquefort cheese will benefit from being wrapped in a damp cloth. It will stay fresh for months if rewrapped each time a piece is cut away.

The molds that form on natural cheeses are unappealing but harmless. If the mold is just on the surface, scrape it off with a small knife. Moisture is what causes the mold to form. Cheeses that tend to mold quickly should be wrapped somewhat loosely in foil, which allows the cheese to breathe and the moisture to escape.

AND EVERYTHING NICE

CHOCOLATE, THE MAGNIFICENT OBSESSION

We are a nation passionate about chocolate, but we are not alone. The Aztecs discovered it and called it food for the gods, the Spanish spiced it, the French court drank it morning, noon, and night, the Belgians shaped and gilded it, the Dutch powdered it for cocoa, the Swiss fondued it, and the English shaped it into bars. They are all as guilty as we.

As we get older we get more sophisticated and discerning about how to spend our chocolate calories. Childhood's milk chocolate has stepped aside. Now only the darkest, richest, silkiest chocolate will do to satisfy our chocolate obsession, for we savor it by the ounce, not the pound.

A CHOCOLATE WHAT'S WHAT

Chocolate is produced from the pods of the cacao tree, which grows only in the hot, rainy climate 20 degrees on either side of the equator. Each tree yields 20 to 30 pods a year, and each pod just 25 to 40 beans. It takes 400 beans to make a pound of chocolate.

The beans are roasted from 30 minutes to 2 hours and then shelled for the nib (the seed with the germ removed). They are pressed and heated until they become liquid, at which point some or all of the cocoa butter can be extracted. The butter's presence in chocolate gives it a silky texture and keeping power. Generally, the more cocoa butter in a chocolate, the better the quality.

Unsweetened chocolate: The chocolate liquor (with about 50 percent cocoa butter). It contains no sugar or added ingredients. Some still call it bitter or baking chocolate, but don't confuse it with bittersweet or Baker's chocolate.

Semisweet and bittersweet chocolate: This is chocolate liquor with cocoa butter, sugar, and vanilla. All brand name semisweet and bittersweet chocolates have these three ingredients in varying amounts. Bittersweet chocolate, of course, has less sugar than semisweet but don't confuse it with unsweetened chocolate, which has none.

Milk chocolate: Chocolate liquor with cocoa butter and sugar, vanilla, and milk solids added. This chocolate is generally for eating, not baking.

Cocoa powder: The dried and pulverized liquor with half or more of the cocoa butter removed. Dutched or Dutch-process cocoa has alkali added, which makes it darker and less acidic. Some cocoa powders have sugar added. Look for unsweetened cocoa powder for the best quality.

Premelted unsweetened baking chocolate: This is a liquid blend of cocoa and vegetable oil. Like most convenience products, it is handy but not the real thing.

White chocolate: This chocolate is not chocolate at all in that it has no chocolate liquor, just cocoa butter, milk solids, sugar, and flavorings. Some white chocolates have more vegetable oil than cocoa butter. Avoid those, for the best white chocolate is all cocoa butter.

Chocolate-flavored chocolate: Called imitation chocolate, compound chocolate, or confectioners' chocolate, this non-chocolate has all vegetable oil rather than cocoa butter. It is added in part or whole to candy and cookies to cut costs and because it is less temperamental than real chocolate.

Coating chocolate: This chocolate is used in candy making for its very high percentage of cocoa butter, which gives the candies a hard, shiny finish. It is magic in the hands of an expert but tricky for the beginner.

KATHLEEN'S DEVIL'S FOOD CAKE

Kathleen King's bake shop took Southampton by storm when it opened awhile back. Bathing suit coverups are put to use when it's time for this devilishly dark cake.

3 ounces good-quality unsweetened chocolate
1 cup (2 sticks) unsalted butter, at room temperature
2 cups (packed) dark brown sugar
3 eggs
2 ¼ cups cake flour
2 teaspoons baking soda
½ teaspoon salt
¼ cup buttermilk
1 cup boiling water
2 teaspoons vanilla extract
Kathleen's Chocolate Icing (recipe follows)

1. Preheat the oven to 375°F. Grease and flour two 9-inch cake pans; set them aside.

2. Place the chocolate in a small heavy saucepan, and melt over low heat, stirring constantly. Remove the pan from the heat and set it aside.

3. Cream the butter and brown sugar together in the bowl of an electric mixer. With the mixer on low speed, add the eggs one at a time, beating well after each addition. Stir in the melted chocolate.

4. Combine the cake flour, baking soda, and the salt. Alternating between the two, add the flour mixture and buttermilk to the chocolate mixture in three stages, ending with flour. Then slowly stir in the boiling water and the vanilla.

5. Pour the batter into the two prepared pans, and bake until a toothpick inserted in the center of a layer comes out clean, 30 minutes.

6. Remove the pans from the oven and let the layers sit for 5 minutes. Then invert the pans over wire racks, releasing the cake, and let the cake cool completely.

7. Using a long thin spatula, cover the top of 1 layer with chocolate icing. Place the second layer on top, and ice the top and sides of the cake.

8 to 10 portions

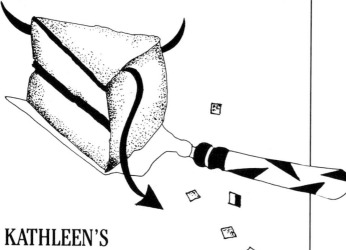

KATHLEEN'S CHOCOLATE ICING

1½ cups semisweet chocolate morsels
8 tablespoons (1 stick) unsalted butter,
  at room temperature
1 teaspoon vanilla extract
1 cup confectioners' sugar

1. Combine the chocolate and butter in a small heavy saucepan, and melt over very low heat.

2. Remove the pan from the heat, stir in the vanilla, and transfer the mixture to a mixing bowl.

3. Add the sugar gradually, beating with an electric mixer. Continue beating until the mixture is smooth; it will be runny.

4. Refrigerate the mixture for 1 hour, beating it every 15 minutes. (The icing will stiffen.)

About 2½ cups

MELTING CHOCOLATE

Chocolate is easily scorched when heated. There are a number of ways to melt chocolate, but for all of them the chocolate must be attended to. Don't walk away. Chocolate melts easiest if grated or chopped—even coarse chopping helps.

DIRECT HEAT: Put the chocolate in a heavy pan and put the pan over very low heat. Stir constantly until melted. This method works best with liquid or butter added to the chocolate to protect it from scorching.

DOUBLE BOILER: Put the chocolate in the top of a double boiler over hot water. Stir constantly and keep the water below a simmer so that no steam or water gets into the chocolate, which would cause it to tighten or stiffen.

MICROWAVE: Put the chocolate in a glass bowl or measuring cup. Microwave on high power for 30 seconds and stir. Continue to microwave and stir at 30-second intervals until the chocolate is smooth.

OVEN: Preheat the oven to 300°F. Put the chocolate in a baking dish, put the dish in the oven, and turn the oven off. Stir and check the chocolate frequently.

CHOCOLATE GATEAU

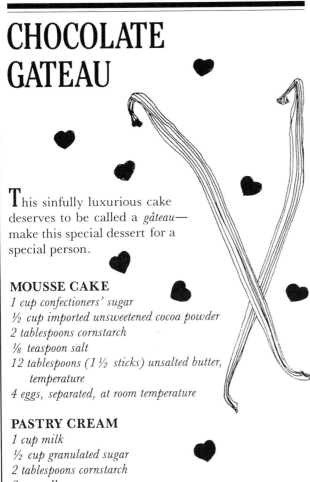

This sinfully luxurious cake deserves to be called a *gâteau*—make this special dessert for a special person.

MOUSSE CAKE

1 cup confectioners' sugar
½ cup imported unsweetened cocoa powder
2 tablespoons cornstarch
⅛ teaspoon salt
12 tablespoons (1 ½ sticks) unsalted butter,
    temperature
4 eggs, separated, at room temperature

PASTRY CREAM

1 cup milk
½ cup granulated sugar
2 tablespoons cornstarch
2 egg yolks
½ vanilla bean
1 tablespoon unsalted butter
⅛ teaspoon salt

GLAZE

½ cup heavy or whipping cream
4 ounces good-quality bittersweet chocolate, broken into
    1-inch pieces

1. Preheat the oven to 325°F. Butter and flour the bottom of an 8-inch round cake pan. Line the bottom with waxed paper. Butter and flour the waxed paper; shake to remove the excess.

2. Prepare the mousse cake: Combine ¾ cup of the confectioners' sugar with the cocoa, cornstarch, and salt in a small bowl. Mix well.

3. Cream the butter with an electric mixer until light. Add the egg yolks one at a time, beating well after each addition. Then add the cocoa mixture 1 tablespoon at a time, and beat until smooth.

4. Beat the egg whites until frothy. Slowly add the remaining ¼ cup confectioners' sugar, beating until the whites are stiff and shiny. Gently fold them into the chocolate mixture until smooth. Transfer the batter to the prepared cake pan.

5. Set the cake pan in a larger baking pan, and fill the larger pan with enough hot water to come halfway up the side of the cake pan. Place the pans in the oven, and bake until a toothpick inserted in the center of the cake comes out clean, 25 minutes. Transfer the cake pan to a wire rack and allow the cake to cool. Then refrigerate it, still in the pan, until firm, 4 hours or as long as overnight.

6. Prepare the pastry cream: Combine the milk, sugar, cornstarch, egg yolks, and the seeds from the vanilla bean in a medium-size saucepan. Place it over low heat and cook, stirring, until the mixture is simmering and thick, 3 to 5 minutes. Cook another minute and remove from the heat. Stir in the butter and salt.

7. Transfer the pastry cream to a bowl, cover it directly with plastic wrap (to prevent a scum from forming on the top), and allow it to cool. Then refrigerate it for 1 hour.

8. Prepare the glaze: Heat the cream almost to a simmer in a heavy saucepan. Add the chocolate and stir until smooth. Remove the pan from the heat and allow the mixture to cool to room temperature; it should be thick but still pourable.

9. Unmold the cake and peel off the waxed paper. Place the cake right side up on a work surface, and using a thin, sharp knife, carefully cut it in half horizontally. Use two spatulas to lift off the top half. Cover the bottom half with the chilled pastry cream, and replace the top half.

10. Set the cake on a wire rack over a baking sheet (to catch the drips). Spoon the glaze over the cake, and spread it over the top and sides. Transfer the cake to a serving platter, and refrigerate until the glaze is set, about 2 hours. Bring the cake back to room temperature before serving.

8 portions

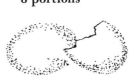

BLACK AND WHITE CHOCOLATE ROLL

We've always loved the tastes of rich dark chocolate and cool whipped cream for their extreme contrasts. This is a great time to flavor both cake and cream with your favorite after-dinner liqueur—amaretto, Frangelico, Grand Marnier, or framboise.

4 tablespoons (½ stick) unsalted butter
2 ounces good-quality imported bittersweet chocolate
1 vanilla bean
4 large eggs
½ cup granulated sugar
⅓ cup unbleached all-purpose flour
⅓ cup plus 1 tablespoon unsweetened cocoa powder
1 teaspoon instant espresso powder
1 tablespoon confectioners' sugar

FILLING
1 vanilla bean
1 ⅓ cups heavy or whipping cream
3 tablespoons granulated sugar

1. Preheat the oven to 375°F. Line a 15½ x 10½-inch jelly roll pan with aluminum foil. Butter and flour the foil.

2. Combine the butter and chocolate in a small saucepan, and melt over low heat, stirring until smooth. Cool to room temperature.

3. Scrape the seeds from the vanilla bean into a mixer bowl. Add the eggs and sugar, and beat until the mixture has tripled in volume and is thick and pale.

4. Blend the flour, ⅓ cup cocoa, and espresso powder in a small bowl. Fold this gently into the beaten eggs. Then slowly drizzle the chocolate mixture into the eggs, folding gently so as not to deflate the volume.

5. Spread the batter in the prepared pan and bake until the top is dry and a toothpick inserted in the center comes out clean, 8 to 10 minutes. Cool on a wire rack for 3 minutes.

6. Spread a clean lint-free towel on a flat surface. Sprinkle it with the remaining 1 tablespoon cocoa and the confectioners' sugar. Invert the cake onto the towel and remove the foil. Starting with a short end, gently roll the cake up, using the towel to lift it. Lift the roll onto a wire rack; let it cool, seam side down.

7. Prepare the filling: Scrape the seeds from the vanilla bean into a mixer bowl, and add the cream and sugar. Whip until stiff.

8. Unroll the cake and spread the filling over it to within 1 inch of the edges. Roll it up and arrange it seam side down on a cake plate. Chill, covered with plastic wrap, until ready to serve.

12 portions

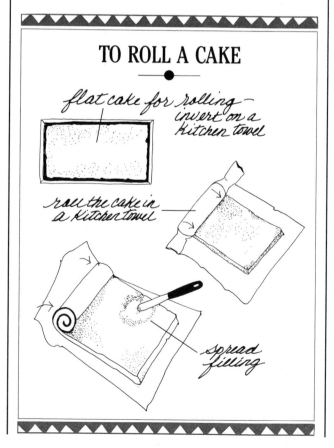

TO ROLL A CAKE

flat cake for rolling—
invert on a kitchen towel

roll the cake in a kitchen towel

spread filling

CHOCOLATE RASPBERRY CAKE A LA SIMCA

Our friend Susy Davidson, a long-time colleague of Simone (Simca) Beck's, shared her version of Simca's classic with us. It's as much a treasure as Simca herself—a great cake from a grand lady for an important occasion! Hats off to both Simca and Susy!

1 pound good-quality semisweet chocolate
3 tablespoons instant espresso powder
½ cup crème de cassis
4 eggs, separated
12 tablespoons (1 ½ sticks) unsalted butter
⅓ cup unbleached all-purpose flour
1 ½ pints fresh raspberries
⅔ cup sugar
Pinch of salt
1 tablespoon water

1. Preheat the oven to 375°F. Butter and flour a 9-inch round cake pan. Line the bottom with waxed paper. Butter and flour the waxed paper; shake to remove the excess.

2. Combine 8 ounces of the chocolate, 2 tablespoons of the espresso powder, and ¼ cup of the cassis in a heavy saucepan, and stir over low heat until the chocolate is melted. Stir to blend the mixture. Remove the pan from the heat and add the egg yolks one at a time, beating well after each addition.

3. Return the pan to the heat and cook, stirring, for 2 minutes. Remove the pan from the heat once more and add the butter, beating it in 1 tablespoon at a time. Stir in the flour.

4. Combine the raspberries, ⅓ cup of the sugar, and 1 tablespoon of the cassis in a bowl. Toss to combine, and set aside.

5. Combine the egg whites and the salt, and beat until they form soft peaks. Sprinkle the remaining ⅓

cup sugar over the whites, and beat until glossy, 30 seconds.

6. Fold the whites, in thirds, into the chocolate mixture. Pour the batter into the prepared pan, and bake until the cake is slightly puffed but not completely cooked in the center, 20 minutes.

7. Allow the cake to cool in the pan for 45 minutes. Then unmold it onto a serving platter. Turn the cake right side up. Leaving a 1-inch border around the edges, scoop out the top ½ inch of cake. Fill the cake with the reserved raspberries, patting them down gently. (Nibble on the scooped-out cake scraps while you finish the cake.)

8. Combine the remaining 8 ounces chocolate with the water, the remaining 1 tablespoon espresso powder, and the remaining 3 tablespoons cassis in a heavy saucepan. Place over low heat and stir until melted and blended. Remove the pan from the heat, and glaze the cake while the icing is still warm, covering the top and the sides.

8 to 10 portions

BABY BROWNIES

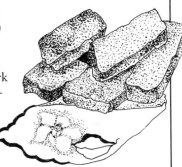

We like these moist dark brownies in miniature—they're neater that way, and it's not so easy to notice how fast they're disappearing.

6 ounces good-quality semisweet chocolate
¼ cup chocolate syrup
8 tablespoons (1 stick) unsalted butter, at room temperature
1 teaspoon vanilla extract
2 eggs, lightly beaten
¾ cup sugar
Pinch of salt
½ cup unbleached all-purpose flour

1. Preheat the oven to 350°F. Butter and flour an 8-inch square baking pan. Set it aside.

2. Melt the chocolate in a small heavy saucepan over low heat, stirring constantly. Add the syrup and stir well.

3. Remove the pan from the heat, and add the butter. Beat until the mixture is smooth. Stir in the vanilla and the eggs; mix thoroughly.

4. In a mixing bowl, sift together the sugar, salt, and flour. Add this to the chocolate mixture and blend thoroughly.

5. Pour the batter into the prepared pan, and bake just until cooked, 30 minutes.

6. Allow the brownies to cool completely in the pan. Then cut them into 1-inch squares and transfer to a serving plate.

64 tiny brownies

> Chocolate is associated with passion—it satisfies like little else. On an annual basis chocolate is a five-billion-dollar industry. Last year, on average, every American man, woman, and child ate eleven pounds of chocolate. We would have guessed more.

ANNE ROSENZWEIG'S CHOCOLATE BREAD PUDDING WITH BRANDY CUSTARD SAUCE

From the day the door first opened we have adored Arcadia, Anne Rosenzweig's Manhattan restaurant. We always finish a meal there with this dessert, which she describes as "a very basic American classic, seemingly unsophisticated and homey but very satisfying," and which she elevates to new heights by using the most luxurious ingredients.

1 loaf brioche (12 inches long), cut into 12 slices
1 cup (2 sticks) unsalted butter, melted
8 ounces good-quality bittersweet chocolate, preferably Caillebaut
3 cups heavy or whipping cream
1 cup milk
1 cup sugar
12 egg yolks
1 teaspoon vanilla extract
Pinch of salt
Brandy Custard Sauce (recipe follows)

1. Preheat the oven to 425°F.

2. Brush the brioche slices with the melted butter, and toast them on both sides in the oven until golden brown.

3. Coarsely chop the chocolate, and put the pieces in a small bowl. Place the bowl in a larger bowl of hot water and set aside, allowing the chocolate to melt slowly.

4. Combine the cream and milk in a saucepan, and heat almost to a boil.

5. While the cream-milk mixture is heating, whisk the sugar and egg yolks together in a large mixing bowl until well blended. Slowly add the hot cream, whisking constantly. Then strain the mixture into another bowl and skim off any foam. Slowly pour the strained mixture into the melted chocolate, whisking constantly. Stir in the vanilla and salt.

6. Arrange the brioche slices in a 12 x 9-inch baking dish, in two overlapping rows. Pour the chocolate mixture over the brioche, and loosely lay a piece of plastic wrap over the dish. Place a smaller dish on top of the plastic wrap, weighting down the brioche to keep it submerged. Add weights such as soup cans to the smaller dish if necessary. Let stand until the bread is soaked through, 1 hour.

7. Preheat the oven to 325°F.

8. Remove the weights (if any), the smaller pan, and plastic wrap. Cover the baking dish with foil, and make a few holes in the foil for steam to escape.

9. Place the baking pan in a larger pan, and fill the larger pan with hot water so that it reaches two thirds of the way up the sides of the baking dish. Transfer the pans to the oven, and bake until the chocolate liquid has been absorbed and the pudding looks glossy, 1¾ hours.

10. Spoon a pool of custard sauce onto each plate. Cut the warm pudding into squares, and arrange a square on the sauce. Serve additional sauce on the side.

6 to 8 portions

BRANDY CUSTARD SAUCE

3 egg yolks
⅓ cup sugar
1 cup heavy or whipping cream
⅓ cup milk
¼ cup brandy
Pinch of salt

1. Fill a large mixing bowl with ice cubes and set aside.

2. Combine the egg yolks and sugar in another mixing bowl, and beat until well blended.

3. Combine the cream and milk in a heavy saucepan, and bring to a boil. Remove the pan from the heat, and gradually add ½ cup of the hot cream to the egg mixture, whisking constantly.

4. Slowly whisk the egg mixture back into the saucepan containing the remaining hot cream, and place the pan over medium-low heat. Whisk constantly until the cream begins to thicken (do not let it boil).

5. Remove the pan from the heat, and stir in the brandy and salt. Strain the mixture into a small bowl and cool it quickly by placing the bowl in the bowl with the ice cubes. Serve chilled.

About 2 cups

CHOCOLATE SOUFFLE CAKE

This is one of the richest and lightest chocolate cakes we know. It's great to balance its velvety sweetness with our spicy Cinnamon Ice Cream. To make it especially festive, garnish your plate with berries—we're partial to strawberries, raspberries, blueberries, and blackberries. Or add flowers—violets or roses are lovely. For extra indulgence, add a dollop of whipped cream!

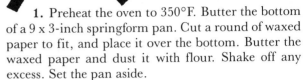

2 ounces good-quality unsweetened chocolate,
*   broken into small pieces*
4 ounces good-quality semisweet chocolate,
*   broken into small pieces*
9 tablespoons unsalted butter,
*   at room temperature*
12 tablespoons sugar
3 tablespoons unbleached all-purpose flour
5 eggs, separated
Pinch of salt
Chocolate Satin Icing (recipe follows)

1. Preheat the oven to 350°F. Butter the bottom of a 9 x 3-inch springform pan. Cut a round of waxed paper to fit, and place it over the bottom. Butter the waxed paper and dust it with flour. Shake off any excess. Set the pan aside.

2. Place both chocolates in the top of a double boiler over simmering water, and stir until melted. Remove the pan from the heat and use a rubber spatula to scrape the chocolate into a medium-size bowl. Allow it to cool for 3 minutes.

3. Gradually add the butter, stirring well. Then add 9 tablespoons of the sugar and the flour. Stir the egg yolks in, one at a time.

4. Place the egg whites in the bowl of an electric mixer. Add the salt and beat until the whites start to hold their shape. Add the remaining 3 tablespoons sugar, and beat until the whites hold their shape but are not too stiff.

5. Using a rubber spatula, gradually and gently fold the whites into the chocolate mixture cup by cup.

6. Place the batter in the prepared springform pan, and smooth the top with the rubber spatula. Bake for 35 minutes.

7. Remove the pan from the oven, and let the cake cool for 15 minutes.

8. Carefully remove the sides of the springform pan. Cover the top with a wire cake rack, and invert the cake and rack together. Carefully remove the bottom of the pan and peel off the waxed paper. Place a second wire cake rack over the bottom of the cake and invert once again, so the top faces up. Cool completely on the rack.

9. To ice the cake, place the cake rack on top of a baking sheet (to catch the drips) and pour the warm icing over the cake. Spread it with a long thin cake icer or spatula, making sure the sides are iced too. Let the cake rest for 2 hours for the icing to set.

10. Carefully transfer the cake to a serving platter, and serve.

8 portions

CHOCOLATE SATIN ICING

4 tablespoons (½ stick) unsalted butter
2 ounces good-quality semisweet chocolate
2 ounces good-quality unsweetened chocolate
3 tablespoons heavy or whipping cream
⅔ cup sifted confectioners' sugar
1 teaspoon vanilla extract

1. Melt the butter and both chocolates in the top of a double boiler over simmering water, whisking constantly.

2. Remove the pan from the heat, and whisk in the cream.

3. Add the confectioners' sugar and vanilla, and whisk until completely smooth.

4. Spread the icing while it is still warm.

About 1¼ cups

AMARETTO SOUFFLE WITH CHOCOLATE SAUCE

Italians love amaretto, and so do we—that's why we put it in both the soufflé and the sauce!

3 tablespoons unsalted butter
3 tablespoons unbleached all-purpose flour
1¼ cups milk
¼ cup amaretto liqueur
⅓ cup sugar
4 egg yolks
4 amaretto cookies, crushed
6 egg whites
Few drops of fresh lemon juice
Amaretto Chocolate Sauce (recipe follows)

1. Preheat the oven to 400°F. Place an oven rack in the lower third of the oven. Butter an 8-cup soufflé dish and sprinkle it with sugar. Turn the dish to coat it evenly, and shake out any excess; set the dish aside.

2. Melt the butter in a medium-size saucepan over low heat. Add the flour, whisking until smooth. Then whisk in the milk and amaretto. Raise the heat to medium.

3. As the mixture starts to thicken, gradually whisk in the sugar. Cook until boiling, stirring to prevent sticking or scorching, 2 to 3 minutes. Set the pan aside and allow the mixture to cool slightly.

4. Whisk the egg yolks into the mixture one at a time. Then stir in the crushed amaretto cookies.

5. Beat the egg whites with the lemon juice until stiff but not dry.

6. Stir one fourth of the egg whites into the soufflé base. Then gently and quickly fold in the remaining whites until the mixture is smooth. Transfer it to the prepared soufflé dish.

7. Bake until the soufflé is puffed, golden, and still slightly wet inside, 30 minutes. Serve it immediately, with a dollop of the chocolate sauce.

8 portions

AMARETTO CHOCOLATE SAUCE

1 cup heavy or whipping cream
½ cup sugar
6 ounces good-quality imported bittersweet chocolate
2 tablespoons unsalted butter
2 tablespoons amaretto liqueur

Combine the cream, sugar, chocolate, and butter in a small saucepan, and stir over low heat until thick and smooth. Remove the pan from the heat, and stir in the amaretto. Cover and keep warm until the soufflé is ready to serve.

About 2 cups

"Too much of a good thing can be wonderful."
—MAE WEST

THE CORDIALS

These sweet liqueurs often add the perfect touch at the end of a special dinner. Sip, and enjoy.

Amaretto: Truly a great American favorite, this sweet almond-flavored liqueur from Italy is ideal for adding to soufflés and chocolate sauces. It's also lovely as an after-dinner drink with little baskets of ripe berries.

Benedictine: This glorious liqueur from a monastery in Normandy is made from a Cognac base, like Grand Marnier. It is probably best known and most often served mixed with brandy for the classic B & B.

Chartreuse: It is hard to resist this voluptuous green liqueur infused with 130 secret herbs by the Carthusian monks in Grenoble. We love to serve this sweet robust nectar after an autumn dinner of game.

Cointreau: Similar in flavor to Triple Sec, this clear liqueur is made from the peels of Curaçao oranges, as is Grand Marnier, but it is not quite as rich or syrupy. It's a lovely addition to a raspberry mousse.

Crème de Menthe: Both green and white, this familiar liqueur evokes the flavor of peppermint. We love the white mixed with brandy for stingers and pour the green over ice to dilute the intense flavor and color.

Drambuie: This velvety spirit from Scotland is based on malt whiskey and aromatic heather honey. Perfect in front of a roaring fire on a cold winter evening.

Frangelico: This lightly sweet and rich liqueur exudes the very essence of toasted hazelnuts. Americans seem to love the nutty flavor in this liqueur and amaretto, perhaps because they are not as cloying as Grand Marnier.

Grand Marnier: Very well known and widely enjoyed in America, this sweet liqueur is an infusion of the finest Cognac with the peels of luscious Curaçao oranges. A delightful complement to a demitasse of strong coffee.

Kahlua: This thick coffee-flavored liqueur evokes memories of our early years in New York when we would drink a Black Russian after a hard day at the office. Mexico provides us with this unique blend derived from a sugarcane alcohol base. Add a bit to hot chocolate for a wonderful mocha drink.

CHOCOLATE MOUSSE

Many years ago a dear friend, Don Forst, served a chocolate mousse that eventually become one of our best-selling desserts at The Silver Palate. Sheila was lucky enough to learn his secrets, and although we may have changed it a bit, it's still the best we know. This mousse can be frozen—so make it ahead and steal spoonfuls until serving time.

1½ pounds semisweet chocolate morsels
½ cup brewed espresso coffee
½ cup Grand Marnier
4 egg yolks
2 cups heavy or whipping cream, cold
¼ cup sugar
8 egg whites
Pinch of salt
½ teaspoon vanilla extract
Candied rosebuds or violets,
    for garnish (optional)

1. Melt the chocolate in a heavy saucepan over very low heat, stirring constantly. Add the espresso, then stir in the Grand Marnier. Let the mixture cool to room temperature.

2. Add the egg yolks, one at a time, beating thoroughly after each addition.

3. Whip 1 cup of the cream until thickened. Gradually add the sugar, beating until the cream is stiff.

4. Beat the egg whites with the salt until they form stiff peaks. Gently fold the egg whites into the whipped cream.

5. Stir about one third of the cream mixture thoroughly into the chocolate mixture. Then scrape the remaining cream mixture over the chocolate base, and gently fold them together. Pour the mousse into individual dessert cups or a serving bowl and refrigerate until set, 2 hours.

6. At serving time, whip the remaining 1 cup cream until thickened. Add the vanilla and whip to soft peaks. Top each portion of mousse with a dollop of whipped cream, and garnish with candied flowers.

8 portions

CHOCOLATE LEAVES

Buy sturdy smooth leaves from a florist (lemon and rose leaves are perfect). Melt semisweet or coating (if you're experienced with it) chocolate until smooth, then using a narrow spatula or a flat brush, paint the underside of the leaves smoothly with chocolate. Leave the edges of the leaves unpainted or you will never get the chocolate off. Let them cool and set, then carefully peel the chocolate from each leaf. The leaves can be used over and over again.

QUATORZE'S CHOCOLATE PRALINE MOUSSE

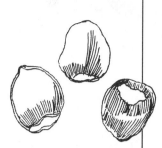

We've always thought our chocolate mousse was the best, but this one—from Peter Meltzer and Mark DiGiulio of Restaurant Quatorze in New York City—gives us a run for the money.

15 ounces good-quality semisweet chocolate
2 ounces good-quality unsweetened chocolate
2 cups heavy or whipping cream
3 eggs, separated
¼ cup confectioners' sugar
½ cup praline paste*
⅛ teaspoon salt
¼ cup brown crème de cacao
1 tablespoon unsalted butter, melted and cooled to room temperature
1 tablespoon brewed espresso or very strong coffee, cooled

1. Break both the chocolates into chunks and place them in the top of a double boiler over simmering water. Heat until melted, stirring occasionally. Set aside and cool to lukewarm.

2. Whip the cream until it is stiff and doubled in volume. Set it aside.

3. Beat the egg whites until they form soft peaks. Then add the confectioners' sugar 1 tablespoon at a time, beating constantly until the whites are stiff but not dry. Set them aside.

4. Combine the praline paste, salt, and crème de cacao in a large mixing bowl. Stir well, and add the egg yolks. Whisk until smooth.

5. Add the melted butter, espresso, and melted chocolate to the praline paste mixture, and blend thoroughly. Then, using a rubber spatula, fold in the whipped cream. Finally, very gently fold in the egg whites.

6. Spoon the mousse into individual bowls or a large serving bowl. Cover, and refrigerate for 8 hours before serving.

8 portions
*Available from specialty food shops and in some supermarkets.

CHOCOLATE TIPS

★

▲ For grated chocolate, refrigerate a large piece of chocolate until hard. Hold it with a paper towel so your hand doesn't warm the chocolate and grate it into a large bowl or over a piece of waxed paper. A rotary grater (such as a Mouli) works well because your hands don't warm the chocolate.

▲ If you need a lot of grated chocolate, cut it into small chunks, put it in the food processor, and process with on/off pulses. The food processor works best with semisweet or bittersweet chocolate. If you are grating or chopping unsweetened choco-

late, it is best to do so by hand.

▲ Semisweet chocolate chips (or morsels) can be substituted for semisweet chocolate.

▲ An acceptable but not great substitute for an ounce of unsweetened chocolate is 3 tablespoons of cocoa mixed with 1 tablespoon of unsalted butter or vegetable shortening. If you need semisweet chocolate, add 3 tablespoons of sugar.

▲ For bittersweet chocolate, combine 1 ounce of unsweetened chocolate and 4 ounces of semisweet chocolate.

TRIPLE CHOCOLATE TERRINE

This is made of three ganaches—bittersweet, milk, and white chocolate—in layers.

3 cups heavy or whipping cream
7 ounces good-quality bittersweet chocolate,
*   broken into 1-inch pieces*
6 ounces good-quality milk chocolate,
*   broken into 1-inch pieces*
4 ounces good-quality white chocolate,
*   broken into 1-inch pieces*
½ vanilla bean
2 cups Chocolate Fudge Sauce (recipe follows)

1. Heat the cream almost to a simmer in a heavy medium-size saucepan. Remove the cream from the heat, and divide it among three mixing bowls in these amounts: 1¼ cups, 1 cup, ¾ cup.

2. Stir the bittersweet chocolate into the 1¼ cups cream, whisking until smooth. Stir the milk choco-

late into the 1 cup cream, whisking until smooth. Stir the white chocolate into the ¾ cup cream, and add the seeds from the vanilla bean; stir until smooth. Cover the three bowls loosely, and refrigerate until the mixtures are thick but still pourable, 3 hours.

3. Line an 8½ x 4½-inch loaf pan with aluminum foil. Leave some foil above the edge of the pan.

4. Transfer the white chocolate mixture to a mixer bowl, and beat until it forms soft peaks—be careful not to overbeat it. Beat the last two or three strokes by hand; the mixture should be thick and firm. Scrape it into the prepared pan, smooth the top, and chill it in the freezer for 5 minutes.

5. Repeat the beating process with the milk chocolate mixture, and spread it over the white chocolate mixture in the loaf pan. Smooth the top, and freeze for 5 minutes.

6. Repeat again with the bittersweet chocolate. Spread it over the milk chocolate mixture, smooth the top, and cover with plastic wrap. Refrigerate until firm, 3 hours.

7. Lift up the foil to unmold the terrine. Remove the foil and cut the terrine into ½-inch-thick slices. Spoon a pool of chocolate sauce onto each plate, and arrange a slice on top. Let it stand for 5 minutes before serving.

16 portions

CHOCOLATE FUDGE SAUCE

2 cups semisweet chocolate morsels
2 tablespoons unsalted butter, melted
½ teaspoon vanilla extract
½ cup heavy or whipping cream

1. Place the chocolate morsels in the top of a double boiler over simmering water. As the chocolate melts, whisk in the butter and vanilla. Then slowly whisk in the cream.

2. Cook, stirring, until smooth, 5 minutes. Remove the pan from the heat and allow the sauce to cool. As it cools, it will thicken.

2 cups

RICH HOT CHOCOLATE

We prefer our hot chocolate made from great-quality chocolate instead of cocoa powder. Try this new basic in the microwave.

1½ to 2 ounces good-quality semisweet chocolate
1 cup milk

1. Coarsely chop the chocolate, and place it in a 2-cup microwave-safe glass measuring cup with a spout. Add the milk.

2. Place the measuring cup, uncovered, in the microwave. Whisking after 1½ minutes, cook the chocolate at medium-high power (70%) until it is melted, well blended, and heated through, 3 to 4 minutes. (You may need to whisk a second time while it is cooking.)

3. Pour into a mug and serve.

1 portion

Note: This recipe was cooked on Medium-High (70% power) in a carousel microwave (650 to 700 watts) using microwave-safe containers.

If your microwave is less powerful, you will have to allow for more cooking time (approximately 1½ times the amount called for—but watch carefully); if it does not have a carousel, you may have to rotate the dish while it is cooking.

INTERNATIONAL HOT CHOCOLATE

Drinking chocolate began with the Aztecs. Montezuma reportedly drank up to fifty cups a day, believing it to be an aphrodisiac. Then again, maybe he just liked the taste. In France chocolate is melted into milk and cream. In Vienna they dollop the drink with whipped cream. In America you may have to face several marshmallows or a candy stick. In Russia and Brazil they add coffee, and in modern Mexico they stir in cinnamon, sherry, and even orange zest.

CANDY BAR HOT CHOCOLATE

Great milk chocolate nut bars are enriched with egg yolks for the most luscious hot chocolate ever. If you're going all out, dollop with whipped cream!

2 egg yolks
2 ounces milk chocolate candy bar with fine nuts (such as
  Toblerone)
1 cup milk

1. Beat the egg yolks in a small bowl, and set them aside.

2. Coarsely chop the chocolate, and place it in a 2-cup microwave-safe glass measuring cup with a spout. Add the milk.

3. Place the measuring cup, uncovered, in the microwave. Whisking once or twice, cook at medium-high power (70%) until the chocolate is melted and well blended, 2½ to 3 minutes.

4. Remove the cup from the microwave and slowly pour the chocolate into the reserved egg yolks, whisking constantly. Return the mixture to the measuring cup and cook in the microwave until heated through, 1 minute.

5. Pour into mugs and serve.

2 portions

Note: This recipe was cooked on Medium-High (70% power) in a carousel microwave (650 to 700 watts) using microwave-safe containers.

If your microwave is less powerful, you will have to allow for more cooking time (approximately 1½ times the amount called for—but watch carefully); if it does not have a carousel, you may have to rotate the dish while it is cooking.

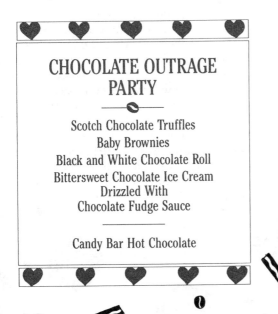

CHOCOLATE OUTRAGE PARTY

Scotch Chocolate Truffles
Baby Brownies
Black and White Chocolate Roll
Bittersweet Chocolate Ice Cream
Drizzled With
Chocolate Fudge Sauce

Candy Bar Hot Chocolate

CHOCOLATE SQUARES WITH MINT CRÈME ANGLAISE

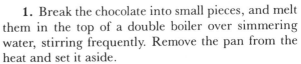

Squares of the richest and smoothest chocolate surrounded by a cool minty pool. What a lovely reason to grow masses of your own fresh mint!

8 ounces good-quality semisweet
  chocolate
1 cup (2 sticks) unsalted butter
5 eggs, separated
½ cup sugar
Pinch of salt
Mint Crème Anglaise
  (recipe follows)
Fresh mint leaves, for garnish

1. Break the chocolate into small pieces, and melt them in the top of a double boiler over simmering water, stirring frequently. Remove the pan from the heat and set it aside.

2. Melt the butter in a small heavy saucepan over low heat, and set it aside.

3. Combine the egg yolks and sugar in a large bowl, and whisk until the mixture is light and falls from the whisk in a ribbon when it is lifted. Set it aside.

4. Beat the egg whites with the salt until they form soft peaks.

5. Stir the melted butter into the chocolate. Then stir in the egg yolk mixture. Add one quarter of the egg whites, and then carefully fold in the remaining whites.

6. Rinse two small (2-cup) bread pans under cold water. Shake dry. Carefully pour in the chocolate mixture. Cover loosely with plastic wrap, then place the pans in the refrigerator, and chill at least 12 hours.

7. Unmold the chocolate loaves, and using a warmed knife, cut them into ½-inch-thick slices. Spoon some Mint Crème Anglaise onto each plate, and arrange two chocolate slices on top. Garnish with fresh mint leaves, and serve.

10 portions

MINT CREME ANGLAISE

2 cups milk
2 cups (loosely packed) fresh mint leaves
6 egg yolks
¼ cup sugar
2 tablespoons green crème de menthe

1. Combine the milk and mint leaves in a saucepan, and bring to a boil. Remove the pan from the heat, cover, and set it aside for 30 minutes.

2. Strain the milk into another saucepan, pressing against the mint leaves to extract as much flavor as possible.

3. Whisk the egg yolks and sugar together in a bowl until the mixture is light and thick.

4. Reheat the milk over medium-low heat and gradually add it to the egg mixture, stirring constantly. Return this to the saucepan and cook over low heat until the mixture has thickened slightly and coats the back of a metal spoon. (Do not allow it to boil, or the sauce will curdle.)

5. Remove the pan from the heat, stir in the crème de menthe, and transfer the mixture to a bowl to cool to room temperature.

1½ to 1¾ cups

CHOCOLATE SCOTCH TRUFFLES

Scotch heightens the flavor of chocolate most beautifully. We like the added surprise of hazelnuts (or walnuts, pecans, or almonds) in the center. Offer these when you're serving a simple fruit dessert; they'll make it very elegant.

1½ pounds good-quality unsweetened chocolate
2 egg yolks
1 cup confectioners' sugar
½ cup heavy or whipping cream
4 tablespoons (½ stick) unsalted butter
¼ cup Scotch whiskey
30 whole shelled hazelnuts
1 cup sifted unsweetened cocoa powder, for dusting

1. Preheat the oven to 375°F.

2. Place 10 ounces of the chocolate in a heavy saucepan, and melt over low heat. Remove the pan from the heat and set it aside.

3. Combine the egg yolks and ½ cup of the confectioners' sugar in a large bowl, and cream until well blended.

4. Combine the cream, butter, and remaining ½ cup sugar in a medium-size saucepan and bring to a boil, stirring until the butter and sugar are thoroughly melted.

5. Slowly pour the hot sugar mixture over the egg yolk mixture, whisking constantly. Mix thoroughly and set aside to cool slightly. Then stir in the melted chocolate and the Scotch; beat for 1 minute.

6. Place the mixture in the refrigerator and chill until firm, 30 to 45 minutes.

7. Meanwhile, place the hazelnuts on a baking sheet and toast them in the oven for 15 minutes. Remove them from the oven and rub handfuls of nuts in a kitchen towel to remove the skins. Set them aside.

8. Roll a spoonful of the chilled chocolate around each hazelnut to form a truffle about 1 inch in diameter. Set them on a baking sheet lined with waxed paper, and chill thoroughly in the refrigerator, 2 to 3 hours.

9. Melt the remaining 14 ounces chocolate in a heavy saucepan over low heat. Remove the pan from the heat.

10. Sprinkle a shallow dish generously with cocoa. Dip each truffle in the melted chocolate, covering it completely. Then lift it out with a fork and roll it in the cocoa. Arrange the truffles on the baking sheet again, and chill before serving.

40 truffles

CHOCOLATE-COVERED FRUIT

For a long time, it has been our belief that the simplest sweet with after-dinner coffee is a perfectly ripe strawberry, raspberry, banana slice, or tangerine section dipped in chocolate. The best dipping chocolate is melted from the best bittersweet chocolate—Caillebaut, Tobler, Suchard, or Ghirardelli. Melt the chocolate in the top of a double boiler over hot, not simmering, water. Pick the fruit up on a toothpick, dip it into the chocolate, and swirl it gently to cover it. Let the excess chocolate drip off, then stick the toothpick with the fruit aloft into a piece of styrofoam. Or you could plant it in the flesh of a canteloupe half or any other firm fruit that will hold the chocolate-covered fruit while it dries. Be sure to choose one that will benefit from chocolate drippings. Put the fruit in the refrigerator to harden and set the chocolate.

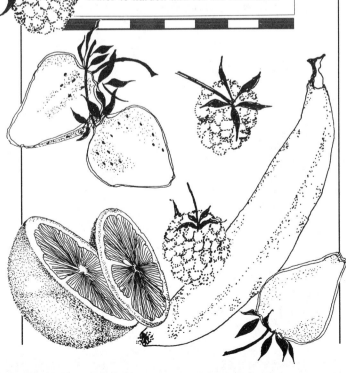

CHOCOLATE FUDGE

This fudge is yummy. Be sure to beat the fudge for the exact time called for, or it will become too hard to spread in the pan.

⅔ cup half-and-half
⅓ cup light corn syrup
2 cups sugar
2 ounces good-quality unsweetened chocolate
4 tablespoons (½ stick) unsalted butter
1 teaspoon vanilla extract
½ cup coarsely chopped walnuts

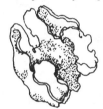

1. Butter an 8-inch square baking pan.
2. Combine the half-and-half, corn syrup, and sugar in a medium-size heavy saucepan, and stir well. Add the chocolate, and place over low heat. Cook, stirring constantly, until the sugar has dissolved and the chocolate has melted.
3. Continue cooking until the mixture begins to boil. Place a candy thermometer in the saucepan, raise the heat slightly, and continue cooking, without stirring, until the temperature reaches 238°F (soft boil point).
4. Remove the pan from the heat and add the butter. With the thermometer still in the saucepan, set the pan aside in a cool place until the temperature has lowered to 150°F, 15 to 20 minutes. Remove the thermometer.
5. Add the vanilla, and beat with a wooden spoon until the chocolate mixture begins to lose its sheen and lightens slightly. This should take 1½ minutes. Then add the walnuts and beat another 30 seconds.
6. Working very quickly, transfer the mixture to the prepared pan and smooth it out to the edges with a rubber spatula. Using a sharp knife, cut the fudge into sixteen pieces. Let it cool completely in the pan before serving.
16 pieces

CAKE AND COFFEE

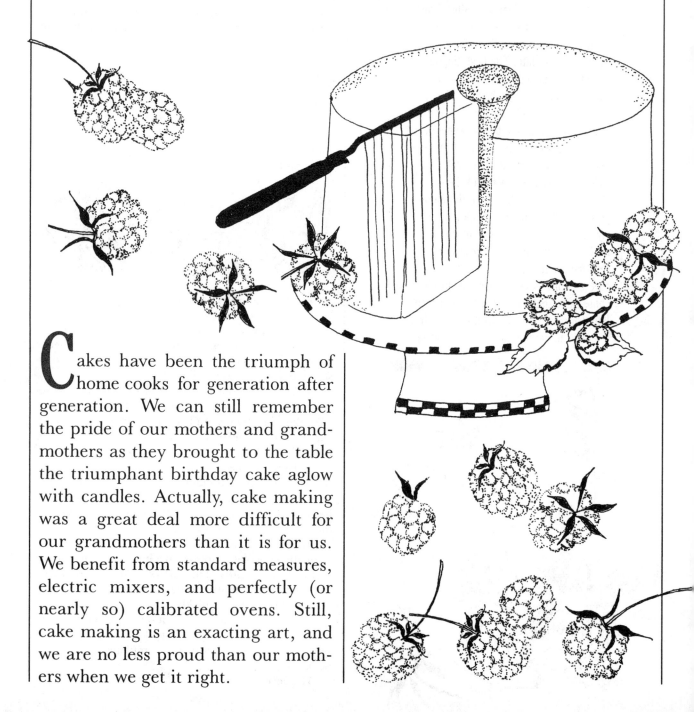

Cakes have been the triumph of home cooks for generation after generation. We can still remember the pride of our mothers and grandmothers as they brought to the table the triumphant birthday cake aglow with candles. Actually, cake making was a great deal more difficult for our grandmothers than it is for us. We benefit from standard measures, electric mixers, and perfectly (or nearly so) calibrated ovens. Still, cake making is an exacting art, and we are no less proud than our mothers when we get it right.

RASPBERRY ANGEL FOOD CAKE WITH RASPBERRY AMARETTO SAUCE

A perfect angel food cake is light, puffy, and cloud-like with a crispy crust—a wonderfully light way to make a menu magical.

10 egg whites, at room temperature
1¼ teaspoons cream of tartar
¼ teaspoon salt
1 teaspoon vanilla extract
½ teaspoon almond extract
1¼ cups sugar
1 cup cake flour
1 cup fresh raspberries
Raspberry Amaretto Sauce (recipe follows)

1. Preheat the oven to 350°F.

2. Beat the egg whites, cream of tartar, and salt in a large bowl with an electric mixer until they form soft peaks. Add the vanilla and almond extracts. Then gradually add the sugar, beating until the whites are stiff, but not dry, and shiny.

3. Sift the flour onto the egg whites and sprinkle the raspberries over the top. Using a rubber spatula, gently fold in the flour and raspberries.

4. Spoon the mixture into an ungreased 10-inch nonstick tube pan, and bake until a toothpick inserted in the cake comes out clean, 40 minutes.

5. Invert the pan onto a cake rack and let it cool completely without removing the cake from the pan.

6. When the cake is cool, invert the pan onto a serving platter. Remove the pan carefully, loosening the cake slightly around the edges if necessary, and serve with the raspberry sauce.

16 portions

RASPBERRY AMARETTO SAUCE

2 cups fresh or frozen raspberries, thawed if frozen
½ cup confectioners' sugar
1 tablespoon fresh lemon juice
¼ cup amaretto liqueur

1. Purée the raspberries in a blender or food processor. Add the confectioners' sugar, lemon juice, and amaretto, and continue to process until smooth.

2. Strain the sauce to remove the seeds, and serve.

1½ cups

BEATING EGG WHITES

The most important thing when beating eggs is to pick the right bowl. Once beaten, the egg whites will have six times more volume, so the bowl must be big enough. The bottom of the bowl should be narrower than the top so that all the egg whites are in motion at the same time. Our first choice is a hammered copper bowl that is not too wide, but we think stainless steel is fine, too. Since copper helps stabilize the whites, we add a pinch of cream of tartar to the whites when we use a stainless steel bowl. Porcelain and glass bowls won't do at all because the egg whites slip down the sides, and plastic bowls have an oily film that deflates the egg whites as fast as you can beat them.

The point of beating egg whites is to get as much air as possible into them and still leave them moist enough to expand even further with heat. French chefs recommend balloon whisks, but we find electric mixers work as well. Most recipes call for egg whites beaten to "soft peaks" or until "stiff but not dry." Soft peaks will flop when you remove the whisk. Stiff peaks will stand up and stay standing. Let your egg whites come to room temperature before beating.

LET'S ALL EAT CAKE

All cakes fall into two basic categories: The first is foam cakes, such as angel food and sponge (or genoise) cakes. These cakes attain their texture and volume from the air that is beaten into the eggs. The second category is butter cakes, which includes pound, carrot, devil's food, and most layer cakes. The butter in these cakes is creamed with sugar before the remaining ingredients are added.

Mixing methods must be followed precisely. Cake making is not the place to let your imagination run wild—that is, until you're an expert.

FOAM CAKES

Foam cakes are made by whipping eggs, often with sugar, so that air, which will give the cake volume, is trapped in the batter. Sponge cakes and angel food cakes are the most popular foam cakes. Light sponge cakes include both egg yolks and whites. The yolks are combined with sugar, and then beat to a frothy lightness. The whites are whipped separately. Angel food cakes are the lightest of all, with perfectly whipped whites (no yolks) to give them volume. It is very important to whip the whites to what is known as a "wet peak." In other words, don't beat them so much that they become dry. Overwhipping and underwhipping are the two most common problems with angel food cake.

For both cakes, the whipping is done first, then the remaining ingredients are carefully folded in.

Sponge cakes freeze well; angel food cakes do not.

BUTTER CAKES

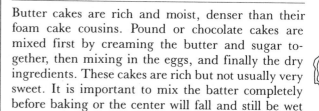

Butter cakes are rich and moist, denser than their foam cake cousins. Pound or chocolate cakes are mixed first by creaming the butter and sugar together, then mixing in the eggs, and finally the dry ingredients. These cakes are rich but not usually very sweet. It is important to mix the batter completely before baking or the center will fall and still be wet when the rest of the cake is done.

All cakes, butter cakes included, should be baked in the center of the oven. When it is done, a yellow cake will be golden in color. To check for doneness, touch the center of the cake; if it springs back and the sides have shrunk from the pan, it is ready. Another sure method for testing cakes is to insert a toothpick into the center; if the toothpick is clean and dry when pulled out, the cake is done.

Remove the cake from the oven and sprinkle some sugar onto a flat plate or baking sheet. Invert the cake onto the sugar and remove the pan. This will flatten the top of the cake for a perfect icing surface.

FRUIT AND VEGETABLE CAKES

Fruits and vegetables supply the liquid in a variation of the basic butter cake. The results are dense, moist

cakes that do not require frosting and will keep at least 1 to 1½ weeks. Our favorites are carrot and apple spice cakes.

Holiday fruitcakes are made with the best-quality dried and candied fruit with just enough batter to hold them together. They are best baked in small pans because they are always very dense. When soaked with brandy or another liqueur, fruitcakes can last a long, long time, just getting "riper" and better with age. Make fruitcakes months in advance of the holiday season. After baking, wrap the cake in cheesecloth and moisten it with brandy or liqueur. Repeat this moistening at least once a month. It's a spectacular gift for the holiday season.

CUPCAKES

Cupcakes are fun! They are perfect kid cakes—just the right size and easy to pack and take along. A standard muffin tin has cups that each hold about ½ cup of batter. We love to line the tins with decorative paper liners and fill them half full with Berta's Carrot Cake or Kathleen's Devil's Food Cake for high, lush cupcakes. Any butter cake recipe will work as well. Cupcakes bake in about two thirds of the time it takes to bake the full cake recipe. Test with a toothpick in the center for doneness. Ice them and have one with a glass of milk for the best feeling of nostalgia.

CHEESECAKES

Cheesecakes are wonderfully silky, rich, creamy cakes so just a sliver will do. When lined with a crust, they can be baked in a springform pan or tart pan with a removable bottom. Without a crust, they must be baked in a cake pan so that the batter doesn't leak through. Unmolding cheesecakes can be somewhat difficult. It's best to cool them completely, then invert onto a lightly sugared plate and invert again onto the serving plate. If the cakes have been chilled, warm the pan briefly before unmolding. Running a knife around the inside of the pan always helps, too.

Cheesecakes are best served completely cooled but not chilled so that the flavors can come through. Be sure to eat them within a week and don't freeze.

GREAT YELLOW CAKE

There are times when cravings for a light, moist yellow cake just have to be appeased. Here's our favorite answer. Smooth chestnut purée and luscious chocolate icing add the right touch of sophistication.

2 cups sugar
4 eggs
1 cup vegetable oil
1 cup dry white wine
2½ cups unbleached all-purpose flour
½ teaspoon salt
2¼ teaspoons baking powder
1 teaspoon vanilla extract
2½ cups Kathleen's Chocolate Icing (see Index), warmed
¾ cup sweetened chestnut purée*
Whole chestnuts preserved in syrup, well drained* (optional garnish)

1. Preheat the oven to 350°F. Grease and flour two 9-inch round cake pans.

2. Beat the sugar and eggs together with an electric mixer on medium speed for 30 seconds. Add the oil, wine, flour, salt, baking powder, and vanilla; beat for 1 minute.

3. Pour the batter into the prepared pans. Place the pans on the middle rack of the oven, and bake until the cake has pulled away from the sides of the pans and a knife inserted in the center comes out clean, 30 minutes.

4. Let the cakes cool in the pans for 5 minutes. Then turn them out onto wire racks and let them cool for at least 2 hours.

5. Arrange 1 cooled cake layer on a platter, and spread some of the warmed chocolate icing over the top. Set the second layer on top of the first, and spread the chestnut purée over the top. Cover the sides of the cake with the remaining chocolate icing. Decorate the top with the chestnuts if desired. Chill the cake, uncovered, for 45 minutes before serving.

8 portions
*Available at specialty food shops.

ORANGE-SCENTED SPONGE CAKE

Our sponge cake is delicious on its own or as a base for fresh fruits and lightly flavored whipped cream, or a scoop of your favorite ice cream.

4 eggs, separated
¾ cup plus 2 tablespoons sugar
½ teaspoon vanilla extract
1 teaspoon orange flower water*
Pinch of salt
¾ cup unbleached all-purpose flour
4 tablespoons (½ stick) unsalted butter, melted and cooled to
*   room temperature*

1. Preheat the oven to 350°F. Butter and flour a 9-inch cake pan.

2. Combine the egg yolks and ¾ cup sugar in a mixing bowl, and whisk until thick and light. Stir in the vanilla and orange flower water.

3. Beat the egg whites and salt with an electric mixer until they form soft peaks. Add the remaining 2 tablespoons sugar, and beat until glossy, 15 to 20 more seconds.

4. Incorporate one third of the whites into the egg mixture. Then sift ¼ cup of the flour over the mixture and fold it in. Repeat, folding in whites and flour until the last batch of flour is nearly incorporated. Then fold in the melted butter.

5. Pour the batter into the prepared pan, and bake just until the cake begins to pull away from the sides of the pan, about 30 minutes. Allow the cake to cool slightly in the pan before unmolding.

8 portions
*Available in specialty food stores.

ROSE LEVY BERANBAUM'S LEMON POPPY SEED POUND CAKE

Rose, who has an extraordinary talent and possesses an eye for the beautiful, says this about her delicious creation: "This is perhaps my favorite way to eat pound cake! The fresh light flavor of lemon blends beautifully with the buttery flavor of pound cake. The lemon syrup tenderizes, adds tartness, and helps to keep the cake fresh for a few days longer than usual. Poppy seeds add a delightful crunch. Lemon blossoms and lemon leaves make a lovely and appropriate garnish."

3 tablespoons milk
3 large eggs
1½ teaspoons vanilla extract
1½ cups sifted cake flour
¾ cup sugar
¾ teaspoon baking powder
¼ teaspoon salt
1 tablespoon (loosely packed) grated lemon zest
3 tablespoons poppy seeds
13 tablespoons unsalted butter, at room temperature

LEMON SYRUP
¼ cup plus 2 tablespoons sugar
¼ cup fresh lemon juice

1. Preheat the oven to 350°F. Grease a 4-cup (8 x 4-inch) or 6-cup loaf pan, line the bottom with parchment or waxed paper, and grease and flour the paper. Or grease and flour a fluted tube pan.

2. Lightly combine the milk, eggs, and vanilla in a medium-size bowl.

3. In a large mixing bowl, combine the cake flour, sugar, baking powder, and salt. Add the lemon zest and poppy seeds. Mix on low speed for 30 seconds to blend. Then add the butter and half the egg mixture. Mix on low speed until the dry ingredients are moistened. Increase the speed to medium (high if you are using a hand mixer), and beat for 1 minute.

4. Scrape down the sides of the bowl. Gradually add the remaining egg mixture in two batches, beating for 20 seconds after each addition, and scraping down the sides of the bowl as necessary.

5. Spoon the batter into the prepared pan, and smooth the surface with a spatula. (The batter will be almost ½ inch from the top of a 4-cup loaf pan. If your pan is slightly smaller, use any excess batter for cupcakes.)

6. Bake, covering the pan loosely with buttered aluminum foil after 30 minutes to prevent over browning, until a toothpick inserted in the center comes out clean, 55 to 65 minutes (35 to 45 minutes in a fluted tube pan).

To get an attractive split down the middle of the crust, wait until the natural split is about to develop (when the cake has cooked for about 20 minutes), and then use a lightly greased sharp knife to make a shallow mark about 6 inches long down the middle of the cake. (This must be done very quickly so that the oven door does not remain open very long, or the cake will fall.) When the cake splits, it will open along the mark.

7. Shortly before the cake is done, prepare the Lemon Syrup: In a small pan over medium heat, stir the sugar and lemon juice together until the sugar has dissolved.

8. As soon as the cake comes out of the oven, place the pan on a wire rack, poke the cake all over with a wire tester or wooden skewer, and brush it with half the syrup. Cool the cake in the pan for 10 minutes.

9. Loosen the sides of the cake with a spatula, and invert it onto a greased wire rack. Poke the bottom of the cake with the wire tester, brush it with some syrup, and reinvert onto a greased wire rack. Brush the sides with the remaining syrup and allow the cake to cool completely.

10. Store the cake for 24 hours, tightly wrapped in plastic wrap (to give the syrup a chance to distribute evenly). Serve at room temperature.

8 portions

Note: Tightly wrapped, the cake will keep for 3 days at room temperature, 1 week in the refrigerator, and 2 months in the freezer.

"Everyone needs a touch of luxury, something grand and pampering."
—BILL BLASS

LADY BALTIMORE CAKE

A true Southern belle crowned, for any special occasion, with a very special seven-minute boiled icing. This is certainly the time to bring out your cake pedestal.

CAKE
2 ½ cups unbleached all-purpose flour
2 ¼ teaspoons baking powder
½ teaspoon salt
4 eggs
1 ½ cups sugar
1 cup vegetable oil
1 cup fresh orange juice

FROSTING
2 egg whites
1 ½ cups sugar
¼ teaspoon baking powder
3 tablespoons fresh orange juice
2 tablespoons fresh lemon juice
2 teaspoons finely grated orange zest
½ cup pecans, toasted (see Index) and finely chopped
½ cup raisins, chopped

Candied Orange Zest (optional garnish; recipe follows), slivered

1. Preheat the oven to 350°F. Butter and flour two 9-inch round cake pans. Line the bottom of each with a circle of waxed paper.

2. Prepare the cake: Toss the flour, baking powder, and salt together in a bowl.

3. In a mixing bowl, cream the eggs and sugar together just until blended. Beat in the oil and orange juice. Then slowly beat in the flour mixture just until smooth.

4. Spoon the batter into the prepared cake pans, and bake until the cake has begun to pull away from the sides of the pans and a toothpick inserted in the center comes out clean, 30 minutes.

5. Cool in the pans on wire racks for 30 minutes. Then remove the cake from the pans and let them cool to room temperature on wire racks.

6. Prepare the frosting: Whisk the egg whites, sugar, baking powder, orange juice, lemon juice, and orange zest together in the top of a double boiler. Cook over boiling water, beating constantly, and carefully, with a hand-held electric mixer for 7 minutes. Remove the pan from the heat. The frosting should be satiny and fluffy.

7. Gently fold the pecans and raisins into the frosting.

8. Spread about one third of the frosting over one cake layer. Place the second layer on top, and spread the remaining frosting over the tops and sides of the cake. Decorate with the candied zest.

8 to 10 portions

CANDIED ORANGE ZEST

These thin strips of orange peel marinated in Grand Marnier are delicious on their own, too, with after-dinner coffee and chocolates.

3 oranges
2 lemons
3 cups water
2 cups sugar
¼ cup Grand Marnier liqueur
¾ cup raw or granulated sugar, for coating

1. Cut the oranges into eight sections and remove the pulp from the peel. Using a sharp paring knife, cut away as much of the white pith as possible from the peel, and cut the remaining zests in half lengthwise.

2. Place the orange zests and half of 1 of the lemons in a large saucepan. Add water to cover, bring to a boil, and boil for 15 seconds. Drain, rinse under cold water, and drain again. Discard the lemon half.

3. Repeat this process two more times, each time covering the zests with fresh water and adding another lemon half.

4. Combine the 3 cups water and the sugar in a saucepan, and cook over medium heat until the sugar has dissolved. Add the zests and the remaining lemon half. Bring to a gentle boil and cook for 15 minutes.

5. Remove the pan from the heat and add the Grand Marnier. Leave the zests in the liquid, loosely covered, for at least 12 hours.

6. Remove the zests from the liquid, and set them on paper towels to drain. Roll them in the sugar, pressing it into the zests. Allow them to dry out slightly before serving. Store the zests in an airtight jar.

4 dozen candied zests

SEPARATING EGGS

We find separating eggs easiest when they are fresh and cold. Crack the egg at the middle and gently pull apart the shell with your thumbs and fingertips. Tip one half of the shell to catch the yolk and let the egg white slip into a bowl. Pass the egg yolk from shell to shell until all the white has run into the bowl, then drop the egg yolk into a second bowl.

Don't let any egg yolk mix with the whites. For egg whites to be beaten to their absolute peaks, they cannot be mixed with any fat—that means not a drop of egg yolk nor a trace of grease on the bowl or beater. We often find we can successfully scoop out a drop or two of yolk using a piece of the shell. If it's more than a drop or if we don't see it soon enough, we start over again.

CAKE BAKING TIPS

★

▲ Have all ingredients at hand and measured (if necessary) before starting the recipe.

▲ Use cake flour when it is called for (it's not the same as self-rising flour). To substitute for cake flour, measure 2 tablespoons of cornstarch into a 1-cup dry measure, then fill the cup with all-purpose flour and blend.

▲ Aluminum pans with a dull finish are best for most cake baking.

▲ Fill cake pans at least half full with batter.

▲ Use vegetable shortening to grease pans.

▲ Bake cakes in the center of the oven.

▲ 350°F is an ideal oven temperature for most cakes. Lower temperatures make a coarse grain and sponge cakes will not rise as high. At 375°F, butter cakes will form a peak in the center and sponge cakes will overbrown.

▲ Don't open the oven door while a cake is baking until you are quite sure it is close to being done.

▲ Cool layer cakes 5 to 10 minutes before removing them from the pans.

▲ Let a cake cool completely before slicing or icing it. It's usually better the next day.

▲ For more flavor, before icing it dab a cake with sugar syrup mixed with a splash of liqueur or liquor.

▲ Wrap unfrosted cakes in plastic wrap, not foil.

▲ To freeze cakes, first wrap securely in plastic wrap, then in heavy foil.

▲ Freeze frosted cakes unwrapped until firm, then wrap them in plastic and aluminum foil and return them to the freezer. Partially thaw the cake before unwrapping.

▲ To cut a round cake, start at the center and work toward the edge.

▲ Fruitcakes and pound cakes are easier to slice when they are cold.

▲ Slice cheesecakes and sticky frosted cakes with a hot wet knife. Have a tall glass of hot water on hand to dip the knife and damp paper towels to wipe it after each slice.

▲ For even slices, cut a whole cake in half, then quarters, then into the desired number of slices.

HELEN'S COCONUT CAKE

Over the years we have seen Phyllis Richman, food critic of the *Washington Post,* at many professional gatherings and have always enjoyed good times and good talk. When we asked if she would share a recipe with us for our cookbook, she sent along this especially luscious coconut cake, created by her mother Helen Chasanow. Says Phyllis, "This has long been a family favorite, and although it has been recreated by many members, my mother had that special touch—she always made it best."

1 cup milk
2 tablespoons unsalted butter
4 eggs
2 cups sugar
2 teaspoons vanilla extract
2 cups sifted unbleached all-purpose flour
2 teaspoons baking powder
¼ teaspoon salt

TOPPING

6 tablespoons (¾ stick) unsalted butter
½ cup plus 2 tablespoons (packed) brown sugar
1 can (4 ounces) shredded Southern-style (not flaked) coconut
(see Note)
1 tablespoon vanilla extract

1. Preheat the oven to 350°F. Butter and flour a 13 x 9-inch baking pan.

2. In a small saucepan, heat the milk and butter until scalding.

3. In the meantime, start beating the eggs with an electric mixer. Add the sugar, and beat well until thick and foamy. With the beater on low speed, gradually add the hot milk mixture and the vanilla.

4. Sift the flour, baking powder, and salt together in a bowl. Beat this into the egg mixture with the mixer on low speed. Pour the batter into the prepared pan.

5. Bake for about 30 minutes, testing with a toothpick after 25 minutes to see if the cake is done (it should come out clean). Cool the cake slightly in the pan.

6. Prepare the topping: Melt the butter in a saucepan, and add the brown sugar. Stir in the coconut and vanilla.

7. Spread the coconut topping over the cake as evenly as possible. Place it under the broiler, 4 to 6 inches from the heat, and broil until the topping is bubbling and brown. Turn the cake if necessary to brown it evenly. Watch very carefully, as it turns from done to burnt in an instant.

8. Let the cake cool to room temperature. Cut it into squares to serve.

12 portions

Note: Use canned coconut, since it tends to be more moist than coconut packaged in bags. A Southern-style shredded coconut makes a crunchier topping than flaked coconut.

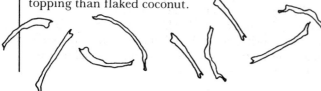

LIGHT LEMON CHEESECAKE

We all love cheesecake, so to justify eating lots we've made ours with a granola crust and lemon yogurt—it's lighter and thinner. Serve it with fresh berries.

1 cup granola
2 tablespoons (packed) light brown sugar
1 tablespoon grated lemon zest
1 tablespoon plus 1 teaspoon unsalted butter
¾ cup lemon yogurt
¾ cup ricotta cheese
½ cup cream cheese, at room temperature
2 teaspoons cornstarch
1 teaspoon vanilla extract
3 eggs
½ cup sugar
3 cups sliced strawberries, for garnish

1. Preheat the oven to 350°F.

2. Combine the granola, brown sugar, and 1 teaspoon of the lemon zest in a food processor, and process until fine. Add the butter and process until the mixture begins to come together.

3. Using the back of a spoon, press the mixture into the bottom and sides of a 9-inch tart pan with removable bottom. Bake the crust for 10 minutes; then remove it from the oven. Leave the oven on.

4. Purée the yogurt, cheeses, cornstarch, and vanilla in a food processor. Add the eggs, sugar, and remaining 2 teaspoons lemon zest. Process until smooth.

5. Gently ladle the filling into the prepared crust, and place the pan on a baking sheet. Bake until set, 30 minutes.

6. Cool the cheesecake on a wire rack, and then refrigerate until chilled, 2 hours.

7. Remove the side of the tart pan and arrange the strawberries on top of the cheesecake before serving.

8 to 10 portions

HOW TO BLANCH ALMONDS

★

Blanch almonds to remove their thin outer skin. Place the almonds in a bowl and pour boiling water just to cover them. Let the almonds sit for only 1 minute (you don't want them to lose their crispness). Drain, rinse under cold water, and drain again. Pat dry and slip the skin off.

FLOUR FACTS

▼

Flour is classified according to the amount of gluten-forming protein in it. Although there are variations from one wheat-growing region to another, hard winter wheat generally produces bread flour with 13 to 15 percent protein (gluten). The high amount of gluten is important for giving bread its stretch.

The wheat grown in the hot months between spring and autumn is "soft," with just 4 to 9 percent protein. The soft wheat is milled for cake and pastry flours where little stretch and a lot of tenderness is required.

All-purpose flour is a blend of the two, with 11 to 12 percent protein, and is used for everything from baking to dredging meat before sautéing to thickening sauces.

Whole-wheat flour is milled with the wheat germ and the bran; the percentage of protein is lower because of these additions, but it is rich in riboflavin, thiamine, niacin, and iron. White flour, except for cake flour, is enriched so that the nutrients are equal to those in whole-wheat flour. Some flour mills add vitamins A and D and calcium as well.

ALMOND SOUR CREAM CHEESECAKE

Simplicity is cheesecake's only secret. You may prefer it feathery light or lusciously heavy; made of cream or cottage cheese or ricotta; with a pastry, bread crumb, or graham cracker crust; with topping or without. We've added almonds to this one, and we think it's sublime!

CRUST
1 package graham crackers, ground (2 cups)
½ cup blanched almonds (see box)
⅓ cup sugar
8 tablespoons (1 stick) unsalted butter, at room temperature

FILLING
1½ pounds cream cheese
½ cup sugar
2 teaspoons fresh lemon juice
½ teaspoon vanilla extract
1 teaspoon almond extract
2 tablespoons amaretto liqueur
3 eggs

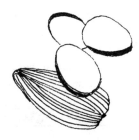

TOPPING

8 ounces sour cream
1 tablespoon sugar
2 tablespoons amaretto liqueur
½ cup slivered blanched almonds, toasted (see Index)

1. Preheat the oven to 375°F.

2. Prepare the crust: Combine the cracker crumbs, almonds, and sugar in a food processor. Add the butter, and process thoroughly.

3. Press the mixture into an 8½-inch springform pan, covering the bottom and reaching nearly halfway up the sides.

4. Prepare the filling: Combine the cream cheese, sugar, lemon juice, vanilla extract, almond extract, and amaretto in the bowl of a food processor, and cream thoroughly. Add the eggs and process until well blended.

5. Pour the mixture into the prepared pan, and bake until the cheesecake has just begun to crack, 45 to 50 minutes. Remove it from the oven and allow it to cool for several minutes. Reduce the oven heat to 350°F.

6. Prepare the topping: Stir the sour cream, sugar, and amaretto together in a bowl, and spoon the mixture over the cheesecake.

7. Return the cheesecake to the oven and bake another 20 minutes. Sprinkle it with the toasted almonds and allow it to cool completely. Refrigerate 4 hours before serving.

8 to 10 portions

ICED COFFEE
★

To make good iced coffee, you must first make good hot coffee. Don't make it too far in advance. Sweeten it if you want, cover it to preserve the aroma, and refrigerate after it has come to room temperature. We like to add a strip or two of lemon peel, a little rum, cooled melted chocolate, or honey. Try a scoop of ice cream—vanilla, chocolate, or coffee.

LITTLE BOSTON CREAM PIES

Individual square Boston cream pies—white cake, custard, and milk chocolate glaze—with a touch of almond.

CUSTARD FILLING

3 egg yolks
5 teaspoons cornstarch
¾ cup sugar
1½ cups milk
¼ teaspoon salt
1 tablespoon unsalted butter, at room temperature
1 teaspoon vanilla extract

CAKE

5 ounces sliced or slivered blanched almonds
½ cup unbleached all-purpose flour
½ teaspoon baking powder
12 tablespoons (1½ sticks) unsalted butter, at room temperature
¾ cup sugar
1 tablespoon amaretto liqueur
½ teaspoon vanilla extract
4 eggs

GLAZE

3 ounces good-quality milk chocolate
3 tablespoons half-and-half
1 tablespoon amaretto liqueur

1. Prepare the custard: Beat the egg yolks in a heavy medium-size saucepan. Add the cornstarch and sugar, and mix well. Then stir in the milk, salt, and butter.

AFTER-DINNER COFFEES

Amaretto Coffee: Stir 1 to 2 tablespoons amaretto liqueur into a cup of strong coffee. Top with whipped cream and garnish with toasted almond slivers.

Belgian Coffee: Fold beaten egg white into whipped cream and put a large dollop in the bottom of a coffee cup. Pour in the coffee. When the froth comes to the top, garnish with grated bittersweet chocolate.

Café Brûlot: Place 3 broken sticks of cinnamon, 2 large strips of orange zest and 1 of lemon zest, 1 teaspoon allspice berries, and 16 demitasse cubes of sugar in a chafing dish or skillet. Pour in 1 cup Cognac or bourbon and heat, without stirring, until the liquor is warm. Light the liquor with a match and stir until the flames die out. Pour in 5 cups hot strong coffee and stir. Strain, then ladle into demitasse cups.

Irish Coffee: Stir 1 to 2 tablespoons Irish whisky and 1 to 2 teaspoons sugar together in the bottom of a coffee cup. Pour in hot strong coffee, stir, and top with whipped cream.

Kahlua Coffee: Stir 1 to 2 tablespoons Kahlua into a cup of strong coffee. Top with whipped cream and sprinkle with grated orange zest or garnish with a chocolate-covered coffee bean.

Viennese Coffee: For each cup of coffee, melt an ounce of semisweet chocolate with a tablespoon of heavy cream in the top of a double boiler over simmering water. Gradually whisk in 1 cup of coffee for each ounce of chocolate and beat until frothy. Pour into cups. Top with whipped cream and garnish with a sprinkle of cinnamon, cocoa, or grated orange zest. For a spicier version, brew the coffee with a few cloves and a cinnamon stick.

---

2. Cook the egg mixture over medium heat, stirring constantly, until it is bubbling and thick, 5 to 7 minutes.

3. Remove the pan from the heat and stir in the vanilla. Transfer the mixture to a glass bowl, cover it with plastic wrap, and refrigerate for 2 to 4 hours.

4. Prepare the cake: Preheat the oven to 375°F. Butter and flour an 8-inch square cake pan.

5. Combine the almonds and 2 tablespoons of the flour in a food processor, and process until fine. Transfer the mixture to a bowl, and stir in the remaining flour and the baking powder.

6. Cream the butter and sugar together in a mixing bowl until light. Add the amaretto and vanilla. Beat in the eggs one at a time. Then slowly fold in the dry ingredients until the mixture is smooth.

7. Spoon the batter into the prepared cake pan, and bake until it is golden and a toothpick inserted in the center comes out clean, 20 minutes. Cool the cake in the pan for 20 minutes. Then remove it from the pan and transfer it to a wire rack to cool.

8. Prepare the glaze: Combine the chocolate and half-and-half in a small saucepan and stir over low heat until smooth. Remove the pan from the heat and slowly stir in the liqueur. Allow the glaze to cool until slightly thickened, 10 to 15 minutes.

9. To assemble the pies, cut the cake into nine squares. Halve each square horizontally and cover the bottom halves with the custard. Replace the tops, and drizzle each one with chocolate glaze. Refrigerate, but bring to room temperature before serving.

9 portions

STRAWBERRY SHORTCAKE

Strawberry shortcake is an American passion. When done properly, it tastes of contrasts—perfect tart juicy berries, thick rich sweet cream, and the sour crumbly texture of a hot biscuit. The result is sweet and tart, warm and cool, soft and crunchy, smooth and crumbly. We are enchanted!

Remember, of course, that perfect berries are called for. Sniff the strawberries: If there is a deep, complex fragrance, the flavor will be good. No aroma, no taste.

Once you've selected your scarlet treasures, don't make the mistake of overworking them. They absorb water so just rinse them quickly and hull them. They must be at room temperature. And the whipped cream must be icy cold. Oh my goodness, is it June yet?

2 pints strawberries, lightly rinsed, hulled, and quartered
¼ cup plus 2 teaspoons sugar
1 cup heavy or whipping cream
¼ teaspoon vanilla extract
8 New Basic Biscuits, the sweet variation (see Index)
3 tablespoons unsalted butter, melted

1. Toss the strawberries in a bowl with the ¼ cup sugar. Let them stand at room temperature for 2 hours, stirring occasionally.

2. Combine the cream with the vanilla and the remaining 2 teaspoons sugar, and whip until thick but soft. Cover the bowl loosely and refrigerate.

3. Just before serving, halve the biscuits and brush the bottoms with melted butter. Spoon some strawberries with their juice and a dollop (or two) of whipped cream on each biscuit bottom. Cover with the biscuit tops at an angle. Serve immediately.

8 portions

EGGQUIVALENTS

Eggs are sized jumbo, extra-large, large, medium, small, and even peewee, and they are weighed in ounces per dozen. An egg's size depends on the hen that laid it—her breed, weight, and age. Most recipes are developed and tested for the ubiquitous large egg, but other sizes can be substituted. Here's how to figure how many of each size to use.

JUMBO	EXTRA-LARGE	LARGE	MEDIUM	SMALL
1	1	1	1	1
2	2	2	2	3
2	3	3	3	4
3	4	4	5	5
4	4	5	6	7
5	5	6	7	8

But you can also figure out how many to use by cup measure. In 1 cup there are:

SIZE	WHOLE	WHITES	YOLKS
Jumbo	4	6	12
Extra-large	4	6	12
Large	5	7	14
Medium	5	8	16
Small	6	9	18

LARRY FORGIONE'S WILD HUCKLEBERRY SHORTCAKE

Larry has been a tremendous force behind the availability of indigenous ingredients in food markets today, which has made the "new American cuisine" distinctive and possible. A dinner at his An American Place in New York City offers a delicious and inventive education on the far-reaching resources our country has to offer.

SHORTCAKE
4 cups unbleached all-purpose flour
¼ cup plus 2 tablespoons sugar
3¼ teaspoons cream of tartar
1¾ teaspoons baking soda
2 teaspoons salt
12 tablespoons (1½ sticks) unsalted butter, cold, cut into
*   small pieces*
1½ cups heavy or whipping cream
4 hard-cooked large egg yolks, mashed

4 tablespoons (½ stick) unsalted butter, melted
3 cups huckleberries, rinsed and picked over
½ cup sugar
1 cup heavy or whipping cream, whipped

1. Preheat the oven to 375°F. Lightly butter a baking sheet.

2. Prepare the shortcake: Sift the flour, sugar, cream of tartar, baking soda, and salt into a bowl. Using your fingertips, work the butter in quickly and lightly. Add the cream and mashed egg yolks, and stir until the dough holds together.

3. Turn the dough out onto a lightly floured work surface and knead it a few times; do not overwork it. Pat or roll it out so that it is ½ to ¾ inch thick.

4. Cut out six rounds using a 3-inch floured cookie cutter. Cut out six more rounds using a 2½-inch cutter, rerolling the scraps of dough if necessary.

5. Place the larger rounds on the prepared baking sheet, and brush each one with 1 teaspoon of the melted butter. Top with the smaller rounds, and brush the tops with melted butter. Bake on the middle shelf of the oven until the biscuits are golden and firm to the touch, 14 to 18 minutes.

6. Meanwhile, bring a saucepan of water to a boil. Plunge the huckleberries into the water for 15 seconds; then drain. Toss the berries and ½ cup sugar together in a bowl, and let them sit while the shortcake bakes.

7. Transfer the shortcake biscuits to dessert plates and carefully separate the layers. Heap some berries onto the bottom layers, and spoon whipped cream onto each. Top with the smaller shortcake layers. Serve immediately, with the remaining whipped cream on the side.

6 portions

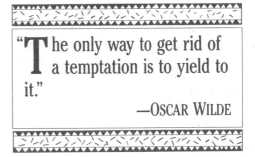

"The only way to get rid of a temptation is to yield to it."

—OSCAR WILDE

BERTA'S CARROT CAKE

Carrot cakes abound, but there's still none better than the one created by Sheila's mother. It has just the right texture and taste—and not too sweet. Try it unfrosted for breakfast. It's a classic for us and it will be for you.

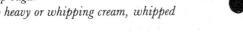

2 cups unbleached all-purpose flour
2 cups granulated sugar
2 teaspoons baking soda
2 teaspoons ground cinnamon
1 cup corn oil
3 eggs, lightly beaten
2 teaspoons vanilla extract
1⅓ cups puréed cooked carrots
1 cup chopped walnuts
1 cup shredded coconut
¾ cup canned crushed pineapple, drained
Cream Cheese Frosting (recipe follows)
Confectioners' sugar, for dusting

1. Preheat the oven to 350°F. Line a 13 x 9-inch layer cake pan with waxed paper, and grease the paper.

2. Sift the flour, sugar, baking soda, and cinnamon together in a large bowl. Add the oil, eggs, and vanilla, and beat well. Then fold in the carrots, walnuts, coconut, and pineapple.

3. Pour the batter into the prepared pan. Place it on the middle rack of the oven and bake until the edges have pulled away from the sides of the pan and a toothpick inserted in the center comes out clean, 1 hour.

4. Cool the cake in the pan for 10 minutes. Then invert it over a cake rack and unmold, remove the waxed paper, and continue to cool for 1 hour.

5. Frost the top and sides of the cooled cake with the cream cheese frosting, and then dust the top with confectioners' sugar.

12 portions

CREAM CHEESE FROSTING

4 ounces cream cheese, at room temperature
3 tablespoons unsalted butter, at room temperature
1½ cups confectioners' sugar
½ teaspoon vanilla extract
Juice of ¼ lemon

1. Cream the cream cheese and butter together in a mixing bowl.

2. Slowly sift in the confectioners' sugar, and continue beating until fully incorporated (there should be no lumps). Stir in the vanilla and lemon juice.

Frosting for a 13 x 9-inch cake

A REALLY GOOD CUP OF COFFEE

Our coffee of choice for years has been dripped through a filter, but whether you make coffee in a percolator or in a drip pot, you can guarantee yourself a good cup by following these simple guidelines:

▲ Start with fresh beans and fresh cold water.

▲ Choose the correct grind for your pot.

▲ Measure the coffee and water accurately.

▲ Wash the coffee maker after every pot.

▲ Don't reheat coffee or leave it on the warmer for hours.

All coffee drinkers have their own formula for the proportion of coffee to water. We go by these measures:

▲ Regular-strength coffee: 1 coffee measure (2 tablespoons) to 6 ounces (¾ cup) water.

▲ Extra-strength coffee: 1 coffee measure (2 tablespoons) to 4 ounces (½ cup) water.

▲ Double-strength coffee: 2 coffee measures (¼ cup) to 6 ounces (¾ cup) water.

APPLE SPICE CAKE

In the fall the orchards are aglow with red, green, and golden globes. Apples have long been the mainstay of winter fruits because of their keeping ability and cooking versatility, and this cake's extra moistness makes it a keeper too!

2 ¼ cups unbleached all-purpose flour
2 ½ teaspoons baking powder
1 teaspoon ground cinnamon
½ teaspoon ground cloves
½ teaspoon ground ginger
Pinch of salt
½ teaspoon baking soda
3 cups finely diced peeled tart apples
⅓ cup raisins
⅓ cup chopped walnuts
12 tablespoons (1 ½ sticks) unsalted butter, at room
    temperature
1 ½ cups (packed) dark brown sugar
1 teaspoon vanilla extract
3 large eggs
½ cup buttermilk
½ cup applesauce

SYRUP
⅓ cup Calvados or applejack
2 tablespoons granulated sugar
1 teaspoon fresh lemon juice
6 strips lemon zest (3 x ½ inches)

1. Preheat the oven to 350°F. Butter and flour a 9-inch tube pan or a 12-cup bundt pan.

2. Using a fork, stir the flour, baking powder, spices, and baking soda together in a bowl.

3. Combine the apples, raisins, and walnuts in another bowl, and add 3 tablespoons of the flour mixture. Toss to coat the fruit and nuts. Set aside.

4. Combine the butter, brown sugar, and vanilla in a mixing bowl and cream until the mixture is light and creamy. Beat in the eggs one at a time. Then stir in the buttermilk and applesauce.

5. Slowly add the flour mixture to the butter mixture, beating just until blended. Then stir in the reserved fruits and nuts. Pour the batter into the prepared pan and smooth the top.

6. Bake until a toothpick inserted in the cake comes out clean, 1 hour. Let the cake cool, still in the pan, for 1 hour.

7. Prepare the syrup: Combine all the ingredients in a small saucepan and heat just to a simmer. When the sugar has dissolved, remove the pan from the heat and set it aside for 15 minutes.

8. Unmold the cake and place it on a serving platter. Prick the cake all over with a wooden skewer. Remove the lemon zest from the syrup, and brush the top and sides of the cake with the syrup until it has all been absorbed.

12 portions

A PROPER CUP OF TEA

To make a proper cup of tea you need a good teapot and loose tea. Fill a kettle with fresh cold water and heat it to a boil. Place the teapot near the kettle to warm. When the water nears the boil, pour a little hot water into the teapot, swirl it around, and pour it out.

Measure the tea leaves—one heaping teaspoon per cup and one for the pot—into the teapot. As soon as the water boils, pour it over the tea. Stir quickly, cover the pot, and put it under a tea cozy or in a warm spot to steep for five to seven minutes.

The proper English pour a little milk into each teacup and it truly does make the tea taste better. Tea calls for cold whole milk, not cream, half-and-half, or skim. Just whole milk.

Stir the tea. The English never do, but it blends the strong settled tea with the weaker tea at the top. Pour through a fine strainer into cups. If you live in a chilly place, heat the cups first by swirling hot water in them and pouring it out.

THE THREE GREAT BRANDIES FROM FRANCE

Armagnac: Gutsy, aromatic, and bursting with fruity virility, this glorious brandy flows from Gascony in southwestern France. The process of distilling Armagnac can be traced back to the twelfth century, but its great character comes from authorized grape varietals, such as Folle Blanche, Saint-Emilion, and Baco. A source of great pride to the fiery Gascony farmers, Armagnac should be savored in small brandy snifters with short stems so that one's hands can cup the glass and warm the spirit.

Cognac: Smoother and considered finer than the spirited Armagnac, Cognac is distilled twice and put to age in Limousin oak barrels and develop its rich amber color. The western region of Grande Champagne is most well known for this sophisticated brandy, which by law is produced only from Folle Blanche, Colombard, and Saint-Emilion grapes.

Swirl it in large brandy snifters and enjoy it after a perfect dinner. The most familiar and best Cognac in America is labeled V.S.O.P for Very Superior Old Pale.

Calvados: While Armagnac and Cognac are distilled from the nectar of grapes, Calvados is born from the fermented juices of the great Normandy apples in a process that dates back to the sixteenth century. The Calvados is put in fine oak casks to age, developing character and complexity. Smooth and dry, this brandy of deep woody flavor and golden color is a favorite of the French. It can also be enjoyed when it is young and the flavor of the apples is more predominant. In Normandy one often sees a typical French workman, dressed in the classic blue uniform, at a bar early in the morning asking for a "Calva" to begin his day. We've tried it once or twice ourselves!

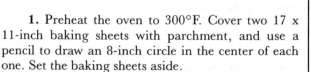

COCONUT CLOUD

A delectable meringue cake is one of the loveliest of light desserts, and this one tastes just as good as it looks. Serve it as is or with a fresh berry purée.

6 egg whites
¼ teaspoon salt
⅜ teaspoon cream of tartar
1½ cups sugar
1 tablespoon white vinegar

3 teaspoons vanilla extract
4 cups heavy or whipping cream
½ cup dark rum
2 cups shredded coconut

1. Preheat the oven to 300°F. Cover two 17 x 11-inch baking sheets with parchment, and use a pencil to draw an 8-inch circle in the center of each one. Set the baking sheets aside.

2. Combine the egg whites, salt, and cream of tartar in a mixing bowl and beat with an electric mixer until foamy (the whites should not look watery).

3. With the beater on medium speed, slowly add the sugar. Then add the vinegar and 1 teaspoon of the vanilla, and beat on high speed until the mixture is very shiny and forms stiff peaks.

4. Fit a pastry bag with a large tip, and fill it with half of the meringue mixture. Beginning in the center of one of the circles on the prepared baking sheets, pipe a spiral to fill the circle completely. Then pipe a coil around the outer edge on top of the first layer, and another coil on top of that one, to form a 1¾-inch rim. This will be the bottom layer.

5. Fill the pastry bag with the remaining meringue mixture, and pipe a spiral on the other baking sheet, filling the circle and making a rim as in Step 4.

6. Bake the meringues for 50 minutes. Then turn the oven off and leave the meringues in the oven for another 25 minutes (to dry out). Set the baked meringues aside in a cool spot.

7. Preheat the broiler.

8. Whip the cream with an electric mixer until thick. Slowly beat in the rum and the remaining 2 teaspoons vanilla, and continue beating until stiff. Gently fold in 1½ cups of the coconut.

9. Spread the remaining ½ cup coconut on a baking sheet and toast it under the broiler, 4 inches from the heat, until just golden, 2 to 3 minutes. Set the coconut aside.

10. Remove one meringue shell from the parchment, carefully peeling it away, and place the shell on a round serving platter. Fill the center of the shell with half the whipped cream mixture. Place the other meringue layer upside down over the bottom shell. Cover the top and sides with the remaining whipped cream. Sprinkle the top with the reserved coconut, and serve.

8 portions

NUTTY AS A FRUITCAKE

In our estimation, this is a fruitcake as it should be: chock-full of dates and walnuts, with a sprinkling of candied cherries for color and only enough "cake" to hold it all together. This is good any time of the year.

8 cups pitted whole dates (about 3 pounds)
8 cups walnut halves (about 1¾ pounds)
1 cup candied cherries (about 6 ounces)
½ cup unbleached all-purpose flour
6 eggs, separated, at room temperature
¾ cup granulated sugar
¾ cup (packed) dark brown sugar
6 tablespoons (¾ stick) unsalted butter, melted
4½ tablespoons heavy or whipping cream
2 tablespoons vanilla extract
2 teaspoons grated orange zest
½ teaspoon almond extract
1½ cups whole-wheat flour
1½ teaspoons baking powder

1. Preheat the oven to 325°F. Butter three 9 x 5 x 3-inch loaf pans. Line the bottoms and sides with aluminum foil, and butter the foil generously.

2. Combine the dates, walnuts, and candied cherries in a very large bowl or roasting pan. Sprinkle with the all-purpose flour and toss to coat well, separating the dates with your fingers.

3. Combine the egg yolks and both sugars in a large mixing bowl; beat until light and fluffy. Beat in the butter, cream, vanilla, orange zest, and almond extract. Mix the whole-wheat flour and baking powder thoroughly in a small bowl; stir this into the batter with a wooden spoon.

4. Beat the egg whites in another large bowl just until they form stiff peaks. Fold a quarter of the whites into the batter, and then fold in the remaining whites. Pour the batter over the fruit mixture and mix well to coat all the fruit and nuts. Spoon it into the prepared pans, mounding the batter slightly in the pans.

5. Cover the pans with buttered aluminum foil and bake for 40 minutes. Remove the foil from the tops and continue baking until the centers are firm to the touch, 15 to 20 minutes.

6. Cool the cakes in the pans on wire racks. Then remove them from the pans and wrap tightly in aluminum foil. The fruitcake can be eaten the next day or stored in a cool place for up to 2 weeks.

About 25 portions

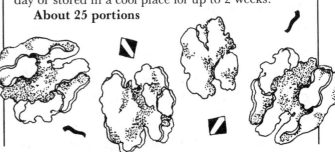

THE FRUIT ORCHARD

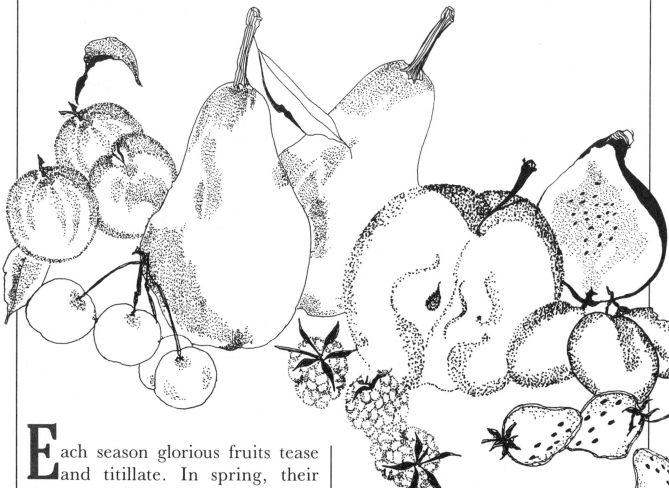

Each season glorious fruits tease and titillate. In spring, their blossoms delight us and we're filled with eager anticipation. We dream of summer's juicy peaches, luscious sweet and pungent berries, jewel-like cooling melons. In autumn, we long to bite into crisp apples, savor a succulent pear, and linger over a velvety persimmon.

Adaptable and giving, fruits en-liven light mousses and soufflés, glistening tarts, cozy cobblers, and homey preserves. They shine on their own or gently poached atop a pool of puréed berries. Whether in the orchard, the berry patch, or the garden, the thrill is there for the asking and the plucking.

MINIATURE PEACH CHARLOTTES

A light, light charlotte that explodes with bourbon and peach flavors. When topped with a Raspberry Peach Sauce, these are glorious treasures.

8 cups water
3¾ cups sugar
2 tablespoons vanilla extract
7 tablespoons bourbon
6 ripe peaches
1 Orange-Scented Sponge Cake (see Index)
3 envelopes unflavored gelatin
⅓ cup warm water
2 cups milk
8 egg yolks
2 cups heavy or whipping cream, cold
Raspberry Peach Sauce (recipe follows)

1. Combine the 8 cups water and 3 cups of the sugar in a large saucepan or soup pot, and heat over low heat, stirring, to dissolve the sugar. Add the vanilla, 4 tablespoons of the bourbon, and the peaches. Bring to a simmer and poach gently until the peaches are very tender but not mealy, 5 to 8 minutes. Using a slotted spoon, remove the peaches and set them aside to cool completely. Reserve the poaching liquid.

2. Peel the cooled peaches and cut them into ¼-inch-thick slices, reserving any juice.

3. Cut the sponge cake in half horizontally. Using a ⅔-cup ramekin as a guide, cut out eight rounds of spongecake.

4. Butter eight ⅔-cup ramekins, and in the bottom of each one arrange peach slices, slightly overlapping, in a spiral. Coarsely chop the remaining peach slices and set aside.

5. Combine the gelatin and warm water in a small bowl, stir, and set aside until the gelatin has dissolved.

6. Heat the milk just to a boil in a small saucepan. Remove it from the heat.

7. Combine the egg yolks with the remaining ¾ cup sugar, and beat with an electric mixer until thick and light. Stir in 2 tablespoons of the bourbon, and then gradually whisk in the hot milk. Return the mixture to the saucepan and cook over low heat,

stirring constantly with a wooden spoon, until it has thickened slightly and coats the back of a spoon, 10 to 15 minutes. Remove the pan from the heat, stir in the softened gelatin and the chopped peaches, and transfer the mixture to a bowl. Set the bowl in a larger bowl filled with ice, and set it aside to chill. Stir the custard from time to time as it begins to set, 20 to 30 minutes.

8. Place 2 cups of the reserved poaching liquid and any juice reserved in Step 2 over high heat and reduce it to 1 cup, 5 to 7 minutes.

9. When the custard has begun to thicken and set, whip 1½ cups of the cream until it forms soft peaks. Fold the custard into the whipped cream, and pour the mixture into the ramekins.

10. Set aside ½ cup of the reduced poaching liquid to use for the Raspberry Peach Sauce. Brush the cake rounds with the remaining poaching liquid, and place them on top of the filled ramekins. Brush the rounds again with the liquid.

11. Chill the ramekins, loosely covered, in the refrigerator for 6 to 8 hours, or overnight. The custard should be completely set.

12. When you are ready to serve the charlottes, whip the remaining ½ cup cream until it forms soft peaks, and stir in the remaining 1 tablespoon bourbon. Unmold the charlottes onto individual plates, surround them with the sauce, and top with a tiny dollop of the bourbon cream.

8 portions

RASPBERRY PEACH SAUCE

1 pint fresh raspberries
½ cup reduced poaching liquid
1 tablespoon bourbon

Purée the raspberries in a food processor. Add the poaching liquid and bourbon, and process until blended.
About 2¼ cups

PEACHES GALORE

A perfectly ripe peach is worth waiting for all summer long. This sweet juicy fruit with downy skin has glorious color—golden yellow with a rosy blush. The ways in which we eat peaches run the gamut from ice cream to pies, cobblers, and crisps, from preserves to flambéed with brandy. Still, the simplest, and perhaps tastiest, way to eat a peach is out of hand.

There are two basic types of peaches—freestone and clingstone. As the names imply, freestones separate from the pit and clingstones cling to it. We see few clingstone peaches at the market because they are firmer and less juicy than freestones. Because of their texture, they can take the heat of canning. There are also semi-freestone peaches, which have more cling than regular freestones.

Peach season runs from June to September with early, middle, and late varieties appearing in their turn. Buy peaches that are somewhat firm but not hard. They should have a creamy yellow color with a good pink blush. Avoid those tinged with green because they were picked underripe and will never ripen well. Smell the peaches and buy those with some peachy fragrance. Since most peaches are bought firm, you will have to wait a few days for them to ripen. Put them in a bowl on the table and enjoy their good looks while they ripen.

It's not necessary to peel a peach for eating, but many desserts do call for peeled fruit. If you need more than just a couple of peeled peaches, you will save yourself some time by blanching them in boiling water for 10 to 20 seconds, then dropping them in ice water. The peel should slip right off.

VARIETIES

Redhaven (freestone): These peaches are one of the most loved for they have plenty of flavor and juice. Their season is August and they are good for eating, cooking, and preserving.

Fairhaven (freestone): This peach is good both for eating and cooking. Its season is just a week or two after that of the Redhaven.

Elberta (freestone): This is the last peach of the season, not making its appearance until September. It is colorful, large, and juicy.

Desert Gold (semi-freestone): One of the earliest peaches, Desert Gold is medium in size and quite firm even when perfectly ripe.

Sunhaven (clingstone): This peach is surprisingly juicy and sweet for a clingstone. Good for both eating and cooking, its season is August.

GINGER ZABAGLIONE WITH POACHED PEACHES

Luscious peaches with the surprise of ginger. Try this zabaglione with fresh fruits and gingerbread, too.

3 cups Ginger Zabaglione (recipe follows)
6 Poached Peaches (recipe follows)
4 pieces crystallized ginger, finely chopped
Grated zest of 1 orange
6 sprigs fresh mint

Divide half the zabaglione among six dessert plates. Place a peach in the center of each plate, and spoon the remaining zabaglione over the peaches. Sprinkle with the chopped ginger and the orange zest, and garnish each plate with a sprig of mint.

6 portions

GINGER ZABAGLIONE

6 egg yolks
6 tablespoons sugar
1 teaspoon ground ginger
1 cup dry Marsala

1. Combine the egg yolks, sugar, and ginger in a medium-size bowl. Whisk well, until pale yellow.

2. Add the Marsala in a slow stream, whisking constantly. Transfer the mixture to a double boiler, and cook over boiling water, whisking constantly, until the zabaglione is frothy and has doubled in volume. It should easily coat the back of a spoon. Remove the pan from the heat and allow the zabaglione to cool to room temperature.

3 cups

Note: For a lighter version, gently fold ½ cup whipped cream into the cooled mixture.

POACHED PEACHES

6 large ripe peaches (about 2½ pounds)
2 cups dry white wine
5 cups water
8 pieces crystallized ginger

1. Carefully peel the peaches with a vegetable peeler or a small sharp knife.

2. Fill a medium-size heavy saucepan with the wine, water, and ginger. Bring to a boil over medium heat.

3. Gently place the peaches in the liquid, reduce the heat to low, and simmer for 15 minutes. Using a slotted spoon, remove the peaches and set them aside to cool. Discard the liquid.

6 portions

SUMMER BERRY MINT TRIFLE

The lightest, freshest, most wonderful trifle we've ever tasted. The mint freshens the strawberries and blueberries to transform a classic into a lovely summer gem.

1 Orange-Scented Sponge Cake (see Index)
½ cup cream or pale sherry
1 quart strawberries, lightly rinsed, drained, and hulled
Confectioners' sugar, to taste
1 pint blueberries, lightly rinsed, drained, and picked over
2½ cups Mint Crème Anglaise (see Index)
1 cup heavy or whipping cream, cold
2 tablespoons confectioners' sugar
Fresh mint leaves, for garnish

1. Cut the cake into 1-inch cubes, and line the bottom of a large glass serving bowl with them. Sprinkle the cake with the sherry, and set aside for 30 minutes.

2. Purée 1 pint of the strawberries in a food processor, and strain them into a bowl. Add confectioners' sugar to taste. Stir well, and pour the purée over the cake.

3. Halve the remaining strawberries. Sprinkle the blueberries and strawberries over the purée.

4. Pour the crème anglaise over all, and place the bowl, loosely covered, in the refrigerator. Chill for 3 to 4 hours.

5. When you are ready to serve the trifle, combine the cream and confectioners' sugar in a mixing bowl, and whip with an electric mixer until the cream forms soft peaks.

6. Dollop the whipped cream over the trifle, garnish with fresh mint leaves, and serve immediately.

8 to 10 portions

CREPES SNOW WHITE

Just imagine sitting at a café on the beach in Cannes, indulging in crepes while gazing at the Mediterranean sunset. These classic French crepes suzette, made by our friend Ellen "Snow" White, are equally memorable.

1 cup (2 sticks) unsalted butter, at room temperature
1 cup confectioners' sugar
1 tablespoon grated orange zest
½ cup fresh orange juice
½ cup Grand Marnier liqueur
2 oranges, peeled, cut into sections, and seeded
12 crepes (recipe follows)

1. Blend the butter and confectioners' sugar together in a mixing bowl. Add the orange zest, juice, and Grand Marnier. Mix thoroughly.

2. Transfer the mixture to a large skillet and cook over low heat for 5 minutes.

3. While the butter mixture is heating, place 2 orange sections on each crepe and fold them into quarters. Add the folded-up crepes to the skillet, and continue cooking over low heat, spooning the liquid over the crepes, for another 5 minutes. Serve immediately.

4 portions

CREPES

It takes a little practice, and you usually toss out the first one, but once you learn to make crepes you'll be able to create many exciting dishes spontaneously.

1 cup unbleached all-purpose flour
1 tablespoon sugar
¼ teaspoon salt
1 cup milk
⅓ cup water
3 eggs
3 tablespoons unsalted butter, melted

1. Combine the flour, sugar, and salt in a food processor and process briefly.

2. With the motor running, add the milk, water, eggs, and butter through the feed tube. Process until smooth.

3. Heat a heavy 7-inch nonstick skillet until quite hot. Pour in 3 tablespoons of the batter, then quickly tilt the pan so the batter spreads evenly, forming a crepe. Cook until lightly brown, 30 to 45 seconds; then turn and cook another 15 seconds.

4. Repeat, using up all the batter. As you finish the crepes, stack them between sheets of waxed paper to prevent them from sticking. Wrap the stacked crepes in plastic wrap. They will keep in the refrigerator for 2 days.

12 crepes

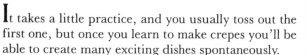

OUR OWN ORCHARDS

We both live on the edge of orchards on weekends in the country—Sheila on her farm in Connecticut and Julee in her cottage on Lake Michigan. Both orchards are rather old. It seems that apple, peach, pear, and plum trees are particularly adept at aging—they just get better looking.

We delight in watching our orchards through every season of the year. The trees welcome spring with their dainty blossoms and fragrance. In summer, their branches tempt us to escape under their cool shadows to read and daydream. As summer moves on, we watch the green fruits ripen day by day until the orchard is a blaze of color. Then we pick bushel baskets full and sauce, purée, and freeze all that we can. When the trees are pruned, we gather the limbs for the best, most fragrant firewood.

CINNAMON APPLE BEIGNETS

Those light, wonderful beignets come to your kitchen straight from New Orleans. Serve them with your hottest, darkest coffee and you'll truly believe you're sitting in a café in the French Quarter.

1 cup unbleached all-purpose flour
Salt
2 tablespoons plus ½ cup sugar
2 tablespoons ground cinnamon
2 eggs, separated
⅔ cup milk
1 tablespoon corn oil
4 McIntosh apples
1 lemon, halved
Vegetable or corn oil for deep-frying

1. Sift the flour, a pinch of salt, the 2 tablespoons sugar, and 1 tablespoon of the cinnamon together in a large bowl. Add the egg yolks and ⅓ cup of the milk, and stir to form a smooth paste.

2. Stir in the remaining ⅓ cup milk and the corn oil. Mix until the batter is smooth. Then set it aside to rest for 30 minutes.

3. Combine the remaining ½ cup sugar with the remaining 1 tablespoon cinnamon in a small bowl, and set it aside.

4. Peel the apples, and rub them with a lemon half to prevent discoloration. Core the apples, and slice them into ¼-inch-thick rings. Squeeze the lemon juice over them and toss.

5. Beat the egg whites and a pinch of salt with an electric mixer until they form stiff peaks. Fold the whites into the batter.

6. Fill a deep-fryer or a deep skillet with oil to a depth of 2 inches, and heat it to 375°F.

7. Dip the apple slices into the batter, coating them well. Remove them from the bowl with a fork, allowing the excess batter to drip off. Cook them in the hot oil, turning once, until well browned on both sides, 3 to 4 minutes.

8. Drain the beignets on paper towels, and sprinkle them immediately with the reserved cinnamon sugar. Serve warm.

4 portions

PEAR AND GINGER COBBLER

Everybody loves a crisp...or a crumble...or a cobbler. It is one of those scrumptious desserts that we find ourselves eating for breakfast the next day, and "evening up" until there's none left.

8 ripe pears, peeled, cored, and cut into ¼-inch-thick slices
1½ tablespoons grated fresh ginger, or more to taste
½ cup plus 3 tablespoons sugar
1 tablespoon fresh lemon juice
Finely grated zest of ½ lemon
2 cups unbleached all-purpose flour
Pinch of salt
1 tablespoon baking powder
2 tablespoons unsalted butter
⅓ cup solid vegetable shortening
1 egg
⅓ cup milk

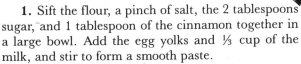

1. Preheat the oven to 425°F. Butter a large (14-inch-long) baking dish or casserole or a 2½- to 3-quart soufflé dish.

2. Combine the pears, ginger, ½ cup sugar, lemon juice, and lemon zest in a large bowl. Toss well to combine, and spoon into the prepared baking dish.

3. In another bowl combine the flour, salt, baking powder, and 1 tablespoon of the sugar. Work the butter and shortening in with a pastry blender, two knives, or your fingertips until the mixture resembles coarse crumbs. Lightly beat the egg and milk together, and then slowly stir this into the mixture. Knead lightly, sprinkling on more flour if necessary to form a smooth, not sticky, dough.

4. Break off portions of the dough and place them on top of the fruit, pressing slightly and flattening the dough. Cover the entire surface with the dough pieces to give a "cobbled" effect.

5. Sprinkle the remaining 2 tablespoons sugar over the dough, and bake until well browned, 35 to 45 minutes. Serve immediately.

6 to 8 portions

COBBLERS

❤

We have always loved homey food—sweet or savory—with a rich and abundant spirit. Our fruit cobblers certainly fit the description. We combine blueberries, strawberries, and raspberries, apples, blackberries, and figs, or pears and ginger with flavorful spices and spoon them into a deep casserole or straight-sided soufflé dish, from 1½ to 3 quarts depending on how many are being served. It takes just a minute to mix up a soft biscuit dough and spoon it over the top. Don't smooth the dough—you want the top to be bumpy and rough (cobbled). Bake until bubbly hot and serve with a pitcher of rich cream. Delicious!

BLUEBERRY, RASPBERRY, AND STRAWBERRY COBBLER

Sheila will never forget the taste of her grandmother's fruit desserts. This combination is splendid in summertime, when flavors are bursting from the berries and nostalgic memories of childhood are in the air.

1 pint blueberries, lightly rinsed, drained, and picked over
1 pint raspberries, lightly rinsed and drained
1 quart strawberries, lightly rinsed, drained, and hulled
½ cup plus 3 tablespoons sugar
1 tablespoon fresh lemon juice
Finely grated zest of ½ lemon
2 cups unbleached all-purpose flour
Pinch of salt
1 tablespoon baking powder
⅓ cup solid vegetable shortening
3 tablespoons unsalted butter
1 egg
⅓ cup milk

1. Preheat the oven to 425°F. Butter a large (14-inch-long) oval baking dish or casserole or a 2½- to 3-quart soufflé dish.

2. Combine the berries, ½ cup sugar, lemon juice, and lemon zest in a large bowl. Toss well to combine, and spoon into the prepared baking dish.

3. In another bowl combine the flour, salt, baking powder, and 1 tablespoon of the sugar. Work the shortening and butter in with a pastry blender, two knives, or your fingertips until the mixture resembles

BERRY CARE

★

If you aren't lucky enough to have a berry patch just out the door, you will have to buy your berries at the market and know what to look for and how to store them. Whenever possible, buy local berries in season. Some berries are available year round, but the quality of out-of-season berries is generally poor. Fresh berries should look plump and shiny and be firm not mushy. If you buy berries by the box, check for signs of mold and any juice stains on the bottom. The best berries have a wonderful fragrance.

When you get the berries home, remove them from the cartons. If you aren't going to use them within several hours, spread them out on paper towels on a baking sheet, cover lightly with plastic wrap, and refrigerate. Rinse berries lightly (never soak) and do it just before you use them. Berries are very fragile and disintegrate to mush if they are wet. If you can't use the most fragile berries—raspberries and strawberries—within two days,

purée them for fresh berry sauce. Delicious!

To freeze berries whole, spread them out on the paper-towel-lined baking sheets and freeze until firm. Pack them lightly in freezer containers (not plastic bags) and label and date them. Frozen berries are good for baking and cooked sauces, but they can't be served as if fresh. When we know the berry season is ending, we like to purée all we can get hold of and freeze them. Come fall and winter we spoon the purée over poached pears and other winter fruit.

When sugaring berries, use a light hand so that you can taste the berry and not just sweetness. Two to three tablespoons per pint should be enough for all but the very tart berries, such as cranberries and gooseberries. Tasteless berries can be revived with a splash of liqueur. We especially like Grand Marnier and Cointreau. But good berries just off the vine are best combined with just a little cream.

coarse crumbs. Lightly beat the egg and milk together, and then slowly stir this into the mixture. Knead lightly, sprinkling on more flour if necessary to form a smooth, not sticky, dough.

4. Break off portions of the dough and place them on top of the fruit, pressing slightly and flattening the dough. Cover the entire surface with the dough pieces to give a "cobbled" effect.

5. Sprinkle the remaining 2 tablespoons sugar over the dough, and bake until well browned, 35 to 45 minutes. Serve immediately.

6 to 8 portions

APPLE, FIG, AND BLACKBERRY COBBLER

Luxurious ripe figs and deep purple blackberries catch the last of Indian summer and combine with autumn's crisp-tasting apples for a tasty cobbler.

6 fresh figs, halved (about 1 ½ cups)
6 apples (McIntosh, Granny Smith, or Golden Delicious),
    peeled, cored, and cut into ¼ -inch-thick wedges
1 pint blackberries, lightly rinsed and drained
½ cup plus 3 tablespoons sugar
1 tablespoon fresh lemon juice
Finely grated zest of ½ lemon
2 cups unbleached all-purpose flour
Pinch of salt
1 tablespoon baking powder
⅓ cup solid vegetable shortening
3 tablespoons unsalted butter
1 egg
⅓ cup milk

1. Preheat the oven to 425°F. Butter a large (14-inch-long) oval baking dish or casserole or a 2½ - to 3-quart soufflé dish.

2. Combine the figs, apples, blackberries, ½ cup sugar, lemon juice, and lemon zest in a large bowl. Toss well to combine, and spoon into the prepared baking dish.

3. In another bowl combine the flour, salt, baking powder, and 1 tablespoon of the sugar. Work the shortening and butter in with a pastry blender, two knives, or your fingertips until the mixture resembles coarse crumbs. Lightly beat the egg and milk together, and then slowly stir this into the mixture. Knead lightly, sprinkling on more flour if necessary to form a smooth, not sticky, dough.

4. Break off portions of the dough and place them on top of the fruit, pressing slightly and flattening the dough. Cover the entire surface with the dough pieces to give a "cobbled" effect.

5. Sprinkle the remaining 2 tablespoons sugar over the dough, and bake until well browned, 35 to 45 minutes. Serve immediately.

6 to 8 portions

RHUBARB STRAWBERRY SAUCE

Tart, crisp, tasty rhubarb and smooth, sweet strawberries are just naturally complementary. When the rhubarb is ready for picking, make a big batch of this sauce. It's great to have around . . . for breakfast or snacking or warmed over gingerbread.

10 large stalks rhubarb, trimmed and cut into 1-inch lengths
4 cups hulled, halved strawberries
1 cup sugar
1 cup fresh orange juice
Finely grated zest of 1 orange
Finely grated zest of 1 lemon
2 teaspoons ground ginger
½ teaspoon salt (optional)
½ vanilla bean, split
    lengthwise

1. Combine all the ingredients in a heavy saucepan. Stir well and bring to a boil over medium heat. Reduce the heat and simmer, stirring once and skimming off any foam that forms on top, until the rhubarb is just tender, 10 to 12 minutes.

2. Remove the vanilla bean and let the mixture cool to room temperature. Then cover and refrigerate. It will keep for two days.

8 cups

Note: Rhubarb leaves are inedible, so be sure to trim the stalks thoroughly before cooking.

CRANBERRY FOOL

Don't be foolish and limit yourself to cranberries. Fools are easy to make. Whip up the liqueur-flavored cream and fold in the ripest of raspberries, strawberries, or blueberries.

2 cups heavy or whipping cream
1 tablespoon sugar
¼ cup Grand Marnier liqueur
1 ½ cups Maple Cranberry Sauce (see Index and Note
    below), cranberry conserve, or whole-berry cranberry sauce

1. In a large bowl, whip the cream with an electric mixer until it starts to thicken. Add the sugar and beat until it thickens more. Then add the Grand Marnier and continue beating until the cream is fluffy and forms peaks.

2. Place the cranberry sauce in a bowl and using a rubber spatula, gently fold in the whipped cream. Do not overmix. The mixture should be pink and white. Refrigerate, loosely covered, until ready to serve.

3. Serve in glass bowls.

6 portions

Note: If you use the Maple Cranberry Sauce recipe for the fool, prepare it without the walnuts.

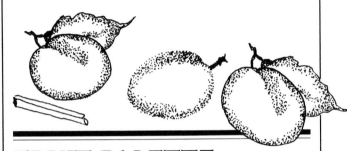

FRUIT PALETTE

An elegant way to serve seasonal fruit. Select a variety of colors and shapes, such as a mixture of plums, grapes, bananas, strawberries, blueberries, tangerines, and raspberries.

1 ½ cups fresh or frozen (thawed) strawberries, hulled
1 cup fresh or frozen (thawed) whole raspberries
½ cup confectioners' sugar
2 tablespoons fresh lemon juice
2 tablespoons Grand Marnier liqueur
¼ teaspoon ground cinnamon
Seasonal fresh fruits, such as decoratively sliced plums, nectarines, and kiwis
Fresh mint leaves, for garnish

1. Combine the berries, confectioners' sugar, lemon juice, Grand Marnier, and cinnamon in a mixing bowl and beat with an electric mixer on low speed until smooth.

2. Divide the sauce among six rimmed dessert plates, and arrange the sliced fruits on top. Garnish with mint leaves, and serve.

2 ¾ cups sauce, 6 portions

LUSCIOUS PLUMS
★

A "plum" is a reward, a well-deserved bonus. So too the fruit—plump, full of flavor, and bursting with juice. Plums are smooth skinned and gloriously colored—red, green, yellow, purple, scarlet, blue, and black. The tastes are varied and distinctive. Plums are cultivated everywhere in Europe, especially Eastern Europe, and in America. Plums are summer fruits, on the market from June to September, with the small purple prune plums appearing last in the fall.

There are basically two types of plums—European and Japanese. European plums are tart and fairly small. Their season is early summer. Japanese types are harvested later in the summer and are large, sweet, and juicy.

Buy plums with rich deep color and skin that is firm but not taut. If overripe, the plums will feel sticky and split easily. Don't buy plums with brown sunburned patches. Firm plums will ripen at room temperature within a day or two, and ripe plums can be stored in the refrigerator for several days. Peeling a plum will make it less tart; if the plum is ripe, the peel should come off easily.

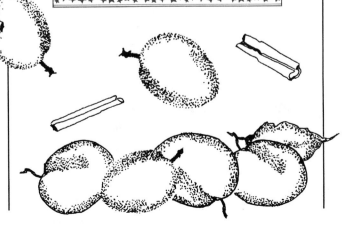

GRAPES

●

Grapes are believed to be the world's oldest fruit, and today they claim the lion's share of the world's fruit industry. Grapes are grown in all areas of the world where it is not extremely cold. In this country, California produces 98 percent of the grapes grown for eating and juice.

Buy grapes with fresh stems and firm fruit. And look for the deepest color for the most sugar. Grapes should be stored in the refrigerator, but warm them to room temperature before serving for the most flavor. Rinse them just before eating, not before, or they will get soft.

A large part of the grape crop is sun-dried for currants, raisins, and sultanas, and another part is grown for juice. But nearly a dozen varieties are raised exclusively for the table. Here are some of the most popular.

SEEDLESS

Perlette: Small green, round to oval grapes. California Perlettes are the earliest grapes of the season, appearing in May and June. Buy them late in the season for the sweetest taste.

Red Flame: A medium-size grape—juicy, crisp, and very sweet. Their season is August to October.

Ruby Red Seedless: Redder, smaller, and less flavorful than the Red Flame. The California season lasts from August to December.

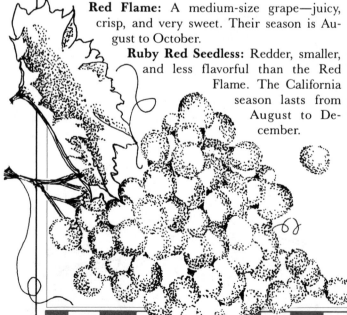

Thompson Seedless: Small, juicy, white-green grapes with a sweet flavor. Thompsons are the best known and most widely distributed of the green grapes. Their California season begins in July and continues until October. We get some Thompsons from South America in late winter.

WITH SEEDS

Almeria: Large oval grapes, crisp and juicy, with sweet winey flavor. The California season extends from late August to midfall.

Black Ribier: Large, blue-black grapes with tart, full-bodied flavor. Their season is August through February.

Cardinal: Deep red grape streaked with green and yellow, Cardinal grapes are round, firm, and loaded with juice. It is the first grape of the season, appearing in May and disappearing by mid-July.

Champagne: Tiny purple Champagne grapes look like miniature grape clusters. They are crisp, sweet, rosy, and delicious. Eat them with the tiny stems. It is one of the few wine grapes that are equally delicious at the table. Their season is late summer to early fall.

Concord: Large, purple-black grape with a tough skin and large seeds. They are most widely used for jams and jellies, but we think they make good eating, too. Slip the skin off if you don't like the tart taste. Their season is very short—just three weeks in early fall.

Flame Tokay: Red, juicy grapes with large seeds. Their flavor is second only to Red Flame. Their season extends from July to October.

Muscat: These grapes are prized in Europe but rarely seen here. They are very large, yellow-green, with a heady, winey flavor—delicious with cheese. Their season is late—October through November.

Red Emperor: A maroon-colored oval grape with juice, crunch, and a cherry-like flavor. Their season is early fall to midwinter, with South American imports appearing from November to February.

LIME MOUSSE

A tart and tasty way to end a meal. For a glamorous presentation, fill balloon wine glasses with the mousse and garnish with berries. Or you could place the mousse in a tart shell and top it with bitter chocolate sauce. Just remember to make it a day ahead.

4 eggs, separated
1½ cups sugar
1 envelope unflavored gelatin
¼ cup cold water
1 teaspoon cornstarch
8 tablespoons fresh lime juice
2 tablespoons finely grated lime zest
4 tablespoons rum (optional)
1½ cups heavy or whipping cream
3 tablespoons confectioners' sugar
Fresh berries, for garnish (optional)

1. Combine the egg yolks and the sugar in a bowl, and beat with an electric mixer until pale yellow. Set aside.

2. Combine the gelatin and the cold water in the top of a double boiler and stir together to soften the gelatin. Place the pan over simmering water and stir until the gelatin has dissolved. Remove the pan from the heat.

3. In a small bowl, combine the cornstarch and 3 tablespoons of the lime juice; stir until smooth. Add the remaining 5 tablespoons lime juice, the lime zest, and the softened gelatin. Stir well.

4. Add the lime mixture to the egg yolk mixture and whisk thoroughly. Transfer to the top of a double boiler and cook over hot (not boiling) water, stirring constantly, until the custard has thickened, about 20 minutes. Add 2 tablespoons of the rum and cook, stirring, 1 minute more. Transfer the custard to a medium-size bowl.

5. Set the bowl with the custard in a larger bowl filled with ice, and chill until the custard is almost set, about 30 minutes.

6. Whip the cream with an electric mixer, gradually adding the remaining 2 tablespoons rum and the confectioners' sugar, until it is stiff. Wash and dry the mixer blades.

7. Beat the egg whites with the mixer in another bowl until stiff.

8. Using a rubber spatula, gently fold the whipped cream and the egg whites into the chilled lime custard. Refrigerate the mousse, loosely covered, until it is thoroughly chilled, at least 4 hours.

9. Serve in individual dessert bowls or in a large serving bowl, garnished with berries.

6 to 8 portions

HOT LEMON MOUSSE

A hot and zesty version of the tangy lemon tart we love so much. For a very special treat, sprinkle with fresh Crystallized Candied Ginger.

4 tablespoons (½ stick) unsalted butter
6 tablespoons fresh lemon juice
⅔ cup sugar
4 egg yolks
Finely grated zest of 2 lemons
5 egg whites
Pinch of salt

1. Butter four 1½-cup ramekins or small soufflé dishes and sprinkle them with sugar.

2. Combine the butter, lemon juice, and ⅓ cup of the sugar in a saucepan. Bring just to a boil, and then remove from the heat. Add the egg yolks one at a time, mixing thoroughly with each addition. Stir in the lemon zest. Cook over medium-low heat, stirring constantly, until the mixture thickens, 7 to 10 minutes. (Do not let it boil or it will curdle.)

3. Preheat the oven to 400°F.

4. Beat the egg whites and salt with an electric mixer until they form soft peaks. Sprinkle the remaining ⅓ cup sugar over the whites and continue beating until glossy, about 30 seconds more.

5. Fold one quarter of the whites into the lemon mixture; then gently fold in the remaining whites until thoroughly blended.

6. Divide the mixture among the ramekins and smooth the tops. Bake until puffed and golden, 12 to 15 minutes. Serve immediately.

4 portions

THE CITRUS GROVE

Citrus fruits were once very rare and a symbol of wealth and power. The fruits arrived in America in the late fifteenth century with the Spanish explorers who kept them on board to combat scurvy. The warmer southern regions of the New World, especially the Caribbean, Florida, and the southwest, were perfect for growing citrus trees.

The first citrus fruit we know of was citron, which was followed by the lemon, lime, orange, grapefruit, and mandarin. Today markets are abundant with pomelos, kumquats, clementines, and blood oranges—each with a slightly different fresh tart taste.

Citrus fruits are wonderfully low in calories and sodium and high in vitamin C. With a fresh flavor and natural sweetness, citrus pulp, zest, and juice can be used in endless ways to enhance dishes.

Finding the best fruit is similar for most citrus varieties. Skin color is not as important as thin skin and heaviness, which indicates the fruit is mature. Many citrus fruits are available all year round, but peak season for most varieities is December to March.

FRUIT	SEASON	BUYING TIPS	STORAGE
CITRON The first citrus fruit—very large and heavy. Most often candied.	February and March	Look for firm, heavy fruit with unblemished skin.	At room temperature up to 3 to 4 days; in plastic bag in refrigerator up to 1 month
GRAPEFRUIT Sweet-tart fruit with yellow to blush yellow skin. Types include white, pink, seedless, Florida, ruby, and star ruby.	Year round	Look for nearly flawless, smooth skin and firm, heavy fruit.	At room temperature up to 1 week; in plastic bag in refrigerator up to 6 weeks
KUMQUAT Tiny fruit the size of a large grape, sweet skin and tart pulp—eat skin and pulp in one bite.	December to February	Look for smooth, unblemished fruit with fresh greens attached.	In refrigerator up to 1 week
LEMON Sunny yellow, sour-tart fruit with high acidity.	Year round	Look for smooth, thin skin with no tinge of green. Avoid bruised or wrinkled fruit.	At room temperature 3 to 4 days; in plastic bag in refrigerator up to 1 month
LIME Green to yellow-green, sour fruit with high acidity.	Year round	Buy fruit with thin, smooth green skin—unshriveled and firm.	At room temperature 3 to 4 days; in plastic bag in refrigerator up to 2 weeks

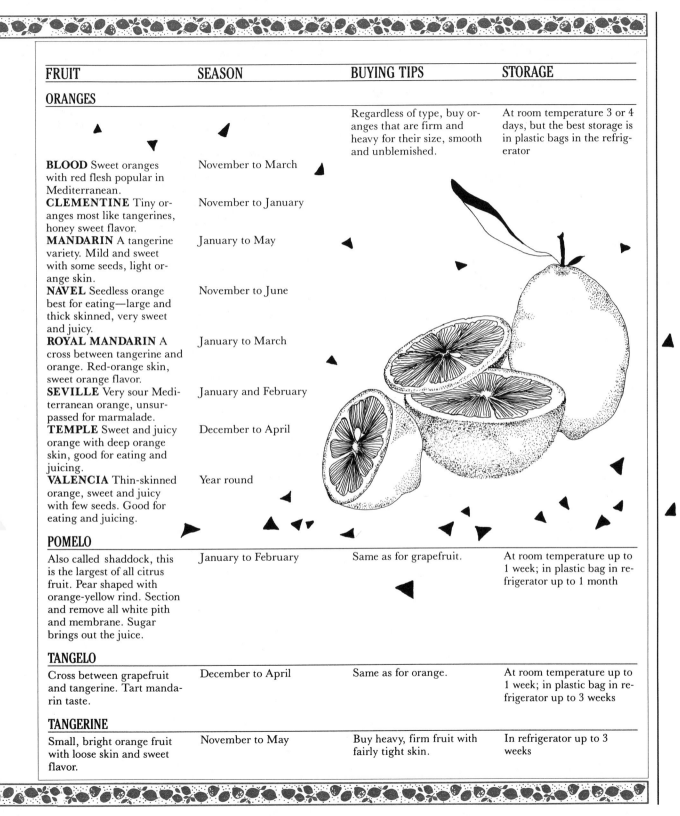

FRUIT	SEASON	BUYING TIPS	STORAGE
ORANGES		Regardless of type, buy oranges that are firm and heavy for their size, smooth and unblemished.	At room temperature 3 or 4 days, but the best storage is in plastic bags in the refrigerator
BLOOD Sweet oranges with red flesh popular in Mediterranean.	November to March		
CLEMENTINE Tiny oranges most like tangerines, honey sweet flavor.	November to January		
MANDARIN A tangerine variety. Mild and sweet with some seeds, light orange skin.	January to May		
NAVEL Seedless orange best for eating—large and thick skinned, very sweet and juicy.	November to June		
ROYAL MANDARIN A cross between tangerine and orange. Red-orange skin, sweet orange flavor.	January to March		
SEVILLE Very sour Mediterranean orange, unsurpassed for marmalade.	January and February		
TEMPLE Sweet and juicy orange with deep orange skin, good for eating and juicing.	December to April		
VALENCIA Thin-skinned orange, sweet and juicy with few seeds. Good for eating and juicing.	Year round		
POMELO			
Also called shaddock, this is the largest of all citrus fruit. Pear shaped with orange-yellow rind. Section and remove all white pith and membrane. Sugar brings out the juice.	January to February	Same as for grapefruit.	At room temperature up to 1 week; in plastic bag in refrigerator up to 1 month
TANGELO			
Cross between grapefruit and tangerine. Tart mandarin taste.	December to April	Same as for orange.	At room temperature up to 1 week; in plastic bag in refrigerator up to 3 weeks
TANGERINE			
Small, bright orange fruit with loose skin and sweet flavor.	November to May	Buy heavy, firm fruit with fairly tight skin.	In refrigerator up to 3 weeks

FROZEN CITRUS SOUFFLES

With the refreshing coolness and zest of citrus, these individual soufflés are the perfect ending to a lavish meal. They can be prepared well ahead of time and make a dazzling impression. Be creative with garnish—you might top them with candied violets.

1 cup heavy or whipping cream
3 egg whites
Pinch of salt
1 cup superfine sugar
1 tablespoon fresh lemon juice
Finely grated zest of 2 oranges
Finely grated zest of 2 lemons
Finely grated zest of 2 limes

1. Butter four ¾-cup ramekins, and sprinkle them with sugar. Tear off strips of waxed paper long enough to wrap around the ramekins, and fold them in half lengthwise. Using string or rubber bands, secure the strips around the ramekins so that they extend 2 to 2½ inches above the rim (see page 447).

2. Whip the cream with an electric mixer until it forms soft peaks. Wash and dry the mixer blades.

3. Beat the egg whites and salt with the mixer until they form soft peaks. Sprinkle the whites with 2 tablespoons of the superfine sugar and beat until glossy, about 30 seconds more.

4. Fold the remaining superfine sugar, the lemon juice, and all but ½ cup of the whipped cream into the whites. Put the remaining whipped cream, loosely covered, in the refrigerator. Stir the three zests together, and fold all but 1 teaspoon of the mixture into the whites.

5. Divide the soufflé mixture among the prepared ramekins, and chill them in the freezer until completely frozen, 2 to 3 hours.

6. Remove the waxed paper strips from the frozen soufflés, and top each soufflé with a dollop of the remaining ½ cup whipped cream. Sprinkle with the reserved teaspoon of citrus zest, and serve.

4 portions

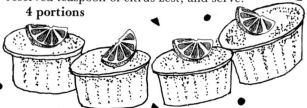

FROZEN STRAWBERRY CASSIS SOUFFLES

A tablespoon of cassis adds a richness to ripe summer or winter strawberries. Try not to refrigerate the berries before using, as they may become watery. Decorate these pink confections with candied roses for Valentine's Day, or scatter pink rose petals around a little saucer under the soufflés.

1 cup heavy or whipping cream
1 quart strawberries, lightly rinsed, drained, and hulled
1 tablespoon crème de cassis
1 cup sugar
3 egg whites
Pinch of salt

1. Butter four ¾-cup ramekins, and sprinkle them with sugar. Tear off strips of waxed paper long enough to wrap around the ramekins, and fold them in half lengthwise. Using string or rubber bands, secure the strips around the ramekins so that they extend 2 to 2½ inches above the rim (see page 447).

2. Whip the cream until it forms soft peaks. Wash and dry the mixer blades.

3. Reserve 6 to 8 of the best-looking strawberries, and purée the rest in a food processor. Stir in the cassis and all but 2 tablespoons of the sugar.

4. Beat the egg whites and salt with the mixer until they form soft peaks. Sprinkle the whites with the remaining sugar and beat until glossy, about 30 seconds more.

5. Fold the strawberry purée and all but ½ cup of the whipped cream into the whites. Put the remaining whipped cream, loosely covered, in the refrigerator.

6. Divide the soufflé mixture among the prepared ramekins, and chill them in the freezer until completely frozen, 2 to 3 hours.

7. Remove the waxed paper strips from the frozen soufflés, and top each soufflé with a dollop of the remaining ½ cup whipped cream. Top with the reserved strawberries, and serve.

6 to 8 portions

SOUFFLES

A soufflé base is similar to a custard, yet soufflés are in a class by themselves. Sweet or savory, soufflés never cease to dazzle. A good soufflé rises above its dish and is slightly moist inside. It will continue to cook on its way to the table, so be sure not to overcook a soufflé or it will be dry inside.

The soufflé base can be made one or even two days in advance. The beaten egg whites, which make the soufflé rise, should be gently folded in at the last minute. Soufflés can be made in all sorts of straight-sided dishes, large and small. Check carefully to be sure the volume of the dish or dishes is suited to the recipe —the unbaked mixture should fill the dish no less than three quarters full. We recommend buttering the sides as well as the bottom of the dish, then dusting with sugar for sweet soufflés or grated Parmesan for savories. Gently scoop the mixture into the prepared mold and bake it in a preheated oven according to the recipe. Wait the cooking time before opening the door, and anticipate raves!

We like to serve sauce or berries with the soufflé by poking a hole in the center with a small spoon and ladling the sauce in.

APRICOTS

★

▲ With Roquefort and whole walnuts
▲ Ripe and sunny with Camembert
▲ Preserves spread over Coeur de Brie on toasted walnut bread
▲ With sweet Gorgonzola
▲ Preserves on fresh cream cheese
▲ With a tangy Cheddar and pistachios

SALLY DARR'S APRICOT SOUFFLES

When the restaurant La Tulipe first opened in New York, we were all thrilled. Sally Darr is a wonderful chef and her husband, John, a most gracious host. Sally's apricot soufflé is the very best! If you're in New York on Valentine's Day, remember La Tulipe— it's super-romantic.

It's important to use California apricots here—no others have their color and flavor. The apricot purée will keep for several weeks in the refrigerator.

8 ounces dried California apricots
2½ cups water
1 cup superfine sugar
3 tablespoons fresh lemon juice
6 large egg whites
Pinch of salt
Confectioners' sugar
1 cup heavy or whipping cream, whipped

1. Combine the apricots and 1½ cups of the water in a 2-quart saucepan, and set aside for 2 hours.

2. Add the remaining 1 cup water to the apricots, and bring to a boil over medium heat. Cover, reduce the heat to low, and cook for 20 minutes.

3. Transfer the mixture to a food processor and process until smooth, stopping once to scrape down the bowl, about 45 seconds. Strain the purée into a large mixing bowl.

4. Stir ¾ cup of the superfine sugar and 2 tablespoons of the lemon juice into the purée. Let the mixture cool and then refrigerate it, covered, for at least 1 hour.

5. Butter eight 1-cup or ten to twelve smaller soufflé molds. Dust them with superfine sugar, and refrigerate the molds for 30 minutes.

6. Beat the egg whites and salt with an electric mixer until they form soft peaks. Gradually beat in the remaining ¼ cup superfine sugar, and then the remaining 1 tablespoon lemon juice. Continue to beat the mixture until it forms stiff, shiny peaks.

7. Stir 1 cup of the egg whites into the apricot purée. Then fold the mixture back into the egg whites with a large rubber spatula. Pour it into the prepared molds, mounding the mixture about 1 inch above the rim.

8. Using a metal spatula, shape the top of the mixture into a cone. Make a spiral groove with your finger about one quarter of the way in from the edge of the mold. Bring the mixture up and let it fall off the end of your finger to form a topknot. Smooth the edge with a small knife, and wipe off the rim of the mold. Refrigerate for up to 1 hour.

9. Meanwhile, preheat the oven to 375°F.

10. Put the soufflés in a shallow baking pan, and pour in enough hot water to reach one third of the way up the sides of the molds. Bake for 30 minutes.

11. Remove the soufflés from the pan, and sift confectioners' sugar over the tops. With a tablespoon, remove the tops of the soufflés, fill the cavities with a bit of whipped cream, and replace the lids lightly. Serve immediately.

8 to 12 portions

FRESH APRICOTS

Apricots arrive early in the bountiful summer fruit season. Their season is brief—from late May to early August. Currently, 97 percent of our domestic crop is grown on about 24,000 acres of the San Joaquin Valley. Sixty percent of the crop is canned and another 25 percent is dried. A scant 6 percent is sold fresh.

To be at their best, apricots must be picked when they are ripe and plump; unfortunately, when they are best for picking, they are at their most fragile for shipping. Many apricots are picked when not fully mature, which is a mistake because they will never ripen properly. They are either hard and bitter or soft and dry. Squeeze them or ask to taste one before you buy. With any luck, they will have been flown in.

To prepare fresh apricots, simply wash and cut in half to remove the pit. A good fresh apricot is truly precious, so serve them simply with just a dollop of yogurt or crème fraîche if you must. If you are so lucky as to have a ripe tree, you can make tarts, soufflés, ice cream, chutney, preserves, wine, and brandied apricots. And be sure to give plenty away to your friends!

BLACKBERRY SOUFFLES

We've made these beautiful soufflés in individual portions and sprinkled them with confectioners' sugar. Just perfect for an Easter dessert.

1 cup blackberries, lightly rinsed
½ cup water
½ cup sugar
1 egg yolk
1 tablespoon heavy or whipping cream
3 egg whites
Few drops of fresh lemon juice
Confectioners' sugar, for dusting

1. Preheat the oven to 400°F. Butter six ½-cup ramekins, and sprinkle them with sugar.

2. In a small saucepan, heat the berries, water, and ¼ cup of the sugar to a simmer. Cover, and simmer 10 minutes.

3. Allow the berries to cool slightly, and then pass them through a food mill. You should have about ¾ cup syrup.

4. Stir the syrup, egg yolk, and cream together in a medium-size bowl.

5. Beat the egg whites and lemon juice with an electric mixer until frothy. Then slowly add the remaining ¼ cup sugar, beating until the whites are stiff but not dry.

6. Stir one quarter of the whites into the syrup mixture. Then gently and quickly fold in the remaining whites until well blended. Arrange the prepared ramekins on a baking sheet and fill them with the soufflé mixture.

7. Bake until puffed, 8 minutes. Sift confectioners' sugar over the top, and serve immediately.

6 soufflés

RED BERRY MOUSSE

End a meal or a day with a lovely blushing-pink cloud of red berries. You'll want to begin picking anew the next morning, for more berry mousse.

1 envelope unflavored gelatin
2 tablespoons cold water
Juice of 1 lemon
Grated zest of 1 lemon
1 pint raspberries, lightly rinsed and drained
1 pint strawberries, lightly rinsed, drained, hulled, and
   quartered
2 tablespoons crème de cassis
2 egg yolks
½ cup sugar
2 cups heavy or whipping cream
Fresh mint sprigs, for garnish

1. Combine the gelatin and water in a small saucepan, and set aside to soak for 5 minutes.

2. Stir the lemon juice into the softened gelatin. Then add the zest, raspberries (reserving a few for garnish), strawberries, and Cassis. Bring gently to a boil, stirring frequently, and then set aside to cool to room temperature.

3. Combine the egg yolks and sugar in a small bowl, and beat until pale yellow. Transfer the mixture to a double boiler and cook over simmering water, whisking, until hot and slightly thickened, 10 to 15 minutes. Set aside this custard to cool.

4. Fold the berry mixture thoroughly into the cooled custard.

5. Whip the cream with an electric mixer until it forms soft peaks, and gently fold it into the mixture. Scoop the mousse into a glass bowl or large individual wine goblets, and refrigerate until set.

6. Garnish with the reserved raspberries and sprigs of mint, and serve.

6 portions

GALETTE OF RHUBARB

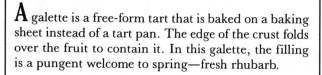

A galette is a free-form tart that is baked on a baking sheet instead of a tart pan. The edge of the crust folds over the fruit to contain it. In this galette, the filling is a pungent welcome to spring—fresh rhubarb.

PASTRY
1 ¼ cups unbleached all-purpose flour
1 tablespoon granulated sugar
¼ teaspoon salt
6 (¾ stick) tablespoons unsalted butter, cold, cut in pieces
1 teaspoon finely grated orange zest
2 tablespoons ice water

5 tablespoons confectioners' sugar
2 ½ cups rhubarb chunks (1-inch chunks), see Note, page 692
Slivered orange zest

1. Prepare the pastry shell: Combine the flour, sugar, and salt in a medium-size mixing bowl, and toss well to blend. Using a pastry blender, 2 knives, or your fingertips, cut in the butter and the orange zest until the mixture resembles coarse crumbs.

2. Sprinkle the water, 1 tablespoon at a time, over the mixture and toss with a fork until the mixture can be gathered into a ball. Knead it once or twice, then flatten it slightly. Cover the dough with plastic wrap and refrigerate for 30 minutes.

3. Meanwhile, preheat the oven to 350°F.

4. Roll out the chilled dough on a lightly floured surface to form an 11-inch circle. Transfer it to a baking sheet.

5. Lightly mark off a 9-inch circle in the center of the dough. Trim away the ragged edges to neaten it up. Sprinkle the marked off area with 3 tablespoons of the confectioners' sugar. Spread the rhubarb evenly over the sugar, then sprinkle on the remaining 2 tablespoons of confectioners' sugar. Top with the slivered orange zest.

6. Fold up the edge of dough to cover the fruit slightly.

7. Bake the galette until the crust is golden and the filling bubbles, 40 minutes. Cool slightly before serving.

Serves 6

BLUSHING PEARS

This is a perfect dessert after an important meal—lovely on individual plates or in a crystal bowl.

½ cup sugar
1 ½ quarts cranberry-raspberry juice
1 cinnamon stick
6 ripe pears, peeled
1 cup heavy or whipping cream
1 pint raspberries

1. Combine the sugar and the juice in a large saucepan, and heat over medium heat, stirring until the sugar has dissolved. Add the cinnamon stick.

2. Bring the mixture to a gentle boil and add the pears. Poach at a low simmer, turning the pears carefully, until they are easily pierced with a knife, about 20 minutes.

3. Allow the pears to cool in the syrup, carefully turning them once or twice. When they are cool, drain them, reserving 3 cups of the syrup.

4. Place the reserved syrup over high heat and reduce it to about 1 cup. Set it aside to cool.

5. Whip the cream until it forms soft peaks. Reserve about ½ cup of the raspberries and stir the rest into the whipped cream. Pour some of the reserved syrup onto each plate, and place a pear on top of it. Pour a little more syrup over the pears, coating them. Add a dollop of raspberry cream to each plate, and sprinkle with the reserved raspberries. Serve immediately.

6 portions

CLEMENTINES ORIENTALES

This compote, with its rum-laced amber syrup, caramel-glazed clementines and kumquats, and sprinkling of little pomegranate rubies, is a stunning finale when served in a large crystal bowl.

SYRUP
1 ¼ cups water
1 cup sugar

CARAMEL
1 cup sugar
¼ cup water

20 kumquats, rinsed, drained, halved
  lengthwise, and seeded
8 clementines, peeled, and halved crosswise
½ cup dark rum
Seeds of ½ pomegranate

1. Prepare the syrup: Combine the water and sugar in a saucepan and heat over medium-low heat until the sugar has dissolved. Simmer for 5 minutes. Then cover the pan and let the syrup simmer as you prepare the caramel.

2. To make the caramel, heat the sugar and water over medium-low heat in a heavy saucepan until the sugar has dissolved. Cook the syrup until it forms an amber-colored caramel, brushing away any crystals that may form on the edge with a wet pastry brush. The mixture will be very hot.

3. Very carefully pour the hot caramel into the simmering syrup (it will spit and sputter). Cook just until smooth. Allow the mixture to cool slightly.

4. Place the kumquats and clementines in a heat-proof bowl, and pour the hot syrup over them. Stir in the rum and pomegranate seeds. Cover, and refrigerate overnight, stirring occasionally.

8 portions

POMEGRANATES WITH CHEESE

- Seeds sprinkled and juice drizzled over L'Explorateur
- Seeds nibbled with sheep's-milk yogurt
- Seeds and juice atop farmer's cheese

MADEIRA

Madeira is produced only on a tiny island of the same name about 400 miles off the Moroccan coast. In the 1800s it was discovered that the wine of this island improved with the long sea voyages necessary for export.

The original wine was made for export from surplus grapes and fortified with additional alcohol to survive the journey in prime condition. Now to produce Madeira, the fermented wine is held in casks for six months; the temperature is gradually increased to 114°F, then allowed to drop back to normal. The effect is the same as was achieved on early ocean voyages to East India. Sweet Madeiras are fortified with brandy before this process, killing the yeast and halting the fermentation. Drier Madeiras are fortified after the process. The wines then age for 18 months and are blended to develop depth of flavor and consistency from year to year.

There are several styles of Madeira, each based on a particular grape variety. The Malvasia grape produces a sweet, rich, dark Madeira called Malmsey. Serve Malmsey at room temperature after a good meal.

The Bual grape produces Bual Madeira. This Madeira is rich and sweet in flavor with a dark color and distinctive aroma. It is an excellent dessert wine.

Verdelho Madeira comes from a grape of the same name. This Madeira is smoky and medium sweet with a gentle fruit flavor. It is excellent added to soups and sauces. Rainwater is a pale Verdelho style of Madeira that was originally lightened by letting rainwater seep into the casks during shipment. It is very popular in the States because of its lighter style.

Sercial Madeira is considered the best of the dry Madeiras. It is somewhat like a German Riesling with its savory spirit and steely acidity. Chill it and serve it as an aperitif.

Madeiras have longer lives than any other wine and the flavor becomes more concentrated with age. Classified according to age, a class-three Madeira will be from three to five years old. Class two contains wine that are seven years of age. All wines of at least ten years are class one. The word "Reserve" on the label indicates the Madeira is blended, the youngest wine in the blend being five years old. "Special Reserve" indicates a blend at least ten years old, and "Extra Reserve" is used for wines at least fifteen years old.

Because it costs twice as much to make a Madeira than a port, a good Madeira is fairly expensive. Look for a minimum age of ten years and you won't be disappointed.

The best Madeira is purely a matter of taste. We consider Sercial and Verdelho, the driest Madeira, best for an apertif. Be sure to chill it well. Madiera served with dessert or after dinner should be at room temperature. For these occasions serve a Malmsey or Bual.

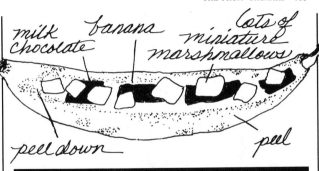

BANANAS FOSTER

We have reinterpreted this classic—created at the Commander's Palace in New Orleans in the 1950s—for a quick, luscious dessert prepared in the microwave.

3 tablespoons banana cordial
¼ cup dark rum
4 tablespoons (½ stick) unsalted butter
¼ cup (packed) dark brown sugar
2 bananas, peeled and halved lengthwise
¼ teaspoon ground cinnamon
Vanilla Vanilla Ice Cream (see Index)

1. Stir the banana cordial and rum together in a small bowl, and set aside.

2. Place the butter in a 9-inch square microwave-safe dish and melt at full power (650 to 700 watts) for 1½ minutes.

3. Stir the brown sugar into the melted butter. Turn the banana halves in the mixture, coating them well, and then arrange them, flat side down, in the dish. Sprinkle with the cinnamon, cover, and return to the microwave. Cook for 1½ minutes.

4. Drizzle the rum mixture over the bananas, recover, and return to the microwave. Cook for 1 minute.

5. Place a scoop of ice cream in the center of each dessert plate and arrange the banana halves around it. Spoon the hot sauce over, and serve immediately.

2 portions

Notes: Traditionally the bananas are flambéed when the rum mixture is added, but microwave cooking may prevent the rum from igniting. The bananas are still delicious.

This recipe was cooked on High (full power, 650 to 700 watts) in a carousel microwave, using microwave-safe containers.

If your microwave is less powerful, you will have to allow for more cooking time (approximately 1½ times the amount called for—but watch carefully); if it does not have a carousel, you may have to rotate the dish while it is cooking.

ANNABEL'S BANANA BOAT

Sheila's daughter, Annabel, has spent many happy hours around her summer campfire eating these yummy treats. She was anxious to share the recipe but it was wintertime, so we decided to try it in the microwave. It's a yummy treat again!

1 bright yellow banana
1 plain Hershey bar (about 2 ounces)
Miniature marshmallows, to taste

1. Starting from the stem end, peel back one third of the banana peel along the concave side to ¾ inch from the bottom, making a flap.

2. With the tip of a teaspoon, scoop out a lengthwise ¼-inch-thick strip of banana so that it resembles a canoe. Eat the scooped-out strip and continue with the recipe.

3. Lay three or four pieces of the chocolate bar along the indentation. Top with as many marshmallows as you can fit.

4. Fold the banana peel flap back over the marshmallows, and wrap the banana tightly with microwave-safe plastic wrap. Cook on medium-high power (70 percent) for 1 minute.

5. Carefully remove the plastic wrap. Place the banana on a plate, peel back the flap, and dig in.

1 portion

Note: This recipe was cooked on Medium-High (70 percent) in a carousel microwave (650 to 700 watts), using microwave-safe containers.

If your microwave is less powerful, you will have to allow for more cooking time (approximately 1½ times the amount called for—but watch carefully); if it does not have a carousel, you may have to rotate the dish while it is cooking.

ISLAND FRUITS

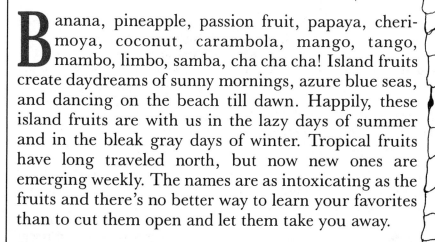

Banana, pineapple, passion fruit, papaya, cherimoya, coconut, carambola, mango, tango, mambo, limbo, samba, cha cha cha! Island fruits create daydreams of sunny mornings, azure blue seas, and dancing on the beach till dawn. Happily, these island fruits are with us in the lazy days of summer and in the bleak gray days of winter. Tropical fruits have long traveled north, but now new ones are emerging weekly. The names are as intoxicating as the fruits and there's no better way to learn your favorites than to cut them open and let them take you away.

MELONS

To be good, a melon must first smell like a melon. Let your nose be your guide when choosing one. Next, the melon should be heavy for its size and have a little give when pressed. A hard melon with little aroma will improve with just a day or two to ripen, but if you can hear the seeds slosh when you shake it, it's been left too long—it's overripe. Ripen melons in a cool dry place and refrigerate them once they are ripe.

There are three classifications for melons. The first is the true cantaloupe of the Charentais variety, usually found only in Europe. It is oblong and green with a netted rind. The flesh is brilliant orange, sweet, and juicy.

The cantaloupe typically found in American markets is technically a muskmelon. There are two kinds—our cantaloupe, with a season from June to September, and the oval muskmelon, which is fragile and only grown locally.

The third group of melons includes Casaba, Crenshaw, Persian, Spanish, and honeydew melons. All are smooth-skinned and less aromatic than other melons.

When the Persian melon is ripe, its gray-green skin turns to gray-gold. The best month for Persian melons is August. Serve chilled or at room temperature with a splash of lime juice.

The Casaba melon has white flesh with a yellow edge next to the seeds. They have little fragrance unless vine-ripened. The best Casaba melons are found in late summer. Buy those that feel slightly sticky and have a little give when pressed.

The Crenshaw melon is large and oval with tapered ends. The skin is golden when ripe.

Because Spanish melons arrive at the market in late December, they are often called Christmas melons. The skin is green and hard and the melons have little fragrance. The yellow flesh is firm but juicy.

Honeydew melons have cool green flesh. When ripe, the skin turns from white to soft gold and feels slightly sticky. Most honeydews are picked green because they are too fragile to transport when ripe. The pink-flesh honeydew ripens more easily than the green honeydew. The skin turns

MELONS WITH CHEESE

▼

- Slice hot-pink watermelons alongside Explorateur with rich black bread

- Slice yellow watermelons, drizzle with Chartreuse, and serve with sweet Gorgonzola

- Scoop out a Charentais melon, drizzle with Beaujolais, add a dollop of fresh chèvre, and garnish with mint

- Fill a Casaba with farmer's cheese and sprinkle with toasted coconut

- Make honeydew balls, dollop with mascarpone, and sprinkle with chopped hazelnuts

- Serve Creamy Havarti with cantaloupe and drizzle with honey

- Place a dollop of creamy Saga Blue inside a halved Charentais melon

- Alternate Casaba wedges with Taleggio wedges

- Sprinkle watermelon balls with a drop of framboise eau-de-vie and serve with fromage blanc

- Serve Pipo Crème with yellow watermelon

golden when ripe and the melons have a strong perfume and give softly when touched. The flesh is not quite as sweet as the green but it is juicier. Look for the "pink flesh" label at your market.

Watermelon season begins each year in the months of May and June with melons from Texas and Florida. These melons have a subtle flavor, light gray-green skin, and weigh between ten and twenty pounds.

The dark green striped watermelons, weighing up to fifty pounds, from Florida, Georgia, and the Carolinas, come to market in early summer. They have a sugary crisp flavor and deep red flesh.

By midsummer local farmers begin to bring in their crops. Crimsons are round and have few seeds. They weigh in at about twenty pounds and have a very crisp texture. The small light green Sugar Babies and the yellow and dark green Cannonballs have sweet juicy flesh and very few seeds.

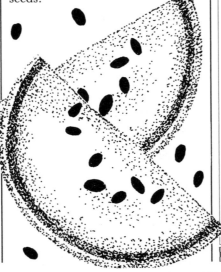

BANANAS

Buy bananas that are firm and plump, green at the stems, and in a bunch. Ripen in a brown paper bag or in a bowl at room temperature. Once they are ripe you can refrigerate them; the skins will turn black but that will not affect the fruit inside. For baking, broiling, or sautéing, catch them when they are still a little green so they

BANANAS AND PLANTAINS WITH CHEESE

- Bake bananas and top with a dollop of mascarpone

- Fry plantains and serve with English Double Gloucester Cheddar cheese

- Slice bananas over farmer's cheese, top with lowfat yogurt, and sprinkle with pumpkin seeds

- Serve fried plantain chips with spicy Gaperon

- Spread cream cheese on toasted Multi-Grain Bread and top with sliced bananas and wildflower honey

- Stir bananas into sheep's-milk yogurt and sprinkle with chopped macadamia nuts

don't cook to mush. Fully ripe bananas are best for mashing, and frozen bananas are a favorite summertime treat.

We no longer see just one type of banana at the market. The most familiar is the Cavendish, or speckled banana. It demands a great deal of care in shipping to prevent bruising. Three medium bananas weigh about one pound.

The Red Cuban banana is short and fat with thick purplish red skin. The fruit is dark and creamy and filled with fine black specks. The flavor is much more intense than the common yellow banana. It is good in fruit salads and blender drinks.

The Chicaditas, or Lady Finger banana, is small, yellow, and very sweet. Another miniature banana, the lemon banana, is small and round with a lemon color and flavor.

The plantain is a vegetable-like banana that is eaten ripe as well as unripe but never raw. The flavor is bland. Unripe, the plantain can be cut into chunks and added to stews or split and fried or grilled. As it ripens and the skin turns to yellow, the plaintain gets creamier when cooked. We like to cook it and mix it with apples or sweet potatoes, or bake it and serve it like a baked potato. When the skin turns black, the plantain most resembles a yellow banana. Try sautéing ripe plantains in butter, then sprinkling them with brown sugar, and browning them under the broiler. Or dip them in flour seasoned with salt and pepper and fry them to serve with black beans.

BANANAS AND . . .

- Slice bananas in a peanut butter sandwich, then grill like a grilled cheese sandwich—Elvis' and our favorite

- Slice red bananas into bowls and top with slightly sweetened whipped cream or yogurt

- Combine bananas with other tropical fruits and add Crystallized Candied Ginger and a splash of rum for an island dessert

- Slice over pancakes and drizzle with maple syrup

- Bananas go well with pineapples, apricots, oranges, strawberries, and raspberries

- Sauté peeled firm bananas just until soft. Heat rum, Armagnac, or Cognac, pour over bananas, and flame

- Brush peeled bananas with butter and broil, turning frequently, until soft. Sprinkle with brown sugar and dollop with sour cream

COCONUT

The fruit of a tropical palm tree, coconuts are available in markets year round, but they are best in the fall and winter because the juices ferment quickly in hot weather. Buy coconuts that feel heavy for their size. Shake them to make sure you can hear the "milk" sloshing inside, and check the "eyes" to make sure they are not wet or moldy.

To prepare coconut, pierce the three eyes with an ice pick or screwdriver. Drain off all the liquid—drink it if you want but do not confuse it with coconut milk. Bake the coconut at 350°F for 15 to 20 minutes, then break it with a hammer into large pieces. Take the meat from the shell and grate it with a little water in the food processor. A medium coconut will yield about 3 cups of grated coconut. The brown skin on the white meat does not have to be removed for it does not affect the flavor. Remove it only if you want snowy white coconut.

To make coconut milk, process the grated coconut with hot water (or milk for coconut cream), then strain and discard the pulp. The milk is the magic ingredient of real curries—it's also delicious in sauces and stirred into spicy rice dishes. The cream makes wonderful puddings, ice creams, and cakes, as well as luscious tropical drinks.

PINEAPPLES

Today ripe pineapples are shipped to stateside markets from Hawaii, the Caribbean, Central America, and Mexico. They are available year round but the peak season is spring.

We find two varieties on the market. The small Red Spanish pineapple ripens to a red-orange color and has a taste that is more acid than sweet.

We much prefer the Cayenne pineapple, which is sweet, soft, and very juicy. Cayennes are picked ripe and shipped "jet fresh" from Hawaii, Mexico, and Central America. They are more expensive than the Red Spanish but well worth the price.

Everyone tries to guess the best ripe pineapple by plucking a leaf, sniffing the aroma, or checking for softness. It's not necessary. Pineapples are field ripened and picked only after the fruit has developed the necessary degree of sugar. A pineapple will not ripen after harvesting. A ripe pineapple can be mostly green or mostly yellow and still be ripe. If kept too long, pineapples get soft and mushy, so buy ones that are firm and plump, with a green crown and shiny skin.

We like to serve pineapple fresh in long wedges, but you can cut rings or chunks if you prefer. First cut off the top and trim the bottom so that it stands upright. Using a sharp knife, cut away the skin, then go back and trim any eyes. Slice in wedges or rings and cut away the core. Cut pineapple can be refrigerated for up to one week.

PINEAPPLES WITH CHEESE

- Melt jalapeño Jack cheese on pineapple slices and country ham atop corn bread

- Serve Pineapple Salsa atop a cheese burrito

- Stir fresh pineapple chunks into fresh ricotta cheese, spoon into a pineapple shell, and sprinkle with poppy seeds

- Serve thinly sliced pineapple on soft raisin pumpernickel spread with Pipo Crème cheese

KIWIS WITH CHEESE

- Sliced with a dollop of Explorateur

- With a log of creamy Caprini

- Layered with fresh chèvre and garnished with a violet

KIWIS

A kiwi looks like an oversize fuzzy brown egg. As curious as it is on the outside, it is gorgeous inside with bright green flesh studded with tiny edible black seeds. The taste is refreshing and plum-like. Since they don't brown when cut and the color is unusual and dramatic, kiwis have come to garnish pastries, cakes, and tarts from coast to coast.

Kiwis are also delicious on their own. We like to cut them in half and eat them right out of the skin with a spoon. Kiwis are also delicious in chicken and seafood salads, in sorbets and ices, and combined with other fruits.

Kiwis don't bruise easily so they are easy to transport and store. We get kiwis from both California and New Zealand—the combination of the two keeps this fruit in the market year round.

Kiwis are cooled upon harvesting and will not ripen until placed in a warm environment. Buy firm kiwis and ripen in a bowl or in a paper bag at room temperature. Kiwis should be soft before you eat them; anything less will make you pucker. Once ripe, they will keep in the refrigerator up to two weeks. Kiwis should be peeled; the skin is edible but unpleasant.

MANGOES

A ripe mango is an unforgettable experience—velvety and juicy, peachy sweet.

Some varieties are round and plump; others are kidney shaped. They weigh anywhere from half a pound to three pounds, and are usually yellow to red orange when ripe but also occasionally green. You should be able to buy mangoes all summer long through September.

With a ripe mango, keep it simple—peel and eat. The flesh does not leave the large central pit without a struggle. You just have to cut around it with a sharp knife. Mango is as good in fruit salads as it is in green and vegetable salads or with grilled pork or chicken. It makes a delicious purée spooned over dessert or cut up and combined with pineapples and strawberries. Mango makes excellent chutney and luscious sorbet when blended with banana.

MANGOES AND PAPAYAS WITH CHEESE

- Serve ripe papayas with dry Jack cheese

- Serve Chèvre Raclette with thin slices of ripe mango

- Serve rich Munster with slices of papaya and macadamia nuts

- Fill a papaya with fresh chèvre and sprinkle with pepper and lemon zest

- Serve Fresh Mango Chutney with Cheddar cheese or Monterey Jack

- Complement a ripe mango with creamy Bleu de Bresse

- Serve a ripe mango with ripe Camembert on sourdough toast

- Find a ripe papaya in winter and enjoy it with Vacherin Mont d'Or

PAPAYAS

Papayas may be a common fruit to the world in general, but not to us. The papayas we see at the market are but one variety of this luscious fruit. Its flesh is yellow-pink to yellow-orange and the fruit has a pocket of small black seeds. The seeds are edible and make a dramatic garnish.

A papaya is ripe when it gives comfortably to thumb pressure. To ripen, keep the fruit out of the sun in a bowl or in a paper bag. Refrigerate when ripe and eat within a day or two.

Papaya is delicious in fruit salads, especially with citrus fruits, or it can be eaten alone with just a drizzle of lime juice. It combines well with meat— grilled pork, smoked turkey and chicken— and seafood; and it makes a terrific salsa.

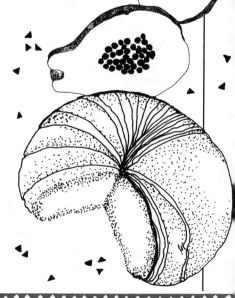

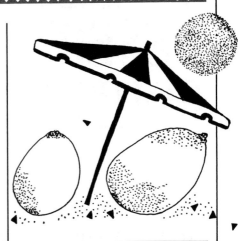

CARAMBOLAS WITH CHEESE

- Serve sliced sweet carambola with a soft blue chèvre

- Serve with sweet Gorgonzola and gingersnap cookies

- Serve the sliced stars dolloped with fresh chèvre and sprinkled with chopped pecans

- Serve sliced with a sharp Farmhouse Cheddar

A LITTLE EXOTICA

Some tropical fruits—such as pineapples, kiwis, and mangoes—have found a permanent place in American markets. Others are up and coming.

Cactus Pear: Also called prickly pear, this fruit is more egg shaped than pear shaped and its thick skin is dotted with prickles. The flesh is most like watermelon and colored exotic red or purple. These are available all year round but are best in early autumn.

Carambola: Also called star fruit, carambola is a bright yellow to green, deeply grooved, oval fruit the size of an orange. Sliced horizontally, the fruit looks like a five-sided star. You will find two varieties at the market—sweet and tart. They should be labeled. The sweet carambola can be eaten out of hand; it is very juicy and crisp and tastes like a most refreshing plum. The tart fruit can be used as you would a lemon.

Cherimoya: This fruit is heart shaped with a bumpy skin and petals. The creamy white flesh is sweet and thick and tastes like a medley of flavors—almost a tropical fruit cocktail. Cherimoyas should be left to ripen until they are soft and custardy and then chilled before eating. Eat them in the skins with a spoon.

Guava: An oval, somewhat pear shaped, perfumy fruit. Not all taste the same—some are tart, some sweet. The ripe fruit will have a slight give when pressed and the skin will turn from green to yellow. Peel and eat out of hand, mix in fruit salad, or purée for a sauce for chicken and pork.

GUAVAS WITH CHEESE

- Swirl puréed ripe guava into creamy mascarpone and sprinkle with chopped pecans

- Swirl guava purée into sheep's-milk yogurt and sprinkle with confectioners' sugar

- Spread guava jelly on cream cheese atop nutty brown bread

PASSION FRUIT WITH CHEESE

- Drizzle this rich nectar onto fresh mascarpone for a spectacular dessert

- Drizzle the juice over golden raspberries and dollop gently with fresh chèvre

Passion Fruit: Some consider passion fruit the best of all tropical fruits, but they are not much to look at, resembling most a puckered up purplish egg. But the fragrance is heady and the taste ambrosial. They are available all year round but are best in the fall. The passion fruit is ripe when you can hear the pulp slosh when you shake it. Eat out of the skin with a spoon or juice them and use the juice as a flavoring for beverages, ice creams, custards, and purées.

DESERT FRUITS

Apricots, dates, and figs are fruits of trees dating back to the beginning of civilization. The trees are baked in the sun, maturing slowly, then gracefully produce fruits for decades. Because these are such fragile fruits, we are more accustomed to eating some of them dried rather than fresh. With recent innovations in shipping and storing, we have had to learn the fresh fruit anew. We sometimes like to serve the same fruit in all its forms— fresh, dried, and cooked. These flavors are rich.

firmer figs can be found, let them ripen at room temperature. Their season extends from late summer to early fall. Store ripe figs in the refrigerator but serve them at room temperature.

Try using fresh figs in recipes calling for apricots. They can be baked or broiled simply with honey, or eaten with fresh chèvre for breakfast. They are also delicious with watercress and endive in a salad.

FIGS

Fresh figs are to us one of the most sensual fruits in the world. The flower grows within the fruit, leaving the tree with no blossoms. What is eaten is actually the pulp surrounding the fleshy blossoms.

Americans are just beginning to appreciate fresh figs—California, of course, leads in production stateside. The rest of the world depends on Spain, Italy, and Turkey for their supplies. We see basically just three varieties in the States: Black Mission figs, which are purple, honey flavored, and rich; Calimyrna figs, which are amber colored and richly flavored; and Kadota figs, which are green, fragrant, with a lighter sweet flavor.

When fully ripe, the fig secretes a sweet sap through the opening on the blossom end. They are very delicate and must be shipped carefully. Look for figs that are soft to the touch without any sour smell, which would indicate that they are overripe. If only

ROASTED FIGS

▼

Thread large ripe figs on skewers and grill them over the coals of a hot fire or under the broiler, basting once or twice with a little brandy.

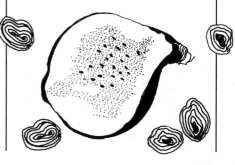

FRESH FIGS WITH CHEESE

- Serve ripe green figs with feta cheese and pistachios

- Quarter ripe purple figs and serve with sweet Gorgonzola

- Serve with fresh chèvre and a grind of black pepper

- Fall in love with ripe figs, Brin d'Amour, and toasted Olive Rosemary Country Bread

- Serve figs with rosy prosciutto and crumble on Roquefort

- Drape figs with pancetta and serve with *mozzarella di bufalo*

- Spoon fig preserves on Robiola del Bek for breakfast

- Mix mascarpone and chopped hazelnuts, then spoon the mixture over halved figs

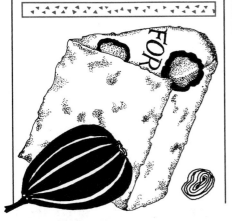

DATES

Dates are called the candy that grows on trees, for they are fully one-half sugar. More than 100 varieties are grown in southern California. They are classed soft, semidry, or dry, depending on how soft they are when ripe. Dates are excellent in baking—contributing both sweetness and richness—in salads, and combined with other fruits. They are a good source of vitamins A and B, calcium, and iron.

DRIED DATES AND APRICOTS WITH CHEESE

- Stuff dates with sweet Gorgonzola

- Serve dried apricots with St.-André, crispy toast, and Brazil nuts

- Arrange dates and apricots with a mild Kasseri

- Serve tangy dried apricots with velvety Reblochon

- Spread Doux de Montagne on buttered raisin pumpernickel with apricots

- Serve thin slices of provolone with dates for dessert

DRIED FRUIT

Dates, figs, apples, peaches, pears, plums, apricots, currants, pineapples, grapes, cherries, blueberries, and cranberries are the fruits most frequently dried. But in Tokyo we've seen lovely bright air-dried slices of strawberry, melon, and kiwi. Perhaps the best is still to come our way.

When fruits are dried in the sun or by hot air, the water content disappears and the flesh and skin darken. Dried fruits have a much higher calorie, nutrient, and sugar content than fresh. The flavor also intensifies and the fiber content increases.

Three varieties of grapes are dried for raisins: the Thompson Seedless, Muscat, and Thompson Black Corinth. Sultanas are dried from green grapes. Most of our currants come from Greece, with those from the Zante Gulf judged the best. Prunes are dried from small purple-black freestone plums.

All dried fruit must be stored tightly covered at room temperature. Dried fruit can be plumped in water, but it's more interesting to use fruit juices, wine, brandy, Cognac, rum, port, Marsala, or Armagnac.

THE ALL-AMERICAN PIE

Simple and homey or rich and fancy, pie is perfect. We all have childhood memories of walking into Grandmother's kitchen and smelling her fresh-baked pies. Or at least we wish we did. Of course, the secret to good pie has remained the same since Grandma was a little girl— fresh, fresh fillings and crisp, flaky pastry. Hot or cold, double-crusted or open-faced, brimming with fruit or creamy custard, topped with ice cream or whipped cream, pies are the quintessential American dessert.

STEPS TO MAKING GREAT CRUST

Some people take easily to making perfect pie crusts; for others it's a struggle. But it need not be. The right ingredients, the right utensils, and definitely the right temperature in the kitchen (cool, not hot) all aid in giving you the magic pastry touch.

The kind of fat used in the pastry dough varies the results slightly. Shortening or lard make a pastry that is tender and flaky. Butter and margarine can be combined with either of them for richer flavor and deeper color.

Pastry flour, a soft wheat flour with less gluten than all-purpose or bread flour, makes the tenderest crusts, but since it is not readily available, we use all-purpose flour in ours with delicious results.

1. Work on a cool surface in a cool kitchen.

2. Make sure all your ingredients are very cold—fat chilled and water iced. The fat and flour should form little nuggets before the water is added for a flaky crust.

3. Quickly work the flour and fat together with a pastry blender, two knives, or your fingertips until the mixture resembles coarse crumbs and remains light and dry. Mixing longer will produce a mealy, tough crust.

4. Stir in ice water one tablespoon at a time until the dough holds together. If too much water is added, the dough will be sticky and the crust tough.

5. Remember, the more you handle the dough the tougher it becomes, so if you use your fingertips to blend it, work quickly.

6. When the dough is mixed, quickly gather it into a rough ball, wrap it, and refrigerate 30 minutes to an hour before rolling it out.

7. Marble is the ideal surface for rolling out pie dough because it remains cool. A wooden table or Formica countertop will also do. Lightly flour the surface and the top of the dough. Rub a bit of flour over the rolling pin. Flatten the dough into a disk and roll lightly from the center to the edge. Lift and turn the dough while rolling, sprinkling lightly with flour if needed. Roll until the dough is about ⅛ inch thick and 1½ to 2 inches larger than the pie plate. If any patching is necessary, lightly moisten the edge of the patch and the hole with water and gently press into place.

8. For a double-crust pie, fit the bottom crust carefully into the pie plate, add the filling, and cover with the top crust. Moisten the crusts where they meet with water, then turn the top crust under the bottom and flute the edge. Cut a few slits in the top to allow the steam to escape.

9. Leave the top crust plain or glaze it for a different effect:
- ▲ Brush lightly with milk or cream for a nice finish.
- ▲ Sprinkle the crust with sugar. Some will melt and some will remain crunchy.
- ▲ Brush with an egg wash (egg mixed with a little water or milk) for rich color and shine.

10. For some pies, the crust is partially or completely baked before the filling is added. It's important to get the bottom crust into the pie plate or tart pan without stretching it or it will shrink when it's baked. Decoratively flute the edge and prick the bottom with a fork to keep the dough from puffing. Cover the pastry with aluminum foil and weight it down with pie weights or a generous handful of dried beans. Then bake it in a preheated oven for the amount of time noted in the recipe.

pastry blender

ball of dough

lightly floured surface

Roll dough away from center in all directions to form a circle of even thickness

You can roll dough between 2 sheets of lightly floured waxed paper.

APPLE OF HER EYE PIE

We like to put Cheddar in the crust of an apple pie so we can taste its sharpness with every bite. It doesn't hurt to serve slices of Cheddar atop, also. Of course make sure that it's the best you can find— aged Canadian, Black Diamond, or Vermont, for instance. It seems that the lighter the color, the sharper the taste.

You can turn this into a Dutch Apple Pie by removing it from the oven 10 minutes before it's finished and pouring 4 tablespoons of heavy cream through a tiny hole in the center of the top crust. It makes it even more wonderful.

PASTRY

3 cups unbleached all-purpose flour
¼ cup sugar
1 teaspoon dry mustard
Pinch of salt
8 tablespoons (1 stick) unsalted butter, cold
⅓ cup solid vegetable shortening, cold
¾ cup shredded sharp Cheddar cheese
6 to 8 tablespoons ice water

FILLING

8 tart apples, such as Granny Smith
4 tablespoons (½ stick)
*   unsalted butter, melted*
½ cup plus 2 tablespoons sugar
2 tablespoons cornstarch
¾ teaspoon ground cinnamon
1 teaspoon grated lemon zest
1 teaspoon vanilla extract

TOPPING

1 teaspoon sugar
Pinch of ground cinnamon

1. Prepare the pastry dough: Combine the flour, sugar, mustard, and salt in a mixing bowl, and toss well to blend. Using a pastry blender, two knives, or your fingertips, cut in the butter and shortening until the mixture forms small clumps. Then add the cheese, and work it in until the mixture resembles coarse crumbs.

2. Sprinkle the water, 2 tablespoons at a time, over the mixture and toss with a fork until the mixture can be gathered into a ball. Knead it once or twice in the bowl and divide it into slightly unequal halves. Wrap both halves, and chill in the refrigerator for 45 minutes.

3. Meanwhile, preheat the oven to 350°F.

4. Prepare the filling: Core, halve, and peel the apples. Cut them into 1-inch chunks. Combine the apples and melted butter in a large bowl. Add the remaining filling ingredients, and toss until the apples are evenly coated.

5. Roll the smaller portion of chilled dough out on a lightly floured surface to form a 12-inch circle. Transfer it to a 10-inch pie plate, and press it into the bottom and sides of the plate. Trim the dough, leaving a 1-inch overhang. Reserve any excess dough.

6. Roll the larger portion of dough out to form a slightly larger circle.

7. Fill the pie plate with the apple mixture, mounding it slightly. Brush the edge of the bottom crust with water. Then transfer the top crust over the apples, tucking it slightly inside the rim. Trim off any excess, allowing a 1-inch overhang. Seal the edges of the crusts together with a fork and crimp decoratively. Trim away any remaining excess pastry.

8. Prepare the topping: Mix together the sugar and cinnamon. Prick the top crust with a fork in several places, and cut a small vent in the center. Brush the top lightly with water, and sprinkle it with the cinnamon sugar. If you like, cut out shapes, such as leaves or apples, from the dough trimmings and decorate the top crust with them.

9. Bake until the filling is bubbling and the top is golden, 1¼ hours.

8 portions

TRADE SECRET

Spice your apple pies Scandinavian-style with ground cardamom instead of cinnamon. It's a nice change.

APPLE ABCs

Apples are as basic to the family of fruits as A is to the alphabet. They are hardy and reliably tasty, never overwhelming but subtly complementary to a multitude of foods. Apples have always been inexpensive. In a pinch of hunger, it's easy to grab an apple and eat it on the spot. With knife in hand, an apple is the perfect dessert—light, juicy, and slightly astringent.

What you want in an apple is freshness, whether you are eating them out of hand or going to cook them. Although some apples are recommended for eating and some for cooking (and some for cider or drying), remember that a mealy, uninspiring apple remains mealy and uninspiring when cooked. Ripe apples are firm, crisp, and deeply colored, whether that be green or red or any of the colors in between. Apples continue to ripen once picked even when refrigerated. Store apples in the refrigerator in perforated bags and don't rinse them until you are ready to eat them.

APPLE	SEASON	REGION	EATING	COOKING
BALDWIN Mottled red, mellow and mildly sweet, crisp and juicy.	November through January	Northeast	Good	Excellent
BLACK TWIG Dull red and green, very firm and crisp.	October	Ozarks/Appalachians; Northeast	Good	Fair
CORTLAND Large, red striped with purple; tart with soft texture. Doesn't brown when cut.	October through December	Northeast; Midwest	Good	Good
COX'S PIPPIN Yellow with yellow flesh, mild flavor.	August through September	Northeast	Good	Good
EMPIRE Brilliant red; sweet, spicy, crisp, and juicy. Makes rosy applesauce.	September through November	Northeast; Midwest	Good	Fair
GOLDEN DELICIOUS Pale yellow to yellow-green; firm, flowery, sweet, and moderately juicy. Keeps its shape in pies; not for applesauce.	September through October	All regions	Fair	Good

APPLE	SEASON	REGION	EATING	COOKING
GOLDEN RUSSET				
Tawny red with sweet flavor. Excellent for storing.	Late October	Northeast; Midwest	Good	Good
GRANNY SMITH				
Freckled apple green; tart to very tart flavor, crisp and juicy.	Year round	Imported from Australia and New Zealand	Excellent	Excellent
GRAVENSTEIN				
Yellow or green striped with red; fairly tart, crisp, and juicy. Makes wonderful applesauce.	August through September	West Coast	Good	Excellent
GRIMES GOLDEN				
Freckled pale yellow; mellow and sweet taste, crisp and juicy.	Late October through November	Appalachians; Midwest	Good	Good
IDA RED				
Deep red, sweet and spicy; crisp. Another keeper.	October through early November	Northeast; Midwest	Excellent	Very Good
JONATHAN				
Small, brilliant red, with sweet-tart flavor, crisp and very juicy. Great for eating and cider making.	September through November	All regions	Excellent	Excellent
LADY APPLE				
Tiny, red to yellow-red; crisp and tart. Dates back to the Renaissance.	September through November	Northeast	Good	Very Good
MACOUN				
Wine red with gray bloom; sweet-tart taste, very crisp and juicy.	October through November	Northeast; Midwest	Excellent	Very Good
MCINTOSH				
Two-toned red and green; fresh sweet-tart taste, crisp and very juicy. Turns to mush quickly when cooked.	September through October	Northeast; Midwest	Excellent	Poor
NEWTOWN PIPPIN				
Pale green to russet yellow; tart to sweet-tart flavor, crisp and juicy. Good pie apple.	September through October	West Coast; Northwest	Good	Good

APPLE	SEASON	REGION	EATING	COOKING
NORTHERN SPY Pale green to yellow striped with red; spicy and sweet-tart, crisp, firm, and juicy. One of the most interesting eating apples.	October through early November	Northeast; Midwest	Good	Excellent
PAULA RED Bright red mottled with yellow, mildly tart and sweet.	September	Northeast; Midwest	Good	Good
RED DELICIOUS Brilliant red streaked with green. Hard skin with sweet, dry flesh. America's most popular eating apple.	September through October	All regions	Fair	Poor
RHODE ISLAND GREENING Large, green to yellow-green; tart to sweet-tart taste, and crisp. Very good pie apple.	September through October	All regions	Good	Excellent
ROME BEAUTY Large and deep red, sweet taste, dry and somewhat mealy texture. Holds its shape in pies.	Late September	All regions	Poor	Good
STAYMAN WINESAP Large, red shaded with green, sweet spicy flavor, crisp and juicy. Makes good applesauce.	October through November	Northeast; East Coast; Midwest	Good	Excellent
WEALTHY Large, red streaked with yellow, sweet, crisp, and juicy.	September through October	Northern Midwest to Rockies	Good	Good
WINESAP Small, deep red, with spicy, sweet-tart taste, crisp and very juicy. Good for storing.	October through November	Northwest; Northeast	Excellent	Very Good
WOLF RIVER Red with yellow blush; sweet and crisp. Good pie apple.	September through October	Midwest	Good	Good
YORK IMPERIAL Deep red striped with green; tart honey flavor, firm and mildly crisp. Old-fashioned apple flavor.	September through November	Mid-Atlantic; Appalachians	Good	Good

CRISPY HOT APPLE TART

We like our apple tarts piping hot from the oven on just a wisp of pastry. Topped with cool double applesauce, the intense flavors and contrasts in temperature elevate this tart to a new high.

5 Granny Smith apples (about 2½ pounds)
3 McIntosh apples (about 1½ pounds)
2 lemons, halved
4 tablespoons apple brandy
4 tablespoons sugar
8 tablespoons apple jelly
½ recipe Adrienne's
    Rough Puff Pastry (see Index)
1 tablespoon ground cinnamon

1. Peel, quarter, and core 2 of the Granny Smith apples and all of the McIntosh apples. Rub a lemon half over the apples to prevent discoloration. Then cut the quartered apples into ⅛-inch-thick slices, place them in a heavy saucepan, and toss them with the juice from 1½ of the lemons.

2. Add 2 tablespoons of the brandy to the apple slices, cover the pan, and place it over low heat. Cook, stirring occasionally to prevent sticking, until the apples are soft, about 15 minutes.

3. Add 1 tablespoon of the sugar and 2 tablespoons of the jelly to the apples, and cook, stirring, until they form a thick purée, 5 minutes. Transfer the applesauce to a bowl, cover, and refrigerate until thoroughly chilled, 2 to 3 hours.

4. Preheat the oven to 400°F.

5. Roll the pastry out on a lightly floured surface to form an 18 x 8-inch rectangle. Transfer it to a heavy baking sheet.

6. Peel, quarter, and core the remaining 3 Granny Smith apples. Rub them with the remaining lemon half to prevent discoloration, and then cut them into very thin (¹⁄₁₆-inch) slices and arrange them, overlapping slightly, on the pastry; cover the pastry completely. Chill the tart in the freezer until firm, about 20 minutes.

7. Combine the remaining 6 tablespoons apple jelly with the remaining 2 tablespoons apple brandy in a small saucepan, and melt over low heat. Brush the melted jelly over the apple tart, transfer it to the oven, and bake until the pastry is well cooked, 25 minutes.

8. Combine the remaining 3 tablespoons sugar with the cinnamon. Remove the tart from the oven, sprinkle it with this mixture, and return it to the oven. Continue to bake the tart until the apples are slightly caramelized, 5 minutes.

9. Serve immediately, topped with the chilled applesauce.

8 portions

PIE TIPS

▲ Pie dough will keep in the refrigerator for up to three days or in the freezer for six months. Thaw frozen dough in the refrigerator, then let stand at room temperature 30 minutes before rolling it out.

▲ Use a pizza wheel to trim rolled pastry or cut lattice strips for the top of a pie.

▲ Most pies should be stored at room temperature, covered loosely with aluminum foil or plastic wrap to keep them crisp. Store custard and cream pies in the refrigerator, but let them warm to room temperature before serving.

▲ The best pans for pies are the old-fashioned lightweight aluminum ones that are fairly deep. The crust is baked crisp with a golden brown color.

SPICED RASPBERRY PIE

A pie with a glimmer of cinnamon and orange in the crust, and with framboise, the very essence of raspberry, in the filling. To us this is the berry at its best, especially when we fully indulge by serving it still warm, with Vanilla Vanilla Ice Cream atop!

PASTRY

1 ½ cups unbleached all-purpose flour
2 teaspoons sugar
½ teaspoon ground cinnamon
½ teaspoon salt
1 teaspoon grated orange zest
5 ½ tablespoons unsalted butter, cold
3 tablespoons solid vegetable shortening, cold
¼ cup ice water

FILLING

1 quart raspberries, lightly rinsed and drained
1 cup sugar
⅓ cup framboise liqueur
¼ cup cornstarch
1 tablespoon fresh lemon juice
Pinch of salt
1 egg yolk
1 teaspoon milk

1. Prepare the pastry dough: Combine the flour, sugar, cinnamon, salt, and orange zest in a large mixing bowl; stir well.

2. Using a pastry blender, two knives, or your fingertips cut the butter and shortening into the dry ingredients until the mixture resembles coarse crumbs.

3. Add the ice water 1 tablespoon at a time, until the mixture can be gathered into a ball. Wrap it in waxed paper and refrigerate for 2 hours.

4. Preheat the oven to 425°F.

5. Prepare the filling: Gently combine the raspberries with the sugar in a medium-size bowl.

6. In a small bowl, stir the framboise and cornstarch together until smooth.

7. Gently add the framboise mixture, lemon juice, and salt to the berries. Set them aside.

8. Roll the chilled dough out on a lightly floured surface to form an 11-inch circle. Transfer it to a 9-inch pie plate, and press it into the bottom and sides. Trim the dough, leaving a 1-inch overhang.

9. Gather up the excess pastry, roll it out in an 11-inch circle, and cut it into ½-inch-wide lattice strips.

10. Carefully spoon the reserved raspberry mixture into the pie shell. Weave the lattice strips over the top, fold the ends over the edge, and trim away any remaining excess pastry. Crimp the edge decoratively.

11. Blend the egg yolk and milk in a small bowl, and carefully brush this glaze over the lattice.

12. Place the pie plate on a baking sheet (to catch any drips), and bake it on the upper rack of the oven for 15 minutes. Then reduce the heat to 350°F, transfer the pie plate to the lower rack, and cook until the crust is golden and the berries are bubbling, 35 to 40 minutes. Serve warm or at room temperature.

8 portions

FRESH SUMMER STRAWBERRY PIE

When June rolls around, go strawberry picking and make this pie, the harbinger of summer. It's great with a topping of lightly sweetened whipped cream.

PASTRY

1 cup unbleached all-purpose flour
¼ cup sugar
¼ teaspoon ground cinnamon
Pinch of salt
⅓ cup unsalted butter, cold, cut into pieces
About 1 tablespoon fresh lemon juice

FILLING

2 pints strawberries, lightly rinsed,
*   drained, hulled, and halved*
¼ cup sugar
¼ cup instant tapioca
2 tablespoons unsalted butter
½ teaspoon ground cinnamon
1 tablespoon fresh lemon juice
½ teaspoon vanilla extract
2 tablespoons (packed) light brown sugar

1. Prepare the pastry: Toss the flour, sugar, cinnamon, and salt together in a bowl. Using a pastry blender, two knives, or your fingertips, cut in the butter until the mixture resembles coarse crumbs. With a fork, stir in just enough lemon juice for the dough to form a mass.

2. Gather the dough into a ball, wrap it with plastic wrap, and refrigerate for 30 minutes.

3. Preheat the oven to 375°F.

4. Prepare the filling: Combine the strawberries, sugar, tapioca, butter, and cinnamon in a medium-size saucepan, and stir over low heat until thick, 5 minutes. Remove the pan from the heat, stir in the lemon juice and vanilla, and set aside.

5. Roll the chilled dough out on a lightly floured surface to form an 11-inch circle. Transfer it to a 9-inch pie plate, and press it into the bottom and sides. Trim the dough, leaving a 1-inch overhang. Fold the overhang back toward the inside, and crimp the edge decoratively.

6. Prick the bottom of the pastry with a fork and line it with aluminum foil, shiny side down. Fill the plate with dried beans or pie weights, and bake the pastry for 15 minutes. Remove it from the oven and reduce the heat to 350°F.

7. Remove the foil and weights, and spoon the filling into the pie shell. Place it on a baking sheet (to catch the drips). Sprinkle the top with the brown sugar. Bake until bubbling, 45 minutes.

8. Cool the pie on a wire rack for 1 hour. Then refrigerate it overnight. Remove the pie 30 minutes before serving.

8 portions

SALLY'S FRESH FRUIT TART

A treasured recipe given to us long ago by a dear friend from Michigan. The tartness of the cheese adds that oh-so-right dimension to fresh fruit.

3 ounces cream cheese, at room temperature
½ cup sugar
1 teaspoon vanilla extract
1 cup heavy or whipping cream
1 New Basic Pie Crust, baked (see Index)
1 cup raspberries, lightly rinsed and drained
1 cup blueberries, lightly rinsed, drained, and picked over
3 tablespoons red currant jelly

1. Combine the cream cheese, sugar, and vanilla in a bowl, and mix until thoroughly blended.

2. Whip the cream with an electric mixer and fold it into the cream cheese mixture.

3. Spoon the filling into the crust, and spread it out evenly. Arrange the raspberries and blueberries decoratively on top.

4. Heat the red currant jelly in a small saucepan until melted. Using a pastry brush, glaze the top of the pie with the jelly. Transfer the pie to the refrigerator and chill, uncovered, 3 to 4 hours.

8 portions

SUMMER'S RIPE BERRIES

❤

ummer's sweet berry season is all too brief. At the very first sign, head to the nearest berry patch or farm stand and claim your share, for nothing beats local sweet berries just hours off the vine. Raspberries, blackberries, blueberries, strawberries—we fight the brambles and thorns to pick our own, brush away the soil, and eat them as we pick—two for us and one for the pail! Whatever your methods, celebrate these fragile fruits with a little cream here, a dash of Grand Marnier there.

BERRY	SEASON	STORAGE	BEST USE
BLACKBERRY Also called dewberry, this berry is plump, juicy, and purple-black in color with sweet-tart taste. Related are boysenberries and loganberries.	May through July	Use within 1 week	Fresh with cream, in ice creams and sorbets, tarts, pies, jams, wine, and vinegar
BLUEBERRY Small, plump, juicy berry with sweet-tart taste and velvety purple-blue color.	June through August	Use within 1 week	Fresh with cream and yogurt, in cobblers, muffins, chutneys, pies, sauces, and vinegars
CRANBERRY Hard, lacquer-red berry with sour-tart taste.	September through January	Use within 1 week, or freeze up to 3 months	In sauces, muffins, pies, tarts, chutneys, and relishes
CURRANT Tiny tart red, black, or white berry. An old favorite regaining its popularity.	July through August	Use within 1 week	In tarts, jams, jellies, puddings, vinegars, and sauces with game
GOOSEBERRY Small sour-tart berry colored silvery green. Berries colored white, yellow, and red are dessert berries and sweeter—but rarely found in States.	July through September	Use within 3 days	In jams and jellies, pies, tarts, puddings, sauces for game and fish
HUCKLEBERRY Tiny deep blue berry with sweet, winey taste.	August through September	Use within 3 days	In jams and jellies, pies, tarts, purées, and sauces
RASPBERRY Fragile, cup-shaped berry with very sweet, winey taste. Colored black, red, or amber.	July through September	Use within 24 hours	Fresh with cream, shortcake, meringues, in mousses, ice creams, sorbets, pies and tarts, purées, sauces, jams and jellies
STRAWBERRY Plump, juicy, heart-shaped berry, colored bright red. America's favorite.	Year round, but April through July for most local berries, which are best	Use within 24 hours	Fresh with cream, shortcake, meringues, in mousses, ice creams, pies (with rhubarb) and tarts, purées, sauces, jams and jellies

MACADAMIA BANANA CREAM PIE

This one is a showstopper. It's very rich from top to bottom—from whipped cream to macadamia nut crust. Be sure to allow the time for the pie to chill fully, for it will be much easier to cut.

CRUST
1 cup chopped unsalted macadamia or cashew nuts
½ cup flaked unsweetened coconut
2 tablespoons light brown sugar
1 egg white

CUSTARD FILLING
3 egg yolks
5 teaspoons cornstarch
¾ cup granulated sugar
1½ cups milk
¼ teaspoon salt
1 tablespoon unsalted butter, at room temperature
1 teaspoon vanilla extract

½ cup heavy or whipping cream
2 bananas
½ cup finely chopped macadamia or cashew nuts

1. Preheat the oven to 375°F.
2. Prepare the crust: Combine the nuts, coconut, and brown sugar in a medium-size bowl.
3. Beat the egg white until stiff, and gently fold it into the nut mixture.
4. Press the mixture evenly into an 8-inch pie plate, making sure the sides are thickish (the crust will shrink while baking). Bake until the crust is lightly browned, 7 minutes.
5. Remove the pie plate from the oven and let it cool on a rack. (The crust will tighten as it cools.)
6. Prepare the custard: Beat the egg yolks in a heavy medium-size saucepan. Add the cornstarch and sugar, and mix well. Then stir in the milk, salt, and butter.
7. Cook the egg mixture over medium heat, stirring constantly, until it is bubbling and thick, 5 to 7 minutes.
8. Remove the pan from the heat and stir in the vanilla. Transfer the mixture to a glass bowl, cover it with plastic wrap, and refrigerate for 2 to 4 hours.

9. Whip the cream with an electric mixer until it forms stiff peaks. Fold the whipped cream into the chilled custard.
10. Peel and slice 1 of the bananas, and arrange it evenly on the bottom of the reserved crust. Spoon the filling into the crust, cover with plastic wrap, and chill for another 2 hours.
11. When you are ready to serve the pie, sprinkle the chopped nuts evenly over the top. Then peel and slice the remaining banana, and arrange the slices in a circle on top of the pie, with a few slices placed decoratively in the center. Serve immediately.

6 to 8 portions

CANDACE'S CHOCOLATE PEANUT BUTTER PIE

Our long-time friend Candace Strong is known for her sit-up-and-take-notice baking for the Kalamazoo Country Club. She likes flavors to really leap out at you, and we do too. This treat is scrumptious—just a thin wedge will do!

CRUST
1⅓ cups graham cracker crumbs
⅓ cup sugar
8 tablespoons (1 stick) unsalted butter, melted

FILLING
12 ounces cream cheese, at room temperature
1½ cups peanut butter
1½ cups sugar
1 cup heavy or whipping cream

TOPPING
½ cup sugar
½ cup heavy or whipping cream
2 ounces good-quality unsweetened chocolate
4 tablespoons (½ stick) unsalted butter
½ teaspoon vanilla extract

1. Preheat the oven to 350°F.

2. Prepare the crust: Combine the graham cracker crumbs, sugar, and melted butter in a mixing bowl, and stir together thoroughly. Press the mixture into the bottom and sides of a 9-inch pie plate.

3. Bake the crust for 8 minutes. Then set it aside to cool completely.

4. Prepare the filling: Mix the cream cheese, peanut butter, and sugar together in a large bowl until well blended.

5. Whip the cream with an electric mixer until stiff, and fold it into the cream cheese mixture. Spoon the filling into the cooled crust.

6. Prepare the topping: Combine the sugar and cream in a saucepan and bring to a boil. Reduce the heat and simmer, without stirring, for 6 minutes.

7. Remove the pan from the heat, add the chocolate and butter, and stir until melted. Then stir in the vanilla.

8. Carefully pour the topping over the pie, and refrigerate, uncovered, for at least 4 hours.

8 portions

Buy cherries that are firm, shiny, and dry. If the cherries are sticky, they are overripe and exuding their juice. Before you eat or cook any cherry, be sure to rinse it well. Most cherries are sprayed with insecticides, which help bring them to market but which shouldn't be ingested. Eat or cook fresh cherries within a day or two of purchase when they are still at their sweetest.

QUEEN ANNE'S CHERRY TART

We've combined regal golden Queen Anne cherries with sweet dark ones, then added kirsch and Cherry Heering to make a very cherry tart. It's a beauty!

PASTRY
1 cup unbleached all-purpose flour
1 tablespoon sugar
¼ teaspoon salt
6 tablespoons (¾ stick) unsalted butter, cut in pieces, cold
1 egg yolk
2 tablespoons ice water

FILLING
1 can (17 ounces) pitted sweet dark cherries in syrup
¼ cup kirsch
¼ cup Cherry Heering
3 tablespoons sugar
1 teaspoon fresh lemon juice
2 tablespoons cornstarch
12 ounces golden (Queen Anne) cherries
2 tablespoons cherry jam

1. Prepare the pastry: Combine the flour, sugar, and salt in a food processor. Add the butter and process until the mixture has the texture of coarse crumbs.

2. With the motor running, add the egg yolk and ice water through the feed tube. Process until the dough forms a ball.

3. Cover the dough with plastic wrap, and refrigerate for 1 hour.

4. Preheat the oven to 425°F.

TARTS

♥

We love our tarts—both sweet and savory. Unlike a pie crust, the tart shell must be firm enough to stand on its own when it's removed from the pan. Sweet tarts are filled with cooked or uncooked fruit, custard, light mousses, or rich pastry creams. Fresh berry or cherry tarts dazzle in the summer.

Tart shells can be made with pie dough or short dough, which is simply a sweeter crust (pâte sucrée) made with flour, butter, sugar, and egg. This firm dough is strong enough to hold its shape when it's baked. Of course, short doughs are not as flaky as pie crust. If you want a flakier crust, make a combination of half pie dough and half short dough.

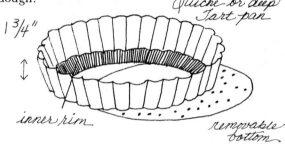

1 3/4"

Quiche or deep
Tart pan

inner rim

removable
bottom

TIPS FOR TARTS

▲ Partially bake the crust for a custard or fruit tart before filling so that the crust remains a separate layer.

▲ Bake unfilled shells in the middle of your oven, but bake the shells with filling in the lower third so that the bottom browns.

▲ Once baked, the shell will shrink from the side of the pan. When the tart is completely cooled, the outside ring can be removed. It's a good idea to leave the bottom of the tart on the pan.

▲ Glaze fresh fruit on a tart by brushing it with melted red currant or apple jelly. If you melt a jelly with seeds for glazing, be sure to press it through a sieve.

▲ Sprinkle sugar over the top of an apple, peach, or pear tart before baking for a nicely glazed finish.

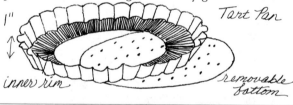

1"

Tart Pan

inner rim

removable
bottom

5. Roll the chilled dough out on a lightly floured surface to form an 11-inch circle. Transfer it to a 9-inch tart pan with a removable bottom, pressing it into the bottom and sides. Trim the dough, leaving a 1-inch overhang. Fold the overhang back toward the inside, and crimp the edge decoratively. Prick the bottom of the pastry with a fork and line it with aluminum foil, shiny side down. Fill the pan with pie weights or dried beans, and bake the pastry until slightly golden, 12 to 14 minutes.

6. Remove the pan from the oven, lift out the foil and weights, and cool the crust completely.

7. Prepare the filling: Set aside ⅓ cup of the syrup from the canned cherries. Combine the remaining syrup with the cherries, kirsch, Cherry Heering, sugar, and lemon juice in a saucepan.

Bring to a boil, then reduce the heat to a simmer.

8. Stir the cornstarch and the reserved ⅓ cup syrup together, and slowly add this to the saucepan. Simmer until the mixture is thick, about 20 minutes. Remove the pan from the heat and allow the mixture to cool completely.

9. Rinse the golden cherries and pat them dry. Cut them in half and remove the pits.

10. Spread the cooled cherry mixture in the prepared tart shell and arrange the golden cherries, skin side up, in a circular pattern covering the top.

11. Melt the cherry jam in a small saucepan, and using a pastry brush, gently paint the golden cherries with the jam—they will shine. Let the tart rest for 1 hour before serving.

8 portions

PEAR SAUCE TART

Poire Williams, a delicious pear brandy, adds sparkle to the taste of this pear tart. Serve it with a dollop of crème fraîche or Vanilla Vanilla Ice Cream.

PASTRY

⅔ cup unbleached all-purpose flour
⅓ cup ground hazelnuts
½ teaspoon salt
5 tablespoons unsalted butter, cold, cut into pieces
½ teaspoon finely grated lemon zest
¼ teaspoon Poire Williams
1 tablespoon cold water
1 tablespoon sugar

PEAR SAUCE

6 Bosc pears, slightly underripe, peeled,
    cored, and quartered
1 lemon, peeled, quartered, and seeded
1 cup sugar
2 tablespoons Poire Williams

PEARS AND TOPPING

Zest of 1 lemon
1 slice fresh ginger (1 inch), peeled
2 cups Champagne
1 ½ cups water
¼ cup fresh lemon juice
1 cup sugar
⅓ cup applesauce
1 cinnamon stick (3 inches long)
2 whole cloves
4 firm but ripe Bosc pears
    (about 2 pounds)
1 tablespoon white wine vinegar
2 tablespoons Poire Williams

1. Prepare the pastry shell: Combine the flour, hazelnuts, and salt in a food processor, and process for 15 to 20 seconds. With the motor off, add the pieces of butter, the lemon zest, and Poire Williams; process for 15 seconds. Gradually add the cold water through the feed tube, ½ teaspoon at a time, turning the motor on and off two or three times; add enough of the water to hold the dough together. Gather the dough into a ball, flatten it slightly, cover with plastic wrap, and refrigerate for 30 minutes.

2. Meanwhile, preheat the oven to 425°F. But-ter a 9-inch tart pan with removable bottom.

3. Roll the chilled dough out on a lightly floured surface to form an 11-inch circle. Transfer it to the tart pan, pressing it into the bottom and sides. Trim the dough, leaving a 1-inch overhang. Fold the overhang back toward the inside, and crimp the edge decoratively.

4. Prick the bottom of the pastry with a fork and line it with aluminum foil, shiny side down. Fill the plate with pie weights or dried beans, and bake the pastry for 15 minutes. Remove the foil and weights, and sprinkle the sugar over the bottom. Return the shell to the oven and bake until golden, another 8 to 10 minutes. Remove the pan from the oven and set it aside to cool.

5. Prepare the sauce: Combine half the pear quarters and 2 of the lemon quarters in a food processor and process for 30 seconds. Transfer the mixture to a heavy saucepan, and repeat with the remaining pears and lemon.

6. Stir the sugar and Poire Williams into the saucepan, and cook over low heat until the mixture begins to color slightly, 30 minutes. Continue cooking over medium-low heat, stirring occasionally, until the mixture has the consistency of thick applesauce, 1 ½ hours. Set it aside to cool.

7. To make the topping, first prepare the poaching liquid: Cut the lemon zest into ⅛-inch-wide julienne strips. Then cut the ginger into ⅛-inch-wide julienne strips. Combine the zest, ginger, Champagne, 1 cup of the water, the lemon juice, ½ cup of the sugar, the applesauce, cinnamon stick, and cloves in a medium-size saucepan. Bring to a boil, reduce the heat, and cover. Simmer for 15 minutes, and set aside.

8. Peel the pears, reserving the peel, and cut them in half lengthwise. Remove the core with a melon baller. Place the pears in a large bowl and add water to cover. Add the vinegar (to keep the pears from discoloring).

9. Combine the pear peels, remaining ½ cup water, remaining ½ cup sugar, and Poire Williams in a saucepan. Bring to a boil, then reduce the heat and simmer for 10 minutes. Strain, and set the liquid aside.

10. Using a slotted spoon, transfer the pears to the reserved poaching liquid. Add the pear peel liquid and bring to a boil. Then reduce the heat, cover, and simmer for 8 minutes. Remove the pan from the heat and allow the pears to cool in the poaching liquid.

11. Transfer the pears to a shallow dish. Return

PEARS

Cool crisp weather always starts us dreaming of pears. A perfectly ripe pear is sheer ambrosia. The perfume is ethereal, the flesh buttery and melting, and there is enough fruit and juice to quench a thirst.

There are more than 5,000 varieties of pears, but just a dozen or so are available nationwide. Pears are not all pear shaped. Some are round and plump, others are perfect bells, and still others are as chubby and knobby as fists. Most pears in our markets are grown in the Northwest and are harvested in September and October. They are then put into cold storage and shipped from winter through late spring.

Pears must be picked when mature but not ripe. If picked too soon, they shrivel; too late, they are bitter and gritty. Buy pears when they are firm but not hard and ripen them out of the sun in a bowl on the table or in a paper bag. Check the stem end for ripeness; if it gives a little when pressed, the pear is ready. Slightly underripe pears are best for cooking because they don't fall apart. If you cut or peel them, rub them with lemon juice to keep them from browning.

VARIETIES

Anjou or D'anjou: Large, russet-colored, egg-shaped pears with tender skin and sweet, winey flavor. They are good for both eating and cooking and available from October through May.

Bartlett: This pear is harvested in mid-August and is available in abundance through November. The Bartlett makes up 75 percent of all of America's pears. They are big and bell shaped. Red Bartletts turn crimson red when ripe; others are picked green and turn yellow-green when ripe. The flavor is sweet and musky. This is a good eating pear.

Bosc: One of the prettiest pears, Boscs have long thin necks with a russet hue over golden skin. The flavor is tart and the texture is buttery and rich. Boscs keep their shape when cooked, but they are also very good eating pears.

Comice: This pear is on the top of our list for eating. The flesh is sweet, juicy, and buttery all at once. It's round and chubby and colored green.

Forelle: Golden yellow with crimson flesh, Forelles look like little Bartletts and are the perfect Christmas pear.

Nelis: Large and roundish like the Comice, this pear is dark green and russeted with a spicy flavor and buttery texture. It's a sweet, juicy eating pear that holds its shape when cooked as well.

Seckel: Seckels are small to tiny with russet skin. The texture is slightly gritty and the flavor, spicy and sweet.

---

the poaching liquid to medium-high heat, bring it to a boil, and reduce to 1½ cups, 10 to 15 minutes. Allow the liquid to cool, then pour it over the pears, cover, and refrigerate until chilled, 4 hours.

12. Assemble the tart: Pour the reserved pear sauce into the prepared shell.

13. Remove the pears from the poaching liquid and slice them crosswise into thin half-moons. Starting at the outside edge of the tart and working inward, arrange the slices in concentric circles or a spiral, overlapping slightly to cover the entire surface.

14. Preheat the broiler.

15. Cover the edge of the crust with a strip of aluminum foil, and place the tart under the broiler until the pears turn golden brown, 4 to 5 minutes. Serve hot or at room temperature.

8 portions

VERY LEMON TART

A burst of sunny citrus is just the way to end those heavy winter meals.

PASTRY

1 cup unbleached all-purpose flour
4 tablespoons (½ stick) unsalted butter, cold, cut into small pieces
½ cup confectioners' sugar
Pinch of salt
2 tablespoons Champagne, sparkling wine, or lemon juice, cold

FILLING

Zest of 2 lemons
⅔ cup granulated sugar
5 egg yolks
½ cup fresh lemon juice
Pinch of salt
8 tablespoons (1 stick) unsalted butter, melted

Crystallized Lemon Zest (recipe follows)

1. Prepare the pastry shell: Combine the flour, butter, confectioners' sugar, and salt in a food processor, and process until the butter is coarsely chopped. With the motor running, pour the Champagne through the feed tube and process until the pastry holds together. Gather the dough into a ball, flatten it slightly, cover with plastic wrap, and refrigerate for 30 minutes.

2. Meanwhile, preheat the oven to 425°F.

3. Roll the chilled dough out on a lightly floured surface to form an 11-inch circle. Transfer it to a 9-inch tart pan with removable bottom, pressing it into the bottom and sides. Trim the dough, leaving a 1-inch overhang. Fold the overhang back toward the inside and crimp the edge decoratively.

4. Prick the bottom of the pastry with a fork and line it with aluminum foil, shiny side down. Fill the plate with dried beans or pie weights. Bake it on the center rack of the oven for 12 minutes. Then remove the foil and weights, return it to the oven, and bake until it is light golden brown, 8 minutes. Remove the pan from the oven and let the crust cool completely.

5. Prepare the filling: Combine the lemon zest and sugar in a food processor, and process until the zest is as fine as the sugar. Add the egg yolks, lemon juice, and salt; process for 5 seconds to blend. With the motor on, pour the hot butter through the feed tube. Transfer the mixture to a stainless steel saucepan.

6. Cook the filling over medium-low heat, stirring constantly with a wooden spoon, until thick, 4 to 5 minutes. Do not let the mixture boil. Set it aside to cool.

7. When you are ready to assemble the tart, preheat the oven to 325°F.

8. Pour the cooled lemon filling into the tart shell, and place the tart pan on a baking sheet (to catch any drips). Bake it in the lower third of the oven until the filling is set, 50 minutes. Sprinkle the tart with the Crystallized Lemon Zest, and let the tart cool completely before removing the sides of the pan. Serve at room temperature.

8 portions

CRYSTALLIZED LEMON ZEST

Peel of 4 lemons
1½ cups cold water
1½ cups sugar
2 tablespoons light corn syrup

1. Combine the lemon peel and 1 cup of the cold water in a saucepan, and bring to a boil. Reduce the heat and simmer until the peel is soft, 15 minutes. Drain the peel, and carefully scrape off any white pith with a spoon. Only the zest should remain. Cut the zest into very thin strips.

2. Combine the lemon strips, 1 cup of the sugar, the remaining ½ cup cold water, and the corn syrup in another saucepan. Cook over medium heat until the mixture is clear and registers 230°F on a candy thermometer. Drain, and set aside to cool.

3. Spread the remaining ½ cup sugar on a flat plate. Roll the lemon strips in the sugar, coating them well. Leave them in a cool place to dry. When they are completely dry, store the strips in an airtight container. (Crystallized lemon zest will last for several weeks.)

4. To use as a garnish, cut the strips into small confetti-like squares.

LEMONS

For every chocoholic in the world, there must be one lemonphile. We always have a large bowl of lemons on the kitchen counter because they are forever in use. They have clearly made their way into every aspect of our cooking.

Ripe lemons are bright yellow, shiny, heavy, and unwrinkled. They also have the highest vitamin C content of any citrus fruit. The best and cheapest are available from December to March.

Lemons are grown in many subtropical regions, including the Mediterranean basin, southern Italy, Israel, and Spain, but the California–Arizona sunbelt produces the largest lemon crop in the world. The most common variety is the Eureka lemon, followed by Lisbon and Villafranca lemons. The most delicious of all—the Meyer—is a cross between an orange and a lemon. This is the lemon tree most Californians grow in their backyards. Sweet lemons—Marrakesh limonette, Mediterranean sweet, and Millsweet—are not easy to find, but if you do come across them, make a pitcher of lemonade and hold the sugar.

KEY LIME CHIFFON PIE

On those dreary damp days, there's nothing that will add a ray of sunshine faster than this pie. Serve it for dessert after a Seafood Gumbo.

SYRUP
1 cup water
½ cup sugar
2 tablespoons julienned lime zest (½ inch long)

CRUST
22 graham cracker squares
¼ cup (packed) light brown sugar
1 tablespoon grated lime zest
5 tablespoons unsalted butter, cut in pieces

FILLING
1 envelope unflavored gelatin
⅓ cup fresh lime juice
½ cup sugar
2 eggs, separated
1 cup heavy or whipping cream
1 teaspoon vanilla extract

1. Prepare the syrup: Combine the water and sugar in a small saucepan and heat to a simmer. Stir in the julienned lime zest, and simmer for 30 minutes. Strain, reserving the zest and syrup separately.

2. Preheat the oven to 375°F.

3. Prepare the crust: Combine the graham crackers, brown sugar, grated lime zest, and butter in a food processor, and process until the mixture holds together. Press the mixture into the bottom and sides of a 9-inch pie plate, and bake for 8 minutes. Set the crust on a wire rack to cool.

4. Prepare the filling: Heat ⅓ cup of the reserved lime syrup in a small saucepan. Remove the pan from the heat and sprinkle the gelatin over the syrup; let it soften for 1 minute. Then stir in the lime juice, ¼ cup of the sugar, and the 2 egg yolks. Stir over low heat until the mixture is thick and frothy, 5 minutes. Set it aside to cool to room temperature.

5. Beat the egg whites and 2 tablespoons of the sugar with an electric mixer until stiff. Transfer the whites to a large bowl. Wash and dry the mixer blades.

6. In another bowl, whip the cream with the electric mixer, vanilla, and remaining 2 tablespoons sugar until thick. Fold the whipped cream into the egg whites, drizzling in the reserved lime mixture at the same time. When the mixture is smooth, spoon it into the prepared crust. Sprinkle the reserved lime julienne on top, and chill, uncovered, until firm, 2 to 3 hours.

8 portions

MERINGUE AND CHIFFON PIES

We like our meringue pies tall, fluffy, and luxurious looking. Completely cover the filling with the meringue, spreading it to the crust, so that it is sealed to the edge when it bakes. If you want the meringue more golden, place it under the broiler, 1 to 2 minutes, watching carefully, just until golden brown.

Delicate, fluffy chiffon pies are ideal luncheon desserts. Typically, citrus fruit is blended with custard, set with gelatin, and lightened with beaten egg whites. These pies are easy to make ahead and keep in the refrigerator. Try a cracker crumb or crunchy nut crust for even greater ease and flavor.

LEMON MERINGUE TARTLETS

These little individual tartlets are just the right finale to a spring dinner.

PASTRY
1 cup unbleached all-purpose flour
¼ cup sugar
⅓ cup unsalted butter
1 egg
2 teaspoons grated lemon zest

FILLING
5 egg yolks
½ cup granulated sugar
6 tablespoons (¾ stick) unsalted butter
¼ cup fresh lemon juice
2 tablespoons grated lemon zest

MERINGUE
2 egg whites
⅛ teaspoon cream of tartar
¼ cup confectioners' sugar
½ teaspoon grated lemon zest

1. Prepare the pastry: Toss the flour and sugar together in a bowl. Using a pastry blender, two knives, or your fingertips, cut in the butter until the mixture resembles coarse crumbs. Then add the egg and lemon zest, stirring until the mixture clumps together. Form the dough into a ball.

2. Divide the dough into eight pieces, and press them into the bottom and sides of eight 3½-inch tartlet pans. Chill the pans for 30 minutes.

3. Preheat the oven to 375°F.

4. Prick the bottoms and sides of the pastry with a fork and line each with aluminum foil, shiny side down. Fill the pans with pie weights or dried beans and transfer them to a baking sheet. Bake until the edges are lightly browned and the pastry is cooked through, 15 minutes. Cool on wire racks.

5. Prepare the filling: Combine all the filling ingredients in a medium-size saucepan and stir over low heat until the mixture is thick, 5 to 7 minutes. Allow it to cool to room temperature.

6. Drop a heaping tablespoon of filling into each tartlet shell, and spread it out to the edges.

7. Prepare the meringue: Beat the egg whites and the cream of tartar with an electric mixer in a mixing bowl until frothy. Slowly add the confectioners' sugar, beating until the whites are stiff. Then beat in the lemon zest.

8. Preheat the broiler.

9. Drop a heaping tablespoon of meringue onto each tartlet, and spread it out to cover the top. Arrange the pans on a baking sheet, and broil just until the meringue is lightly browned, less than 1 minute.

10. Set the tartlets aside to cool slightly, and then refrigerate until chilled, 2 hours.

8 tartlets

WALNUT PECAN TART

Top this great nut combination with whipped cream or Vanilla Vanilla Ice Cream.

PASTRY
1 cup unbleached all-purpose flour
Pinch of salt
2 tablespoons sugar
8 tablespoons (1 stick) unsalted butter, cold, cut into pieces
1 egg yolk
1 tablespoon fresh lemon juice

FILLING
2 cups sugar
½ cup water
1 cup heavy or whipping cream
2 eggs
2½ cups walnut halves
2½ cups pecan halves

1. Prepare the pastry: Combine the flour, salt, and sugar in a food processor. Add the butter and process with several quick pulses to coat the butter with flour. Then add the egg yolk and lemon juice, and process until the pastry is thoroughly blended and forms a smooth ball. Dust it with flour and cover with plastic wrap. Chill in the refrigerator for 30 minutes.

2. Roll the chilled dough out on a lightly floured surface to form a 12-inch circle (keeping the surface and the rolling pin well floured, as the pastry will easily become sticky). Carefully transfer the pastry to a 10-inch tart pan wtih removable bottom. Press it into the bottom and sides of the pan, trim the edges, and place it in the freezer for 15 minutes.

3. Preheat the oven to 375°F.

4. Prick the bottom of the chilled tart shell with a fork, and line it with a piece of aluminum foil. Fill the plate with pie weights or dried beans, and bake until the pastry is well set and the edges are lightly browned, 12 to 15 minutes. Then remove the foil and weights, return it to the oven, and bake until the bottom has begun to brown, about 5 minutes. Remove the pan from the oven and set it aside. Lower the oven temperature to 350°F.

5. Prepare the filling: Combine the sugar and water in a heavy saucepan and cook over low heat until the sugar has dissolved. Then raise the heat to medium-high and cook just until it has begun to turn a light caramel color. Immediately remove the pan from the heat and set it aside to cool slightly.

6. Carefully stir the cream into the caramel (it may sputter). Allow the mixture to cool completely.

7. Beat the eggs until frothy. With the electric mixer running, carefully pour the cooled caramel into the eggs, and mix thoroughly. Then stir in the walnuts and pecans, and pour the filling into the prepared pastry shell. Bake until the filling is set and the top is lightly browned, 35 to 40 minutes. Allow the tart to cool slightly, and then serve.

10 to 12 portions

TRADE SECRET

 To make your own superfine sugar, whirl sugar cubes or granulated sugar in a food processor until powdery.

MINCEMEAT TARTLETS

We've lightened the usual mincemeat pie by wrapping it all up in delicate phyllo pastry. Serve these hot and crispy, right from the oven.

2 tart apples, cored, peeled, and cut into large chunks
1 orange, unpeeled, cut into large chunks, and seeded
Zest of 1 lemon
½ cup golden raisins
½ cup dark raisins
½ cup cider vinegar
¾ cup (packed) dark brown sugar
1 teaspoon ground cinnamon
1 teaspoon ground cloves
1 teaspoon allspice
1 cup coarsely chopped walnuts
2 tablespoons Cognac
1 package (1 pound) phyllo dough, thawed if frozen
8 tablespoons (1 stick) unsalted butter, melted
½ cup granulated sugar

1. Combine the apple and orange chunks with the lemon zest in a food processor, and coarsely chop. Transfer the mixture to a large bowl, and stir in both raisins.

2. Bring the vinegar to a boil in a large saucepan, and add the brown sugar, spices, and the apple mixture. Reduce the heat to low and simmer, stirring occasionally, for 30 minutes. Remove the pan from the heat, stir in the walnuts and Cognac, and set it aside to cool completely.

3. Preheat the oven to 425°F.

4. Cut the phyllo sheets onto 12 x 8-inch rectangles. Work with one piece at a time, covering the rest with a lightly dampened kitchen towel to keep them from drying out.

5. Place a sheet of phyllo on a work surface, and brush it with melted butter. Sprinkle with ½ teaspoon of the sugar. Place another piece of phyllo on top, and butter and sprinkle it with sugar. Repeat two more times, making four layers.

6. Place ½ cup of the mincemeat in the center of the phyllo and flatten it out slightly. Cover it with a piece of phyllo, and brush it with melted butter; sprinkle with ½ teaspoon sugar. Repeat the layers three times, again making four layers.

7. Fold the lengthwise edges in, creating a ½-inch-thick border. Fold the ends under, and place the package, seam side down, on a baking sheet.

8. Repeat Steps 5 through 7, creating five more mincemeat tartlets and placing them on the baking sheet. Brush them with the remaining melted butter, and bake until golden and crispy, 40 to 45 minutes. Serve hot.

6 tartlets

MERINGUE TORTE WITH HAZELNUTS AND CHOCOLATE

Truly a spectacular dessert. Easily prepared, save this one for autumn and winter entertaining as meringues tend to become sticky in the heat.

1 cup superfine sugar (see Trade Secret)
2 tablespoons cornstarch
6 egg whites
Pinch of salt
1 cup hazelnuts, toasted (see Index) and finely chopped
9 ounces good-quality semisweet chocolate
2 cups heavy or whipping cream
¼ cup confectioners' sugar

1. Preheat the oven to 300°F. Butter and flour two heavy baking sheets. Butter three 8-inch pastry rings or the sides of three springform pans; set them aside.

2. Combine ¾ cup of the superfine sugar with the cornstarch in a small bowl, and set it aside.

3. Beat the egg whites and salt with an electric mixer until they form soft peaks. Sprinkle them with the remaining ¼ cup superfine sugar and beat until glossy, about 30 seconds more. Sift the reserved sugar-cornstarch mixture over the whites and fold together. Then fold in the hazelnuts. Wash and dry the mixer blades.

4. Place the prepared pastry rings on the prepared baking sheets. Divide the meringue mixture among the pastry rings and spread it out evenly. Bake until the meringues are slightly colored and are beginning to pull away from the sides of the molds, about 1 hour. Allow them to cool slightly in the molds; then remove the molds and cool completely on wire racks.

5. Melt 8 ounces of the chocolate over very low heat, stirring constantly. Invert each meringue layer (smooth bottom up) and spread it evenly with chocolate. Let the chocolate set slightly.

6. Whip the cream with the electric mixer until it forms soft peaks. Sift the confectioners' sugar over it, and beat until it forms firm peaks.

7. Spread the whipped cream evenly over the meringue layers, and place the layers on top of one another. Grate the remaining 1 ounce chocolate, and sprinkle it over the torte.

8 to 10 portions

PUMPKIN PECAN TORTE

Combine two autumnal flavor favorites for a simple but sophisticated dessert. It's light and luscious any time of the year!

CRUST

1 ½ cups pecans, toasted (see Index)
2 tablespoons granulated sugar
2 tablespoons unbleached all-purpose flour
1 egg white

FILLING

1 ½ cups cooked puréed pumpkin
1 cup (packed) light brown sugar
½ cup milk
1 teaspoon ground cinnamon
½ teaspoon salt
½ teaspoon allspice
½ teaspoon ground nutmeg
3 eggs, separated
1 envelope unflavored gelatin
¼ cup warm water
Pinch of salt
2 tablespoons granulated sugar

1 cup heavy or whipping cream
2 tablespoons confectioners' sugar
¼ cup bourbon
⅓ cup chopped toasted pecans (see Index)

1. Preheat the oven to 350°F.

2. Prepare the crust: Combine the pecans and the sugar in a food processor, and process until pecans are finely chopped. Add the flour and egg white, and process until well mixed.

3. Press the pecan mixture into the bottom and sides of an 8½-inch springform pan (moistening your fingers with water if necessary). Bake until the crust pulls away from the sides, about 15 minutes. Set it aside to cool.

4. Prepare the filling: Combine the pumpkin, brown sugar, milk, cinnamon, salt, allspice, and nutmeg in a saucepan and heat just to a boil. Remove the pan from the heat and add the egg yolks one at a time, incorporating well after each addition.

5. Combine the gelatin and the warm water in a small bowl, and set aside for 3 minutes.

6. Stir the softened gelatin into the pumpkin mixture, and transfer it to a mixing bowl. Set it in a larger bowl filled with ice, and stir occasionally as the mixture cools and begins to set, 20 to 30 minutes.

7. Beat the egg whites and salt with an electric mixer until they form soft peaks. Sprinkle the granulated sugar over the whites and continue beating until they are glossy, 15 to 20 seconds more. Wash and dry the mixer blades.

8. Just as the pumpkin mixture is beginning to set, fold in the egg whites. Pour the mixture into the prepared crust, tap the pan lightly to eliminate any bubbles, and chill, uncovered, until thoroughly set, at least 6 hours.

9. To serve, whip the cream to soft peaks with the electric mixer and stir in the confectioners' sugar and bourbon. Top each slice with a dollop of the bourbon cream, and sprinkle with the chopped pecans.

8 to 10 portions

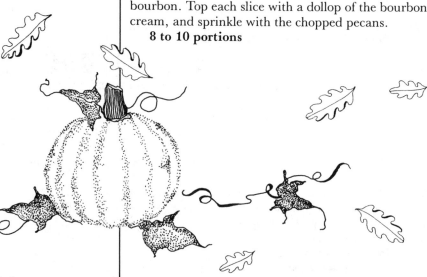

NUTS ABOUT NUTS

We love the nuts in our lives—at a baseball game, on an airplane, at the circus, in a bar, or at a cocktail party. But nuts go far beyond snack food. They are a traditional pastry and dessert ingredient, complementing other flavors of citrus, fruit, and chocolate or taking center stage. And we are just beginning to discover how versatile they are in side dishes, entrées, soups, stews, and sandwiches.

BUYING, STORING, AND PREPARING NUTS

You can buy nuts raw, dry- or oil-roasted, and smoked, in the shell or out, whole, in halves, chopped, slivered, sliced, or ground, with skins or without, salted, sugared, or spiced, loose in barrels or packed in cellophane bags, cans, or jars.

Nuts in shells store better than shelled nuts, those in skins better than without, and whole nuts better than sliced or chopped. Nuts in their shells are best stored in a cool, dry place. Because part of every nut is oil or fat, they do turn rancid over time. Most shelled nuts will keep for several months if kept dry and cool, but they will last even longer in the refrigerator and up to a year in the freezer.

Shells Off. Thin nut shells, like peanuts, will give if pressed with your fingers. Harder shells should be opened with a nutcracker. Crack the nut all around in little bits to keep the meat intact. To open Brazil nuts and black walnuts, you'll need a hammer. Two pounds of nuts in the shell generally yields one pound shelled.

Blanching. Blanching nuts removes the thin papery skin, which has flavor and color but not always the taste or appearance you would like. To blanch nuts, put up to ¼ pound of them in a bowl and cover with boiling water. Let stand for only 1 minute (you don't want the nuts to lose their crispness), then drain and cool in cold water. Pop the nuts out of their skins with your fingers or rub them with a kitchen towel. Spread on paper towels to dry.

Toasting Nuts and Seeds. Toasting nuts brings out their flavor and aroma. Spread nuts, whole or cut up, in a single layer on a baking sheet and toast in a 350°F oven until fragrant and golden brown, 3 to 5 minutes. Shake the pan once or twice so that they brown evenly. Check the nuts after 3 minutes. As soon as they begin to color they will toast very quickly. Be sure not to let them burn.

Slicing, Chopping, and Grinding. Slicing nuts requires a sharp heavy knife and a firm surface. Slice nuts before you toast them because toasting makes them dry and brittle.

To chop nuts, hold the knife point to the cutting surface with one hand and chop up and down with the other hand on the knife handle. A quick turn in the food processor will also do the trick.

Grinding nuts is tricky because the oil and nutmeat separate if they are too finely ground. For pastry, it is very important that the ground nuts be light and dry, not oily. Use a nut grater or grinder and grind just a few nuts at a time. Or grind the nuts in a food processor, then sift the nuts through a sieve.

IN A NUTSHELL

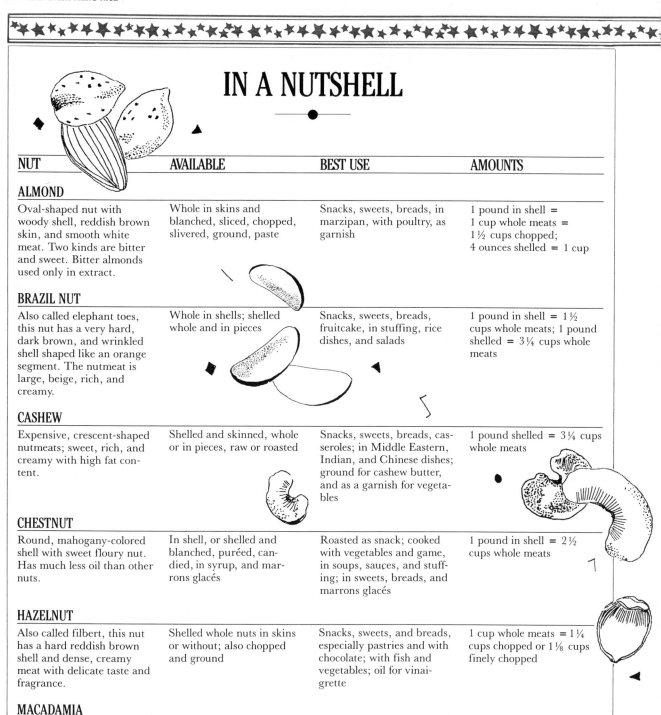

NUT	AVAILABLE	BEST USE	AMOUNTS
ALMOND Oval-shaped nut with woody shell, reddish brown skin, and smooth white meat. Two kinds are bitter and sweet. Bitter almonds used only in extract.	Whole in skins and blanched, sliced, chopped, slivered, ground, paste	Snacks, sweets, breads, in marzipan, with poultry, as garnish	1 pound in shell = 1 cup whole meats = 1½ cups chopped; 4 ounces shelled = 1 cup
BRAZIL NUT Also called elephant toes, this nut has a very hard, dark brown, and wrinkled shell shaped like an orange segment. The nutmeat is large, beige, rich, and creamy.	Whole in shells; shelled whole and in pieces	Snacks, sweets, breads, fruitcake, in stuffing, rice dishes, and salads	1 pound in shell = 1½ cups whole meats; 1 pound shelled = 3¼ cups whole meats
CASHEW Expensive, crescent-shaped nutmeats; sweet, rich, and creamy with high fat content.	Shelled and skinned, whole or in pieces, raw or roasted	Snacks, sweets, breads, casseroles; in Middle Eastern, Indian, and Chinese dishes; ground for cashew butter, and as a garnish for vegetables	1 pound shelled = 3¼ cups whole meats
CHESTNUT Round, mahogany-colored shell with sweet floury nut. Has much less oil than other nuts.	In shell, or shelled and blanched, puréed, candied, in syrup, and marrons glacés	Roasted as snack; cooked with vegetables and game, in soups, sauces, and stuffing; in sweets, breads, and marrons glacés	1 pound in shell = 2½ cups whole meats
HAZELNUT Also called filbert, this nut has a hard reddish brown shell and dense, creamy meat with delicate taste and fragrance.	Shelled whole nuts in skins or without; also chopped and ground	Snacks, sweets, and breads, especially pastries and with chocolate; with fish and vegetables; oil for vinaigrette	1 cup whole meats = 1¼ cups chopped or 1⅛ cups finely chopped
MACADAMIA Large, light tan, unevenly round, creamy nut. Rich, sweet, and buttery flavor.	Shelled only, roasted, raw, or chopped	Snacks, sweets, breads, salads, with fish and poultry	4 ounces = 1 cup whole meats

NUT	AVAILABLE	BEST USE	AMOUNTS
PEANUT			
Technically a legume, the peanut is America's favorite nut. Two bean-shaped nuts covered with papery skin in thin, tan shell.	Raw or roasted in shells, shelled and raw, roasted, and roasted and salted	Snacks, ground for butter, in casseroles, sauces, soups, and stews; cooking oil withstands high heat without burning	1 ½ pound in shell = 1 pound shelled meats
PECAN			
Semihard round shells with curly irregular halves of meat. Sweet taste and rich texture. Can be substituted for walnuts.	In shells; shelled in halves, pieces, and chopped; raw and roasted salted and unsalted	Snacks, sweets, breads, with chocolate, in ice cream, in soups and stews for thickening	2 pounds in shell = 1 pound shelled = 4 cups whole meats
PINE NUT			
Also called pignoli. This nut is small, pellet-shaped, and creamy white with sweet, rich flavor and high amount of oil. Nuts are harvested from pine cones and are expensive.	Shelled whole nuts; less expensive if bought loose (check Italian markets) than in tiny spice bottles	In Mediterranean cuisine—pesto, stuffing, sauces, soups, stews, rice dishes, pastries, and cookies	1 ½ ounces = ¼ cup
PISTACHIO			
Small nut with smooth thin shell and pale green meat covered with reddish skin. Mild flavor.	In shells raw or roasted and salted; shelled raw and roasted salted and unsalted	Snacks, in Middle Eastern pastries, halvah, ice cream, sausages, stuffing, and pâté	3 pounds in shell = 1 pound shelled meats
BLACK WALNUT			
Thinner nut than regular walnut with dark skin, very hard black shell, and stronger flavor.	In shells and shelled raw	Sweets, candy, ice cream, bread	4 ounces shelled = 1 cup
WALNUT			
Specifically the English or Persian walnut, this nut has a hard, round, tan shell with irregular curly nutmeat halves. Mild, sweet flavor, rich in oil.	In shells; shelled in halves, pieces, and chopped; also pickled	Snacks, sweets, breads, ground for butter, in stuffing, rice dishes, pâté, with poultry, game, vegetables; oil for vinaigrette	1 pound in shell = 2 cups meats

COOKIES AND MILK

We were always getting caught with our hands in the cookie jar as children, and we still are. Cookies just don't seem to let you grow up. Ever since the Dutch brought their *koekjes* to the New World, Americans have been wild about cookies. We've raided every nation's cookie jar for the best—tea biscuits from England, tuiles from France, shortbread from Scotland, Christmas cookies from Germany and Austria, and almond cakes from China. And in our inimitable American fashion, we've thrown into the cookie dough everything from peanut butter to chocolate, then dunked the results in milk. Today, that's the way the cookie crumbles.

OLD-FASHIONED CHOCOLATE CHIP COOKIES

The original Toll House recipe with just a bit of updating. We also like these done in miniature—the size of a quarter. They're so crisp... we just never tire of them with a big glass of cold milk or icy lemonade.

1 cup plus 2 tablespoons unbleached all-purpose flour
½ teaspoon baking soda
Pinch of salt
8 tablespoons (1 stick) unsalted butter, at room temperature
6 tablespoons granulated sugar
6 tablespoons (packed) light brown sugar
½ teaspoon vanilla extract
1 large egg
1 cup semisweet chocolate morsels

1. Preheat the oven to 375°F. Lightly grease baking sheets.

2. Stir the flour, baking soda, and salt together in a small bowl.

3. Combine the butter, both sugars, and vanilla in a mixing bowl, and beat until light. Beat in the egg. Slowly add the flour mixture, beating until smooth. Then stir in the chocolate morsels.

4. Drop the batter by rounded dessert spoonfuls, 3 inches apart, onto the prepared baking sheets. Bake 5 minutes. Remove the baking sheets from the oven, rap them twice on the counter or stove top, and return them to the oven. Bake until the cookies are dry on top and golden, about 4 minutes. Transfer the cookies to a wire rack to cool.

2 dozen cookies

GINGERSNAPS

By far the snappiest ginger cookies we've yet made —ginger addicts take note! A stack of these interlaced with ginger-flavored whipped cream makes a great "ice box dessert."

2 cups (4 sticks) unsalted butter, at room temperature
2 ½ cups (packed) dark brown sugar
3 eggs
¾ cup molasses
4 ½ cups unbleached all-purpose flour
¼ cup ground ginger
1 ½ teaspoons ground cinnamon
1 ½ teaspoons baking soda
½ teaspoon salt

1. Cream the butter and brown sugar together in a large mixing bowl until light. Beat in the eggs, and then the molasses.

2. Sift the flour, ginger, cinnamon, baking soda, and salt together in another bowl. Using a wooden spoon, stir into the butter-sugar mixture until completely incorporated.

3. Cover the bowl with plastic wrap and set it aside for 30 minutes. (The batter may be made ahead to this point and frozen for later use.)

4. Preheat the oven to 325°F. Line baking sheets with parchment paper.

5. Place 3 to 4 large spoonfuls of batter into a pastry bag fitted with a plain large round tip, and pipe 1-inch drops, 2 inches apart, onto the prepared baking sheets. If you don't have a pastry bag, drop the batter onto the baking sheets by the teaspoonful.

6. Dip your finger in warm water, and press the cookie drops down flat. Bake until browned, 10 to 13 minutes.

7. Carefully lift the parchment off the hot baking sheets and transfer it to a cool surface. When the cookies are firm, remove them from the parchment.

About 6 dozen cookies

BAKING GREAT COOKIES

A new baking sheet on the market called Cushionaire is made of two sheets of metal with air in between. They are great for meringues because they don't overbrown the bottom. If you stack two baking sheets together, you will get the same results. Although nonstick pans produce a slightly different result in cookie baking, they are so easy to use that we always have a couple in the kitchen.

▲ Cookies baked on greased pans spread more and are thinner than those baked on ungreased pans.

▲ Do not regrease a hot baking sheet. Let it cool, wipe it clean, and begin afresh.

▲ Baking parchment or aluminum foil-covered pans will keep certain cookies, such as molasses and oatmeal, moist and less likely to burn on the bottom. Cut sheets of parchment or foil ahead of time and simply change the sheet with each batch.

BAKING

▲ Preheat your oven at least 30 minutes before baking.

▲ Use a kitchen timer. An overbaked cookie is dry and tastes stale.

▲ Check cookies for doneness 2 to 3 minutes before the recipe indicates. Ovens vary and different baking sheets affect results, so keep a sharp eye on them for the first batch or two.

COOLING AND STORING

▲ Cool cookies on wire racks without touching each other to keep them from sticking together.

▲ Store completely cooled cookies in airtight jars or tins topped with plastic wrap before closing.

▲ Store delicate cookies between sheets of waxed paper.

▲ Cookies can be frozen up to two months if securely wrapped. Thaw at room temperature.

▲ Store just one kind of cookie in a container. Don't mix them up or they'll all taste just the same.

Soft, warm cookies right out of the oven are one of life's great treats. As long as you have good recipes and the best ingredients, it's quite simple to make divine cookies. There are more kinds of cookies than any other baked goody because of all the different shapes, sizes, textures, and flavors possible. While technique is easy and equipment minimal, a few general rules for good cookie baking should be followed.

▲ Read the entire recipe through.

▲ Assemble all the ingredients before you begin.

▲ Cream the butter and sugar together thoroughly, but mix in the dry ingredients gently or your cookies will be too tough to crumble.

PANS

Choose your pans carefully for they will affect the color, shape, and height of your cookies. Make sure the baking sheets and pans are smaller than the inside of your oven so the heat can circulate evenly. When baking more than one sheet at a time, switch them halfway through baking if one is baking faster than the other.

We prefer heavy-gauge aluminum, turned steel, or blue steel pans. They darken as they age, which is good, and should not be scrubbed shiny clean. Just wipe them after baking and put them in the oven to dry.

PINWHEEL COOKIES

The cookie that makes grown-ups and kids go in circles: crisp light chocolate and vanilla swirls. If you make these, you'll never grow old!

⅔ cup unsalted butter, at room temperature
⅔ cup sugar
½ vanilla bean, cut lengthwise
1 egg
1¾ cups unbleached all-purpose flour
¼ cup imported unsweetened cocoa

1. Cream the butter and sugar together in a mixing bowl until light. Scrape out and add the seeds from the vanilla bean, and then beat in the egg until the mixture is smooth. Set aside ¾ cup of the batter.

2. Add 1 cup of the flour to the remaining batter, beating until smooth. Roll the dough out between two sheets of waxed paper to form a 12 x 8-inch rectangle. Transfer the wrapped dough to a baking sheet, and remove the top sheet of waxed paper.

3. Beat the remaining ¾ cup flour and the cocoa into the reserved ¾ cup batter. Roll the dough out between two sheets of waxed paper as in Step 2. Remove the top sheet, and invert the dough onto the first rectangle. Refrigerate for 15 minutes.

4. Remove the top sheet of waxed paper, and starting on a long side, roll the dough up tightly, jelly-roll fashion. Refrigerate it, wrapped in the bottom sheet of waxed paper, for 1 hour.

5. Preheat the oven to 375°F. Lightly grease baking sheets.

6. Remove the waxed paper and cut the roll into ¼-inch-thick slices. Arrange them, 2 inches apart, on the prepared baking sheets and bake until pale golden, 12 minutes. Cool the cookies on wire racks.

4 dozen cookies

LACY OATMEAL COOKIES

If you've never been caught with your hand in the cookie jar, then you haven't had a cookie this good. Brown sugar adds a great flavor to these classic favorites.

1½ cups quick-cooking rolled oats
¾ cup unbleached all-purpose flour
½ teaspoon ground cinnamon
½ teaspoon baking soda
8 tablespoons (1 stick) unsalted butter, at room temperature
½ cup (packed) light brown sugar
½ cup granulated sugar
1 egg
1 teaspoon vanilla extract
½ cup dried currants
¼ cup chopped walnuts

1. Preheat the oven to 350°F. Lightly grease baking sheets.

2. Toss the oats, flour, cinnamon, and baking soda together in a bowl.

3. Cream the butter and both sugars together in a mixing bowl until light. Beat in the egg and vanilla. Then slowly beat in the dry ingredients, then the currants, and walnuts.

4. Drop the batter by rounded teaspoonfuls, 2 inches apart, onto the prepared baking sheets and bake until golden, 10 minutes. Leave the cookies on the baking sheets for 2 minutes; then transfer them to wire racks to cool.

4½ dozen cookies

WHO STOLE THE COOKIE FROM THE COOKIE JAR?

❤

Cookies can be classified into six groups: bar, drop, rolled, pressed, molded or shaped, and refrigerated. Bar and drop cookies are made with a soft dough. All others are made with a stiff dough; they are usually less sweet and often have a higher proportion of fat than soft-dough cookies.

BAR COOKIES

Bar cookies vary greatly depending on the dough used for the base, the filling, and the topping. A simple one-layer bar cookie is best typified by the brownie. It is fully baked in one step. A two-layered bar cookie is baked in two steps. First a soft dough is patted into the prepared pan and baked. Then the topping is spread over the dough and baked again. A three-layer bar cookie begins with the layer of baked soft dough. Then a simple filling, like chocolate chips, is spread over the dough and returned to the oven to melt, creating the second layer. Finally, the topping is added and the pan goes back into the oven.

Although it's tempting to dig right into a pan of bar cookies, be sure to cool them completely before cutting. A simple trick for neat bar cookies is to trim all the sides about ¼ inch before cutting into squares or rectangles. Bar cookies do not keep very well, so bake them as close to serving as possible.

DROP COOKIES

Drop cookies are fun and easy to make—perfect for the beginner. The batter is quickly mixed and then the soft dough is dropped from a spoon onto baking sheets. Be sure to allow plenty of room between cookies for them to spread out. If the recipe calls for flattening the mound, slightly moisten the bottom of a glass or the palm of your hand and press lightly.

ROLLED COOKIES

We love these cookies for the variety of shapes they can be cut into. Wrap the chilled dough first to firm it slightly—15 minutes is about right. The chilling relaxes the gluten and produces a more tender cookie. Too much chilling hardens the butter and shortening, and you'll have to work the dough hard to roll it out, which will make a tougher cookie.

To roll the dough, sprinkle a surface very lightly with flour. If the dough has a lot of butter in it, roll the dough between two sheets of floured waxed paper. To cut shapes, start from the edge of the dough and work toward the center so that fewer scraps remain. When rerolling scraps, only reflour the surface if necessary and do it lightly.

PRESSED COOKIES

Pressed cookies are most often made with a stiff dough and they will not spread much at all when baked. If you do not have a cookie press to squeeze out the dough, a pastry bag with a shaped tip can be used. These cookies are nice garnished with a small nut or glazed cherry at the center before baking.

MOLDED OR SHAPED COOKIES

Our favorite molded cookie is the tuile. They're wonderfully decorative and impressive when they're huge—4 to 5 inches in diameter—and delightful when tiny alongside a mousse. No matter what the size, they are a bit tricky to make. Tuiles should be baked a few at a time because they must be molded while they are still warm. If pressed over the bottom of an upside-down custard cup, the tuile becomes a crisp little bowl for a scoop of ice cream or spoonful of fresh berries. For light airy cookies, shape them over a rolling pin; for tighter cigars, roll them around the handle of a wooden spoon.

REFRIGERATED COOKIES

If you ever need 100 cookies or more or you need a batch at a moment's notice, this is the dough to choose. Make up individual rolls, wrap in plastic wrap, and freeze. The dough will keep up to three months, but most are chilled overnight in the refrigerator and sliced and baked the next day. These lovely cookies can be sliced thin and baked crisp or sliced thick for soft cookies. They are wonderful with ice cream, sorbets, and fruit desserts and perfect for packing in a tin and sending as a gift.

ORANGE TUILES

drape hot tuiles over a rolling pin to shape

Tuiles make a dramatic appearance as part of dessert. Grand Marnier, orange flower water, and orange zest make these very special—lovely with a rich espresso. Just be prepared to work fast when they come out of the oven, as they must be shaped when they're very hot.

⅓ cup unbleached all-purpose flour
⅔ cup confectioners' sugar
Pinch of salt
2 teaspoons Grand Marnier liqueur
1 teaspoon orange flower water*
2 egg whites, lightly beaten
Finely grated zest of 2 oranges
1 cup sliced blanched almonds
8 tablespoons (1 stick) unsalted butter, at room temperature

1. Preheat the oven to 400°F. Lightly butter a heavy baking sheet.

2. Sift the flour, confectioners' sugar, and salt together in a large bowl. Make a well in the center, and add the Grand Marnier, orange flower water, egg whites, orange zest, and almonds. Mix thoroughly. Then add the butter and stir until smooth.

3. Drop the batter by teaspoonfuls, at least 3 inches apart, onto the prepared baking sheet. Using a fork dipped in cold water, spread the batter out slightly. Only three or four will fit on the baking sheet.

4. Bake until the cookies are golden brown, 6 to 8 minutes. Remove them immediately and drape them over a rolling pin. Allow them to cool on the pin. Remove the cooled, shaped cookies very carefully.

5. Repeat with the remaining batter. Store the cookies in a large plastic container with a tight seal.

12 cookies
*Available in specialty food shops.

LEMON LACE COOKIES

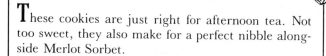

These cookies are just right for afternoon tea. Not too sweet, they also make for a perfect nibble alongside Merlot Sorbet.

1 cup unbleached all-purpose flour, sifted
¼ teaspoon salt
1 cup finely chopped blanched almonds
¾ cup (packed) light brown sugar
½ cup light corn syrup
8 tablespoons (1 stick) unsalted butter
1 teaspoon lemon extract
Finely grated zest of 2 lemons
1 tablespoon fresh lemon juice

1. Preheat the oven to 350°F. Lightly butter heavy baking sheets.

2. Combine the flour, salt, and almonds in a large bowl, and stir thoroughly.

3. Combine the brown sugar, corn syrup, and butter in a heavy saucepan and bring to a boil. Remove the pan from the heat and stir in the flour mixture and the lemon extract, zest, and juice.

4. Drop the batter by ½ teaspoonfuls about 2 inches apart on the prepared baking sheets. Bake just until they are lightly browned at the edges, 9 to 10 minutes. Allow the cookies to cool slightly on the baking sheet before transferring them to wire racks to cool completely.

3 dozen cookies

LEMON SENSE

▲ Lemons will keep at least 3 to 4 days at room temperature or up to four weeks in the refrigerator.

▲ If a recipe calls for both lemon juice and zest, pour the lemon juice over the zest to keep it moist and flavorful.

▲ Lemon juice and lemon zest freeze well.

▲ To extract the most juice, have the lemons at room temperature and roll them under your palm on a countertop before squeezing.

▲ Grate or remove the zest first, then squeeze for juice.

▲ To remove the zest in strips, use a very sharp paring knife, a vegetable peeler, or a special tool called a lemon zester. Remove only the colored part of the peel, leaving the bitter white pith on the lemon. If necessary, turn the strips over and scrape away any white with a sharp knife.

▲ Do not cut lemons with carbon steel knives or cook with lemon in aluminum pots.

▲ Thin-skinned lemons are the juiciest.

▲ Buy a good lemon juicer—a French wood cone or corrugated cone in a bowl. In an emergency, squeeze a lemon half around the tines of a fork.

COCONUT RAISIN MACAROONS

Golden in color and golden in raisins, these chewy macaroons could just become a habit. Remember to be ever so gentle when folding the ingredients into the egg whites.

2 egg whites
Pinch of salt
⅔ cup sugar
1 teaspoon vanilla extract
1 ½ cups shredded coconut
¼ cup golden raisins

1. Preheat the oven to 325°F. Butter heavy baking sheets and cover them with waxed paper. Lightly butter the waxed paper.

2. Beat the egg whites and salt with an electric mixer until they form soft peaks. Sprinkle 1 tablespoon of the sugar over the whites, and beat until the peaks are glossy, several seconds longer.

3. Toss together the vanilla, coconut, and raisins in a small mixing bowl. Using a rubber spatula, gently fold the remaining sugar and the coconut mixture into the egg whites.

4. Drop the batter by tablespoonfuls, 1 inch apart, onto the prepared baking sheets. Bake just until golden, about 15 minutes. Transfer them to a wire rack to cool.

20 to 25 cookies

JUNE'S MERINGUES

Molly and Annabel Lukins love to make these meringues, originally created by Julee's mother, June. That's what sharing recipes is all about! These are wonderful when topped with crushed strawberries and a dollop of whipped cream.

6 egg whites, at room temperature
⅛ teaspoon cream of tartar
2 cups sugar
1 teaspoon vanilla extract
1 tablespoon white vinegar

1. Preheat the oven to 275°F. Grease 2 baking sheets.

2. Beat the egg whites with an electric mixer in a large mixing bowl until foamy. Add the cream of tartar and continue beating until the whites are somewhat stiff.

3. Gradually beat the sugar into the egg whites. Then add the vanilla and vinegar, and beat until the whites are very stiff and shiny, about 10 minutes more.

4. Place about ½ cup of the meringue on 1 of the prepared baking sheets. Using your hands, pull the meringue into a peak to resemble a large chocolate kiss. Smooth the sides. Repeat with the remaining meringue.

5. Bake until the meringues are lightly colored, about 45 minutes. Cool completely on wire racks.

8 large meringues

MERINGUE TIPS

▲ Make sure the bowl, beater, and your hands are bone dry.

▲ Separate the eggs while they are cold—it's easier—but let the egg whites come to room temperature before starting.

▲ Add the sugar very slowly while beating the egg whites. We adore the taste of just a touch of vinegar.

▲ Beat the meringue until shiny and very stiff but not dry. If underbeaten, the meringue will weep (egg white will run out at the edges). If overbeaten, the meringue will clump together instead of spreading evenly and will bake flat with beads of sugar on the top.

TRADE SECRET

Freshly grated lemon or orange zest adds zip to all cookies.

LEMON SHORTBREAD

Lots of lemon zest makes these bars perfect for teatime or for pairing with a rich chocolate mousse.

*12 tablespoons (1½ sticks) unsalted butter, at room
   temperature*
½ cup confectioners' sugar
1½ cups unbleached all-purpose flour
¼ teaspoon salt
½ teaspoon vanilla extract
2 tablespoons grated lemon zest
2 tablespoons granulated sugar

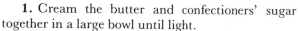

1. Cream the butter and confectioners' sugar together in a large bowl until light.

2. Sift the flour and salt together in another bowl, and add to the butter mixture. Then add the vanilla and the lemon zest, and blend thoroughly.

3. Gather the dough into a ball, wrap it in waxed paper, and refrigerate for 4 to 6 hours.

4. Remove the dough from the refrigerator and allow it to soften slightly.

5. Press the dough into an 8-inch-square cake pan. Sprinkle it with the sugar, and refrigerate, uncovered, for 45 minutes.

6. Meanwhile, preheat the oven to 325°F.

7. Bake until the shortbread is just starting to color slightly, 20 minutes. Remove the pan from the oven and allow it to cool; then cut the shortbread into 4 x 1-inch bars.

16 bars

KAY'S SANDIES

One of those childhood packaged cookies that we craved until Julee's mother-in-law, Kay, made these crisp nutty wonders. Now we're spoiled . . .

1 cup (2 sticks) unsalted butter, at room temperature
⅓ cup granulated sugar
2 tablespoons light brown sugar
2 teaspoons water
2 teaspoons vanilla extract
2 cups sifted unbleached all-purpose flour
1 cup chopped pecans
3 tablespoons confectioners' sugar

1. Combine the butter and both sugars in a mixing bowl, and cream until smooth and pale yellow.

2. Stir in the water and vanilla. Then add the flour and pecans, mixing until the dough is thick and creamy.

3. Wrap the dough in waxed paper, and chill in the refrigerator for 3 to 4 hours.

4. Preheat the oven to 325°F.

5. Remove the dough from the refrigerator and allow it to soften slightly.

6. Shape the dough into balls the size of a rounded teaspoonful, and drop them onto baking sheets, 2 inches apart. Flatten them slightly with the tines of a fork. Bake until pale golden, 20 minutes.

7. Allow the cookies to cool slightly on the baking sheets, and then roll them in the confectioners' sugar. Set them on wire racks to cool completely.
3 dozen cookies

STEFFI BERNE'S HAZELNUT LACE COOKIES

Every year at Christmastime Steffi bakes the most wonderful cookies for a holiday Champagne and dessert party. As she packs them away in cookie jars, the big question is: How many will be left for the night of the party? They are irresistible!

⅓ cup light corn syrup
4 tablespoons (½ stick) unsalted butter
⅓ cup (packed) light brown sugar
½ cup finely chopped hazelnuts, skins removed (see Note)
½ cup unbleached all-purpose flour
Pinch of salt

1. Adjust the oven racks to divide the oven into thirds. Preheat the oven to 375°F. Line baking sheets with parchment.

2. Combine the syrup, butter, and brown sugar in a heavy saucepan and heat over medium-low heat, stirring, until the butter has melted.

3. Remove the pan from the heat and allow it to cool slightly. Stir in the nuts, flour, and salt. The mixture should not be too hot.

4. Using a measuring spoon and a small rubber spatula, drop the batter by level ½ teaspoonfuls, about 3 inches apart, on the lined baking sheets. Bake two sheets at a time, one on the upper and one on the lower rack, until the cookies have spread out very thin and appear lacy and light brown, 7 to 8 minutes total. After 4 minutes, switch the baking sheets to ensure even baking.

5. Remove the sheets from the oven and immediately slide the parchment onto a flat surface. Let the cookies cool until firm, 3 minutes. Then use a metal spatula to carefully transfer them to a wire rack to cool completely.

6 dozen very thin cookies

Note: To skin hazelnuts, place them in a single layer on a baking sheet and bake in a 350°F oven, shaking the pan occasionally, for 10 to 15 minutes. Do not let them burn (this can happen very quickly). Transfer the nuts to a dish towel and let them steam briefly. Then rub them in the towel until the skin flakes off. Cool completely before using.

PEANUT BUTTER COOKIES

We all remember peanut butter cookies from our childhood—keep them in a cookie jar for your children too! The Cookie Monster is alive and well.

8 tablespoons (1 stick) unsalted butter, at room temperature
½ cup chunky peanut butter
¾ cup (packed) light brown sugar
2 tablespoons maple syrup
1 egg, lightly beaten
1 teaspoon vanilla extract
1 ½ cups unbleached all-purpose flour
¾ teaspoon baking soda
½ cup salted peanuts, coarsely chopped

1. Preheat the oven to 375°F.

2. In a mixer bowl, cream the butter, peanut butter, and brown sugar together until light. Then beat in the maple syrup, egg, and vanilla.

3. In another bowl, toss the flour with the baking soda and peanuts. Slowly beat this into the liquid ingredients.

4. Drop the mixture by rounded tablespoonfuls, 3 inches apart, on baking sheets. Flatten them slightly with the tines of a fork. Bake until pale golden, 7 to 8 minutes. Remove the cookies from the baking sheets and cool on a wire rack.

2 dozen cookies

THE PROOF OF THE PUDDING IS IN THE CREME BRULEE

We are crazy for custards, passionate about puddings, and fascinated by flans. Bread pudding comforts and crème brûlée beguiles. It's amazing but true that a basic formula of milk, eggs, and sugar is transformed into so many creamy sweets from every corner of the world. Each has just a little different formula, its own cooking method, and often one or two subtle added ingredients that make it extraordinary. Custard is one of the most elusive and magical of the kitchen arts, but when the result is a great one, everybody knows it.

THE BASIC COMFORT FOOD

❤

We remember years ago our mothers making chocolate and butterscotch puddings for dessert. Whenever we were in need of comfort, they seemed to do the trick. But sweet puddings are a relatively modern invention since sugar as we know it only became available in the late eighteenth century. Early English puddings were actually sausages. In New England, the colonists ate pudding as a savory first course, and Indian pudding was made with cornmeal, a truly native American ingredient. Today pudding can be both sweet and savory. We've taken poetic license with our recipes and have both lightened and updated these old favorites.

RICE PUDDING

One of our favorites, rice pudding has very simple ingredients. We combine Italian Arborio rice (the risotto rice) with milk, sugar, hazelnuts, and sweet dried currants plumped in Frangelico. During the long, slow baking, the pudding thickens and becomes deliciously creamy. Be creative with these puddings: Substitute cream for milk, light brown sugar for white, and add raisins soaked in rum or other dried fruit plumped in orange liqueur with lots of orange zest. Use the basic method as your artist's palette and serve up your own creation hot or chilled with a little cream drizzled over the top.

BREAD PUDDING

All bread puddings start with the same basic ingredients—day-old bread, milk or cream, eggs, sugar, and flavorings. Stale or dry bread really is best for the pudding since much of the moisture has evaporated, leaving the bread to soak up the flavored cream like a sponge.

Any type of bread will do, but we love puddings made with eggy challah and brioche. For variety, we sometimes bake the pudding in a loaf pan, slice it thin, and fan the slices on dessert plates. (Be sure the pudding is well chilled before slicing.) Brandy or whiskey sauces are delicious with bread pudding, but for a lighter, eye-catching dessert, we spoon a fresh raspberry or strawberry sauce under or over it.

CUSTARDS

Creamy and comforting, these are made basically with eggs, sugar, milk or cream, and a dazzle of spices or special flavorings. The fat in the cream can make these desserts very rich. We've compromised and used half-and-half in our ginger custard—just a little wicked. Custards are baked in a water bath, which creates steam inside the oven and prevents the top of the custard from forming a crust or cracking. Serve custard hot, warm, or chilled.

FLAN (Crème Caramel)

Flan is a custard baked in a ramekin lined with caramelized sugar. After the custard is baked and chilled, it is inverted onto a plate. The caramel oozes off the top, forming a luscious sauce. The custard may be heated on top of the stove before pouring into ramekins, but with our Orange Flan we just whisk the custard ingredients together, pour them into a caramel-coated pan, and bake the dessert in a hot water bath. Fresh orange juice and Grand Marnier add delightful flavor.

CREME BRULEE

This is undoubtedly the ultimate baked custard. We lightened ours with half-and-half and added the surprise of fresh berries. The custard is baked in a water bath well ahead of time and then thoroughly chilled. Shortly before serving, the tops are sprinkled with sugar and the dishes placed under a broiler until the sugar melts and caramelizes. They must be watched carefully so that they don't burn, and they should be served within 15 minutes or the sugar will begin to weep.

CHALLAH BREAD PUDDING WITH WHISKEY SAUCE

A very moist bread pudding—the kind you slice with a knife and serve with a warm, creamy whiskey sauce. This can be either elegant or comfy, depending on your mood.

4 tablespoons (½ stick) unsalted butter, at room temperature
12 slices day-old challah or other egg bread, crusts removed
3 cups milk
4 large eggs
3 egg yolks
⅓ cup Irish whiskey or bourbon
⅔ cup sugar
1½ teaspoons vanilla extract
1 cup Whiskey Sauce (recipe follows)

1. Preheat the oven to 350°F.

2. Butter the bread on both sides, and set it aside.

3. In a large mixing bowl, whisk together the milk, whole eggs, egg yolks, whiskey, sugar, and vanilla.

4. Place a layer of buttered challah in the bottom of a 9 x 5-inch loaf pan. Be sure the entire surface is covered, with no spaces between the slices. Continue layering the challah slices until they reach 1 inch from the top of the pan. Slowly pour the milk mixture over the challah, letting the bread absorb the liquid. When no more liquid can be absorbed, stop adding the milk mixture.

5. Place the loaf pan in the center of a deep ovenproof pan. Pour boiling water into the pan until it reaches halfway up the sides of the loaf pan. Place the pan on the center rack of the oven, and bake until the pudding is just set, 45 minutes. Remove the pan carefully from the oven and cool the loaf pan on a wire rack.

6. To serve, place a thick slice of warm bread pudding on a plate, and top it with Whiskey Sauce.

6 to 8 portions

WHISKEY SAUCE

5 large egg yolks
½ cup sugar
¼ cup Irish whiskey or bourbon

1. Beat the egg yolks and sugar in a bowl with an electric mixer until pale yellow. Add the whiskey and beat until well mixed.

2. Transfer the mixture to the top of a double boiler and place it over cold water. Cook, stirring constantly, over medium-high heat until the water in the bottom pot reaches the boiling point and the mixture in the top part is thick and creamy.

3. Serve hot or cold. Whisk before serving.

1 cup

FRUITY CREME BRULEE

Fresh berries add new lightness and texture to this glisteningly rich basic.

1 pint blueberries (picked over) and/or raspberries, lightly rinsed and drained
3 cups half-and-half
¼ cup sugar
3 whole eggs
2 egg yolks
1 teaspoon vanilla extract
Confectioners' sugar, for dusting

1. Line the bottom of eight ½-cup ramekins with the berries, and set them aside.

2. Preheat the oven to 300°F.

3. Heat the half-and-half in a heavy saucepan over medium-low heat just to the boiling point.

4. Meanwhile, whisk the sugar, whole eggs, and egg yolks together in a large bowl until the mixture is light and frothy.

5. Slowly whisk the hot half-and-half into the egg mixture; mix thoroughly, and strain the mixture back into the saucepan. Using a wooden spoon, stir the mixture over low heat until it just coats the back of the spoon. Add the vanilla.

6. Divide the custard among the berry-lined ramekins, and set them in a baking dish. Pour hot water into the dish until it reaches two thirds of the way up the sides of the ramekins. Place the dish in the oven, and bake until a skewer inserted in the center of one of the custards comes out clean, about 35 to 40 minutes.

7. Remove the ramekins from the water bath and allow them to cool slightly. Then cover and refrigerate until chilled, 2 hours.

8. To serve, preheat the broiler.

9. Sift a light layer of confectioners' sugar over the ramekins, and place them under the broiler just until the sugar caramelizes, 2 to 4 minutes. Serve immediately.

8 portions

GINGER CUSTARD

A traditionally soothing custard is sparkled by the bite of fresh and crystallized ginger.

3 cups half-and-half
10 slices (¼-inch thick) peeled fresh ginger
¾ cup finely chopped Crystallized Candied Ginger (recipe follows)
3 whole eggs
2 egg yolks
¼ cup sugar
½ teaspoon ground ginger
1 cup heavy or whipping cream, whipped

1. Heat the half-and-half in a heavy saucepan over medium-low heat just to the boiling point. Add the fresh ginger slices and remove from the heat. Cover the pan and set it aside for 30 minutes.

2. Divide ½ cup of the crystallized ginger among eight ½-cup ramekins, lining the bottoms.

3. Preheat the oven to 300°F.

4. Whisk the whole eggs, egg yolks, sugar, and ground ginger together in a large bowl.

5. Heat the half-and-half just to a boil again. Slowly strain it into the egg mixture (discard the fresh ginger); combine thoroughly. Then whisk the mixture back into the saucepan and cook over low heat, stirring constantly with a wooden spoon, until the custard just coats the back of the spoon. Be careful not to allow the mixture to boil.

6. Divide the custard among the ginger-lined ramekins, and set them in a baking dish. Pour hot water into the dish until it reaches two thirds of the way up the sides of the ramekins. Place the dish in the oven, and bake until a skewer inserted in the center of one of the custards comes out clean, about 30 minutes.

7. Serve the custard warm or chilled, with a dab of whipped cream on top, sprinkled with the remaining ¼ cup crystallized ginger.

8 portions

CRYSTALLIZED CANDIED GINGER

*2 cups peeled and diagonally sliced fresh ginger (¼ -inch-
thick slices)*
Salt
4 cups water
1 cup sugar, plus extra for coating

1. Place the ginger slices in a medium-size saucepan and add cold water to cover. Stir in a pinch of
salt, and bring to a boil. Reduce the heat and simmer
for 30 minutes. Then drain the ginger, rinse it under
cold water, and drain again.

2. Repeat this process three more times, each
time using fresh cold water and another pinch of salt.

3. Return the ginger to the saucepan and add the
4 cups water and 1 cup sugar. Bring to a boil. Then
lower the heat and simmer until a thick syrup coats
the ginger, 1 ¼ hours.

4. Sprinkle a ¼ -inch layer of sugar on a small
baking sheet. Using a fork, lift the ginger slices out of
the saucepan and turn them in the sugar, coating
them well. Transfer the ginger to a wire rack to cool
and dry for at least 1 hour.

5. Store the ginger in a covered jar (it will keep
for several months if airtight).

About 2 cups

HAZELNUT RISOTTO PUDDING

This elegant and earthy version
of the nursery-room classic would
be cause for celebration at any
black-tie dinner.

½ cup dried currants
½ cup Frangelico liqueur
4 cups milk
5 tablespoons sugar
½ teaspoon vanilla extract
¼ cup Arborio rice
⅓ cup hazelnuts, toasted (see Index) and coarsely chopped
1 cup heavy or whipping cream

1. Combine the currants and Frangelico in a
small bowl, and soak, loosely covered, for 8 hours or
overnight.

2. Preheat the oven to 350°F.

3. Butter a 3-quart baking dish and pour in the
milk. Add the sugar, vanilla, and rice, and mix
thoroughly.

4. Bake, uncovered, stirring every 15 to 20 minutes, until the rice is cooked and almost all the liquid
has been absorbed, about 2 hours.

5. Drain the currants, and stir them into the
pudding along with the hazelnuts. Serve hot or
chilled, with heavy cream drizzled over.

4 portions

ORANGE FLAN

We have always loved the silky, velvety texture of
flan. The orange flavors in this one are like a kiss of
sunshine in the middle of winter. A perfect dessert
when you're serving Catalan Pheasant Stew.

CARAMEL
½ cup sugar
3 tablespoons water

CUSTARD
1 cup fresh orange juice
5 whole eggs, lightly beaten
2 egg yolks, lightly beaten
½ cup sugar
2 tablespoons heavy or whipping cream
1 tablespoon Grand Marnier liqueur
½ teaspoon vanilla extract

1. Preheat the oven to 350°F.

2. Prepare the caramel: Combine the sugar and water in a small heavy saucepan and cook over medium heat until the mixture is thick, bubbling, and just amber colored. As it cooks, brush down any crystals forming on the sides of the pan with a wet pastry brush (or keep the pan covered for the first 5 minutes). The mixture will be very hot.

3. Pour the hot caramel into a dry 4- to 5-cup ring mold. Wearing pot holders or mitts, swirl the ring mold to coat the bottom and part of the sides with caramel. Set aside.

4. Prepare the custard: Whisk the orange juice, whole eggs, yolks, sugar, cream, Grand Marnier, and vanilla together in a bowl just until smooth.

5. Pour the mixture into the caramel-coated mold. Set the mold in a larger pan, and pour enough hot water in the larger pan to reach halfway up the sides of the mold.

6. Bake until the top of the custard is firm to the touch, about 30 minutes. Let it cool to room temperature, and then refrigerate it until chilled, 2 hours.

7. Unmold the flan onto a large platter. Slice and serve, spooning caramel over each serving.

6 to 8 portions

MASCARPONE COEUR A LA CREME

The perfect way to say I love you—with a bit of sweet creamy mascarpone cheese and the gentle bite of chèvre. Our Blueberry Sauce, made with red wine vinegar, is the perfect foil.

12 ounces mascarpone cheese
8 ounces farmer's cheese
3 tablespoons soft mild chèvre
3 tablespoons confectioners' sugar
1 cup heavy or whipping cream
Blueberry Sauce (recipe follows)

1. Dampen and thoroughly wring out a double thickness of cheesecloth, and use it to line a 7- to 8-inch coeur à la crème mold; leave enough cloth overhanging to fold over the top. Set the mold aside.

2. Combine the three cheeses in a food processor and process until smooth. Add the confectioners' sugar and process again. Then, with the motor still running, add the cream through the feed tube and process until it is thoroughly incorporated.

3. Fill the prepared mold with the cheese mixture, cover it with the overhanging cheesecloth, and place the mold in a shallow pan (to contain the liquid given off by the cheese). Refrigerate until firmly set, 24 hours.

4. To serve, open the cheesecloth wrapping and invert the coeur à la crème onto a large round serving platter. Carefully remove the cheesecloth, and surround with the sauce.

6 portions

BLUEBERRY SAUCE

4 cups fresh or frozen (thawed) blueberries
½ cup sugar
2 tablespoons red wine vinegar
¼ teaspoon ground cinnamon
¼ teaspoon ground nutmeg
⅛ teaspoon ground mace
⅛ teaspoon ground cloves

1. Place the blueberries in a medium-size heavy saucepan. Add all the remaining ingredients, and toss gently.

2. Cook over medium heat, stirring frequently, for 15 minutes. Then raise the heat and boil for 5 minutes. Finally, reduce the heat to medium again and cook, stirring frequently, for 10 minutes.

3. Remove the sauce from the heat and allow it to cool to room temperature. Refrigerate until chilled, 2 hours.

2 cups

THE SODA FOUNTAIN

We are still screaming for ice cream, and it doesn't sound like the clamor is letting up. Each American eats about 32 quarts a year, which makes ice cream by far America's favorite sweet. And in the last ten years, we have seen an explosion of flavors, textures, and colors the likes of which we've never seen before. Keeping pace are the large number of faster, simpler ice cream machines on the market. Even with a hundred flavors, we want it our way. To us that means intense: not just chocolate, but bitter chocolate; lemon—not just tart, but creamy too; double vanilla; and sorbets the very essence of fruits and wines.

BITTERSWEET CHOCOLATE ICE CREAM

The rich consistency of this ice cream comes from creating a perfectly smooth custard base. Using the microwave eliminates the guessing about when it's thick enough or stirred enough—and dramatically reduces the cooking time. Adding the buttermilk heightens the chocolate flavor.

4 extra-large egg yolks
¾ cup sugar
1 cup milk
1 cup heavy or whipping cream
7 ounces good-quality bittersweet chocolate, broken into small
  pieces
¾ cup buttermilk

1. Using an electric mixer, cream the egg yolks and sugar in a bowl until the mixture is thick and light.

2. Combine the milk and cream in a 6-cup microwave-safe casserole, and cook at full power (650 to 700 watts), uncovered, for 2 minutes.

3. With the mixer running, slowly add the hot milk-cream mixture to the egg yolks, and blend until smooth.

4. Transfer the mixture to the casserole and return it, uncovered, to the microwave. Whisking once a minute, cook until the mixture is thick and coats the back of a spoon, 3 minutes.

5. Remove the casserole from the microwave and add the chocolate, whisking until melted and smooth. Then whisk in the buttermilk.

6. Allow the custard to cool to room temperature.

Then refrigerate it, loosely covered, until chilled, a minimum of 3 hours.

7. Transfer the mixture to an ice cream maker and freeze according to manufacturer's directions.

1 quart

Note: This recipe was cooked on High (full power, 650 to 700 watts) in a carousel microwave, using microwave-safe containers.

If your microwave is less powerful, you will have to allow for more cooking time (approximately 1½ times the amount called for—but watch carefully); if it does not have a carousel, you may have to rotate the dish while it is cooking.

VANILLA VANILLA ICE CREAM

If you love vanilla ice cream, we've created a taste you won't forget! Make a New Basic "black cow" by pouring cold, tangy root beer over a scoop of vanilla—or try a scoop of vanilla, some chocolate syrup, and a bit of seltzer for a good old-fashioned soda-fountain soda.

6 egg yolks
¾ cup sugar
1¼ cups milk
1¼ cups heavy or
  whipping cream
1½ large vanilla beans
  (1 large bean is 6 inches long)
½ teaspoon vanilla extract
Pinch of salt

1. Cream the egg yolks and sugar together in a mixing bowl until thick and light.

2. Combine the milk and cream in a 2-quart microwave-safe casserole. Cut the vanilla beans in half lengthwise, and scrape the seeds into the bowl. Add the beans, extract, and salt. Cook, uncovered, at full power (650 to 700 watts) for 3 minutes.

3. Remove the vanilla beans. With a mixer running on low speed, slowly add the milk mixture to the egg yolk mixture, stirring until smooth. Return the mixture to the casserole.

4. Whisking once a minute, cook until the custard is thick and coats the back of a spoon, 3½ minutes. Do not overcook it.

5. Allow the custard to cool to room temperature. Then refrigerate it, loosely covered, until chilled, a minimum of 3 hours.

6. Freeze in an ice cream maker according to manufacturer's directions.

5 cups

Note: This recipe was cooked on High (full power, 650 to 700 watts) in a carousel microwave, using microwave-safe containers.

If your microwave is less powerful, you will have to allow for more cooking time (approximately 1½ times the amount called for—but watch carefully); if it does not have a carousel, you may have to rotate the dish while it is cooking.

The creamy smoothness in ice cream is butterfat. The higher the butterfat content, the richer and smoother the ice cream. The FDA stipulates that to be called ice cream, vanilla ice cream must have at least 10 percent butterfat and chocolate 8 percent (the other 2 percent is made by the fat in chocolate). Many ice creams just reach those percentages, but premium ice cream goes far beyond—up to 22 percent.

SWEET STRAWBERRY ICE CREAM

All you need is a sugar cone and some sprinkles!

1 pint strawberries, hulled and quartered
¾ cup sugar
4 egg yolks
1 cup milk
1 cup heavy or whipping cream
¼ cup crème de cassis

1. Combine the berries and ¼ cup of the sugar in a 2-quart microwave-safe casserole, and toss well to combine. Cook at full power (650 to 700 watts), uncovered, for 8 minutes. Cool to room temperature, then cover, and refrigerate.

2. Using an electric mixer, cream the egg yolks with the remaining ½ cup sugar in a mixing bowl until thick and light. Set the mixture aside.

3. Combine the milk and cream in a 2-quart microwave-safe casserole, and cook, uncovered, for 2 minutes.

4. With a mixer running on low speed, slowly add the milk mixture to the egg mixture, stirring until smooth. Return it to the casserole.

5. Whisking once a minute, cook until the custard is thick and coats the back of a spoon, 2 minutes. Do not overcook it.

6. Allow the custard to cool to room temperature. Then refrigerate it, loosely covered, until chilled, a minimum of 3 hours.

7. Stir the reserved berries and the cassis into the custard, and freeze in an ice maker according to manufacturer's directions.

About 5 cups

Note: This recipe was cooked on High (full power, 650 to 700 watts) in a carousel microwave, using microwave-safe containers.

If your microwave is less powerful, you will have to allow for more cooking time (approximately 1½ times the amount called for—but watch carefully); if it does not have a carousel, you may have to rotate the dish while it is cooking.

SODA FOUNTAIN TREATS

SUNDAES

▲ Sweet Strawberry Ice Cream with fresh strawberries macerated in Grand Marnier

▲ Bittersweet Chocolate Ice Cream with minty fudge sauce

▲ Sweet Strawberry Ice Cream with Rhubarb Strawberry Sauce

▲ Peaches and Cream Ice Cream with sliced ripe peaches and a dash of peach brandy

▲ Vanilla Vanilla Ice Cream with hot Chocolate Fudge Sauce and Spanish peanuts

▲ Cinnamon Ice Cream with warm maple syrup and toasted pecans

▲ Bittersweet Chocolate Ice Cream with ribbons of dark and white chocolate sauces sprinkled with fresh raspberries

▲ Peaches and Cream Ice Cream topped with raspberry sauce and fresh raspberries

▲ Lemonade Ice Cream with Chartreuse and a sprig of lemon balm

▲ Brown Sugar Ice Cream with warm caramel sauce and toasted almonds

▲ Blackberry Sherbet with fresh blackberries and raspberries

▲ Persimmon Sorbet with chopped candied ginger

▲ Merlot Sorbet with raspberries, blackberries, and blueberries

SODAS

▲ Merlot Sorbet in a red wine spritzer

▲ Sweet Strawberry Ice Cream with strawberry soda and sliced fresh strawberries

▲ Vanilla Vanilla Ice Cream with cream soda

▲ Brown Sugar Ice Cream in root beer

▲ Sunny Lemon Sherbet with lemonade, club soda, and a sprig of mint

▲ Peaches and Cream Ice Cream in peach soda

▲ Blackberry Sherbet in raspberry soda

▲ Papaya Colada Sorbet in pineapple juice with club soda

BROWN SUGAR ICE CREAM

The tartness of sour cream softened by the sweetness of brown sugar makes every single bite of this ice cream sublime. Try a dollop on fresh fruit.

2 cups whole milk
6 egg yolks
⅔ cup (packed) dark brown sugar
1 teaspoon vanilla extract
1 cup sour cream

1. Heat the milk to a boil in a heavy saucepan. Then cover the pan and remove it from the heat.

2. Whisk the egg yolks and brown sugar together in a bowl until thickened. Stir in the vanilla.

3. Slowly pour the hot milk into the egg mixture, whisking constantly. Return the mixture to the saucepan and cook over low heat, stirring with a wooden spoon, until it has thickened slightly and coats the back of a spoon (do not allow it to boil).

4. Allow the custard to cool to room temperature. Then refrigerate it, loosely covered, until chilled, a minimum of 3 hours.

5. Freeze the mixture in an ice cream maker according to manufacturer's directions just until it begins to set. Then add the sour cream and continue freezing until it is set.

1 quart

The ice cream machine freezes liquid while constantly breaking down the ice crystals into fine fragments and aerating the mixture. Ice cream will keep its consistency in the freezer, but to enjoy that fine texture, sorbets and ices should be eaten while they are fresh.

CHUNKY BLACK CHERRY ICE CREAM

Filled with chunks of dark black cherries, this ice cream is better still if you wait until the summer cherries are in season, pit them, and add as many as you like.

2 cans (17 ounces each) pitted sweet dark
  cherries in extra-heavy syrup
4 egg yolks
½ cup sugar
1 cup milk
1 cup heavy or whipping cream

1. Drain the cherries, reserving ¾ cup of the syrup. Combine the reserved syrup and half the cherries in a food processor, and coarsely purée.

2. Transfer the mixture to a 2-quart microwave-safe casserole and cook, uncovered, at full power (650 to 700 watts) until slightly thickened, 10 minutes. Cool to room temperature, then cover, and refrigerate.

3. Cut the remaining cherries in half, place in a bowl, then cover, and refrigerate. (If you have fresh cherries, here's the place to use them.)

4. Using an electric mixer, cream the egg yolks and sugar together in a mixing bowl until thick and light.

5. Combine the milk and cream in a microwave-safe 6-cup casserole and cook, uncovered, for 2 minutes.

6. With the mixer running on low speed, slowly add the milk mixture to the egg yolk mixture, stirring until smooth. Return the mixture to the 6-cup casserole.

7. Cook, whisking once a minute, until the custard is thick and coats the back of a spoon, 2 minutes. Do not overcook.

8. Allow the custard to cool to room temperature. Then refrigerate it, loosely covered, until well chilled, a minimum of 3 hours.

9. Stir the cooked and uncooked cherries into the chilled custard, and freeze in an ice cream maker according to manufacturer's directions.

5 cups

Note: This recipe was cooked on High (full power, 650 to 700 watts) in a carousel microwave, using microwave-safe containers.

If your microwave is less powerful, you will have to allow for more cooking time (approximately 1½ times the amount called for—but watch carefully); if it does not have a carousel, you may have to rotate the dish while it is cooking.

CHERRIES AND . . .

▲ Mix fresh cherries with fresh chèvre and sugar to taste for dessert.

▲ Add sweet cherries to fruit salads at the last minute so that the color doesn't run.

▲ Look for dried cherries from Michigan to cook up in sauces, breads, muffins, cakes, and cookies. They can be eaten out of hand, too.

▲ Top Vanilla Vanilla Ice Cream with ripe Bing cherries.

PEACHES AND CREAM ICE CREAM

Keen! Wait, if you can, for the sweet ripe peaches of summer.

1 ½ cups peach nectar or juice
4 egg yolks
½ cup sugar
1 cup milk
1 cup heavy or whipping cream
1 cup chopped fresh ripe or
   drained canned peaches
6 tablespoons peach schnapps

1. Cook the peach nectar, uncovered, in a 2-quart microwave-safe casserole at full power (650 to 700 watts) until reduced to about ⅔ cup, 15 minutes. Cool to room temperature. cover, and refrigerate.

2. Using an electric mixer, cream the egg yolks and sugar together in a bowl until thick and light.

3. Combine the milk and cream in a 2-quart microwave-safe casserole and cook, uncovered, 2 minutes.

4. With the mixer running on low speed, slowly add the milk mixture to the egg mixture, stirring until smooth. Return the mixture to the casserole.

5. Stirring once a minute, cook until the custard is thick and coats the back of a spoon, 2 minutes. Do not overcook.

6. Allow the custard to cool to room temperature. Then refrigerate, loosely covered, until chilled, a minimum of 3 hours.

7. Stir the peaches, schnapps, and reduced peach nectar into the chilled custard, and freeze in an ice cream maker according to manufacturer's directions.

5 cups

Note: This recipe was cooked on High (full power, 650 to 700 watts) in a carousel microwave, using microwave-safe containers.

If your microwave is less powerful, you will have to allow for more cooking time (approximately 1 ½ times the amount called for—but watch carefully); if it does not have a carousel, you may have to rotate the dish while it is cooking.

CINNAMON ICE CREAM

When visions of sugarplums abound and summer fruit is far away, this should satisfy those creamy cravings.

3 cups heavy or whipping cream
1 cup milk
¾ cup sugar
1 large vanilla bean (6 inches long), halved lengthwise
2 teaspoons ground cinnamon
4 egg yolks
Cinnamon sticks, for garnish

1. Combine the cream, milk, sugar, vanilla bean, and ground cinnamon in a heavy saucepan, and cook, stirring occasionally, over medium-low heat until the sugar has dissolved and the mixture is hot. Remove the pan from the heat.

2. Remove the vanilla bean and scrape the seeds from the bean back into the cream mixture.

3. Whisk the egg yolks in a bowl, and slowly add 1 cup of the hot cream mixture, whisking constantly until smooth. Then slowly pour the egg mixture back into the remaining cream mixture, whisking constantly.

4. Place the saucepan over medium heat, and stir constantly until the mixture thickens, 10 to 15 minutes; do not boil. Pour the mixture through a fine-mesh strainer into a bowl. Allow the custard to cool to room temperature, and then refrigerate it, loosely covered, until chilled, 2 hours.

5. Pour the chilled custard into the bowl of an ice cream maker and freeze according to manufacturer's directions.

6. To serve, place a cinnamon stick on top of each scoop.

1 quart

LEMONADE ICE CREAM

When we get nostalgic for those long summer afternoons and fresh lemonade, it's a treat to make this ice cream. Wonderful served with hot fudge sauce or scooped into a sugar cone.

2 cups whole milk
6 egg yolks
⅔ cup sugar
1 teaspoon lemon extract
Finely grated zest of 3 lemons
2 tablespoons fresh lemon juice
¼ cup undiluted frozen lemonade concentrate

1. Heat the milk to a boil in a heavy saucepan. Then cover the pan and remove it from the heat.

2. Whisk the egg yolks and sugar together in a bowl until thick and light.

3. Slowly pour the hot milk into the egg mixture, whisking constantly. Return the mixture to the saucepan and cook over low heat, stirring with a wooden spoon, until it has thickened slightly and coats the back of a spoon (do not allow it to boil or it will curdle). Stir in the lemon extract, zest, and juice.

4. Allow the custard to cool to room temperature. Then refrigerate it, loosely covered, until chilled, a minimum of 3 hours.

5. Freeze the mixture in an ice cream maker according to manufacturer's directions just until it has begun to set. Then add the lemonade concentrate and continue freezing until it is set. Cover and freeze in the freezer for at least 1 hour before serving.

1 quart

GOOD HUMORED BAKED ALASKAS WITH CHOCOLATE SAUCE

Creamy vanilla ice cream filled with orange sherbet atop sponge cake, under a mountain of meringue. We love that contrast of sweet cream with tart orange, hot and cold, and cloud-like meringue with dark chocolate.

1 Orange-Scented Sponge Cake (see Index)
1 quart Vanilla Vanilla Ice Cream (see page 755)
¼ cup chopped Candied Orange Zest (see Index)
½ pint orange sherbet

MERINGUE
4 egg whites, at room temperature
Pinch of salt
¼ teaspoon cream of tartar
⅔ cup superfine sugar (see Note)

Chocolate Orange Sauce, warm (recipe follows)

1. Cut the cooled sponge cake in half horizontally. Cut out three 3½-inch rounds from each half, and place them on a heavy baking sheet.

2. Using a large (4-ounce) ice cream scoop, scoop out six rounds of vanilla ice cream. Using a small scoop or a melon baller, create a deep hollow in the center of the rounds, and sprinkle about 2 teaspoons of the orange zest into each hollow. Fill the hollows with a small scoop of orange sherbet, invert the ice cream balls onto the cake rounds, and freeze thoroughly, 2 hours.

3. Prepare the meringue: Beat the egg whites and salt with an electric mixer until foamy. Add the cream of tartar and continue beating until they form soft peaks. Then sprinkle the superfine sugar over the whites and beat until they are thick and glossy, about 30 seconds more.

4. Cover the cake and ice cream rounds completely with the meringue, either piping it on with a pastry bag fitted with a ½-inch star tip or spreading it on with a spoon or knife. Freeze them thoroughly, 2 hours.

5. Preheat the oven to 500°F.

6. Bake the Alaskas until the tips of the meringue

COOL CONFUSION

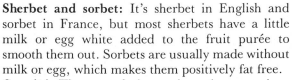

Sherbet and sorbet: It's sherbet in English and sorbet in France, but most sherbets have a little milk or egg white added to the fruit purée to smooth them out. Sorbets are usually made without milk or egg, which makes them positively fat free.

Granité: The same fruit or wine mixture as in a sorbet but with a coarser, more granular texture. Granités are not whirled in an ice cream maker but frozen in a steel pan or bowl and only occasionally stirred, which makes the ice crystals larger.

Frappé: Simply a fruit sherbet or sorbet frozen hard and pressed through a sieve when it's thawed a little so that it's slushy instead of firm.

Ice: Fruit juice, sweetener, and water frozen in an ice-cream machine. The fruit flavors are simple and the mixture is a little more watery than that of sorbet.

---

are well browned, about 4 minutes. Serve immediately, surrounded by a pool of the warm chocolate sauce.

6 portions

Note: If you don't have superfine sugar, pulse granulated sugar or sugar cubes in the food processor until it is fine but not powdery, 15 to 30 seconds.

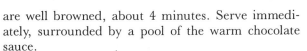

CHOCOLATE ORANGE SAUCE

3 ounces good-quality semisweet chocolate
1 ounce good-quality unsweetened chocolate
¾ cup fresh orange juice
4 tablespoons (½ stick) unsalted butter, at room temperature

1. Combine both chocolates and the orange juice in a small heavy saucepan, and stir constantly over low heat until melted; do not overheat.

2. Add the butter and incorporate it thoroughly. (This sauce can be made ahead and reheated at serving time.)

1½ cups

BLACKBERRY SHERBET

Blackberries at their most exciting. This is a sherbet you'd better hide until serving time, or there won't be any left.

3 cups blackberries
1 cup crème de cassis
2 tablespoons fresh lemon juice
½ cup sugar
¼ cup heavy or whipping cream

1. Place all the ingredients in a blender or food processor, and process until smooth.

2. Pour the purée through a strainer into a bowl to remove the seeds. Then refrigerate it, loosely covered, until chilled, a minimum of 1 hour.

3. Freeze in an ice cream maker according to manufacturer's directions.

3 cups

SORBETS

▲

Sorbets are a magician's trick of undiluted flavor and ice. A wine sorbet serves as a pause between courses to refresh and stimulate the palate or as an elegant dessert scooped into goblets and topped with bursting ripe berries. The sorbet is as good as the wine that goes into it. We like Merlot for its mellow softness and Beaujolais for its fruitiness.

Fruit sorbets are one of the best ways we know to present perfectly ripe fruit. It's very chic—and even though it takes a little extra effort to present two or three fruit sorbets in oval scoops on a gorgeous plate, it's worth it. Pampering is in!

SUNNY LEMON SHERBET

Tangy, zesty, and light, this sherbet is the perfect ending to a rich meal. Serve with Lemon Lace Cookies.

4 cups water
2 cups sugar
Finely minced zest of 3 lemons
½ cup fresh lemon juice
½ cup heavy or whipping cream

1. Combine the water, sugar, and two thirds of the lemon zest in a saucepan and heat to a simmer. Cover, and simmer 10 minutes. Stir in the remaining lemon zest and the lemon juice, and allow the mixture to cool to room temperature.

2. Whisk the cream into the mixture, and refrigerate it until chilled, a minimum of 2 hours.

3. Freeze in an ice cream maker according to manufacturer's directions. (For a granité, freeze the mixture in your freezer. Place it in a shallow pan and freeze for 4 to 5 hours, checking the consistency and whisking, once every hour, until smooth. When it is slush-like, transfer it to a serving bowl and refrigerate for 30 minutes; then serve.)

6 cups

PERSIMMON SPICE SORBET

The flavor of this unusual fruit is complemented by a double dose of ginger—fresh and crystallized—and Armagnac. It is a sweet and soothing finale.

1 cup water
1 cup sugar
5 medium-size ripe persimmons, skinned,
*   pitted, and puréed (about 3 cups)*
6 tablespoons Armagnac
¼ cup very finely minced Crystallized
*   Candied Ginger (see Index)*
1 tablespoon minced fresh ginger
½ teaspoon ground cinnamon

1. Combine the water and sugar in a saucepan and cook over medium-low heat just until the sugar has dissolved. Allow the mixture to cool to room temperature. Refrigerate, loosely covered, until chilled, a minimum of 2 hours.

2. Pour the sugar syrup into a large bowl, and add the remaining ingredients. Stir until smooth.

3. Freeze in an ice cream maker according to manufacturer's directions.

5 to 6 cups

PAPAYA COLADA SORBET

The flavors of a Caribbean vacation are brought to mind while eating this sorbet. Serve it with Gingersnaps.

1 cup water
1 cup sugar
4 ripe papayas, peeled, seeded, and puréed (about 3 cups)
½ cup cream of coconut*
5 tablespoons rum
2 teaspoons finely minced lemon zest

1. Combine the water and sugar in a saucepan and cook over medium-low heat until the sugar has dissolved. Allow the mixture to cool to room temperature.

2. Pour the sugar syrup into a large bowl, and add the remaining ingredients. Stir until smooth. Refrigerate the mixture, loosely covered, until chilled, a minimum of 2 hours.

3. Freeze in an ice cream maker according to manufacturer's directions.

About 5 cups

*Available in many supermarkets and specialty food stores.

SUNDAE SWEET SUNDAE

★

Bittersweet Chocolate Ice Cream
Baby Brownies

★

Vanilla Vanilla Ice Cream
Orange Tuiles

★

Sweet Strawberry Ice Cream
Lemon Shortbread Bars

★

Sugar Cones ✳ Sprinkles ✳ Whipped Cream ✳ Cherries

MERLOT SORBET

Delicious served between courses to cleanse the palate.

3 cups water
1 ½ cups sugar
1 ¼ cups Merlot wine

1. Combine the water and sugar in a saucepan and heat to a simmer. Cover, and simmer 5 minutes. Stir in the wine, and set it aside to cool to room temperature. Then refrigerate it, loosely covered, until chilled, a minimum of 2 hours.

2. Freeze in an ice cream maker according to manufacturer's directions. (For a granité, freeze the mixture in your freezer. Place it in a shallow pan and freeze for 4 to 5 hours, checking the consistency and whisking, once every hour, until smooth. When it is slush-like, transfer it to a serving bowl and refrigerate for 30 minutes; then serve.)

5 cups

THE NEW BASICS

MICROWAVE MIRACLES

Of all the subjects in our book, microwave cooking was the most difficult for us. Until this point neither our recipes nor our philosophies seemed suited to this new type of cooking. Our love for and continuing curiosity about the latest fresh ingredients seemed to be miles away from all the new meals-in-a-minute packaged for the microwave. But with microwaves in close to 80 percent of all American households, we could not ignore their importance. We truly needed to develop a more knowledgeable point of view.

So although our expectations were limited, we began experimenting with different foods and preparations in the microwave, and—lo and behold—we experienced far better results than we expected. Results were not uniformly good across the board but they were certainly fine in specific areas. Bottom line: We'll never replace our conventional ovens with microwaves, but we're now convinced the microwave is a great appliance when used for the right purpose.

In testing recipes, we also considered the time factor. Our goal was not to substitute convenience for quality. This proved very interesting, because while most dishes cook in the microwave in less time, some, risotto for example, do not—but the results are excellent and constant stirring is eliminated.

On the other hand, after spending so many years simmering jams, marmalades, and chutneys in large pots for hours, we were delighted with the fresh fruit and vegetable chutneys turned out in less than 20 minutes in the microwave. It's amazing to think that you can run out the kitchen door, pick fresh berries, mix up a recipe, and serve fresh preserves for breakfast—dazzling in flavor with no loss of freshness and color. This is when the microwave excitement started for us. It's hard now to buy a jar of mango chutney when fresh mangoes are in the market.

Kiwi, too, became cause for excitement. We added lime and cooked up a savory marmalade just right for scones and biscuits at teatime. We then tried pineapples in a spicy chutney to top off grilled fish. These condiments, once secondary in importance, became stars. We no longer had to worry about chutneys and jams sticking to the bottom of the pot, and all their fresh flavors and colors were preserved.

We delighted in making our own ketchup and tomato paste. Even though they took longer to cook than the microwave preserves, it was still a fraction of the time it would have taken to cook them on top of the stove, and the flavor and color were dazzling. Our applesauce from the microwave also has never seemed better.

In the microwave, beans and grains cook to just the right consistency—not at all mushy—and retain their distinctive characteristics. Custard bases for ice cream, which usually require long stirring and a bit of guessing, were a joy to prepare.

We were even able to make an excellent Coq au Vin, and Chicken With Salsa epitomized the very best of microwave cooking.

THE RIGHT EQUIPMENT

All microwave ovens are not alike. They vary not only in wattage but also in size and features. We feel a simple carousel oven with variable power serves well for all recipes.

House power varies from one home to another and voltage may also be different during peak consumption hours. For these reasons, cooking times given in a recipe are not always accurate. Make sure you check the food and determine when it is done; don't depend on the clock.

MICROWAVE TIPS

▲ Remember that cooking times vary according to the wattage of your oven. Always check 1 or 2 minutes before the cooking time has elapsed and decide if more time is needed.

▲ Most dishes reheat beautifully in the microwave.

▲ The microwave cooks too quickly to tenderize red meat. It is best used for poultry, fish, and vegetables.

▲ Round dishes heat food more evenly. The square corners on a dish receive more energy and the food in those corners will overcook.

▲ Cut food in same-size pieces so they cook in the same time.

▲ Prick tight skins on vegetables such as potatoes, eggplant, and squash to let the steam escape.

▲ Foods with high sugar content, like jams, jellies, and syrups, jell before the fruit has a chance to lose its fresh-fruit flavor.

▲ Sugar caramelizes easily in the microwave without fuss or mess.

▲ Sauces made with cornstarch will thicken without lumps or the raw starch taste sometimes found in stovetop sauces.

▲ Polenta and risotto cook wonderfully in the microwave without constant stirring. Stir twice or according to the recipe and serve a deliciously easy dish.

▲ Vegetables retain their natural fresh color and texture when cooked in the microwave.

▲ Fish cooks in its own juices and will be moist and tender.

▲ Chocolate melts easily and there is less danger of scorching.

▲ Custards and puddings will be smooth and creamy with just an occasional stir.

▲ To clarify butter, cut 1 stick (½ cup) of unsalted butter into teaspoon slices in a 2-cup glass measure. Microwave on high power for 1½ minutes. Skim the foam off the top and pour the clear clarified butter into a clean container. Discard the white solids at the bottom of the cup. Refrigerate or freeze until ready to use.

▲ To toast nuts or seeds microwave ¼ cup of nuts or seeds and 1 teaspoon of butter on high power for 5 minutes, stirring once after 2 minutes.

When following a microwave recipe, it is important to pay close attention to the weights of ingredients, sizes of dishes, and cooking times. Adding another quarter pound of chicken or using a dish that is an inch too small will make a difference. You can still use the recipe, but you will have to adjust the cooking time. And don't assume you can double or halve the recipe and cook it in the same amount of time. Unlike cooking in a conventional oven, one potato takes 5 to 8 minutes to bake in the microwave, but two potatoes may take twice as long.

You probably will not need to buy a whole new set of dishes for microwave cooking. Check your cupboards first for covered glass and ceramic dishes. We find that simple straight-sided glass casseroles with rounded corners produce the best results. You cannot use metal or metal pans in the microwave so make sure dishes don't have any metal bases, handles, glazes, or decorations. Glass dishes are good because you can see what's happening with the food all the way through. Dishes should be large enough to hold the food; but for sauces, jams, and jellies, the dish has to be large enough to allow the food to boil up. The volume of the dish must be correct or the timing will be off.

Glass measuring cups of various sizes are useful for sauces and soups because you can watch the boil or reduction without opening the door. Plastic wrap and waxed paper labeled safe for the microwave can act as covers. If you want to contain the moisture and steam in a dish, cover it tightly with plastic wrap and leave a small vent in one corner.

Most of our microwave recipes are cooked in the following containers:

▲ Glass measures: 2 and 4 cup
▲ Covered glass or ceramic casseroles: 1½, 2, 2½, 3, and 4 quart
▲ Glass pie plates: 9 and 10 inch

If a recipe says "cover" or "cover tightly," we prefer to use a casserole with a lid. If that's not possible, we cover the dish tightly with plastic wrap and vent it. For "cover loosely," we drape a piece of plastic wrap or waxed paper over the top. If a recipe doesn't say a dish is to be covered, then cook it uncovered. Read the recipe carefully—a dish may be covered initially and uncovered later on.

Our microwave recipes were tested in a full-power carousel microwave of 650 to 700 watts, using microwave-safe containers, plastic wrap, and paper towels. Recipes were cooked on High (full) power unless otherwise indicated. If your microwave has less than 650 watts, you must cook the dish longer, and if your microwave does not have a carousel, you will have to rotate the dish during the cooking time. Carousels can be purchased in most housewares stores and are a worthwhile investment. We feel they are very important for even cooking.

ARRANGING

The food closest to the outside edge of a dish cooks fastest. If you have uneven pieces of meat or vegetables, place the thickest ends at the edge of the plate. When microwaving chicken, put the thick ends of the drumsticks and thighs at the outside and the thin breast pieces at the center. If you have foods that are small and all the same size, arrange them in a circle around the edge of the dish so that they all cook in the same time.

SAFETY TIPS

▲ If your microwave does not have a carousel or glass bottom liner, be sure to put a plate or paper towel underneath any food. Don't put food directly on the surface of the oven.

▲ Don't use the microwave as a timer. If it's on, always have something in it.

▲ We do not recommend cooking egg dishes in the microwave because we prefer the results from conventional preparation. Still, if you must: Never cook a whole egg in its shell—it will explode. To keep the yolk from exploding in a baked or poached egg, pierce the membrane twice with the tip of a knife.

▲ We do not recommend deep-frying in the microwave. A container filled with hot oil is dangerous and very awkward to handle in the oven, and there is no way to control the temperature of the oil.

▲ Do not experiment with different containers or use your own paper bag for popping corn. Use only those containers and bags designated safe for microwaves.

▲ Have pot holders nearby when removing dishes from the microwave. Dishes that cook a long time can be very, very hot.

▲ Do not use dishes with metal fittings and never use glassware that has been broken and repaired.

▲ Plastic storage containers can be used for reheating food, but those not specifically designated "microwave safe" may become warped.

THE FOOD WE LOVE IN THE MICROWAVE

Throughout the book are scattered recipes that we created for and that work best in the microwave. Check the index for any you are interested in making. Those that appear in this chapter are followed by their page number.

BEGINNINGS

Date and Olive Wrap-Arounds: A neat one-bite hors d'oeuvre that softens the dates, leaves the olives firm, and crisps the bacon.

Cream of Fennel Soup: Fresh fennel retains its anise flavor and delicate color in this smooth, creamy soup.

Spring Herb Soup: Fresh dill and parsley burst forth with the flavors of springtime in this quick soup.

Billi Bi: Mussels are cooked to perfection in the microwave, intensely flavoring this soup from the sea.

Welsh Rabbit: Cheese melts beautifully without separating in this piquant dish.

VEGETABLES

Stuffed Artichokes: Artichokes are quickly prepared and full of flavor without losing their velvety texture. The cheese filling melts in just 3 minutes.

Little French Beets: Cooked within 15 minutes, sweet ruby red beets complement slightly bitter radicchio in our multitextured side dish.

Billionaire's Broccoli: Garlic is cooked tender and sweet to enhance the tiny, delicate broccoli florets.

Curried Carrots and Lentils: The textures of carrots and lentils combine wonderfully in this quick-cooking curry.

Elegant Eggplant Caviar: A whole eggplant cooks in just 10 minutes, retaining its golden interior, and is combined with chopped fresh vegetables and spices for a Provençal flavor.

Marinated White Eggplant: The dazzling white color and creamy texture makes this quickly prepared vegetable perfect with grilled food.

Sweet Onion Relish: This spicy onion condiment is prepared in just 10 minutes.

Three Pepper Sauces: Sweet peppers and complementing vegetables are quickly cooked for gem-like purées—perfect for saucing crab cakes and vegetable terrines.

Real Hot Pepper Chutney: Peppers, ginger, and raisins retain their flavors—hot and sweet—and beautiful colors in this three-alarm chutney.

Butternut Timbales: Squash cooks in just 6 minutes for these delicate timbales—just right with roasts.

Spaghetti Squash Casserole: A whole spaghetti squash is baked in 18 minutes, pulled into glorious strands, and combined with tomatoes and easy-melting cheeses. The texture of the squash is ideal in this preparation.

Tomato Time Ketchup: The ripe flavor and deep red color of our fresh tomato ketchup bring back the summer harvest in all its glory.

Fresh Tomato Paste: Fresh tomato paste cooked down from five pounds of ripe tomatoes. Although the cooking time is longer than that of most microwave preparations, it's but a fraction of most conventional recipes and well worth every minute.

Kay's Fresh Tomato Juice: Ripe tomatoes, fresh vegetables, and herbs are cooked in 9 minutes to make the brightest, freshest tomato juice possible.

BEANS AND GRAINS

Pinto Bean Chili: Beans cook in the microwave in less than half the time of those cooked on top of the stove, and we love the texture.

Limas and Spinach: Limas, fennel, and spinach all retain their individual flavors and textures in this quick vegetable dish.

Barley Pilaf: Barley with perfect texture, not at all mushy, is enhanced with mushrooms and pecans.

Kasha Varnishkes: We toast buckwheat groats and cook them to the ideal texture in less than 10 minutes for the great dish grandma used to make.

Fresh Tomato Risotto: Creamy and toothsome, risotto in the microwave is heavenly.

Duck and Olive Risotto: This robust risotto is enlivened with pungent olives and velvety duck.

SEAFOOD

Steamed Littlenecks: In 12 minutes this meal of littleneck clams is perfectly cooked with plump and delicate texture.

Shrimp on a Bed of Leeks: Both vegetables and shrimp maintain their clear, crisp flavors and textures in this delicate entrée—prepared in less than 15 minutes.

Fruits of the Sea Salad: Both shellfish and fresh fish are beautifully suited to the quick-cooking microwave.

John Dory on a Bed of Greens: This sweet fish is delicately cooked on a bouquet of spinach and basil in 4 minutes. It is light, flaky, moist, and delicious.

POULTRY

Chicken With Salsa: Chicken and vegetables are arranged on a dinner plate and cooked in 3 minutes. Moist, tender poultry is very well suited to the microwave.

Chicken With Julienne of Vegetables: Fresh vegetables and skinless, boneless chicken breasts are moist, tender, and low in calories.

Coq au Vin: This French classic is easily interpreted into a new basic in less than 30 minutes with all of the original's lush flavor.

Wild Duck With Lentils: Without much fat, these ducks stay moist accompanied by a classic lentil garnish.

Hens Southwestern Style: Rock Cornish hens are moist and succulent, spiced with the flavors of the Southwest—ready in 12 minutes.

MEAT

Not So Sloppy Joe: Actually a neat preparation, this all-in-one dish can be brought directly to the table and spooned onto rolls or corn bread.

Speedy Short Ribs: Conventionally a long-simmering dish, these little ribs are prepared in a rich sauce, spiked with tangerine, and cooked in less than half the time.

Braised Lamb Shanks: This moist, tender cut is perfect for braising with sweet peppers.

FRUITS

Chunky Applesauce: Just the perfect texture—not too soft, not too crunchy—this applesauce cooks in 10 minutes (see facing page).

Apple Thyme Jelly: We love this jelly infused with thyme—excellent in autumn when apple cider is pressed (see facing page).

Apricot Marmalade: The flavor of dried apricots becomes brilliant in our quick-cooking marmalade made in 8 minutes (see page 773).

Four-Berry Preserve: Four fresh berries make the freshest preserves with no fuss in 15 minutes (see page 772).

Dried Cherry Chutney: The wonderful dried cherries from Michigan are spiced with fresh ginger and fruit juices to make a glorious chutney in 15 minutes (see page 774).

Kiwi Lime Marmalade: A luscious new use for the kiwi. Kiwi combined with lime makes a delightful preserve, sparkling in flavor and color—in just 11 minutes (see page 773).

Mango Chutney: All the flavors of our fresh mango chutney are enhanced in this microwave preparation—it's ready in just 7 minutes (see page 772).

Hot-Pepper and Orange Preserve: The chile peppers are fiery and bright red, the oranges fresh as the sunrise. Cook for 6 minutes and serve this HOT treat with cornbread.

Pineapple Chutney: Fresh pineapple cooks into another excellent, full-flavored microwave chutney (see page 773).

DESSERTS

Chunky Black Cherry Ice Cream: Cherry syrup is quickly reduced in the microwave to intensify the flavor of our smooth custard base.

Bittersweet Chocolate Ice Cream: A velvety custard and melted chocolate base is simply prepared for our ice cream.

Peaches and Cream Ice Cream: Rich, thick peach nectar heightens the flavor of our creamy custard base, prepared in the microwave for summer's favorite ice cream.

Sweet Strawberry Ice Cream: Fresh berries are cooked to a glistening concentrate for the richest of fruit ice creams.

Vanilla Vanilla Ice Cream: Our rich microwave custard is infused with whole vanilla beans for the dazzling flavor of homemade vanilla ice cream.

Annabel's Banana Boat: Chocolate melts and ripe bananas soften to just the right point in 1 minute.

Bananas Foster: Delightful flavors of the Old South slather these perfectly baked bananas.

Mincemeat: All the flavors of lean stew meat, the best apple pie spices, candied fruits, and marmalades are cooked in the microwave for this classic holiday pie filling (see page 774).

Rich Hot Chocolate: The microwave melts chocolate to perfection for this wonderful drink prepared right in the mug.

Candy Bar Hot Chocolate: From candy shop to mug, we enriched this simple microwave hot chocolate with egg yolks and popped it back into the microwave to heat it through.

ABOUT OUR MICROWAVE RECIPES

Our recipes were cooked on High (full power, 650 to 700 watts) in a carousel microwave, using microwave-safe containers.

If your microwave is less powerful, you will have to allow for more cooking time (approximately 1½ times the amount called for—but watch carefully); if it does not have a carousel, you may have to rotate the dish while it is cooking.

CHUNKY APPLESAUCE

Although it tastes old-fashioned, our applesauce is made the most modern way we know. It has a freshness that long stewing cannot maintain.

2 McIntosh apples
2 Granny Smith or other tart apples
1 cup water
Juice of ½ lemon
½ cup sugar
½ teaspoon ground cinnamon

1. Halve and core the McIntosh apples; peel them if you like. Cut each one into 6 wedges.

2. Halve and core the Granny Smith apples; peel them if you like. Cut them into 1-inch chunks.

3. Combine the apples, water, and lemon juice in a deep microwave-safe 2½-quart casserole.

4. Toss the sugar and cinnamon together in a small bowl, and stir this into the apple mixture.

5. Cook, uncovered, at full power (650 to 700 watts) for 5 minutes. Stir, pressing the apples into the liquid, and return to the microwave. Cook for another 5 minutes.

6. Using a potato masher, coarsely mash the apples, stirring them into the liquid. Allow the applesauce to cool to room temperature, and then cover and refrigerate.

4 portions

APPLE THYME JELLY

A delicate flavor—just perfect for glazing a simple lamb or pork roast.

2 cups apple cider
3½ cups sugar
2 teaspoons fresh thyme leaves
1 pouch (3 ounces) liquid fruit pectin

1. Combine the cider, sugar, and thyme in a 4-quart microwave-safe bowl, and stir well.

2. Cook, uncovered, at full power (650 to 700 watts) for 10 minutes. Stir, return to the microwave, and cook until the sugar has dissolved and the mixture has reached a full rolling boil, about 5 more minutes.

3. Stir the pectin into the mixture, return it to the microwave, and cook for 1½ minutes.

4. Skim any foam off the surface, and pack the jelly into sterilized jars according to the manufacturer's directions.

1 quart

FOUR-BERRY PRESERVE

When fresh berries are in season, this is the preserve to make—the flavors just burst forth. No pectin is necessary as the cranberries and blueberries have lots of their own. Serve this often!

1 cup blackberries, lightly rinsed and drained
1 cup halved hulled strawberries
½ cup cranberries, lightly rinsed, drained, and picked over
½ cup blueberries, lightly rinsed, drained, and picked over
2 cups sugar

1. Stir all the ingredients together in a 4-quart microwave-safe bowl.

2. Cook, uncovered, at full power (650 to 700 watts) for 10 minutes. Stir well, return to the microwave, and cook another 5 minutes.

3. Allow the preserves to cool slightly; then cover and refrigerate. They will keep for 1 week, tightly covered, in the refrigerator.

2 cups

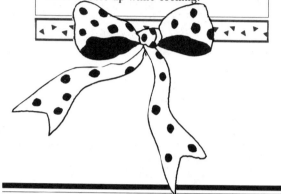

For jams, chutneys, and so on cooked in the microwave, make sure you use a container of the recommended size—the mixtures bubble up while cooking.

MANGO CHUTNEY

You have never eaten a mango chutney like this! It's fresh, spicy, and a beautiful bright gold color. The microwave seems to make this possible. Try making this—it takes less than 10 minutes. You'll never go back to the jars.

1 mango (10 to 12 ounces)
½ cup sugar
¼ cup finely chopped red onion
2 tablespoons white vinegar
2 tablespoons finely chopped green bell pepper
1 tablespoon grated fresh ginger
½ teaspoon ground ginger
⅛ teaspoon ground turmeric
⅛ teaspoon ground cloves
Freshly ground black pepper, to taste

1. Peel, halve, and seed the mango, and cut it into ½-inch cubes.

2. Combine the mango with all the other ingredients in a deep 1½-quart microwave-safe casserole. Stir thoroughly.

3. Cook, uncovered, at full power (650 to 700 watts) for 7 minutes.

4. Allow the chutney to cool slightly; then cover tightly and refrigerate. It will keep for 1 week in the refrigerator.

1 cup

APRICOT MARMALADE

Recalling the flavor of English bitter orange marmalade, this version features apricot flavor bursting forth with the same dramatic intensity. Serve with toasted Walnut Raisin Whole-Wheat Bread.

6 ounces dried apricot halves (about 30)
¼ cup plus 2 tablespoons sugar
Zest of 1 lemon, slivered
1 cup water
1 tablespoon fresh lemon juice

1. Combine the apricot halves and ¼ cup sugar in a food processor, and coarsely purée.
2. Stir the apricot purée, remaining 2 tablespoons sugar, lemon zest, water, and lemon juice together in a 1-quart microwave-safe measuring cup.
3. Cook, uncovered, at full power (650 to 700 watts) for 8 minutes.
4. Cover the marmalade loosely and allow it to cool to room temperature. Then cover tightly and refrigerate. It will keep for 1 week in the refrigerator.

1½ cups

KIWI LIME MARMALADE

This makes kiwis taste as great as they look—even greater. The fresh taste of lime is sublime, and the colors are bright and true. Serve this with toasted Hot and Sassy Corn Bread.

4 kiwis, peeled and trimmed
Zest of 1 lime, slivered
¾ cup sugar
2 tablespoons fresh lime juice

1. Quarter the kiwis lengthwise, and then cut them crosswise into ½-inch cubes.
2. Combine the kiwis with all the remaining in-

gredients in a deep 2½-quart microwave-safe casserole, and stir well.

3. Cook, uncovered, at full power (650 to 700 watts) for 5 minutes. Stir, return to the microwave, and cook until thick, another 6 minutes.
4. Allow the marmalade to cool to room temperature; then cover tightly and refrigerate. It will keep for 1 week in the refrigerator.

1 cup

PINEAPPLE CHUTNEY

This chutney can make a summer fiesta out of the simplest meal, such as lamb riblets or grilled fish. Just make sure you choose a ripe pineapple!

2 cups diced fresh pineapple (½-inch dice)
1¼ cups sugar
½ cup golden raisins
½ cup white vinegar
¼ cup minced crystallized ginger
2 tablespoons diced red bell pepper
2 tablespoons minced onion
2 tablespoons fresh lime juice
Zest of 1 lime, slivered
1 clove garlic, minced
¼ teaspoon ground cinnamon
⅛ teaspoon cayenne pepper

1. Stir all the ingredients thoroughly in a deep microwave-safe 1½-quart casserole.
2. Cook, uncovered, at full power (650 to 700 watts) for 8 minutes. Stir, return to the microwave, and cook another 8 minutes.
3. Allow the chutney to cool slightly; then cover tightly and refrigerate. It will keep for 2 days in the refrigerator.

2 cups

4. Cook, uncovered, for 10 minutes. Stir, return to the microwave, and cook to a full rolling boil, another 5 minutes.

5. Allow the mincemeat to cool to room temperature. If you are not using it immediately, divide it in half and freeze.

7 cups, enough for 2 pies

MINCEMEAT

During the holiday season, when time is at a premium, prepare this luscious mincemeat—a rich combination of meat, fruits, and spices—in the microwave. It cooks up in a fraction of the time, leaving you plenty of extra to wrap gifts.

1 pound lean stew beef, cut into 1½-inch cubes
2 cups water
⅔ cup apple cider
1½ cups (packed) dark brown sugar
2 teaspoons ground cinnamon
2 teaspoons ground nutmeg
1 teaspoon ground cloves
1 cup mixed candied fruit
1 cup raisins
½ cup dried currants
¾ cup apple butter
¾ cup strawberry jam
¾ cup orange marmalade
¾ cup cherry jam
1 cup canned sour cherries, drained and coarsely chopped
⅓ cup white wine or cider vinegar
¼ cup undiluted frozen orange juice concentrate
3 tablespoons unsalted butter, melted
1 teaspoon salt

1. Combine the beef and water in a 2-quart microwave-safe casserole with a lid. Cover, and cook at full power (650 to 700 watts) for 20 minutes. Stir, turning the meat, re-cover, and cook until tender, another 20 minutes. Allow the meat to cool slightly, reserving any liquid.

2. Combine the cider, brown sugar, cinnamon, nutmeg, and cloves in a 3-quart microwave-safe casserole and cook, uncovered, for 4 minutes. Stir until the sugar has dissolved, and set aside.

3. Mince the beef, candied fruit, and raisins, preferably by hand or through the large holes of a meat grinder (do not use a food processor). Add the minced mixture to the cider mixture, along with any reserved meat cooking liquid, and stir well. Then stir in all the remaining ingredients until smooth.

DRIED CHERRY CHUTNEY

While working on the recipes for this book, we discovered the marvelous dried pitted cherries from Michigan. They are available at specialty food stores and are so good that we think they'll be found all over the country soon. Here we've used them in a chutney spiced with fresh ginger and red pepper. This is a great alternative to cranberry sauce at Thanksgiving.

2 cups pitted dried cherries
1¼ cups sugar
¾ cup white vinegar
¼ cup finely chopped celery
¼ cup minced fresh ginger
6 tablespoons apple juice
3 tablespoons fresh lemon juice
½ teaspoon crushed dried red pepper flakes

1. Combine all the ingredients in a microwave-safe 2-quart casserole, and stir well.

2. Cook, uncovered, at full power (650 to 700 watts) for 6 minutes. Stir, making sure the sugar has dissolved, and return to the microwave. Cook another 8 minutes.

3. Allow the chutney to cool to room temperature; then cover tightly and refrigerate. It will keep for 1 week in the refrigerator.

2 cups

THE BASICS

♥ ♥ ♥

NEW BASIC TOMATO SAUCE

This tomato sauce is easy to prepare year round. It freezes very well, and the recipe can be doubled—so you can have some on hand any time a basic sauce is called for.

2 cans (35 ounces each) plum tomatoes
¼ cup olive oil
1 cup chopped onions
½ cup finely chopped carrot
4 cloves garlic, finely chopped
¼ cup dry red wine
2 tablespoons tomato paste
½ cup chopped fresh Italian (flat-leaf) parsley
1 tablespoon dried oregano
2 teaspoons dried basil
½ teaspoon ground nutmeg
½ teaspoon freshly ground black pepper
Salt, to taste
Pinch of dried red pepper flakes (optional)

1. Drain the tomatoes, reserving 1 cup of the juice. Crush the tomatoes with the back of a spoon, and set aside.

2. Heat the oil in a saucepan over medium-low heat. Add the onions, carrot, and garlic. Cook, stirring, until the onions and garlic have wilted, about 10 minutes.

3. Add the tomatoes, reserved juice, wine, tomato paste, and remaining ingredients. Cover, and cook over medium heat for 15 minutes, stirring once.

4. Remove the cover and simmer another 45 minutes, stirring occasionally.

6 cups

HOMEMADE MAYONNAISE

Marvelous with cold poached salmon and other seafood salads, there are those times when a commercial mayonnaise just won't do. Add fresh herbs and seasonings for creative variations.

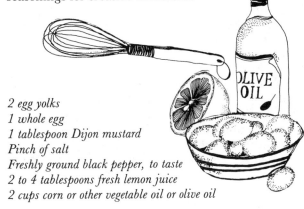

2 egg yolks
1 whole egg
1 tablespoon Dijon mustard
Pinch of salt
Freshly ground black pepper, to taste
2 to 4 tablespoons fresh lemon juice
2 cups corn or other vegetable oil or olive oil

1. Combine the egg yolks, whole egg, mustard, salt, pepper, and 2 tablespoons of the lemon juice in a food processor; process for 1 minute.

2. With the motor running, gradually add the oil through the feed tube in a slow, steady stream. When the mayonnaise is thoroughly blended, turn the processor off and scrape down the sides of the bowl. Taste the mayonnaise and correct the seasonings if necessary; if you are using vegetable oil, you will probably need the remaining 2 tablespoons lemon juice.

3. Scrape the mayonnaise into a container, cover, and refrigerate (it will keep for 5 days). Let it return to room temperature before stirring and using.

3 cups

BEARNAISE SAUCE

This classic sauce really becomes exciting when you use fresh tarragon instead of dried. It makes all the difference in the world!

As soon as the sauce is thickened, set the pan in a bowl of ice-cold water to stop the cooking. Your béarnaise sauce should not separate if you do it this way.

2 tablespoons white wine vinegar
2 tablespoons dry white wine
1 tablespoon chopped shallots
1 tablespoon chopped fresh tarragon leaves or 1 teaspoon dried
8 tablespoons (1 stick) unsalted butter
3 egg yolks
Salt and freshly ground black pepper, to taste

1. Combine the vinegar, wine, shallots, and tarragon in a small saucepan. Place over high heat and boil until reduced by half, about 1 minute. Remove the pan from the heat and allow it to cool to room temperature.

2. Melt the butter in a small saucepan.

3. Fill the bottom of a double boiler with water and bring it almost to a boil. Lower the heat so that the water is hot but not boiling.

4. Combine the egg yolks and the reserved shallot mixture in the top of the double boiler, and place the top over the bottom. Gradually whisk in the melted butter in a slow, steady stream. Continue whisking until the sauce has thickened. Season to taste with salt and pepper. Serve immediately.

1½ cups

HOLLANDAISE SAUCE

Hollandaise, like mayonnaise, is an emulsion—but in this case the egg yolks hold butter, not oil, in suspension. The trick here is to keep the egg yolks at a low, even heat as the melted butter is slowly added.

8 tablespoons (1 stick) unsalted butter
3 egg yolks
2 tablespoons fresh lemon juice
Pinch of cayenne pepper
Salt and ground white pepper, to taste

1. Melt the butter in a small saucepan. Set it aside to cool to room temperature.

2. Fill the bottom of a double boiler with water, and bring it almost to a boil. Then lower the heat so that the water is hot but not boiling.

3. Mix the egg yolks and lemon juice together in the top of the double boiler. Then place the top over the bottom and whisk until smooth. Gradually whisk in the butter in a slow, steady stream. Add the cayenne, and salt and white pepper. Continue whisking until the sauce is thick. Serve immediately.

1 cup

Note: If the sauce should separate or curdle, add 1 ice cube and whisk briskly until it has melted. This will bring the sauce back together.

REMOULADE SAUCE

This basic is delicious tossed over julienned celery root, dolloped on cold poached lobster or on crab cakes. Cornichons and capers add a piquant flavor.

1 egg yolk
2 tablespoons Dijon mustard
2 tablespoons whole-grain mustard
1 tablespoon fresh lemon juice
1 teaspoon white wine vinegar
2 tablespoons chopped cornichons
2 tablespoons chopped capers, drained
1 tablespoon chopped fresh tarragon leaves
1 tablespoon chopped fresh parsley
½ teaspoon freshly ground black pepper
¼ teaspoon salt
Dash of Tabasco sauce
1 cup corn oil
2 tablespoons whole capers, drained

1. Combine the egg yolk, both mustards, lemon juice, and vinegar in a food processor and process for 30 seconds.

2. Add the cornichons, chopped capers, tarragon, parsley, pepper, salt, and Tabasco. Process for 30 seconds.

3. With the motor running, slowly add the oil through the feed tube; process until thick. Transfer the sauce to a bowl and fold in the whole capers. Cover, and refrigerate for at least 1 hour before serving. It will keep for about 6 hours in the refrigerator.

1¾ cups

BECHAMEL SAUCE

The basic white sauce, versatile enough to layer on lasagne or moussaka, or to use as the basis for a creamy cheese sauce.

4 tablespoons (½ stick) unsalted butter
3 tablespoons unbleached all-purpose flour
1½ cups milk
Pinch of paprika
Pinch of ground nutmeg
Salt and ground white pepper, to taste

1. Melt the butter in a heavy saucepan. Add the flour and cook, stirring, over low heat for 3 minutes. Raise the heat to medium and slowly add the milk, stirring constantly with a wire whisk.

2. Continue whisking until the sauce thickens, about 5 minutes. Add the paprika, nutmeg, and salt and white pepper. Stir well, and remove from the heat.

1¾ cups

MORNAY SAUCE

When you want to dress up a fresh head of cauliflower or broccoli spears, call upon this classic cheese sauce. It also makes a superb macaroni and cheese and adds a creamy touch to a broiled fleshy, white fish fillet.

4 tablespoons (½ stick) unsalted butter
3 tablespoons unbleached all-purpose flour
1½ cups milk
⅓ cup grated Gruyère cheese
Pinch of paprika
Pinch of ground nutmeg
Salt and ground white pepper, to taste

1. Melt the butter in a heavy saucepan. Add the flour and cook, stirring, over low heat for 3 minutes. Raise the heat to medium and slowly add the milk, stirring constantly with a wire whisk.

2. Continue whisking until the sauce begins to thicken, about 3 minutes. Slowly sprinkle in the Gruyère, stirring as you add it. When all the cheese has been added and has melted in, add the paprika, nutmeg, and salt and white pepper. Stir well, and remove from the heat.

About 2 cups

CREME FRAICHE

More tart than whipped heavy cream and a bit richer than sour cream, crème fraîche is a delicious addition to sauces and is just the right topping for rich chocolate desserts.

½ cup heavy or whipping cream (not ultra-pasteurized)
½ cup sour cream

Whisk the creams together in a small bowl. Pour the mixture into a jar, cover, and let stand in a warm place for 12 hours. Then stir, and refrigerate for 24 hours.

1 cup

BEURRE BLANC

Beurre blanc is lovely with fish fillets and luscious on a plate topped with lightly steamed asparagus.

1 tablespoon finely minced shallots
2 tablespoons white wine vinegar
1½ tablespoons dry vermouth
1½ tablespoons fresh lemon juice
½ cup heavy or whipping cream
1 cup (2 sticks) unsalted butter, at room temperature
Salt and ground white pepper, to taste

1. Combine the shallots, vinegar, vermouth, and lemon juice in a saucepan. Cook rapidly over high heat until the liquid has almost all evaporated, 1 to 2 minutes.

2. Add the cream and cook over medium heat until the mixture has reduced and thickened slightly, 1 to 2 minutes. Remove the pan from the heat and set it aside until you are ready to serve the sauce.

3. Just before serving, place the sauce in the top of a double boiler over hot, not boiling, water. Add the butter and salt and white pepper, whisk just until the butter has melted. Serve immediately.

1 cup

BEURRE NOIR

This basic "black" butter sauce is perfect with delicate-flavored fish such as skate or sole.

4 tablespoons (½ stick) unsalted butter
1 tablespoon white wine vinegar
1 tablespoon fresh lemon juice
1 teaspoon capers, drained
1 tablespoon chopped fresh Italian (flat-leaf) parsley

1. Melt the butter in a saucepan and cook it over medium heat until it turns a light brown. Watch carefully so it doesn't burn. Pour the butter into a bowl and set it aside.

2. Add the vinegar, lemon juice, and capers to

the saucepan. Cook rapidly over high heat until the liquid has almost entirely evaporated. Return the butter to the pan, add the parsley, stir, and serve immediately.

⅓ cup

CLARIFIED BUTTER

Clarified butter can be heated, without burning, to higher temperatures than regular butter.

8 tablespoons (1 stick) unsalted butter

1. Melt the butter over low heat in a small heavy saucepan.

2. Remove the pan from the heat and set it aside for 5 minutes.

3. Using a spoon, carefully remove and discard the foamy white butterfat that has risen to the top. Spoon or pour off the clear liquid. This is the clarified butter. Discard the solids that remain on the bottom of the pan. Allow the clarified butter to cool, and then cover and refrigerate. (The butter will keep for several weeks.)

About ⅓ cup

HERB BUTTER

Add this summer-garden flavor to corn on the cob; use it in place of garlic butter for hot herb bread; or place a slice on grilled chicken or fish.

8 tablespoons (1 stick) unsalted butter, at room temperature
1½ teaspoons fresh tarragon or ½ teaspoon dried
1½ teaspoons fresh thyme leaves or ½ teaspoon dried
1½ teaspoons fresh oregano or ½ teaspoon dried
¼ teaspoon freshly ground black pepper
3 tablespoons chopped fresh Italian (flat-leaf) parsley

1. Combine all the ingredients in a food processor and process until well blended (you may have to turn the motor off and scrape down the sides of the bowl once or twice).

2. Serve immediately in individual ramekins. Or transfer the butter to a sheet of plastic wrap and roll it up in the wrap to form a sausage shape. Twist the ends closed and refrigerate until firm, 1 hour, or freeze. To serve, unwrap the butter and slice it into ⅛-inch-thick rounds.

¾ cup

SEASONED BREAD CRUMBS

It's a good idea to make a couple batches of these crumbs at one time. They freeze well and homemade does make a difference.

1 loaf French bread, 1 day old
1½ teaspoons dried thyme leaves
1½ teaspoons dried oregano
1½ teaspoons dried basil
½ teaspoon freshly ground black pepper

1. Preheat the broiler.

2. Slit the bread in half lengthwise and cut it crosswise into cubes. Place the cubes on a baking sheet and toast under the broiler until golden. Set the cubes aside to cool and dry out completely.

3. Combine the bread cubes and all the remaining ingredients and process until coarse crumbs are formed. Remove, and store in an airtight jar.

1½ cups

Note: For topping vegetable gratins, mix two thirds crumbs to one third freshly grated Parmesan cheese.

RED WINE MINT SAUCE

We have mellowed the flavor of a classic mint sauce by adding red wine and orange zest. Still just right with lamb, this more delicate version can even be splashed over a bowl of ripe melon balls and strawberries.

½ cup dry red wine
3 tablespoons confectioners' sugar
¾ cup red wine vinegar
Finely grated zest of 1 orange
¼ cup loosely packed, coarsely chopped fresh mint leaves
1½ teaspoons dried mint leaves
¼ teaspoon freshly ground black pepper

1. Heat the wine in a small saucepan over low heat. Add the confectioners' sugar, and swirl the pan over the heat until the sugar has dissolved. Then transfer the mixture to a bowl, add the vinegar, and allow to cool slightly.

2. Bring a small saucepan of water to a boil, add the orange zest, and cook for 15 seconds. Drain the zest in a fine-mesh sieve, and add it to the vinegar mixture. Stir in the remaining ingredients.

3. Chill the sauce in the refrigerator for at least 1 hour before serving. This will keep for 2 to 3 days.

About 1 cup

LEMON MARMALADE

Just the right bite for coating the bottom of tart shells to be filled with fruit. This marmalade also stands on its own with toasted Irish soda bread, and it's a refreshing surprise with smoked salmon and herbed cream cheese.

8 lemons
1½ cups sugar

1. Using a vegetable peeler or a small sharp

knife, remove all the lemon zest and cut it into thin slivers.

2. Juice the lemons, and combine the juice, zest, and sugar in a large saucepan. Cook over low heat, stirring constantly, until thick and syrupy, about 30 minutes.

3. Allow the marmalade to cool before serving. It will keep, covered and refrigerated, for 1 to 2 weeks.

1 cup

MAPLE CRANBERRY SAUCE

Tart crisp red cranberries are mellowed with maple syrup, orange zest, and walnuts in a chunky sauce that is just the right accent for roast chicken, hearty game dishes, and of course, for your Thanksgiving bird.

12 ounces fresh cranberries (1 bag), well rinsed
1 cup pure maple syrup
1 cup raspberry-cranberry juice
Grated zest of 1 orange
1 cup walnut halves

1. Combine the cranberries, maple syrup, juice, and orange zest in a heavy saucepan. Bring to a boil, then lower the heat to medium and cook until the cranberries pop open, about 10 minutes.

2. Carefully skim off any foam that has formed on the surface of the cranberry mixture, and stir in the walnuts. Allow the sauce to cool; then cover and refrigerate. This sauce will keep for 3 to 4 days.

10 to 12 portions

PAPAYA SALSA

This native tropical American fruit, with its sweet and tart flavor, adds a festive note to snapper, grilled chicken, or grilled shrimp.

2 ripe papayas (about 1 pound each)
1 fresh jalapeño or serrano pepper
1 large clove garlic, finely minced
½ cup finely chopped red onion
¼ cup coarsely chopped cilantro (fresh coriander)
Grated zest of 2 limes
½ cup fresh lime juice

1. Peel the papayas, remove the seeds, and cut the pulp into ¼- to ½-inch cubes. Place them in a medium-size bowl.

2. Carefully seed and finely chop the jalapeño pepper. (You should have about 1 tablespoon.) Add it to the papaya, along with the remaining ingredients. Toss together gently. Serve this salsa within 4 to 6 hours for a really fresh taste.

1 quart

SORREL SALSA

Finely chopped fresh sorrel, with its tart lemony flavor, is the perfect contrast to red onion and tomatoes. Fabulous anywhere you want a bright accent.

1 large bunch sorrel, rinsed and thoroughly dried
3 ripe plum tomatoes, cored, seeded, and coarsely chopped
½ cup chopped red onion
2 tablespoons extra virgin olive oil
1 teaspoon fresh lemon juice
Salt and freshly ground black pepper, to taste

1. Remove the tough stems and coarsely chop the sorrel leaves. (You should have about 4 cups.)

2. Combine the sorrel and all the remaining ingredients in a bowl, and let the mixture sit for 15 to 20 minutes before serving.

3 cups

PRESERVED LEMONS

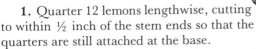

The time spent in nurturing these lemons is well worthwhile. Once they are well preserved—in two to three weeks—they will last for months in the refrigerator. Since the skins are permeated by the brine, it is best to use lemons with thin smooth skins. (The juice and skin are used in cooking, but the pulp is discarded.)

15 lemons
5 to 6 tablespoons coarse (kosher) salt
3 cinnamon sticks

1. Quarter 12 lemons lengthwise, cutting to within ½ inch of the stem ends so that the quarters are still attached at the base.
2. Sprinkle the cut surfaces with coarse salt.
3. Sprinkle 2 tablespoons of the coarse salt in the bottom of a 6-cup covered glass jar.
4. Place 4 of the quartered lemons in the jar, and press them into the bottom, flattening them slightly. Sprinkle with a thin layer of salt. Place a cinnamon stick on top.
5. Repeat twice, for a total of three layers of lemons, salt, and cinnamon.
6. Press down on the lemons to release the juice. Squeeze the remaining 3 lemons into the jar so that the juice comes nearly to the top of the lemons. Discard these last lemons.
7. Cover the jar and refrigerate. Turn once a day for at least 2 weeks. Rinse the lemons before using.

12 lemons

BERTA'S CHICKEN STOCK

The recipe for this all-purpose chicken soup comes from Sheila's mother, Berta. She's nurtured her family on it for years. Strain the soup to use as a stock. If a rich stock is needed, cook strained stock over medium-high heat until reduced by half.

1 chicken (4 to 5 pounds), preferably a stewing hen
3 quarts water
1 teaspoon salt
1 large or 2 medium onions
4 ribs celery with leaves
8 sprigs fresh dill
4 carrots, peeled
3 parsnips, peeled
Salt and freshly ground black pepper, to taste

1. Rinse the chicken well and trim off all excess fat. Cut the chicken into quarters and place them in a large soup pot. Add the water and salt, and bring to a boil. Skim off the foam as it collects on the surface.
2. Add the onions, celery, and dill. Cover, reduce the heat, and simmer for 1 hour.
3. Cut the carrots and parsnips in half and add them to the stock. Simmer until the chicken is fork-tender, about 1 hour.
4. Remove the chicken from the pot and reserve it for another use. Discard the carrots and parsnips. Strain the stock through a fine-mesh sieve into a bowl, and allow it to cool; then refrigerate or freeze.

About 8 cups regular stock or 4 cups reduced rich stock

CHICKEN BOUILLON CUBES

Long slow simmering and then reduction give this chicken stock the intensity necessary for highly flavored bouillon cubes. Just one cube added to a simple sauce creates a great depth of taste.

4 pounds chicken wings and backs
2 carrots, peeled and cut into 2-inch pieces
2 ribs celery, cut into 2-inch pieces
1 leek (white part and 3 inches green), well rinsed and cut
*   into 1-inch pieces*
1 onion, halved
2 bay leaves
2 large sprigs parsley
2 large sprigs dill
1 teaspoon very coarsely ground black pepper
4 quarts water

1. Combine all the ingredients in a large soup pot or kettle, and bring to a boil. Skim the foam as it collects on the surface. Lower the heat, and simmer for 2 hours.

2. Strain the stock (you should have 9 to 10 cups). Return the stock to a smaller saucepan and bring it to a boil, skimming off any fat. Lower the heat and simmer until the liquid is a deep caramel color, syrupy, and reduced to about 1½ cups, 2 hours. Turn the heat very low during the last 30 minutes, and keep a close watch.

3. Pour the reduced stock into an 8-inch square cake pan, and cool to room temperature. Refrigerate, covered, until very firm, 8 hours or overnight.

4. Cut the stock into sixteen squares, and wrap each in plastic wrap or foil. Freeze for future use.

16 cubes

Note: For a quick stock, dissolve 1 cube in 1 cup boiling water. Season with ⅛ teaspoon salt, and pepper to taste.

VEAL STOCK

This fairly simple way to prepare veal stock may become one of your favorite New Basics for use in sauces and stews. The marrow from the veal bones gives it great flavor. For an even richer stock, return the strained stock to a simmer and reduce it further.

1 large onion, unpeeled
6 whole cloves
5 pounds veal bones
1½ pounds veal shoulder
2 carrots, peeled
4 ribs celery
1 bay leaf
½ teaspoon dried thyme leaves
10 peppercorns
4 quarts water
Salt, to taste

1. Stud the onion with the cloves.

2. Place all the ingredients in a soup pot and bring to a boil, skimming off any foam that rises to the surface. Reduce the heat and simmer, uncovered, for 5 hours.

3. Strain the stock and let it cool to room temperature.

4. If you are going to use the stock right away, set it aside for 15 minutes to allow the fat to rise to the surface. Then degrease the stock completely, scooping the fat off with a shallow metal spoon.

5. If you are not going to use it immediately, refrigerate the cooled stock, and remove the hardened layer of fat from the top before you use the stock or before you freeze it.

2½ quarts

BEEF STOCK

The recipe for this flavorful stock comes from Felipe Rojas-Lombardi, chef-owner of The Ballroom restaurant, one of New York's shining lights.

2 large onions (about 1¾ pounds), unpeeled, cut into 8 pieces each
½ pound leeks (white part and 3 inches green), well rinsed and cut into thirds
½ head garlic, unpeeled (halve a whole head crosswise)
4 ribs celery with leaves, rinsed and cut into pieces
1 carrot, unpeeled, sliced
3 pounds beef bones, preferably marrow and knuckle
4 pounds veal bones, preferably shin, knuckle, and feet
1 pound oxtail, cut into small pieces
1½ gallons cold water
4 whole cloves
1 bay leaf
12 black peppercorns
½ bunch (¼ ounce) fresh thyme
1 fresh hot chile pepper, such as jalapeño or serrano, or ½ hot dried chile (optional)

1. Place a rack in the upper third of the oven, and preheat it to 500°F.

2. Arrange all the vegetables in a large deep roasting pan, making sure they cover the bottom completely. Arrange the beef and veal bones and the oxtail over the vegetables, and roast on the upper rack of the oven for 1 hour.

3. Remove the pan from the oven, and transfer

all the bones and vegetables to a large soup pot. Pour off all the fat from the roasting pan. Add 1 quart of the water to the pan, and bring it to a full boil over high heat, scraping up all the browned bits in the pan. Pour this into the soup pot.

4. Add the remaining 1¼ gallons water, cloves, bay leaf, peppercorns, thyme, and chile pepper. Bring to a boil, skimming off any foam that rises to the surface. Then lower the heat, stir, and cover. Simmer for 5 hours.

5. Remove the pot from the heat, and let the stock cool to room temperature undisturbed.

6. Strain the stock into a large bowl through a fine-mesh sieve or a strainer lined with a double layer of cheesecloth.

7. If you are going to use the stock right away, set it aside for 15 minutes to allow the fat to rise to the surface. Then degrease the stock completely, scooping the fat off with a shallow metal spoon.

8. If you are not going to use it immediately, refrigerate the cooled stock, and remove the hardened layer of fat from the top before you use the stock or before you freeze it.

About 4 quarts

FISH STOCK

The flavor of this fish stock is enhanced by adding fennel, orange and lemon zest, and all the good herbs of Provence. Make extra and freeze it for future use.

2 tablespoons unsalted butter
2 leeks (white part and 3 inches green), rinsed and chopped
1 fennel bulb or 2 ribs celery, coarsely chopped
2 strips orange zest (each 2 inches long)
2 strips lemon zest (each 2 inches long)
2 bay leaves
4 sprigs rosemary
4 sprigs basil
1 teaspoon dried thyme, crumbled
1 teaspoon fennel seeds, crushed
1 tablespoon unbleached all-purpose flour
4 cups water
1 cup dry white wine
1 pound fish trimmings (heads, tails, skin, bones)
1 teaspoon salt

1. Melt the butter in a large saucepan. Add the leeks, fennel, orange and lemon zest, bay leaves, herbs and spices, and cook 10 minutes. Stir in the flour, and cook 1 minute.

2. Add the water, wine, fish trimmings, and salt, and heat to a boil. Reduce the heat and simmer 30 minutes. Strain, and allow to cool before refrigerating or freezing.

4 to 5 cups

VEGETABLE BROTH

The intense flavor of fresh vegetables makes for a wonderful broth. This broth substitutes easily in any recipe calling for chicken or beef stock.

2 cups sliced carrots
2 cups coarsely chopped leeks
1½ cups chopped celery with leaves
1½ cups coarsely chopped zucchini
1½ cups coarsely chopped green beans
1 cup coarsely chopped peeled parsnips
1 cup coarsely chopped green bell peppers
12 ounces fresh spinach, rinsed and trimmed
4 sprigs dill
2 bay leaves
1½ teaspoons salt
1 teaspoon freshly ground black pepper
3 quarts water

1. Combine all the ingredients in a large soup pot and bring to a boil. Then reduce the heat and simmer, uncovered, for 30 minutes. Remove the pot from the heat and let it sit another 30 minutes.

2. Strain the stock and discard the vegetables. Return it to the heat, and reduce at a low boil for 15 minutes. Cool completely before refrigerating or freezing.

6 cups

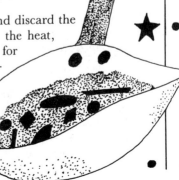

TIPS FOR PUFF PASTRY

❤

▲ Be sure the butter for folding in is cold yet pliable.

▲ Preheat the oven for at least 30 minutes.

▲ Resting time between turns should be not less than 20 minutes and not more than 30 minutes.

▲ Puff pastry freezes beautifully—both after its last turns and after it's been cut into shapes before baking.

ADRIENNE'S ROUGH PUFF PASTRY

Our friend Susy Davidson began making this pastry, a somewhat simpler version of the classic, while working with her colleague Adrienne at *Cook's* magazine. The result is every bit as delicious as the more time-consuming version. Puff pastry should be prepared in a cool kitchen.

2 cups unbleached all-purpose flour
1 teaspoon salt
1½ cups (3 sticks) unsalted butter, very cold,
  cut into pieces
6 tablespoons ice water
½ teaspoon fresh lemon juice

1. Combine the flour and salt in a food processor, and process to blend. Add the butter, and pulse on and off until it is in small pieces (about the size of a dried split pea), about 10 pulses. Add 4 tablespoons of the ice water and the lemon juice, and pulse just to blend, about 10 pulses more.

2. Turn the mixture out onto a cool (marble would be perfect), lightly floured surface. Gather the dough into a loose ball, and then using the heel of your hand, smear the dough away from you, about ¼ cup at a time. Repeat until all the dough has been smeared. (This will blend in the butter and make the pastry flakier.) Gather the dough back into a loose ball, using a dough scraper. Add the remaining 2 tablespoons ice water if necessary to make a dough that barely holds together.

3. Roll the dough out to form a 14 x 7-inch rectangle. Fold the top third of the dough down and the bottom third up to meet it, edges touching in the center (your rectangle should now be 14 x 3½ inches). Then fold one half over the other (for a 7 x 3½-inch rectangle), and pound lightly with the rolling pin to seal the fold. (The dough will be very crumbly at this point; it will come together as you work with it.)

4. Turn the pastry so the folded edges are on your right, and roll it out again to form a 14 x 7-inch rectangle. Fold the top third of the pastry down and the bottom third up to meet it, as in Step 3. Fold it in half (7 x 3½-inch rectangle) and pound it gently with the rolling pin to seal. Cover the dough well with plastic wrap and chill it in the freezer until very firm, about 20 minutes.

5. Repeat Steps 3 and 4, and return the pastry to the freezer for 20 minutes.

6. Now the pastry is ready to use. (If you aren't using it immediately, keep the pastry, well wrapped, in the refrigerator. It also may be frozen.)

About 1 pound

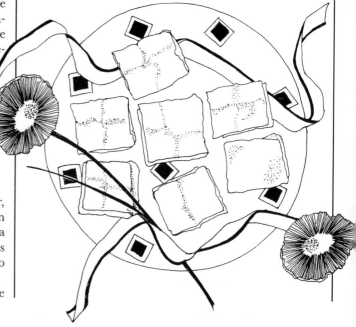

NEW BASIC PIE CRUST

pastry blender

ball of dough

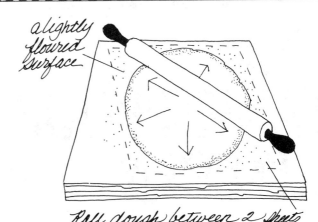

a lightly floured surface

Roll dough evenly from center in all directions to form a circle of even thickness —

Roll dough between 2 sheets of lightly floured waxed paper

This basic pie crust works well for both sweet and savory pies and tarts. When needing sweet, add sugar. When needing savory, sprinkle in some herbs or spices instead. Be sure to add them gingerly.

2½ cups unbleached all-purpose flour
1 teaspoon salt
2 teaspoons granulated sugar (for a sweet filling); 1
*   tablespoon of a fresh herb or 1 to 2 teaspoons of a dried*
*   herb or spice (for a savory filling)*
8 tablespoons (1 stick) unsalted butter, cold, cut into pieces
6 tablespoons solid vegetable shortening, cold
5 to 6 tablespoons ice water

1. Combine the flour and salt in a mixing bowl. Add the sugar if you are going to be making a sweet (dessert) pie or the herb or spice for a savory pie or tart. Add the butter and shortening, and working quickly, use a pastry blender, two knives, or your fingertips to cut in the ingredients until the mixture resembles coarse crumbs.

2. Sprinkle the ice water over the mixture 1 or 2 tablespoons at a time, and toss after each addition. When you can gather the dough into a ball, you've added enough water (usually 5 to 6 tablespoons). Transfer the dough onto a cool (marble would be perfect) lightly floured surface, and using the heel of your hand, smear the dough away from you, about ¼ cup at a time. Repeat until all the dough has been smeared. (This will blend in the butter and shortening and make the pastry flakier.) Gather the dough into a ball, using a dough scraper, then divide the ball in half. Flatten each half slightly, wrap them in waxed paper, and refrigerate for 30 minutes to 1 hour. (You can freeze the dough at this point. Wrap it well in plastic wrap.)

3. The pastry is now ready to use.

4. To blind bake a bottom crust: Preheat the oven to 375°F.

5. Roll 1 ball of chilled dough out on a lightly floured surface to form an 11-inch circle. Transfer it to a 9-inch pie plate, and press it into the bottom and sides. Trim the dough, leaving a 1-inch overhang. Fold the overhang back toward the inside, and crimp the edge decoratively.

6. Prick the bottom of the pastry with a fork and line it with aluminum foil, shiny side down. Fill the plate with pie weights or dried beans, and bake the pastry for 8 minutes. Then remove the foil and weights and return the pastry to the oven; bake until golden brown, 10 to 13 minutes. Set aside to cool.

7. To partially bake a bottom crust: Follow the directions in Steps 4, 5, and 6 through removing the weights and foil. Then brush the crust with the white from 1 egg and return it to the oven for 2 minutes more. It is now ready to be filled before the final baking.

Crust for one 9-inch double-crust pie or two single-crust pies

THE PANIC-PROOF KITCHEN

Without a guide to follow, it can take years of frustration to achieve a well-stocked kitchen. Although no one needs every kitchen gadget or new food product on the market, there are certain essentials that will make your cooking easier and more enjoyable.

TO EQUIP A KITCHEN

We've planned three stages of equipment purchases for achieving the ultimate dream kitchen.

The first stage is the most essential, and lists the items you'll need for an efficient Basic Kitchen.

The second stage will certainly result in the Complete Kitchen. This is the kitchen for accomplished home cooks.

The Professional Kitchen, the third and final stage, is a luxury, but as you become more proficient, you may want to add at least some of these items for they will enable you to make just about anything you want at home.

A word of caution: In our experience, this year's hot and trendy cooking gadget ends up in the back of the broom closet next year. Think carefully before you buy.

THE BASIC KITCHEN

The basic pots and pans that we use most frequently and that have the greatest versatility are available in several materials. We recommend stainless steel with aluminum or copper bases, enamel-coated cast iron, and glass ceramic that is stove-top, oven, and microwave proof. We don't recommend buying prepackaged starter sets of pots—they are expensive and never deliver the quality you need.

POTS AND PANS

3 saucepans, 1 quart, 2 quart, and 3 quart, all with tight-fitting lids and ovenproof handles, and between 3½ and 4 inches deep.

2 saucepots, 2½ quart and 5 quart ovenproof pots with tight-fitting lids and 2 easy-to-grip ovenproof handles. Saucepots should be 4 to 5 inches deep.

1 stockpot, 8 quart, with tight-fitting lid

2 skillets or frying pans, 8 inches and 10 inches with lids and ovenproof handles. Preferably, the 10 inch pan will be nonstick SilverStone.

1 dutch oven or casserole, 3 quart with lid

1 microwave-safe casserole, 2½ to 3 quart with lid

1 glass ceramic baking dish, 13 x 9 x 2 inches

1 shallow roasting pan, about 15 x 10 x 2 inches

1 deep, large roasting pan with rack, about 16 x 11½ x 5 inches

1 vegetable steamer, preferably the collapsible kind that fits into pots of different sizes

COPPER

We have always loved copper pots and pans. They are both highly functional and beautiful. Copper conducts heat evenly, which is essential for cooking sauces and other delicate dishes, and it cools down quickly. Most of the copper pans available are lined on the inside with tin. This surface doesn't last forever, however. If you see copper showing through the tin lining, you must send them out to be relined.

Unfortunately for most home cooks, copper pots and pans are extremely expensive. If you can afford two or three pans, we would recommend buying an 8- or 9-inch saucepan about 4 inches deep with a long handle. This is a great all-purpose pan for sauces, such as béchamel and hollandaise. The second pan should be a 16-inch oval roasting or gratin pan with two small handles—wonderful for bringing dishes directly from oven to table. The third would be an unlined 2- to 3-quart copper mixing bowl, ideal for whisking egg whites to delicate peaks.

Keep your copper well polished and don't store it behind closed doors!

UTENSILS

1 set of 4 nested mixing bowls, preferably stainless steel

1 set of measuring spoons, preferably stainless steel. The set should have ¼ teaspoon, ½ teaspoon, 1 teaspoon, and 1 tablespoon measurements.

2 sets of measuring cups: 1 set for liquid and the other for dry. Liquid measures are glass or plastic with markings on the side and are available in 1-, 2-, and 4-cup sizes. Dry measures are sets of 4 cups: ¼ cup, ⅓ cup, ½ cup, and 1 cup. We prefer these in stainless steel.

1 instant meat thermometer, preferably with a large dial for easier reading, measuring 100° to 200°F

1 mercury oven thermometer. We find it essential to keep an oven thermometer in the oven as a double check on the thermostat. Too hot or too cold ovens are often the cause for a recipe's not turning out.

1 metal spatula

1 hard rubber spatula for nonstick surfaces

1 soup ladle

1 standing 4-sided grater

1 potato ricer or masher

1 long-handled fork

1 carving fork

1 stainless-steel wire whisk, 8 inches long

1 bulb baster

1 bottle opener

1 heavy can opener

1 corkscrew

1 food mill

1 citrus zester

1 small citrus grater

1 long-handled stainless-steel slotted spoon

3 long-handled wooden spoons

2 long-handled stainless-steel spoons

2 flexible rubber spatulas, 1 large and 1 small

1 small citrus juicer

2 wire-mesh strainers, 1 large (8 inches wide) and 1 small

1 stainless-steel colander, 8 inches wide and with legs

1 rotary egg beater

1 kitchen tongs

1 funnel

1 nutcracker

1 vegetable peeler

1 kitchen timer

1 pepper grinder

1 sturdy wooden chopping board, preferably butcher block

1 salad spinner

1 filter coffee pot

1 teakettle

1 dozen thin wooden skewers, at least 6 inches long

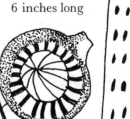

KNIVES

Invest in high-quality knives and keep them sharp and carefully stored. These are really your most essential tools. We prefer high-carbon stainless-steel knives.

2 paring knives, 3½ inches long
1 cook's knife, 6 inches long
1 chef's knife, 8 inches long
1 carving knife, 10 inches long
1 serrated bread knife, 8 inches long
1 sharpening steel, 10 inches long

RANGE

There are pros and cons to both gas and electric stoves. We definitely prefer a gas cook top because the heat can be regulated instantly. We often think electric wall ovens are preferable because the temperature seems to us more consistent and you don't have to bend into a low oven. Temperatures in gas ovens are apt to be uneven and fluctuate as much as 50°F.

EQUIPMENT

1 heavy-duty blender
1 countertop toaster oven
1 small kitchen scale with readings for both pounds and grams and measuring at least up to 5 pounds
1 electric hand mixer

BAKING EQUIPMENT

5 cake pans, preferably with non-stick surfaces, of the following sizes:
  2 round cake pans, 9 inches
  1 springform pan, 9 inches
  1 rectangular baking pan, 13 x 9 inches
  1 square baking pan, 9 inches
2 loaf pans, 9 x 5 x 3 inches
1 baking sheet (rimless), preferably nonstick
1 baking sheet (with rim), 18 x 12 x 1 inch
1 ovenproof glass pie plate, 9 inches
2 muffin tins, 12 cups each, with ½-cup capacity
1 flour sifter
1 heavy rolling pin
1 wire rack
1 pastry brush

THE COMPLETE KITCHEN

Add the following items to the Basic Kitchen list:

POTS AND PANS

1 small saucepan, 1 cup
1 double boiler with lid, glass is best
1 large dutch oven or casserole with lid, 6 quarts
1 microwave-safe glass ceramic casserole with lid, 5 quarts
1 oval roasting pan, 12 inches
3 glass ceramic baking dishes of assorted sizes for gratins and lasagne
1 stainless-steel fish poacher, 15 inches
1 deep-fat fryer with removable basket
1 wok
1 omelet pan

UTENSILS

1 extra set of 4 nested mixing bowls, preferably stainless steel
1 stainless-steel wire whisk, 10 inches
1 large spaghetti fork
1 deep-fat thermometer
6 thin metal skewers for trussing poultry
1 pair kitchen shears
1 pair poultry shears
1 pair long chopsticks
1 trussing needle
1 pizza-cutting wheel
1 apple corer
1 smooth-bottomed meat pounder
1 egg slicer
1 extra pepper grinder
1 griddle, preferably cast iron
1 ice cream scoop

KNIVES

1 grapefruit knife
1 boning knife, 5 inches
1 chef's knife, 10 inches

EQUIPMENT

1 food processor, 7-cup capacity
1 carousel microwave oven, 650 to 700 watts
1 standing mixer, 4- to 5-quart capacity
1 electric coffee grinder
1 waffle iron
1 electric juicer
1 ice cream maker
1 pressure cooker
1 chafing dish

BAKING EQUIPMENT

1 palette knife for icing cakes
1 pastry blender
1 jelly-roll pan, 12 x 8 x 1 inch
2 ovenproof glass pie plates, 8 and 10 inches
1 fluted tart pan with removable bottom, 9 inch diameter and 1 inch deep
4 tart pans with removable bottoms, 2½ to 3 inch diameter and 1 inch deep
1 soufflé dish, 2 quart
2 loaf pans, 8½ x 4½ x 2½ inches
8 ovenproof ramekins, ¾-cup capacity
1 set cookie cutters
1 pastry bag with decorating tips
1 pastry scraper, (metal or plastic)

THE PROFESSIONAL KITCHEN

Add the following items to those in the Basic and Complete Kitchen lists:

POTS AND PANS

2 saucepans with lids, 1 and 2 quart
1 large stockpot with lid, 10 to 12 quart
1 large skillet, 13½ inches
1 sauté pan with lid, 10 inch diameter and 2¼ inches deep
1 fish poacher, 24 inches
1 crepe pan, 6½ inches

UTENSILS

1 meat grinder
1 mortar and pestle
1 set ring molds in assorted sizes
1 clay pot cooker
1 nutmeg grater
1 candy thermometer
1 long-handled ladle, 2-cup capacity
1 extra-long spatula for fish
1 double-mesh strainer or chinois
1 ivory or mother-of-pearl caviar spoon

KNIVES

1 narrow slicer, 12 inches
1 cleaver
1 oyster and clam knife

RANGE

1 gas range with 6 burners, a double oven, griddle, and salamander

EQUIPMENT

1 electric meat slicer
1 standing mixer, 10-quart capacity

BAKING EQUIPMENT

2 fluted tart pans with removable bottoms, 8 and 10 inch diameter and 2 inches deep
1 charlotte mold
1 marble pastry slab
1 ladyfinger pan
1 madeleine pan
1 coeur à la crème mold

If you like French and Italian cooking, add also:
1 mandoline slicer
1 crescent-shaped knife or mezzaluna
1 pasta maker
1 double-handled cheese knife

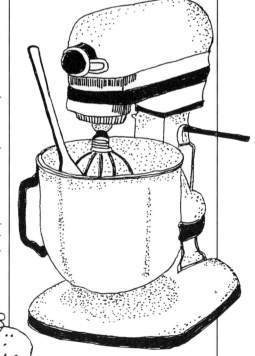

BASIC PANTRY

I t may seem overwhelming at first glance, but once you stock a basic pantry you can consider yourself set. All you need to do in the future is replace what is used up. Don't buy jumbo sizes—remember, the fresher, the better. Initially choose brands you are familiar with and always buy those of high quality, but keep an eye out for new products coming into the market. Once you have your basic pantry, enjoy all the pleasures of shopping for glorious fresh ingredients as you need them.

A basic pantry should always have a wide selection of dried herbs and spices. Be sure to store yours in a cool place out of the light. If kept over the stove or in a spice rack on the wall, they begin to oxidize and lose flavor quickly.

Shelf-stable ingredients (dry goods) are a must to stock up on. Choose interesting varieties of flours, beans, and rice. Nuts are great to have on hand, as are various condiments that can be used for cooking as well as spontaneous hors d'oeuvres. Canned broths, tomatoes, oils, and vinegars are always needed. Go through your cupboards with our list in hand, take inventory, and begin refining. In a very short time, you will have the ideal pantry.

DRY HERBS AND SPICES

Allspice, ground and whole berries
Aniseed
Basil
Bay leaves
Caraway seeds
Cardamom
Celery seeds
Chervil
Chili powder
Cinnamon, ground and sticks
Cloves, ground and whole
Cumin, seeds and ground
Curry powder
Dill
Fennel seeds
Ginger, ground and crystallized
Juniper berries
Mace
Marjoram
Mint
Mustard seeds
Nutmeg, ground and whole
Oregano
Paprika, sweet and hot
Pepper: cayenne, dried red flakes, and hot red pepper sauce
Peppercorns: dried black and white, and green packed in water
Pickling spices
Poppy seeds
Rosemary
Saffron threads
Sage
Salt: table and coarse or kosher
Savory
Sesame seeds
Tarragon
Thyme
Turmeric

BASIC PANTRY

Baking powder, double acting
Baking soda
Beans, canned: red kidney, cannellini, chick-peas
Beans, dried: red kidney, Great Northern or navy, lima, lentils, split peas, black, black-eyed peas, pinto
Bouillon cubes and powder: beef, chicken, vegetable (use in a pinch when no broth or stock is available)
Bread crumbs, unseasoned
Broths: chicken and beef
Capers: nonpareil and regular
Chocolate: unsweetened squares, semisweet morsels, semisweet squares
Clam juice
Cocoa, unsweetened
Coconut, shredded
Coffee, beans and instant espresso
Cornstarch
Cream of tartar
Dried fruits: raisins, currants, apricots
Extracts: vanilla, almond, lemon, orange, hazelnut
Flour: unbleached all-purpose, cake, whole-wheat, cornmeal—white and yellow. If you want to do a variety of baking, add rye flour, bran, cracked wheat, wheat germ, semolina, oat bran.
Gelatin, powdered and unflavored
Honey: strained clover for cooking, unstrained for spreading and eating
Horseradish
Ketchup
Liqueur: Cognac or brandy, Grand Marnier, port
Milk: sweetened condensed and evaporated

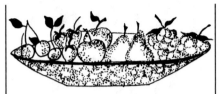

Mustards: Dijon, whole-grain, dried (we prefer Coleman's)
Nuts: almonds—whole and sliced; hazelnuts; peanuts; pecans; pine nuts (pignoli); pistachios; walnuts
Oils: olive oil—regular and extra virgin; vegetable; safflower or peanut; Asian sesame
Olives: green martini, pitted black, imported black
Pasta, dried: spaghetti, angel hair, linguine, fettuccine, tagliatelli, macaroni, penne, rigatoni
Peanut butter
Pickles: sweet gherkins, cornichons
Preserves: fruit jams, red currant jelly for sauces and glazing
Rice: long-grain converted, wild, basmati, Arborio
Soy sauce
Sugars: granulated, superfine, confectioners', brown—light and dark
Syrups: corn—light and dark; maple; molasses
Tabasco sauce
Tea, an assortment
Teriyaki sauce
Tomatoes: whole plum, tomato paste, tomato purée
Vinegars: white wine, red wine, cider, white all-purpose, rice wine, balsamic
Wines: dry sherry, Madeira, Marsala, dry Burgundy, dry Chardonnay
Worcestershire sauce
Yeast, dry active

NEW BASIC PANTRY

Anchovies, flat fillets
Artichoke hearts
Bamboo shoots
Biscuits and crackers, an assortment
Chestnuts in glass jars
Chile oil
Chile peppers, dried whole
Chopped clams or whole baby clams, canned
Escargots, canned
Espresso coffee, beans
Hearts of palm
Hoisin sauce
Liqueurs: kirsch, peach schnapps, Cointreau, amaretto, crème de menthe
Mushrooms, dried: shiitake, porcini, morels
Mustards: herb and honey
Oils: walnut and hazelnut
Olives: Niçoise, green Picholine, Calamata
Oyster sauce
Pesto in jars
Sun-dried tomatoes packed in oil
Sweet sauces: an assortment of fudge and berry sauces
Tuna
Vanilla beans
Vinegars: sherry, herb and fruit vinegars, aged balsamico
Water chestnuts

BASIC REFRIGERATED GOODS

Butter, unsalted
Cheeses: cream, 1 large chunk Parmesan
Creams: whipping cream, half-and-half, sour cream, crème fraîche
Eggs, large
Mayonnaise
Milk: regular, skim
Yeast, compressed cake (optional)

GLOSSARY OF COOKING TERMS

AGE
To leave meat to hang after the animal is killed, bringing out the flavor and tenderizing the meat.

AL DENTE
Slightly underdone with a chewy consistency, from the Italian phrase "to the tooth." Usually applied to the cooking of pasta, but can also apply to vegetables that are blanched, not fully cooked.

ASPIC
A jelly made from clarified meat, fish, or vegetable stock.

AU JUS
Roasted beef or lamb (usually) served with natural pan juices that accumulate during cooking.

BAIN-MARIE
What we call a hot water bath. Used to keep food warm on top of the stove or to cook custards and baked eggs in the oven without curdling or cracking.

BAKE
To cook by free-circulating dry air. It is very important to preheat the oven before putting in food. Do not crowd the food in the oven but give it room to cook evenly.

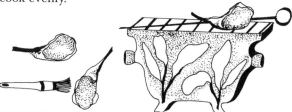

BARBECUE
To cook poultry or meats over natural woods or charcoal on a grill, in open pits, or on a spit over intense heat, marinating first, then basting with a piquant sauce.

BARD
To cover meat entirely with a thin layer of fat to keep it from drying out during cooking.

BASTE
To keep foods moist during cooking by spooning, brushing, or drizzling with a sauce, pan juice, or wine. A bulb baster is convenient to use.

BEAT
To mix ingredients rapidly so that air is incorporated, resulting in a smooth cream mixture.

BEURRE MANIE
Equal amounts of soft butter and flour mixed together and then added in small amounts as a thickener to hot soups or sauces.

BIND
To add an ingredient such as an egg, which holds the other ingredients together.

BISQUE
A seafood-base soup that is rich and creamy, such as Lobster Bisque.

BISTRO
A French restaurant or café specializing in country or less fancy local fare. Originally it meant a quick meal, but today many bistros feature full-course but simple meals.

BLANCH
To plunge vegetables, seafood, or fruit into boiling water for a very brief period of time to bring out the color, loosen skins for peeling, or mellow flavors. We like to blanch vegetables for crudités and refresh them under cold water.

BLANQUETTE
A stew or ragout made of veal, poultry, or fish cooked in wine or broth, then finished with heavy cream.

BLEND
To combine ingredients together to a desired consistency, usually until smooth.

BOIL
To heat water or other liquids to 212°F at sea level. When water boils, its surface is covered with bubbles.

BOLOGNESE
Cooking from the area of Bologna, Italy. Bolognese sauce is a thick sauce made from meat, vegetables, and tomatoes often finished with a little cream or milk.

BONE
To remove the bones from meat, fish, poultry or game, often with a thin boning knife.

BOUQUET GARNI
A small bundle of herbs, usually parsley, thyme, and bay leaves, wrapped with cheesecloth and added to a soup or stew for flavor.

BOURRIDE
Fish soup that has been strained and bound together with aïoli (garlic mayonnaise).

BRAISE
To brown meat in fat over high heat, then cover and cook slowly in the oven in a small amount of liquid. This method is ideal for tougher cuts of meat, firm-fleshed fish, and certain vegetables.

BRANDADE
A somewhat smooth mixture from Provence of salt cod, olive oil, and milk or cream. Variations include garlic, truffle, crawfish, or potato.

BREAD
To dredge or coat with bread crumbs. For example, fish or chicken is dipped in buttermilk, coated with crumbs and pan-fried or baked.

BROCHETTE
Meat, fish, and vegetables threaded on a skewer and then baked, broiled, or grilled.

BROIL
To cook with intense direct heat either on a grill or under a broiler. The high heat seals in the juices, browns the outside, and keeps the food tender.

BROWN
To cook food quickly in a preheated hot oven, broiler, or hot skillet to "brown" the outside and seal in the juices.

BRUISE
To crush an aromatic food slightly in order to release flavor. Most often used for garlic and ginger.

CANDY
To cook and coat ingredients in a sugar syrup.

CARAMELIZE
To dissolve sugar and water slowly, then heat until it turns caramel brown.

CHIFFONADE
Very finely shredded or sliced leafy vegetables, often used as garnish.

CHOP
To cut food into pieces, which can range from small (finely chopped) to large (coarsely chopped) in size.

CHOWDER
A hearty, highly flavored soup usually made from either corn or shellfish and thickened with potatoes.

CHUTNEY
A mixture of fruit and/or vegetables cooked with vinegar, sugar, and spices, used as a condiment—most often with meat, poultry, or curries.

CLARIFY
To clear stock by straining through cooked egg whites; or to make butter clear by heating, separating, and discarding milk solids.

COBBLER
A deep-dish pie made of various fruits with a top crust only. The crust is made from biscuit dough spooned on top. When baked, the biscuit is rough, or "cobbled."

CODDLE
To poach in slowly simmering water, as a coddled egg.

COURT BOUILLON

A broth made of wine, water, herbs, and spices used for poaching fish or as a base for fish soups. Onions studded with whole cloves, celery with leaves, and carrots are often added for flavor.

CRACKLINGS

The crisp brown bits that remain when all the fat is rendered from duck and chicken skin or pork rinds. These are often used for "crackling" corn bread.

CREAM

To mix a softened ingredient, like butter, alone or with other ingredients, such as sugar, until well blended and completely soft.

CREME FRAICHE

A dairy product that is similar in taste and texture to sour cream but a bit more tart. Widely available in specialty food stores or very easily made at home (see Index).

CREME PATISSIERE

A cooked, creamy custard thick enough to be used for pastry fillings.

CRIMP

To decorate the edge of a pie crust by pinching dough together with the fingers.

CUBE

To cut food into cube-shaped pieces, ranging in size from ¼ inch to 1 inch.

CURDLE

The separation that occurs in egg- or cream-based mixtures when they are heated too quickly.

CURE

To preserve meats by either smoking, drying, pickling, or salting.

CUT

To combine butter or vegetable shortening with dry ingredients until the mixture resembles coarse meal by using two dinner knives, a pastry blender, or the fingers.

DASH

A small quantity. Often used when measuring Tabasco sauce, one or two quick shakes yields a dash.

DEGLAZE

To add broth, wine, or water to a pan in which food, usually meat or poultry, has been cooked, stirring and scraping up and dissolving the browned bits from the bottom of the pan. Once the food has cooked, remove it from the pan, add the liquid and heat, stirring the juices and scraping the bits remaining in the pan until the liquid is reduced to the desired consistency.

DEGREASE

To carefully skim the layer of fat from the top of a soup, sauce, or stock. If possible, chill the mixture to solidify the fat, which will then be easier to remove.

DEVEIN

To remove the intestinal tract of a shrimp. After a shrimp has been shelled, make a slit lengthwise on the outermost curve with a knife and remove the intestinal tract. Rinse under cold water.

DEVIL

To mix (usually) cooked chopped foods into a sauce of wine or vinegar that has been spiced with a combination of "hot" ingredients, such as dry mustard, hot paprika, and Tabasco sauce.

DICE

To cut into equal-size small cubes from ¼ inch to ½ inch.

DILUTE

To make a sauce or stock less strong by adding more liquid.

DOT

To scatter small pieces of butter, usually about ¼ inch square, here and there over the top layer of a prepared dish.

DRAIN

To remove liquid or fat from food through a strainer or by absorption on paper toweling.

DREDGE

To lightly coat food, usually with flour or bread crumbs. Fill a paper bag with flour and spices and shake ingredient to be cooked in the mixture. Always shake off excess before browning.

DRIPPINGS

The juices, fat, and brown bits that are left in a pan after meat or poultry has been roasted or sautéed. Skimmed of fat, the drippings are often used for sauces and gravies.

DRIZZLE

To slowly pour a very thin stream of liquid lightly over food.

DUST

To sprinkle very lightly with sugar or flour.

DUXELLES

A finely chopped mixture of mushrooms, shallots, and herbs sautéed and often used for stuffings.

EVISCERATE

To remove entrails from animals, fish, or fowl.

FEIJOADA

A Brazilian dish of pork, sausages, onions, celery, bacon, pepper, and black beans. Similar to French cassoulet.

FILLET

To cut meat, chicken, or fish from the bones.

FLAKE

To test the flesh of a fish to see if it is done by lightly breaking away a small piece with a fork. It should separate easily.

FLAMBE

To pour brandy or liqueur over food, warm it, and ignite with a match.

FLUTE

To decorate the edge of a pastry shell in a scalloped pattern.

FOLD

To incorporate one ingredient into another without stirring or beating but instead by gently lifting from underneath with a rubber spatula.

FRICASSEE

To cook food gently covered in liquid and vegetables after it has been browned. When cooking is complete, the remaining liquid is made into a sauce.

FRITTER

A small piece of meat, vegetable, or fruit dipped in a batter and then deep-fried.

FRY

To cook food in hot fat in a skillet over high heat until brown and crisp. The process is a bit longer than for sautéing and is ideal for less delicate foods. Foods to be fried are often dipped in flour or batter first.

GARNISH

To decorate food with fresh herbs, edible flowers, fresh vegetables, or fruit to enhance the look of the dish.

GAZPACHO

A cold soup originating in Spain. The traditional soup has cucumber, tomato, onion, sweet pepper, and garlic, though there are many varieties.

GRATE

To change a solid food to fine shreds by rubbing it against a hand grater or placing it in a food processor.

GRATIN

Food, most often vegetables, topped with grated cheese or bread crumbs, drizzled with oil or butter, baked in a shallow "gratin" dish, and browned under a broiler.

GREASE

To lightly coat a pan with some fat to prevent foods from sticking and to help in browning.

GRILL

To cook on a rack over very hot coals or under a broiler in order to seal in juices.

GRIND

To use a mortar and pestle, a food processor, or a meat grinder to transform a solid piece of food into fine pieces.

HORS D'OEUVRE

A bite-size savory canapé, either cold or hot, served with cocktails or before dinner.

HULL

To pluck out the green stem and leaves of berries, most commonly strawberries.

HUSK

To remove the outside leaves from an ear of corn.

JULIENNE

To cut fresh vegetables or other foods into thin matchstick-size strips of uniform length.

KNEAD

To work dough, after blending ingredients, with the palms of your hands on a lightly floured surface, making it smooth and elastic.

LARD

To place thin strips of fat through non-fatty meat to add moistness. Usually done with a larding needle.

LEAVEN

To cause a mixture to rise while it is baking by adding baking powder, baking soda, or yeast.

LINE

To cover the surface of a baking sheet or roasting pan with waxed or parchment paper to prevent sticking.

MACERATE

To cover fruits or vegetables with a liquid, often a liqueur or lemon juice and sugar, and let them rest until the flavor has been absorbed and the fruits or vegetables softened.

MARINATE

To tenderize and flavor food by placing it in a seasoned liquid, usually composed of some combination of vinegar, lemon juice, wine, oil, herbs, and/or spices.

MELT

To change solids into liquids by use of slow heat. Most commonly used in reference to butter and chocolate.

MERINGUE

Egg whites beaten stiffly with sugar and then baked in a slow oven. Used to form dessert shells, cookies, or topping decorations.

MILANESE

Literally "from Milan," the term is used to describe food that has been dipped in flour, then egg, then bread crumbs, and sautéed in butter.

MINCE

To cut or chop into very fine pieces, no larger than ⅛ inch square.

MIX

To stir ingredients together with a spoon or fork.

MULL

To infuse hot wine or cider with herbs and spices.

PAELLA

Originally from Spain, a dish traditionally consisting of rice, saffron, tomatoes, sausages, chicken, vegetables, and shellfish. Outside of tradition, it can include any ingredients desired.

PAN-BROIL

To cook on top of the stove in a preheated heavy skillet over high heat, pouring off fat or liquid as it accumulates.

PARBOIL

To partially cook in boiling water or broth. Often vegetables are parboiled and finished off with a quick sauté.

PARE

To use a thin knife to remove skin or rind from fruits and vegetables.

PATE A CHOUX

A dough used for gougères, cream puffs, profiteroles, and éclairs. Little puffs are sometimes filled with a savory mixture for hors d'oeuvres.

PHYLLO

A tissue-thin leaf or sheet of dough, usually layered to make Greek dishes or strudel pastries.

PICKLE

A method of preserving fresh vegetables, fruits, and meats in a salty or highly acidic brine. Most usually refers to cucumber pickles.

PILAF

A rice dish highly seasoned with herbs and spices and often combined with nuts, dried fruits, poultry, and vegetables.

PINCH

The amount of a dry ingredient you can hold between your thumb and finger.

PIPE

To decorate food with a purée or stiff, smooth mixture by forcing it through a pastry bag.

PIPERADE

A long-simmering mixture of sweet peppers, tomatoes, onion, and garlic cooked in olive oil.

PIT

To remove the pits from fruit. With small fruits, such as cherries, a special pitter is often used.

PLANK

To secure food, most often fillets of salmon, to a wooden plank before grilling.

PLUMP

To soak dried fruits in broth or liquid until they swell and are rehydrated.

POACH

To cook food gently in simmering liquid that does not boil. For best results, food should be started in warm liquid and then slowly brought to a simmer.

THE WINE DICTIONARY

Acidity: The quality that gives freshness, tang, and protection from bacterial spoilage in wine.

Aroma: The impression made on the nose by the fruit from which the wine is made. Wines with aroma are generally young and have retained some of the original grape sugar.

Balance: A term to describe the degree of harmony achieved by different ingredients of a wine—the acidity, fruit, sugar, etc. No one part should stand above the rest. A good wine is well balanced.

Body: A characteristic given to wine by the amount of alcohol and tannin it possesses, which gives the wine enough substance to fill the mouth with flavor.

Bouquet: A good wine should be clean in scent with no whiff of moldiness. As the wine sits open, the esters and ethers from the bottle vaporize and produce this scent. The lingering odor that comes later is the aroma.

Breathing: When wine comes in contact with the air, it oxidizes and allows the chemical components to vaporize and create the bouquet. Generally, young red wines with high tannin need more airing than other wines. Give the bottle an hour or two to develop and show to its best advantage.

Brüt: The word on a bottle of Champagne that indicates the wine is very dry. Confusing is the fact that it is more dry than one labeled Extra-Sec or Extra Dry.

Decant: To pour wine from its bottle to another container from which it will be served. This procedure separates the wine from its sediment and aerates it, helping to create the bouquet.

Dry: When all of the sugar in the grape has completely fermented into alcohol, the wine will be dry and not sweet.

Extra-Sec or Dry: These words printed on a bottle of Champagne indicate that the wine is only fairly dry. Look for Brüt if you want Champagne without that touch of sweetness.

Flowery: A term used to describe a taste reminiscent of flowers that is found in young wines. Few wines have this quality.

Fruity: This term indicates the aroma and taste of fruit—berries, apples, even herbs—found mostly in young wines.

Heavy: A wine that is very full bodied but without distinction is called heavy.

Light: This term is used to describe red wines that are low in alcohol content and tannin, though very pleasant in most cases.

Round: A wine that is round is in perfect balance —it is harmonious and big. When tasted, it will give a sense of "roundness" in the way it fills your mouth.

Sec: This is the French word for dry, although when printed on a bottle of Champagne, it indicates the wine will tend toward sweetness.

Soft: When a wine is termed soft, it is firm, not hard and not rough. Some wines that mature quickly will achieve this quality at a young age; others need years to develop softness. When a wine is soft, it is ready to drink for it will not keep long at that point.

Tannin: The organic compounds imparted during fermentation by the grape skins, seeds, stems, and if the wine is aged in oak barrels, from them too. Tannin gives the wine its complexity and enables it to age properly. As the wine ages, the astringent quality of tannin softens, giving the wine a mellower flavor.

Thin: A thin wine lacks character, alcohol, flavor, and body.

Varietal Wine: This is an American term for wine made from the grape variety named on the label. It must contain at least 75 percent of the grape in its blend.

Velvety: A wine that is velvety will be mature, full bodied, and smooth.

POUND

To flatten or tenderize meat, often between sheets of waxed paper, with a heavy mallet or saucepan. Boneless chicken breasts and veal for scallopine are often prepared in this way.

PREHEAT

To set an oven or broiler at the desired temperature 15 to 30 minutes before use so that the desired temperature is reached before food is put in to cook. With pizza, we preheat the oven for 1 hour before cooking.

PRICK

To pierce food or pastry with the tines of a fork to prevent it from bursting or rising during baking.

PROOF

To test yeast to see if it is active. Dissolve the yeast in warm liquid mixed with a little sugar. Let stand in a warm place for 5 to 10 minutes. If the yeast is active, it will bubble and foam.

PUFF PASTRY

Light, flaky pastry of many thin layers. The basic dough is flour, butter, water, and salt but egg yolks may be added. The layers are made by repeated rolling and folding of the dough.

PUREE

To mash solid food or pass it through a food mill or food processor until it is smooth.

RAGOUT

A highly flavored stew of seafood, meat, or poultry combined with vegetables and liquid.

RECONSTITUTE

To rehydrate dry food by soaking in liquid.

REDUCE

To thicken or concentrate a sauce by boiling down, which lessens the volume and intensifies the flavor.

REFRESH

To run hot vegetables under cold water or to plunge them into cold water to stop the cooking process and retain color.

REMOULADE

Homemade mayonnaise with the addition of mustard, pickles, capers, and herbs. Anchovy and chopped hard-cooked egg may also be added. Used as an accompaniment to meat, fish, and shellfish.

RENDER

To liquefy a solid fat over low heat.

RICE

To push a soft cooked food, usually potatoes, through a mesh strainer or a potato ricer.

ROAST

To cook by the free circulation of dry heat, often beginning with a very hot oven to seal in juices and then lowering the heat to complete the cooking. Roasting can also be done on a spit.

ROUX

A mixture of melted butter and flour cooked over low heat to make a base for thickening a sauce. Flour should always be cooked at least 2 minutes, stirring constantly, so the floury taste is eliminated.

SAUTE

To cook food in butter or fat in a skillet until lightly browned. Sautéing is usually a quick process so food should be sliced thin and should be tender.

SAVORY

A nonsweet food, often served as an hors d'oeuvre. In England, savories are often served after dessert to ready the palate for brandy and Cognac.

SCALD

To cook a liquid, most often milk or cream, over low heat until just before it boils. Look for small bubbles around the edge of the liquid.

SCALLOP

To attractively finish a pie crust edge. Also to bake a dish, such as scalloped potatoes, with cream or a creamy sauce; or a thin small piece of meat, such as a veal scallop; or a type of shellfish.

SCORE

To make very thin slashes along the surface of fish or meat to help tenderize it.

SCRAMBLE

To prepare eggs by gently stirring with a fork while cooking.

SEAR

To brown the surface of meat very quickly in a hot oven, under a broiler, or in a pan over high heat on top of the stove to seal in juices.

SHRED

To tear or cut into long thin pieces.

SIFT

To pass dry ingredients, most often flour, through a fine-mesh strainer to remove lumps and lighten the texture.

SIMMER

To cook liquid alone or along with other ingredients over low heat, never boiling. A few small bubbles may appear on the surface.

SKIM

To spoon off fat or scum that rises to the surface of a cooked liquid.

SLIVER

To cut food into long thin strips.

SNIP

To cut herbs such as chives into small bits with a scissors.

SOUFFLE

A baked food, either a dessert or entrée, made light and fluffy by the addition of beaten egg whites before cooking.

SPIT-ROAST

To cook meats, often whole meats, on a metal rod rotating over a hot fire.

STEAM

To cook food, covered, over a small amount of boiling water. This is the best low-fat method of cooking, especially ideal for vegetables.

STEEP

To place dry ingredients, such as tea leaves, into a warm liquid to infuse the liquid with flavor or color.

STEW

To slowly cook meats and vegetables in liquid in a covered pan, either in the oven or on top of the stove.

STIR

To blend a mixture together using a spoon in a circular motion.

STIR-FRY

To quickly sauté meat or vegetables while stirring constantly in a hot wok or skillet.

STOCK

A long-simmering, well-flavored broth made from meat, poultry, fish, or vegetables with the addition of herbs and spices. When simmering stock on the back burner, add peels from vegetables and stems from herbs for additional flavor and color. Strain before use.

STRAIN

To remove solids from liquids by pouring through a colander or sieve.

STUD

To insert seasonings, such as whole cloves or garlic, into the surface of a food to infuse it with flavor.

STUFF

To fill a cavity with a well-flavored mixture. This applies to poultry, fish, meat, vegetables, and bread—to name a few. Always let stuffing come to room temperature before using it and stuff meats, poultry, and fish just before cooking.

TEMPER

To moderate and balance a cool ingredient before adding it gradually to a hot ingredient, or vice versa, to avoid separation and curdling.

TOAST

To brown by baking, as for nuts and seeds, or to brown by placing food under direct heat, as for bread.

TOSS

To quickly and gently mix ingredients, such as a salad or a pasta dish, together using a large spoon and fork.

TRUSS

To tie the legs and wings of poultry close to the body with string in preparation for roasting. If poultry is stuffed, the cavity is closed with skewers laced together so that the stuffing remains enclosed.

VINAIGRETTE

A dressing made from a mixture of vinegar, oil, salt, and pepper. Mustard, garlic, shallots, anchovies, or egg can also be added. Use as dressing for salads and other cold dishes.

WHIP

To beat rapidly, either by hand or with an electric mixer, to add air and increase volume.

WHISK

A looped wire kitchen utensil attached to a handle, used to mix or "whisk" sauces, dressings, eggs, and other liquid ingredients with a swift, circular motion.

ZEST

To remove in fine strips the outermost colored peel, or zest, of citrus fruits, being careful not to incorporate the bitter white pith just underneath the surface.

ZESTER

A small utensil used specifically to remove the outermost layer of citrus fruits.

CONVERSION CHART

U.S. WEIGHTS AND MEASURES

1 pinch = less than ⅛ teaspoon (dry)
1 dash = 3 drops to ¼ teaspoon (liquid)
3 teaspoons = 1 tablespoon = ½ ounce (liquid and dry)
2 tablespoons = 1 ounce (liquid and dry)
4 tablespoons = 2 ounces (liquid and dry) = ¼ cup
5⅓ tablespoons = ⅓ cup
16 tablespoons = 8 ounces = 1 cup = ½ pound
16 tablespoons = 48 teaspoons
32 tablespoons = 16 ounces = 2 cups = 1 pound
64 tablespoons = 32 ounces = 1 quart = 2 pounds
1 cup = 8 ounces (liquid) = ½ pint
2 cups = 16 ounces (liquid) = 1 pint
4 cups = 32 ounces (liquid) = 2 pints = 1 quart
16 cups = 128 ounces (liquid) = 4 quarts = 1 gallon
1 quart = 2 pints (dry)
8 quarts = 1 peck (dry)
4 pecks = 1 bushel (dry)

APPROXIMATE EQUIVALENTS

1 quart (liquid) = about 1 litre
8 tablespoons = 4 ounces = ½ cup = 1 stick butter
1 cup all-purpose presifted flour = 5 ounces
1 cup stoneground yellow cornmeal = 4½ ounces
1 cup granulated sugar = 8 ounces
1 cup brown sugar = 6 ounces
1 cup confectioners' sugar = 4½ ounces
1 large egg = 2 ounces = ¼ cup = 4 tablespoons
1 egg yolk = 1 tablespoon + 1 teaspoon
1 egg white = 2 tablespoons + 2 teaspoons

TEMPERATURES: °FARENHEIT (F) TO °CELSIUS(C)

−10°F = −23.3°C (freezer storage)
  0°F = −17.7°C
 32°F =   0°C (water freezes)
 50°F = 10°C
 68°F = 20°C (room temperature)
100°F = 37.7°C
150°F = 65.5°C
205°F = 96.1°C (water simmers)
212°F = 100°C (water boils)
300°F = 148.8°C
325°F = 162.8°C
350°F = 177°C (baking)
375°F = 190.5°C
400°F = 204.4°C (hot oven)
425°F = 218.3°C
450°F = 232°C (very hot oven)
475°F = 246.1°C
500°F = 260°C (broiling)

CONVERSION FACTORS

If you need to convert measurements into their equivalents in another system, here's how to do it.

ounces to grams: multiply ounce figure by 28.3 to get number of grams

grams to ounces: multiply gram figure by .0353 to get number of ounces

pounds to grams: multiply pound figure by 453.59 to get number of grams

pounds to kilograms: multiply pound figure by 0.45 to get number of kilograms

ounces to milliliters: multiply ounce figure by 30 to get number of milliliters

cups to liters: multiply cup figure by 0.24 to get number of liters

Fahrenheit to Celsius: subtract 32 from the Fahrenheit figure, multiply by 5, then divide by 9 to get Celsius figure

Celsius to Fahrenheit: multiply Celsius figure by 9, divide by 5, then add 32 to get Fahrenheit figure

inches to centimeters: multiply inch figure by 2.54 to get number of centimeters

centimeters to inches: multiply centimeter figure by .39 to get number of inches

BIBLIOGRAPHY

Adams, John F. *The Epicurean Gardener*. New York: E.P. Dutton, 1988

Anderson, Frederick O. *How to Grow Herbs for Gourmet Cooking*. New York: Hawthorn Books, 1967.

Andrews, Jean. *Peppers: The Domesticated Capsicums*. Austin, Texas: University of Texas Press, 1984.

Artusi, Pellegrino. *Italianissimo: Italian Cooking at Its Best*, trans. Elisabeth Abbott. New York: Liveright, 1975.

Audubon Society Staff and Lincoff, Gary H. *The Audubon Society Field Guide to North American Mushrooms*. New York: Alfred A. Knopf, 1981.

Bacon, Josephine. *The Citrus Cookbook*. Boston: The Harvard Common Press, 1983.

Baird, Charlotte. *Apples, Peaches and Pears*. Toronto: James Lorimer & Co., 1977.

Barer-Stein, Thelma. *You Eat What You Are*. Toronto: The Canadian Publishing Company, 1979.

Barret, Judith, and Wasserman, Norma. *Risotto: The Classic Rice Dish of Northern Italy*. New York: Charles Scribner's Sons, 1987.

Barzini, Luigi. *The Italians*. New York: Atheneum, 1977.

Beard, James. *Barbecue with Beard*. New York: Warner Books, 1976.

Beard, James. *James Beard's American Cookery*. New York: Little, Brown & Co., 1972.

Beck, Bruce. *Produce: A Fruit & Vegetable Lovers' Guide*. New York: Friendly Press, 1984.

Berg, Donald. *The Kitchen Gardener's Guide*. Berkeley: Ten Speed Press, 1987.

Bernard, Françoise. *Les Recettes Faciles de Françoise Bernard*. Paris: Hachette, 1965.

Berry, Naomi, and Bellini, Beppe. *Food Alla Florentine*. Garden City, New York: Doubleday & Co., 1972.

Bertholle, Louisette. *French Cuisine for All*. Garden City, New York: Doubleday & Co., 1980.

Bianchini, Francesco; Corbetta, Francesco; and Pistoia, Marelena. *The Complete Book of Fruits & Vegetables*. New York: Crown Publishers, 1973.

Bianco, Marie. "Wild About Mushrooms." *Newsday*, January 25, 1989, pp. D12–15.

Boursier, Helen T. "Cranberries." *Cape Cod Life*, October 1984, p. 7.

Boxer, Arabelle, and Back, Philippa. *The Herb Book*. London: Octopus Books, Ltd., 1980.

Bremness, Lesley. *The Complete Book of Herbs*. New York: Viking, 1988.

Brennan, Georgeanne, and Glenn, Charlotte. *Peppers: Hot & Chile*. Berkeley: Aris Books, 1988.

Brennan, Georgeanne; Cronin, Isaac; and Glenn, Charlotte. *The New American Vegetable Cookbook*. Berkeley: Aris Books, 1985.

Brody, Jane. *Jane Brody's Nutrition Book*. New York: Bantam Books, 1984.

Bugialli, Giuliano. *Bugialli on Pasta*. New York: Simon & Schuster, 1988.

Bugialli, Giuliano. *The Fine Art of Italian Cooking*. New York: Times Books, 1977.

Burpee, Lois. *Lois Burpee's Gardeners' Companion & Cookbook*. New York: Harper & Row, 1983.

Buszek, Beatrice. *The Blueberry Connection*. Nova Scotia, Canada: Cranberrie Cottage, 1979.

Camp, Raymond. *Game Cookery in America and Europe*. Los Angeles: HP Books, 1983.

Carluccio, Antonio. *A Taste of Italy*. Boston: Little, Brown & Co., 1986.

Casella, Dolores. *The Complete Vegetable Cookbook*. Port Washington, New York: David White, Inc., 1983.

Chardenon, Ludo. *In Praise of Wild Herbs*, trans. Susan Kinnell and John Frederick. Santa Barbara, California: Capra Press, 1984.

Charpentier, Henri. *Food & Finesse: The Bride's Bible*. W.B. Conkey Company, 1945.

Clarke, Ethne. *The Art of the Kitchen Garden*. New York: Alfred A. Knopf, 1988.

Colchie, Elizabeth Schneider. "All About Apples." *Food & Wine*, October 1982, p. 23.

Cooper, Jilly, and Hartman, Tom, eds. *Violets & Vinegar: An Anthology of Women's Writings & Sayings*. New York: Stein & Day, 1982.

Cost, Bruce. *Ginger East to West: A Cook's Tour with Recipes, Techniques & Lore*. Berkeley: Aris Books, 1984.

Courtine, Robert. *Zola at Table*. Paris: Editions Robert Laffont, 1978.

Creasy, Rosalind. *The Complete Book of Edible Landscaping*. San Francisco: Sierra Club Books, 1982.

D'Andrea, Jeanne. *Ancient Herbs in the J. Paul Getty Museum*. Malibu: J. Paul Getty Museum, 1982.

Dariaux, Genevieve Antoine. *Entertaining with Elegance*. Garden City, New York: Doubleday & Co., 1965.

David, Elizabeth, *French Country Cooking*. New York: Horizon Press, 1968.

David, Elizabeth. *Italian Food*. New York: Harper & Row, 1987.

Davidson, Alan. *Mediterranean Seafood.* London: Penguin, 1972.

Davidson, Alan. *North Atlantic Seafood.* New York: Viking, 1979.

Day, Avanelle. *The Spice Cookbook.* Port Washington, New York: David White, Inc., 1964.

de Amezua, Clara Maria G. *The Regional Cooking of Spain.* Madrid: Editorial Castalia, 1980.

de Groot, Roy Andries. *Feasts for All Seasons.* New York: Alfred A. Knopf, 1966.

de Groot, Roy Andries. *Revolutionizing French Cooking.* New York: McGraw-Hill, 1975.

Del Conte, Anna. *Gastronomy of Italy.* New York: Prentice Hall, 1988.

della Croce, Julia. *Pasta Classica: The Art of Italian Pasta Cooking.* San Francisco: Chronicle Books, 1987.

Del Nero, Constance Arkin, and Del Nero, Rosario. *Risotto: A Taste of Milan.* New York: Harper & Row, 1988.

Dinnage, Paul. *The Book of Fruit and Fruit Cookery.* London: Sedgwick & Jackson, 1981.

Duijker, Hubrecht. *The Good Wines of Bordeaux.* New York: Crescent Books, 1980.

Durrell, Gerald. *My Family and Other Animals.* New York: Viking, 1963.

Ellwanger, George. *The Garden's Story: Pleasures and Trials of an Amateur Gardener.* New York: D. Appleton & Co., 1889.

Ensrud, Barbara. *The Pocket Guide to Wine.* New York: Putnam Publishing Group, 1980.

Ferrari, Ambra. *Emilia in Bocca.* Palermo, Italy: Edizioni e Ristampe Siciliane, 1987.

Ford, Ford Madox. *Provence.* New York: Ecco Press, 1935.

Foster, Don, and Foster, Marge. *Tapas, Wines, and Good Times.* Chicago: Contemporary Books, 1986.

Gewanter, Vera. *A Passion for Vegetables.* New York: Viking, 1980.

Giobbi, Edward, and Wolff, Richard. *Eat Right, Eat Well: The Italian Way,* ed. Judith B. Jones. New York: Alfred A. Knopf, 1985.

Grigson, Jane. *Jane Grigson's Fruit Book.* New York: Atheneum, 1982.

Grimaldi, Gianni. *Liguria in Bocca.* Palermo, Italy: La Nuòva Edrisi, 1987.

Hall, Nancy, and Hall, Walter. *The Wild Palate.* Emmaus, Pennsylvania: Rodale Press, 1980.

Halpin, Anne Moyer. *Gourmet Gardening.* Emmaus, Pennsylvania: Rodale Press, 1981.

Hampstead, Marilyn. *The Basil Book.* New York: Pocket Books, 1984.

Harris, Lloyd J. *The Book of Garlic.* Berkeley: Aris Books, 1974.

Heaten, Rose Henniker. *The Perfect Hostess.* New York: E.P. Dutton, 1931.

Hendrickson, Audra, and Hendrickson, Jack. *The Carrot Cookbook.* Pownal, Vermont: Storey Communications, 1987.

Heriteau, Jacqueline. *The How to Grow and Cook It Book of Vegetables, Herbs, Fruits and Nuts.* New York: Hawthorn Books, 1970.

Hirasuna, Delphine, and Hirasuna, Diane J. *Vegetables.* New York: Chronicle Books, 1985.

Hoge, Tom. *Potato Cookery.* New York: Cornerstone Library, 1980.

Hutson, Lucinda. *The Herb Garden Cookbook.* Austin, Texas: Texas Monthly Press, 1987.

Jenkins, Nancy Harmon. "Growing U.S. Taste for Mushrooms." *The New York Times,* October 23, 1985, pp. C5–6.

Johnston, Mireille. *The Cuisine of The Sun: Classical French Cooking from Nice and Provence.* New York: Random House, 1979.

Kasper, Lynn. "Hot Chiles & Sweet Peppers." *Bon Appetit,* October 1981, p. 32.

Kennedy, Diana. *Nothing Fancy: Recipes and Recollections of Soul-Satisfying Food.* Garden City, New York: Doubleday & Co., 1984.

Keys, Ancel, and Keys, Margaret. *The Benevolent Bean.* New York: Noonday, 1972.

King, Shirley. *Saucing the Fish: A Chef's Collection of Recipes for Stylish Fish Dishes.* New York: Simon & Schuster, 1986.

Klein, Maggie Blyth. *The Feast of the Olive: Cooking with Olives and Olive Oil.* Berkeley: Aris Books, 1983.

Krutch, Joseph Wood. *The Twelve Seasons.* New York: William Sloan Associates, 1949.

Kuper, Jessica. *The Anthropologists' Cookbook.* London: Routledge & Kegan Paul, 1978.

Lang, Jenifer Harvey, ed. *Larousse Gastronomique.* New York: Crown Publishers, 1988.

Lantermo, Alberta. *Piemonte in Bocca.* Palermo, Italy: Edizioni e Ristampe Siciliane, 1986.

Lappé, Frances Moore. *Diet for a Small Planet.* New York: Ballantine Books, 1972.

Larkcom, Joy. *The Salad Garden.* New York: Viking, 1984.

Lichine, Alexis. *Alexis Lichine's New Encyclopedia of Wines and Spirits.* New York: Alfred A. Knopf, 1981.

Longone, Janice B. "Mother Maize & King Corn: The Persistence of Corn in the American Ethos." Ann Arbor, Michigan: The William L. Clements Library, The University of Michigan, 1980.

Lubbock, Sir John. *Pleasures of Life.* New York: H.M. Caldwell Co., 1887.

Marcus, George, and Marcus, Nancy. *Forbidden Fruits & Forgotten Vegetables.* New York: St. Martin's Press, 1982.

Mariani, John. *The Dictionary of American Food & Drink.* New Haven, Connecticut: Ticknor & Fields, 1985.

McClane, Alan. *McClane's North American Fish Cooking.* New York: Holt, Rinehart & Winston, 1981.

McGee, Harold J. *On Food & Cooking: The Science and Lore of the Kitchen.* New York: Charles Scribner's Sons, 1984.

Murdich, Jack. *Buying Produce: The Greengrocer's Guide to Selecting & Storing Fresh Fruits & Vegetables.* New York: Hearst Books, 1986.

Murray, Thomas J. *Oysters & Fish.* New York: Frederick A. Stokes & Brother, 1888.

Muscatine, Doris; Amerine, Maynard A.; and Thompson, Bob, eds. *The University of California/Sotheby Book of California Wine.* Berkeley: University of California Press/Sotheby Publications, 1984.

National Gardening Association. *The Complete Guide to Growing America's Favorite Fruits & Vegetables.* Reading, Massachusetts: Addison-Wesley, 1985.

Pappas, Lou Seibert. *The Elegant, Economical Egg Cookbook.* San Francisco: 101 Productions, 1983.

Parker, Lonnie, and Jenkins, David. *Mushrooms: A Separate Kingdom.* Birmingham, Alabama: Oxmoor House, 1979.

Pellegrini, Angelo M. *The Unprejudiced Palate.* New York: Macmillan Company, 1948.

Peterson, Maude Gridley. *How to Know Wild Fruits.* New York: Dover Publications, 1973.

Pettingill, Amos. *The White Flower Farm Garden Book.* New York: Alfred A. Knopf, 1971.

Plotkin, Fred. *The Authentic Pasta Book.* New York: Simon & Schuster, 1985.

Read, Jan, and Manyon, Maite. *The Wine & Food of Spain.* Boston: Little, Brown & Co., 1987.

Reardon, Joan, and Ebling, Ruth. *Oysters: A Culinary Celebration.* Orleans, Massachusetts: Parnassus Imprints, 1984.

Rinzler, Carol Ann. *The Complete Book of Food: A Nutritional, Medical & Culinary Guide.* New York: Pharos Books, 1987.

Riotte, Louise. *Sleeping with a Sunflower: A Treasury of Old-Time Gardening Lore.* Pownal, Vermont: Storey Communications, 1987.

Roden, Claudia. *Everything Tastes Better Outdoors.* New York: Alfred A. Knopf, 1984.

Romer, Elizabeth. *Italian Pizza and Hearth Breads.* New York: Clarkson N. Potter, 1987.

Romer, Elizabeth. *The Tuscan Year.* New York: Atheneum, 1985.

Root, Waverley, *Food.* New York: Simon & Schuster, 1980.

Root, Waverley, ed. *Herbs & Spices: A Guide to Culinary Seasoning,* rev. ed. New York: Alfred van der Marck Editions, 1985.

Rosengarten, Frederic, Jr. *The Book of Edible Nuts.* New York: Walker & Co., 1983.

Rubin, Cynthia, and Rubin, Jerome. *Cherry Cookbook.* Boston: Emporium Publications, 1974.

Sanders, Rosanne. *The Apple Book.* New York: Philosophical Library, 1988.

Sax, Richard. "Veal Quick." *Gentlemen's Quarterly,* August 1984, p. 21.

Scaravelli, Paola, and Cohen, Jon. *Cooking from an Italian Garden: Classic Meatless Recipes from Antipasto to Dessert.* New York: Harvest/HBJ, 1985.

Schneider, Elizabeth. *Uncommon Fruits & Vegetables: A Commonsense Guide.* New York: Harper & Row, 1986.

Schulz, Phillip Stephen. *Cooking with Fire & Smoke.* New York: Simon & Schuster, 1986.

Shepherd, Renee. *Recipes from a Kitchen Garden.* Felton, California: Shepherd's Garden Publishing, 1987.

Simon, Andre L. *A Concise Encyclopedia of Gastronomy: Birds and Their Eggs.* London: The Wine & Food Society, 1940.

Simon, Andre L. *A Concise Encyclopedia of Gastronomy: Cereals.* London: The Wine & Food Society, 1940.

Simon, Andre L. *A Concise Encyclopedia of Gastronomy: Fish.* London: The Wine & Food Society, 1940.

Sinnes, A. Cort. *The Grilling Book: The Techniques, Tools, and Tastes of the New American Grill.* Berkeley: Aris Books, 1985.

Spurrier, Steven. *The Wine Cellar Book.* Boston: Salem House Publishers, 1986.

Standard, Stella. *Whole Grain Cooking.* New York: The John Day Company, 1951.

Stewart, Donald Ogden. *Perfect Behavior.* New York: George H. Doran and Co., 1922.

Stone, Sally, and Stone, Martin. *The Brilliant Bean.* New York: Bantam Books, 1988.

Tatum, Billy Joe. *Wild Foods Field Guide and Cookbook.* New York: Workman Publishing, 1976.

Tobias, Doris. "Pepper Perfect." *W,* October 15–22, 1980, pp. 7–8.

Toklas, Alice B. *The Alice B. Toklas Cookbook.* New York: Harper & Row, 1984.

Toklas, Alice B. *Aromas and Flavors of Past & Present.* New York: Harper & Brothers, 1958.

Tolley, Emelie, and Mead, Chris. *Herbs: Gardens, Decorations, and Recipes.* New York: Clarkson N. Potter, 1985.

Visser, Margaret. *Much Depends on Dinner.* New York: Grove Press, 1987.

Vyncky, Virginia Vass. "The Green Giant." *Chicago Sun-Times,* April 28, 1988, pp. 34–35.

Whiteaker, Stafford. *The Compleat Strawberry.* New York: Crown Publishers, 1985.

Williams, Lonnie, and Warner, Karen. *Oysters: A Connoisseur's Guide & Cookbook.* San Francisco: 101 Productions, 1987.

Woolfolk, Margaret. *Cooking with Berries.* New York: Clarkson N. Potter, 1979.

Wynne, Peter. *Apples: History, Folklore, Horticulture and Gastronomy.* New York: Hawthorn Books, 1975.

INDEX

B

C

Porgy

I loves you Bass!

G

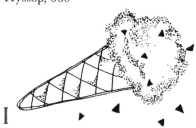

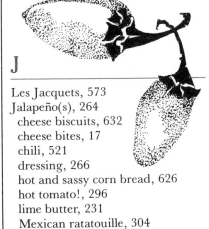

J

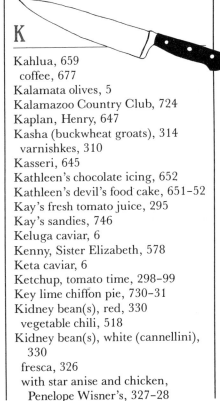

K

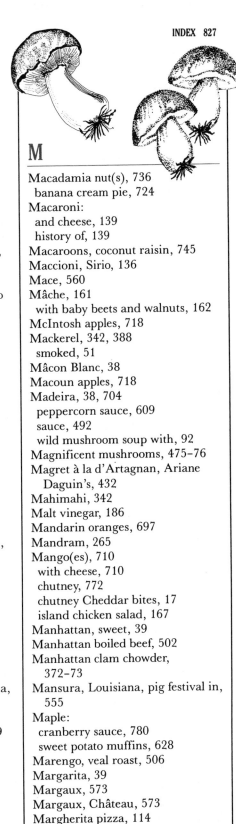

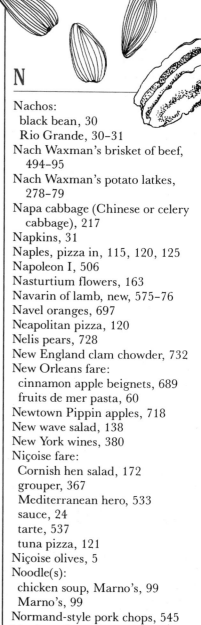

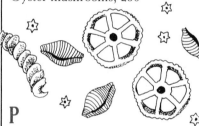

Q

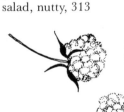

R

U

V

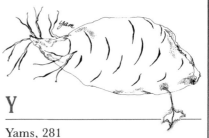

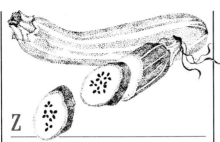

Z